Exploring Psychology

Alexej Jawlensky, *Kopf*

Fourth Edition

Exploring Psychology

David G. Myers

Hope College, Holland, Michigan

WORTH PUBLISHERS

To Carol, with love

Exploring Psychology, *Fourth Edition*

Manufactured in the United States of America
Library of Congress Catalog Card Number: 98-85010

ISBN: 1-57259-416-0 (Paper edition)
ISBN: 1-57259-656-2 (Cloth edition)
Printing: 1 2 3 4 5—03 02 01 00 99

Executive editor: Catherine Woods
Project director: Penny Bice
Development editors: Betty Probert, Christine Brune
Design: Malcolm Grear Designers
Design director: Jennie Nichols
Production editors: Laura Rubin, Elizabeth Geller
Production managers: Sarah Segal, Patricia Lawson
Photo editor: Joan Meisel
Graphics art manager: Demetrios Zangos
Illustrations: Shawn Kenney, Bonnie Hofkin, and Demetrios Zangos

Composition and separations: TSI Graphics, Inc.
Printing and binding: R.R. Donnelley and Sons

Cover and frontispiece: *Kopf*, by Alexej Jawlensky, 1920,
watercolor on paper, Christie's Images.
Illustration credits begin on page IC-1, and constitute
an extension of the copyright page.

All royalties from the sale of this book are assigned to the
David and Carol Myers Foundation, which exists to receive
and distribute funds to other charitable organizations.

Worth Publishers
33 Irving Place
New York, New York 10003

Contents in Brief

Contents

CHAPTER 3

The Developing Person 79

CHAPTER 4

Sensation and Perception 125

CHAPTER 5

States of Consciousness 169

CHAPTER 9
Motivation 311

CHAPTER 10
Emotions, Stress, and Health 347

CHAPTER 11
Personality 389

APPENDIX A

APPENDIX B

Preface

Like the human beings whom psychologists study, textbooks, too, develop with age. From its conception in 1982 and through the first several editions of its childhood and youth, this book, like the field it reports, has matured. Today's psychological science is more attuned to gender and cultural diversity, evolutionary and genetic influences, and the neuroscience revolution. We today can also harness new ways to present information, both in books and via electronic media. These changes are exhilarating! Keeping up with new discoveries and technologies fills each day and connects me with many colleagues and friends.

The thousands of instructors and millions of students who have studied this book have contributed immensely to its development. Much of this has occurred spontaneously, through correspondence and conversations. I look forward to continued feedback as we strive, over future editions, to create an ever better book.

Throughout its four editions, however, my vision for *Exploring Psychology* has not wavered: *to merge rigorous science with a broad human perspective in a book that engages both mind and heart.* My aim has been to create a state-of-the-art introduction to psychology, written with sensitivity to students' needs and interests. I aspire to help students gain insight into, and appreciate the wonder of, important phenomena of their lives. I also want to convey the inquisitive, caring spirit in which psychologists *do* psychology. The study of psychology, I believe, enhances our abilities to restrain intuition with critical thinking, judgmentalism with compassion, and illusion with understanding.

Believing with Thoreau that "Anything living is easily and naturally expressed in popular language," I seek to communicate psychology's scholarship with crisp narrative and vivid storytelling. Writing as a solo author, I hope to tell psychology's story in a way that is warmly personal as well as rigorously scientific. I love to reflect on connections between psychology and other realms, such as literature, philosophy, history, religion, sports, politics, and popular culture. And I love to provoke thought, to play with words, and to laugh.

Big Changes in the Fourth Edition

This new edition retains its predecessor's voice, and much of its content and organization. However, every page has been updated. The result is several hundred new references and many new sections and examples reflecting the psychology of the late 1990s. This edition also *looks* new. Its thoughtfully revised art program, including easier-to-read graphs, and many improved photos, should help it *work* better than ever.

More Extensive Gender and Cultural Diversity Coverage

Thorough coverage of gender and cultural diversity is integrated throughout every chapter of the book. Topics range from the first chapter's discussions of the social-cultural perspective, of cultural and gender variations, and of "human diversity and kinship," through the last chapter's discussion of cultural and gender roles. In between are dozens more gender- and culture-related topics, including those itemized below and on the next page.

For this and succeeding editions I also am working to offer a world-based psychology for our worldwide student readership. Thus, I continually search the world for research findings and text and photo examples, conscious that readers may be in Melbourne, Sheffield, Vancouver, or Nairobi. North American and European examples come easily, given that I reside in the United States, maintain contact with colleagues in Canada, subscribe to several European periodicals, and live periodically in the United Kingdom. But this edition also offers more than 40 mentions of Australia and New Zealand. Thanks to increased migration and the growing global economy, we are all citizens of a shrinking world. Thus, American students, too, benefit from information and examples that internationalize their world-consciousness. And if psychology seeks to explain *human* behavior (not just American or Cana-

Coverage of the Psychology of Women and Men

Coverage of **the psychology of women and men** can be found on the following pages:

Abortion stress, pp. 370–371
Behavioral effects of gender, pp. 29–30
Biological sex/gender, p. 80
Dieting, p. 324
Dream content, p. 181
Eating disorders, p. 319
Emotion detecting, p. 306
Emotional expression, p. 352
Empty nest, p. 118
Freud's views, pp.392–393, 394–395, 396–397
Gender and child-rearing, pp. 97–98
Generic pronoun "he," p. 286
Happiness, p. 363
Heart disease, pp. 372–373
Hormones and
  aggression, p. 514
  sexual behavior, pp. 328–329
  sexual development, pp. 80, 100–101
Immune system, p. 374
Intelligence, pp. 304–306
Leadership, p. 342
Genital arousal in REM sleep, p. 175
Maturation, p. 101
Menarche, p. 100
Menopause, p. 110
Midlife crisis, pp. 136–137
Pornography, pp. 329–330
Psychological disorders, rates of, pp. 456–457
  depression, pp. 442, 446, 447
Rape, pp. 214, 518–519
Sexual disorders, pp. 330–331
Sexual fantasies, pp. 171–172
Sexuality, pp. 326–332
Sexual orientation, pp. 332–336
Social clock, p. 115
Social connectedness, pp. 105–106
Suicide, p. 444
Weight discrimination, pp. 320–321
Women and work, pp. 118–119
Women in psychology, pp. 4, 7

Coverage of Culture and Multicultural Experience

From Chapter 1 to Chapter 14, coverage of **culture and multicultural experience** permeates the book in the following discussions:

dian or Australian behavior), the broader the scope of studies presented, the more accurate is our picture of this world's people. My aim is to expose all students to the world beyond their own country. Thus, I continue to welcome input and suggestions from readers everywhere.

Increased Evolution and Behavior Genetics Coverage

The evolutionary and behavior genetics perspectives on psychology are now introduced in the first chapter, and coverage of these issues is extensively integrated throughout the book. Chapter 2 offers a new main section on "Genetics and Behavior," which includes subsections on evolutionary psychology and behavior genetics. This new section introduces students to basic concepts of evolution and behavior genetics that will recur throughout the book.

The integrated coverage of evolution and genetics appears in almost every chapter. For example, Chapter 3 (The Developing Person) discusses "The Genetics of Life" and "Sex Chromosomes, Sex Hormones, and Gender." Chapter 8 (Thinking, Language, and Intelligence) includes a lengthy section on "Genetic and Environmental Influences on Intelligence."

New discoveries from the neuroscience frontier have also been added, building on Chapter 2's axiom that *"everything psychological is simultaneously biological."* Rather than pack all this information into an early chapter or two, much of it is more palatably disseminated throughout the book. Chapter 2, "Biology and Behavior," thus aims not to overwhelm students with biology, but to introduce important concepts and to whet readers' appetite for more.

Evolution and Behavior Genetics Coverage

Figure 7.17 The effects of context on memory Words heard underwater are best recalled underwater; words heard on land are best recalled on land. (Adapted from Godden & Baddeley, 1975)

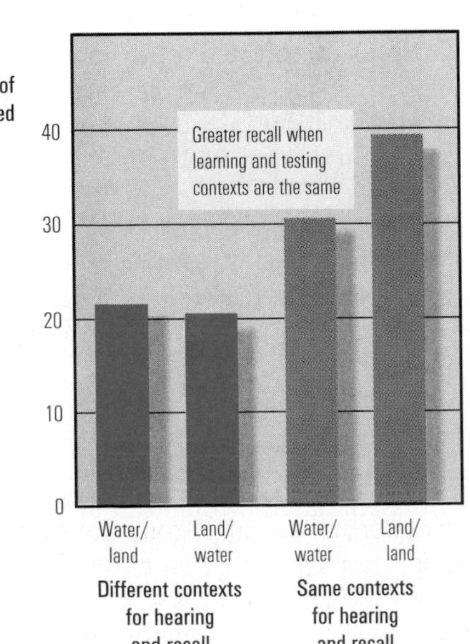

Thoughtfully Revised Art Program

The art for this edition has been carefully and creatively revised, with clearer, more helpful labels, and improved color and design of each figure. Improved labeling of graphs, such as in Figure 7.17 at left, will help students learn to read graphs and interpret data more effectively. Figure 8.6 at right exemplifies the creative combination of well-labeled art with illustrative photos. In addition, the faces pictured in our vastly improved photo program accurately reflect this book's diverse readership.

New Electronic Teaching and Learning Opportunities

Using the best of the World Wide Web and CD-ROM technology, Worth Publishers has created a new teaching and learning application. ***MyersPlus for Exploring Psychology*** neatly integrates an instructor's content with the ancillaries and even more new resources in an easy-to-navigate, browser-like environment.

The CD-ROM component of *MyersPlus* includes a syllabus maker, video clips, critical thinking exercises, animated activities, quizzes, Web links, material from our printed Instructor's Resources and selected text illustrations. The Web component will offer periodic updates with new materials. Instructors or

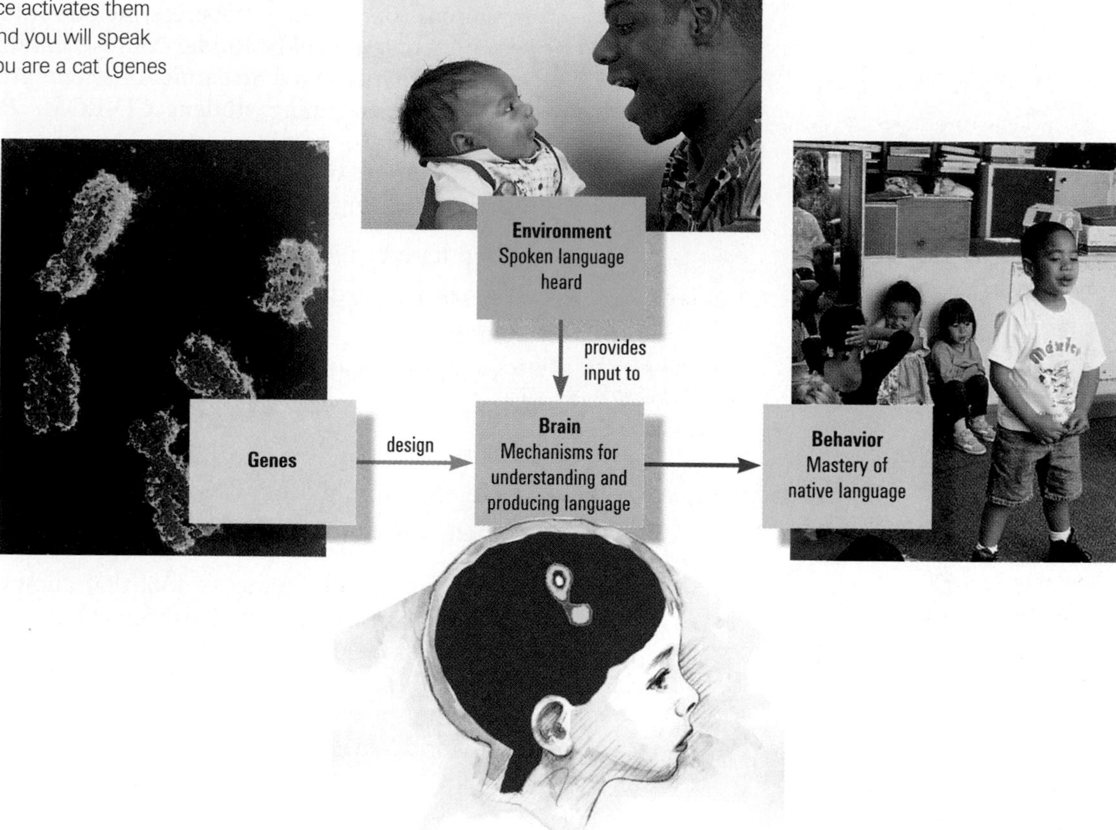

Figure 8.6 Nature and nurture Genes design the mechanisms for a language, and experience activates them as it modifies the brain. Grow up in Paris and you will speak French (environment matters), but not if you are a cat (genes matter).

students who do not have a CD-ROM drive may download the *MyersPlus for Exploring Psychology* application and view content via the Web at

www.worthpublishers.com/exploring

MyersPlus enables instructors to:

- create an online syllabus that will then be used by the application to organize the wealth of CD-ROM and Web content,
- integrate their own content, such as course notes and Web links,
- receive periodic content updates via the Web throughout the school year,
- create annotated study or lecture aids for online "review" sessions or classroom presentations, and
- maintain a mailing list of students and colleagues.

MyersPlus allows students to:

- work through fun activities that help teach key concepts from the course,
- hone their critical thinking skills with exercises designed especially for *MyersPlus*,
- quiz themselves after completing study of each chapter in the book, and
- pursue areas of special interest via Web links for more information.

I am pleased to be part of an unprecedented collaborative effort to provide teaching resources and interactive learning opportunities for introductory psychology. Our team of psychology educators is working with Peregrine Publishers to create a one-stop Web site, ***The Psychology Place*** (www.psychplace.com). Instructors will find continuously updated teaching resources, including news, teaching tips and thought-provoking Op-Ed essays from prominant colleagues for discussion. Student resources include interactive learning activities, online experiments, a Weekly Riddle contest, carefully reviewed "Best of the Web" links, and hyperlinked *Scientific American* articles.

Our award-winning student CD-ROM, ***PsychQuest*** (by Thomas Ludwig, Hope College), provides active learning of important concepts for higher student interest and better retention. *PsychQuest* contains eight modules, each exploring a high-interest topic:

- depth perception in sports,
- psychoactive drugs,
- memory,
- weight regulation,
- depression,
- chronic stress,
- stereotyping, and
- mate selection.

PsychQuest is an interactive tool that allows students to explore various psychological research topics, participate in experiments and simulations, quiz themselves on content, and link to its World Wide Web component for additional information. Each module is designed to foster critical thinking and stimulate interest in key issues in psychology by relating psychological concepts to real-world issues.

Successful SQ3R Study Aids

1. *Exploring Psychology's complete system of learning aids includes numbered "preview questions," which appear in this format throughout the book.*

In the margins of this book, students will find interesting and informative review notes and quotes from researchers and others that will encourage them to be active learners and apply what they are learning.

Exploring Psychology has retained its popular system of study aids, integrated into an SQ3R structure that augments the narrative without disrupting it. Each chapter opens with a chapter outline that enables students to quickly *survey* its major topics. Numbered preview *questions* at the start of each new major topic define the learning objectives that will guide students as they *read. Rehearse It* quizzes at the end of each major section will stimulate students to rehearse what they have learned (see sample at right from Chapter 1). These test items offer a novel combination of crisp review of key ideas and practice with the multiple-choice test format. The chapter-ending *Review* answers each of the numbered preview questions and is followed by answers for each of the Rehearse It multiple-choice questions. All key terms are defined in the margins for ready reference while students are being introduced to the new term in the narrative (see sample at left). Key terms are also boldfaced in the Review section at the end of the chapter. Periodic "Thinking Critically," "Close-Up," and "Psychology Applied" boxes encourage development of critical thinking skills as well as application of the new concepts. A "Critical Thinking Exercise" at the end of each chapter allows practice of new skills as well as review of important chapter topics. The "Tips For Studying Psychology" section at the end of Chapter 1 explains the SQ3R-based system of study aids, suggesting how students can survey, question, read, rehearse, and review the material for maximum retention.

key terms Look for complete definitions of each important term in the margin near its introduction in the narrative.

REHEARSE IT!*

1. Psychology is the science of behavior and mental processes. The perspective in psychology that focuses on how behavior and thought differ from situation to situation and from culture to culture is the
   a. cognitive perspective.
   b. behavioral perspective.
   c. social-cultural perspective.
   d. neuroscience perspective.

2. In the history of psychology, one of the main debates has been over the nature-nurture issue. Nature is to nurture as
   a. personality is to intelligence.
   b. biology is to experience.
   c. intelligence is to biology.
   d. psychological traits are to behaviors.

3. The behavioral perspective in psychology emphasizes observable responses and how they are acquired and modified. A behavioral psychologist would be most likely to study
   a. the effect of school uniforms on classroom behaviors.
   b. the hidden meaning in children's themes and drawings.
   c. the age at which children can learn algebra.
   d. whether certain mathematical abilities appear to be inherited.

4. A psychologist who treats emotionally troubled adolescents at the local mental health agency is most likely to be a/an
   a. research psychologist.
   b. psychiatrist.
   c. industrial/organizational psychologist.
   d. clinical psychologist.

5. A psychologist who conducts basic research to expand psychology's knowledge base would be most likely to
   a. design a computer screen with limited glare and assess the effect on computer operators' eyes after a day's work.
   b. treat older people who are overcome by depression.
   c. observe 3- and 6-year-old children solving puzzles and analyze differences in their abilities.
   d. interview children with behavioral problems and suggest treatments.

*You can use these Rehearse It questions to gauge whether you are ready for the next section. The answers are at the end of the chapter.

Goals for the Fourth Edition

Throughout this revision, I have steadfastly followed eight principles:

1. ***To exemplify the process of inquiry*** I strive to show students not just the outcome of research, but how the research process works. Throughout, the book tries to excite readers' curiosity. It invites them to imagine themselves as participants in classic experiments. Several chapters introduce research stories as mysteries that progressively unravel as one clue after another falls into place. (See, for example, the historical story of research on the brain's processing of language—page 60.)
2. ***To teach critical thinking*** By presenting research as intellectual detective work, I exemplify an inquiring, analytical mind-set. Whether students are studying development, cognition, or statistics, they will become involved in, and see the rewards of, critical reasoning. Moreover, they will discover how an empirical approach can help them evaluate competing ideas and claims for highly publicized phenomena—ranging from subliminal persuasion, ESP, and facilitated communication to astrology, basketball streak-shooting, and repressed and recovered memories.
3. ***To put facts in the service of concepts*** My intention is not to fill students' intellectual file drawers with facts, but to reveal psychology's major concepts—to teach students how to think and to offer psychological ideas worth thinking about. In each chapter I place emphasis on those concepts I hope students will carry with them long after they complete the course. Always, I try to follow Albert Einstein's dictum: "Everything should be made as simple as possible, but not simpler."

4. ***To be as up-to-date as possible*** Few things dampen students' interest as quickly as the sense that they are reading stale news. While retaining psychology's classic studies and concepts, I also present the discipline's most important recent developments. Fully 24 percent of the references in this edition are dated 1994 to 1998.
5. ***To integrate principles and applications*** Throughout—by means of anecdotes, case histories, and the posing of hypothetical situations—I relate the findings of basic research to their applications and implications. Where psychology can illuminate pressing human issues—be they racism and sexism, health and happiness, or violence and war—I have not hesitated to shine its light.
6. ***To enhance comprehension by providing continuity*** Many chapters have a significant issue or theme that links subtopics, forming a thread that ties the chapter together. Chapter 6, "Learning" conveys the idea that bold thinkers can serve as intellectual pioneers. Chapter 8, "Thinking, Language, and Intelligence," raises the issue of human rationality and irrationality. Chapter 12, "Psychological Disorders," conveys empathy for, and understanding of, troubled lives. "The uniformity of a work," observed Edward Gibbon, "denotes the hand of a single artist." Because the book has a single author, other threads, such as behavior genetics and cultural diversity, weave throughout the whole book, and students hear a consistent voice.
7. ***To reinforce learning at every step*** Everyday examples and rhetorical questions encourage students to process the material actively. Concepts presented earlier are frequently applied, and thereby reinforced, in later chapters. For instance, in Chapter 4, "Sensation and Perception," students learn that much of our information processing occurs *outside* of our conscious awareness. Ensuing chapters reinforce this concept. The SQ3R system of pedagogical aids augments learning without interrupting the text narrative. A marginal glossary helps students master important terminology. Major sections begin with numbered preview questions and end with Rehearse It sections for self-testing on key concepts. End-of-chapter reviews repeat the preview questions and answer them, incorporating all key terms from that section for further review.
8. ***To convey respect for human unity and diversity*** Time and again, readers will see evidence of our human kinship—our shared biological heritage, our common mechanisms of seeing and learning, hungering and feeling, loving and hating. They will also better understand the dimensions of our diversity—our *individual* diversity in development and aptitudes, temperament and personality, and disorder and health; and our *cultural* diversity in attitudes and expressive styles, child-rearing and care for the elderly, and life priorities.

The Supplements Package

Exploring Psychology is accompanied by widely acclaimed materials to enhance teaching and learning. Please see pages xvi–xviii, "New Electronic Teaching and Learning Opportunities," for a description of our new ***MyersPlus for Exploring Psychology*** CD-ROM/Web application, ***The Psychology Place*** Web site, and our new ***PsychQuest*** student CD-ROM.

For students who desire additional help mastering the text, there is Richard O. Straub's (University of Michigan, Dearborn) ***Study Guide***. Each chapter follows the text's SQ3R format to guide students at each step of their study. For each section of the text chapter, an explanation is provided of the idioms and other phrases potentially unfamiliar to students for whom

English is a second language. Several new Internet activities, called "Web Sightings," have been included, along with new crossword puzzles and pedagogically effective new fill-in-the-blank flow charts. The study guide is also computerized in a highly interactive program for use in the Windows or Macintosh formats.

The ***Instructor's Resources***, created by Martin Bolt (Calvin College) for *Exploring Psychology*, has been hailed as the finest set of psychology teaching resources ever assembled. With 20 percent new items in this edition, it features dozens of ready-to-use demonstration handouts and video and film suggestions, along with learning objectives, lecture/discussion ideas, student projects, and classroom exercises, all of which incorporate numerous Internet exercises. Martin Bolt's ***Lecture Guides***, which come in both printed and easily modifiable WordPerfect formats, offer instructors an additional resource for lecture preparation. A complete set of ***transparency images***, from this book and other sources, is also available.

PsychSim 4, developed by Thomas Ludwig (Hope College), brings some of psychology's most important concepts and methods to life. *PsychSim 4* (available on CD-ROM or floppies) contains 19 programs for use in the Windows and Macintosh formats. Some simulations engage the student as experimenter—conditioning a rat, electrically probing the hypothalamus, or working in a sleep lab. Others engage the student as subject—responding to tests of memory or visual illusions, or interpreting facial expressions. Still others provide a dynamic tutorial/demonstration of, say, hemispheric processing or cognitive development principles. Student worksheets are provided. *PsychSim 4* is significantly enhanced over the earlier, award-winning *PsychSim*.

The ***Test Banks***, by John Brink (Calvin College), provide over 4000 multiple-choice questions, plus essay questions. Each question is keyed to a learning objective, page-referenced to the textbook, and rated in level of difficulty. Optional questions are also included for the *PsychQuest* and *PsychSim* programs, and for *The Brain* and *The Mind* modules (see below). User-friendly computerized test generation is also available.

Our ***Psychology Videodisc*** contains 26 brief, exciting video clips and animated segments, as well as hundreds of still images. This videodisc is accompanied by an extensive *Instructor's Guide*, by Martin Bolt and Richard O. Straub, complete with bar codes, descriptions of each item and suggestions for how to incorporate the material into your lecture, and a subject index that references and cross-references all items by topic. Thomas Ludwig's accompanying presentation software package, which includes a barcode generator, is also available for use on IBM-PC or Macintosh computers.

We also have available a *Study Guide* and a *Faculty Guide* designed for use with this text and with the *Discovering Psychology* telecourse, narrated by Philip Zimbardo and produced by the Annenberg/CPB Project.

In addition, Worth Publishers has produced **38 video modules from *The Mind* series**, in association with WNET. These modules were edited by Frank J. Vattano (Colorado State University) with the consultation of Charles Brewer (Furman University) and myself. Rather than displace the instructor, as do longer films, these brief clips (which can be dubbed onto individual cassettes) dramatically enhance and illustrate lectures. They do so in ways that written and spoken words cannot—by introducing students to a split-brain patient being tested, a sleeping subject being monitored in a lab, a patient suffering the ravages of schizophrenia, and so forth. In addition to the 38 modules on videocassettes, Worth Publishers also offers ***The Mind laser disc***, with 14 highlights from *The Mind* modules. The laser disc is accompanied by a bar-coded *Faculty Guide*.

The new **Second Edition of *The Brain* teaching modules** by Frank J. Vattano, Thomas L. Bennet, and Michelle Butler (all of Colorado State University) is also available with this text. Accompanied by a *Faculty Guide* keyed specifically to the chapters in this book, these video modules effectively capture students' interest and vividly illustrate the important role of biological processes in human behavior. There are 11 new and 12 significantly updated modules in addition to nine from the original series.

Worth Publishers has created the **Scientific American Frontiers Video Collection for Introductory Psychology**. These 25 video segments, each 8 to 25 minutes long, are another excellent resource for stimulating class discussion and interest on a variety of topics.

In Appreciation

If it is true that "whoever walks with the wise becomes wise" then I am wiser for all the wisdom and advice received from colleagues. With the aid of several hundred consultants and reviewers over the last decade, this has become a better, more accurate book than one author alone (this author, at least) could write. My indebtedness continues to each of the teacher-scholars whose influence I acknowledged in the three previous editions.

My gratitude now extends to the colleagues who contributed criticism, corrections, and creative ideas to this new edition. For their expertise and encouragement, I thank the following reviewers:

David Baskind, *Delta College*

Linda Brunton, *Columbia State Community College*

Terry Darling, *Spring Arbor College*

Timothy K. Daugherty, *Valparaiso University*

George Demakis, *Elmhurst College*

Douglas N. Dunham, *Northwest Missouri State University*

Paul Fenton, *University of Wisconsin, Stout*

Peter Flynn, *Northern Essex Community College*

Sam Gaft, *Macomb Community College*

Patrick M. Ghezzi, *University of Nevada, Reno*

Vernon Haynes, *Youngstown State University*

Robert D. Johnson, Jr., *Pierce College*

Robert Kraft, *Otterbein College*

Carole Ann Pierce, *Austin Community College*

Holly R. Straub, *University of South Dakota*

Patrick S. Williams, *University of Houston, Downtown*

Jan Yeaman, *Spring Arbor College*

Charles Brewer (Furman University) enhanced this book with meticulous critiques, probing questions, and spirit-sustaining encouragement through its early editions, and has continued to help define priorities as a special consultant.

At Worth Publishers a host of people played key roles in creating this fourth edition. Christine Brune, chief editor for the first three editions and associate editor for this fourth edition, is a wonder worker. She offers just the right mix of encouragement, gentle admonition, attention to detail, and passion for excellence. An author could not ask for more. But for this fourth edition I have had more—the additional support of Betty Probert. Her wise and sensitive editing helped us take our game to a new level. Betty also ably edited and produced the enormous supplements package.

Others at Worth also played essential roles. Worth president Susan Driscoll, managing editor Suzanne Thibodeau, and psychology executive editor Catherine Woods helped construct and execute the plan for this new edition and its teaching and learning supplements. Copyeditor Nancy Fleming sensitively finetuned the final manuscript. Production editors Elizabeth Geller and Laura Rubin effectively guided the transformation of manuscript into book. The hard work of Project Director Penny Bice, Production Manager Sarah Segal, Supplements Production Manager Stacey Alexander, and others made for a smooth and timely production process. And psychology marketing manager Kate Steinbacher has led the effort to make this new edition available to psychology instructors. To all of them I am deeply grateful for an extraordinary effort.

At Hope College the supporting team members for this edition included Gretchen Rumohr-Voskuil, who researched countless bits of information, proofed hundreds of pages, and prepared the name index. With good cheer, Kathy Adamski served ably as administrative assistant. Typesetters Phyllis and Richard Vandervelde met or exceeded all deadlines, often by working into the wee hours to enter or revise every one of the more than 300,000 words, and finally to code them for electronic delivery.

Again, I gratefully acknowledge the influence of my writing coach, poet Jack Ridl, whose influence lingers in the voice you will be hearing in the pages that follow. He more than anyone cultivated my delight in dancing with the language and taught me to approach writing as a craft that shades into art.

After hearing countless dozens of people say that this book's supplements have taken their teaching to a new level, I reflect on how fortunate I am to be a part of a team on which everyone has produced on-time work marked by the highest professional standards. For their remarkable talents, their dedication, and their friendship, I thank Martin Bolt, John Brink, Thomas Ludwig, and Richard Straub. Rick Straub also authored the critical thinking exercises that appear at the end of each chapter.

Finally, my gratitude extends to the students and instructors who have written to offer suggestions, or just an encouraging word. It is for them, and those about to begin their study of psychology, that I have done my best to introduce the field I love.

Those who paint the Golden Gate Bridge never finish. So it is with this book. The ink is barely dry before one begins envisioning the next edition. By the time you read this, I will be gathering information for the fifth edition. Your input will again influence how this book continues to evolve. So, please, do share your thoughts.

David Myers

Hope College
Holland, Michigan 49422-9000
USA
E-mail: myers@hope.edu

CHAPTER
1

Introduction: Thinking Critically With Psychology

Hoping to satisfy their curiosity about people and to remedy their woes, millions of people turn to "psychology." They listen to talk shows featuring over-the-air counseling, read magazine columns on harnessing psychic powers, attend seminars on how to stop smoking through hypnosis, and browse self-help books on the meaning of dreams, the secrets of ecstatic love, and the roots of personal happiness.

Others, intrigued by claims of psychological truth, wonder: Do mothers and infants bond in the first hours after birth? Should we trust memories of child sexual abuse "recovered" in adulthood—and prosecute the alleged predators? Are children whose parents encourage independence more driven to achieve? Does handwriting give clues to personality? Does psychotherapy help?

For these questioners, as for most people whose exposure to psychology comes from popular books, magazines, and TV, psychologists analyze personality, offer counseling, and dispense child-rearing advice.

Do they? Yes, and much more. Consider some of psychology's questions, questions that from time to time you may wonder about:

> Have you ever found yourself reacting to something just as one of your parents would—perhaps in a way you vowed you never would—and then wondered how much of your personality you inherited? To what degree are you really like your mother or your father? *To what extent is your parents' influence transmitted through their genes? To what extent through the environment they gave you?*
>
> Have you ever played peekaboo with a 6-month-old infant and wondered why the baby finds the game so delightful? The baby reacts as though, when you momentarily move behind a door, you actually disappear—only to reappear later out of thin air. *What do babies actually perceive and think?*
>
> Have you ever awakened from a nightmare and, with a wave of relief, wondered why we have such crazy dreams? *How often, and why, do we dream?*
>
> Have you ever wondered what makes for school and work success? Are some people just born smarter? *Does brute intelligence explain why some people get richer, think more creatively, or relate more sensitively?*
>
> Do you ever get depressed or anxious and wonder whether you'll ever feel "normal"? *What triggers our bad moods—and our good ones?*
>
> Have you ever worried about how to act among people of a different culture, race, or sex? *In what ways are we alike as members of the human family? How do we differ?*

Such questions provide grist for psychology's mill, for psychology is a science that seeks to answer all sorts of questions about us all: how we think, feel, and act.

A smile is a smile the world around
Throughout this book, you will see examples of our cultural and gender diversity as well as the similarities that define our shared human nature. Men and women in different cultures show differences in when and how often they smile, but a smile *means* the same thing anywhere in the world.

What Is Psychology?

Psychology's Roots

1. *How did the science of psychology develop?*[1]

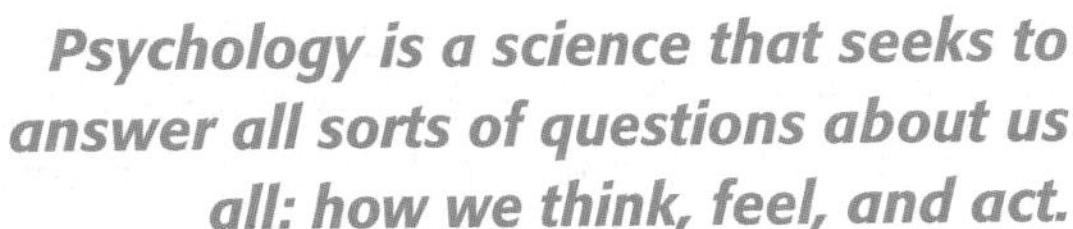

Psychology is a science that seeks to answer all sorts of questions about us all: how we think, feel, and act.

To be human is to be curious about ourselves and the world around us. Psychology's ancestors therefore date to the world's early writings. Before 300 B.C., the Greek naturalist and philosopher Aristotle theorized about learning and memory, motivation and emotion, perception and personality. Today we chuckle at some of his guesses, like a meal making us sleepy by causing gas and heat to collect around the source of our personality, the heart. But credit Aristotle with asking the right questions.

At the dawn of modern science in the 1600s, British philosophers adopted a down-to-earth approach to knowledge, rooted in observation. One of them, John Locke, rejected the notion of inborn ideas. At birth the mind is, he said, but a "white paper" upon which experience writes.

In 1831, an indifferent student but ardent collector of beetles, mollusks, and shells set sail on what was to prove a historic round-the-world voyage. The 22-year-old voyager was Charles Darwin, and for some time afterward, he pondered the incredible species variation he had encountered, including tortoises on one island that would differ from those on other islands of the region. His 1859 *Origin of Species* explained this diversity of life by proposing an evolutionary process. From among chance variations in organisms, he believed, nature selects those that best enable an organism to survive and reproduce in a particular environment. Darwin's big idea—"the single best idea anyone has ever had," says philosopher Daniel Dennett (1996)—is called *natural selection*, and it is still with us some 140 years later, having become an organizing principle of biology. Evolution also has become an important principle for psychology. This would surely have pleased Darwin, for he believed his theory explains not only animal structures (such as why polar bear coats are white) but also animal behaviors (such as the emotional expressions associated with lust and rage).

Thinking about thinking continued to evolve until the birth of psychology as we know it, on a December day in 1879. In a small room on the third floor of a shabby building at Germany's University of Leipzig, two young men were helping a long-

[1]A preview question will appear at the beginning of each major section of a chapter. Search actively for the answer to the question as you read through the section. Answers are available in the form of a numbered chapter review at the end of the chapter.

psychology the science of behavior and mental processes.

Information sources are cited in parentheses, with name and date, then provided fully in the References section at the book's end.

faced, austere, middle-aged professor, Wilhelm Wundt, create an experimental apparatus. Their machine measured the time lag between people's hearing a ball hit a platform and their pressing a telegraph key (Hunt, 1993). Later, they compared this to the time required for slightly more complex tasks. Wundt was seeking to measure the "atoms of the mind"—the fastest and simplest mental processes. Thus began what many consider psychology's first experiment, launching the first psychological institute, staffed by Wundt and psychology's first graduate students.

The young science of psychology thus evolved from the more established fields of biology and philosophy. Wundt was both a physiologist and a philosopher. Darwin was an English naturalist. Ivan Pavlov, who pioneered the study of learning, was a Russian physiologist. Sigmund Freud, renowned personality theorist, was an Austrian physician. Jean Piaget, this century's most influential observer of children, was a Swiss biologist. William James, author of an important 1890 psychology textbook, was an American philosopher. This list of pioneering psychologists—"Magellans of the mind," as Morton Hunt (1993) calls them—illustrates that psychology has its origins in many countries (Figure 1.1).

So what is psychology? With activities ranging from recording nerve-cell activity to psychotherapy, psychology is not easily defined. Psychology began as the science of mental life. Wundt's basic research tool became introspection—self-examination of one's own emotional states and mental processes. Wundt focused on *inner* sensations, feelings, and thoughts. Thus, until the 1920s, psychology was defined as "the science of mental life."

Psychology is less a set of findings than a way of asking and answering questions.

From the 1920s into the 1960s, American psychologists, led by flamboyant and provocative John Watson, dismissed introspection and redefined psychology as "the science of observable behavior." After all, they said, science is rooted in observation. You cannot observe a sensation, a feeling, or a thought, but you *can* observe people's *behavior* as they respond to different situations.

In the 1960s, psychology began to recapture its initial interest in mental processes through studies of how our minds process and retain information—how we perceive, think, and remember. To encompass psychology's concern both with observable behavior and with inner thoughts and feelings, **psychology** has become *the science of behavior and mental processes.*

Throughout this book, important concepts appear in bold type. As you study, you can find these terms with their definitions in a nearby margin and also at the end of the book in the Glossary section.

Let's unpack this definition. *Behavior* is anything an organism *does*—any action we can observe and record. Yelling, smiling, blinking, sweating, talking, and questionnaire-marking are all observable behaviors. *Mental processes* are the internal subjective experiences we infer from behavior—sensations, perceptions, dreams, thoughts, beliefs, and feelings.

For many psychologists, the key word in psychology's definition is *science*. Psychology, as I will emphasize throughout this book, is less a set of findings than a way of asking and answering questions. As a science, psychology aims to sift opinions and evaluate ideas with careful observation and rigorous analysis. In its quest to describe and explain nature (human nature included), psychological science welcomes hunches and plausible-sounding theories. And it puts them to the test. If a theory works—if the data support its predictions—so much the better for it. If the predictions fail, the theory gets rejected or revised.

My aim in this text, then, is not merely to report results but to show you how we play the game. How do research psychologists sift contesting opinions and ideas? And how might all of us, whether scientists or simply curious people, think smarter when describing and explaining the events of our lives?

Of course, psychology also has content: Its scientific sifting of ideas has produced a smorgasbord of concepts and findings from which we can only sample the fare. Once aware of psychology's well-researched ideas—about how body and mind connect, how a child's mind grows, how we construct our perceptions, how we remember (and misremember) our experiences, how people across the world differ (and are alike)—your mind may never again be quite the same.

"Once expanded to the dimensions of a larger idea, [the mind] never returns to its original size."

Jurist Oliver Wendell Holmes
1841–1935

Figure 1.1 A timeline of psychology's pioneers, 1879–1913

Hermann Ebbinghaus in Germany reports the first experiments on memory (1885).

Alfred Binet (shown) and **Theodore Simon** devise the first intelligence test for use with Parisian schoolchildren (1905).

Margaret Floy Washburn, the first woman to receive a Ph.D. in psychology, synthesizes research on animal behavior in *The Animal Mind* (1008).

Wilhelm Wundt establishes the first psychology laboratory at the University of Leipzig, Germany (1879).

Edward L. Thorndike in the United States conducts the first experiments on animal learning (1898).

American Psychological Association is founded (1892).

1875 1880 1885 1890 1895 1900 1905 1910 1915

G. Stanley Hall, a student of Wundt's, establishes the first American psychology laboratory at Johns Hopkins University (1883).

Sigmund Freud in Austria introduces his psychoanalytic theory in *The Interpretation of Dreams* (1900).

John B. Watson in the United States champions psychology as the science of behavior (1913).

William James publishes the widely used *Principles of Psychology* in the United States (1890).

Mary Whiton Calkins creates paired-associates technique for studying memory; becomes president of American Psychological Association (1905).

Ivan Pavlov in Russia begins to publish his classic studies of animal learning (1906).

nature-nurture issue the longstanding controversy over the relative contributions of genes and experience to the development of psychological traits and behaviors.

Psychology's Perspectives

2. *What theoretical perspectives do psychologists take?*

During its short history, psychology has wrestled with some issues that will reappear throughout this book. One such issue concerns the relative contributions of biology and experience. Today's psychologists explore this **nature-nurture** debate by asking, for example:

- Are intelligence, personality, obesity, and psychological disorders influenced more by heredity or by environment?
- Is children's grammar innate or shaped by experience?
- Are eating and sexual behavior more "pushed" by inner biology or "pulled" by external incentives?
- Is depression a brain disorder or a thought disorder?
- How are humans alike (thanks to their common biology) and different (thanks to their differing cultures)?
- Are gender differences biologically predisposed or socially constructed?

Like peas in a pod Because identical twins have the same genes, they are ideal participants in studies designed to shed light on hereditary and environmental influences on temperament, intelligence, and other traits. Studies of identical and fraternal twins provide a rich array of findings—described in later chapters—that underscore the importance of both nature and nurture.

Over and over again we will see the nature-nurture tension dissolve: Nurture works on what nature endows. Unlike reptiles, our species is biologically endowed with an enormous capacity to learn and adapt. Moreover, every psychological event (every thought, every emotion) is simultaneously a biological event. Thus depression can be *both* a thought disorder and a brain disorder.

Psychologists' theoretical perspectives (Table 1.1) influence not only whether they emphasize nature or nurture but also what sorts of questions they ask. Take an emotion such as anger.

Table 1.1 Psychology's Current Perspectives

Perspective	Focus	Sample Questions
Neuroscience	How the body and brain create emotions, memories, and sensory experiences	How are messages transmitted within the body? How is blood chemistry linked with moods and motives?
Evolutionary	How natural selection favors traits that promote the perpetuation of one's genes	How does evolution influence behavior tendencies?
Behavior genetics	How much our genes, and our environment, influence our individual differences	To what extent are psychological traits such as intelligence, personality, sexual orientation, and depression attributable to our genes? To our environment?
Behavioral	How we learn observable responses	How do we learn to fear particular objects or situations? What is the most effective way to alter our behavior, say, to lose weight or stop smoking?
Cognitive	How we process, store, and retrieve information	How do we use information in remembering? Reasoning? Solving problems?
Social-cultural	How behavior and thinking vary across situations and cultures	How are we—as Africans, Asians, Australians, or North Americans—alike as members of one human family? As products of different environmental contexts, how do we differ?

basic research pure science that aims to increase the scientific knowledge base.

applied research scientific study that aims to solve practical problems.

clinical psychology a branch of psychology that studies, assesses, and treats people with psychological disorders.

psychiatry a branch of medicine dealing with psychological disorders; practiced by physicians who sometimes provide medical (for example, drug) treatments as well as psychological therapy.

Someone working from a *neuroscience perspective* might study the brain circuits that trigger the physical states of being "red in the face" and "hot under the collar."

Someone working from an *evolutionary perspective* might analyze how anger has facilitated the survival of one's genes.

Someone working from a *behavior genetics perspective* might study how heredity and experience influence our individual differences in temperament.

Someone working from a *behavioral perspective* might study the facial expressions and body gestures that accompany anger, or might attempt to determine which external stimuli result in angry responses or aggressive acts.

Someone working from a *cognitive perspective* might study how our interpretation of a situation affects our anger and how our anger affects our thinking.

Someone working from a *social-cultural perspective* might explore which situations produce the most anger and how expressions of anger vary across cultural contexts.

Such perspectives needn't contradict one another. Rather, they are complementary outlooks on the same biological state. It's like explaining why grizzly bears hibernate. Is it because their inner physiology drives them to do so? Because cold environments hinder food gathering during winter? Both perspectives are useful, and they are complementary because "everything is related to everything else" (Brewer, 1996).

Although psychology's perspectives can shed light on many issues, we need to keep in mind psychology's limits. Don't expect psychology to answer the ultimate questions posed by Russian novelist Leo Tolstoy (1904): "Why should I live? Why should I do anything? Is there in life any purpose which the inevitable death that awaits me does not undo and destroy?" Instead, expect that psychology will help you understand why people think, feel, and act as they do. Then you should find the study of psychology both fascinating and useful.

Psychology's Subfields

3. *What are psychology's specialized subfields?*

Picturing a chemist at work, you probably envision a white-coated scientist surrounded by glassware and high-tech equipment. Picture a psychologist at work and you would be right to envision

- a white-coated scientist probing a rat's brain.
- an intelligence researcher measuring how quickly an infant becomes bored with (looks away from) a familiar picture.
- an executive proposing a new "healthy life-styles" employee-training program.
- someone at a computer keyboard, analyzing data on whether adopted teens have temperaments more like their adoptive or biological parents.
- a traveler en route to collecting data on human values and behaviors in different cultures.
- a therapist listening carefully to a client's depressed thoughts.

Drawing by Handelsman; ©1986 The New Yorker Magazine, Inc.

"I'm a social scientist, Michael. That means I can't explain electricity or anything like that, but if you ever want to know about people I'm your man."

The cluster of subfields that we call psychology has less unity than most other sciences. But there is a payoff: Psychology is a meeting ground for different disciplines and is thus a perfect home for those with wide-ranging interests. In their diverse activities, from biological experimentation to cultural comparisons, psychologists share a common quest: describing and explaining behavior and the mental processes that underlie it.

Psychology: A science and a profession In their laboratories and consulting rooms, psychologists study and treat a wide range of human conditions. Here you see a psychologist, testing a child, a laboratory experiment designed to test social judgment, and a face-to-face encounter typical of psychotherapy.

Some psychologists conduct **basic research** that builds psychology's knowledge base. In the pages that follow we will meet a wide variety of such researchers: *biological psychologists* exploring the links between brain and mind; *developmental psychologists* studying our changing abilities from womb to tomb; *personality psychologists* investigating our inner traits.

Other psychologists conduct **applied research** that tackles practical problems. For example, *industrial/organizational psychologists* study and advise on behavior in the workplace. They use psychology's concepts and methods to help organizations and companies select and train their employees, boost morale and productivity, and design products and implement systems and assess people's responses to them.

Although most psychology texts focus on the basic research of psychological science, psychology is also a helping profession devoted to such practical issues as how to have a happy marriage, how to overcome anxiety or depression, and how to raise thriving children. **Clinical psychologists** study, assess, and treat troubled people. After graduate school training, they administer and interpret tests, provide psychotherapy, manage mental health programs, and conduct research. By contrast, **psychiatrists**, who also often provide psychotherapy, are medical doctors licensed to prescribe drugs and otherwise treat physical causes of psychological disorders. In both of these mental health professions, some practitioners are influenced by Sigmund Freud's *psychoanalytic perspective*, which saw problems arising from unconscious desires, repressed traumas, or unresolved childhood conflicts.

Today, psychology's researchers and students, like its historic pioneers, are citizens of many lands. Worldwide, the number of psychologists—now well over 500,000—has doubled since 1980 (Rosenzweig, 1992). Sixty-three nations, from Argentina to Zimbabwe, participate in the International Union of Scientific Psychology (Pawlik & d'Ydewalle, 1996).

Although men still outnumber women in psychology, the balance is shifting. In Britain, 51 percent of recent doctorates have gone to women, as have 61 percent in the United States (Cantor, 1995; Colley, 1995; NRC, 1995). In both countries, women earn more than 7 in 10 undergraduate psychology degrees. In Canada, 69 percent of students receiving professional training in psychology are women, as are 70 percent in The Netherlands, 73 percent in Denmark, and 89 percent in Spain (Adair & others, 1996; Foltved, 1996; Sanchez & others, 1996; van Drunen, 1996). What a change from the turn of the century, when Harvard University denied Mary Whiton Calkins the Ph.D. she had earned, because she was a woman. (Calkins refused Harvard's offer of a doctorate from Radcliffe College, its undergraduate sister school for women, and she went on to become the first woman to be elected president of the American Psychological Association.)

I see you! A *biological psychologist* might view this child's delighted response as evidence of brain maturation. A *cognitive psychologist* might see it as a demonstration of the baby's growing knowledge of his surroundings. For a *cross-cultural psychologist*, the role of grandparents in different societies might be the issue of interest.

REHEARSE IT!

1. Psychology is the science of behavior and mental processes. The perspective in psychology that focuses on how behavior and thought differ from situation to situation and from culture to culture is the
   - **a.** cognitive perspective.
   - **b.** behavioral perspective.
   - **c.** social-cultural perspective.
   - **d.** neuroscience perspective.
2. In the history of psychology, one of the main debates has been over the nature-nurture issue. Nature is to nurture as
   - **a.** personality is to intelligence.
   - **b.** biology is to experience.
   - **c.** intelligence is to biology.
   - **d.** psychological traits are to behaviors.
3. The behavioral perspective in psychology emphasizes observable responses and how they are acquired and modified. A behavioral psychologist would be most likely to study
   - **a.** the effect of school uniforms on classroom behaviors.
   - **b.** the hidden meaning in children's themes and drawings.
   - **c.** the age at which children can learn algebra.
   - **d.** whether certain mathematical abilities appear to be inherited.
4. A psychologist who treats emotionally troubled adolescents at the local mental health agency is most likely to be a/an
   - **a.** research psychologist.
   - **b.** psychiatrist.
   - **c.** industrial/organizational psychologist.
   - **d.** clinical psychologist.
5. A psychologist who conducts basic research to expand psychology's knowledge base would be most likely to
   - **a.** design a computer screen with limited glare and assess the effect on computer operators' eyes after a day's work.
   - **b.** treat older people who are overcome by depression.
   - **c.** observe 3- and 6-year-old children solving puzzles and analyze differences in their abilities.
   - **d.** interview children with behavioral problems and suggest treatments.

You can use these Rehearse It questions to gauge whether you are ready for the next section. The answers are at the end of the chapter.

Why Do Psychology?

"What good fortune for those in power that people do not think."

Adolf Hitler
1889–1945

Although in some ways we outsmart the smartest computers, our intuition often goes awry. To err is human. Enter psychological science. With its procedures for gathering and sifting evidence, science restrains error. As we familiarize ourselves with its strategies and incorporate its underlying principles into our daily thinking, we can think smarter. *Psychologists use the science of behavior and mental processes to better understand why people think, feel, and act as they do.*

The Scientific Attitude

4. *What attitudes characterize scientific inquiry?*

Underlying all science is a hard-headed curiosity, a passion to explore and understand without fooling or being fooled. Some questions (Is there life after death?) are beyond science. To answer them either way requires a leap of faith. With many other ideas, the proof is in the pudding. No matter how sensible or crazy-sounding an idea, the hard-headed question is, Does it work? When put to the test, can its predictions be confirmed?

This scientific approach has a long history. How to evaluate a self-proclaimed prophet? Moses had an answer: Put the prophet to the test. If the predicted event "does not take place or prove true," then so much the worse for the prophet (Deuteronomy 18:22). Magician James Randi uses Moses' approach when testing those claiming to see auras around people's bodies:

> **Randi:** *Do you see an aura around my head?*
> **Aura-seer:** *Yes, indeed.*
> **Randi:** *Can you still see the aura if I put this magazine in front of my face?*
> **Aura-seer:** *Of course.*
> **Randi:** *Then if I were to step behind a wall barely taller than I am, you could determine my location from the aura visible above my head, right?*

Randi tells me that no aura-seer has yet agreed to take this simple test.

The Amazing Randi The magician James Randi, shown here with the "Alexander the Man Who Knows" machine, is an exemplar of skepticism. He has tested and effectively debunked a variety of psychic phenomena.

When subjected to such scrutiny, crazy-sounding ideas sometimes find support. More often, it relegates crazy-sounding ideas to the mountain of forgotten claims of perpetual motion machines, miracle cancer cures, and out-of-body travels into centuries past. To sift reality from fantasy, sense from nonsense, therefore requires a scientific attitude: being skeptical but not cynical, humbly open but not gullible.

As scientists, psychologists aim to approach the world of behavior with a curious *skepticism*. They persistently ask two questions: What do you mean? and How do you know? Consider some familiar claims. Can a theater owner make you hungry by flashing an imperceptibly brief message—EAT POPCORN? Do lie detectors tell the truth? Can astrologers analyze your character and predict your future based on the position of the planets at your birth? As you will see in the chapters that follow, we can test all such claims. In the arena of competing ideas, skeptical testing can reveal which ones best match the facts. "To believe with certainty," says a Polish proverb, "we must begin by doubting."

"A skeptic is one who is willing to question any truth claim, asking for clarity in definition, consistency in logic, and adequacy of evidence."

Philosopher Paul Kurtz
The Skeptical Inquirer
1994

Putting a scientific attitude into practice also requires *humility* because it means that we may have to reject our own ideas. In the last analysis, what matters is not my opinion or yours but whatever truths nature reveals in response to our questioning. If animals or people don't behave as our ideas predict, then so much the worse for our ideas. As Agatha Christie's Miss Marple explained, "It wasn't what I expected. But facts are facts, and if one is proved to be wrong, one must just be humble about it and start again." This is the humble attitude expressed in one of psychology's early mottos: "The rat is always right."

Historians of science tell us that these attitudes of curious skepticism and open-minded humility helped make modern science possible. Many of its founders were people whose religious convictions made them humble before nature and skeptical of any human authority (Hooykaas, 1972; Merton, 1938). Of course, scientists, like anyone else, can have big egos and may cling stubbornly to their preconceptions. We all view nature through the spectacles of our preconceived ideas. Still, the ideal that unifies psychologists with all scientists is the skeptical yet humble scrutiny of competing ideas.

"My deeply held belief is that if a god anything like the traditional sort exists, our curiosity and intelligence are provided by such a god. We would be unappreciative of those gifts . . . if we suppressed our passion to explore the universe and ourselves."

Carl Sagan
Broca's Brain
1979

Critical Thinking

Skepticism and humility, aided by scientific principles for sifting reality from illusion, prepare us to think smarter. Smart thinking, called **critical thinking**, examines assumptions, discerns hidden values, evaluates evidence, and assesses conclusions. Whether reading news reports or listening to conversation, critical thinkers ask questions. They wonder, How do they know that? What axe is this person grinding? Is the conclusion based on mere anecdote and gut feelings or on trustworthy evidence? Does the evidence justify a cause-effect conclusion? What alternative explanations are possible? Carried to an extreme, healthy skepticism can degenerate into a negative cynicism that scorns any unproven idea. But a critical attitude can also produce humility—an awareness of our own vulnerability to error and an openness to surprises and new perspectives.

Throughout this book, you will encounter Thinking Critically boxes. The first one appears on page 22. Each highlights careful thinking about some interesting or important issue.

Has psychology's own critical inquiry indeed been open to surprising findings? The answer, as ensuing chapters illustrate, is plainly yes. Believe it or not. . .

- massive losses of brain tissue early in life may have minimal long-term effects (see page 62).
- within days, newborns can recognize their mother's odor and voice (see page 82).
- on average, any two children from the same family (children reared under the same parental philosophy and in the same schools, neighborhood, and social class) have personalities nearly as different as any two children picked from the population at random (see page 72).

critical thinking thinking that does not blindly accept arguments and conclusions. Rather, it examines assumptions, discerns hidden values, evaluates evidence, and assesses conclusions.

hindsight bias the tendency to believe, after learning an outcome, that one would have foreseen it. (Also known as the *I-knew-it-all-along phenomenon.*)

- prolonged stress hinders the body's disease-fighting immune system, making people more vulnerable to physical illness (see page 374).
- diverse groups—men and women, old and young, rich and working class, those with disabilities and without—report roughly comparable levels of personal happiness (see page 361).
- electroconvulsive ("shock") therapy is often a very effective treatment for severe depression (see page 486).

And has critical inquiry convincingly debunked popular presumptions? The answer, as ensuing chapters also illustrate, is again yes. The available evidence *contradicts* beliefs that . . .

- men in their early forties, as part of their passage to middle adulthood, undergo a traumatic midlife crisis (see page 115).
- most mothers are depressed for a time after their children grow up and leave home (see page 118).
- some people seldom dream; sleepwalkers are acting out their dreams; sleeptalkers are verbalizing their dreams (see Chapter 5).
- our past experiences are all recorded in our brains; with brain stimulation or hypnosis, one can "play the tape" and relive long-buried or repressed memories (see Chapter 7).
- most people suffer from unrealistically low self-esteem (see page 410).
- opposites attract (see Chapter 14).

As you will see, careful research disputes all these popular beliefs.

What About Intuition and Common Sense?

5. ***What leads people to overestimate the value of common sense and underestimate the usefulness of psychological science?***

Skeptical inquiry and humility before nature are well and good for science. But don't intuition and plain common sense suffice for everyday life? In sifting reality from illusion, do we need the scientific attitude that drives critical thinking?

Some doubt it. They say psychology merely documents what people already know and dresses it in jargon: "So what else is new—you get paid for using fancy methods to prove what my grandmother knew?"

Others scorn a scientific approach because of their faith in human intuition. Advocates of "intuitive management" urge us to tune into our hunches. When hiring, firing, and investing, we should distrust statistical predictors and listen to our premonitions. We should follow *Star Wars'* Luke Skywalker by trusting the force within.

Actually, notes writer Madeline L'Engle, "The naked intellect is an extraordinarily inaccurate instrument." Intuition and common sense sometimes blunder. Like after-the-fact pundits, we sometimes err in presuming we could have foreseen what we know happened.

The limits of intuition Personnel interviewers tend to be overconfident of their gut feelings about job applicants. Their confidence stems partly from their recalling cases where their favorable impression proved right, and from their ignorance about rejected applicants who succeeded elsewhere.

Did We Know It All Along? The Hindsight Bias

Psychologists Paul Slovic and Baruch Fischhoff (1977) and Gordon Wood (1979) have shown how scientific results and historical happenings can indeed *seem* like obvious common sense. They discovered that events that don't seem obvious beforehand do seem so in hindsight. A curious thing happens once

people learn the outcome of an experiment or a historical episode: It suddenly seems less surprising to them than to people asked to guess the outcome. Finding out that something has happened makes it seem inevitable. After the next stock market swing, many investment gurus will say, "The market was obviously overdue for a correction." Psychologists call this 20/20 hindsight vision the **hindsight bias**, also known as the *I-knew-it-all-along phenomenon*.

This phenomenon is easy to demonstrate by giving half the members of a group some purported psychological finding and the other half an opposite result. For example, if you were in the first group, you might read, "Psychologists have found that separation weakens romantic attraction. As the saying goes, 'Out of sight, out of mind.'" Could you imagine why this might be true? Most people can, and nearly all will then regard the finding as unsurprising.

But what if you had read the opposite: "Psychologists have found that separation strengthens romantic attraction. As the saying goes, 'Absence makes the heart grow fonder.'" People given this result can also easily explain it, and they overwhelmingly see it as unsurprising common sense. Obviously, when both a supposed finding and its opposite seem like common sense, there is a problem.

"Life is lived forwards, but understood backwards."

Søren Kierkegaard
1813–1855

Consider hindsight bias in a medical context. To doctors given case information plus an autopsy report, a cause of death may seem obvious—something they easily could have foreseen, knowing the symptoms. But it is not so obvious to doctors told the same symptoms without the autopsy report (Dawson & others, 1988).

We often experience hindsight bias while looking back on history. In contrast to other people's preelection uncertainty, people questioned *after* a presidential election exude confidence that they could have told you how it would turn out (Powell, 1988). Similarly, many people who had expected O. J. Simpson's first jury to declare him guilty found on reflection that the announced verdict was unsurprising (Bryant & Brockway, in press). How easy it is to seem astute when drawing the bull's eye after the arrow has struck.

***Common sense describes what* has happened *more easily than it predicts what* will happen.**

From our vantage point, it may in hindsight seem obvious that Eastern European countries would exchange communism for democracy. But it wasn't obvious to United Nations ambassador Jeanne Kirkpatrick in 1980 when she warned, "The history of this century provides no grounds for expecting that radical totalitarian regimes will transform themselves." The point is *not* that common sense is usually wrong but that it is often after-the-fact reasoning. Common sense describes what *has happened* more easily than it predicts what *will happen*. As Dr. Watson said to Sherlock Holmes, "Anything seems commonplace, once explained."

Nevertheless, Grandmother is often right—as baseball great Yogi Berra once said, "You can observe a lot by watching." (We have Berra to thank for other gems, such as "Nobody ever comes here—it's too crowded" and "If the people don't want to come out to the park, nobody's gonna stop 'em.") Because we're all behavior-watchers, it would be surprising if many of psychology's findings had *not* been foreseen.

But sometimes Grandmother's intuition has it wrong. Informed by countless casual observations, our intuition may tell us that familiarity breeds contempt, that dreams predict the future, and that emotional reactions coincide with menstrual phase. As we will see in later chapters, the available evidence suggests that these common-sense ideas are wrong, wrong, and wrong. Throughout this book we will see how research has both inspired and overturned popular ideas—about aging, about sleep and dreams, about personality. And we will also see how it has surprised us with discoveries about animal abilities, about how the brain's chemical messengers control our moods and memories, about the effects of stress on our capacity to fight disease.

Overconfidence

Our everyday thinking is limited not only by our after-the-fact common sense but also by our human tendency toward overconfidence. As Chapter 8 explains, we tend to think we know more than we do. Asked how sure we are of our answers to factual questions (Is Boston north or south of Paris?), we tend to be more confident than correct.[2] Or consider these three anagrams, which Richard Goranson (1978) asked people to unscramble.

WREAT → WATER ETRYN → ENTRY GRABE → BARGE

Reflect for a moment: About how many seconds do you think it would have taken you to unscramble each of these?

Once people know the target word, hindsight makes it seem obvious—so much so that they become overconfident. They think they would have seen the solution in only 10 seconds or so, when in reality the average subject spent 3 minutes, as you also might, given an anagram without the solution: OCHSA (see page 15 to check your answer).

Are we any better at predicting our social behavior? To find out, Robert Vallone and his associates (1990) had students predict at the beginning of the school year whether they would drop a course, vote in an upcoming election, call their parents more than twice a month, and so forth. On average, the students felt 84 percent confident in making these self-predictions. Later quizzes about their actual behavior showed their predictions were correct only 71 percent of the time. Even when they were 100 percent sure of themselves, their self-predictions erred 15 percent of the time.

Overconfidence stems partly from our human tendency to seek information that *confirms* our ideas (a phenomenon that Chapter 8 will label *confirmation bias*). When assessing our ideas, we prefer to look at evidence that might confirm rather than disconfirm them. Reflecting on many experiments, P. C. Wason (1981) reports that once people have a wrong idea they often will not budge from their illogic: "Ordinary people evade facts, become inconsistent, or systematically defend themselves against the threat of new information relevant to the issue."

The point to remember: Hindsight and overconfidence bias lead us to overestimate our intuition. But scientific inquiry, fed by skepticism and humility, helps us sift reality from illusion.

"It ain't so much the things we don't know that get us into trouble. It's the things we know that just ain't so."

Artemus Ward
1834–1867

"We don't like their sound. Groups of guitars are on their way out."

Decca Records, in turning down a recording contract with the Beatles

"Computers in the future may weigh no more than 1.5 tons."

Popular Mechanics
1949

"They couldn't hit an elephant at this dist–."

General John Sedgwick's last words, uttered during a U.S. Civil War battle, 1864

[2]Boston is south of Paris.

6. As scientists, psychologists view theories with skepticism and humility. This means that they
- **a.** approach research with a negative cynicism.
- **b.** assume that an article published in a reputable journal must be true.
- **c.** realize that some issues should not be studied.
- **d.** persistently ask questions and are willing to reject ideas that cannot be verified by research.

7. A newspaper article describes how a "cure for cancer has been found." A critical thinker probably will
- **a.** immediately dismiss the article as untrue because there is no evidence to back up the facts.
- **b.** accept the information as a wonderful breakthrough.
- **c.** question the article, evaluate the evidence, and assess the conclusions.
- **d.** question the article but quickly accept it as true due to the author's excellent reputation.

8. Psychology tells us what we already know from common sense, say some skeptics. Hindsight bias refers to our tendency to
- **a.** perceive events as obvious or inevitable after the fact.
- **b.** assume that two events happened because we wished them to happen.
- **c.** overestimate our abilities to predict the future.
- **d.** make judgments that fly in the face of common sense.

theory an explanation using an integrated set of principles that organizes and predicts observations.

hypothesis a testable prediction, often implied by a theory.

replication repeating the essence of a research study, usually with different subjects in different situations, to see whether the basic finding generalizes to other subjects and circumstances.

How Do Psychologists Ask and Answer Questions?

Psychologists arm their scientific attitude with the scientific method: They make observations, form theories, and then refine their theories in the light of new observations.

The Scientific Method

6. *What is the place of theory in the scientific method?*

In everyday conversation, we tend to use "theory" to mean "mere hunch." In science, "theory" is linked with observation. A scientific **theory** *explains* through an integrated set of principles that *organizes* and *predicts* observable behaviors or events. By organizing isolated facts, a theory simplifies things. There are now so many known facts about behavior—Nobel-laureate psychologist Allen Newell (1988) estimated 3000 (including 29 that govern behavior while typing at a keyboard)—that we could never hope to remember them all. By linking observations and bridging them to deeper principles, a theory offers a useful summary. G. E. Morton (1994) likens theory construction to solving a connect-the-dots puzzle; as lines are drawn linking the isolated dots, a coherent picture emerges even before the dots are all connected.

"The real purpose of the scientific method is to make sure Nature hasn't misled you into thinking you know something you don't actually know."

Robert M. Pirsig
Zen and the Art of Motorcycle Maintenance
1974

A good theory of depression, for example, will first help us organize countless observations concerning depression into a much shorter list of principles. Say we observe over and over that depressed people describe themselves—their past, present, and future—in gloomy terms. We might therefore theorize that low self-esteem contributes to depression. So far so good: Our self-esteem principle neatly summarizes a long list of facts about depressed people.

Yet no matter how reasonable a theory may sound—and low self-esteem certainly seems a reasonable explanation of depression—we must put it to the test. A good theory doesn't just sound appealing. It must imply testable predictions, called **hypotheses**. By enabling us to test and reject or revise the theory, such predictions give direction to research. They specify in advance what results would support the theory and what results would disconfirm it. To test our self-esteem theory of depression, we might give people a test of self-esteem on which they respond to statements such as "I have good ideas." Then we could see whether, as we hypothesized, people who report poorer self-images are indeed more depressed (Figure 1.2, page 14).

In testing our theory, we should be aware that it can bias our observations. Having theorized that depression springs from low self-esteem, we may see what we expect to see. We may be tempted to perceive depressed people's comments as self-disparaging.

As one check on their biases, psychologists report their research precisely enough to allow others to **replicate** (repeat) their observations. If other researchers re-create the essence of a study with different subjects and materials and get similar results, then our confidence in the reliability of our finding grows. The first study of hindsight bias aroused psychologists' curiosity. Now, after many successful replications with differing people and questions, we feel quite sure of the phenomenon's power.

In the end, our theory will be useful if it (1) effectively *organizes* a range of observations and (2) implies clear *predictions* that anyone can use to check the theory or to derive practical applications. (If we boost people's self-esteem, will their depression lift?) Eventually, our research will probably lead to a revised

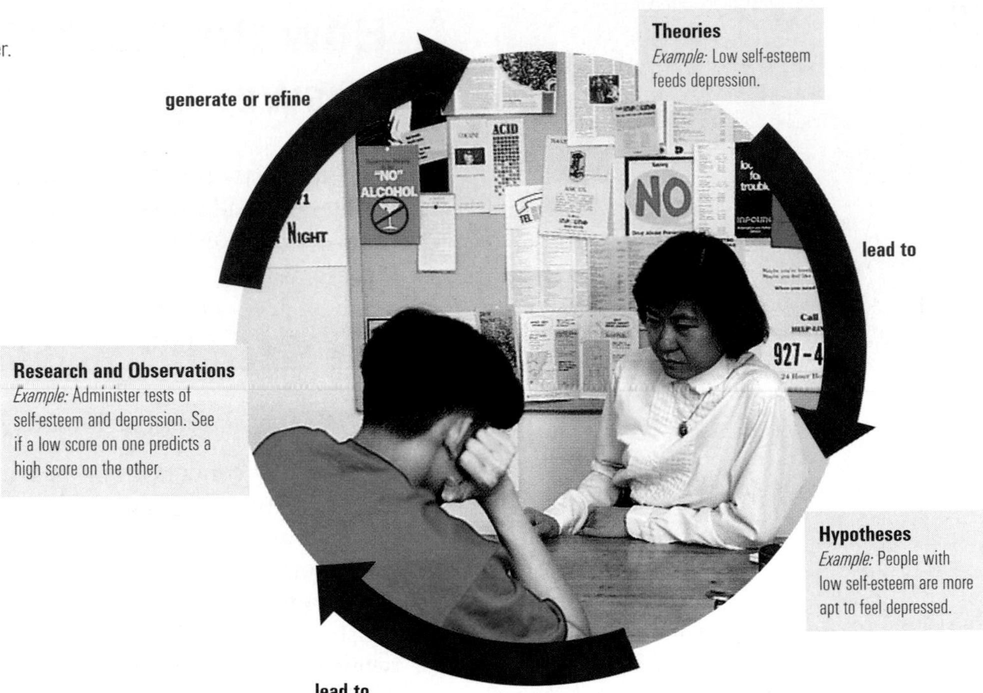

Figure 1.2 The scientific method A self-correcting process for asking questions and observing nature's answer.

theory (such as the one on page 448) that better organizes and predicts what we know about depression.

Good theories explain by
1. organizing and linking observed facts.
2. implying hypotheses that offer testable predictions and, sometimes, practical applications.

To describe, predict, and explain behavior and mental processes, psychologists use three strategies: They *describe* behavior using case studies, surveys, and naturalistic studies. They *predict* behavior from studies that detect *correlations*. And they seek cause-effect *explanations* through *experiments* that manipulate one or more factors under controlled conditions.

Description

7. *How do psychologists observe and describe behavior?*

The starting point of any science is description. In everyday life, all of us observe and describe people, often forming hunches about why they behave as they do. Professional psychologists are doing much the same, only more objectively and systematically.

The Case Study

Among the oldest research methods is the **case study**, in which psychologists study one or more individuals in great depth in the hope of revealing things true of us all. Some examples: Much of our early knowledge about the brain came from case studies of individuals who suffered a particular impairment after damage to a certain brain region. Sigmund Freud constructed his theory of personality from a handful of case studies. Developmental psychologist Jean Piaget taught us about children's thinking after carefully observing and questioning his own three children. Studies of a few chimpanzees have revealed their capacity for understanding and simple language. Intensive case studies are sometimes very revealing.

"'Well my dear,' said Miss Marple, 'human nature is very much the same everywhere, and of course, one has opportunities of observing it at closer quarters in a village.'"

Agatha Christie
The Tuesday Club Murders
1933

The case of the conversational chimpanzee In intensive case studies of chimpanzees, psychologists have explored the intriguing question of whether language is uniquely human. Here Nim Chimpsky signs "hug" as his trainer, psychologist Herbert Terrace, shows him the puppet Ernie. But is Nim really capable of using language? We'll explore that issue in Chapter 8.

Although case studies can also suggest hypotheses for further study, they sometimes have a problem: Any given individual may be atypical, making the case misleading. Our tendency to leap to conclusions from unrepresentative information is a common source of mistaken judgment. Indeed, anytime a researcher mentions a finding ("Smokers die younger: 95 percent of men over 85 are nonsmokers") someone is sure to offer a contradictory case ("Well, I have an uncle who smoked two packs a day and lived to be 89"). Anecdotal cases—dramatic stories, personal experiences, even psychological case examples—have a way of overwhelming general truths. Numbers are numbing (in one study of 1300 dream reports concerning a kidnapped child, only 5 percent correctly envisioned the child as dead—see page 162). Anecdotes are alarming ("But I know a man who dreamed his sister was in a car accident, and two days later she was badly injured").

The point to remember: Individual cases can suggest fruitful ideas. But to discern the general truths that cover individual cases, we must turn to other methods of answering questions.

Solution to anagram on page 12: CHAOS.

The Survey

The **survey** method, which is commonly used in both descriptive and correlational studies, looks at many cases in less depth. A survey asks people to report their behavior or opinions. Questions about everything from sexual practices to political opinions get put to the public. It's hard to think of a significant question that survey researchers have not asked. In the United States, for example, recent Harris and Gallup surveys have revealed that 72 percent of people think there is too much TV violence, 89 percent say they face high stress, 95 percent believe in God, and 96 percent would like to change something about their appearance.

Wording Effects

Asking questions is tricky because even subtle changes in the order or wording of questions can have big effects. Should cigarette ads or pornography be allowed on television? People are much more likely to approve "not allowing" such things than "forbidding" or "censoring" them. In a recent national survey, only 27 percent of Americans approved of "government censorship" of media sex and violence, though 66 percent approved of "more restrictions on what is shown on television" (Lacayo, 1995). People are similarly much more approving of "aid to the needy" than of "welfare," of "affirmative action" than of "preferential treatment," and of "revenue enhancers" than of "taxes." Because wording questions is such a delicate matter, critical thinkers will reflect on how the phrasing of a question might have affected the opinions respondents expressed.

Sampling

In everyday experience we are exposed to a biased sample of people. We associate mostly with those who share our attitudes and habits. Thus, when we are guessing how many people hold a particular belief, those who think as we do come to mind most readily. This tendency to overestimate others' agreement with us is the **false consensus effect** (Ross & others, 1977). Vegetarians will think more people are vegetarians than will meat-eaters, and conservatives will perceive more support for conservative views than will liberals. To restrain this bias, we can gather a more representative sample of people.

Most surveys sample a target group. If you wished to survey the students at your college or university, you could question them all, but there probably are too many to do so. Instead, you could survey a representative sample of the total student **population**—the whole group you wanted to study and describe.

case study an observation technique in which one person is studied in depth in the hope of revealing universal principles.

survey a technique for ascertaining the self-reported attitudes or behaviors of people, usually by questioning a representative, random sample of them.

false consensus effect the tendency to overestimate the extent to which others share our beliefs and behaviors.

population all the cases in a group, from which samples may be drawn for a study.

random sample a sample that fairly represents a population because each member has an equal chance of inclusion.

naturalistic observation observing and recording behavior in naturally occurring situations without trying to manipulate and control the situation.

correlation a statistical measure that indicates the extent to which two factors vary together and thus how well either factor predicts the other.

How could you make your sample representative of this population? By making it a **random sample**, one in which every person in the entire group has an equal chance of participating.

To sample the students at your institution randomly, you would *not* send them all a questionnaire. (The conscientious people who return it would not be a random sample.) Rather, you would aim for a representative sample by, say, using a table of random numbers to pick participants from a student listing and then making sure you get responses from nearly everyone whose number was drawn. Large, representative samples are better than small ones, but it is better to have a small, representative sample of 100 than a haphazard, unrepresentative sample of 500.

The random-sampling principle also works in national surveys. Imagine that you had a giant barrel containing 60 million white beans thoroughly mixed with 40 million red beans. A scoop that randomly sampled 1500 of them would contain about 60 percent white and 40 percent red beans, give or take 2 or 3 percent. Sampling voters in a national election survey is like sampling the beans; 1500 randomly sampled people, drawn from all areas of a country, provide a remarkably accurate snapshot of the opinions of a nation.

Because gathering a random sample can be a huge task, some survey takers don't make the effort. Shere Hite's book *Women and Love* reported survey findings based on only a 4.5 percent response rate from mailings to an unrepresentative sample of 100,000 women. The response was doubly unrepresentative because not only did she have a modest, self-selected return, but also the women initially contacted were members of women's organizations. Nonetheless, "It's 4500 people. That's enough for me," reported Hite. And it was apparently enough for *Time* magazine, which made a cover story of her findings—that 70 percent of women married 5 or more years were having affairs, and that 95 percent of women felt emotionally harassed by the men they love (Wallis, 1987). Evidently it didn't matter that on less publicized surveys, *randomly* sampled American women express much higher levels of satisfaction: Half or more report feeling "very happy" or "completely satisfied" with their marriage; only 3 percent say they are "not at all happy" (Peplau & Gordon, 1985). And only 1 in 7 reports having had an affair during her current marriage—a level of faithfulness replicated in British, French, and Danish surveys (Greeley, 1991, 1994). Without random sampling, large samples such as Hite's—including call-in phone samples—merely give better estimates of a misleading number.

"How would you like me to answer that question? As a member of my ethnic group, educational class, income group, or religious category?"

You can forecast the weather by taking a haphazard sample—by looking at the clouds and holding your finger in the wind—or you can look at weather maps based on comprehensive reporting. You can describe human experience using common sense, dramatic anecdotes, personal experience, and haphazard samples. But for an accurate picture of the experiences and attitudes of a whole population, there's only one game in town—the representative survey.

The point to remember: Before believing survey findings, think critically: Consider the sample. You cannot compensate for an unrepresentative sample by adding more people.

We can extend this point to everyday thinking as we generalize from samples we observe. We meet a few students and attend a few classes during a visit to a college and infer from those instances how friendly the campus is and how good the teaching is. We observe the weather during a week-long visit to Scotland and then tell our friends about the climate there.

It is often tempting to overgeneralize from such select samples, especially so when they are vivid cases. Given (a) a statistical summary of a professor's student evaluations and (b) the vivid comments of two irate students, an administrator's impression of the professor may be influenced as much by the two unhappy students as by the many favorable evaluations in the statistical summary. Driving into Chicago from the south, many people see the miles of tene-

Naturalistic observation Some psychologists study human and animal behavior in natural environments. As University of St. Andrews psychologist Richard Byrne observes an adult gorilla, recording its behavior on a hand-held computer, a curious infant approaches and investigates his camera lens cap.

ment houses near the highway and think, "What an unfortunate city this is." Standing in the checkout line at the supermarket, George sees the woman in front of him pay with government-provided food stamps and then watches with dismay as she drives away in a BMW. In each of these situations, the temptation to generalize from a few vivid but unrepresentative cases is nearly irresistible.

The point to remember: The best basis for generalizing is not from the exceptional cases one finds at the extremes, but from a representative sample of cases.

Naturalistic Observation

Watching and recording the behavior of organisms in their natural environment is known as **naturalistic observation**. Naturalistic observations range from watching chimpanzee societies in the jungle, to unobtrusive measures of parent-child interactions in different cultures, to recording students' self-seating patterns in the lunchrooms of multiracial schools.

Like the case study and survey methods, naturalistic observation does not *explain* behavior. It *describes* it. Nevertheless, description can be revealing. We once thought, for example, that only humans use tools. Then naturalistic observation revealed that chimpanzees sometimes insert a stick in a termite mound and withdraw it, eating the stick's load of termites. Chimps and baboons also use deception to achieve their aims. Psychologists Andrew Whiten and Richard Byrne (1988) repeatedly saw one young baboon pretending to have been attacked by another as a tactic to get its mother to drive the other baboon away from its food.

Through naturalistic observations we have also learned that Scandinavians, North Americans, and the British prefer more personal space than do Latin Americans, Arabs, and the French (Sommer, 1969). If someone invades our *personal space*—the portable buffer zone we like to maintain around our bodies—we feel uncomfortable. At a social gathering, a Mexican seeking a comfortable conversation distance may waltz around a room with a backpedaling American. (You can demonstrate this at a party by playing space invader as you talk with someone.) To the American, the Mexican may seem intrusive; to the Mexican, the American may seem cold and standoffish.

Correlation

8. *Why do correlations permit prediction but not explanation? How accurately does the naked eye detect correlations?*

Describing behavior is a first step toward predicting it. When surveys and naturalistic observations reveal that one trait or behavior accompanies another, we say the two correlate. A **correlation** is a statistical measure of relationship: It reveals how closely two things vary together and thus how well either one *predicts* the other. Knowing how much aptitude test scores *correlate* with school grades tells us how well the scores *predict* grades.

A positive correlation (between 0 and +1.00) indicates a direct relationship, meaning that two things increase together or decrease together. Some examples:

- According to some studies, the amount of violence viewed on television correlates about +.3 with aggressive social behavior; people's TV-viewing habits therefore modestly predict their aggressiveness (or vice versa).
- Genetically identical twins correlate about +.6 on tests of extraversion, which means that the outgoingness of either twin gives a reasonable clue to that of the other (Bouchard & others, 1990).

illusory correlation the perception of a relationship where none exists.

- University of Michigan surveys of 71,000 representatively sampled high school seniors revealed that the more hours students worked on a job, the less they slept and exercised and the more they used cigarettes, alcohol, and other drugs (ISR, 1994).

A *negative* correlation—equally predictive—indicates an *inverse* relationship: As one thing increases, the other decreases. Our earlier findings on self-esteem and depression illustrate a negative correlation: People who score *low* on self-esteem tend to score *high* on depression. Negative correlations could go as low as –1.00, which means that, like people on the opposite ends of a teeter-totter, one set of scores goes down precisely as the other goes up.

Though informative, psychology's correlations usually leave most of the variation among individuals unpredicted. As we will see, there is a correlation between parents' abusiveness and their children's later abusiveness when they become parents. But this does not mean most abused children become abusive. The correlation simply indicates a statistical relationship: Although most abused children do not grow into abusers, nonabused children are even less likely to become abusive.

Likewise, early crime correlates with later crime. Boys arrested by age 14 are 18 times more likely to become chronic offenders than are boys who have not been arrested by that age, and chronic offenders are 14 times more likely to commit violent offenses. Yet two-thirds of boys arrested only once do *not* go on to commit violent crimes (Forgatch, 1995). Correlations point us toward predictions, but usually imperfect ones.

Illusory Correlations

Correlations make visible relationships that the naked eye would miss. They also help us stop "seeing" relationships that actually don't exist. A perceived correlation that does not really exist is an **illusory correlation**. When we *believe* there is a relationship between two things, we are likely to *notice* and *recall* instances that confirm our belief (Troilier & Hamilton, 1986).

We are, it seems, very, very good at detecting patterns, whether they're there or not, and not so good at testing our hypotheses.

Illusory correlations help explain many a superstitious belief, such as the presumption that more babies are born when the moon is full or that infertile couples who adopt (Figure 1.3) become more likely to conceive (Gilovich, 1991). Such illusory thinking helps explain why for so many years people believed (and many still do) that sugar made children hyperactive, that getting cold and wet predisposed a cold, and that weather changes trigger arthritis pain. Physician Donald Redelmeier, working with Amos Tversky (1996; Kolata, 1996), a psychologist who specialized in "debugging human intuition," followed 18 arthritis patients for 15 months. The researchers recorded both the patients' pain reports and the daily temperature, humidity, and barometric pressure. Despite patients' beliefs, the weather was uncorrelated with their discomfort, either on the same day or up to two days earlier or later. Shown columns of random numbers labeled "arthritis pain" and "barometric pressure," even college students saw a correlation where there was none. We are, it seems, very, very good at detecting patterns, whether they're there or not, and not so good at testing our hypotheses.

Because we are sensitive to dramatic or unusual events, we are especially likely to notice and remember the occurrence of two such events in sequence—say, a premonition of an unlikely phone call followed by the call. When the call does not follow the premonition, we are less likely to note and remember the nonevent.

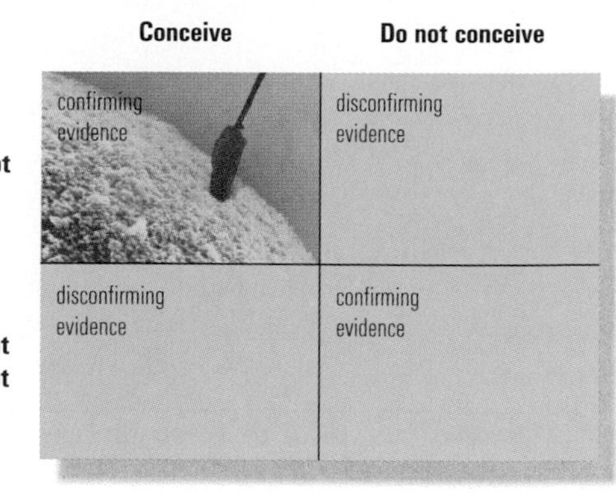

Figure 1.3 Illusory correlation Many people believe infertile couples become more likely to conceive a child after adopting a baby. Their belief arises from their attention being drawn to such cases. The many couples who adopt without conceiving or conceive without adopting grab less attention. To determine whether there actually is a correlation between adoption and conception, we need data from all four cells in this figure. (From Gilovich, 1991)

Likewise, instances of positive-thinking people being cured of cancer impress those who believe that positive attitudes counter disease. But to assess whether positive thinking actually affects cancer, we need three more types of information. First, we need an estimate of how many positive thinkers *were not* cured. Then we need to know how many people with cancer were and were not cured among those not using positive thinking. Without these comparison figures, positive examples of a few hope-filled people tell us nothing about the actual correlation between attitudes and disease. (As Chapter 10 explains, emotions do influence health and illness.)

The point to remember: When we notice random coincidences, we may forget that they are random and see them as correlated. Thus, we can easily deceive ourselves by seeing what is not there.

Perceiving Order in Random Events

Illusory correlations arise from our natural eagerness to make sense of our world. Given even random data, we look for order, for meaningful patterns. And we usually find it, because *random sequences often don't look random.* Consider the following sequences of heads (H) and tails (T): HHHTTT and HTTHTH and HHHHHH. If someone flipped a coin six times, would one sequence be more likely than the other two?

Daniel Kahneman and Amos Tversky (1972) found that most people believe HTTHTH would be the most likely random sequence. Actually, all possible sequences are equally likely (or, you might say, equally unlikely) to occur. A bridge or poker hand of 10 through Ace, all of hearts, would seem extraordinary; actually, it would be no more or less likely than any other specific hand of cards (Figure 1.4).

Figure 1.4 Two random sequences Your chances of being dealt either of these hands is precisely the same: 1 in 2,598,960.

Psychologists Thomas Holtgraves and James Skeel (1992) exposed people's perceptions of randomness in their bets placed in Indiana's Pick-3 Lottery. You can play, too: Pick any three-digit number from zero to 999.

Did your number have a repeated digit (as in 525)? Probably not. Only 14 percent of 2.24 million number strings chosen in July 1991 had a repeated digit. Although repeated digits actually occur in 28 percent of the available numbers, such numbers *look* less random (and people prefer to bet random-looking series). In actual random sequences, seeming patterns and streaks (such as repeating digits) occur more often than people expect. Thus, shown random data, scientists and psychics alike can often "see" an interesting pattern (Guion, 1992). To demonstrate this phenomenon for myself (as you can do), I flipped a coin 51 times, with the results shown on page 20.

1. H	9. T	17. T	24. T	31. T	38. T	45. T
2. T	10. T	18. T	25. T	32. T	39. H	46. H
3. T	11. T	19. H	26. T	33. T	40. T	47. H
4. T	12. H	20. H	27. H	34. T	41. H	48. T
5. H	13. H	21. T	28. T	35. T	42. H	49. T
6. H	14. T	22. T	29. H	36. H	43. H	50. T
7. H	15. T	23. H	30. T	37. T	44. H	51. T
8. T	16. H					

Bizarre-looking, perhaps. But actually no more unlikely than any other number sequence.

Looking over the sequence, patterns jump out: Tosses 10 to 22 provided an almost perfect pattern of pairs of tails followed by pairs of heads. On tosses 30 to 38 I had a "cold hand," with only one head in nine tosses. But my fortunes immediately reversed with a "hot hand"—seven heads out of the next nine tosses.

What explains these patterns? Was I exercising some sort of paranormal control over my coin? Did I snap out of my tails funk and get into a heads groove? No such explanations are needed, for these are the sort of streaks found in any random data. Comparing each toss to the next, 23 of the 50 comparisons yielded a changed result—just the sort of near 50-50 result we expect from coin tossing. Despite the seeming patterns in these data, the outcome of one toss gives no clue to the outcome of the next toss.

The failure to recognize random occurrences for what they are can predispose people to seek extraordinary explanations for ordinary events. Imagine that on one warm spring day 4000 college students gather for a coin-tossing contest. Their task is to flip heads. On the first toss, 2000 students do so and remain standing for a second round. As you might expect, about 1000 of these progress to a third round, 500 to a fourth, 250 to a fifth, 125 to a sixth, 62 to a seventh, 31 to an eighth, 15 to a ninth, and 8 amazing individuals, having flipped heads nine times in a row with ever-increasing displays of concentration and effort, remain standing for the tenth round.

By now, the crowd of losers is in awestruck silence as these expert coin tossers prepare to display their amazing ability yet again. The proceedings are temporarily halted so that a panel of impartial scientists can observe and document the incredible achievement of these gifted individuals. Alas, on succeeding tosses half of those remaining flip a tail, until all have sat down. "But, of course," their admirers say, "coin tossing is a highly sensitive skill. The tense, pressured atmosphere created by the scientific scrutiny has disturbed their fragile gift."

Some happenings, though, seem so extraordinary that we struggle to conceive an ordinary, chance-related explanation (as applies to our coin tosses). In such cases, statisticians often are less mystified. When Evelyn Marie Adams won the New Jersey lottery *twice*, newspapers reported the odds of her feat as 1 in 17 trillion. Bizarre? Actually, 1 in 17 trillion are the odds that a given person who buys a single ticket for two New Jersey lotteries will win both times. But statisticians Stephen Samuels and George McCabe (1989) report that, given the millions of people who buy U.S. state lottery tickets, it was "practically a sure thing" that someday, somewhere, someone would hit a state jackpot twice. Indeed, say fellow statisticians Persi Diaconis and Frederick Mosteller (1989), "with a large enough sample, any outrageous thing is likely to happen."

Given enough random events, something weird will happen Evelyn Marie Adams was the beneficiary of one of those extraordinary, chance events when she won the New Jersey lottery a second time.

We all experience enough events that we're sure to feel astonished now and then. One day when my daughter bought two pairs of shoes, we later were astounded to discover that the two brand names were her first and last names. Checking out a photocopy counter from our library, I confused the clerk when giving him my six-digit department charge number—which just happened at that moment to be identical to the counter's one-in-a-million number on which the last user had finished. Ron Vachon was astounded while sitting among thousands

Correlation need not mean causation Length of marriage correlates with hair loss in men. Does this mean that marriage causes men to lose their hair (or that balding men make better husbands)? In this case, as in many others, a third factor obviously explains the correlation: Golden anniversaries and baldness both accompany aging.

of fans at a September 1990 baseball game in Boston. Oakland A's outfielder Rickey Henderson hit two foul balls right to him, on successive pitches. That something like that should have happened to Vachon (who dropped them both) was incredibly unlikely. That it sometime would happen to someone was not. An event that happens to but one in 1 billion people every day occurs about six times a day, 2000 times a year. For two provocative instances of random sequences that don't look random, see Thinking Critically: Hot and Cold Streaks in Basketball and the Stock Market.

Correlation and Causation

So far we've seen that correlations help us predict and restrain the illusions of our flawed intuition. Viewing violence correlates with (and therefore predicts) aggression. But does it *cause* aggression? Does low self-esteem *cause* depression? If, based on the correlational evidence, you assume that they do, you have much company. Perhaps the most irresistible thinking error made both by laypeople and by professional psychologists is to assume that correlation proves causation. No matter how strong the relationship, it does not! If watching TV violence correlates positively with aggressiveness, does this mean that watching TV violence influences aggressive behavior? It may. Or does it mean that aggressive people prefer violent programs?

And what about the negative correlation between self-esteem and depression? Perhaps low self-esteem does cause depression. But as Figure 1.5 suggests, we'd get the same coincidence of low self-esteem and depression if depression caused people to be down on themselves or if something else—a third factor such as heredity or brain chemistry—caused both low self-esteem and depression. Among men, length of marriage correlates positively with hair loss—because both are associated with a third factor, age.

Consider this finding from a recent survey of 12,118 adolescents: The more teens feel loved by their parents, the less likely they are to behave in unhealthy ways—having early sex, smoking, abusing alcohol and drugs, exhibiting violence (Resnick & others, 1997). "Adults have a powerful effect on their children's behavior right through the high school years," gushed an Associated Press story on the study. But the correlation comes with no built-in cause-effect arrow. Thus, the AP could as well have said, "Well-behaved teens feel their parents' love and approval; out-of-bounds teens more often think their parents are disapproving jerks."

The point to remember: Correlation may hint at possible cause-effect relationships. But it does not provide a causal explanation. Knowing that two events are correlated need not tell us anything about causation. *Correlation does not prove causation.* Remember this principle and you will be wiser as you see reports of scientific studies in the news and in this book.

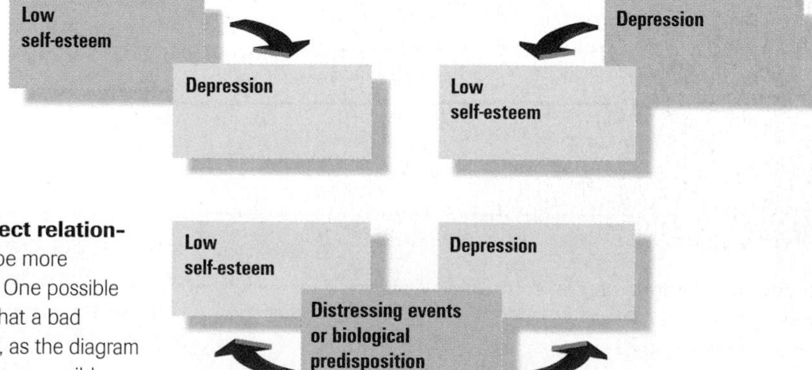

Figure 1.5 **Three possible cause-effect relationships** People low in self-esteem tend to be more depressed than those high in self-esteem. One possible explanation of this negative correlation is that a bad self-image causes depressed feelings. But, as the diagram indicates, other cause-effect relationships are possible.

THINKING CRITICALLY

Hot and Cold Streaks in Basketball and the Stock Market

Misinterpreting random sequences is common in sports and investing. In both arenas, the statistical facts collide with common-sense intuition.

Basketball Players' "Hot Hands"

Every basketball player and every fan intuitively "knows" that players have hot and cold streaks. Players who have "hot hands" can't seem to miss. Those who have "cold" ones can't find the center of the hoop. When Thomas Gilovich, Robert Vallone, and Amos Tversky (1985) interviewed Philadelphia 76ers, the players estimated they were about 25 percent more likely to make a shot after they had just made one than after a miss. In one survey, 9 in 10 basketball fans agreed that a player "has a better chance of making a shot after having just *made* his last two or three shots than he does after having just *missed* his last two or three shots." Believing in shooting streaks, players will feed the ball to a teammate who has just made two or three shots in a row. Many coaches will bench the player who has just missed three in a row.

The only trouble is (believe it or not), it isn't true. When Gilovich and his collaborators studied detailed individual shooting records, they found that the 76ers—and the Boston Celtics, the New Jersey Nets, the New York Knicks, and Cornell University's men's and women's basketball players—were equally likely to score after a miss and after a basket. A typical 50 percent shooter averages 50 percent after just missing three shots, and 50 percent after just making three shots. It works with free throws, too. Celtics star Larry Bird made 88 percent of his free throws after making a free throw and 91 percent after missing. (Did this reduce Larry Bird to a mere puppet, manipulated by statistical laws? No, his skill was reflected in his 90 percent average.)

Why, then, do players and fans alike believe that players are more likely to score after scoring and to miss after missing? It's because streaks do occur, more than people expect in random sequences. In any series of 20 shots by a 50 percent shooter (or 20 flips of a coin), there is a 50-50 chance of 4 baskets (or heads) in a row, and it is quite possible that 1 person out of 5 will have a streak of 5 or 6 baskets. Players and fans notice these random streaks and so form the myth that "when you're hot, you're hot" (Figure 1.6).

Mutual Funds: Does Past Performance Predict Future Returns?

The same misinterpretation of random sequences occurs when investors believe that a mutual fund that has had a string of good years will likely outperform one that has had a string of bad years. Based on that assumption, investment magazines report mutual funds' past performance. But, as economist Burton Malkiel (1989, 1995) documents, past performances of mutual funds do *not* predict their future performance. If on January 1 of each year since 1980 we had bought the previous year's top-performing funds, our hot funds would not have beaten the next year's market average. Putting our money on the *Forbes* "Honor Roll" of funds each year would have gotten us an annual return since 1975 of 13.5 percent (compared with the market's overall 14.9 percent annual return). Of the top 81 Canadian funds during 1994, 40 performed above average and 41 below average during 1995 (Chalmers, 1995).

When funds have streaks of several good years, we may nevertheless be fooled into thinking that past success predicts future success. "Randomness is a difficult notion for people to accept," notes Malkiel. "When events come in clusters and streaks, people look for explanations and patterns. They refuse to believe that such patterns—which frequently occur in random data—could equally well be derived from tossing a coin. So it is in the stock market as well."

The point to remember: Whether watching basketball, choosing stocks, or flipping coins, remember that our intuition often deceives us. Random sequences frequently don't look random. Expect streaks.

Figure 1.6 Who is the chance shooter? Here are 21 consecutive shots, each scoring either a basket or a miss, by two players who each make 11. Within this sample of shots, which player's sequence looks more like what we would expect in a random sequence? (See page 25.) (Adapted from Barry Ross, *Discover*, 1987)

Player A

Player B

REHEARSE IT!

9. In psychology a good theory implies hypotheses, or predictions that can be tested. When hypotheses are tested, the result is typically
- **a.** increased skepticism.
- **b.** rejection of the merely theoretical.
- **c.** confirmation or revision of the theory.
- **d.** personal bias on the part of the investigator.

10. Psychology's basic *research strategies* are description, correlation, and experimentation. Which of the following would you use in an attempt to predict college grades from high school grades?
- **a.** a case study
- **b.** naturalistic observation
- **c.** correlational research
- **d.** experimental research

11. You wish to take an accurate poll in a certain country by questioning people who truly represent the country's adult population. Therefore, you need to make sure the people are
- **a.** at least 30 percent urban dwellers.
- **b.** registered voters.
- **c.** a very large sample of the population.
- **d.** a random sample of the population.

12. Suppose a psychologist finds that the *more* natural childbirth training classes a woman attends, the *less* pain medication she requires during childbirth. The relationship between the number of training sessions and the amount of pain medication required is a
- **a.** positive correlation (direct relationship).
- **b.** negative correlation (inverse relationship).
- **c.** cause-effect relationship.
- **d.** controlled experiment.

13. Some people wrongly perceive that their dreams predict future events. This is an example of a/an
- **a.** negative correlation.
- **b.** positive correlation.
- **c.** illusory correlation.
- **d.** naturalistic correlation.

14. Knowing that two events are correlated does not tell us what is the cause and what is the effect. However, it does provide
- **a.** a basis for prediction.
- **b.** an explanation of events.
- **c.** proof that as one increases, the other also increases.
- **d.** an indication that an underlying third factor is at work.

Experimentation

9. *How do experiments clarify or reveal cause-effect relationships?*

Happy are they "who have been able to perceive the causes of things," remarked the Roman poet Virgil. We endlessly wonder and debate *why* people act as they do. As I write, the day's newspapers are filled with such wonderings: Why do people smoke? Have babies as unmarried teens? Do stupid things when drunk? Psychology can't answer these questions directly, but it has helped us to understand what influences aggression, drug use, sexual attitudes, and thinking when drinking.

In everyday life, many factors influence behavior. To isolate cause and effect—to explain what helps cause, say, depression—psychologists conduct **experiments**. Experiments enable a researcher to focus on the possible effects of one or more factors by (1) *manipulating the factors of interest* and (2) *holding constant ("controlling") other factors*. Imagine that some researchers wanted to study the effect of alcohol consumption on thinking ability. Before giving a thinking test, they would *manipulate* alcohol consumption (by giving some people a strong-tasting drink laced with alcohol, others the same-tasting drink without alcohol). By randomly assigning people to the two conditions, which otherwise are similar, they would hold all other factors constant. This would eliminate alternative explanations for why thinking might vary with drinking.

If behavior changes when we vary an experimental factor, such as alcohol, then the factor is having an effect. To repeat: Unlike correlational studies, which uncover naturally occurring relationships, an experiment manipulates a factor to see its effect. To illustrate, let's consider two actual experiments.

experiment a research method in which the investigator manipulates one or more factors (independent variables) to observe their effect on some behavior or mental process (the dependent variable) while controlling other relevant factors by random assignment of subjects.

Do Black Sports Uniforms Affect Perceptions?

Cornell University psychologists Mark Frank and Thomas Gilovich (1988) noticed that in virtually all cultures from central Africa to Asia to Western Europe, black clothing connotes evil. In movies, the bad guys wear black.

experimental condition the condition of an experiment that exposes subjects to the treatment (to one version of the "independent variable").

control condition the condition of an experiment that contrasts with the experimental treatment and serves as a comparison for evaluating the effect of the treatment.

random assignment assigning subjects to experimental and control conditions by chance, thus minimizing preexisting differences between those assigned to the different groups.

independent variable the experimental factor that is manipulated; the variable whose effect is being studied.

dependent variable the experimental factor—in psychology, the behavior or mental process—that is being measured; the variable that may change in response to manipulations of the independent variable.

operational definition a statement of the procedures (operations) used to define research variables.

Summarizing these varied observations, Frank and Gilovich proposed a simple, small-scale theory: Black garb suggests evil, cuing us to *perceive* people dressed in black as evil and cuing those who wear black to *act out* their evil image. Knowing that a useful theory must offer testable predictions, the researchers derived several hypotheses. First, they predicted that people unfamiliar with football and hockey would rate the black uniforms of National Football League and National Hockey League teams as seeming more evil than nonblack uniforms. Indeed, for both sports, people rated black uniforms as bad, mean, and aggressive.

Second, Frank and Gilovich hypothesized, and found, a positive correlation between the wearing of black uniforms and total penalties for aggressive play. In all but one of the 17 seasons between 1970 and 1986, the football teams with black uniforms were penalized a disproportionate number of yards. Likewise, in 16 consecutive hockey seasons during the 1970s and 1980s, the teams wearing black uniforms spent more time in the penalty box. Moreover, when the Pittsburgh Penguins switched to black uniforms during the middle of the 1979–1980 season, their penalties increased from an average of 8 minutes per game to 12 minutes. So, in these two sports at least, there definitely has been a correlation between teams wearing black uniforms and penalized play.

Remember, a correlation is simply a relationship between two factors—in this case, uniform color and penalties. Correlation cannot prove a cause-effect relationship. Maybe there is no cause-effect connection; maybe organizations wanting an aggressive image simply choose black outfits and hire aggressive players. (For a motorcycle gang, white outfits just won't do.) But can you imagine *possible* causes of this correlation? Frank and Gilovich suggested two: The correlation could occur because referees *perceive* acts by players in black as more violent than similar acts by players not wearing black. Or, players who wear black uniforms might *enact* the expected tough image.

The color effect is not race-related. Instead, believes cross-cultural researcher John Williams (1992), it stems from our ancestors' associations with the black of night and light of day. Thus, in many African societies, "black" magic is bad magic.

In experimenting to evaluate these two possibilities, Frank and Gilovich found, first, that uniform color did indeed affect perceptions. They videotaped two staged football plays in which black- or white-clad defenders either drove the ball carrier back several yards and then threw him to the ground or hit the ball carrier violently in midair. The experimenters then manipulated the jersey-color factor. They randomly assigned people to either an experimental condition or a control condition. In the **experimental condition**, raters saw the same videotape in full color. With the color on, the raters (fans and professional referees) were more likely to judge the tackles as aggressive and illegal when committed by players wearing black (Figure 1.7). For comparison, the experimenters took the color out of the picture to create a **control condition**—a condition that contrasts with the experimental treatment. When all the players' jerseys appeared dull gray, raters judged the tackles of the white- and black-clad defenders as equally illegal. Thus, the control condition of an experiment provides a baseline against which we can compare the effect of the treatment used in the experimental condition.

Note the distinction between random sampling in surveys and random assignment in experiments. Random sampling *helps us generalize to a larger population.* Random assignment *controls extraneous influences, which helps us infer cause and effect.*

Note that a key feature of experiments is **random assignment**. If enough individuals of different ages and opinions are randomly assigned to two groups, the random assignment will roughly equalize the two groups in age, opinion, and every other characteristic that could possibly affect the results. With random assignment, we can say that if the two groups behave or feel differently at the end of the experiment, it very probably is due to the manipulated factor. Without random assignment, the groups might differ in ways that could affect the results. If the researchers asked people from one university dormitory to view the color video and asked people from another dormitory to view the no-color video, they wouldn't know whether the color or the dorm population made the difference.

Note the importance of random assignment. If people had chosen their jersey color, the results might merely reflect a greater natural aggressiveness among those who prefer black jerseys.

In a second experiment, Cornell University students came to a study of "the psychology of competition." Frank and Gilovich randomly assigned them to

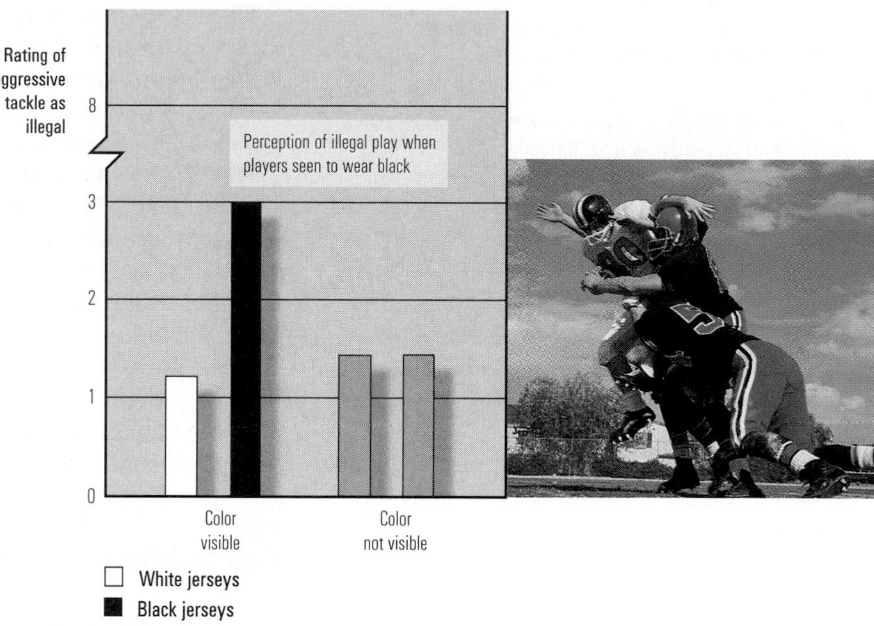

Figure 1.7 **Perceptions of violence** People judged videotaped midair tackles as more likely illegal when enacted by a player wearing black—but only when the color of the jersey was visible. (From Frank & Gilovich, 1988)

Answer to Figure 1.6 (page 22): Player B, whose outcomes may look more random, actually has fewer streaks than would be expected by chance. For these players, chance shooting, like chance coin tossing, should produce a change in outcome about 50 percent of the time. But 70 percent of the time (14 times out of 20) Player B's outcome changes on successive shots. Player A is scoring as we would expect from a 50 percent shooter; 10 times out of 20, Player A's next outcome is different.

wear either black or white jerseys and then invited them to choose some games. The students who donned black jerseys rather than white preferred more aggressive games. On average, wearing black affected not only perceptions but behavior as well.

The Frank and Gilovich experiments were fairly simple. They manipulated just one factor, jersey color. We call this experimental factor the **independent variable** because we can vary it independently of the other factors, such as the age or size of the players. Experimenters examine the effect of one or more independent variables on some measurable behavior, called the **dependent variable** because it can vary *depending* on what takes place during the experiment.

Both variables are given precise **operational definitions**. Operational definitions specify the procedures that manipulate the independent variable or measure the dependent variable. Thus they answer the "What do you mean?" question with an exactness that allows others to repeat the study. In Frank and Gilovich's first experiment (to test perception), the dependent variable was the subjects' ratings of illegal aggression. Table 1.2 shows the independent and dependent variables in their second experiment (to test behavior).

Let's recap: An experiment has at least two different conditions, a comparison or control condition and an experimental condition. Random assignment equates the conditions before any treatment effects. In this way, an experiment tests the effect of at least one independent variable (the experimental factor) on at least one dependent variable (the measured response).

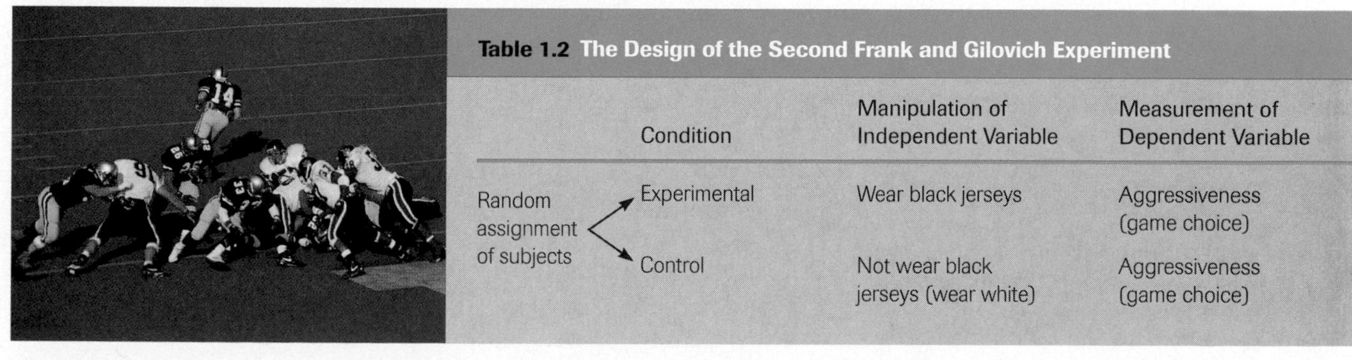

Table 1.2 **The Design of the Second Frank and Gilovich Experiment**

	Condition	Manipulation of Independent Variable	Measurement of Dependent Variable
Random assignment of subjects	Experimental	Wear black jerseys	Aggressiveness (game choice)
	Control	Not wear black jerseys (wear white)	Aggressiveness (game choice)

Note, too, that in this series of studies a very simple theory, inspired by everyday observations, generated hypotheses. These predictions were confirmed by the correlation between uniforms and penalties, which in turn stimulated experiments that examined causation. Table 1.3 compares the features of psychology's research methods.

How freely can we generalize Frank and Gilovich's findings? Surely we don't perceive Catholic priests and nuns as aggressive, nor does it seem that wearing black causes them to act aggressively. Frank and Gilovich wonder: Do the effects occur only in situations involving competition and aggressive confrontation? As often happens, answering one question has led to asking another. Scientific inquiry is a voyage of discovery toward a horizon, beyond which yet another horizon beckons.

"In solving one discovery we never fail to get an imperfect knowledge of others of which we had no idea before, so that we cannot solve one doubt without creating several new ones."

Joseph Priestly
Experiments and Observations on Different Kinds of Air
1775–1786

These concepts—experimental and control conditions, independent and dependent variables, random assignment—are important, yet easily confused. So let's put them to work with another intriguing set of experiments.

Can Subliminal Tapes Improve Your Life?

A new generation of entrepreneurs would have you believe so. Mail-order catalogs, cable television ads, and bookstores offer tapes with imperceptibly faint messages that will "reprogram your unconscious mind for success and happiness." While underachieving students listen to soothing music, subliminal messages (below one's threshold for hearing) persuade the unconscious that "I am a good student. I love learning." Procrastinators can be similarly reprogrammed to think "I set my priorities. I get things done ahead of time!"

Is there *anything* to these wild and sometimes wacky claims? Might positive subliminal messages help us, even a little? In Chapter 4, we will see that subliminal sensation is for real. We do process much information without conscious awareness. And under certain conditions, a stimulus too weak to recognize can briefly affect us.

But does this subtle, fleeting effect extend to the powerful, enduring influence claimed by the subliminal tape merchants? Anthony Greenwald and his colleagues (1991) decided to find out. They randomly assigned eager university students to listen daily for five weeks to commercial subliminal tapes designed to improve either self-esteem or memory. Then the researchers

Table 1.3 Comparing Research Methods

Research Method	Basic Purpose	How Conducted	What Is Manipulated
Descriptive	To observe and record behavior	Case studies, surveys, and naturalistic observations	Nothing
Correlational	To detect naturally occurring relationships; to assess how well one variable predicts another	Computing statistical association, sometimes among survey responses	Nothing
Experimental	To explore cause and effect	Manipulating one or more factors and using random assignment to eliminate preexisting differences among subjects	The independent variable(s)

placebo [pluh-SEE-bo] an inert substance or condition that may be administered instead of a presumed active agent, such as a drug, to see if it triggers the effects believed to characterize the active agent.

double-blind procedure an experimental procedure in which both the subject and the research staff are ignorant (blind) about whether the subject has received the treatment or a placebo. Commonly used in drug-evaluation studies.

In this experiment, what was the independent variable? The dependent variable? (See page 28.)

manipulated an experimental factor. On half the tapes the researchers switched the labels. People given these tapes *thought* they were receiving affirmations of self-esteem when they actually were hearing the memory enhancement tape. Or they got the memory tape but *thought* their self-esteem was being recharged (Figure 1.8).

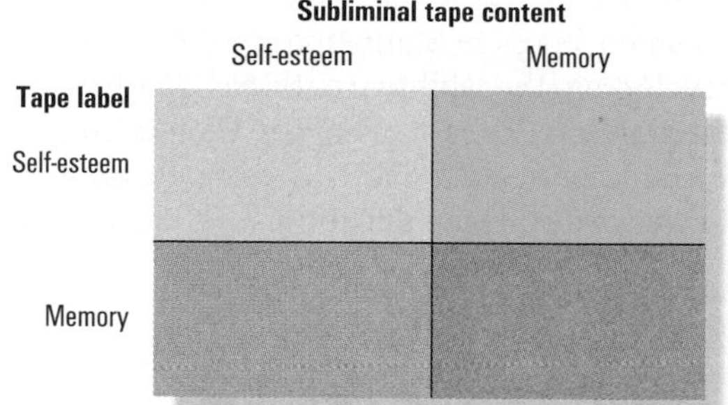

Figure 1.8 Design of the subliminal tapes experiment Students' self-esteem and memory abilities were assessed before and after listening to subliminal tapes purporting to increase either self-esteem or memory. Half the students, however, received deliberately mislabeled tapes.

Were the tapes effective? Scores on both self-esteem and memory tests, taken before and after the five weeks, revealed no effects. Zilch. Nevertheless, those who *thought* they had heard a memory tape *believed* that their memories had improved. Same for those who thought they had heard a self-esteem tape. Although the tapes had no effects, people *perceived* themselves receiving the benefits they expected. Reading this research, we can hear echoes of the testimonies that adorn the mail-order tape catalogs. Having bought something that is not supposed to be heard, and having indeed not heard it, many customers are impressed. "I really know that your tapes were invaluable in reprogramming my mind," wrote one thankful customer.

Our natural tendencies to try new remedies when we are in an emotional down can further distort a testimony. When our emotions rebound to normal, we attribute the rebound to something we have done. If three days into a cold we start taking vitamin C tablets and find our cold symptoms lessening, the pills may seem more potent than they are (an illusion of control). If, after doing exceptionally poorly on the first exam, we listen to a "peak learning" subliminal tape and then improve on the next exam, we may be deceived into crediting the tape rather than realizing that our performance has simply returned to our average. In the 1700s, even bloodletting *seemed* effective. Sometimes people improved after the treatment; when they didn't, the practitioner inferred the disease was too far advanced to be reversed. So, whether or not a remedy is effective, enthusiastic users will probably endorse it. To find out whether it actually is effective, we must experiment.

And that is precisely how we evaluate new drug treatments and new methods of psychological therapy (see Chapter 13). In many of these studies, the subjects are *blind* (uninformed) about what treatment, if any, they are receiving. One group might receive the treatment (say, a particular subliminal message or a new drug). Others receive a pseudotreatment—an inert **placebo** (a tape without the expected message or a pill with no drug in it). Often neither the subject nor the research assistant who collects the data will know which condition the subject is in. This **double-blind procedure** allows researchers to check a treatment's actual effects apart from their subjects' and their own enthusiasm for it. In one ten-year period, 16 double-blind experiments evaluated subliminal self-help tapes. Their results were uniform: Not one found any therapeutic effect (Greenwald, 1992).

Whether or not a remedy is effective, enthusiastic users will probably endorse it. To find out whether it actually is effective, we must experiment.

Among the general public there is surprising ignorance of the importance of controlled experiments. A 1995 science literacy survey asked people to imagine testing a new drug to combat high blood pressure (Miller & Pifer, 1996). Would it make more sense to give it to 1000 individuals and see what happened, or to give it to half of them and compare their reactions to those who got no drug? One-third preferred to give the drug to all 1000 people, reasoning that the greater the number of people tested, the more reliable the finding. Among those who preferred the option with the control group, 30 percent did so to save lives: "If the drug kills people, it kills only half as many." Remember: Psychology's most powerful tool for sorting reality from wishful thinking and evaluating cause and effect is the control group.

Experiments can also help us evaluate social programs. Do early childhood education programs boost impoverished children's chances for success? What are the effects of different antismoking appeals? Do school sex-education programs reduce teen pregnancies? To answer such questions, we can experiment: If a treatment is welcomed but resources are scarce, we could use a lottery to randomly assign some people (or regions) to experience the new program and others to a control condition. If the treated and untreated groups later differ, then we can be more confident that the treatment works.

Using the principles discussed in this chapter can also help us think critically—to see more clearly what we might otherwise miss or misinterpret and to generalize more accurately from our observations. People do think smarter when they understand and use the principles of research methods and statistics (Fong & others, 1986; Lehman & others, 1988; VanderStoep & Shaughnessy, 1997). It requires training and practice, but developing the ability to think clearly and critically is part of becoming an educated person. The report of the Project on Redefining the Meaning and Purpose of Baccalaureate Degrees (1985) eloquently asserts why there are few higher priorities in a college education:

> If anything is paid attention to in our colleges and universities, thinking must be it. Unfortunately, thinking can be lazy. It can be sloppy. . . . It can be fooled, misled, bullied. . . . Students possess great untrained and untapped capacities for logical thinking, critical analysis, and inquiry, but these are capacities that are not spontaneous: They grow out of wide instruction, experience, encouragement, correction, and constant use.

Answer to question on page 27: In the subliminal tapes experiment, the primary independent variable was the type of subliminal message, self-esteem versus memory. (This experiment actually had a second independent variable as well: people's beliefs about which tape they received.) The primary dependent variable was improvement on the self-esteem and memory measures.

REHEARSE IT!

15. A researcher wants to determine whether noise level affects the blood pressure of elderly subjects. In one group she varies the level of noise in the environment and records blood pressures. In this experiment the level of noise is the

- **a.** control condition.
- **b.** dependent variable (the factor being measured).
- **c.** independent variable (the factor being manipulated).
- **d.** cause of any blood pressure variations.

16. To test the effect of a new drug on depression, we randomly assign subjects to control and experimental conditions. Those in the experimental condition take a pink pill containing the new medication; the control group takes a pink pill that contains no medication. Which statement is true?

- **a.** The medication is the dependent variable.
- **b.** Depression is the independent variable.
- **c.** The subjects in the control group take a placebo.
- **d.** Neither the experimental nor the control group is told the purpose of the experiment.

17. To eliminate the biasing effect of a researcher's positive expectations on the outcome of a health clinic's research experiment

- **a.** subjects are randomly assigned to the control and experimental groups (random assignment).
- **b.** neither the subjects nor the researcher will know whether a given subject has been assigned to the experimental or control condition (double-blind procedure).
- **c.** the experimental subjects are carefully matched for age, sex, income, and level of education with subjects in the control group (controlled selection).
- **d.** experimental subjects are chosen by selecting every tenth person in an alphabetical listing of all the clinic's patients (random selection).

18. Description is to explanation as case study is to

- **a.** correlation.
- **b.** naturalistic observation.
- **c.** experiment.
- **d.** survey.

Frequently Asked Questions About Psychology

We have seen how case studies, surveys, and naturalistic observations allow us to describe behavior. We have noted that correlational studies assess the relationship between two factors, indicating how well we can predict one thing, knowing another. We have examined the logic that underlies experiments, which use control conditions and random assignment of subjects to isolate the

culture the enduring behaviors, ideas, attitudes, and traditions shared by a large group of people and transmitted from one generation to the next.

effects of an independent variable on a dependent variable. And we have reflected on how a scientific approach can restrain the biases of our unaided intuition.

This is reasonable preparation for understanding what lies ahead and for thinking critically about psychological matters. Yet, knowing this much, students often approach psychology with a mixture of curiosity and apprehension. So before we plunge in, let's confront some typical questions and concerns.

10. *Can Laboratory Experiments Relate to Everyday Life?*

When you see or hear a report of psychological research, do you ever wonder whether people's behavior in the laboratory has "external validity"—whether it predicts their behavior in real life? Does detecting the blink of a faint red light in a dark room have anything useful to say about flying a plane at night? Does our tendency to remember best the first and last items in a list of unrelated words tell us anything about how we remember the names of people we meet at a party? After viewing a violent, sexually explicit film, does an angered man's increased willingness to push buttons he thinks will electrically shock a woman really say anything about whether violent pornography makes men more likely to abuse women?

As psychologists, our concerns lie less with particular behaviors than with general principles that help explain many behaviors.

Before you answer, consider the intent of laboratory experiments. Far from considering artificiality a problem, the experimenter intends the laboratory environment to be a simplified reality—one in which important features of everyday life can be simulated and controlled. Just as an aeronautical wind tunnel enables an engineer to re-create atmospheric forces under controlled conditions, a laboratory experiment enables a psychologist to re-create psychological forces under controlled conditions.

The experiment's purpose, as Douglas Mook (1983) has noted, is not to re-create the exact behaviors of everyday life but to test theoretical principles. *It is the resulting principles—not the specific findings—that help explain everyday behaviors.* When psychologists apply laboratory research on aggression to actual violence, they are applying theoretical *principles* of aggressive behavior, principles refined through many experiments. Similarly, it is the principles of the visual system, developed from experiments in artificial settings (such as looking at red lights in the dark), that we apply to more complex behaviors such as night flying.

The point to remember: As psychologists, our concerns lie less with particular behaviors than with general principles that help explain many behaviors. The controlled simplicity of an experiment enables the study of cause-effect relationships.

A cultured greeting Because culture shapes people's understanding of social behavior, actions that seem ordinary to us may seem quite odd to visitors from far away. Yet underlying these differences are powerful similarities. Schoolchildren everywhere greet their teachers with respect, although not necessarily with the formality of this young Japanese schoolchild.

11. *Doesn't Behavior Depend on One's Culture and Gender?*

If culture shapes behavior, what can psychological studies done in one culture—often with white North Americans—really tell us about people in general? As we will see time and again, **culture**—shared ideas and behaviors that one generation passes on to the next—matters. Our culture influences our standards of promptness and frankness, our attitudes toward premarital sex and differing body shapes, our tendencies to be casual or formal, and much more. Being aware of such differences can restrain our assuming that others will—or should—think and act as we do. Given the growing mixing and clashing of cultures, the need for such awareness becomes urgent.

As you will see throughout this book, gender matters, too. Researchers report gender differences in what we dream, in how we express and detect emotions, and in our risk of alcoholism, depression, and eating disorders. Studying such differences is not only interesting but also potentially beneficial. Many researchers believe, for example, that women converse more readily to build relationships and that men talk more to give information and advice (Tannen, 1990). Knowing this difference can help prevent conflicts and misunderstandings on the job and in everyday relationships.

Likewise, it's important to remember that psychologically as well as biologically, women and men are overwhelmingly similar. Whether female or male, we learn to walk at about the same age; experience the same sensations of light and sound; feel the same pangs of hunger, desire, and fear; and exhibit similar overall intelligence and happiness. Moreover, we tend to exhibit and perceive the very behaviors our culture expects of males and females. Biology determines our sex, and then culture further bends the genders.

Psychologically as well as biologically, women and men are overwhelmingly similar.

Yet our shared biological heritage unites us as members of a universal human family. The same underlying processes guide people everywhere. The variation in languages—spoken and gestured—may impede communication across cultures. Yet all languages share deep principles of grammar, and people from opposite sides of the globe can communicate with a smile or a frown. People in different cultures vary in feelings of loneliness, yet across cultures shyness and low self-esteem magnify loneliness (Jones & others, 1985). Japanese prefer their fish raw and North Americans prefer theirs cooked, but the same principles of hunger and taste influence both when they sit down to a meal. It is truly said that we are each in certain respects like all others, like some others, and like no other. Studying people of all races and cultures helps us discern our similarities *and* our differences.

The point to remember: Even when specific attitudes and behaviors vary across cultures, as they often do, the underlying processes are much the same. (See Close-Up: Human Diversity and Human Kinship.) A children's song says it well: "We're all the same and different."

"All people are the same; only their habits differ."

Confucius
551–479 B.C.

12. *Why Do Psychologists Study Animals?*

Many psychologists study animals because they find them fascinating. Psychologists also study animals to learn about people, by doing experiments that are permissible only with animals. Human physiology resembles that of many other animals. That is why animal experiments have led to treatments for human diseases—insulin for diabetes, vaccines to prevent polio and rabies, transplants to replace defective organs.

Likewise, the processes by which humans see, exhibit emotion, and become obese operate in rats and monkeys. To discover more about the basics of human learning, researchers are even studying sea slugs. To understand how a combustion engine works, you would do better to study a lawn mower's engine than a Mercedes'. Humans, like Mercedes, are more complex. But it is precisely the simplicity of the sea slug's nervous system that makes it so revealing of the neural mechanisms of learning.

13. *Is It Ethical to Experiment on Animals?*

If we share important similarities with other animals, then should we not respect them? "We cannot defend our scientific work with animals on the basis of the similarities between them and ourselves and then defend it morally on the basis of differences," notes Roger Ulrich (1991). The animal protection movement protests the use of animals in psychological, biological, and medical

CLOSE-UP

Human Diversity and Human Kinship

Whatever our differences, we are the leaves of one tree. We in the human family share not only a common biological heritage—cut us and we bleed—but also common behavioral tendencies. Our shared brain architecture predisposes us to sense the world, develop language, and feel hunger through identical mechanisms. Coming from opposite sides of the globe, we know how to read one another's smiles and frowns. Whether our last name is Wong, Nkomo, Gonzales, or Smith, we fear strangers beginning at about 8 months of age and as adults prefer the company of individuals whose attitudes and attributes are similar to our own. Regardless of our culture or gender, we regard female features that signify youth and health—and reproductive potential—as attractive. Whether we live in the Arctic or the tropics, we prefer sweet tastes to sour, we divide the color spectrum into similar colors, and we feel drawn to behaviors that produce and protect offspring. As members of one species, we affiliate, conform, reciprocate favors, punish offenses, organize hierarchies of status, and grieve a child's death. A visitor from outer space could drop in anywhere and find humans dancing and feasting, singing and worshipping, playing sports and games, laughing and crying, living in families, and forming groups. To be human is to be more alike than different. Taken together, such universal behavioral tendencies define human nature.

These behavioral similarities arise from our biological similarity. Genetically, we are all very similar to one another. Of our genetic differences, only 6 percent is differences among races. Only 8 percent is differences among groups within a race. The rest—over 85 percent—is individual variation within local groups. The average genetic difference between two Icelandic villagers or between two Kenyans is much greater than the difference between the two groups. Thus, notes geneticist Richard Lewontin (1982), if after a worldwide catastrophe only Icelanders or Kenyans survived, the human species would suffer only "a trivial reduction" in its genetic diversity.

Among our similarities, the most important—the behavioral hallmark of our species—is our enormous capacity to learn and adapt. Ironically, this fundamental likeness enables human diversity. We all are driven to eat, but depending on our culturally learned tastes, we may have a yen for fish eyes, fried insects, or chicken legs. Go barefoot for a summer and you will develop toughened, calloused feet—a biological adaptation to friction. Meanwhile, your shoed neighbor will remain a tenderfoot. Is the difference between the two of you an effect of environment? Yes, of course. Is it also the product of a biological mechanism? Yes again. Our shared biology enables our adaptive diversity (Buss, 1991).

As citizens in a multicultural world, we need to appreciate our similarities. We also need to understand our differences. At various points throughout this book we will examine our *individual differences* in traits such as temperament, intelligence, personality, psychological disorder, and health. Depending on their experiences in particular environments, one person may become aggressive, another gentle; one may value freedom, another order and control; one may prize individuality, another the social ties that bind people together. We will also glimpse a second dimension of diversity—our *group differences* in tendencies ranging from concern about body weight, to expressing anger, to individualism. Here again, our shared biology enables our adaptive diversity: Where famine threatens, plump is beautiful; where food is abundant, slender is chic.

"Whatever I do or think as a black can never be more than a variant of what all people do and think. . . . All races are composed of human beings."

Shelby Steele
The Content of Our Character
1990

research—some 20 million U.S. animals annually, according to the National Academy of Sciences (1991), plus 3 million British and 2 million Canadian animals (Mukerjee, 1997). Researchers remind us that these 25 million animals are less than 1 percent of the 6 billion animals killed annually in these countries as a source of food (which means the average person eats 20 animals a year). While researchers each year conduct experiments on some 200,000 dogs and cats cared for under humane regulations, humane animal shelters are forced to kill 50 times that many.

Mobilization for Animals, a network of animal protection organizations, has nevertheless been concerned. It has declared that animals used in psychological experiments are shocked "until they lose the ability to even scream in pain,

Justifiable experimentation Is it right to use animals to advance our understanding of humans? For animal rights activists, no purpose justifies hurting, frightening, or (as here) manipulating an animal. For most psychologists and medical researchers, animal research is ethically justified so long as researchers observe strict standards and inflict no unnecessary pain.

. . . [are] deprived of food and water to suffer and die slowly from hunger and thirst, . . . [are] put in total isolation chambers until they are driven insane or even die from despair and terror," and are made "the victims of extreme pain and stress, inflicted upon them out of idle curiosity." Psychologists Caroline Coile and Neal Miller (1984) analyzed every animal research article published in the American Psychological Association's journals during the preceding five years. They found no study in which any of these allegations were true. Even when researchers used shock, it usually was of a mild intensity that humans can easily endure on their fingers. Only 7 percent of psychology's studies involved animals, 95 percent of which were rats, mice, rabbits, or birds. About 10 percent of these animal studies involved electric shock (Coile & Miller, 1984; Gallup & Suarez, 1985). In British psychology departments, where animal use has dropped by two-thirds since 1977, electric shock has been used in only 4 percent of animal studies—all involving rats (Thomas & Blackman, 1991).

Animal protection organizations, such as Psychologists for the Ethical Treatment of Animals, advocate naturalistic observation of animals rather than laboratory manipulation. However, say researchers, this is not the morality of good versus evil but of compassion (for animals) versus compassion (for people). How many of us would have attacked Pasteur's experiments with rabies, which in causing some dogs to suffer led to a vaccine that spared millions of people, and dogs, from agonizing death? And would we really wish to have deprived ourselves of the animal research that led to effective methods of training retarded children; of relieving fears and depression; and of controlling obesity, alcoholism, and stress-related pain and disease?

"Please do not forget those of us who suffer from incurable diseases or disabilities who hope for a cure through research that requires the use of animals."

Paraplegic psychologist Dennis Feeney (1987)

Out of the heated debate on this subject, two issues emerge. The basic one is whether it is right to place the well-being of humans above that of animals. In experiments on stress and cancer, is it right that mice get tumors so that people might not? Is the human use of other animals as natural and moral as the behavior of carnivorous hawks, cats, and whales? (Animals themselves do not assign rights to other animals lower on the food chain.)

If we give human life first priority, the second issue is the priority given the well-being of animals. What safeguards should protect animals? Most researchers today feel ethically obligated to enhance the well-being of captive animals and protect them from needless suffering. They also believe that humane care is good science, because pain and stress would distort animals' behavior during experiments. Thus, they welcomed national animal protection legislation updated by the United States in 1985 and by Britain in 1986, and they supported the accompanying regulations and laboratory inspections (Cherfas, 1990; Johnson, 1990).

"The greatness of a nation can be judged by the way its animals are treated."

Mahatma Gandhi
1869–1948

"I believe that to prevent, cripple, or needlessly complicate the research that can relieve animal and human suffering is profoundly inhuman, cruel, and immoral."

Psychologist Neal Miller (1983)

Ironically, animals have themselves benefited from animal research. Studies have helped improve their care and management in laboratories, zoos, and natural habitats. By revealing our behavioral kinship with animals and the remarkable intelligence of some animals, experiments have also increased our empathy with them. At its best, a psychology that is concerned for humans and sensitive to animals can serve the welfare of both.

14. *Is It Ethical to Experiment on People?*

If the image of animals or people receiving supposed electric shocks troubles you, you may find it reassuring that most psychological research involves no such stress. Blinking lights, flashing words, and pleasant social interactions are the rule.

Occasionally, though, researchers temporarily stress or deceive people. This is done only when judged essential to a justifiable end, such as understanding and controlling violent behavior or studying mood swings. Such experiments wouldn't work if the participants knew all there was to know about the experiment beforehand. Either the procedures would be ineffective or the participants, wanting to be helpful, might try to confirm the researchers' predictions.

Ethical principles developed by the American Psychological Association (1992) and the British Psychological Society (1993) urge investigators to (1) obtain the informed consent of potential participants, (2) protect them from harm and discomfort, (3) treat information about individual participants confidentially, and (4) fully explain the research afterward. Moreover, most universities today screen research proposals through an ethics committee that safeguards participants' well-being.

15. *Is Psychology Free of Value Judgments?*

"It is doubtless impossible to approach any human problem with a mind free from bias."

Simone de Beauvoir
The Second Sex
1953

Psychology is definitely not value-free. Values affect what we study, how we study it, and how we interpret results. Consider: Researchers' values influence their choice of research topics—whether to study worker productivity or worker morale, sex discrimination or gender differences, conformity or independence. Values can also color "the facts." Our preconceptions can bias our observations and interpretations; sometimes we see what we want or expect to see (Figure 1.9). Even the words we use to describe a phenomenon can reflect our values. Whether we label the sex acts we do not practice as "perversions" or as "sexual variations" conveys a value judgment. The same holds true in everyday speech, as when one person's "terrorists" are another's "freedom fighters," or one person's "faith" is another's "fanaticism." Our labeling someone as "firm" or "stubborn," "careful" or "picky," "discreet" or "secretive" reveals our feelings. Both in and out of psychology, labels describe and labels evaluate.

Figure 1.9 What do you see? People interpret ambiguous information to fit their preconceptions. Did you see a duck or a rabbit? What influenced your first impression? (From Shepard, 1990)

Popular applications of psychology also contain hidden values. When people defer to "professional" guidance about how to live—how to raise children, how to achieve self-fulfillment, what to do with sexual feelings, how to get ahead at work—they are accepting value-laden advice. A science of behavior and mental processes can help us reach our goals, but it cannot decide them.

So, is psychology potentially dangerous? If some people see psychology as mere common sense, others have an opposite concern—that it is becoming dangerously powerful. Might psychology be used to manipulate people? Might it become the tool of someone seeking to create a totalitarian *Brave New World* or *1984?*

Knowledge is a power that, like all powers, we can use for good or evil. Nuclear power has been used to light up cities—and to demolish them. Persuasive power has been used to educate people—and to deceive them. The power of mind-altering drugs has been used to restore sanity—and to destroy it.

Although psychology has the power to deceive, it strives to enlighten. Psychologists are exploring ways to enhance learning, creativity, and compassion. And psychology speaks to many of the world's great problems—war, overpopulation, prejudice, family dysfunction, crime—all of which involve attitudes and behaviors. Psychology also speaks to humanity's deepest longings—for food and water, for love, for happiness. Psychology cannot address all the great questions of life, but it speaks to some mighty important ones.

REHEARSE IT!

19. In a laboratory experiment, features of everyday life can be simulated, manipulated, and controlled. The laboratory environment is designed to help us

a. exactly re-create the events of everyday life.
b. re-create psychological forces under controlled conditions.
c. create opportunities for naturalistic observation.
d. minimize the use of animals and humans in psychological research.

20. Which of the following is true regarding gender differences and similarities?

a. Differences between the genders outweigh any similarities.
b. Despite some gender differences, the underlying processes of human behavior are the same.
c. Both similarities and differences between the genders depend more on biology than on environment.
d. Gender differences are so numerous, it is difficult to make meaningful comparisons.

21. The animal protection movement has protested the use of animals in all fields of scientific research. In defending their experimental research with animals, psychologists have noted that

a. animals' physiology and behavior can tell us much about our own.
b. they do not torture or needlessly exploit animals.
c. advancing the well-being of humans justifies animal experimentation.
d. all of the above.

Tips for Studying Psychology

16. *How do psychological principles help you as a student?*

The investment you are making in studying psychology has the potential to enrich your life and enlarge your vision. Although many of life's significant questions are beyond psychology, some very important ones are illuminated by even a first course in psychology. Through painstaking research, psychologists have gained insights into brain and mind, depression and joy, dreams and memories. Even the unanswered questions can enrich us, by renewing our sense of mystery about "things too wonderful" for us yet to understand. What is more, your study of psychology can help teach you *how to ask important questions*—how to think critically as you evaluate competing ideas and pop psychology's claims.

Having your life enriched and your vision enlarged (and getting a decent grade, too) requires effective study. As we will see in Chapter 7, Memory, to master any subject you must *actively process* it. Your mind is not like your stomach, something to be filled passively; it is more like a muscle, which grows stronger with exercise. Countless experiments reveal that people learn and remember material best when they put it in their own words, rehearse it, and then review and rehearse it again.

The **SQ3R** study method incorporates these principles (Robinson, 1970). SQ3R is an acronym for its five steps: *S*urvey, *Q*uestion, *R*ead, *R*ehearse, *R*eview.

To study a chapter, first *survey*, taking a bird's-eye view as you note its headings. Notice how the chapter is organized.

As you prepare to read each section, use its heading or the preview question to form a *question* that you should answer. For this section, you might have asked, "How can I most effectively and efficiently master the information in this book?"

Then *read*, actively searching for the answer. At each sitting, read only as much of the chapter as you can absorb without tiring. Usually, a single main chapter section will do—the Frequently Asked Questions section you just finished, for example. Relating what you are reading to your own life will improve

SQ3R a study method incorporating five steps: *Survey*, *Question*, *Read*, *Rehearse*, *Review*.

understanding and retention. Reading the occasional Close-Up, Psychology Applied, and Thinking Critically boxes will also help.

Having read a section, *rehearse* in your own words what you read. Test yourself by trying to answer your question, rehearsing what you can recall, then glancing back over what you can't recall.

Finally, *review:* Read over any notes you have taken, again with an eye on the chapter's organization, and quickly review the whole chapter.

Survey, question, read, rehearse, review. This book's chapters are organized to facilitate your use of the SQ3R study system. Each chapter begins with a chapter outline that aids your *survey*. Headings and preview *questions* suggest issues and concepts you should consider as you *read*. The material is organized into sections of readable length, and the end of a section is the time to *rehearse* what you have learned. The chapter summaries *review* the chapter's essentials and list key terms to help you check your mastery of important concepts. Survey, question, read. . . .

Five additional study tips may further boost your learning:

1. *Distribute your study time.* One of psychology's oldest findings is that "spaced practice" promotes better retention than "massed practice." You'll remember material better if you space your time over several study periods rather than cram it into one long study blitz. Better to give your study of this text one hour a day, with one day off a week, than six hours at a time. Doing this requires a disciplined approach to managing your time. (Richard Straub explains time management in *Discovering Psychology*, the study guide that accompanies this text.) For example, rather than trying to read an entire chapter in a single sitting, read just one section and then turn to something else.
2. *Learn to think critically.* Whether reading or in class, note people's *assumptions and values*. What perspective or bias underlies an argument? *Evaluate evidence*. Is it anecdotal? Correlational? Experimental? *Assess conclusions*. Are there alternative explanations?
3. *In class, listen actively.* As psychologist William James urged a century ago, "No reception without reaction, no impression without . . . expression." Listen for the main ideas and subideas of a lecture. Write them down. Ask questions during and after class. In class, as in your private study, process the information actively and you will understand and retain it better.
4. *Overlearn.* Psychology tells us that overlearning improves retention. Most of us are prone to overestimating how much we know. You may understand a chapter as you read it, but by devoting extra study time to testing yourself and reviewing what you think you know, you will retain your new knowledge long into the future.
5. *Be a smart test-taker.* If a test contains both multiple-choice questions and an essay question, turn first to the essay. Read the question carefully, noting exactly what the instructor is asking. On the back of a page, pencil in a list of points you'd like to make and then organize them. Before writing, put aside the essay and work through the multiple-choice questions. (As you do so, your mind may continue to mull over the essay question. Sometimes the objective questions will bring pertinent thoughts to mind.) Then reread the essay question, rethink your answer, and start writing. When finished, proofread to eliminate spelling and grammatical errors that make you look less competent than you are. When reading multiple-choice questions, don't confuse yourself by trying to imagine how each of the alternatives might be right. Try instead to recall the answer *before* reading the alternatives given. Answer the question as if it were a fill-in-the-blank; first cover the answers and complete the sentence in your mind, and then find the alternative that best matches your own answer.

While exploring psychology, you will learn much more than effective study techniques. Psychology deepens our appreciation for how we humans perceive, think, feel, and act. By so doing it can indeed enrich our lives and enlarge our vision. Through this book I hope to help guide you toward that end. As educator Charles Eliot said a century ago: "Books are the quietest and most constant of friends, and the most patient of teachers."

REVIEWING ■ *Introduction: Thinking Critically With Psychology*

What Is Psychology?

1. ***How did the science of psychology develop?***

Beginning with the first psychological laboratory, founded in 1879 by German philosopher and physiologist Wilhelm Wundt, **psychology's** modern roots can be found in many disciplines and countries. Psychology's historic perspectives and current activities lead us to define the field as the science of behavior and mental processes.

2. ***What theoretical perspectives do psychologists take?***

There are many disciplines that study human nature. Psychology is one. Within psychology, the *neuroscience, behavioral, evolutionary, behavior genetics, cognitive,* and *social-cultural perspectives* are complementary. Where psychologists stand on the *nature-nurture issue* depends partly on their perspective. Each perspective has its own purposes, questions, and limits; together they provide a fuller understanding of mind and behavior.

3. ***What are psychology's specialized subfields?***

Psychologists' activities are widely varied, ranging from the **basic research** conducted by biological, developmental, or personality psychologists and the **applied research** of industrial/organizational psychologists to the diagnoses and therapies of **clinical psychologists** and **psychiatrists**.

Why Do Psychology?

4. ***What attitudes characterize scientific inquiry?***

Scientific inquiry begins with an attitude—an eagerness to skeptically scrutinize competing ideas and an open-minded humility before nature. Putting ideas, even crazy-sounding ideas, to the test helps us winnow sense from nonsense. The curiosity that drives us to test ideas and to expose their underlying assumptions carries into everyday life as **critical thinking**.

5. ***What leads people to overestimate the value of common sense and to underestimate the usefulness of psychological science?***

If intuition and common sense were trustworthy, we would have less need for scientific inquiry and critical thinking. But without such thinking we readily succumb to **hindsight bias**, or the *I-knew-it-all-along phenomenon.* Learning the outcome of a study (or of an everyday happening) can make it seem like obvious common sense. But things seldom seem so obvious before the fact. We also are routinely overconfident of our judgments, thanks partly to our bias to seek information that confirms them. Such biases lead us to overestimate our unaided intuition. Although limited by the testable questions it can address, a scientific approach can help us sift reality from illusion, taking us beyond the horizons of our intuition and common sense.

How Do Psychologists Ask and Answer Questions?

6. ***What is the place of theory in the scientific method?***

Research stimulates the construction of **theories**, which organize the observations and imply predictive **hypotheses**. These hypotheses (predictions) are then tested to validate and refine the theory and to suggest practical applications. Research findings are considered reliable if they can be **replicated**.

7. ***How do psychologists observe and describe behavior?***

Through individual **case studies, surveys** among **random samples** of a **population**, and **naturalistic observations**, psychologists observe and describe behavior and mental processes. In generalizing from observations, remember: Do not overestimate the extent to which others agree with us (the **false consensus effect**) and keep in mind that representative samples are a better guide than vivid examples.

8. ***Why do correlations permit prediction but not explanation? How accurately does the naked eye detect correlations?***

The strength of the relationship between one factor and another is expressed in their **correlation**. Correlations help us to see relationships that the naked eye might miss and to discount **illusory correlations** and random events that might otherwise look significant. Knowing how closely two things are positively or negatively correlated tells us how much one predicts the other. But correlation is only a measure of relationship; it does not reveal cause and effect.

9. ***How do experiments clarify or reveal cause-effect relationships?***

To discover cause-effect relationships, psychologists conduct **experiments**. By constructing a controlled reality, experimenters can manipulate one or more factors and discover how these **independent variables** affect a particular behavior, the **dependent variable**, as specified by **operational definitions**. In many experiments, control is achieved by **randomly assigning** people to either an **experimental condition**, in which they are exposed to the treatment, or to a **control condition**, in which they experience no treatment or a different version of the treatment. Sometimes a pseudotreatment—a **placebo**—is given to the control group. To ensure the reliability of the results, a **double-blind procedure** may be employed.

Frequently Asked Questions About Psychology

10. *Can laboratory experiments relate to everyday life?*

By intentionally creating a controlled, artificial environment in the lab, researchers aim to test theoretical principles. These principles help us to understand, describe, explain, and predict everyday behaviors.

11. *Doesn't behavior depend on one's culture and gender?*

Although attitudes and behaviors vary across **cultures**, the principles that underlie them vary much less. Cross-cultural psychology explores both our cultural differences and the universal similarities that define our human kinship. Gender is also a fact of life. Although gender differences tend to capture attention, it is important to remember the much greater similarities between men and women.

12. *Why do psychologists study animals?*

Some psychologists study animals out of an interest in animal behavior. Others do so because knowledge of the physiological and psychological processes of animals permits a better understanding of the similar processes operating in humans.

13. *Is it ethical to experiment on animals?*

Only about 7 percent of all psychological experiments involve animals, and under ethical and legal guidelines these animals rarely experience pain. Nevertheless, animal rights groups raise an important issue: Is an animal's temporary suffering justified if it leads to the relief of human suffering?

14. *Is it ethical to experiment on people?*

Occasionally researchers temporarily stress or deceive people in order to learn something important. Professional ethical standards provide guidelines for the treatment of human as well as animal participants.

15. *Is psychology free of value judgments?*

Psychology is not value-free. Psychologists' own values influence their choice of research topics, their theories and observations, their labels for behavior, and their professional advice.

Knowledge is power that can be used for good or evil. Applications of psychology's principles have so far been mostly for the good, and psychology addresses some of humanity's greatest problems and deepest longings.

Tips for Studying Psychology

16. *How do psychological principles help you as a student?*

Experiments have shown that learning and memory are enhanced by active study. The **SQ3R** study method applies the principles derived from these experiments.

CRITICAL THINKING EXERCISE by Richard O. Straub

Now that you have read and reviewed Chapter 1, take your learning a step further by testing your critical thinking skills on this scientific problem-solving exercise. For an introduction to these exercises, turn to Appendix B before you begin working.

Philip, who teaches first grade, believes that educational television programs such as *Sesame Street* promote reading ability in young children. He announces his hunch to his students and tells their parents about his idea during a meeting between parents and teachers. Some parents respond enthusiastically when he asks for volunteers to participate in a three-month experiment to test his hypothesis. Ten volunteers are assigned to the experimental group and are instructed to have their children watch the one-hour *Sesame Street* program each day after school. The parents of 10 other students, who are picked at random from the remaining members of the class, receive the same instructions, except that the program they watch is a one-hour noneducational cartoon. After the three-month period, Philip administers a standardized reading test to both groups. He is delighted to find that the average test score of the students in the experimental group is substantially higher than that of the students in the comparison group.

1. What is the focal behavior of the study?
2. What is Philip's hypothesis?
3. What is the independent variable?
4. What is the dependent variable?
5. List three variables that are controlled in the experiment.
6. List three variables that are not controlled and explain how they might have affected Philip's findings.
7. Was the research a valid test of Philip's hypothesis? Explain your reasoning.

Check your progress on becoming a critical thinker by comparing your answers with the sample answers found in Appendix B.

REHEARSE IT ANSWER KEY

1. c., **2.** b., **3.** a., **4.** d., **5.** c., **6.** d., **7.** c., **8.** a., **9.** c., **10.** c., **11.** d., **12.** b., **13.** c., **14.** a., **15.** c., **16.** c., **17.** b., **18.** c., **19.** b., **20.** b., **21.** d.

CHAPTER
2

Biology and Behavior

1. *Why do psychologists study biology?*

No principle is more central to today's psychology, or to this book, than this: *Everything psychological is simultaneously biological.* Your every idea, every mood, every urge is a biological happening. You are a body. You think, feel, and act with your body. You relate to the world through your body. (Try laughing, crying, or loving without it.) Your body—your genes, your brain, your body chemistry, your inner organs, your appearance—is you. Without your body, you are, indeed, nobody. Although we find it convenient to talk separately of biological and psychological influences on behavior, let us not forget: To think, feel, or act without a body is as plausible as running without legs.

As we finish this century, scientific attention is riveted on the most amazing parts of our body—our brain, its component neural systems, and their genetic blueprints. The brain's ultimate challenge is to understand itself. How does the brain organize and communicate with itself? How does heredity prewire the brain, and how does experience modify it? How does the brain process the information needed for a basketball player's jump shot? A poet's rhythm of words? A lover's memory of the first kiss?

We have come far since the early 1800s, when a German physician named Franz Gall invented *phrenology*, an ill-fated theory that bumps on the skull could reveal our mental abilities and character traits. At one point, Britain had 29 phrenological societies, and phrenologists traveled North America giving skull readings (Hunt, 1993).

Despite its wrong-headedness, phrenology correctly focused attention on the idea that various brain regions have particular functions. In little more than a century, we have also realized that the body is composed of cells; that among these are nerve cells that conduct electricity and "talk" to one another by sending chemical messages across a tiny gap that separates them; that specific brain systems serve specific functions (though not the functions Gall supposed); and that from the information processed in these different brain systems, we construct our experience of sights and sounds, meanings and memories, pain and passion. You and I are privileged to live in a time when discoveries about the interplay of our biology and behavior are occurring at an exhilarating pace.

Throughout this book you will find examples of how our biology underlies our behavior and mental processes. By studying the links between biological activity and psychological events, **biological psychologists** are gaining a better

A wrong-headed theory Despite initial acceptance of Gall's speculations, bumps on the skull tell us nothing about how the brain works. Nevertheless, some of his assumptions have been found to hold true: Different parts of the brain do control different aspects of behavior.

understanding of sleep and dreams, depression and schizophrenia, hunger and sex, stress and disease. We therefore begin our study of psychology with a look at its biological roots.

Neural Communication

Each of us is a system composed of subsystems that are in turn composed of even smaller subsystems. Cells organize to form body organs such as the stomach, heart, and brain, which form larger systems for digestion, circulation, and information processing, which are part of an even larger system—you, which in turn forms a part of your family, community, and culture. For a deep understanding of behavior, we must study how biological, psychological, and social systems work and interact. We are bio-psycho-social systems.

In this book we start small and build—to the brain in this chapter, and to the environmental and cultural influences that interact with our biology in later chapters. At all levels, psychologists examine how we process information—how we get information in; how we organize, interpret, and store it; and how we use it. For scientists, it is a happy fact of nature that the information systems of humans and other animals operate similarly—so similarly, in fact, that you could not distinguish between small samples of brain tissue from a human and a monkey. This similarity allows researchers to study relatively simple animals, such as squids and sea slugs, to discover how their neural systems operate, and to study mammals' brains to understand the organization of our own. Human brains are more complex, but they follow principles that govern the rest of the animal world.

Figure 2.1 **A motor neuron**

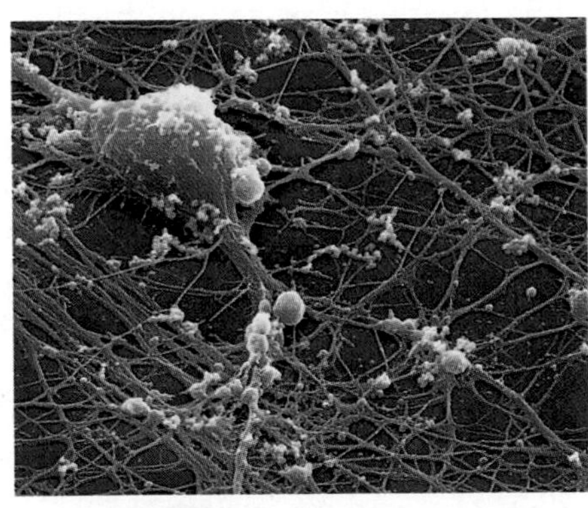

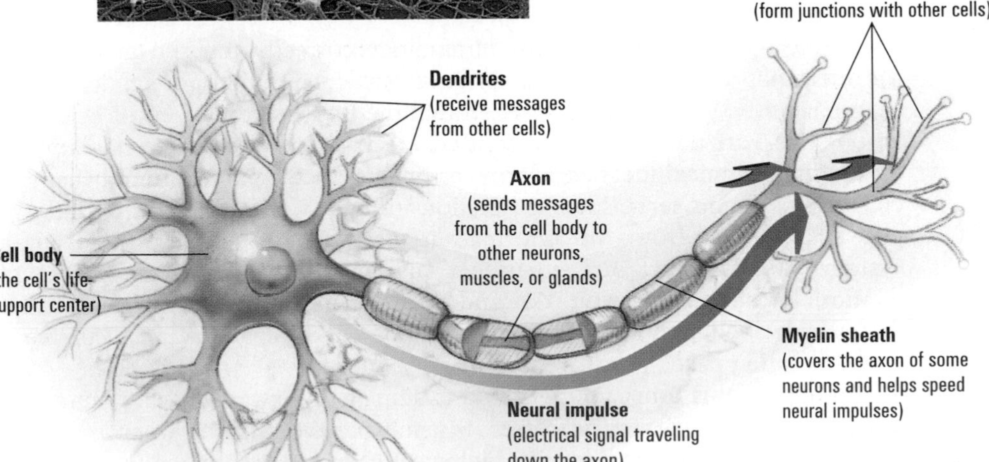

Neurons

2. *What are neurons, and how do they transmit information?*

Our body's neural information system is complexity built from simplicity. Its building blocks are **neurons**, or nerve cells. Each neuron consists of a cell body and its branching fibers (Figure 2.1). The fibers are of two types: The bushy **dendrites** receive information. The **axon** passes it along to other neurons or to muscles or glands. Unlike the short dendrites, axons may be very long, projecting several feet through the body. A neuron that carries orders to a leg muscle has a cell body and an axon that are roughly on the scale of a basketball attached to a rope 4 miles long. A layer of fatty tissue, called the **myelin sheath**, insulates the axons of some neurons and helps speed their impulses. The importance of the myelin sheath can be seen in the disease multiple sclerosis, in which the myelin sheath degenerates, with a resulting slowdown of communication to muscles and loss of muscle control.

A neuron fires an impulse when it receives a signal from adjacent neurons or from sensory receptors stimulated by pressure, heat, light, or chemical messages. The neural impulse, called the **action potential**, is a brief electrical

biological psychology a branch of psychology concerned with the links between biology and behavior. (Some biological psychologists call themselves *behavioral neuroscientists, neuropsychologists, behavior geneticists, physiological psychologists,* or *biopsychologists.*)

neuron a nerve cell; the basic building block of the nervous system.

dendrite the bushy, branching extensions of a neuron that receive messages and conduct impulses toward the cell body.

axon the extension of a neuron, ending in branching terminal fibers, through which messages are sent to other neurons or to muscles or glands.

myelin [MY-uh-lin] **sheath** a layer of fatty tissue segmentally encasing the fibers of many neurons; makes possible vastly greater transmission speed of neural impulses.

action potential a neural impulse; a brief electrical charge that travels down an axon. The action potential is generated by the movement of positively charged atoms in and out of channels in the axon's membrane.

threshold the level of stimulation required to trigger a neural impulse.

synapse [SIN-aps] the junction between the axon tip of the sending neuron and the dendrite or cell body of the receiving neuron. The tiny gap at this junction is called the *synaptic gap* or *cleft.*

neurotransmitters chemical messengers that traverse the synaptic gaps between neurons. When released by the sending neuron, neurotransmitters travel across the synapse and bind to receptor sites on the receiving neuron, thereby influencing whether it will generate a neural impulse.

charge that travels down the axon, rather like a line of dominoes falling, each one tripping the next.

Depending on the type of fiber, the neural impulse travels at speeds ranging from a sluggish 2 miles per hour to, in some myelinated fibers, a breakneck 200 or more miles per hour. But even this top speed is 3 million times slower than the speed of electricity through a wire. We measure brain activity in milliseconds (thousandths of a second) and computer activity in nanoseconds (billionths of a second). That helps to explain why, unlike the nearly instantaneous reactions of a high-speed computer, it may take a quarter-second or more for you to react to a sudden event, such as a child darting in front of your car.

The neuron, a miniature decision-making device, receives signals on its dendrites and cell body from hundreds or even thousands of other neurons. Some of these signals are *excitatory*, rather like pushing a neuron's accelerator. Other signals are *inhibitory*, rather like pushing its brake. The combined signals trigger an impulse if excitatory signals minus inhibitory signals exceed a minimum intensity, called the **threshold**. If excitatory inputs exceed the threshold, the neuron transmits a neural impulse (the action potential) down its axon, which branches into junctions with hundreds or thousands of other neurons and with muscles and glands.

Increasing the stimulus above the threshold, however, will not increase the impulse's intensity. (The neuron's reaction is an *all-or-none response*; like guns, neurons either fire or they don't.) Nor does the strength of the stimulus affect the impulse's speed.

How then do we detect the intensity of a stimulus? How do we distinguish a gentle touch from a firm hug? A strong stimulus cannot trigger a stronger or faster impulse in a neuron—squeezing a trigger harder won't make a bullet go faster. But a strong stimulus can trigger more neurons to fire, and to fire more often.

"I sing the body electric."

Walt Whitman
"Children of Adam"
1855

How Neurons Communicate

3. *How do nerve cells communicate?*

Neurons interweave so intricately that even with a microscope it is hard to see where one neuron ends and another begins. A hundred years ago many scientists believed that the branching axon of one cell fused with the dendrites of another in an uninterrupted fabric.

We now know that the axon terminal of one neuron is separated from the receiving neuron by a tiny gap less than a millionth of an inch wide. This junction is called the **synapse**, and the gap is called the *synaptic gap* or *cleft*. To the Nobel laureate, Spanish neuroanatomist Santiago Ramùn y Cajal (1832–1934), these near-unions of neurons—"protoplasmic kisses," he called them—were another of nature's marvels. How does the nerve impulse execute the protoplasmic kiss? How does it cross the tiny synaptic gap? The answer is one of the important scientific discoveries of our age.

"All information processing in the brain involves neurons 'talking to' each other at synapses."

Neuroscientist Solomon H. Snyder (1984)

When the action potential reaches the knoblike terminals at an axon's end, it triggers the release of chemical messengers, called **neurotransmitters** (Figure 2.2, page 42). Within 1/10,000th of a second, the neurotransmitter molecules cross the synaptic gap and bind to *receptor sites* on the receiving neuron—as precisely as a key fits a lock. For an instant, the neurotransmitter unlocks tiny channels at the receiving site. This allows electrically charged atoms to enter the receiving neuron, thereby either exciting or inhibiting its readiness to fire.

Most neurons have a resting rate of random firing that increases or decreases with input from other neurons and from chemicals that affect their sensitivity. Roughly speaking, the neuron is democratic: If it receives many more excitatory than inhibitory messages, the cell fires often. More electrical impulses flash down

Figure 2.2 **How neurons communicate**

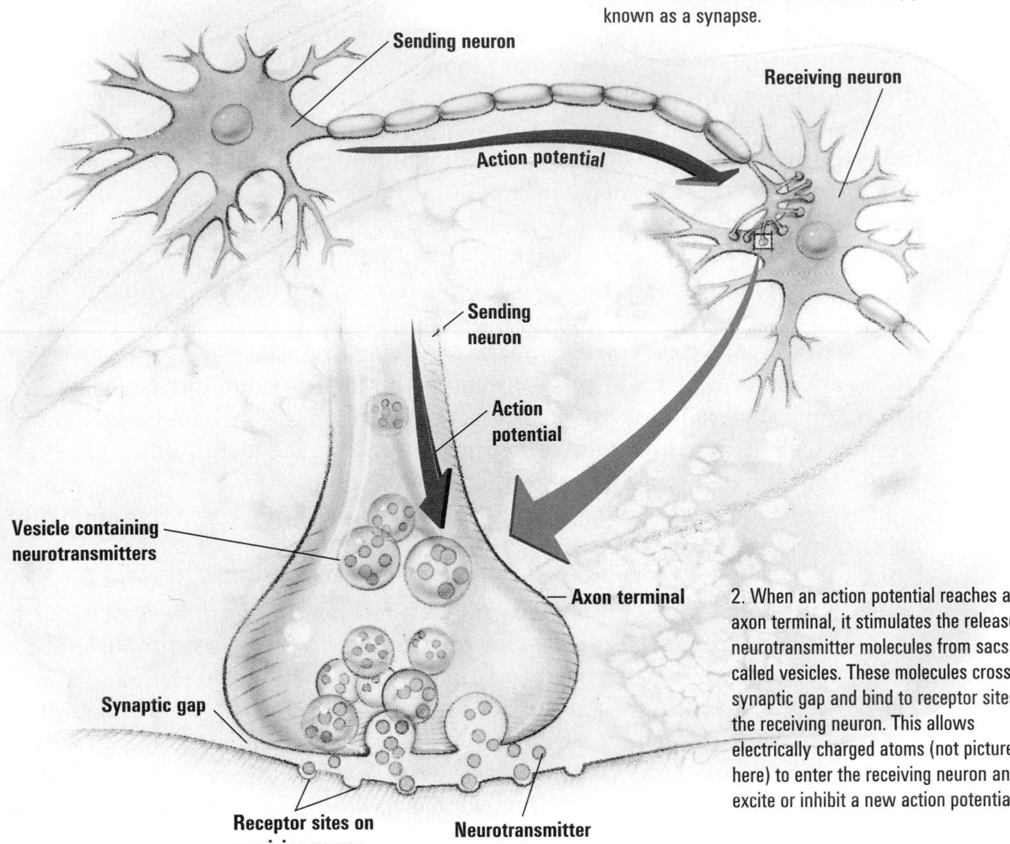

its axon, releasing more packets of neurotransmitters, which diffuse across their synaptic gaps to other neurons.

How Neurotransmitters Influence Us

4. *How do neurotransmitters influence human behavior?*

The discovery of dozens of different neurotransmitters has raised questions: Are certain neurotransmitters found only in specific places? What are their effects? Can we boost or diminish these effects through drugs or diet? Could such changes affect our moods, memories, or mental abilities?

Later chapters explain the role of neurotransmitters in depression and euphoria, hunger and thinking, addictions and therapy. For now, let's glimpse how neurotransmitters influence our motions and emotions. We now know that a particular neural pathway in the brain may use only one or two neurotransmitters, and that particular neurotransmitters may have particular effects on behavior and emotions. One of the best understood neurotransmitters, **acetylcholine (ACh)**, is the messenger at every junction between a motor neuron and muscle. With powerful electron microscopes, neurobiologists can magnify thinly sliced specimens of tissue enough to see the sacs that store and release ACh molecules. When ACh is released to the muscle cells, the muscle contracts.

"When it comes to the brain, if you want to see the action, follow the neurotransmitters."

Neuroscientist Floyd Bloom (1993)

If the transmission of ACh is blocked, muscles cannot contract. Curare, a poison that certain South American Indians have put on the tips of their hunting darts, occupies and blocks ACh receptor sites, leaving the neurotransmitter unable to affect the muscles. Struck by one of these darts, an animal becomes paralyzed. Botulin, a poison that can form in improperly canned food, causes paralysis by blocking ACh release from the sending neuron. The venom of the black widow spider causes a synaptic flood of ACh. The result? Violent muscle contractions, convulsions, and possible death.

Molecules and muscles When your body moves, a flood of acetylcholine molecules triggers the muscle action.

The Endorphins

An exciting discovery about neurotransmitters occurred when Candace Pert and Solomon Snyder (1973) attached a radioactive tracer to morphine, allowing them to see exactly where in an animal's brain it was taken up. Pert and Snyder discovered that morphine, an opiate drug that elevates mood and eases pain, was taken up by receptors in areas linked with mood and pain sensations.

It was hard to imagine why the brain would contain these "opiate receptors" unless it had its own naturally occurring opiates. Why would the brain have a chemical lock, unless it also had a corresponding key? Researchers soon confirmed that

acetylcholine [ah-seat-el-KO-leen] **(ACh)** a neurotransmitter that, among its functions, triggers muscle contraction.

endorphins [en-DOR-fins] "morphine within"—natural, opiatelike neurotransmitters linked to pain control and to pleasure.

Physician Lewis Thomas, on the endorphins: ***"There it is, a biologically universal act of mercy. I cannot explain it, except to say that I would have put it in had I been around at the very beginning, sitting as a member of a planning committee."***

The Youngest Science
1983

the brain does indeed contain several types of neurotransmitter molecules similar to morphine. Named **endorphins** (short for *endo*genous [produced within] *morphine*), these natural opiates are released in response to pain and vigorous exercise (Farrell & others, 1982; Lagerweij & others, 1984). They may therefore help explain all sorts of good feelings, such as the "runner's high," the painkilling effects of acupuncture, and the indifference to pain in some severely injured people, such as David Livingstone reported in his 1857 *Missionary Travels*:

> I heard a shout. Starting, and looking half round, I saw the lion just in the act of springing upon me. I was upon a little height, he caught my shoulder as he sprang, and we both came to the ground below together. Growling horribly close to my ear, he shook me as a terrier does a rat. The shock produced a stupor similar to that which seems to be felt by a mouse after the first shake of the cat. It caused a sort of dreaminess in which there was no sense of pain nor feeling of terror, though [I was] quite conscious of all that was happening. . . . This peculiar state is probably produced in all animals killed by the carnivora; and if so, is a merciful provision by our benevolent Creator for lessening the pain of death.

How Drugs Alter Neurotransmission

If indeed the endorphins lessen pain and boost mood, why not flood the brain with artificial opiates, thereby intensifying the brain's own "feel-good" chemistry? One problem is that when flooded with opiate drugs such as heroin and morphine, the brain may stop producing its own natural opiates. When the drug is withdrawn, the brain may be deprived of any form of opiate. For a drug addict, the result is agony that persists until the brain resumes production of its natural opiates or receives more artificial opiates. As we will see in later chapters, mood-altering drugs, from alcohol to nicotine to heroin, share a common effect: They trigger unpleasant, lingering aftereffects. For suppressing the body's own neurotransmitter production, nature charges a price.

Neurotransmitter research is enabling the creation of new therapeutic drugs such as those used to alleviate depression. *Agonists* work by mimicking a particular neurotransmitter (Figure 2.3b). An agonist is a drug molecule that is similar enough to the neurotransmitter to mimic its effects. This may, for example, produce a temporary "high" by amplifying normal sensations of arousal or pleasure (as with opiate drugs). *Antagonists* work by blocking neurotransmitters (Figure 2.3c). An antagonist is a drug molecule that is enough like the natural neurotransmitter to occupy its receptor site and block its effect but not similar enough to stimulate the receptor (rather like coins from another country that fit into, but won't operate, a soda or candy machine). Some poison and snake venoms paralyze by blocking acetylcholine receptors that produce muscle movement. Other drugs are neither agonists nor antagonists but work by hampering the neurotransmitter's natural breakdown or its reabsorption.

Figure 2.3 Agonists and antagonists

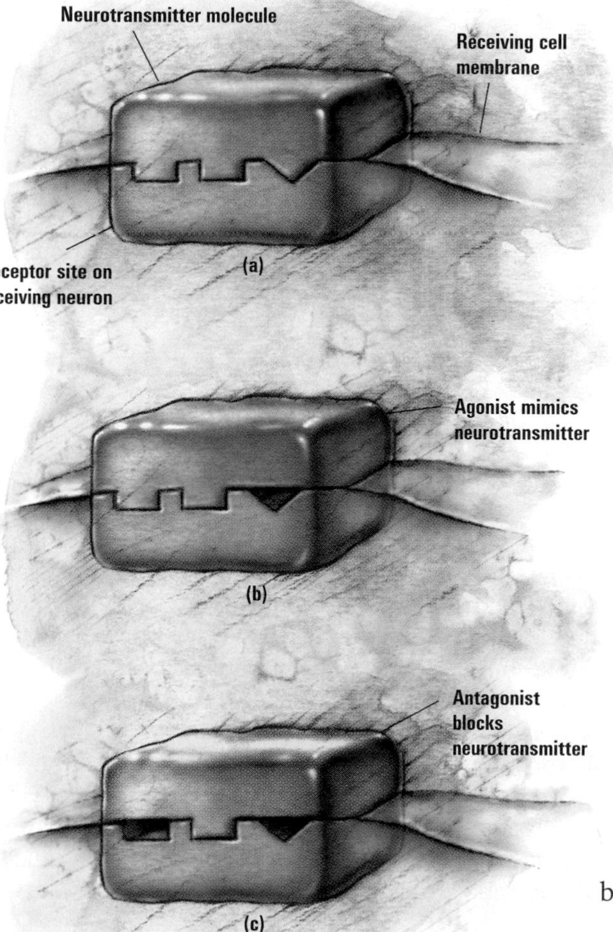

This neurotransmitter molecule has a molecular structure that precisely fits the receptor site on the receiving neuron, much like a key fits a lock.

This agonist molecule is similar enough in structure to the neurotransmitter molecule that it mimics its effects on the receiving neuron. Morphine, for instance, mimics the action of endorphins by stimulating receptors in brain areas involved in mood and pain sensations.

This antagonist molecule has a structure similar enough to the neurotransmitter to occupy its receptor site and block its action, but not similar enough to stimulate the receptor. An example is venom that paralyzes its victims by blocking ACh receptors involved in muscle movement.

Designing a drug can be harder than it sounds. A *blood-brain barrier* enables the brain to fence out unwanted chemicals circulating in the blood, and some chemicals don't have the right shape to slither through this barrier. Scientists know, for example, that the tremors of Parkinson's disease result from the death of nerve cells that produce a neurotransmitter called *dopamine*. Giving the patient dopamine as a drug doesn't help, though, because dopamine cannot cross the blood-brain barrier. But L-dopa, a raw material the brain can convert to dopamine, can sneak through. Given L-dopa, patients gain better muscular control.

REHEARSE IT!

1. The neuron fiber that carries messages to other neurons is the

a. dendrite.
b. axon.
c. cell body.
d. myelin.

2. The neuron's response to stimulation is an *all-or-none* response, meaning that the intensity of the stimulus determines

a. whether or not an impulse is generated.
b. how fast an impulse is transmitted.
c. how intense an impulse will be.
d. whether the stimulus is excitatory or inhibitory.

3. There is a minuscule space between the axon of a sending neuron and the dendrite or cell body of a receiving neuron. This small space is called the

a. axon terminal.
b. sac or vesicle.
c. synaptic gap.
d. threshold.

4. When the action potential reaches the axon terminal of a neuron, it triggers the release of chemical messengers called

a. ions.
b. synapses.
c. neural impulses.
d. neurotransmitters.

5. When the transmission of acetylcholine (ACh) is blocked,

a. death from convulsions may result.
b. the brain is flooded with substitute excitatory neurotransmitters, causing a brief "rush."
c. paralysis may result.
d. the brain starts producing antagonists, resulting in depression.

6. Endorphins are released in the brain in response to

a. morphine or heroin.
b. pain or vigorous exercise.
c. antagonists.
d. all of the above.

The Nervous System

5. *What are the major divisions of the nervous system, and what are their basic functions?*

Neurons communicating with other neurons form our body's primary information system, the **nervous system** (Figure 2.4). The brain and spinal cord form the **central nervous system (CNS)**. The **peripheral nervous system (PNS)** links the central nervous system with the body's sense receptors, muscles, and glands. The sensory and motor axons carrying this PNS information are bundled into the electrical cables that we know as **nerves**. The optic nerve, for example, bundles nearly a million axon fibers into a single cable carrying the information that each eye sends to the brain.

Information travels in the nervous system through three types of neurons. The **sensory neurons** send information from the body's tissues and sensory organs inward to the brain and spinal cord, which process the information. This processing involves a second class of neurons, the central nervous system's own **interneurons**, which enable its internal communication. The central nervous system then sends instructions out to the body's tissues via the **motor neurons**.

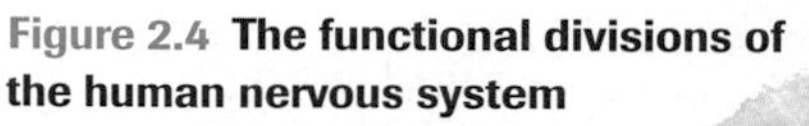

Figure 2.4 **The functional divisions of the human nervous system**

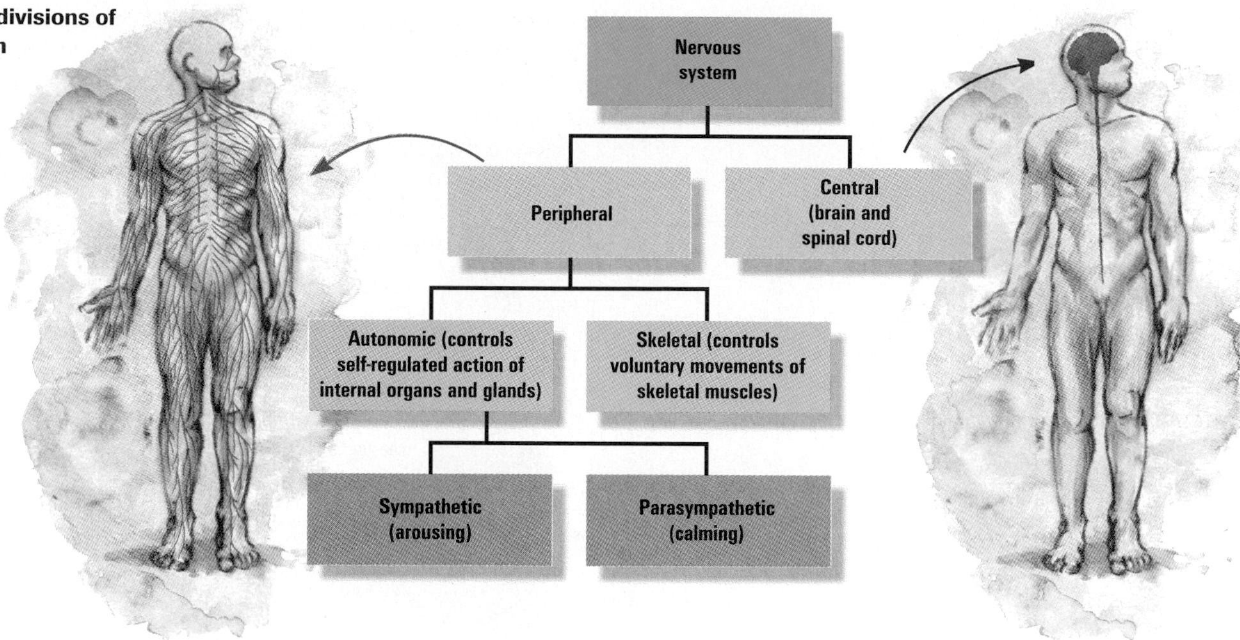

Our complexity, though, resides mostly in our interneuron systems. Our nervous system has a few million sensory neurons, a few million motor neurons, and billions and billions of interneurons.

nervous system the body's speedy, electrochemical communication system, consisting of all the nerve cells of the peripheral and central nervous systems.

central nervous system (CNS) the brain and spinal cord.

peripheral nervous system (PNS) the sensory and motor neurons that connect the central nervous system (CNS) to the rest of the body.

nerves neural "cables" containing many axons. These bundled axons, which are part of the peripheral nervous system, connect the central nervous system with muscles, glands, and sense organs.

sensory neurons neurons that carry incoming information from the sense receptors to the central nervous system.

interneurons central nervous system neurons that internally communicate and intervene between the sensory inputs and motor outputs.

motor neurons the neurons that carry outgoing information from the central nervous system to the muscles and glands.

skeletal nervous system the division of the peripheral nervous system that controls the body's skeletal muscles.

autonomic [aw-tuh-NAHM-ik] **nervous system** the part of the peripheral nervous system that controls the glands and the muscles of the internal organs (such as the heart). Its sympathetic division arouses; its parasympathetic division calms.

sympathetic nervous system the division of the autonomic nervous system that arouses the body, mobilizing its energy in stressful situations.

parasympathetic nervous system the division of the autonomic nervous system that calms the body, conserving its energy.

The Peripheral Nervous System

Our peripheral nervous system has two components—skeletal and autonomic. The **skeletal nervous system** controls the voluntary movements of our skeletal muscles. As you reach the bottom of this page, the skeletal nervous system will report to your brain the current state of your skeletal muscles and carry instructions back, triggering your hand to turn the page.

Our **autonomic nervous system** controls the glands and the muscles of our internal organs. Like an automatic pilot, it may sometimes be consciously overridden. But usually it operates on its own (autonomously) to influence our internal functioning, including our heartbeat, digestion, and glandular activity.

The autonomic nervous system is a dual system (Figure 2.5, page 46). The **sympathetic nervous system** arouses us for defensive action. If something alarms or enrages you, the sympathetic system will accelerate your heartbeat, slow your digestion, raise the sugar level in your blood, dilate your arteries, and cool you with perspiration, making you alert and ready for action. When the stress subsides, the **parasympathetic nervous system** produces opposite effects. It conserves energy as it calms you by decreasing your heartbeat, lowering your blood sugar, and so forth. In everyday situations, the sympathetic and parasympathetic nervous systems work together to keep us in a steady internal state. At this very moment your parasympathetic system is maintaining your heart rate and digestion.

The Central Nervous System

From the simplicity of neurons "talking" to other neurons arises the complexity of the central nervous system's spinal cord and brain that enables our humanity—our thinking, feeling, and acting. Tens of billions of neurons, each in communication with thousands of other neurons, yield an ever-changing wiring diagram that dwarfs a powerful computer.

reflex a simple, automatic, inborn response to a sensory stimulus, such as the knee-jerk response.

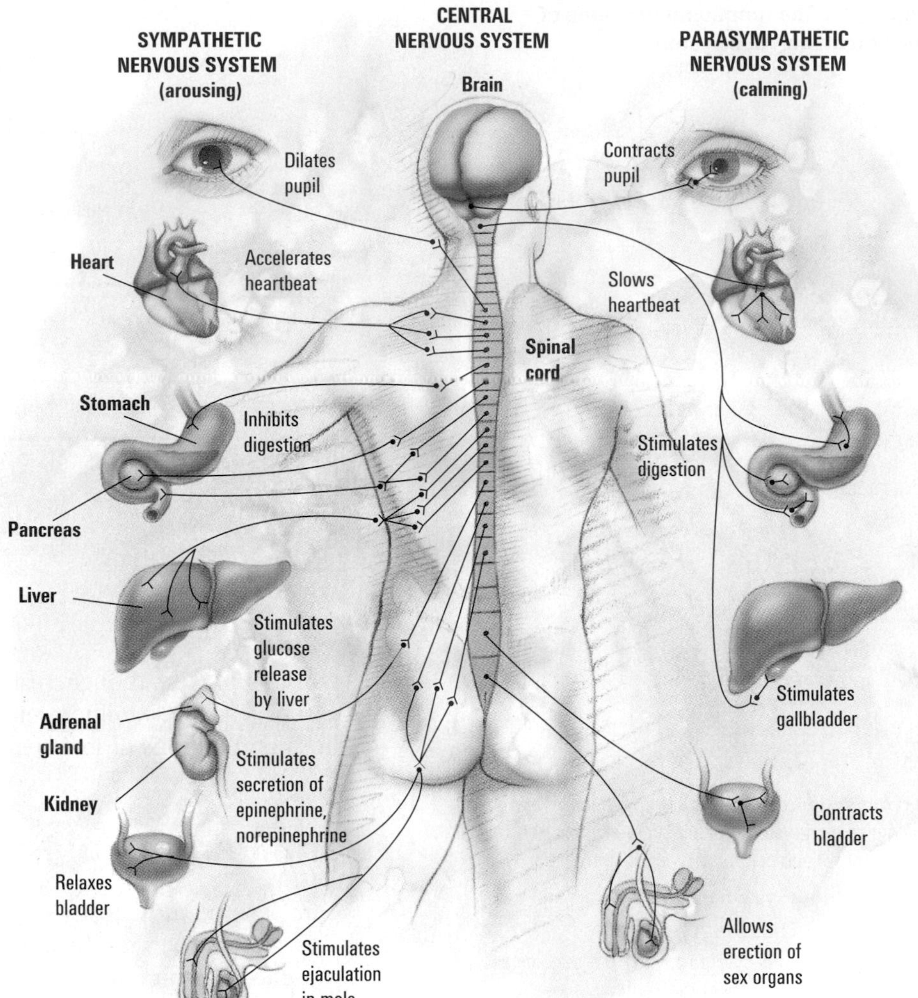

Figure 2.5 **The dual functions of the autonomic nervous system**
The autonomic nervous system controls the more autonomous (or self-regulating) internal functions. Its sympathetic division arouses and expends energy. Its parasympathetic division calms and conserves energy, allowing routine maintenance activity. For example, sympathetic stimulation accelerates heartbeat, while parasympathetic stimulation slows it.

Spinal Cord and Brain

The spinal cord is an information highway connecting the peripheral nervous system to the brain. Ascending neural tracts send up sensory information, and descending tracts send back motor-control information. A look at the neural pathways governing our **reflexes**, our automatic responses to stimuli, illustrates the spinal cord's work. A simple spinal-reflex pathway is composed of a single sensory neuron and a single motor neuron, which often communicate through an interneuron. The knee-jerk response is one example; a headless warm body could do it.

Another such pathway makes up the pain reflex (Figure 2.6). When your fingers touch a hot stove, neural activity excited by the heat travels via sensory neurons to interneurons in your spinal cord. These interneurons respond by activating motor neurons to the muscles in your arm, causing you to jerk your hand away.

Because the simple pain-reflex pathway runs through the spinal cord and out, you jerk your hand from a candle's flame *before* your brain receives and responds to the information that causes you to feel pain. Information travels to and from the brain by way of the spinal cord. Were the top of your spinal cord severed, you would not feel such pain. Or pleasure. Your brain would literally be out of touch with your body. Thus, you would lose all sensation and voluntary movement in body regions whose sensory and motor neurons connect with the spinal cord below its point of injury. Male paraplegics (whose legs are paralyzed) are usually

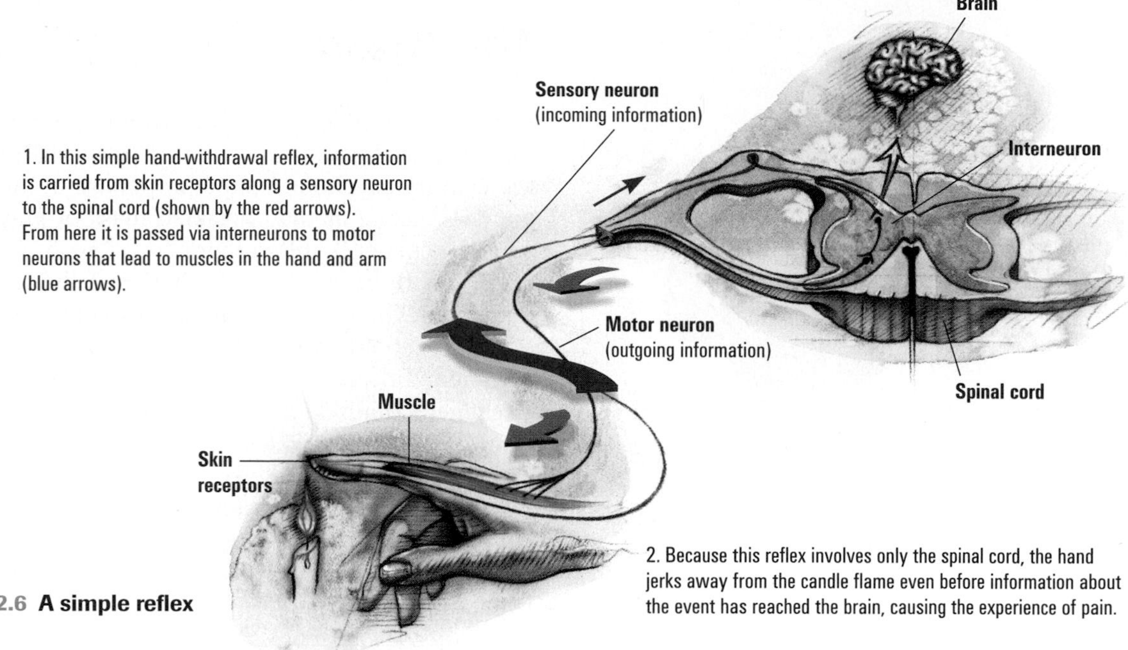

Figure 2.6 A simple reflex

capable of an erection (a simple reflex) if their genitals are stimulated. But, depending on where and how completely the spinal cord is severed, they may be genitally unresponsive to erotic images and have no genital feeling (Kennedy & Over, 1990).

To produce bodily pain or pleasure, the sensory information must reach the other part of your central nervous system, your brain. There you receive information, interpret it, and decide how to respond. In doing so, your brain functions rather like a computing machine. Consider, for example, how the brain processes a seemingly simple operation like shooting a basket. It receives images of the basket from the two eyes, computes their difference, and instantly infers how far the basket must be to project such a difference. As basketball star Michael Jordan shoots a falling-away jump shot, his agile brain performs an incredible number of instant computations, adjusting for body position and movement, distance, and angle. As we will see, this is but one of many feats of this information-processing system that we call the brain.

REHEARSE IT!

7. Information travels to and from the brain mostly by way of the spinal cord. The neurons of the spinal cord are called

a. motor neurons.
b. sensory neurons.
c. sending neurons.
d. interneurons.

8. The autonomic nervous system controls internal functions, such as heart rate and glandular activity. The word "autonomic" means

a. peripheral.
b. voluntary.
c. self-regulating.
d. arousing.

9. Usually, the sympathetic nervous system arouses us for action and the parasympathetic nervous system calms us down. Together the two systems make up the

a. autonomic nervous system.
b. skeletal nervous system.
c. central nervous system.
d. peripheral nervous system.

10. The neurons of the spinal cord are part of the

a. skeletal nervous system.
b. central nervous system.
c. autonomic nervous system.
d. peripheral nervous system.

The Brain

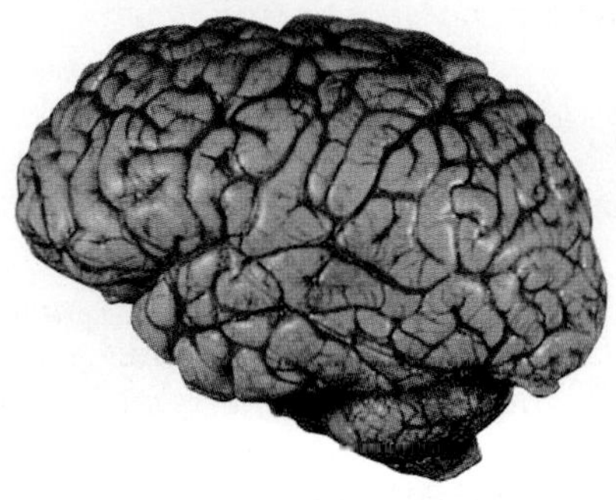

The human brain This small, wrinkled organ is far more complex than the most sophisticated computer. What you see here is only a portion of the brain's outer layer. Most of its surface lies hidden within its convoluted folds.

In a jar on a display shelf in Cornell University's psychology department resides the well-preserved brain of Edward Bradford Titchener, a great turn-of-the-century psychologist and proponent of the study of consciousness. Imagine yourself gazing at that wrinkled mass of grayish tissue. Is there any sense in which Titchener is still in there?[1]

You might answer that, without the living whir of electrochemical activity, there could be nothing of Titchener in his preserved brain. Consider then an experiment about which the inquisitive Titchener himself might have daydreamed. Imagine that just moments before his death, someone removed Titchener's brain from his body and kept it alive by pumping enriched blood through it as it floated in a tank of cerebral fluid. Would Titchener now still be in there? Further imagine, to carry our fantasy to its limit, that someone transplanted the still-living brain into the body of a badly brain-damaged person. To whose home should the recovered patient return?

That we can imagine such questions illustrates how convinced we are that we live in our heads. And for good reason. The brain enables the mind to see, hear, remember, think, feel, speak, and dream. Indeed, say neuroscientists, *the mind is what the brain does*. But precisely where and how are mind functions tied to the brain?

"I am a brain, Watson. The rest of me is a mere appendix."

Sherlock Holmes
in Arthur Conan Doyle's
"The Adventure of the Mazarin Stone"

Lower-Level Brain Structures

If you could open the skull and look inside, the first thing you might notice is the brain's size. In dinosaurs, the brain represented 1/100,000th of the body's weight; in whales, it represents 1/10,000th; in elephants, 1/600th; in humans, 1/45th. It looks as though a principle is emerging. But keep reading. In mice the brain is 1/40th the body's weight, and in marmosets, 1/25th. So there are exceptions to the rule of thumb that the ratio of brain to body weight provides a clue to a species' intelligence.

More useful clues to an animal's capacities come from the brain's structures. In primitive vertebrate (backboned) animals, such as sharks, the brain primarily regulates basic survival functions: breathing, resting, and feeding. In lower mammals, such as rodents, a more complex brain enables emotion and greater memory. In advanced mammals, such as humans, the brain processes more information, enabling us to act with foresight.

Brain evolution has not greatly altered the basic mechanisms for survival. Rather, new brain systems evolved on top of the old, much as the earth's landscape covers the old with the new. Digging down, one discovers the fossil remnants of the past—brainstem components still performing much as they did for our distant ancestors. Let's now explore the brain, starting with the brainstem and working up.

THE FAR SIDE

"The picture's pretty bleak, gentlemen. . . . The world's climates are changing, the mammals are taking over, and we all have a brain about the size of a walnut."

The Brainstem

6. What are the functions of the brainstem and its associated structures?

The **brainstem** is the brain's basement, its oldest and innermost region. It begins where the spinal cord enters the skull and swells slightly, forming the **medulla**, which controls your heartbeat and breathing. If the top of a cat's

1 Carl Sagan's *Broca's Brain* inspired this question.

brainstem the oldest part and central core of the brain, beginning where the spinal cord swells as it enters the skull; it is responsible for automatic survival functions.

medulla [muh-DUL-uh] the base of the brainstem; controls heartbeat and breathing.

reticular formation a nerve network in the brainstem that plays an important role in controlling arousal.

thalamus [THAL-uh-muss] the brain's sensory switchboard, located on top of the brainstem; it directs messages to the sensory receiving areas in the cortex and transmits replies to the cerebellum and medulla.

brainstem is severed from the rest of the brain above it, the animal will still breathe and live—and even run, climb, and groom (Klemm, 1990). But with the brainstem cut off from the brain's higher region, the cat won't purposefully run or climb to get food.

Here in the brainstem is also the crossover point, where most nerves to and from each side of the brain connect with the body's opposite side. This peculiar cross-wiring is but one of many surprises the brain has to offer.

Inside the brainstem, the **reticular** ("netlike") **formation**, a finger-shaped network of neurons, extends from the spinal cord right up to the thalamus (Figure 2.10). As the spinal cord's sensory input travels up to the thalamus, some of it branches off to the reticular formation, which filters incoming stimuli and relays important information to other areas of the brain. Among its other functions, the reticular formation helps control arousal.

In 1949, Giuseppe Moruzzi and Horace Magoun discovered that electrically stimulating the reticular formation of a sleeping cat almost instantly produced an awake, alert animal. Magoun also severed a cat's reticular formation from higher brain regions without damaging the nearby sensory pathways. The effect? The cat lapsed into a coma from which it never awakened. The conclusion? The reticular formation is involved in arousal.

The Thalamus

Atop the brainstem sits a joined pair of egg-shaped structures called the **thalamus** (Figure 2.10). This is the brain's sensory switchboard: It receives information from the sensory neurons and routes it to the higher brain regions that deal with seeing, hearing, tasting, and touching. We can think of the thalamus as being to neural traffic what London is to England's train traffic: Sensory input passes through it en route to various destinations. The thalamus also receives some of the higher brain's replies, which it directs to the cerebellum and medulla.

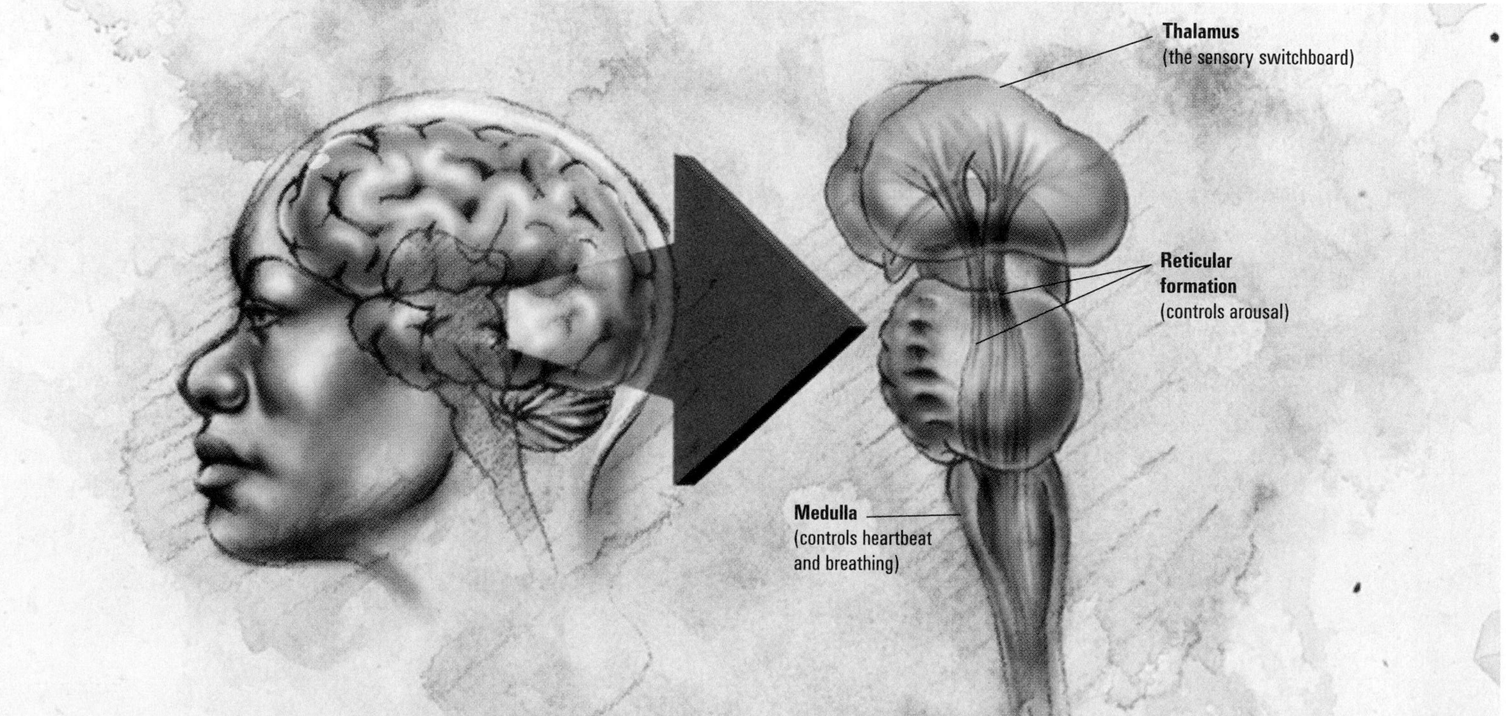

Figure 2.10 **The brainstem and thalamus** The brainstem, including the medulla, is an extension of the spinal cord. The thalamus is attached to its top, and the reticular formation passes through both structures.

CLOSE-UP

The Tools of Discovery

It is exciting to consider how fast and how far the neurosciences have progressed within a lifetime. Some of the effects of brain diseases and injuries were recorded more than 5000 years ago, and two centuries ago physicians began systematically to record the results of such damage. Even so, the human brain lay largely beyond the reach of science. The neuron was too small to study with the naked eye, its impulses too faint to record with ordinary electrodes. We were able to feel bumps on the skull, dissect and analyze lifeless brains, and observe the effects of specific brain diseases and injuries. But there were no tools high-powered yet gentle enough to explore the living brain. Now, that has changed. Whether in the interests of science or medicine, we can selectively **lesion** (destroy) tiny clusters of normal or defective brain cells, leaving their surroundings unharmed. We can probe the brain with tiny electrical pulses. We can snoop on the messages of individual neurons and on the mass action of billions of them. We can see color representations of the brain's energy-consuming activity. These new tools and techniques have made possible a neuroscientific revolution.

Modern researchers can now eavesdrop on the brain. The tips of modern microelectrodes are so small they can detect the electrical pulse in a single neuron, making possible some astonishingly precise findings. For example, we can now detect exactly where in a cat's brain the information goes after someone strokes the animal's whisker.

Electrical activity in the brain's billions of neurons sweeps in regular waves across its surface. The **electroencephalogram (EEG)** is an amplified tracing of such waves by an instrument called an electroencephalograph. Studying an EEG of the gross activity of the whole brain is like studying the activity of a car engine by listening to the hum of its motor. However, by presenting a stimulus repeatedly and having a computer filter out brain activity unrelated to the stimulus, one can identify the electrical wave evoked by the stimulus (Figure 2.7).

Other new windows into the brain give us a Supermanlike ability to see inside the brain without lesioning it. For example, the **CT (computed tomography) scan** examines the brain by taking x-ray photographs that can reveal brain damage.

Even more dramatic is the **PET (positron emission tomography) scan** (Figure 2.8). The PET scan depicts the activity of different brain areas by showing each area's consumption of the brain's chemical fuel, the sugar glucose (see illustration, page 59). Active neurons burn more glucose. When a person is given a temporarily radioactive form of glucose, the PET scan locates and measures

Figure 2.7 An electroencephalograph providing amplified tracings of waves of electrical activity in the brain Here it is detecting brain response to sound, making possible an early evaluation of what may be a hearing impairment.

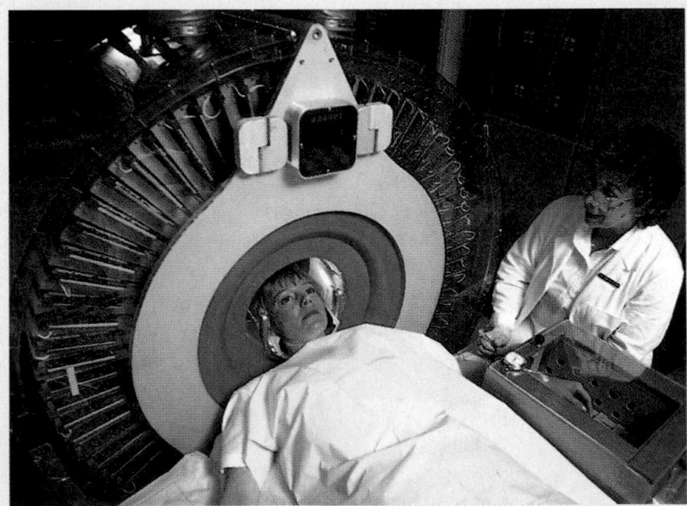

Figure 2.8 The PET scan To obtain a PET scan, researchers inject someone with a low and harmless dose of a short-lived radioactive sugar. Detectors around the subject's head pick up the release of gamma rays from the sugar, which has concentrated in active brain areas. A computer then processes and translates these signals into a map of the brain at work.

the radioactivity, thereby detecting where this "food for thought" goes. In this way, researchers can see which brain areas are most active as the person performs mathematical calculations, listens to music, or daydreams.

Another new way of looking into the living brain exploits the fact that the centers of atoms, including those in our brains, spin like tops. In **MRI (magnetic resonance imaging)** scans, the head is put in a strong magnetic field, which aligns the spinning atoms. Then a brief pulse of radio waves disorients the atoms momentarily. When the atoms return to their normal spin, they release detectable signals, which become computer-generated images of their concentrations. The result is a detailed picture of the brain's soft tissues. For example, MRI scans reveal enlarged fluid-filled brain areas in some patients who have schizophrenia, a disabling psychological disorder (Figure 2.9).

By taking pictures less than a second apart, MRI scans can now show the brain lighting up (with increased oxygen-laden bloodflow) as a person performs different mental functions. As a person sees a light turn on, a *functional MRI* (also called *fast* or *dynamic MRI*) machine detects blood rushing to the back of the brain, which processes visual information (Figure 2.16, page 57). Ask the person to solve a verbal analogy problem, and the part of the brain's left side near the front will light up. Such snapshots of the brain's mind-making activity provide new insights into how and where the brain divides its labor.

These new brain-imaging instruments are doing for psychological science what the microscope did for biology and the telescope for astronomy—they are triggering a scientific revolution. To be learning about the neurosciences now is like studying world geography while Magellan was exploring the seas. Every year the explorers announce new discoveries, which also generate new interpretations of old discoveries. A small sampling of new revelations:

- PET scans show that the brain areas that light up when people silently say the name of an animal differ from those that light up when they say the name of a tool (Martin & others, 1996).
- MRI scans reveal a larger-than-average neural area in the left brain of musicians who display perfect pitch (Schlaug & others, 1995).
- MRI scans of bilingual people's brains reveal that first and second languages are represented in common areas if the second language was learned early, and in differing areas if the second language was learned late (Kim & others, 1997).
- Functional MRI scans reveal that, during a rhyming task, men's brains have a distinctively active left brain area, whereas women's brains are active on both sides (Shawitz & others, 1995).

Such data from different brain-imaging techniques are appearing faster than anyone can read and remember them. Researchers are now assembling this information in computer databases. Clearly, this has been the "decade of the brain" (as declared by the U.S. Congress), the golden age of brain science.

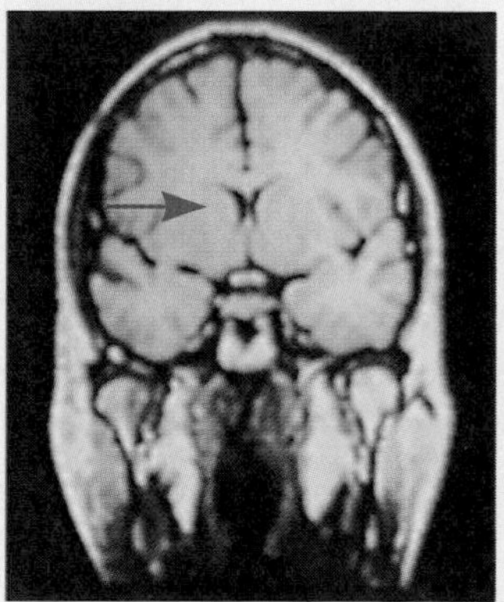

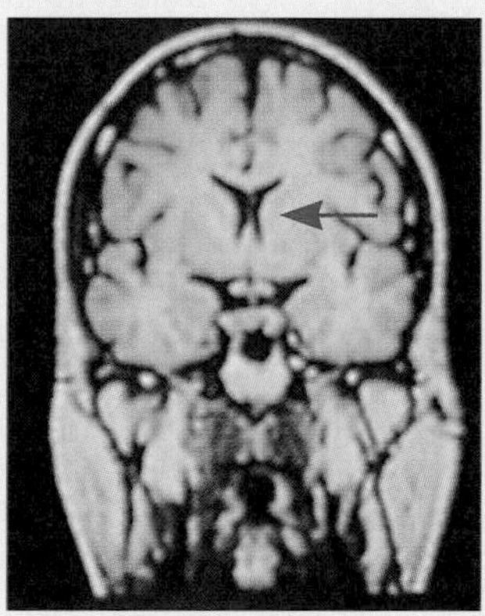

Figure 2.9 MRI scan of a healthy individual (left) and a schizophrenia patient (right) Note the enlarged fluid-filled brain region in the image on the right.

lesion [LEE-zhuhn] tissue destruction. A brain lesion is a naturally or experimentally caused destruction of brain tissue.

electroencephalogram (EEG) an amplified recording of the waves of electrical activity that sweep across the brain's surface. These waves are measured by electrodes placed on the scalp.

CT (computed tomography) scan a series of x-ray photographs taken from different angles and combined by computer into a composite representation of a slice through the body. Also called *CAT scan.*

PET (positron emission tomography) scan a visual display of brain activity that detects where a radioactive form of glucose goes while the brain performs a given task.

MRI (magnetic resonance imaging) a technique that uses magnetic fields and radio waves to produce computer-generated images that distinguish among different types of soft tissue; allows us to see structures within the brain.

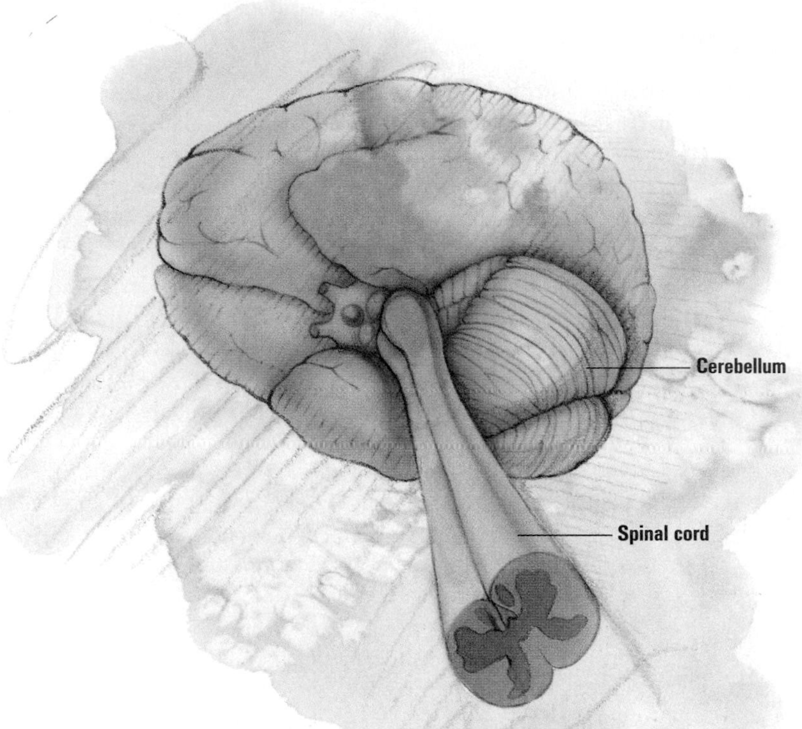

Figure 2.11 The cerebellum Hanging at the back of the brain, this "little brain" coordinates our movements.

The Cerebellum

Extending from the rear of the brainstem is the **cerebellum**, meaning "little brain," which is rather what its two wrinkled hemispheres look like (Figure 2.11). As we will see in Chapter 7, the cerebellum influences one type of learning and memory. But its most obvious function is coordinating voluntary movement. If you injured your cerebellum, you would probably have difficulty walking, keeping your balance, or shaking hands. Your movements would be jerky and exaggerated.

Note that these lower brain functions all occur without any conscious effort. This illustrates another of this book's recurring themes: *Our brain processes much information outside of our awareness.* We are aware of the *results* of our brain's labor (say, our current visual experience) but not of *how* we construct the visual image. Likewise, whether we are asleep or awake, our brainstem manages its life-sustaining functions, freeing our higher brain regions to dream, to think, to talk, to savor a memory.

You can challenge your understanding of the essential functions of lower-level brain areas by considering these questions: Within what brain region would damage be most likely to disrupt your ability to skip rope? Your ability to sense tastes or sounds? In what brain region would damage perhaps leave you in a coma? Without the very breath and heartbeat of life? (See page 54.)

REHEARSE IT!

11. The brainstem is the oldest and innermost region of the brain. The part of the brainstem that controls heartbeat and breathing is the

a. cerebellum. **c.** cortex.
b. medulla. **d.** thalamus.

12. The part of the brain that coordinates voluntary movement is the

a. cerebellum. **c.** thalamus.
b. medulla. **d.** reticular formation.

13. The lower brain structure that governs arousal is the

a. spinal cord. **c.** reticular formation.
b. cerebellum. **d.** medulla.

14. The thalamus receives information from the sensory neurons and routes it to the higher brain regions that control the senses. The thalamus functions like a

a. memory bank. **c.** breathing regulator.
b. pleasure center. **d.** switchboard.

The Limbic System

7. *What are the functions of limbic system structures?*

At the border (*limbus*) of the brain's older parts and the cerebral hemispheres is a doughnut-shaped neural system called the **limbic system** (Figure 2.12). We will see in Chapter 7 how one limbic system component, the *hippocampus*, processes memory. (Animals or humans who lose their hippocampus to surgery or injury are unable to lay down new memories of facts and experiences.) For now, let's look at the limbic system's links to emotions such as fear and anger and to basic motives such as those for food and sex. As we will see, the limbic system's influence on emotions and motives occurs partly through its control of the body's hormones.

cerebellum [sehr-uh-BELL-um] the "little brain" attached to the rear of the brainstem; it helps coordinate voluntary movement and balance.

limbic system a doughnut-shaped system of neural structures at the border of the brainstem and cerebral hemispheres; associated with emotions such as fear and aggression and drives such as those for food and sex. Includes the hippocampus, amygdala, and hypothalamus.

amygdala [ah-MIG-dah-la] two almond-shaped neural clusters that are components of the limbic system and are linked to emotion.

hypothalamus [hi-pō-THAL-uh-muss] a neural structure lying below (*hypo*) the thalamus; it directs several maintenance activities (eating, drinking, body temperature), helps govern the endocrine system via the pituitary gland, and is linked to emotion.

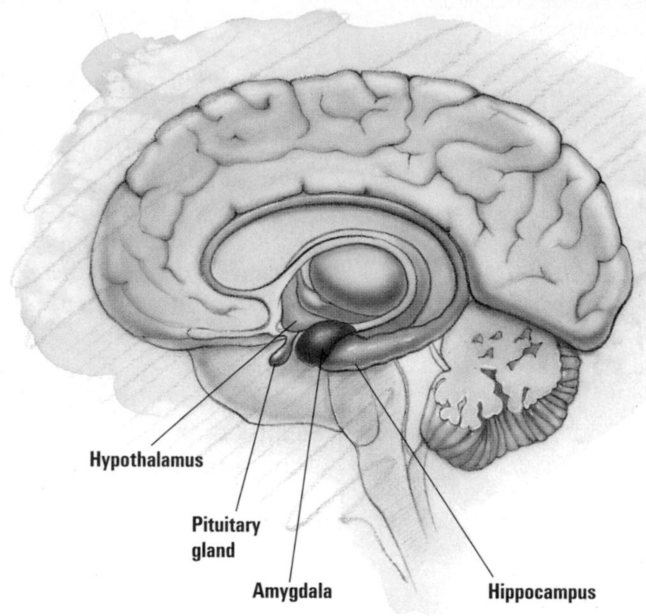

Figure 2.12 The limbic system As a group, the parts of the limbic system form a doughnut-shaped neural system that borders the brain's older parts and the cerebral hemispheres. Although part of the endocrine system (see page 67), not the brain, the pituitary gland is controlled by the limbic system's hypothalamus, just above it.

The Amygdala

Two almond-shaped neural clusters in the limbic system, called the **amygdala**, influence aggression and fear. In 1939, psychologist Heinrich Klüver and neurosurgeon Paul Bucy surgically lesioned the part of a rhesus monkey's brain that included the amygdala. The operation transformed the normally ill-tempered monkey into the most mellow of creatures. Poke it, pinch it, do virtually anything that normally would trigger a ferocious response and still the animal remained placid. In later studies with other wild animals, including the lynx, wolverine, and wild rat, researchers noted the same effect. What then might happen if we electrically stimulated the amygdala in a normally placid domestic animal such as a cat? Do so in one spot and the cat prepares to attack, hissing with its back arched, its pupils dilated, its hair on end. Move the electrode only slightly within the amygdala and the cat cowers in terror when caged with a small mouse.

Aggression as a brain state Back arched and fur fluffed, this fierce cat is ready to attack. Electrical stimulation of a cat's amygdala provokes reactions such as the one shown here, suggesting its role in emotions such as rage. Which division of the autonomic nervous system is activated by such stimulation? (See page 57.)

These experiments testify to the amygdala's role in such emotions as rage and fear, not to mention the perception of such emotions in others (Adolphs & others, 1994). Still, we must be careful not to think of the amygdala as *the* control center for aggression and fear. The brain is *not* neatly organized into structures that correspond to our categories of behavior. Aggressive and fearful behavior involve neural activity in all levels of the brain. Even within the limbic system, stimulating neural structures other than the amygdala can evoke such behavior. Similarly, if you put a charge to your car's dead battery you can activate your car's engine, but that doesn't mean that the battery by itself runs the car. It is merely one link in an integrated system.

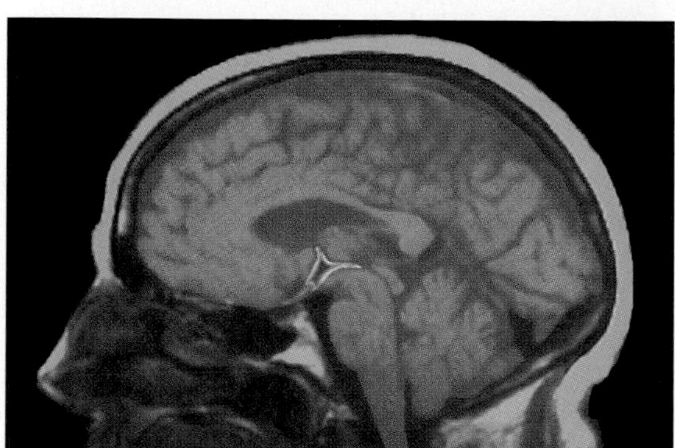

The hypothalamus This small but important structure, colored red in this MRI brain scan photograph, helps keep the body's internal environment in a steady state by regulating thirst, hunger, and body temperature. Its activity also influences experiences of pleasureful reward.

The Hypothalamus

Another of the limbic system's fascinating structures lies just below (*hypo*) the thalamus, and so is called the **hypothalamus**. By lesioning or stimulating different areas in the hypothalamus, neuroscientists have isolated within it neural networks that perform specific bodily maintenance duties. Some of these neural clusters influence hunger; still others regulate thirst, body temperature, and sexual behavior.

The hypothalamus monitors blood chemistry and takes orders from other parts of the brain. Thinking about sex (in your brain's cerebral cortex) can stimulate your hypothalamus to secrete hormones. Through these hormones, the

cerebral [seh-REE-bruhl] **cortex** the intricate fabric of interconnected neural cells that covers the cerebral hemispheres; the body's ultimate control and information-processing center.

glial cells non-neural nervous system cells that support, nourish, and protect neurons.

frontal lobes the portion of the cerebral cortex lying just behind the forehead; involved in speaking and muscle movements and in making plans and judgments.

parietal [puh-RYE-uh-tuhl] **lobes** the portion of the cerebral cortex lying at the top of the head and toward the rear; includes the sensory cortex.

occipital [ahk-SIP-uh-tuhl] **lobes** the portion of the cerebral cortex lying at the back of the head; includes the visual areas, which receive visual information from the opposite visual field.

temporal lobes the portion of the cerebral cortex lying roughly above the ears; includes the auditory areas, each of which receives auditory information primarily from the opposite ear.

hypothalamus controls the adjacent "master gland," the pituitary (Figure 2.12), which influences hormone release by other glands, which the hypothalamus monitors. (Note the interplay between the nervous and hormonal systems: The brain influences the hormone [endocrine] system, which in turn influences the brain.) The powerful little hypothalamus also exerts control by triggering autonomic nervous system activity. On page 67 we will take a closer look at the *endocrine system*, our slower, *chemical* communication system.

The story of a remarkable discovery about the hypothalamus illustrates how progress in scientific research often occurs—when curious, open-minded investigators make an unexpected observation. Two young McGill University neuropsychologists, James Olds and Peter Milner (1954), were trying to implant electrodes in the reticular formations of white rats when they made a magnificent mistake. In one rat, they incorrectly placed an electrode in what was later discovered to be a region of the hypothalamus (Olds, 1975). Curiously, the rat kept returning to the place on its tabletop enclosure where it had been stimulated by this misplaced electrode, as if it were seeking more stimulation. Upon discovering their mistake, the alert investigators recognized that they had stumbled upon a brain center that provides a pleasurable reward.

Answers to questions on page 52: the cerebellum, the thalamus, the reticular formation, and the medulla.

In a meticulous series of experiments, Olds (1958) then went on to locate other "pleasure centers," as he called them. (What the rats actually experience only they know, and they aren't telling. Not wanting to attribute human feelings to the rat, today's scientists refer to reward centers, not "pleasure centers.") When rats were allowed to trigger their own stimulation in these areas by pressing a pedal, they would sometimes do so at a feverish pace—up to 7000 times per hour—until they dropped from exhaustion. Moreover, they would do anything to get this stimulation, even cross an electrified floor that a starving rat would not cross to reach food (Figure 2.13).

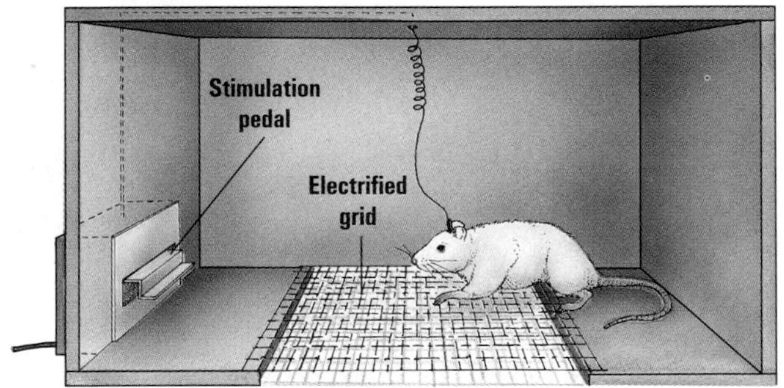

Figure 2.13 Rat with an implanted electrode With an electrode implanted in a reward center of its hypothalamus, the rat readily crosses an electrified grid, accepting the painful shocks, to press a lever that sends electrical impulses to its "reward centers."

Similar reward centers in or near the hypothalamus were later discovered in many other species, including goldfish, dolphins, and monkeys. In fact, animal research reveals both a general reward system that triggers the release of the neurotransmitter dopamine, and specific centers associated with the pleasures of eating, drinking, and sex. Animals, it seems, come equipped with built-in systems that reward activities essential to survival.

"If you were designing a robot vehicle to walk into the future and survive, . . . you'd wire it up so that behavior that ensured the survival of the self or the species—like sex and eating—would be naturally reinforcing."

Candace Pert (1986)

These dramatic findings made people wonder whether humans, too, might have limbic centers for pleasure. Indeed they do. One neurosurgeon has used electrodes to calm violent patients. Stimulated patients report mild pleasure; unlike rats, they are not driven to a frenzy by it (Deutsch, 1972; Hooper & Teresi, 1986). Some researchers also believe that addictive disorders, such as alcoholism, drug abuse, and food binging, may stem from a *reward deficiency syndrome*—a genetically disposed deficiency in the natural brain systems for pleasure and well-being that leads people to crave substances that provide missing pleasure or to relieve negative feelings (Blum & others, 1996).

REHEARSE IT!

15. The limbic system, a doughnut-shaped structure at the border of the brain's older parts and the cerebral hemispheres, is associated with basic motives, emotions, and memory functions. Two parts of the limbic system are the amygdala and the

a. reticular formation. **c.** thalamus.
b. hippocampus. **d.** medulla.

16. A ferocious response to electrical brain stimulation would lead you to suppose that the electrode had been touching the

a. medulla. **c.** hippocampus.
b. pituitary. **d.** amygdala.

17. The reward centers discovered by Olds and Milner were located in regions of the

a. cerebral cortex. **c.** hypothalamus.
b. brainstem. **d.** spinal cord.

18. The neural structure that most directly regulates eating, drinking, and body temperature is the

a. cerebellum. **c.** thalamus.
b. hypothalamus. **d.** amygdala.

The Cerebral Cortex

The people who first dissected and labeled the brain used the language of scholars—Latin and Greek. Their words are actually attempts at graphic description: For example, cortex *means "bark,"* cerebellum *is "little brain," and* thalamus *is "inner chamber."*

The **cerebral cortex** is an intricate covering of interconnected neural cells that, like bark on a tree, forms a thin surface layer on the cerebral hemispheres. It is our body's ultimate control and information-processing center.

With the elaboration of the cerebral cortex, tight genetic controls relax and the organism's adaptability increases. Thus, frogs and other amphibians have a small cortex and operate extensively on preprogrammed genetic instructions. The larger cortex of mammals offers increased capacities for learning and thinking, enabling them to be more adaptable.

Structure of the Cortex

8. *How is the cerebral cortex organized?*

Opening a human skull and exposing the brain, we would see a wrinkled organ, shaped rather like the meat of an oversized walnut. Without these wrinkles a flattened cortex would require triple the area—roughly that of a very large pizza—to fit inside the skull.

Eighty percent of the brain's weight lies in the ballooning left and right cerebral hemispheres, which are mostly filled with axon connections between the brain's surface and its other regions. The thin surface layer of the cerebral hemispheres is the cerebral cortex, a one-eighth-inch-thick sheet of cells composed of some 30 billion nerve cells and around 300 trillion synaptic connections. Being human takes a lot of nerve. Supporting these billions of nerve cells are 9 times as many **glial cells**—"glue cells" that guide neural connections, provide nutrients and insulating myelin, and mop up electrically charged atoms and neurotransmitters. By chatting with neurons, some researchers now believe, glial cells may also participate in information and memory (Travis, 1994).

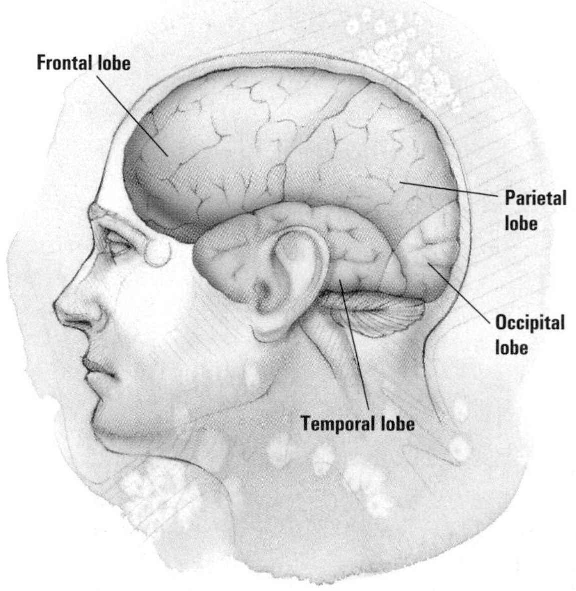

Figure 2.14 The basic subdivisions of the cortex

We can view each brain hemisphere as divided into four regions, or *lobes*. Starting at the front of your brain and going around over the top, there are the **frontal lobes** (behind your forehead), the **parietal lobes** (at the top and to the rear), the **occipital lobes** (at the back of your head), and the **temporal lobes** (just above your ears). These lobes are convenient geographic subdivisions separated by prominent folds (Figure 2.14). Each lobe carries out many functions, and some functions require the interplay of several lobes. A big part of what makes us distinctively human is our large frontal lobes.

Functions of the Cortex

9. *What are the functions of the cerebral cortex?*

More than a century ago, autopsies of partially paralyzed or speechless people revealed damage to specific areas of the cortex. But this rather crude evidence did not prove that specific parts of the cortex perform specific functions. After all, if control of speech and movement were diffused across the cortex, damage to almost any area might produce the same effect. A television would go dead with its power cord cut, but we would be deluding ourselves if we were to think we had "localized" the source of the picture in the cord. This analogy suggests how easy it is to err when trying to localize brain functions.

Motor Functions

In 1870, German physicians Gustav Fritsch and Eduard Hitzig applied mild electrical stimulation to the cortexes of dogs and made an important discovery: They could make different body parts move. The effects were selective: Stimulation caused movement only when applied to an arch-shaped region at the back of the frontal lobe, running roughly from ear to ear across the top of the brain. This arch we now call the **motor cortex** (Figure 2.15). Moreover, when the researchers stimulated specific parts of this region in the left or right hemisphere, specific body parts moved on the *opposite* side of the body.

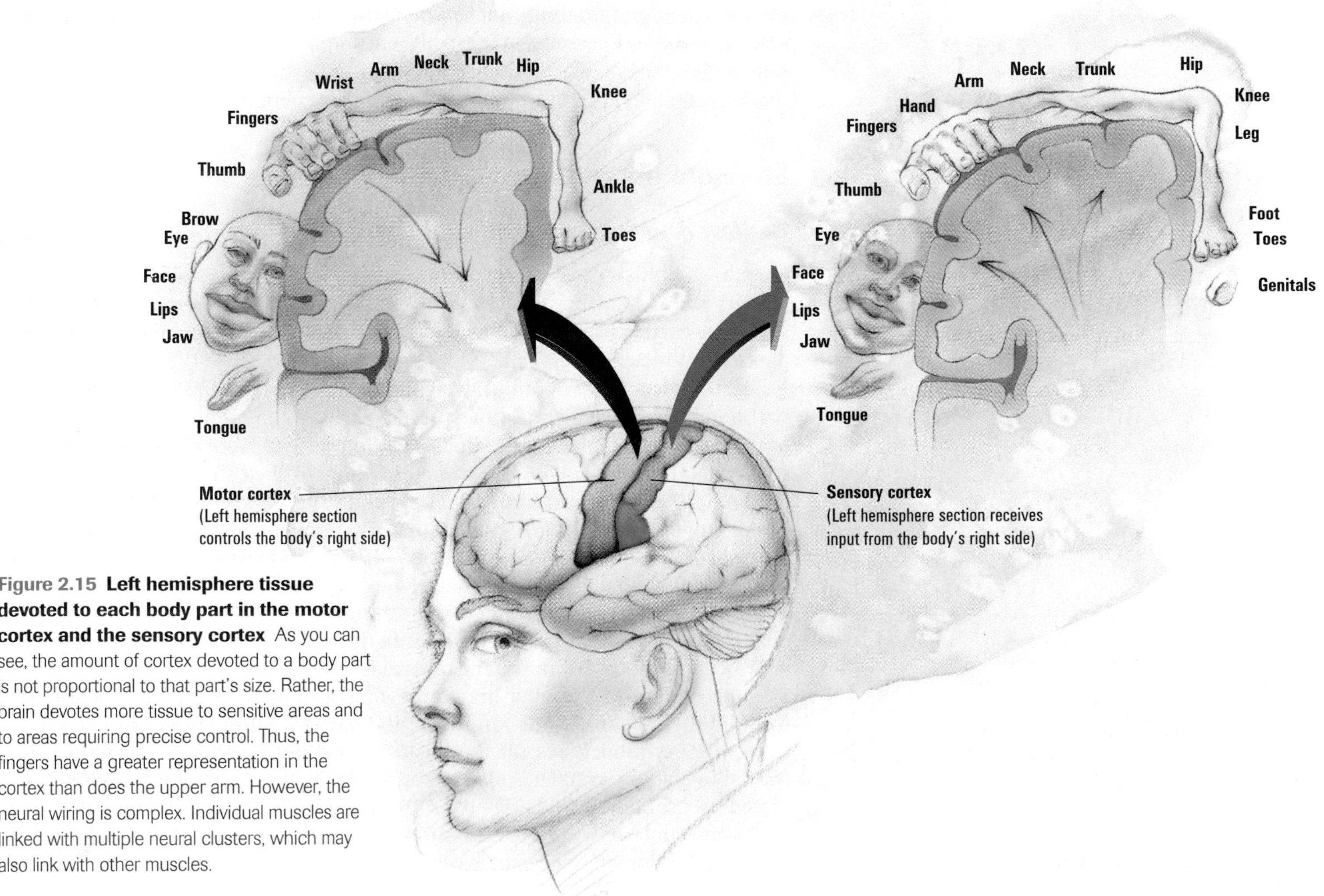

Figure 2.15 **Left hemisphere tissue devoted to each body part in the motor cortex and the sensory cortex** As you can see, the amount of cortex devoted to a body part is not proportional to that part's size. Rather, the brain devotes more tissue to sensitive areas and to areas requiring precise control. Thus, the fingers have a greater representation in the cortex than does the upper arm. However, the neural wiring is complex. Individual muscles are linked with multiple neural clusters, which may also link with other muscles.

motor cortex an area that is located at the rear of the frontal lobes and that controls voluntary movements.

sensory cortex the area that is located at the front of the parietal lobes and that registers and processes body sensations.

A half-century ago, neurosurgeons Otfrid Foerster in Germany and Wilder Penfield in Montreal mapped the motor cortex in hundreds of wide-awake patients. The surgeons needed to know the possible side effects of removing different parts of the cortex. So, before putting the knife to the brain, they would painlessly (the brain has no sensory receptors) stimulate different cortical areas and note body responses. Like Fritsch and Hitzig, they found that when they stimulated different areas of the motor cortex at the back of the frontal lobe, different body parts moved. They were therefore able to map the motor cortex according to the body parts it controlled (Figure 2.15). Interestingly, those areas of the body requiring precise control, such as the fingers and mouth, occupied the greatest amount of cortical space.

Neuroscientist José Delgado demonstrated the mechanics of motor behavior. In one monkey, he evoked a smiling response over 400,000 times. In a human patient, stimulation of a certain spot on the left motor cortex triggered the right hand to make a fist. Asked to keep the fingers open during the next stimulation, the patient, whose fingers closed despite his best efforts, remarked, "I guess, Doctor, that your electricity is stronger than my will" (Delgado, 1969, p. 114). More recently, scientists have been able to predict a monkey's arm motion a tenth of a second before it moves—by repeatedly measuring motor cortex activity preceding specific arm movements (Gibbs, 1996).

The cat on page 53 is aroused via its sympathetic nervous system.

More recent research reveals that the precise muscle-to-brain connections are not so simple as the early brain stimulation studies suggested. In one study, researchers traced these connections using functional MRI scans to observe where the brain lights up when specific muscles are moved (Sanes & others, 1995). They found that a given finger or wrist movement, for example, would activate multiple and overlapping sites. Although it's true that certain areas of the cortex control certain areas of the body and that some areas require more brain tissue than others, the wiring pattern is complex—complex enough to enable the many different muscle combinations needed to produce specific gestures.

Sensory Functions

If the motor cortex sends messages out to the body, where do *incoming* messages reach the cortex? Penfield identified a cortical area that specializes in receiving information from the skin senses and from the movement of body parts. This area, parallel to the motor cortex and just behind it at the front of the parietal lobes, we now call the **sensory cortex** (Figure 2.15). Stimulate a point on the top of this band of tissue, and the person may report being touched on the shoulder; stimulate some point on the side, and the person may feel something on the face.

The more sensitive a body region, the greater the area of the sensory cortex devoted to it; your supersensitive lips project to a larger brain area than do your toes (Figure 2.15). Similarly, rats have a large area of the brain devoted to whisker sensations, owls to hearing sensations, and so forth. If a monkey or a human loses a finger, the region of the sensory cortex devoted to receiving input from that finger branches to receive sensory input from the adjacent fingers, which now become more sensitive (Fox, 1984). As this illustrates, the brain is sculpted not only by our genes (nature) but also by our experience (nurture).

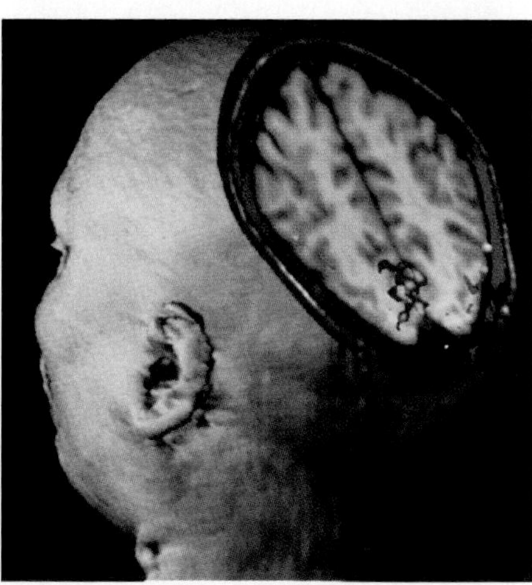

Figure 2.16 **New technology shows the brain in action** In this composite sketch and photograph, a functional MRI scan shows the visual cortex activated (color representation of increased bloodflow) as researchers shine a light into a subject's eyes. If the light is switched off, the region instantly calms down.

Further exploration identified areas where the cortex receives input from the other senses. At this moment you are receiving visual information in the occipital lobes at the very back of your brain (Figure 2.16). Stimulated there, you might see flashes of light or dashes of color. So, in a sense, we *do* have eyes in the back of our head. From your occipital lobes, the visual information you are now processing goes to other portions of the brain (called *association areas*) that specialize in tasks such as identifying words, detecting emotions, and recognizing faces.

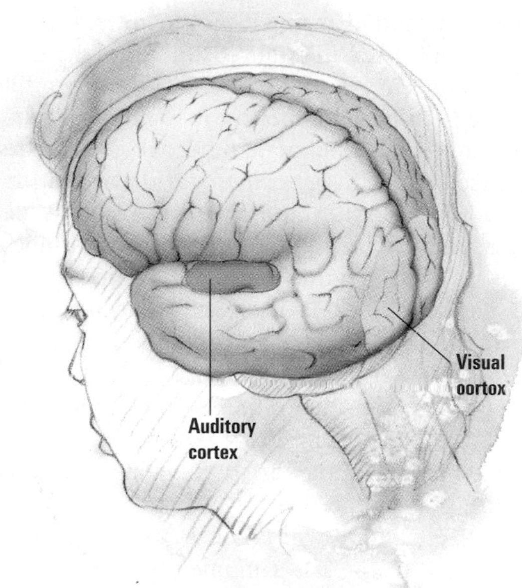

Figure 2.17 The visual cortex and auditory cortex
The occipital lobes at the rear receive input from the eyes. An auditory area of the temporal lobes receives information from the ears.

Any sound you are hearing you processed with the auditory areas in your temporal lobes (Figure 2.17). Most of this auditory information travels a circuitous route from one ear to the auditory receiving area above your opposite ear. Stimulated there, you might hear a sound.

Association Functions

So far, we have pointed out small areas of the cortex that either receive sensory information or direct muscular responses. In humans, that leaves some three-fourths of the thin wrinkled layer, the cerebral cortex, uncommitted to sensory or motor functioning. Neurons in these **association areas** (the tan areas in Figure 2.18) integrate information. They associate various sensory inputs with stored memories—an important part of thinking.

Electrically probing the association areas doesn't trigger any observable response. So, unlike our mapping of the sensory and motor areas, we can't so neatly specify the functions of the association areas. Their silence seems to be what someone had in mind when formulating one of pop psychology's most widespread myths: that we ordinarily use only 10 percent of our brains. This myth—"one of the hardiest weeds in the garden of psychology," writes Donald McBurney (1996, p. 44)—implies that if we could activate our whole brain, we would be far smarter than those who drudge along on 10 percent brain power. But from observing surgically lesioned animals and brain-damaged humans, we know that the association areas are not dormant. (The brain has no appendix—no apparently purposeless tissue.) Rather, the association areas interpret, integrate, and act on information processed by the sensory areas.

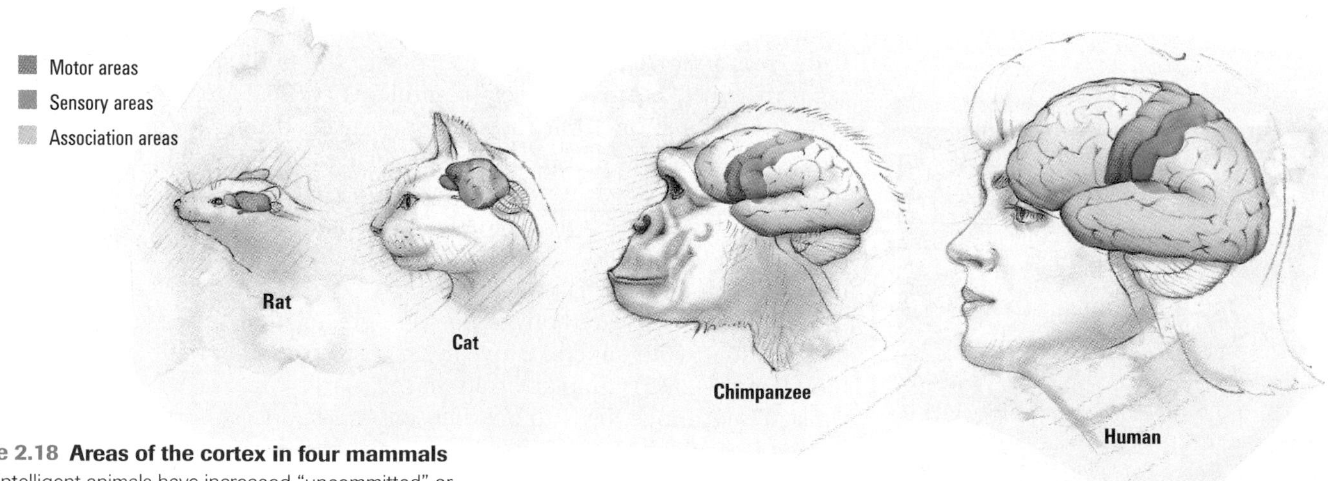

Figure 2.18 Areas of the cortex in four mammals
More intelligent animals have increased "uncommitted" or association areas of the cortex. These vast areas of the brain are responsible for integrating and acting on information received and processed by sensory areas.

Association areas in the frontal lobes enable judging, planning, and the processing of new memories. People with damaged frontal lobes may have intact memories, score high on intelligence tests, and be able to bake a cake—yet be unable to plan ahead to *begin* baking the cake for a birthday party.

association areas areas of the cerebral cortex that are not involved in primary motor or sensory functions; rather, they are involved in higher mental functions such as learning, remembering, thinking, and speaking.

aphasia impairment of language, usually caused by left hemisphere damage either to Broca's area (impairing speaking) or to Wernicke's area (impairing understanding).

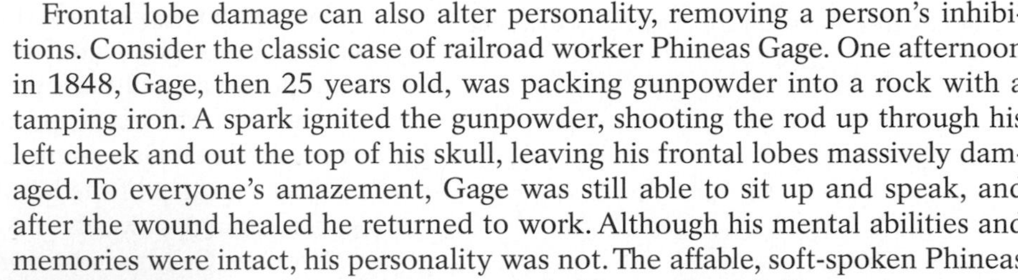

Frontal lobe damage can also alter personality, removing a person's inhibitions. Consider the classic case of railroad worker Phineas Gage. One afternoon in 1848, Gage, then 25 years old, was packing gunpowder into a rock with a tamping iron. A spark ignited the gunpowder, shooting the rod up through his left cheek and out the top of his skull, leaving his frontal lobes massively damaged. To everyone's amazement, Gage was still able to sit up and speak, and after the wound healed he returned to work. Although his mental abilities and memories were intact, his personality was not. The affable, soft-spoken Phineas Gage was now an irritable, profane, dishonest person who eventually lost his job and ended up earning his living as a fairground exhibit. This person, said his friends, was "no longer Gage." With his frontal lobes ruptured, Gage's moral compass became disconnected from his behavior.

Phineas Gage reconsidered Using measurements of his skull (which was kept as a medical record) and modern neuroimaging techniques, researcher Hanna Damasio and her colleagues (1994) have reconstructed the probable path of the rod through Gage's brain.

The association areas of the other lobes also perform mental functions. For example, an area on the underside of the right temporal lobe enables us to recognize faces. If a stroke or head injury destroyed this area of your brain, you would still be able to describe facial features and to recognize someone's gender and approximate age, yet be strangely unable to identify the person as, say, Nelson Mandela or your next-door neighbor or even your spouse. But by and large, complex mental functions such as learning and memory don't reside in any one place. There is no one spot in a rat's small association cortex that, when damaged, will obliterate its ability to learn or remember a maze. Such functions seem spread throughout much of the cortex.

Language

Complex human abilities, such as language, result from the intricate coordination of many brain areas. For example, consider the curious finding that damage to any one of several cortical areas can cause **aphasia**, an impaired use of language. It is even more curious that some people with aphasia can speak fluently but are unable to read (despite good vision), while others can comprehend what they read but are unable to speak. Still others can write but not read, read but not write, read numbers but not letters, or sing but not speak. These observations are puzzling because we think of speaking and reading, or writing and reading, or singing and speaking as merely different examples of the same general ability.

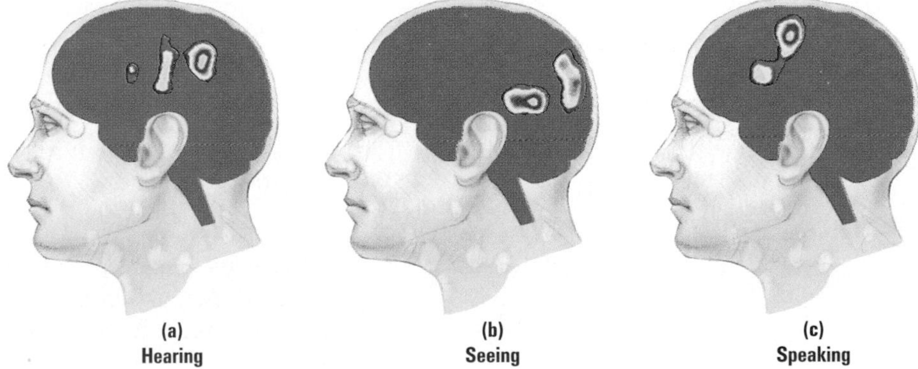

Brain activity when hearing, seeing, and speaking words PET scans detect the activity of different areas of the brain by measuring their relative consumption of a temporarily radioactive form of the brain's normal fuel, glucose. These PET scans show levels of increased brain activity in specific areas: **(a)** when hearing a word—auditory cortex and Wernicke's area; **(b)** when seeing a word—visual cortex and angular gyrus; and **(c)** when repeating a word—Broca's area and the motor cortex. The red blotches show where the brain is rapidly consuming glucose.

Broca's area an area of the frontal lobe, in the left hemisphere for most people, that directs the muscle movements involved in speech.

Wernicke's area an area of the left temporal lobe involved in language comprehension.

Researchers began to sort out how the brain processes language after a discovery by French physician Paul Broca in 1865. Broca discovered that after damage to a specific area of the left frontal lobe, later called **Broca's area**, a person would struggle to form words, yet often would be able to sing familiar songs with ease. A decade later, German investigator Karl Wernicke discovered that after damage to a specific area of the left temporal lobe (**Wernicke's area**) people could speak only meaningless words and were unable to comprehend others' words.

Norman Geschwind assembled these clues into an explanation of how we use language. When you read aloud, the words (1) register in the visual area; (2) are relayed to the angular gyrus, an area that transforms the words into an auditory code; which is (3) received and understood in the nearby Wernicke's area; and then (4) sent to Broca's area; which (5) controls the motor cortex, creating the pronounced word (Figure 2.19). Depending on which link in this chain is damaged, a different form of aphasia occurs. Damage to the angular gyrus leaves the person able to speak and understand but unable to read. Damage to Wernicke's area disrupts understanding. Damage to Broca's area disrupts speaking. The general principle bears repeating: *Complex abilities result from the intricate coordination of many brain areas.*

Said differently, the brain operates by dividing its mental functions—speaking, perceiving, thinking, remembering—into subfunctions. Our conscious experience *seems* indivisible. Right now you are experiencing a whole visual scene as if your eyes were video cameras projecting the scene into your brain. Actually, as you will see in Chapter 4, your brain breaks vision into specialized subtasks such as discerning color, depth, movement, and form. (After a localized stroke that destroys one of these neural work teams, people may lose just one aspect of vision, such as the ability to perceive movement.) These specialized neural networks, each having simultaneously done its own thing, then feed their information to "higher-level" networks that combine the atoms of experience and relay them to progressively higher-level association areas, enabling us to recognize a face as "Grandmother." The same is true of reading a word: The brain computes the word's form, sound, and meaning using different neural networks (Posner & Carr, 1992). Think about it: *What you experience as a continuous, indivisible stream of perception is actually but the visible tip of the information-processing iceberg, most of which lies beneath the surface of your conscious awareness.*

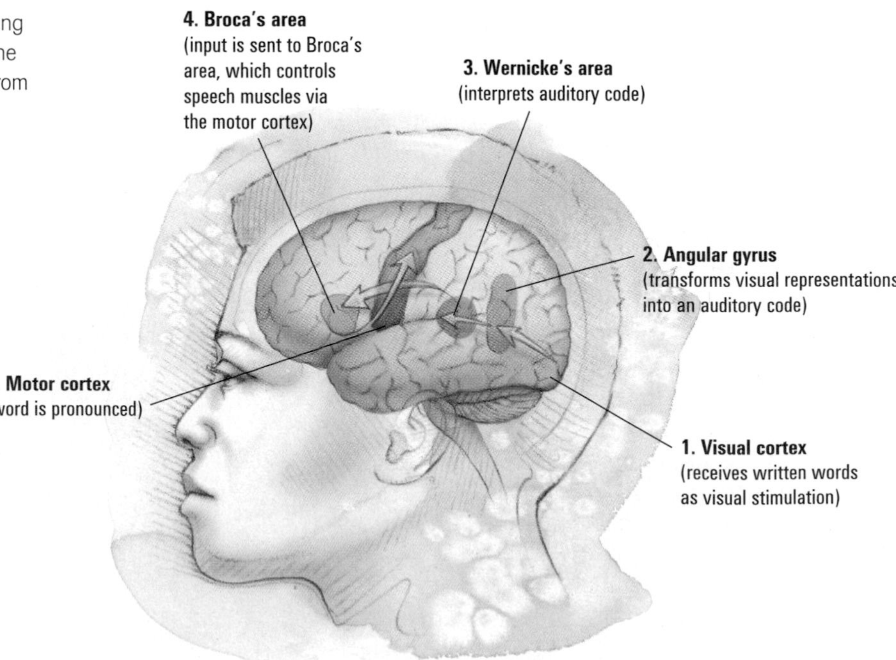

Figure 2.19 **Specialization and integration** Reading aloud requires the coordination of several brain areas. The arrows show the movement of information in the brain from the time a word is read until it is spoken.

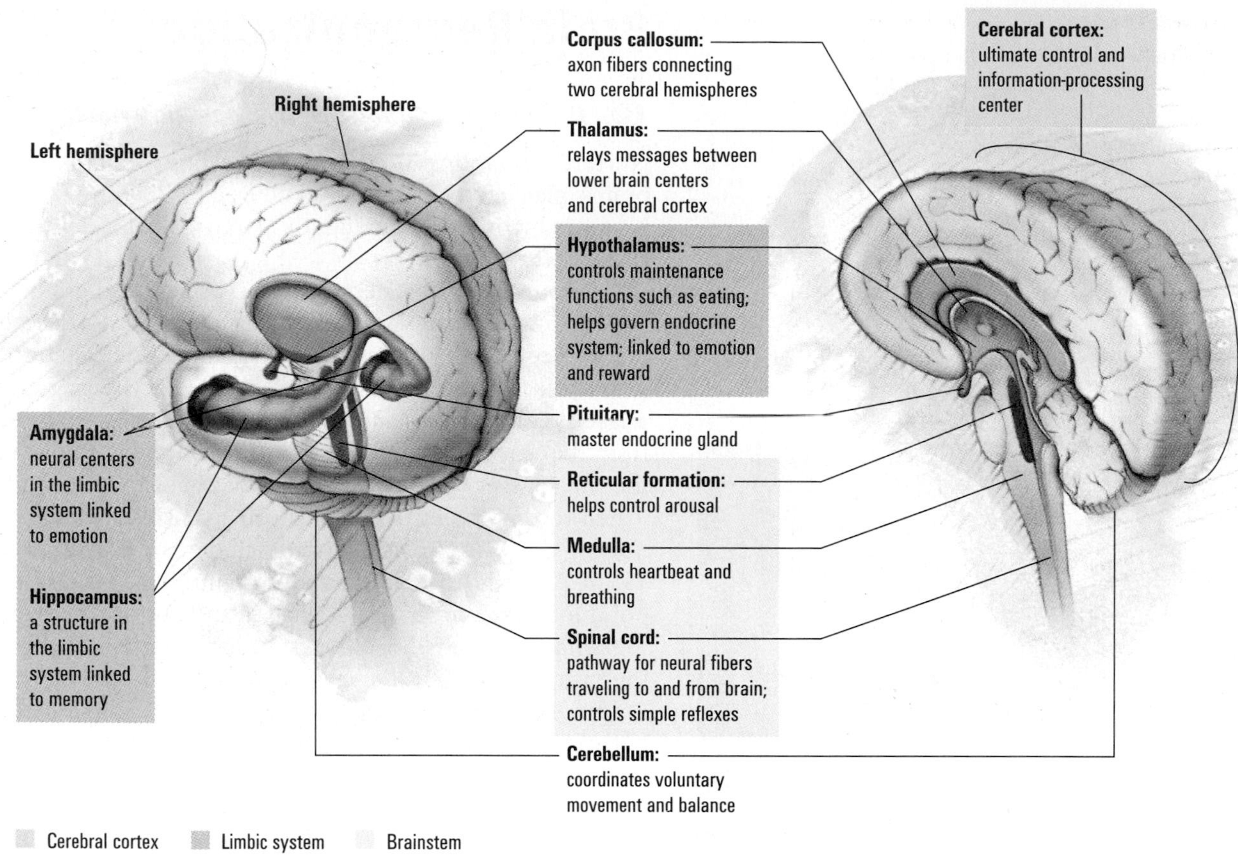

Figure 2.20 Brain structures and their functions

To review, the mind's subsystems are localized in particular brain regions (Figure 2.20), yet the brain acts as a unified whole. Moving your hand; recognizing faces; even perceiving color, motion, and depth all depend on specific neural networks. Yet complex functions such as language, learning, and loving involve the coordination of many brain areas. Both principles—specialization and integration—appear in research on the two brain hemispheres.

REHEARSE IT!

19. The motor cortex is the brain region that controls voluntary muscle movement. If a neurosurgeon stimulated your right motor cortex, you would most likely

a. see light.
b. hear a sound.
c. feel a touch on the right arm.
d. move your left leg.

20. The sensory cortex registers and processes body sensations, with the more sensitive body regions having the greatest representation. Which of the following has the greatest representation?

a. knee
b. toes
c. fingers
d. thumb

21. About three-fourths of the cerebral cortex is not committed to any specific sensory or muscular function. The "uncommitted" areas are called

a. occipital lobes.
b. fissures.
c. association areas.
d. Wernicke's area.

22. Judging and planning are enabled by the

a. occipital lobes.
b. parietal lobes.
c. frontal lobes.
d. temporal lobes.

23. The area in the brain that, if damaged, might impair your speech is

a. Wernicke's area.
b. Broca's area.
c. the left occipital lobe.
d. the angular gyrus.

plasticity the brain's capacity for modification, as evident in brain reorganization following damage (especially in children) and in experiments on the effects of experience on brain development.

corpus callosum [KOR-pus kah-LOW-sum] the large band of neural fibers connecting the two brain hemispheres and carrying messages between them.

split brain a condition in which the two hemispheres of the brain are isolated by cutting the connecting fibers (mainly those of the corpus callosum) between them.

Brain Reorganization

10. *Is the brain capable of reorganizing itself if damaged?*

Nurture's sculpting of the ever-changing brain is evident in studies of the brain's **plasticity**. Most severed neurons will not regenerate—if your spinal cord is severed, you are permanently paralyzed. But neural tissue can reorganize in response to damage.

In one experiment, neuroscientists severed the neural pathways for incoming information from a monkey's arm. The area of the sensory cortex that formerly received this input gradually shifted its function and began to respond when researchers touched the animal's face (Pons & others, 1991). Similarly, if a laser beam damages a spot in a cat's eye, the brain area that received input from that spot will soon begin responding to stimulation from nearby areas in the cat's eye. If blind people use one finger to read Braille, the brain area dedicated to that finger expands (Barinaga, 1992a). PET scans also reveal activation of the *visual* cortex when blind people read Braille (Sadato & others, 1996). Among deaf people who communicate with sign language, it is the temporal lobe area normally dedicated to auditory information that waits in vain for stimulation. Finally, it looks for other signals to process, such as those from the visual system.

Brain plasticity Believe it or not, this 4-year-old is functioning with only half a brain. Her right hemisphere was surgically removed to eliminate seizures. Now neurons in her left hemisphere have made countless new connections to take over the tasks once performed by her right hemisphere.

Thus, the brain may not be as "hard-wired" as once thought. Unlike fixed computer circuits, brain hardware changes with time. In response to changing stimulation, the brain can either rewire itself with new synapses or (according to another theory) select new uses for its prewired circuits (Gazzaniga, 1992). When one brain area is damaged, other areas may in time reorganize and take over some of its functions. If neurons are destroyed, nearby neurons may partly compensate for the damage by making new connections that replace the lost ones. These new connections are one way the brain struggles to recover from a minor stroke. They are also the brain's way of partially compensating for the gradual loss of neurons with age.

Our brains are most plastic when we are young children (Kolb, 1989). Children are born with a surplus of neurons. If an injury destroys one part of a child's brain, the brain will compensate by putting other surplus areas to work. Thus, if the speech areas of an infant's left hemisphere are damaged, the right hemisphere will take over much of its language function. After age 5, left hemisphere damage permanently and severely disrupts language.

As an extreme example of plasticity, consider a 5-year-old boy whose severe seizures, caused by a deteriorating left hemisphere, require removing the *entire* hemisphere. What hope for the future would such a child have? Is there any chance he might attend school and lead a normal life, or would he suffer permanent retardation?

Astonishingly, one such individual was at last report an executive. Half his skull is filled with nothing but cerebrospinal fluid—functionally it might as well be sawdust—yet he has scored well above average on intelligence tests, has completed college, and has attended graduate school (Smith & Sugar, 1975; A. Smith, 1987). Although paralyzed on the right side, this man (along with other such cases of "hemispherectomy") testifies to the brain's extraordinary powers of reorganization when damaged before it is fully developed.

Our Divided Brains

For more than a century, clinical evidence has shown that the brain's two sides serve differing functions. Accidents, strokes, and tumors in the left hemisphere generally impair reading, writing, speaking, arithmetic reasoning, and understanding. Similar lesions in the right hemisphere usually do not have such dramatic effects. Small wonder, then, that the left hemisphere became known as the "dominant" or "major" hemisphere and its silent companion to the right as the "subordinate" or "minor" hemisphere. The left, verbal hemisphere is rather like the moon's facing side—the one easiest to observe and study. The other side is there, of course, but less visibly noticeable. (With some left-handers, speech is processed in the right hemisphere—see page 65.) Fascinating experiments on the brain's two hemispheres reveal, however, that each serves important functions.

Splitting the Brain

11. *What is a split brain, and what does it reveal about brain functioning?*

In 1961, two Los Angeles neurosurgeons, Philip Vogel and Joseph Bogen, were considering surgery for several patients who suffered from uncontrolled epilepsy. The surgeons speculated that major epileptic seizures were caused by an amplification of abnormal brain activity that reverberated between the two hemispheres. They therefore wondered whether they might control severe epilepsy by cutting communication between the hemispheres. To do so, the surgeons would have to sever the **corpus callosum**, the wide band of axon fibers connecting the two hemispheres (Figure 2.21).

Corpus callosum

Figure 2.21 The corpus callosum This wide band of neural fibers connects the two brain hemispheres. To photograph the half-brain shown here, the hemispheres were separated by cutting through the corpus callosum and lower brain regions.

They had reason to believe such an operation would not be incapacitating. Psychologists Roger Sperry, Ronald Myers, and Michael Gazzaniga had divided the brains of cats and monkeys in this manner, without serious ill effects. So Vogel and Bogen operated. The result? The seizures were nearly eliminated and the patients were surprisingly normal, their personalities and intellect hardly affected. Waking from the surgery, one patient even managed to quip that he had a "splitting headache" (Gazzaniga, 1967).

THE FAR SIDE

Innocent and carefree, Stuart's left hand didn't know what the right was doing.

If you chatted with one of these **split-brain** patients you probably would not notice anything unusual. You could understand why only a decade earlier neuropsychologist Karl Lashley had jested that maybe the corpus callosum served only "to keep the hemispheres from sagging." But surely a broad band of 200 million nerve fibers capable of transferring more than a billion bits of information per second between the hemispheres must have a more significant purpose. It does, and the ingenious testing of these patients by psychologists Sperry and Gazzaniga revealed its purpose and provided a key to understanding the two hemispheres' special functions.

After one of the split-brain operations, the patient could not identify a familiar unseen object, such as a spoon, placed in his left hand. He denied it was there. This came as no surprise to Sperry or Gazzaniga. They knew that information from the left hand went to the right hemisphere, and their animal experiments suggested that the right hemisphere would be unable to send this information to the left hemisphere (which in most humans controls speech).

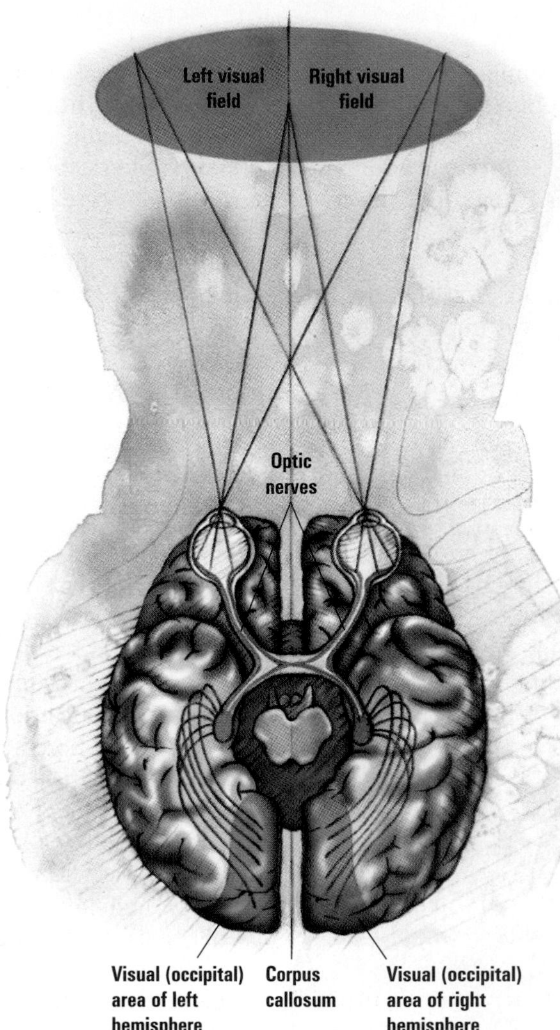

Figure 2.22 **The information highway from eye to brain** Information from the left half of your field of vision goes to your right hemisphere, and information from the right half of your visual field goes to your left hemisphere. (Note, however, that each eye receives sensory information from both the right and left visual fields.) The data received by either hemisphere are quickly transmitted to the other across the corpus callosum. In a split-brain patient with a severed corpus callosum, this information sharing does not take place.

More extraordinary results came when Sperry and Gazzaniga conducted some perceptual tests.

Our eyes connect to our brains in such a way that, when we look straight ahead, the left half of our field of vision transmits through both eyes to our right hemisphere (Figure 2.22). Likewise, the right side of our field of vision transmits only to our left hemisphere. One woman, who had lost a vision-related part of her *right* hemisphere following a massive stroke but was otherwise normal, sometimes complained that nurses had not put dessert or coffee on her tray. A nurse would then turn the woman's head so that the tray came into view in the right half of her field of vision (where her *left* visual cortex could detect it). She then would say, "Oh, there it is—it wasn't there before" (Sacks, 1985, p. 77).

In most of us with healthy, intact brains, information presented only to our right hemisphere is quickly sent to our left hemisphere, which names it. But what happens in a person whose corpus callosum has been severed? To find out, experimenters ask a split-brain patient to look at a designated spot. Then they send information to either the left or right hemisphere (by flashing it to the spot's right or left). Finally, they quiz each hemisphere separately.

See if you can guess the results of an experiment using this procedure (Gazzaniga, 1967). While the patients stared at a dot, the word HEART was flashed across the visual field with HE in the left visual field and ART in the right. First, what did the patients *say* they saw? Second, asked to identify with their *left* hands what they had seen, did they *point* to HE or ART?

As Figure 2.23, page 65 shows, the patients *said* they saw ART and so were startled when their left hands *pointed* to HE. When given an opportunity to express itself, each hemisphere reported only what it had seen.

Question: If we flashed a red light to the right hemisphere of a split-brain patient and a green light to the left hemisphere, would each hemisphere observe its own color? Would the person be aware that the colors differ? What would the person report seeing? (Answers on page 67.)

"Do not let your left hand know what your right hand is doing."

Matthew 6:3

Similarly, when a picture of a spoon was flashed to their right hemisphere, the patients could not say what they saw. But when asked to identify what they had seen by feeling with their left hand an assortment of objects hidden behind a screen, they readily selected the spoon. If the experimenter said, "Right!" the patient might reply, "What? Right? How could I possibly pick out the right object when I don't know what I saw?" It is, of course, the left hemisphere doing the talking here, bewildered by what its other half knows. It is as if the patients have "two separate inner visual worlds," noted Sperry (1968). In a split brain each hemisphere truly has a mind of its own.

The left hemisphere, which acts as the brain's press agent, does mental gymnastics to rationalize reactions it does not understand. If the patient followed an order sent to the right hemisphere ("Walk"), the interpretive left hemisphere would offer a ready explanation ("I'm going into the house to get a Coke"). Thus, Michael Gazzaniga (1988) concluded that the left hemisphere is an "interpreter" that instantly constructs theories to explain our behavior.

Outside the laboratory, a few split-brain patients have been for a time bothered by the unruly independence of their left hand, which would unbutton a shirt while the right hand buttoned it. It was as if each hemisphere was thinking "I've half a mind to wear my green (blue) shirt today." Indeed, said Sperry (1964), split-brain surgery leaves people "with two separate minds." (Reading these reports, I fantasize a split-brain person enjoying a solitaire game of "rocks, paper, and scissors"—left versus right hand.)

Figure 2.23 Testing the divided brain When an experimenter flashes the word HEART across the visual field of a split-brain patient, the patient reports seeing the portion of the word transmitted to her left hemisphere. However, if asked to indicate with her left hand what she saw, she points to the portion of the word transmitted to her right hemisphere. (From Gazzaniga, 1983)

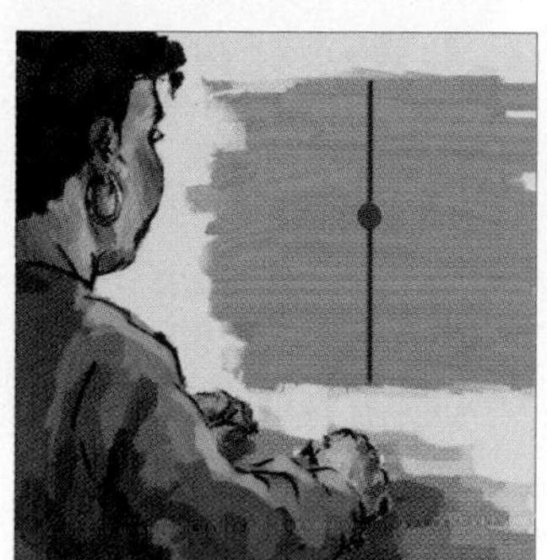

"Look at the dot."

Two words separated by red dot appear projected in front of person.

"What word did you see?"

or

"Point with your left hand to the word you saw."

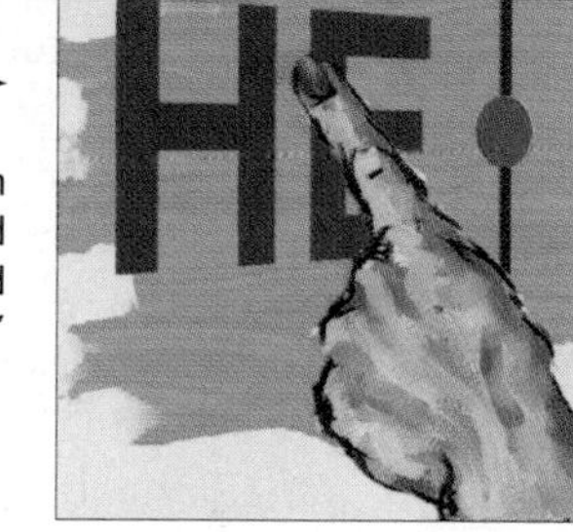

Studying Hemispheric Differences in the Intact Brain

What about the 99.99+ percent of us with undivided brains? Have scientists found our hemispheres similarly specialized? They have indeed, in several different types of studies. For example, when a person performs a *perceptual* task, brain waves, bloodflow, and brain glucose consumption reveal increased activity in the *right* hemisphere; when a person speaks or calculates, activity increases in the *left* hemisphere.

The mind seeking to understand the brain—that is indeed the ultimate scientific challenge.

On occasion, hemispheric specialization has been even more dramatically shown by briefly sedating an entire hemisphere. To check for the locus of language before surgery, a physician may inject a sedative into the neck artery that feeds blood to the hemisphere on its side of the body. Before the drug is injected, the patient is lying down, arms in the air, conversing easily. Can you predict what happens when the drug flows into the artery going to the left hemisphere? Within seconds, the right arm falls limp and, assuming that the person's left hemisphere controls language, the subject becomes speechless until the drug wears off. When the drug goes into the artery to the right hemisphere, the *left* arm falls limp, but speech is still possible.

Tests reveal that about 95 percent of right-handers process speech primarily in the left hemisphere (Springer & Deutsch, 1985). Left-handers are more diverse. More than half process speech in the left hemisphere, as right-handers do. About one-quarter process language in the right hemisphere; the other quarter use both hemispheres more or less equally. Such left-handers may therefore require better communication between the hemispheres. This might explain the discovery that the corpus callosum averages 11 percent larger in left-handers (Witelson, 1985).

Other tests confirm hemispheric specialization. Most people recognize a picture faster and more accurately when it is flashed to the right hemisphere. But they recognize a word faster and more accurately when it is flashed to the left hemisphere. If a word is flashed to your right hemisphere, perception takes a fraction of a second longer—the length of time it takes to send the information through the corpus callosum to the more verbal left hemisphere.

Finally, which hemisphere would you suppose enables sign language among the deaf? Is it the right hemisphere, because of its visual-spatial superiority? Or the left, because of its preparedness to process language? Studies reveal that, just as hearing people use the left hemisphere to process speech, deaf people use the left hemisphere to read signs (Corina & others, 1992). A stroke in the left hemisphere therefore disrupts a deaf person's signing, much as it would disrupt a hearing person's speaking. To the brain, language is language, whether spoken or signed.

So, a variety of observations—of people with split brains and people with normal brains—converge beautifully. There is now little doubt that we have unified brains with specialized parts. Although language requires the left hemisphere, the right hemisphere helps us modulate our speech to make meaning clear—as when

THINKING CRITICALLY

Left Brain/Right Brain

"Error flies from mouth to mouth, from pen to pen, and to destroy it takes ages."

Voltaire, 1694–1778

You've heard or read it many times: Some people are "left-brained," others "right-brained." Leaping from the new research on split and intact brains, educators, management advisers, and self-help writers urge us to harness the undeveloped half of our brain. Are you lacking in creativity, music appreciation, or emotional empathy? Well, get your brain in balance. Awaken your dormant right hemisphere. Advocate "whole brain" education in your schools. Unleash intuitive, right-brained management from the chains of cold logic and statistics. Try *Drawing on the Right Side of the Brain* (the title of a million-copy bestseller translated into 10 languages).

What should we make of all this? By calling my friend Elsie "right-brained" have I explained why she's such a zany free spirit? And why her "left-brained" husband Bill is so coolly analytical? We've seen that research does show that each hemisphere serves special functions. But neuroscientists offer a caution flag: Beware the fad of locating complex human abilities such as science or art in either hemisphere. "The left-right dichotomy in cognitive mode is an idea with which it is very easy to run wild," warned Sperry (1982). Complex activities such as doing science or creating art require the integrated activity of both hemispheres. Even when we just read a story, both hemispheres are active and communicating—the left processing the words and finding meaning, the right appreciating humor, imagery, and emotional content (Hellige, 1993; Levy, 1985).

Why, then, do the popularizations of brain research so greatly exaggerate the findings? In *The Left-Hander Syndrome*, University of British Columbia psychologist Stanley Coren (1993) illustrates how journalism often oversimplifies and embellishes science. He recalls hearing a convention talk by Doreen Kimura, a psychologist at the University of Western Ontario in London, Ontario. Kimura reported that melodies fed to the left ear were more easily recognized than melodies fed to the right ear. Knowing that the left ear sends most of its information to the right hemisphere, she concluded that, among her right-handed student volunteers, the right brain was better at recognizing melodies.

A few days later, the *New York Times* reported that "Doreen Kimura, a psychologist from London, Ontario, has found that *musical ability* is controlled by the right side of the brain" (italics highlight the embellishment). Apparently drawing from the *Times* story, a syndicated newspaper story then reported that "London psychologist, Dr. Doreen Kimura, claims that musicians are right-brained!" (But Kimura studied university students, not musicians.) Later, a follow-up newspaper article further distorted the study: "An English psychologist has finally explained why there are so many great left-handed musicians."

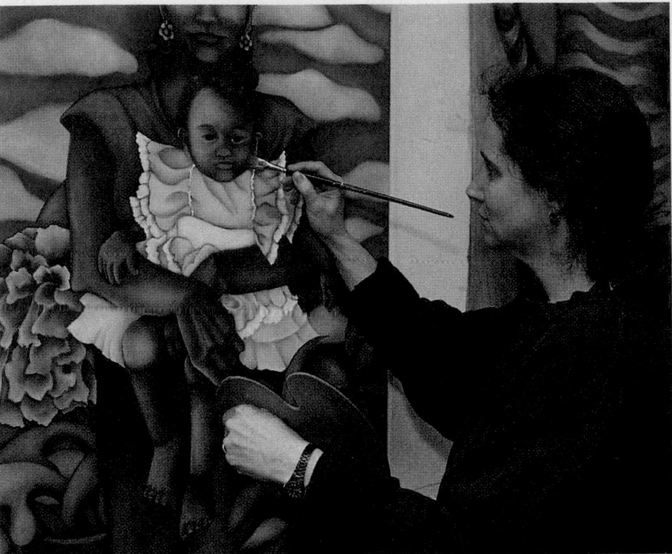

Left brain/right brain Is the artist a "right-brained" person? Such notions distort scientific findings regarding the cerebral hemispheres. While some areas of each hemisphere specialize in different tasks, the brain's two sides cooperate to enable the person in whatever he or she does.

Knowing that Kimura is not English, did not study musicians, and did not study left-handers, Coren recalled the words of an American editor: "Everything you read in the newspaper is absolutely true, except for the rare story of which you happen to have first-hand knowledge."

What can happen is this: As information flows from scientist to reader, it gets simplified and embellished, much as gossip does in passing from one person to the next. A TV network picks up an interesting finding, then reduces it to a 30-second report with an 11-second sound bite from the researcher. This alerts a major newspaper to a story angle, which in turn gets picked up by popular science magazines and, eventually, by supermarket magazines and tabloids.

At each step, notes Coren, "Ideas become more speculative and more distant from the actual research. . . . After a while, the neuropsychologist is no longer even visible in the communication chain." Eventually, the rumors grow, accumulate, and evolve into scientific myths that become "'accepted truths,' which show up in conversation and writing in sentences that begin with, 'As everybody knows . . . ,' or 'Scientists have shown that. . . .'" In the end, sighs Coren, the public myth drowns the weak voices of dissenting scientists.

The moral is not to disbelieve everything you read. Rather, beware that reporters want their stories to be newsworthy. At their best, their ideal (and mine, in writing this book) is to extract the essence—to simplify without oversimplifying. At their worst, they distort pretzel-shaped findings into a breadstick-shaped story: Some people are left-brained, others right-brained. . . .

Answers to questions on page 64: Yes. No. Green.

"If the human brain were so simple that we could understand it, we would be so simple that we couldn't."

Emerson M. Pugh, quoted by George E. Pugh
The Biological Origin of Human Values
1977

we ask "What's that in the road ahead?" instead of "What's that in the road, a head?" (Heller, 1990). From looking at the two hemispheres, which look alike to the naked eye, who would suppose that they contribute so uniquely to the harmony of the whole?

From nineteenth-century phrenology to today's neuroscience we have come a long way. Yet what is unknown still dwarfs what is known. We can describe the brain. We can learn the functions of its parts. We can study how the parts communicate. But how does this electrochemical whir give rise to a feeling of elation, a creative idea, or a memory of Grandmother's freshly baked cookies? The mind seeking to understand the brain—that is indeed the ultimate scientific challenge.

REHEARSE IT!

24. Plasticity refers to the brain's ability to reorganize itself after damage. Especially plastic are the brains of

a. split-brain patients. **c.** young children.
b. young adults. **d.** right-handed people.

25. The brain structure that enables the right and left hemispheres to communicate is

a. the medulla. **c.** Wernicke's area.
b. Broca's area. **d.** the corpus callosum.

26. An experimenter flashes the word HERON across the visual field of a split-brain patient. HER is transmitted to his right hemisphere and ON to his left hemisphere. When asked to indicate what he saw, the patient

a. *says* he saw HER but *points* to ON.
b. *says* he saw ON but *points* to HER.
c. *says* he saw HERON but *points* to HER.
d. *says* he saw HERON but *points* to ON.

27. The study of split-brain patients has allowed us to observe the special functions of each hemisphere of the brain. The left hemisphere excels in

a. processing language.
b. visual perceptions.
c. recognition of emotion.
d. recognition of faces.

28. Damage to the brain's right hemisphere is most likely to reduce a person's ability to

a. recite the alphabet rapidly.
b. recognize a picture.
c. understand verbal instructions.
d. solve arithmetic problems.

The Endocrine System

12. *How does the endocrine system transmit information?*

Interconnected with the nervous system is the second of the body's communication systems, the slower **endocrine system** (Figure 2.24, page 68). The endocrine system's glands secrete **hormones**, chemical messengers that are produced in one tissue and travel through the bloodstream and affect other tissues, including the brain. Hormones acting on the brain influence our interest in sex, food, and aggression.

Some hormones are chemically identical to neurotransmitters (those chemical messengers that diffuse across a synapse and excite or inhibit an adjacent neuron). The endocrine system and nervous system are therefore kindred systems: They both secrete molecules that activate receptors elsewhere. But unlike the messages of the speedy nervous system, which zip from eyes to brain to hand in a fraction of a second, endocrine messages use the slow lane. If the nervous system's communication delivers messages rather like e-mail, the endocrine system is the body's snail mail. Several seconds or more may elapse

endocrine [EN-duh-krin] **system** the body's "slow" chemical communication system; a set of glands that secrete hormones into the bloodstream.

hormones chemical messengers, mostly those manufactured by the endocrine glands, that are produced in one tissue and affect another.

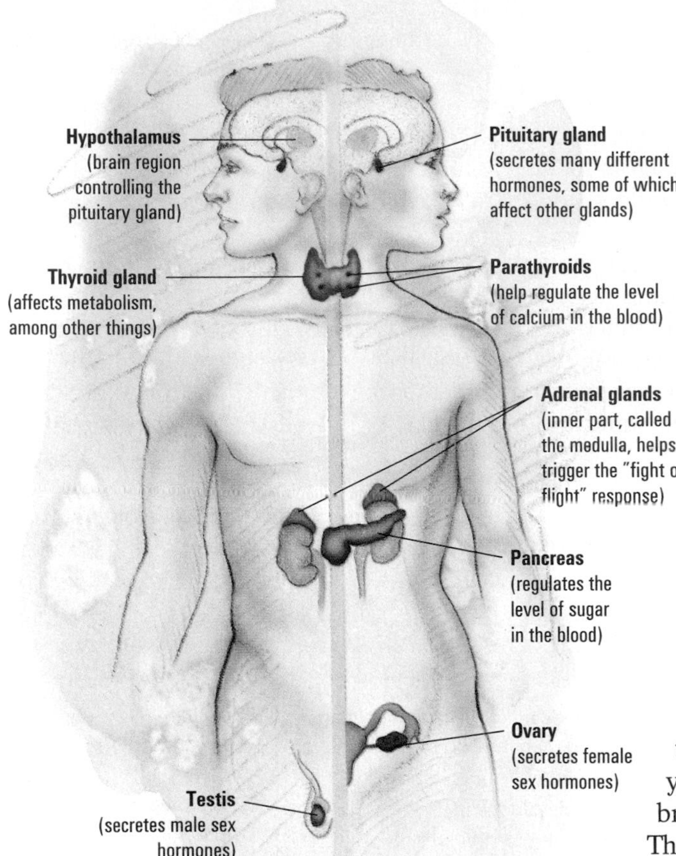

Figure 2.24 **The body's major endocrine glands**

before the bloodstream carries a hormone from an endocrine gland to its target tissue. But these endocrine messages are often worth waiting for because their effects are usually longer-lasting than the effects of a neural message.

The endocrine system's hormones influence many aspects of our lives, from growth to reproduction, from metabolism to mood, keeping everything in balance while we respond to stress, exertion, and internal thoughts. In a moment of danger, for example, the autonomic nervous system will order the **adrenal glands** on top of the kidneys to release *epinephrine* and *norepinephrine* (also called *adrenaline* and *noradrenaline*). These hormones increase heart rate, blood pressure, and blood sugar, providing us with a surge of energy. When the emergency passes, the hormones and the feelings of excitement—linger a while.

The most influential endocrine gland is the **pituitary gland**, a pea-sized structure located in the base of the brain, where it can be controlled by the adjacent hypothalamus. The pituitary releases hormones that influence growth. Its secretions also influence the release of hormones by other endocrine glands. This makes the pituitary a sort of master gland. For example, under the brain's influence, the pituitary triggers your sex glands to release sex hormones, which may in turn influence your brain and behavior.

This feedback system (brain → pituitary → other glands → hormones → brain) illustrates the intimate connection of the nervous and endocrine systems. The nervous system directs endocrine secretions, which affect the nervous system. Conducting and coordinating this whole electrochemical orchestra is that maestro we call the brain.

Autonomic arousal The adrenal glands of these rafters are surely releasing epinephrine and norepinephrine.

REHEARSE IT!

29. The endocrine system, the second and slower bodily communication system, produces chemical messengers that travel through the bloodstream and affect other tissues. These chemical substances are

a. hormones.
b. neurotransmitters.
c. endorphins.
d. glands.

30. The pituitary gland releases hormones that influence growth and the activity of other glands. The pituitary gland is part of the

a. endocrine system.
b. peripheral nervous system.
c. sympathetic nervous system.
d. central nervous system.

adrenal [ah-DREEN-el] **glands** a pair of endocrine glands just above the kidneys. The adrenals secrete the hormones epinephrine (adrenaline) and norepinephrine (noradrenaline), which help to arouse the body in times of stress.

pituitary gland the endocrine system's most influential gland. Under the influence of the hypothalamus, the pituitary regulates growth and controls other endocrine glands.

chromosomes threadlike structures made of DNA molecules that contain the genes.

DNA (deoxyribonucleic acid) a complex molecule containing the genetic information that makes up the chromosomes.

genes the biochemical units of heredity that make up the chromosomes; a segment of DNA capable of synthesizing a protein.

Genetics and Behavior

13. ***How do evolutionary psychologists use natural selection to explain universal behavioral tendencies? How do behavior geneticists explain individual differences?***

Behind the story of our human brain—surely the most awesome thing on earth—are the blueprints that design both our universal human attributes and our individual traits. When egg and sperm unite, the 23 **chromosomes** carried in the egg pair up with the 23 chromosomes brought to it by the sperm. These 46 chromosomes contain the master plan for your development. Each chromosome is composed of a coiled chain of a molecule called **DNA (deoxyribonucleic acid)**. DNA in turn is made of thousands of **genes**. Our genes are the biochemical units of heredity that by synthesizing specific proteins make each of us a distinctive human being. The genes we share are what make us people rather than dogs or tulips (Figure 2.25).

More than 98 percent of our genes are identical to those of chimpanzees, making them as close to us as a fox is to a dog (de Waal, 1995). But what a difference that 2 percent makes—enabling not only our art and science but also our power to destroy all our achievements.

As we will see in chapters to come, one of psychology's really big questions concerns the extent to which our genes provide the blueprints not only for our bodies but for our behaviors. Clearly, genes do predispose certain behaviors. Dog breeders, as Robert Plomin and his colleagues (1997) remind us, have given us sheepdogs that herd, retrievers that retrieve, trackers that track, and pointers that point. They also have given us placid spaniels and aggressive bulldogs. Psychologists, too, have bred dogs, mice, and rats whose genes predispose them to be serene or reactive, quick-learners or slow-learners.

Everyone agrees that the tight genetic leash that predisposes an ant's nest-building, a dog's retrieving, or a cat's pouncing, is looser on humans. Our genes endow us with a capacity to learn and to adapt to life on the tundra or in the jungle. But to what extent do our genetic predispositions explain both our shared human nature and our individual differences?

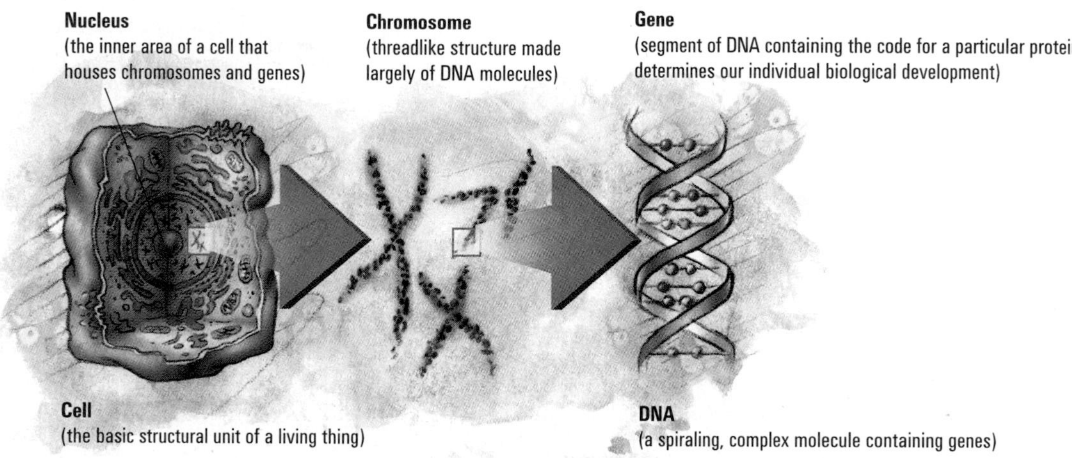

Figure 2.25 **The genes: Their location and composition** Contained in the nucleus of each of the trillions of cells in your body are chromosomes. Each chromosome contains a coiled chain of the molecule DNA. Genes are DNA segments that form templates for the production of proteins. By directing the manufacture of proteins, the genes determine our individual biological development.

Evolutionary Psychology: Explaining Universal Behaviors

In some ways, we differ from others in our culture, and certainly from people shaped by other cultures. Yet in the big picture our lives are remarkably alike. As humans, we all face certain questions: Who is my ally, who my foe? What food should I eat? With whom should I mate?

evolutionary psychology the study of the evolution of behavior using the principles of natural selection, which presumably favor behavioral tendencies that contribute to the preservation and spread of one's genes.

behavior genetics the study of the power and limits of genetic and environmental influences on behavior.

identical twins twins who develop from a single zygote (fertilized egg) that splits in two, creating two genetic replicas.

fraternal twins twins who develop from separate zygotes. They are genetically no closer than brothers and sisters, but they share the fetal environment.

At the dawn of human history, some individuals answered those questions more successfully than others. Those disposed to eat food that nourished rather than poisoned them more often survived to contribute their genes to later generations. Similarly successful were those who mated with someone with whom they could produce and nurture offspring. Individuals not disposed to eat and mate in such ways tended, over generations, to have their genes removed from the human gene pool. As further random variations occurred, those that had an adaptive edge continued to be selected. The result, say **evolutionary psychologists**, was not only bodies but behavioral tendencies and ways of thinking that prepared our Stone Age ancestors to survive, reproduce, and send their genes into the future. Nature selected the fittest adaptations.

As inheritors of this genetic legacy, we therefore love the taste of sweets and fats, which once were hard to come by, but which prepared our ancestors to survive famines. (Today, with famine rare in Western cultures, and sweets and fats beckoning us from store shelves, fast-food outlets, and vending machines, obesity is a growing problem.) Evolution has been important to biology for a long time. It has only recently been incorporated into psychology's spotlight of understanding as a perspective that can address some very important issues. Darwin (1859) anticipated this "second Darwinian revolution"—the application of evolutionary principles to psychology. In concluding his book *Origin of Species*, he foresaw "open fields for far more important researches. Psychology will be based on a new foundation . . ." (p. 346).

Psychologists, as we shall see, have used evolutionary principles to explore questions such as these:

- Why do infants come to fear strangers about the time they become mobile?
- Why are most parents so passionately devoted to their children?
- Why do we display greater empathy and helpfulness toward those who think, look, and act as we do?
- Why do men tend to find healthy-looking younger women attractive, and why are men with status and resources appealing to women?
- Why are men quicker than women to perceive friendliness as sexual interest, to initiate sexual relations, and to feel jealous rage over their mate's having sex with someone else?

The answer to these and other questions, say evolutionary psychologists, is that nature selects behavioral tendencies that increase the likelihood of sending one's genes into the future. As mobile gene machines, we are predisposed by nature to have longings and make choices that worked for our ancestors. For possible explanations of *why* such behaviors were genetically successful, stay tuned. Future chapters will offer some answers.

Behavior Genetics: Explaining Individual Differences

While evolutionary psychologists explore the behavioral implications of Darwin's big idea in hopes of explaining our universal human tendencies, **behavior geneticists** explore our differences from one another. How much are we shaped by our genetic blueprint? By our upbringing? By our culture and current circumstances? By how our environment reacts to our genetic traits?

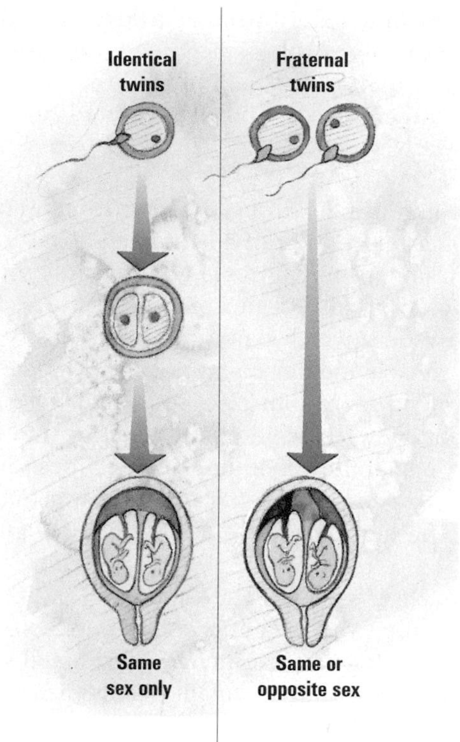

Figure 2.26 **Same egg, same genes; different eggs, different genes** Identical twins develop from a single fertilized egg, fraternal twins from two.

Studying the Genetic Factor

To answer such questions, behavior geneticists harness powerful methods such as these:

Twin Studies

To discern the effect of heredity, it would be nice if we could hold shared environment constant while varying heredity. Happily for our purposes, nature has given us ready-made subjects for this experiment: identical versus fraternal twins. **Identical twins**, who develop from a single fertilized egg that splits in two, are genetically identical (Figure 2.26). They are—millions and millions of them—nature's own human clones. (The possibility of laboratory human cloning raises new ethical issues but hardly new psychological issues.)

Fraternal twins, who develop from separate eggs, are genetically no more similar than ordinary brothers and sisters. A person whose identical twin had Alzheimer's disease has a 60 percent risk of sharing the disease; with an affected fraternal twin, the risk is 30 percent (Plomin & others, 1997). Such a difference suggests a genetic influence.

Behavior geneticists ask: Are identical twins, being genetic clones of one another, more similar than fraternal twins? Studies of nearly 13,000 pairs of Swedish identical and fraternal twins, of 7000 Finnish twin pairs, and of 3810 Australian twin pairs provide a consistent answer: On both extraversion (outgoingness) and neuroticism (emotional instability), identical twins are much more similar than fraternal twins. Genes matter.

Other dimensions of personality also reflect genetic influences. John Loehlin and Robert Nichols (1976) gave a battery of questionnaires to 850 U.S. twin pairs. Once again, identical twins were much more similar, and in a variety of ways—in abilities, personality, even interests. However, the identical twins, more than fraternal twins, also reported being treated alike. So, did their experience rather than their genes account for their similarity? No, said Loehlin and Nichols. Identical twins whose parents treated them alike were *not* psychologically more alike than identical twins who were treated less similarly.

Curiously, twinning rates vary by race. The rate among Caucasians is roughly twice that of Asians and half that of Africans (Diamond, 1986).

Separated Twins

Imagine a science fiction experiment in which a mad scientist decides to separate identical twins at birth and rear them in differing environments. In reality, circumstances occasionally set up just these conditions.

In 1979, University of Minnesota psychologist Thomas Bouchard read a newspaper account of the reunion of 39-year-old twins who had been separated from infancy. Seeing a scientific opportunity, he flew them to Minneapolis for extensive tests. Bouchard was looking for differences. What "the Jim twins," Jim Lewis and Jim Springer, presented were amazing similarities (Holden, 1980a,b). Both had married and divorced women named Linda and had later married women named Betty. One had a son James Alan, the other a son James Allan. Both had dogs named Toy, chain-smoked Salems, served as sheriff's deputies, drove Chevrolets, chewed their fingernails to the nub, enjoyed stock car racing, had basement workshops, and had built circular white benches around trees in their yards. They also had similar medical histories: Both gained 10 pounds at about the same time and then lost it. Both suffered what they mistakenly believed were heart attacks. Both began having late-afternoon headaches at age 18.

Twins Lorraine and Levinia Christmas, driving to deliver presents to each other near Flitcham, England, collided (Shepherd, 1997).

Identical twins Oskar Stohr and Jack Yufe presented equally striking similarities. One was raised by his grandmother in Germany as a Catholic and a Nazi, while the other was raised by his father in the Caribbean as a Jew. Nevertheless, they share traits and habits galore. They like spicy foods and sweet liqueurs, have a habit of falling asleep in front of the television, flush the toilet before using it, store rubber bands on their wrists, and dip buttered toast in their coffee. Stohr is domineering toward women and yells at his wife, as did Yufe before he and his wife separated.

"In some domains it looks as though our identical twins reared apart are . . . just as similar as identical twins reared together. Now that's an amazing finding and I can assure you none of us would have expected that degree of similarity."

Thomas Bouchard (1981)

Aided by publicity in magazine and newspaper stories, Bouchard and his colleagues (1990; DiLalla & others, in press) have located and studied 69 pairs of identical twins reared apart. They continue to be impressed by the similarities not only of tastes and physical attributes but also of personality, abilities, attitudes, interests, and even fears. In Sweden, which has a national registry of 25,000 pairs of adult twins, Nancy Pedersen and her co-workers (1988) identified 99 separated identical twin pairs and more than 200 separated fraternal twin pairs. Compared with equivalent samples of identical twins reared together, the separated identical twins had more dissimilar personalities. Still, separated twins were more alike when genetically identical than when fraternal. And separation shortly after birth (rather than, say, at age 8) didn't amplify their personality differences.

Coincidences are not unique to twins. Patricia Kern of Colorado was born March 13, 1941, and named Patricia Ann Campbell. Patricia DiBiasi of Oregon also was born March 13, 1941, and named Patricia Ann Campbell. Both had fathers named Robert, worked as bookkeepers, and have children ages 21 and 19. Both studied cosmetology, enjoy oil painting as a hobby, and married military men, within 11 days of each other. They are not genetically related. (From an AP report, May 2, 1983)

The cute stories do not impress Bouchard's critics. They contend that if any two strangers of the same sex and age were to spend hours comparing their behaviors and life histories, they would probably discover many coincidental similarities. Even the more impressive data from the personality assessments are clouded by the reunion of many of the separated twins for some years before being tested. Moreover, adoption agencies tend to place separated twins in similar homes. When environments are similar, the impact of environment looks smaller relative to heredity. As twins age, differing experiences often make their personality differences more noticeable (McCartney & others, 1990). Nevertheless, the twin studies illustrate why scientific opinion has shifted toward a greater appreciation of genetic influences.

Adoption Studies

Another of nature's experiments, adoption, creates two groups of relatives: genetic relatives (biological parents and siblings) and environmental relatives (adoptive parents and siblings). For any given trait we can therefore ask whether adopted children are more like their adoptive parents, who contribute a home environment, or their biological parents, who contributed their genes. While sharing the same home environment, do adopted siblings come to share traits? The stunning finding from studies of hundreds of adoptive families—toppling many of our cherished notions about parental influence—is that people who grow up together do not much resemble one another in personality, whether biologically related or not (Rowe, 1990). If parental nurture mattered as much as most people suppose, then shouldn't people be more alike if reared in the same home?

Affable by nature? Identical twins Gerald Levey and Mark Newman were separated at birth and raised in different homes. When reunited at age 31, they discovered that they both volunteered as firefighters. Research has shown remarkable similarities in the life choices of separated identical twins, lending support to the idea that genes influence personality.

What we have here is developmental psychology's biggest puzzle: Why are children in the same family so different? Why do the shared genes and the shared family environment (the family's social class, the parents' personalities and marital status, day care versus home care, the neighborhood) have so little discernible effect on children's personalities? Is it because each sibling nevertheless experiences a different environment—differing peer influences and life events (Dunn & Plomin, 1990; Hetherington & others, 1993)? Is it because siblings—despite sharing half their genes—have very different combinations of genes (Lykken & others, 1992)? Does parental influence therefore affect an easygoing child one way, a reactive child another? "Child-rearing is not something a parent does to a child," notes Judith Rich Harris (1999). "It is something the parent and the child do together. . . . I

Family ties Studies of adoptive families have provided new clues to hereditary and environmental influences. How similar would you expect adopted children to be to their adoptive parents? To their biological parents?

would have been pegged as a permissive parent with my first child, a bossy one with my second."

Adoption studies show that, although the personalities of adopted children do not much resemble those of their adoptive parents, adoption matters (Brodzinsky & Schechter, 1990). First, the home environment influences adopted children's values, beliefs, and social attitudes. Second, in adoptive homes, child neglect and abuse and even parental divorce are rare. (Adoptive parents are carefully screened; natural parents are not.) So it is not surprising that, despite somewhat greater risk of psychological disorder, most adopted children thrive, especially when adopted as infants (Benson & others, 1994; Wierzbicki, 1993). They score higher than their biological parents on intelligence tests. Seven in eight report feeling strongly attached to one or both parents. And they generally become happier and more stable people than they would have been in a stressed or neglectful environment. In a Swedish study, infant adoptees grew up with fewer problems than were experienced by children whose biological mothers had initially registered them for adoption but then decided to raise the children themselves (Bohman & Sigvardsson, 1990). Children need not resemble their adoptive parents to have benefited from adoption.

Heritability

Using twin and adoption studies, behavior geneticists can mathematically estimate the **heritability** of any trait—the extent to which variation among individuals is due to their differing genes.

So, to what extent are we the product of our genes? The answer varies with the trait. But we will see that on traits as widely varying as sleep needs, obesity, happiness, intelligence, personality, and sexual orientation, the genetic influence is considerable. Yet the bio-psycho-social perspective reminds us that genes always are expressed in a particular environment. Genes and environment, nature and nurture, work together like two hands clapping, with the environment reacting to and shaping what nature predisposes. Thus, asking whether your intelligence or personality is more a product of your genes or your environment is like asking whether the area of a field is more the result of its length or its width.

"The same fire that tempers steel melts butter."
Anonymous

We could, however, ask whether the differing areas of *various* fields are more the result of differences in their length or width. For psychological traits, human differences are nearly always the result of both genetic and environmental influences. Thus (to give a preview of coming attractions) eating disorders are genetically influenced; some individuals are more at risk than others. But culture also bends the twig, for eating disorders are a contemporary Western cultural phenomenon. Likewise, criminal and aggressive tendencies are known to be genetically influenced. Yet genetic changes cannot explain the explosion in juvenile violence since 1960.

If genetic influences help explain individual differences in traits such as aggressiveness, can the same be said of group differences between men and women, or between people of different races? Not necessarily. Individual differences in height and weight are highly heritable. Yet nutritional rather than genetic influences explain why, as a group, today's adults are taller and heavier than those of a century ago. As with height and weight, so with personality and intelligence scores: Heritable individual differences need not imply heritable group differences.

heritability the proportion of variation among individuals that we can attribute to genes.

We have glimpsed the truth of our overriding principle: Everything psychological is simultaneously biological. This chapter has focused on some ways in which our thoughts, feelings, and actions arise from our specialized yet integrated brain, which is designed by our evolutionary history and genetic blueprints. Chapters to come will further explore the significance of the biological revolution in psychology. We will see, for example, how

- brain development underlies a child's mental development.
- genes and experience jointly influence our personality, emotions, gender, and intelligence.
- our sense organs and our brain enable us to see and hear.
- the brain records memories.
- abnormal brain anatomy and chemistry influence depression and schizophrenia, and how biological treatments can alleviate these conditions.
- our brain and body work to create our experiences of hunger and sexuality, anger and fear, sleep and dreams.
- mind and body together influence our vulnerability to disease and our capacity for healing.
- our species' evolution may predispose us to hurt, help, or love certain others.

REHEARSE IT!

31. When the egg and sperm unite, each contributes

a. one chromosome pair.
b. 23 chromosomes.
c. 23 chromosome pairs.
d. an *XY* chromosome.

32. Evolutionary psychologists focus on the

a. ways in which we differ from one another.
b. links between biology and behavior.
c. natural selection of the fittest adaptations.
d. random assignment of genes over several generations.

33. Fraternal twins result when

a. a single egg is fertilized by a single sperm and then splits.
b. a single egg is fertilized by two sperm and then splits.
c. two eggs are fertilized by two sperm.
d. two eggs are fertilized by a single sperm.

34. Adoption studies seek to reveal genetic influences on personality mainly by

a. comparing adopted children with nonadopted children.
b. evaluating whether adopted children more closely resemble their adoptive parents or their biological parents.
c. studying the effect of prior neglect on adopted children.
d. studying the effect of one's age at adoption.

35. The heritability of a trait may vary, depending on the range of populations and environments studied. To say that the heritability of intelligence is 60 percent means that 60 percent of

a. intelligence is due to genetic factors.
b. the similarities among groups of people are attributable to genes.
c. the *variation* in intelligence within a group of people is attributable to genetic factors.
d. intelligence is due to the mother's genes and the rest is due to the father's genes.

REVIEWING ■ *Biology and Behavior*

1. ***Why do psychologists study biology?***

   As a first step in understanding our behavior and mental processes, **biological psychologists** examine the biological roots of how we think, feel, and act.

Neural Communication

2. ***What are neurons, and how do they transmit information?***

   The body's neural circuitry consists of billions of nerve cells, called **neurons**. A neuron receives signals from external stimuli and from other neurons through its branching **dendrites** and cell body, combines these signals in the cell body, and, if the signals exceed a certain **threshold**, transmits an electrical impulse (the **action potential**) down its **axon**, which may be covered by a **myelin sheath**.

3. ***How do nerve cells communicate?***

   When electrical signals reach the end of the axon, they stimulate the release of chemical messengers called **neurotransmitters**. These molecules pass on their excitatory or inhibitory messages as they traverse the tiny gap (**synapse**) between neurons and combine with receptor sites on neighboring neurons.

4. ***How do neurotransmitters influence human behavior?***

   Dozens of different neurotransmitters have been discovered, and the functions of some, such as **acetylcholine (ACh)**, have become well-understood. Learning about **endorphins**, the feel-good neurotransmitters, has helped us understand how drugs affect our brain chemistry. Some drugs (agonists) mimic particular neurotransmitters; others (antagonists) block them.

The Nervous System

5. ***What are the major divisions of the nervous system, and what are their basic functions?***

   The **nervous system** consists of the **central nervous system (CNS)** and the **peripheral nervous system (PNS)**. The **interneurons** in the brain and spinal cord (the CNS) communicate with the **sensory** and **motor neurons** that form **nerves** in the PNS. The peripheral nervous system has two main divisions. The **skeletal nervous system** directs voluntary movements and **reflexes**. The **autonomic nervous system**, through its **sympathetic** and **parasympathetic divisions**, controls our involuntary muscles and the glands of the internal organs.

The Brain

6. ***What are the functions of the brainstem and its associated structures?***

   Within the **brainstem**, the **medulla** controls heartbeat and breathing and the **reticular formation** controls arousal and attention. The **cerebellum**, which is attached to the rear of the brainstem, coordinates muscle movement. On top of the brainstem is the **thalamus**, the brain's sensory switchboard. Methods of studying the brain include **lesioning**, **electroencephalograms (EEGs)**, and **CT**, **PET**, and **MRI scans**.

7. ***What are the functions of limbic system structures?***

   The **limbic system** has been linked primarily to memory, emotions, and drives. For example, one of its neural centers, the **amygdala**, is involved in aggressive and fearful responses. Another, the **hypothalamus**, has been linked to various bodily maintenance functions and to pleasurable rewards. The hypothalamus also controls the endocrine system.

8. ***How is the cerebral cortex organized?***

   The **cerebral cortex** is a thin, wrinkled sheet of neurons with trillions of interconnections. **Glial cells** support, nourish, and protect the neurons. Each of the hemispheres it covers can be viewed as having four geographical areas: the **frontal**, **parietal**, **occipital**, and **temporal lobes**, which are separated by prominent folds.

9. ***What are the functions of the cerebral cortex?***

   Small, well-defined regions within the cerebral lobes control muscle movement (the **motor cortex**) and receive information from the body senses (the **sensory cortex**). However, most of the cortex—its **association areas**—is uncommitted to such functions and is therefore free to process other information.

   Some brain regions are known to serve specific functions. In general, however, human emotions, thoughts, and behaviors result from the intricate coordination of many brain areas. Language, for example, depends on a chain of events in several brain regions, particularly **Broca's area** and **Wernicke's area**. Damage to an area of the brain involved in language may cause one of several types of **aphasia**.

Brain Reorganization

10. ***Is the brain capable of reorganizing itself if damaged?***

    If one hemisphere is damaged early in life (in the first five years), the other will pick up many of its functions, thus demonstrating the brain's **plasticity**. Unfortunately, the brain is less plastic later in life. However, nearby neurons can often at least partially compensate for damaged ones, as when a patient recovers from a minor stroke.

11. ***What is a split brain, and what does it reveal about brain functioning?***

    A **split brain** is one whose **corpus callosum**, the wide band of nerve fibers connecting the two brain hemispheres, has been severed. Clinical observations long ago revealed that the left cerebral hemisphere is crucial for language. More recent experiments on split-brain patients have refined our knowledge of each hemisphere's special functions. By testing the two hemispheres separately, researchers have confirmed that for most people the left hemisphere is indeed the more verbal and that the right hemisphere excels in visual perception and the recognition of emotion. Studies of normal people with intact brains confirm that each hemisphere makes unique contributions to the integrated functioning of the brain.

The Endocrine System

12. ***How does the endocrine system transmit information?***

Hormones released by the glands of the **endocrine system** travel through the bloodstream and affect other tissues, including the brain. The endocrine system's master gland, the **pituitary**, influences hormone release by other glands. The **adrenal glands** are activated in stressful times by the autonomic nervous system.

Genetics and Behavior

13. ***How do evolutionary psychologists use natural selection to explain universal behavioral tendencies? How do behavior geneticists explain individual differences?***

Genes, which make up our **chromosomes**, are segments of complex **DNA (deoxyribonucleic acid)** molecules. These biochemical units of heredity provide the blueprint for protein molecules, the building blocks of our physical and behavioral development. **Evolutionary psychologists** study how natural selection has shaped our universal behavioral tendencies. **Behavior geneticists** explore our individual differences. Using methods such as twin and adoption studies, they identify the **heritability** of various traits and disorders. Studies of the inheritance of temperament, and of **identical** and **fraternal twins** and adopted children, provide scientific support for the idea that nature *and* nurture influence one's developing personality. Researchers agree that genes and environment, biological and social factors, direct our life courses as their effects intertwine.

CRITICAL THINKING EXERCISE by Richard O. Straub

Now that you have read and reviewed Chapter 2, take your learning a step further by testing your critical thinking skills on this pattern-recognition exercise.

Playing a musical instrument is a complicated skill that involves every major aspect of behavior and cognition. To be proficient, musicians must have honed their fine motor skills. In addition, many aspects of thinking come into play, including *memory* of how to play the instrument and of musical scales and time signatures, and the planning and *decision making* inherent in translating a piece of sheet music into sound. The musician's *motivation* and *emotion* are equally important influences on a musical performance.

In this exercise you will develop a map describing how various parts of the brain enable a musician to perform a piece of music. Identify three lower-level brain structures and three upper-level structures; then describe how each structure is involved in musical performance.

1. Lower-Level Brain Structure
   a. ______________________________
   b. ______________________________
   c. ______________________________
2. Description of How the Lower-Level Structure Is Involved in Musical Performance
   a. ______________________________
   b. ______________________________
   c. ______________________________
3. Upper-Level Brain Structure
   a. ______________________________
   b. ______________________________
   c. ______________________________
4. Description of How the Upper-Level Structure Is Involved in Musical Performance
   a. ______________________________
   b. ______________________________
   c. ______________________________

Check your progress in becoming a critical thinker by comparing your answers to the sample answers found in Appendix B.

REHEARSE IT ANSWER KEY

1. b., **2.** a., **3.** c., **4** d., **5.** c., **6.** b., **7.** d., **8.** c., **9.** a., **10.** b., **11.** b., **12.** a., **13.** c., **14.** d., **15.** b., **16.** d., **17.** c., **18.** b., **19.** d., **20.** d., **21.** c., **22.** c., **23.** b., **24.** c., **25.** d., **26.** b., **27.** a., **28.** b., **29.** a., **30.** a., **31.** b., **32.** c., **33.** c., **34.** b., **35.** c.

FOR FURTHER INFORMATION

For more information on evolutionary psychology see:

For more information on neuroscience see:

For more information on behavior genetics see:

CHAPTER 3

The Developing Person

In mid-1978, the newest astonishment in medicine, covering all the front pages, was the birth of an English baby nine months after conception in a dish. The older surprise, which should still be fazing us all, is that a solitary sperm and a single egg can fuse and become a human being. . . . This has been going on under our eyes for so long a time that we've gotten used to it; hence the outcries of amazement at this really minor technical modification of the general procedure—nothing much, really, beyond relocating the beginning of the process from the fallopian tube to a plastic container.

Lewis Thomas
The Medusa and the Snail
1979

The developing person is no less a wonder after birth than in the womb. As we journey through life from womb to tomb, when and how do we change? Usually we notice how we differ. To **developmental psychologists**, who study physical, mental, and social changes throughout the human life cycle, our commonalities are just as important. Virtually all of us began walking around age 1 and talking by age 2. As children we all engaged in social play in preparation for life's serious work. As adults, we all smile and cry, love and loathe, and occasionally ponder the fact that someday we will die.

Human development is a lifelong process. Psychology's developmental perspective examines how people are continually developing, from infancy through old age. Much of its research centers on three major issues:

1. *Nature/nurture:* How much is human development influenced by our genetic inheritance (our *nature*) and how much by our experience (the *nurture* we receive)?
2. *Continuity/stages:* Is development a gradual, continuous process like riding an escalator, or does it proceed through a sequence of separate stages, like climbing rungs on a ladder?
3. *Stability/change:* Do our early personality traits persist through life, or do we become different persons as we age?

We considered the nature/nurture issue in some detail in Chapter 2. At the end of this chapter, we will reflect once more on the continuity and stability issues.

Prenatal Development and the Newborn

1. ***How does life develop before birth?***

The Genetics of Life

"From the very moment that the sperm hits the egg, a precarious trip on the thin edge of biological extinction has begun."

Ralph Blair
Nevertheless Joy!
1989

Nothing is more natural than a species reproducing itself. Yet nothing is more wondrous. Consider human reproduction. The process starts when a woman's ovary releases a mature egg, a cell roughly the size of the period at the end of this sentence, and when the 200 million or more sperm deposited during intercourse begin their race upstream toward it.

Like space voyagers approaching a huge planet, the sperm approach a cell 85,000 times their own size. The relatively few sperm that make it to the egg release digestive enzymes that eat away the egg's protective coating, allowing a sperm to penetrate (Figure 3.1). But the egg is hardly passive. Rather, as soon as one sperm begins to penetrate, the egg's surface blocks out all other sperm. Meanwhile, fingerlike projections sprout around the successful sperm and pull it inward. The egg nucleus and the sperm nucleus move toward each other and, before half a day elapses, fuse. The two have become one.

Figure 3.1 **The union of egg and sperm** **(a)** A hoard of sperm cells surrounds an ovum. **(b)** As one sperm penetrates the egg's jellylike outer coating, a series of chemical events begins that will cause sperm and egg to fuse into a single cell. If all goes well, that cell will subdivide again and again to emerge 9 months later as a 100-trillion-cell human being.

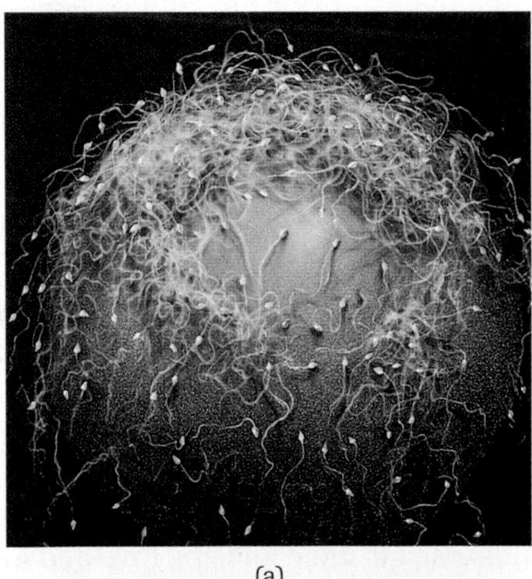

(a)

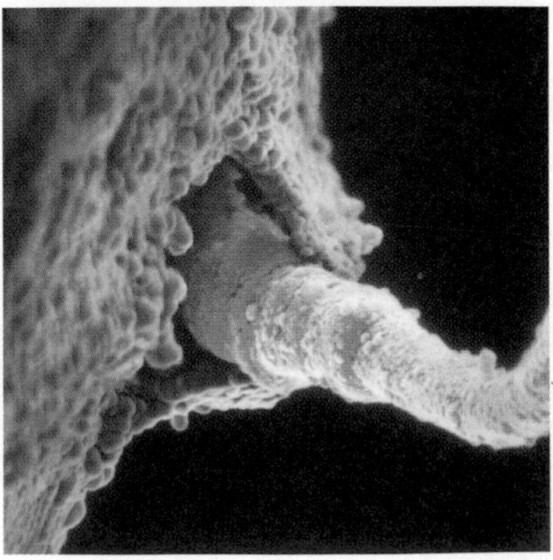

(b)

Sex Chromosomes, Sex Hormones, and Gender

Males and females are variations on a single form. Eight weeks after conception, you were anatomically indistinguishable from the other sex. Then, your genes activated your sex. Your twenty-third pair of chromosomes, the sex chromosomes, determined your sex. The member of the pair that came from your mother was an ***X* chromosome**. Thus, of your 46 chromosomes, 45 are unisex. From your father, you received the forty-sixth—either an *X* chromosome, making you a girl, or a ***Y* chromosome**, making you a boy. The *Y* chromosome contains a single gene that throws a master switch triggering the testes to develop and produce the principal male hormone, **testosterone**, which in turn triggers the development of external male sex organs. The fourth and fifth months of prenatal development are a key time for sexual differentiation, which also involves differing brain-wiring patterns for males and females.

What do you suppose happens when glandular malfunction or hormone injections expose a female embryo to excess testosterone? These genetically female infants are born with masculine-appearing genitals, which can be corrected surgically. Until puberty, such females tend to act in more aggressive "tomboyish" ways than is typical of most girls, and they dress and play in ways more typical of boys than of girls (Berenbaum & Hines, 1992; Ehrhardt, 1987). Given a choice of toys, they (like boys) play with cars and blocks rather than with dolls and crayons. Some develop into lesbians, but most—like nearly all girls with traditionally feminine interests—become heterosexual.

Is their behavior due to the prenatal hormones? If so, may we conclude that biological sex differences produce behavioral **gender** differences? Experiments with many species, from rats to monkeys, confirm that female embryos given male hormones later appear more masculine and exhibit more aggressive behavior (Hines & Green, 1991). Because these girls frequently look masculine and are known to be "different," perhaps people also treat them more like boys. Early exposure to sex hormones thus affects us both directly (physically) and indirectly—by influencing experiences that shape us. Biological appearances have social consequences.

developmental psychology a branch of psychology that studies physical, cognitive, and social change throughout the life span.

***X* chromosome** the sex chromosome found in both men and women. Females have two *X* chromosomes; males have one. An *X* chromosome from each parent produces a female.

***Y* chromosome** the sex chromosome found only in males. When paired with an *X* sex chromosome from the mother, it produces a male child.

testosterone the most important of the male sex hormones. Both males and females have it, but the additional testosterone in males stimulates the growth of the male sex organs in the fetus and the development of the male sex characteristics during puberty.

gender in psychology, the characteristics, whether biologically or socially influenced, by which people define male and female.

zygote the fertilized egg; it enters a 2-week period of rapid cell division and develops into an embryo.

embryo the developing human organism from about 2 weeks after fertilization through the second month.

fetus the developing human organism from 9 weeks after conception to birth.

teratogens agents, such as chemicals and viruses, that can reach the embryo or fetus during prenatal development and cause harm.

fetal alcohol syndrome (FAS) physical and cognitive abnormalities in children caused by a pregnant woman's heavy drinking. In severe cases, symptoms include noticeable facial misproportions.

Prenatal development

zygote:	*conception to 2 weeks*
embryo:	*2 weeks through 8 weeks*
fetus:	*9 weeks to birth*

Prenatal Development

Fewer than half of all fertilized eggs, called **zygotes**, survive beyond the first 2 weeks (Grobstein, 1979). But for you and me, good fortune prevailed. Beginning as one cell, each of us became two cells, then four—each cell just like the first. Then, within the first week, when this cell division had produced a zygote of some 100 cells, the cells began to *differentiate*—to specialize in structure and function. How identical cells do this—as if one decides "I'll become a head, you become intestines!"—is a scientific puzzle that developmental biologists are just beginning to solve.

About 10 days after conception, the increasingly diverse cells attach to the mother's uterine wall, beginning approximately 37 weeks of the closest human relationship. When the zygote's outer part attaches to the uterine wall, it becomes the placenta, through which nourishment passes. In this second prenatal stage, the inner cells become the **embryo** (Figure 3.2). During the next 6 weeks, the embryo's body organs begin to form and function. The heart begins to beat and the liver begins to make red blood cells.

By 9 weeks after conception, the embryo looks unmistakably human and is now a **fetus**. By the end of the sixth month, internal organs such as the stomach have become sufficiently formed and functional to allow a prematurely born fetus a chance of survival.

At each prenatal stage, genetic *and* environmental factors affect development. The placenta screens out many potentially harmful substances, while allowing nutrients and oxygen to pass through. But some toxins slip by the placental screen, and devastating effects may follow if the placenta admits **teratogens**—harmful agents such as certain viruses and drugs. For example, a pregnant woman never smokes alone. When she puffs on a cigarette, she and her fetus both experience reduced blood oxygen and a shot of nicotine. If she is a heavy smoker, her newborn probably will be underweight, sometimes dangerously so. If she is a heroin addict, her baby will be born a heroin addict. If she carries the AIDS virus, her baby may also.

When a pregnant woman takes a drink, alcohol enters her bloodstream—and her fetus's—and depresses activity in both their central nervous systems. If she drinks heavily, her baby will be at risk for birth defects and mental retardation. For 1 in 750 infants, the effects are visible as **fetal alcohol syndrome (FAS)**, marked by a small, misproportioned head and lifelong brain abnormalities, making it now the leading cause of mental retardation (Niccols, 1994; Streissguth & others, 1991). Although there is no known safe amount of alcohol for a pregnant woman—even moderate drinking can affect the fetal brain (Braun, 1996)—children of alcoholic mothers are especially at risk. About 4 in 10 alcoholic mothers who drink during pregnancy have babies who suffer the enduring damage of fetal alcohol syndrome.

(a)

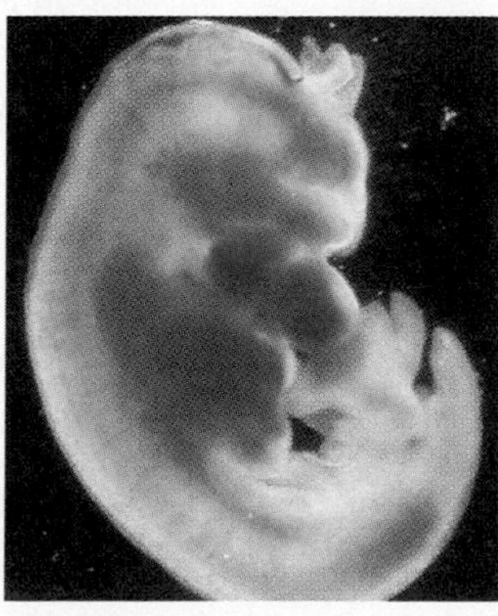
(b)

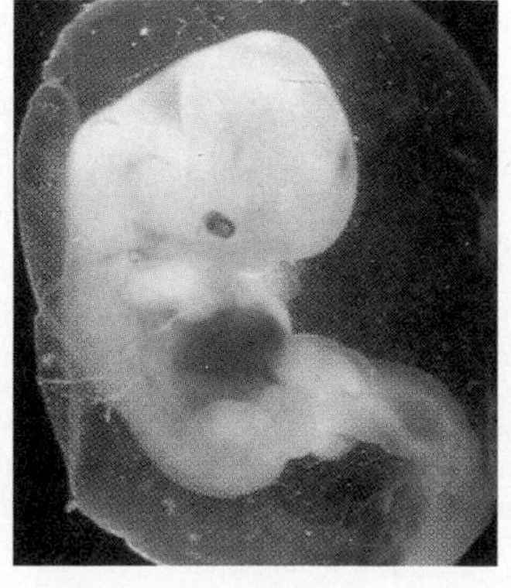
(c)

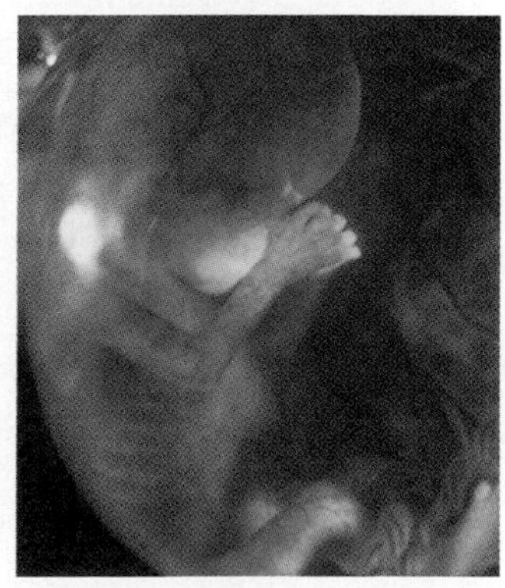
(d)

Figure 3.2 **Prenatal development (a)** The embryo grows and develops rapidly. At 40 days, the spine is visible and the arms and legs are beginning to grow. **(b)** Five days later, the inch-long embryo's proportions have begun to change. The rest of the body is now bigger than the head, and the arms and legs have grown noticeably. **(c)** By the end of the second month, when the fetal period begins, facial features, hands, and feet have formed. **(d)** As the fetus enters the fourth month, its 3 ounces could fit in the palm of your hand.

The Competent Newborn

2. *What are some of the newborn's abilities?*

Having survived prenatal hazards, newborns come equipped with reflexes ideally suited for survival. Infants will withdraw a limb to escape pain. Put a cloth over their faces, interfering with their breathing, and they will turn their heads from side to side and swipe at it. New parents are often awed by the coordinated sequence of reflexes by which babies get food. The **rooting reflex** illustrates this: When something touches their cheeks, babies will open their mouths and vigorously "root" for a nipple. Finding one, they will automatically close on it and begin sucking—which itself requires a coordinated sequence of tonguing, swallowing, and breathing. Failing to find satisfaction, the hungry baby may cry—a behavior parents are predisposed to find highly unpleasant to hear and very rewarding to relieve.

Moreover, psychologists have discovered that infants are born preferring sights and sounds that facilitate social responsiveness. Newborns turn their heads in the direction of human voices. They gaze longer at a drawing of a human face (Figure 3.3) than at a bull's-eye pattern; yet they gaze more at a bull's-eye pattern—which has contrasts much like that of the human eye—than at a solid disk (Fantz, 1961). They prefer to look at objects 8 to 12 inches away, which, wonder of wonders, just happens to be the approximate distance between a nursing infant's eyes and its mother's (Maurer & Maurer, 1988).

Figure 3.3 Newborns' preference for faces When shown these two stimuli in the first week of life, Italian newborns spent nearly twice as many seconds looking at the facelike image. (Umiltà & others, 1996)

Babies' perceptual abilities are continuously developing during the first months of life. Within days of birth, babies can distinguish their mother's odor. The infant's brain is an absorbent sponge, its neural networks stamped immediately with the smell of its mother's body. Thus, a week-old nursing baby, placed between a gauze pad from its mother's bra and one from another nursing mother, will usually turn toward the smell of its own mother's pad (MacFarlane, 1978). At 3 weeks of age, an infant given a pacifier that turns on recordings, sometimes of its mother's voice and sometimes of a female stranger's, will suck more vigorously when it hears its now-familiar mother's voice (Mills & Melhuish, 1974). Newborns can also learn to turn their heads to the left or right to receive a sugar solution when their forehead is stroked (Lancioni, 1980). So not only can young infants see what they need to see, and smell and hear well, but they are already using their sensory equipment to learn.

REHEARSE IT!

1. Developmental psychologists tend to focus on three major issues. Which of the following is not one of those issues?
   - **a.** nature/nurture
   - **b.** uniqueness/commonality
   - **c.** stability/change
   - **d.** continuity/stages
2. The fertilized egg will develop into a boy if it receives
   - **a.** an *X* chromosome from its mother.
   - **b.** an *X* chromosome from its father.
   - **c.** a *Y* chromosome from its mother.
   - **d.** a *Y* chromosome from its father.
3. The 9 months of prenatal development prepare the individual for survival outside the womb. The body organs first begin to form and function during the period of the ________; within 6 months, during the period of the ________, the organs are sufficiently functional to allow a chance of survival.
   - **a.** zygote; embryo
   - **b.** zygote; fetus
   - **c.** embryo; fetus
   - **d.** placenta; fetus
4. Teratogens are chemicals that pass through the placenta's screen and may harm an embryo or fetus. Which of the following is *not* a teratogen?
   - **a.** oxygen
   - **b.** heroin
   - **c.** alcohol
   - **d.** nicotine
5. Stroke a newborn's cheek and he or she will root for a nipple. This illustrates
   - **a.** a reflex.
   - **b.** sensorimotor learning.
   - **c.** perceptual ability.
   - **d.** a gender difference.

rooting reflex a baby's tendency, when touched on the cheek, to open the mouth and search for the nipple.

maturation biological growth processes that enable orderly changes in behavior, relatively uninfluenced by experience.

Infancy and Childhood

During infancy, a baby grows from newborn to toddler, and during childhood from toddler to teenager. Beginning with infancy and childhood and continuing with adolescence through old age, we will see how people of all ages develop—physically, cognitively, and socially.

"It is a rare privilege to watch the birth, growth, and first feeble struggles of a living human mind."

Annie Sullivan, in Helen Keller's *The Story of My Life* 1903

Physical Development

3. *How do the brain and motor skills develop during infancy and childhood?*

Brain Development

While you resided in your mother's womb, your body was forming nerve cells at the rate of about one-quarter million per *minute*. On the day you were born, you had essentially all the brain cells you will ever have. However, at birth your nervous system was immature: After birth, the neural networks that eventually enabled you to walk, talk, and remember had a wild growth spurt (Figure 3.4).

Figure 3.4 **Drawings of human cerebral cortex sections** In humans, the brain is immature at birth. As the child matures, the neural networks grow increasingly more complex.

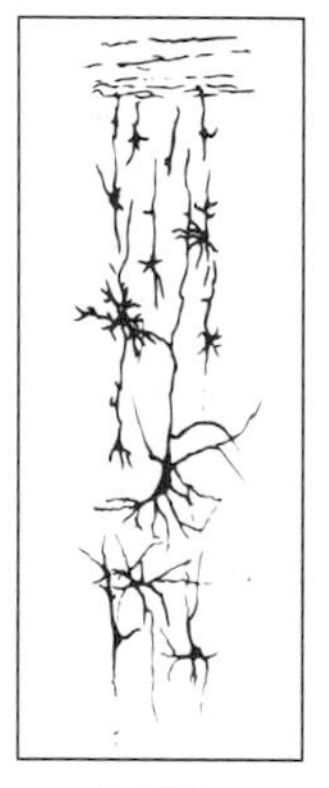
At birth

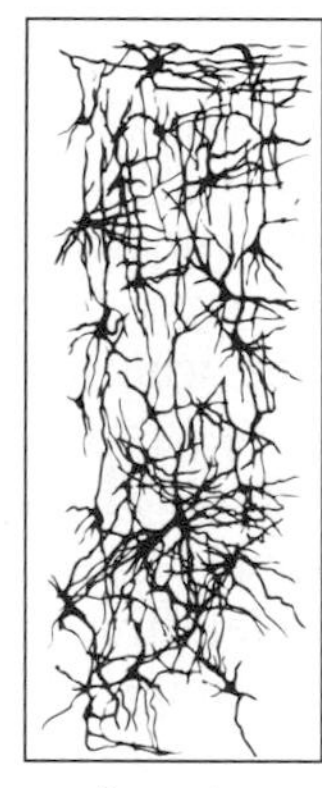
3 months

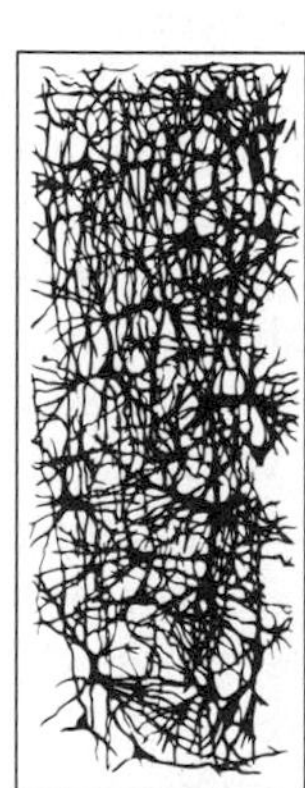
15 months

As a flower unfolds in accord with its genetic blueprint, so do we experience an orderly sequence of genetically designed biological growth processes called **maturation**. Maturation decrees many of our commonalities: standing before walking, using nouns before adjectives. Although extreme deprivation or abuse will retard development, the genetic growth tendencies are inborn. Maturation sets the basic course of development and experience adjusts it.

Maturation and Infant Memory

The lack of neural connections helps explain why our earliest memories seldom predate our third birthdays (Howe & Courage, 1993; Nelson, 1993). For example, children who gain a baby brother or sister at age 4 or later will usually recall the event as adults, but not if they were under age 3 when the baby was born. Preschoolers who experienced an emergency fire evacuation caused by a burning popcorn maker were able 7 years later to recall the alarm and what caused it—*if* they were 4 to 5 years old at the time. Those who experienced the event as 3-year-olds could not remember the cause and usually misrecalled being already outside when the alarm sounded (Pillemer, 1995).

Experience and Brain Development

Experience helps develop the brain's neural connections. Although "forgotten," early learning helps prepare our brains for thought and language and for later experiences.

How do early experiences leave their "marks" in the brain? Mark Rosenzweig and David Krech reared some young rats in solitary confinement and others in a communal playground (Figure 3.5, page 84). Rats living in the enriched environment usually developed a heavier and thicker brain cortex. Rosenzweig (1984; Renner & Rosenzweig, 1987) reported being so surprised by these effects of experience on brain tissue that he repeated the experiment several times before publishing his findings. The effects are great enough that, shown brief video clips of rats in a novel situation, you could actually identify whether their rearing was impoverished or enriched (Renner & Renner, 1993). Such results have helped encourage improvement in the environments provided for laboratory, farm, and

The brain's development does not end with childhood. Throughout life our neural tissue is changing. Sights and smells, touches and tugs activate and strengthen some neural pathways while others weaken from disuse.

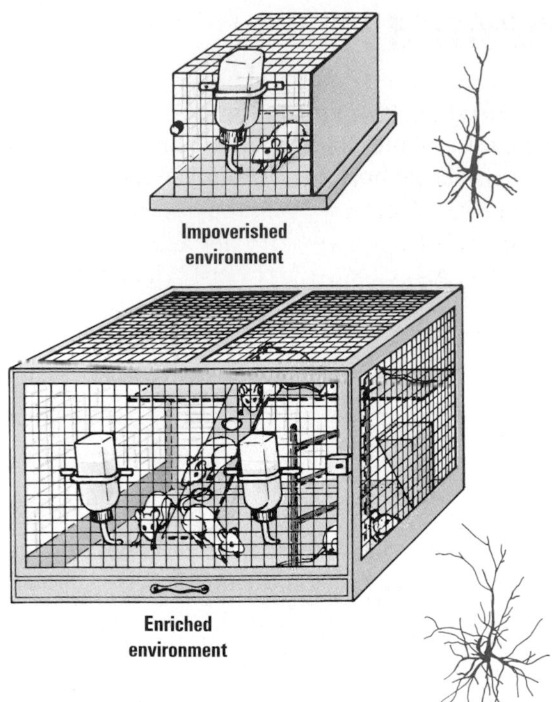

Figure 3.5 **Experience affects brain development** Mark Rosenzweig and David Krech reared rats either alone in an environment without playthings or with others in an environment enriched with playthings that were changed daily. In 14 of 16 repetitions of this basic experiment, the rats placed in the enriched environment developed significantly more cerebral cortex (relative to the rest of the brain's tissue) than did those in the impoverished environment. An artist has illustrated a typical brain cell from a rat reared in each condition. (From "Brain changes in response to experience" by M. R. Rosenzweig, E. L. Bennett, and M. C. Diamond. Copyright © 1972 Scientific American, Inc. All rights reserved.)

zoo animals—and for children in institutions. Several research teams have found that infant rats and premature babies benefit from the stimulation of touch or massage (Field & others, 1986; Meaney & others, 1988). "Handled" infants of both species gain weight more rapidly and develop faster neurologically.

The brain's development does not end with childhood. Throughout life our neural tissue is changing. Sights and smells, touches and tugs activate and strengthen some neural pathways while others weaken from disuse. Like pathways through a forest, less traveled paths are abandoned, popular paths are broadened. Our genes dictate our overall brain architecture, but experience directs the details. If a monkey is trained to push a lever with a finger several thousand times a day, the brain tissue that controls the finger changes to reflect the experience. Human brains work similarly. The wiring of Eric Clapton's brain reflects the thousands of hours he has spent practicing guitar. Similarly, while learning to keyboard or in-line skate or perform a laboratory task, we perform with increasing skill as our brain incorporates the learning. Experience nurtures nature.

Motor Development

As the infant's muscles and nervous system mature, more complicated skills emerge. With minor exceptions, the sequence of physical (motor) development is universal. Babies roll over before they sit unsupported, and they creep on all fours before they walk. These behaviors reflect not imitation but a maturing nervous system; blind children, too, crawl and walk.

But there are individual differences in the timing of this sequence. In the United States, for example, 25 percent of all babies walk by age 11 months, 50 percent within a week after their first birthday, and 90 percent by age 15 months (Frankenburg & others, 1992).

There are also cultural differences in timing. Although such differences could be genetic, experiments reveal that experience does predict motor behavior. Consider Ugandan babies, for example, who usually walk by 10 months. Unlike babies from other cultures who spend much of the day lying in a crib, Ugandan babies experience more intimate and rhythmic physical contact while being carried on the back (Bril, 1986). Two-week-old babies wave their arms more if they can see them, suggesting that they are learning to visually control their movements (van der Meer & others, 1995). Although 3-month-old infants still cannot efficiently reach and grab something, their seemingly spontaneous

Triumphant toddlers Roll, crawl, walk, run—the sequence of these motor development milestones is the same the world around, though babies reach them at varying ages.

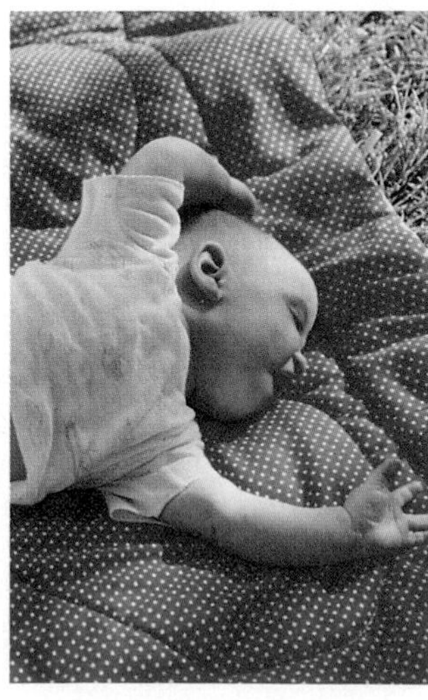

kicking movements become more purposeful and coordinated when they activate a mobile (Thelen, 1994, 1995).

But nature (genes) plays a major role, too. Identical twins typically begin sitting up and walking on nearly the same day (Wilson, 1979). Biological maturation—including the rapid development of the cerebellum at the brain's rear—creates a readiness to learn walking within 2 or 3 months of age 1. Experience before that time has a limited effect. This is true for other physical skills, including bowel and bladder control. Until the necessary muscular and neural maturation occurs, no amount of pleading, harassment, or punishment will produce successful toilet training.

Cognitive Development

4. *How did Piaget view the mind's development, and what are current researchers' views?*

"Who knows the thoughts of a child?" wondered poet Nora Perry. As much as anyone of his generation, developmental psychologist Jean Piaget (pronounced Pee-ah-ZHAY) knew. His interest began in 1920, when he was working in Paris to develop questions for children's intelligence tests. While administering tests to find out at what age children could answer certain questions correctly, Piaget became intrigued by children's *wrong* answers. Where others saw childish mistakes, Piaget saw intelligence at work. The errors made by children of a given age, he noted, were often strikingly similar.

Piaget became intrigued by children's wrong answers. Where others saw childish mistakes, Piaget saw intelligence at work.

The half century Piaget spent with children convinced him that the child's mind is not a miniature model of the adult's. Young children understand the world in ways radically different from those of adults, a fact we sometimes overlook when teaching children. Piaget was not the first to say this. The philosopher Jean Jacques Rosseau (1798) believed that "childhood has its own way of seeing, thinking, and feeling, and there is nothing more foolish than the attempt to put ours in its place." Just as Copernicus revolutionized our understanding of the solar system, Piaget revolutionized our understanding of children's minds, suggests William Damon (1995). Until Piaget, most people—forgetting their own preschool days—assumed children "simply knew less, not *differently*, than adults." Thanks partly to Piaget, we now understand that "children reason in wildly illogical ways about problems whose solutions are self-evident to adults" (Brainerd, 1996).

Piaget further believed that the child's mind develops through a series of stages, in an upward march from the newborn's simple reflexes to the adult's abstract reasoning power. An 8-year-old child therefore comprehends things that a 3-year-old cannot. An 8-year-old might grasp the analogy "getting an idea is like having a light turn on in your head," but trying to teach the same analogy to a 3-year-old would be fruitless.

Piaget felt that the driving force behind this intellectual progression is our unceasing struggle to make sense of our experience. Piaget's core idea is that "children are active thinkers, constantly trying to construct more advanced understandings of the world" (Siegler & Ellis, 1996). To this end, the maturing brain builds concepts, which Piaget called **schemas**. Schemas (or schemes) are mental molds into which we pour our experience. By adulthood we have built countless schemas that range from knowing how to tie a knot to our concept of love.

schema a concept or framework that organizes and interprets information.

Two-year-old Antonia has learned the schema for "cow" from her picture books.

Antonia sees a moose and calls it a "cow." She is trying to assimilate this new animal into an existing schema. Her mother tells her, "No, it's a moose."

Antonia accommodates her schema for large, shaggy animals and continues to modify that schema to include "mommy moose," "baby moose," etc.

Pouring experience into mental molds We use our existing schemas to assimilate new experiences. But sometimes we need to accommodate (adjust) our schemas to include new experiences.

An impossible object Look carefully at the "devil's tuning fork" above. Now look away—no, better first study it some more—and then look away and draw it. . . . Not so easy, is it? Because this tuning fork is an impossible object, you have no schema for such an image.

Piaget's Theory and Current Thinking on Cognitive Stages

Cognition refers to all the mental activities associated with thinking, knowing, remembering, and communicating. Piaget described cognitive development as occurring in four stages—sensorimotor, preoperational, concrete operational, and formal operational (Table 3.1). Developing children, he believed, experience spurts of change followed by greater stability as they move from one developmental plateau to the next. Each plateau has distinctive characteristics that permit specific kinds of thinking. To appreciate how the mind of a child grows, let's look at each of Piaget's stages in the light of current thinking about cognitive development.

Sensorimotor Stage

During Piaget's **sensorimotor stage**, from birth to nearly age 2, babies understand the world through their sensory and motor interactions with objects—through looking, touching, mouthing, and grasping. At first they seem unaware that things continue to exist apart from their perceptions.

Table 3.1 **Piaget's Stages of Cognitive Development**

Typical Age Range	Description of Stage	Developmental Phenomena
Birth to nearly 2 years	*Sensorimotor* Experiencing the world through senses and actions (looking, touching, mouthing, and grasping)	• Object permanence • Stranger anxiety
About 2 to 6 years	*Preoperational* Representing things with words and images but lacking logical reasoning	• Pretend play • Egocentrism • Language development
About 7 to 11 years	*Concrete operational* Thinking logically about concrete events; grasping concrete analogies and performing arithmetical operations	• Conservation • Mathematical transformations
About 12 through adulthood	*Formal operational* Abstract reasoning	• Abstract logic • Potential for mature moral reasoning

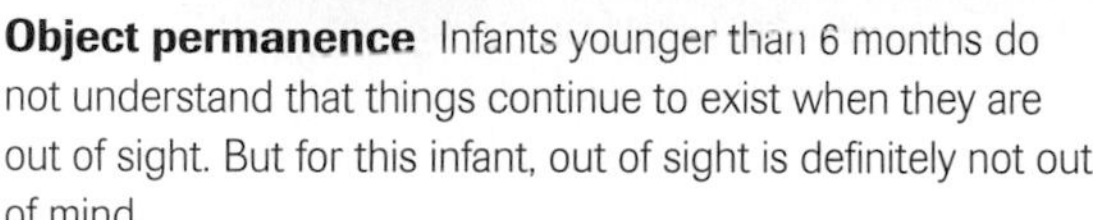
Object permanence Infants younger than 6 months do not understand that things continue to exist when they are out of sight. But for this infant, out of sight is definitely not out of mind.

In one of his tests, Piaget would show an infant an appealing toy and then flop his beret over it to see whether the infant searched for the toy. Before the age of 6 months, the infant did not. Infants lack **object permanence**—the awareness that objects continue to exist when not perceived. They live in the present: What is out of sight is out of mind. By 8 months, infants begin to exhibit memory for things no longer seen. Hide a toy and an infant will momentarily look for it. Within another month or two, the infant will look for it even after being restrained for several seconds.

But today's researchers wonder: Do children's cognitive abilities really grow through distinct stages? Does object permanence in fact blossom by 8 months, much as a tulip blossoms in spring? Today's researchers see development as more continuous than did Piaget. For example, they now view object permanence as unfolding gradually, beginning with young infants' looking for a toy where they saw it hidden a second before.

Consider some simple experiments:

- Andrew Meltzoff and Richard Borton gave 1-month-old babies one of two pacifiers to suck on without letting them see the objects (**Figure 3.6**). When later shown both pacifiers, the infants *looked* mostly at the nipple they had *felt* in their mouth. Follow-up studies revealed the same amazing result with infants as young as 12 hours old (Kaye & Bower, 1994).
- Infants look longer when viewing an unexpected scene of a car seeming to pass through a solid object or of a ball stopping in midair (Bailargeon, 1992, 1994; Wellman & Gelman, 1992).
- Babies exhibit not only an intuitive grasp of simple laws of physics, they also comprehend number. Karen Wynn (1992, 1995) showed 5-month-old infants one or two objects. Then she hid the objects behind a screen, sometimes removing or adding one through a trap door (**Figure 3.7, page 88**). When she lifted the screen, the infants sometimes did a double take, staring longer when shown a wrong number of objects. Clearly, infants comprehend more than Piaget realized.

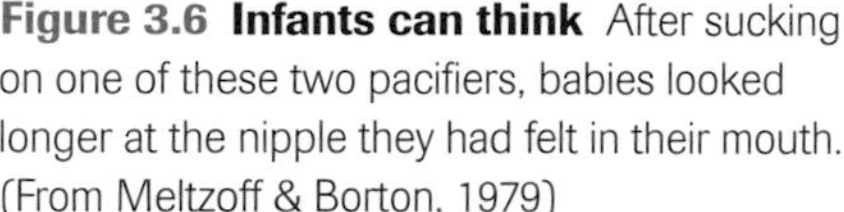
Figure 3.6 Infants can think After sucking on one of these two pacifiers, babies looked longer at the nipple they had felt in their mouth. (From Meltzoff & Borton, 1979)

Preoperational Stage

Piaget believed that during the preschool period and up to about age 6 or 7, children are in a **preoperational stage**—too young to perform mental operations. For a 5-year-old, the quantity of milk that is "too much" in a tall, narrow glass may become an acceptable amount if poured into a short, wide glass. This is because the child focuses only on the height dimension and is incapable of performing the *operation* of mentally pouring it back. The child lacks the concept of **conservation**—the principle that quantity remains the same despite changes in shape.

Piaget did not view the stage transitions as abrupt; even so, symbolic thinking appears at an earlier age than he supposed. Judy DeLoache (1987) discovered

cognition all the mental activities associated with thinking, knowing, remembering, and communicating.

sensorimotor stage in Piaget's theory, the stage (from birth to about 2 years of age) during which infants know the world mostly in terms of their sensory impressions and motor activities.

object permanence the awareness that things continue to exist even when not perceived.

preoperational stage in Piaget's theory, the stage (from about 2 to 6 or 7 years of age) during which a child learns to use language but does not yet comprehend the mental operations of concrete logic.

conservation the principle (which Piaget believed to be a part of concrete operational reasoning) that properties such as mass, volume, and number remain the same despite changes in the forms of objects.

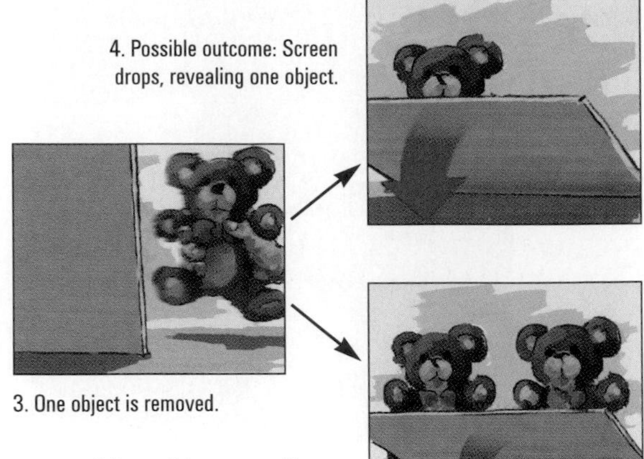

Figure 3.7 Baby mathematics Shown a numerically impossible outcome, infants stare longer. (From Wynn, 1992)

Question: If most 2½-year-olds do not understand how miniature dolls and toys can symbolize real objects, should anatomically correct dolls be used when questioning such children about alleged physical or sexual abuse? Judy DeLoache (1995) reports that "very young children do not find it natural or easy to use a doll as a representation of themselves."

this when she showed a group of 2½-year-olds a model of a room and hid a model toy in it (say, a miniature stuffed dog behind a miniature couch). The children could easily remember where to find the miniature toy. But they could not readily use that model to locate an actual stuffed dog behind a couch in a real room. Three-year-olds—only 6 months older—usually went right to the actual stuffed animal in the real room, showing that they *could* think of the model as a symbol for the room.

Seen through the eyes of Piaget, preschool children are still unable to reason and to take another's point of view. Although aware of themselves, of time, and of the permanence of objects, they are, he said, **egocentric**: They cannot perceive things from another's point of view. Asked to "show Mommy your picture," 2-year-old Gabriella holds the picture up facing her own eyes. Three-year-old Rebecca hides under a table, assuming that if she can't see someone's eyes they can't see her. Children's conversations also reveal their egocentrism, as one young boy demonstrated (Phillips, 1969, p. 61): *"Do you have a brother?" "Yes." "What's his name?" "Jim." "Does Jim have a brother?" "No."*

Piaget's test of conservation This preoperational child does not yet understand the principle of conservation of substance. Closed beakers with identical volumes seem suddenly to hold different amounts after one is merely inverted.

Preschool TV-watchers who block your view of the television assume that you see what they see. Preschoolers who ask a question while you are on the phone assume that you hear no more than they hear. When relating to a young child, remember that such behaviors reflect a cognitive limitation: The egocentric preschooler is not intentionally "selfish" or "inconsiderate" but rather has difficulty taking another's viewpoint. Parents who abuse their children generally have no understanding of these limits.

Although still egocentric, preschoolers begin forming a "theory of mind." They seek to understand what made a playmate angry, when a sibling will share, and what might make a parent buy a toy. The preschooler's growing ability to tease, empathize, and persuade stems from a growing ability to take another's perspective. Between ages 3 and 5, for example, children come to realize that others may hold false beliefs. University of Toronto researchers Jennifer Jenkins and Janet Astington (1996) showed children a Band Aids (plasters) box and asked them what was inside. The children naturally expected Band Aids, and so they were surprised when they discovered that the box actually contained pencils. Asked what another child who had never seen the box would think was inside, 3-year-olds typically answered "pencils." By age 4 to 5, the children's theory of mind had leapt forward, and they delighted in anticipating their friends' false belief that the box would hold Band Aids.

Even as adults, we never completely lose our early egocentrism. Once we know a problem's solution, we instantly find it difficult to appreciate how hard the problem may be for others. We also have a curious tendency to overestimate others' agreement with our opinions—a phenomenon social psychologists

egocentrism in Piaget's theory, the inability of the preoperational child to take another's point of view.

concrete operational stage in Piaget's theory, the stage of cognitive development (from about 6 or 7 to 11 years of age) during which children gain the mental operations that enable them to think logically about concrete events.

call the "false consensus effect" (see page 15). And we imagine that others notice us more than they do. Thomas Gilovich (1996) demonstrated this "spotlight effect" by having individual Cornell University students don Barry Manilow T-shirts before entering a room with other students. Feeling self-conscious, the T-shirt wearers guessed that nearly half of their peers would take note of the shirt as they walked in. In reality, only 23 percent did. So, next time you have a bad hair day, relax. Fewer people notice than you imagine.

The abilities to perform mental operations, to think symbolically, and to take another's perspective are not absent in the preoperational stage and then miraculously present at some later time. Rather, these abilities begin early and develop gradually.

By age 7, children become more capable of verbal thinking and of using it to work out solutions to problems. They do this, noted the Russian psychologist Lev Vygotsky (1896–1934), by no longer thinking aloud. Instead they internalize their culture's language and rely on inner speech. Second-graders who mutter to themselves while doing math problems grasp third-grade math better the following year (Berk, 1994). Whether out loud or inaudibly, talking to themselves helps children control their behavior and emotions and master new skills. "I think I can, I think I can," says *The Little Engine That Could*, illustrating the commonality of private speech in children's literature.

Private speech A badger starring in a series of children's books sings to herself—in this case, to help her cope with the jealousy she feels toward her younger sister, who is soon to celebrate a birthday.

Concrete Operational Stage

By about 6 or 7 years of age, said Piaget, children enter the **concrete operational stage**. Given concrete materials, they begin to grasp that a given quantity remains the same no matter how its shape changes. They can mentally pour milk back and forth between glasses of different shapes. They also enjoy jokes that allow them to use their new concepts, such as conservation:

> Mr. Jones went into a restaurant and ordered a whole pizza for his dinner. When the waiter asked if he wanted it cut into 6 or 8 pieces, Mr. Jones said, "Oh, you'd better make it 6, I could never eat 8 pieces!" (McGhee, 1976)

During the concrete operational stage, said Piaget, children fully gain the mental ability to comprehend mathematical transformations and conservation. When my daughter Laura was 6, I was astonished at her inability to reverse arithmetic operations—until considering Piaget. Asked, "What is eight plus four?" she required 5 seconds to compute "twelve," and another 5 seconds to then compute twelve minus four. By age 8, she could reverse the process and answer the second question instantly.

If Piaget was correct—if children construct their understandings and think differently than adults do—what are the implications for parents and teachers? Piaget contended that learning grows from children's *interactions* with the world. Thus, children are not passive receptacles waiting to be filled with a teacher's knowledge. Building on what children already know, teachers should engage children in concrete demonstrations and stimulate them to think for themselves. Future parents and teachers, remember: Young children are incapable of adult logic. Understand how children think. Realize that what is simple and obvious to you—that, say, subtraction is the reverse of addition—may be incomprehensible to a 6-year-old. Accept children's cognitive immaturity as adaptive—as nature's strategy for keeping children close to protective adults and providing time for learning and socialization (Bjorklund & Green, 1992).

Dennis the Menace

"Cut it up into a LOT of slices, Mom. I'm really hungry!"

Formal Operational Stage

By age 12, reasoning expands from the purely concrete (involving actual experience) to encompass abstract thinking (involving imagined realities and symbols). As they approach adolescence, said Piaget, many children become capable of

formal operational stage in Piaget's theory, the stage of cognitive development (normally beginning about age 12) during which people begin to think logically about abstract concepts.

stranger anxiety the fear of strangers that infants commonly display, beginning by about 8 months of age.

attachment an emotional tie with another person; shown in young children by their seeking closeness to the caregiver and showing distress on separation.

solving hypothetical propositions and deducing consequences: *If* this, *then* that. Systematic reasoning, which Piaget called **formal operational** thinking, is now within their grasp. Consider this simple problem:

> If John is in school, then Mary is in school. John is in school. What can you say about Mary?

Formal operational thinkers have no trouble answering correctly; nor do most 7-year-olds (Suppes, 1982). This illustrates why, once again, critics say the rudiments of Piaget's cognitive stages begin earlier than he realized.

Reflections on Piaget's Theory

Piaget's stage theory is controversial. In some ways it gets high marks. Studies around the globe, from aboriginal Australia to Algeria to North America, reveal that human cognition everywhere unfolds basically in the sequence he proposed (Segall & others, 1990). Today's researchers do, however, see development as more continuous than did Piaget. By detecting the beginnings of each type of thinking at earlier ages, they have revealed conceptual abilities that Piaget missed. Moreover, they see formal logic as a smaller part of cognition than did Piaget.

What remains of Piaget's ideas about the child's mind? Plenty. "Assessing the impact of Piaget on developmental psychology is like assessing the impact of Shakespeare in English literature," mused Harry Beilin (1992). Piaget identified important cognitive milestones and stimulated interest in how the mind develops. What Piaget emphasized was less the ages at which children typically reach specific milestones than their sequence—which is pretty much as he described (Lourenco & Machado, 1996). He would not be surprised that today we are adapting his ideas to accommodate new findings—as part of our own cognitive development.

REHEARSE IT!

6. The orderly sequence of biological growth is called maturation. Maturation explains why
- **a.** children differ greatly in temperament.
- **b.** most children have begun walking by about 12 months.
- **c.** enriching experiences may affect brain tissue.
- **d.** differences between the sexes are minimal.

7. Most of us remember nothing before our third birthday because
- **a.** we are not born with enough brain cells to form memories.
- **b.** we were not given the extra "handling" and environmental stimulation we needed.
- **c.** the connections between our brain cells had not yet become complex enough to form permanent memories.
- **d.** we do not enter the memory stage until our third year.

8. As the infant's muscles and nervous system mature, more complicated skills emerge. Which of the following is true of motor-skill development?
- **a.** It is determined solely by genetic factors.
- **b.** The sequence, but not the timing, is universal.
- **c.** Maturation has a limited effect if the environment is not right.
- **d.** Environment creates a readiness to learn.

9. According to Piaget, the preoperational stage extends from about age 2 to 6. During this period the young child's thinking is
- **a.** abstract.
- **b.** negative.
- **c.** conservative.
- **d.** egocentric.

10. The principle of conservation explains why a pint of milk remains a pint, whether poured into a tall thin glass or a round goblet. Children acquire the mental operations necessary to understand conservation during
- **a.** infancy.
- **b.** the sensorimotor stage.
- **c.** the preoperational stage.
- **d.** the concrete operational stage.

11. Piaget's stage theory continues to inform our understanding of cognitive development in childhood. However, many researchers believe that
- **a.** Piaget's "stages" begin earlier and development is more continuous than Piaget realized.
- **b.** children do not progress as rapidly as Piaget predicted.
- **c.** few children really progress to the concrete operational stage.
- **d.** there is no way of testing much of Piaget's theoretical work.

Stranger anxiety A newly emerging ability to evaluate people as unfamiliar and possibly threatening helps protect babies during the second 6 months of life.

Social Development

5. ***How do the bonds of attachment form, and with what effects later in life?***

Babies are social creatures from birth. In all cultures, infants develop an intense bond with those who care for them. Beginning with newborns' attraction to humans in general, infants soon come to prefer familiar faces and voices and then to coo and gurgle when given their mother's or father's attention. Soon after object permanence emerges and children become mobile enough to crawl into danger, a curious thing happens: They develop a fear of strangers, called **stranger anxiety**. Watch how infants of different ages react when handed over to a stranger. Beginning at 8 or 9 months, they often will cry and reach for their familiar caregivers. "I can't stand being without you!" the infants' distress seems to say. After about 8 months of age, children have schemas for familiar faces; when they cannot assimilate an approaching new face into these remembered schemas, they become distressed (Kagan, 1984). This illustrates an important principle: The brain, the mind, and social-emotional behavior develop together.

At 12 months, many infants cling tightly to a parent when frightened or expecting separation. Reunited, they shower the parent with smiles and hugs. No social behavior is more striking than this intense and mutual infant-parent bond, called **attachment**—a powerful survival impulse that keeps infants close to their caregivers.

Origins of Attachment

A number of elements work to create the parent-infant bond. Infants become attached to those—typically their parents—who are comfortable, familiar, and responsive to their needs.

Body Contact

For many years, developmental psychologists reasoned that infants became attached to those who satisfied their need for nourishment. It made perfect sense. But an accidental finding revealed that this explanation is incomplete. During the 1950s, University of Wisconsin psychologist Harry Harlow bred monkeys for his learning studies. To equalize the infant monkeys' experiences and to prevent the spread of disease, he separated the monkeys from their mothers shortly after birth and raised them in sanitary, individual cages, which included a cheesecloth baby blanket (Harlow & others, 1971). Surprisingly, the infants became intensely attached to their blankets: When the blankets were taken to be laundered, the monkeys became distressed.

Harlow soon recognized that this attachment to the blanket contradicted the idea that attachment derives from the association with nourishment. But could he show this more convincingly? To pit the drawing power of a food source against the contact comfort of the blanket, Harlow created two artificial mothers. One was a bare wire cylinder with a wooden head, the other a cylinder wrapped with terry cloth. He could associate either with nourishment by attaching a bottle.

When reared with both a nourishing wire mother and a nonnourishing cloth mother, the monkeys overwhelmingly preferred the cloth mother (Figure 3.8). Like human infants clinging to their mothers, the monkeys would cling to their cloth mothers when anxious. They also used her as a secure base from which to venture into the environment, as if attached to the mother by an invisible elastic band that stretches so far and then pulls the infant back. Further studies

Figure 3.8 **Harlow's mothers** Psychologist Harry Harlow reared monkeys with two artificial mothers—one a bare wire cylinder with a wooden head and an attached feeding bottle, the other a cylinder with no bottle but covered with foam rubber and wrapped with terry cloth. Harlow's discovery surprised many psychologists: The monkeys much preferred contact with the comfortable cloth mother, even while feeding from the nourishing mother.

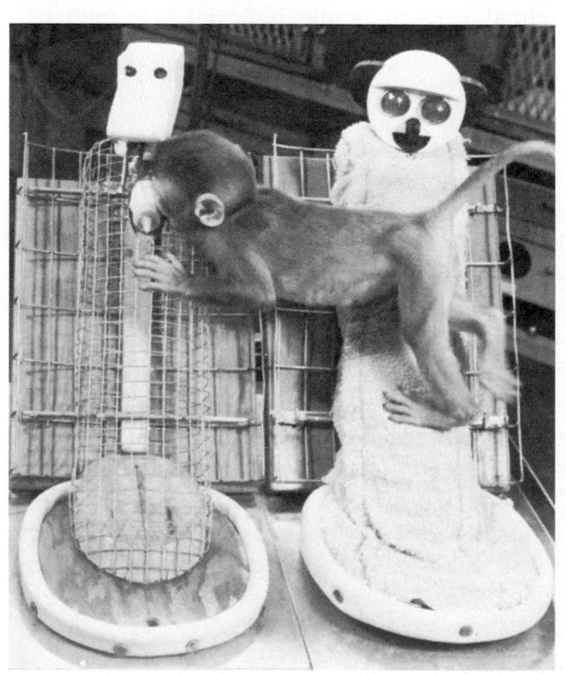

critical period an optimal period shortly after birth when an organism's exposure to certain stimuli or experiences produces proper development.

imprinting the process by which certain animals form attachments during a critical period very early in life.

temperament a person's characteristic emotional reactivity and intensity.

revealed that other qualities—rocking, warmth, and feeding—could make the cloth mother even more appealing.

Human infants, too, become attached to parents who are soft and warm and who rock, feed, and pat. All this should reassure the fathers of breast-fed infants: Attachment does not depend on feeding alone.

Moreover, for humans, too, attachment consists of one person providing another with a *secure base* from which to explore the world and a *safe haven* in times of stress. As we mature, our attachments change. Our secure base and safe haven shift from parents to peers and partners. But at all ages we are social creatures. We gain strength when someone says to us, by words and actions, "I am here. I will be here. I am interested in what you do and what you think and feel. I will actively support you" (Crowell & Waters, 1994). We are "happiest and able to deploy [our] talents to best advantage," said attachment researcher John Bowlby (1979), when we know that one or more trusted friends will stand behind us, come what may.

Lee Kirkpatrick (1994) reports that for some people a perceived relationship with God functions as do other attachments—by providing a secure base for exploration and a safe haven when threatened.

Familiarity

Another key to attachment is familiarity. As we noted earlier, nature opens windows of opportunity for wiring the brain for vision or language, then slams them shut. In many animals, attachments based on familiarity likewise form during a sensitive, **critical period**—an optimal period shortly after birth when certain events must take place if proper development is to occur (Bornstein, 1989). The first moving object a gosling, duckling, or chick sees during the hours shortly after hatching is normally its mother. Thereafter the young fowl follows her, and her alone.

Konrad Lorenz (1937) explored this rigid attachment process, called **imprinting**. He wondered what ducklings would do if *he* was the first moving creature they observed. What they did was follow him around: Everywhere that Konrad went, the ducks were sure to go. Further tests revealed that although baby birds imprint best to their own species, they also will imprint to a variety of moving objects—an animal of another species, a box on wheels, a bouncing ball (Colombo, 1982; Johnson, 1992). Once formed, this attachment is difficult to reverse.

Thus, children like to reread the same books, rewatch the same movies, reenact the same family traditions. They prefer to eat familiar foods, live in the same familiar neighborhood, attend school with the same old friends. Familiarity breeds content.

THE FAR SIDE

When imprinting studies go awry . . .

Temperament

In studies the world over, some babies seem more disposed to forming a secure attachment. Placed in a strange situation (usually a laboratory playroom), about 60 percent of infants show *secure attachment*. In their mother's presence they play comfortably, happily exploring their new environment. When she leaves, they are distressed; when she returns, they seek contact with her. Other infants show *insecure attachment*. They are less likely to explore their surroundings and may even cling to their mother. When she leaves, they either cry loudly and remain upset or seem indifferent to their mother's going and returning (Ainsworth, 1973, 1989; Kagan, 1995; van IJzendoorn & Kroonenberg, 1988). What accounts for these differences?

Might the infants' differing behavior patterns be inborn? An infant's **temperament** includes the inborn rudiments of personality, especially the child's emotional excitability. From the first weeks of life, "difficult" babies are more irritable, intense, and unpredictable. "Easy" babies are cheerful, relaxed, and predictable in feeding and sleeping (Chess & Thomas, 1987).

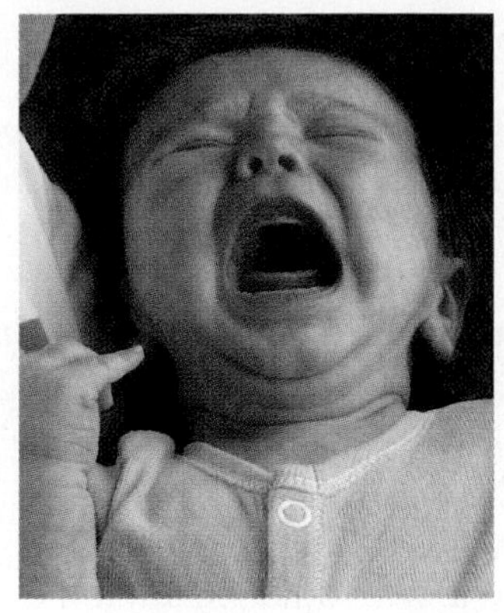

Temperament Some babies are predisposed to be emotionally reactive, others to react calmly. Caregiving that is responsive to a child's needs usually enables the parent and child to form a secure bond.

Heredity also seems to predispose human differences in physiological reactions. Anxious, high-strung human infants have high and variable heart rates and a reactive nervous system (Kagan & others, 1992). They become more physiologically aroused when facing new or strange situations. Those who remain more anxious as children are more likely as young adults to live with their parents (Gest, 1997). Compared with fraternal twins, identical twins are more likely to have similar temperaments (Emde & others, 1992; Gabbay, 1992; Robinson & others, 1992).

Genetic influences also seem to help explain why several studies find newborn and infant Asian infants calmer, more placid, and less reactive than Caucasian infants. That should not stun us, say Jerome Kagan and his colleagues (1994), because Europeans and Asians were "reproductively isolated for about 30,000 years, or about 1500 generations." In animal experiments, one can selectively breed obvious trait differences after "only 15 to 20 generations." There's a practical moral here, says Kagan (1995): We "should not automatically assume that every anxious child had an insensitive parent but should entertain the possibility that temperament" also makes the child.

Responsive Parenting

But there is more to infant attachment differences than inherited temperament. Another possible influence on attachment is the mother's behavior. Mary Ainsworth (1979) observed mother-infant pairs at home during their first 6 months and then later observed the 1-year-old infants in a "strange situation" without their mothers. Sensitive, responsive mothers—mothers who noticed what their babies were doing and who responded appropriately—had infants who usually became securely attached. Insensitive, unresponsive mothers—mothers who attended to their babies when they felt like doing so but ignored them at other times—had infants who often became insecurely attached. Harlow's monkey studies, in which the artificial mothers were the ultimate in unresponsiveness, produced even more striking effects. When put in strange situations without their artificial mothers, the deprived infants were more than distressed—they were terrified (Figure 3.9).

Figure 3.9 **Social deprivation and fear** Monkeys raised by artificial mothers were terror-stricken when placed in strange situations without their surrogate mothers. (Today's climate of greater respect for animal welfare prevents such primate studies.)

To see whether human infants' attachments are also a product of parenting and not just of biologically disposed temperaments, Dutch researcher Dymphna van den Boom (1990) varied parenting while controlling temperament. (Pause and think: If you were the researcher, how might you have done this?)

Van den Boom's solution was to randomly assign one hundred 6- to 9-month-old temperamentally difficult infants to either an experimental condition, in which mothers received personal training in sensitive responding, or to an untreated control condition. At age one, 68 percent of the experimental condition infants were rated securely attached, as were only 28 percent of the control condition infants.

As the attachments of early childhood eventually relax, children become familiar with a wider range of situations and communicate with strangers more freely. Whether children are raised entirely at home or also in a day-care center, whether they live in North America, Guatemala, or the Kalahari Desert, anxiety over separation from parents peaks at around 13 months and then gradually declines (Figure 3.10, page 94).

Does this mean that our need for and love of others also fades away? Hardly. Yet much of the life cycle story boils down to a poignant rhythm of attachment and separation—from the attachment of fetal life to the separation of birth, from infant attachment to adolescent separation, from the attachments of marriage and parenthood to the separation of death.

Figure 3.10 **Infants' distress over separation from parents** In an experiment, groups of infants who had and had not experienced day care were left by their mothers in an unfamiliar room. In both groups, the percentage who cried when the mother left peaked at about 13 months. (From Kagan, 1976)

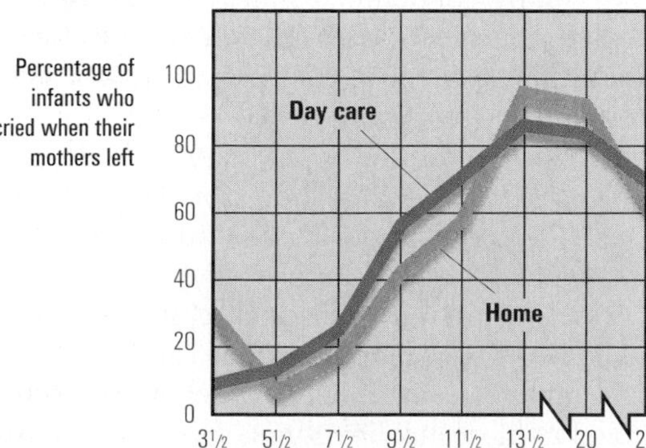

Effects of Attachment

Does a trusting, secure attachment have lasting benefits? And does the quality of an infant's attachment predict the child's social competence in the years that follow?

Secure Attachment Predicts Social Competence

At the University of Minnesota, Alan Sroufe and his colleagues (1983) identified infants who were securely attached at 12 to 18 months of age. When Sroufe restudied these infants as 2- to 3-year-olds, he saw them functioning more confidently than other toddlers. Given challenging tasks, they were more enthusiastic and persistent. With other children they were more outgoing and responsive.

Developmental theorist Erik Erikson (1902–1994), influenced by conversations with his wife, Joan, said that securely attached children approach life with a sense of **basic trust**—a sense that the world is predictable and reliable. Erikson attributed basic trust not to one's continuing positive environment or inborn temperament, but to early parenting. He theorized that infants blessed with sensitive, loving caregivers form a lifelong attitude of trust rather than fear. Erikson would not have been surprised that as adults, our romantic love styles exhibit either secure, trusting attachment; insecure, anxious attachment; or the avoidance of attachment (Feeney & Noller, 1990; Shaver & Hazan, 1993; Simpson & others, 1992). Our early attachment styles, it seems, form a foundation for our future relationships. "What is learned in the cradle," says a French proverb, "lasts to the grave."

"Out of the conflict between trust and mistrust, the infant develops hope, which is the earliest form of what gradually becomes faith in adults."

Erik Erikson (1983)

Deprivation of Attachment

If secure attachment nurtures social competence, what happens when circumstances prevent children from forming attachments? In all of psychology, no research literature is more saddening. Babies reared in institutions without the stimulation and attention of a regular caregiver, or locked away at home under conditions of abuse or extreme neglect, are often withdrawn, frightened, even speechless. Those who were abandoned in Romanian orphanages "look frighteningly like Harlow's monkeys" (Carlson, 1995). Adopted during infancy or childhood into a loving home, they usually progress rapidly, especially in their cognitive development. Nevertheless, they frequently bear scars from their early mistreatment (Malinosky-Rummell & Hansen, 1993; Rutter, 1979).

So, too, did Harlow's monkeys if reared in total isolation, without even an artificial mother. As adults they either cowered in fright or lashed out in aggression when placed with other monkeys their age. Upon reaching sexual maturity, most were incapable of mating. Artificially impregnated females often were neglectful, abusive, or even murderous toward their first-born offspring.

Most abusive human parents, too, report having been neglected or battered as children (Kempe & Kempe, 1978). Many condemned murderers report the same. One study of 14 young men awaiting execution for juvenile crimes found that all but two had histories of brutal physical abuse (Lewis & others, 1988). The unloved often become the unloving.

So, do most victims of child abuse become abusive? Is today's victim predictably tomorrow's predator? No. Most abused children do *not* later become violent criminals or abusive parents. But 30 percent of those abused do abuse their children—a rate four times higher than the national rate of child abuse (Kaufman & Zigler, 1987; Widom, 1989a,b). Moreover, young children terrorized through sexual abuse, physical abuse, or wartime atrocities (being beaten, witnessing torture, and living in constant fear) may suffer other scars—often nightmares, depression, and a troubled adolescence involving substance abuse, binge eating, or aggression (Kendall-Tackett & others, 1993; Polusny & Follette, 1995; Trickett & McBride-Chang, 1995).

basic trust according to Erik Erikson, a sense that the world is predictable and trustworthy; said to be formed during infancy by appropriate experiences with responsive caregivers.

Such experiences can leave footprints on the brain. When normally placid golden hamsters are repeatedly threatened and attacked while young, the effects linger into their adult lives. They grow up to be cowards when caged with same-size hamsters or bullies when caged with weaker ones (Ferris, 1996). Such animals show changes in such brain chemicals as serotonin, which calms aggressive impulses. Abused children who become aggressive teens and adults have been found to have a similarly sluggish serotonin response.

Children and Divorce

Nearly half the marriages in Western countries (slightly more than half in the United States, somewhat less in Canada, Britain, and elsewhere) end in divorce. That's double the proportion of 30 years ago. This fact makes people wonder and worry: Are children casualties of divorce? Does the stress of divorce and its aftermath erode children's well-being?

To glimpse possible effects of divorce, a research team led by sociologist Andrew Cherlin and others (1991, 1995) compared children before and after divorce. This monumental study began when researchers interviewed 17,414 women—the mothers of 98 percent of all British children born during the first full week of March 1958. Knowing that some of the children would experience parental divorce, Cherlin and his co-workers studied them as 7-year-olds and again as 11- , 16- , and 23-year-olds. For example, when the children reached age 23, the intrepid researchers traced and interviewed 12,537 of the original sample. These follow-up interviews enabled them to focus on those who at age 7 had lived with two biological parents. The researchers could then compare children whose parents had divorced with those whose parents had not divorced during the ensuing 9 years. Their finding: Children whose parents had divorced experienced more problems.

Controlling for predivorce family problems did *not* weaken the divorce effect, report Cherlin and colleagues. Even after adjusting for emotional problems and school achievement at age 7, the odds of psychological problems were 39 percent greater among 16-year-olds whose parents had divorced in the intervening years. Curiously, a parental death (which can feel less rejecting and involves less conflict) had "a substantially weaker effect."

To be sure, predivorce stress may also be toxic. Children can benefit when they and a custodial parent escape from an abusive situation. But on balance, report Mavis Hetherington and her colleagues (1989, 1992), divorce places "children at increased risk for developing social, psychological, behavioral and academic problems." Compared with those who grew up in intact two-parent families, children of divorce grow up with a diminished feeling of well-being. As adults they are more likely to divorce and less likely to say they are "very happy."

But are their problems caused by divorce per se? Consider the results of one study of more than 17,000 children by the U.S. Census Bureau for the National Center for Health Statistics (1991). The researchers knew that intact and divided families can differ in many ways (parental education, race, income, and so forth), so they statistically adjusted their results to remove such influences. Still, children of divided parents were about twice as likely to experience a variety of social, psychological, or academic problems. As Figure 3.11 (page 96) shows, however, most of them do fine—especially if endowed with an easygoing temperament and the love and support of relatives and friends.

Parents struggle with conflicting advice and with the stresses of child-rearing. Indeed, the investment in raising a child buys many years not only of joy and love but of worry and irritation. Yet for most parents, a child is one's biological and social legacy—one's personal investment in the human future. To paraphrase

. . . the investment in raising a child buys many years not only of joy and love but of worry and irritation. Yet for most parents, a child is one's biological and social legacy—one's personal investment in the human future.

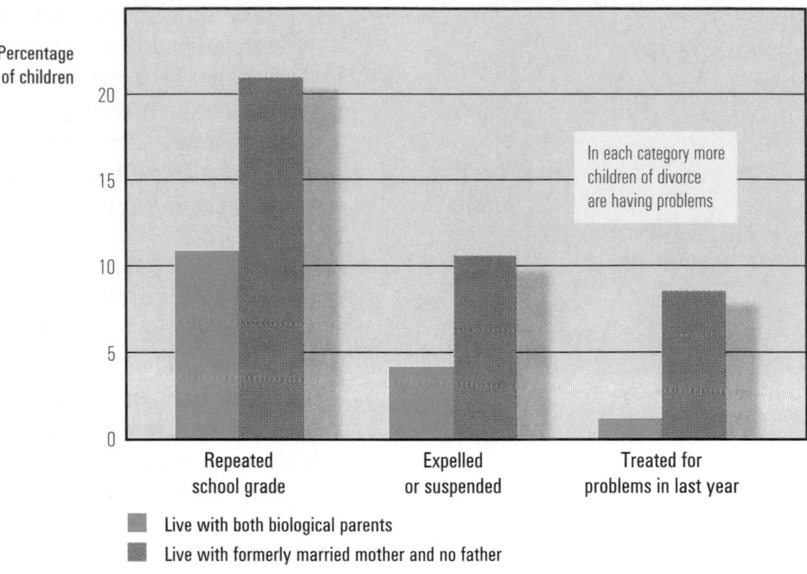

Figure 3.11 Percentage of children experiencing school problems in the previous year In the 1988 National Health Survey, children living with both their biological parents had fewer problems. (Conducted by the U.S. Census Bureau for the National Center for Health Statistics, 1991)

psychiatrist Carl Jung, we reach backward into our parents and forward into our children, and through their children into a future we will never see, but about which we must therefore care.

Culture and Child Rearing

6. *How do parenting styles and values vary among cultures?*

Parenting styles vary. Some parents spank, some reason. Some parents are strict, some are lax. Some parents seem indifferent to their children, some liberally hug and kiss them. Such differences reflect differing parental values. Social values differ not only from expert to expert but also from one time and place to another. Do you prefer children who are independent or children who respect authority?

If you live in Western Europe or North America, the odds are you prefer the former. Most parents in Western societies want their children to think for themselves. "You are responsible for yourself," our families and schools tell us. "Follow your conscience. Be true to yourself. Define your gifts. Satisfy your personal needs." But cultural values change over time. A half-century ago, Western parents placed greater priority on obedience, respect, and sensitivity to others (Alwin, 1990; Remley, 1988). "Be true to your traditions," they taught their children. "Be loyal to your heritage and country. Show respect toward your parents and superiors."

Parental involvement promotes development Parents in every culture facilitate their children's discovery of their world, but cultures differ in what they deem important. Asian cultures place more emphasis on school and hard work than does North American culture. This may help explain why Japanese and Taiwanese children get higher scores on mathematics achievement tests.

Unlike most Westerners, who now raise their children to be independent, many Asians and Africans live in communal cultures, which focus on cultivating emotional closeness. Rather than being given their own bedrooms and sent off to day care or nursery school, infants typically sleep with their mothers and spend their days close to a family member (Morelli & others, 1992; Whiting & Edwards, 1988). Children of communal cultures grow up with a stronger sense of "family self"—a feeling that what shames the child shames the family. Compared with Westerners, people in Japanese and Chinese cultures, for example, exhibit greater shyness toward strangers and greater concern for social harmony and loyalty (Bond, 1988; Cheek & Melchior, 1990; Triandis, 1994). "My parents will be disappointed in me" is a concern of 7 percent of American and Italian teenagers, 14 percent of Australian teens, but nearly 25 percent of teens in Taiwan and Japan (Atkinson, 1988).

gender identity one's sense of being male or female.

gender-typing the acquisition of a traditional masculine or feminine role.

social learning theory the theory that we learn social behavior by observing and imitating and by being rewarded or punished.

Across place and time, children have thrived under various child-rearing systems. Upper-class British parents traditionally left routine caregiving to nannies, before sending their children off to boarding school. Their children generally grew up to be pillars of British society, just like their parents. In some preindustrial societies, babies spend the day on their mother's back—with lots of body contact but little face-to-face and language interaction. When the mother becomes pregnant, the toddler is weaned and handed over to someone else, often an older sibling or a grandmother. Today's North American parents give their children lots of cuddles and hugs—more so than at the beginning of this century. Although children do better when treated warmly than when treated coldly, such diversity in child-rearing cautions us against presuming that our culture's way is the only way to rear successful children.

Mindful of how others differ from us, we often fail to notice the similarities predisposed by our shared biology. Cross-cultural research helps us appreciate both our cultural diversity *and* our human kinship. Compared with person-to-person differences within groups, differences between groups are small. Thus, regardless of our culture, we humans share the same life cycle. We all speak to our infants in similar ways and respond similarly to their coos and cries (Bornstein & others, 1992a,b). Across the world, parents who are warm and supportive have children who feel better about themselves and are less hostile than do punitive and rejecting parents (Rohner, 1986; Scott & others, 1991).

"When someone has discovered why men on Bond Street wear black hats he will at the same moment have discovered why men in Timbuctoo wear red feathers."

G. K. Chesterton
1874–1936

The available data so far come from the United States. But "it bodes well," say the researchers, "that developmental processes are alike in many subgroups of *Homo sapiens*." In surface ways we may differ, but as members together of one species we seem subject to the same psychological forces. As members of different ethnic and cultural groups, our languages vary, yet they reflect universal principles of grammar (Chapter 8). Our tastes vary, yet they reflect common principles of hunger (Chapter 9). Our social behaviors vary, yet they reflect pervasive principles of human influence (Chapter 14).

Gender and Child Rearing

7. *What social influences help explain gender differences?*

What biology initiates, environment accentuates. Society assigns each of us—even those few whose biological sex is ambiguous at birth—to a *gender*, the social category of male or female. The inevitable result is our strong **gender identity**, our sense of being male or female. To varying extents, we also become **gender-typed.** That is, some boys more than others exhibit traditionally masculine traits and interests, and some girls more than others become distinctly feminine.

Social learning theory assumes that children learn gender-linked behaviors by observing and imitating and by being rewarded or punished. "Nicole, you're such a good mommy to your dolls"; "Big boys don't cry, Alex." The modeling and rewarding is not done by parents alone, because differences in the way parents rear boys and girls are not enough to explain gender-typing (Lytton & Romney, 1991). "Boys who are reared in fatherless homes are no less masculine," notes Judith Harris (1998), "than boys and girls who are provided with a Dan Quayle–approved parental pair." Even when their families discourage traditional gender-typing, children organize themselves into "boy worlds" and "girl worlds," each guided by rules for what boys and girls do.

This mother seems unaware of the social learning of gender.

"We don't believe in pressuring the children. When the time is right, they'll choose the appropriate gender."

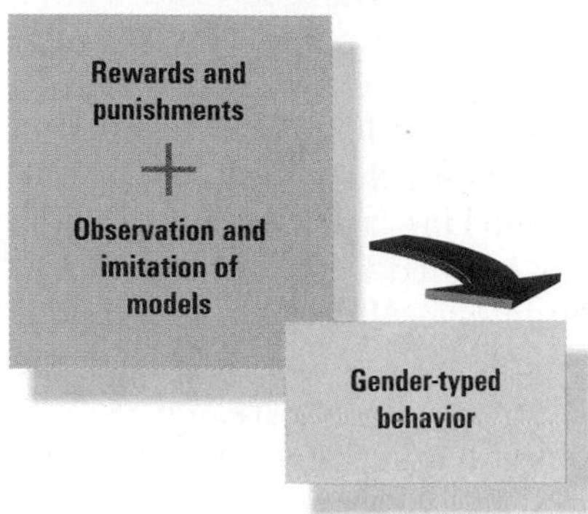

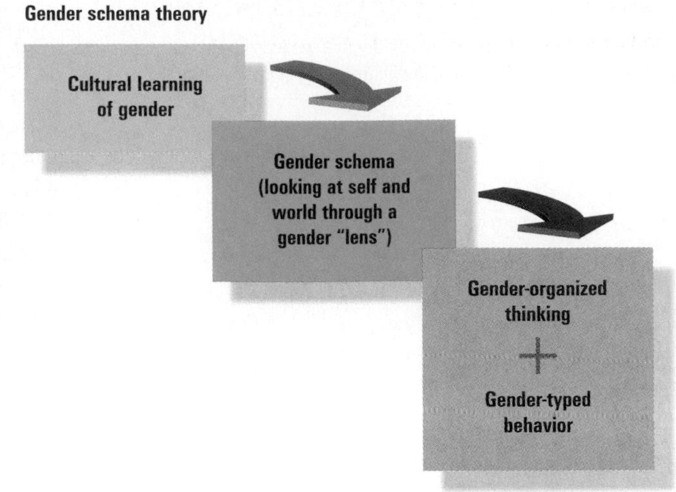

Figure 3.12 **Two theories of gender-typing** Social learning theory proposes that gender-typing evolves through imitation and reinforcement. In gender schema theory, one's concept of maleness and femaleness influences one's perceptions and behavior.

Gender schema theory combines social learning theory with cognition: Out of children's struggles to comprehend the world come concepts, or schemas, including a schema for their own gender (Bem, 1987, 1993). Gender becomes a lens (a schema) through which children view their experience (Figure 3.12). By age 3, language forces them to begin organizing their worlds on the basis of gender. English, for example, uses the pronouns *he* and *she*; other languages classify objects as masculine ("*le* train") or feminine ("*la* table"). Through language, dress, toys, and songs, social learning shapes gender schemas. Children then compare themselves with their concept of gender ("I am male—thus, masculine, strong, aggressive," or "I am female—therefore, feminine, sweet, and helpful") and adjust their behavior accordingly.

REHEARSE IT!

12. After about 8 months of age, infants develop schemas for familiar objects. Faced with a new babysitter, they will show distress, a behavior referred to as

a. conservation.
b. stranger anxiety.
c. imprinting.
d. maturation.

13. Body contact facilitates attachment between infant and parent. In a series of experiments, Harry Harlow found that monkeys raised with artificial mothers tended when afraid to cling to

a. the wire mother.
b. the cloth mother.
c. whichever mother held the feeding bottle.
d. none of the artificial mothers.

14. From the very first weeks of life, infants differ in their characteristic emotional reactions, with some infants being intense and anxious, while others are easygoing and relaxed. These differences are usually explained as differences in

a. attachment. **c.** temperament.
b. imprinting. **d.** parental responsiveness.

15. Children who in infancy formed secure attachments to their parents

a. are likely to become good parents.
b. prefer the company of adults to that of their peers.
c. usually become socially competent youngsters.
d. have less stranger anxiety.

16. Social values vary from culture to culture. Western cultures are to __________ as Asian and African cultures are to __________.

a. obedience; social harmony
b. independence; emotional closeness
c. loyalty; interdependence
d. respect; morality

17. Psychologists differentiate between our biological sex and our gender. As a consequence of the gender assigned to us by society, we develop a gender identity, which means that we

a. exhibit traditional masculine or feminine roles.
b. are socially categorized as male or female.
c. have a sense of being male or female.
d. have an ambiguous biological sex.

gender schema theory the theory that children learn from their cultures a concept of what it means to be male and female and that they adjust their behavior accordingly.

adolescence the transition period from childhood to adulthood, extending from puberty to independence.

Adolescence

How will you look back on your life 10 years from now? Are you making choices that someday you will recollect with satisfaction? In one survey, adults' most common regret was not having taken their education more seriously (Kinnier & Metha, 1989).

Among developmental psychologists, the view that childhood fixes our traits has given way to an awareness that development is *lifelong*. As today's life-span perspective emerged, psychologists began to look at how maturation and experience shape us in infancy and childhood—*and* in adolescence and beyond. At a 5-year high school reunion, friends may be surprised at the divergence of their paths. A decade after college, two former soul mates may have trouble keeping a conversation going. As long as we live, we develop.

Adolescence is life between childhood and adulthood. It starts with the physical beginnings of sexual maturity and ends with the social achievement of independent adult status, a period that in the Western world roughly corresponds to the teen years.

Adolescence is a time of transition. At earlier times in Western societies (and in some developing countries today), adolescence was but a brief interlude between the dependence of childhood and the responsibilities of adulthood (Baumeister & Tice, 1986). Adult status and responsibilities were bestowed shortly after sexual maturity, often marked by an elaborate initiation. The new adult worked, married, and had children.

But thanks to improved nutrition, sexual maturity began occurring earlier. And thanks to compulsory schooling, adult independence began occurring later. As a result, the brief interlude between biological maturity and social independence has widened to a considerable gap (Figure 3.13). That gap is adolescence.

To G. Stanley Hall (1904), one of the first psychologists to describe adolescence, the tension between biological maturity and social dependence created a period of "storm and stress." Indeed, after age 30, many people look back on their teenage years as a time they would not like to relive, a time when the social approval of peers was imperative, one's sense of direction in life was in flux, and alienation from parents was deepest (Macfarlane, 1964). Humorist Dave Barry (1996) is one such person:

> When my dad pulled up, wearing his poodle hat and driving his Nash Metropolitan—a comically tiny vehicle resembling those cars outside supermarkets that go up and down when you put in a quarter, except the Metropolitan looked sillier and had a smaller motor—I was mortified. I might as well have been getting picked up by a flying saucer piloted by some bizarre multi-tentacled stalk-eyed slobber-mouthed alien being that had somehow got hold of a Russian hat. I was horrified at what my peers might think of my dad; it never occurred to me that my peers didn't even notice my dad, because they were too busy being mortified by THEIR parents.

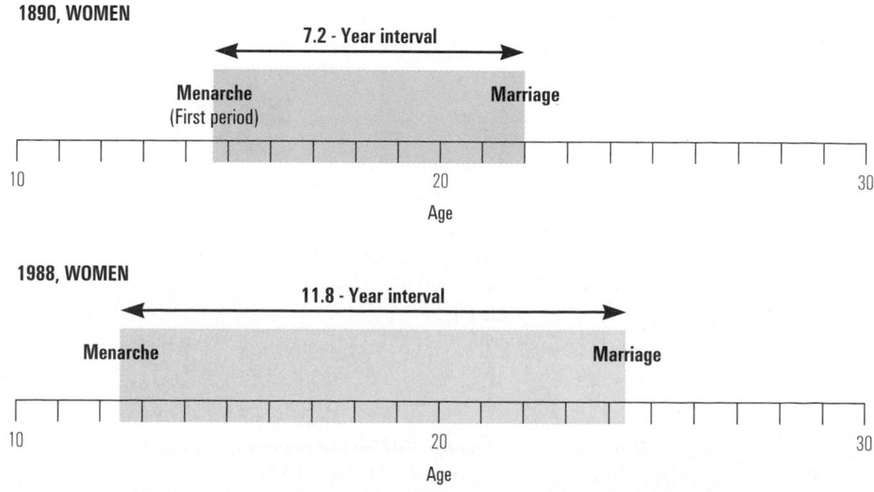

Figure 3.13 **Adolescence is being stretched from both ends** In the 1890s the average interval between a woman's first menstrual period and marriage was about 7 years; today it is nearly 12 years. (Guttmacher Institute, 1994)

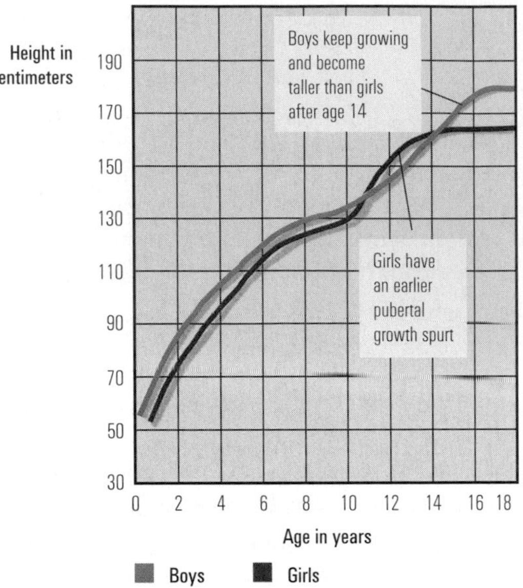

Figure 3.14 **Height differences** Throughout childhood, boys and girls are similar in height. At puberty, girls surge ahead briefly, but then boys overtake them at about age 14. (Data from Tanner, 1978)

Of course eventually my father stopped being a hideous embarrassment to me, and I, grasping the Torch of Dorkhood, became a hideous embarrassment to my son.

Today's psychologists note that adolescence is, indeed, often marked by mood swings. Yet for many it is also as Tolstoy described it—a time of vitality without the cares of adulthood, a time of rewarding friendships, a time of heightened idealism and a growing sense of life's exciting possibilities (Coleman, 1980). These psychologists would not be surprised that 9 of 10 high school seniors agree with the statement, "On the whole, I'm satisfied with myself" (*Public Opinion*, 1987).

Physical Development

8. *What major physical changes occur during adolescence?*

Adolescence begins with **puberty**, when one is becoming sexually mature. Puberty follows a surge of hormones, which may intensify moods and which trigger a 2-year period of rapid physical development that usually begins in girls at about age 11 and in boys at about age 13. About the time of puberty, boys' growth propels them to greater height than their female counterparts (Figure 3.14). During this growth spurt, the reproductive organs and external genitalia—the **primary sex characteristics**—develop dramatically. So do **secondary sex characteristics**, the nonreproductive traits such as breasts and hips in girls, facial hair and deepened voice in boys, pubic and underarm hair in both sexes (Figure 3.15). A year or two before puberty, however, boys and girls often feel the first stirrings of attraction toward those of the other (or their own) sex (McClintock & Herat, 1996).

The landmarks of puberty are the first ejaculation in boys, which usually occurs by about age 14, and the first menstrual period in girls, by about age 13. The first menstrual period, called **menarche** (meh-NAR-key), is a memorable event, one that is recalled by nearly all adult women. Most experience and later recall a mixture of feelings—pride, excitement, embarrassment, and apprehension (Greif & Ulman, 1982; Woods & others, 1983). For the first few months

Figure 3.15 **Body changes at puberty** At about age 11 in girls and age 13 in boys, a surge of hormones triggers a variety of physical changes.

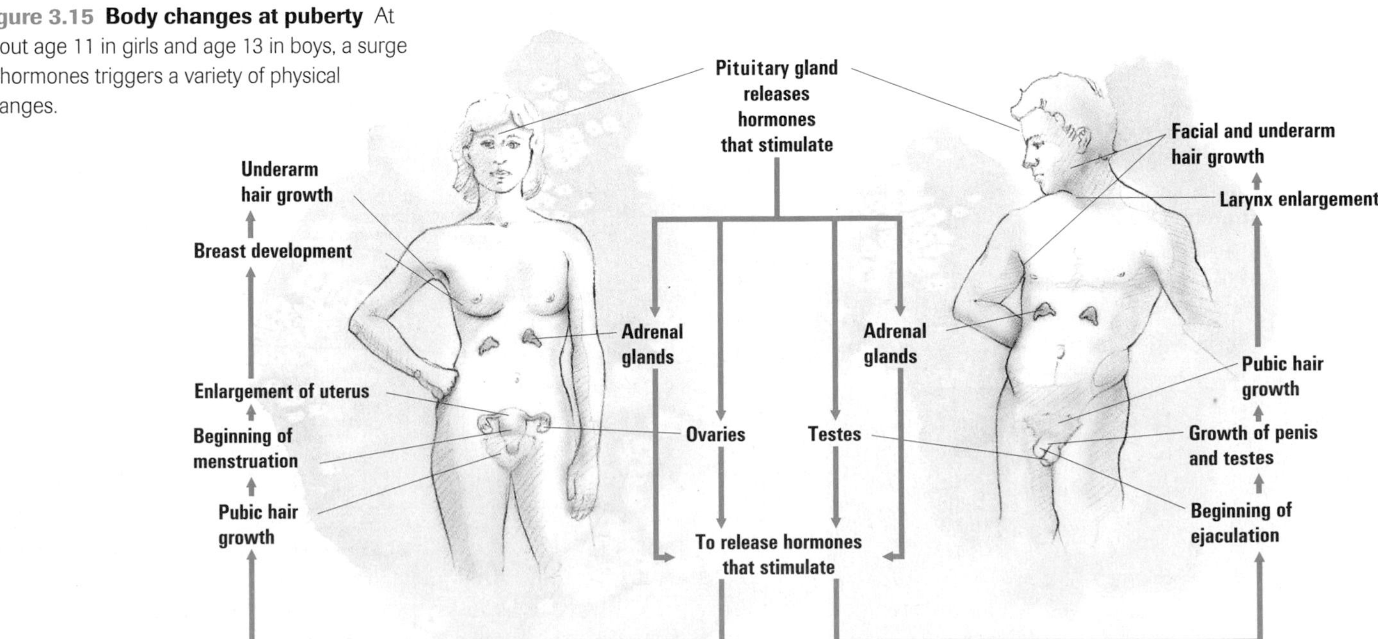

puberty the period of sexual maturation, during which a person becomes capable of reproducing.

primary sex characteristics the body structures (ovaries, testes, and external genitalia) that make sexual reproduction possible.

secondary sex characteristics nonreproductive sexual characteristics, such as female breasts and hips, male voice quality, and body hair.

menarche [meh-NAR-key] the first menstrual period.

many keep it a secret from friends; while most discuss it with their mothers, very few discuss it with their fathers (Brooks-Gunn, 1989). Girls prepared for menarche usually experience it as a positive life transition. And a transition it is. Regardless of their age, girls afterward increasingly see and present themselves as different from boys and function more independently of their parents (Golub, 1983). Most men similarly recall their first ejaculation, which usually occurs as a nocturnal emission (Fuller & Downs, 1990).

As in the earlier life stages, the *sequence* of physical changes (for example, breast buds and visible pubic hair before menarche) is far more predictable than their *timing*. Some girls start their growth spurt at 9, some boys as late as age 16. Such variations have little effect on height at maturity, but they may have psychological consequences. Studies performed in the 1950s by Mary Cover Jones and her colleagues revealed that early maturation pays dividends for boys. Early-maturing boys, being stronger and more athletic during their early teen years, tend to be more popular, self-assured, and independent. For girls, early maturation can be stressful (Caspi & Moffitt, 1991; Stattin & Magnusson, 1990). If a young girl's body is out of sync with her emotional maturity and with what her friends are experiencing, she may begin associating with older adolescents or may suffer teasing. It's not only when we mature that counts, but how people react to our genetically influenced physical development. Remember: *Heredity and environment interact.*

Cognitive Development

9. How did Piaget and Kohlberg describe cognitive and moral development during adolescence?

"When the pilot told us to brace and grab our ankles, the first thing that went through my mind was that we must all look pretty stupid."

Jeremiah Rawlings, age 12, after a 1989 DC-10 crash in Sioux City, Iowa

Adolescents' developing ability to reason gives them a new level of social awareness and moral judgment. As young teenagers become capable of thinking about their thinking, and of thinking about other people's thinking, they begin imagining what other people are thinking about *them*. (Adolescents might worry less about what others think of them if they knew how similarly self-preoccupied their peers are.) As their cognitive abilities mature, many adolescents begin to think about what is ideally possible, and they begin to criticize their society, their parents, and even their own shortcomings.

As young teenagers become capable of thinking about their thinking, and of thinking about other people's thinking, they begin imagining what other people are thinking about them.

Developing Reasoning Power

During the early teen years, reasoning is often self-focused. Adolescents may think their private experiences are unique. They may assume their parents just can't understand what it feels like to be dating or to hate school: "But, Mother, *you* don't really know how it feels to be in love" (Elkind, 1978).

Gradually, though, most achieve the intellectual summit that Piaget called *formal operations*. Preadolescents reason concretely, but adolescents become more capable of abstract logic. They can reason hypothetically and deduce consequences: *If* this, *then* that. We can see this new abstract reasoning power as adolescents ponder and debate human nature, good and evil, truth and justice. Having perhaps envisioned God as an old man in the clouds when they were first capable of symbolic thinking in early childhood, they may now seek a deeper conception of God and existence (Elkind, 1970; Worthington, 1989). Adolescents' logical thinking also enables them to detect inconsistencies in others' reasoning and between their ideals and their actions. Indeed, their newfound ability to spot hypocrisy can lead to heated debates with parents and silent vows never to lose sight of their own ideals (Peterson & others, 1986).

"Ben is in his first year of high school, and he's questioning all the right things."

Demonstrating their reasoning ability Although on opposite sides of the abortion debate, these teens demonstrate their newfound ability to think logically about abstract topics. According to Piaget, they are in the final cognitive stage, formal operations.

Developing Morality

A crucial task of childhood and adolescence is learning right from wrong and developing character—the psychological muscles for controlling impulses. To be a moral person is to *think* morally and *act* accordingly. "It is a delightful harmony when doing and saying go together," said the French essayist Montaigne. But such harmony often eludes us. "To put one's thoughts into action," noted the German poet Goethe, is "the most difficult thing in the world."

Piaget (1932) believed that children's moral judgments build on their cognitive development. Agreeing with Piaget, Lawrence Kohlberg (1981, 1984) sought to describe the development of *moral reasoning*, the thinking that occurs as we consider right and wrong. Kohlberg posed moral dilemmas to children, adolescents, and adults. He then analyzed their answers for evidence of stages of moral thinking. Ponder for a moment his best-known dilemma:

> In Europe, a woman was near death from a very bad disease, a special kind of cancer. There was one drug that the doctors thought might save her. It was a form of radium that a druggist in the same town had recently discovered. The drug was expensive to make, but the druggist was charging 10 times what the drug cost him to make. He paid $200 for the radium and charged $2000 for a small dose of the drug. The sick woman's husband, Heinz, went to everyone he knew to borrow the money, but he could get together only about $1000, which was half of what it cost. He told the druggist that his wife was dying and asked him to sell it cheaper or let him pay later. But the druggist said, "No, I discovered the drug and I'm going to make money from it." Heinz got desperate and broke into the man's store to steal the drug for his wife.

What do you think: Should Heinz have stolen the drug? Why was what he did right or wrong? Kohlberg would not have been interested in whether you judged Heinz's behavior as right or wrong—either answer could be justified—but rather in your reasoning. We all are moral philosophers, Kohlberg proposed, and our moral reasoning helps guide our judgments and behavior. Kohlberg himself discussed with a friend the moral dilemma of suicide before, nearing 60 and racked by pain, he committed suicide (Hunt, 1993).

Kohlberg argued that as we develop intellectually we pass through as many as six stages of moral thinking, moving from the simplistic and concrete toward more abstract and principled reasoning. He clustered these six stages into three basic levels: preconventional, conventional, and postconventional.

"This might not be ethical. Is that a problem for anybody?"

- **Preconventional morality** Before age 9, most children have a preconventional morality of self-interest: They obey either to avoid punishment ("If you let your wife die, you will get in trouble") or to gain concrete rewards ("If you save your wife, you will be a hero").

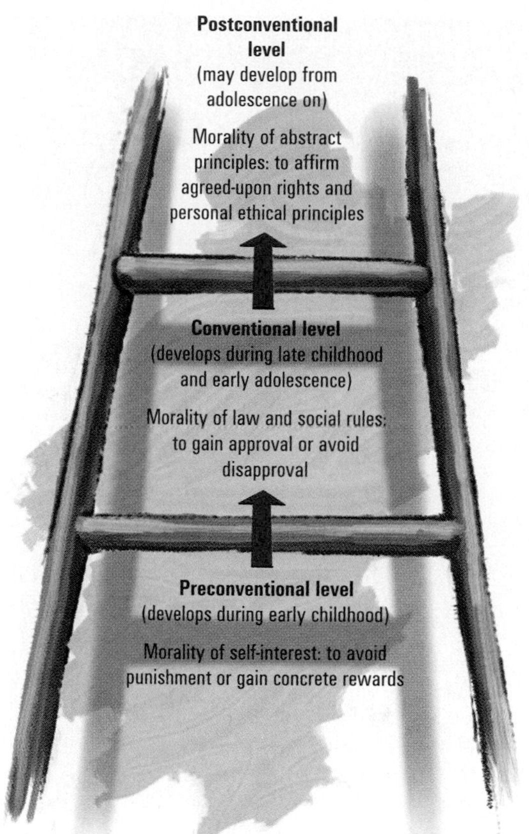

Figure 3.16 Kohlberg's moral ladder Why is it wrong to steal or cheat on an exam? As moral development progresses, the focus of concern moves from the self to the wider social world. Kohlberg contended that postconventional moral thinking, embodied by Martin Luther King, Jr., may be rejected by those who do not comprehend it.

- **Conventional morality** By early adolescence, morality usually evolves to a more conventional level that upholds laws and social rules simply because they are the laws and rules. Being able to take others' perspectives, adolescents may approve actions that will gain social approval or that will help maintain the social order ("If you steal the drug, everyone will think you are a criminal").
- **Postconventional morality** Those who develop the abstract reasoning of formal operational thought may come to a third level. Postconventional morality affirms people's agreed-upon rights ("People have a right to live") or follows what one personally perceives as basic ethical principles ("If you steal the drug, you won't have lived up to your own ideals").

Kohlberg's controversial claim was that these levels form a moral ladder (Figure 3.16). The rungs extend from a young child's immature, preconventional morality at the bottom to an adult's self-defined ethical principles at the top. As with all stage theories, the sequence does not vary. We begin on the bottom rung and ascend to varying heights.

Research confirms that children in various cultures do progress from the level Kohlberg called preconventional into the stages of his conventional level (Edwards, 1981, 1982; Snarey, 1985, 1987). And as our *thinking* matures, our *behavior* also becomes less selfish and more caring (Krebs & Van Hesteren, 1994; Miller & others, 1996). However, the postconventional level appears mostly in the European and North American educated middle class, which prizes individualism—giving priority to one's own goals rather than group goals (Eckensberger, 1994; Miller & Bersoff, 1995). Critics therefore contend that the theory is biased against the moral reasoning of those in communal societies such as China and India—and also against women, whose morality may be less a matter of abstract, impersonal principles and more a matter of caring relationships.

We can stimulate children's moral reasoning through discussions of moral issues and their implications. We can teach children empathy for others' feelings. And we can teach them the self-discipline needed to restrain their impulses—to delay small gratifications now for the sake of bigger gratifications later. Those who learn to delay gratification become more socially responsible, academically successful, and productive (Funder & Block, 1989; Mischel & others, 1988, 1989).

> ***"I am a bit suspicious of any theory that says that the highest moral stage is one in which people talk like college professors."***
>
> James Q. Wilson
> *The Moral Sense*
> 1993

Social Development

Theorist Erik Erikson (1963) contended that each stage of life has its own "psychosocial" task, a crisis that needs resolution. Young children wrestle with issues of *trust* (page 94), then *autonomy* (independence), then *initiative* (Table 3.2, page 104). School-age children develop *competence*, the sense that they are able and productive human beings. In adolescence, the task is to synthesize past, pres-ent, and future possibilities into a clearer sense of self. Adolescents wonder "Who am I as an individual? What do I want to do with my life? What values should I live by? What do I believe in?" Erikson called this quest to define one's sense of self more deeply the adolescent's "search for identity."

> ***"I am becoming still more independent of my parents; young as I am, I face life with more courage than Mummy; my feeling for justice is immovable, and truer than hers. I know what I want, I have a goal, an opinion, I have a religion, and love. Let me be myself and then I am satisfied. I know that I'm a woman, a woman with inward strength and plenty of courage."***
>
> Anne Frank
> *Diary of a Young Girl*
> 1947

Forming an Identity

10. *What is involved in the adolescent's search for identity?*

To refine their sense of identity, adolescents in Western cultures usually try out different "selves" in different situations—perhaps acting out one self at home, another with friends, and still another at school and work. If two of these situations

Table 3.2 Erikson's Stages of Psychosocial Development

Identity Stage (approximate age)	Issues	Description of Task
Infancy (to 1 year)	*Trust vs. mistrust*	If needs are dependably met, infants develop a sense of basic trust.
Toddlerhood (1 to 2 years)	*Autonomy vs. shame and doubt*	Toddlers learn to exercise will and do things for themselves, or they doubt their abilities.
Preschooler (3 to 5 years)	*Initiative vs. guilt*	Preschoolers learn to initiate tasks and carry out plans, or they feel guilty about efforts to be independent.
Elementary school (6 years to puberty)	*Competence vs inferiority*	Children learn the pleasure of applying themselves to tasks, or they feel inferior.
Adolescence (teen years into 20s)	*Identity vs. role confusion*	Teenagers work at refining a sense of self by testing roles and then integrating them to form a single identity, or they become confused about who they are.
Young adulthood (20s to early 40s)	*Intimacy vs. isolation*	Young adults struggle to form close relationships and to gain the capacity for intimate love, or they feel socially isolated.
Middle adulthood (40s to 60s)	*Generativity vs. stagnation*	The middle-aged discover a sense of contributing to the world, usually through family and work, or they may feel a lack of purpose.
Late adulthood (late 60s and up)	*Integrity vs. despair*	When reflecting on his or her life, the older adult may feel a sense of satisfaction or failure.

overlap—as when a teenager brings home friends with whom he is Joe Cool—the discomfort can be considerable. The teen asks, "Which self should I be? Which is the real me?" Often, this role confusion is resolved by the gradual reshaping of a self-definition that unifies the various selves into a consistent and comfortable sense of who one is—an **identity**.

But not always. Erikson noticed that some adolescents forge their identity early, simply by taking on their parents' values and expectations. (Traditional, less individualistic cultures tell adolescents who they are rather than letting them decide on their own.) Other adolescents may adopt a negative identity that defines itself in opposition to parents and society but in conformity with a particular peer group—complete, perhaps, with shaved head or pierced body parts. Still others never quite seem to find themselves or to develop strong commitments. For most, the identity question—Who am I?—continues past the teen years and reappears at turning points during adult life.

The late teen years, when many people begin attending college or working full time, provide new opportunities for trying out possible roles. As seniors, many students have achieved a clearer identity than they had as first-year students (Waterman, 1988). Their identity typically incorporates an increasingly positive self-concept. In several nationwide studies, researchers have given young Americans tests of self-esteem. (Sample item: "I am able to do things as well as most other people.") Between ages 13 and 23, the self-concept usually becomes more positive, especially among boys and among those who belong to a satisfying peer group. A clearer, more self-affirming identity is forming, and with it comes a greater sense of control over one's future (Baumgardner, 1990; O'Malley & Bachman, 1983; Strange & Forsyth, 1993).

Who shall I be today? By varying the way they look, adolescents try out different "selves." Although we eventually form a consistent and stable sense of identity, the "self" we present may change with the situation.

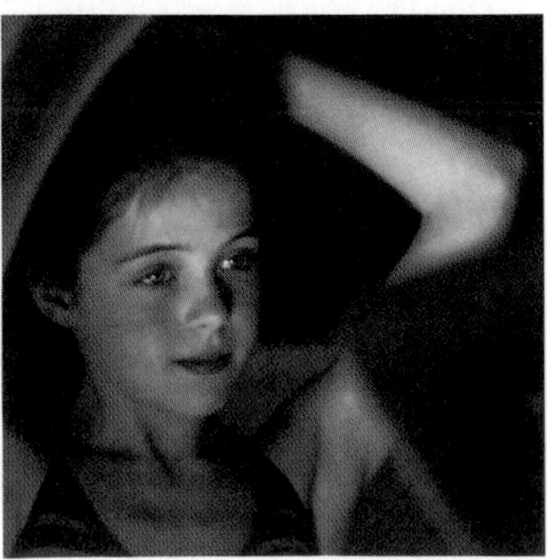

identity one's sense of self; according to Erikson, the adolescent's task is to solidify a sense of self by testing and integrating various roles.

intimacy in Erikson's theory, the ability to form close, loving relationships; a primary developmental task in late adolescence and early adulthood.

Developing Intimacy

Erikson contended that the adolescent identity stage is followed in young adulthood by a developing capacity for **intimacy**, the ability to form emotionally close relationships. Once you have a clear and comfortable sense of who you are, said Erikson, you are ready for close relationships.

11. ***Do males and females differ in their social relations?***

Gender and Social Connectedness

To Carol Gilligan and her colleagues (1982, 1990), the "normal" struggle to create one's separate identity describes individualist males more than relationship-oriented females. Gilligan believes females differ from males both in being less concerned with viewing themselves as separate individuals and in being more concerned with "making connections."

These gender differences surface early, in children's play. Boys typically play in large groups with an activity focus and little intimate discussion. Girls play in smaller groups, often with one friend. Girls' play is less competitive than boys' and more imitative of social relationships (Lever, 1978). In play and in later achievement settings, females are more open and responsive to feedback than are males (Maccoby, 1990; Roberts, 1991). As teens, girls spend more time with friends and less time alone (Wong & Csikszentmihalyi, 1991).

The gender difference in connectedness carries into adulthood. Women, being more *interdependent*, use conversation to explore relationships; men use it to convey solutions (Tannen, 1990). Women emphasize caring and provide most of the care to the very young and the very old. Although 69 percent of people say they have a close relationship with their father, 90 percent feel close to their mother (Hugick, 1989). Men, like empowered people generally, emphasize freedom and self-reliance. (That helps explain why at all ages men assign less importance to religion and pray less often than their female counterparts [Benson, 1992].)

"What's the difference between a man and E.T.? E.T. phoned home."

Anonymous

Women also have closer relationships with each other. Study after study finds the bonds and feelings of support stronger among women than among men (Rossi & Rossi, 1990). Women's ties, as mothers, daughters, sisters, and grandmothers, bind families together. As friends, women are more intimate than men; they talk more often and more openly (Berndt, 1992; Dindia & Allen, 1992).

When surveyed, women are far more likely than men to describe themselves as having empathy. If you are empathic, you identify with others. You rejoice with those who rejoice and weep with those who weep. You imagine what it must feel like to live with that problem, what it must be like to try so hard to impress people, what a thrill it must be to win that award. Physiological measures of empathy, such as one's heart rate while seeing another's distress, reveal a much smaller gender gap than reported in surveys (Eisenberg & Lennon, 1983). Nevertheless, females are more likely to *express* empathy—to cry and to report distress when observing someone in distress.

Gender and human bonds
Empathy, social support, and talk about relationships often seem to come more "naturally" to females.

Moreover, studies consistently find females better at reading people's emotional cues (Hall, 1987). Shown a silent, 2-second film clip of an upset woman's face, women are better than men at sensing whether she is criticizing someone for being late or discussing a divorce. Women's nonverbal sensitivity, perhaps a by-product of their roles, helps explain their greater emotional responsiveness in positive and negative situations (Grossman & Wood, 1993; Sprecher & Sedikides, 1993; Stoppard & Gruchy, 1993). It also helps explain why both men and women report their friendships with women to be more intimate, enjoyable, and nurturing (Rubin, 1985; Sapadin, 1988). When wanting understanding and someone with whom to share worries and hurts, both men and women usually turn to women.

Separating from Parents

As adolescents seek to form their own identities, they begin to separate themselves from their parents (Paikoff & Brooks-Gunn, 1991). The preschooler who can't be close enough to mother, who loves to touch and cling to her, becomes the 14-year-old who wouldn't be caught dead holding hands with mom. Arguments occur more often, usually over small things such as household chores, bed time, and homework (Tesser & others, 1989).

For a minority of parents and their adolescents, differences mean estrangement. But for most, disagreement at the level of bickering is not destructive.

- A study of 6000 adolescents in 10 countries, from Australia to Bangladesh to Turkey, found that most liked their parents (Offer & others, 1988). "We usually get along but . . . ," adolescents often report (Galambos, 1992; Steinberg, 1987).
- In one survey of 25,000 middle-class teens worldwide, more than 80 percent rated family relationships as an "important" guiding principle for their lives, and more than half said it was *most* important—more significant than their "relationship with friends," "having fun," or "making the world a better place" (Stepp, 1996).
- A Gallup poll (1996) of American teens reported that 97 percent said they got along "fairly" or "very" well with their parents. Most, however, reported getting along better with Mom than with Dad. Positive relations with parents support positive peer relations. High school girls who have the most affectionate relationships with their mothers tend also to enjoy the most intimate friendships with girlfriends (Gold & Yanof, 1985). And teens who feel close to their parents tend to be healthy and happy and to do well in school (Resnick & others, 1997). Of course, we can state this correlation the other way: Misbehaving teens are more likely to have tense parental relationships and to say their parents are jerks.

In Western cultures, adolescence is typically a time of growing peer influence and diminishing parental influence, especially on matters of personal taste and life-style. Asked in a 1997 survey if they "ever had a serious talk" with their

DOONESBURY

Parent–adolescent relations For a relative few, adolescence means estrangement from parents.

child about illegal drugs, 85 percent of American parents answered yes. But the teens often tuned out their parents' earnest advice, for only 45 percent could recall such a talk (Morin & Brossard, 1997). Instead, what their friends are—what "everybody's doing"—they often become.

Peer influences on development may actually exceed parental influences, argues Judith Harris (1998). Consider:

- Preschoolers who disdain a certain food despite parents' urgings often will eat the food if put at a table with a group of children who like it.
- Immigrant children develop language and accents more like those of their peers than of their parents. Moreover, put immigrant children in peer groups of nonimmigrants and they will quickly lose their parents' culture. "When in Rome, they become Romans," notes Harris. "Even if their parents happen to be British or Chinese or Mesquakie."
- Direct parental influences on smoking are less important than many people suppose. Rather, teens who start smoking typically have friends who model smoking, who suggest its pleasures, and who offer cigarettes.
- Nazi youth group members mostly came from emotionally supportive, middle-class homes, according to behavior geneticist David Rowe (1990, 1994). What corrupted them was not bad parenting but the "heavier weight" of cultural change around them.

"A child's goal is not to become a successful adult, any more than a prisoner's goal is to become a successful guard. A child's goal is to be a successful child. . . . Because the guards have power over them, prisoners try to keep on reasonably good terms with their guards. But what really matters to most of them is how they are regarded by their fellow prisoners."

Judith Rich Harris
The Nurture Assumption (1998)

As people mature in young adulthood, emotional ties between parents and children continue to loosen. During their early twenties, many still lean heavily on their parents. (From 1970 to 1994, the percentage of American 18- to 24-year-olds living with parents increased from 47 to 53 percent.) By their late twenties, most feel more comfortably independent of their parents and better able to empathize with them as fellow adults (Frank, 1988; White, 1983). As the twentieth century winds down, this graduation from adolescence to adulthood is taking longer. From Europe to Australia, adolescents are taking longer to finish college, to leave the nest, to establish their careers. Since 1960, Americans' average age at first marriage has increased by nearly 4 years (to 26 for men, 24 for women).

Adolescent Sexuality and Pregnancy

12. *What factors influence teen pregnancy?*

Adolescents' physical maturation fosters a sexual dimension to their emerging identity. How and when sexuality is expressed differs with time and culture. In the United States, about half of ninth- to twelfth-graders report having had sexual intercourse, as do 42 percent of Canadian 16-year-olds (Boroditsky & others, 1995; MMWR, 1995). Teen intercourse rates are higher in Western Europe but much lower in Arab and Asian countries. In one survey, only 2.5 percent of 4688 unmarried Chinese students entering Hong Kong's six universities reported having had sexual intercourse (Meston & others, 1996). These varying sexual standards from country to country help explain cultural differences in rates of nonmarital childbearing (Figure 3.17).

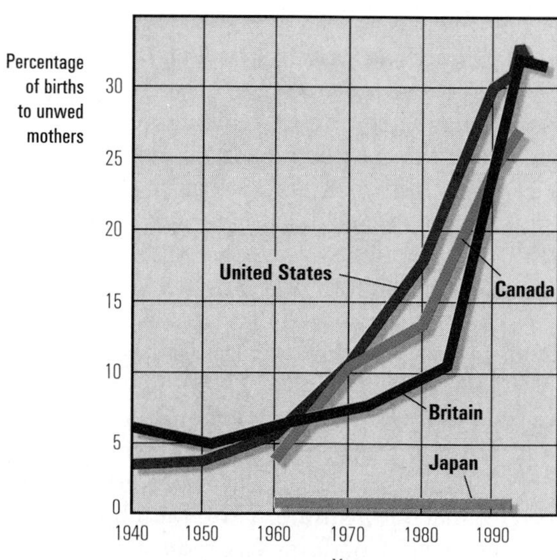

Figure 3.17 Cultural differences in births to unwed parents Since 1960, the percentage of babies born to unmarried Canadian, British, and American women—one-third of whom were teens—has more than quintupled. This increase stems from two trends: a decreasing birthrate among married women and a doubling of the birthrate among unmarried women. (Data from National Center for Health Statistics; Bureau of the Census [1996], Table 1330; and British Central Statistical Office, 1993)

The increased adolescent pregnancy rate and the often impoverished futures of teen mothers and of children in father-absent homes have prompted new research on teen sexuality and adolescents' use of contraceptives. Short of "just saying no," contraceptives are the surest strategy of preventing pregnancy. Although the number of American teenagers using condoms doubled during the 1980s, half of teen sexual acts were unprotected. Only one-third of sexually active male teens used condoms consistently (Sonenstein, 1992). Why? Among the contributing factors are these:

"Will your child learn to multiply before she learns to subtract?"

Anti–teen-pregnancy poster, Children's Defense Fund

1. ***Ignorance*** In eight surveys, fewer than half the adolescents could correctly identify the safe and risky times of the menstrual cycle (Morrison, 1985). Half of sexually active Canadian teen girls have mistaken ideas about which birth control methods will protect them from pregnancy and sexually transmitted diseases (STDs) (Immen, 1995). Thus, most unwed teens report surprise at finding themselves pregnant (Brooks-Gunn & Furstenberg, 1989).
2. ***Guilt related to sexual activity*** Although sexual inhibitions reduce sexual activity, they also result in lack of planned birth control for those who do engage in sex (Gerrard & Luus, 1995). Not wanting to appear deliberately sexual or promiscuous, teens may hesitate to carry and produce a condom. When, as sometimes happens, passion overwhelms intentions, the result may be conception.
3. ***Minimal communication about birth control*** Many teenagers are uncomfortable discussing contraception with parents, partners, and peers (Kotva & Schneider, 1990; Milan & Kilmann, 1987). Teens are more likely to use contraceptives if they talk freely with friends or parents and are in an exclusive relationship with a partner with whom they communicate openly.
4. ***Alcohol use*** Sexually active teens are typically alcohol-using teens (National Research Council, 1987). By depressing brain centers that control judgment, inhibition, and self-awareness, alcohol tends to break down normal restraints, a phenomenon well known to sexually coercive males (page 193).
5. ***Mass media norms of unprotected promiscuity*** The Planned Parenthood Federation (1986) has complained that television and movies help define sexual norms, which today are "Go for it *now*. . . ." An average hour of prime-time television on the three major U.S. networks contains approximately 15 sexual acts, words, and innuendos. Nearly all of these instances involve unmarried partners, and few communicate any concern for birth control or sexually transmitted disease (Sapolsky & Tabarlet, 1991). Planned Parenthood contends that repeated portrayals of unsafe sex, without consequence, amounts to a campaign of sex disinformation.

"All of us who make motion pictures are teachers, teachers with very loud voices."

Film producer George Lucas, Academy Award ceremonies 1992

With teen pregnancy having risen despite increased sex education, the U.S. national health objectives for the year 2000 include a dual aim: increasing condom use to 90 percent among those sexually active, and reducing from approximately 70 percent to under 40 percent the proportion of 17-year-olds who have had intercourse (Centers for Disease Control, 1992). Sex education is similarly shifting toward a two-pronged emphasis on both contraception ("safe sex") and commitment ("saved sex").

The shift to include teen abstinence within comprehensive sex education is also a response to increased rates of sexually transmitted disease (STD)—12 million cases annually in the United States, not including bacterial diseases such as chlamydia, syphilis, and gonorrhea (Guttmacher Institute, 1993). More than 60 percent of these new infections occur in persons under 25. Because of their less mature biological development and fewer protective antibodies, teenage girls seem to be especially vulnerable to STD and associated risks of becoming infertile and developing certain cancers (Guttmacher Institute, 1994; Morell, 1995).

The rapid spread of STDs is not surprising. Condoms can reduce the risk of HIV transmission by two-thirds, although they do not always prevent transmission (condoms can leak HIV) (Weller, 1993). With certain other STDs, notably the human papilloma virus which is responsible for most genital cancers, condoms are virtually useless (Medical Institute, 1994).

Throughout history, the pendulum of sexual values has swung—from the European eroticism of the early 1800s to the conservative Victorian era of the late 1800s, from the libertine flapper era of the 1920s to the family values of the 1950s. With new 1990s voices decrying family disintegration and calling for a balance between sexual expression and restraint, the pendulum may have begun a new swing toward commitment. In West Germany, the percentage of teens who link sex with committed love is up significantly since 1970 (Schmidt & others, 1994). And would you agree or disagree that "if two people like each other, it's all right for them to have sex even if they've known each other for a very short time"? The percentage of first-year American college and university students who agree dropped from 52 percent in 1987 to 42 percent in 1996 (Sax & others, 1996).

REHEARSE IT!

18. Adolescence is marked by the onset of

a. an identity crisis. **c.** separation anxiety.
b. puberty. **d.** parent-child conflict.

19. The adolescent growth spurt is marked by dramatic developments in the sex characteristics. Primary sex characteristics relate to __________; secondary sex characteristics refer to __________.

a. ejaculation; menarche
b. breasts and facial hair; ovaries and testes
c. emotional maturity; hormone surges
d. reproductive organs; nonreproductive traits

20. According to Piaget, the ability to think logically about abstractions indicates

a. concrete operational thought.
b. egocentrism.
c. formal operational thought.
d. conservation.

21. According to Kohlberg, preconventional morality focuses on __________; conventional morality is more concerned with __________.

a. upholding laws and social rules; self-interest
b. self-interest; basic ethical principles
c. upholding laws and social rules; basic ethical principles
d. self-interest; upholding laws and social rules

22. Erik Erikson contends that each stage of life has its own special psychosocial task or challenge. The primary task during adolescence is to

a. attain formal operations.
b. forge an identity.
c. develop a sense of intimacy with another person.
d. live independent of parents.

23. The differences among individuals of each sex are much greater than the differences between men and women. Nevertheless, women more than men exhibit a concern for

a. independence and self-reliance.
b. social connections.
c. competitive achievement.
d. social stereotyping.

24. Aside from abstinence, contraception is the surest way of preventing pregnancy. More than half of all sexually active teens, however, either do not use contraceptives or do not use them regularly. Factors contributing to the epidemic of teen pregnancies include ignorance about reproduction and contraception, insufficient communication about contraception, and

a. the "just say no" attitude.
b. the unavailability of abortion.
c. the absence of guilt feelings about sexual activity.
d. alcohol use.

Adulthood

"I am still learning."

Michelangelo
1560, at age 85

At one time, psychologists viewed adulthood, especially the center-of-life years between adolescence and old age, as one long plateau. No longer. Those who follow the unfolding of people's adult lives now believe development continues. Physically, cognitively, and especially socially, people at age 50 differ from their 25-year-old selves.

It's harder to generalize about adulthood stages than about life's early years. During adulthood, age only modestly correlates with people's traits. If you know that James is a 1-year-old and Jamal is a 10-year-old, you could say a great deal about each child. Not so with adults who differ by a similar number of years. The boss may be 30 or 60; the marathon runner may be 20 or 50; your classmates may be teenagers or grandparents. Likewise, a 19-year-old can be a parent who supports a child or a child who gets an allowance. Yet our life courses are in some ways similar. Our bodies, our minds, and our relationships undergo some changes in common with those of childhood friends, who in other ways now seem so very different.

menopause the time of natural cessation of menstruation; also refers to the biological changes a woman experiences as her ability to reproduce declines.

Physical Changes

13. *What major physical changes occur during middle and late adulthood?*

Although few of us are aware of it at the time, our physical abilities peak in early adulthood. Muscular strength, reaction time, sensory keenness, and cardiac output all crest by the mid-twenties. Like the declining daylight after the summer solstice, declining physical prowess begins imperceptibly. Athletes are often the first to notice. World-class sprinters and swimmers peak in their teens or early twenties. Women, because they mature earlier than men, also peak earlier. But most people—especially those whose daily lives do not require peak physical performance—hardly perceive the early signs of decline.

Physical Changes in Middle Adulthood

Middle-aged athletes know all too well that physical decline gradually accelerates (Figure 3.18). As a 55-year-old who regularly plays basketball, I now find myself occasionally wondering whether my team really needs me down court. But even diminished vigor is sufficient for normal activities. Moreover, during early and middle adulthood, physical vigor has less to do with age than with a person's health and exercise habits. Many of today's physically fit 50-year-olds run 4 miles with ease, while sedentary 25-year-olds find themselves huffing and puffing up two flights of stairs. Even many 70-year-olds don't yet feel old. How old does a person have to be before you think of him or her as old? The average 18- to 29-year-old says 67. The average person 60 and over says 76 (Yankelovich, 1995).

Figure 3.18 **The slow decline of the body's physical capacities during adulthood** (Adapted from Insel & Roth, 1976)

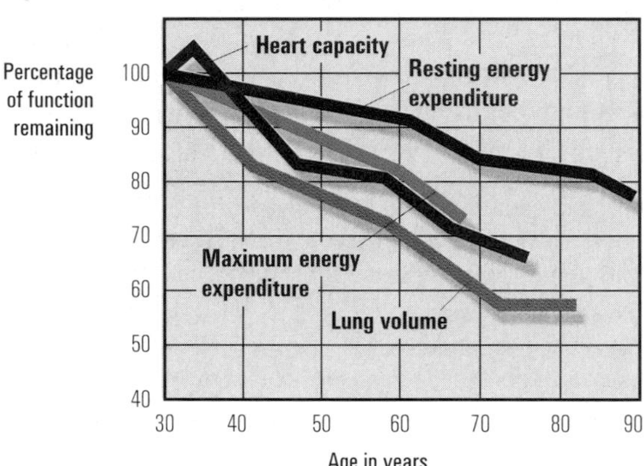

For women, the foremost biological sign of aging is **menopause**, the ending of the menstrual cycle, usually beginning within a few years of age 50. Menopause and its physical symptoms, such as hot flashes in some women, accompany a reduction in the hormone estrogen. Like the stereotype of adolescent storm and stress, the image of menopausal emotionality and depression clashes with reality: Menopause usually does *not* create psychological problems for women. One survey of 2500 middle-aged Massachusetts women, another that followed 541 middle-aged Pennsylvania women for 3 years, and yet another that followed 3049 middle-aged women over 10 years all found them no more or less depressed if experiencing menopause (Busch & others, 1994; Matthews, 1992; McKinlay & others, 1987a,b).

A woman's expectations and attitudes regarding menopause influence its emotional impact. Does she see menopause as a sign that she is losing her femininity and sexual attractiveness and growing old? Or does she look on it as liberation from contraceptives, menstrual periods, fears of pregnancy, and children's demands? Social psychologist Jacqueline Goodchilds (1987) quipped: "If the truth were known, we'd have to diagnose [older women] as having P.M.F.—Post-Menstrual Freedom."

Men experience no equivalent to menopause—no cessation of fertility, no sharp drop in sex hormones. But they do experience a more gradual decline in sperm count, testosterone level, and speed of erection and ejaculation. Some may also experience psychological distress related to their perception of decreased virility and declining physical capacities. Nevertheless, after middle age most men and women remain capable of satisfying sexual activity.

Physical Changes in Later Life

Is old age "more to be feared than death" (Juvenal, *Satires*)? Or is life "most delightful when it is on the downward slope" (Seneca, *Epistulae ad Lucilium*)? What is it like to grow old?

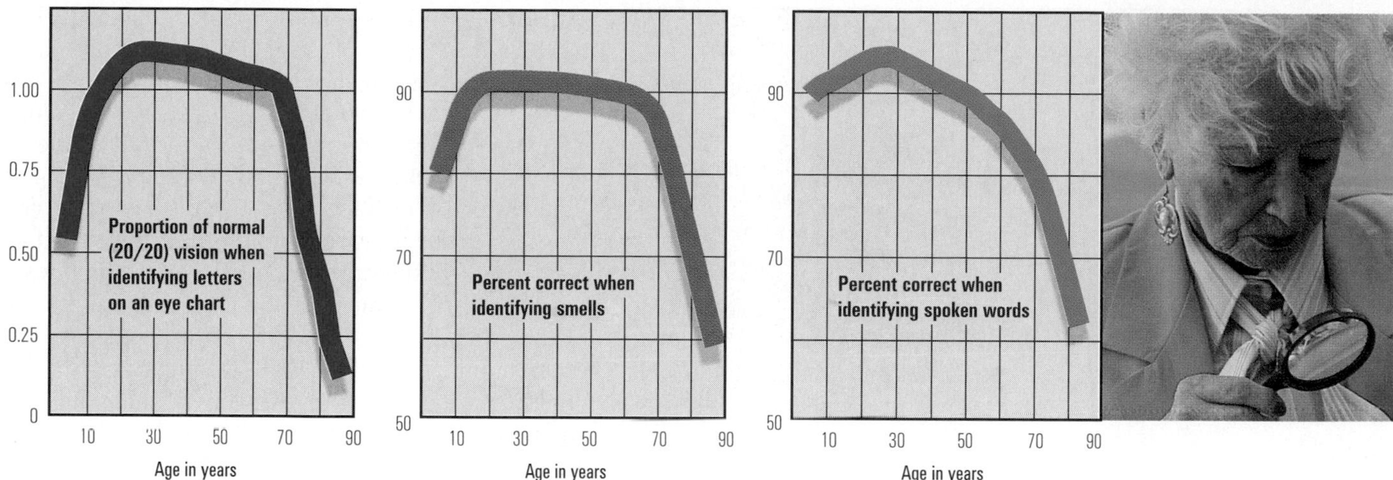

Figure 3.19 The aging senses Sight, smell, and hearing all decline in later life. (From Doty & others, 1984)

Sensory Abilities

As we have seen, physical decline begins in early adulthood, but not until later life do people become acutely aware of it. As visual sharpness diminishes and adaptation to changes in light level slows, older people have more accidents. Most stairway falls taken by older persons occur on the top step, precisely where the person typically descends from a window-lit hallway into the darker stairwell (Fozard & Popkin, 1978). By using what we know about aging when designing environments, we could reduce such accidents (National Research Council, 1990). Muscle strength, reaction time, and stamina also diminish noticeably, as do hearing, distance perception, and the sense of smell (Figure 3.19). In later life, the stairs get steeper, the newsprint gets smaller, and people seem to mumble more. My 88-year-old father speaks for many nearing life's end: "Growing old is the nuts."

With age, the eye's pupil shrinks and its lens becomes less transparent, reducing the amount of light reaching the retina. In fact, a 65-year-old retina receives only about one-third as much light as its 20-year-old counterpart (Kline & Schieber, 1985). Thus, to see as well as a 20-year-old when reading or driving, a 65-year-old needs three times as much light—a reason for buying cars with untinted windshields. This also explains why older people sometimes ask younger people, "Don't you need better light for reading?"

Keeping the biological clock running smoothly How quickly people age depends in part on their health habits. As this cheerful group makes clear, the more active people remain, the more vigor they retain.

Health

For those growing older, there is both bad and good news about health. The bad news: The body's disease-fighting immune system weakens, making the elderly more susceptible to life-threatening ailments such as cancer and pneumonia. It's as if the very old have a very mild case of AIDS—the immune deficiency that hampers the body's ability to fight infections.

The good news: Thanks to a lifetime's accumulation of antibodies, older people *less* often suffer short-term ailments, such as common flu and cold viruses. For example, those over 65 are half as likely as 20-year-olds and one-fifth as likely as preschoolers to suffer upper respiratory flu each year (National Center for Health Statistics, 1990). This is one reason why older workers have lower absenteeism rates (Rhodes, 1983).

By slowing neural processing, aging levies a tax on the brain. During the early years of life, up to the teen years, we process information more and more speedily (Fry & Hale, 1996; Kail, 1991). But compared with teens and young adults, older people take a bit more time to react, to solve perceptual puzzles, even to remember names (Bashore, 1994; Salthouse, 1992, 1994). And car accident rates per mile increase after age 70. By age 75, they reach the relatively high teenage level (National Research Council, 1990), as Figure 3.20 indicates. Speed slows especially

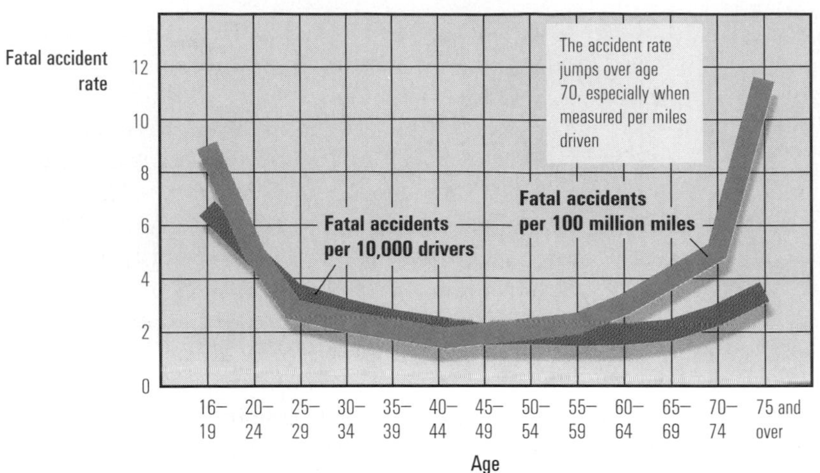

Figure 3.20 Age and fatal accidents Slowing reactions contribute to increased accident risks among those 70 and older (Stock, 1995). Would you favor driver exams based on performance, not age, to screen out those whose slow reactions or mental confusion indicate accident risk?

If—as now seems likely—it becomes possible to discern by brain scans or genetic testing those likely to suffer Alzheimer's disease, would you want to take the test? If so, at what age would you take it?

when the task becomes complex (Cerella, 1985; Poon, 1987). At video games, most 70-year-olds are no match for a 20-year-old. As we age, we become aware of a growing gap between what we were and what we are becoming.

During aging, brain regions important to memory begin to atrophy (Schacter, 1996). Beginning in young adulthood, there is also a small, gradual loss of brain cells, contributing to a 5 percent or so reduction of brain weight by age 80. But the proliferation of neural connections, especially in people who remain active, helps compensate for the cell loss (Coleman & Flood, 1986). This helps explain the common finding that adults who remain active—physically, sexually, and mentally—retain more of their capacity for such activities in later years (Jarvik, 1975; Pfeiffer, 1977). "Use it or lose it" is sound advice. We are more likely to rust from disuse than to wear out from overuse.

Some adults do, unfortunately, suffer a substantial loss of brain cells. A series of small strokes, a brain tumor, or alcoholism can progressively damage the brain, causing that mental erosion we call *dementia*. So, too, can the most feared of all brain ailments, **Alzheimer's disease**, which strikes 3 percent of the world's population by age 75. Alzheimer's symptoms are *not* the same as normal aging. (Occasionally forgetting where you laid the car keys or struggling over someone's name is no cause for alarm; forgetting who a friend is does suggest Alzheimer's.) Underlying the symptoms of Alzheimer's is a deterioration of neurons that produce the neurotransmitter acetylcholine. Deprived of this vital chemical messenger, memory and thinking suffer. Up to age 95, the incidence of mental disintegration doubles roughly every 5 years (Figure 3.21).

Alzheimer's destroys even the brightest of minds. First memory, then reasoning and language deteriorate. Robert Sayre (1979) recalls his father shouting at his afflicted mother to "think harder" when she could not remember where she had put something, while his mother, confused, embarrassed, on the verge of tears, randomly searched the house. But if you lose it, you can't use it. As Alzheimer's runs its course, after 5 to 20 years, the patient becomes emotionally flat, then disoriented, then incontinent, finally mentally vacant—a sort of living death, a mere body stripped of its humanity. Caregiving family members of increasingly confused and helpless sufferers themselves often become the disease's exasperated and exhausted victims.

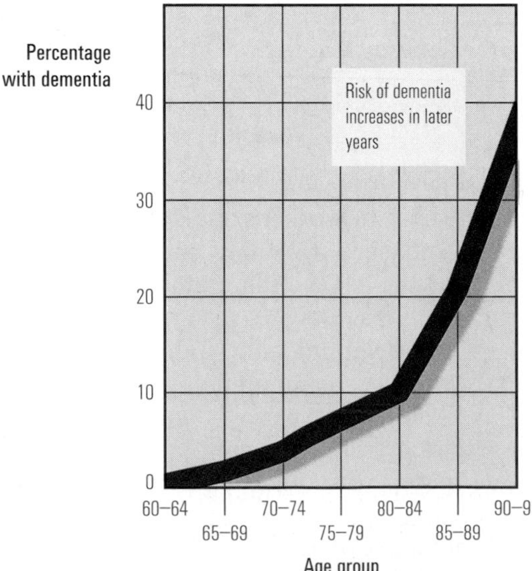

Figure 3.21 Incidence of dementia (mental disintegration) by age Risk of mental loss due to Alzheimer's disease or a series of strokes doubles about every 5 years in later life. (From Jorm & others, 1987, based on 22 studies in industrial nations)

Cognitive Changes

14. *How are memory and intelligence influenced by aging?*

One of the most controversial questions in the study of the human life span is whether adult cognitive abilities, such as memory, creativity, and intelligence, parallel the gradually accelerating decline of physical abilities. Employers, for example, may wonder whether they should encourage their senior workers to retire—or capitalize on their experience. People generally perceive the elderly as mentally less sharp (Kite & Johnson, 1988). Is this stereotype accurate? Is there truth in the proverb, "You can't teach an old dog new tricks"? Or does more truth lie with another proverb: "You're never too old to learn"?

Aging and Memory

Early adulthood is the peak time for some types of learning and remembering. In one experiment, Thomas Crook and Robin West (1990) invited 1205 people to learn some names. Fourteen videotaped people said their names, using a

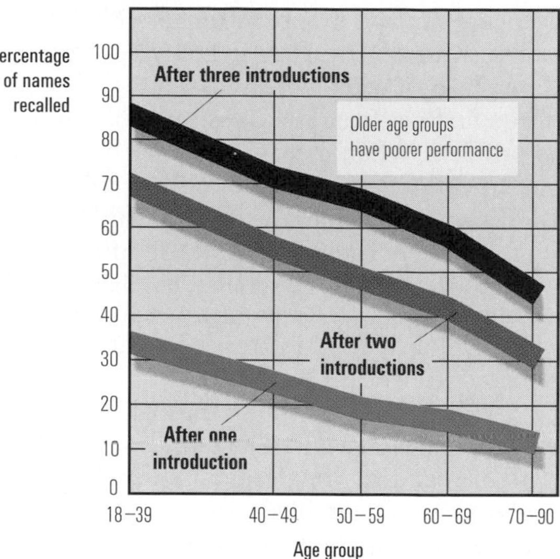

Figure 3.22 Tests of recall Recalling new names introduced once, twice, or three times is easier for younger adults than for older ones. (Data from Crook & West, 1990)

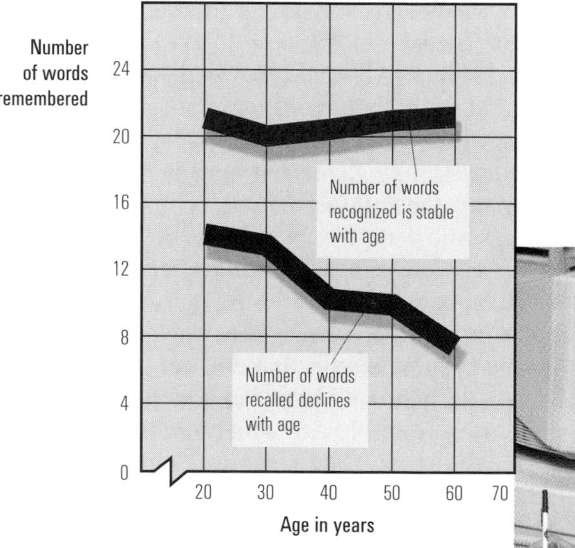

Figure 3.23 Recall and recognition in adulthood In this experiment, the ability to *recall* new information declined during early and middle adulthood, but the ability to *recognize* new information did not. (From Schonfield & Robertson, 1966)

common format: "Hi, I'm Larry." Then the same individuals reappeared and said, for example, "I'm from Philadelphia"—thus providing a visual and voice cue for remembering the person's name. As Figure 3.22 shows, everyone remembered more names after a second and third replay of the introductions, but younger adults' recall for the names consistently surpassed that of older adults. Within hours after Prime Minister Margaret Thatcher announced her resignation, young and old British people recalled how they heard the news. When asked again 11 months later, 90 percent of the younger group but only 42 percent of the older group told the same story (Cohen & others, 1994).

But consider another experiment. David Schonfield and Betty-Anne Robertson (1966) asked adults of various ages to learn a list of 24 words. Without giving any clues, the researchers asked some to recall as many words as they could from the list. As Figure 3.23 shows, younger adults had better recall. Others, given multiple-choice questions that asked them simply to *recognize* the words they had seen, exhibited no memory decline with age. Recognition memory is especially good when older adults are tested early rather than late in the day (May & others, 1993). So, how well older people remember depends: Are they being asked simply to *recognize* what they have tried to memorize (minimal decline) or to *recall* it without clues (greater decline)?

Part of the memory difficulty older adults complain of may be normal forgetfulness. When a 20-year-old mislays her car keys, she gets frustrated; when her grandfather mislays his, he gets frustrated and blames his age. But forgetting seems also to depend on the type of information. If you are asked to recall meaningless information—nonsense syllables or unimportant events—then the older you are, the more errors you are likely to make. However, if the information is meaningful, older people's rich web of existing knowledge helps them to catch it. Thus, their capacity to learn and remember skills and *meaningful* material shows less decline (Graf, 1990; Labouvie-Vief & Schell, 1982; Perlmutter, 1983).

Aging and Intelligence

What happens to our broader intellectual powers as we age? Do they gradually decline, as does our ability to recall new material? Or do they remain constant, as does our ability to recognize meaningful material? The evolving answer to this question makes an interesting research story that illustrates psychology's self-correcting process (Woodruff-Pak, 1989).

Phase I: Cross-Sectional Evidence for Intellectual Decline

In **cross-sectional studies**, researchers test and compare people of various ages. When giving intelligence tests to representative samples of people, researchers consistently find that older adults give fewer correct answers than do younger adults. David Wechsler (1972), creator of the most widely used adult intelligence test, therefore concluded that "the decline of mental ability with age is part of the general [aging] process of the organism as a whole."

Phase II: Longitudinal Evidence for Intellectual Stability

Colleges began giving intelligence tests to entering students about 1920, making it possible to retest older people who had taken an intelligence test years earlier. Several psychologists saw their chance to study intelligence **longitudinally**, by retesting the same people over a period of years. What they expected

Alzheimer's disease a progressive and irreversible brain disorder characterized by gradual deterioration of memory, reasoning, language, and, finally, physical functioning.

cross-sectional study a study in which people of different ages are compared with one another.

longitudinal study research in which the same people are restudied and retested over a long period.

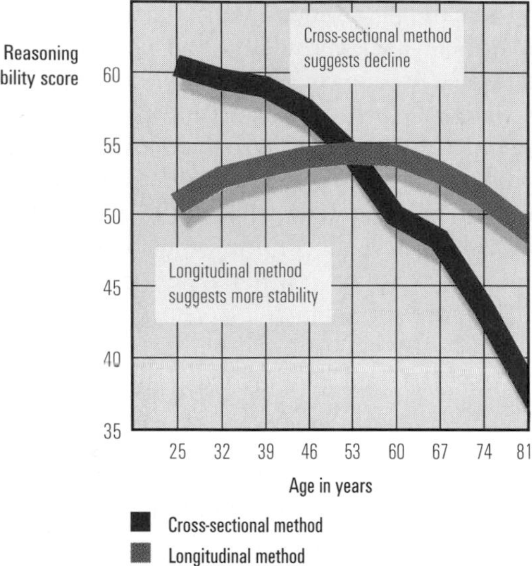

Figure 3.24 Cross-sectional versus longitudinal testing of intelligence at various ages In this test of one type of verbal intelligence (inductive reasoning), the cross-sectional method produced declining scores with age. The longitudinal method (in which the same people were retested over a period of years) produced a slight *rise* in scores well into adulthood. (Adapted from Schaie, 1994)

to find was a decrease in intelligence after about age 30 (Schaie & Geiwitz, 1982). What they actually found was a surprise: Until late in life, intelligence remained stable (Figure 3.24). On some tests, it even increased.

How then are we to account for the findings from the cross-sectional studies? In retrospect, researchers saw the problem. When a cross-sectional study compares 70-year-olds and 30-year-olds, it compares people not only of two different ages but of two different eras. It compares generally less-educated people (born, say, in the early 1900s) with better-educated people (born after 1950), people raised in large families with people raised in smaller families, people growing up in less affluent families with people raised in more affluent families.

Phase III: It All Depends

But the controversy continues. For one thing, longitudinal studies have their own pitfalls. Those who survive to the end of longitudinal studies may be bright, healthy people whose intelligence is least likely to decline. (Perhaps people who died younger and were removed from the study had declining intelligence.) If so, such studies underestimate the average decline in intelligence.

Research is further complicated by the finding that intelligence is not a single trait (see Chapter 8). Intelligence tests that assess speed of thinking may place older adults at a disadvantage because of their slower neural mechanisms for processing information. But slower need not mean less intelligent. Given other tests that assess general vocabulary, knowledge, and ability to integrate information, older adults generally hold their own.

German researcher Paul Baltes (1993, 1994) has developed "wisdom" tests that assess traits such as expertise and sound judgment on important matters of life. His results suggest that older adults more than hold their own on such tests. Thus, despite 30-year-olds' quick-thinking smarts, we usually select older people to be president of the company, the college, or the country. To be growing older is, in some ways, to be still growing. Age is sage. To paraphrase one 60-year-old, "Forty years ago I had a great memory, but I was a fool."

To be growing older is, in some ways, to be still growing. Age is sage.

So, whether intelligence increases or decreases with age depends on the type of intellectual performance we measure. **Crystallized intelligence**—one's accumulated knowledge as reflected in vocabulary and analogies tests—*increases* up to old age. **Fluid intelligence**—one's ability to reason speedily and abstractly, as when solving novel logic problems—*decreases* with age (Cattell, 1963; Horn, 1982). We can see this pattern in the intelligence scores of a national sample of adults. After adjustments for education, verbal scores (reflecting crystallized intelligence) held relatively steady from ages 20 to 74. Nonverbal, puzzle-solving intelligence declined (Figure 3.25).

"In youth we learn, in age we understand."

Marie Von Ebner-Eschenbach
Aphorisms
1883

Figure 3.25 Intelligence and age After adjustments for education, verbal intelligence scores hold steady with age, while nonverbal intelligence scores decline. (Intelligence scores from standardization sample of the Wechsler Adult Intelligence Scale, based on norms for 25- to 34-year-olds.) (Adapted from Kaufman & others, 1989)

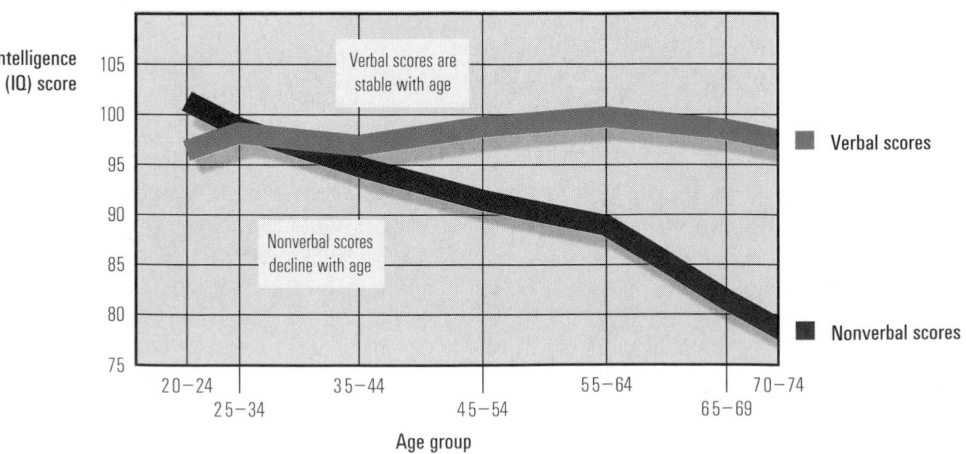

crystallized intelligence one's accumulated knowledge and verbal skills; tends to increase with age.

fluid intelligence one's ability to reason speedily and abstractly; tends to decrease during late adulthood.

social clock the culturally preferred timing of social events such as marriage, parenthood, and retirement.

This helps explain why mathematicians and scientists produce much of their most creative work during their late twenties or early thirties, whereas those in literature, history, and philosophy tend to produce their best work in their forties, fifties, and beyond, after accumulating more knowledge (Simonton, 1988, 1990). For example, poets (who depend on fluid intelligence) reach their peak output earlier than prose authors (who need a deeper knowledge reservoir)—a finding observed in every major literary tradition, for both living and dead languages. So, whether intellectual performance increases or decreases with age depends on how we assess it.

Social Changes

"Midway in the journey of our life I found myself in a dark wood, for the straight way was lost."

Dante
The Divine Comedy
1300–1321

Many differences between younger and older adults are created not by the physical and cognitive changes that accompany aging but by life events associated with family relationships and work. A new job means new relationships, new expectations, and new demands. Marriage brings the joy of intimacy and the stress of merging your life with another's. The birth of a child introduces responsibilities and significantly alters your life focus. The death of a loved one creates an irreplaceable loss and a need to reaffirm your own life. Do these normal events of adult life shape a predictable sequence of life changes?

Adulthood's Ages and Stages

15. ***Why are age-based stage theories of adult development considered controversial?***

Some psychologists have argued that as people enter their forties, they undergo a "midlife transition" to middle adulthood, which for many is a crisis, a time of great struggle or even of feeling struck down by life. But the fact—reported by large samples of people—is that job dissatisfaction, marital dissatisfaction, divorce, anxiety, and suicide do *not* surge during the early forties (Hunter & Sundel, 1989). Divorce, for example, is most common among those in their twenties, suicide among those in their seventies and eighties. Moreover, one study of emotional instability in nearly 10,000 men and women found "not the slightest evidence" that distress peaks anywhere in the midlife age range (Figure 3.26).

Figure 3.26 **Early-forties midlife crises?** Among 10,000 people responding to a national health survey, there was no early-forties increase in emotional instability ("neuroticism") scores. (From McCrae & Costa, 1990)

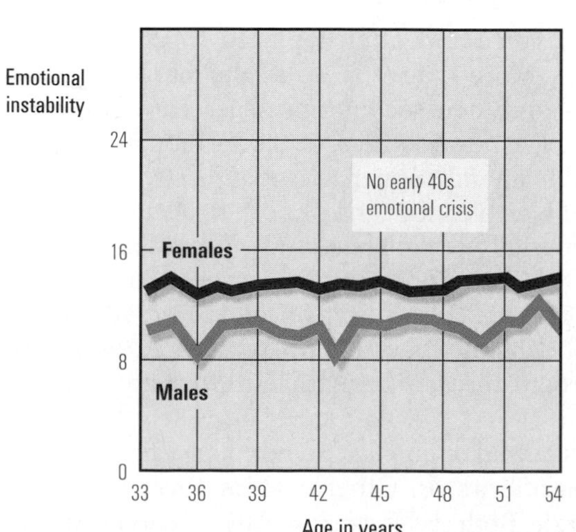

There is another reason skeptics question age-linked stages such as "midlife crisis." The **social clock**—the cultural prescription of "the right time" to leave home, get a job, marry, have children, and retire—varies from culture to culture and era to era. In Jordan, 40 percent of brides are in their teens; in Hong Kong, only 3 percent are (United Nations, 1992). In Western Europe, fewer than 10 percent of men over 65 remain in the work force, as do 16 percent in the United States, 36 percent in Japan, and 69 percent in Mexico (Davies & others, 1991). In contemporary Western nations, the 1950s sequence from student to worker to wife to at-home mom to older worker has loosened and the age at marriage has increased. Modern women occupy these roles in any order or all at once. Given variations in the social clock and individual experience, stage theory critics are suspicious of any neat timetable of adult ages and stages.

More important than one's chronological age are life events. Marriage, parenthood, vocational changes, divorce, nest-emptying, relocation, and retirement mark transitions to new life stages whenever they occur—and increasingly they are occurring at unpredictable ages. The social clock is still ticking, but people feel freer to be out of sync with it.

Adulthood's Commitments

16. ***What do psychologists view as adulthood's two primary commitments?***

Two basic aspects of our lives do, however, dominate adulthood. Erik Erikson called them *intimacy* (forming close relationships) and *generativity* (being productive and supporting future generations). Researchers have chosen various terms—*affiliation* and *achievement*, *attachment* and *productivity*, *commitment* and *competence*. But Sigmund Freud (1935) put it most simply: The healthy adult, he said, is one who can *love* and *work*. For most adults, love centers on family commitments toward partner, parents, and children. Work encompasses our productive activities, whether for pay or not.

Love

Across time and place, human societies have nearly always included a relatively monogamous bond between men and women and a bond between parents and their children. We flirt, fall in love, and marry—one person at a time. "Pair-bonding is a trademark of the human animal," notes anthropologist Helen Fisher (1993). The arrangement makes sense from an evolutionary perspective: Parents who cooperated to nurture their children to maturity were more likely to have their genes passed along to posterity than parents who didn't.

The bond of love is most satisfying and enduring when marked by a similarity of interests and values, a sharing of emotional and material support, and intimate self-disclosure (see Chapter 14). Women's marital satisfaction, even more than men's, is colored by their mate's social support (Acitelli & Antonucci, 1994). Happiness is having a reassuring, respectful, caring, and mutually confiding partner.

"One can live magnificently in this world if one knows how to work and how to love."

Leo Tolstoy
1856

Marriage bonds are usually stronger when couples marry after age 20 and are well educated. Compared with their counterparts of 30 years ago, people in Western countries *are* better educated and marrying later. Ironically, however, people are divorcing more. When marrying, whether for the first time or the second, nearly everyone hopes for an enduring bond. We also now have high expectations for our mate, whom we anticipate being a wage-earner, caregiver, intimate friend, and warm and responsive lover. Partly as a result of these rising expectations, as well as women's lessened economic dependence, marriages today are twice as likely to end in divorce as they were in 1960. To judge from the divorce rate—recall that both Canada and the United States now have about one divorce for every two marriages—marriage has become a union that often defies management (Bureau of the Census, 1996). In Europe, divorce is only slightly less common.

Love Intimacy, attachment, commitment—love by whatever name—is central to healthy and happy adulthood.

Although rocked by increased divorce and often replaced by cohabitation, the institution of marriage endures. More than 9 in 10 adults marry. Of those who divorce, 75 percent remarry—and their second marriages are virtually as happy as the average first marriage (Vemer & others, 1989). Although the relatively few people who feel trapped in an unhappy marriage typically feel miserable, most married Europeans and North Americans of both sexes feel happier than those who are unmarried, especially when compared with others who are separated and divorced (Inglehart, 1990). For example, surveys of more than 32,000 Americans since 1972 reveal that 23 percent of unmarried adults and 40 percent of married adults report being "very happy" (NORC, 1997). Lesbian women in couples, too, report greater well-being than those who are alone (Wayment & Peplau, 1995).

Marriages that last are not always devoid of conflict. Some couples fight but also shower one another with affection afterwards. Other couples never raise their voices yet also seldom praise or nuzzle. Both styles can last. After observing the in-

THINKING CRITICALLY

Trial Marriages—Do They Reduce Divorce?

Changing sexual values are evident in changing norms regarding cohabitation. In 1958, the University of Illinois fired a professor who suggested, through the student newspaper, the desirability of young people testing their love relationship before venturing into marriage. When Barnard College sophomore Linda Leclair in 1968 moved in with her boyfriend, a Columbia University junior, a student-faculty committee debated Leclair's fate for several months. They eventually decided that she could remain a student, but they denied her the use of the cafeteria, snack bar, and recreation room.

Today, most universities look the other way. Cohabitation has become commonplace. The number of cohabiting unmarried couples in the United States tripled during the 1970s and has more than doubled again since 1980 (Bureau of the Census, 1996). Similar trends have occurred since 1960 throughout much of Western Europe. In Australia, 56 percent of couples who married in 1992 had lived together before marrying—nearly four times the percentage who did so in 1975 (McLennan, 1995).

Many people see premarital cohabitation as a trial period that serves to weed out unsuccessful unions before marriage occurs. In one survey of nearly 300,000 first-year U.S. college students, 51 percent agreed that "a couple should live together before marriage" (Astin & others, 1989). Might those who are sexually experienced and thoroughly familiar with the living habits of their partner indeed be less likely to stumble into an ill-fated marriage? Does test-driving life together before committing reduce the risk of divorce?

It seems not. Eight studies concur that, compared with couples who do not cohabit with their spouses-to-be, those who do have higher divorce rates. A U.S. survey of 13,000 adults found that couples who lived together before marriage were one-third more likely to separate or divorce within a decade (Bumpass & Sweet, 1989). A 1990 Gallup survey of still-married Americans also found that 21 percent of those who had not cohabited before marrying, and 40 percent of those who had, said they might divorce (Greeley, 1991). A Canadian national survey of 5300

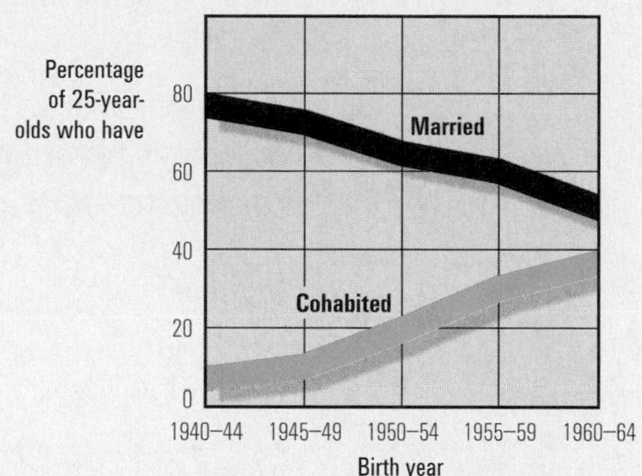

U.S. rates of cohabitation and marriage by age 25 From the U.S. National Survey of Families and Households. (From Bumpass & Sweet, 1989)

women found that those who cohabited were 54 percent more likely to divorce within 15 years (Balakrishan & others, 1987). And a Swedish study of 4300 women found cohabitation linked with an 80 percent greater risk of divorce (Bennett & others, 1988).

Can you imagine why? (Remember: A correlation between cohabitation and divorce risk need not imply that cohabitation is a *cause* of future divorce.) William Axinn and Arland Thornton (1992) report data that support two explanations.

First, cohabitation attracts people who are more open to terminating unsatisfying relationships. The very idea of cohabitation presumes that intimate relationships need not be permanent. It sees love as conditional rather than committed. If either partner becomes dissatisfied, he or she can seek bliss elsewhere. People who cohabit therefore bring a more individualistic ethic to marriage, are more likely to see close relationships as temporary and fragile, and are more accepting of divorce.

Second, the experience of cohabitation increases acceptance of divorce. Over time, those who cohabit tend to become more approving of dissolving an unfulfilling union. This divorce-accepting attitude increases the odds of later divorce.

teractions of 2000 couples, John Gottman (1994) reported a better indicator of likely marital success: at least a 5 to 1 ratio of positive to negative interactions. Stable marriages provide five times more instances of smiling, touching, complimenting, and laughing than of sarcasm, criticism, and insults. And if you want to predict which newlyweds will stay together, do not pay attention to how passionately they are in love. The couples who make it are more often those who restrain the number of putdowns that, unchecked, can take over a relationship (Notarius & Markman, 1993). To prevent a cancerous negativity, successful couples learn to fight fair (to state feelings without insulting) and to steer conflict away from chaos with comments like "I know it's not your fault" or "Be quiet for a moment and listen."

Thought question: Does marriage correlate with happiness because marital support and intimacy breed happiness, because happy people more often marry and stay married, or both?

Often, love bears children. The most enduring of life changes, having a child, is for most people a happy event. As children begin to absorb time, money, and emotional energy, however, satisfaction with the marriage itself may decline. This is especially likely among employed women who, more than they expected, bear the traditional burden of increased chores at home (Belsky & others, 1986; Hackel & Ruble, 1992). Efforts to create an equitable relationship can pay double dividends, making for more satisfying marriages, which also breed better parent-child relations (Erel & Burman, 1995).

Seven national surveys reveal that the empty nest is for most people a happy place.

Another significant event in family life happens when children leave home. If you have left home, consider your parents' experience: Did they suffer the "empty nest syndrome"—a feeling of distress focusing on a loss of purpose and relationship? Or did your parents discover renewed freedom, relaxation, and satisfaction with their own relationship?

Seven national surveys reveal that the empty nest is for most people a happy place (Adelmann & others, 1989; Glenn, 1975). Compared with middle-aged women who still have children at home, those whose nest has emptied report greater happiness and greater enjoyment of their marriage. Many parents therefore experience what sociologists Lynn White and John Edwards (1990) call a "postlaunch honeymoon," especially if they maintain close relationships with their children.

Work

For most adults, a large part of the answer to "Who are you?" depends on the answer to "What do you do?" For most adults, to feel productive and competent is to raise children and to undertake a career. Career choices are hard to predict, especially in today's changing work environment. During the first 2 years of college or university, most students cannot predict their later career path. Most shift from their initially intended majors, many find their postcollege employment in fields not directly related to their majors, and most will change careers (Rothstein, 1980).

Does work, including a career, indeed contribute to self-fulfillment and life satisfaction, as Freud supposed? One approach to answering this question has been to compare the roughly equal numbers of North American women who are or are not employed. From their studies at the Wellesley College Center for Research on Women, Grace Baruch and Rosaline Barnett (1986) conclude that what matters is not which roles a woman occupies—whether it be as paid worker, wife, and/or mother—but the quality of her experience in those roles. Happiness is about having work that fits your interests and provides you with a sense of competence and accomplishment; having a partner who

Job satisfaction and life satisfaction Work provides people with a sense of identity and competence and opportunities for accomplishment. Perhaps this is why a challenging and interesting occupation enhances people's happiness.

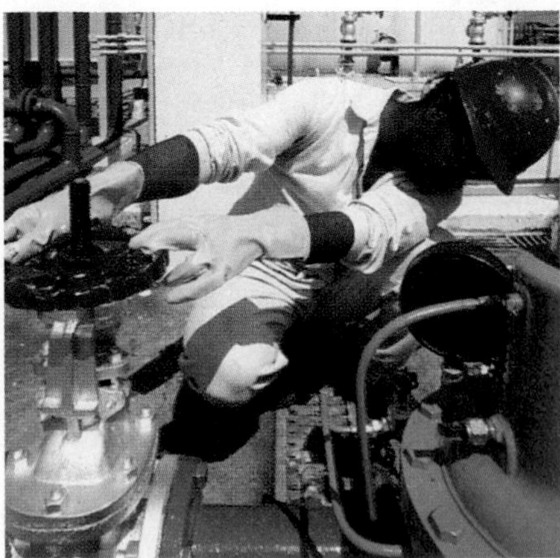

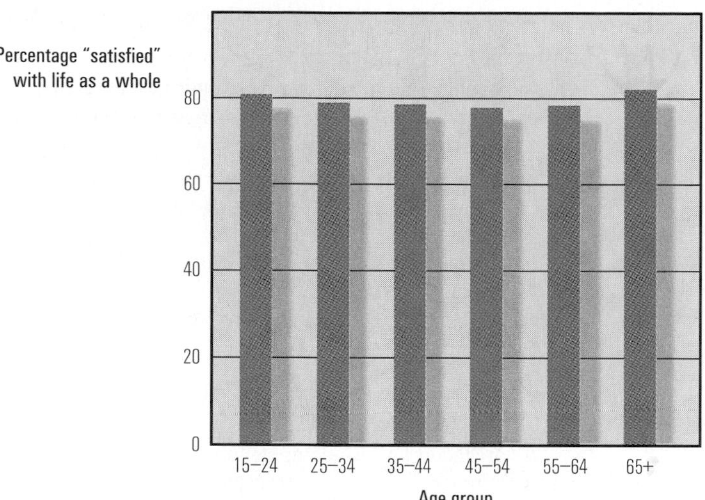

Figure 3.27 Age and life satisfaction With early adult tasks behind them, many older adults have more time to pursue personal interests. No wonder their satisfaction with life remains high, especially if they are healthy and active. As this graph based on multinational surveys shows, age differences in life satisfaction are trivial. (Data from Inglehart, 1990)

is a close, supportive companion and who sees you as special; and/or having loving children whom you like and feel proud of.

Well-Being Across the Life Span

To live is to grow older, which means that we all can look backward with satisfaction or regret, and forward with hope or dread. When people are asked what they would have done differently if they could relive their lives, their most common answer is "taken my education more seriously and worked harder at it." Other regrets—"I should have told my father I loved him," "I regret that I never went to Europe"—also focus less on mistakes made than on the things one *failed* to do (Gilovich & Medvec, 1995).

In later life, income shrinks, work is taken away, the body deteriorates, recall fades, energy wanes, family members and friends die or move away, and the great enemy, death, looms ever closer. Small wonder that many presume the over-65 years to be the worst of times (Freedman, 1978). But they are not. People of all ages report similar feelings of happiness and satisfaction with life. Ronald Inglehart (1990) confirmed this when he amassed interviews conducted during the 1980s with representative samples of nearly 170,000 people in 16 nations. As Figure 3.27 illustrates, older people report as much happiness and satisfaction with life as younger people do. Given that growing older is one sure consequence of living, an outcome most of us prefer to its alternative, we can all take comfort in this finding.

Death and Dying

Grief is especially severe when the death of a loved one comes suddenly and before its expected time on the social clock.

Most of us will suffer and cope with the deaths of relatives and friends. Usually, the most difficult separation is from one's spouse—a loss suffered by five times more women than men. Grief is especially severe when the death of a loved one comes suddenly and before its expected time on the social clock. The accidental death of a child or the sudden illness that claims a 45-year-old spouse may trigger a year or more of mourning flooded with memories, eventually subsiding to a mild depression that sometimes continues for several years (Lehman & others, 1987). AIDS, which so often strikes down people in midlife and younger, has left countless grief-stricken partners experiencing such bereavement (Folkman & others, 1996).

The normal range of reactions to a loved one's death is wider than most people suppose. Some cultures encourage public weeping and wailing; others hide grief. Within any culture some individuals grieve more intensely and openly. Contrary to a popular myth, those who express the strongest grief immediately do not purge their grief more quickly (Bonanno & others, 1995; Wortman & Silver, 1989). Given similar losses, some people grieve hard and long, others more lightly and briefly.

We can be grateful for the waning of death-denying attitudes. Facing death with dignity and openness helps people complete the life cycle with a sense of life's meaningfulness and unity—the sense that their existence has been good and that life and death are parts of an ongoing cycle. Although death may be unwelcome, life itself can be affirmed even at death. This is especially so for people who review their lives not with despair but with what Erik Erikson called a sense of *integrity*—a feeling that one's life has been meaningful and worthwhile.

"Do not go gentle into that good night,
Old age should burn and rave at close of day;
Rage, rage against the dying of the light."

Dylan Thomas
"Do Not Go Gentle into That Good Night"
1952
Poem written to his father as he lay dying peacefully

"Consider, friend, as you pass by, as you are now, so once was I. As I am now, you too shall be. Prepare, therefore, to follow me."

Scottish tombstone epitaph

REHEARSE IT!

25. By age 75, a person has experienced declining heart and muscular strength and losses in sight and hearing. However, this older adult is *less* likely than younger people to suffer from

a. Alzheimer's disease.
b. accidents and falls.
c. short-term illnesses such as the flu.
d. chronic illnesses such as diabetes.

26. Some types of learning and remembering peak in early adulthood. By age 65, a person would be most likely to experience a decline in the ability to

a. recall and list all the items in the chapter glossary.
b. select the correct definition in a multiple-choice question.
c. evaluate whether a statement is true or false.
d. exercise sound judgment in answering an essay question.

27. In longitudinal studies the same people are retested at different ages. Longitudinal research suggests that intelligence

a. steadily declines with age.
b. peaks at age 25.
c. generally increases in later life.
d. remains stable until very late in life.

28. Most middle-aged adults define themselves in terms of their career. Which of the following has research shown to be true of women and work?

a. Women who work for wages are happier than those who do not.
b. Women whose roles are wife and mother are happier than those who also work for wages.
c. The quality of a woman's experience in her role matters more than the role she occupies.
d. A woman's age determines which role makes her happier.

29. Freud defined the healthy adult as one who is able to love and work. Erikson agreed, observing that the adult struggles to attain intimacy and

a. affiliation. **c.** competence.
b. identity. **d.** generativity.

30. Contrary to what many people assume

a. older people are much happier than adolescents.
b. men in their forties express much greater dissatisfaction with life than do women of the same age.
c. people of all ages report similar levels of happiness.
d. those whose children have recently left home–the empty nesters–have the lowest level of happiness of all groups.

Reflections on the Major Developmental Issues

We began our survey of developmental psychology by identifying three pervasive issues: (1) whether development is steered more by genes or by experience, (2) whether development is a gradual, continuous process or a series of discrete stages, and (3) whether development is characterized more by stability over time or by change. It is time to reflect on the latter two issues.

Continuity and Stages

17. *What conclusions can we draw from research on the issues of continuity versus stages and of stability versus change?*

Adults are vastly different from infants. But do they differ as a giant redwood differs from its seedling—a difference created by gradual, cumulative growth? Or do they differ as a butterfly differs from a caterpillar—a difference of distinct stages?

Generally speaking, researchers who emphasize experience and learning see development as a slow, continuous shaping process. Those who emphasize biological maturation tend to see development as a sequence of genetically predetermined stages or steps; although progress through the various stages may be quick or slow, everyone passes through the stages in the same order.

Are there clear-cut stages of psychological development, as there are physical stages such as crawling before walking? We have considered the stage theories of Jean Piaget on cognitive development, Lawrence Kohlberg on moral development, and Erik Erikson on psychosocial development. And we have seen their stage theories criticized: Young children have some abilities that Piaget attributed to later stages. Kohlberg's work appears biased by a worldview characteristic of educated males in individualistic cultures. The ideas of Erikson are contradicted by research showing that adult life does not progress through a fixed, predictable series of steps.

Although research casts doubt on the idea that life proceeds through neatly defined, age-linked stages, the concept of stage remains useful. There are spurts of brain growth during childhood and puberty that correspond roughly to Piaget's stages (Thatcher & others, 1987). And stage theories contribute a developmental perspective on the whole life span, by suggesting how people of one age think and act differently when they arrive at a later age.

Stability and Change

This leads us to the final question: Over time, are people's personalities consistent, or do they change? If reunited with a long-lost grade school friend, would you instantly recognize that "it's the same old Andy"? Or does a person during one period of life seem like a different person at a later period?

Researchers who have followed lives through time have found evidence for both stability and change. There is continuity to personality and yet, happily for troubled children and adolescents, human development is life: The struggles of the present may be laying a foundation for a happier tomorrow. More specifically, researchers generally agree on the following points:

1. The first 2 years of life provide a poor basis for predicting a person's eventual traits (Kagan, 1978, 1988). Even children and adolescents often change: Many confused and troubled children have blossomed into mature, successful adults (Macfarlane, 1964; Thomas & Chess, 1986). As people grow older, however, continuity of personality does gradually increase (Costa & McCrae, 1989; Stein & others, 1986).
2. Some characteristics, such as temperament, are more stable than others, such as social attitudes (Moss & Susman, 1980). But attitudes, too, become more stable with age (Krosnick & Alwin, 1989).
3. In some ways, we all change with age. Most shy, fearful toddlers begin opening up by age 4, and during adulthood most of us mellow. In the years after college, most people become calmer and more self-disciplined (McCrae & Costa, 1994). Many a 20-year-old goof-off has matured into a 40-year-old business or cultural leader. Such changes can occur without changing a person's position *relative* to others of the same age.

"At 70, I would say the advantage is that you take life more calmly. You know that 'this, too, shall pass'!"

Eleanor Roosevelt
1954

Finally, we should remember that life contains *both* stability and change. Stability enables us to depend on others, motivates our concern for the healthy development of children, and provides our identity. Change motivates our concerns about present influences, sustains our hope for a brighter future, and enables us to adapt and grow with experience.

REHEARSE IT!

31. Developmental researchers who emphasize learning and experience tend to believe in __________; those who emphasize biological maturation tend to believe in __________.

a. nature; nurture
b. continuity; stages
c. stability; change
d. randomness; predictability

32. Although development is lifelong, there is stability of personality over time. For example,

a. most personality traits emerge in infancy and persist throughout life.
b. temperament tends to remain stable throughout life.
c. few people change significantly after adolescence.
d. people tend to undergo greater personality changes as they age.

REVIEWING ■ *The Developing Person*

Prenatal Development and the Newborn

1. ***How does life develop before birth?***

By studying the human life span from conception to death, **developmental psychologists** examine how we develop physically, cognitively, and socially. The life cycle begins when one sperm cell unites with an egg. Their nuclei fuse to form a **zygote**, which attaches to the uterine wall after about 10 days. The ***X*** (female) or ***Y*** (male) **chromosome** inherited from the father determines the child's sex; the *Y* chromosome triggers the release of **testosterone**. The resulting biological characteristics, along with socially influenced characteristics, determine the child's **gender**. During the next 6 weeks, the developing **embryo** begins to form body organs and by 9 weeks becomes a **fetus** that is recognizably human. Along with nutrients, **teratogens** ingested by the mother can reach the developing child and place it at risk for birth defects and mental retardation, as found in babies born with **fetal alcohol syndrome**.

2. ***What are some of the newborn's abilities?***

Researchers have discovered that newborns are surprisingly competent. They are born with sensory equipment and reflexes such as the **rooting reflex** that facilitate their interacting with adults and securing nourishment.

Infancy and Childhood

3. ***How do the brain and motor skills develop during infancy and childhood?***

Within the brain, nerve cells form before birth and, sculpted by experience, their interconnections continue to multiply after birth. Infants' more complex physical skills—sitting, standing, walking—develop in a predictable sequence whose actual timing is a function of individual **maturation** rate.

4. ***How did Piaget view the mind's development, and what are current researchers' views?***

Jean Piaget's observations of children convinced him—and almost everyone else—that the mind of a child is not that of a miniature adult. Piaget theorized that the mind develops by forming **schemas** that help us organize and interpret our experiences. In this way, children's **cognition** progresses from the **sensorimotor** simplicity of the infant to more complex stages of thinking. For example, by about 8 months, an infant develops **object permanence**.

Piaget believed that **preoperational** children are **egocentric** and unable to perform simple logical operations. However, he thought that at about age 6 or 7 children become capable of performing **concrete operations** such as those required to comprehend the principle of **conservation**. And by adolescence, most youth develop a capacity for more abstract, **formal operational** thinking. Recent research shows that young children are more capable, and development more continuous, than Piaget believed.

5. ***How do the bonds of attachment form, and with what effects later in life?***

Although the experiences of infancy are not consciously remembered for long and their effects may be reversed by later experiences, they can nevertheless have a lasting influence on social development. **Attachment** style in infancy predicts later social development. Infants become attached to their parents not simply because they gratify biological needs but, more important, because they are comfortable, familiar, and responsive. In many animals, this attachment process, called **imprinting**, occurs during a **critical period**. If denied responsive care, or if abused, both monkey and human infants may become pathetically withdrawn, anxious, and eventually abusive. Once an attachment forms, infants who are separated from their caregivers will, for a time, display **stranger anxiety**. Human infants who display secure attachment to their mothers—and thus develop a sense of **basic trust**—generally become socially competent preschoolers. Infants' differing attachment styles reflect both their individual **temperament** and their caregivers' responsiveness.

6. ***How do parenting styles and values vary among cultures?***

Decisions about child rearing involve value judgments about what traits to encourage in children. Cultural differences, such as between the communalism of Asian families and the individualism of Euro-American families, illustrate the impact of parental values.

7. ***What social influences help explain gender differences?***

Cultural socialization, through **social learning** and **gender schemas**, helps explain why some children have a stronger **gender identity** and become more **gender-typed** than others.

Adolescence

8. ***What major physical changes occur during adolescence?***

Adolescence begins at **puberty** with the onset of rapid growth and developing sexual maturity, and extends to adult independence. During this period, both **primary** and **secondary sex characteristics** develop dramatically. Girls, for example, experience **menarche** by about age 13. Boys seem to benefit from "early" maturation, girls from "late" maturation.

9. ***How did Piaget and Kohlberg describe cognitive and moral development during adolescence?***

Piaget theorized that adolescents develop the capacity for formal operations, which enables them to reason abstractly. However, most developmentalists now believe that the rudiments of logic appear earlier than Piaget believed.

Following Piaget's lead, Lawrence Kohlberg contended that moral thinking likewise proceeds through a sequence of stages, from a preconventional morality of self-interest, to a conventional morality concerned with gaining others' approval or doing one's duty, to (in some people) a postconventional morality of agreed-upon rights or universal ethical principles. But morality also lies in actions. Moreover, say Kohlberg's critics, the postconventional level represents the perspective of individualist, middle-class males.

10. ***What is involved in the adolescent's search for identity?***

Erik Erikson theorized that a chief task of adolescence is to form one's **identity**, or sense of self. This often means "trying on" a number of different roles. For many people the struggle for identity continues in the adult years as new relationships emerge—as the capacity for **intimacy** develops—and new roles are assumed.

11. ***Do males and females differ in their social relations?***

Males and females differ in their social connectedness. Boys define themselves apart from their caregivers and playmates, girls through their social ties. Women typically become more caring, empathic, and sensitive to nonverbal cues, and men more independent and self-reliant.

12. ***What factors influence teen pregnancy?***

Teens are vulnerable to pregnancy when ignorant or blindly optimistic about the risks of pregnancy, when inhibited from using birth control by guilt and minimal communication with parents and partners, and when under the influence of alcohol and mass media modeling of impulsive sex.

Adulthood

13. ***What major physical changes occur during middle and late adulthood?***

The barely perceptible physical declines of early adulthood begin to accelerate during middle adulthood. For women, a significant physical change of adult life is **menopause**. In men and women after 65, perceptual acuity, strength, and stamina decline, but short-term ailments such as colds and the flu are fewer. Neural processes slow, but the brain remains healthy, except for those who suffer brain disease, such as the progressive deterioration of **Alzheimer's disease**.

14. ***How are memory and intelligence influenced by aging?***

As the years pass, recall begins to decline, especially for meaningless information, but recognition memory remains strong. Research on how intelligence changes with age has progressed through several phases: **cross-sectional studies** suggesting a steady intellectual decline after early adulthood; **longitudinal studies** suggesting intellectual stability until very late in life; and today's view that **fluid intelligence** declines in later life but **crystallized intelligence** does not.

15. ***Why are age-based stage theories of adult development considered controversial?***

Several theorists maintain that adults progress through an orderly sequence of age-related stages. Erikson proposes that after the formation of an identity, the young adult must deal with intimacy, achieve generativity in middle adulthood, and gain a sense of integrity in later adulthood. Others contend that moving from one stage to the next entails recurring times of crisis. Critics contend that people are not so predictable, that the **social clock** is no longer fixed; life events influence adult development in unanticipated ways and vary with culture. Moreover, feelings of well-being are remarkably stable across the life span.

16. ***What do psychologists view as adulthood's two primary commitments?***

Adulthood's two major commitments are love (intimate relationships, especially with family) and work (productive activity, or what Erikson called "generativity").

Reflections on the Major Developmental Issues

17. ***What conclusions can we draw from research on the issues of continuity versus stages and of stability versus change?***

Although the stage theories of Piaget, Kohlberg, and Erikson have been modified in the light of later research, the theories usefully alert us to differences among people of different ages. The discovery that people's traits continue to change in later life has helped create the new emphasis that development is lifelong. Nevertheless, research demonstrates that there is also an underlying consistency in most people's temperament and personality traits, especially after infancy and early childhood.

CRITICAL THINKING EXERCISE by Richard O. Straub

Now that you have read and reviewed Chapter 3, take your learning a step further by testing your critical thinking skills on this creative problem-solving exercise.

Erik Erikson, whose psychosocial theory emphasizes each person's relationship to the social environment, identified eight important crises, or challenges, in life and, hence, eight stages of development. Each challenge can be resolved positively, in a growth-promoting way, or negatively, in a way that disrupts healthy development. Consider how the particular circumstances of a person's life might make it easier, or more difficult, for that individual to resolve each of Erikson's crises in a positive way. For example, in what ways is development harder for children with physical disabilities? Will these children need greater self-confidence simply because everyday tasks are more difficult? What about children who are gifted athletically? Will their talents be a stimulus to their emerging sense of competence? In what way is the search for identity different for today's teenagers than it was for their grandparents? What impact might a messy divorce, being laid off from work, or being a member of an ethnic minority have on a person's ability to meet the psychosocial challenges of adulthood?

For each of the following stages of the life span, briefly describe the psychosocial challenge proposed by Erikson. Then identify several ways in which a person's life circumstances might affect his or her ability to meet the challenge successfully. To stretch your creative imagination, try to identify developmental obstacles and supports from several different domains (biological, environmental, social, and so forth).

1. Infancy and toddlerhood
2. Preschool and elementary school years
3. Adolescence and young adulthood
4. Middle and late adulthood

Check your progress on becoming a critical thinker by comparing your answers with the sample answers found in Appendix B.

REHEARSE IT ANSWER KEY

1. b., **2.** d., **3.** c., **4.** a., **5.** a., **6.** b., **7.** c., **8.** b., **9.** d., **10.** d., **11.** a., **12.** b., **13.** b., **14.** c., **15.** c., **16.** b., **17.** c., **18.** b., **19.** d., **20.** c., **21.** d., **22.** b., **23.** b., **24.** d., **25.** c., **26.** a., **27.** d., **28.** c., **29.** d., **30.** c., **31.** b., **32.** b.

CHAPTER 4

Sensation and Perception

In the outer world, innumerable stimuli bombard your body. In a silent, cushioned, inner world of utter darkness floats your brain. These facts raise a question that predates psychology by thousands of years and helped inspire its beginnings a century ago: *How does the world out there get in?*

To modernize the question: How do we construct our representations of the external world? How do we represent a campfire's flicker, crackle, and smoky scent as patterns of active neural connections? And how from this living neurochemistry do we create our conscious experience of the fire's motion and temperature, its aroma and beauty?

To represent the world in our head, we must detect physical energy from the environment and encode it as neural signals, a process traditionally called **sensation**. And we must select, organize, and interpret our sensations, a process traditionally called **perception**. In our everyday experiences, sensation and perception blend into one continuous process. In this chapter, we slow down that process to study its parts.

We will start with the sensory receptors and work up to higher levels of processing. Psychologists refer to sensory analysis that starts at the entry level as **bottom-up processing**. Then we will focus on how our minds interpret what our senses detect. We construct perceptions drawing not only on sensations coming "up" to the brain but also on our experience and expectations, a process we call **top-down processing**.

Failures of perception may occur anywhere between sensory detection and perceptual interpretation. For example, the eyes of a person born with cataracts may be unable to detect light, rendering the brain's higher-level visual processing equipment useless. Brain-damaged patients reveal the importance of other links in the sensation-perception chain. After losing a temporal lobe area essential to recognizing faces, patient "E. H." suffers from a condition called *prosopagnosia*. She has complete sensation but incomplete perception. She can sense visual information—indeed may accurately report the features of a face—yet she cannot recognize it. Shown an unfamiliar face, she is unreactive. Shown a familiar face, her autonomic nervous system responds with measurable perspiration. Still, she hasn't a clue who the person is. Shown her own face in a mirror, she is again stumped. Because of her brain damage, she is unable to process top-down—she cannot relate her stored knowledge to the sensory input.

What's going on here? Our sensory and perceptual processes work together to help us sort out the complex images in this Bev Doolittle painting, "The Forest Has Eyes." Bottom-up processing enables our sensory systems to detect the lines, angles, and colors that form the horses, rider, and surroundings. Top-down processing causes us to consider the painting's title, notice the apprehensive expressions, and then direct our attention to aspects of the painting that will give those observations meaning. (Detail, "The Forest Has Eyes" by Bev Doolittle © The Greenwich Workshop, Inc., Irumbull, CT)

Sensing the World: Some Basic Principles

Consider how sensory systems inform organisms:

- A frog, which feeds on flying insects, has eyes with receptor cells that fire only in response to small, dark, moving objects. A frog could starve to death knee-deep in motionless flies. But let one zoom by and the frog's "bug detector" cells snap awake.
- A male silkworm moth has receptors so sensitive to the odor of the female sex-attractant that a single female silkworm moth need release only a billionth of an ounce per second to attract every male silkworm moth within a mile. Which is why there continue to be silkworms.
- We humans are similarly designed to detect what are, for us, the important features of our environments. Our ears are most sensitive to the sound frequencies of the human voice.

The shades on our senses are open just a crack, allowing us only a restricted awareness of the vast sea of energy that surrounds us.

Nature's sensory gifts suit each recipient's needs.

Thresholds

We exist in a sea of energy. At this moment, you and I are being struck by x-rays and radio waves, ultraviolet and infrared light, and sound waves of very high and very low frequencies. But to all of them we are blind and deaf. The shades on our senses are open just a crack, allowing us only a restricted awareness of this vast sea. **Psychophysics** is the study of how this physical energy relates to our psychological experience. What stimuli can we detect? At what intensity? How sensitive are we to changing stimulation?

sensation the process by which our sensory receptors and nervous system receive and represent stimulus energies from our environment.

perception the process of selecting, organizing, and interpreting sensory information, enabling us to recognize meaningful objects and events.

bottom-up processing analysis that begins with the sense receptors and works up to the brain's integration of sensory information.

top-down processing information processing guided by higher-level mental processes, as when we construct perceptions drawing on our experience and expectations.

psychophysics the study of relationships between the physical characteristics of stimuli, such as their intensity, and our psychological experience of them.

absolute threshold the minimum stimulation needed to detect a particular stimulus.

subliminal below one's absolute threshold for conscious awareness.

Absolute Thresholds

1. ***What is an absolute threshold, and are we influenced by stimuli below it?***

To some kinds of stimuli we are exquisitely sensitive. Standing atop a mountain on an utterly dark, clear night, we can, given normal senses, see a candle flame atop another mountain 30 miles away. In a silent room, we can hear a watch ticking 20 feet away. We can feel the wing of a bee falling on our cheek. We can smell a single drop of perfume in a three-room apartment (Galanter, 1962).

Our awareness of these faint stimuli illustrates our **absolute threshold**—the minimum stimulation necessary to detect a particular stimulus (light, sound, pressure, taste, odor). Psychologists usually measure absolute threshold by recording the stimulation needed for detection 50 percent of the time. To test your absolute threshold for sounds, a hearing specialist would expose each of your ears to varying sound levels. For each pitch, the hearing test defines where half the time you correctly detect the sound and half the time you do not. For each of the senses, that 50–50 point defines your absolute threshold.

Subliminal Stimulation

How to think uncritically without psychology: James Vicary, an unemployed marketing researcher, masterminded the EAT POPCORN subliminal advertising hoax with the help of uncritical reporters and broadcasters. Vicary reportedly collected big fees from advertising firms for his promised services—and then disappeared (Rogers, 1993, 1994).

In 1956, controversy erupted over a false report that New Jersey movie audiences were unwittingly being influenced by imperceptible flashed messages to DRINK COCA-COLA and EAT POPCORN (Pratkanis, 1992). Many years later, the controversy erupted anew. Advertisers were said to manipulate consumers by imperceptibly printing the word *sex* on crackers and by embedding erotic images in liquor ads. Rock recordings were said to contain "satanic messages" that could be heard if the recordings were played backwards and that, even when played in a forward direction, could unconsciously persuade the unwitting listener (see the Thinking Critically box).

"The heart has its reasons which reason does not know."

Blaise Pascal
Pensees
1670

In a more straightforward effort to trespass on our unconscious, entrepreneurs offer to help us lose weight, stop smoking, or improve our memories with audiotapes. These tapes contain soothing ocean sounds that mask unheard messages such as, "I am thin," "Smoke tastes bad," or "I do well on tests. I have total recall of information." Claims like these make two assumptions: that unconsciously we can sense **subliminal** (literally, "below threshold") stimuli (Figure 4.1), and that, without our awareness, these stimuli have extraordinary suggestive powers.

Can we be affected by stimuli too weak for us *ever* to notice? Recent experiments hint that, under certain conditions, the answer may be yes. One experiment subliminally flashed either emotionally positive scenes (such as kittens or a romantic couple) or negative scenes (such as a werewolf or a dead body) an instant before participants viewed slides of nine people (Krosnick & others, 1992). Although the participants consciously perceived only a flash of light, they gave more positive ratings to people whose photos had been associated with positive scenes. People somehow looked nicer if their photo immediately followed unperceived kittens rather than an unperceived werewolf. Chinese characters, too, seem nicer if preceded by a flashed but unperceived smiling face rather than a scowling face (Murphy & Zajonc, 1993). Sometimes we *feel* what we do not know and cannot describe. An imperceptibly brief stimulus evidently triggers a weak response that evokes a feeling, though not a conscious awareness of the stimulus.

Figure 4.1 Subliminal stimuli and absolute threshold Do I smell it or not? When stimuli are detectable less than 50 percent of the time they are "subliminal." Absolute threshold is the intensity at which we can detect a stimulus half the time.

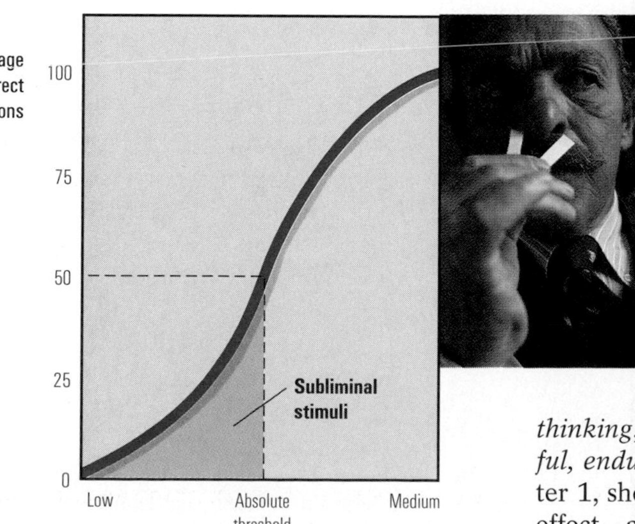

But does the fact of subliminal *sensation* verify entrepreneurial claims of subliminal *persuasion*? Can advertisers really manipulate us with "hidden persuasion"? The near-consensus among research psychologists is no. The laboratory research reveals a *subtle, fleeting* effect on *thinking*, but the subliminal tape hucksters claim something different: a *powerful, enduring* effect on *behavior*. Experiments, such as one described in Chapter 1, show that commercial subliminal tapes have no effect beyond a placebo effect—an effect of one's belief in them (Moore, 1988; Pratkanis & others, 1994; Smith & Rogers, 1994).

THINKING CRITICALLY

Unconscious Influence: Backward Messages in Rock Albums

The influences on how we think and act are often subtle, even unrecognized. Might it therefore be possible for unperceived backward messages, implanted on rock albums, to corrupt unwitting listeners? In the 1980s, concerns about such messages led to political efforts in the Canadian parliament and several U.S. states to contain the supposed powers of "backmasking."

Are such concerns warranted? Assuming that backward messages exist, could they have any influence? If indeed people are unconsciously influenced by a message they can't perceive, how might psychologists detect such influence?

Confronted with such questions and armed with the methods of psychological science, University of Lethbridge psychologists John Vokey and Don Read (1985) decided to investigate. They began by recording some simple sentences from Lewis Carroll's "Jabberwocky" and from the Twenty-third Psalm and then rerecorded them in reverse. This recording retained the pauses and pitches, producing a string of sounds rather like a foreign language.

But it was gibberish. Listeners could not detect whether a given word was or wasn't present, whether they had heard a declarative sentence or a question, or whether the sentence was meaningful or nonsensical. When simple messages such as "Jesus loves me, this I know" were played backward, people couldn't surpass chance when guessing whether the words were satanic, Christian, pornographic, advertising, or from a nursery rhyme.

Might meaningless backward information nevertheless have a subtle influence? Research psychologists have invented clever methods for uncovering such influences, including one that uses homophones—words that sound alike but differ in spelling and meaning. Imagine, for example, hearing the sentence, "Climbing a mountain is a remarkable *feat*." Later, even after you had forgotten the sentence, you would be more likely to spell the italicized word as f-e-a-t rather than f-e-e-t. This effect occurs without people realizing why they have chosen a particular spelling. But you must hear the homophone normally, not backward. When Vokey and Read buried the homophone in a backward message, the unconscious influence disappeared.

In continued quest of unconscious influence, Ian Begg and his McMaster University colleagues (1993) adapted "the illusory truth effect"—the tendency for repeated statements, such as "The most prevalent infection in the world today is cholera," to seem true. The phenomenon disappears, Begg and his colleagues found, when the statements are played backward.

So, once again, a popular idea collapsed when tested experimentally. Those concerned about backward messages in rock music can relax. Rock's influence doesn't leak through as messages played backward.

Shortly after news of the supposed EAT POPCORN effect swept North America, the Canadian Broadcasting Corporation used a popular Sunday night TV show to flash a subliminal message 352 times (*Advertising Age*, 1958). Asked to guess the message, none of the almost 500 letter-writers did so. Nearly half, however, did report feeling strangely hungry or thirsty during the show. But this was merely an effect of expectations. The actual message was TELEPHONE NOW. The effect of these 352 subliminal messages on Canadian telephone usage? Zilch.

Difference Thresholds

2. *How is our threshold for detecting differences affected by the magnitude of the stimuli?*

To function effectively, we need absolute thresholds low enough to allow us to detect important sights, sounds, textures, tastes, and smells. We also need to detect small differences among stimuli. A musician must detect minute discrepancies in an instrument's tuning. A wine taster must detect the slight flavor difference between two vintage wines. Parents must detect the sound of their own child's voice amid other children's voices.

The **difference threshold** (also called the *just noticeable difference*, or *jnd*) is the minimum difference a person can detect between any two stimuli 50 percent of the time. The difference threshold increases with the magnitude of the stimulus. Thus, if you add 10 grams to a 100-gram weight, you will detect the difference; add 10 grams to a 1-*kilogram* weight and you will not, be-

The LORD is my shepherd;
I shall not want.
He maketh me to lie down
in green pastures:
he leadeth me
beside the still waters.
He restoreth my soul:
he leadeth me
in the paths of righteousness
for his name's sake.
Yea, though I walk through the valley
of the shadow of death,
I will fear no evil:
for thou art with me;
thy rod and thy staff
they comfort me.
Thou preparest a table before me
in the presence of mine enemies:
thou anointest my head with oil,
my cup runneth over.
Surely goodness and mercy
shall follow me
all the days of my life:
and I will dwell
in the house of the LORD
for ever.

The difference threshold In this computer-generated copy of the Twenty-third Psalm, each line of the typeface changes imperceptibly. How many lines are required for you to experience a just noticeable difference?

difference threshold the minimum difference that a person can detect between two stimuli 50 percent of the time. We experience the difference threshold as a just noticeable difference. (Also called *just noticeable difference* or *jnd*.)

Weber's law the principle that, for a difference to be perceived, two stimuli must differ by a constant minimum percentage (rather than a constant amount).

sensory adaptation diminished sensitivity as a consequence of constant stimulation.

cause the difference threshold has increased. More than a century ago, Ernst Weber noted that regardless of their magnitude, two stimuli must differ by a constant proportion for their difference to be perceptible. This principle—that the difference threshold is not a constant amount but some constant *proportion* of the stimulus—is so simple and so widely applicable that we still refer to it as **Weber's law**. The exact proportion varies, depending on the stimulus. For the average person to perceive their differences, two lights must differ in intensity by at least 8 percent. Two objects must differ in weight by at least 2 percent. And two tones must differ in frequency by only 0.3 percent (Teghtsoonian, 1971).

Weber's law is a rough approximation that works well for nonextreme sensory stimuli. It also parallels some of our life experiences. If the price of a 50-cent chocolate bar goes up by 5 cents, shoppers might notice the change; similarly, it might take a $5000 price hike in a $50,000 Mercedes to raise the eyebrows of its potential buyers. In both cases, the price went up by 10 percent. Weber's principle: Our thresholds for detecting differences are a roughly constant proportion of the size of the original stimulus.

Sensory Adaptation

3. *What function does sensory adaptation serve?*

Entering your neighbor's living room, you smell an unpleasant odor. You wonder how she tolerates the stench, but within minutes you no longer notice it. Jumping into a swimming pool, you shiver and complain how cold it is. A short while later a friend arrives and you exclaim, "C'mon in. Water's fine!" These examples illustrate **sensory adaptation**—our diminishing sensitivity to an unchanging stimulus. (To experience this phenomenon, move your watch up your wrist an inch: You will feel it—but only for a few moments.) After constant exposure to a stimulus, our nerve cells fire less frequently.

"We need above all to know about changes; no one wants or needs to be reminded 16 hours a day that his shoes are on."

Neuroscientist David Hubel (1979)

Why, then, if we stare at an object without flinching, does it not vanish from sight? Because, unnoticed by us, our eyes are always moving, quivering just enough to guarantee that retinal stimulation continually changes.

For 9 in 10 people—but, curiously, for only 1 in 3 schizophrenia patients—this eye flutter turns off when the eye is following a moving target (Holzman & Matthysse, 1990).

What if we could stop our eyes from moving? Would sights seem to vanish? To find out, psychologists have devised ingenious instruments for maintaining a constant image on the retina. Imagine that we fitted a volunteer, Mary, with one of these instruments—a miniature projector mounted on a contact lens. When Mary's eye moves, the image from the projector moves as well. Thus, everywhere that Mary looks the scene is sure to go.

"My suspicion is that the universe is not only queerer than we suppose, but queerer than we can suppose."

J. B. S. Haldane
Possible Worlds
1927

If we project the profile of a face through such an instrument, what will Mary see? At first she will see the complete profile. But within a few seconds, as her sensory receptors begin to fatigue, things get weird. Bit by bit, the image vanishes, only later to reappear and then disappear—in recognizable fragments or as a whole.

Although sensory adaptation reduces our sensitivity, it offers an important benefit: It enables us to focus our attention on *informative* changes in our environment without being distracted by the uninformative constant stimulation of garments, odors, and street noise. Our sensory receptors are alert to novelty; bore them with repetition and they free our attention for more important things. This reinforces a fundamental lesson: We perceive the world not exactly as it is, but as it is useful for us to perceive it.

Our sensory receptors are alert to novelty; bore them with repetition and they free our attention for more important things.

Sensory thresholds and adaptation are not the only commonalities among the senses. All the senses receive sensory stimulation, transform it into neural information, and deliver that information to the brain. How do the senses work? How do we see? Hear? Smell? Taste? Feel pain? Let's start with vision, the sense people tend to prize the most.

REHEARSE IT!

1. To construct meaning out of our external environment, we select, organize, and interpret sensory information. This is the process of
   a. sensation.
   b. persuasion.
   c. encoding.
   d. perception.
2. Sensation is to __________ as perception is to __________.
   a. absolute threshold; difference threshold
   b. bottom-up processing; top-down processing
   c. interpretation; detection
   d. conscious awareness; persuasion
3. The absolute threshold is the minimum stimulation that a person can detect 50 percent of the time. Knowing your absolute threshold for sound tells you
   a. the smallest difference you can detect between two sounds.
   b. how likely you are to hear a particular faint sound.
   c. why you become used to background noise.
   d. whether you are being affected by subliminal stimulation.
4. People wonder whether subliminal stimuli, such as undetectably faint sights or sounds, influence us. Subliminal stimuli are
   a. too weak to be processed by the brain in any way.
   b. consciously perceived only 50 percent of the time.
   c. strong enough to affect our behavior.
   d. below the absolute threshold for conscious awareness.
5. To be perceived as different, two lights must differ in intensity by at least 8 percent. This illustrates a general principle called Weber's law, which states that for a difference to be perceived, two stimuli must differ by
   a. a fixed or constant amount.
   b. a constant minimum percentage.
   c. a constantly changing amount.
   d. more than 7 percent.
6. Confronted with an unchanging stimulus, we experience sensory adaptation. Sensory adaptation explains why we
   a. perceive subliminal stimuli.
   b. notice only large differences between two stimuli.
   c. soon get used to an unpleasant smell.
   d. have difficulty keeping our eyes completely still when staring at an object.
7. Sensory adaptation reduces our sensitivity to some stimuli in the environment. However, sensory adaptation has survival benefits. It helps us focus on
   a. the world as it really is.
   b. underlying phenomena and stimuli.
   c. constant features of the environment.
   d. important changes in the environment.

Vision

"The most commonplace crime is often the most mysterious. . . . Life is infinitely stranger than anything which the mind of man could invent."

Sherlock Holmes
In Arthur Conan Doyle's *A Study in Scarlet*
1888

Part of your taken-for-granted genius is your body's ability to convert one sort of energy to another. Our sensory systems convert stimulus energy into neural messages. Your eyes, for example, receive light energy and manage an amazing feat: They transduce (transform) the energy into neural messages that the brain processes into what you consciously see. Let's consider how that happens.

The Stimulus Input: Light Energy

4. How does the eye transform light energy into neural messages?

Scientifically speaking, what strikes our eyes is not color but pulses of electromagnetic energy that our visual system experiences as color. What we see as visible light is but a thin slice of the whole spectrum of electromagnetic radiation. As Figure 4.2 illustrates, this *electromagnetic spectrum* ranges from the imperceptibly short pulses or waves of gamma rays to the narrow band that we see as visible light to the long waves of radio transmission.

Two physical characteristics of light (and sound) help determine our sensory experience of them. Light's **wavelength**—the distance from one wave peak to the next (Figure 4.3a)—determines its **hue** (the color we experience, such as blue or green). **Intensity**, the amount of energy in light waves (determined by a wave's *amplitude*, or height), influences brightness (Figure 4.3b). To understand *how* we transform physical energy into a sensation of color, we first need to understand our mind's window, the eye.

wavelength the distance from the peak of one light or sound wave to the peak of the next. Electromagnetic wavelengths vary from the short blips of cosmic rays to the long pulses of radio transmission.

hue the dimension of color that is determined by the wavelength of light.

intensity the amount of energy in a light or sound wave, which we perceive as brightness or loudness, as determined by the wave's amplitude.

accommodation the process by which the eye's lens changes shape to focus the image of objects on the retina.

retina the light-sensitive inner surface of the eye, containing the receptor rods and cones plus layers of neurons that begin the processing of visual information.

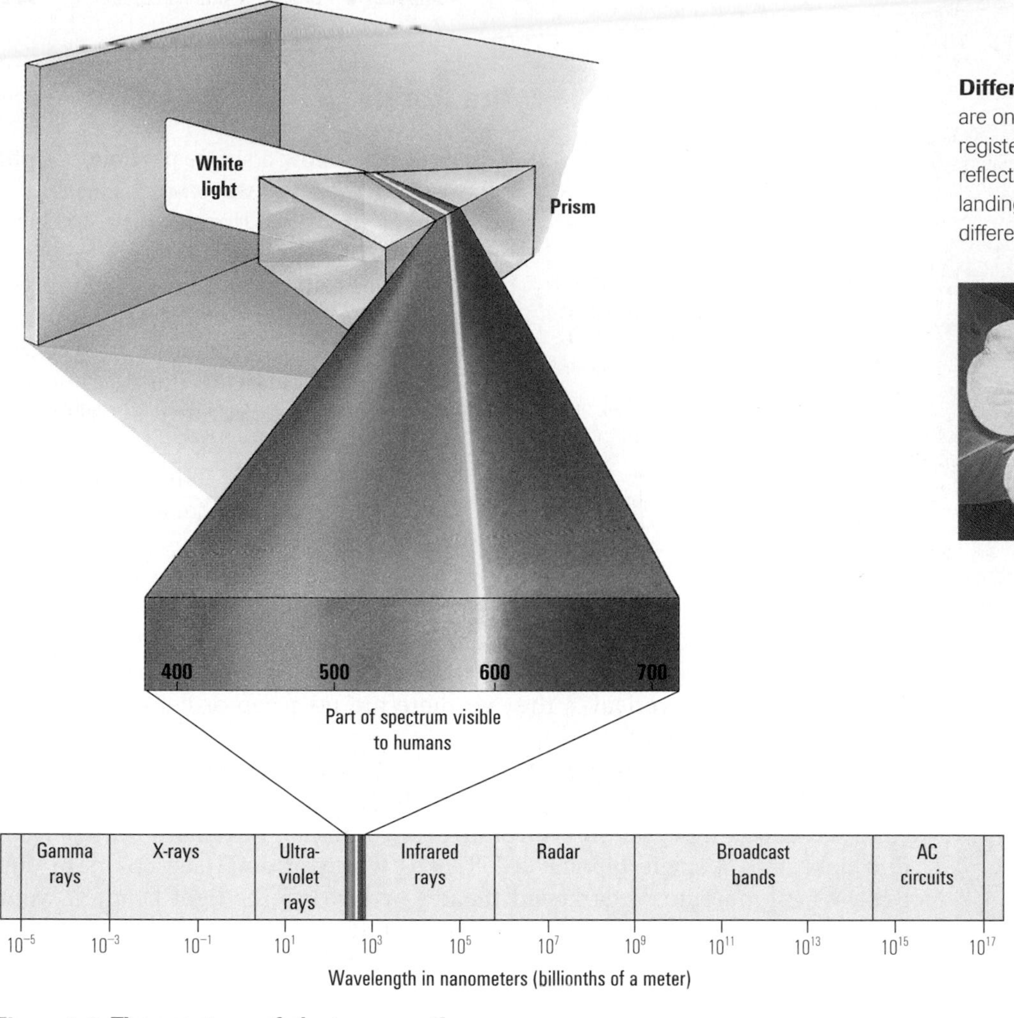

Figure 4.2 The spectrum of electromagnetic energy This spectrum ranges from gamma rays as short as the diameter of an atom to radio waves over a mile long. The narrow band of wavelengths visible to the human eye (shown enlarged) extends from the shorter waves of blue-violet light to the longer waves of red light. Other organisms are sensitive to differing portions of the spectrum. For instance, bees cannot see red but can see ultraviolet light (see photos).

Differing eyes When it comes to vision, humans and bees are on a different wavelength. Compare the way a flower is registered by a human's and a bee's eye. The bee detects reflected ultraviolet wavelengths, enabling it to see the pollen landing field. The differing ecological niches occupied by different species demand sensitivity to different stimuli.

Human Eye

Bee's Eye

The Eye

Light enters the eye through the *cornea*, a transparent protector, then travels through the *pupil*, a small adjustable opening (Figure 4.4, page 132). The pupil's size, and therefore the amount of light entering the eye, is regulated by the *iris*, a colored muscle surrounding the pupil. Behind the pupil is a *lens* that focuses the incoming rays into an image on a light-sensitive surface. It does so by changing its curvature in a process called **accommodation**. The eyeball's light-sensitive surface on which the rays focus is the **retina**, a multilayered tissue.

For centuries, scientists have known that when the image of a candle passes through a small opening, its mirror image appears inverted on a dark wall behind (as in Figure 4.4). This fact had scholars baffled. If the retina receives an upside-down image, how can we see the world right side up?

Eventually scientists discovered that the retina doesn't read the image as a whole. Rather, its millions of receptor cells convert light energy into neural impulses. These impulses are sent to the brain and constructed *there* into a perceived, upright-seeming image.

Figure 4.3 The physical properties of waves (a) Waves vary in wavelength, the distance between successive peaks. Frequency, the number of complete wavelengths that can pass a point in a given time, depends on the wavelength. The shorter the wavelength, the higher the frequency. **(b)** Waves also vary in amplitude, the height from peak to trough. Wave amplitude determines the intensity of colors and sounds.

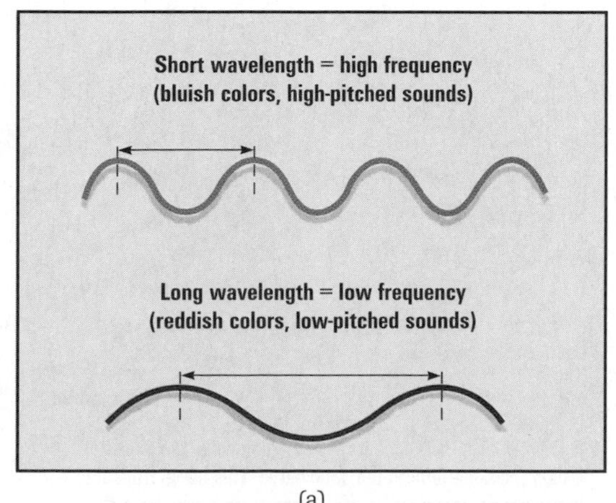

(a)

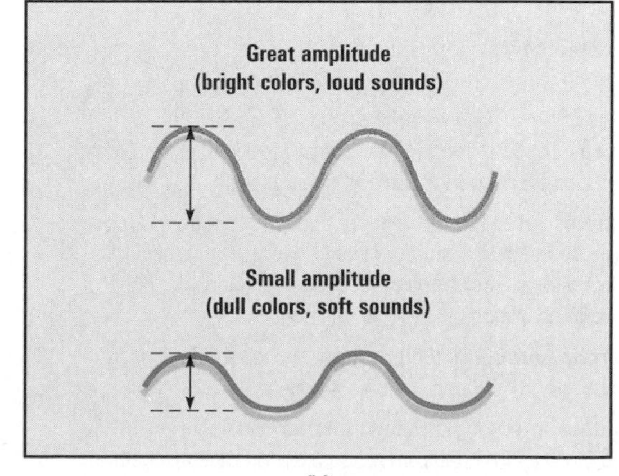

(b)

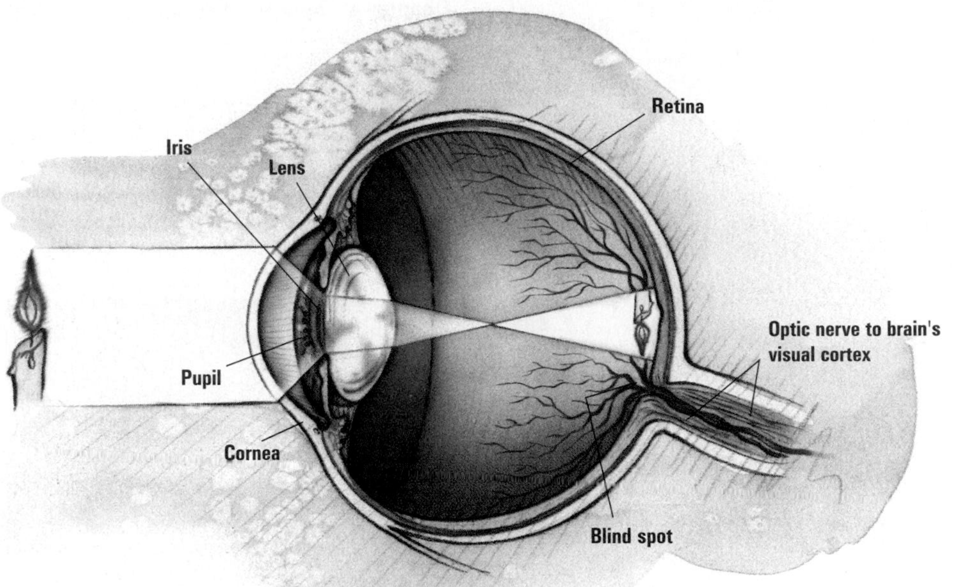

Figure 4.4 **The eye** Light rays reflected from the candle pass through the cornea, pupil, and lens. The curvature and thickness of the lens change to bring either nearby or distant objects into focus on the retina. Light rays travel in straight lines. So rays from the top of the candle strike the bottom of the retina and those from the left side of the candle strike the right side of the retina. The candle's retinal image is thus upside-down and reversed.

Knowing just this much about the eye, can you imagine why a cat sees so much better at night than you do? (See p. 134.)

The Retina

If we were to follow a single particle of light energy into the eye, we would see that it first makes its way through the retina's outer layer of cells to its buried receptor cells, the **rods** and **cones** (Figure 4.5). Light energy striking the rods and cones produces chemical changes that generate neural signals. These signals activate the neighboring *bipolar cells*, which in turn activate the neighboring *ganglion cells*. The axons from the network of ganglion cells converge like the strands of a rope to form an **optic nerve** that carries information to the brain. Nearly a million messages can be sent by the optic nerve at once, through nearly 1 million ganglion fibers. (The auditory nerve, which enables hearing, carries much less information through its mere 30,000 fibers.) Where the optic nerve leaves the eye there are no receptor cells—creating a **blind spot** (Figure 4.6).

Rods enable black-and-white vision; cones enable you to see color. As illumination diminishes, the cones become ineffectual. The rods, however, remain sensitive in dim light, because several rods will funnel their faint energy from dim light onto a single bipolar cell. That is why you don't see colors in dim light. When you enter a darkened theater or turn off the light at night, your pupils dilate to allow more light to reach the rods in the retina's periphery. Typically it takes 20 minutes or more before our eyes fully adapt.

Figure 4.5 **The retina's reaction to light**

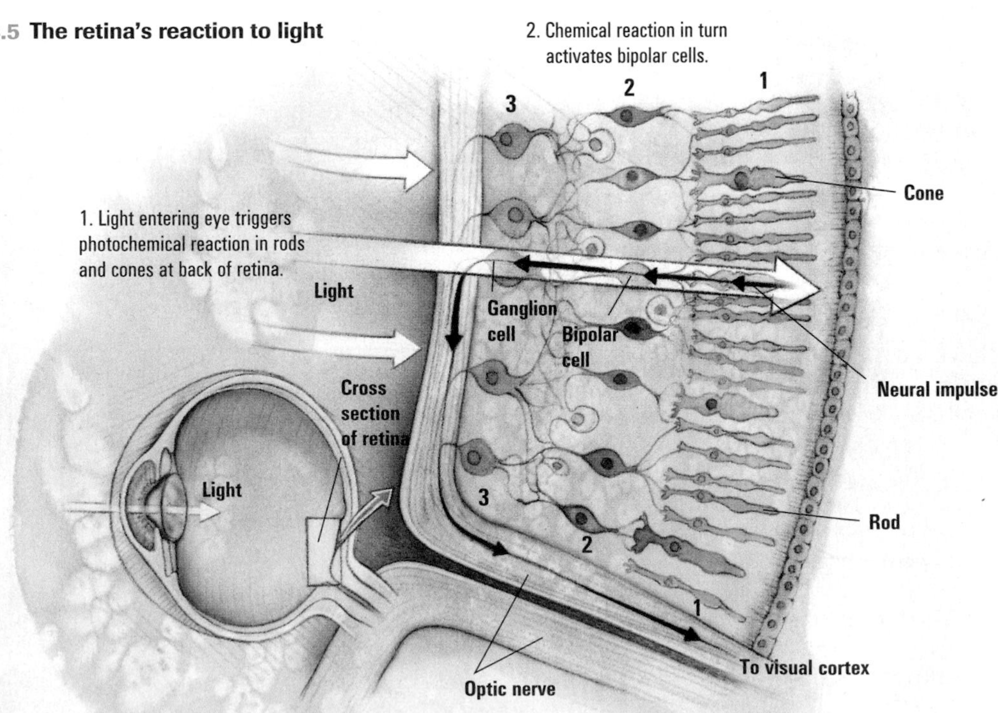

rods retinal receptors that detect black, white, and gray; necessary for peripheral and twilight vision.

cones receptor cells that are concentrated near the center of the retina and that function in daylight or in well-lit conditions. The cones detect fine detail and give rise to color sensations.

optic nerve the nerve that carries neural impulses from the eye to the brain.

blind spot the point at which the optic nerve leaves the eye, creating a "blind" spot because no receptor cells are located there.

Rod-shaped rods and cone-shaped cones As the scanning electron microscope shows, rods and cones are well named. Rods are more sensitive to light than are the color-sensitive cones, which is why the world looks colorless at night. Some nocturnal animals, such as toads, mice, rats, and bats, have retinas made up almost entirely of rods, allowing them to function well in dim light. These creatures probably have very poor color vision.

Receptors in the Human Eye

	Cones	Rods
Number	6 million	120 million
Location in retina	Center	Periphery
Sensitivity in dim light	Low	High
Color sensitive?	Yes	No

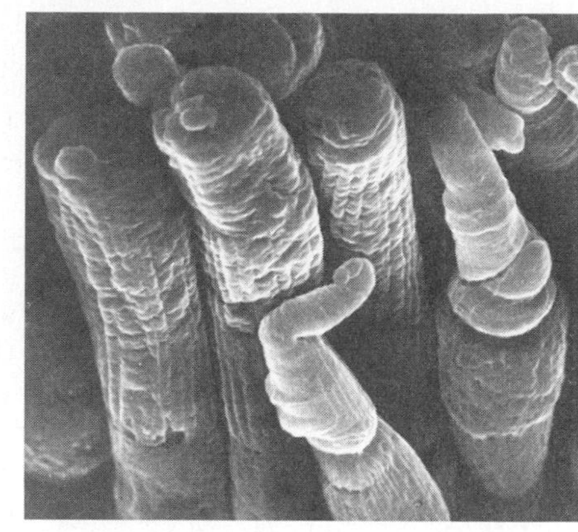

Turn your eyes to the left, close them, and then gently rub the right side of your right eyelid with your fingertip. Note the patch of light to the left, moving as your finger moves. Why do you see light? Why at the left? (See p. 134.)

You can demonstrate *dark adaptation* by closing or covering one eye for up to 20 minutes, then making the room light not quite bright enough to read this book with your open eye. Now open the dark-adapted eye and read. This period of dark adaptation is yet another instance of the remarkable adaptiveness of our sensory systems, for it parallels the average natural twilight transition between the sun's setting and darkness.

Figure 4.6 The blind spot Where the optic nerve leaves the eye (Figure 4.5), there are no receptor cells. This creates a blind spot in our vision. To demonstrate, close your left eye, look at the spot, and move the page to a distance from your face (about a foot) at which the car disappears. In everyday vision the blind spot doesn't impair your vision because your eyes are moving and because one eye catches what the other misses.

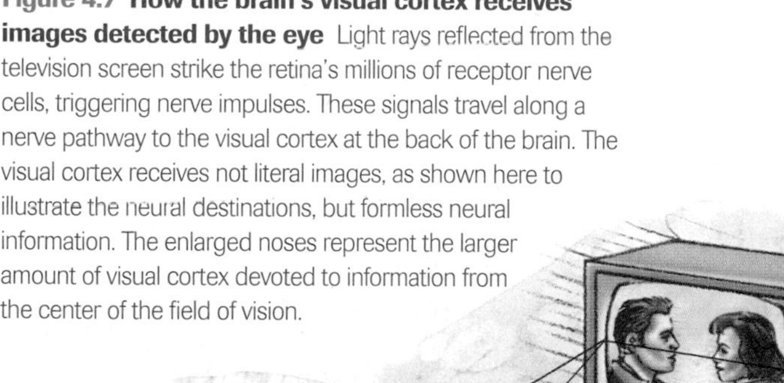

Figure 4.7 How the brain's visual cortex receives images detected by the eye Light rays reflected from the television screen strike the retina's millions of receptor nerve cells, triggering nerve impulses. These signals travel along a nerve pathway to the visual cortex at the back of the brain. The visual cortex receives not literal images, as shown here to illustrate the neural destinations, but formless neural information. The enlarged noses represent the larger amount of visual cortex devoted to information from the center of the field of vision.

Visual Information Processing

5. How is visual information processed in the brain?

Visual information percolates through progressively more abstract levels. At the entry level, the retina's neural layers are not just passing along electrical impulses; they also help to encode and analyze the sensory information before routing it to the cortex. The information from the retina's nearly 130 million receptor rods and cones is received and transmitted by the million or so ganglion cells, whose fibers make up the optic nerve. But most information processing occurs in the brain. Any given area of the retina relays its information to a corresponding location in the visual cortex at the back of the brain (**Figure 4.7**).

Feature Detection

When individual ganglion cells register information in their region of the visual field, they send signals to the visual cortex. Nobel prize winners David Hubel and Torsten Wiesel (1979) demonstrated that when certain cortical neurons,

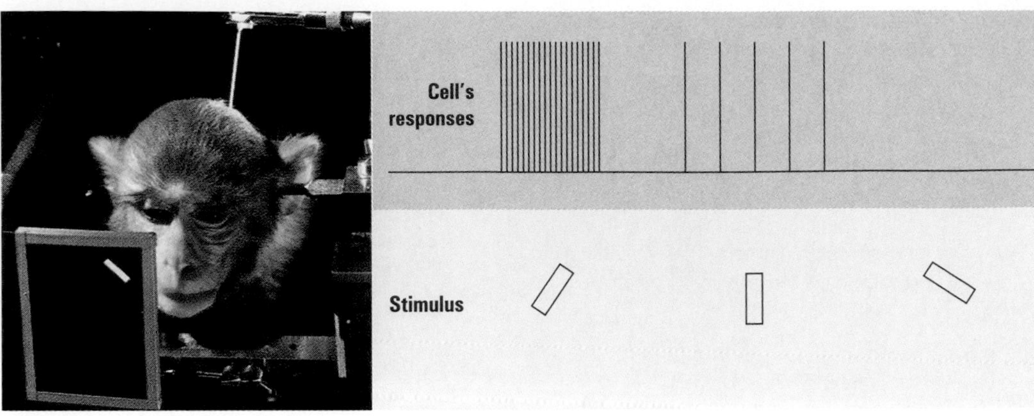

Figure 4.8 **Electrodes record how individual cells in this monkey's visual cortex respond to different visual stimuli** Hubel and Wiesel won the Nobel prize for their discovery that most cells in the visual cortex respond only to particular features—for example, to the edge of a surface or to a line at a 30-degree angle in the upper right part of the field of vision. More complex features trigger higher-level detector cells, which integrate information from these simpler ones.

Going left or right? In the semifinal game of the 1996 European Cup, German goalie Andreas Kopke anticipates the direction of Gareth Southgate's tiebreaker kick for England. Before Southgate's foot connects with the ball, Kopke's visual system has processed information from Southgate's eyes, posture, and movement, activating "going right" supercells. Kopke blocks the kick and Germany wins.

called **feature detectors**, receive this information, they respond to specific features of a scene—to particular edges, lines, angles, and movements. From these elements the brain assembles the perceived image.

For example, Hubel and Wiesel report that a given brain cell might respond maximally to a line flashed at a 2 o'clock tilt (Figure 4.8). If the line is tilted further—say, to a 3 o'clock or 1 o'clock position—the cell quiets down. Thus, the feature detector cells record amazingly specific features taken in by the eye. Feature detector cells pass this information to other cells that respond only to more complex patterns. The basic idea is that perceptions arise from the interaction of many neuron systems, each performing a simple task.

The visual cortex passes this information along to the temporal and parietal cortex, which includes higher-level brain cells that respond to specific visual scenes, such as a face or an arm movement in a particular direction. Psychologist David Perrett and his colleagues (1988, 1992, 1994) report that for biologically important objects and events, monkey brains (and surely ours as well) have a "vast visual encyclopedia" distributed as cells that respond to one stimulus but not to others. Perrett has identified nerve cells that specialize in responding to a specific gaze, head angle, posture, or body movement. Other supercell clusters integrate this information and fire only when the cues collectively indicate the direction of someone's attention and approach. This instant analysis, which aided our ancestors' survival, also helps a goalie anticipate the direction of an impending soccer kick and a pedestrian anticipate another pedestrian's next movement.

Answer to question on p. 132: There are at least two reasons: A cat's pupils can open much wider than yours, letting in more light; and a cat has a higher proportion of light-sensitive rods (Moser, 1987). But there is a trade-off: With fewer cones, a cat can't see details or color as well as you do.

Answer to question on p. 134: Your retinal cells are so responsive that even pressure triggers them. But your brain interprets their firing as light. Moreover, it interprets the light as coming from the left—where light normally comes from when it activates the right side of the retina.

Parallel Processing

Neural impulses travel a million times slower than a computer's internal messages, yet the brain humbles any computer by recognizing a familiar face instantly. Unlike most computers, which do step-by-step serial processing, our brains engage in **parallel processing**, which means we can do several things at once. The brain divides a visual scene into subdimensions such as color, depth, movement, and form and works on each aspect simultaneously (Livingstone & Hubel, 1988).

The distribution of visual tasks to different neural work teams explains a strange phenomenon. After a stroke, people may lose just one aspect of vision. A person may perceive color but not movement. If something moves, it disappears until it stops. Other brain-damaged patients can tell you all about the subdimensions of an object or person (a rose's color or a woman's height) but cannot name the object or the person. This reminds us once again of the startling truth: Our brains do many things at once, automatically and without our awareness.

Senses other than vision also process information with similar speed and intricacy. Opening the back door, you recognize the aroma wafting from the

Parallel processing Studies of brain-damaged patients suggest that the brain delegates the work of processing color, motion, form, and depth to different areas. After taking a scene apart, how does the brain integrate these subdimensions into the perceived image? The answer to this question is the Holy Grail of vision research.

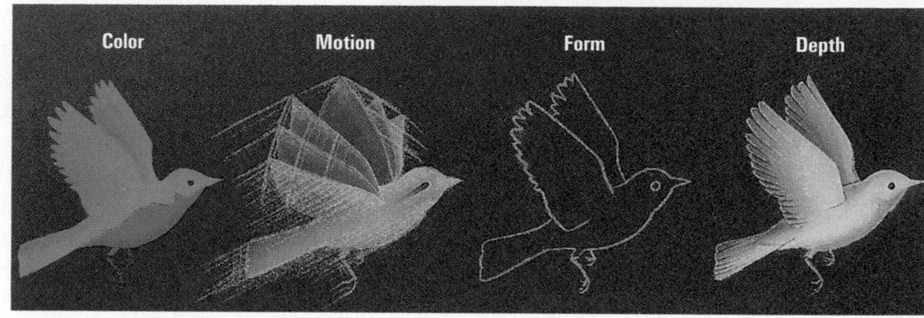

"I am fearfully and wonderfully made."

King David
Psalms 139:14

kitchen even before you step inside. Answering the phone, you recognize the friend calling from the moment she says "Hi." Within a fraction of a second after such events stimulate the senses, millions of neurons have simultaneously coordinated in extracting the essential features, comparing them with past experience, and identifying the stimulus (Freeman, 1991).

This scientific understanding of sensory information processing illustrates neuropsychologist Roger Sperry's (1985) reflection: The "insights of science give added, not lessened, reasons for awe, respect, and reverence." Think about it: As you look at someone, the visual information is sent to your brain as millions of neural impulses, then constructed into its component features, and finally, in some as yet mysterious way, composed into a meaningful perceived image, which is then compared with previously stored images and recognized as, for example, your grandmother. The whole process (Figure 4.9) is as complex as taking a car apart, piece by piece, transporting it to a different location, then having specialized workers reconstruct it. That all of this happens instantly, effortlessly, and continuously is indeed awesome.

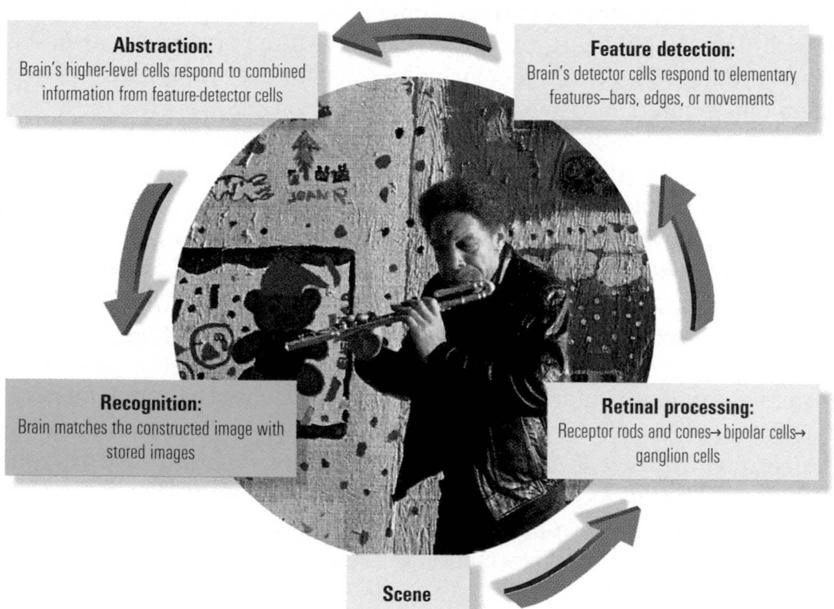

Figure 4.9 **A simplified summary of visual information processing**

Color Vision

6. What theories contribute to our understanding of color vision, and how are we affected by color constancy?

People talk as though objects possess color. We say, "The tomato is red." Perhaps you have pondered the old question, "If a tree falls in the forest and no one hears it, does it make a sound?" We can ask the same of color: If no one sees the tomato, is it red?

The answer is no. First, the tomato is everything *but* red, because it *rejects* (reflects) the long wavelengths of red. Second, the tomato's color is our mental construction. As Isaac Newton (1704) noted, "The [light] rays are not coloured." Color, like all aspects of vision, resides not in the object but in the theater of our brains. Even while dreaming, we may perceive things in color.

In the study of vision, one of the most basic and intriguing mysteries is how we see the world in color. How, from the light energy striking the retina, does the brain manufacture our experience of color—and of such a multitude of colors? Our difference threshold for colors is so low that we can discriminate some 7 million different color variations (Geldard, 1972).

"Only mind has sight and hearing; all things else are deaf and blind."

Epicharmus
Fragments
550 B.C.

feature detectors nerve cells in the brain that respond to specific features of the stimulus, such as shape, angle, or movement.

parallel processing processing several aspects of a problem simultaneously; the brain's natural mode of information processing for many functions, including vision.

Figure 4.10 **The three primary colors of light** The primary colors of light mix to create other colors. For example, red and green combine to create yellow. All three—red, green, and blue—combine to create white.

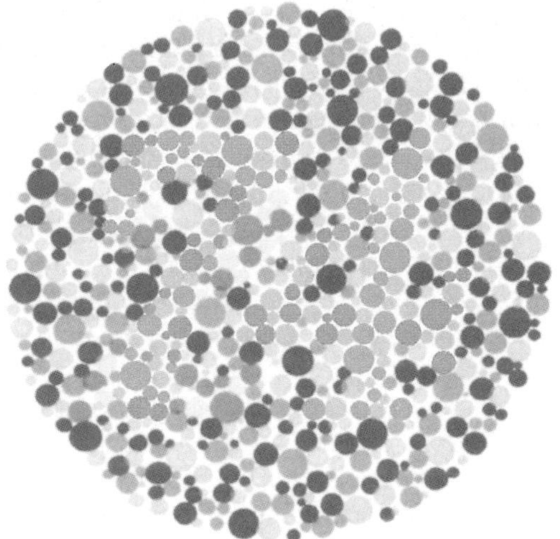

Figure 4.11 **Color-deficient vision** People who suffer red-green blindness have trouble perceiving the number within the design.

"Is it not stirring to understand how the world actually works—that white light is made of colors, that color measures light waves, that transparent air reflects light . . . ? It does no harm to the romance of the sunset to know a little about it."

Carl Sagan, *Skies of Other Worlds*, 1988

At least most of us can. For about 1 person in 50, vision is color-deficient—and that person is usually male, because the defect is genetically sex-linked. To understand why some people have color-deficient vision, we must first understand how normal color vision works.

Modern detective work on the mystery of color vision began in the nineteenth century when Hermann von Helmholtz built on the insights of an English physicist, Thomas Young. Young and Helmholtz recognized that any color can be created by combining the light waves of three primary colors—red, green, and blue (Figure 4.10). So, they inferred that the eye must have three types of receptors, one for each primary color of light.

Many years later, researchers measured the response of various cones to different color stimuli and confirmed the **Young-Helmholtz trichromatic (three-color) theory**, which simply states that the retina has three types of color receptors, each especially sensitive to one of three colors. And surprise! Those colors are, indeed, red, green, or blue. When we stimulate combinations of these cones, we see other colors. For example, there are no receptors especially sensitive to yellow. Yet when both red- and green-sensitive cones are stimulated, we see yellow.

Most color-deficient people are not actually "colorblind." Rather, they simply lack functioning red- or green-sensitive cones. Their vision is dichromatic instead of trichromatic, making it difficult to distinguish red and green, as in Figure 4.11 (Boynton, 1979). Dogs, too, lack receptors for the wavelengths of red, giving them only limited, dichromatic color vision (Neitz & others, 1989).

Soon after Young and Helmholtz proposed the trichromatic theory, physiologist Ewald Hering pointed out that other parts of the color vision mystery remained unsolved. For example, we see yellow when mixing red and green light. But how is it that those blind to red and green can often still see yellow? And why does yellow appear to be a pure color and not a mixture of red and green, as purple does of red and blue?

Hering found a clue in the well-known occurrence of *afterimages*. When you stare at a green square for a while and then look at a white sheet of paper, you see red, green's *opponent color*. Stare at a yellow square and you will later see its opponent color, blue, on the white paper (as in the flag demonstration in Figure 4.12). Hering surmised that there were two additional color processes, one responsible for red versus green perception, and one for blue versus yellow.

A century later, researchers confirmed Hering's **opponent-process theory**. *After* leaving the receptor cells, visual information is analyzed in terms of the opponent colors red and green, blue and yellow, and also black and white. In the retina and in the thalamus (where impulses from the retina are relayed en route to the visual cortex) some neurons are turned "on" by red but turned "off" by green. Others are turned on by green but off by red (DeValois & DeValois, 1975). Opponent processes explain afterimages, such as in the flag demonstration, in which we tire our green response by staring at green. When we then stare at white (which contains all colors, including red), only the red part of the green/red pairing will fire normally.

The present solution to the mystery of color vision is therefore roughly this: Color processing occurs in two stages. The retina's red, green, and blue cones respond in varying degrees to different color stimuli, as the Young-Helmholtz trichromatic theory suggested. Their signals are then processed by the nervous system's opponent-process cells, en route to the visual cortex.

Young-Helmholtz trichromatic (three-color) theory the theory that the retina contains three different color receptors—one most sensitive to red, one to green, one to blue—which when stimulated in combination can produce the perception of any color.

opponent-process theory the theory that opposing retinal processes (red-green, yellow-blue, white-black) enable color vision. For example, some cells are stimulated by green and inhibited by red; others are stimulated by red and inhibited by green.

color constancy perceiving familiar objects as having consistent color, even if changing illumination alters the wavelengths reflected by the object.

Color Constancy

Our experience of color depends on something more than the wavelength information received by our trichromatic cones and transmitted through the opponent-process cells.

That something more is the surrounding *context*. If you view only part of a tomato, its color will seem to change as the light changes. But if you see the

Figure 4.12 Afterimage effect Stare at the center of the flag for a minute and then shift your eyes to the dot in the white space beside it. What do you see? (After tiring your neural response to black, green, and yellow, you should see their opponent colors.)

Figure 4.13 Color depends on context In this painting by Joseph Albers (1975), the unchanging line seems to vary from gray to yellow as its surrounding context changes.

whole tomato as one item in a bowl of fresh vegetables, its color will remain roughly constant as the lighting and wavelengths shift—a phenomenon known as **color constancy**. Dorothea Jameson (1985) notes that a chip colored blue under indoor lighting matches the wavelengths reflected by a gold chip in the sunlight. Yet bring a bluebird indoors and it won't look like a goldfinch. Likewise, a green leaf hanging from a brown branch may, when the illumination changes, now reflect the same light energy that formerly came from the brown branch. Yet to us the leaf stays greenish and the branch stays brownish. Put on yellow-tinted ski goggles and the snow, after a second, looks as white as before.

We take this color constancy for granted, but the phenomenon is remarkable. It demonstrates that our experience of color comes not just from the object—the color is not in the isolated leaf—but from everything around it as well. You and I see color thanks to our brains' computations of the light reflected by any object *relative to its surrounding objects*.

In an unvarying context, we maintain color constancy. But what if we change the context? Because the brain computes the color of an object relative to its context, the perceived color changes (as is dramatically apparent in Figure 4.13). This principle—that we perceive objects not in isolation but in their environmental context—is especially significant for artists, interior decorators, and clothing designers. The perceived color of a wall or of a swatch of paint on a canvas is determined not just by the paint in the can but by the surrounding colors.

REHEARSE IT!

8. Two physical characteristics of light help determine our sensory experience of it. The characteristic that determines the color we experience is

a. intensity. **b.** wavelength. **c.** amplitude. **d.** hue.

9. The blind spot is located in the area of the retina in which

a. there are rods but no cones.
b. there are cones but no rods.
c. the optic nerve leaves the eye.
d. the bipolar cells meet the ganglion cells.

10. Rods and cones are the eye's receptor cells. Cones are especially sensitive to __________ light and are responsible for our __________ vision.

a. bright; black-and-white **b.** dim; color **c.** bright; color **d.** dim; black-and-white

11. According to Hubel and Wiesel, the brain includes cells that respond maximally to certain bars, edges, and movements. These cells are called

a. rods and cones. **b.** feature detector cells. **c.** bug detectors. **d.** ganglion cells.

12. Unlike most computers, the brain is capable of simultaneously processing separate aspects of an object or problem. We call this ability

a. parallel processing. **b.** feature detection. **c.** recognition. **d.** accommodation.

13. Researchers today believe that the Young-Helmholtz and Hering theories together account for color vision. The Young-Helmholtz theory shows that the eye contains __________ and the Hering theory accounts for the brain having __________.

a. opposing retinal processes; three pairs of color receptors
b. opponent-process cells; three types of color receptors
c. three pairs of color receptors; opposing retinal processes
d. three types of color receptors; opponent-process cells

14. We perceive tomatoes and stringbeans as consistently red and green, respectively, even though shifting illumination may alter their reflective wavelengths. This demonstrates the phenomenon of

a. afterimages. **b.** color constancy. **c.** trichromatic vision. **d.** color processing.

visual capture the tendency for vision to dominate the other senses, as when we perceive voices in films as coming from the screen we see rather than from the projector behind us.

audition the sense of hearing.

frequency the number of complete wavelengths that pass a point in a given time (for example, per second).

pitch a tone's highness or lowness; depends on frequency.

middle ear the chamber between the eardrum and cochlea containing three tiny bones (hammer, anvil, and stirrup) that concentrate the vibrations of the eardrum on the cochlea's oval window.

inner ear the innermost part of the ear, containing the cochlea, semicircular canals, and vestibular sacs.

cochlea [KOHK-lee-uh] a coiled, bony, fluid-filled tube in the inner ear through which sound waves trigger nerve impulses.

The Other Senses

For humans, vision is the major sense. More of our brain cortex is devoted to vision than to any other sense. Moreover, when there is a conflict between visual and other sensory information, vision tends to dominate or "capture" the other senses. This phenomenon of **visual capture** is an everyday experience. When viewing a movie for which the projector provides the sound, we nevertheless perceive the sound as coming from the screen, where we *see* the actors talking. While viewing a roller coaster ride on a giant wraparound movie screen, we may brace ourselves, even though our other senses tell us we're not moving. In both cases, vision has captured the other senses.

Yet without our senses of hearing, touch, taste, smell, and body motion and position, our capacities for experiencing the world would be vastly diminished.

Hearing

7. How does the ear transform sound energy into neural messages?

Like our other senses, our hearing, or **audition**, is highly adaptive. We hear a wide range of sounds, but we are best able to hear sounds having frequencies within a range that corresponds to the range of the human voice. We also are remarkably sensitive to faint sounds, an obvious boon to our ancestors' survival when hunting or being hunted. (If our ears were much more sensitive, we would hear a constant hiss from the movement of air molecules.) Moreover, we are acutely sensitive to differences in sounds. We can easily detect differences among thousands of human voices, which helps us instantly recognize the voice of almost anyone we know.

For hearing, as for seeing, one fundamental question remains—How do we do it? How do we transform sound energy into neural messages that the brain interprets as a particular sound coming from a particular place?

The Stimulus Input: Sound Waves

Hit a piano key and the resulting stimulus energy is sound waves—jostling molecules of air, each bumping into the next, like a shove being transmitted through the crowded exit tunnel of a concert hall. The resulting waves of compressed and expanded air are like the ripples on a pond circling out from where a tossed stone has broken the surface of the water. The strength, or amplitude, of sound waves determines their *loudness*. Waves also vary in length, and therefore in **frequency** (recall Figure 4.3, page 131). Their frequency determines their **pitch**: The longer the waves (the lower their frequency), the lower the pitch; the shorter the waves (the higher their frequency), the higher the pitch. A piccolo produces much shorter sound waves than does a kettledrum.

Decibels are the measuring unit for sound energy. The absolute threshold for hearing is arbitrarily defined as 0 decibels. Every 10 decibels correspond to a tenfold increase in sound. Thus, normal conversation (60 decibels) is about 10,000 times louder than a soft whisper (20 decibels). And a tolerable 90-decibel sound is a trillion times louder than the faintest detectable sound. When prolonged, however, exposure to sounds above 85 decibels can produce hearing loss (Figure 4.14).

Figure 4.14 The intensity of some common sounds

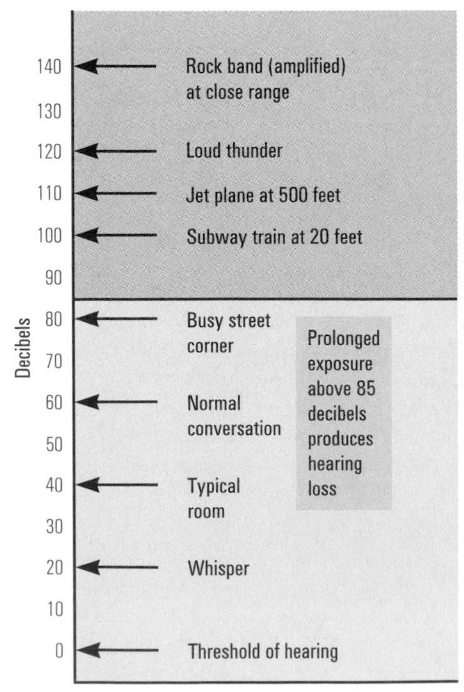

The thunder that follows such lightning has an intensity of 120 decibels at close range.

The sounds of music A guitar's short, fast waves create higher pitches than a drum's longer, slower waves. Differences in the wave's height or amplitude create differing loudness.

The Ear

To hear, we must somehow convert sound waves into neural activity. The human ear accomplishes this feat through an intricate mechanical chain reaction (Figure 4.15). First, the visible outer ear channels sound waves through the auditory canal to the *eardrum*, a tight membrane that vibrates with the waves. The **middle ear** transmits the eardrum's vibrations through a piston made of three tiny bones (the *hammer, anvil*, and *stirrup*) to a snail-shaped tube in the **inner ear** called the **cochlea** (KOHK-lee-uh). The incoming vibrations cause the cochlea's membrane (the *oval window*) to vibrate the fluid that fills the tube. This motion causes ripples in the *basilar membrane*, which is lined with *hair cells*, so named because of their tiny hairlike projections. At the end of this sequence, the rippling of the basilar membrane bends these hair cells, rather like the wind bending a wheat field. This hair cell movement triggers impulses in the adjacent nerve fibers, which converge to form the auditory nerve. Through this mechanical chain of events, sound waves cause the hair cells of the inner ear to send neural messages up to the temporal lobe's auditory cortex. From vibrating air to moving piston to fluid waves to electrical impulses to the brain: We hear.

Brief exposure to extremely intense sounds, such as gunfire near one's ear, and prolonged exposure to intense sounds, such as amplified music, can damage receptor cells and auditory nerves (Backus, 1977; West & Evans, 1990). Although rock and roll may be here to stay, the sad truth for some rock musicians is that their hearing may not be. For others, hearing loss, especially for the higher frequencies, accompanies the biology of aging. To many adults, chirping birds seem quieter, and soft conversation becomes frustratingly unintelligible.

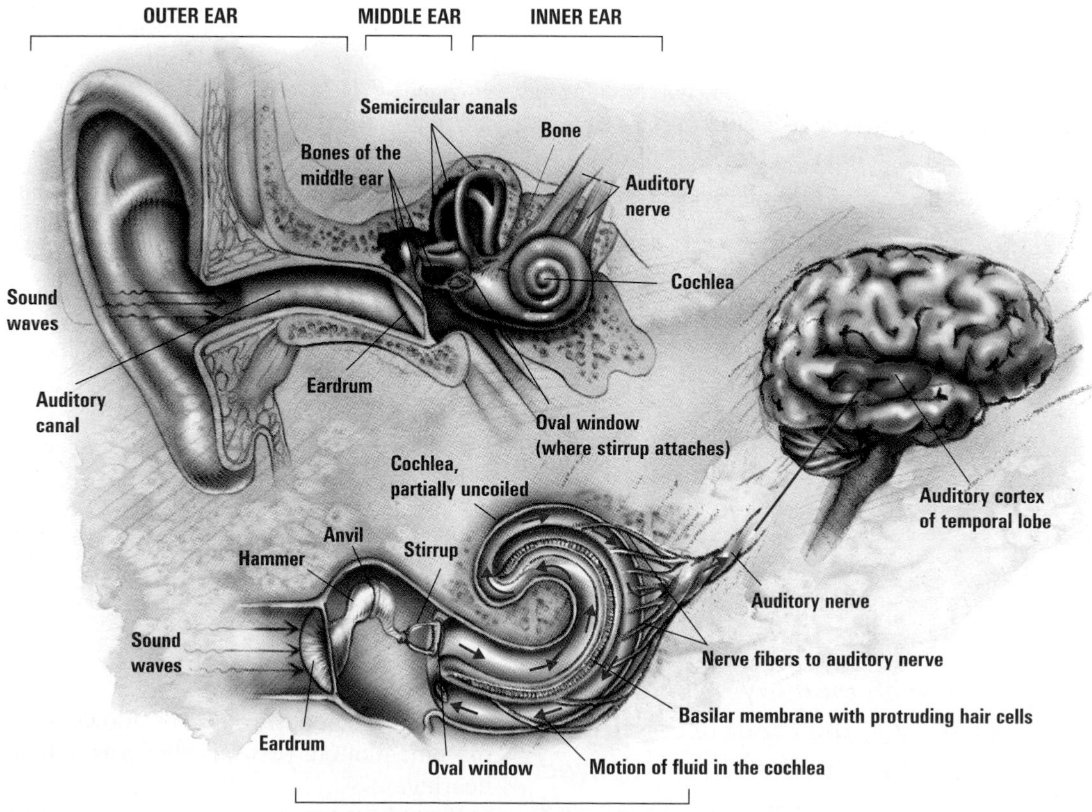

Figure 4.15 **How we transform sound waves into nerve impulses that our brain interprets (a)** The outer ear funnels sound waves to the eardrum. The bones of the middle ear amplify and relay the eardrum's vibrations through the oval window into the fluid-filled cochlea. **(b)** The resulting pressure changes in the cochlear fluid cause the basilar membrane to ripple, bending the hair cells on the surface. Hair cell movements trigger impulses at the bases of the nerve cells, whose fibers converge to form the auditory nerve. (For clarity, the cochlea is shown partially uncoiled.)

CLOSE-UP

Living in a Silent World

Those who live with hearing loss are a diverse group. Some are profoundly deaf; others have limited hearing. Some were deaf "prelingually" (before developing language); others have known the hearing world. Some communicate with sign language and identify with the language-based culture of deafness; others, especially those postlingually deaf, are "oral" and converse with the hearing world by reading lips. Still others move between the deaf and hearing cultures. Those who grow up around other deaf people more often identify with the deaf community and feel positive self-esteem. Deaf children raised in a signing household, whether by deaf or hearing parents, also express higher self-esteem and feel more accepted (Bat-Chava, 1993, 1994).

Among deaf children, about one-fourth attend residential schools, half attend special education programs in public schools, and the remaining fourth are partially or wholly mainstreamed into regular classrooms, sometimes aided by sign language interpreters (Kirk & Gallagher, 1989). Among the deaf as among the hearing, some of these students are slow learners, others are brilliant. Essentially all children, whether deaf or hearing, whether signers or speakers, display a remarkable ability to learn language (Meier, 1991).

Cracking the code With the help of a computer at the Lexington Center in New York, this profoundly deaf young man is learning to speak. The computer screen displays for him the position of his teacher's tongue, the vibration of her nose, and the intensity of her voice. By matching her speech patterns, this boy will learn to speak more clearly.

Still, all deaf people face challenges (Braden, 1994). Because academic subjects are rooted in spoken languages, school achievement may suffer. The social challenges are even greater. Unable to communicate in customary ways, deaf children and their playmates struggle to coordinate their play. Adolescents may experience social exclusion and resulting low self-confidence. Even adults whose hearing becomes impaired later in life may find the difficulties of social interaction producing a sort of shyness. "It's almost universal among the deaf to want to cause hearing people as little fuss as possible," reports Henry Kisor (1990, p. 244), a Chicago newspaper editor and columnist who lost his hearing at age 3. "We can be self-effacing and diffident to the point of invisibility. Sometimes this tendency can be crippling. I must fight it all the time."

I know. My recently deceased mother, with whom we communicated by writing notes on an erasable "magic pad," lived her last decade in a silent world, withdrawn from the stress and strain of trying to interact with people outside a small circle of family and old friends. With my own hearing now declining on a trajectory toward hers, I find myself sitting front and center at plays and meetings, seeking quiet corners in restaurants, using a special volume-controllable telephone, and asking my wife to make necessary calls to friends whose accents differ from ours. But the greatest frustration comes when, with or without a hearing aid, I can't hear the joke that everyone else is guffawing over; when, after repeated tries, I just can't catch that exasperated person's question and can't fake my way around it; when I can't hear the low frequencies of the bass that my son is playing in the school orchestra; when family members give up and say, "Oh, never mind" after trying three times to tell me something unimportant.

As my mother aged, she came to feel that seeking social interaction was just not worth the effort. But for newspaper columnist Kisor, communication is worth the effort. "So, for the most part, I will grit my teeth and plunge ahead" (p. 246). To reach out, to connect, to communicate with others, even across a chasm of silence, is to affirm our humanity as social creatures.

With auditory as with visual information, the brain uses parallel processing—by putting specialized neural teams to work simultaneously on different subtasks.

How Do We Locate Sounds?

As the placement of our eyes allows us to sense depth visually (page 149), the placement of our two ears allows us to enjoy stereophonic ("three-dimensional") hearing.

For at least two reasons, two ears are better than one. If a car to the right honks, your right ear receives a more *intense* sound slightly *sooner* than your left ear. Because sound travels 750 miles per hour and our ears are but 6 inches apart, the loudness difference and time lag are extremely small. But our sensitive auditory system can detect such minute differences (Brown & Deffenbacher, 1979; Middlebrooks & Green, 1991). A just noticeable difference in the direction from which two sounds come corresponds to a time difference of just 0.000027 second!

With auditory as with visual information, the brain uses parallel processing—by putting specialized neural teams to work simultaneously on different subtasks. Owls (and probably humans, too) process timing differences in one neural pathway and intensity differences in another before merging their information to pinpoint a sound's location (Konishi, 1993).

Touch

8. *How do we sense touch and feel pain?*

The precious sense of touch As William James wrote in his *Principles of Psychology* (1890), "Touch is both the alpha and omega of affection."

If you had to give up one sense, which would it be? If you could retain only one sense, which would it be?

Touch would be a good candidate for retention. Right from the start, touch is essential to our development. Infant rats deprived of their mothers' grooming touch produce less growth hormone and have a lower metabolic rate—a good way to keep alive until the mother returns, but a reaction that stunts growth if she's delayed. Infant monkeys allowed to see, hear, and smell—but not touch—their mothers are desperately unhappy; much less so are those separated by a screen with holes that allow touching. As we noted in Chapter 3, premature babies gain weight faster and go home sooner if stimulated by hand massage. As lovers, we yearn to touch—to kiss, to stroke, to snuggle.

Dave Barry is perhaps right to say of the skin that it "keeps people from seeing the inside of your body, which is repulsive, and it prevents your organs from falling onto the ground." But skin does more. Our "sense of touch" is actually a mix of at least four distinct skin senses—pressure, warmth, cold, and pain. Touching various spots on the skin with a soft hair, a warm or cool wire, and the point of a pin reveals that some spots are especially sensitive to pressure, others to warmth, others to cold, still others to pain. Within the skin are different types of specialized nerve endings.

Surprisingly, there is no simple relationship between what we feel at a given spot and the type of specialized nerve ending found there. Only pressure has identifiable receptors. The relationship between warmth, cold, and pain and the receptors that respond to them remains a mystery. Other skin sensations are variations of the basic four (pressure, warmth, cold, and pain):

- Stroking adjacent pressure spots creates a tickle.
- Repeated gentle stroking of a pain spot creates an itching sensation.
- Touching adjacent cold and pressure spots triggers a sense of wetness, which you can experience by touching dry, cold metal.

Be thankful for pain. Pain is your body's way of telling you that something has gone wrong.

Pain

Be thankful for occasional pain. Pain is your body's way of telling you that something has gone wrong. It draws your attention to a burn, a break, or a rupture and tells you to change your behavior immediately. The rare people who are born without the ability to feel pain may experience severe injury without ever being alerted by pain's danger signals. Usually, they die by early adulthood. Without the discomfort that makes us occasionally shift position, their joints fail from excess strain. Without pain, the effects of unchecked infections and injuries accumulate (Neese, 1991). More numerous are those who endure chronic pain. The suffering

"When belly with bad pains doth swell, It matters naught what else goes well."

Sadi
The Gulistan
1258

gate-control theory the theory that the spinal cord contains a neurological "gate" that blocks pain signals or allows them to pass on to the brain. The "gate" is opened by the activity of pain signals traveling up small nerve fibers and is closed by activity in larger fibers or by information coming from the brain.

sensory interaction the principle that one sense may influence another, as when the smell of food influences its taste.

of people with persistent or recurring backaches, arthritis, headaches, and cancer-related pain prompts us to try to understand pain.

Pain is a property not only of the senses—of the region where we feel it—but of the brain as well. As the dreamer may see with eyes closed and the listener may hear a ringing during utter silence, so some 7 in 10 amputees may feel pain or movement in their nonexistent limbs (Melzack, 1992, 1993). (An amputee may also try to step off a bed onto a phantom limb or to lift a cup with a phantom hand.) These *phantom limb sensations* indicate that with pain, as with sights and sounds, the brain can misinterpret the spontaneous central nervous system activity that occurs in the absence of normal sensory input. To see, hear, and feel, we require not a body but a brain.

Unlike vision, however, the pain system is not located in a simple neural cord running from a sensing device to a definable area in the brain. Moreover, there is no one type of stimulus that triggers pain (as light triggers vision), and there are no special receptors (like the retina's rods and cones) for pain. At low intensities, the stimuli that produce pain cause other sensations, including warmth or coolness, smoothness or roughness.

Putting pain out of mind Just before this photo was taken, Kerri Strug had sprained her left ankle so severely that she would be unable to do gymnastics for months afterwards. Yet with this near-perfect vault, she helped carry her team to a 1996 Olympic gold medal. Because pain is a phenomenon of the conscious brain, athletes sometimes endure serious injuries while focusing their attention outside their bodies.

Although no theory of pain explains all the available findings, psychologist Ronald Melzack and biologist Patrick Wall's (1965, 1983) **gate-control theory** provides a useful model. Melzack and Wall believe that the spinal cord contains a sort of neurological "gate" that either blocks pain signals or allows them to pass on to the brain. The spinal cord contains small nerve fibers that conduct most pain signals and larger fibers that conduct most other sensory signals. When tissue is injured, the small fibers activate and open the neural gate, and you feel pain. Large-fiber activity closes the pain gate, turning pain off.

Thus, one way to treat chronic pain is to stimulate (electrically, by massage, or even by acupuncture) "gate-closing" activity in the large neural fibers. Rubbing the area around your stubbed toe creates competing stimulation that will block some of the pain messages. Placing ice on a bruise serves not only to control swelling but also to trigger cold messages that close the gate on the pain signals. Some arthritic patients and people with lower back pain wear a small portable electrical stimulation unit next to a painful area. When the unit stimulates nerves in the area, the patient feels a vibrating sensation rather than pain (Murphy, 1982).

Melzack and Wall believe the pain gate can also be closed by information from the brain. These brain-to-spinal-cord messages help explain some striking psychological influences on pain. When we are distracted from pain signals and soothed by the release of endorphins, our experience of pain may be greatly diminished. Sports injuries may go unnoticed until the after-game shower. During a 1989 basketball game, Ohio State University player Jay Burson broke his neck—and kept playing. Clearly, there is more to pain than what stimulates the sense receptors.

There is also more to our memories of pain than the pain we experience. In experiments, and after medical procedures, people overlook a pain's duration. Their memory snapshots instead record its peak moment and how much pain they felt at the end. Daniel Kahneman and his co-researchers (1993) discovered this when they asked people to immerse one hand in painfully cold water for 60 seconds, and then the other hand in the same painfully cold water for 60 seconds followed by a slightly less painful 30 seconds more. Curiously, when asked which trial they would prefer to repeat, most preferred the longer trial, with more net pain—but less pain at the end. When patients recalled the pain of a colon examination a month later, their memories were similarly dominated by the final (and the worst) moments, not by how long the pain had lasted.

"From there to here, from here to there, funny things are everywhere."

Dr. Seuss
One Fish, Two Fish, Red Fish, Blue Fish
1960

For medical personnel, the implication is clear: It's better to taper down a painful procedure than to switch it off abruptly. In one experiment, a physician did this for some patients undergoing colon exams—lengthening the discomfort by a minute, though with milder pain (Kahneman, in press). Although this discomfort added to the net pain experience, patients given the "taper down" treatment later recalled the exam as less painful than those whose pain ended abruptly.

Pain Control

If pain is where body meets mind—if it is indeed a physical and a psychological phenomenon—then it should be treatable both physically and psychologically.

The widely practiced Lamaze method of childbirth combines several of these pain control techniques. Among them are relaxation (through deep breathing and muscle relaxation), counterstimulation (through gentle massage), and distraction (through focusing attention on, say, a pleasant photograph).

Although Lamaze training reduces labor pain, most Lamaze patients request a local anesthetic during labor. Some—having expected a "natural, painless birth"—feel needless guilt and failure (Melzack, 1984). Melzack therefore advocates—as does the Lamaze program itself—childbirth training that prepares a woman "to cope with an event which is often extremely painful and, at the same time, one of the most fulfilling peak experiences in her life."

Distracting people with pleasant images ("Think of a warm, comfortable environment") or drawing their attention away from the painful stimulation ("Count backward by 3's") is an especially effective way to increase pain tolerance (Fernandez & Turk, 1989; McCaul & Malott, 1984). The principle works in health-care situations. A well-trained nurse may distract needle-shy patients by chatting with them and asking them to look away when inserting the needle.

Taste

9. *How do we experience taste and smell?*

Our sense of taste involves four basic sensations—sweet, sour, salty, and bitter (McBurney & Gent, 1979). All other tastes are mixtures of these. Investigators have, however, been frustrated in their search for specialized nerve fibers for each of the four basic taste sensations.

The joy of taste Four taste sensations—salty, sweet, sour, and bitter—combine with odors to produce a multitude of flavors.

Taste is a chemical sense. Inside the little bumps on the top and sides of your tongue are 200 or more taste buds. Each contains a pore that catches food chemicals. These molecules are sensed by 50 taste receptor cells that project antennalike hairs into the pore. Some of these receptors respond mostly to sweet-tasting molecules, others to salty- , sour- , or bitter-tasting ones. It doesn't take much to trigger a response. When a stream of water is pumped across the tongue, the addition of a concentrated salty or sweet taste for but one-tenth of a second gets noticed (Kelling & Halpern, 1983). When a friend asks for "just a taste" of your soft drink, you can squeeze off the straw after a mere fraction of a second.

Taste receptors reproduce themselves every week or two, so if you burn your tongue with hot food it matters little. However, as you grow older, the number of taste buds decreases, as does taste sensitivity (Cowart, 1981). (No wonder adults enjoy strong-tasting foods that children resist.) Smoking and alcohol use accelerate the decline in taste buds and sensitivities.

Although taste buds are essential for taste, there is more to taste than meets the tongue. Hold your nose, close your eyes, and have someone feed you various foods. A piece of apple may then be indistinguishable from a piece of raw potato; a piece of steak may taste like cardboard. To savor a taste, we normally breathe the aroma through our nose—which is why eating is not much fun when you have a bad cold, and why people who lose their sense of smell may think they have also lost their sense of taste. Smell not only adds to our perception of taste, it also changes it. A drink's strawberry odor enhances our perception of its sweetness. This is **sensory interaction** at work—the principle that one sense may influence another. Smell plus taste equals flavor. Similarly, we correctly perceive the location of the voice directly in front of us partly because we also *see* that the person is in front of us, not behind, above, or beneath us.

Smell

Breaths come in pairs—inhale, exhale—except at two moments: birth and death. Each day, as you inhale and exhale nearly 20,000 breaths of life-sustaining air, you bathe your nostrils in a stream of scent-laden molecules. More than you

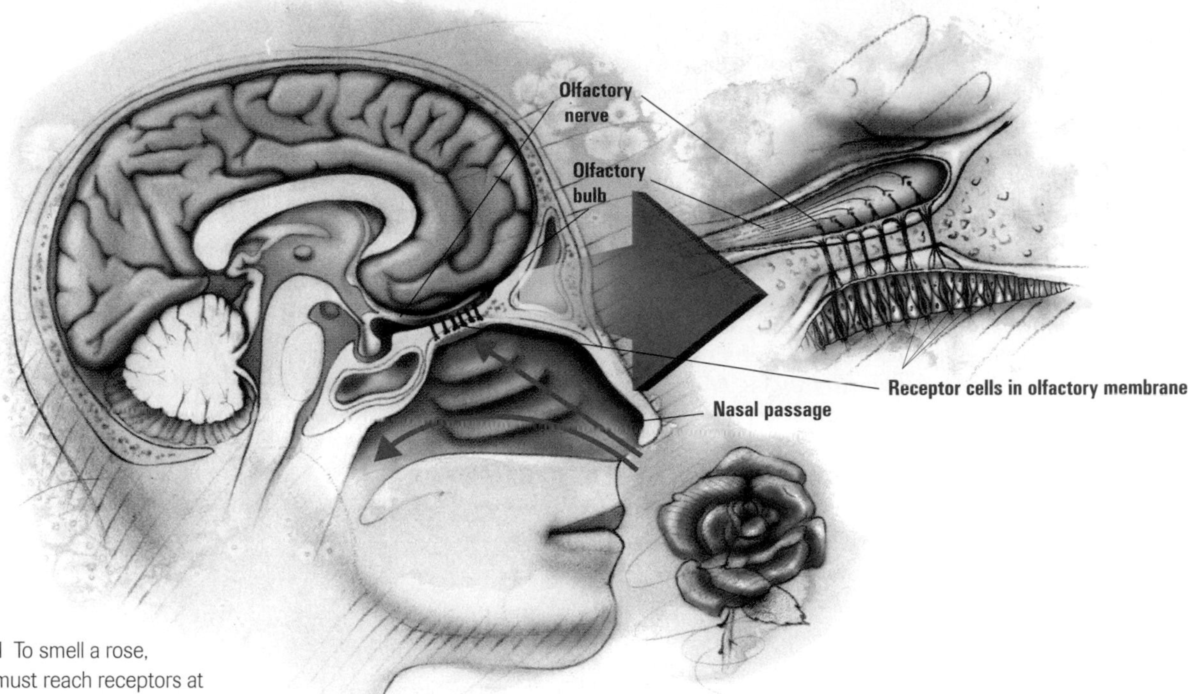

Figure 4.16 The sense of smell To smell a rose, airborne molecules of its fragrance must reach receptors at the top of the nose. Sniffing swirls air up to the receptors, enhancing the aroma. The receptor cells send messages to the brain's olfactory bulb, and then onward to the temporal lobe's primary smell cortex and to the parts of the limbic system involved in memory and emotion.

may realize, your resulting experiences of smell (*olfaction*) are intimate ones. To smell someone, you inhale something of the person.

Like taste, smell is a chemical sense. We smell something when air-carried molecules of a substance reach a tiny cluster of 5 million receptor cells at the top of each nasal cavity (Figure 4.16). These olfactory receptor cells, waving like sea anemones on a reef, respond selectively to the aroma of cake baking, to a wisp of smoke, to a friend's fragrance, and they instantly alert the brain through their axon fibers. Even nursing infants and mothers have a literal chemistry to their relationship, as they quickly learn to recognize each other's scents (McCarthy, 1986). Aided by smell, a mother fur seal returning to a beach crowded with pups will find her own. Our own sense of smell is less impressive than the acuteness of our seeing and hearing. Looking out across a garden we see its forms and colors in exquisite detail and hear its singing birds, yet smell little of it without jamming our nose into the flowers.

Precisely how olfactory receptors work is a mystery. Unlike light, which can be separated into its spectral colors, an odor cannot be separated into more elemental odors. Thus, the olfaction system has no parallel to the retina, which detects myriad colors with sensory cells dedicated to red, green, or blue. Olfactory receptors recognize odors individually.

Odor molecules come in so many shapes and sizes that it takes lots of different receptors to detect them. A large family of 1000 genes—some 1 percent of all our genes—design receptor proteins that recognize particular molecules (Axel, 1995). As a key slips into a lock, so odor molecules slip into these receptors. Yet we seem not to have a distinct receptor for each of the some 10,000 odors we can detect. This suggests that some odors trigger a combination of receptors, whose activity the olfactory cortex interprets.

The ability to identify scents peaks in early adulthood and gradually declines thereafter (Figure 4.17).

Odors also have the power to evoke memories and feelings. They do so thanks to a hotline between the brain area that gets information from the nose and the brain's ancient limbic centers associated with memory and emotion. Smell is primitive. Eons before the elaborate analytical areas of our cerebral cortex had fully evolved, our mammalian ancestors were sniffing for food and predators.

Figure 4.17 Age, sex, and sense of smell Among the 1.2 million people who responded to a *National Geographic* scratch and sniff survey, women and younger adults most successfully identified six sample odors. (From Wysocki & Gilbert, 1989)

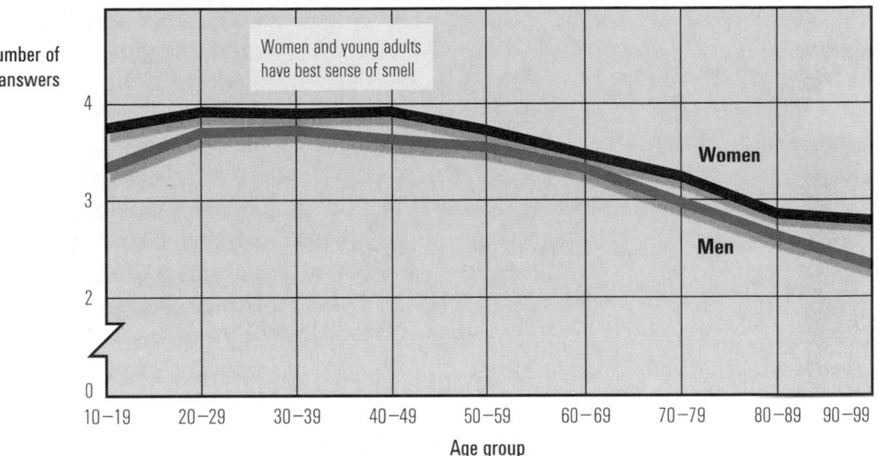

In *Remembrance of Things Past*, the French novelist Marcel Proust described how the aroma and flavor of a bit of cake soaked in tea resurrected long-forgotten memories of his aunt's bedroom in the old family house. "The smell and taste of things," he noted, "bears unfaltering, in the tiny and almost impalpable drop of their essence, the vast structure of recollection."

Laboratory studies confirm that, though it's difficult to recall odors by name, we do indeed have a remarkable capacity to recognize long-forgotten odors and their associated personal episodes (Engen, 1987; Schab, 1991). Students who do a word exercise while smelling the aroma of chocolate remember the words better the next day if the chocolate aroma is again present (Schab, 1990). And pleasant odors evoke pleasant memories (Ehrlichman & Halpern, 1988). The smell of the sea, the scent of a perfume, or an aroma like the floorwax smell in Grandma's kitchen bring to mind happy times. Such is the power of odors to switch on memories and to retrieve associated emotions.

Body Position and Movement

10. *How do we sense our body's position and movement?*

Mechanisms that normally give us an accurate experience of the world can, under special conditions, fool us. Understanding how we get fooled provides clues to how our perceptual system works.

With only the five familiar senses we have so far considered, we would be helpless. We could not put food in our mouths, stand up, or reach out and touch someone. To know just how to move your arms to grasp someone's hand, you first need to know the current position of your arms and hands and then be aware of their changing positions as you move them. To take just one step requires feedback from and instructions to some 200 muscles.

Humans come equipped with millions of such position and motion sensors. They are all over our bodies—in the muscles, tendons, and joints—and they are continually providing our brains with information. If we twist our wrists one degree, the sensors immediately report it. This sense of our body parts' position and movement is **kinesthesis** (kin-ehs-THEE-sehs).

Have you ever considered life without kinesthesis, without, say, being able to sense the positions of your limbs when awakening during the night? Such is the experience of Christina, whose nerve fibers carrying information from muscles, tendons, and joints were destroyed by disease, leaving her floppy as a rag doll (Sacks, 1985). What does it feel like? Like she is disembodied, her body dead, not real, not hers. Against all odds, Christina has, however, learned to walk and eat—by visually attending to her limbs and directing them accordingly.

A companion **vestibular sense** monitors the head's (and thus the body's) position and movement. The biological gyroscopes for this sense of equilibrium are

kinesthesis [kin-ehs-THEE-sehs] the system for sensing the position and movement of individual body parts.

vestibular sense the sense of body movement and position, including the sense of balance.

in the inner ear. The *semicircular canals*, which look like a three-dimensional pretzel (Figure 4.15, page 139), and the *vestibular sacs*, which connect the canals with the cochlea, contain substances that move when the head rotates or tilts. This movement stimulates hairlike receptors, which send the brain messages that enable us continually to sense our body position and maintain our balance.

If you've been twirling around and come to an abrupt halt, neither the fluid in your semicircular canals nor your kinesthetic receptors immediately return to their neutral state. The aftereffect fools your dizzy brain with the sensation that you're still spinning. This illustrates a principle that underlies perceptual illusions: Mechanisms that normally give us an accurate experience of the world can, under special conditions, fool us. Understanding how we get fooled provides clues to how our perceptual system works.

REHEARSE IT!

15. The amplitude of a light wave determines our perception of brightness. The amplitude of a sound wave determines our perception of

a. loudness. **c.** audition.
b. pitch. **d.** frequency.

16. The frequency of sound waves determines their pitch. The __________ the waves are, the lower their frequency is and the __________

a. shorter; higher **c.** lower; longer
b. longer; lower **d.** higher; shorter

17. Sound waves pass through the auditory canal to a tight membrane. Vibrations of this membrane are transmitted by three tiny bones to a snail-shaped tube in the inner ear, where the waves are converted into neural activity. This tube is called the

a. anvil. **c.** cochlea.
b. basilar membrane. **d.** eardrum.

18. At least four skin senses—pressure, warmth, cold, and pain—make up our sense of touch. Of all the skin senses, the only one that has its own identifiable receptor cells is

a. pressure. **c.** cold.
b. warmth. **d.** pain.

19. There is no one type of stimulus that triggers pain and no one definable spot in the brain that interprets pain. Although no theory fully explains our experience of pain, the gate-control theory is useful. According to this theory,

a. special pain receptors send signals directly to the brain.
b. pain is a property of the senses, not of the brain.
c. small nerve fibers in the spinal cord conduct most pain signals.
d. the stimuli that produce pain are unrelated to other sensations.

20. The taste of the food we eat is greatly enhanced by its smell or aroma. One sense influencing another is referred to as

a. sensory adaptation. **c.** gate-control theory.
b. chemical sensation. **d.** sensory interaction.

21. Kinesthesis is the body's way of sensing its position and movement. The receptors for our companion vestibular sense are in the

a. skin. **c.** inner ear.
b. brain. **d.** skeletal muscles.

Perceptual Organization

11. *What did the Gestalt psychologists contribute to our understanding of perception?*

We have examined the processes by which we sense sights and sounds, tastes and smells, touch and movement. Now our central question is, how do we see not just shapes and colors, but a rose in bloom, a familiar face, a sunset? How do we hear not just a mix of pitches and rhythms, but a child's cry of pain, the hum of distant traffic, a symphony? In short, how do we *organize* and *interpret* our sensations so that they become meaningful perceptions?

Early in the twentieth century, a group of German psychologists became intrigued with how the mind organizes sensations into perceptions. Given a clus-

gestalt an organized whole. Gestalt psychologists emphasize our tendency to integrate pieces of information into meaningful wholes.

figure-ground the organization of the visual field into objects (the *figures*) that stand out from their surroundings (the *ground*).

grouping the perceptual tendency to organize stimuli into coherent groups.

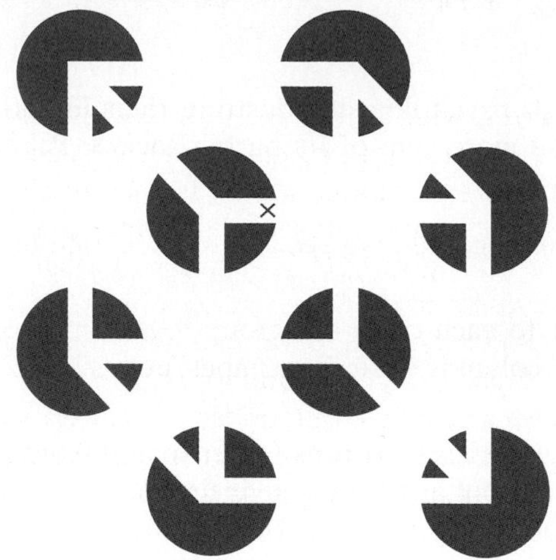

Figure 4.18 A Necker cube What do you see: circles with gray lines, or a cube? If you stare at the cube, you may notice that it reverses location, moving the tiny *X* in the center from the front edge to the back. At times the cube may seem to float in front of the page, with circles behind it; other times the circles may become holes in the page through which the cube appears, as though it were floating behind the page. Because attention is selective, you see only one interpretation at a time. (From Bradley & others, 1976)

ter of sensations, the human perceiver organizes them into a **gestalt**, a German word meaning a "form" or a "whole." The Gestalt psychologists provided compelling demonstrations of gestalt perception and described principles by which we organize our sensations into perceptions.

For example, look at Figure 4.18. Note that the individual elements of the figure are really nothing but eight blue circles, each containing three converging white lines. But when we view them all together, we see a *whole* form, a "Necker cube." As the Gestalt psychologists were fond of saying, in perception the whole may exceed the sum of its parts. There is far more to perception than meets the senses.

As you read about the Gestalt psychologists' organizational principles, keep in mind the fundamental truth they illustrate: Our brains do more than merely register information about the world. Perception is not just opening a shutter and letting a picture print itself on the brain. Always, we are filtering sensory information and inferring perceptions in ways that make sense to us. Mind matters.

Form Perception

12. ***How do the principles of figure-ground and grouping contribute to our perception of form?***

Imagine that you wanted to design a video/computer system that, like your eye/brain system, could read handwritten addresses or recognize faces at a glance. (Postal services are, in fact, hoping to develop such a scanner.) What abilities would it need?

Figure and Ground

Figure 4.19 Reversible figure and ground Monkey experiments suggest that brain activity changes as the perceived image shifts from faces to vase (Barinaga, 1997).

To start with, the system would need to recognize the addresses and faces as distinct from their backgrounds. Likewise, our first perceptual task is to perceive any object, called the *figure*, as distinct from its surroundings, called the *ground*. Among the voices you hear at a party, the one you attend to becomes the figure, all others part of the ground. As you read, the words are the figure; the white paper, the ground. In Figure 4.19, the **figure-ground** relationship continually reverses—but always we organize the stimulus into a figure seen against a ground. (Is it a vase, or profiles of a younger Prince Phillip and Queen Elizabeth?) Such reversible figure and ground illustrations demonstrate again that the same stimulus can trigger more than one perception. Curiously, though, if you do not *know* the figure is reversible, it likely will not reverse (Rock & others, 1994).

Grouping

Having discriminated figure from ground, we (and our video/computer system) must then organize the figure into a meaningful form. Some basic features of a scene—such as color, movement, and light-dark contrast—we process instantly and automatically (Treisman, 1987). To bring order and form to these basic sensations, our minds follow certain rules for **grouping** stimuli together (Figure 4.20).

Figure 4.20 Organizing stimuli into groups There are many ways we could perceive the stimuli shown here, and yet people everywhere see them similarly. The Gestalt psychologists believed this shows that the brain uses "rules" to order sensory information into wholes.

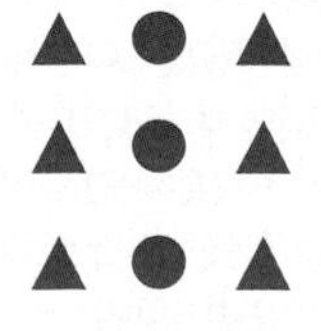

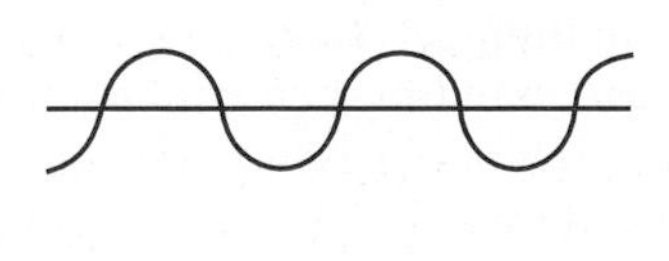

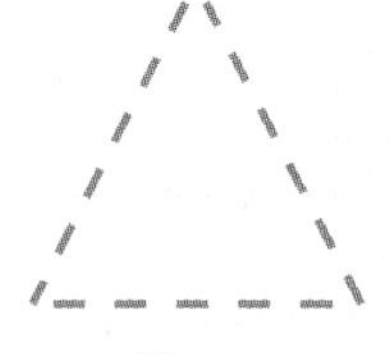

Figure 4.21 Grouping principles You probably perceive this doghouse as a gestalt–a whole (though impossible) structure. Actually, your brain imposes this sense of wholeness on the picture. As the photo on page 155 shows, gestalt grouping principles such as closure and continuity are at work here. (Reprinted from GAMES Magazine [810 Seventh Avenue, New York, NY 10019]. Copyright © 1983 PSC Games Limited Partnership)

These rules, identified by the Gestalt psychologists, illustrate their idea that the perceived whole differs from the mere sum of its parts (Rock & Palmer, 1990):

Proximity We group nearby figures together. We see not six separate lines, but three sets of two lines.

Similarity Figures that are similar to each other we group together. We see the triangles and circles as vertical columns of similar shapes, not as horizontal rows of dissimilar shapes.

Continuity We perceive smooth, continuous patterns rather than discontinuous ones. This pattern could be a series of alternating semicircles, but we perceive it as two continuous lines—one wavy and one straight.

Closure We fill in gaps to create a complete, whole object. We easily fill the gaps in this figure's outline and see a complete triangle.

Connectedness We perceive spots, lines, or areas as a single unit when uniform and linked.

These grouping principles usually help us perceive reality. Sometimes, however, they can lead us astray, as when viewing the doghouse in Figure 4.21.

Depth Perception

13. *Why do we see the world in three dimensions?*

From the two-dimensional images that fall on our retinas we somehow organize three-dimensional perceptions. Seeing objects in three dimensions, called **depth perception**, allows us to estimate their distance from us. At a glance, we estimate the distance of an oncoming car or the height of a cliff. This ability is partly innate. Eleanor Gibson and Richard Walk (1960) discovered this using a miniature cliff with a drop-off covered by sturdy glass. The inspiration for these experiments occurred to Gibson as she was eating a picnic lunch on the rim of the Grand Canyon. She wondered: Would a toddler peering over the rim perceive the dangerous drop-off and draw back?

Figure 4.22 Visual cliff Eleanor Gibson and Richard Walk devised this miniature cliff with a glass-covered drop-off to determine whether crawling infants and newborn animals can perceive depth. Even when coaxed, infants are reluctant to venture onto the glass over the cliff.

Back in their Cornell University laboratory, Gibson and Walk placed 6- to 14-month-old infants on the edge of a safe canyon—a **visual cliff** (Figure 4.22). Their mothers then coaxed them to crawl out on the glass. Most refused to do so, indicating that they could perceive depth. Perhaps by crawling age they had *learned* to perceive depth. Yet newborn animals with virtually no visual experience—including young kittens, a day-old goat, and newly hatched chicks—responded similarly. Each species, by the time it is mobile, has the perceptual abilities it needs. What is more, during the first month of life, human infants turn to avoid objects coming directly at them but are unbothered by objects approaching at an angle that would not hit them (Ball & Tronick, 1971).

Although biological maturation predisposes our wariness of heights, experience amplifies it. Infants' wariness increases with crawling experience, at whatever age crawling begins. Given the enhanced locomotion made possible by a walker, infants become even more wary of heights (Campos & others, 1992).

How do we do it? How do we transform two-dimensional retinal images into three-dimensional perceptions? Some depth cues—**binocular cues**—require both eyes. Others—**monocular cues**—are available to each eye separately.

depth perception the ability to see objects in three dimensions although the images that strike the retina are two-dimensional; allows us to judge distance.

visual cliff a laboratory device for testing depth perception in infants and young animals.

binocular cues depth cues, such as retinal disparity and convergence, that depend on the use of two eyes.

monocular cues distance cues, such as linear perspective and overlap, available to either eye alone.

retinal disparity a binocular cue for perceiving depth; the greater the disparity (difference) between the two images the retina receives of an object, the closer the object is to the viewer.

Binocular Cues

If you could pull out your eyeballs and switch their positions (leaving their neural wiring intact), you would reverse the retinal disparity, making all objects reversed in depth. Close objects would appear distant, and distant objects would appear close (Wolf, 1996).

Because our eyes are about 2½ inches apart, our retinas receive slightly different images of the world. When the brain compares these two images, the difference between them—their **retinal disparity**—provides an important cue to the relative distance of different objects. When you hold your finger directly in front of your nose, your retinas receive quite different views. (You can see this if you close one eye and then the other, or create a finger sausage as in Figure 4.23.) At a greater distance—say, when you hold your finger at arm's length—the disparity is smaller.

The creators of three-dimensional (3-D) movies simulate retinal disparity by photographing a scene with two cameras placed a few inches apart (a feature we might want to build into our video/computer). When viewed through spectacles or a device that allows the left eye to see only the image from the left camera and the right eye only the image from the right camera, the 3-D effect mimics normal retinal disparity. Computer-generated 3-D images do the same.

Figure 4.23 The floating finger sausage Hold your two index fingers about 5 inches in front of your eyes, with their tips half an inch apart. Now look beyond them and note the weird result. Move your fingers out farther and the retinal disparity—and the finger sausage—will shrink.

Can you find the three-dimensional Greek letter psi (ψ) in the 3-D stereogram in Figure 4.24? Cross your eyes slightly (or look at a pencil tip 3 inches or so above the page). As the two dots at the top of the stereogram become three, the psi image will appear (at which point you will no longer feel that your eyes are crossed). The image looks so real you may be able to measure its distance from the page with a ruler.

But note that you cannot trace the outline of the 3–D image on the page—because it isn't on the page. Note also that if you close one eye, the image immediately disappears, again illustrating that it doesn't really exist, except in your brain. The perceived depth, from two slightly different images lying one on top of the other, occurs as each eye focuses on one image and the brain integrates the two versions into a single 3-D image. This dramatically illustrates this chapter's fundamental lesson: Perception is not merely projecting the world onto our brains. Rather, sensations are disassembled into information bits that the brain reassembles into its own functional model of the external world. *Our brains construct our perceptions.*

Figure 4.24 Two eyes + brain = depth If you are having trouble seeing the 3-D image, try holding the picture close to your face, so that the center of it touches your nose, then slowly move it backward without changing the focus of your eyes. Less than a foot from your face, with your eyes feeling slightly crossed, the 3-D image should emerge. The image appears because the picture contains two views of the psi, from slightly different angles. When the brain fuses these two into one, you see the image in three dimensions. (For a really great effect, blink and the Ψ may reverse from behind to in front of the page, or vise versa.)

Another binocular cue to distance is **convergence**, a neuromuscular cue from the greater inward turn when the eyes view a near object. By noting the angle of convergence, the brain can compute whether you are focusing on this printed page or on the person across the room.

Relative size

Interposition

Monocular Cues

Try this: With both eyes open, hold two pens or pencils in front of you and touch their tips together. Now do so with one eye closed. Does the task become noticeably more difficult? This demonstrates the importance of binocular cues in judging the distance of nearby objects. Two eyes are better than one. How then do we judge whether a person is 10 or 100 meters away? In both cases, the retinal disparity while looking straight ahead is slight. At such distances we depend on monocular cues such as the following:

Relative size If we assume that two objects are similar in size, we perceive the one that casts the smaller retinal image as farther away.

Interposition If one object partially blocks our view of another, we perceive it as closer. The painting below purposely confuses figure and ground by interposition.

Relative height We perceive objects higher in our field of vision as farther away. (This reverses above the horizon, as when we perceive a higher bird as closer.) Relative height may contribute to the illusion that vertical dimensions are longer than identical horizontal dimensions. Measure the image and see.

Relative motion As we move, stable objects appear to move relative to us. If while riding in a train you fix your gaze on some object—say, a house—the objects closer than the house (the fixation point) appear to move backward. The nearer an object is, the faster it seems to move. (This is also called *motion parallax*.)

Objects beyond the fixation point appear to move with you at a decreasing speed as the object gets farther away. Your brain uses these speed and direction clues to compute the objects' relative distances.

Linear perspective Parallel lines, such as railroad tracks, appear to converge with distance. The more the lines converge, the greater their perceived distance. Linear perspective can contribute to rail-crossing accidents, by leading people to overestimate a train's distance (Leibowitz,

Relative height

Relative motion Direction of passenger's motion

convergence a binocular cue for perceiving depth; the extent to which the eyes converge inward when looking at an object.

relative size a monocular cue for perceiving distance; when we assume two objects are the same size, the one that produces the smaller image appears more distant.

interposition a monocular cue for perceiving distance; we perceive an object partially blocking our view of another object as closer.

relative height a monocular cue for perceiving distance; higher objects appear more distant.

relative motion a monocular cue for perceiving distance; when we move, objects at different distances change their relative positions in our visual image, with those closest moving most. (Also called *motion parallax*.)

linear perspective a monocular cue for perceiving distance; we perceive the converging of what we know to be parallel lines as indicating increasing distance.

relative brightness a monocular cue for perceiving distance; dimmer objects appear more distant.

perceptual constancy perceiving objects as unchanging (having consistent lightness, color, shape, and size) even as illumination and retinal images change.

Linear perspective

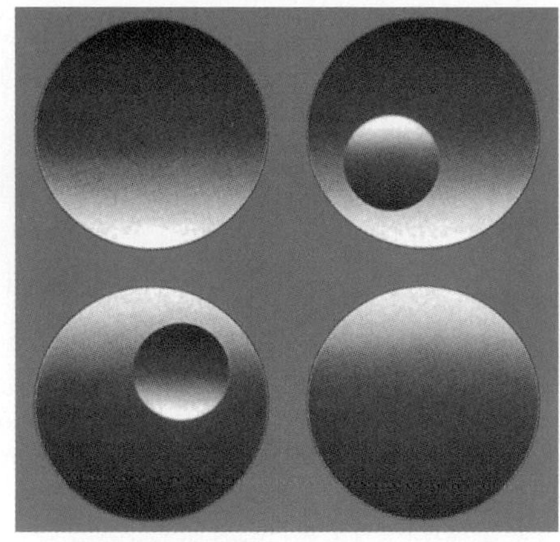

Relative brightness

(From "Perceiving Shape from Shading" by Vilayanur S. Ramachandran. Copyright © 1988 by Scientific American, Inc. All rights reserved)

1985). (A train's massive size also makes it appear to be moving more slowly than it is.)

Relative brightness Nearby objects reflect more light to our eyes. Thus, given two identical objects, the dimmer one seems farther away. This illusion also contributes to accidents, as when a fog-shrouded vehicle, or one with only its parking lights on, seems farther away than it is.

To convey depth on a flat canvas (Figure 4.25), artists use such monocular cues, as do people who must gauge depth with but one eye. In 1960, the University of Washington football team won the year's biggest game, thanks partly to the superb ball throwing of Bob Schloredt. Schloredt, who was obviously skilled at judging his receiver's distance, used monocular cues for distance because he is blind in his left eye.

Figure 4.25 **Perspective techniques** By the time that "Bristol, Broad Quay" was painted (c. 1730, Anonymous), techniques for depicting three dimensions on a flat surface were well established. Note the effective use of distance cues such as interposition, linear perspective, and relative size and height.

Perceptual Constancy

14. ***How do perceptual constancies help us to organize our sensations into meaningful perceptions?***

So far we have noted that our video/computer system must first perceive objects as we do—as having a distinct form, location, and perhaps motion. Its next task is even more challenging: to recognize the object without being deceived by changes in its size, shape, brightness, or color. **Perceptual constancy** allows us to perceive an object as unchanging even though the stimuli we receive from it change. You glance at someone ahead of you on the sidewalk and instantly recognize a classmate. In less time than it takes to draw a breath, information reaching your eyes has been sent to your brain, where work teams comprising millions of neurons have extracted the essential features, compared them with stored images, and identified the person.

Recall the famous EAT POPCORN/DRINK COCA-COLA subliminal persuasion hoax described on page 127. For several reasons, we know that such an experiment could never have occurred. We know this not only because the reported site—the Fort Lee, New Jersey, theater—could not have held the number of people supposedly tested, and not only because the theater manager at the time denied such an experiment was ever conducted, but also because of what we know about stroboscopic movement. The briefest possible movie image, a 1/24th-second frame, would not *have been subliminal (Rogers, 1994).*

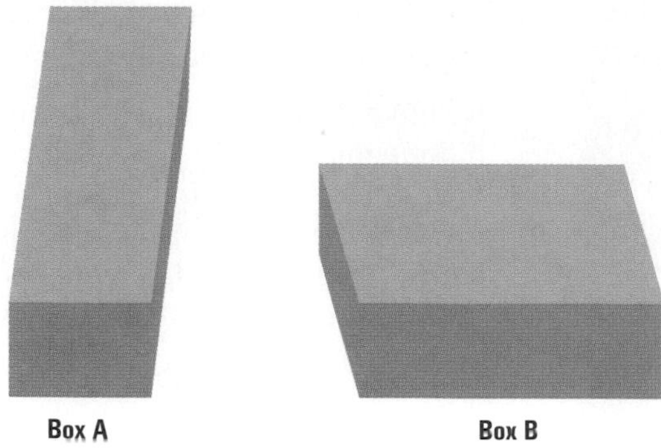

Figure 4.26 Perceiving shape Do the tops of boxes A and B have different dimensions? They appear to. But—believe it or not—they are identical. (Measure and see.) With both boxes we adjust our perceptions relative to our viewing angle. (From Shepard, 1981)

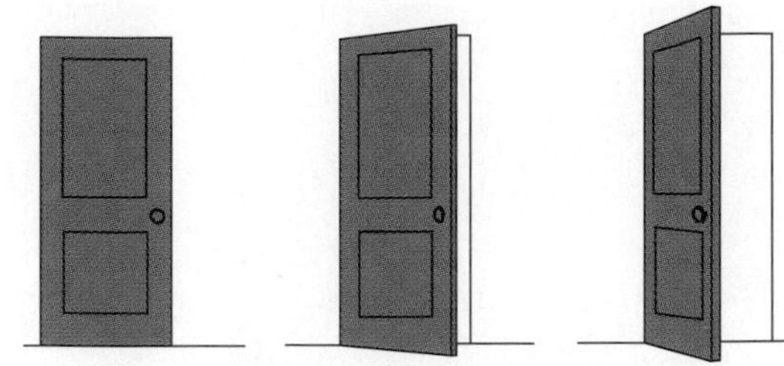

Figure 4.27 Shape constancy A door casts an increasingly trapezoidal image on our retinas as it opens, yet we still perceive it as rectangular.

Shape and Size Constancies

Sometimes an object's actual shape is unchanging, but the object *seems* to change shape with our viewing angle (Figure 4.26). More often, thanks to *shape constancy*, we perceive familiar objects as having a constant form even while our retinal images of them change. When a door opens, it casts a changing shape on our retinas, yet we manage to perceive the door as having a constant doorlike shape (Figure 4.27).

Thanks to *size constancy* we perceive objects as having a constant size, even while our distance from them varies. Size constancy allows us to perceive a car as big enough to carry people, even when we see its tiny image from two blocks away. This illustrates the close connection between an object's perceived *distance* and perceived *size*. Perceiving an object's distance gives us cues to its size. Likewise, knowing its general size—that the object is, say, a car—provides us with cues to its distance.

Size-Distance Relationship

The marvel of size perception is how effortlessly it occurs. Given the perceived distance of an object and the size of its image on our retinas, we instantly and unconsciously infer the object's size. Although the monsters in Figure 4.28(a) cast the same retinal images, linear perspective tells our brain that the monster in pursuit is farther away. We therefore perceive it as larger.

(a)

(b)

Figure 4.28 The interplay between perceived size and distance (a) The monocular cues for distance make the pursuing monster look larger than the pursued. It isn't. (From Shepard, 1990) **(b)** This visual trick, called the Ponzo illusion, is based on the same principle as the fleeing monsters. The two orange bars cast identical-size images on our retinas. But experience tells us that a more distant object can create the same-size image as a nearer one only if it is actually larger. As a result, we perceive the bar that seems more distant as larger.

This interplay between perceived size and perceived distance helps explain several well-known illusions. For example, can you imagine why the moon looks up to 50 percent larger near the horizon than when high in the sky? For at least 22 centuries, scholars have wondered and argued about reasons for the *moon illusion* (Hershenson, 1989). One reason is that cues to objects' distances at the horizon make the moon behind them seem farther away (Kaufman & Rock, 1962). Thus, the moon on the horizon seems larger, like the distant monster in Figure 4.28(a) and the distant bar in the *Ponzo illusion* in Figure 4.28(b). Take away these distance cues—by looking at the horizon moon (or each monster or each bar) through a paper tube—and it immediately shrinks.

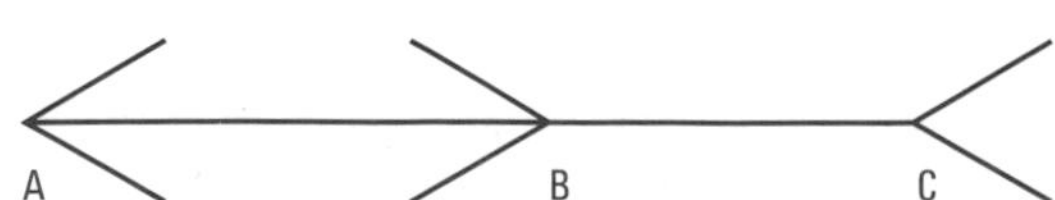

The size-distance relationship helps us understand a famous illusion: To the left is an adaptation of a classic illusion created in 1889 by Franz Müller-Lyer. Does either line segment—AB or BC—appear longer? To most people the two segments appear the same length. Surprise! They are not. As your ruler can verify, line AB is a full one-third longer than line BC. Why do our eyes deceive us?

(a)

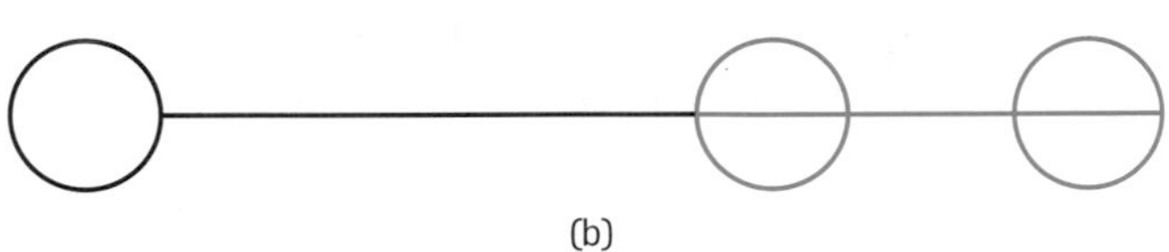

(b)

Figure 4.29 The Müller-Lyer illusion (a) Richard L. Gregory (1968) suggested that the corners in our rectangularly carpentered world teach us to interpret "outward" or "inward" pointing arrowheads at the ends of a line as a cue to the line's distance from us and so to its length. The red line defined by the corner at the ticket booth looks shorter than the red line defined by the corner to the left. But if you measure them, you will see that both are the same length. **(b)** There is more to the Müller-Lyer illusion than size constancy, however, for if we replace the arrowheads with circles and judge whether the black or blue line segment seems longer, we still get much the same effect. Here the two line segments are equal. Most people judge the black line as longer, apparently because they perceptually adjust the lengths of the lines toward the distance separating the figures. (From Day, 1984)

One explanation for such illusions draws on our experience with the corners of rooms or buildings. This experience prompts us to interpret the vertical line on the ticket booth in Figure 4.29(a) as closer to us and therefore shorter, and the vertical line by the door as farther away and therefore longer, although the two lines are equal. Thus, what appears as an illusion when isolated in a line drawing actally enables correct depth perception in our three-dimensional world.

Size-distance relationships also explain why in Figure 4.30 the same-age girls seem so different in size. As the diagram reveals, the girls are actually about the same size, but the room is distorted. Viewed with one eye through a peephole, its trapezoidal walls produce the same images as those of a normal rectangular room viewed with both eyes. Presented with the camera's one-eyed view, the brain makes the reasonable assumption that the room *is* normal and that each of the girls is therefore the same distance from us. But given the different sizes of the images on the retina, our brain ends up calculating that the girls are very different in size.

Our occasional misperceptions demonstrate the workings of our normally effective perceptual processes. The perceived relationship between distance and size is generally valid, but under special circumstances it can lead us astray—as when helping to create the moon illusion, the Müller-Lyer illusion, and the Ames illusion. Using distance cues to assess perceived size triggers illusions only if we are not familiar with the object or if the distance cues are misleading. When we correctly interpret the distance cues—which we normally do—we perceive the size of objects correctly.

Lightness Constancy

White paper reflects 90 percent of the light falling on it; black paper, only 10 percent. In sunlight the black paper may reflect 100 times more light than does the white paper indoors, but it still looks black (McBurney & Collings, 1984). This illustrates *lightness constancy* (also called *brightness constancy*); we perceive an object as having a constant lightness even while its illumination varies. Perceived lightness depends on *relative luminance*—the amount of light an object reflects relative to its surroundings. If you view sunlit black paper through a narrow tube so nothing else is visible, it may look gray, because in bright sunshine it reflects a fair amount of light. View it

Figure 4.30 The Ames room This distorted room, designed by Adelbert Ames, appears to have a normal rectangular shape when viewed through a peephole with one eye. The girl in the near corner appears disproportionately large because we judge her size based on the false assumption that she is the same distance away as the girl in the far corner.

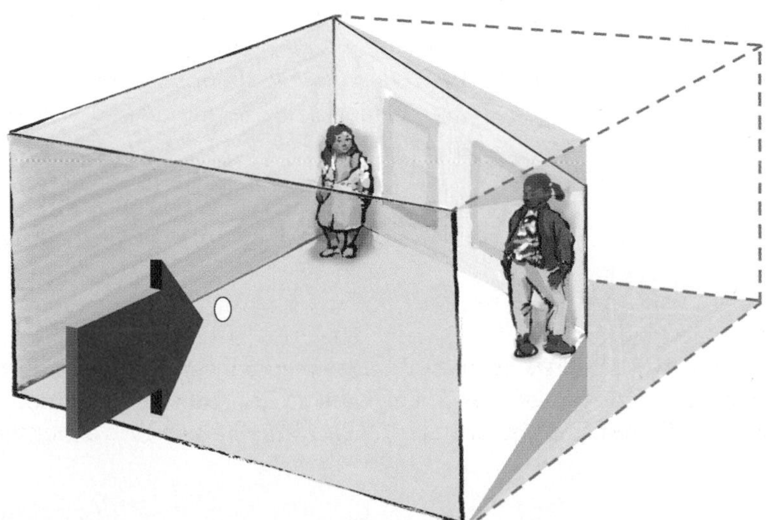

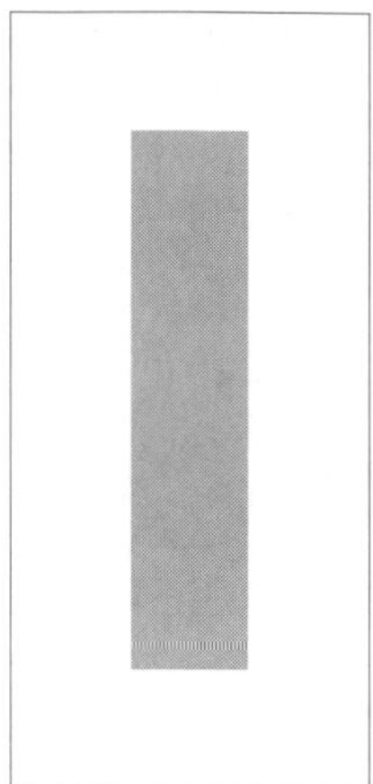

Figure 4.31 Brightness contrast Although the interior rectangles are in fact identical, we perceive the right one as lighter because of the contrast with its dark surroundings. Like the effect of context on color perception (Figure 4.13), this phenomenon has great significance for artists and interior designers.

without the tube and it is again black, because it reflects much less light than the objects around it. The phenomenon is similar to that of color constancy (pages 136–137). A red apple in a fruit bowl retains its redness as the light changes, because our brain computes the light reflected by any object relative to its surrounding objects.

If perceived lightness stays roughly constant, given an unchanging context, what happens when the surrounding context changes? As Figure 4.31 shows, the brain computes brightness and color relative to surrounding objects. Thus, perceived lightness changes with context.

Form perception, depth perception, motion perception, and perceptual constancy illustrate how we organize our visual experiences. Perceptual organization applies to other senses, too. It explains why we perceive the clock's steady tick not as a tick-tick-tick but as grouped sounds, say, TICK-tick, TICK-tick. Listening to an unfamiliar language, we have trouble hearing where one word stops and the next one begins. Listening to our own language, we automatically hear distinct words. This, too, is a form of perceptual organization. But it is more, for we even organize a string of letters—THEDOGATEMEAT—into words that make an intelligible phrase, more likely "The dog ate meat" than "The do gate me at" (McBurney & Collings, 1984). This process involves not only organization but interpretation—finding meaning in what we perceive.

REHEARSE IT!

22. Gestalt psychologists identified the principles by which we organize our perceptions. Our tendencies to fill in the gaps and to perceive a pattern as continuous are two different examples of the organizing principle called

a. figure-ground. **c.** shape constancy.
b. depth perception. **d.** grouping.

23. In their experiments, Gibson and Walk used a visual cliff to test depth perception in infants and young animals. Their results suggest that

a. infants have not yet developed depth perception.
b. crawling infants perceive depth.
c. depth perception depends on experience.
d. humans differ significantly from animals in being able to perceive depth in infancy.

24. The images that fall on our retinas are two-dimensional, or flat. Yet we perceive the world as having three-dimensional depth. Depth perception underlies our ability to

a. discriminate figure from ground.
b. perceive objects as having a constant shape or form.
c. judge distances.
d. fill in the gaps in a figure.

25. In estimating distances we use both binocular cues, which depend on both eyes, and monocular cues, which are available to either eye alone. Examples of monocular cues are interposition and

a. closure. **c.** linear perspective.
b. retinal disparity. **d.** convergence.

26. In the Müller-Lyer illusion, we misperceive the length of the lines between arrowheads. We do so partly because

a. distance cues do not help us assess size.
b. the visual distance cues (implied by the arrowheads) mislead us.
c. the perceived relationship between distance and size is generally illusory.
d. of our linear perspective.

27. Form perception and perceptual constancy are organizing principles that apply to hearing as well as vision. For example, in listening to a concerto, you follow the solo instrument and perceive the orchestra as accompaniment; this illustrates the organizing principle of

a. figure-ground. **c.** grouping.
b. shape constancy. **d.** depth or distance perception.

Interpretation

Philosophers have debated the origins of our perceptual abilities: Is it nature or nurture? German philosopher Immanuel Kant (1724–1804) maintained that knowledge comes from our *inborn* ways of organizing sensory experiences.

Indeed, we come equipped to process sensory information. But British philosopher John Locke (1632–1704) argued that through our experiences we also *learn* to perceive the world. Indeed, we learn to link an object's distance with its size. But just how important is experience? How radically does it shape our perceptual interpretations?

Sensory Restriction and Restored Vision

15. ***What does research on sensory restriction and restored vision reveal about the effects of experience on perception?***

"Let us then suppose the mind to be, as we say, white paper void of all characters, without any ideas: How comes it to be furnished? . . . To this I answer, in one word, from EXPERIENCE."

John Locke
An Essay Concerning Human Understanding
1690

Writing to John Locke (1690), William Molyneux wondered whether "a man *born* blind, and now adult, taught by his *touch* to distinguish between a cube and a sphere" could, if made to see, visually distinguish the two. Locke's answer was no, because the man would never have *learned* to see the difference.

Molyneux's hypothetical case has since been put to the test with dozens of adults who, though blind from birth, have gained sight (Gregory, 1978; von Senden, 1932). Most of these people were born with cataracts—clouded lenses that enabled them to see only diffused light, rather as you or I might see a diffuse fog through a Ping-Pong ball sliced in half. When their cataracts were surgically removed, the patients could distinguish figure from ground and could sense colors—suggesting that these aspects of perception are innate. But much as Locke supposed, the formerly blind patients often could not visually recognize objects that were familiar by touch.

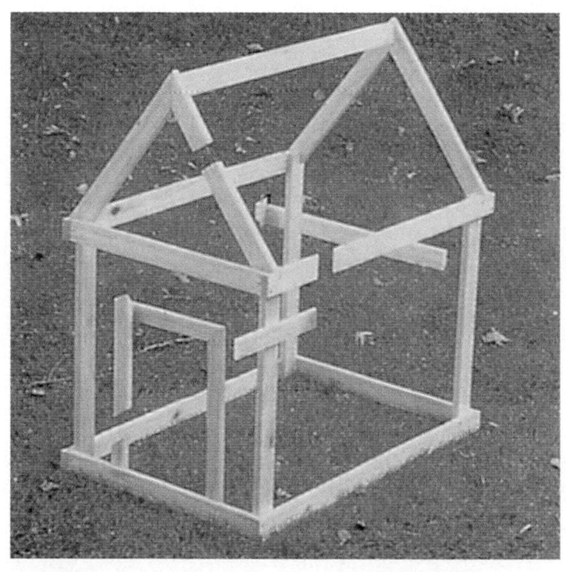

The Solution Another view of the impossible doghouse in Figure 4.21 (page 148) reveals the secrets of this illusion. From the photo angle in Figure 4.21, the grouping principle of closure leads us to perceive the boards as continuous. (Reprinted from GAMES Magazine [810 Seventh Avenue, New York, NY 10019]. Copyright © 1983 PSC Games Limited Partnership.)

Seeking to gain more control than is provided by clinical cases, researchers have conducted Molyneux's imaginary experiment with infant kittens and monkeys. In one experiment, they outfitted them with goggles through which the animals could see only diffuse, unpatterned light (Wiesel, 1982). After infancy, when their goggles were removed, these animals exhibited perceptual limitations much like those of humans born with cataracts. Their eyes had not degenerated; their retinas still relayed signals to their visual cortex. But lacking stimulation, the cortical cells had not developed normal connections. Thus, the animals remained functionally blind to shape.

In both humans and animals, a similar period of sensory restriction does no permanent harm if it occurs later in life. Cover the eye of an animal for several months during adulthood, and vision will be unaffected after removing the eye patch. Remove cataracts that develop after early childhood, and a human, too, will enjoy normal vision. The effects of visual experiences during infancy in cats, monkeys, and humans suggest there is a *critical period* (page 92) for normal sensory and perceptual development. Experience guides the organization of the brain's neural connections.

Perceptual Adaptation

16. ***How adaptable is our perception?***

Given a new pair of glasses, we may feel slightly disoriented and dizzy. Within a day or two, we adjust. Our **perceptual adaptation** to changed visual input makes the world seem normal again. Now imagine a far more dramatic new pair of glasses—one that shifts the apparent location of objects 40 degrees to the left. When you first put them on and toss a ball to a friend, it sails off to the left. Walking forward to shake hands with the person, you veer to the left.

Could you adapt to this distorted world? Chicks cannot. When fitted with such lenses, they continue to peck where food grains *seem* to be (Hess, 1956;

perceptual adaptation in vision, the ability to adjust to an artificially displaced or even inverted visual field.

Perceptual adaptation "Oops, missed," thinks Dr. Hubert Dolezal as he views the world through inverting goggles. Remarkably, people can learn to adapt to an upside-down visual world.

Rossi, 1968). But humans adapt to distorting lenses quickly. Within a few minutes your throws would again be accurate, your stride on target. Remove the lenses and you would experience an aftereffect: At first your throws would err in the *opposite* direction, sailing off to the right; but again, within minutes you would readapt.

Indeed, given an even more radical pair of glasses—one that literally turns the world upside down—you could still adapt. Turn-of-the-century psychologist George Stratton (1896) experienced this when he invented, and for eight days wore, optical headgear that flipped left to right *and* up to down, making him the first person to experience a right-side-up retinal image while standing upright.

At first, Stratton was disoriented. When he wanted to walk, he had to search for his feet, which were now "up." Eating was nearly impossible. He became nauseated and depressed. But Stratton persisted, and by the eighth day he could comfortably reach for something in the right direction and walk without bumping into things. When Stratton finally removed the headgear, he readapted quickly.

Later experiments replicated Stratton's experience (Dolezal, 1982; Kohler, 1962). After a period of adjustment, people wearing the optical gear have even been able to ride a motorcycle, ski the Alps, and fly an airplane. Is this because through experience they perceptually reinvert their upside-down world to an upright position? No, the street, ski slopes, and runway still seem above their heads. But by actively moving about in this topsy-turvy world, they adapt to the context and learn to coordinate their movements.

Perceptual Set

17. *How do our assumptions, expectations, and contexts affect our perceptions?*

As everyone knows, to see is to believe. As many people also know, but do not fully appreciate, to believe is to see. Our experiences, assumptions, and expectations may give us a **perceptual set**, or mental predisposition, that greatly influences what we perceive. Is the image in the center picture of Figure 4.32 a man playing the saxophone or a woman's face? What we see in such a drawing can be influenced by first viewing either of the two unambiguous versions (Boring, 1930).

"The temptation to form premature theories upon insufficient data is the bane of our profession."

Sherlock Holmes
In Arthur Conan Doyle's *The Valley of Fear*
1914

Everyday examples of perceptual set abound. In 1972, a British newspaper published genuine, unretouched photographs of a "monster" in Scotland's Loch Ness—"the most amazing pictures ever taken," stated the paper. If this information creates in you the same perceptual set it did in most of the paper's readers, you, too, will see the monster in the photo in Figure 4.33(a). But when

Figure 4.32 **Perceptual set** What do you see in the center picture: a male saxophonist or a woman's face? Glancing first at one of the two unambiguous versions of the picture is likely to influence your interpretation. (From Shepard, 1990)

(a)

(b)

Figure 4.33 **Believing is seeing** What do you perceive in these photos? **(a)** Is this Nessie, the Loch Ness monster, or a log? **(b)** Are these flying saucers or clouds? We often perceive what we expect to see.

Steuart Campbell (1986) approached the photos with a different perceptual set, he saw a curved tree trunk—very likely the same tree trunk others had seen in the water the day the photo was shot. Moreover, with this different perceptual set, you may now notice that the object is floating motionless, without any water disturbance or wake around it—hardly what we would expect of a lively monster.

Our perceptual set can influence what we hear as well as what we see. Witness the kindly airline pilot who, on a takeoff run, looked over at his depressed co-pilot and said, "Cheer up." The co-pilot heard the usual "Gear up" and promptly raised the wheels—before they had left the ground (Reason & Mycielska, 1982). When listening to rock music played backward, people often perceive an evil message *if* specifically told what to listen for (Vokey & Read, 1985). When observing political campaign debates, most people perceive their favorite candidate as being the better debater (Gallup, 1992). Clearly, much of what we perceive comes not just from the world "out there" but also from what's behind our eyes and between our ears.

Much of what we perceive comes not just from the world "out there" but also from what's behind our eyes and between our ears.

Even when listening to Disney movies, sex-preoccupied viewers have perceived supposedly subliminal messages, such as the letters *S-E-X* in a cloud of dust stirred up by Simba in *The Lion King* or "All good teenagers take off your clothes," murmured by a voice in *Alladin*. The latter message was first perceived by a testosterone-laden male university student, who told his sister, who told her mother, who wrote to *Movie Guide*, whose report (later retracted) was picked up by the American Life League newsletter, whose allegation was reported by Virginia's *Newport News*, from which it was picked up by the Associated Press. "If somebody is seeing something, that's their perception," responded Rick Rhoades, a spokesperson for Disney, which was inundated with protest letters. "There's nothing there" (Bannon, 1995). Some things must be believed to be seen.

What determines our perceptual set? Our preexisting schemas for male saxophonists and women's faces, for monsters and tree trunks, for airplane lights and UFOs—all help us interpret ambiguous sensations with top-down processing.

Context Effects

A given stimulus may trigger radically different perceptions, partly because of our differing schemas but also because of the immediate context. Some examples:

- Imagine hearing a noise interrupted by the words "eel is on the wagon." Likely, you would actually perceive the first word as *wheel*. Given "eel is on the orange," you would hear *peel*. This curious phenomenon, discovered by

perceptual set a mental predisposition to perceive one thing and not another.

Richard Warren, suggests that the brain can work backward in time to allow a later stimulus to determine how we perceive an earlier one. The context creates an expectation that, top-down, influences our perception as we match our bottom-up signal against it (Grossberg, 1995).

- Did the pursuing monster in Figure 4.28(a) on page 152 look aggressive? Did the pursued one seem frightened? If so, you are experiencing a context effect. The two monsters are the same.
- Is the "Magician's Cabinet" in **Figure 4.34** sitting on the floor or hanging from the ceiling? How we perceive it depends on the context defined by the bunnies.
- Did the speaker say "cults and sects" or "cults and sex"? Did the critic advocate "attacks" or "a tax" on our politicians? In both instances, we must discern the meaning from the surrounding words.

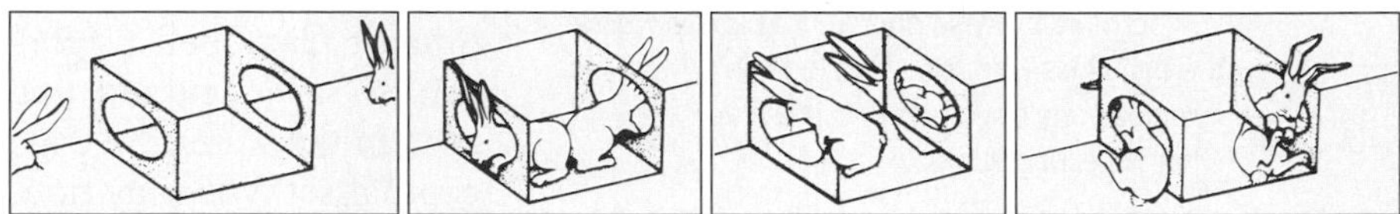

Figure 4.34 **Context effects: The Magician's Cabinet** Is the box in the far left frame lying on the floor or hanging from the ceiling? What about the one on the far right? In each case, the context defined by the inquisitive bunnies guides our perceptions. (From Shepard, 1990)

Even hearing sad rather than happy music can predispose people to perceive a sad meaning in spoken homophone words—*mourning* rather than *morning*, *die* rather than *dye*, *pain* rather than *pane* (Halberstadt & others, 1995).

In Seattle's county hospital where I was once an orderly, we occasionally faced the task of transporting a dead body through crowded hallways without alarming the patients or their visitors. Our solution was to exploit the "Kulechov effect" by creating a context that matched people's schemas for sleeping and sedated patients: With the body's face uncovered and the sheet turned down in normal fashion, we could wheel an apparently "sleeping" body past the unsuspecting.

The effects of perceptual sets and context show how experience helps us construct perception. "We hear and apprehend only what we already half know," said Thoreau. The river of perception is fed by two streams, sensation and cognition. To return to the question—Is perception innate or learned?—we can answer simply: It's both. "Simple" perceptions are the brain's creative products.

Culture and context effects What is above the woman's head? In one study, nearly all those questioned from East Africa thought she was balancing a metal box or can on her head and that the family was sitting under a tree. Westerners, to whom corners and boxlike architecture are more common, were more likely to perceive the family as being indoors, with the woman sitting under a window. (Adapted from Gregory & Gombrich, 1973)

PSYCHOLOGY APPLIED

The Human Factor in Operating Machines

I love our VCR, though I still haven't figured out how to make it "express record." Our stove is wonderful, except for the moments I spend puzzling over which control works which burner. The push-bar doors on our campus buildings are safe and easy, though occasionally frustrating when I push the wrong end. The extra buttons on my computer-linked phone are handy, though when transferring a call I still must look up which button to press.

Human factors psychologists help to design appliances, machines, and work settings that harness rather than confound our natural perceptions. Psychologist Donald Norman (1988) suggests how simple design changes could reduce some of our frustrations. For example, by exploiting "natural mapping," we could design stove controls that require no labels.

Understanding human factors can do more than design for reduced frustration; it can help avoid disaster. After beginning commercial flights in the late 1960s, the Boeing 727 was involved in several landing accidents caused by pilot error. Psychologist Conrad Kraft (1978) noted a common setting for these accidents: All took place at night, and all involved landing short of the runway after crossing a dark stretch of water or unilluminated ground. Kraft reasoned that, beyond the runway, city lights would project a larger retinal image if on a rising terrain. This would make the ground seem farther away than it was. By re-creating these conditions in flight simulations, Kraft discovered that pilots were deceived into thinking they were flying safely, higher than their actual altitudes (Figure 4.35). Aided by Kraft's finding, the airlines began corrective measures (such as requiring the co-pilot to monitor the altimeter and call out altitudes) and the accidents diminished.

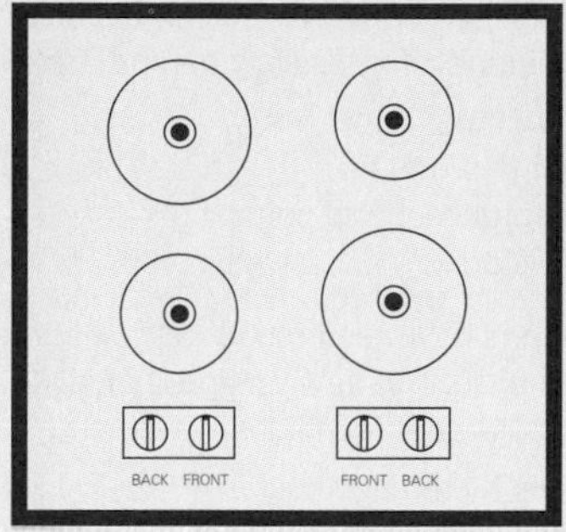

(a) Traditional labeling

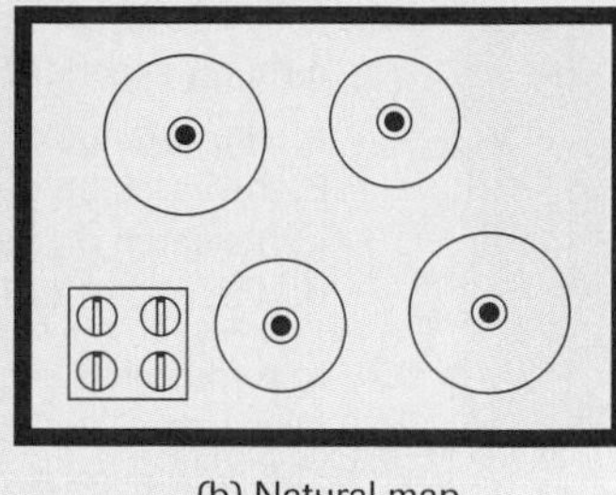

(b) Natural map

(a) With traditionally positioned stove controls a person must read the labels to figure out which knob works which burner. **(b)** By positioning the controls in a natural map, which the brain understands at a glance, we can eliminate the need to ponder written instructions just to boil water.

Figure 4.35 Human factors solution Lacking distance cues when approaching a runway from over a dark surface, pilots simulating a night landing tended to fly too low. (From Kraft, 1978)

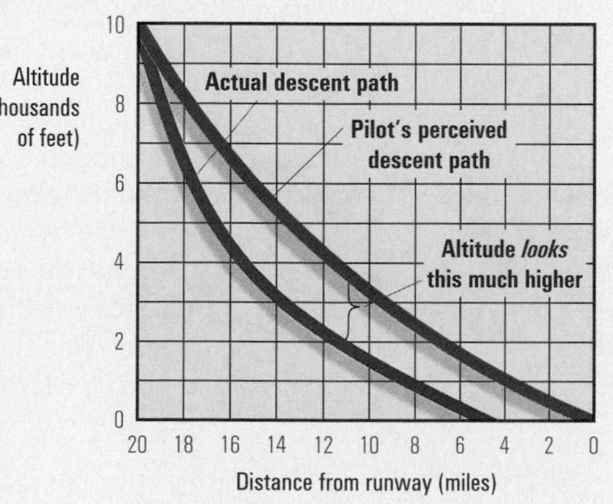

28. Locke believed that our perception of the world is learned through experience. Support for his view can be found in
    a. the writings of Immanuel Kant.
    b. research on depth perception.
    c. research on perceptual set and context.
    d. theories of color vision.

29. In some cases, surgeons have restored vision to patients who have been blind from birth. The newly sighted individuals were able to sense colors but had difficulty
    a. recognizing objects by touch.
    b. recognizing the shapes of objects.
    c. distinguishing figure from ground.
    d. distinguishing between bright and dim light.

30. Experiments in which subjects wear glasses that displace or invert their visual fields show that, after a period of disorientation, the subjects learn to function quite well. This ability is called
    a. visual capture.
    b. perceptual set.
    c. sensory restriction.
    d. perceptual adaptation.

31. Our perceptual set influences what we perceive. This mental predisposition reflects our
    a. experiences, assumptions, and expectations.
    b. perceptual adaptation.
    c. objectivity, realism, and intelligence.
    d. perceptual constancy.

Is There Perception Without Sensation?

Can we perceive only what we sense? Or, without sensory input, are we capable of extrasensory perception? Half of Americans say they believe in **extrasensory perception (ESP)**, and another quarter aren't sure—beliefs similar to those expressed by Japanese university students (McAneny, 1996; Nishizawa, 1996). The media overflow with reports of psychic wonders: crimes solved, dreams come true, futures foretold. Paranormal television (such as "Unsolved Mysteries" and "X-Files") and movies (such as *Close Encounters* and *The Exorcist*) are big business. The dial-a-psychic industry now tops $100 million a year (Emery, 1995; *Fortune*, 1995). Are there indeed people who can read minds, see through walls, or foretell the future?

If ESP is real, we would need to overturn the scientific understanding that we are creatures whose minds are tied to our physical brains and whose perceptual experiences of the world are built of sensations.

In laboratory experiments, **parapsychologists**—those who study paranormal (literally, beyond the normal) happenings—have sometimes been astonished at psychics who seem capable of discerning the contents of sealed envelopes, influencing the roll of a die, or drawing a picture of what someone else is viewing at an unknown remote location. But other research psychologists and scientists—including 96 percent of the scientists in the National Academy of Sciences—are skeptical (McConnell, 1991). If ESP is real, we would need to overturn the scientific understanding that we are creatures whose minds are tied to our physical brains and whose perceptual experiences of the world are built of sensations. Sometimes new evidence does overturn our scientific preconceptions. So let's look at some claims for ESP and then see why scientists remain dubious.

Claims of ESP

18. *What types of ESP have been proposed, and why are most research psychologists skeptical?*

Claims of paranormal phenomena include astrological predictions, psychic healing, reincarnation, communication with the dead, and out-of-body frequent-flyer programs. Of these, the most respectable, testable, and—for a chapter on perception—relevant claims are for three varieties of ESP:

extrasensory perception (ESP) the controversial claim that perception can occur apart from sensory input. Said to include *telepathy, clairvoyance*, and *precognition.*

parapsychology the study of paranormal phenomena, including ESP.

Which supposed psychic ability does the sportscaster claim?

Telepathy, or mind-to-mind communication—one person sending thoughts to another or perceiving another's thoughts.

Clairvoyance, or perceiving remote events, such as sensing that a friend's house is on fire.

Precognition, or perceiving future events, such as a political leader's death or a sporting event's outcome.

On stage, the "psychic," like a magician, controls what the audience sees and hears. In the laboratory, the experimenter controls what the psychic sees and hears. Consider one careful experiment conducted by Bruce Layton and Bill Turnbull (1975) at the University of North Carolina. Layton and Turnbull had a computer generate a randomized 100-item list of the digits *1, 2, 3, 4*, and *5* for each of their 179 participants. They gave each student such a list in a sealed envelope and asked the student to guess which number was in each of the 100 positions.

By chance, 1 guess in 5, or 20 guesses out of the 100, should be correct. When told beforehand that ESP was beneficial, subjects averaged 20.66 correct out of 100. When told that ESP was harmful, they averaged only 19.49 correct. The difference might seem trivial—indeed, you would never notice so small an effect while observing an experiment. But a statistical analysis revealed that a difference that large among so many participants would seldom occur by chance. So Layton and Turnbull concluded that an ESP effect had occurred.

Bolstered by such experiments, believers in ESP accuse research psychologists of the same sort of skepticism that led eighteenth-century scientists to scoff at the idea that meteorites come from outer space. Novelist Arthur Koestler, who on his death in 1983 left a bequest to fund a British professorship in parapsychology, registered similar complaints. He once commented that today's skeptical scientists resemble the Italian philosophers who refused to look at Jupiter's moons through Galileo's telescope—because they "knew" that such moons did not exist. Stubborn skepticism sometimes blinds people to surprising truth.

"A man does not attain the status of Galileo merely because he is persecuted; he must also be right."

Stephen Jay Gould
Ever Since Darwin
1973

Skepticism About ESP

The skeptics reply that an uncritical mind is a gullible mind. Time and again, they point out, so-called psychics have exploited unquestioning audiences with amazing performances in which they *appeared* to communicate with the spirits of the dead, read minds, or levitate objects—only to have it revealed that their acts were a hoax, nothing more than the illusions of stage magicians. Indeed, many psychic deceptions have been exposed by magicians, who resent the exploitation of their art in the name of psychic powers.

People's gullibility illustrates how tempting it is to label phenomena *they* don't understand as beyond explanation: "What other explanation could there possibly be but ESP?" asks the awestruck observer.

In 1996, Psychic Friends Network owner Michael Lasky spent $500,000 to purchase Eddie Murray's 500th home-run baseball (Dodd, 1996). One couldn't help but wonder not only about the poor souls whose money Lasky was spending, but why his psychics hadn't just told him when and where to sit to catch it himself.

"A psychic is an actor playing the role of a psychic."

Psychologist-Magician Daryl Bem (1984)

Premonitions or Pretensions?

Can psychics see into the future? Although one might wish for a psychic stock forecaster, the tallied forecasts of "leading psychics" reveal meager accuracy. Between 1978 and 1985, the New Year's predictions of the *National Enquirer*'s favorite psychics yielded 2 accurate predictions out of 486 (Strentz, 1986). During the early 1990s, tabloid psychics were all wrong in predicting surprising events (Madonna did not become a gospel singer, Bill Cosby has not become an ambassador to South Africa, Queen Elizabeth did not abdicate her throne to enter a convent). And they missed all the big-news unexpected events, such as specific terrorist bombings, Saddam Hussein's assault on Kuwait, and the O. J. Simpson case. Before 1994, psychics offered many other predictions about Michael Jackson—that he would marry Oprah Winfrey, become a traveling evangelist, and undergo a "complete sex change operation and insist that everyone call him Michelle"—but they missed their chance to predict his marriage to Lisa Marie Presley (CSICOP, 1994).

Analyses of psychic visions offered to police departments reveal that these, too, are no more accurate than guesses made by others (Reiser, 1982). Psychics working with the police do, however, generate dozens or even hundreds of predictions. This increases the odds of an occasional correct guess, which psychics can then report to the media. As a Spanish proverb says, "A person who talks a lot is sometimes right." Moreover, vague predictions can later be interpreted ("retrofitted") to match events, which provide a perceptual set for interpreting them. Nostradamus, a sixteenth-century French psychic, explained in an unguarded moment that his ambiguous prophecies "could not possibly be understood till they were interpreted after the event and by it." Police departments are wise to all this. When Jane Ayers Sweat and Mark Durm (1993) asked the police departments of America's 50 largest cities whether they ever used psychics, 65 percent said they never had. Of those that had, not one had found it helpful.

Are the spontaneous "visions" of ordinary people any more accurate? Consider our dreams. Do they foretell the future, as about half of university students believe (Messer & Griggs, 1989)? Or do they only seem to because we are more likely to recall or reconstruct dreams that seem to have come true? Sixty years ago, two Harvard psychologists (Murray & Wheeler, 1937) tested the prophetic power of dreams. After aviator Charles Lindbergh's baby son was kidnapped and murdered but before the body was discovered, the researchers invited the public to report their dreams about the child. Of the 1300 dream reports submitted, how many accurately envisioned the child dead? A mere 5 percent. And how many also correctly anticipated the body's location—buried among trees? Only 4 of the 1300. Although this number was surely no better than chance, to those 4 dreamers the accuracy of their *apparent* precognitions must have seemed uncanny.

More recent experiments in which people attempted to send mental images to dreamers produced some intriguing initial results, but these could not be replicated even with the same subjects. Dream telepathy experiments therefore were discontinued (Hyman, 1986).

Every day each of us imagines many events. Occasionally an unlikely imagined event is bound to occur and to astonish us when it does. If you tell everyone in a group of 100 people to think "heads" before each tosses six coins, someone is likely to get all heads (whether thinking of heads or not) and to feel eerie afterwards. As Chapter 1 explained, random sequences will sometimes contain weird conjunctions or streaks. Given the billions of events that occur in the world each day, and given enough days, some stunning coincidences are sure to occur. "Time converts the improbable to the inevitable," notes Stephen Jay Gould.

"There comes a point where one has to accept the message of the data, that absence of evidence is evidence of absence."

Frank Close
Too Hot to Handle: The Race for Cold Fusion
1991

Finally, consider this, say the skeptics: If ESP existed, then surely someone out there could, when feeling the psychic spirit stirring, occasionally pick winning lottery numbers or black jack outcomes (becoming fabulously wealthy or generous over time). And why doesn't some psychic make billions playing the stock market? But after tens of thousands of experiments, *there has never been discovered a reproducible ESP phenomenon, nor any individual who can convincingly demonstrate psychic ability*. A National Research Council investigation of ESP similarly concluded that "the best available evidence does not support the contention that these phenomena exist" (Druckman & Swets, 1988). And in 1995, a report commissioned by the Central Intelligence Agency (CIA) evaluated 10 years of military testing of psychic spies (a program previously abandoned by the CIA for having produced nothing). After $20 million had been invested, the program again produced nothing. Given so many disappointing laboratory results and

To refute those who say there is no ESP, one need only produce a single person who can demonstrate a single reproducible ESP phenomenon. As yet, no one has exhibited any such power.

BIZARRO

The "Bizarro" cartoon by Dan Piraro is reprinted by permission of Chronicle Features.

Which supposed psychic ability does Psychic Pizza claim?

vague or erroneous psychic visions, the psychic spy program was scrapped (Hyman, 1996; Waller, 1995).

One skeptic, magician James Randi, has offered $10,000 to anyone who can demonstrate "*any* paranormal ability" before a group of competent experts. With pledges from others, that offer—"to anyone who proves a genuine psychic power under proper observing conditions"—has now been upped to $1.1 million (Randi, 1997). Large as this sum is, the scientific seal of approval would be worth far more to anyone whose claims could be authenticated. So far, no winners have emerged, though Randi's offer has been publicized for three decades and dozens of people have been tested, sometimes under the scrutiny of an independent panel of judges.

To refute those who say there is no ESP, one need only produce a single person who can demonstrate a single reproducible ESP phenomenon. As yet, no one has exhibited any such power. Lacking such, and faced with increasing skepticism, the Parapsychological Association has lost membership, and several major parapsychological laboratories lost their funding and closed during the 1980s (Hess, 1993).

Thinking Critically About ESP

In times past, there have been all kinds of crazy ideas—that bumps on the head reveal character traits, that bloodletting is a cure-all, that each sperm cell contains a miniature person inside. When faced with such claims—or with claims of mind-reading or out-of-body travel or communication with the dead—how can we separate crazy ideas from those that sound crazy but are true? At the heart of science we find a simple answer: Test them to see if they work. If they do, so much the worse for our skepticism. If they don't, so much the worse for the ideas.

"At the heart of science is an essential tension between two seemingly contradictory attitudes—an openness to new ideas, no matter how bizarre or counterintuitive they may be, and the most ruthless skeptical scrutiny of all ideas, old and new."

Carl Sagan (1987)

This scientific attitude appears in the agreement of believers and skeptics that what parapsychology needs to give it credibility is a reproducible phenomenon and a theory to explain it. Could the Layton and Turnbull clairvoyance experiment (in which students beat chance in guessing numbers in sealed envelopes) provide such a reproducible phenomenon? The skeptical editor of the *Journal of Experimental Social Psychology*, to which Layton and Turnbull submitted their results for publication, wondered. So he and the authors reached an unusual agreement: The researchers would repeat their experiment, and the journal would then publish the results of both, regardless of the new outcome. (As this illustrates, both ESP researchers and skeptics genuinely seek truth.) The result of the second experiment? Layton and Turnbull summarized honestly and succinctly: "No [statistically] significant effects were present."

"Doubt is the key to knowledge."

Iranian Proverb

Knowing how easily people are deceived, and lacking reproducible results, most research psychologists remain skeptical. Indeed, they are dismayed by all the shows, books, and magazines on paranormal topics. But some are newly intrigued by findings recently published by social psychologist Daryl Bem and parapsychologist Charles Honorton (1994) using the "ganzfeld procedure." The procedure would place you in a reclining chair, play hissing white noise through headphones, and shine diffuse red light through Ping-Pong ball halves strapped over your eyes. Ostensibly, this reduction of external distractions would put you in an ideal state to receive others' thoughts, which you may hear as small voices from within. Building on earlier studies using this procedure, Bem and Honorton isolated a "sender" and "receiver" in separate, shielded chambers and had the sender concentrate for half an hour on one of four randomly selected visual images. The receivers were then asked which of four images best matched the images they experienced during the session. Over 11

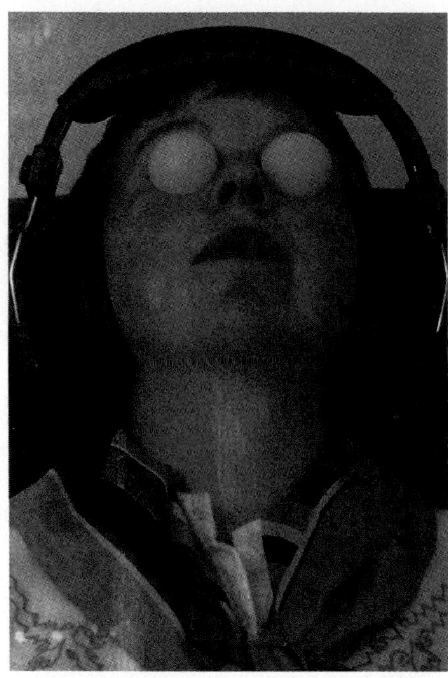

The ganzfeld procedure Hoping to detect faint telepathy signals, some parapsychologists use sensory deprivation to minimize distractions.

studies, the receivers beat chance (25 percent accurately matched) by a small but reliable margin (32 percent accurately matched). University of Edinburgh parapsychologist Richard Morris and his students (1995, 1996) have reported similar results.

Recall that psychology-based critical inquiry asks two questions: What do you mean? And how do you know (what's your evidence)? Parapsychologists say these ganzfeld tests of ESP offer clear answers to both questions. Skeptic Ray Hyman (1994, 1996) grants that their methodology surpasses that of previous ESP experiments, but he questions certain procedural details that may have introduced bias. Intrigued, other researchers are now at work replicating these experiments. Will this be the first reliable ESP phenomenon? Or one more dashed hope, one more "phenomenon" that later will be refuted and abandoned? Stay tuned, and remember: The scientific attitude blends curious skepticism with open-minded humility. It demands that extraordinary claims be supported by clear and reliable evidence. (If at 5′7″ and age 54 I claim to be able to dunk a basketball, the burden of proof would be on me to show that I can do it, not on you to prove that I couldn't.) Given such evidence, science is open to nature's occasional surprises.

The scientific attitude blends curious skepticism with open-minded humility. It demands that extraordinary claims be supported by clear and reliable evidence.

As critical thinkers, we can share this attitude. We can be open to new ideas without being gullible, be discerning without being cynical. We can be critical thinkers, yet—knowing that our understanding of nature is incomplete—we can agree with Shakespeare's Hamlet that "there are more things in heaven and earth, Horatio, than are dreamt of in your philosophy."

Why are so many people predisposed to believe that ESP exists? In part, such beliefs may stem from understandable misperceptions, misinterpretations, and selective recall. But for some people there also exists an unsatisfied hunger for wonderment, an itch to experience the magical. In Britain and the United States, the founders of parapsychology were mostly people who, having lost their religious faith, were searching for a scientific basis for believing in the meaningfulness of life and the possibility of life after death (Alcock, 1985; Beloff, 1985). In the upheaval since the collapse of autocratic rule in Russia, there has come an "avalanche of the mystical, occult, and pseudoscientific" (Kapitza, 1991). "Extrasensorial" healers, astrologers, and seers fascinate the awestruck public.

"I have uttered what I did not understand, things too wonderful for me."

Job 42:3

To feel awe and to gain a deep reverence for life, we need look no further than our own perceptual system and its capacity for organizing formless nerve impulses into colorful sights, vivid sounds, and evocative smells. Within our ordinary perceptual experiences lies much that is truly extraordinary—surely much more than has so far been dreamt of in our psychology. A century of research has revealed many of the secrets of sensation and perception, but for future generations of researchers there remain profound and genuine mysteries to solve.

32. More than half of Americans believe in the reality of ESP (extrasensory perception). The response of psychologists to these claims has been to

a. deny the possibility of perception apart from sensation.
b. doubt the existence of mysteries and extraordinary phenomena.
c. test and critique ESP claims.
d. devise a theory that explains why ESP exists.

33. The most testable varieties of ESP involve perceiving future events, mind-to-mind communication, and perceiving remote events. In order, these refer to

a. clairvoyance, telepathy, and precognition.
b. telepathy, clairvoyance, and precognition.
c. precognition, telepathy, and clairvoyance.
d. precognition, clairvoyance, and telepathy.

REVIEWING ■ *Sensation and Perception*

Sensing the World: Some Basic Principles

Sensation—receiving and representing stimulus energies from our environment—involves **bottom-up processing**. **Perception**—the process of selecting, organizing, and interpreting sensory information—involves **top-down processing**. **Psychophysics** is the study of how sensations are perceived.

1. ***What is an absolute threshold, and are we influenced by stimuli below it?***

Each species comes equipped with sensitivities that enable it to survive and thrive. We sense only a portion of the sea of energy that surrounds us, but to this portion we are exquisitely sensitive. Our **absolute threshold** for any stimulus is the minimum stimulation that is detectable 50 percent of the time. Although recent experiments reveal that we can process some information from **subliminal** (subthreshold) stimuli, the restricted conditions under which this occurs would not enable unscrupulous opportunists to exploit us with subliminal messages.

2. ***How is our threshold for detecting differences affected by the magnitude of the stimuli?***

To survive and thrive, an organism must have **difference thresholds** low enough to detect minute changes in important stimuli. In humans, a difference threshold (also called a *just noticeable difference*, or *jnd*) is a constant proportion of the magnitude of the stimulus—a principle known as **Weber's law**.

3. ***What function does sensory adaptation serve?***

The phenomenon of **sensory adaptation** helps to focus our attention on changing stimulation by diminishing our sensitivity to constant or routine odors, sounds, and so forth.

Vision

4. ***How does the eye transform light energy into neural messages?***

Each of our senses receives stimulation, transforms it into neural signals, and sends these neural messages to the brain. The energies we experience as visible light are a thin slice from the broad spectrum of electromagnetic radiation. The perceived **hue** and brightness of light depend on its **wavelength** and **intensity**. After entering the eye and being focused by a cameralike lens (through the process of **accommodation**), light waves strike the **retina**. The retina's light-sensitive **rods** and color-sensitive **cones** convert the light energy into neural impulses, which travel along the **optic nerve** to the brain. The point at which the optic nerve leaves the eye is the **blind spot**.

5. ***How is visual information processed in the brain?***

Nerve cells in the retina process information before routing it to the brain. Within the cortex, individual **feature detector** cells respond to specific aspects of the visual stimulus, and their information is pooled by higher level brain cells for interpretation. Subdimensions of vision (color, movement, depth, and form) are processed separately and simultaneously, illustrating our brain's capacity for **parallel processing**.

6. ***What theories contribute to our understanding of color vision, and how are we affected by color constancy?***

Research on how we see color supports two nineteenth-century theories. First, as the **Young-Helmholtz trichromatic (three-color) theory** suggests, the retina contains three types of cones. Each is most sensitive to the wavelengths of one of the three primary colors (red, green, or blue). Second, as **opponent-process theory** maintains, the nervous system codes the color-related information from the cones into pairs of opponent colors, as demonstrated by the phenomenon of afterimages and as confirmed by measuring opponent processes within the retina and within visual neurons of the thalamus. The phenomenon of **color constancy** under varying illumination shows that our brains construct our experience of color.

The Other Senses

7. ***How does the ear transform sound energy into neural messages?***

Although vision tends to dominate our other senses (**visual capture**), our other senses, including hearing (**audition**), are highly adaptive. The pressure waves we experience as sound vary in **frequency** and amplitude, and correspondingly in perceived **pitch** and loudness. Through a mechanical chain of events, these sound waves traveling down the auditory canal cause minuscule vibrations in the eardrum. Transmitted via the bones of the **middle ear** to the fluid-filled **cochlea** in the **inner ear**, these vibrations create movement in tiny hair cells, triggering neural messages to the brain. We localize sound by detecting minute differences in the loudness and timing of the sounds received by each ear.

8. ***How do we sense touch and feel pain?***

Our sense of touch is actually four senses—pressure, warmth, cold, and pain—that combine to produce other sensations, such as a tickle. One theory of pain is that a "gate" in the spinal cord either opens in response to pain signals traveling up small nerve fibers, which then pass on to the brain, or closes to prevent their passage (**gate-control theory**). Because pain is both a physiological and a psychological phenomenon, it often can be controlled through a combination of physical and psychological treatments.

9. ***How do we experience taste and smell?***

Taste, a chemical sense, is a composite of four basic sensations—sweet, sour, salty, and bitter—and of the aromas that interact with information from the taste buds. Like taste, smell is a chemical sense. The fact that our sense of smell affects our taste illustrates **sensory interaction**.

10. ***How do we sense our body's position and movement?***

Our effective functioning requires a **kinesthetic sense**, which notifies the brain of the position and movement of body parts, and a **vestibular sense**, which monitors the position and movement of the whole body.

Perceptual Organization

11. ***What did the Gestalt psychologists contribute to our understanding of perception?***

The early Gestalt psychologists were impressed with the seemingly innate way in which we organize fragmentary sensory data into whole perceptions (**gestalts**). They studied how our minds structure the information that comes to us.

12. ***How do the principles of figure-ground and grouping contribute to our perception of form?***

To recognize an object, we must first perceive it (see it as a **figure**) as distinct from its surroundings (the **ground**). We must also organize the figure into a meaningful form. Several gestalt principles of **grouping**—proximity, similarity, continuity, closure, and connectedness—describe this process.

13. ***Why do we see the world in three dimensions?***

Research on the **visual cliff** reveals that many species perceive the world in three dimensions at, or very soon after, birth. We transform two-dimensional retinal images into three-dimensional **depth perceptions** by use of **binocular cues** (such as **retinal disparity** and **convergence**) and **monocular cues** (such as **interposition, relative size, relative height, relative motion,** [also called *motion parallax*], **relative brightness**, and **linear perspective**).

14. ***How do perceptual constancies help us to organize our sensations into meaningful perceptions?***

Because of size, shape, and lightness constancy, objects appear to have unchanging characteristics regardless of their true distance from us or their actual shape or illumination. These **perceptual constancies** explain several of the well-known visual illusions, such as the Müller-Lyer and moon illusions.

Interpretation

15. ***What does research on sensory restriction and restored vision reveal about the effects of experience on perception?***

For many species, infancy is a critical period during which experience must activate the brain's innate visual mechanisms. Although cataract removal may restore eyesight to adults who were blind from birth, these people remain unable to perceive the world normally. Generally, they can distinguish figure from ground and can perceive colors but they are unable to recognize shapes and forms. In controlled experiments, infant animals have been reared with severely restricted visual input. When their visual exposure is returned to normal, they, too, suffer enduring visual handicaps.

16. ***How adaptable is our perception?***

Human vision is remarkably **adaptable**. For example, given glasses that shift the world slightly to the left or right, or even turn it upside down, people manage to adapt their movements and, with practice, to move about with ease.

17. ***How do our assumptions, expectations, and contexts affect our perceptions?***

Clear evidence that perception is influenced by our learned assumptions and beliefs as well as by sensory input comes from the many demonstrations of **perceptual set**. Contexts plus the ideas we have stored in memory help us to interpret otherwise ambiguous stimuli. This helps explain why some of us "see" monsters, faces, and UFOs that others do not.

Is There Perception Without Sensation?

18. ***What types of ESP have been proposed, and why are most research psychologists skeptical?***

Parapsychologists have tried to document several forms of **ESP**—telepathy, clairvoyance, and precognition. But for several reasons, especially the lack of a reproducible ESP effect, most research psychologists remain skeptical. New studies using the ganzfeld procedure have recently raised hopes of a measurable telepathy phenomenon. Follow-up studies should soon indicate the phenomenon's reliability.

CRITICAL THINKING EXERCISE by Richard O. Straub

Now that you have read and reviewed Chapter 4, take your learning a step further by testing your critical thinking skills on the following practical problem-solving exercise.

The World Wide Web has become a distinct publishing genre with its own language and set of evolving rules and conventions. Although Web sites come in nearly every conceivable shape, size, and style, some are more informative, entertaining, or persuasive than others. Successful sites are visually pleasing and easy to navigate, and they convey information efficiently.

As with the perception of any complex visual stimulus, our brains construct our perception of a Web site according to basic principles of perceptual organization and interpretation. These principles include those by which we group stimuli together into recognizable forms, those that enable the perception of depth and distance, and those by which our brains compute motion. The principle of stroboscopic movement, for example, states that our brains will interpret a rapid series of slightly varying images as movement. On a Web site, such images form the basis for animation and special video effects, which add visual appeal and offer another venue for transmitting information. Motion on a Web page, such as a blinking "New" button, also attracts attention and conveys importance.

Now, suppose you have been commissioned by a local company to consult on the design of their home page. You are the "psychology expert" and need to explain how the following five major perceptual principles are involved in designing an effective Web site. First indicate what the principle enables the brain to perceive, and then explain how it can be exploited to enhance the effectiveness of a Web site.

1. *Figure and ground:*
2. *Similarity:*
3. *Relative brightness:*
4. *Size-distance relationship:*
5. *Culture and perception:*

Check your progress on becoming a critical thinker by comparing your answers to the sample answers in Appendix B.

REHEARSE IT ANSWER KEY

1. d., **2.** b., **3.** b., **4** d., **5.** b., **6.** c., **7.** d., **8.** b., **9.** c., **10.** c., **11.** b., **12.** a., **13.** d., **14.** b., **15.** a., **16.** b., **17.** c., **18.** a., **19.** c., **20.** d., **21.** c., **22.** d., **23.** b., **24.** c., **25.** c., **26.** b., **27.** a., **28.** c., **29.** b., **30.** d., **31.** a., **32.** c., **33.** c.

CHAPTER
5

States of Consciousness

Now playing at an inner theater near you: the premiere showing of some sleeping person's vivid dream. This never-before-seen mental movie features captivating characters wrapped in a plot so original and unlikely, yet so intricate and real-seeming, that the viewer later marvels at its creation. Awakening from a troubling dream, wrenched by its emotions, who among us has not wondered about this weird state of consciousness? How does our brain so creatively, colorfully, and completely construct this alternative conscious world? In the shadowland between our dreaming and waking consciousness, we may even wonder for a moment which realm represents reality. And what shall we make of other altered states of consciousness—of daydreaming, hypnosis, drug-altered hallucinations, and near-death visions?

But first questions first: What is consciousness? In every science there are concepts so fundamental they are nearly impossible to define. Biologists agree on what is alive but not on precisely what life is. In physics, matter and energy elude simple definition. To psychologists, consciousness is similarly a fundamental yet slippery concept.

Waking Consciousness

1. *What is consciousness and how does it function?*

At its beginning, psychology was sometimes defined as "the description and explanation of states of consciousness" (Ladd, 1887). But the difficulty of scientifically studying consciousness led many psychologists during the first half of the twentieth century to turn to direct observations of behavior—an approach favored by an emerging school of psychology called *behaviorism* (page 214). At midcentury, psychology was no longer defined as the study of consciousness or "mental life" but rather as the science of behavior. Psychology had nearly lost consciousness. Consciousness was viewed as resembling a car's speedometer: "It doesn't make the car go, it just reflects what's happening" (Seligman, 1991, p. 24).

By 1960, mental concepts had begun to reenter psychology. Advances in neuroscience made it possible to relate brain activity to various mental states—

"Psychology must discard all reference to consciousness."

Behaviorist John B. Watson (1913)

As two behaviorists pass in the hall, one says: "You feel fine this morning. How do I feel?"

waking, sleeping, dreaming. Researchers were also beginning to study consciousness altered by hypnosis and drugs. Psychologists of all persuasions were affirming the importance of mental processes (cognition). Psychology was regaining consciousness.

For most psychologists today, **consciousness** is our awareness of ourselves and our environment. When we learn a complex concept or behavior—say, driving a car—consciousness focuses our concentration on the car and the traffic. This awareness varies with our attentional spotlight. With practice, driving becomes automatic and does not require our undivided attention—freeing our consciousness to focus on other tasks. If I call your attention to the weight of your body pressing on your buttocks as you sit reading, you will momentarily stop reading.

Selective Attention

Perceptions come to us moment by moment, one perception vanishing as the next appears. When you were looking at the Necker cube and figure-ground demonstrations in Chapter 4, you could *know* that two interpretations were possible, yet at any moment you consciously experienced only one of them. This illustrates an important principle: Our conscious attention is *selective*.

Selective attention means that at any moment we focus our awareness on only a limited aspect of all that we are capable of experiencing. Until reading this sentence, you have been unaware that your shoes are pressing against your feet or that your nose is in your line of vision. Now, suddenly, your attentional spotlight shifts and your feet feel encased, your nose stubbornly intrudes on the page before you. While attending to these words, you've also been blocking from awareness information coming from your peripheral vision. But you can change that. While staring at the X below, notice what surrounds the book (the edges of the page, your desk top, and so forth).

X

Attention With experience, tasks such as driving become mostly automatic, freeing our conscious attention for other matters. However, in heavy traffic, a driver immersed in a phone conversation may have difficulty attending to the challenges of driving.

Another example of selective attention is the *cocktail party effect*—the ability to attend selectively to only one voice among many. Imagine hearing two conversations over a headset, one in each ear, and being asked to repeat the left-ear message as it is spoken. When you pay attention to what's being said in your left ear, you won't perceive what is said in your right ear. If later you are asked what language your right ear heard, you may draw a blank (though you could report the speaker's gender and loudness). At the level of conscious awareness, whatever has your attention pretty much has your undivided attention.

Can unnoticed stimuli affect us? Indeed yes. In one experiment, women students listened through headphones as a prose passage played in one ear. Their task was to repeat its words out loud and to check them against a written transcript (Wilson, 1979). Meanwhile, some simple, novel tunes played in the other ear. The tunes were not subliminal—the women could hear them easily. But with their attention selectively focused on the passage, the women were no more aware of the tunes than you normally are of your shoes. Thus, when they later heard these tunes interspersed among new ones, they could not recognize them (just as people cannot recall a conversation to which they paid no attention). Nevertheless, when asked to rate their fondness for each tune, they *preferred* the ones previously played. Their preferences revealed what their conscious memories could not. Although perception requires attention, even unattended stimuli sometimes have subtle effects.

consciousness our awareness of ourselves and our environment.

selective attention the focusing of conscious awareness on a particular stimulus, as in the cocktail party effect.

Consciousness Our awareness of ourselves and our environment is but the visible surface of our brain's information processing.

Levels of Information Processing

Conscious awareness enables us to exert voluntary control and to communicate our mental states to others, yet consciousness is but the tip of the information-processing iceberg. Several of this book's other chapters (Sensation and Perception; Learning; Memory; Thinking, Language, and Intelligence; Emotions, Stress, and Health) reveal that we process much information outside our awareness. We register and react to stimuli we do not consciously perceive. We perform well-learned tasks automatically, as when keyboarding without attending to where the letters are. When we meet someone, we instantly and unconsciously react to the person's gender, race, and appearance, and then become aware of our response. We change our attitudes and reconstruct our memories with no awareness of doing so. Our past influences us in ways we don't know (Greenwald & Banaji, 1995).

Unlike the processing of subconscious information, which occurs simultaneously on many parallel tracks, conscious processing takes place in sequence (serially). Moreover, consciousness is relatively slow and has limited capacity. Consciousness is like a chief executive officer, whose many assistants automatically take care of routine business. Consider your hands. When not under conscious control, they have a life of their own, scanning your body for imperfections, grooming, gesturing. Traveling a familiar route, your hands do the driving while your mind engages in conversation. Running on automatic pilot allows consciousness—the mind's CEO—to monitor the whole system and deal with new challenges.

Unlike the processing of subconscious information, which occurs simultaneously on many parallel tracks, conscious processing takes place in sequence (serially).

Novel tasks require our conscious attention. When we first arrive in a country where people drive on the other side of the road, driving commands our full attention. Or try this: If you are right-handed, you can move your right foot in a smooth counterclockwise circle, and you can write the number 3 repeatedly with your right hand—but not at the same time. (If you are musically inclined, try something equally difficult: Tap a steady three times with your left hand while tapping four times with your right hand.) Both tasks require conscious attention, which can be in only one place at a time. If time is nature's way of keeping everything from happening at once, then consciousness is nature's way of keeping us from thinking and doing everything at once.

Looking into the inner world Daydreams and fantasies are a constructive part of everyone's repertory of behavior. For these Dutch commuters, daydreams may release tension, increase creativity, illuminate solutions to problems—and even lessen boredom.

Daydreams and Fantasies

2. *What are the functions of daydreams and fantasies?*

In James Thurber's classic story "The Secret Life of Walter Mitty," the bland existence of mild-mannered Walter Mitty is spiced with gratifying fantasies. As he drives past a hospital, Mitty imagines himself as Dr. Mitty, rushing to an operating room where two renowned specialists plead for his help. Again and again, the bumbling Walter Mitty relieves the tedium of his life by imagining himself as the triumphant Walter Mitty—now the world's greatest target shooter, now a heroic pilot.

Thurber's story became a classic because most of us can identify with Walter Mitty. From interview and questionnaire studies with hundreds of adults, clinical psychologist Jerome L. Singer (1975) reported that nearly everyone has daydreams or waking fantasies every day—on the job, in the classroom, walking down the street—in fact, almost anywhere at any time. Compared with older adults, young adults spend more time daydreaming and admit to more sexual fantasies (Cameron & Biber, 1973; Giambra, 1974). About 95 percent of both men and women say they have had sexual fantasies. But men (whether gay or straight) fantasize about sex more often, more physically, and less romantically—and prefer books and videos accordingly (Leitenberg & Henning, 1995). Sexual fantasies do *not* indicate sexual problems or dissatisfaction. (If anything, sexually active and satisfied people have more sexual fantasies.)

fantasy-prone personality someone who imagines and recalls experiences with lifelike vividness and who spends considerable time fantasizing.

circadian rhythm [ser-KAY-dee-an] the biological clock; cyclical bodily rhythms (for example, of temperature and wakefulness).

Not all daydreaming is as overtly escapist or dramatic as Walter Mitty's. Mostly it involves the familiar details of our lives—perhaps imagining an alternative approach to a task we are performing, or picturing ourselves explaining to an instructor why a paper will be late, or replaying in our minds personal encounters that we relish or wish had gone differently.

Some individuals—perhaps 4 percent of the population—fantasize so vividly they are called **fantasy-prone personalities**. One study of 26 such women found that as children they had enjoyed unusually intense make-believe play with their dolls, stuffed animals, or imaginary companions (Wilson & Barber, 1983). As adults, they reported spending more than half their time fantasizing. They would relive experiences or imagine scenes so vividly that occasionally they later had trouble sorting out their remembered fantasies from their memories of actual events. When watching or imagining violent or scary scenes, they sometimes felt ill. Many reported profound mystical or religious experiences. Three-fourths had experienced orgasms solely by sexual fantasy.

Are the hours we spend in fantasy merely a way of escaping rather than facing reality? Sometimes. But daydreaming can also be adaptive. Some daydreams help us prepare for future events by keeping us aware of unfinished business and serving as mental rehearsals. Playful fantasies enhance the creativity of scientists, artists, and writers. For children, daydreaming in the form of imaginative play feeds social and cognitive development—a fact that makes the diversion of television watching a matter of concern to some developmental psychologists (Singer, 1986).

"When I examined myself, and my methods of thought, I came to the conclusion that the gift of fantasy has meant more to me than my talent for absorbing positive knowledge."

Albert Einstein
1879–1955

"The art of living requires us to steer a course between the two extremes of external and internal stimulation."

Psychologist Jerome L. Singer (1976)

Daydreams may also substitute for impulsive behavior. People who are prone to delinquency and violence or who seek the artificial highs of dangerous drugs have fewer vivid fantasies (Singer, 1976). Perhaps Walter Mitty's imaginative reveries not only rescued him from boredom but also allowed him to indulge his impulses within the safety of his inner world.

Consciousness occurs in varied states. We have not only normal seeing and hearing, reasoning and remembering, daydreams and fantasies, but also the altered consciousness of sleep, hypnotic states, chemically induced hallucinations, and near-death visions.

REHEARSE IT!

1. Consciousness involves selective attention to ongoing perceptions. An example of selective attention is the "cocktail party effect," which is the ability to

a. drink without becoming intoxicated.
b. follow many voices simultaneously.
c. attend to but one voice among many other voices.
d. be affected by unnoticed stimuli.

2. Most people daydream every day. These daydreams serve several functions: They provide an escape from reality, they help us prepare for the future, they enhance creativity, and they may substitute for

a. a rich, complete life.
b. impulsive behavior.
c. night dreams.
d. meditative time.

Sleep and Dreams

Sleep—sweet, renewing, mysterious sleep. Sleep—the irresistible tempter to whom we must all succumb. Sleep—the mantle that covers human thought. What is it? Why must we have it? Why do we spend a third of our lives—some 25 years, on average—sleeping? What and why do we dream?

Such questions have intrigued humans for centuries. Now, some of these mysteries are being solved. In laboratories throughout the world, thousands have slept attached to recording devices while others observe. By recording sleepers' brain waves and muscle movements, by observing and awakening them from time to time, the sleep-watchers glimpse things that a thousand years of common sense never told us. Perhaps you can anticipate some of their discoveries. Are the following statements true or false?

"I love to sleep. Do you? Isn't it great? It really is the best of both worlds. You get to be alive and unconscious."

Comedian Rita Rudner, 1993

1. Sleepwalkers are acting out their dreams (page 175).
2. When people dream of performing some activity, their limbs often move in concert with the dream (page 175).
3. Some people dream every night; others seldom dream at all (page 176).
4. After two or three sleepless days, a person's performance on a brief but demanding task suffers (page 178).
5. Sleep experts recommend treating insomnia with an occasional sleeping pill (page 179).

All these statements (adapted from Palladino and Carducci [1983]) are false. Let's see why.

Biological Rhythms and Sleep

3. *What is our daily biological rhythm, and what is the rhythm of our sleep?*

The rhythm of the day parallels the rhythm of life—from our waking to a new day's birth to our nightly return to what Shakespeare called "death's counterfeit." Our bodies synchronize with the cycle of day and night through a biological clock called the **circadian rhythm** (from the Latin *circa*, "about," and *dies*, "day"). Our body temperature, for example, rises as morning approaches, peaks during the day, dips for a time in early afternoon (when many people take siestas), and then begins to drop again before we go to sleep. Awake at 4:00 A.M., with a depressed body, we may fret over concerns: Does a lovers' spat signal a split? Does a child's moodiness mean more trouble ahead? By midday, our body energized, we fret less. Pulling an all-nighter, we feel groggiest about 4:00 A.M., but we feel a second wind as our normal wake-up time arrives.

Recent evidence suggests that thinking is sharpest and memory most accurate when people are at their daily peak in circadian arousal. University students often are "evening persons," report Cynthia May and Lynne Hasher (1997). Their performance typically improves across the day. Older adults tend to be "morning persons," with performance declining as the day wears on.

If we stay up late and sleep in on weekends, our biological clock begins to reset itself. When the weekend ends, the result may be "Sunday night insomnia" and "Monday morning blues."

A transcontinental flight disrupts our circadian rhythm and we experience jet lag, mainly because we are awake when our circadian rhythm cries, "Sleep!" If we stay up late and sleep in on weekends, our biological clock begins to reset itself. When the weekend ends, the result may be "Sunday night insomnia" and "Monday morning blues." (Those who sleep till noon on Sunday and then go to bed just 11 hours later in preparation for the new workweek often find sleep elusive.)

If our natural circadian rhythm were attuned to a 23-hour cycle, would we instead need to discipline ourselves to stay up later at night and sleep in longer in the morning? Do older adults, who typically prefer an earlier bedtime than university students, have a shorter circadian rhythm?

Mysteriously, young adults isolated without clocks or daylight typically adopt a 25-hour day. This helps explain why many people find it easier to jet west, with an extended day, than east; why rotating shift workers adapt better to progressively later shifts than to earlier shifts; why until our later years we must discipline ourselves to get to bed on time and force ourselves to get up. When placed under constant illumination, most animals, too, exceed a 24-hour day.

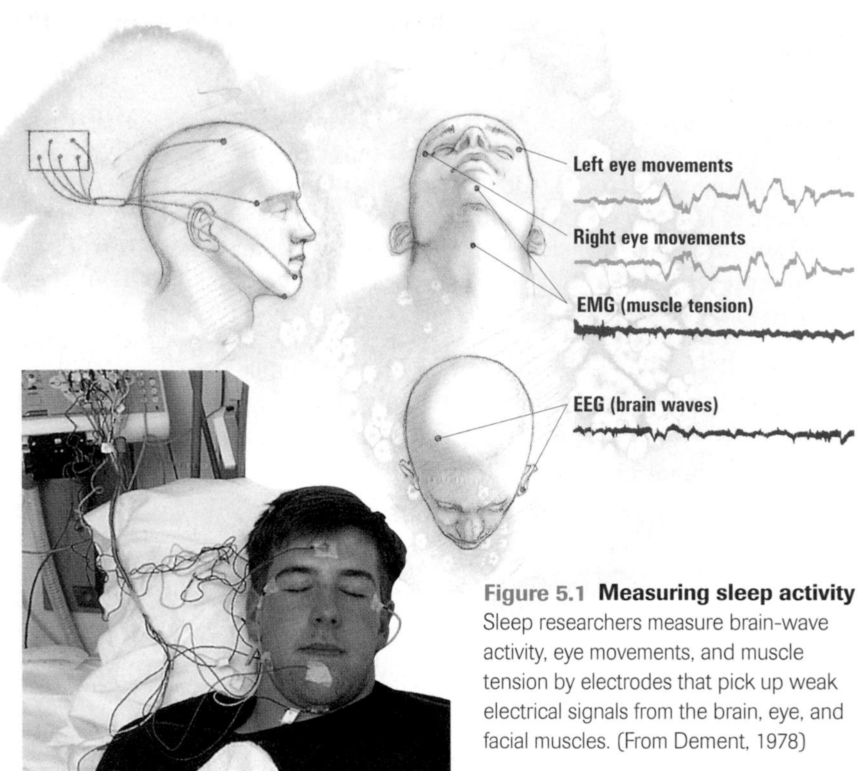

Figure 5.1 Measuring sleep activity Sleep researchers measure brain-wave activity, eye movements, and muscle tension by electrodes that pick up weak electrical signals from the brain, eye, and facial muscles. (From Dement, 1978)

The Stages of Sleep

Our circadian rhythm influences when we sleep. There is also a biological rhythm *during* our sleep. Throughout the night we pass through a cycle of five distinct sleep stages. This elementary fact was unknown until 8-year-old Armond Aserinsky went to bed one night in 1952. His father, Eugene, a University of Chicago graduate student, needed to test an electroencephalograph he had been repairing during the day (Aserinsky, 1988; Seligman & Yellen, 1987). He placed electrodes near Armond's eyes to record the rolling eye movements believed to occur during sleep. Before long, the machine went wild, tracing deep zigzags on the graph paper. Aserinsky thought the machine was still broken. But as the night proceeded, the activity periodically recurred, indicating, Aserinsky finally realized, fast, jerky eye movements accompanied by energetic brain activity. When he awakened Armond during one such episode, the boy reported he was having a dream. Aserinsky had discovered what we now know as **REM sleep** (*r*apid *e*ye *m*ovement sleep).

To find out if similar cycles occur during adult sleep, Nathaniel Kleitman (1960) and Aserinsky pioneered procedures that have now been used with thousands of volunteers. To appreciate both their methods and findings, imagine yourself as a participant. As the hour grows late, you yawn in response to reduced brain metabolism. Yawning stretches your neck muscles and increases your heart rate, thus increasing the bloodflow to your brain and your alertness (Moorcroft, 1993). When you are ready for bed, the researcher glues electrodes to your scalp (to detect your brain waves), just outside the corners of your eyes (to detect eye movements), and on your chin (to detect muscle tension) (Figure 5.1). Other devices allow the researcher to record your heart rate, your respiration rate, and even the degree of your genital arousal.

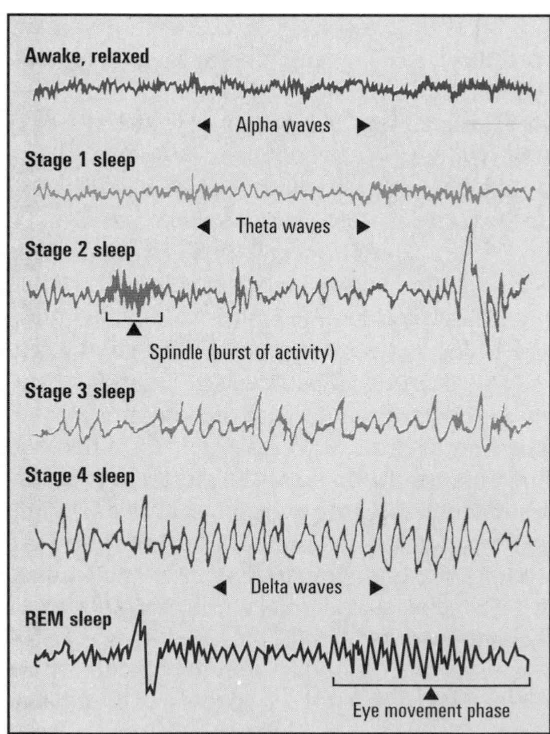

Figure 5.2 Brain waves and sleep stages The regular alpha waves of an awake, relaxed stage are quite different from the slower, larger delta waves of deep Stage 4 sleep. Although the rapid REM sleep waves resemble the near-waking theta waves of Stage 1, the body is more aroused during REM sleep than during Stage 1 sleep. (From Dement, 1978)

When you are in bed with your eyes closed, the researcher in the next room sees on the EEG the relatively slow **alpha waves** of your awake but relaxed state (Figure 5.2). As you adapt to all this equipment and grow tired, you slip into sleep and begin your dive toward deeper and deeper levels. Your breathing rate slows and your brain waves slow further and show the irregular theta waves of Stage 1 sleep. During this brief light sleep, you may experience fantastic images, which are like **hallucinations**—sensory experiences that occur without a sensory stimulus. You may have a sensation of falling (at which moment your body may suddenly jerk) or of floating weightlessly. Such "hypnogogic" sensations may later be incorporated into memories. People who claim to have been abducted by aliens, for example, commonly recall being floated off their beds.

Soon, you relax more deeply and begin about 20 minutes of Stage 2 sleep, characterized by the periodic appearance of *sleep spindles*—bursts of rapid, rhythmic brain-wave activity. Although you can still be awakened without too much difficulty during this phase, you are now clearly asleep. Sleeptalking—usually garbled or nonsensical—can occur during this or any other sleep stage (Mahowald & Ettinger, 1990).

Then for the next few minutes you go through the transitional Stage 3 to the deep sleep of Stage 4. First in Stage 3, and increasingly in Stage 4, your brain emits large, slow **delta waves**. These stages together are therefore called *slow-wave sleep*. They last for about 30 minutes, during which you are hard to awaken. Curiously, it is at the end of the deep sleep of Stage 4 that children may wet the bed or begin walking in their sleep. About 20 percent of 3- to 12-year-

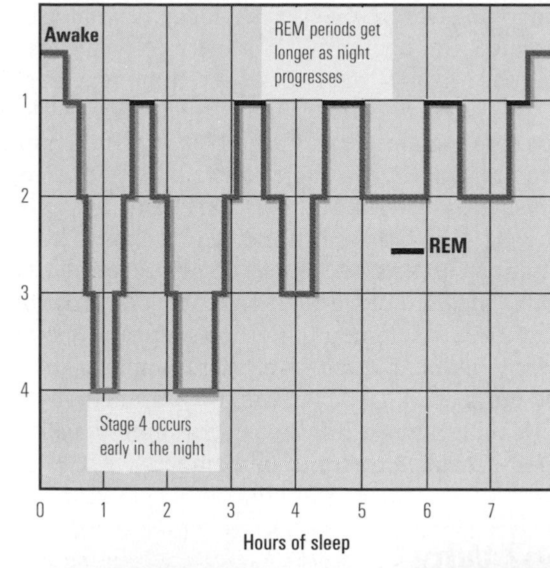

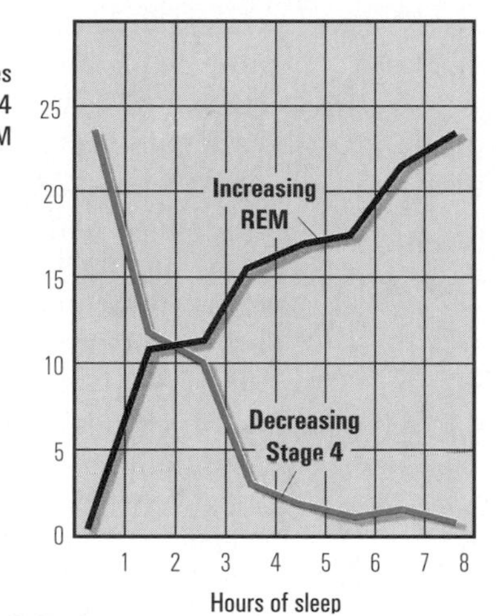

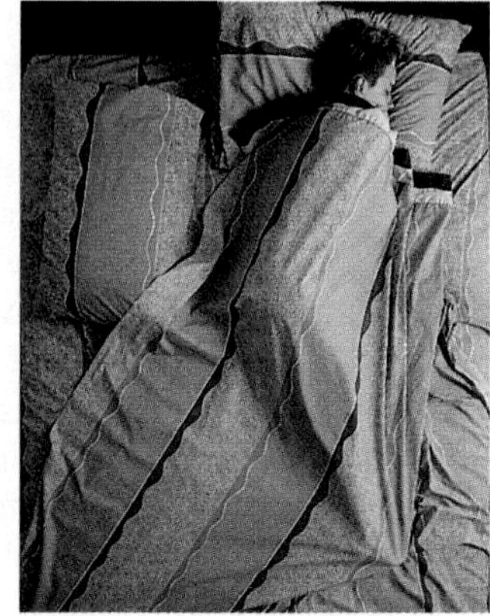

Figure 5.3 **The stages in a typical night's sleep** Most people pass through the 5-stage sleep cycle several times, with the periods of Stage 4 sleep and then Stage 3 sleep diminishing and REM sleep periods increasing in duration as the night wears on. The second graph plots this increasing REM sleep and decreasing Stage 4 sleep based on data from 30 young adults. (Cartwright, 1978; Webb, 1992)

olds have at least one episode of sleepwalking, usually lasting 2 to 10 minutes; some 5 percent have repeated episodes (Giles & others, 1994). Identical twins share sleepwalking tendencies more often than fraternal twins do, suggesting a genetic influence (Hublin & others, 1997).

Even when you are deeply asleep, your brain somehow processes the meaning of certain stimuli. You move around on your bed, but you manage not to fall out of it. If you sleep with your babies, you will not roll over and suffocate them. The occasional roar of passing vehicles may leave deep sleep undisturbed, but the cry from a baby's nursery quickly interrupts it. So does the sound of your name—a stimulus humans are ever alert for. EEG recordings confirm that the brain's auditory cortex responds to sound stimuli even during sleep (Kutas, 1990). All this reminds us of one of this book's basic lessons: *We process most information outside of conscious awareness.*

REM Sleep

About an hour after you first fall asleep, a strange thing happens. Rather than continuing in deep slumber, you ascend from your initial sleep dive. Returning through Stage 3 and Stage 2 (where you spend about half your night), you enter the most intriguing sleep phase of all—REM sleep (Figure 5.3). For about 10 minutes, your brain waves become rapid and saw-toothed, more like those of the nearly awake Stage 1 sleep. But unlike Stage 1 sleep, REM sleep is a time when your heart rate rises, your breathing becomes rapid and irregular, and every half minute or so your eyes dart around in a momentary burst of activity behind closed lids. Because anyone watching a sleeper's eyes can notice these REM bursts, it is amazing that science was ignorant of REM sleep until 1952.

During REM sleep, your genitals become aroused and you have an erection or increased vaginal lubrication. The common "morning erection" stems from the night's last REM period, often just before waking. Except during very scary dreams, genital arousal always occurs, regardless of whether the dream's content is sexual (Karacan & others, 1966). In young men, sleep-related erections outlast REM periods, lasting 30 to 45 minutes on average (Karacan & others, 1983; Schiavi & Schreiner-Engel, 1988). A typical 25-year-old man therefore has an erection during nearly half his night's sleep, a 65-year-old man for one-quarter. Many men troubled by "erectile disorder" (impotence) have morning erections, which suggests that their problem is not with their genitals.

Although your brain's motor cortex is active during REM sleep, your brainstem blocks its messages, leaving your muscles relaxed—so relaxed that, except for an occasional finger, toe, or facial twitch, you are essentially paralyzed. Moreover, you cannot easily be awakened. Thus, REM sleep is sometimes called *paradoxical sleep*; internally the body is aroused while externally it appears calm.

REM sleep rapid eye movement sleep, a recurring sleep stage during which vivid dreams commonly occur. Also known as *paradoxical sleep* because the muscles are relaxed (except for minor twitches) but other body systems are active.

alpha waves the relatively slow brain waves of a relaxed, awake state.

hallucinations false sensory experiences, such as seeing something in the absence of an external visual stimulus.

delta waves the large, slow brain waves associated with deep sleep.

People rarely snore during dreams. When REM starts, snoring stops.

More intriguing than the paradoxical nature of REM sleep is what the rapid eye movements usually announce: the beginning of a dream. Even those who claim they never dream will, more than 80 percent of the time, recall a dream after being awakened during REM sleep. Unlike the fleeting images of Stage 1 sleep, REM sleep dreams are often emotional and usually storylike. (People occasionally recall dreams when awakened from stages other than REM sleep, but these dreams often contain a single vague image, such as, "I was trying to borrow something from someone.")

As the night wears on, variations on this sleep cycle repeat themselves about every 90 minutes. During the night, deep Stage 4 sleep gets progressively briefer and then disappears, and the REM sleep period gets longer. By morning, 20 to 25 percent of our average night's sleep—some 100 minutes—has been REM sleep. This means that those who say, "I never dream" actually spend about 600 hours a year experiencing some 1500 dreams, or more than 100,000 dreams over a typical lifetime—dreams they rarely remember.

"Boy are my eyes tired! I had REM sleep all night long."

Do We Need Sleep? Why?

4. How does sleep loss affect us? What is the function of sleep?

Sleep commands roughly one-third of our lives. Deprived of it, we begin to feel terrible; our bodies yearn for it. It takes an alarm to awaken us; sleep beckons while we listen to a lecture; we lack the vigor needed for peak functioning.

Allowed to sleep unhindered, most humans will sleep 9 to 10 hours a night, reports Stanley Coren (1996). Given such sleep, they do not become groggy. Rather, long sleepers awake refreshed, sustain better moods, and perform more efficient and accurate work than do people who get less sleep. People who sleep less than 7 hours often show signs of sleep deprivation—depressed immune systems, poorer judgments, irritability, and more accidents. As a demonstration of the costs of widespread sleep deprivation among today's adolescents and adults, Coren capitalized on a naturally occurring experiment that manipulates sleep length—the "spring forward" to daylight time and "fall backward" to standard time. Searching millions of records, he found that in both Canada and the United States, accidents increase immediately after the shortened sleep associated with the spring time change. In Canada, for example, traffic accidents during 1991 and 1992 were 7 percent higher the Monday after the spring time change than on the Monday before, and they were 7 percent lower on the Monday following the extra sleep bestowed by the fall time change (Figure 5.4).

Figure 5.4 **Canadian traffic accidents, 1991 and 1992** The Monday after the spring time change, when people lose sleep, accidents increased as compared with the Monday before. After the fall time change, they dropped. (Adapted from Coren, 1996)

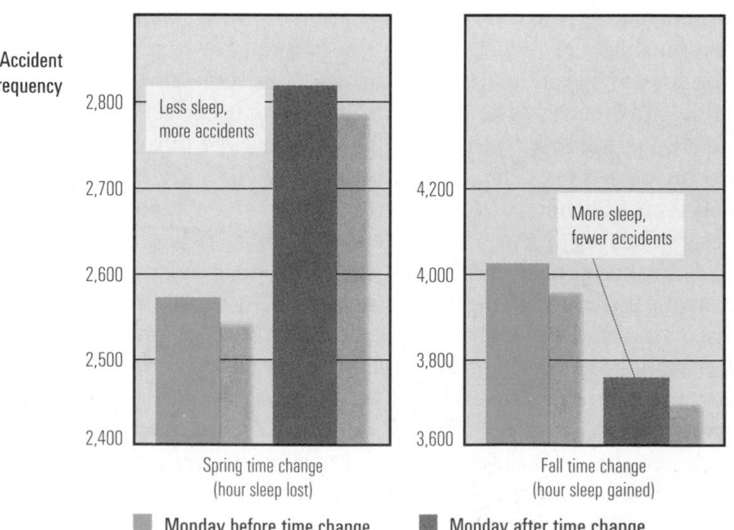

Obviously, we need sleep—enough, says sleep researcher William Moorcroft (1993), so that you will not feel tired the next day. But why? It seems an easy question to answer: Just keep people awake for several days and note how they deteriorate. If you were a volunteer in such an experiment, how do you think it would affect your body and mind?

Of course, you would become terribly drowsy at times—especially during the hours when your biological clock programs you to sleep. But could lack of sleep physically damage you? Would it noticeably alter your biochemistry or body organs? Would you become emotionally disturbed? Intellectually disoriented?

Owing to modern light bulbs, shift work, and social diversions, people in industrialized nations are able to sleep less than they did a century ago. Thomas Edison (1948, pp. 52, 178), inventor of the light bulb, was pleased to accept credit for this. For him, lost sleep meant more time and opportunity.

When I went through Switzerland in a motor-car, so that I could visit little towns and villages, I noted the effect of artificial light on the inhabitants. Where water power and electric light had been developed, everyone seemed normally intelligent. When these appliances did not exist, and the natives went to bed with the chickens, staying there till daylight, they were far less intelligent.

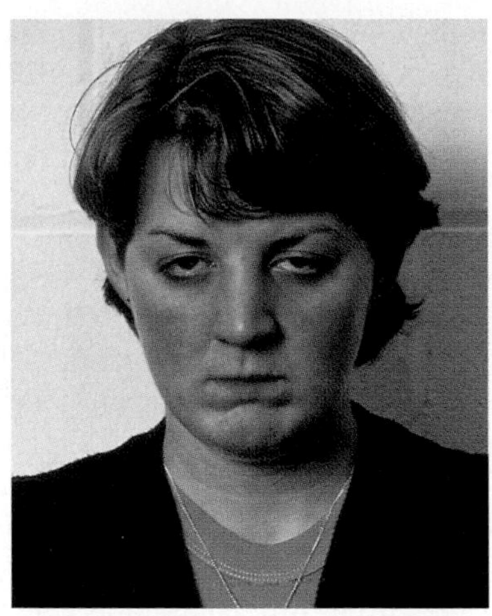

Sleepless and suffering This fatigued, sleep-deprived person may also experience a depressed immune system, impaired concentration, and greater vulnerability to accidents.

The Effects of Sleep Loss

Actually, a major effect of lessened sleep, as fatigued college students know, is sleepiness, and sometimes a general malaise (Mikulincer & others, 1989). People today more than ever suffer from sleep patterns that thwart their having an energized feeling of well-being. Teenagers typically need 8 or 9 hours sleep, but they now average nearly 2 hours less sleep a night than their counterparts of 80 years ago (Holden, 1993; Maas, 1998). Many fill this need by using homeroom for their first siesta and after-lunch study hall for a slumber party. As sleep researcher William Dement (1990) laments, "The national sleep debt is larger and more important than the national debt." (To test whether you are one of the many sleep-deprived college students, see Table 5.1.)

Table 5.1 Are You Sleep Deprived?

Cornell University psychologist James Maas reports that most college students suffer the consequences of less-than-needed sleep. To see if you are in that group, answer the following true-false questions:

True	False	
☐	☐	1. I need an alarm clock in order to wake up at the appropriate time.
☐	☐	2. It's a struggle for me to get out of bed in the morning.
☐	☐	3. Weekday mornings I hit the snooze bar several times to get more sleep.
☐	☐	4. I feel tired, irritable, and stressed out during the week.
☐	☐	5. I have trouble concentrating and remembering.
☐	☐	6. I feel slow with critical thinking, problem solving, and being creative.
☐	☐	7. I often fall asleep watching TV.
☐	☐	8. I often fall asleep in boring meetings or lectures or in warm rooms.
☐	☐	9. I often fall asleep after heavy meals or after a low dose of alcohol.
☐	☐	10. I often fall asleep while relaxing after dinner.
☐	☐	11. I often fall asleep within five minutes of getting into bed.
☐	☐	12. I often feel drowsy while driving.
☐	☐	13. I often sleep extra hours on weekend mornings.
☐	☐	14. I often need a nap to get through the day.
☐	☐	15. I have dark circles around my eyes.

If you answered "true" to three or more items, you probably are not getting enough sleep. To determine your sleep needs, Maas recommends that you "go to bed 15 minutes earlier than usual every night for the next week—and continue this practice by adding 15 more minutes each week—until you wake without an alarm clock and feel alert all day." (Quiz reprinted with permission from James B. Maas, *Power sleep: Revolutionary strategies that prepare your mind and body for peak performance.* [New York: Villard, 1998].)

"The average sleep requirement for college students is well over eight hours. . . . Here at Stanford . . . we found that 80 percent were dangerously sleep deprived. Tiger Woods said that one of the best things about his choice to leave Stanford for the professional golf circuit was that he could now get enough sleep."

Sleep researcher William Dement (1997)

Some sleep-loss effects are more subtle. One such effect is suppression of the disease-fighting immune system (Irwin & others, 1994; Beardsley, 1996). In rats, sleep deprivation increases the pathogens normally suppressed by the immune system. In humans, sleep deprivation suppresses immune cells that fight off viral infections. When infections do set in, immune-boosting sleep typically increases.

Other sleep-loss effects include impaired creativity and concentration, slight hand tremors, irritability, slowed performance, and occasional misperceptions on monotonous tasks (Horne, 1989; Koslowsky & Babkoff, 1992). These effects can be devastating for some tasks, such as driving and piloting. Some 30 percent of Australian highway deaths occur when drivers fall asleep on long, monotonous roads (Maas, 1998). "Rest. That's what I need is rest," said Eastern Airlines Captain James Reeves to the control tower on a September 1974 morning—30 minutes before crashing his airliner at low altitude, killing the crew and all 68 passengers (Moorcroft, 1993). Consider also the *Exxon Valdez* oil spill; Union Carbide's Bhopal, India, disaster; and the Three Mile Island and Chernobyl nuclear accidents—they all occurred after midnight, when operators were likely to be drowsiest. Apparently asleep, the *Exxon Valdez* mate at the helm was unresponsive to clear signals to turn his vessel back into the shipping lanes.

The current record holder, Robert ("Ramblin Rob") McDonald, reportedly stayed awake for 18 days and 22 hours in a 1986 rocking chair marathon.

On short, highly motivating tasks, however, sleep deprivation has little effect. When 17-year-old Randy Gardner made his way into the *Guinness Book of World Records* by staying awake for 11 days, he suffered hallucinations and speech and movement problems, and at times had to keep moving to stay awake. Nevertheless, during his final night of sleeplessness, Gardner managed to beat researcher Dement 100 straight times in a pinball game. He then slept 15 hours and awoke feeling fine (Coren, 1996; Gulevich & others, 1966).

A few of the unanswered questions about sleep: Why do we sleep more when we are young? Why do some animals sleep most of the day, others not at all? Why, when REM sleep paralyzes our muscles, do we twitch and jerk? Most important, what is sleep's function? (Adapted from UCLA Brain Research Institute, 1989)

Sleep Theories

Why, then, must we sleep? We have few answers, but sleep may have evolved for at least two reasons: First, sleep suits our ecological niche. When darkness precluded our ancestors' hunting and food gathering and made travel treacherous, they were better off asleep in a cave, out of harm's way. Animals with the least reason to fear predation or the most need to graze tend to sleep less. Elephants and horses sleep 3 to 4 hours a day, gorillas 12 hours, cats 15 hours, and bats 20 hours.

"Sleep faster, we need the pillows."

Yiddish Proverb

Second, sleep helps us recuperate. It helps restore body tissues, especially those of the brain. As we sleep, our brain is actively repairing and reorganizing itself and consolidating memories. Our lowered body temperature during sleep also conserves energy for the daytime hours.

Sleep may also play a role in the growth process. During deep sleep, the pituitary gland releases a growth hormone. As adults grow older, they release less of this hormone and they spend less time in deep sleep (Pekkanen, 1982). These physiological discoveries are only beginning to solve the ongoing riddle of sleep. As researcher Dement (1978, p. 83) deadpanned, "We have miles to go before we sleep."

Sleep Disorders

5. *What are the major sleep disorders?*

The idea that "everyone needs 8 hours of sleep" is untrue. Newborns spend nearly two-thirds of their day asleep, most adults no more than one-third. Age-related differences in average time spent sleeping are rivaled by differences in the normal amount of sleep among individuals at any age. Some people thrive with fewer than 6 hours of sleep per night; others regularly sleep 9 hours or

insomnia a sleep disorder involving recurring problems in falling or staying asleep.

narcolepsy a sleep disorder characterized by uncontrollable sleep attacks. The sufferer may lapse directly into REM sleep, often at inopportune times.

sleep apnea a sleep disorder characterized by temporary cessations of breathing during sleep and consequent momentary reawakenings.

1993 Time/CNN poll:
"How many hours do you sleep each night?"

Under six	*12%*
Six	*26%*
Seven	*30%*
Eight	*28%*
Over eight	*3%*

"The lion and the lamb shall lie down together, but the lamb will not be very sleepy."

Woody Allen
In the Movie *Love and Death*
1975

"In 1757 Benjamin Franklin gave us the axiom, 'Early to bed, early to rise, makes a man healthy, wealthy, and wise.' It would be more accurate to say 'consistently to bed and consistently to rise . . .'"

James B. Maas
Power Sleep
1998

more. Sleep patterns may be genetically influenced. When Wilse Webb and Scott Campbell (1983) checked the pattern and duration of sleep among fraternal and identical twins, only the identical twins were strikingly similar.

Whatever their normal need for sleep, some 10 to 15 percent of adults complain of **insomnia**—persistent problems in falling or staying asleep. True insomnia is not the occasional inability to sleep that we experience when anxious or excited. For a stressed organism, alertness is natural and adaptive. Moreover, from middle age on, sleep is seldom uninterrupted. Occasional awakenings become the norm, not something to fret over or treat with medication.

Sometimes people fret unnecessarily about their sleep. Scientists have learned to doubt people's fretful sleep reports (Coren, 1996). In laboratory studies, insomnia complainers do get less sleep than others, but they typically overestimate, by about double, how long it took them to fall asleep, and they underestimate by nearly half how long they actually slept. Even if we've been awake only an hour or two, we may *think* we've had little sleep, because it's the waking part we remember. When researchers awaken people repeatedly during the night, some recall having slept soundly.

The most common quick fixes for true insomnia—sleeping pills and alcohol—can aggravate the problem. Both reduce REM sleep and can leave a person with next-day blahs. With continued use, one needs bigger doses to get an effect, and when the drug is discontinued, the insomnia may worsen. Scientists are searching for natural chemicals that are abundant during sleep and might be synthesized as a sleep aid without side effects. In the meantime, sleep experts offer other natural alternatives:

- Relax before bedtime, using dimmer light.
- Avoid caffeine (this includes chocolate) after late afternoon and avoid rich foods before bedtime. A glass of milk may help. (Milk provides raw materials for the manufacture of serotonin, a neurotransmitter that facilitates sleep.)
- Sleep on a regular schedule (rise at the same time even after a restless night) and avoid naps. A regular sleep schedule boosts daytime alertness, too, as shown in a recent experiment in which University of Arizona students slept 7.5 hours a night on either a varying or consistent schedule (Manber & others, 1996).
- Exercise regularly but not in the late evening. (Late afternoon is best.)
- Reassure yourself that the temporary loss of sleep causes no great harm, certainly nothing worth losing sleep over. "Sleep is like love or happiness," notes Wilse Webb (1992, p. 170). "If you pursue it too ardently it will elude you."
- If nothing else works, aim for less sleep; go to bed later or get up earlier.

More rare but also more severe than insomnia are the sleep disorders narcolepsy and sleep apnea. People with **narcolepsy** (from *narco*, "numbness," and *lepsy*, "seizure") suffer periodic, overwhelming sleepiness. This usually lasts less than 5 minutes but sometimes occurs at the most inopportune times, perhaps just after taking a terrific swing at a softball or when laughing loudly or shouting angrily (Dement, 1978). In severe cases, the person may collapse directly into a brief period of REM sleep, with its accompanying loss of muscular tension. Those who suffer from narcolepsy—1 in 2000 people, estimates the Stanford University Center for Narcolepsy (1996)—must live with extra caution. As a traffic menace, "snoozing is second only to boozing," says the American Sleep Disorders Association, and those with narcolepsy are especially at risk (Aldrich, 1989).

The National Heart, Lung, and Blood Institute reports that 1 in 25 people (mostly overweight men) suffer from **sleep apnea**—a treatable disorder that was unknown before modern sleep research. They intermittently stop breathing during sleep. (*Apnea* means "stopping respiration.") After an airless minute or so, decreased blood oxygen arouses the sleeper to awaken and snort in air for a

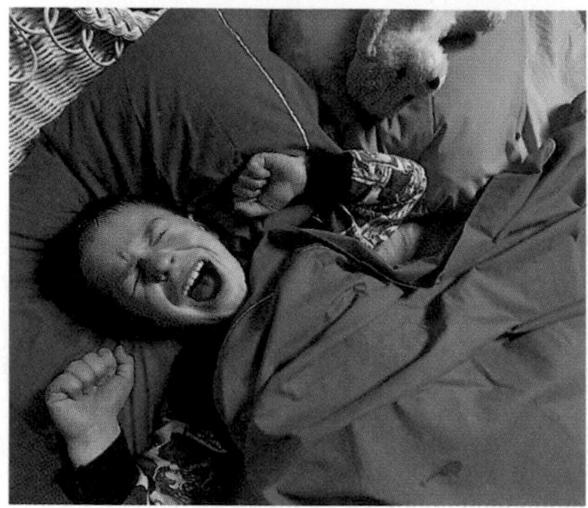

Night terrors and nightmares Night terrors occur within 2 or 3 hours of falling asleep, during Stage 4 sleep. Nightmares occur toward morning, during REM sleep. (From Hartmann, 1984)

few seconds. The process can repeat more than 400 times a night, depriving the person of slow-wave sleep. Apart from complaints of sleepiness and irritability during the day—and their mates' complaints about their loud "snoring"—apnea sufferers are often unaware of their disorder.

Other sleepers, mostly children, experience **night terrors**. The person might sit up or walk around, talk incoherently, experience a doubling of heart and breathing rates, and appear terrified (Hartmann, 1981). The night-terror sufferer seldom awakens fully and recalls little or nothing the next morning—at most, a fleeting, frightening image. Night terrors are not nightmares (which, like other dreams, typically occur during early morning REM sleep). As with sleepwalking, night terrors usually occur during the first few hours of sleep and begin during Stage 4 sleep. Family members usually guide a sleepwalker back to bed or try to awaken and reassure the person with night terrors. As we grow older, we have less of the deep Stage 4 sleep, which also usually means an end to night terrors and sleepwalking.

REHEARSE IT!

3. Our body temperature tends to rise and fall in sync with a biological clock, which is referred to as
- **a.** the circadian rhythm.
- **b.** narcolepsy.
- **c.** REM sleep.
- **d.** hypnogogic sensations.

4. Stage 1 sleep is a twilight zone of light sleep. During Stage 1 sleep, a person is most likely to experience
- **a.** sleep spindles.
- **b.** hallucinations.
- **c.** night terrors or nightmares.
- **d.** rapid eye movements.

5. In the deepest stage of sleep–surprisingly, the stage when people sleepwalk–the brain emits large, slow delta waves. This deep stage of sleep is called
- **a.** Stage 2.
- **b.** Stage 4.
- **c.** REM sleep.
- **d.** paradoxical sleep.

6. An electroencephalograph shows that during sleep we pass through a cycle of five stages, each with characteristic brain waves. As the night progresses, the REM stage
- **a.** gradually disappears.
- **b.** becomes briefer and briefer.
- **c.** remains about the same.
- **d.** becomes progressively longer.

7. Two relatively rare sleep disorders are narcolepsy and sleep apnea. With narcolepsy, the person ______________; with sleep apnea, the person ______________.
- **a.** has persistent problems falling asleep; experiences a doubling of heart and breathing rates
- **b.** experiences a doubling of heart and breathing rates; has persistent problems falling asleep
- **c.** intermittently stops breathing; suffers periodic, overwhelming sleepiness
- **d.** suffers periodic, overwhelming sleepiness; intermittently stops breathing

8. Various theories have been proposed to explain why we need sleep. They include all but which of the following?
- **a.** Sleep has survival value.
- **b.** Sleep helps us recuperate.
- **c.** Sleep rests the eyes.
- **d.** Sleep plays a role in the growth process.

Dreams

Discovering the link between REM sleep and increased dreaming opened a new era in dream research. Instead of relying on someone's hazy recall hours or days after having a dream, researchers could catch dreams as they happened. They could awaken people during a REM sleep period, or within 3 minutes afterward, and hear a vivid dream account.

night terrors a sleep disorder characterized by high arousal and an appearance of being terrified; unlike nightmares, night terrors occur during Stage 4 sleep, within 2 or 3 hours of falling asleep, and are seldom remembered.

manifest content according to Freud, the remembered story line of a dream (as distinct from its latent content).

What We Dream

6. *What do we dream?*

REM dreams—"hallucinations of the sleeping mind"—are vivid, emotional, and bizarre. Several times a night, you are the creator and producer of a surrealistic mental movie, in which events frequently occur in a jumbled sequence, scenes change suddenly, people appear and disappear, and physical laws, such as gravity, may be violated. Yet dreams are so vivid we may confuse them with reality. Occasionally, we may be sufficiently aware during a dream to wonder whether we are, in fact, dreaming. When experiencing such *lucid dreams*, some people are able to test their state of consciousness. If they can perform some absurd act, such as floating in the air, then they know they are dreaming.

"I do not believe that I am now dreaming, but I cannot prove that I am not."

Philosopher Bertrand Russell
1872–1970

Although we are more likely to be awakened by our most emotional dreams and to remember them, many dreams are rather ordinary. When awakened during REM sleep, people report dreams with sexual imagery less often than you might think. Some 1 in 8 dreams among young men and 1 in 25 among young women have sexual overtones (Domhoff, 1996).

Six years of our life we spend dreaming, most of which is anything but sweet.

More commonly, we dream of daily life events, such as a meeting at work or taking an exam. In the month after the San Francisco earthquake, 4 in 10 college students in the area (but only 1 in 20 students elsewhere) had one or more nightmares about an earthquake (Wood & others, 1992). Six years of our life we spend dreaming, most of which is anything but sweet: People commonly dream of repeatedly failing in an attempt to do something; of being attacked, pursued, or rejected; or of experiencing misfortune (Hall & others, 1982).

The story line of our dreams—what Sigmund Freud called their **manifest content**—often incorporates experiences and preoccupations from the day's events, especially in our first dreams of the night. People in hunter-gatherer societies often dream of animals; urban Japanese rarely do (Mestel, 1997). The sensory stimuli of our sleeping environment may also intrude. A particular odor or the telephone's ringing may be instantly and ingeniously woven into the dream story. In one experiment, William Dement and Edward Wolpert (1958) lightly sprayed cold water on dreamers' faces. Compared with sleepers who did not get the cold water treatment, these sleepers were more likely to dream about water—about a waterfall, a leaky roof, or even about being sprayed by someone. Even while in REM sleep, focused on internal stimuli, we maintain some awareness of changes in our external environment.

Would you suppose that people dream if blind from birth? Studies of blind people in France, Hungary, and Egypt all found them dreaming of using their nonvisual senses—hearing, touching, smelling, tasting (Buquet, 1988; Taha, 1972; Vekassy, 1977).

So, could we learn a foreign language by listening to tapes during sleep? If only it were so easy. While sleeping we can learn to associate a sound with a mild electric shock (and to react to the sound accordingly). But we do not remember taped information played while we are soundly asleep (Eich, 1990; Wyatt & Bootzin, 1994). In fact, experiences that occur during the 5 minutes just before falling asleep are typically lost from memory (Roth & others, 1988). This explains why sleep apnea patients, who repeatedly awaken with a gasp and then immediately fall back to sleep, do not recall the episodes. It also explains why dreams that momentarily awaken us are mostly forgotten by morning. To remember a dream, get up and stay awake for a while.

A popular sleep myth: If you dream you are falling and hit the ground (or if you dream of dying), you die. (Unfortunately, those who could confirm these ideas are not around to do so. Some people, however, have had such dreams and are alive to report them.)

Why We Dream

7. *What is the function of dreams?*

In his landmark book *The Interpretation of Dreams*, published in 1900, Freud offered "the most valuable of all the discoveries it has been my good fortune to make." He argued that by fulfilling wishes, a dream provides a psychic safety

A night of solid sleep (and dreaming) does, it seems, have an important place in a student's life. As we sleep, our brains are consolidating the day's important memories.

valve that discharges otherwise unacceptable feelings. According to Freud, a dream's manifest content is but a censored, symbolic version of its **latent content**, which consists of unconscious drives and wishes that would be threatening if expressed directly. Although most dreams have no overt sexual imagery, Freud nevertheless believed that most adult dreams can be "traced back by analysis to *erotic wishes*." In Freud's view, a gun, for example, might be a disguised representation of a penis.

Although Freud considered dreams the key to understanding our inner conflicts, his critics say that it's time to wake up from Freud's dream theory, because dream interpretation actually is one of Freud's greatest failures. Some critics contend that even if dreams were symbolic, they could be interpreted as one wishes. Others maintain that there is nothing hidden in dreams. A dream about a gun, they say, is a dream about a gun. Legend has it that even Freud, who loved to smoke cigars, remarked that "sometimes, a cigar is just a cigar."

"For what one has dwelt on by day, these things are seen in visions of the night."

Menander of Athens
342–292 B.C.
Fragments

Freud's theory of dreams is giving way to newer theories. One of these sees dreams as *information processing*: Dreams may help sift, sort, and fix in memory our day's experiences. Following stressful experiences or intense learning periods, REM sleep increases (Palumbo, 1978). What is more, there is "consistent and compelling evidence" that REM sleep facilitates memory (McGrath & Cohen, 1978). In experiments, people have heard unusual phrases or learned to find hidden visual images before bedtime. If awakened every time they began REM sleep, they remembered less the next morning than if awakened during other sleep stages (Empson & Clarke, 1970; Karni & Sagi, 1994). A night of solid sleep (and dreaming) does, it seems, have an important place in a student's life. As we sleep, our brains are consolidating the day's important memories.

Another explanation of dreams proposes that they may also serve a physiological function. Perhaps dreaming—or the associated brain activity of REM sleep—provides the sleeping brain with periodic stimulation. As you may recall from Chapter 3, stimulating experiences develop and preserve the brain's neural pathways. This theory makes sense from a developmental point of view. Infants, whose neural networks are just developing, spend a great deal of time in REM sleep.

Nocturnal mysteries Marc Chagall's "I and the Village" captures the surrealism of many dreams. Psychologists study and debate why the brain creates such flights of fancy.

Still other physiological theories propose that dreams erupt from neural activity that spreads upward from the brainstem (Antrobus, 1991; Hobson, 1988). According to one version, this neural activity is random, and dreams are the brain's attempt to make sense of it. Much as a neurosurgeon can produce hallucinations by stimulating different parts of a patient's cortex, so can stimulation originating within the brain. Psychologists Martin Seligman and Amy Yellen (1987) note that the seconds-long bursts of rapid eye movements during REM sleep coincide with bursts of activity in the visual cortex. If awakened during one of these bursts of brain activity, people report vivid experiences, usually dramatic hallucinations.

Given these visual scenes, our cognitive machinery—influenced by its culture, age, gender, and current concerns—weaves a story line. The emotion-related limbic system also becomes active during REM sleep. PET scans taken of sleeping people (if you can imagine sleeping while lying in a brain-scanning machine) reveal increased activity in several brain areas, especially the amygdala (Maquet & others, 1996). Add its activity to the brain's commotion and—voila!—we dream.

This speculative theory, then, is that dreams spring from the mind's relentless effort to make sense of unrelated visual bursts, which are given their emotional tone by the limbic system. This helps explain many of our dream experiences, such as the sudden and bizarre changes in scene (triggered by a new visual burst). Dream reports by Seligman's University of Pennsylvania students confirm that the most vivid dream images are the surprising, discontinuous aspects

latent content according to Freud, the underlying but censored meaning of a dream (as distinct from its manifest content). Freud believed that a dream's latent content functions as a safety valve.

REM rebound the tendency for REM sleep to increase following REM sleep deprivation (created by repeated awakenings during REM sleep).

hypnosis a social interaction in which one person (the hypnotist) suggests to another (the subject) that certain perceptions, feelings, thoughts, or behaviors will spontaneously occur.

of the dream; the other, less vivid images are those we presumably conjure up to string the visual bursts together.

The function of dreams provokes vigorous debate, but the disputants all agree that we *need* REM sleep. Deprived of it by repeated awakenings, people return more and more quickly to the REM stage after falling back to sleep. When finally allowed to sleep undisturbed, they literally sleep like babies, with increased REM sleep—a phenomenon called **REM rebound**. The withdrawal of REM-suppressing sleeping medications also increases REM sleep, but with accompanying nightmares.

Most other mammals also experience REM sleep and REM rebound. Animals' need for REM sleep suggests that its causes and functions are deeply biological. That REM sleep occurs in mammals (and not in animals such as fish, whose behavior is less influenced by learning) also fits the information-processing theory of dreams. All of which serves to remind us once again of another basic lesson: *Biological and psychological explanations of behavior are partners, not competitors.*

"When people interpret [a dream] as if it were meaningful and then sell those interpretations, it's quackery."

Sleep researcher J. Allan Hobson (1995)

But if dreams serve physiological functions and lack the disguised meanings that Freud supposed, are they psychologically meaningless? Are they as nonsensically random as Alice's dreams of Wonderland? Not necessarily. Every psychologically meaningful experience involves an active brain. Moreover, say advocates of dream reflection, dreams may be akin to abstract art—amenable to more than one meaningful interpretation, yet illuminating to ponder.

REHEARSE IT!

9. According to Sigmund Freud, dreams are the key to the understanding of our inner conflicts. In interpreting dreams, Freud was most interested in their

a. information-processing function.
b. physiological function.
c. manifest content, or story line.
d. latent content, or symbolic meaning.

10. Some theories of dreaming propose that dreams serve a physiological purpose. One such theory suggests that dreams

a. are the brain's attempt to make sense of random neural activity.
b. enable neurons to make new connections.
c. are manifestations of the sensory stimuli that intrude on our sleep.
d. prevent the brain from being disturbed by periodic stimulations.

11. The tendency for REM sleep to increase following REM sleep deprivation is referred to as

a. paradoxical sleep.
b. deep sleep.
c. REM rebound.
d. slow-wave sleep.

Hypnosis

8. *What do hypnotized people experience, and how do they behave?*

Imagine you are about to be hypnotized. The hypnotist invites you to sit back, fix your gaze on a spot high on the wall, and relax. In a quiet, low voice the hypnotist suggests, "Your eyes are growing tired. . . . Your eyelids are becoming heavy . . . now heavier and heavier. . . . They are beginning to close. . . . You are becoming more deeply relaxed. . . . Your breathing is now deep and regular. . . . Your muscles are becoming more and more relaxed. Your whole body is beginning to feel like lead."

After a few minutes of this hypnotic induction, your eyes are probably closed and you may undergo **hypnosis**—a social interaction in which one person (the

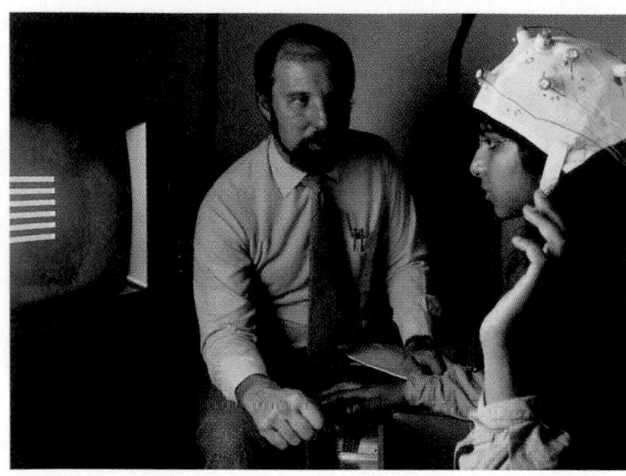

Subject to influence As a deeply hypnotized woman sits before a TV screen, researcher David Spiegel asks her to imagine that a cardboard box is blocking the screen. When a stimulus appears on the screen, her brain waves do not display the normal response. Such findings, Spiegel argues, suggest that hypnosis can alter brain functioning.

hypnotist) suggests to another (the subject) that certain perceptions, feelings, thoughts, or behaviors will spontaneously occur. When the hypnotist suggests, "Your eyelids are shutting so tight that you cannot open them even if you try," your eyelids may seem beyond your control and may remain closed. Told to forget the number 6, you may be puzzled when you count 11 fingers on your hands. Invited to smell a sensuous perfume that is actually ammonia, you may linger delightedly over its pungent odor. Asked to describe a nonexistent picture the hypnotist claims to be holding, you may talk about it in detail. Told that you cannot see a certain object, such as a chair, you may indeed report that it is not there, although, curiously, you manage to avoid the chair when walking around.

And if instructed to forget all these happenings once you are out of the hypnotic state, you may later report **posthypnotic amnesia**, a temporary memory loss rather like being unable to recall a familiar name. Although people *say* they don't remember "forgotten" material, subtle tests lead skeptics to doubt their reported amnesia (Coe, 1989a). The material must be "in there," for it can affect later behavior and be recalled at a prearranged signal (Kihlstrom, 1985; Spanos & others, 1985).

Also working against the respectability of hypnosis, note skeptics, were the grand claims made by its practitioners. Supposedly, mesmerized people could see with the backs of their heads, perceive others' internal organs, and communicate with the dead. Researchers now agree that hypnotized persons can perform no such feats. Like unhypnotized people, those under hypnosis cannot leap tall buildings, run faster than a speeding bullet, or display superhuman strength. In experiments, their strength, stamina, learning, and perceptual abilities are like those of motivated unhypnotized people (Druckman & Bjork, 1994). Hypnotized people may surprise you by, say, extending their arms for 6 minutes straight or by assuming the form of a "human plank"—but unhypnotized people can also perform these feats. (See Figure 5.5.)

Before considering whether the hypnotic state is actually an *altered* state of consciousness, let's first consider some areas of general agreement. Then, with the facts of hypnosis in mind, we can ponder two perplexing questions: What is hypnosis? And what does hypnosis tell us about human consciousness?

Figure 5.5 **The "amazing" hypnotized "human plank"** Actually, unhypnotized people can also perform this feat.

Facts and Falsehoods

Can Hypnosis Work for Anyone?

Those who study hypnosis agree that its power resides not in the hypnotist but in the subject's openness to suggestion (Bowers, 1984). To some extent, nearly everyone is suggestible. When people standing upright with their eyes closed are told repeatedly that they are swaying back and forth, most will indeed sway a little. In fact, postural sway is one of the items on the Stanford Hypnotic Susceptibility Scale that assesses a person's hypnotizability. During the assessment, a hypnotist gives a brief hypnotic induction and then presents a series of suggested experiences that range from easy (one's outstretched arms will move together) to difficult (with eyes open one will see a nonexistent person).

Those who are highly hypnotizable—say, the 20 percent who can carry out a suggestion not to smell or react to a bottle of ammonia held under the nose—are still likely to be the most hypnotizable 25 years later (Piccione & others, 1989). These hypnotically susceptible people, like the fantasy-prone people described earlier, frequently become deeply absorbed in imaginative activities (Lynn & Rhue, 1986; Silva & Kirsch, 1992). Typically, they have rich fantasy lives and easily become absorbed in the imaginary events of a novel or movie. Many

"Excellent hypnotic subjects choose to become absorbed in suggestions in the same way that many people become absorbed in movies and novels."

Nicholas P. Spanos
Multiple Identities and False Memories
1996

researchers therefore refer to hypnotic "susceptibility" as hypnotic *ability*, a label with more positive connotations. Few of us would care to be "susceptible" to hypnosis, but most of us would be glad to have the "ability" to focus our attention totally on a task, to become imaginatively absorbed in it, to entertain fanciful possibilities. And that is what fantasy-prone people with hypnotic ability can do.

Can Hypnosis Enhance Recall of Forgotten Events?

Can hypnotic procedures enable people to relive earlier experiences? To recall kindergarten classmates? To retrieve forgotten or suppressed details of a crime? Should testimony obtained under hypnosis be admissible in court?

Most people believe—wrongly, as Chapter 7 will explain—that our experiences are all "in there," that our brains record everything that happens to us and can recall it when we break through our own defenses (Loftus, 1980). Most university students, for example, agree that "under hypnosis a person [can] recall childhood events with very high accuracy" (Furnham, 1993). Testimonies to this come from *age regression* demonstrations, in which people supposedly relive experiences from their childhood. But 60 years of research dispute claims of age regression: Hypnotized people are *not* more genuinely childlike than unhypnotized people who are asked to feign childlike behavior (Nash, 1987). Age-regressed people act as they *believe* children would, but they typically miss the mark by outperforming real children of the specified age (Silverman & Retzlaff, 1986). Age-regressed people may, for example, *feel* childlike and may print much as they know a 6-year-old would, but they sometimes do so with perfect spelling and typically without any change in their adult brain waves, reflexes, and perceptions.

On rare occasions, the relaxed, focused state of hypnosis has enabled witnesses to produce leads in criminal investigations. One instance occurred in 1977, when 26 children and their bus driver, Ed Ray, were kidnapped and forced into an abandoned trailer truck buried 6 feet underground. After their rescue, Ray, under hypnosis, recalled all but one digit of the kidnapper's license plate. With this crucial information, police tracked down the abductors. This anecdote is atypical, and it is unclear whether hypnosis enabled the memory retrieval. Nevertheless, many researchers believe that hypnotic procedures may have some value—or at least do little harm—when used as an investigative tool.

Hypnotically refreshed memories combine fact with fiction.

The problem comes in putting on the witness stand someone whose memories are "hypnotically refreshed." Researchers have found that hypnotically refreshed memories combine fact with fiction. Thus, American, Australian, and British courts increasingly ban testimony from witnesses who have been hypnotized (Druckman & Bjork, 1994; Gibson, 1995; McConkey, 1995).

Hypnosis has unpredictable effects. Sometimes the relaxed reflection boosts recall. But often hypnosis contaminates memory with false recollections or increases confidence in false memories (Lynn & others, 1997; McConkey, 1992). When pressed under hypnosis to recall details, perhaps to "zoom in on your visual memory screen," people use their imaginations to construct their memories. Without either person being aware of what is going on, the hypnotist's hints—"Did you hear loud noises?"—can become the subject's pseudomemory. Previously hypnotized witnesses may end up testifying confidently to events they never experienced (Laurence & Perry, 1988). And whether hypnotized or not, highly hypnotizable (fantasy-prone) people are especially vulnerable to false memory suggestions (Barnier & McConkey, 1992).

So, hypnosis cannot change the rules by which we form, store, and retrieve memories. "Hypnosis is not a psychological truth serum," concludes researcher Kenneth Bowers (1987), "and to regard it as such has been a source of considerable mischief."

posthypnotic amnesia supposed inability to recall what one experienced during hypnosis; induced by the hypnotist's suggestion.

Most reports of UFOs have come from people who are predisposed to believe in aliens, are fantasy prone, and have undergone hypnosis.

It distresses memory researchers that many therapists do not appreciate the unreliability of hypnotically induced memories. When hypnosis researcher Michael Yapko (1994) surveyed 869 therapists attending various therapy conventions, 47 percent agreed that "psychotherapists can have greater faith in details of a traumatic event when obtained hypnotically than otherwise." And 54 percent agreed that "hypnosis can be used to recover memories of actual events as far back as birth." Such ignorance "of the facts" left Yapko aghast: "I am deeply concerned that psychotherapy patients will be led to believe destructive ideas that are untrue . . . all in the name of 'psychotherapy.'"

See Chapter 7 for a more detailed discussion of how people may construct false memories.

Striking examples of memories created under hypnosis come from the tens of thousands of people who since 1980 have reported being abducted by UFOs, abused in satanic cults, or adulated during a past life. Under hypnosis, one woman

> remembered a light and a voice calling her out of bed. She obeyed against her will and went to a muddy field as a saucer-shaped craft neared the ground. Through the windows she saw beings and a piercing sound prevented her from moving. A warm beam of light then pulled her inside the craft. She found herself inside a white hospital room. Two small beings with tiny mouths and compelling eyes, dressed as if in motorcycle jackets, told her without speaking to undress and lie down on a table. She resisted but eventually gave in . . . at last the doctor entered and gave her an injection. He then inserted a needle into her navel. . . . One being . . . undressed himself and rubbed her with a jelly. It warmed her [and he] then raped her. (Bullard, 1987)

Studies reveal that most reports of UFOs have come from people who are predisposed to believe in aliens, are fantasy prone, and have undergone hypnosis (Newman & Baumeister, 1996; Nickell, 1996).

Can Hypnosis Force People to Act Against Their Will?

Researchers Martin Orne and Frederick Evans (1965) demonstrated that hypnotized people *could* be induced to perform an apparently dangerous act. For example, the participants followed a request to dip a hand briefly in fuming acid and then throw the "acid" in a research assistant's face. When interviewed a day later, they exhibited no memory of their acts and emphatically denied they would follow orders to commit such actions.

Had hypnosis given the hypnotist a special power to control these people against their will? To find out, Orne and Evans unleashed that enemy of so many illusory beliefs—the control group: Orne asked some additional people to *pretend* they had been hypnotized. The laboratory experimenter, unaware that these control subjects had not been hypnotized, treated all participants in the same manner. The result? All the *un*hypnotized participants (perhaps believing that the laboratory context assured safety) performed the same acts as the hypnotized ones. Similarly, most hypnotized subjects can be induced to deface a sacred book, and a few will even cooperate in stealing an exam or selling illegal drugs. But people asked to simulate hypnosis are no less likely to perform the same acts (Levitt, 1986).

This illustrates a principle that Chapter 14 emphasizes: An authoritative person in a legitimate context can induce people—hypnotized or not—to perform some unlikely acts. Hypnosis researcher Spanos (1982) put it simply: "The overt behaviors of hypnotic subjects are well within normal limits."

Can Hypnosis Be Therapeutic?

posthypnotic suggestion a suggestion, made during a hypnosis session, to be carried out after the subject is no longer hypnotized; used by some clinicians to help control undesired symptoms and behaviors.

Hypnotherapists do nothing magical. Rather, they try to help patients harness their own healing powers (Baker, 1987). **Posthypnotic suggestions** (suggestions to be carried out after the hypnosis session has ended) have helped alleviate

THINKING CRITICALLY

Hypnotic Age Regression: A True Story

Remembrances of Christmases Past?

What shall we make of a clever study by Robert True (1949)? He regressed hypnotized volunteers back to their Christmases and birthday parties at ages 10, 7, and 4. In each case, he asked them what day of the week it was. Without hypnosis, the odds that a person could name offhand the day of a long-ago date are but 1 in 7. Remarkably, the hypnotized subjects' answers were 82 percent correct.

Other investigators were unable to replicate True's results. When Martin Orne (1982) asked True why, he replied that *Science*, the journal that published his article, had shortened his key question to "What day is this?" Actually, he had asked his age-regressed subjects, "Is it Monday? Is it Tuesday?" and so forth until the subject stopped him with a yes. When Orne asked True if he knew the actual day of the week while posing the questions, True granted that he did but was puzzled why Orne would ask.

Can you see why? True's experiment appears to be a beautiful example of how hypnotists can subtly influence their subjects' memories (and, more generally, of how experimenters can subtly communicate their expectations). "Given the eagerness of the hypnotized subject to fulfill the demands placed upon him," surmised Orne, it takes only the slightest change of inflection (in asking "Is it Wednesday?") for the subject to respond, "Yes."

The final blow to True's experiment came when Orne simply asked ten 4-year-olds what day of the week it was. To his surprise, none knew. If 4-year-olds typically do not know the day of the week, then True's adults were reporting information they probably didn't know when they were 4.

Remembrances of Lives Past?

If people's hypnotic regressions to childhood are partly imagined, then how believable are claims of hypnotic "regression to past lives"? Can the 20 to 30 percent of Americans who believe in reincarnation (Gallup & Newport, 1991; *George*, 1996) find support in such reports? Were 36 percent of university students correct to agree, in a survey by Scott Brown and others (1996), that "certain people can be age regressed to recall past lives"?

Nicholas Spanos (1987–1988; Spanos & others, 1991) reported that, when hypnotized, fantasy-prone people who believe in reincarnation will offer vivid details of "past lives." But they nearly always report being their same race—unless the researcher has informed them that different races are common. They often report being someone famous rather than one of the countless "nobodies." Some contradict one another by claiming to have been the same person, such as Joan of Arc (Reveen, 1987–1988). Moreover, they typically do not know things that any person of that historical time would have known. One subject who "regressed" to a "previous life" as a Japanese fighter pilot in 1940 could not name the emperor of Japan and did not know that Japan was already at war. Hypnotic regressions to past lives thus offer no credible evidence of reincarnation.

Will the real Joan of Arc please stand up? Under hypnosis, people who claim to remember a past life will often report being someone famous.

headaches, asthma, warts, and stress-related skin disorders. One woman, who had suffered open sores all over her body for more than 20 years, was asked to imagine herself swimming in shimmering, sunlit liquids that would cleanse her skin and to experience her skin as smooth and unblemished. Within 3 months her sores had disappeared (Bowers, 1984).

dissociation a split in consciousness, which allows some thoughts and behaviors to occur simultaneously with others.

When hypnosis is applied to self-control problems such as nail biting and smoking, the most hypnotizable people show no greater benefit than those least hypnotizable. This suggests that the benefits are not a result of the hypnosis per se (Bowers & LeBaron, 1986). Should we also then question whether hypnosis is the therapeutic agent when we hear of improvements in problems unrelated to willpower, such as skin disorders? Do the benefits of hypnosis surpass those of merely encouraging people to relax and form positive images? The answer remains in doubt. For example, hypnosis speeds the disappearance of warts, but in controlled studies, so do the same positive suggestions given without hypnosis (Spanos, 1991, 1996).

Can Hypnosis Alleviate Pain?

Yes, hypnosis *can* relieve pain (Druckman & Bjork, 1994; Kihlstrom, 1985). When unhypnotized subjects put their arms in an ice bath, they feel intense pain within 25 seconds. When hypnotized subjects do the same after being given suggestions to feel no pain, they indeed report feeling little pain. As some dentists know, even light hypnosis can reduce fear, and thus hypersensitivity to pain. Nearly 10 percent of us can become so deeply hypnotized that even major surgery can be performed without anesthesia. And half of us can gain some pain relief from hypnosis.

The Lamaze method of childbirth Like hypnosis, the Lamaze method involves breathing and concentration techniques that draw attention away from pain. Women for whom the method works tend to have high hypnotic ability (Venn, 1986).

How can this be? One theory of hypnotic pain relief proposes **dissociation**, a split between different levels of consciousness. Hypnosis, it suggests, dissociates the sensation of the pain stimulus (of which the subject is still aware) from the emotional suffering that defines our pain experience. The ice water therefore feels very cold but not painful.

Another theory proposes that hypnotic pain relief is due to selective attention, as when an injured athlete, caught up in the competition, feels little or no pain until the game ends. Support for this view comes from several studies showing that hypnosis relieves pain no better than does merely relaxing and distracting people (Chaves, 1989). With their attention distracted during hypnosis, some women can experience childbirth with minimal pain; but so can some women without hypnosis, especially if given childbirth training (D'Eon, 1989).

Both views of pain assume that at some level a hypnotized person does experience the pain stimulus. Indeed, people who report feeling no pain nevertheless may respond with a pounding heart to electric shock or a surgeon's knife. Similar disparities between self-reports and behavior involve seeing and hearing. Following a suggestion of deafness, hypnotized people will deny being able to hear their own voices. But when they hear their voice over a headset with a half-second delay, they respond as unhypnotized people do: The delayed feedback disrupts their ability to speak fluently. If told they are colorblind, hypnotized people do not respond to colorblindness tests as do people with actual color-deficient vision. In each of these cases, the hypnotized subjects *report* perceiving no pain, sound, or color. Yet the stimuli have quite obviously registered within their sensory systems. Thus, hypnosis does *not* block sensory input. What people *say* they experience just doesn't fit with their behavior.

Hypnotic subjects, say skeptics, are imaginative actors caught up in playing the role of hypnotic subject.

The unanswered question of how hypnosis relieves pain—by *dissociating* the pain sensation from conscious awareness, or merely by focusing *attention* on other things—brings us to the basic issue: Is hypnosis a unique psychological state?

Explaining the Hypnotized State

9. Should hypnosis be considered an extension of normal consciousness or an altered state?

We have seen that hypnosis involves heightened suggestibility. We have also seen that hypnotic procedures do not endow a person with special powers. But they can sometimes enhance recall of real (and unreal) past events, aid in overcoming psychologically influenced ailments, and help alleviate pain. So, just what is hypnosis? Does it qualify as an altered—out-of-the-ordinary—state of consciousness?

Hypnosis as a Social Phenomenon

Explaining hypnosis How can she do it? How can this hypnotized young woman show no reaction to the terrible smell of ammonia? Divided-consciousness theory and social influence theory offer possible explanations.

In some way attention is being diverted from a very aversive stimulus. How?

Divided-consciousness theory:
hypnosis has caused a split in awareness

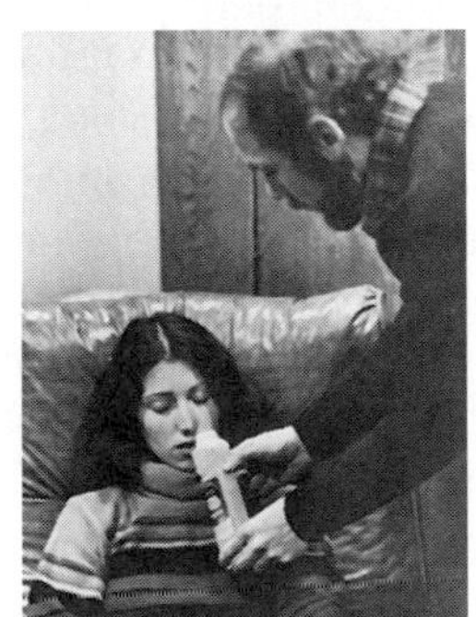

Social influence theory:
the subject is so caught up in the hypnotized role that she can ignore the odor

Skeptics note that hypnosis is not a unique physiological state. Moreover, behaviors produced through hypnotic procedures can also be produced without them. This suggests that hypnotic phenomena may reflect the workings of normal consciousness (Lynn & others, 1990; Spanos & Coe, 1992).

In Chapter 4 we saw how powerfully our interpretations influence ordinary perceptions. Especially in the case of pain, for which the effects of hypnosis seem most dramatic, our perceptions follow our attention. Moreover, imaginative people can manufacture vivid perceptions without hypnosis. Perhaps, then, "hypnotized" people are just acting the role of "good hypnotic subjects" and allowing the hypnotist to direct their fantasies.

It's not that people are consciously faking hypnosis. Rather, they're doing and reporting what's expected of them. Like actors who get caught up in their roles, they begin to feel and behave in ways appropriate to the hypnotic role. The more they like and trust the hypnotist and feel motivated to demonstrate hypnotic behavior, the more they do so (Gfeller & others, 1987). If told later to scratch their ear when they hear the word *psychology*, subjects will likely do so only if they think the experiment is still under way (and scratching is therefore expected). If an experimenter eliminates the motivation for acting hypnotized—by stating that hypnosis reveals "gullibility"—subjects become unresponsive.

Based on such findings, advocates of the *social influence theory* contend that hypnotic phenomena are *not* unique to hypnosis. They argue that hypnotic phenomena—like behavior associated with other supposed altered states, such as dissociative identity disorder (page 438) and spirit or demon possession—are an extension of everyday social behavior (Spanos, 1994, 1996). Hypnotic subjects, say skeptics, are imaginative actors caught up in playing the role of hypnotic subject.

Hypnosis as Divided Consciousness

Most hypnosis researchers grant that normal social and cognitive processes play a part in hypnosis, but they believe hypnosis is more than imaginative acting. For one thing, hypnotized subjects will *sometimes* carry out suggested behaviors on cue, even when they believe no one is watching. Their doing so shows that more may be at work than merely trying to be a "good subject." Moreover, many practitioners remain convinced that certain phenomena *are* unique to hypnosis. What else explains hypnotic experiences such as pain

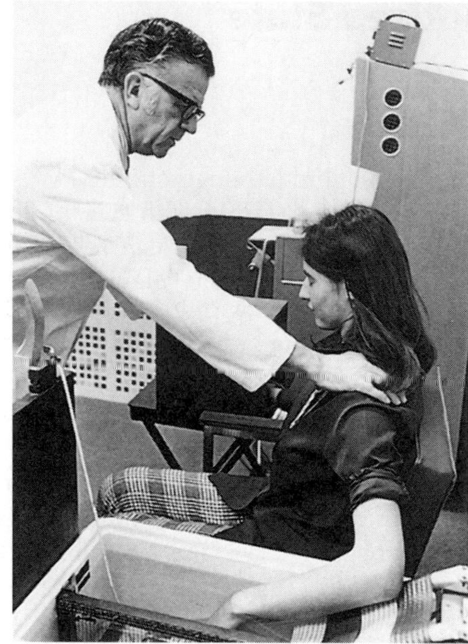

Demonstrating the "hidden observer" A hypnotized subject being tested by Ernest Hilgard exhibits no pain when her arm is placed in an ice bath. But asked to press a key if some part of her feels the pain, she does so. To Hilgard, this suggests that hypnosis divides consciousness into one part that is unaware of pain and another part—a "hidden observer"—that is aware of it.

reduction and compelling hallucinations (Bowers, 1990)? Skeptics reply that hypnotists' livelihoods depend on maintaining an aura of mysterious power (Coe, 1989b).

To veteran researcher Ernest Hilgard (1986, 1992), hypnosis involves not only social influence but also a special state of dissociated consciousness. Hilgard views hypnotic dissociation as a vivid form of everyday mind splits. Putting a child to bed, we might read *Goodnight Moon* for the fourteenth time while mentally organizing a busy schedule for the next day.

With practice, it is even possible to read and comprehend a short story while copying dictated words, much as you can doodle while listening to a lecture, or much as a skilled pianist can converse while playing a familiar piece (Hirst & others, 1978). Thus, when hypnotized subjects write answers to questions about one topic while talking or reading about a different topic, they display an accentuated form of normal cognitive dissociation. So, when today's researchers refer to a "hypnotic state," note Irving Kirsch and Steven Jay Lynn (1995), they merely refer to the subjective experience of hypnosis and not to a unique trance state.

Hypnotized subjects, as noted earlier, report far less pain than others when they place their arms in ice water. But when asked to press a key if "some part" of them does feel the pain, they invariably press the key. To Hilgard, this suggests that a dissociated consciousness, a **hidden observer**, is passively aware of what is happening.

The *divided-consciousness theory* of hypnosis provoked controversy, because what the "hidden observer" reports varies with what the experimenter seems to want. But this much seems clear: You and I process much information without conscious awareness. We have seen other examples of unconscious information processing in the chapter on sensation and perception, and we will see more in later chapters on learning, memory, and thinking. Without doubt, there is much more to thinking and acting than we are conscious of. Our information processing *is* divided into simultaneous conscious and subconscious realms.

"The total possible consciousness may be split into parts which co-exist but mutually ignore each other."

William James
Principles of Psychology
1890

Then again, there is also little doubt that social influences do play an important role in hypnosis. So, might the two views—social influence and divided consciousness—be bridged? Each position has its supporters, and some now believe that they both have merits. For example, researchers John Kihlstrom and Kevin McConkey (1990) believe there is no contradiction between the two approaches, which are converging toward a "unified account of hypnosis." Hypnosis, they suggest, is an extension *both* of normal principles of social influence *and* of everyday splits in consciousness.

REHEARSE IT!

12. Hypnotism is a social interaction in which a hypnotist suggests to a subject that certain perceptions, feelings, thoughts, or behaviors will spontaneously occur. Subjects who are hypnotizable and will carry out a hypnotic suggestion usually

a. are fantasy-prone.
b. have low self-esteem.
c. are good at playing a role.
d. are female.

13. Although experts differ in their understandings of hypnotism, most agree that hypnotism can be effectively used to

a. elicit testimony about a "forgotten" event.
b. re-create childhood experiences.
c. relieve pain.
d. alter personality.

14. Ernest Hilgard believes hypnosis is not merely an extension of normal social influence but involves dissociation, which means

a. nonconformity to social pressure.
b. a state of paradoxical sleep.
c. a state of divided consciousness.
d. conscious enactment of a hypnotic role.

hidden observer Hilgard's term for a hypnotized subject's awareness of experiences, such as pain, that go unreported during hypnosis.

psychoactive drug a chemical substance that alters perceptions and mood.

tolerance the diminishing effect with regular use of the same dose of a drug, requiring the user to take larger and larger doses before experiencing the drug's effect.

withdrawal the discomfort and distress that follow discontinuing the use of an addictive drug.

physical dependence a physiological need for a drug, marked by unpleasant withdrawal symptoms when the drug is discontinued.

psychological dependence a psychological need to use a drug, such as to relieve negative emotions.

Drugs and Consciousness

10. *What are psychoactive drugs?*

If there is controversy about whether hypnosis alters consciousness, there is little dispute that drugs do. **Psychoactive drugs** are chemicals that change perceptions and moods. An imaginary drug user's day dramatizes the widespread use of legal psychoactive drugs: It begins with a wake-up cup of strong coffee. By midday, several cigarettes and a prescription tranquilizer have calmed the nerves. An early exit from work makes time for a happy-hour drink, providing a relaxing and sociable prelude to a dental appointment, where nitrous oxide makes an otherwise painful experience mildly pleasurable. A diet pill before dinner helps stem the appetite, and its stimulating effects can later be partially offset with a sleeping pill. Before drifting off into REM-depressed sleep, our hypothetical drug user is dismayed by a news report of "rising drug abuse."

"Just tell me where you kids got the idea to take so many drugs."

Dependence and Addiction

Continued use of a psychoactive drug produces **tolerance**: The user requires larger and larger doses to experience the drug's effect. A person who rarely drinks alcohol might get tipsy on one can of beer, but an experienced drinker may not get tipsy until the second six-pack (Figure 5.6). Despite the connotations of "tolerance," alcoholics' brains, hearts, and livers suffer damage from the excessive alcohol they are "tolerating."

Users who stop taking psychoactive drugs may experience the undesirable side effects of **withdrawal**. As the body responds to the drug's absence, the user may feel physical pain and intense cravings. This indicates a **physical dependence** on the drug. People can also develop **psychological dependence**, particularly for stress-relieving drugs. Although such drugs may not be physically addictive, they nevertheless become an important part of the user's life, often as a way of relieving negative emotions. With either physical addiction or psychological dependence, the user's primary focus becomes obtaining and using the drug.

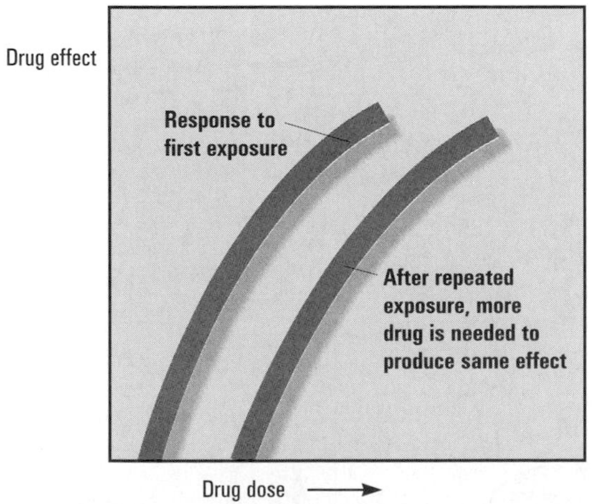

Figure 5.6 **Drug tolerance** With repeated exposure to a psychoactive drug, the drug effect lessens. Thus, it takes bigger doses to get the desired effect.

Misconceptions About Addiction

An "addiction" has traditionally meant a craving for a substance, with physical symptoms such as aches, nausea, and distress following sudden withdrawal. In recent pop psychology, the supposedly irresistible seduction of addiction has been extended to cover many behaviors formerly considered bad habits or even sins. Has the concept been stretched too far? Are addictions as irresistible as commonly believed? Many drug researchers believe the following three myths about addiction are false:

1. *Addictive drugs quickly corrupt; for example, morphine taken to control pain is powerfully addictive and often leads to heroin abuse.* After taking a psychoactive drug, some people—perhaps 10 percent—do indeed have a hard time using it in moderation or stopping altogether. However, there are many more controlled, occasional users than addicts of drugs such as alcohol, marijuana, and cocaine (Gazzaniga, 1988; Siegel, 1990). Moreover, people typically don't become addicted when using drugs medically. Those given morphine to control pain rarely develop the cravings of the addict who uses morphine as a mood-altering drug (Melzack, 1990).

2. *Addictions can't be overcome voluntarily; therapy is a must.* Some addicts do benefit from treatment programs. Alcoholics Anonymous, for example, has

supported many people in overcoming their alcohol dependence. But, say critics, the recovery rates of treated and untreated groups differ less than one might suppose.

Moreover, viewing addiction as a disease, as diabetes is a disease, can undermine self-confidence and the will to change cravings that, without treatment, "one can't fight." And that, critics say, would be unfortunate, for many people do voluntarily stop using addictive drugs, without treatment. Some 70 percent of smokers who seek treatment for their addiction later return to smoking, whereas most of America's 41 million ex-smokers kicked the habit on their own (see Chapter 10). Half of the U.S. soldiers in Vietnam tried heroin or opium, and 20 percent became regular users. And, of nearly 500 men whose urine revealed narcotic use upon their departure from Vietnam, one-third did try narcotics again (Robins & others, 1974). Yet, removed from the war's stressful setting and all the stimulus cues associated with their drug use (the place, the friends, the circumstances), only 7 percent of the 500 became readdicted.

3. *We can extend the concept of addiction to cover not just drug dependencies, but a whole spectrum of repetitive, pleasure-seeking behaviors.* We can, and we have, but should we? The addiction-as-disease-needing-treatment idea has been suggested for a host of driven behaviors, including overeating, shopping, exercise, gambling, work, and sex. Initially, we may use the term metaphorically ("I'm a ski addict"), but when people begin taking the metaphor as reality, addiction becomes an all-purpose excuse. Those who embezzle to feed their "gambling addiction" or who abuse or betray to indulge their "sex addiction" can then seek sympathy and treatment rather than judgment and jail. As Washington, D.C., Mayor Marion Barry replied when asked why he lied about being "chemically dependent," "That was the disease talking. I did not purposely do that to you. I was a victim" (Leo, 1991).

Bookstores now carry whole sections of books on addictive relationships, also known as "co-dependence." A supposedly co-dependent person—usually a woman—is said to be addicted to, or dependent on, a dysfunctional partner, at the cost of losing her own identity and self-fulfillment. Indeed, daughters of alcoholic parents may learn to meet exploitive people's expectations (Lyon & Greenberg, 1991). And women who live with a substance abuser do experience great stress and sometimes help hide the abuser's addiction from public view. But, say critics, our individualistic culture often stretches "co-dependence" to include the lost freedoms of normal, mutually dependent wife-husband or parent-child relationships (Kaminer, 1992). Moreover, the co-dependent person often is *blamed*, and the dysfunctional partner's shame becomes hers as well. If people derive meaning from supporting and loving a troubled family member, are they really blameworthy or socially ill?

Sometimes, though, behaviors such as gambling do become compulsive and dysfunctional, much like abusive drug-taking. Is there justification for stretching the addiction concept to cover social behaviors? Debates over the addiction-as-disease model continue.

CALVIN AND HOBBES

depressants drugs (such as alcohol, barbiturates, and opiates) that reduce neural activity and slow body functions.

stimulants drugs (such as caffeine, nicotine, and the more powerful amphetamines and cocaine) that excite neural activity and speed up body functions.

hallucinogens psychedelic ("mind-manifesting") drugs, such as LSD, that distort perceptions and evoke sensory images in the absence of sensory input.

Varieties of Psychoactive Drugs

There are at least three categories of psychoactive drugs:

- **Depressants**, or "downers," calm neural activity and slow body functions.
- **Stimulants**, or "uppers," temporarily excite neural activity and arouse body functions.
- **Hallucinogens** distort perceptions and evoke sensory images in the absence of sensory input.

Drugs in all three categories do their work at the brain's synapses, by stimulating, inhibiting, or mimicking the activity of neurotransmitters, the brain's chemical messengers.

Depressants

11. ***What are depressants, and what are their effects?***

Let's look first at drugs such as alcohol, barbiturates (tranquilizers), and opiates, which slow body functions.

Alcohol

True or false? In large amounts, alcohol is a depressant; in small amounts, it is a stimulant.

A University of Illinois campus survey showed that before sexual assaults, 80 percent of the male assailants and 70 percent of the female victims had been drinking (Camper, 1990).

False. Small doses of "spirits" may, indeed, enliven a drinker, but they do so by slowing brain activity that controls judgment and inhibitions. If provoked, people under alcohol's influence respond more aggressively than usual. If asked to help, people under alcohol's influence respond more helpfully than usual. In everyday life, alcohol *increases* both harmful tendencies—as when sexually coercive college men try to disinhibit their dates by getting them to drink (Abbey, 1991; Mosher & Anderson, 1986)—and helpful tendencies, as when restaurant patrons tip more when tipsy (M. Lynn, 1988). Thus, alcohol makes us more aggressive or helpful or more self-disclosing or more sexually daring—when such tendencies are already present. The urges you feel when sober are the same ones you are more likely to act upon when intoxicated. Many college students understand this. In one survey of 1900 students at 12 colleges, 33 percent of men and 17 percent of women acknowledged having in the last year "let themselves drink more than normal in order to make it easier for them to have sex with someone" (Anderson & Mathieu, 1996).

Alcohol* increases *both harmful tendencies–as when sexually coercive college men try to disinhibit their dates by getting them to drink–and helpful tendencies, as when restaurant patrons tip more when tipsy.

Low doses of alcohol relax the drinker by slowing sympathetic nervous system activity. With larger doses, alcohol can become a staggering problem: Reactions slow, speech slurs, and skilled performance deteriorates. As Shakespeare foresaw (in *Macbeth*), alcohol releases "the desire but takes away the performance."

These effects contribute to alcohol's worst consequences—to several hundred thousand lives claimed worldwide in alcohol-related accidents and violent crimes each year. Accidents occur despite drinkers' belief (when sober) that driving impaired is wrong and despite their insisting they wouldn't do so. Yet under alcohol's influence, people's moral judgments become more immature, their qualms about drinking and driving lessen—and virtually all will drive home from a bar, even if given a breathalyzer test and told they are intoxicated (Denton & Krebs, 1990; MacDonald & others, 1995).

Don't drink and drive With billboards like this one that shows the appalling consequences of driving under the influence of alcohol, Mothers Against Drunk Driving (MADD) has vigorously promoted awareness of the dangers of alcohol abuse. They have also lobbied for stiffer penalties for drunk drivers.

Alcohol not only affects judgment, it affects memory. It impairs neither short-term recall for what just happened nor existing long-term memories. Rather, it disrupts the *processing* of recent experiences into long-term memories. Thus, the day after being intoxicated, heavy drinkers may not recall whom they met or what they said or did the night before. This memory blackout stems partly from an inability to transfer memories from the intoxicated to the sober state (Eich, 1980). Blackouts after drinking may also result from alcohol's suppression of REM sleep. (Recall that people deprived of REM sleep have difficulty fixing their day's experiences into permanent memories.)

Alcohol has another intriguing effect on consciousness: It reduces self-awareness (Hull & others, 1986). Compared with people who feel good about themselves, those who want to suppress their awareness of failures or shortcomings are more likely to drink. The Nazi doctors who selected "unfit" concentration camp inmates for the gas chambers often did so while drunk, or got drunk afterwards (Lifton, 1986).

Alcohol also focuses attention on the immediate situation and away from future consequences. This facilitates urges that the individual might otherwise resist (Steele & Josephs, 1990). Thus, sexually active university students are less likely to use condoms when intoxicated (MacDonald & others, 1996; in press). And in surveys, over half of rapists acknowledge drinking before committing their offense (Seto & Barbaree, 1995).

As with other psychoactive drugs, alcohol's behavioral effects stem not only from its alteration of brain chemistry but also from the user's expectations. Many studies have found that when people *believe* that alcohol affects social behavior in certain ways and *believe*, rightly or wrongly, that they have been drinking alcohol, they will behave accordingly (Leigh, 1989). In one experiment, David Abrams and Terence Wilson (1983) gave Rutgers University men who volunteered for a study on "alcohol and sexual stimulation" either an alcoholic or a nonalcoholic drink. (Both drinks had a strong taste that masked any alcohol.) In each group, half the participants thought they were drinking alcohol and half thought they were not. After being shown an erotic movie clip, the men who *thought* they had consumed alcohol were more likely to report having strong sexual fantasies and feeling guilt-free. Being able to *attribute* their sexual responses to alcohol released their inhibitions—whether they actually had drunk alcohol or not. If, as commonly believed, liquor is the quicker pick-her-upper, the effect lies partly in that powerful sex organ, the mind.

This research illustrates an important principle: A drug's psychological effects are powerfully influenced by the user's expectations. And that explains why drug experiences vary with cultures (Ward, 1994). If one culture assumes that a particular drug produces euphoria (or aggression or sexual arousal) and another does not, each culture may find its expectations fulfilled.

Fact: *College and university students drink more alcohol than their nonstudent peers, and spend more on alcohol than on books and other beverages combined. Fraternity and sorority members drink three times as much as other students (Atwell, 1986; Malloy & others, 1994). Although few university students believe they have an alcohol problem, many meet the criteria for alcohol abuse (Marlatt, 1991). As students mature, they drink less.*

Fact: *In a Harvard School of Public Health survey of 18,000 students at 140 colleges and universities, almost 9 in 10 students reported abuse by intoxicated peers, including sleep and study interruption, insults, sexual advances, and property damage (Wechsler & others, 1994).*

Fact: *Alcohol kills more people than all illegal drugs combined. So does tobacco (Siegel, 1990).*

Barbiturates

The **barbiturate** drugs, or *tranquilizers*, mimic the effects of alcohol. Because they depress sympathetic nervous system activity, barbiturates such as Nembutal and Seconal are sometimes prescribed to induce sleep or reduce anxiety. In larger doses, they can lead to impaired memory and judgment. In combination with alcohol—as when people take a sleeping pill after an evening of heavy drinking—the total depressive effect on body functions can be lethal. With sufficient doses, barbiturates by themselves can also cause death, which makes them the drugs often chosen by those attempting suicide.

barbiturates drugs that depress the activity of the central nervous system, reducing anxiety but impairing memory and judgment.

opiates opium and its derivatives, such as morphine and heroin; they depress neural activity, temporarily lessening pain and anxiety.

amphetamines drugs that stimulate neural activity, causing speeded-up body functions and associated energy and mood changes.

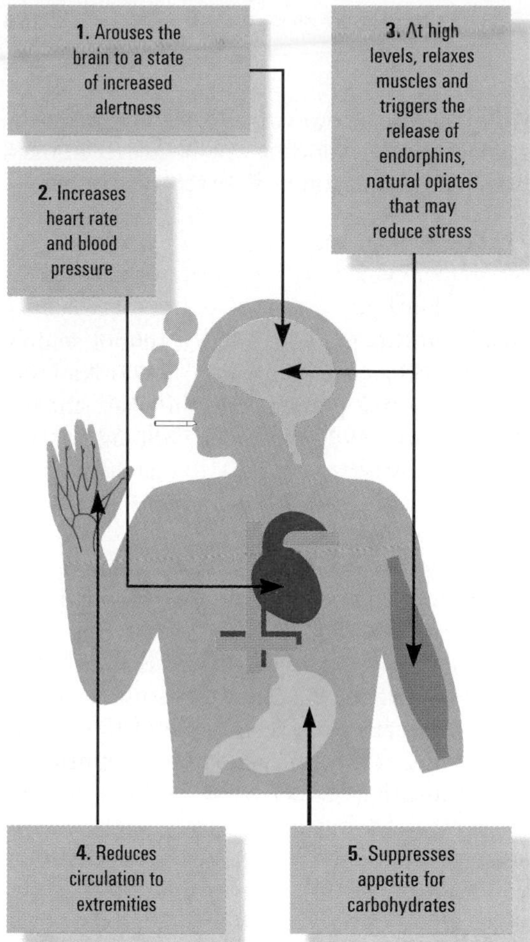

Figure 5.7 Where there's smoke . . . : The physiological effects of nicotine Nicotine reaches the brain within 7 seconds, twice as fast as intravenous heroin. Within minutes, the amount in the blood soars. Nicotine stimulates neurons by mimicking the action of the neurotransmitter acetylcholine and produces the effects shown here.

Opiates

The **opiates**—opium and its derivatives, morphine and heroin—also depress neural functioning. The pupils constrict, the breathing slows, and the user becomes lethargic. For a few hours, blissful pleasure replaces pain and anxiety. But for pleasure one pays a price, which for the heroin user is the gnawing craving for another fix, the need for progressively larger doses, the week-long physical anguish of withdrawal—and for some, the ultimate price: death by overdose.

The pathway to addiction is treacherous. When repeatedly flooded with artificial opiates, the brain eventually stops producing its own opiates, the endorphins. If the drug is then withdrawn, the brain lacks the normal level of these painkilling neurotransmitters. The result is the agony of withdrawal.

Stimulants

12. *What are stimulants, and what are their effects?*

The most widely used stimulants are caffeine, nicotine, the powerful **amphetamines**, and the even more powerful cocaine. Stimulants speed up body functions, hence the nickname "speed" for amphetamines. Strong stimulants increase heart and breathing rates. The pupils dilate, appetite diminishes (because blood sugar rises), and energy and self-confidence rise. For these reasons, people use stimulants to stay awake, lose weight, or boost mood or athletic performance. As with other drugs, the benefits come with a price. When drug stimulation ends, the user experiences a compensating slowdown and may "crash" into tiredness, headaches, irritability, and depression. Like the depressants, stimulants, including coffee, can be addictive (Silverman & others, 1992).

Nicotine

Each year throughout the world, the tobacco industry kills some 3 million of its best customers—equivolent to 20 loaded jumbo jets daily (Peto & others, 1992, 1994). And the worst is yet to come. Given present trends, estimates a 1994 World Health Organization report, *half a billion* people alive today will be killed by tobacco. Thus, the elimination of smoking would do more to increase life expectancy than any other preventive measure. Smoking's addictiveness and destructiveness have prompted psychologists to study why people smoke and how we might help people to quit.

Cost analysis shows that smokers repay society for the health, disability, and fire-risk costs of their habit by dying earlier, saving Social Security and retirement pension payments (Manning & others, 1989).

Of the millions of people who try to lick their addiction each year, only 8 percent succeed, according to a 1994 Centers for Disease Control report. Once addicted to nicotine, a smoker finds it hard to quit because tobacco is as addictive as heroin or cocaine. The smoking habit is tough to break because the craving, hunger, and irritability that accompany nicotine withdrawal are aversive states that a cigarette relieves (Figure 5.7). After an hour or a day without smoking, the habitual smoker finds a cigarette powerfully reinforcing. Given low-nicotine cigarettes, the smoker will light up more of them to maintain a roughly constant level of nicotine in the blood.

1996 Gallup Poll asked of smokers: "All things considered, would you like to give up smoking, or not?"

Yes	*73%*
No	*26%*

Smoking not only terminates the aversive craving, it also is pleasurable. Nicotine triggers the release of epinephrine and norepinephrine, which in turn diminish appetite and boost alertness and mental efficiency. More important, nicotine stimulates the central nervous system to release neurotransmitters that calm anxiety and reduce pain sensitivity (Pomerleau & Pomerleau, 1984). These rewards of smoking, combined with the relief smoking provides from the discomfort of withdrawal, keep people smoking even when they wish they could stop—indeed, even when they

The recipe for Coca-Cola originally included an extract of the coca plant, creating a cocaine tonic for tired elderly people. Between 1896 and 1905, Coke was indeed "the real thing."

know they are committing slow-motion suicide. However, a 1990 report by the Centers for Disease Control found that half of all Americans who have ever smoked have quit. More than 90 percent did so on their own, often after repeated attempts.

Cocaine

In national surveys, 3 percent of adults and 6 percent of high school seniors have reported trying cocaine in the preceding year (Johnston, 1997; National Institute on Drug Abuse, 1992). Of the seniors, 2 percent said they had smoked *crack*, a potent form of cocaine. By the early 1990s, the decade-long cocaine epidemic had begun to subside somewhat. Credit goes partly to increased treatment and awareness but also to the impoverishment, imprisonment, and death of so many cocaine victims (Hamid, 1992).

Cocaine addiction is a fast track from euphoria to crash. When animals and people chew coca leaves, only small amounts of cocaine enter the bloodstream, and they do so gradually, without seeming ill effects (Siegel, 1990). But when extracted cocaine is sniffed ("snorted"), and especially when it is injected or smoked ("free-based"), it enters the bloodstream quickly. The result: a "rush" of euphoria that lasts 15 to 30 minutes. Because the rush depletes the brain's supply of the neurotransmitters dopamine, serotonin, and norepinephrine, a crash of agitated depression occurs as the drug's effect wears off (Figure 5.8). Crack works even faster and produces a briefer but more intense high, a more intense crash, and a craving for more crack, which wanes after several hours and then returns several days later (Gawin, 1991).

To explore dopamine's role in cocaine addiction, researchers created a strain of mice in which they had "knocked out" the gene for a protein that mops up and recycles the excess dopamine released by a nerve cell (Giros & others, 1996). Like cocaine-hyped mice, these mice became hyperactive. They passed through a photocell beam five times as often as other mice. Moreover, cocaine did not affect the "knockout" mice. This suggests that cocaine raises dopamine

Figure 5.8 **Cocaine euphoria and crash**

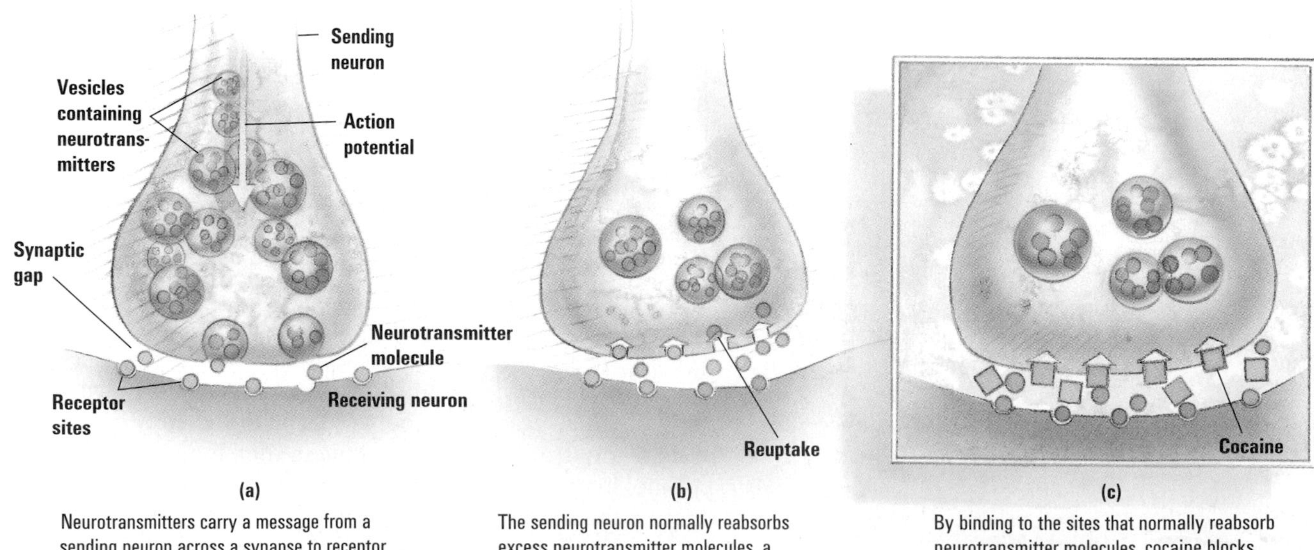

(a) Neurotransmitters carry a message from a sending neuron across a synapse to receptor sites on a receiving neuron.

(b) The sending neuron normally reabsorbs excess neurotransmitter molecules, a process called reuptake.

(c) By binding to the sites that normally reabsorb neurotransmitter molecules, cocaine blocks reuptake of dopamine, norepinephrine, and serotonin (Ray & Ksir, 1990). The extra neurotransmitter molecules therefore remain in the synapse, intensifying their normal mood-altering effects and producing a euphoric rush. When the cocaine level drops, the absence of these neurotransmitters produces a crash.

LSD (*lysergic acid diethylamide*) a powerful hallucinogenic drug; also known as acid.

near-death experience an altered state of consciousness reported after a close brush with death (such as through cardiac arrest); often similar to drug-induced hallucinations.

concentrations by binding to the mop-up site, thus blocking its reuptake of dopamine. This effectively locks neural switches in the brain's reward pathway into the "on" position (Landry, 1997).

By manipulating dopamine, the seeming master molecule of addiction, regular cocaine users become hooked. Monkeys have become so strongly addicted that they will press a lever more than 12,000 times to gain each cocaine injection (Siegel, 1990). Human and animal cocaine users may experience emotional disturbance, suspiciousness, convulsions, cardiac arrest, or respiratory failure. In situations that trigger aggression, ingesting cocaine may increase aggressive reactions. Caged rats fight when given foot shocks, and they fight even more when given cocaine and foot shocks. One experiment asked people how much electric shock an opponent should receive during a laboratory competition. Cocaine users who had ingested high-dose cocaine rather than a placebo set higher levels (Licata & others, 1993).

As with all psychoactive drugs, cocaine's psychological effects depend not only on the drug's dosage and form but also on one's expectations, one's personality, and the situation. Given a placebo, cocaine users who *think* they are taking cocaine often have a cocainelike experience (Van Dyke & Byck, 1982).

Hallucinogens

13. *What are hallucinogens, and what are their effects?*

Hallucinogens are psychoactive drugs that distort perceptions and evoke vivid images in the absence of sensory input (which is why these drugs are also called *psychedelics*, meaning "mind-manifesting"). Some hallucinogens are natural substances, such as marijuana. Others are synthetic. Of the synthetics, the two best known are LSD and PCP ("angel dust"), a potent and illegal painkiller that has highly unpredictable and sometimes devastating psychological effects.

LSD

The first "acid trip" was taken in 1943 by chemist Albert Hofmann, the creator of **LSD** (*lysergic acid diethylamide*). After accidentally ingesting some of the chemical, Hofmann reported that he "perceived an uninterrupted stream of fantastic pictures, extraordinary shapes with intense, kaleidoscopic play of colors" (Siegel, 1984). LSD and other powerful hallucinogens are chemically similar to (and therefore block the actions of) a subtype of the neurotransmitter serotonin (Jacobs, 1987). The emotions of an LSD trip vary from euphoria to detachment to panic.

As with all drug use, a person's current mood and expectations color the LSD experience. Despite emotional variations, the resulting perceptual distortions and hallucinations have common features. The experience typically begins with simple geometric forms, such as a lattice, a cobweb, or a spiral. The next phase consists of more meaningful images; some may be superimposed on a tunnel or funnel, others may involve the replay of past emotional experiences. When the hallucinogenic experience peaks, people frequently feel separated from their bodies and experience dreamlike scenes as if they were real—so real that users may become panic-stricken or may harm themselves.

These hallucinatory sensations are strikingly similar to the **near-death experience** reported by about one-third of those who survive a brush with death, as when revived from cardiac arrest (Moody, 1976; Ring, 1980; Schnaper, 1980). Psychologist Ronald Siegel (1980) reports that one may experience visions of tunnels and bright lights or beings of light (Figure 5.9), a replay of old memories, and out-of-body sensations. Siegel (1982) notes that whether you provoke your brain to hallucinate by loss of oxygen, sensory deprivation, or drugs, "it will hallucinate in basically the same way."

Figure 5.9 **Near-death vision or hallucination?** Psychologist Ronald Siegel (1977) reports that people under the influence of hallucinogenic drugs often see "a bright light in the center of the field of vision. . . . The location of this point of light create[s] a tunnel-like perspective." Susan Blackmore (1991, 1993) offers an explanation of similar light during a near-death experience: As oxygen deprivation turns off the brain's inhibitory cells, neural activity increases in the visual cortex. The result is a growing patch of light, which looks much like what you would see moving through a tunnel. (From "Hallucinations" by R. K. Siegel. Copyright © 1977 Scientific American, Inc. All rights reserved.)

Given that oxygen deprivation and other insults to the brain are known to produce hallucinations, it is difficult to resist wondering whether near-death experiences are manufactured by the brain under stress. Patients who have experienced temporal lobe seizures have reported similarly profound mystical experiences, as have solitary sailors and polar explorers while enduring monotony, isolation, and cold (Suedfeld & Mocellin, 1987). Fantasy-prone persons are especially susceptible—or should we say *open*—to near-death and other out-of-body experiences, such as believing one has encountered or been abducted by aliens (Ring, 1992; Wilson & Barber, 1983).

Marijuana

Marijuana consists of the leaves and flowers of the hemp plant, which for 5000 years has been cultivated for its fiber. Marijuana's major active ingredient is **THC**, the everyday name of the complex organic molecule delta-9-tetrahydrocannabinol. Whether smoked or eaten, THC produces a mix of effects that makes the drug difficult to classify. (Smoking gets the drug into the brain in about 7 seconds; this produces a greater effect than does eating the drug, which causes its peak concentration to be reached at a slower, unpredictable rate.) Like alcohol, marijuana relaxes, disinhibits, and may produce a euphoric high. But marijuana also acts as a mild hallucinogen by amplifying sensitivity to colors, sounds, tastes, and smells.

As with other drugs, the marijuana user's experience varies, depending on the situation. If the person feels anxious or depressed, taking the drug may intensify these feelings. In other situations, using marijuana can be not only pleasurable but therapeutic. For those who suffer the pain of glaucoma (caused by pressure within the eyeball) or the nausea that sometimes accompanies cancer chemotherapy, marijuana may spell relief (Fackelmann, 1997). Such benefits have motivated legislation legalizing the drug for such patients.

A review of marijuana research published by the National Academy of Sciences (1982) also identified some not-so-pleasant consequences. Like alcohol, marijuana impairs the motor coordination, perceptual skills, and reaction time necessary for safe driving and machine operation. "THC causes animals to misjudge events," reports Ronald Siegel (1990, p. 163). "Pigeons wait too long to respond to buzzers or lights that tell them food is available for brief periods; and rats turn the wrong way in mazes." Marijuana also disrupts memory formation and interferes with immediate recall of information learned only a few minutes before. Such cognitive effects outlast the period of smoking (Pope & Yurgelun-Todd, 1996; Smith, 1995). Clearly, being stoned is not conducive to learning.

Unlike alcohol, which the body eliminates within hours, THC and its by-products linger in the body for a month or more. Thus, contrary to the usual tolerance phenomenon, regular users may achieve a high with smaller amounts of the drug than occasional users would take to get the same effect.

Uncertainty persists about marijuana's physical effects, but medical research suggests that long-term marijuana use may depress male sex hormone and sperm levels and damage the lungs more than does cigarette smoking (Wu & others, 1988). Large doses hasten the loss of brain cells (Landfield & others, 1988). Although marijuana is not as addictive as cocaine or nicotine, it changes brain chemistry much as do cocaine and heroin, and it may make the brain more susceptible to cocaine and heroin addiction (Tanda & others, 1997; Rodriquez & others, 1997). One study that followed 654 junior high students into their early twenties found that adolescents who heavily used marijuana developed more health and family problems than did nonusers (Newcomb & Bentler, 1988).

Despite their differences, the psychoactive drugs summarized in Table 5.2 share a common feature: They trigger negative aftereffects that offset their immediate positive effects. The aftereffects illustrate a more general principle that

THC the major active ingredient in marijuana; triggers a variety of effects, including mild hallucinations.

Table 5.2 **A Guide to Selected Psychoactive Drugs**

Drug	Type	Pleasurable Effects	Adverse Effects
Alcohol	Depressant	Initial high followed by relaxation and disinhibition	Depression, memory loss, organ damage, impaired reactions
Heroin	Depressant	Rush of euphoria, relief from pain	Depressed physiology, agonizing withdrawal
Cocaine	Stimulant	Rush of euphoria, confidence, energy	Cardiovascular stress, suspiciousness, depressive crash
Nicotine	Stimulant	Arouses and relaxes, sense of well-being	Heart disease, cancer (from tars)
Marijuana	Mild hallucinogen	Enhances sensation, relieves pain, distorts time, relaxed high	Lowered sex hormones, disrupted memory, lung damage

"How strange would appear to be this thing that men call pleasure! And how curiously it is related to what is thought to be its opposite, pain! . . . Wherever the one is found, the other follows up behind."

Plato
Phaedo
Fourth Century B.C.

emotions tend to produce opposing emotions, which linger after the original emotions disappear. With repetition, the opposing emotions grow stronger. This principle parallels that of drug-induced pleasures; the pleasures wane as the drug exacts its compensatory price. That helps explain both tolerance and withdrawal. As the opposing, negative aftereffects get stronger, the user requires larger and larger doses to achieve the desired high (tolerance), causing the aftereffects to worsen in the drug's absence (withdrawal). This in turn creates a need to switch off the withdrawal symptoms by taking yet more of the drug.

Influences on Drug Use

14. *Why do people use psychoactive drugs?*

Drug use by North American youth increased during the 1970s. Then, thanks to drug education and the media's deglamorization of drug use, it declined sharply until the early 1990s. Since then, with the cultural anti-drug voice softened and countered by the reglamorization of drugs in some music and films, drug use has rebounded, renewing public concern. Consider the trends:

- In the University of Michigan's annual survey of 16,000 high school seniors, the proportion who believed there is "great risk" in regular marijuana use rose from 35 percent in 1978 to 79 percent in 1991, then dropped to 58 percent in 1997 (Johnston, 1997).
- After peaking in 1978, marijuana use by this age group declined until 1992, but has been rising since then (Figure 5.10)
- In the UCLA/American Council on Education annual survey of new college and university students, support for the legalization of marijuana dropped from 53 percent in 1977 to 17 percent in 1989, and rebounded to 33 percent in 1996 (Sax & others, 1996).

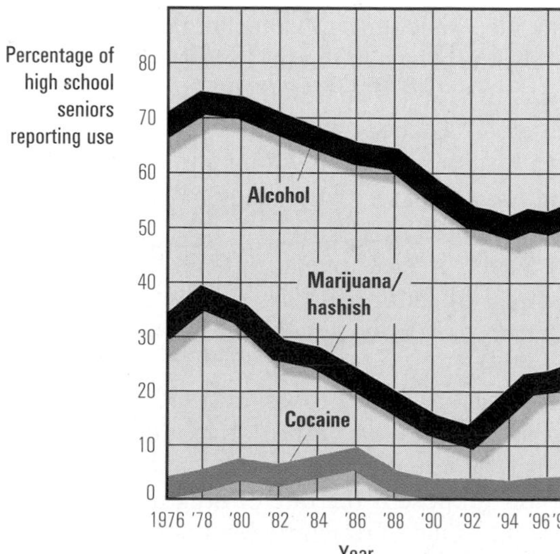

Figure 5.10 Trends in drug use The percentage of high school seniors who report having used alcohol, marijuana, or cocaine during the past 30 days declined from the late 1970s to 1992. Since then, drug use has been increasing and drug merchandise has become more openly available in stores and at concerts. (From Johnston, 1997)

Similar attitude and usage changes since the late 1970s appear in surveys of Canadian teens (Smart & others, 1991).

Other studies reveal a changing national attitude toward alcohol. As much as any time since Prohibition, health- and safety-conscious people see alcohol less as a cheerful beverage than as a drug to be shunned (Gallup, 1996). The number of new U.S. collegians who reported abstinence from beer during the past year increased from 25 percent in 1981 to 47 percent in 1996.

Effectively inform people about the health hazards of taking drugs and—without therapy, support groups, or medicines—many will simply stop.

Still, many people continue to use psychoactive drugs. For some adolescents, occasional drug use represents thrill-seeking. Why do other adolescents become regular drug users?

Genetic Influences

In the case of alcohol, some people may be biologically vulnerable. For example, evidence accumulates that heredity influences alcoholic tendencies:

- Adopted individuals are more susceptible to alcoholism if one or both of their biological parents has a history of alcoholism (Mirin & Weiss, 1989).
- Having an alcoholic identical twin puts a male at especially increased risk for alcohol problems (Heath & others, 1989; McGue & others, 1992; Prescott & others, 1994).
- Boys who at age 6 are excitable, impulsive, and fearless (genetically influenced traits) are more likely as teens to smoke, drink, and use other drugs (Masse & Tremblay, 1997).
- Compared with children of nonalcoholics, children of alcoholics have a higher tolerance for multiple alcoholic drinks taken over an hour or two (Schuckit & Smith, 1996).
- Researchers have bred rats and mice that prefer alcoholic drinks to water (Azar, 1995; Holden, 1991; Goldman, 1996).
- Molecular geneticists have identified a gene on chromosome 11 that is more common among alcoholics, especially severe alcoholics (Noble, 1993).

Psychological and Cultural Influences

Psychological and social factors may also have an important influence. In their studies of youth and young adults, Michael Newcomb and L. L. Harlow (1986) found that one psychological factor is the feeling that one's life is meaningless and directionless, a common feeling among school dropouts who subsist without job skills, without privilege, with little hope. When young unmarried adults leave home, alcohol and other drug use increases; when they marry and have children, it decreases (Bachman & others, 1997).

Some warning signs of alcoholism:
- *Drinking binges*
- *Regretting things done or said when drunk*
- *Feeling low or guilty after drinking*
- *Failing to honor a resolve to drink less*
- *Drinking to alleviate depression or anxiety*
- *Avoiding family or friends when drinking*

Other studies reveal that heavy users of alcohol, marijuana, and cocaine often have experienced significant stress or failure and are depressed. By temporarily dulling the pain of self-awareness, alcohol may offer a way to avoid having to cope with depression, anger, anxiety, or insomnia.

Especially for teenagers, drug use also has social roots, evident in differing rates of drug use across cultural groups. Alcohol and other drug addiction rates are extremely low among the Amish, Mennonites, Mormons, and Orthodox Jews (Trimble, 1994). And what do you suppose is the rate of drug usage among African-American students—low or high? One of psychology's best-kept secrets is that, contrary to popular stereotypes, African-American high school seniors "report the lowest rates of use for virtually all drugs" (Johnston & others, 1994, 1996). For example, nearly a third of white seniors, but only 13 percent of black seniors, report recent heavy drinking. Monthly smoking rates are 38 percent among white seniors but only 14 percent among black seniors. Although these data exclude high school dropouts, independent government studies of drug use in households nationwide and among 12,272 high schoolers in all 50 states con-

In the real world, alcohol accounts for one-sixth or less of beverage use. In television's world, alcohol drinking occurs more often than the combined drinking of coffee, tea, soft drinks, and water (Gerbner, 1990).

Annual Beer and Wine Consumption, Liters per Person

	Beer	*Wine*
France	*41*	*67*
Germany	*143*	*25*
Italy	*23*	*57*
New Zealand	*110*	*15*
Australia	*102*	*19*
U.K.	*106*	*12*
United States	*87*	*7*
Sweden	*59*	*12*

Source: Australian Social Trends, 1995.

Humorist Dave Barry (1995) recalling why he smoked his first cigarette the summer he turned fifteen: "Arguments against smoking: It's a repulsive addiction that slowly but surely turns you into a gasping, gray-skinned, tumor-ridden invalid, hacking up brownish gobs of toxic waste from your one remaining lung."

"Arguments for smoking: Other teen-agers are doing it."

"Case closed! Let's light up!"

firms the finding: African-American teens have sharply lower rates of drinking, smoking, and cocaine use (Bass & Kane-Williams, 1993; Kann & others, 1993). (Curiously, however, cocaine-related arrests and emergency room visits occur more often among African-Americans [Bennett & DiIulio, 1996].)

Social influences are transmitted largely through the peer culture. By their words and examples, peers influence attitudes about drugs. They also provide the drugs and the parties for their use. If an adolescent's friends use drugs, the odds are that he or she will, too. If the friends don't, the temptation may not even arise.

Peer influence is a matter not just of what friends do and say but also of what adolescents *believe* their friends are doing and favoring. Young adolescents consume more alcohol when, as often happens, they overestimate their friends' use (Aas & Klepp, 1992; Graham & others, 1991). At the university level, drinking dominates social occasions partly because students overestimate their fellow students' enthusiasm for alcohol use (Prentice & Miller, 1993; Self, 1994). Thinking that few students share their concerns about the risks associated with alcohol, most students surrender to the perceived norm.

Those who use drugs are more likely to stop if their drug use was peer influenced (Kandel & Raveis, 1989). When the friends stop or the social network changes, usage typically ceases. As noted earlier, more than 9 in 10 soldiers who became drug-addicted while in Vietnam ceased their drug use after returning home. Teenagers who come from happy families and do well in school seldom use drugs, largely because they rarely associate with those who do (Oetting & Beauvais, 1987, 1990). As always with correlations, the traffic between friends' and one's own drug use may be two-way: Our friends influence us, but we also select as friends those who share our likes and dislikes.

The findings suggest three possible channels of influence for drug prevention and treatment programs: (1) education about the long-term costs of a drug's temporary pleasures, (2) efforts to boost people's self-esteem and purpose in life, and (3) attempts to modify peer associations, or to "inoculate" youth against peer pressures, by training "refusal skills."

REHEARSE IT!

15. Depressants are drugs that reduce neural activity and slow down body functions. The depressants include alcohol, barbiturates,

a. and opiates.
b. cocaine, and morphine.
c. caffeine, nicotine, and marijuana.
d. and amphetamines.

16. Alcohol is a depressant that, in significant doses, powerfully affects behavior. For example, drinking alcohol may make a person more helpful or more self-disclosing; conversely, it may make a person more aggressive or more sexually daring. These alcohol effects result from

a. alcoholic blackouts or memory losses.
b. deprivation of REM sleep.
c. sensory arousal and hallucination.
d. the lowering of inhibitions.

17. Nicotine, caffeine, amphetamines, and cocaine stimulate neural activity, speed up body functions, and

a. induce sensory hallucinations.
b. interfere with memory.
c. induce a temporary sense of well-being.
d. lead to heroin use.

18. About one-third of those who have survived a brush with death have reported near-death experiences, which are strikingly similar to the hallucinations evoked by

a. amphetamines.
b. barbiturates.
c. LSD.
d. marijuana.

19. Smoking marijuana can relieve certain kinds of pain and nausea. It also

a. impairs motor coordination, perception, reaction time, and memory.
b. inhibits people's emotions.
c. increases male sex hormone levels.
d. stimulates brain cell development.

20. Drug use by young North Americans generally declined from the late 1970s until the early 1990s. *Social* explanations for drug use today focus on the powerful effect of peer influence. An important *psychological* contributor to drug use is

a. inflated self-esteem.
b. the feeling that life is meaningless and directionless.
c. academic and job pressures.
d. overprotective parents.

REVIEWING ▪ *States of Consciousness*

Waking Consciousness

1. ***What is consciousness and how does it function?***

Psychology has returned to the study of **consciousness**—our awareness of ourselves and our environment. At any moment our **selective attention** makes us conscious of a very limited amount of all that we are capable of experiencing, as when we attend to one voice among many at a party (the cocktail party effect). Speedy, parallel processing handles subconscious information, conscious processing is serial and much slower.

2. ***What are the functions of daydreams and fantasies?***

Virtually everyone daydreams, especially **fantasy-prone** people and especially in times when attention can be freed from the tasks at hand. Daydreaming can be adaptive; it can help us prepare for future events and may substitute for impulsive behavior.

Sleep and Dreams

3. ***What is our daily biological rhythm, and what is the rhythm of our sleep?***

Our daily schedule of waking and sleeping is timed with a body clock known as the **circadian rhythm**. Each night's sleep also has a rhythm of its own. Beginning with the **alpha waves** of the awake but relaxed state, it cycles from transitional Stage 1 sleep, in which **hallucinations** may occur, to deep Stage 4 sleep, characterized by **delta waves**, and back up to the more internally active **REM sleep** stage. (also called *paradoxical sleep*). Periods of Stage 4 sleep progressively shorten and periods of dream-laden REM sleep lengthen through the night.

4. ***How does sleep loss affect us? What is the function of sleep?***

Sleep deprivation impairs concentration, creativity, and the body's ability to fight disease. But depriving people of sleep has not conclusively revealed why, physiologically, we need sleep. Several theories have been proposed. One is that sleep has evolutionary value. Others are that sleep is linked with the release of pituitary growth hormone and that it may help to restore brain tissues and consolidate memories.

5. ***What are the major sleep disorders?***

The disorders of sleep include **insomnia** (recurring wakefulness), **narcolepsy** (uncontrollable lapsing into REM sleep), **sleep apnea** (the temporary cessation of breathing while sleeping), and **night terrors** (high arousal and terrified appearance occurring during Stage 4 sleep).

6. ***What do we dream?***

Although conscious thoughts can occur during any sleep stage, waking people during REM sleep yields predictable "dreamlike" reports; waking them during other sleep stages yields only an occasional fleeting image. Our dreams are mostly of ordinary events; they often relate to everyday experiences and more frequently involve anxiety or misfortune than triumphant achievements.

7. ***What is the function of dreams?***

Freud believed that a dream's **manifest content**, or story line, is a censored version of its **latent content**, which gratifies our unconscious wishes. Newer explanations of why we dream suggest that dreams (1) help process information from the day and fix it in memory, (2) serve a physiological function, and/or (3) are the brain's efforts to string periodic hallucinations (from activity bursts in the visual cortex) into a story line. Despite their differences, most theorists agree that REM sleep and its associated dreams serve an important function, as shown by the **REM rebound** that occurs following REM deprivation.

Hypnosis

8. ***What do hypnotized people experience, and how do they behave?***

Psychologists agree that **hypnosis** is a social interaction in which the hypnotist suggests to a subject that certain perceptions, feelings, thoughts, or behaviors will occur spontaneously. They also agree that people are suggestible in varying degrees, and that, although hypnotic procedures may help someone to recall past events, the hypnotist's beliefs frequently work their way into the subject's recollections. They further agree that hypnotized people can no more be made to act against their will than can nonhypnotized people. Hypnosis can be at least temporarily therapeutic (through **posthypnotic suggestion**), and hypnotizable people can enjoy significant pain relief (perhaps through **dissociation**). They do not believe, however, that **posthypnotic amnesia** really occurs.

9. ***Should hypnosis be considered an extension of normal consciousness or an altered state?***

There is debate whether hypnosis is a by-product of normal social and cognitive processes or an altered state of consciousness, perhaps involving a dissociation between levels of consciousness (the **hidden observer**).

Drugs and Consciousness

10. ***What are psychoactive drugs?***

Psychoactive drugs are perception- and mood-altering substances. A surprising number of these drugs, such as caffeine, nicotine, and alcohol, are legal and a part of everyday life. The use of psychoactive drugs often leads to **tolerance** and **physical** and/or **psychological dependence**. Users who are physically dependent will experience **withdrawal** when they try to stop taking the drug. The three types of psychoactive drugs are **depressants, stimulants**, and **hallucinogens**.

11. ***What are depressants, and what are their effects?***

Alcohol, **barbiturates**, and the **opiates** are examples of depressants, which dampen neural activity and slow down body functions. Alcohol seems to enliven by disinhibiting both harmful and helpful tendencies and by impairing judgment. Alcohol also disrupts the processing of recent experiences into long-term memory and reduces self-awareness. User expectation strongly influences alcohol's behavioral effects. Barbiturates can be especially dangerous in combination with alcohol. The harmful aftereffects of opiates oppose and offset the temporary pleasure they induce.

12. ***What are stimulants, and what are their effects?***

Caffeine, nicotine, the **amphetamines**, and cocaine are examples of stimulants, which stimulate neural activity and arouse body functions. The reinforcing effects of nicotine make smoking a difficult habit to kick, but increased knowledge of its devastating health effects has led to a decreasing percentage of Americans who smoke. All stimulants, but especially cocaine and crack, produce a crash of agitated depression as the drug wears off. This reinforces the use of increased amounts of the drug to get out of the depression, leading regular cocaine and crack users to become addicted. As with nearly all psychoactive drugs, stimulants act at the synapses by influencing the brain's neurotransmitters, and their effects depend on dosage and the user's personality and expectations.

13. ***What are hallucinogens, and what are their effects?***

LSD (*lysergic acid diethylamide*) and marijuana are examples of hallucinogens, which distort perception and evoke sensory images without sensory input. Both LSD and marijuana can distort the user's judgments of time and, depending on the setting in which they are taken, can alter sensation and perception. Similar hallucinations are reported in **near-death experiences**, perhaps as a result of oxygen deprivation in the brain. Although **THC**, the major active ingredient in marijuana, can be therapeutic for those enduring glaucoma or chemotherapy, it corrodes health, judgment, and memory.

14. ***Why do people use psychoactive drugs?***

Drug use among teenagers and young adults declined during the 1980s and early 1990s and has been increasing since. Nevertheless, psychological factors (such as stress, depression, and feelings of hopelessness) and social factors (such as peer pressure) combine to lead many people to experiment with—and become dependent on—drugs. Some people also appear to have a greater biological susceptibility to dependence on drugs such as alcohol.

CRITICAL THINKING EXERCISE by Richard O. Straub

Now that you have read and reviewed Chapter 5, take your learning a step further by testing your critical thinking skills on the following creative problem solving exercise.

Rapid eye movement, or REM sleep, is the recurring stage during which vivid dreaming occurs. Theories of why people dream range from Freud's belief that dreams are a psychic safety valve, to the role that dreaming may play in information processing, to the possibility that dreams merely erupt from random neural activity in the brain. Although *why* we dream continues to be debated, that people *need* REM sleep is not. Periods of REM deprivation are invariably followed by increased amounts of REM sleep.

In this exercise, imagine that your middle-aged aunt is worried about her sleep. She claims that she sleeps only three or four hours a night, feels alert only in the morning, and has stopped dreaming altogether. Fearing that her loss of sleep and dreaming will lead to psychological problems, she has tried napping during the day to "catch up," late-night aerobics to tire herself out, and even having a "nightcap or two" before going to bed. Although she claims her insomnia is affecting her health and mood, you haven't noticed any changes in either. Moreover, she seems to have no difficulty concentrating while conversing.

1. Are your aunt's concerns valid? Should she be worried about her insomnia?
2. If your aunt would like to improve her sleep patterns, what steps should she take?
3. Is it likely that your aunt has stopped dreaming altogether? How can she find out for sure?
4. Suppose that your aunt is correct in her belief that she has stopped dreaming. What are some of the probable effects of such a condition according to Freud? According to a physiological psychologist? A cognitive psychologist?

Check your progress on becoming a critical thinker by comparing your answers to the sample answers found in Appendix B.

REHEARSE IT ANSWER KEY

1. c., **2.** b., **3.** a., **4.** b., **5.** b., **6.** d., **7.** d., **8.** c., **9.** d., **10.** a., **11.** c., **12.** a., **13.** c., **14.** c., **15.** a., **16.** d., **17.** c., **18.** c., **19.** a., **20.** b.

CHAPTER 6

Learning

1. ***What is learning?***

When a chinook salmon first emerges from its egg in the gravel bed of a stream, its genes provide many of the behavioral instructions it needs for life. It instinctively knows how and where to swim, what to eat, and how to protect itself from predators. Following this built-in plan, the young salmon soon begins a trek to the sea. After some 4 years in the ocean, the mature salmon returns to its birthplace. It navigates hundreds of miles to the mouth of its home river and then, guided by the scent of its home stream, begins an upstream odyssey to its ancestral spawning ground. Once there, the salmon seeks out the exact conditions of temperature, gravel, and water flow that will facilitate its breeding, and then mates and dies.

Unlike the salmon, we are not born with a genetic blueprint for life. Much of what we do we must learn from experience. Although we struggle to find the life direction a salmon is born with, our learning gives us more flexibility. We can learn how to build grass huts or submarines or space stations and thereby adapt to almost any environment. Indeed, nature's most important gift to us may be our *adaptability*—our capacity to learn new behaviors that enable us to cope with changing circumstances.

No topic is closer to the heart of psychology than is **learning**, *a relatively permanent change in an organism's behavior due to experience*. In earlier chapters we considered the learning of moral ideas, of visual perceptions, of a drug's expected effect. In later chapters we will consider how learning shapes our thought and language, our motivations and emotions, our personalities and attitudes.

Learning in all such realms breeds hope. What is learnable we can potentially teach—a fact that encourages parents, educators, coaches, and animal trainers. What has been learned we can potentially change by new learning—an assumption that underlies counseling, psychotherapy, and rehabilitation programs. No matter how unhappy, unsuccessful, or unloving we are, that need not be the end of our story.

By definition, experience is key to learning. More than 200 years ago, philosophers such as John Locke and David Hume echoed Aristotle's conclusion from 2000 years earlier: We learn by association. Our minds naturally connect events that occur in sequence: We *associate* them. If, after seeing and smelling freshly baked bread, you eat some and find it satisfying, then the next time you see and smell fresh bread, your experience will lead you to expect

learning a relatively permanent change in an organism's behavior due to experience.

associative learning learning that certain events occur together. The events may be two stimuli (as in classical conditioning) or a response and its consequences (as in operant conditioning).

classical conditioning a type of learning in which an organism comes to associate stimuli. A neutral stimulus that signals an unconditioned stimulus (UCS) begins to produce a response that anticipates and prepares for the unconditioned stimulus. (Also called *Pavlovian conditioning.*)

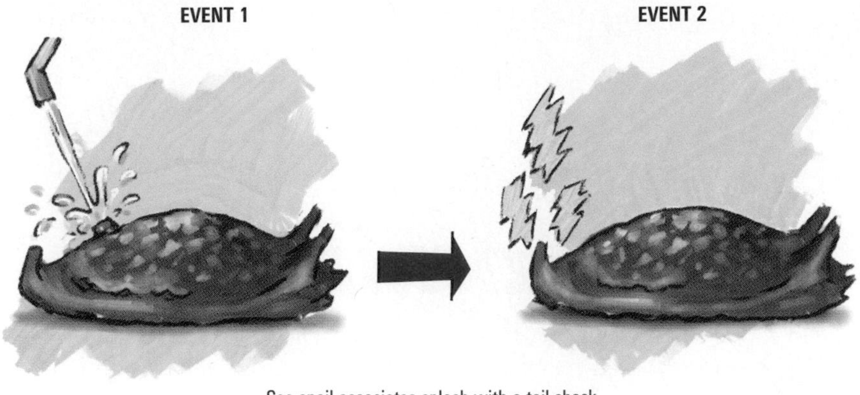

Sea snail associates splash with a tail shock

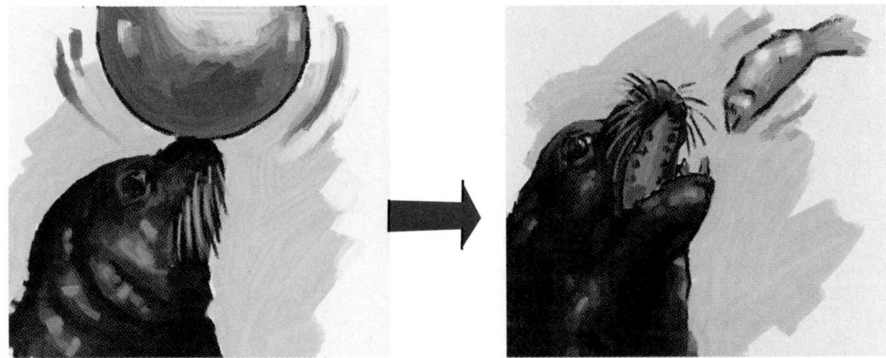

Seal learns to expect a snack for its showy antics

Figure 6.1 **Associative learning: Learning to associate two events**

Figure 6.2 **Classical conditioning**

Two related events:

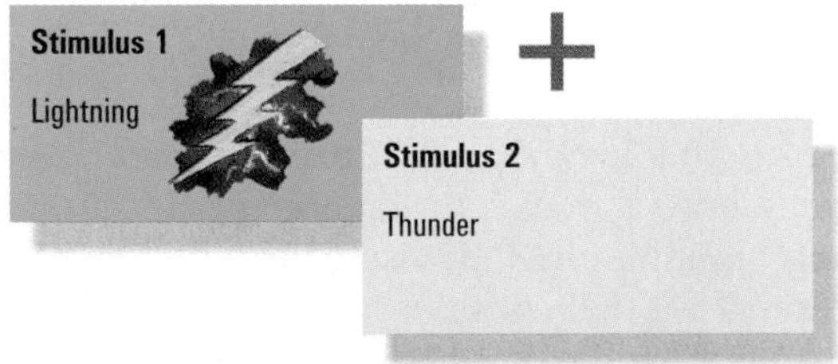

Result after repetition:

Which type of conditioning does the sea snail illustrate? What about the seal? (See page 208.)

that eating some will be satisfying again. And if you associate a sound with a frightening consequence, then your fear may be aroused by the sound itself. As one 4-year-old exclaimed after watching a TV character get mugged, "If I had heard that music, I wouldn't have gone around the corner!" (Wells, 1981).

Simpler animals can learn simple associations. When disturbed by a squirt of water, the sea snail *Aplysia* will protectively withdraw its gill. If the squirts continue, as happens naturally in choppy water, the withdrawal response diminishes. (The snail's response "habituates.") But if the sea snail repeatedly receives an electric shock just after being squirted, its withdrawal response to the squirt alone becomes stronger. The animal associates the squirt with the impending shock. More complex animals can learn more complex associations, especially those that bring favorable consequences. Seals in an aquarium will repeat behaviors, such as slapping and barking, that prompt people to toss them a herring.

By linking two events that occur close together, both the sea snail and the seals exhibit **associative learning**. The sea snail associates the squirt with impending shock; the seal associates slapping, barking, or balancing a ball on its nose with receiving a herring (Figure 6.1). In both cases, the animals learned something important to their survival: to associate the past with the immediate future.

Conditioning is the process of learning associations. In *classical conditioning*, we learn to associate two stimuli. We learn that a flash of lightning signals an impending crack of thunder, and so we start to brace ourselves when lightning flashes nearby (Figure 6.2).

In *operant conditioning*, we learn to associate a response and its consequence. We learn that pushing a vending machine button relates to the delivery of a candy bar (Figure 6.3).

Figure 6.3 Operant conditioning

To simplify things, we will consider these two types of associative learning separately. Often, though, they occur together in the same situation. A clever Japanese rancher reportedly herds cattle by outfitting them with electronic pagers, which he calls from his portable phone. After a week of training, the cows learned to associate two stimuli—the beep on their pager and the arrival of food (classical conditioning). But they also learned to associate their hustling to the food trough with the pleasure of eating (operant conditioning).

The concept of conditioning by association, however, leaves many questions: What principles influence the learning and the loss of associations? How can we apply these principles? And what really are the associations: Does the beep on the cow's pager evoke a cognitive representation of food, to which the cow responds by coming to the trough? Or does it make little sense to explain conditioned associations in terms of cognitive processes?

Conditioning is not the only form of learning. Complex animals, such as chimpanzees, sometimes learn behaviors merely by observing others perform them. If one animal watches another learn to solve a puzzle that gains a food reward, the observing animal may perform the trick more quickly.

In all these ways—by classical and operant conditioning and by observation—we humans learn and adapt to our environments. As this chapter will explain, we learn to expect and prepare for significant events such as food or pain (classical conditioning). We also learn to repeat acts that bring good results and to avoid acts that bring bad results (operant conditioning). By watching others, we gain new behaviors indirectly (observational learning). And, through language, we also learn things we have neither experienced nor observed. Of all the world's creatures, we humans are the most capable of changing our behavior through learning.

Of all the world's creatures, we humans are the most capable of changing our behavior through learning.

Classical Conditioning

2. How does classical conditioning demonstrate learning by association?

Although the idea of learning associations had long generated philosophical discussion, it was only in the early twentieth century that psychology's most famous research verified it. For many people, the name Ivan Pavlov rings a bell. His experiments are classics, and the phenomenon he explored we justly call **classical conditioning** (or *Pavlovian conditioning*).

Most people would be unable to name the order of the songs on a favorite CD. Yet hearing the end of one piece cues (by association) an anticipatory mental representation of the next. Likewise, when singing your national anthem, you associate the end of each line with the beginning of the next. (Pick a line out of the middle and notice how much harder it is to recall the previous line.)

Pavlov's Experiments

Pavlov was driven by a lifelong passion for research. After receiving a medical degree at age 33, he spent the next two decades studying the digestive system, work that earned him Russia's first Nobel prize in 1904. But it was his novel experiments on learning, to which he devoted the last three decades of his life, that earned this feisty scientist his place in history.

Ivan Pavlov "Experimental investigation . . . should lay a solid foundation for a future true science of psychology" (1927).

Pavlov's new direction came when his creative mind seized on an incidental finding. After studying salivary secretion in dogs, he knew that when he put food in a dog's mouth the animal would invariably salivate. He also noticed that when he worked with the same dog repeatedly, the dog began salivating to stimuli associated with food—to the mere sight of the food, to the food dish, to the presence of the person who regularly brought the food, or even to the sound of that person's approaching footsteps. Because these "psychic secretions" interfered

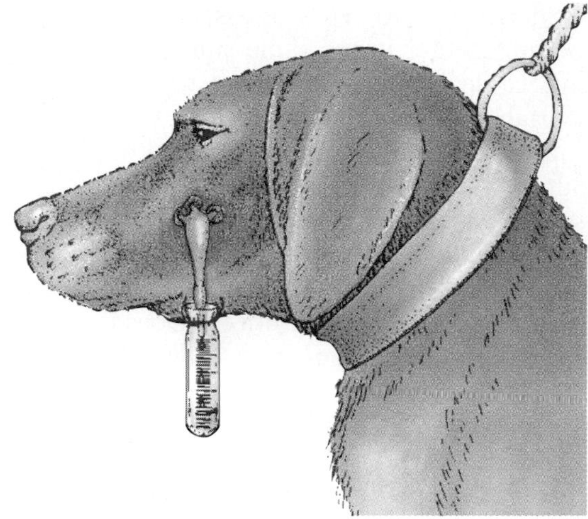

Figure 6.4 Pavlov's device for recording salivation The dog's saliva was collected drop by drop in a tube. (Adapted from Goodwin, 1991)

with his experiments on digestion, Pavlov considered them an annoyance—until he realized they pointed to a simple but important form of learning. From that time on, Pavlov studied learning, which he hoped might enable him to better understand the brain's workings.

At first, Pavlov and his assistants tried to imagine what the dog was thinking and feeling as it drooled in anticipation of the food. This only led them into fruitless debates. So to attack the phenomenon more objectively, they experimented. They paired various neutral stimuli with food in the mouth to see if the dog would begin salivating to the neutral stimuli alone. To eliminate the possible influence of extraneous stimuli, they isolated the dog in a small room, secured it in a harness, and attached a device that diverted its saliva to a measuring instrument (Figure 6.4). From an adjacent room they could present food—at first by sliding in a food bowl, later by blowing meat powder into the dog's mouth at a precise moment. If a neutral stimulus—something the dog could see or hear—now regularly signaled the arrival of food, would the dog associate the two stimuli? If so, would it begin salivating to the neutral stimulus in anticipation of the food?

The answers proved to be yes. Just before placing food in the dog's mouth to produce salivation, Pavlov sounded a tone. After several pairings of tone and food, the dog began salivating to the tone alone, in anticipation of the meat powder. Using this procedure, Pavlov conditioned dogs to salivate to other stimuli—a buzzer, a light, a touch on the leg, even the sight of a circle.

Answers to questions on page 206. The sea snail illustrates classical conditioning. The seal illustrates operant conditioning.

Because salivation in response to food in the mouth was unlearned, Pavlov called it an **unconditioned response (UCR)**. Food in the mouth automatically, *unconditionally*, triggers a dog's salivary reflex (Figure 6.5). Thus, Pavlov called the food stimulus an **unconditioned stimulus (UCS)**.

Salivation in response to the tone was *conditional* upon the dog's learning the association between the tone and the food. This learned response we therefore call the **conditioned response (CR)**. The previously neutral tone stimulus that now triggered the conditional salivation we call the **conditioned stimulus (CS)**. It's easy to distinguish these two kinds of stimuli and responses. Just remember: conditioned = learned; *un*conditioned = *un*learned.

Figure 6.5 Pavlov's classic experiment Pavlov presented a neutral stimulus (a tone) just before an unconditioned stimulus (food in mouth). The neutral stimulus then became a conditioned stimulus, producing a conditioned response.

BEFORE CONDITIONING

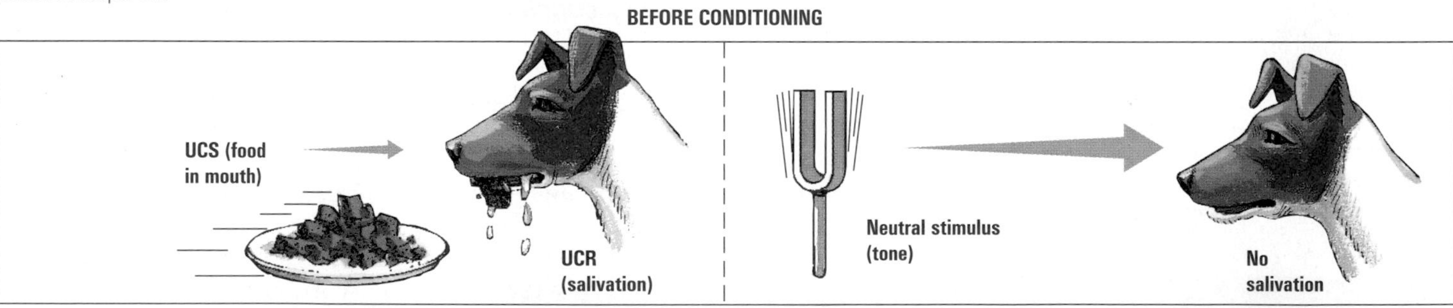

An unconditioned stimulus (UCS) produces an unconditioned response (UCR).

A neutral stimulus produces no salivation response.

DURING CONDITIONING

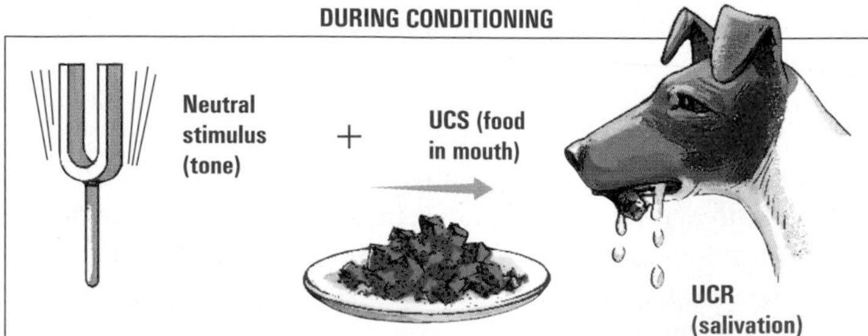

The unconditioned stimulus is repeatedly presented just after the neutral stimulus. The unconditioned stimulus continues to produce an unconditioned response.

AFTER CONDITIONING

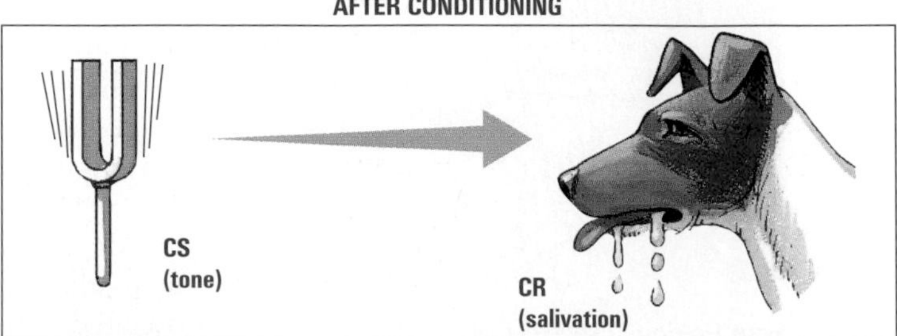

The neutral stimulus alone now produces a conditioned response (CR), thereby becoming a conditioned stimulus (CS).

unconditioned response (UCR) in classical conditioning, the unlearned, naturally occurring response to the unconditioned stimulus (UCS), such as salivation when food is in the mouth.

unconditioned stimulus (UCS) in classical conditioning, a stimulus that unconditionally—naturally and automatically—triggers a response.

conditioned response (CR) in classical conditioning, the learned response to a previously neutral conditioned stimulus (CS).

conditioned stimulus (CS) in classical conditioning, an originally neutral stimulus that, after association with an unconditioned stimulus (UCS), comes to trigger a conditioned response.

acquisition the initial stage in classical conditioning; the phase associating a neutral stimulus with an unconditioned stimulus so that the neutral stimulus comes to evoke a conditioned response.

extinction the diminishing of a conditioned response; occurs in classical conditioning when an unconditioned stimulus (UCS) does not follow a conditioned stimulus (CS).

Check yourself: If the aroma of cake baking sets your mouth to watering, what is the UCS? The CS? The CR? (See page 211)

Remember:
***UCS** = **U**n**C**onditioned **S**timulus*
***UCR** = **U**n**C**onditioned **R**esponse*
***CS** = **C**onditioned **S**timulus*
***CR** = **C**onditioned **R**esponse*

If this demonstration of associative learning was so simple, what did Pavlov do for the next three decades? How did his research factory generate 532 papers on salivary conditioning (Windholz, 1997)? He and his associates explored the causes and effects of classical conditioning. Their experiments identified five major conditioning processes: acquisition, extinction, spontaneous recovery, generalization, and discrimination.

Acquisition

3. *How do the processes of acquisition, extinction, spontaneous recovery, generalization, and discrimination affect a CR?*

To understand the **acquisition**, or initial learning, of the stimulus-response relationship, Pavlov and his associates first had to confront the question of timing: How much time should elapse between presenting the neutral stimulus (the tone, the light, the touch, or whatever) and the unconditioned stimulus? They found that, in most cases, the answer was not much. With many species and procedures, half a second works well. What do you suppose would happen if the food (UCS) appeared *before* the tone (CS) rather than after? Would conditioning occur?

Not likely. Although there are exceptions, conditioning seldom occurs when the UCS comes before the CS. This finding fits the presumption that classical conditioning is biologically adaptive. It helps organisms *prepare* for good or bad events. Pavlov's tone (CS) signals an important biological event—the arrival of food (UCS). To a deer in the forest, the sound of a snapping twig (CS) may come to signal a predator (UCS). If the good or bad event had already occurred, the CS would not likely signal anything significant.

Michael Domjan (1992, 1994) showed how the CS signals an important biological event by conditioning the sexual arousal of male Japanese quail. The researchers turned on a red light before presenting an approachable female. Over time, as the red light continued to herald a female's impending arrival, it caused the male quail to become excited (and to copulate with her more quickly when she arrived). Moreover, the male quail developed a general liking for their cage's red-light district.

In humans, too, objects, smells, and sights associated with sexual pleasure become conditioned stimuli for sexual arousal. Psychologist Michael Tirrell (1990) recalls: "My first girlfriend loved onions, so I came to associate onion breath with kissing. Before long, onion breath sent tingles up and down my spine. Oh what a feeling!" (Questions: What is the unconditioned stimulus here? What is the conditioned response? See Figure 6.6.) In laboratory experiments, even a geometric figure can become sexually arousing if repeatedly associated with an erotic stimulus (Byrne, 1982). (Note that in this case the figure is a CS, which gains its power to arouse by repeated pairing with a naturally erotic stimulus.)

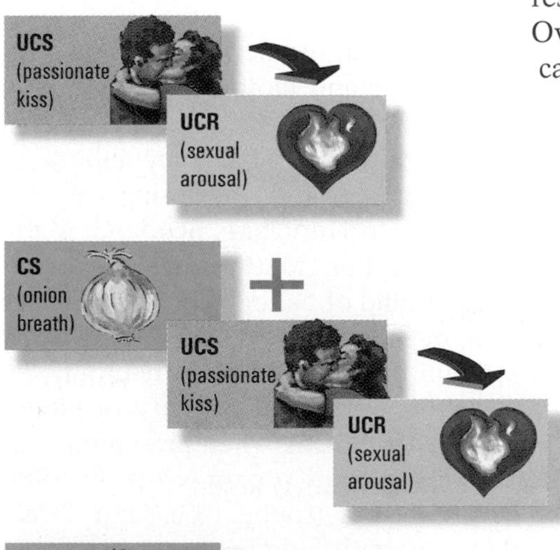

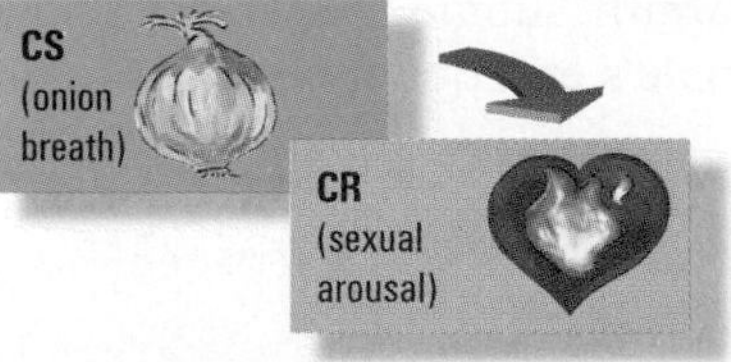

Figure 6.6 **An unexpected CS** Onion breath does not usually produce sexual arousal. But when repeatedly paired with a passionate kiss it can become a CS and do just that.

Extinction and Spontaneous Recovery

After conditioning, what happens if the CS occurs repeatedly without the UCS? Will the CS continue to elicit the CR? Pavlov found that when he sounded the tone again and again without presenting food, the dogs salivated less and less. Their declining salivation illustrates **extinction**, the diminished responding that occurs when the CS (tone) no longer signals the associated UCS (food).

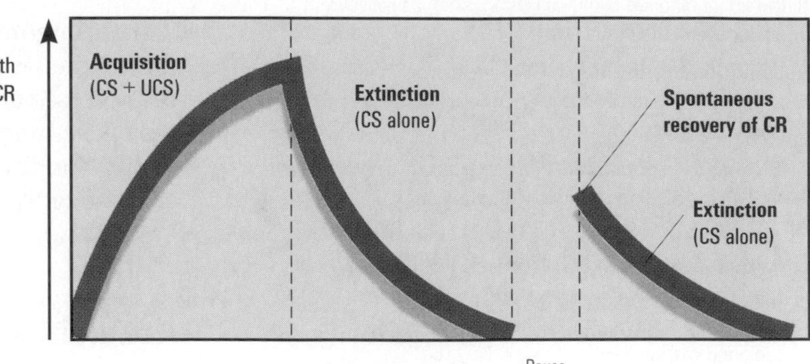

Figure 6.7 Idealized curve of acquisition, extinction, and spontaneous recovery The rising curve shows that the CR rapidly grows stronger as the CS and UCS are repeatedly paired (acquisition), then wanes as the CS is presented alone (extinction). After a rest pause, the CR reappears (spontaneous recovery).

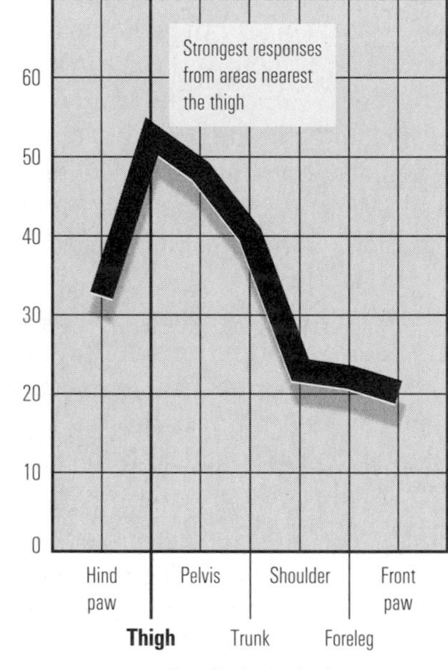

Figure 6.8 Generalization Pavlov demonstrated generalization by attaching miniature vibrators to various parts of a dog's body. After conditioning salivation to stimulation of the thigh, he stimulated other areas. The closer a stimulated spot was to the thigh, the stronger the conditioned response. (From Pavlov, 1927)

Pavlov found, however, that if he allowed several hours to elapse before sounding the tone again, the salivation to the tone would reappear spontaneously (Figure 6.7). This **spontaneous recovery**—the reappearance of a (weakened) CR after a rest pause—suggested to Pavlov that extinction was suppressing the CR rather than eliminating it.

After breaking up with his fire-breathing heartthrob, Tirrell also experienced extinction and spontaneous recovery. He recalls that "the smell of onion breath (CS), no longer paired with the kissing (UCS), lost its ability to shiver my timbers. Occasionally, though, after not sensing the aroma for a long while, smelling onion breath awakens a small version of the emotional response I once felt."

Generalization

Pavlov and his students noticed that a dog conditioned to the sound of one tone also responded somewhat to the sound of a different tone never paired with food. Likewise, a dog conditioned to salivate when rubbed would also salivate some when scratched (Windholz, 1989) or when stimulated on a different body part (Figure 6.8). This tendency to respond to stimuli similar to the CS is called **generalization**.

Generalization can be adaptive, as when toddlers taught to fear moving cars in the street respond similarly to trucks and motorcycles. So automatic is the process that one tortured Argentine writer still recoils with fear when he sees black shoes—his first glimpse of his torturers when they approached his cell. And a year after being shot in the shoulder and ribs during the 1995 massacre of 16 five-year-olds and their teacher in Dunblane, Scotland, Matthew Birnie similarly showed evidence of generalization. Matthew still responded with terror to the sight of toy guns and the sound of balloons popping, festive trappings that were excluded from his sixth birthday party (Craig & Shields, 1996).

Because of generalization, stimuli that are similar to naturally disgusting or appealing objects will, by association, evoke some disgust or liking. Normally desirable foods, such as fudge, are unappealing when presented in a disgusting form, as when shaped to resemble dog feces (Rozin & others, 1986). We perceive adults with childlike facial features (round face, large forehead, small chin, large eyes) as having childlike warmth, submissiveness, and naiveté (Berry & McArthur, 1986). In both cases, people's emotional reactions to one stimulus generalize to similar stimuli.

Discrimination

Pavlov's dogs also learned to respond to the sound of a particular tone and *not* to other tones. **Discrimination** is the learned ability to *distinguish* between a conditioned stimulus (which predicts the UCS) and other irrelevant stimuli.

spontaneous recovery the reappearance, after a rest period, of an extinguished conditioned response.

generalization the tendency, once a response has been conditioned, for stimuli similar to the conditioned stimulus to evoke similar responses.

discrimination in classical conditioning, the ability to distinguish between a conditioned stimulus and other stimuli that do not signal an unconditioned stimulus.

Like generalization, discrimination has survival value. Slightly different stimuli are at times followed by vastly different consequences. Being able to recognize these differences is adaptive. Confronted by a pit bull, your heart may race; confronted by a cocker spaniel, it does not. Facing an approaching group of skinheads, you may cross the street to avoid them; approaching some bald gentlemen, you don't.

Updating Pavlov's Understanding

4. ***Do cognitive processes and biological constraints affect classical conditioning?***

Pavlov's disdain for "mentalistic" concepts such as consciousness has given way to a growing realization that he underestimated the importance of cognitive processes (thoughts, perceptions, expectations) and of biological constraints on an organism's learning capacity.

"All brains are, in essence, anticipation machines."

Daniel C. Dennett
Consciousness Explained
1991

Cognitive Processes

Pavlov and other early researchers believed that the learned behaviors of various organisms could be reduced to mindless mechanisms. The idea that rats and dogs exhibit cognition therefore struck many psychologists as unnecessary. No longer. Robert Rescorla and Allan Wagner (1972) argued that when two significant events occur close together in time, an animal learns the *predictability* of the second event. If a shock always is preceded by a tone, and then sometimes also by a light that accompanies the tone, a rat will react with fear to the tone but not to the light. Although the light always is followed by the shock, the tone better predicts impending shock. The more predictable the association, the stronger the conditioned response. It's as if the animal learns an *expectancy*, an awareness of how likely it is that the UCS will occur.

Answer to questions on page 209: The cake (and its taste) are the UCS. The associated aroma is the CS. Salivation to the aroma is the CR.

This principle helps explain why classical conditioning treatments that ignore cognition often have limited success. For example, therapy for alcoholics sometimes includes giving them alcohol spiked with a nauseating drug. Will they then associate alcohol with sickness? If classical conditioning were merely a matter of "stamping in" stimulus associations, we might hope so, and—to some extent—this does occur (as we will see on page 469). However, alcoholics are aware that they can blame their nausea on the drug, not on the alcohol. This cognition often weakens the association between alcohol and sickness. So, even in classical conditioning, it is not only the simple CS–UCS association but also the thought that counts.

Biological Predispositions

Ever since Darwin, scientists have assumed that animals share both a common evolutionary history and resulting commonalities in their makeup and functioning. Pavlov, for example, believed that the basic laws of learning were essentially similar in all animals, so it should make little difference whether one studied pigeons or people. Moreover, it seemed that any natural response could be conditioned to any neutral stimulus. As learning researcher Gregory Kimble proclaimed in 1956, "Just about any activity of which the organism is capable can be conditioned and . . . these responses can be conditioned to any stimulus that the organism can perceive" (p. 195).

More than the early behaviorists realized, an animal's capacity for conditioning is constrained by its biology.

John Garcia As the laboring son of California farmworkers, Garcia attended school only in the off-season during his early childhood years. After entering junior college in his late twenties, and earning his Ph.D. in his late forties, he received the American Psychological Association's Distinguished Scientific Contribution Award "for his highly original, pioneering research in conditioning and learning" and was elected to the National Academy of Sciences.

Twenty-five years later, Kimble (1981) humbly acknowledged that "half a thousand" scientific reports had proven him wrong. More than the early behaviorists realized, an animal's capacity for conditioning is constrained by its biology. The biological predispositions of each species dispose it to learn the particular associations that enhance its survival. Environments are not the whole story.

The person most responsible for challenging the prevailing behaviorist environmentalism was John Garcia. While researching the effects of radiation on laboratory animals, Garcia and Robert Koelling (1966) noticed that rats began to avoid drinking water from the plastic bottles in the radiation chambers. They wondered whether classical conditioning might be the culprit. Might the rats have linked the plastic-tasting water (a CS) to the radiation (UCS) that induced the sickness (UCR)?

To test their hunch, Garcia and Koelling gave the rats a particular taste, sight, or sound (CS) and later also gave them radiation or drugs (UCS) causing nausea (UCR). Two startling findings emerged: First, even if sickened as late as several hours after tasting a particular flavor, the rats thereafter avoided that flavor. This appeared to violate the notion that for conditioning to occur, the UCS must follow the CS immediately.

Second, the sickened rats developed aversions to the tastes but not to the sights or sounds. This contradicted the idea that any perceivable stimulus could serve as a CS. But it made adaptive sense, because for rats the easiest way to identify tainted food is to taste it. (If sickened after sampling a new food, they thereafter avoid the food—which makes it difficult to eradicate a population of "bait shy" rats by poisoning.) Birds, which hunt by sight, appear biologically primed to develop aversions to the *sight* of tainted food (Nicolaus & others, 1983).

Nature prepares the members of each species to learn those things crucial to their survival.

Humans, too, seem biologically prepared to learn some things rather than others. If you get violently ill 4 hours after eating contaminated mussels, you will likely develop an aversion to the taste of mussels, but not to the sight of the associated restaurant, its plates, the people you were with, or the music you heard there. We also more readily learn to fear snakes and spiders than to fear flowers (Cook & others, 1986). Again, it makes sense: Such animals harm us more frequently than do flowers.

All these cases support Darwin's principle that natural selection favors traits that aid survival. Nature prepares the members of each species to learn those things crucial to their survival. Someone who readily learns a taste aversion is unlikely to eat the same toxic food again and is more likely to survive and leave descendants. Indeed, all sorts of bad feelings, from nausea to anxiety to pain, serve good purposes. Like the low-oil light on a car dashboard, each alerts the body to a threat (Neese, 1991).

Taste aversion If you became violently ill after eating mussels, you likely would have a hard time eating them again. Their smell and taste would have become a CS for nausea. This learning occurs readily because our biology prepares us to learn taste aversions to toxic foods.

Garcia and Koelling's provocative findings stimulated new research, which confirmed their surprising findings and extended them to other species. In one well-known study, coyotes and wolves that were tempted into eating sheep carcasses laced with a sickening poison developed an aversion to sheep meat (Gustavson & others, 1974, 1976). Two wolves that were later penned with a live sheep seemed actually to fear it.

Such research suggests possible humane ways for controlling predators and agricultural pests. This is but one instance in which psychological research that began with the discomfort of some laboratory animals enhanced the welfare of many more animals. In this case, the research saved the sheep from the coyotes. The coyotes in turn were saved from angry ranchers and farmers who, with their livestock no longer endangered, were less adamant about destroying the coyotes. Later experiments revealed that conditioned taste aversion could successfully prevent baboons from raiding African gardens, racoons from attacking chickens, and ravens and crows from feeding on crane eggs—all while preserving predators who occupy an important ecological niche (Garcia & Gustavson, 1997).

"Once bitten, twice shy."

G. F. Northall
Folk-Phrases
1894

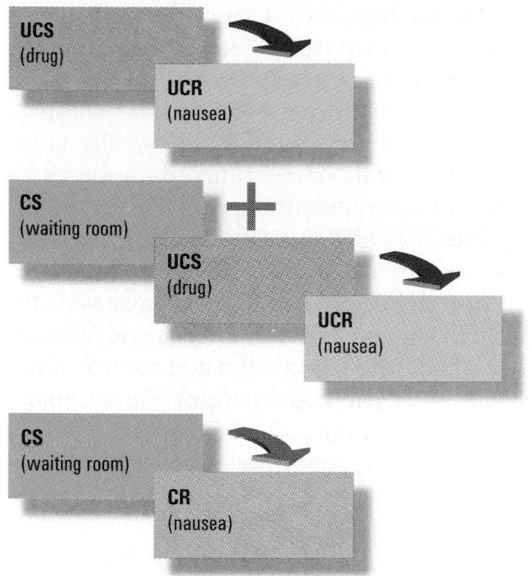

Nausea conditioning among cancer patients

Has research on biological constraints compelled researchers to abandon the search for universal principles of learning that generalize across species? No, biological predispositions affirm a deeper principle: *Learning enables animals to adapt to their environments.* Adaptation shows us why animals would be responsive to stimuli that announce significant events, such as food or pain. Animals are predisposed to associate a CS with a UCS that follows predictably and immediately—for causes often immediately precede effects.

Adaptation also helps explain exceptions such as the taste-aversion finding. In this case, effect need not follow cause immediately—bad food usually causes sickness quite a while after it has been consumed. Similarly, cancer patients who suffer nausea and vomiting beginning more than an hour following chemotherapy often develop classically conditioned nausea to stimuli associated with taking the drug. (Under normal circumstances, such revulsion to sickening stimuli is adaptive.) The conditioned stimuli evoke the associated nausea. Thus, merely returning to the clinic's waiting room or seeing the nurses can provoke sick feelings (Burish & Carey, 1986; Davey, 1992).

Pavlov's Legacy

5. ***Why is Pavlov's work important?***

What, then, remains of Pavlov's ideas about conditioning? A great deal. All the researchers we have met so far in this chapter agree that classical conditioning is a basic form of learning. Judged by today's knowledge of cognitive processes and biological predispositions, Pavlov's ideas were incomplete. But if we see further than Pavlov did, it is because we stand on his shoulders.

Why is Pavlov's work so important? If he had taught us only that old dogs can learn new tricks, his experiments would long ago have been forgotten. Why should anyone care that a dog can be conditioned to drool at the sound of a tone? The importance lies first in this fact: Many other responses to many other stimuli can be classically conditioned in many other organisms—in fact, in every species tested, from earthworms to fish to dogs to monkeys to people (Schwartz, 1984). Thus, classical conditioning is one way that virtually all organisms learn to adapt to their environment.

Second, Pavlov showed us how an internal process such as learning can be studied objectively. Pavlov was proud that his methods involved virtually no subjective judgments or guesses about what went on in the dogs' minds. The salivary response is an overt behavior measurable as so many drops or cubic centimeters of saliva. Pavlov's success therefore suggested a scientific model for how the young discipline of psychology might proceed—by isolating the elementary building blocks of complex behaviors and studying them with objective laboratory procedures.

Applications of Classical Conditioning

In later chapters on motivation, emotion, psychological disorders, therapy, and health, you will see how Pavlov's principles of classical conditioning apply to human health and well-being. For example, former crack cocaine users often feel a craving when they again encounter cues (people, places) associated with previous highs. Thus, drug counselors advise addicts to steer clear of settings associated with the euphoria of previous drug use. And, as you will see, counselors also attempt to give alcoholics experiences that reverse their positive associations with alcohol (page 469). Classical conditioning even works on the body's disease-fighting immune system. When, say, a

PSYCHOLOGY APPLIED

Rape as Classical Conditioning

"A burnt child dreads the fire," says a medieval proverb. Experiments with dogs reveal that, indeed, if a painful stimulus is sufficiently powerful, a single event is sometimes enough to traumatize the animal when it again faces the situation. The human counterparts to these experiments can be tragic, as illustrated by one woman's experience of being attacked and raped, and thereby conditioned to a life of fear. Her fear (CR) is most powerfully associated with particular locations and people (CS), but it generalizes to other places and people. Note, too, how her traumatic experience has robbed her of the normally relaxing associations with such stimuli as home and bed.

> Four months ago I was raped. In the middle of the night I awoke to the sound of someone outside my bedroom. Thinking my housemate was coming home, I called out her name. Someone began walking slowly toward me, and then I realized. I screamed and fought, but there were two of them. One held my legs, while the other put a hand over my mouth and a knife to my throat and said, "Shut up, bitch, or we'll kill you." Never have I been so terrified and helpless. They both raped me, one brutally. As they then searched my room for money and valuables, my housemate came home. They brought her into my room, raped her, and left us both tied up on my bed.
>
> We never slept another night in that apartment. We were too terrified. Still, when I go to bed at night—always with the bedroom light left on—the memory of them entering my room repeats itself endlessly. I was an independent person who had lived alone or with other women for four years; now I can't even think about spending a night alone. When I drive by our old apartment, or when I have to go into an empty house, my heart pounds and I sweat. I am afraid of strangers, especially men, and the more they resemble my attackers the more I fear them. My housemate shares many of my fears, and is frightened when entering our new apartment. I'm afraid to stay in the same town, I'm afraid it will happen again, I'm afraid to go to bed. I dread falling asleep.

Eleven years later this woman could report that her conditioned fears are gradually extinguishing:

> The frequency and intensity of my fears have subsided. Still, I remain cautious about personal safety and occasionally have nightmares about my experience. But more important is my renewed ability to laugh, love, and trust—both old friends and new. Life is once again joyful. I have survived.

Source: From personal correspondence, with permission.

particular taste accompanies a drug that influences immune responses, the taste by itself may come to produce an immune response (page 376).

Pavlov's work provided a basis for John Watson's idea that human behavior, though biologically influenced, is mainly a bundle of conditioned responses.

In searching for laws underlying learning, psychologist John B. Watson (1913) urged his colleagues to discard reference to inner thoughts, feelings, and motives. Psychology should therefore study how organisms respond to stimuli in their environments, said Watson. "Its theoretical goal is the prediction and control of behavior." Simply said, psychology should be an objective science based on *observable behavior*. This view, which influenced North American psychology during the first half of this century, Watson called **behaviorism**.

In one famous study, Watson and Rosalie Rayner (1920; Harris, 1979) showed how specific fears might be conditioned. Their subject was an 11-month-old infant named Albert. Like most infants, "Little Albert" feared loud noises but not white rats. Watson and Rayner presented him with a white rat and, as he reached to touch it, struck a hammer against a steel bar just behind his head. After seven repetitions of seeing the rat and then hearing the frightening noise, Albert burst into tears at the mere sight of the rat (making this an ethically troublesome study by today's standards). What is more, five days later Albert showed generalization of his conditioned response by reacting with fear to a rabbit, a dog, and a sealskin coat, but not to dissimilar objects such as toys.

Although Little Albert's fate is unknown, Watson's is not. After losing his professorship at Johns Hopkins University over an affair with Rayner (whom he later married), he became the J. Walter Thompson advertising agency's resident psychologist. There he used his knowledge of associative learning to conceive many successful campaigns, including one for Maxwell House that helped make the "coffee break" an American custom (Hunt, 1993).

Although some psychologists had difficulty repeating Watson and Rayner's findings with other children, the work with Little Albert has had legendary significance for many psychologists. Some have wondered if

behaviorism the view that psychology (1) should be an objective science that (2) studies behavior without reference to mental processes. Most research psychologists today agree with (1) but not with (2).

John B. Watson Watson (1924) admitted to "going beyond my facts" when offering his famous boast: "Give me a dozen healthy infants, well-formed, and my own specified world to bring them up in and I'll guarantee to take any one at random and train him to become any type of specialist I might select—doctor, lawyer, artist, merchant-chief, and, yes, even beggar-man and thief, regardless of his talents, penchants, tendencies, abilities, vocations, and race of his ancestors."

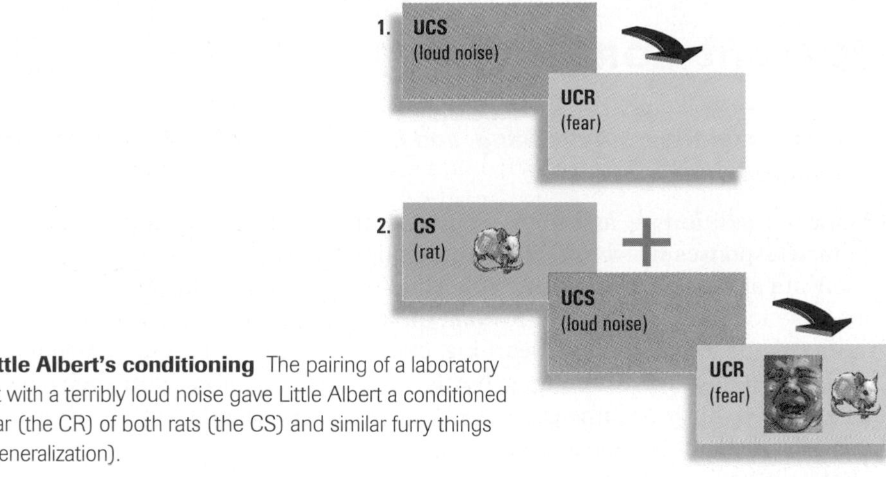

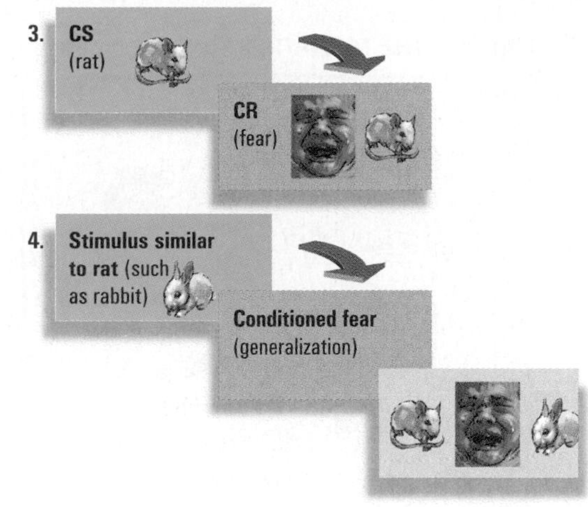

Little Albert's conditioning The pairing of a laboratory rat with a terribly loud noise gave Little Albert a conditioned fear (the CR) of both rats (the CS) and similar furry things (generalization).

each of us might not be a walking repository of conditioned emotions. Might our less adaptive emotions be controlled by the application of extinction procedures or by conditioning new responses to emotion-arousing stimuli? One therapist told a patient, who for 30 years had feared going into an elevator alone, to force himself to enter 20 elevators a day. Within 10 days, his fear nearly vanished (Ellis & Becker, 1982). In Chapter 13 we will see more examples of how psychologists use behavioral techniques to treat emotional disorders.

REHEARSE IT!

1. Learning is defined as "a relatively permanent change in behavior due to

a. instinct."
b. mental processes."
c. experience with the environment."
d. education or schooling."

2. Associative learning involves learning that certain events occur together. Two forms of associative learning are classical conditioning, in which the organism associates ____________, and operant conditioning, in which the organism associates ____________.

a. two responses; a response and a consequence
b. two stimuli; two responses
c. two stimuli; a response and a consequence
d. two responses; two stimuli

3. Working with dogs, Pavlov paired a tone or other neutral stimulus with food in the mouth. The dogs then came to salivate when presented with the neutral stimulus alone. Salivation in response to food in the mouth occurs naturally in dogs, without conditioning; food is therefore the unconditioned stimulus (UCS). Salivation in response to a tone must be learned; the tone is therefore a

a. conditioned stimulus.
b. unconditioned stimulus.
c. conditioned response.
d. unconditioned response.

4. Dogs can learn to respond to one kind of stimulus and not to another—for example, to salivate at the sight of a circle (the CS) but not a square. Distinguishing between a CS and an irrelevant stimulus is

a. generalization.
b. discrimination.
c. acquisition.
d. spontaneous recovery.

5. Early behaviorists believed that for conditioning to occur the unconditioned stimulus (UCS) must immediately follow the conditioned stimulus (CS). ____________ demonstrated this was not always so.

a. The Little Albert experiment
b. Pavlov's experiments with dogs
c. Watson's behaviorism theory
d. Garcia and Koelling's taste-aversion studies

6. Research by Garcia and Koelling showed that rats developed aversions to certain tastes but not to sights or sounds, thus supporting

a. Pavlov's demonstration of generalization.
b. Darwin's principle that natural selection favors traits that aid survival.
c. Watson's view that study should be limited to observable behavior.
d. Kimble's original view that organisms can be conditioned to any stimulus.

7. Watson and Rayner classically conditioned a small child named Albert to fear a white rat. After Watson paired the rat with a frightening noise, Little Albert cried when the rat was presented (even without the noise). The child later showed fear in response to a rabbit, a dog, and a sealskin coat. Little Albert's fear of objects resembling the rat illustrates

a. extinction.
b. generalization of the conditioned response.
c. spontaneous recovery.
d. discrimination between two stimuli.

DENNIS THE MENACE

"I think Mom's using the can opener."

Operant Conditioning

6. *What is operant conditioning, and how does it differ from classical conditioning?*

Classical conditioning associates neutral stimuli with important stimuli that produce responses which often are automatic. It's one thing to teach an animal to salivate at the sound of a tone or a child to fear cars in the street; it's something else to teach an elephant to walk on its hind legs or a child to say *please*. Another type of associative learning explains—and trains—such behaviors. Through **operant conditioning**, subjects associate behaviors with their consequences. Thus, they become more likely to repeat rewarded (reinforced) behaviors and less likely to repeat punished behaviors.

Both classical and operant conditioning involve acquisition, extinction, spontaneous recovery, generalization, and discrimination. Yet their difference is straightforward: Classical conditioning forms associations between stimuli (a CS and the UCS it signals). It also involves **respondent behavior**—behavior that occurs as an *automatic* response to some stimulus (such as salivating in response to meat powder and later in response to a tone). Operant conditioning involves **operant behavior**, so called because the act *operates* on the environment to produce rewarding or punishing stimuli. We can therefore distinguish classical from operant conditioning by asking: *Is the organism learning associations between events that it doesn't control (classical conditioning)? Or is it learning associations between its behavior and resulting events (operant conditioning)?*

In operant conditioning, acquisition is the strengthening of a reinforced response. Extinction occurs when a response is no longer reinforced. Generalization and discrimination occur as organisms response to various stimuli that do or do not signal that a behavior will be reinforced.

Skinner's Experiments

B. F. Skinner (1904–1990) was a college English major and an aspiring writer who, seeking a new direction, entered graduate school in psychology. He went on to become modern behaviorism's most influential and controversial figure. Skinner's work elaborated a simple fact of life that turn-of-the-century psychologist Edward L. Thorndike called the **law of effect**: Rewarded behavior is likely to recur. Using Thorndike's law of effect as a starting point, Skinner developed a "behavioral technology" that enabled him to teach pigeons such unpigeonlike behaviors as walking in a Figure 8, playing Ping-Pong, and keeping a missile on course by pecking at a target on a screen.

For his pioneering studies with rats (and later with pigeons), Skinner designed the now famous **Skinner box** (Figure 6.9). The box is typically a soundproof chamber with a bar or a key that an animal presses or pecks to release a food or water reward, and with a device that records these responses.

Experiments by Skinner and other operant researchers did far more than teach us how to pull habits out of a rat. They explored the precise conditions that foster efficient and enduring learning.

Figure 6.9 **A Skinner box** Inside the box, the rat presses a bar for a food reward. Outside, a measuring device records the animal's accumulated responses.

Shaping

In his experiments, Skinner used **shaping**, a procedure in which rewards such as food gradually guide an animal's behavior toward a desired behavior. Imagine that you wanted to condition a rat to press a bar. After observing how the animal naturally behaves before training, you would build on its existing behaviors. You might give the rat a food reward each time it approaches the bar. Once the rat is approaching regularly, you would require it to move closer before rewarding it, then closer still; finally, you would require it to touch the bar before you gave it the food. With this method of *successive approximations*, you reward responses

A discriminating creature University of Windsor psychologist Dale Woodyard uses a food reward to train this manatee to discriminate among objects of different shapes, colors, and sizes. A manatee can remember such responses for as long as a year.

that are ever-closer to the final desired behavior, and you ignore all other responses. In just this way, researchers and animal trainers gradually *shape* complex behaviors.

By shaping nonverbal organisms to discriminate between stimuli, a psychologist can also determine what they perceive. Can a dog distinguish colors? Can a baby discriminate sounds? If we can shape them to respond to one stimulus and not to another, then obviously they can perceive the difference. Experiments show that some animals are remarkably capable of forming concepts; they demonstrate this by discriminating between classes of events or objects. If an experimenter reinforces a pigeon for pecking after seeing a human face, but not after seeing other images, the pigeon will learn to recognize a face (Herrnstein & Loveland, 1964). After being trained to discriminate among flowers, people, cars, and chairs, pigeons can usually identify in which of these categories a new pictured object belongs (Bhatt & others, 1988; Wasserman, 1993). With training, pigeons have even been taught to discriminate between Bach's music and Stravinsky's (Porter & Neuringer, 1984).

In the shaping procedure, the trainer builds on the organism's existing behaviors by expecting and immediately rewarding successively closer approximations of a desired behavior. In everyday life, too, we continually reward and shape the behavior of others, said Skinner, but we often do so unintentionally. Sometimes we unthinkingly reward behaviors we find annoying. Billy's whining, for example, annoys his mystified parents, but look how they typically deal with Billy.

Billy: *Could you tie my shoes?*

Father: *(Continues reading paper.)*

Billy: *Dad, I need my shoes tied.*

Father: *Uh, yeah, just a minute.*

Billy: *DAAAAD! TIE MY SHOES!*

Father: *How many times have I told you not to whine? Now, which shoe do we do first?*

In everyday life, we continually reward and shape the behavior of others. . . . Sometimes we unthinkingly reward behaviors we find annoying.

Or consider the way some teachers use rewards. On a wall chart, the teacher pastes gold stars after the names of children scoring 100 percent on spelling tests. All children take the same tests. As everyone can then see, some children, the academic all-stars, easily get 100 percent. The others, no matter how hard they try or how much they improve, get no reward. The teacher would be better advised to apply the principles of operant conditioning—to reward all spellers for gradual improvements (successive approximations toward fulfilling their own potential).

Principles of Reinforcement

7. What are the basic types of reinforcers?

So far, we have referred rather loosely to the power of "rewards." This idea gains a more precise meaning in Skinner's concept of the **reinforcer**, any event that increases the frequency of a preceding response. A reinforcer may be a tangible reward. It may be praise or attention. Or it may be an activity—being able to use the car when the dishes are done or to have a break after an hour of study.

Most people think of reinforcers as rewards. Actually, there are two basic kinds of reinforcers. One type (positive reinforcer) strengthens a response by *presenting* a stimulus after a response. Food is a positive reinforcer for animals; attention, approval, and money are positive reinforcers for most people. The other type (negative reinforcer) strengthens a response by reducing or *removing*

operant conditioning a type of learning in which behavior is strengthened if followed by reinforcement or diminished if followed by punishment.

respondent behavior behavior that occurs as an automatic response to some stimulus.

operant behavior behavior that operates on the environment, producing consequences.

law of effect Thorndike's principle that behaviors followed by favorable consequences become more likely.

Skinner box a chamber containing a bar or a key that an animal can manipulate to obtain a food or water reinforcer, with attached devices to record the animal's rate of bar pressing or key pecking. Used in operant conditioning research.

shaping an operant conditioning procedure in which reinforcers guide behavior toward closer and closer approximations of a desired goal.

reinforcer in operant conditioning, any event that *strengthens* the behavior it follows.

primary reinforcer an innate reinforcer, such as one that satisfies a biological need.

secondary reinforcer a conditioned reinforcer; an event that gains its reinforcing power through its association with a primary reinforcer.

continuous reinforcement reinforcing the desired response every time it occurs.

partial reinforcement reinforcing a response only part of the time; results in slower acquisition of a response but much greater resistance to extinction than does continuous reinforcement.

fixed-ratio schedule in operant conditioning, a schedule of reinforcement that reinforces a response only after a specified number of responses.

HI AND LOIS

an aversive stimulus. (Negative reinforcers, like negative numbers, subtract something.) Imagine that alien invaders put you in an electrified cage, but that you could reduce or remove the electric shock by pressing a bar. You would surely press the bar and be (negatively) reinforced for doing so. When a barely awake person pushes the snooze button, the silencing of the annoying alarm is similarly a reinforcer. When someone stops nagging or whining, that, too, is a reinforcer. (Note that contrary to popular usage, a negative reinforcer is not a punishing event; it is the *removal* of a punishing event.)

So imagine that whenever Billy throws a tantrum, his parents give in for the sake of peace and quiet. The child's tantrums will be reinforced when the parents give in. And the parents' behavior will be reinforced when Billy stops screaming. Or imagine a worried student who, after goofing off and getting a bad exam grade, studies harder for the next exam. The student's studying may be reinforced by reduced anxiety and by a better grade. Whether it works by giving something positive or by reducing something negative, *a reinforcer is any consequence that strengthens behavior.*

Primary and Secondary Reinforcers

Primary reinforcers—getting food or being relieved of electric shock—are innately satisfying. **Secondary reinforcers** are learned. They get their power through association with primary reinforcers. If a rat in a Skinner box learns that a light reliably signals that food is coming, the rat will work to turn on the light. The light has become a secondary reinforcer associated with food. Our lives are filled with secondary reinforcers—money, good grades, a pleasant tone of voice, a word of praise—each of which has been linked with more basic rewards. Secondary reinforcers greatly enhance our ability to influence one another.

Positive reinforcement An A grade positively reinforces this boy's effort, as do his classmates' smiles and his teacher's praise.

Immediate and Delayed Reinforcers

Let's return to the imaginary shaping experiment in which you were conditioning a rat to press a bar. Before performing this "wanted" behavior, the hungry rat will engage in a sequence of "unwanted" behaviors—scratching, sniffing, and moving around. Whichever of these behaviors immediately precedes the food reinforcer becomes more likely to recur. If you delay the reinforcement of bar pressing for longer than 30 seconds, allowing other behaviors to intervene and be reinforced, virtually no learning of the bar pressing will occur.

Unlike rats, humans do respond to reinforcers that are greatly delayed: the paycheck at the end of the week, the grade at the end of the semester, the trophy at the end of the season. Indeed, to function effectively we must learn to postpone immediate rewards for greater long-term rewards. Four-year-old children who in laboratory testing show an ability to delay gratification—who'd sooner have a big reward tomorrow than a small one right now—become more socially competent and more likely to be high achievers as adolescents (Mischel & others, 1989). A big part of maturity—and of gaining the most rewarding life—is learning to delay gratification.

To function effectively we must learn to postpone immediate rewards for greater long-term rewards.

"Oh, not bad. The light comes on, I press the bar, they write me a check. How about you?"

But to our detriment, small but immediate reinforcements are sometimes more alluring than big but delayed reinforcements. Smokers, alcoholics, and other drug users may know that their immediate pleasure—the kick that often comes within seconds—is more than offset by future ill effects. Still, immediate reinforcement prevails. Thus, hangovers do not prevent further drinking, and drugs such as nicotine and cocaine that provide the most immediate reinforcement are the most strongly addictive (Marlatt, 1991). Likewise, for many teens the immediate gratification of risky, unprotected sex in passionate moments prevails over the delayed gratifications of safe sex or saved sex (Loewenstein & Furstenberg, 1991). And the hour-long enjoyment of staying up to watch another TV show may seem to outweigh the prospect of tomorrow's day-long sluggishness.

Reinforcement Schedules

8. *How do different reinforcement schedules affect behavior?*

So far, most of our examples assume **continuous reinforcement**: The desired response is reinforced every time it occurs. Under such conditions, learning occurs rapidly. But when the reinforcement stops—when we disconnect the food delivery chute—extinction also occurs rapidly. The rat soon stops pressing the bar. If a normally dependable candy machine fails to deliver a chocolate bar twice in a row, we stop putting money into it (although a week later we may exhibit spontaneous recovery by trying again).

In real life, continuous reinforcement is rare. A salesperson does not make a sale with every pitch, nor does an angler get a bite with every cast. But they persist because their efforts have occasionally been rewarded. Researchers have explored several **partial reinforcement** schedules in which responses are sometimes reinforced, sometimes not (Nevin, 1988). Initial learning is typically slower with partial reinforcement, which makes continuous reinforcement preferable until a behavior is mastered. But partial reinforcement produces greater persistence—greater *resistance to extinction*—than is found with continuous reinforcement. Imagine a pigeon that has learned to peck a key to obtain food. When the experimenter gradually fades out the delivery of food until it occurs only rarely and unpredictably, pigeons may peck 150,000 times without a reward (Skinner, 1953). With partial reinforcement, hope springs eternal.

Figure 6.10 Partial reinforcement schedules Skinner's laboratory pigeons produced these response patterns to each of four reinforcement schedules. (Reinforcers are indicated by diagonal marks.) For people, as for pigeons, reinforcement linked to number of responses (a ratio schedule) produces a higher response rate than reinforcement linked to amount of time elapsed (interval schedule). But the predictability of the reward also matters. A predictable (fixed) schedule produces a higher response rate than an unpredictable (variable) schedule. (Adapted from "Teaching Machines" by B. F. Skinner. Copyright © 1961, Scientific American, Inc. All rights reserved.)

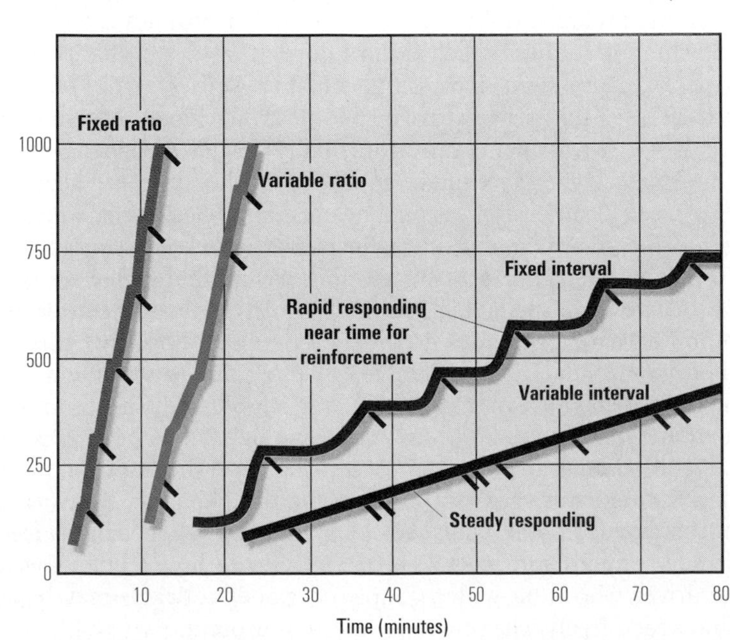

Corresponding human examples come readily to mind. Slot machines reward gamblers occasionally and unpredictably. This partial reinforcement affects them much as it affects pigeons: They keep trying, sometimes interminably. There is also a valuable lesson here for parents. *Occasionally* giving in to children's tantrums for the sake of peace and quiet puts the child on a partial reinforcement schedule. That's the very best procedure for making a behavior persist.

Skinner (1961) and his collaborators compared four schedules of partial reinforcement. Some are rigidly fixed, some unpredictably variable.

Fixed-ratio schedules reinforce behavior after a set number of responses. Like people paid on a piecework basis—say, for every 30 pieces—laboratory animals may be reinforced on a fixed ratio of, say, one reinforcer for every 30 responses. Once conditioned, the animal will pause only briefly after a reinforcer and will then return to a high rate of responding (Figure 6.10). Because resting while on a fixed-ratio schedule reduces rewards, employees often find such arrangements tiring. Unions have therefore pressured employers to replace piecework pay with hourly wage schedules.

"The charm of fishing is that it is the pursuit of what is elusive but attainable, a perpetual series of occasions for hope."

Scottish Author John Buchan
1875–1940

Variable-ratio schedules provide reinforcers after an unpredictable number of responses. This is what gamblers and fly casters experience—unpredictable reinforcement—and what makes gambling and fishing behavior so hard to extinguish. Like the fixed-ratio schedule, it produces high rates of responding, because reinforcers increase as the responding increases.

Fixed-interval schedules reinforce the first response after a fixed time period. Like people checking more frequently for the mail as the delivery time approaches, pigeons on a fixed-interval schedule peck a key more frequently as the anticipated time for reward draws near, producing a choppy stop-start pattern (see Figure 6.10).

Variable-interval schedules reinforce the first response after *varying* time intervals. Like the unpredictable pop quiz that reinforces studying or the "Hello" that finally rewards persistence in redialing a busy phone number, variable-interval schedules tend to produce slow, steady responding. This makes sense, because there is no knowing when the waiting will be over. Should the pop quiz become predictable, students will begin the stop-start work pattern that characterizes fixed-interval schedules.

Question: Airline frequent-flyer programs that offer a free flight after every 25,000 miles of travel use which reinforcement schedule? Door-to-door salespeople are reinforced by which schedule? (See page 223.)

Animal behaviors differ, yet Skinner (1956) contended that these reinforcement principles of operant conditioning are universal. It matters little, he said, what response, what reinforcer, or what species you use. The effect of a given reinforcement schedule is pretty much the same: "Pigeon, rat, monkey, which is which? It doesn't matter. . . . Behavior shows astonishingly similar properties."

Punishment

9. *How does punishment affect behavior?*

The effect of **punishment** is opposite that of reinforcement. Reinforcement increases a behavior; punishment decreases it. Thus, a punisher is an aversive consequence that *decreases* the frequency of a preceding behavior. Swift and sure punishers can powerfully restrain unwanted behavior. The dog that learns to come running at the sound of the electric can opener will learn to hide if its master starts running the can opener to attract and catch it for banishment to the basement. The rat that is shocked after touching the forbidden object and the child who loses a treat after running into the street will learn not to repeat the behavior.

Boys Town psychologist Robert Larzelere (1994, 1996) notes a problem with human punishment studies, which often find that spanked children are at increased risk for aggression, depression, and low self-esteem. Well, yes, says Larzelere, just as people who have received radiation treatments are more likely to die of cancer, and people who have undergone psychotherapy are more likely to suffer depression—because they had preexisting problems that triggered the treatments. If one adjusts for preexisting cancer or depression—or antisocial behavior—then radiation, psychotherapy, or an occasional single swat or two of misbehaving 2- to 6-year-olds looks more effective, if the swat is combined with a generous dose of reasoning and positive parenting.

Punishment tells you what not to do; reinforcement tells you what to do.

Nevertheless, say advocates of nonviolent parenting, punishment has drawbacks. Punished behavior is not forgotten; it is suppressed. This temporary suppression may (negatively) reinforce the punishing behavior. The child swears, the parent swats, the parent hears no more swearing from the child, and the parent feels the punishment was successful in stopping the behavior. But was it? If the punishment is avoidable, the punished behavior may reappear in safe settings. The child may simply learn not to swear around the house but to swear elsewhere. The driver who is hit with a couple of speeding tickets may buy a radar detector and speed freely when no radar patrol is around.

variable-ratio schedule in operant conditioning, a schedule of reinforcement that reinforces a response after an unpredictable number of responses.

fixed-interval schedule in operant conditioning, a schedule of reinforcement that reinforces a response only after a specified time has elapsed.

variable-interval schedule in operant conditioning, a schedule of reinforcement that reinforces a response at unpredictable time intervals.

punishment an aversive event that *decreases* the behavior that it follows.

The problem with punishment Swift and sure punishment can decrease unwanted behavior, but it can also evoke undesired responses, such as anger, fear, or resistance.

Punishment may also increase aggressiveness by demonstrating that aggression is a way to cope with problems. This helps explain why so many aggressive delinquents and abusive parents come from abusive families (Straus & Gelles, 1980). Moreover, punishment can create fear; the person receiving the punishment may associate the fear not only with the undesirable behavior but also with the person who administers it or with the situation in which it occurs. Thus, a child may come to fear the punitive teacher and want to avoid school. For such reasons, most European countries have banned hitting children in schools and childcare institutions (Leach, 1993, 1994). The Scandinavian countries and Austria have further outlawed physical punishment by parents, thereby extending to children the same legal protection given to spouses.

Even when punishment suppresses unwanted behavior, it often does not guide one toward more desirable behavior. Punishment tells you what *not* to do; reinforcement tells you what *to* do. Thus, punishment combined with reinforcement is usually more effective than punishment alone. This approach has been used with children who bite themselves or bang their heads. They may be mildly punished (say, with a squirt of water in the face) whenever they bite themselves but also be rewarded with positive attention and food when they behave well. The approach also works in the classroom. The teacher whose feedback on a paper says, "No, but try this . . . " and "Yes, that's it!" reduces unwanted behavior by reinforcing alternative behaviors.

Parents of delinquent youth often lack this awareness of how to reinforce desirable behavior without screaming or hitting (Patterson & others, 1982). Training programs for such parents help them reframe contingencies from dire threats to positive incentives—from "You clean up your room this minute or no dinner!" to "You're welcome at the dinner table after you get your room cleaned up." When you stop to think about it, many threats of punishment are just as forceful, and perhaps more effective, if rephrased positively. Thus, "If you don't get your homework done, there'll be no TV" would better be phrased as, "After you have finished your homework, you can watch TV." Most psychologists therefore favor an emphasis on reinforcement rather than on punishment. Catch people doing something right and affirm them for it.

REHEARSE IT!

8. Salivating in response to a tone paired with food is a (an) __________; pressing a bar to obtain food is a(an) __________.

a. primary reinforcer; secondary reinforcer
b. secondary reinforcer; primary reinforcer
c. operant behavior; respondent behavior
d. respondent behavior; operant behavior

9. Thorndike's law of effect states that "rewarded behavior is likely to recur." This law became the basis for operant conditioning and the "behavioral technology" developed by

a. Ivan Pavlov. **c.** B. F. Skinner.
b. John Garcia. **d.** John B. Watson.

10. B. F. Skinner taught rats to press a bar to obtain a food pellet. To guide the rat's natural behavior toward the desired behavior, he used

a. shaping. **c.** taste aversion.
b. punishment. **d.** discrimination.

11. A reinforcer is any stimulus presented after a response that increases the frequency of that response. Imagine that your dog barks at every noise it hears. The barking disturbs you, so you put the dog outside when it starts to bark. The stopping of the barking is for you the termination of an aversive stimulus, or a

a. positive reinforcer. **c.** punishment.
b. negative reinforcer. **d.** primary reinforcer.

12. Continuous reinforcement—reinforcement of the desired response every time it occurs—makes for rapid learning and for rapid extinction when reinforcement stops. A partial reinforcement schedule that reinforces a response at unpredictable times—perhaps after 1 day or 2 days or even 15 days—is a

a. fixed-interval schedule. **c.** fixed-ratio schedule.
b. variable-interval schedule. **d.** variable-ratio schedule.

13. A medieval proverb notes that "a burnt child dreads the fire." In behavioral terms, the burning is an example of a

a. primary reinforcer. **c.** punisher.
b. negative reinforcer. **d.** positive reinforcer.

cognitive map a mental representation of the layout of one's environment. For example, after exploring a maze, rats act as if they have learned a cognitive map of it.

latent learning learning that occurs but is not apparent until there is an incentive to demonstrate it.

Updating Skinner's Understanding

Skinner granted the existence of private processes and the biological underpinnings of behavior. Nevertheless, many psychologists criticized him for discounting the importance of cognition and of biology.

Cognition and Operant Conditioning

10. ***Do cognitive processes and biological constraints affect operant conditioning?***

A mere 8 days before dying of leukemia, Skinner (1990) stood before the American Psychological Association convention for one final critique of "cognitive science," which he viewed as a throwback to turn-of-the-century introspectionism. Skinner died resisting the growing belief that cognitive processes—thoughts, perceptions, expectations—have a necessary place in the science of psychology and even in our understanding of conditioning. Yet we have seen several hints that cognitive processes might be at work in operant learning. For example, animals on a fixed-interval reinforcement schedule respond more and more frequently as the time approaches when a response will produce a reinforcer. The animals behave as if they expect that repeating the response will soon produce the reward. To a behaviorist, however, talk of "expectations" is unnecessary; it is enough to say that responses that are reinforced under certain conditions recur when those conditions recur.

For more information on animal behavior, see books by (I am not making this up) Robin Fox and Lionel Tiger.

Other evidence of cognitive processes comes from studies of rats in mazes. Rats exploring a maze, with no obvious reward, are like people driving around a new town. The rats seem to develop a **cognitive map**, a mental representation of the maze. This occurs even if the rats are carried passively through the maze in a wire basket. When an experimenter then places a reward in the maze's goal box, the rats immediately perform as well as rats that have been reinforced with food for running the maze.

During their explorations, the rats seemingly experience **latent learning**—learning that becomes apparent only when there is some incentive to demonstrate it. The unavoidable conclusion: Learning can occur without reinforcement. As the cognitive mapping experiments suggest, there is more to learning than associating a response with a consequence. There is also cognition. In Chapter 8 we will encounter striking evidence of animals' cognitive abilities in solving problems and using aspects of language.

Biological Predispositions

As with classical conditioning, operant conditioning is constrained by an animal's natural predispositions. When you reinforce a hamster's behavior with food, you can easily condition it to dig or to rear up, because these are among the animal's natural behaviors when searching for food. But it is harder to use food reinforcers to shape hamster behaviors, such as face washing, that aren't normally associated with food or hunger (Shettleworth, 1973). Similarly, pigeons easily learn to flap their wings to avoid shock and to peck to obtain food, because they naturally flee with their wings and eat with their beaks. But they have a hard time learning to peck to avoid shock or to flap to obtain food (Foree & LoLordo, 1973). Biological constraints predispose organisms to learn associations that are naturally adaptive.

"Never try to teach a pig to sing. It wastes your time and annoys the pig."

Mark Twain

Natural athletes Animals can most easily learn and retain behaviors that draw on their biological predispositions, such as cats' inborn tendency to leap high and land on their feet.

Skinner's former associates, Keller Breland and Marian Breland (1961), came to appreciate biological predispositions while using operant procedures to train animals for circuses, TV shows, and movies. The Brelands had originally assumed that operant principles would work on almost any response that any animal could make. But after training 6000 animals of 38 different species, from chickens to whales, they concluded that biological predispositions were more important than they had supposed. In one act, they trained pigs to pick up large wooden "dollars" and deposit them in a piggy bank. After learning this behavior, however, the animals began to drift back to their natural ways. They would drop the coin, push it with their snouts as pigs are prone to do, pick it up again, and then repeat the sequence—delaying their food reinforcer. As this "instinctive drift" illustrates, "misbehaviors" occurred when the animals reverted to their biologically predisposed patterns.

Skinner's Legacy

B. F. Skinner was one of the late twentieth century's most controversial intellectual figures. He stirred a hornet's nest by repeatedly insisting that external influences, not internal thoughts and feelings, shape behavior and by urging the use of operant principles to influence people's behavior at school, work, and home. Recognizing that behavior is shaped by its consequences, he believed we should administer rewards in ways that promote more desirable behavior.

Answer to question on page 220: Frequent-flyer programs use a fixed-ratio schedule. Door-to-door salespeople are reinforced on a variable-ratio schedule (after varying numbers of rings).

Skinner's critics objected, saying that he dehumanized people by neglecting their personal freedom and by seeking to control their actions. Skinner's reply: People's behavior is already haphazardly controlled by external consequences, so why not administer those consequences for human betterment? In place of the punishments used in homes, schools, and prisons, would not reinforcers be more humanitarian? And if it is humbling to think that we are shaped by our histories, this very idea also gives us hope that we can shape our future.

Applications of Operant Conditioning

11. ***How might educators, business managers, and other individuals apply operant conditioning?***

We have seen applications of operant conditioning principles, and in later chapters we will see how psychologists apply these principles to problems ranging from high blood pressure to social withdrawal. Reinforcement technologies are also at work in schools, businesses, and homes.

B. F. Skinner "I am sometimes asked, 'Do you think of yourself as you think of the organisms you study?' The answer is yes. So far as I know, my behavior at any given moment has been nothing more than the product of my genetic endowment, my personal history, and the current setting" (1983).

At School

A generation ago, Skinner and others advocated teaching machines and textbooks that would shape learning in small steps and provide immediate reinforcement for correct responses. These machines and texts, they said, would revolutionize education and free teachers to concentrate on their students' special needs.

To envision Skinner's dream, imagine two math teachers. Faced with a class of academically diverse students, Teacher A gives the whole class the same math lesson. The teacher knows that some students already understand the concepts and that others will be frustrated by their inability to comprehend. But with so many different children, how can one teacher guide them individually? When test time comes, the whiz kids breeze through unchallenged, and the slower learners again experience failure. Faced with a similar class, Teacher B paces the material according to each

Computer-assisted learning Computers have helped realize Skinner's goal of individually paced instruction with immediate feedback.

student's rate of learning and provides prompt feedback with positive reinforcement to slow and fast learners. Does the individualized instruction of Teacher B sound like an impossible ideal?

Although the predicted revolution has not occurred, to the end of his life Skinner (1986, 1988, 1989) believed the ideal was achievable. "Good instruction demands two things," he said. "Students must be told immediately whether what they do is right or wrong and, when right, they must be directed to the step to be taken next." To do this, and to free teachers for uniquely human tasks, computers were his final hope. For reading and math drills, the computer could be Teacher B—engaging the student actively, pacing material according to the student's rate of learning, quizzing the student to find gaps in understanding, providing immediate feedback, and keeping flawless records for the supervising teacher. With online testing systems improving and more and more interactive student software and Internet resources becoming available, we are closer than ever before to achieving Skinner's ideal.

At Work

Believing that reinforcers influence productivity, business managers have capitalized on psychological research. Many companies now enable their employees to share profits, or even to participate in company ownership. When workers' productivity boosts rewards for all, their motivation, morale, and cooperative spirit often increase (Deutsch, 1991). Reinforcement for jobs well done is especially effective in boosting productivity when the desired performance is *well-defined and achievable*. The message for managers? Reward specific behaviors, not vaguely defined merit. Criticism, too, triggers the least resentment and the greatest performance boost when it is considerate and specific (Baron, 1988).

Drawing by Ziegler; © 1989 The New Yorker Magazine, Inc.

It's also a good idea to make the reinforcement *immediate*. Thomas Watson, who led IBM during its tremendous growth, would write out a check on the spot for achievements he observed (Peters & Waterman, 1982). But rewards need not be material, nor should they be so big that they become political and a source of discouragement to those who don't receive them. An effective manager may simply walk the floor and praise people for good work, or write unexpected notes of appreciation for a completed project. As Skinner said, "How much richer would the whole world be if the reinforcers in daily life were more effectively contingent on productive work?"

At Home

We can use operant conditioning in parenting. Parent training researchers Michelle Wierson and Rex Forehand (1994) remind us that when parents say "get ready for bed" and then concede to protesting or defiance, they reinforce unwanted behaviors. Eventually, exasperated, they may yell at the child or make a menacing gesture, at which point the child's fearful compliance reinforces the parents' angry behavior. Over time, a destructive parent-child relationship develops. To disrupt this cycle, they have these recommendations for parents:

- Give children attention and other reinforcers when they are behaving *well*. Target a specific behavior, reward it, and watch it increase.
- Ignore whining. If whining has triggered attention in the past, it may temporarily increase when ignored. Over time, if not reinforced, it will diminish.

- When children misbehave or are defiant, don't yell or hit. Simply explain the misbehavior and give them "time-out"—remove them from reinforcing surroundings for a specified time.

We can use operant conditioning on ourselves, by reinforcing our most desired behaviors and extinguishing those undesired.

Finally, we can use operant conditioning on ourselves, by reinforcing our most desired behaviors and extinguishing those undesired. To take charge of your own behavior, psychologists suggest these step-by-step procedures:

1. State your goal—say, to stop smoking, eat less, or study or exercise more—in measurable terms, and make your intention public. You might, for example, aim to boost your study time by an hour a day and announce that goal to your friends.
2. Record how often you engage in the behavior you wish to promote and note how this behavior is being reinforced. You might log your current study time, noting under what conditions you do and don't study. (When I began writing textbooks, I logged my time and was astonished to discover how much time I was wasting.)
3. Begin systematically to reinforce the desired behavior. To increase your study time, allow yourself a snack (or some other reinforcing activity) only after specified periods of study. Agree with your friends that you will join them for weekend activities only if you have met your weekly studying goal.
4. As your new behaviors become more habitual, gradually reduce the incentives while giving yourself a mental pat on the back.

"O! This learning, what a thing it is."

William Shakespeare
The Taming of the Shrew
1597

Contrasting Conditioning Techniques

The last three decades of research have changed psychologists' views of both classical and operant conditioning (summarized in Table 6.1). Learning, like so much else, depends on both nature and nurture. Biological predispositions make learning some associations easier than learning others, yet animals exhibit more sophisticated cognitive processes than once seemed likely.

Table 6.1 Comparison of Classical and Operant Conditioning

	Classical Conditioning	Operant Conditioning
The response	Involuntary, automatic.	"Voluntary," operates on environment.
Acquisition	Associating events; CS announces UCS.	Associating response with a consequence (reinforcer or punisher).
Extinction	CR decreases when CS is repeatedly presented alone.	Responding decreases when reinforcement stops.
Cognitive processes	Subjects develop expectation that CS signals the arrival of UCS.	Subjects develop expectation that a response will be reinforced or punished; they also exhibit latent learning, without reinforcement.
Biological predispositions	Natural predispositions constrain which stimuli can easily be associated.	Organisms best learn behaviors similar to their natural behaviors; unnatural behaviors instinctively drift back toward natural ones.

Michael the model The number of NBA players with shaved heads the season before Michael Jordan shaved his: 6; the number in the 1997 season: 76. (*Harper's Index*, 1997)

Learning by Observation

12. *What is observational learning?*

From drooling dogs, running rats, and pecking pigeons we have learned much about the basic processes of learning. But conditioning principles alone do not tell us the whole story. Among higher animals, especially humans, learning need not occur through direct experience. **Observational learning**, in which we observe and imitate others' behaviors, also plays a big part. A child need not burn his fingers on a hot stove to learn not to touch it; observing his sister do so is enough.

The process of observing and imitating a specific behavior is often called **modeling**. By observing and imitating models we learn all kinds of social behaviors. By 9 months of age, infants will imitate novel play behaviors, and by 14 months they will imitate acts modeled on television (Meltzoff, 1988a,b,c). To persuade children to smoke, expose them to parents, older youth, and attractive media models who smoke. To encourage children to read, read to them and surround them with books and people who read them. To increase the odds of your children practicing your religion, worship and attend religious activities with them.

"Children need models more than they need critics."

Joseph Joubert
Pensées
1842

Bandura's Experiments

Picture this scene from a famous experiment devised by Albert Bandura, the pioneering researcher of observational learning (Bandura & others, 1961). A preschool child is at work on a drawing. An adult in another part of the room is working with some Tinker Toys. The adult then gets up and for nearly 10 minutes pounds, kicks, and throws a large inflated Bobo doll around the room, while yelling such remarks as, "Sock him in the nose. . . . Hit him down. . . . Kick him."

After observing this outburst, the child is taken to another room where there are many appealing toys. Soon the experimenter interrupts the child's play and explains that she has decided to save these good toys "for the other children." She now takes the frustrated child to an adjacent room containing a few toys, including a Bobo doll. Left alone, what does the child do?

Compared with children not exposed to the adult model, children who observed the aggressive outburst were much more likely to lash out at the doll. Apparently, observing the adult model beating up the doll lowered their inhibitions. But something more than lowered inhibitions was at work, for the children also imitated the very acts they had observed and used the very words they had heard.

Albert Bandura "Learning would be exceedingly laborious, not to mention hazardous, if people had to rely solely on the effects of their own actions to inform them what to do" (1977).

Applications of Observational Learning

The bad news from such studies is that antisocial models—in one's family or neighborhood, or on TV—may have antisocial effects (pages 515–520). This helps us understand how abusive parents might have aggressive children and why men who beat their wives often had wife-battering fathers. The lessons we learn as children are not easily unlearned as adults, and they are sometimes

observational learning learning by observing and imitating the behavior of others.

modeling the process of observing and imitating a behavior.

prosocial behavior positive, constructive, helpful behavior. The opposite of antisocial behavior.

visited on future generations. Critics note that the intergenerational transmission of abuse could be genetic. But with monkeys, at least, we know it can be environmental. In study after study, young monkeys subjected to high levels of aggression when reared apart from their mothers grew up to be perpetrators of aggression (Chamove, 1980). Monkey see, monkey do.

The good news is that **prosocial** (positive, helpful) models can have prosocial effects. People who exemplify nonviolent, helpful behavior can prompt similar behavior in others. Mahatma Gandhi and Martin Luther King, Jr., both drew on the power of modeling, making nonviolent action a powerful force for social change. Parents are powerful models. Research indicates that European Christians who risked their lives to rescue Jews from the Nazis usually had a close relationship with at least one parent who modeled a strong moral or humanitarian concern, as did the civil rights activists of a generation ago (London, 1970; Oliner & Oliner, 1988).

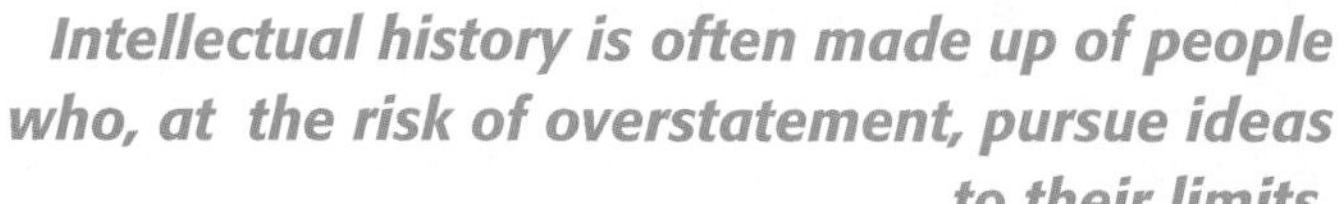

Models are most effective when their actions and words are consistent. Sometimes, however, models say one thing and do another. Many parents seem to operate according to the principle "Do as I *say*, not as I do." Experiments suggest that children learn to do both (Rice & Grusec, 1975; Rushton, 1975). When exposed to a hypocrite, they tend to imitate the hypocrisy by doing what the model did and saying what the model said.

What determines whether we will imitate a model? Bandura believes part of the answer is reinforcements and punishments—those received by the model as well as by the imitator. We look and we learn. By looking, we learn to anticipate a behavior's consequences in situations like those we are observing. By watching TV programs, children may "learn" that physical intimidation is an effective way to control others, that free and easy sex brings pleasure without the misery of unwanted pregnancy or disease, or that men are supposed to be tough and women gentle. We are especially likely to imitate those we perceive as similar to ourselves, as successful, or as admirable.

Although our knowledge of learning principles comes from the work of thousands of investigators, this chapter has focused on the ideas of a few pioneers—Pavlov, Watson, Skinner, and Bandura. They illustrate the impact that can result from single-minded devotion to a few well-defined problems and ideas. These researchers defined the issues and impressed on us the importance of learning. As their legacy demonstrates, intellectual history is often made by people who, at the risk of overstatement, pursue ideas to their limits.

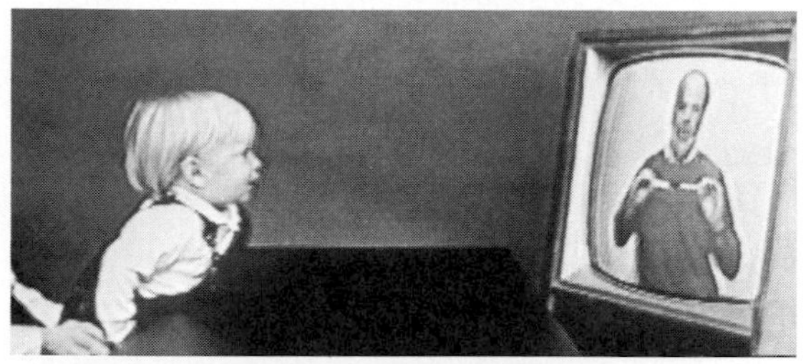

Learning from observation This 14-month-old boy in Andrew Meltzoff's laboratory is imitating behavior he has seen on TV. In the top photo the infant leans forward and carefully watches the adult pull apart a toy. In the middle photo he has been given the toy. In the bottom photo he pulls the toy apart, imitating what he has seen the adult do.

A model grandma This boy is learning to cook by observing his grandmother. As the sixteenth-century proverb states, "Example is better than precept."

REHEARSE IT!

14. Although Skinner disputed the idea, most researchers today believe that cognitive processes can play an important role in learning. Evidence for the effect of cognition (thoughts, perceptions, and expectations) comes from studies in which rats

a. spontaneously recover previously learned behavior.
b. develop cognitive maps.
c. exhibit respondent behavior.
d. generalize responses.

15. Animals, like people, can learn from experience, with or without reinforcement. After being carried passively through a maze and being given no reward, rats demonstrated their prior learning of the maze: In later trials involving food rewards, they immediately did as well as rats that had been reinforced for running the maze. The rats that had learned without reinforcement demonstrate

a. modeling. **c.** shaping.
b. biological predisposition. **d.** latent learning.

16. Children learn many social behaviors by imitating parents and other models. This type of learning is called

a. observational learning. **c.** operant conditioning.
b. reinforced learning. **d.** classical conditioning.

17. Parents are powerful models of behavior. They are *most* effective in getting their children to imitate them if

a. their words and actions are consistent.
b. they have outgoing personalities.
c. the father works and the mother stays home to care for the children.
d. they carefully explain why a behavior is acceptable in adults but not in children.

18. Bandura believes that modeling is not automatic. Whether a child will imitate a model depends in part on the

a. child's closeness to the model.
b. child's ability to distinguish right from wrong.
c. rewards and punishments received by the model and by the imitator.
d. child's age in relation to that of the model.

REVIEWING ▪ *Learning*

1. ***What is learning?***

All animals, especially humans, adapt to their environments aided by **learning**. Through **associative learning**, we come to link certain events. The process of learning associations between events is called conditioning. Through classical conditioning, we learn to anticipate important events, such as impending food or pain. Through operant conditioning, we learn to repeat acts that bring desired results and to avoid acts that bring punishment. Through observational learning, we learn from the experience and example of others.

Classical Conditioning

2. ***How does classical conditioning demonstrate learning by association?***

Although associative learning had been discussed for centuries, it remained for Ivan Pavlov to capture the phenomenon of **classical conditioning**. (also called *Pavlovian conditioning*). Pavlov repeatedly presented a neutral stimulus (such as a tone) just before an **unconditioned stimulus** (**UCS**, such as food) triggered an **unconditioned response** (**UCR**, such as salivation). After several repetitions, the tone alone (now the **conditioned stimulus—CS**) began triggering a **conditioned response** (**CR**, such as salivation). Further experiments on acquisition revealed that classical conditioning was usually greatest when the CS was presented just before the UCS, thus preparing the organism for what was coming.

3. ***How do the processes of acquisition, extinction, spontaneous recovery, generalization, and discrimination affect a CR?***

The first stage in response learning involves the association of a CS with the UCS (**acquisition**). Responses are subsequently weakened if they are not reinforced (**extinction**), but they may reappear after a rest pause (**spontaneous recovery**). Responses may be triggered by stimuli similar to the conditioned stimulus (**generalization**) but not by dissimilar stimuli (**discrimination**).

4. ***Do cognitive processes and biological constraints affect classical conditioning?***

Early optimism that learning principles would generalize from one response to another and from one species to another has been tempered. Conditioning principles, we now know, are cognitively and biologically constrained. In classical conditioning, animals learn when to "expect" an unconditioned stimulus. Moreover, biological predispositions make learning some associations easier than learning others. For example, rats are biologically disposed to learn associations between, say, a peculiar taste and a sickness-producing drink, which they will then avoid. But they don't learn to avoid a sickening drink announced by a noise.

5. ***Why is Pavlov's work important?***

Pavlov's conditioning principles generalize to many species and are applicable to humans, especially to the learning of emotions such as fear. His objective methods illustrated how psychology could proceed as a science.

Pavlov's work laid a foundation for John B. Watson's emerging belief that, to be an objective science, psychology should study only overt behavior, without considering unobservable mental activity. Watson called this position **behaviorism**.

Operant Conditioning

6. ***What is operant conditioning, and how does it differ from classical conditioning?***

Through classical (Pavlovian) conditioning, an organism associates different stimuli that it does not control and responds automatically (**respondent behavior**). Through **operant conditioning**, the organism associates its **operant behaviors** with their consequences. Expanding on Edward Thorndike's **law of effect**, B. F. Skinner and other researchers found that the behavior of rats or pigeons placed in a **Skinner box** can be **shaped** by rewarding closer and closer approximations of the desired behavior.

7. ***What are the basic types of reinforcers?***

   Reinforcers can be positive (when presented after a response) or negative (when an aversive stimulus is withdrawn); **primary** (unlearned) or **secondary** (learned through association with primary reinforcers); and immediate or delayed. Regardless of type, all reinforcers strengthen the behaviors that they follow.

8. ***How do different reinforcement schedules affect behavior?***

   Partial reinforcement schedules (**fixed-interval, fixed-ratio, variable-interval**, and **variable-ratio**) produce slower acquisition of the target behavior than does **continuous reinforcement**. They also produce greater resistance to extinction.

9. ***How does punishment affect behavior?***

   Like reinforcement, **punishment** is most swiftly effective when strong, immediate, and consistent. Although punishment decreases the frequency of the behavior it follows, it is not simply the logical opposite of reinforcement, for punishment can result in several undesirable side effects, such as increased aggression and fear of the punisher.

10. ***Do cognitive processes and biological constraints affect operant conditioning?***

    Many psychologists have criticized behaviorists such as Skinner for underestimating the importance of cognitive and biological processes in operant conditioning. Research on **cognitive mapping** and **latent learning** points to the importance of cognitive processes in learning. Research has also made it clear that biological predispositions constrain what an animal can be taught.

11. ***How might educators, business managers, and other individuals apply operant conditioning?***

    Operant principles are applied successfully in schools, in the workplace, and at home. Computer-assisted instruction both shapes and reinforces learning; immediate reinforcement boosts worker productivity; individuals can strengthen their own desired behavior and extinguish unwanted behavior.

Learning by Observation

12. ***What is observational learning?***

    Observational learning results from watching others' behavior and imitating it. In experiments, children tend to imitate what a **model** both does and says, whether the behavior is **prosocial** or antisocial. Such experiments have stimulated research on social modeling in the home, on television, and within peer groups.

CRITICAL THINKING EXERCISE by Richard O. Straub

Now that you have read and reviewed Chapter 6, take your learning a step further by testing your critical thinking skills on the following pattern-recognition exercise.

Psychologists believe that children learn to control their bladders during sleep through classical conditioning, a type of learning in which an organism comes to associate different events. Normally, a wet bed or diaper causes a child to awaken. Through repeated pairings, bladder tension becomes associated with the sensation of wetness and children wake up when they sense that the bladder is full.

Imagine that you are baby-sitting a 6-year-old bed-wetter who has not yet learned the connection between bladder tension and wetness. In desperation, the child's parents consult a behavioral psychologist who has developed a classical conditioning technique for controlling bed-wetting, using a special sheet containing fine electric wires. When a sleeping child wets the bed, the urine (which conducts electricity) immediately completes an electrical circuit and causes a loud bell to ring, awakening the child. Over time, bladder tension becomes associated with the bell and the child is conditioned to wake up before actually wetting the bed.

Although the parents have read a pamphlet that explains the basic principles underlying the conditioning technique, they are seeking your help in understanding exactly *why* it works.

1. Can you identify the components of classical conditioning for children who learn to wake up before they wet the bed *without* special training?

   Unconditioned stimulus

   Unconditioned response

   Conditioned stimulus

   Conditioned response

2. Can you identify the components of classical conditioning for children who are conditioned to wake up through use of the special sheet and bell?

   Unconditioned stimulus

   Unconditioned response

   Conditioned stimulus

   Conditioned response

3. Does the classical conditioning explanation of how children learn on their own to wake up before wetting the bed make sense? Can you explain this learning, using principles of operant conditioning?

Check your progress on becoming a critical thinker by comparing your answers to the sample answers found in Appendix B.

REHEARSE IT ANSWER KEY

1. c., **2.** c., **3.** a., **4.** b., **5.** d., **6.** b., **7.** b., **8.** d., **9.** c., **10.** a., **11.** b., **12.** b., **13.** c., **14.** b., **15.** d., **16.** a., **17.** a., **18.** c.

CHAPTER
7

Memory

Imagine your life without memory. There would be no savoring the remembrances of joyful moments, no guilt or misery over painful recollections. Each moment would be a fresh experience. But each person would be a stranger, every language foreign, each task—dressing, cooking, biking—a novel challenge.

Your memory is your mind's storehouse, the reservoir of your accumulated learning. To the Roman statesman Cicero, memory was "the treasury and guardian of all things." To a psychologist, **memory** is any indication that learning has persisted over time. It is our ability to store and retrieve information.

The Phenomenon of Memory

Conversing with John, a former graduate student, you would be impressed by his wit, his intelligence (he might explain his master's thesis), and his skill at tasks such as typing. It might be some time before you noticed that John suffers a tragic defect, caused by a brain injury suffered in a motorcycle accident. John cannot form new memories. Although he remembers his life before the accident, John otherwise lives in an eternal present. Each morning when his rehabilitation therapist greets him, she must reintroduce herself. She must listen patiently as over and over he retells anecdotes from his preaccident life. Each time the need arises, he inquires, "Where is the bathroom?" and is told anew.

At the other extreme are some special people who would be medal winners in a memory Olympics, such as the Russian journalist Shereshevskii, or S, as psychologist Alexander Luria (1968) called him. S's memory not only allowed him merely to listen while other reporters were scribbling notes, it also earned him a place in virtually every modern book on memory. You and I can repeat back a string of about seven digits—almost surely no more than nine. S could repeat up to 70 digits or words, provided they were read about 3 seconds apart in an otherwise silent room. Moreover, he could recall them backward as easily as forward. His accuracy was unerring, even when he was asked to recall a list as much as 15 years later, after having memorized hundreds of other lists. "Yes, yes," he might recall. "This was a series you gave me once when we were in your apartment. . . . You were sitting at the table and I in the rocking chair. . . . You were wearing a gray suit and you looked at me like this."

memory the persistence of learning over time through the storage and retrieval of information.

flashbulb memory a clear memory of an emotionally significant moment or event.

encoding the processing of information into the memory system, for example, by extracting meaning.

storage the retention of encoded information over time.

retrieval the process of getting information out of memory storage.

long-term memory the relatively permanent and limitless storehouse of the memory system.

short-term memory activated memory that holds a few items briefly, such as the seven digits of a phone number while dialing, before the information is stored or forgotten.

Do these memory feats make your own memory seem feeble? If so, consider your capacity for remembering countless voices, sounds, and songs; tastes, smells, and textures; faces, places, and happenings. Imagine viewing more than 2500 slides of faces and places, for only 10 seconds each, and later seeing 280 of these slides one at a time, paired with a previously unseen slide. If you are like the subjects in this experiment by Ralph Haber (1970), you would recognize 90 percent of those you saw before.

Or consider the vividness of your memories of unique and highly emotional moments in your past—perhaps a car accident, your first romantic kiss, your first day as an immigrant in a new country, or your surroundings when you heard some tragic news. One of my vivid memories is of my only hit in an entire season of Little League baseball. Most Americans over 50 feel sure of exactly what they were doing when they heard the news of President Kennedy's assassination (Brown & Kulik, 1982). Few San Francisco Bay Area residents will hesitate in recalling exactly where they were when the 1989 earthquake struck. Perhaps you recall with similar clarity receiving the news of Princess Diana's death. This clarity for our memories of surprising, significant events leads some psychologists to call them **flashbulb memories**, because it's as if the brain commands, "Capture this!"

Which is more important—your experiences or your memories of them?

Memory lost and found Larry Treadgold, an engineer, invented a paging system that serves as a kind of artificial memory for his son Adrian. Brain-injured in an auto accident, the young man can speak, understand, and retain information for as long as he pays attention. But as soon as he is distracted, the information fades. The paging system allows a central computer to take over memory functions, reminding him, for example, to "take your 8:00 A.M. medications; call 123-4567 to confirm." If Adrian fails to confirm, the computer continues to page him and eventually contacts an emergency number.

How do we accomplish such memory feats? How can we remember things we have not thought about for years, yet forget the name of someone we met a minute ago? How are memories stored in our brains? Why can even our flashbulb memories sometimes prove dead wrong? (Hours after the space shuttle *Challenger* explosion, people recalled where they had heard the news. Yet they were sometimes wildly inaccurate when again recalling their whereabouts one to three years later [McCloskey & others, 1988; Neisser & Harsch, 1992].) How can we improve our memories? These will be our questions as we review a century of research on memory.

Forming Memories: An Example

History is sometimes determined by what people can remember about events. On June 17, 1972, police caught five men trying to tap the telephones of the Democratic National Committee in the Washington, D.C., Watergate Office Building. In 1973, when President Nixon's legal counsel, John Dean, testified before a U.S. Senate committee investigating White House involvement in what came to be called "the Watergate scandal," his recall of conversations with the

THE FAR SIDE

More facts of nature: All forest animals, to this very day, remember exactly where they were and what they were doing when they heard that Bambi's mother had been shot.

president was so impressive that some writers called him "the human tape recorder." Ironically, it was later revealed that a secret taping system had actually recorded the conversations that Dean recounted, providing a rare opportunity to compare an eyewitness's recollections with the actual event. Dean's recollection of the essentials proved correct. The highest-ranking members of the White House staff went to prison for doing what John Dean said they did, and President Nixon was forced to resign.

However, when Ulric Neisser (1981) compared the details in the tapes with the testimony, he discovered that John Dean was far from a human tape recorder. For example, Dean recalled that entering a September 15 meeting with President Nixon and his chief-of-staff, Robert Haldeman,

> the president asked me to sit down. Both men appeared to be in very good spirits and my reception was very warm and cordial. The president then told me that Bob—referring to Haldeman—had kept him posted on my handling of the Watergate case. The president told me I had done a good job and he appreciated how difficult a task it had been and the president was pleased that the case had stopped with [his reelection committee's attorney] Liddy.

But almost every detail Dean recalled was wrong. The tape of the meeting revealed that the president did not ask Dean to sit down. He did not say Dean had done a good job. He did not say anything about Liddy or the indictments.

Dean's memory was better for a March 15 conversation during which he delivered a well-prepared report to the president on the unraveling of the White House cover-up. The tape caught Dean actually saying, "We have a cancer within, close to the presidency, that is growing. It is growing daily . . . because (1) we are being blackmailed, (2) people are going to start perjuring themselves." In his later congressional testimony, Dean *recalled* "telling the president that there was a cancer growing on the presidency and . . . that it was important that this cancer be removed immediately because it was growing more deadly every day."

How could John Dean have been so right in his basic understanding of the Watergate discussions, yet, except for the March 15 conversation, so wrong in recalling the details of most conversations? Why are you likely later in this chapter to misrecall this sentence: *"The angry rioter threw the rock at the window"*? To understand Dean's memory (and our own), we need a model of memory.

A human tape recorder? John Dean is shown here testifying before the Senate Watergate Committee. When his testimony was compared with the White House tapes, Dean's memory was found to be accurate for the substance of most conversations but not for the details.

Memory as Information Processing

1. *How do psychologists describe the human memory system?*

Human memory is in some ways like a computer information-processing system. To remember any event requires that we *get information into our brain* (**encoding**), *retain* that information (**storage**), and later *get it back out* (**retrieval**). Consider how a computer encodes, stores, and retrieves information. First, it translates input (keystrokes) into an electronic language, much as the brain encodes sensory information into a neural language. The computer permanently stores vast amounts of information on a disk. From this information storehouse it can retrieve a file or document into a working memory, which also can receive new information from the keyboard. Part of this working memory is visible on the screen.

Similarly, we store vast amounts of information in **long-term memory**. (Our memories are, however, less literal and more fragile than a computer's.) From our memory storehouse we can retrieve information into an active working memory, part of which is displayed on our mental screen as **short-term memory**.

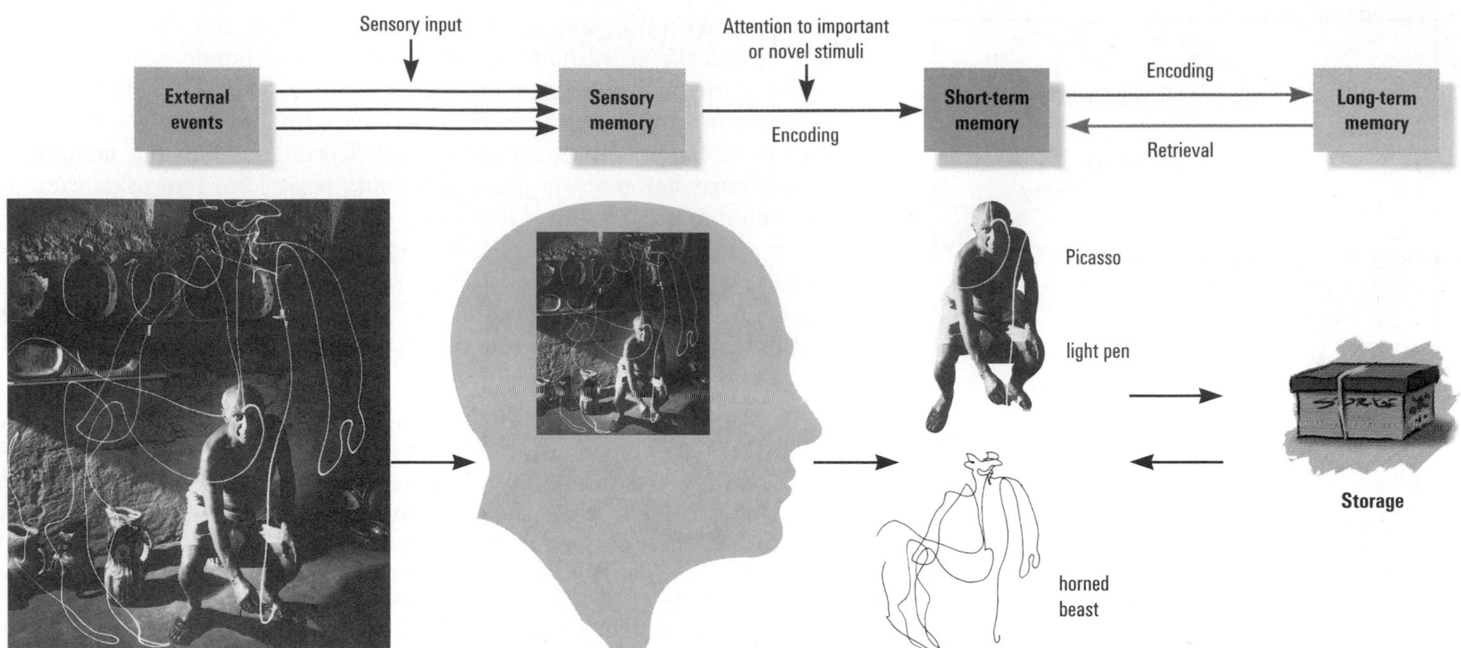

Figure 7.1 A simplified memory model Sensory memory registers incoming information, allowing your brain to capture for a fleeting moment the artist Picasso and his fanciful light-pen drawing. The parts of this sensory input that you most closely attend to get encoded and displayed "on screen" in your short-term memory. From there it may be encoded for long-term storage, and later retrieved, enabling you, an hour from now, to call up a crude image of the picture.

We cannot focus on everything at once, but we do register a vast amount of information in **sensory memory**. Then we shine the flashlight beam of attention on certain incoming stimuli, often novel or changing stimuli that fill our on-screen, short-term memory (Figure 7.1)

Encoding: Getting Information In

2. ***How do the sights, sounds, and other sensations we experience get selectively encoded and transferred into the memory system?***

Some encoding occurs automatically, freeing your attention to simultaneously process information that requires effort. Thus, your memory for the route you walked to class yesterday was handled by **automatic processing**. Your learning this chapter's concepts requires **effortful processing** (Figure 7.2)

Figure 7.2 Automatic versus effortful processing Some information, such as this chapter's concepts, requires effort to encode and remember. Other information, like what you ate for dinner yesterday, you process automatically.

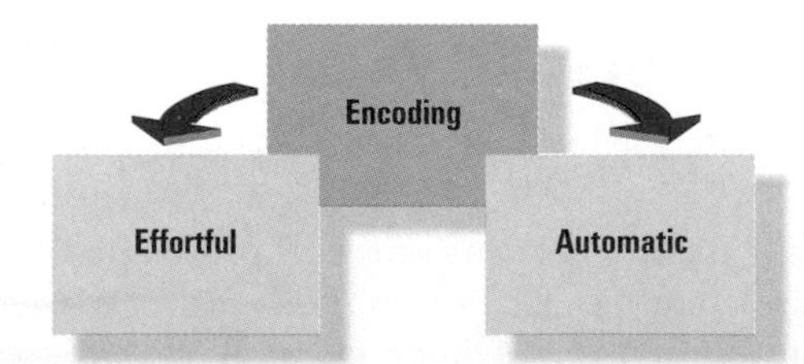

Automatic Processing

With little or no effort, you encode an enormous amount of information about *space*, *time*, and *frequency*: During an exam, you may recall the place on the textbook page where forgotten material appears. To guess where you left your coat, you can re-create a sequence of the day's events. You may realize that "this is the third time I've run into you this afternoon." Memories like these form almost automatically. In fact, not only does automatic processing occur effortlessly, it is difficult to shut off. When you hear or read a word in your native language, whether an insult or a compliment, it is virtually impossible not to register its meaning automatically.

Some types of automatic processing we learn. For example, learning to read reversed sentences at first requires effort:

.citamotua emoceb nac gnissecorp luftroffE

After practice, effortful processing becomes more automatic, much as reading from right to left becomes easy for students of Hebrew (Kolers, 1975).

sensory memory the immediate, initial recording of sensory information in the memory system.

automatic processing unconscious encoding of incidental information such as space, time, and frequency and of well-learned information such as word meanings.

effortful processing encoding that requires attention and conscious effort.

rehearsal the conscious repetition of information, either to maintain it in consciousness or to encode it for storage.

spacing effect the tendency for distributed study or practice to yield better long-term retention than is achieved through massed study or practice.

Effortful Processing

3. *How much does rehearsal aid in forming memories?*

We encode and retain vast amounts of information automatically, without any intentional effort. Other types of information we remember only with effort and attention. When learning novel information such as names, we can boost our memory through **rehearsal**, or conscious repetition. This was shown long ago by the pioneering researcher of verbal memory, German philosopher Hermann Ebbinghaus (1850–1909). Ebbinghaus did for the study of memory what Ivan Pavlov did for the study of conditioning. Impatient with philosophical speculations about memory, Ebbinghaus wanted to study it scientifically. To do so, he decided to study his own learning and forgetting of novel verbal materials.

Where could Ebbinghaus find verbal material that was not familiar? His solution was to form a list of all possible nonsense syllables created by sandwiching a vowel between two consonants. Then, for a particular experiment, he would randomly select a sample of the syllables. To get a feel for how Ebbinghaus tested himself, rapidly read aloud, eight times over, the following list (from Baddeley, 1982). Then recall the items:

> JIH, BAZ, FUB, YOX, SUJ, XIR, DAX, LEQ, VUM,
> PID, KEL, WAV, TUV, ZOF, GEK, HIW.

After learning such a list, Ebbinghaus could recall few of the syllables the following day. But were they entirely forgotten? As Figure 7.3 portrays, the more frequently he repeated the list aloud on day 1, the fewer repetitions he required to relearn the list on day 2. Here, then, was a simple beginning principle: *The amount remembered depends on the time spent learning.* Even after we learn material, additional rehearsal (*overlearning*) increases retention. Thus, John Dean almost perfectly recalled his "cancer on the presidency" remarks because he had written them out and rehearsed them several times before uttering them to President Nixon.

The point to remember is that for novel verbal information, practice—effortful processing—does indeed make perfect. That helps us understand some other interesting phenomena:

- The *next-in-line effect*: When people go around a circle reading words or saying their names, their poorest memories are for what was said by the person just before them (Bond & others, 1991; Brenner, 1973). When we are next in line, we focus on our own performance and often fail to process the last person's words.
- Information presented in the seconds just before sleep seldom is remembered (Wyatt & Bootzin, 1994). When our consciousness fades before we've processed the information, all is lost. (The *hour* before sleep, as we will see, is well remembered.)
- Taped information played during sleep is registered by the ears but is not remembered (Wood & others, 1992). Without opportunity for rehearsal, "sleep learning" does not occur.

We also retain information better when rehearsal is distributed over time (as when learning classmates' names), a phenomenon called the **spacing effect** (Dempster, 1988). Harry Bahrick and Lynda Hall (1991) noted the effect of spaced rehearsal in a study of adults' memory of high school algebra. Those who took algebra only once forgot most of what they learned over the next half-century. Others—after doing no better in high school—rehearsed their algebra knowledge while taking higher-level math courses. For the rest of their lives these people remembered most of their high school algebra, especially if their college math was spaced over several semesters rather than massed into a single

Figure 7.3 **Ebbinghaus's retention curve** Ebbinghaus found that the more times he practiced a list of nonsense syllables on day 1, the fewer repetitions he required to relearn it on day 2. Said simply, the more time we spend learning novel information, the more we retain. (From Baddeley, 1982)

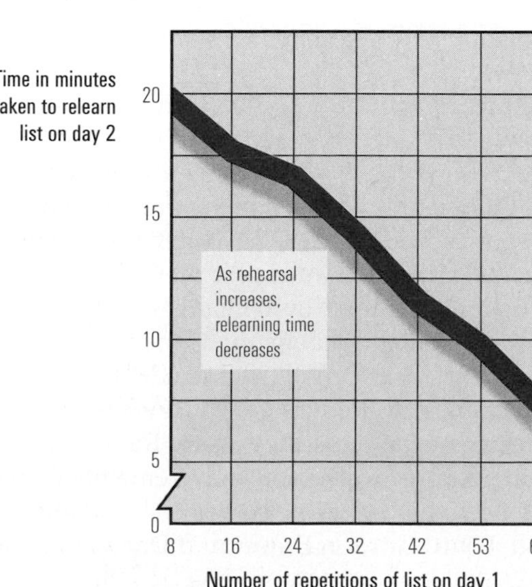

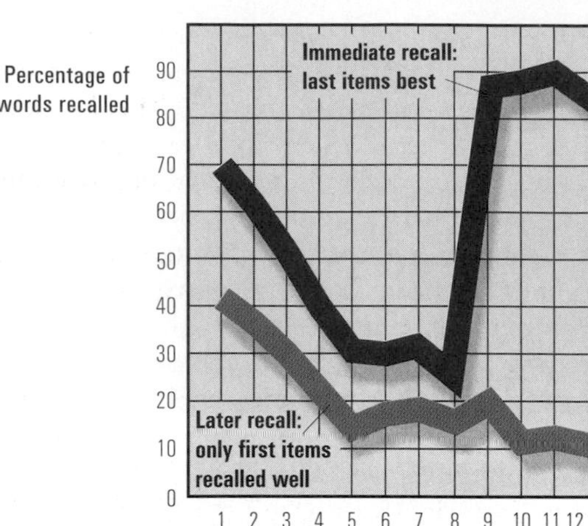

Figure 7.4 The serial position effect After being presented with a list of words or names, people immediately recall the last items well (perhaps because they are still "on screen"), and quite often the first few items nearly as well. But later they recall the first items best. (From Craik & Watkins, 1973)

year. In the first century, the Roman philosopher Seneca anticipated the finding that spaced study beats cramming: "The mind is slow in unlearning what it has been long in learning."

A phenomenon you have surely experienced further illustrates the benefits of rehearsal. Experimenters have shown people a list of items (words, names, dates) and then immediately asked them to recall the items in any order. As people struggle to recall the list, they often demonstrate the **serial position effect**: They remember the last and first items better than they do those in the middle (Figure 7.4). Perhaps because they are still in short-term memory, the last items are briefly recalled especially quickly and well. But after a delay—after attention has shifted from the last items—recall is best for the first items. As an everyday parallel, imagine that as you are being introduced to several people, you repeat (rehearse) all their names from the beginning as you meet each person. By the end, you will have spent more time rehearsing the earlier names than the later names; thus, the next day you will probably recall the earlier names better. Also, learning the first few names may interfere with your learning the later ones.

Rehearsal will not encode all information equally well. Sometimes merely repeating information, such as the new phone number we are about to dial, is not enough to store it for later recall (Craik & Watkins, 1973; Greene, 1987). How, then, do we encode information for processing into long-term memory? Processing our sensory input is like sorting through the day's mail: Some items we instantly discard. Others we process more thoughtfully: We open, read, and retain them. Our memory system processes information not just by repetitive rehearsal but by encoding its significant features.

Encoding Strategies

4. What methods of effortful processing aid in forming memories?

We process information in three key ways—by encoding its meaning, by visualizing it, and by mentally organizing it. To some extent we do these things automatically. But in each case there are effortful strategies for enhancing memory.

Encoding Meaning

Do you recall (from page 233) the sentence about the rioter? Can you complete the sentence: "The angry rioter threw . . ."?

Here is another sentence I will ask you about later: The fish attacked the swimmer.

When processing verbal information for storage, we usually encode its meaning (semantically). For example, we associate it with what we already know or imagine. Whether we hear "eye-screem" as "ice cream" or "I scream" depends on how the context and our experience guide us to interpret the sounds.

Perhaps, then, like the subjects in an experiment by William Brewer (1977), you recalled the rioter sentence as the meaning you encoded when you read it (for example, "The angry rioter threw the rock through the window") and not as written ("The angry rioter threw the rock *at* the window"). As such recall indicates, we tend not to remember things exactly as they were. Rather, *we remember what we encoded.* Studying for an exam, you may remember your lecture notes rather than the lecture itself. Likewise, as we hear or read about a situation, our minds construct a model of it. Gordon Bower and Daniel Morrow

How many Fs are in the following sentence? Finished files are the results of years of scientific study combined with the experience of years. (See page 239.)

serial position effect our tendency to recall best the last and first items in a list.

imagery mental pictures; a powerful aid to effortful processing, especially when combined with semantic encoding.

(1990) liken our minds to theater directors who, given a raw script, imagine a finished stage production. Asked later to recall what we heard or read, we recall not the literal text but the mental model we constructed from it. This helps us understand John Dean's misrecollections of precisely what President Nixon said and did, and Dean's better recall of the *meaning* that he encoded from his conversations with the president.

To experience the importance of meaning for verbal memory, put yourself in the place of the students whom John Bransford and Marcia Johnson (1972) asked to remember the following recorded passage:

> The procedure is actually quite simple. First you arrange things into different groups. Of course, one pile may be sufficient depending on how much there is to do. . . . After the procedure is completed one arranges the materials into different groups again. Then they can be put into their appropriate places. Eventually they will be used once more and the whole cycle will then have to be repeated. However, that is part of life.

When the students heard the paragraph you have just read, without a meaningful context, they remembered little of it. When told that the paragraph was about washing clothes (something meaningful to them), they remembered much more of it—as you probably could now after rereading it.

Such research suggests the benefits of rephrasing what we read and hear into meaningful terms. From his experiments on himself, Ebbinghaus estimated that, compared with learning nonsense material, learning meaningful material required but one-tenth the effort. As memory researcher Wayne Wickelgren (1977, p. 346) noted, "The time you spend thinking about material you are reading and relating it to previously stored material is about the most useful thing you can do in learning any new subject matter."

"A thing when heard, remember, strikes less keen on the spectator's mind than when 'tis seen."

Horace
Ars Poetica
8 B.C.

Encoding Imagery

We struggle to memorize formulas, definitions, and dates, yet we can easily picture where we were yesterday, who was with us, where we sat, and what we wore. Your earliest memories—probably of something that happened when you were about 3 or 4—almost surely involve visual **imagery**, or mental pictures.

In a variety of experiments, researchers have documented the benefits of mental images. For example, we remember words that lend themselves to picture images better than we remember abstract, low-imagery words. (When I quiz you later, which three of these words will you most likely recall: *typewriter, void, cigarette, inherent, fire, process*?) Similarly, you probably still recall the sentence about the rock-throwing rioter, not only because of the meaning you encoded but also because the sentence lent itself to a visual image. As the example suggests, and as some memory experts believe, memory for concrete nouns is aided by encoding them *both* semantically and visually (Marschark & others, 1987; Paivio, 1986). Two codes are better than one.

Thanks to the durability of our most vivid images, we recall our experiences with mental snapshots of their best or worst moments. Thus, the best moment of a pleasure or joy, and the worst moment of a pain or frustration, often colors our memories more than does its duration (Fredrickson & Kahneman, 1993). Recalling the high points while forgetting the mundane moments may explain a phenomenon that Terrence Mitchell and others (1997) call "rosy retrospection": People tend to recall events such as a camping holiday more positively than they evaluated them at the time. The visit to Disney World is remembered less for the muggy heat and long lines than for the exciting rides, fun foods, and enchanting surroundings.

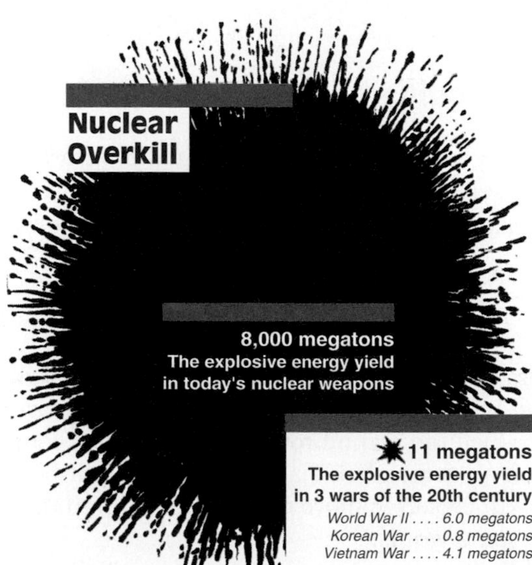

The imagery principle Abstract ideas become memorable when carried by visual images. Numerical facts about the power of today's nuclear weapons are forgettable; tie them to an image that visually illustrates the trend and the message is more memorable. (From Sivard, 1996)

"You simply associate each number with a word, such as 'table' and 3,476,029."

Imagery is at the heart of many memory aids. **Mnemonic** (nih-MON-ik) devices (so named after the Greek word for memory) were developed by ancient Greek scholars and orators as aids to remembering lengthy passages and speeches. Using the *method of loci*, they imagined themselves moving through a familiar series of locations, associating each place with a visual representation of the to-be-remembered topic. Then, when speaking, the orator would mentally revisit each location and retrieve the associated image.

A variation on this method uses vivid stories to organize words to be memorized. Gordon Bower and Michael Clark (1969) used lists of unrelated nouns, asking one group simply to study the lists and another group to invent stories using the nouns. (A sample made-up story: "A LUMBERJACK DARTed out of a forest, SKATEd around a HEDGE past a COLONY of DUCKs. He tripped on some FURNITURE, tearing his STOCKING while hastening toward the PILLOW where his MISTRESS lay.") After working through 12 lists of 10 words each, the group that merely studied each list struggled to recall 13 percent of the words; the group that invented vivid stories recalled an astounding 93 percent.

Other mnemonic devices involve both acoustic and visual codes. For example, the *peg-word system* requires that you first memorize a jingle:

> One is a bun; two is a shoe;
> Three is a tree; four is a door;
> Five is a hive; six is sticks;
> Seven is heaven; eight is a gate;
> Nine is swine; ten is a hen.

Without much effort, you will soon be able to count by peg-words instead of numbers: bun, shoe, tree . . . and then to visually associate the peg-words with to-be-remembered items. Now you are ready to challenge anyone to give you a grocery list to remember. Carrots? Imagine them stuck into a bun. Milk? Fill the shoe with it. Paper towels? Drape them over the tree branch. Think "bun, shoe, tree" and you see their associated images: carrots, milk, paper towels. With few errors (Bugelski & others, 1968), you will be able to recall the items in any order and to name any given item. Such mnemonic systems are often the secret behind the feats of memory experts who repeat long lists of names and objects.

Organizing Information for Encoding

Meaning and imagery enhance memory in part by helping us organize information. When Bransford and Johnson's laundry paragraph (page 237) became meaningful, its sentences formed a sequence. Mnemonic devices help organize material for later retrieval.

Chunking

To experience the importance of organization, glance for a few seconds at row 1 of Figure 7.5, then look away and try to reproduce what you saw. It's nearly impossible. But you can easily reproduce the second row, which is no less complex. Similarly, row 4 is much easier to remember than row 3, although both contain the same letters. And the sixth cluster is more easily remembered than the fifth, although both contain the same words.

As this demonstrates, we organize easily remembered information into meaningful units, or chunks. **Chunking** information into meaningful units occurs so naturally that we take it for granted. Consider your ability to reproduce perfectly the 150 or so line segments that make up the sixth cluster of phrases in Figure 7.5. Surely it would astonish an illiterate person or someone unfamiliar with English.

1. [illegible]
2. K L C I S N E

3. KLCISNE NVESE YNA NI CSTTIH TNDO
4. NICKELS SEVEN ANY IN STITCH DONT

5. NICKELS SEVEN ANY IN STITCH DONT
SAVES AGO A SCORE TIME AND
NINE WOODEN FOUR YEARS TAKE

6. DONT TAKE ANY WOODEN NICKELS
FOUR SCORE AND SEVEN YEARS AGO
A STITCH IN TIME SAVES NINE

Figure 7.5 **Effects of chunking on memory** When we organize information into meaningful units, such as letters, words, and phrases, we recall it more easily. (From Hintzman, 1978)

mnemonics [nih-MON-iks] memory aids, especially those techniques that use vivid imagery and organizational devices.

chunking organizing items into familiar, manageable units; often occurs automatically.

Figure 7.6 An example of chunking—for those who read Chinese After looking at these characters, can you reproduce them exactly? If so, you are literate in Chinese.

You or I might feel similar admiration for the ability of someone literate in Chinese to glance at Figure 7.6 and then to reproduce all the strokes; or for chess masters who, after a 5-second look at the board during a game, can recall the exact positions of most of the pieces (Chase & Simon, 1973); or for varsity basketball players who, given a 4-second glance at a basketball play, can recall the positions of the players (Allard & Burnett, 1985). Like the experienced chess masters and athletes, we all remember information best when we can organize it into personally meaningful arrangements.

Chunking also aids our recall of unfamiliar material. One mnemonic technique organizes it into a more familiar form by creating words (called *acronyms*) or sentences from the first letters of the words to be remembered. Should you ever need to recall the names of North America's five Great Lakes, just remember HOMES (*H*uron, *O*ntario, *M*ichigan, *E*rie, *S*uperior). Want to remember the colors of the rainbow in order of wavelength? Think of ROY G. BIV (*r*ed, *o*range, *y*ellow, *g*reen, *b*lue, *i*ndigo, *v*iolet).

Hierarchies

When people develop expertise in an area, they process information not only in chunks but also in hierarchies composed of a few broad concepts divided and subdivided into narrower concepts and facts. By organizing their knowledge in such ways, experts can retrieve information efficiently. This chapter therefore aims not only to teach you the elementary facts of memory but also to help you organize these facts around broad principles, such as encoding; subprinciples, such as automatic and effortful processing; and still more specific concepts, such as meaning, imagery, and organization (Figure 7.7)

Answer to question on page 236: Partly because your initial processing of the letters was primarily acoustic rather than visual, you probably missed some of the six Fs, *especially those that sound like a* V *rather than an* F.

Gordon Bower and his colleagues (1969) demonstrated the benefits of hierarchical organization by presenting words either randomly or grouped into categories. When the words were hierarchically organized, recall was two to three times better. Such results show the benefits of organizing what you study—of giving special attention to chapter outlines, headings, topic sentences, and summary paragraphs. If you can master a chapter's concepts with their overall organization, your recall should be good at test time. Taking lecture and text notes in outline format—a type of hierarchical organization—may also prove effective.

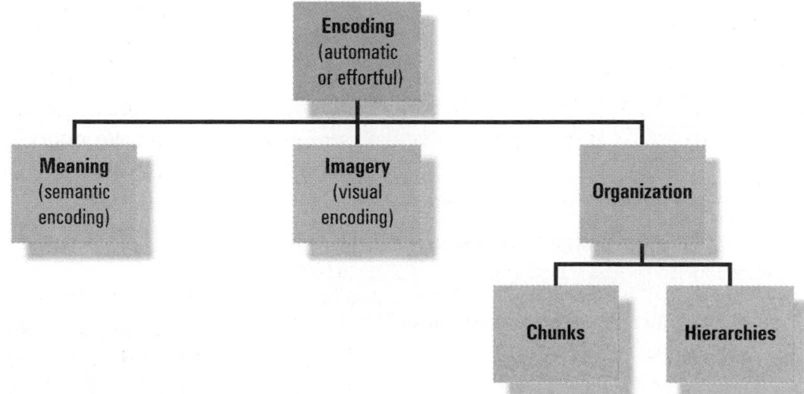

Figure 7.7 Organization benefits memory When we organize words or concepts into hierarchical groups, as here, we remember them better than when we see them presented randomly.

Forgetting as Encoding Failure

"Happiness is nothing more than health and a poor memory."

Physician Albert Schweitzer (1875–1965)

Amidst all the applause for memory—all the efforts to understand it, all the books on how to improve it—have any voices been heard in praise of forgetting? William James (1890, p. 680) was such a voice: "If we remembered everything, we should on most occasions be as ill off as if we remembered nothing."

To discard the clutter of useless or out-of-date information—where we parked the car yesterday, a friend's old phone number, restaurant orders already cooked and served—is surely a blessing (Bjork, 1978). The Russian memory whiz S, whom we met at the beginning of the chapter, was haunted by his junk heap of memories, which continually dominated his consciousness. He had difficulty thinking abstractly—generalizing, organizing, evaluating. A good memory is helpful, but so is the ability to forget.

What causes forgetting? One answer is that we failed to encode the information (Figure 7.8). Thus, it never entered long-term memory. Brain areas that jump into action when young adults are encoding new information are less responsive among older adults. This impaired encoding helps explain age-related memory decline (Grady & others, 1995).

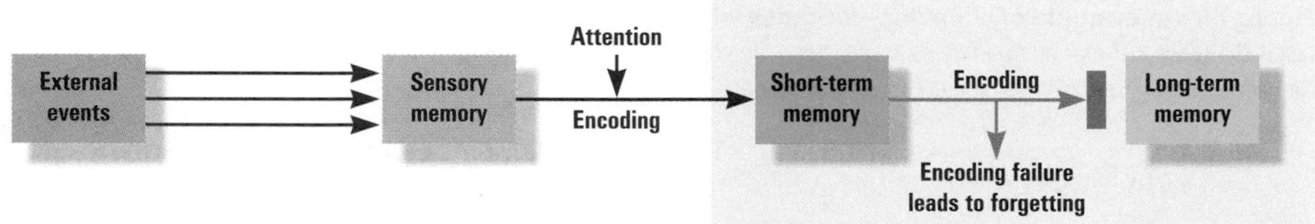

Figure 7.8 **Forgetting as encoding failure**

But no matter how young we are, we cannot attend to more than a few of the myriad sights and sounds that continually bombard us. Thus, much of what we sense we never notice. Consider something you have looked at countless times: What letters accompany the number 5 on your telephone? Or where is the number 0 on your calculator? For most people these are surprisingly difficult questions.

If you live in North America, Britain, or Australia, you have probably also looked at thousands of pennies in your lifetime. You can surely recall the features (color and size) you use to distinguish coins. But can you recall what the side with the head looks like? If not, let's make the memory test easier: If you are familiar with U.S. coins, can you recognize the real thing in Figure 7.9? Raymond Nickerson and Marilyn Adams (1979) discovered that most people cannot. Likewise, few British people can draw from memory the one-pence coin they have seen thousands of times (Richardson, 1993). The details of a penny are not very meaningful—nor are they essential for distinguishing pennies from other coins—and few of us have made the effort to encode them. As we noted earlier, we encode some information automatically; other types of information require effortful processing. Without effort, many memories never form.

Figure 7.9 **Test your memory** Which one of these pennies is the real thing? (If you live outside the United States, try drawing your own country's penny.) (From Nickerson & Adams, 1979) (See page 244.)

REHEARSE IT!

1. Many people have vivid memories of highly emotional moments—for example, what they were doing when they heard the news of an assassination; what kind of morning it was when they brought the new baby home from the hospital. These clear memories of emotional moments are called
   a. short-term memories.
   b. flashbulb memories.
   c. inaccurate memories.
   d. effortful memories.
2. Human memory involves information processing. We take information in, retain it, and later get it back out. In psychological terms, these steps are
   a. retrieval, encoding, and storage.
   b. encoding, storage, and retrieval.
   c. storage, encoding, and retrieval.
   d. retrieval, storage, and encoding.
3. In his research on verbal memory, Hermann Ebbinghaus tested his ability to recall a list of nonsense syllables. He found that the more often he repeated the list aloud, the fewer repetitions he required to relearn the list. This increase in retention was due to additional rehearsal, or
   a. automatic processing.
   b. retrieval.
   c. overlearning.
   d. the flashbulb effect.
4. Rehearsal is the conscious repetition of information a person wants to remember, either in the short or long term. Rehearsal is part of
   a. automatic processing.
   b. effortful processing.
   c. forgetting.
   d. retrieval.
5. Psychologists have found that when people are shown a list of words and are immediately tested, they tend to recall the first and last items on the list more readily than those in the middle (called the serial position effect). When people are *re*tested after a delay, they are most likely to recall
   a. the first items on the list.
   b. the first and last items on the list.
   c. a few items at random.
   d. the last items on the list.
6. Many people use visual imagery to help them remember material that would otherwise be difficult to master. Memory aids that use visual imagery, peg-words, or other organizational devices are called
   a. acronyms.
   b. nonsense material.
   c. mental pictures.
   d. mnemonics.
7. Chunking is a way of organizing information into familiar and manageable units. A related technique involves organizing material into broad categories, which are then divided into subcategories. This technique, used in chapter outlines and organizational charts, is called
   a. serial position.
   b. peg-words.
   c. hierarchial organization.
   d. mental pictures.
8. In some cases, forgetting may be due to encoding failure. That is, meaningless information may not be transferred from
   a. the environment into sensory memory.
   b. sensory memory into long-term memory.
   c. long-term memory into short-term memory.
   d. short-term memory into long-term memory.

Storage: Retaining Information

If you experience something that you later recall, you must, somehow, have stored and retrieved it. What is stored in long-term memory lies dormant, waiting to be reawakened by a cue. What is our memory storage capacity? Let's start with the first memory store noted in Figure 7.1 on page 234, our fleeting sensory memory.

K	Z	R
Q	B	T
S	G	N

Figure 7.10 Momentary photographic memory When George Sperling flashed a group of letters similar to this for 1/20th of a second, people could recall only about half of the letters. But when signaled to recall a particular row *immediately* after the letters had disappeared, they could do so with near-perfect accuracy.

Sensory Memory

5. *How does sensory memory work?*

Consider what one intriguing memory experiment revealed about our sensory memory—the initial recording of sensory information in the memory system. As part of his doctoral research, George Sperling (1960) showed people three rows of three letters each for only 1/20th of a second (Figure 7.10). It was harder than reading by flashes of lightning. After the nine letters disappeared from the screen, the subjects could recall only about half of them.

Why? Was it because they had insufficient time to glimpse them? No, Sperling cleverly demonstrated that even at faster than lightning-flash speed, people actually *can* see and recall all the letters, but only momentarily. Rather than ask them to recall all nine letters at once, Sperling would sound a high, medium, or

"Each of us finds that in [our] own life every moment of time is completely filled. [We are] bombarded every second by sensations, emotions, thoughts . . . nine-tenths of which [we] must simply ignore. The past [is] a roaring cataract of billions upon billions of such moments: any one of them too complex to grasp in its entirety, and the aggregate beyond all imagination. . . . At every tick of the clock, in every inhabited part of the world, an unimaginable richness and variety of 'history' falls off the world into total oblivion."

English Novelist-Critic C. S. Lewis
1967

low tone immediately *after* flashing the nine letters. This cue directed the subject to report only the letters of the top, middle, or bottom row, respectively. Now the subjects rarely missed a letter, showing that all nine letters were momentarily available for recall.

Sperling's experiment revealed that we have a fleeting photographic memory called **iconic memory**. For an instant, the eyes register an exact representation of a scene and we can recall any part of it in amazing detail—but only for a few tenths of a second. If Sperling delayed the tone signal by as much as a second, the iconic memory was gone and the subjects once again recalled only about half the letters. The visual screen clears quickly, as it must, lest new images be superimposed over old ones.

We also have an impeccable, though fleeting, memory for auditory sensory images, called **echoic memory** (Cowan, 1988; Lu & others, 1992). However, even if partially interpreted, the auditory echo disappears more slowly than the visual echo. The last few words spoken seem to linger for 3 or 4 seconds. Sometimes, just as you ask, "What did you say?" you can hear in your mind the echo of what was said.

Short-Term Memory

6. *What are the limits of short-term memory?*

Among the vast amounts of information registered by our sensory memory, we illuminate some with our attentional flashlight. We also retrieve information from long-term storage for "on-screen" display. But unless we meaningfully encode or rehearse that information, it quickly disappears. During your finger's trip from the phone book to the phone, your memory of a telephone number will disappear unless you work to maintain it in consciousness.

To find out how quickly a short-term memory will disappear, Lloyd Peterson and Margaret Peterson (1959) asked people to remember three consonants, such as *CHJ*. To prevent subjects' rehearsal of the letters, the researchers asked them to start at, say, 100, and count aloud backwards by threes. With the help of a friend, you can demonstrate the result shown in Figure 7.11. After 3 seconds people recalled the letters only about half the time; after 12 seconds they seldom recalled them at all. Without active processing, short-term memories have a limited life.

Short-term memory is limited not only in duration but also in capacity. It typically stores but seven or so chunks of information (give or take two). This recall capacity has been enshrined in psychology as "the Magical Number Seven, plus or minus two" (Miller, 1956).

Both children and adults have short-term recall for roughly as many words as they can speak in 2 seconds (Cowan, 1994; Hulme & Tordoff, 1989). The basic principle: At any given moment, we can consciously process only a very limited amount of information.

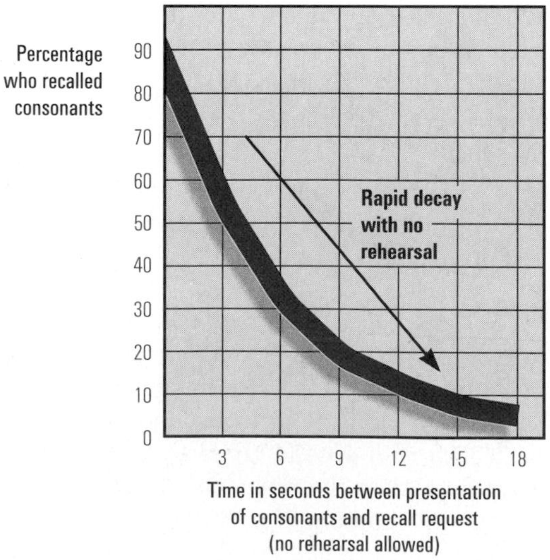

Figure 7.11 Short-term memory decay Unless rehearsed, verbal information may be quickly forgotten. (From Peterson & Peterson, 1959)

Long-Term Memory

7. *How large and durable is our long-term memory?*

In Arthur Conan Doyle's *A Study in Scarlet*, Sherlock Holmes offers a popular theory of memory capacity:

> I consider that a man's brain originally is like a little empty attic, and you have to stock it with such furniture as you choose. . . . It is a mistake to think that that little

iconic memory a momentary sensory memory of visual stimuli; a photographic or picture-image memory lasting no more than a few tenths of a second.

echoic memory a momentary sensory memory of auditory stimuli; if attention is elsewhere, sounds and words can still be recalled within 3 or 4 seconds.

room has elastic walls and can distend to any extent. Depend upon it, there comes a time when for every addition of knowledge you forget something that you knew before.

Contrary to Sherlock Holmes's belief, our capacity for storing long-term memories is essentially limitless. By one careful estimate, the average adult has about a billion bits of information in memory. Allowing for all the brain must do to encode, store, retrieve, and manipulate this information, its storage capacity is probably a thousand to a million times greater (Landauer, 1986). So our brains are *not* like attics, which once filled can store more only if we discard old items.

Clark's Nutcracker Among animals, one contender for champion memorist would be a mere birdbrain—the Clark's Nutcracker—which during winter and early spring can locate up to 6000 caches of buried pine seeds. (From Shettleworth, 1993)

The point is vividly illustrated by those whose efforts have enabled phenomenal memory feats. Consider Rajan Mahadevan, a Florida State University graduate student from India. Give him any string of 10 digits from the first 30,000 or so digits of pi and, after a few moments of mental search for the string, he'll pick up the series from there, firing numbers like a machine gun. He also can repeat 50 random digits—backwards (Thompson & others, 1993). It's no genetic gift, he says; anyone could learn to do it. But given the genetic influence on so many human traits, and knowing that Rajan's father memorized Shakespeare's complete works, one wonders.

How precise and durable are our stored memories? Ebbinghaus (1885) learned lists of nonsense syllables and measured how much he retained when relearning each list, from 20 minutes to 30 days later. His famous "forgetting curve" (Figure 7.12) indicates that much of what we learn we may quickly forget. Many later experiments allow us to state the forgetting curve as one of psychology's laws: The course of forgetting is initially rapid, then levels off with time (Wixted & Ebbesen, 1991).

Harry Bahrick (1984) confirmed Ebbinghaus's finding. He examined the forgetting curve for Spanish vocabulary learned in school. By using the cross-sectional method (page 113), he compared the knowledge of Spanish among people who had just taken Spanish with the knowledge of those who had studied it up to 50 years before. Compared with those just completing a high school or college Spanish course, those who had been out of school for 3 years had forgotten much of what they had learned (Figure 7.13, page 244). However, after roughly 3 years, forgetting leveled off; what people remembered then, they still remembered 25 years later, even if they had not used their Spanish at all.

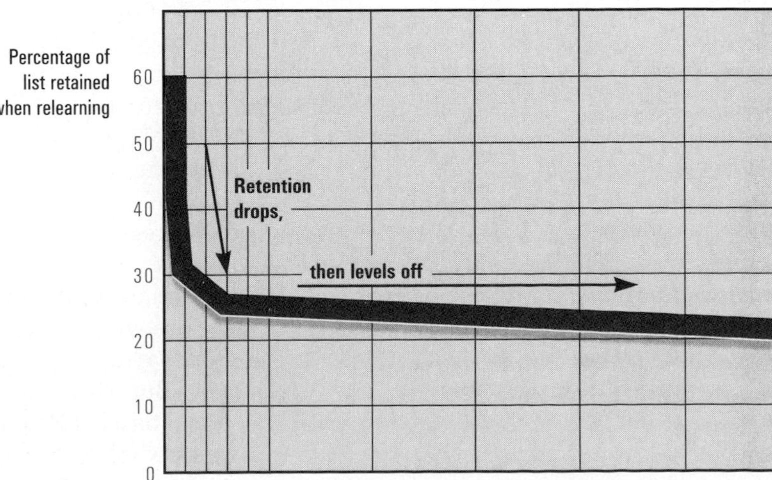

Figure 7.12 **Ebbinghaus's forgetting curve** After learning lists of nonsense syllables, Ebbinghaus studied how much he retained up to 30 days later. He found that memory for novel information fades quickly, then levels out. (Adapted from Ebbinghaus, 1885)

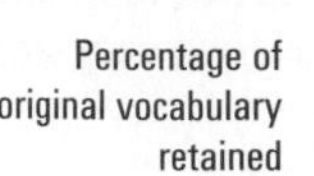

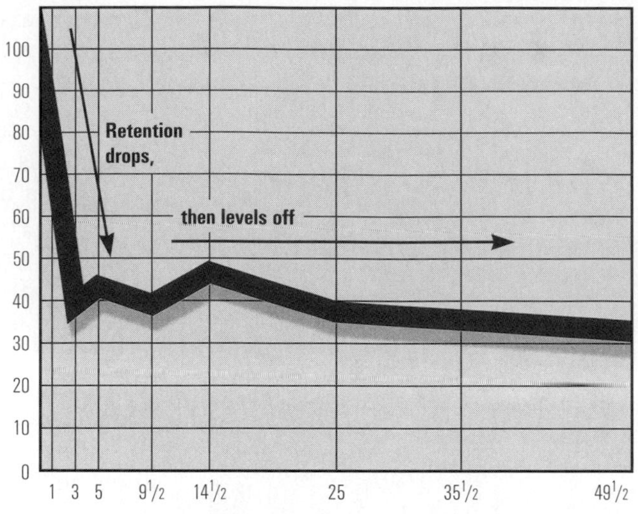

Figure 7.13 The forgetting curve for Spanish learned in school Compared with people just completing a Spanish course, those 3 years out of the course remembered much less. Compared with the 3-year group, however, those who studied Spanish even longer ago did not forget much more. (Adapted from Bahrick, 1984)

How many of the six quiz words on page 238 can you now recall? Of these, how many are high-imagery words? How many are low-imagery?

Answer to question on page 240: The first penny (a) is the real penny.

"Our memories are flexible and superimposable, a panoramic blackboard with an endless supply of chalk and erasers."

Elizabeth Loftus and Katherine Ketcham
The Myth of Repressed Memory (1994)

Storing Memories in the Brain

8. *How are memories recorded in the brain?*

I marvel at my 88-year-old mother-in-law, a retired pianist and organist. Her brain is aging, and her blind eyes can no longer read music. But let her sit at a keyboard and she will flawlessly play any of hundreds of hymns, including ones she hasn't thought of for 20 years. Watching her fingers cover the keyboard in effortless precision I wonder: How and where has her brain stored these thousands of sequenced notes? For a time, it was thought that brain stimulation during surgery provided evidence that our whole past, and not just well-practiced music, is "in there," in complete detail, just waiting to be relived. Even today, 6 in 10 university students agree that "everything we learn is permanently stored, although sometimes inaccessible" (Brown & others, 1996). Perhaps some of them have heard of the brain surgery experiments described on page 57. To predict possible side effects of such surgery, Wilder Penfield (1969) helped map the brain's motor cortex by electrically stimulating wide-awake patients. Occasionally, Penfield's patients would report hearing things, such as "a mother calling her little boy." Penfield assumed that he was activating long-lost experiences etched permanently on the brain.

Scrutinizing these famous reports, memory researchers Elizabeth Loftus and Geoffrey Loftus (1980) discovered that these flashbacks were extremely rare, occurring in only a handful of Penfield's 1100 stimulated patients. Moreover, the content of these few recollections suggested that the experiences were not being relived but were being invented. As if they had been dreaming, people would recall being in locations they had never visited. Although the brain's storage capacity may be essentially unlimited, Penfield's evidence did *not* suggest that we store most information with the exactness of a tape recorder. Rather, say memory researchers, forgetting occurs as new experiences interfere with our retrieval (page 253) and as the physical memory trace gradually decays.

But what exactly is the "memory trace"? Since 1980, new clues to the physical basis of long-term memory have surfaced rapidly. While cognitive psychologists study our memory "software," neuroscientists are gaining new insights into our memory "hardware"—how and where we physically store information in our brains.

long-term potentiation (LTP) an increase in a synapse's firing potential after brief, rapid stimulation. Believed to be a neural basis for learning and memory.

For several decades, neuroscientists have searched the brain for physical evidence of memory. The search has at times been exasperating. One psychologist, Karl Lashley (1950), trained rats to solve a maze, then cut out pieces of the rats' cortexes and retested their memory of the maze. Eventually, he hoped to locate where memory of the maze was stored. Alas, no matter what part of the cortex he removed, the rats retained at least a partial memory of how to solve the maze. Lashley's conclusion: Memories do not reside in single, specific spots.

Are memories instead rooted in the brain's ongoing electrical activity? If so, then temporarily shutting down that activity should eliminate them, much as a power failure eliminates the settings on an electronic clock. To test this, Ralph Gerard (1953) trained hamsters to turn right or left to get food. Then he lowered their body temperature until the brain's electrical activity ceased. When the hamsters were revived and their brains were active again, would they remember which way to turn? Yes. Their long-term memories survived the electrical blackout. "I must admit that memories are more of a spiritual than a physical reality," said one memory researcher in commenting on the elusiveness of the memory trace, with tongue only partly in cheek. "When you try to touch them, they turn to mist and disappear" (Loftus & Ketcham, 1994, p. 4).

While cognitive psychologists study our memory "software," neuroscientists are gaining new insights into our memory "hardware"—how and where we physically store information in our brains.

Synaptic Changes

Other neuroscientists are, however, beginning to touch memories by exploring changes within and between single neurons. Memories begin as impulses whizzing through brain circuits, somehow leaving permanent neural traces. Where does the neural change occur? The available clues point to the synapses—the sites where nerve cells communicate with one another through their neurotransmitter messengers (Alkon & others, 1991). Recall from Chapter 3 how experience modifies the brain's neural networks. Given increased activity in a particular pathway, neural interconnections form or strengthen.

Eric Kandel and James Schwartz (1982) observed actual changes in the sending neurons. As we saw in Chapter 6, pairing electric shock with a squirt of water allowed them to classically condition a sea snail to withdraw its gills, much as a shell-shocked soldier jumps at the sound of a snapping twig. By observing the snails' neural connections before and after conditioning, the researchers pinpointed changes. When learning occurs, the snail releases more of the neurotransmitter serotonin at certain synapses, and these synapses become more efficient at transmitting signals.

Increased synaptic efficiency makes for more efficient neural circuits. In experiments, rapidly stimulating certain memory-circuit connections has increased their sensitivity for hours or even weeks to come. (The sending neuron now needs less prompting to release its neurotransmitter, and receptor sites may increase.) This prolonged strengthening of potential neural firing, called **long-term potentiation (LTP)**, provides a neural basis for learning and remembering associations. We know now that drugs that block LTP interfere with learning (Lynch & Staubli, 1991). Mutant mice engineered to lack an enzyme needed for LTP cannot learn their way out of a maze (Silva & others, 1992). And rats given a drug that enhances LTP will learn a maze with half the usual number of mistakes (Service, 1994). These findings raise hopes that researchers may someday discover a drug to enhance human memory, especially for those whose memory is fading.

Passing an electric current through the brain won't disrupt old memories after long-term potentiation has occurred. But the current will wipe out very recent experiences. Such is the experience both of laboratory animals and of

amnesia the loss of memory.

implicit memory retention without conscious recollection (of skills and dispositions). (Also called *nondeclarative memory.*)

explicit memory memory of facts and experiences that one can consciously know and "declare." (Also called *declarative memory.*)

hippocampus a neural center located in the limbic system that helps process explicit memories for storage.

depressed people given electroconvulsive therapy (page 486). A blow to the head can do the same. When football players who have been dazed or momentarily knocked unconscious are interviewed a few minutes later, they typically cannot recall the name of the play during which the incident occurred (Yarnell & Lynch, 1970). Likewise, a boxer knocked out in round 2 may have no memory of the round. (They are like sleepers who cannot remember what they heard just before losing consciousness.) The information in short-term memory before the blow did not have time to consolidate into long-term memory.

Drugs that block neurotransmitters also disrupt information storage (Squire, 1987). For example, alcohol impairs memory formation by disrupting serotonin's messenger activity (Weingartner & others, 1983). The morning after a night of heavy drinking, a person may have trouble remembering the previous evening.

Stress Hormones and Memory

The naturally stimulating hormones that humans and animals produce when excited or stressed make more glucose energy available to fuel brain activity. This hormone surge signals the brain that something important has happened. The arousal sears the events onto the brain. Conversely, people given a drug that blocks stress hormones will later have more trouble remembering the details of an upsetting story (Cahill, 1994). The absence of emotion means weaker memories.

Emotion-triggered hormonal changes help explain why we long remember exciting or shocking events, such as our first kiss, a political assassination, or an earthquake.

Emotion-triggered hormonal changes help explain why we long remember exciting or shocking events, such as our first kiss, a political assassination, or an earthquake. People who have suffered traumatic experiences often relive the experience with vivid flashbacks. And people who experienced the 1989 San Francisco Bay earthquake had perfect recall a year and a half later of where they were and what they were doing (as they had recorded within a day or two). Others' memories for the circumstances under which they *heard* about the quake were prone to errors (Neisser & others, 1991; Palmer & others, 1991). (A second reason for the durability of dramatic experiences is our reliving and rehearsing them.) The point to remember, according to James McGaugh (1994), is that "stronger emotional experiences make for stronger, more reliable memories." After traumatic experiences—a wartime ambush, a house fire, a rape—vivid recollections of the horrific event intrude again and again, as if they were burned in.

Stress hormones and memory When we are greatly aroused, our stress hormones help make memories indelible.

Storing Implicit and Explicit Memories

After a memory-to-be enters the cortex through the senses, it wends its way into the brain's depths. Where it goes depends on the type of information, as dramatically illustrated in the special **amnesic** patients similar to John, whom we met at the beginning of this chapter.

Neurologist Oliver Sacks (1985, pp. 26–27) describes another such patient. Jimmie, a brain-damaged man, had no memories—thus, no sense of elapsed time—beyond his brain damage in 1945. Asked in 1975 to name the U.S. president, he replied, "FDR's dead. Truman's at the helm."

When Jimmie gave his age as 19, Sacks thrust a mirror at him: "Look in the mirror and tell me what you see. Is that a 19-year-old looking out from the mirror?"

Jimmie turned ashen, gripped the chair, cursed, then became frantic: "What's going on? What's happened to me? Is this a nightmare? Am I crazy? Is this a joke?" When his attention was diverted to some children playing baseball, his panic ended, the dreadful mirror swiftly forgotten.

Flipping through a *National Geographic*, Sacks showed Jimmie a photo. "What is this?" he asked.

"It's the moon," Jimmie replied.

"No, it's not," Sacks answered. "It's a picture of the earth taken from the moon."

"Doc, you're kidding? Someone would've had to get a camera up there!"

"Naturally."

"Hell! You're joking—how the hell would you do that?" Jimmie's wonder was that of a bright young man from 50 years ago reacting with amazement to his travel back to the future.

We seem to have two memory systems operating in tandem. Whatever has destroyed the amnesics' conscious recall has not destroyed their unconscious capacity for learning.

Careful testing of these unique people reveals something even stranger: Although incapable of recalling new facts or anything they have recently done, Jimmie and other similarly amnesic people can learn. They can be classically conditioned. Shown hard-to-find figures in pictures (where's Waldo?), they can quickly spot them again later. They can learn to read mirror-image writing or do a jigsaw puzzle, and they have even been taught complicated job skills (Schacter, 1992, 1996; Squire, 1987). *They do all these things with absolutely no memory of having learned them.*

Consider what happens when such patients have learned to solve a Tower of Hanoi puzzle, which requires moving rings from one pole to another until they are stacked in order of size. Amnesia victims will deny having seen the puzzle before, insist it is silly for them to try, and then, like practiced experts, proceed to solve it.

These curious findings make it hard to argue that memory is a single, unified system. Instead, we seem to have two memory systems operating in tandem (**Figure 7.14**). Whatever has destroyed the amnesics' conscious recall has not destroyed their unconscious capacity for learning. They can learn *how* to do something—called **implicit memory** (*nondeclarative memory*). But they cannot know and declare *that* they know—called **explicit memory** (*declarative memory*). Having read a story once, they will read it faster a second time, showing implicit memory. But there will be no explicit memory, for they cannot recall having seen the story before. Having played golf on a new course, they will forget it completely, yet their game will improve with experience on the course. If repeatedly shown the word *perfume*, they would not recall having seen it. But if asked the first word that comes to mind in response to the letters *per*, they surprise themselves by readily displaying their learning. Strangely, they retain their past without recalling it.

Types of long-term memories
- Explicit (declarative) — With conscious recall
  - Facts—general knowledge ("semantic memory")
  - Personally experienced events ("episodic memory")
- Implicit (nondeclarative) — Without conscious recall
  - Skills—motor and cognitive
  - Dispositions—classical and operant conditioning effects

Figure 7.14 Memory subsystems We process and store our explicit and implicit memories separately. Thus, one may lose explicit memory (becoming amnesic), yet display implicit memory for material one cannot consciously recall.

The two-track memory system reinforces an important principle introduced in Chapter 4's description of parallel processing: Mental feats such as vision, thinking, and memory may seem to be single abilities, but they are not. Rather, we split information into different components for separate and simultaneous processing.

The Hippocampus

These remarkable patients provoke our wondering: Do our explicit and implicit memory systems involve separate brain regions? Scans of the brain in action, and autopsies of amnesic patients, reveal that new explicit memories of names, images, and events are layed down via a limbic system structure called the **hippocampus**. When people recall words (using explicit memory) the

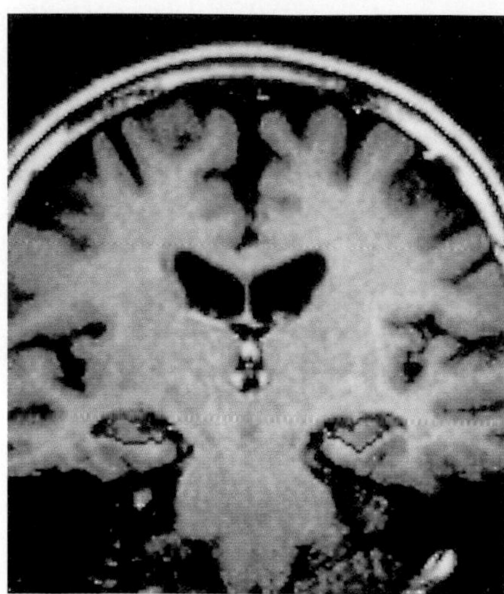

Figure 7.15 The hippocampus Explicit memories for facts and episodes are processed in the hippocampus (circled red in the MRI scan) and fed to other brain regions for storage.

hippocampus lights up on a PET scan (Squire, 1992) (Figure 7.15). Chickadees and other birds (recall the Clark's Nutcracker, page 243) can store food in hundreds of places and return to these unmarked caches months later, but not if their hippocampus has been removed (Sherry & Vaccarino, 1989). Like the cortex, the hippocampus is lateralized, and damage to the left and right sides seems to produce different results. Patients with left hippocampus damage have trouble remembering verbal information, but they have no trouble recalling visual designs and locations. Those with right hippocampus damage have the reverse problem (Schacter, 1996). The hippocampus seems to act as a temporary storage and play-back system. It reactivates neurons that fired when we experienced an event, as if helping the brain strengthen connections among them (Skaggs & McNaughton, 1996).

Our neural librarian then assigns different information to different regions. Brain scans reveal that, once stored, our mental encores of past experience activate various parts of the frontal and temporal lobes (Fink & others, 1996; Gabrieli & others, 1996; Markowitsch, 1995). Calling up a telephone number and holding it in working memory activates a region of the left frontal cortex; recall of a birthday scene would more likely activate the right hemisphere.

"[Brain scanning] technologies are revolutionizing the study of the brain and mind in the same way that the telescope revolutionized the study of the heavens."

Endel Tulving (1996)

The Cerebellum

Although your hippocampus is a temporary processing site for your explicit memories, you could lose it and still lay down memories for skills and conditioned associations. Hoping to locate such implicit memories, psychologist Richard Thompson and his fellow sleuths David Krupa and Judith Thompson studied how a rabbit's brain learns to associate a tone with an impending air puff in the eye (and thus to blink in anticipation of the puff). First, they traced the pathway connecting the brain's reception of the tone with the blink response. They discovered that it runs to the brainstem through a part of the cerebellum (at the back of the head), and that if they cut this pathway, the learned response would be lost. That was like cutting the cords to your stereo speakers, which would confirm the cord's part in the electronic path but might still leave you wondering where the music is stored. Their next step was to administer a drug during the rabbits' eye-blink training, temporarily deadening different parts of the neural pathway. This pinpointed the implicit memory—in the cerebellum. The rabbits failed to display the learned response only when the cerebellum was deactivated during training (Krupa & others, 1993). Human patients with a damaged cerebellum are likewise incapable of eye-blink conditioning (Daum & Schugens, 1996).

The dual explicit-implicit memory system helps explain infantile amnesia: The reactions and skills we learned during infancy reach far into our future, yet as adults we recall nothing (explicitly) of our first three years. Our conscious minds are blank, not only because we index so much of our explicit memory by words that nonspeaking children have not learned, but also because the hippocampus is one of the last brain structures to mature.

recall a measure of memory in which the person must retrieve information learned earlier, as on a fill-in-the-blank test.

recognition a measure of memory in which the person need only identify items previously learned, as on a multiple-choice test.

relearning a memory measure that assesses the amount of time saved when learning material for a second time.

REHEARSE IT!

9. Sensory information is initially recorded in our sensory memory. This memory may be visual (__________ memory) or auditory (__________ memory).
   a. implicit; explicit
   b. iconic; echoic
   c. declarative; nondeclarative
   d. long-term; short-term

10. Our capacity for storing long-term memories is essentially limitless. However, our short-term memory for new information is limited. When confronted with a list of novel items, most people can immediately recall
    a. only the first items on the list.
    b. a series of about 20 items.
    c. a series of about 7 items.
    d. only meaningful items.

11. The average adult probably has about a billion bits of information in long-term memory, which has a capacity perhaps a thousand to a million times greater than that. Evidence suggests that the best way to learn and remember new information is to
    a. undergo hypnosis.
    b. undergo electrical stimulation of the motor cortex.
    c. systematically forget or discard old memories.
    d. relate new information to old.

12. Ebbinghaus found that retention of novel information such as nonsense syllables drops off quickly; 3 days after such a learning session, we have forgotten much of what we learned. Ebbinghaus's "forgetting curve" shows that as time goes on, our retention of the nonsense syllables tends to
    a. increase slightly.
    b. decrease noticeably.
    c. decrease greatly.
    d. level out.

13. Researchers have found that long-term potentiation (LTP) provides a neural basis for learning and memory. LTP refers to
    a. emotion-triggered hormonal changes.
    b. the role of the hippocampus in processing explicit memories.
    c. an increase in a synapse's firing potential after brief, rapid stimulation.
    d. aging people's potential for learning.

14. An amnesic patient who has suffered damage to the hippocampus typically has difficulties in learning new facts and recalling recent events. However, the person may well be able to recall the more distant past and certain well-learned skills, such as how to ride a bicycle or hem a dress. Memories of skills are
    a. explicit memories.
    b. implicit memories.
    c. iconic memories.
    d. echoic memories.

15. The physical basis of memory—how and where memories are physically stored in the brain—is not yet well understood. However, research suggests that the hippocampus, a neural center in the limbic system of the brain, plays an important role. The hippocampus may function as
    a. a way station between short- and long-term explicit memories.
    b. a computer's hard disk.
    c. the cortex.
    d. a processing center for implicit memories.

Retrieval: Getting Information Out

9. *How do we get information out of memory?*

To most people, memory is **recall**, the ability to retrieve information not in conscious awareness. To a psychologist, memory is any sign that something learned has been retained. So *recognizing* or more quickly *relearning* information also indicates memory.

Long after you cannot recall most of the people in your high school graduating class, you may still be able to recognize their yearbook pictures from a photographic lineup and pick their names from a list of names. Harry Bahrick and his colleagues (1975) reported that people who graduated 25 years earlier could not *recall* many of their old classmates, but they could *recognize* 90 percent of their pictures and names.

Remembering things past Even if Madonna and Paul Newman had not become famous, their high school classmates would most likely still recognize their yearbook photos.

Relearning speed can reveal memory. If you once learned something and then forgot it, you probably will relearn it more quickly than when you learned it originally. When you study for a final exam or resurrect a language used in early childhood, the relearning is easier. Tests of **recognition** and of time spent **relearning** reveal that we remember more than we can recall. Although older people often find it increasingly difficult to *recall* names and information, they have fewer difficulties *recognizing* such (see page 113).

The speed and vastness of our recognition memory dwarfs any librarian's ability to call up information. "Is your friend wearing a new or an old outfit?"

Multiple-choice questions test our
a. recall.
b. recognition.
c. relearning.
Fill-in-the-blank questions test our ________.
(See page 253.)

"Old." "Is this seconds-long movie clip from a film you've ever seen?" "Yes." "Have you ever before seen this person—this minor variation on the same old human features (two eyes, one nose, and so on)?" "No." Before the mouth can form our answer to any of millions of such questions, the mind knows, and knows that it knows.

Retrieval Cues

To retrieve a fact from a library, you need a way to access it. In recognition tests, retrieval cues (such as photographs) provide reminders of information (classmates' names) we could not otherwise recall. Retrieval cues also guide us to where to look. If you want to know what the pyramid on the back of an American dollar signifies, you might look in *Collier's Encyclopedia* under "dollar," "currency," or "money." But your efforts would be futile. To get the information you want, you would have to look under "Great Seal of the United States" (Hayes, 1981). Like information stored in encyclopedias, memories are inaccessible unless we have the right cues for retrieving them. Do you recall the gist of the second sentence I asked you to remember (on page 236)? If not, does the word *shark* help? Experiments show that *shark* more readily retrieves the image you stored than does the sentence's actual word, *fish* (Anderson & others, 1976).

Seeing the word *rabbit* → Activates concept → Primes spelling the spoken word *hair/hare* as *h-a-r-e*

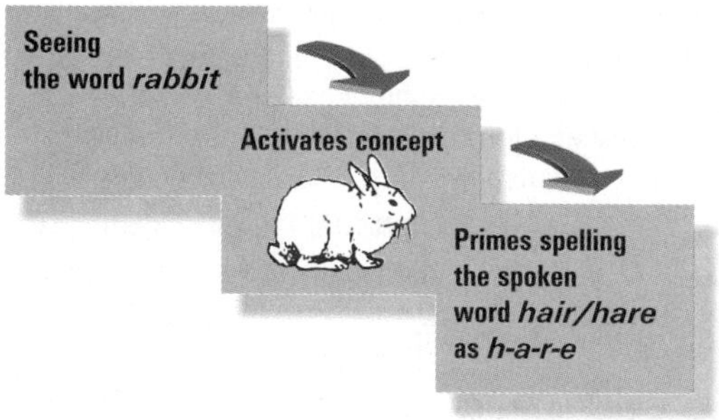

Figure 7.16 Priming: Awakening associations After seeing or hearing *rabbit*, we are later more likely to spell the spoken word *hair/hare* as *h-a-r-e*. The spreading of associations unconsciously activates related associations. This phenomenon is called priming. (Adapted from Bower, 1986)

You can think of a memory as held in storage by a web of associations. To retrieve a specific memory, you first need to identify one of the strands that leads to it, a process called **priming**. Philosopher-psychologist William James referred to priming as the "wakening of associations." Often our associations are activated, or primed, without our awareness. As Figure 7.16 indicates, seeing or hearing the word *rabbit* primes associations with *hare* even though we may not recall having seen or heard *rabbit*.

Priming has been called "memory without remembering." If, walking down a hallway, you see a missing-child poster, you will then be more likely to interpret an ambiguous adult-child interaction as a possible kidnapping (James, 1986). Although you don't consciously remember the poster, it primes your interpretation. (As we saw in Chapter 4, even subliminal stimuli can briefly prime responses to later stimuli.)

Mnemonic devices provide us with handy retrieval cues: ROY G. BIV; HOMES; bun, shoe, tree.

Retrieval cues often prime our memories for earlier experiences. The best retrieval cues come from the associations formed at the time we encode a memory. Before the Watergate hearings, John Dean refreshed his memory "by going through every single newspaper article outlining what had happened and then placing myself and what I had done in a given sequence in time" (Neisser, 1981).

Context Effects

It does help to put yourself back in the context where you experienced something. Duncan Godden and Alan Baddeley (1975) discovered this by having scuba divers listen to a list of words in two different settings, either 10 feet underwater or sitting on the beach. As Figure Figure 7.17 illustrates, the divers recalled more words when they were retested in the same place.

You have probably experienced similar context effects. Returning to where you once lived or to the school you once attended may flood you with retrieval cues and memories. Taking an exam in the same room where you are taught may help a little. In several experiments, Carolyn Rovee-Collier (1993) found that a familiar context activates memories even in 3-month-olds. After learning that kicking would move a crib mobile (via a connecting ribbon from the ankle), the infants kicked more when again tested in the same crib with the same bumper.

priming the activation, often unconsciously, of particular associations in memory.

déjà vu that eerie sense that "I've experienced this before." Cues from the current situation may subconsciously trigger retrieval of an earlier experience.

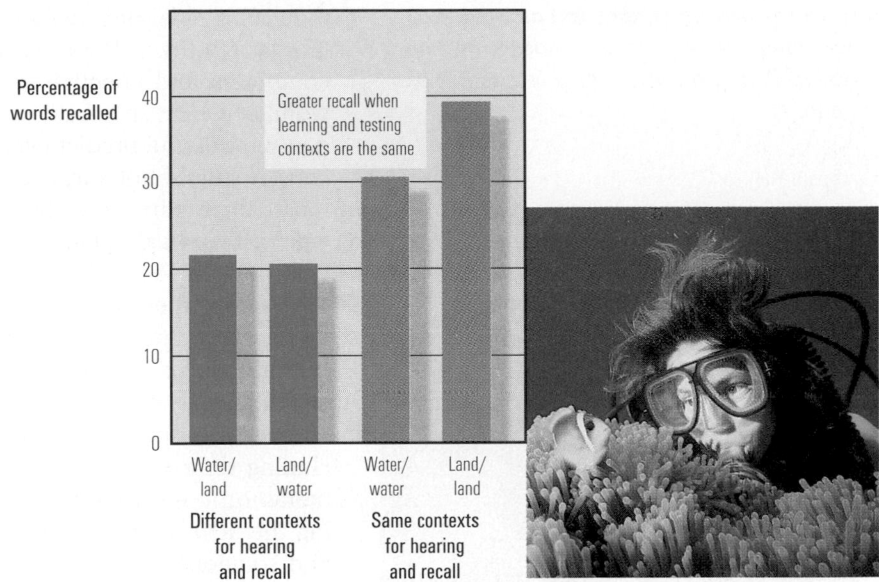

Figure 7.17 The effects of context on memory Words heard underwater are best recalled underwater; words heard on land are best recalled on land. (Adapted from Godden & Baddeley, 1975)

Sometimes, being in a context similar to one we have been in before may trigger the experience of **déjà vu** (French for "already seen")—that eerie sense that "I've been in this exact situation before." People often wonder, "How could I recognize a situation that I'm experiencing for the first time?" Those who suppose something paranormal is occurring may think of reincarnation ("I must have experienced this in a previous life") or precognition ("I viewed this scene in my mind before experiencing it"). If we pose the question differently ("Why do I feel as if I recognize this situation?"), we can see how our memory system might produce déjà vu (Alcock, 1981). If we have previously been in a similar situation, the current situation may be loaded with cues that unconsciously retrieve the earlier experience. Thus, if in such a context you see a stranger who looks and walks like one of your friends, the similarity may give rise to an eerie feeling of recognition. Because the feeling conflicts with your knowing that the person is a stranger, you may think, "I've seen that person in this situation before."

CALLAHAN

"I wonder if you'd mind giving me directions. I've never been sober in this part of town before."

Moods and Memories

Associated words, events, and contexts are not the only retrieval cues. Events in the past may have aroused a specific emotion, which later can prime us to recall its associated events. Cognitive psychologist Gordon Bower (1983) explained it this way: "A specific emotional state is like a specific room in a library into which the subject places memory records, and he can most easily retrieve those records by returning to that same room or emotional state." What we learn in one state—be it joyful or sad, drunk or sober—is sometimes more easily recalled when we are again in the same state, a subtle phenomenon called *state-dependent memory*. What is learned when depressed, high, or drunk is not recalled well in *any* state (depression and certain drugs interfere with encoding), but it's recalled slightly better when again drunk, high, or depressed. Someone who hides money when drunk may forget the location until drunk again.

More striking is the way our memories are biased by our moods (Eich, 1995; Ellis & Ashbrook, 1989; Matt & others, 1992). We seem to associate good or bad events with their accompanying emotions. Thus, the emotions become retrieval cues; when again feeling good or bad, we more easily recall associated good or bad times. If people are put in a buoyant mood—whether under hypnosis or just by the day's events (a World Cup soccer victory for the Ger-

"When a feeling was there, they felt as if it would never go; when it was gone, they felt as if it had never been; when it returned, they felt as if it had never gone."

George MacDonald
What's Mine's Mine
1886

Mood and memory Elated, we remember other happy times. Mood serves as a retrieval cue, activating other memories tinged with the same emotion. These memories help sustain the current mood.

man subjects of one study)—they recall the world through rose-colored glasses (Forgas & others, 1984; Schwarz & others, 1987). They judge themselves to be competent and effective, other people to be benevolent, life in general to be wonderful. Put in a bad mood by negative events, the very same people suddenly recall and predict everything more negatively.

So it should not surprise us that in some studies *currently* depressed people recall their parents as having been rejecting, punitive, and guilt-promoting, whereas *formerly* depressed people describe their parents much as do those who have never suffered depression (Lewinsohn & Rosenbaum, 1987; Lewis, 1992). Our memories are somewhat **mood-congruent**. Being depressed sours memories by priming negative associations, which we use to explain our current mood. No wonder Robert Bornstein and others (1991) report that adolescents' ratings of parental warmth give little clue to how the same adolescents will rate their parents six weeks later. When teenagers are down, their world, including their parents, seems inhuman; as their mood brightens, their parents metamorphose from devils into angels. (The phenomenon is worth remembering the next time you hear someone in a bad mood recalling bitter memories, and someone giddy with love recalling only good times.) You and I may nod our heads knowingly. Yet, in a good or bad mood, we persist in attributing to reality our own changing judgments and memories.

Moods also influence how we *interpret* other people's behavior. In a bad mood we read someone's look as a glare; in a good mood we encode the same look as interest. How we perceive the world depends on our mood. Passions exaggerate.

Your mood's effect on encoding and retrieval helps explain why moods persist. When happy, you recall happy events, which helps prolong the good mood. When depressed, you recall sad events, which in turn darkens your interpretations of current events. As we will see in Chapter 12, this process maintains depression's vicious cycle.

Forgetting as Retrieval Failure

10. *What causes retrieval failure?*

We have seen that forgetting occurs when we fail to encode information and when our stored memories decay. Forgotten events are like books you can't find in your library—some because you never acquired them, others because they were discarded.

There is a third possibility: Even if the book is stored and available, it may be inaccessible. Perhaps you don't have the information needed to look it up and retrieve it. Information sometimes gets into our brain and, though we know it is there, we cannot get it out (Figure 7.18). A person's name may lie poised on the tip of the tongue, waiting to be retrieved. When people who cannot recall information get retrieval cues ("It begins with an *M*"), they often remember what they could not recall. Retrieval problems lie behind the occasional memory failures of older adults. (As Chapter 3 noted, older people tend to recall

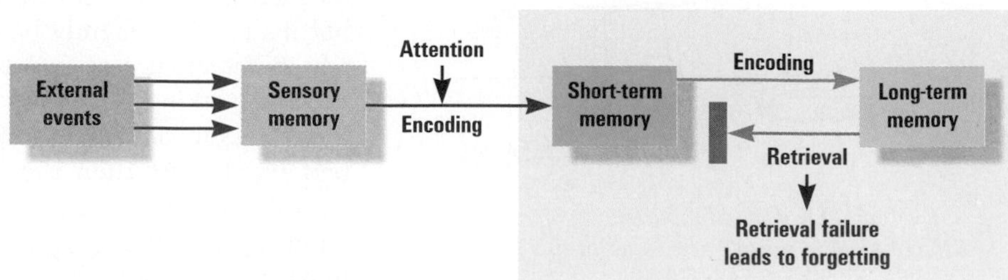

Figure 7.18 **Retrieval failure** Forgetting can result from failure to retrieve information from long-term memory.

mood-congruent memory the tendency to recall experiences that are consistent with one's current good or bad mood.

proactive interference the disruptive effect of prior learning on the recall of new information.

retroactive interference the disruptive effect of new learning on the recall of old information.

less than younger adults do, but they usually remember as well as younger people when given reminders or a recognition test.)

Interference

Learning some items may interfere with retrieving others, especially when the items are similar. If someone gives you a phone number to remember, you may be able to recall it later. But if two more people give you their numbers, each successive number will be more difficult to recall. Such **proactive** (*forward-acting*) **interference** occurs when something you learned earlier disrupts recall of something you experience later. As you collect more and more information, your mental attic never fills, but it certainly gets cluttered.

For example, after buying a new combination lock or receiving a new phone number, you may find the old number sequence interfering with the new one. Benton Underwood (1957) found that people who learn different lists of words on successive days have more and more difficulty remembering each new list the next day. This proactive interference explains why Ebbinghaus, after memorizing countless lists of nonsense syllables during his career, could remember only about one-fourth of a new list of syllables on the day after he learned it—far fewer than you as a novice could remember after learning a single list.

Retroactive (*backward-acting*) **interference** occurs when new information makes it harder to recall something you learned earlier (Figure 7.19). For example, the learning of new students' names typically interferes with a professor's recall of names learned in previous classes.

Answers to questions on page 250: Multiple-choice questions test recognition. Fill-in-the-blank questions test recall.

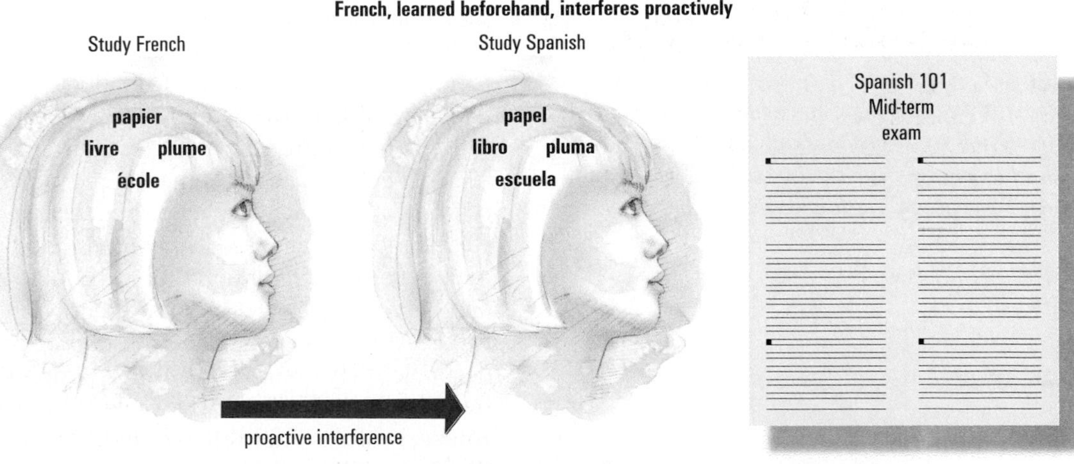

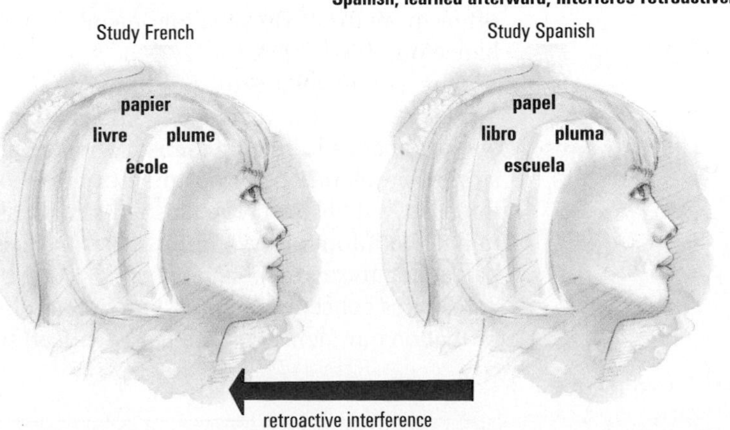

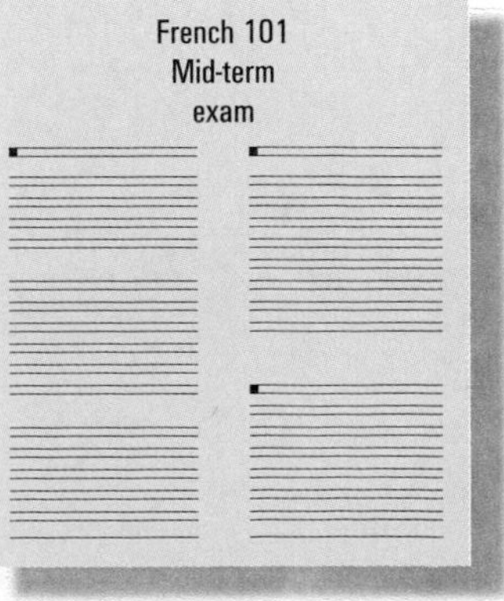

Figure 7.19 **Proactive and retroactive interference**

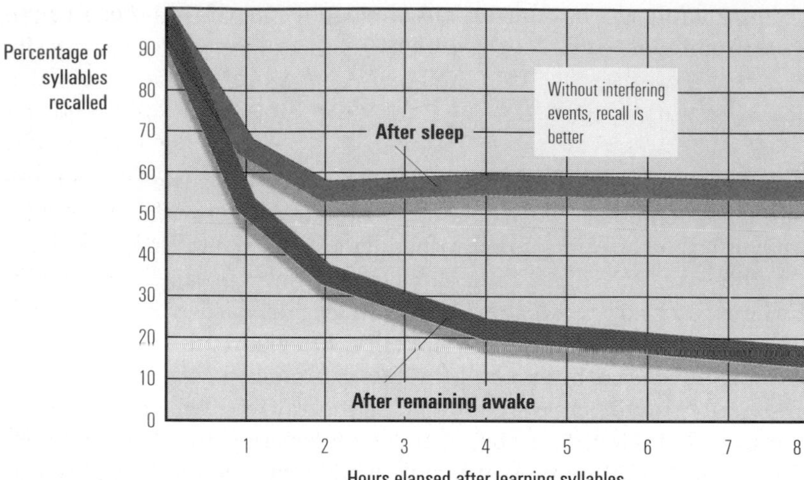

Figure 7.20 Retroactive interference More forgetting occurred when a person stayed awake and experienced other new material. (From Jenkins & Dallenbach, 1924)

You can minimize retroactive interference by reducing the number of interfering events—say, by going to sleep shortly after learning new information. This is what John Jenkins and Karl Dallenbach (1924) found in a classic experiment. Day after day, two people each learned some nonsense syllables, then tried to recall them after up to 8 hours of being awake or asleep at night. As Figure 7.20 shows, forgetting occurred more rapidly after being awake and involved with other activities. The investigators surmised that "forgetting is not so much a matter of the decay of old impressions and associations as it is a matter of interference, inhibition, or obliteration of the old by the new" (1924, p. 612). Later experiments have confirmed that the hour before a night's sleep (but not the minute before sleep) is a good time to commit information to memory (Fowler & others, 1973).

Although interference is an important cause of forgetting, we should not overstate the point. Sometimes old information facilitates our learning of new information. Knowledge of Latin may help us to learn French—a phenomenon called *positive transfer*. It's when the old and new information compete with each other that interference occurs.

Motivated Forgetting

The huge cookie jar in our kitchen was jammed with freshly baked chocolate chip cookies. Still more spread across the cooling racks on the counter. Twenty-four hours later, not a crumb was left. Who had taken them? My wife, three children, and I were the only people in the house during that time. So while memories were still fresh, I conducted a little memory test. Andy acknowledged wolfing down as many as 20. Peter admitted eating 15. Laura guessed that she had stuffed her then-6-year-old body with 15 cookies. My wife, Carol, recalled eating 6, and I remembered consuming 15 and taking 18 more to the office. Collectively, we sheepishly accepted responsibility for 89 cookies. Still, we had not come close; 160 cookies had been baked.

"[It is] necessary to remember that events happened in the desired manner. And if it is necessary to rearrange one's memories . . . then it is necessary to forget that one has done so. The trick of doing this can be learned like any other mental technique. . . . It is called doublethink."

George Orwell
Nineteen Eighty-Four
1948

In experiments that parallel the cookie-memory phenomenon, Michael Ross and his colleagues (1981) found that people unknowingly revise their own histories. After Ross persuaded a group of people that frequent tooth brushing is desirable, they (more than other people) recalled having frequently brushed their teeth in the last two weeks. Having taken a highly touted study skills course, students later inflated their estimates of self-improvement. By *de*flating their evaluations of their previous study habits they convinced themselves that they had really benefited (Conway & Ross, 1984). To remember our past is often to revise it. By recalling events in a desired manner we protect and enhance our self-images.

Why do our memories fail us? Why did my family and I not encode, store, and retrieve all the instances of our cookie-eating? As Figure 7.21 reminds us, we automatically encode sensory information in amazing detail. So was it a storage problem? Might our memories of cookies, like Ebbinghaus's memory of nonsense syllables, have vanished almost as fast as the cookies themselves? Or might the information still be intact but irretrievable because it would be embarrassing to remember?[1]

With his concept of **repression**, Sigmund Freud proposed that with painful information our memory systems are indeed self-censoring. To protect our self-con-

repression in psychoanalytic theory, the basic defense mechanism that banishes anxiety-arousing thoughts, feelings, and memories from consciousness.

[1]One of my cookie-scarfing sons, on reading this in his father's textbook years later, confessed that he also had fibbed a little.

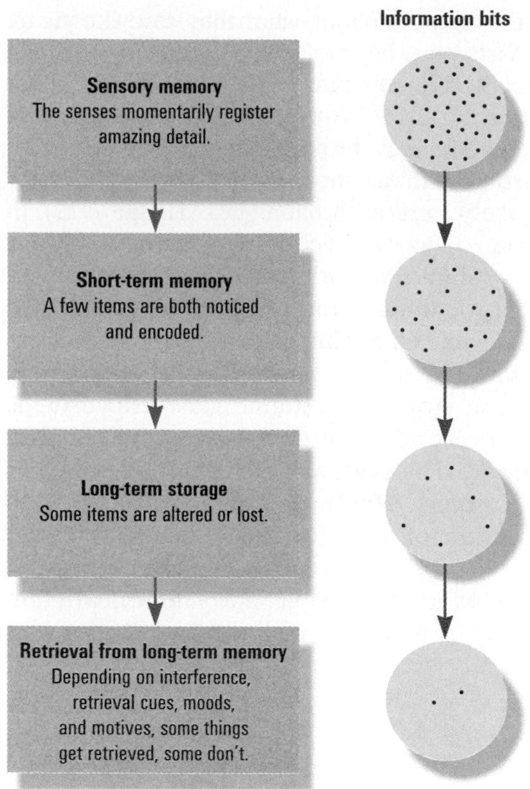

Figure 7.21 When do we forget? Forgetting can occur at any memory stage. As we process information, we filter, alter, or lose much of it.

cepts and to minimize anxiety, we supposedly repress painful memories. But the submerged memory still lingers, said Freud, and with patience and effort may be retrieved during therapy or by some later cue. One reported case involved a woman with an intense, unexplained fear of running water. An aunt solved the mystery one day by whispering, "I have never told." The words relit a blown-out candle in the mind, cuing the woman's memory of an incident when, as a disobedient young child, she wandered away from a family picnic and became trapped under a waterfall—until being rescued by her aunt, who promised not to tell her parents (Kihlstrom, 1990). Such stories have fed the now-common belief, shared by 9 in 10 university students, that "memories for painful experiences are sometimes pushed into the unconsciousness" (Brown & others, 1996). Repression is central to Freud's psychology and has been part of psychology's lore. Therapists assume it. People believe it. Yet increasing numbers of memory researchers think repression rarely, if ever, occurs. As we will see, people do forget negative (and positive) experiences. Do they repress them? Stay tuned.

Memory Construction

11. *How accurate are our memories?*

Picture yourself having this pleasant experience:

> You enter a restaurant and are seated at a table with a white tablecloth. You study the menu. You tell the waiter that you want prime rib, medium rare, a baked potato with sour cream, and a salad with blue cheese dressing. You also order some red wine from the wine list. A few minutes later the waiter returns with your salad. Later he brings the rest of the meal, which you enjoy, except that the prime rib is a bit overdone.

Were I immediately to quiz you on this paragraph (from Hyde, 1983), you could surely retrieve considerable detail. For example, without looking back, answer the following questions:

1. What kind of salad dressing did you order?
2. Was the tablecloth red checked?
3. What did you order to drink?
4. Did the waiter give you a menu?

You were probably able to recall exactly what you ordered, and maybe even the color of the tablecloth. Does retrieval therefore consist merely of "reading" the information stored in our brain's library? We do have an enormous capacity for storing and reproducing the incidental details of our daily experience. But we often construct our memories as we encode them, and we may also alter our memories as we withdraw them from the memory bank. Like a scientist who infers a dinosaur's appearance from its remains, we infer our past from stored information plus what we now assume. Did the waiter give you a menu? Not in the paragraph given. Nevertheless, many people answer yes. By filtering information and filling in missing pieces, our schemas for restaurants direct our memory construction.

Like a scientist who infers a dinosaur's appearance from its remains, we infer our past from stored information plus what we now assume.

Misinformation and Imagination Effects

In more than 200 experiments, involving more than 20,000 people, Elizabeth Loftus has shown how eyewitnesses similarly reconstruct their memories when questioned. In one experiment with John Palmer, Loftus showed a film of a

Accident

Leading question:
"About how fast were the cars going when they *smashed* into each other?"

Memory construction

Figure 7.22 **Memory construction** When people who saw the film of a car accident were asked a leading question, they recalled a more serious accident than they had witnessed. (From Loftus, 1979)

traffic accident and then quizzed the viewers about what they saw (Loftus & Palmer, 1974). Those asked, "How fast were the cars going when they *smashed* into each other?" gave higher speed estimates than those asked, "How fast were the cars going when they *hit* each other?" A week later, the researchers asked the viewers if they recalled seeing any broken glass. Compared with those who had been asked the question with *hit*, those asked the question with *smashed* were more than twice as likely to recall broken glass (Figure 7.22). In fact, the film showed no broken glass.

In many follow-up experiments around the world, people have witnessed an event, received or not received misleading information about it, and then taken a memory test. The repeated result is a **misinformation effect**: After exposure to subtle misinformation, many people misremember. They have misrecalled a yield (give way) sign as a stop sign, hammers as screwdrivers, Coke cans as peanut cans, *Vogue* magazine as *Mademoiselle*, "Dr. Henderson" as "Dr. Davidson," breakfast cereal as eggs, and a clean-shaven man as a man with a mustache (Loftus & others, 1992). As a memory fades with time following an event, the injection of misinformation becomes easier (Loftus, 1992).

So unwitting is the misinformation effect that people later find it nearly impossible to discriminate between their memories of real and suggested events (Schooler & others, 1986). This difficulty was strikingly true among those who three years later misrecalled their whereabouts on hearing of the space shuttle *Challenger*'s explosion (Neisser & Harsch, 1992). When shown their own handwritten accounts from the day after, many were surprised. Some were so sure of their false memories that they insisted their original version must have been flawed.

As people recount an experience, they fill in their memory gaps with plausible guesses and assumptions. After more retellings, they often recall these guessed details, now absorbed into their memories, as if they actually observed them (Roediger & others, 1993). Others' vivid retellings may also implant false memories.

"Memory is insubstantial. Things keep replacing it. Your batch of snapshots will both fix and ruin your memory. . . . You can't remember anything from your trip except the wretched collection of snapshots."

Annie Dillard
"To Fashion a Text"
1988

Even repeatedly *imagining* nonexistent events can create false memories. In one experiment by Maryanne Garry and others (1996), university students noted whether they had experienced certain childhood events, such as breaking a window with their hand. Two weeks later, half were asked to imagine themselves experiencing four of these events—for example, running, tripping, falling, and cutting their hand as it crashed through a window. After vividly imagining the fictional event, one-fourth of them became more likely to believe that such may actually have happened during their childhood.

In similar experiments, Ira Hyman and his co-workers (1995, 1996) invited Western Washington University students to recall actual childhood events (reported to the researchers by their parents), along with a suggested false event, such as spilling a punch bowl at a wedding. By a third interview (after encouragement to think about the events between interviews), one-fourth of the students had constructed false memories. They were asked, for example, to recall something that happened "when you were six years old and you were attending a wedding." One student recalled, "It was an outdoor wedding and I think we were running around and knocked something over like the punch bowl or something and made a big mess and of course got yelled at for it." Elizabeth Loftus and Jacqueline Pickrell (1995) confirmed this result. When they asked students to recall one false and three actual childhood events, one-fourth remembered the suggested nonevent. The take-home point: Given time, the mind's search for a fact may create a fiction.

Given time, the mind's search for a fact may create a fiction.

misinformation effect incorporating misleading information into one's memory of an event.

source amnesia attributing to the wrong source an event that we experienced, heard about, read about, or imagined. (Also called *source misattribution.*) Source amnesia, along with the misinformation effect, is at the heart of many false memories.

Psychologists are not immune to memory construction:

- Frederick Bartlett, a pioneer in studies of memory construction, recalled two decades later the "brilliant afternoon in May 1913" when the Cambridge University experimental psychology lab was opened. His colleague, Sir Godfrey Thompson, remembered that it poured rain (Ross, 1996).
- Another memory researcher, Ulric Neisser (1982), vividly recalls hearing the announcement of the bombing of Pearl Harbor as an interruption to a baseball game broadcast. Years later he realized that American baseball games aren't played in December, when the bombing occurred. Although he knows the memory is false, he still "recalls" the incident.
- The psychologist Jean Piaget was startled as an adult to learn that his vivid, detailed memory of his nursemaid's thwarting his kidnapping was utterly false. Piaget apparently constructed the memory from the many retellings of the story he had heard (later confessed by the nursemaid to have been false).

"Memory isn't like reading a book; it's more like writing a book from fragmentary notes."

Psychologist John F. Kihlstrom (1994)

Memory construction helps explain why John Dean's recollections of the Watergate conversations were a mixture of real and imagined events. It explains why "hypnotically refreshed" memories of crimes so easily incorporate errors, some of which originate with the hypnotist's leading questions. ("Did you hear loud noises?") It explains why dating partners who fall in love *over*estimate their first impressions of one another, while those who break up *under*estimate their earlier liking (McFarland & Ross, 1987). It also explains why people who are asked how they felt 10 years ago about marijuana or gender issues recall attitudes closer to their current views than those they actually reported a decade earlier (Markus, 1986).

Source Amnesia

Australian psychologist Donald Thompson found his own work on memory distortion haunting him when authorities brought him in for questioning about a rape. Although he was a near-perfect match to the victim's memory of the rapist, he had an airtight alibi. Just before the rape occurred Thompson was being interviewed on live television, and he could not possibly have made it to the crime scene. Then it came to light that the victim had been watching the interview—ironically about face recognition—and had experienced **source amnesia** (also called *source misattribution)*, confusing her memories of Thompson and the rapist (Schacter, 1996).

DOONESBURY

When we encode memories, we distribute different aspects of them to different parts of our brains. One of the frailest parts of a memory is its source. Thus, we may recognize someone but have no idea where we have seen the person. We retain the image but not the context in which we acquired it. Note that Piaget remembered, but attributed his memory to the wrong source (to his own experience rather than to his nursemaid's stories).

Debra Poole and Stephen Lindsay (1995) replicated Piaget's source amnesia by having preschoolers interact with "Mr. Science," who engaged them in demonstrations such as blowing up a balloon with baking soda and vinegar. Three months later, their parents on three successive days read them a story about themselves and Mr. Science. The stories described some things they had experienced and some they had not. When asked by a new interviewer what Mr. Science had done with them, 4 in 10 children spontaneously recalled Mr. Science doing things that were only mentioned in the story.

Authors and songwriters sometimes suffer source amnesia. They think an idea came from their own creative imagination, when in fact they are unintentionally adopting something they earlier read or heard.

Ronald Reagan's occasional source misattributions illustrated how fiction can be remembered as fact. During his three U.S. presidential campaigns, he told and retold a story of heroic sacrifice. A World War II gunner was terrified when his plane was hit by anti-aircraft fire and he could not eject from his seat. "Never mind, son," said his commander, "we'll ride it down together." With misty eyes, Reagan would conclude by telling how the brave commander received the Congressional Medal of Honor posthumously. A curious journalist later checked the 434 World War II Congressional Medal recipients. Finding no similar story, he kept digging until he found the episode—in a 1944 movie, *A Wing and a Prayer* (Loftus & Ketcham, 1994).

Children's Eyewitness Recall

Because memory is reconstruction as well as reproduction, we cannot be sure whether a memory is real by how real it feels. Unreal memories feel like real memories. If memories can be sincere, yet so sincerely wrong, might children's recollections of sexual abuse err? Who is most often victimized—abused children whose recollections are disbelieved or those falsely accused whose reputations are ruined?

At issue is the credibility of children's reports. As we have seen, interviewers who ask leading questions can plant false memories of a story they expect to hear. We also know that children sometimes are credible eyewitnesses in criminal cases but that they tend to be suggestible. In 15 of 18 studies, preschoolers were more suggestible than were older children or adults. In one study of nearly 2000 people who had watched a film clip while visiting a San Francisco science museum, younger children were especially susceptible to the misinformation effect (Loftus & others, 1992). But the belief that children routinely confuse reality with fantasy is not supported by research. If questioned about their experiences in words they understand, children often freely recall what happened and who did it (Goodman & others, 1990). Children are especially credible when involved adults have not talked with them prior to the interview and when their disclosure is made in a first interview with a neutral person who asks nonleading questions.

Because memory is reconstruction as well as reproduction, we cannot be sure whether a memory is real by how real it feels. Unreal memories feel like real memories.

As a father, Stephen Ceci (1993) thinks "it would be truly awful to ever lose sight of the enormity of child abuse." Yet Ceci and Maggie Bruck's (1993, 1995) studies have sensitized them to children's suggestibility. In one study, they asked 3-year-olds to show on anatomically correct dolls where a pediatrician had touched them. Fifty-five percent of the children who had not received genital examinations showed either genital or anal touching.

In another study, Ceci and Bruck had a child choose a card from a deck of possible happenings and an adult then read from the card. For example, "Think real hard, and tell me if this ever happened to you. Can you remember going to the hospital with the mousetrap on your finger?" After 10 weekly interviews, with the same adult repeatedly asking children to think about several real and fictitious events, a new adult asked the same question. The stunning result: 58 percent of preschoolers produced false (often vivid) stories regarding one or more events they had never experienced. Here is one from a boy who initially had denied the mousetrap incident (Ceci & others, 1994):

> My brother Colin was trying to get Blowtorch [an action figure] from me, and I wouldn't let him take it from me, so he pushed me into the wood pile where the mousetrap was. And then my finger got caught in it. And then we went to the hospital, and my mommy, daddy, and Colin drove me there, to the hospital in our van, because it was far away. And the doctor put a bandage on this finger.

"[The] research leads me to worry about the possibility of false allegations. It is not a tribute to one's scientific integrity to walk down the middle of the road if the data are more to one side."

Stephen Ceci (1993)

Given such detailed stories, professional psychologists who specialize in interviewing children were often fooled. They could not reliably separate real from false memories. Nor could the children themselves. The above child, reminded that his parents had several times told him that the mousetrap incident never happened, protested, "But it really did happen. I remember it!"

Repressed or Constructed (False) Memories of Abuse?

In 1974, 4-year-old Rachel (not her real name) and two others were molested by Rachel's uncle. Rachel told her mother, who informed the mother of one of the others, who proceeded to stab and kill the uncle. Seventeen years later, psychologist Linda Meyer Williams (1994) tracked down Rachel and 128 other women who were recorded as having experienced child sex abuse (sexual intercourse or fondling). When asked whether she had ever been sexually abused as a child or whether any family members had ever gotten into trouble for their sexual behavior, Rachel calmly said no, then added: "Oh wait a minute. . . . My uncle sexually assaulted someone. . . . I never met my uncle (my mother's brother), he died before I was born. You see, he molested a little boy. When the little boy's mother found out that her son was molested, she took a butcher knife and stabbed my uncle in the heart, killing him." Rachel was but one of 49 victims—38 percent of those interviewed—who did not spontaneously recall the specific reported incident of their own abuse. (Most did recall other traumatic sexual experiences.)

So forgetting such events does happen. What does this mean for the scores of alleged victims who have come forward claiming to have *recovered* memories of abuse? Since 1991 in the state of Washington, for example, 682 people who claim repressed memories of sexual abuse and other crimes have sought money for their therapy bills from the state's victim compensation fund (Hallinan, 1997).

Ellen Bass and Laura Davis (1988), authors of the incest-recovery manual *The Courage to Heal*, encouraged people's recovering and reporting such memories. They offered a long list of incest-survivor characteristics, including feelings of shame, powerlessness, unworthiness, vulnerability, perfectionism, and deficient goals and motivation. If you have some of these feelings, some therapists have said, don't be surprised if you have no memory of sexual abuse, because "denial" and "repression" are common. "If you are unable to remember any specific instances . . . but still have a feeling that something abusive happened to you, it probably did," say Bass and Davis (pp. 21–22). "If you think you were abused and your life shows the symptoms, then you were."

Believing this, some therapists have reasoned with patients that "people who've been abused often have your symptoms, so you probably were abused. Let's see if, aided by hypnosis or drugs, or helped to dig back and visualize your trauma, you can recover it." In one survey of British and American doctoral-level therapists, 7 in 10 said they had used such techniques to help clients recover suspected repressed memories of childhood sexual abuse (Poole & others, 1995).

As we might expect from the research on source amnesia and the misinformation effect, many patients exposed to such techniques do form an image of a threatening person. With further visualization, the image grows more vivid, leaving the patient stunned, angry, and ready to confront or sue the equally stunned and devastated parent or other relative, who, as the therapist has predicted, vigorously denies the accusation. One woman in her 32nd therapy session recalled that her father had abused her at age 15 months. After such aided recall, actress Roseanne Barr Arnold (1991) claimed to recall sexual abuse.

In one survey of British and American doctoral-level therapists, 7 in 10 said they had used drugs, hypnosis, or visualization techniques to help clients recover suspected repressed memories of childhood sexual abuse.

Persuading adult women that their fathers or mothers were incestuous is understandably tearing families apart. Thousands of such families have sought advice from the False Memory Syndrome Foundation. The Foundation takes its name from the term John Kihlstrom (1996) defines as a disruptive condition in which a person's identity and relationships center around a false but strongly believed memory of traumatic experience. The person resists disconfirming information and may become so focused on the memory as to avoid coping with the real problems. In the mid-1990s, the False Memory Syndrome Foundation was tracking 700 suits against accused parents and 200 against therapists (Freyd, 1996). Seven in 10 accused people report their accusers are women ages 31 to 50; of those accusers, 71 percent have siblings who do not believe the accusation (FMS, 1996).

Without questioning the professionalism of most therapists, the skeptics say that the uncorroborated accusations suggested by some therapists are a 1990s reenactment of the 1700s witch trials. Consider Beth Rutherford, who remembered under her therapist's guidance that her clergyman father had regularly raped her between the ages of 7 and 14, and that he twice impregnated her and forced her to abort the fetus with a coat hanger. After the father had to resign over the allegations, medical examination revealed that 22-year-old Rutherford was actually a virgin who had never been pregnant. She then sued the therapist and received a $1 million settlement (Loftus, 1997). Clinicians who use "memory work" techniques such as "guided imagery," hypnosis, and dream analysis to recover such memories "are nothing more than merchants of mental chaos, and, in fact, constitute a blight on the entire field of psychotherapy," say some scientific critics (Loftus & others, 1995). Irate clinicians respond that those who dispute recovered memories of abuse are adding to abused women's trauma and playing into the hands of child molesters.

"Spend time imagining that you were sexually abused, without worrying about accuracy, proving anything, or having your ideas make sense. As you give rein to your imagination, let your intuitions guide your thoughts."

Wendy Maltz
The Sexual Healing Journey
1991

The trouble with inferring child abuse from adult symptoms is that the symptom list is "general enough to include everybody at least sometimes," notes Carol Tavris (1993). People feel unworthy, ashamed, and perfectionistic for so many reasons that the symptoms hardly prove any one cause.

In an effort to find a sensible common ground that might resolve this ideological battle, study panels have been convened and public statements made by the American Medical, Psychological, and Psychiatric Associations; the Australian Psychological Society; the British Psychological Society; and the Canadian Psychiatric Association. Those committed to protecting abused children and those committed to protecting wrongly accused adults agree on the following:

- *Incest and child abuse happen.* And they happen more often than we once supposed. Although there is no characteristic "survivor syndrome" (Kendell-Tackett & others, 1993), sexual abuse can leave its victims predisposed to problems ranging from sexual dysfunction to depression (Briere & Runtz, 1993; Trickett & Putnam, 1993).
- *Forgetting happens.* Like Rachel, notes Elizabeth Loftus (1995), many of the women interviewed by Linda Meyer Williams either were very young when abused or may not have understood the meaning of their experience—circumstances under which forgetting is "utterly common." Forgetting of isolated past events, both negative and positive, is an ordinary part of everyday life.

- *Recovered memories are commonplace.* Cued by a remark or an experience, we recover memories of long-forgotten events, both pleasant and unpleasant. What is debated is whether the unconscious mind sometimes forcibly represses painful experiences and, if so, whether these can be retrieved by certain therapist-aided techniques.
- *Memories "recovered" under hypnosis or the influence of drugs are especially unreliable.* (Recall from Chapter 5 the ease with which "age-regressed" hypnotized subjects incorporate suggestions into their memories, even memories of "past lives.")
- *Memories of things happening before age 3 are also unreliable.* People don't reliably recall happenings of any sort from their first three years—a phenomenon called infantile amnesia.
- *Memories, whether real or false, can be emotionally upsetting.* If a false memory of abuse becomes a real part of one's history, the client as well as the family may suffer. Like real traumas, such experiences can then cause lasting suffering.

Without knowing a person's initial experience (as we do in memory experiments) it is difficult to assess the validity of a person's memory. As Mark Pendergrast (1996) notes, "It is ironic that no one can ethically conduct an experiment to replicate what is happening throughout the UK and the US in private therapy settings." Nevertheless, to many memory researchers, the idea that people literally record, then repress, then recover painful experiences is scientifically naive. All the ingredients for cooking false memories are potentially present in the therapy setting, notes Stephen Lindsay (1995): a credible authority, repeated suggestions, imagination-enhancing techniques, and affirmation for one's budding suspicions.

To more closely approximate therapist-aided recall, Elizabeth Loftus and her colleagues (1996) have experimentally implanted false memories of childhood traumas. In one study, she had a trusted family member recall for a teenager three real childhood experiences and a false one—a vivid account of the child's being lost for an extended time in a shopping mall at age 5 until being rescued by an elderly person. Two days later, one subject, Chris, said, "That day I was so scared that I would never see my family again." Two days after that he began to visualize the flannel shirt, bald head, and glasses of the old man who supposedly had found him. Told the story was made up, Chris was incredulous: "I thought I remembered being lost . . . and looking around for the guys. I do remember that, and then crying, and Mom coming up and saying, 'Where were you? Don't you . . . ever do that again.'"

Such is the memory construction process by which people can recall being abducted by UFOs, victimized by a satanic cult, molested in a crib, or living a past life. Thousands of seemingly healthy people, notes Loftus, "speak in terror-stricken voices about their experience aboard flying saucers. They *remember*, clearly and vividly, being abducted by aliens. Or consider the fact that thousands of reasonable, normally functioning human beings relate in calm voices and with deeply felt conviction their past-life experiences. They *remember* having lived before" (Loftus & Ketcham, 1994, p. 66). There are likewise cases of medically certified virgins who *remember* being raped during satanic ritual abuse, and many thousands more who *remember* seeing babies murdered and eaten (but where, wonder skeptics, including the FBI, are the police reports of the missing babies?) (Pendergrast, 1996; Spanos & others, 1994).

Loftus knows firsthand the phenomenon she studies. At a recent family reunion, an uncle told her that at age 14, she found her mother's drowned body. Shocked, she denied it. But the uncle was adamant, and over the next three days she began to wonder if *she* had a repressed memory. "Maybe that's why I'm so obsessed with this topic." As the now-upset Loftus pondered her uncle's suggestion, she "recovered" an

Elizabeth Loftus "People in general and jurors in particular have a lot of misconceptions about the way memory works" (quoted by Monaghan, 1992).

image of her mother lying in the pool, face down, and of herself finding the body. "I started putting everything into place. Maybe that's why I'm such a workaholic. Maybe that's why I'm so emotional when I think about her even though she died in 1959."

Then her brother called and said there was a mistake. The uncle had remembered what other relatives now confirmed. It was Aunt Pearl, not Loftus, who had found the body (Loftus & Ketcham, 1994; Monaghan, 1992).

But then again, after being molested by a male baby-sitter at age 6 (and not forgetting), Loftus also knows firsthand the reality of sexual abuse. That makes her wary of those whom she sees as trivializing real abuse by suggesting and seeking out uncorroborated traumatic experiences, then accepting them uncritically as fact. The enemies of the truly victimized are not only those who prey and those who deny, she says, but those whose writings and allegations "are bound to lead to an increased likelihood that society in general will disbelieve the genuine cases of childhood sexual abuse that truly deserve our sustained attention" (Loftus, 1993).

So, does repression ever occur? Or is this concept—the cornerstone of Freud's theory and of so much popular psychology—a myth? In Chapter 11, we return to this hotly debated issue. As we will see, this much now appears certain: The most common response to a traumatic experience (witnessing the murder of a parent, experiencing the horrors of a Nazi death camp, being terrorized by a hijacker or wartime battle) is not banishment of the experience into an active but inaccessible unconscious. Rather, such experiences are typically etched on the mind as vivid, persistent, haunting memories. "The things we remember best," noted Baltasar Gracian in 1647, "are those better forgotten."

REHEARSE IT!

16. To measure long-term memory, psychologists test a person's ability to *recall* information. They also test ability to *recognize* what has been learned, and they measure *relearning* time. A psychologist who asks you to write down as many objects as you can remember having seen a few minutes earlier is testing your

a. recall. **c.** recall and recognition.
b. recognition. **d.** relearning.

17. To gain access to a memory, a person activates an association that leads to that memory. The association may be activated by a specific odor, visual image, or mnemonic; all of these are examples of

a. relearning. **c.** declarative memories.
b. déjà vu. **d.** retrieval cues.

18. To retrieve a memory, it sometimes helps to return to the setting where the event occurred. In some cases, retrieval may be enhanced by a context similar to one you have already experienced. The resulting feeling that "you've been there before" is referred to as

a. déjà vu. **c.** relearning.
b. mood-congruent memory. **d.** the misinformation effect.

19. When happy, we tend to recall happy times. When depressed, we more often recall depressing events. This tendency to recall experiences that are consistent with our current emotions is called

a. mnemonics. **c.** repression.
b. chunking. **d.** mood-congruent memory.

20. Experiments show that the hour before sleep is a good time to memorize information. For example, studying a vocabulary list before going to sleep minimizes the disrupting effects of all the other new words and terms that might, in the course of a school day, claim our attention. Going to sleep after learning new material minimizes

a. the misinformation effect. **c.** retroactive interference.
b. amnesia. **d.** proactive interference.

21. Because we often alter information as we encode it and because we tend to fill in memory gaps with our assumptions about events, our memories are generally not exact reproductions of events. One reason for this memory reconstruction is

a. proactive interference. **c.** retroactive interference.
b. the misinformation effect. **d.** the eyewitness recall effect.

22. Aspects of our memories are distributed to different parts of the brain. Thus, while we may recognize a face in the crowd, we may not be able to recall where we know the person from. This is called

a. the misinformation effect. **c.** source amnesia.
b. amnesia. **d.** repression.

23. People unknowingly revise or rearrange their memories of events. According to Sigmund Freud, painful or unacceptable memories are self-censored, or blocked from consciousness, through a mechanism called

a. repression. **c.** anxiety.
b. proactive interference. **d.** memory decay.

Thinking and memory Most of what we know is not the result of efforts to memorize. We learn because we're curious and because we spend time thinking about our experiences. Actively thinking as we read, by rehearsing and relating ideas, yields the best retention.

Improving Memory

12. ***How might we apply memory principles to everyday situations, such as remembering a person's name or even the material of this chapter?***

Now and then we are dismayed at our forgetfulness—at our embarrassing inability to recall someone's name, at forgetting to bring up a point in conversation, at forgetting to bring along something important, at finding ourselves standing in a room unable to recall why we are there (Herrmann, 1982). What can we do to minimize such lapses? Much as biology benefits medicine and botany benefits agriculture, so can the psychology of memory benefit education. Sprinkled throughout this chapter and summarized here for easy reference are concrete suggestions for improving memory. The SQ3R study technique introduced in Chapter 1 incorporates several of these strategies.

SQ3R: *S*urvey, *Q*uestion, *R*ead, *R*ehearse, *R*eview

Study repeatedly to boost long-term recall. Overlearn. To learn a name, say it to yourself after being introduced; wait a few seconds and say it again; wait longer and say it again. To provide many separate study sessions, make use of life's little intervals—riding on the bus, walking across campus, waiting for class to start.

Spend more time rehearsing or actively thinking about the material. Speed-reading (skimming) complex material—with minimal rehearsal—yields little retention. Rehearsal and critical reflection help more. It pays to study actively!

"Knit each new thing on to some acquisition already there."

William James
Principles of Psychology
1890

Make the material personally meaningful. To build a network of retrieval cues, take thorough text and class notes in your own words. Mindlessly repeating information is relatively ineffective. Better to form images, understand and organize information, relate the material to what you already know or have experienced, and put it in your own words. Without such cues, you may be stuck when a question uses phrasing different from the rote forms you memorized. To increase retrieval cues, form as many associations as possible.

To remember a list of unfamiliar items, use mnemonic devices. Associate items with peg-words. Make up a story that incorporates vivid images of the items. Chunk information into acronyms.

Refresh your memory by activating retrieval cues. Mentally re-create the situation and the mood in which the original learning occurred. Return to the same location. Jog your memory by allowing one thought to cue the next.

Minimize interference. Study before sleeping. Don't study in close proximity topics that are likely to interfere with each other, such as Spanish and French.

Test your own knowledge, both to rehearse it and to help determine what you do not yet know. If you must later recall information, do not be lulled into overconfidence by your ability to *recognize* it. Test your recall. Outline sections on a blank page. Define concepts listed at each chapter's end *before* turning back to their definitions. Take practice tests; the study guides that accompany many texts, including this one, can help.

REVIEWING ■ *Memory*

The Phenomenon of Memory

1. ***How do psychologists describe the human memory system?***

   Memory is the persistence of learning over time. We are particularly likely to remember vivid events that form **flashbulb memories**. The computer is one convenient model for thinking about human memory. Both systems must **encode**, **store**, and **retrieve** information. Both feature **long-term memory**, from which we can activate information into a working memory; in computers, part of this working memory is displayed on screen. On-screen memory is similar to our **short-term memory**; unless used or rehearsed, it quickly disappears. We experience **sensory memory** when sensory information is immediately recorded in our memory system.

Encoding: Getting Information In

2. ***How do the sights, sounds, and other sensations we experience get selectively encoded and transferred into the memory system?***

   Some types of information, notably concerning space, time, and frequency, we encode mostly automatically (**automatic processing**). Other types of information, including much of our processing of meaning, imagery, and organization, require **effortful processing**.

3. ***How much does rehearsal aid in forming memories?***

   Without **rehearsal**, much information (such as a new phone number) is lost within three seconds. The more we rehearse information, the better we retain it—especially if our rehearsal is spaced out over time (**spacing effect**) rather than massed. When learning a list of words or names, our later recall is often best for those learned first, which we may have rehearsed more (the **serial position effect**).

4. ***What methods of effortful processing aid in forming memories?***

   Effortful encoding of meaning, **imagery**, and organization enhances long-term retention. **Mnemonic** devices exploit the memorability of visual images and of information that is organized into chunks (**chunking**). Organizing information into hierarchies also aids memory.

Storage: Retaining Information

5. ***How does sensory memory work?***

   We have a precise but fleeting **iconic** (photographic) **memory** for visual stimuli and a slightly longer-lasting **echoic memory** for auditory stimuli.

6. ***What are the limits of short-term memory?***

   In the short run, our memory span for information just presented is very limited—up to about seven items, depending on the information and how it is presented.

7. ***How large and durable is our long-term memory?***

   Our capacity for storing information permanently is essentially unlimited. Nevertheless, most of what we learn is soon forgotten; the brain does not store information with the durability and exactness of a tape recorder.

8. ***How are memories recorded in the brain?***

   The search for the physical basis of memory has recently focused on brain circuits, synapses (through **long-term potentiation [LTP]**), neurotransmitters, and hormones. As demonstrated in studies of people with **amnesia**, one brain structure, the **hippocampus**, processes **explicit memories** (also called *declarative memories*); **implicit memories** (also called *nondeclarative memories*) involve different brain mechanisms. This suggests a dual memory system.

Retrieval: Getting Information Out

9. ***How do we get information out of memory?***

   To be remembered, information that is "in there" must be retrieved, as measured by **recall**, **recognition**, or **relearning**. This occurs with the aid of associations (cues) formed through **priming**; for example, sometimes a familiar context causes us to believe we have experienced an event before (**déjà vu**). Our memory is often **mood-congruent**. Mood can serve as a retrieval cue, leading us to recall happy times when happy, sad times when sad. Moods can also interfere with our recall, as when preoccupation with our feelings—sad or happy—makes us less attentive to new information.

10. ***What causes retrieval failure?***

    One explanation of forgetting is that we fail to encode information for entry into our memory system. Without effortful processing, much of what we sense we never notice or process. Some of what we encode is altered or lost in memory storage. Retrieval failure may be caused by **proactive** or **retroactive interference**, by insufficient cues, or even by motivated forgetting (**repression**).

11. ***How accurate are our memories?***

    Memories are not stored as exact copies, and they certainly are not retrieved as such. Rather, we construct our memories, using both stored and new information. Thus, when eyewitnesses are subtly exposed to **misinformation** after an event, they often believe they saw the misleading details as part of the event. This seems especially true of young children. **Source amnesia** (also called *source misattribution*) occurs when we misattribute an event or statement.

Improving Memory

12. ***How might we apply memory principles to everyday situations, such as remembering a person's name or even the material of this chapter?***

    The psychology of memory suggests concrete strategies for improving memory, which are incorporated into the SQ3R method. These include repeated, spaced study; active rehearsal; encoding of well-organized, vivid, meaningful associations; mnemonic techniques; the return to contexts and moods that are rich with associations; minimizing interference; and self-testing and rehearsal.

CRITICAL THINKING EXERCISE by Richard O. Straub

Now that you have read and reviewed Chapter 7, take your learning a step further by testing your critical thinking skills on the following practical problem-solving exercise.

Naomi happened to be driving into the parking lot of a mall just as another shopper was being carjacked. She caught a quick glimpse of a running man who seemed to be carrying a handgun. When the police arrived at the scene, Naomi couldn't say much about the gunman's appearance. Nevertheless, they took her to headquarters and showed her hundreds of mug-book photographs. After many frustrating hours during which Naomi was repeatedly shown a photo of a man named Raymond but was unable to identify anyone conclusively, the investigator handed her Raymond's photo and said, "We know this man visited the mall the night of the crime. Did you see him running in the parking lot?" When Naomi said she wasn't sure, she was allowed to leave and asked to think more carefully about what she had seen that night.

Three weeks later, Naomi was asked to pick the aggressor from a five-man lineup that included Raymond. Although she remembered feeling uncertain of the identity of the man when she was first questioned, Naomi was surprised at how easily and confidently she picked Raymond from the lineup now.

1. What's going on in this situation? What problem are the police trying to solve?
2. Why couldn't Naomi identify the gunman right after she witnessed the crime?
3. What is wrong with the police questioning procedures described here?

Check your progress on becoming a critical thinker by comparing your answers to the sample answers found in Appendix B.

REHEARSE IT ANSWER KEY

1. b., **2.** b., **3.** c., **4.** b., **5.** a., **6.** d., **7.** c., **8.** d., **9.** b., **10.** c., **11.** d., **12.** d., **13.** c., **14.** b., **15.** a., **16.** a., **17.** d., **18.** a., **19.** d., **20.** c., **21.** b., **22.** c., **23.** a.

CHAPTER
8

Thinking, Language, and Intelligence

Throughout history, we humans have deplored our foolishness and celebrated our wisdom. The poet T. S. Eliot was struck by "the hollow men . . . Headpiece filled with straw." But Shakespeare's Hamlet extolled the human species as "noble in reason! . . . infinite in faculties! . . . in apprehension how like a god!" In the preceding chapters, we, too, have sometimes marveled at our capabilities, sometimes at our propensity to err.

We have studied the human brain—a mere three pounds of tissue containing circuitry more complex than the planet's telephone networks. We have marveled at the competence of newborn infants. We have appreciated the human sensory system, which disassembles visual stimuli into millions of nerve impulses, distributes them for parallel processing, and then reassembles them into clear and colorful perceived images. We have acknowledged the seemingly limitless capacity of human memory and the ease with which we process information, consciously and unconsciously. Little wonder, then, that our species has the genius to invent the camera, the car, and the computer; to unlock the atom and crack the genetic code; to travel into space and probe the oceans' depths.

At the same time, we have seen that our species is kin to the other animals, influenced by principles that produce learning in rats and pigeons. We have noted that we assimilate reality into our preconceptions and succumb to perceptual illusions. We have seen how easily we deceive ourselves about pseudopsychic claims, hypnotic regression, and false memories. Little wonder, then, that we sometimes imagine we can read minds and travel outside our bodies; that we form distorted images of other ethnic, age, and gender groups; that we operate on the same biological principles as other creatures.

In this chapter, we encounter further instances of these two images of the human condition—the rational and the irrational. We will see how we form concepts, solve problems, and make judgments. We will look at our flair for language and ask whether our species alone is capable of language. We will consider the roots of our intelligence. In the end, we will reflect on how deserving we are of our name, *Homo sapiens*—wise human.

Thinking

Previous chapters explained how we receive, perceive, store, and retrieve information. Now we consider how our cognitive system uses this information. Thinking, or **cognition**, refers to all the mental activities associated with

cognition all the mental activities associated with thinking, knowing, and remembering.

concept a mental grouping of similar objects, events, or people.

prototype the best example of a category; matching new items to the prototype provides a quick and easy method for including items in a category (as when comparing feathered creatures to a prototypical bird, such as a robin).

algorithm a methodical, logical rule or procedure that guarantees solving a particular problem. Contrasts with the usually speedier—but also more error-prone—use of *heuristics*.

heuristic a rule-of-thumb strategy that often allows us to make judgments and solve problems efficiently; usually speedier but also more error-prone than *algorithms*.

insight a sudden and often novel realization of the solution to a problem; it contrasts with strategy-based solutions.

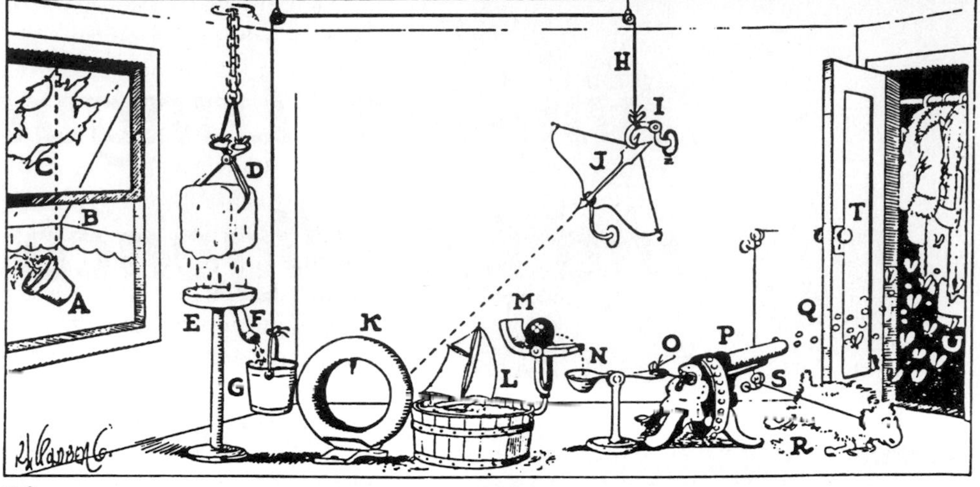

THE PROFESSOR EMERGES FROM THE GOOFY BOOTH WITH A DEVICE FOR THE EXTERMINATION OF MOTHS.
START SINGING. LADY UPSTAIRS, WHEN SUFFICIENTLY ANNOYED, THROWS FLOWER POT (A) THROUGH AWNING (B). HOLE (C) ALLOWS SUN TO COME THROUGH AND MELT CAKE OF ICE (D). WATER DRIPS INTO PAN (E) RUNNING THROUGH PIPE (F) INTO PAIL (G). WEIGHT OF PAIL CAUSES CORD (H) TO RELEASE HOOK (I) AND ALLOW ARROW (J) TO SHOOT INTO TIRE (K). ESCAPING AIR BLOWS AGAINST TOY SAILBOAT (L) DRIVING IT AGAINST LEVER (M) AND CAUSING BALL TO ROLL INTO SPOON (N) AND PULL STRING (O) WHICH SETS OFF MACHINE GUN (P) DISCHARGING CAMPHOR BALLS (Q). REPORT OF GUN FRIGHTENS LAMB (R) WHICH RUNS AND PULLS CORD (S), OPENING CLOSET DOOR (T). AS MOTHS (U) FLY OUT TO EAT WOOL FROM LAMB'S BACK THEY ARE KILLED BY THE BARRAGE OF MOTH BALLS.
IF ANY OF THE MOTHS ESCAPE AND THERE IS DANGER OF THEIR RETURNING, YOU CAN FOOL THEM BY MOVING.

Cognition Cognitive psychologists study the mental activities by which we process and communicate information. In his cartoons, Rube Goldberg delighted in our cognitive powers to imagine complex machines that accomplish tiny tasks.

thinking, knowing, remembering, and communicating. *Cognitive psychologists* study these mental activities, including the logical and sometimes illogical ways in which we create concepts, solve problems, make decisions, and form judgments. We begin this chapter with the building blocks of thinking.

Concepts

1. *What are the functions of concepts?*

To think about the countless events, objects, and people in our world, we simplify things. We form **concepts**—mental groupings of similar objects, events, and people. The concept *chair* sums up a variety of items—a baby's high chair, a reclining chair, the chairs around a dining room table, a dentist's chair.

Imagine life without concepts. We would need a different name for every object and idea. We could not ask a child to "throw the ball" because there would be no concept of *ball*. Instead of saying, "They were angry," we would have to describe facial expressions, vocal intensities, gestures, and words. Concepts such as *ball* and *angry* provide much information with a minimum of cognitive effort.

Other species, too, are capable of feats of concept formation. Pigeons demonstrate the surprising intelligence of bird brains by sorting objects according to their perceptual or functional similarity. Shown pictures of cars, cats, chairs, and flowers, they readily learn to identify the categories. Shown a picture of a never-before-seen chair, the pigeon will reliably peck a key that represents "chairs" (Wasserman, 1995).

To simplify things further, humans organize concepts into hierarchies. Cab drivers organize their cities into geographical sectors, which subdivide into neighborhoods and again into blocks. The earliest naturalists simplified and ordered the overwhelming complexity of some 5 million living species by clustering them into two basic categories—the plant and animal kingdoms. Then they divided these basic categories into smaller and smaller subcategories—vertebrates, bony fish, and Atlantic salmon, for instance.

"Attention, everyone! I'd like to introduce the newest member of our family."

A bird and a . . . ? If asked to imagine a bird, most people quickly come up with a mental picture that is something like this robin. It takes them a bit longer to conceptualize a penguin as a bird because it doesn't match their prototype of a small, feathered, flying creature.

We form some concepts by definition. Told the rule that a triangle has three sides, we thereafter classify all three-sided geometric forms as triangles. By definition, a bird is an animal that has wings and feathers and hatches from an egg. More often, we form our concepts by developing **prototypes**—a best example of a particular category (Rosch, 1978). The more closely something matches our prototype of a concept, the more readily we recognize it as an example of the concept. A robin and a goose both satisfy our rule for *bird*. Yet people agree more quickly that "A robin is a bird" than that "A goose is a bird." For most of us, the robin is the birdier bird; it more closely resembles our bird prototype. Likewise, "maternal love" and "self-love" both qualify as love. But people more instantly agree that "maternal love is a type of love," because it better matches their love prototype (Fehr & Russell, 1991).

If something fails to match our prototype, we may have trouble classifying it. Thus, we might be slow to recognize nonflying penguins and kiwis as birds. Similarly, we are slow to perceive an illness when our symptoms don't fit one of our disease prototypes (Bishop, 1991). People whose heart attack symptoms don't match their prototype of a heart attack may not seek help. And when discrimination doesn't fit our prejudice prototypes—of white against black, male against female, young against old—we often fail to notice it. People more easily detect male prejudice against female than female against male or female against female (Inman & Baron, 1996).

Solving Problems

2. *What strategies do we use to solve problems, and what obstacles hinder our problem solving?*

One tribute to our rationality is our ability to form and use concepts. Another is our skill at solving problems as we cope with novel situations. Some problems we solve through trial and error—Thomas Edison tried thousands of light bulb filaments before stumbling upon one that worked. For other problems, we may follow an **algorithm**, a step-by-step procedure that guarantees a solution. Told to find another word using all the letters in SPLOYOCHYG, we could try each letter in each position, but generating and examining the 907,208 resulting combinations would take too long. Because step-by-step algorithms can be laborious (well-suited to computers), we often solve problems with simple rule-of-thumb strategies, called **heuristics**. Thus, in rearranging the letters of SPLOYOCHYG, we might exclude letter combinations such as two *y*'s together. By using rule-of-thumb heuristics and then applying trial and error, you may hit upon the answer (page 270).

Heuristic searching To search for horseradish in a supermarket, you could search every aisle (an algorithm) or check the mustard, spice, and gourmet sections (heuristics). The heuristic approach is often speedier, but an algorithmic search is exhaustive.

Sometimes we are unaware of using any problem-solving strategy; the answer just comes to us. We can all recall occasions when we puzzled over a problem for some time. Then, suddenly, the pieces fell together and we perceived the solution. This facility for sudden flashes of inspiration we call **insight**. Ten-year-old Johnny Appleton displayed insight in solving a problem that had stumped construction workers: how to rescue a young robin that had fallen into a narrow 30-inch-deep hole in a cement block wall. Johnny's solution: to slowly pour in sand, giving the bird enough time to keep its feet on top of the constantly rising sand (Ruchlis, 1990).

We humans aren't the only creatures that display insight. German psychologist Wolfgang Köhler (1925) observed apparent insight while studying chimpanzees brought to an island off the coast of Africa. In one experiment with a caged chimp named Sultan, Köhler placed a piece of fruit and a long stick well beyond reach, and a short stick inside the cage. Spying the short stick, Sultan grabbed it and tried to reach the fruit with it. But the stick, by design, was too

confirmation bias a tendency to search for information that confirms one's preconceptions.

fixation the inability to see a problem from a new perspective; an impediment to problem solving.

functional fixedness the tendency to think of things only in terms of their usual functions; an impediment to problem solving.

representativeness heuristic a rule of thumb for judging the likelihood of things in terms of how well they seem to represent, or match, particular prototypes; may lead one to ignore other relevant information.

short. After several unsuccessful attempts, the chimp dropped the stick and paused to survey the situation. Then suddenly, as if thinking "Aha!" Sultan jumped up, seized the short stick again and used it to pull in the longer stick—which he then used to reach the fruit. Sultan's actions displayed animal cognition, claimed Köhler, and showed that there is more to learning than conditioning.

Thanks to problem solving shaped by reinforcements, forest-dwelling chimpanzees have become natural tool users (Boesch-Achermann & Boesch, 1993). They can select appropriate branches or stones to use as hammers in cracking nuts. They can also break off a reed or a stick, strip the twigs and leaves, carry it to a termite mound, fish for termites by twisting it just so, and then carefully remove it without scraping off many termites. One anthropologist, trying to mimic the chimpanzee's deft termite fishing, failed miserably.

In human experience, insight provides a sense of satisfaction. After solving a difficult problem or discovering how to resolve a conflict, we feel happy. The joy of a joke may similarly lie in our capacity for insight—our sudden comprehension of an unexpected ending or a double meaning. We find double meaning in the story of Professor Smith, who complained to his colleagues that student interruptions had become a problem: "The minute I get up to speak, some fool begins to talk."

Answer to SPLOYOCHYG anagram on page 269: PSYCHOLOGY.

Obstacles to Problem Solving

Confirmation Bias

A major obstacle to problem solving is our eagerness to search for information that confirms our ideas, a phenomenon known as **confirmation bias**. In an experiment with British university students, Peter Wason (1960) demonstrated our reluctance to seek information that might disprove our beliefs. Wason gave students the three-number sequence 2-4-6 and asked them to guess the rule he had used to devise the series. (The rule was simple: any three ascending numbers.) Before submitting their answers, the students generated their own sets of three numbers, and each time Wason told them whether or not their sets conformed to his rule. Once they had done enough testing to feel *certain* they had the rule, they were to announce it.

"The human understanding, when any proposition has been once laid down . . . forces everything else to add fresh support and confirmation."

Francis Bacon
Novum Organum
1620

The result? Seldom right but never in doubt: Most of the students convinced themselves of a wrong rule. Typically, they formed a wrong idea ("Maybe it's counting by twos") and then searched only for confirming evidence (by testing 6-8-10, 100-102-104, and so forth). Such experiments reveal that we seek evidence that will verify our ideas more eagerly than we seek evidence that might refute them (Klayman & Ha, 1987; Skov & Sherman, 1986). Business managers, for example, are more likely to follow the successful careers of those they once hired than to track the achievements of those they rejected, which helps them confirm their perceived hiring ability.

Fixation

Another obstacle to problem solving is **fixation**—the inability to see a problem from a fresh perspective. Once we incorrectly represent the problem, it's hard to restructure how we approach it. Try to solve the matchstick problem in Figure 8.1. If your attempts to solve the problem were fixated on two-dimensional solutions, then the three-dimensional solution shown in Figure 8.3 (page 272) will have eluded you.

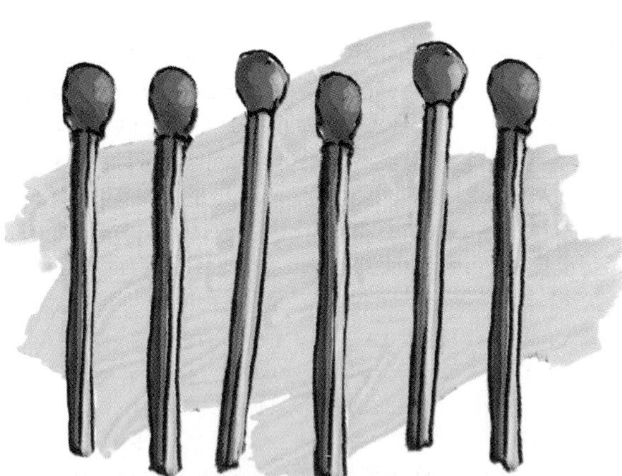

Figure 8.1 **The matchstick problem** How would you arrange six matches to form four equilateral triangles? (From "Problem Solving" by M. Scheerer. Copyright © 1963 by Scientific American, Inc. All rights reserved.)

Flexible, rational thinking becomes even more difficult in times of stress and tension (Janis, 1989). During international crises, views of an enemy become fixed in simplified good-versus-bad terms. During personal crises, too, thinking

Figure 8.2 The candle-mounting problem Using these materials, how would you mount the candle on a bulletin board? (From Duncker, 1945)

often becomes rigid. One Korean War paratrooper readying for a mission was given the last parachute—a left-handed one. "It's the same as the others," explained the ordnance sergeant, "but the rip cord hangs on the left side of the harness." At 8000 feet, the soldiers jumped one by one, and all went well—except for this one man who fell straight to his death. Investigators discovered that under the stress of the jump the man had become fixated on the familiar way to open a chute. The right side of his uniform, where normally he found the rip cord, was completely torn off. Even his chest flesh had been gouged by his bloody right hand. Inches to the left was the rip cord, apparently untouched (Csikszentmihalyi, 1990).

Another type of fixation goes by the awkward but appropriate label **functional fixedness**. This is our tendency to perceive the functions of objects as fixed and unchanging. A person may ransack the house for a screwdriver when a dime would have done the job. Try to solve the candle-mounting problem in Figure 8.2. You will probably experience functional fixedness because most people think of the matchbox as having only the function of holding matches. Its use in solving the problem is shown in Figure 8.4. Perceiving and relating familiar things in new ways is part of creativity.

Making Decisions and Forming Judgments

3. ***How are our decisions and judgments influenced by heuristics, overconfidence, and framing?***

When making each day's hundreds of tiny judgments and decisions—Is it worth the bother to take an umbrella? Can I trust this person? Should I shoot the basketball or pass to the player who's hot?—we seldom take the time and effort to reason systematically. Usually, we follow our intuition. After interviewing policymakers in government, business, and education, social psychologist Irving Janis (1986) concluded that they "often do not use a reflective problem-solving approach. How do they usually arrive at their decisions? If you ask, they are likely to tell you . . . they do it mostly by the *seat of their pants*."

"In creating these problems, we didn't set out to fool people. All our problems fooled us, too."
Amos Tversky (1985)

Using and Misusing Heuristics

Those mental shortcuts we call heuristics often help us make reasonable seat-of-the-pants decisions. Thanks to the mind's automatic information processing, intuitive judgments are instantaneous. But the price we pay for this efficiency can sometimes be costly bad judgments. To gain an idea of how heuristics determine our intuitive judgments—and how they occasionally lead smart people into dumb decisions—consider two heuristics identified by cognitive psychologists Amos Tversky and Daniel Kahneman (1974): *representativeness* and *availability*.

"The information-processing shortcuts—called heuristics—which are normally both highly efficient and immensely time-saving in day-to-day situations, work systematically against us in the market-place. . . . The tendency to underestimate or altogether ignore past probabilities in making a decision is undoubtedly the most significant problem of intuitive predictions."
David Dreman
Contrarian Investment Strategy: The Psychology of Stock Market Success
1979

The Representativeness Heuristic

To judge the likelihood of things in terms of how well they represent particular prototypes is to use the **representativeness heuristic**. To illustrate, consider:

> A stranger tells you about a person who is short, slim, and likes to read poetry, and then asks you to guess whether this person is more likely to be a professor of classics at an Ivy League university or a truck driver. Which would be the better guess? (Adapted from Nisbett & Ross, 1980)

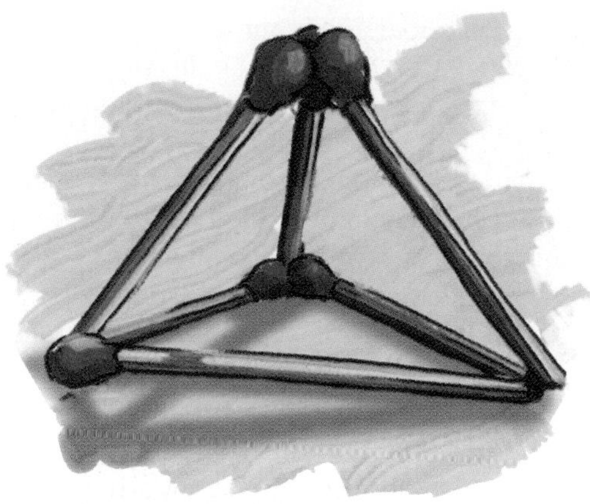

Figure 8.3 **Solution to the matchstick problem** To solve this problem, you must break the fixation of limiting your considerations to two-dimensional solutions. (From "Problem Solving" by M. Scheerer. Copyright © 1963 by Scientific American, Inc. All rights reserved.)

Figure 8.4 **Solution to the candle-mounting problem** Solving this problem requires recognizing that a box need not always serve as a container. (From Duncker, 1945)

If you are like most people, you answered "professor" because the description seems more *representative* of Ivy League scholars than of truck drivers. The representativeness heuristic enabled you to make a snap judgment. But it also led you to ignore other relevant information, such as the total number of classics professors versus the number of truck drivers. When I help people think through this question, their own reasoning usually leads them to an answer that contradicts their immediate intuition. The typical conversation goes something like this:

> **Question:** *First, let's figure out how many professors fit the description. How many Ivy League universities do you suppose there are?*
>
> **Answer:** *Oh, about 10, I suppose.*
>
> **Question:** *How many classics professors would you guess there are at each?*
>
> **Answer:** *Maybe four.*
>
> **Question:** *Okay, that's 40 Ivy League classics professors. What fraction of these are short and slim?*
>
> **Answer:** *Let's say half.*
>
> **Question:** *And, of these 20, how many like to read poetry?*
>
> **Answer:** *I'd say half—10 professors.*
>
> **Question:** *Okay, now let's figure how many truck drivers fit the description. How many truck drivers do you suppose there are?*
>
> **Answer:** *Maybe 400,000.*
>
> **Question:** *What fraction are short and slim?*
>
> **Answer:** *Not many—perhaps 1 in 8.*
>
> **Question:** *Of these 50,000, what percentage like to read poetry?*
>
> **Answer:** *Truck drivers who like poetry? Maybe 1 in 100—oh, oh, I can see where this is going—that leaves me with 500 short, slim, poetry-reading truck drivers.*
>
> **Question:** *Yup. So, although the person I've described may be much more representative of classics professors than of truck drivers, this person is still (even if we accept your stereotypes) 50 times more likely to be a truck driver than a classics professor.*

This illustrates people's illogical use of the representativeness heuristic. To judge the likelihood of something, we intuitively compare it with our mental representation of that category—of, say, what truck drivers are like. If the two match, then that fact usually overrides other considerations of statistics or logic.

The Availability Heuristic

The **availability heuristic** operates when we base our judgments on the availability of information in our memories. If instances of an event are easily available—if they come to mind readily—we presume such events are common. The faster people can remember an instance of some event ("a broken promise"), the more they expect it to recur (MacLeod & Campbell, 1992). Usually, cognitively available events *are* more likely to recur—but not always. To see this, make a guess: In written English does the letter *k* appear more often as the first or third letter?

Because words beginning with *k* come to mind more easily than words having *k* as their third letter, most people guess that *k* occurs more frequently as the first letter. Actually, *k* is two to three times more likely to appear as the third letter. So far in this chapter, words such as *know, kingdom*, and *kin* are outnumbered 43 to 23 by words such as *make, likely, asked*, and *acknowledged.*

availability heuristic estimating the likelihood of events based on their availability in memory; if instances come readily to mind (perhaps because of their vividness), we presume such events are common.

The availability heuristic affects our social judgments, as Ruth Hamill and her co-workers demonstrated (1980). They presented people with a single, vivid case of welfare abuse, in which a long-term welfare recipient had several

THINKING CRITICALLY

Risks—When Statistics Clash With Heuristics

"Most people reason dramatically, not quantitatively," said Oliver Wendell Holmes. With horrific television and magazine images of air crashes in mind, many people, petrified of air travel, prefer the safety of their own cars. One Gallup study (*Gallup Report*, 1989) found that, of those who do fly, 44 percent reported feeling fearful and 63 percent had "lost confidence" in airline safety.

Ironically, the statistical reality is that air travel is safer than ever. Mile for mile, U.S. travelers during the 1980s were 26 times more likely to die in a car crash than on a commercial flight (National Safety Council, 1991). In the 27 months following March 22, 1992, major U.S. airlines carried more than 1 billion passengers on *16 million* flights without a single death (Tolchin, 1994). For most air travelers, the most dangerous part of the journey is the drive to the airport. When a friend tells me of revising her will before flying, I cannot resist saying, "Much better to have done so before you drove to Kansas." For even if she were to board a random jet every day, she would (if her experience matched the average) have to live 21,000 years before crashing to her death (Barnett, 1996).

Still, when overall statistics vie with vivid images of helpless crash victims, many people find the memorable instances more persuasive. It's like judging the likelihood of shark attacks after watching the movie *Jaws*: Regardless of statistics, memorable images have a way of heightening swimmers' feelings of risk. People may *know* their fears are irrational, but no matter. The available images of a plane death—which is 6900 times more likely to make the *New York Times* front page than a cancer death (Barnett, 1990)—protrude into consciousness. Even smokers (whose habit shortens their lives by about five years) may senselessly fret before flying (which shortens the average person's life by one day).

The 1988 terrorist bomb that exploded Pan Am Flight 103 and the 1996 fiery explosion of TWA flight 800 caused many would-be international vacationers to stay home and brave the more dangerous highways. The same fearful public continues to smoke billions of cigarettes a year, guzzle alcohol, and devour foods that put people at risk for the greatest of killers—heart disease. All because people's *perceptions* of risk are virtually unrelated to actual risk (Slovic, 1987)—a phenomenon due partly to our greater fear of things we cannot control and partly to our overestimating the likelihood of dreaded, publicized, and cognitively available events. Thus, the public dreads a catastrophic nuclear accident (which after Chernobyl we can readily visualize). Yet it accepts the less dramatic risks of coal-generated power, which quietly fuels acid rain and global warming.

The point to remember: Whether making travel plans or choosing foods, defining safety standards or evaluating environmental hazards, smart thinkers should define risks based not on mentally available media images but on statistical reality.

Vivid events are more available to memory Photos of this July 1994 crash etched a sharper image in many minds than did the 16 million consecutive fatality-free flights on U.S. airlines during the preceding 27 months. Because such vivid happenings are more available to memory, they seem more common than they really are.

"The human understanding is most excited by that which strikes and enters the mind at once and suddenly, and by which the imagination is immediately filled and inflated. It then begins almost imperceptibly to conceive and suppose that everything is similar to the few objects which have taken possession of the mind."

Francis Bacon
Novum Organum
1620

unruly children. Statistically, this case was exceptional: Most people who receive welfare did so for four years or less (Duncan & others, 1988). Yet when the statistical reality was pitted against the single vivid case, the memorable case had greater influence on people's opinions about welfare recipients.

In everyday life, too, a memorable picture sometimes overwhelms a thousand statistics. When a little girl named Jessica McClure fell into a Texas well, the attention of hundreds of millions of people worldwide was riveted on her three-day rescue. During those three days, more than 100,000 invisible children—mere statistics on some world health ledger—died of preventable starvation, diarrhea, and disease (Gore, 1992).

overconfidence the tendency to be more confident than correct—to overestimate the accuracy of one's beliefs and judgments.

framing the way an issue is posed; how an issue is framed can significantly affect decisions and judgments.

belief perseverance clinging to one's initial conceptions after the basis on which they were formed has been discredited. (Confirmation bias—searching for belief-support information—contributes to belief perseverance.)

Overconfidence

Our use of intuitive heuristics when forming judgments, our eagerness to confirm the beliefs we already hold, and our knack for explaining away failures combine to create **overconfidence**, a tendency to overestimate the accuracy of our knowledge and judgments.

Overconfidence plagues decisions outside the laboratory, too. People are also more confident than correct when answering such questions as, "Is absinthe a liqueur or a precious stone?" On questions where only 60 percent of people answer correctly, they typically feel 75 percent confident. Even when people feel 100 percent certain of their answers to such questions, they err about 15 percent of the time (Fischhoff & others, 1977). (Absinthe is a licorice-flavored liqueur.)

It was an overconfident Hitler who invaded Russia, an overconfident Lyndon Johnson who waged war with North Vietnam, an overconfident Saddam Hussein who marched into Kuwait. Stockbrokers and investment managers market their services with confidence that they can outperform the market average in picking stocks, despite overwhelming evidence to the contrary (Malkiel, 1985, 1995). A purchase of stock X, recommended by a broker who judges this to be the time to buy, is always balanced by a sale made by someone who judges this to be the time to sell. Despite their confidence, they can't both be right.

Predict your own behavior When will you finish reading this chapter?

Roger Buehler and his colleagues (1994) were struck by how routinely planners exhibit overconfidence in estimating how quickly and inexpensively they can do a project. In 1957, planners predicted the Sydney Opera House would be completed in 1963 for $7 million. A reduced version actually opened in 1973 at a cost of $102 million. Buehler reports that students, too, are routinely overconfident of how quickly they can do assignments and write papers. Students typically expect to finish projects ahead of schedule. But projects generally get finished after about twice as many days as predicted. Although people know they have often underestimated completion times, they remain overly confident of their next prediction.

"When you know a thing, to hold that you know it; and when you do not know a thing, to allow that you do not know it; this is knowledge."

Confucius
551–479 B.C.
Analects

Overconfidence has adaptive value. Failing to appreciate one's potential for error when making military, economic, or political judgments can have devastating consequences, but so can lack of self-confidence. People who err on the side of overconfidence live more happily and find it easier to make tough decisions (Baumeister, 1989; Taylor, 1989). Moreover, when given prompt and clear feedback on the accuracy of their judgments—as weather forecasters are after each day's predictions—people soon learn to assess their accuracy more realistically (Fischhoff, 1982). The wisdom to know when we know a thing and when we do not is born of experience.

Framing Decisions

A further test of rationality is whether the same issue, presented in two different but logically equivalent ways, will elicit the same answer. For example, whether a surgeon tells someone that 10 percent of people die while undergoing a particular surgery or that 90 percent survive, the information is the same. But the effect is not. The risk seems greater to people who hear that 10 percent will die (Marteau, 1989). This impact of the way we present an issue is called **framing**.

Whether a surgeon tells someone that 10 percent of people die while undergoing a particular surgery or that 90 percent survive, the information is the same. But the effect is not.

Similarly, consumers respond more positively to ground beef described as "75 percent lean" rather than "25 percent fat" (Levin & Gaeth, 1988). People are more bothered by some students cheating if told that 65 percent of their class had cheated than if told that 35 percent had not cheated (Levin & others, 1988). People express more surprise when a "1 in 20" event happens than

"This CD player costs less than players selling for twice as much."

when an equivalent "10 in 200" event happens (Denes-Raj & others, 1995). And 9 in 10 college students rate a condom as effective if it has a supposed "95 percent success rate" in stopping the AIDS virus; only 4 in 10 think it successful when given a "5 percent failure rate" (Linville & others, 1992).

Consider how the framing effect influences economic and business decisions:

- Merchants mark up their "regular prices" to appear to offer huge savings on "sale prices." A $100 coat marked down from $150 by Store X can seem like a better deal than the same coat priced regularly at $100 by Store Y (Urbany & others, 1988).
- Many people find taking a 7 percent pay cut in a period of zero inflation much more objectionable than a 5 percent pay raise when inflation is 12 percent (Kahneman & others, 1986).
- Federal Express doesn't charge extra to pick up at your door; instead, they offer a "drop-off discount." Likewise, my dentist doesn't charge more if we don't pay on the spot, though she does offer a 5 percent discount for immediate cash payment. FedEx and my dentist both understand that a fee framed as a forfeited discount irritates customers less than one framed as a surcharge, although they add up to the same thing.

That people's judgments flip-flop so dramatically is startling. It suggests that our judgments and decisions may not be well reasoned, and that those who understand the power of framing can use it to influence important decisions—for example, by framing survey questions to support or reject a particular viewpoint. (Recall from Chapter 1 the potentially powerful effects of subtle wording differences.)

"Once you have a belief, it influences how you perceive all other relevant information. Once you see a country as hostile, you are likely to interpret ambiguous actions on their part as signifying their hostility."

Political scientist Robert Jervis (1985)

The Belief Perseverance Phenomenon

4. *How do our preexisting beliefs influence our decision making?*

An additional source of irrationality is our tendency, called **belief perseverance**, to cling to our beliefs in the face of contrary evidence. Belief perseverance often fuels social conflict. Charles Lord and his colleagues (1979) revealed how this happens when they studied people with opposing views of capital punishment. People on both sides studied two supposedly new research findings, one supporting and the other refuting the claim that the death penalty deters crime. Each side was more impressed by the study that supported its beliefs, and each readily disputed the other study. Thus, showing the pro– and anti–capital-punishment groups the *same* mixed evidence actually *increased* their disagreement.

Belief perseverance Do risk-prone or cautious people make better firefighters? Once we've formed opinions on a question such as this and developed reasons for our views, we tend to cling to our beliefs—even if the basis for our opinion is undermined.

For those who wish to rein in the belief perseverance phenomenon, a simple remedy exists: *Consider the opposite.* When Lord and his colleagues (1984) repeated the capital-punishment study, they asked some of their participants to be "as *objective* and *unbiased* as possible." The plea did nothing to reduce the biased evaluation of evidence. They asked another group to consider "whether you would have made the same high or low evaluations had exactly the same study produced results on the *other* side of the issue." Having imagined and pondered *opposite* findings, these people were much less biased in their evaluations of the evidence.

If ambiguous evidence gets interpreted as supporting a person's preexisting belief, would the belief be demolished by information that clearly discredits its basis? Not necessarily. Craig Anderson and Lee Ross discovered that changing a false belief can be surprisingly difficult once a person has ideas that support it. In one study with Mark Lepper (1980), they asked people to consider whether risk-prone people or cautious people are better firefighters. Then they told half the people about a risk-taker who was an excellent fire fighter and about a cautious person who was a poor firefighter. From these cases, the participants surmised that risk-prone people tend to be better firefighters. "Risk-takers are braver" was a typical explanation. The researchers gave the other participants two cases suggesting the opposite conclusion, that cautious people are better firefighters. These participants typically reasoned, "Cautious people think before they act. They're less likely to make foolish mistakes."

"I'm happy to say that my final judgment of a case is almost always consistent with my prejudgment of the case."

The researchers then discredited the basis for the beliefs by truthfully informing both groups that the cases were simply made up for the experiment. Did discrediting the evidence undermine the participants' newly formed beliefs? Not by much, because they held on to their explanations for why these new beliefs made sense. Although the evidence was gone, their theory survived.

The more we come to appreciate why our beliefs might be true, the more tightly we cling to them. Once people have explained to themselves why they believe that a child is "gifted" or "learning disabled," or that candidate X or Y will be more likely to preserve peace or start a war, or that women or men are naturally superior, they tend to ignore evidence undermining that belief. Prejudice therefore persists.

"To begin with, it was only tentatively that I put forward the views I have developed . . . but in the course of time they have gained such a hold upon me that I can no longer think in any other way."

Sigmund Freud
Civilization and Its Discontents
1930

We have seen how our irrational thinking can plague our efforts to solve problems, make wise decisions, form valid judgments, and reason logically. From this we might conclude that our heads are indeed filled with straw. All in all, these and many other findings suggest "bleak implications for human rationality" (Nisbett & Borgida, 1975). Still, let us not forget that our cognition is effective and wonderfully efficient: It enables our survival and our inventive genius.

Moreover, even the most sophisticated computers are dwarfed by the most ordinary of human mental abilities—recognizing a face, distinguishing a cat from a dog, knowing whether the word *line* refers to a rope or a fragment of poetry or a social come-on. A computer's capabilities exceed our own at tasks that use its unique strengths—vast memory and precise logic and retrieval. But computers have not duplicated the wide-ranging intelligence of a human mind, which can *all at once* converse naturally, recognize a caricaturized face, use common sense, experience emotion, and consciously reflect on its own existence.

"Even though I am not religious, the amazement and wonder I have about the human mind is closer to religious awe than dispassionate analysis."

Bill Gates
1997

Computer logic William McCune of Argonne National Laboratory has created a computer reasoning program. In 1996 it solved a problem that had stumped mathematicians for 60 years, offering a proof that would have been called creative if a human had thought of it. (From Kolata, 1996)

REHEARSE IT!

1. We use the concept "bird" to think and talk about a variety of creatures, all of which have wings and feathers. A concept is
   - **a.** a mental grouping of similar things.
   - **b.** an example of insight.
   - **c.** a fixation on certain characteristics.
   - **d.** another word for "prototype."
2. Sometimes we solve problems through trial and error, trying hundreds or even thousands of solutions before finding one that works. At other times we are more methodical or systematic. The most systematic procedure for solving a problem is
   - **a.** heuristics.
   - **b.** an algorithm.
   - **c.** insight.
   - **d.** intuition.
3. A major obstacle to problem solving is confirmation bias, the tendency to search for information that confirms our preconceptions while ignoring information that might prove us wrong. Another obstacle to problem solving is fixation, which is
   - **a.** an error we make when we base our judgments on certain vivid memories.
   - **b.** the art of framing the same question in two different ways.
   - **c.** the inability to view a problem from a new perspective.
   - **d.** a rule of thumb for judging the likelihood of an event in terms of our mental image of it.
4. You move into a new neighborhood and notice that your next-door neighbor is very neatly dressed, wears glasses, and is reading a Greek play. Given a choice between her being a librarian and a store clerk, you incorrectly guess that she is a librarian. Your incorrect judgment is probably due to
   - **a.** the availability heuristic.
   - **b.** confirmation bias.
   - **c.** overconfidence.
   - **d.** the representativeness heuristic.
5. After a New York City bombing by foreign-born terrorists in 1993, many observers incorrectly assumed that the 1995 bombing of a federal building in Oklahoma City was probably the work of foreign-born terrorists. This assumption illustrates
   - **a.** belief perseverance.
   - **b.** the availability heuristic.
   - **c.** functional fixedness.
   - **d.** confirmation bias.
6. The way an issue is posed can affect our decisions and judgments. For example, one study found that people perceived student cheating to be worse if told that 65 percent of students had cheated than if told that 35 percent of students had not cheated. In this case people's reactions were influenced by
   - **a.** belief perseverance.
   - **b.** fixation.
   - **c.** confirmation bias.
   - **d.** framing.

Language transmits culture The actual words and grammar may differ from culture to culture, but every society has a history that it transmits in story form to its children. Here, a group of Ivory Coast boys listen as an elder retells a tribal legend.

Language

The most tangible indication of our thinking power is **language**—our spoken, written, or gestured words and the ways we combine them as we think and communicate. Humans have long and proudly proclaimed that language sets us above all other animals. "When we study human language," asserted linguist Noam Chomsky (1972), "we are approaching what some might call the 'human essence,' the qualities of mind that are, so far as we know, unique" to humans. To cognitive scientist Steven Pinker (1990), language is "the jewel in the crown of cognition." When the human vocal tract evolved the capacity to utter vowels, our capacity for language exploded, catapulting our species forward (Diamond, 1989). Whether spoken, written, or signed, language enables us to communicate complex ideas from person to person and to transmit civilization's accumulated knowledge across generations.

Language Development

5. *When do children acquire language, and how does it develop?*

Make a quick guess: How many words did you learn in one average day during the years between your first birthday and your high school graduation?

The average secondary school graduate knows some 80,000 words (Miller & Gildea, 1987). That averages (after age 1) to nearly 5000 words learned each year, or 13 each day! How you did it—how the 5000 words a year you learned could so far outnumber the roughly 200 words a year that your schoolteachers consciously taught you—is one of the great human wonders. Before children can add 2 + 2, they are creating their own original and grammatically appropriate sentences. Most parents would have trouble stating the rules of syntax. Yet

language our spoken, written, or gestured words and the ways we combine them to communicate meaning.

Although you probably know 80,000 words, you use only 150 words for about half of what you say.

their preschoolers comprehend and speak with a facility that puts to shame a college student struggling to learn a foreign language or a scientist struggling to simulate natural language on a computer. How does our astonishing facility for language unfold, and how can we explain it?

Acquiring Language

Children's language development moves from simplicity to complexity. Infants start without language (*in fantis* means "not speaking"). Yet by 4 months of age, babies can read lips and discriminate speech sounds. They prefer to look at a face that matches a sound, so we know they can recognize that *ah* comes from wide open lips and *ee* from a mouth with corners pulled back (Kuhl & Meltzoff, 1982). At about this age, babies enter a **babbling stage** in which they spontaneously utter a variety of sounds such as *ah-goo*.

Babbling is not an imitation of adult speech, for it includes sounds from various languages, even sounds that do not occur in the household's language. From this early babbling, a listener could not identify an infant as being, say, French, Korean, or Ethiopian. Deaf infants babble (repeat syllablelike gestures), too (Petitto & Marentette, 1991). It seems, then, that before nurture molds our speech, nature enables a wide range of possible sounds.

Babbling eventually comes to resemble the characteristic sounds and intonations of the household language. By the time infants are about 10 months old, their babbling has changed so that a trained ear can identify the language of the household (de Boysson-Bardies & others, 1989). Sounds outside the infant's native tongue begin to disappear. And infants gradually lose their ability to discriminate sounds they never hear. Clever experiments by Janet Werker (1989) reveal that at 6 months infants can perceive subtle sound differences in other languages, but by 12 months they cannot (Figure 8.5). Without exposure to other languages, we became functionally deaf to speech sounds not found in our native language. Thus, by adulthood those who speak only English cannot discriminate certain Japanese sounds. Nor can Japanese adults with no training in English distinguish between the English *r* and *l* (Japanese has a consonant midway between *r* and *l*). Thus, *la-la-ra-ra* may sound like the same repeated syllable to a Japanese adult (believe it or not). Japanese also has no *p* or *f*. So, *please* sounds very much like *freeze*, which may explain why Yoshihiro Hattori, a Japanese exchange student mistaken for a burglar, failed to understand a gun-toting Louisiana homeowner's order to *freeze* and was tragically shot to death.

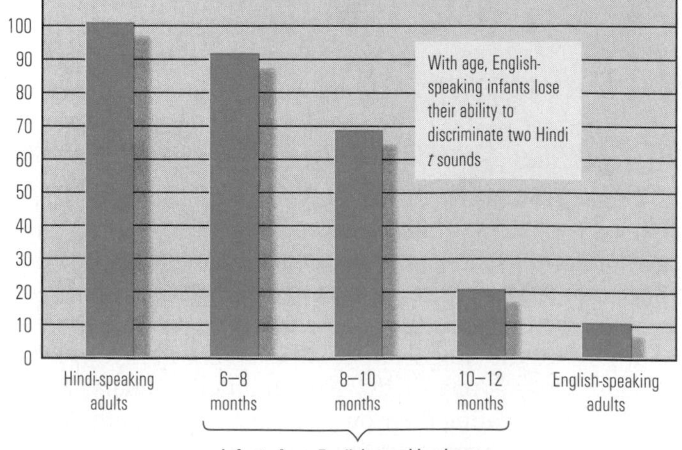

Figure 8.5 Testing for speech sound perception We are all born with the ability to recognize speech sounds from all the world's languages. In Janet Werker's lab, an infant is reinforced with applause and by activating toy animals when he looks to the right after hearing a changed sound (as in *ba, ba, ba, ba, da, da*). Adult Hindi-speakers and young infants from English-speaking homes can easily discriminate two Hindi *t* sounds not spoken in English. By about age 1, however, English-speaking listeners rarely perceive the sound difference. (Adapted from Werker, 1989)

babbling stage beginning at 4 months, the stage of speech development in which the infant spontaneously utters various sounds at first unrelated to the household language.

one-word stage the stage in speech development, from about age 1 to 2, during which a child speaks mostly in single words.

two-word stage beginning about age 2, the stage in speech development during which a child speaks mostly two-word statements.

telegraphic speech during the two-word stage, speech patterns in which the child speaks like a telegram—"go car"—using mostly nouns and verbs and omitting "auxiliary" words.

Around the first birthday (the exact age varies from child to child), most children enter the **one-word stage**. Having already learned that sounds carry meanings, they begin to use sounds to communicate meaning. Their first words usually contain only one syllable—*ma* or *da*, for instance—and may be barely recognizable. But family members quickly learn to understand the infant's language, and gradually it conforms more and more to the family's language.

Most of the child's first words refer to things that move or can be played with—a dog or a ball, for example, rather than the table or crib that just sits there (Nelson, 1973). At this one-word stage, an inflected word may equal a sentence. "Doggy!" may mean "Look at the dog out there!"

Children typically use more and more single words during the second year. Before their second birthday, they usually enter the **two-word stage**, when they start uttering two-word sentences (Table 8.1). Language at this stage is characterized by **telegraphic speech**: Like telegrams (TERMS ACCEPTED. SEND MONEY), this early form of speech contains mostly nouns and verbs (*Want juice*). Also like telegrams, it follows rules of syntax; the words are in a sensible order. The English-speaking child typically says adjectives before nouns—*big doggy* rather than *doggy big*.

There seems to be no "three-word stage." Once children move out of the two-word stage, they quickly begin uttering longer phrases (Fromkin & Rodman, 1983). Although the sentences may still sound like a telegraphed message, they continue to follow the rules of syntax (*Mommy get ball*). By early elementary school, the child understands complex sentences and begins to enjoy the humor conveyed by double meanings: "You never starve in the desert because of all the sand-which-is there."

"Got idea. Talk better. Combine words. Make sentences."

A cultural universal: In every language, the commonest words are the shortest. As a word or phrase is used more and more, it often gets shortened. Television *becomes* TV, compact disc *becomes* CD *(Triandis, 1994).*

Explaining Language Development

Those who study language acquisition inevitably wonder how we do it. Attempts to answer this question have sparked a spirited intellectual controversy. The nature-nurture debate surfaces again and, here as elsewhere, appreciation for innate predisposition has grown.

Behaviorist B. F. Skinner (1957) believed that we can explain language development with familiar learning principles, such as association (of the sights of things with the sounds of words); imitation (of the words and syntax modeled by others); and reinforcement (with success, smiles, and hugs when the child says something right). Thus, Skinner (1985) argued, babies learn to talk

Table 8.1 Summary of Language Development

Month (approximate)	Stage
4	Babbles many speech sounds.
10	Babbling reveals household language.
12	One-word stage.
24	Two-word, telegraphic speech.
24+	Language develops rapidly into complete sentences.

in many of the same ways that animals learn to peck keys and press bars: "Verbal behavior evidently came into existence when, through a critical step in the evolution of the human species, the vocal musculature became susceptible to operant conditioning."

Linguist Noam Chomsky (1959, 1987) thinks Skinner was naive. Surely, says Chomsky, a Martian scientist observing children in a single-language community would conclude that language is almost entirely inborn. It isn't, because children do learn the language used in their environment. But the rate at which they acquire words and grammar without being taught is too extraordinary to be explained solely by learning principles. Children create all sorts of sentences they have never heard and, therefore, could not be imitating. There are 3,628,800 ways to arrange this sentence's 10 words. Only a handful of them make any sense. Yet any 4-year-old could pick them out from among the 3,628,700+ nonsensical orderings.

Thanks to our inborn universal grammar, we readily learn whatever language we hear. It happens so naturally—as naturally as birds learning to fly—that training hardly helps.

Moreover, many of the errors young children make result from overgeneralizing logical grammatical rules, such as adding *-ed* to make the past tense (from de Cuevas, 1990):

> **Child:** *My teacher holded the baby rabbits and we petted them.*
>
> **Mother:** *Did you say your teacher held the baby rabbits?*
>
> **Child:** *Yes.*
>
> **Mother:** *Did you say she held them tightly?*
>
> **Child:** *No, she holded them loosely.*

Chomsky (1987) likens the behaviorist view of how language develops to filling a bottle with water. He instead views language development as "helping a flower to grow in its own way." It is, he believes, akin to sexual maturation: Given adequate nurture, it just "happens to the child." All human languages have the same grammatical building blocks, such as nouns and verbs, subjects and objects, negations and questions, singular and plural word forms. Our 5000 human languages are therefore dialects of the "universal grammar" for which our brains are prewired. Thanks to our inborn universal grammar, we readily learn whatever language we hear. It happens so naturally—as naturally as birds learning to fly—that training hardly helps. Just expose children to language and they will soak it up. If not exposed to a language, a group of children will make up their own. Without exposure to language, deaf children, too, will spontaneously create one with gestures, complete with sophisticated grammar (Horgan, 1995; Pinker, 1995).

Other worlds may have languages that, for us humans, are unlearnable, but our world does not. Chomsky maintains that our language acquisition capacity is like a box—a "language acquisition device"—in which grammar switches are thrown as children experience their language. Thus, English-speaking children learn to put the object of a sentence last ("She ate an apple"). Japanese-speaking children put the object before the verb ("She an apple ate"). We are born with the hardware and an operating system; experience writes the software (Figure 8.6).

Cognitive scientists still debate how much of our language capacity is inborn (Shanks, 1993). With experience (but with no "inborn" linguistic rules), computers can learn to form past-tense verbs appropriately. They can learn, for example, to change words ending in *ow* to *ew*, as in *throw/threw*. To some scientists, this suggests the brain could be a blanker slate than Chomsky believes.

The scholars agree, however, that life's first years are critical. Those who learn a second language as adults usually speak it with the accent of their first language.

Figure 8.6 Nature and nurture Genes design the mechanisms for a language, and experience activates them as it modifies the brain. Grow up in Paris and you will speak French (environment matters), but not if you are a cat (genes matter).

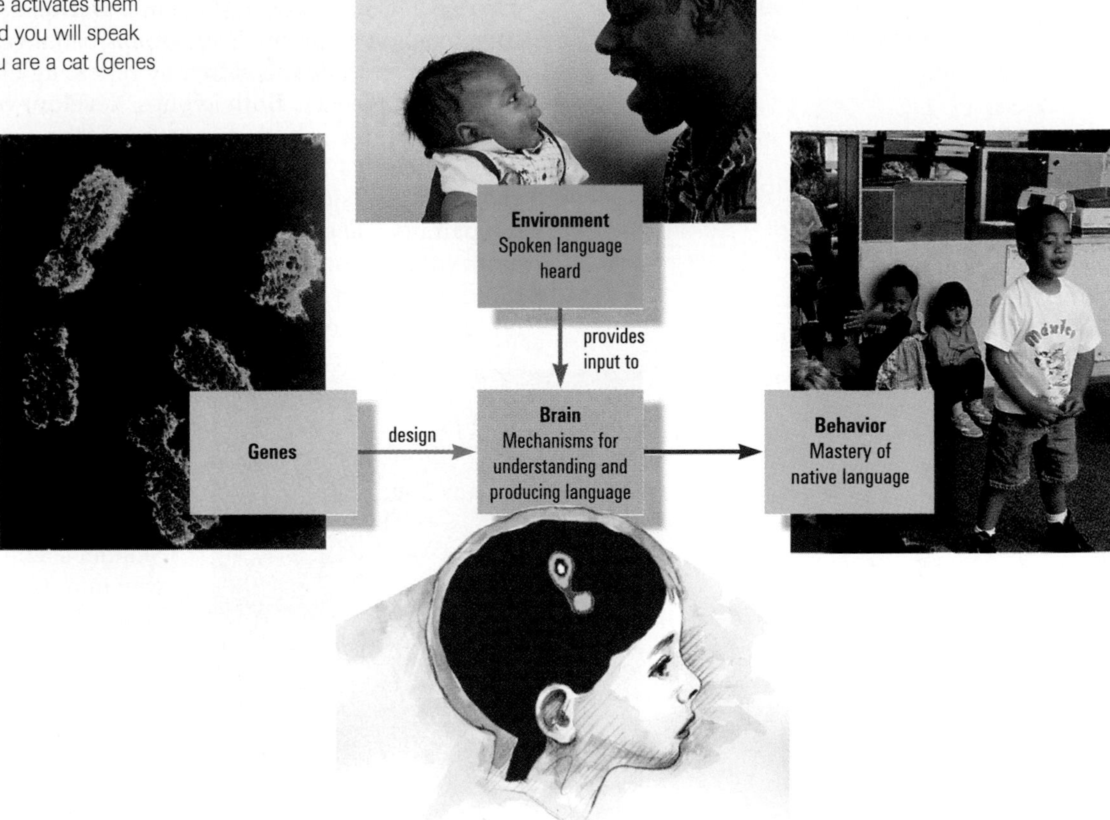

Figure 8.7 New language learning gets harder with age Young children have a readiness to learn language. Ten years after coming to the United States, Asian immigrants took a grammar test. Those who arrived before age 8 understood grammar as well as native speakers. Those who arrived later did not. (From Johnson & Newport, 1991)

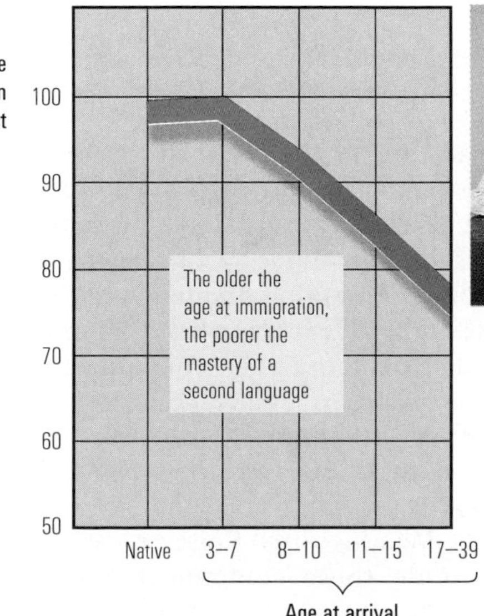

Do they master the foreign grammar better than the accent? To find out, Jacqueline Johnson and Elissa Newport (1991) gave Korean and Chinese immigrants to the United States a grammar test, requiring them to identify each of 276 sentences ("Yesterday the hunter shoots a deer") as grammatically correct or incorrect. Some of the test-takers had immigrated in early childhood, others as adults. Regardless of their age at immigration, each had been in the United States for approximately 10 years. Nevertheless, as Figure 8.7 reveals, those who learned their second language early learned it best. Chomsky would say that once the grammar switches are thrown during a child's developing years, mastering another grammar becomes more difficult. It's rather like Michael Jordan's ill-fated attempt to master the visual-motor connections of baseball hitting long after the normal window of opportunity for acquiring such skills.

Learning is already throwing switches during the first year. When you or I listen to an unfamiliar language, the syllables all run together. Someone unfamiliar with English might, for example, hear the "United Nations" as the Uneye Tednay Shuns. Before our first birthday, our brains were discerning word breaks by statistically analyzing which syllables most often go together. Jenny Saffran and her colleagues (1996) showed this by exposing 8-month-old infants to a computer voice speaking an unbroken, monotone string of nonsense syllables (*bidakupadotigolabubidaku . . .*). After just two minutes of exposure, the infants were able to recognize (as indicated by their attention) three-syllable sequences that appeared repeatedly.

"Childhood is the time for language, no doubt about it. Young children, the younger the better, are good at it; it is child's play. It is a onetime gift to the species."

Lewis Thomas
The Fragile Species
1992

The impact of early experience is also evident among the deaf. Hearing children of hearing-speaking parents, and deaf children of deaf-signing parents, have much in common. Both groups babble as infants—hearing children by repeating sounds, deaf children by repeating elementary sign gestures (Petitto & Marentette, 1991). Both groups develop vocabularies, at comparable rates (Meier, 1991). For both groups, later-than-usual exposure to language (at age 2 or 3) unleashes their brain's idle language capacity, producing a rush of language. But consider the 90+ percent of deaf children born to hearing-nonsigning parents. These children typically do not experience language during their early years. Compared with deaf children exposed to sign language from birth, those who learn to sign as teens or adults are like immigrants who learn English after childhood. They can master the basic words and how to order them, but they never become as fluent as native signers in producing and comprehending subtle grammatical differences (Newport, 1990).

No means NO! No matter how you say it Deaf children of deaf-signing parents and hearing children of hearing parents have much in common. They develop language skills at about the same rate, and they are equally effective at opposing parental wishes and demanding their way.

To summarize, children's genes design complex brain wiring that prepares them to learn language as they interact with their caregivers. Skinner's emphasis on learning helps explain why infants acquire the language they hear and how they add new words to their vocabularies. Chomsky's emphasis on our built-in readiness to learn grammar rules helps explain why preschoolers acquire language so readily and use grammar so well. Once again, we see biology and experience working together.

Returning to our debate about humanity's thinking powers, let's pause to issue a report card. On decision making and judgment, our error-prone species might rate a C+. On problem solving, where humans are inventive yet vulnerable to fixation, we would probably receive better marks, perhaps a B+. On cognitive efficiency, our fallible but quick heuristics earn us an A. And when it comes to learning and using language, the awestruck experts would surely award the human species an A+.

Animal Language

6. *Is language unique to humans, or do other species also have language?*

If in our use of language we humans are, as the psalmist rhapsodized, "little lower than God," where do other animals fit in the scheme of things? Are they "little lower than human"? In part, the answer lies in the extent to which other species share our capacity for language.

Smart bird brain Alex, an African gray parrot trained and tested by University of Arizona professor Irene Pepperberg (1994), displays numerical competence when shown novel assortments of objects. Asked, for example, "How many red blocks?" or "How many blue balls?" Alex answers correctly more than 80 percent of the time.

Without doubt, animals communicate. Vervet monkeys have different alarm cries for different predators: a barking call for a leopard, a coughing for an eagle, and a chuttering for a snake. Hearing the leopard alarm, other vervets climb the nearest tree. Hearing the eagle alarm, they rush into the bushes. Hearing the snake chutter, they stand up and scan the ground (Byrne, 1991). Whales also communicate, with clicks and wails. But do these communications make up a language?

The Case of the Apes

The greatest challenge to humanity's claim to be the only language-using species has come from reports of apes that "talk" with people. Genetically speaking, our closest relatives are the chimpanzees, and the chimpanzees' closest relatives are not other apes, but us (Sagan & Druyan, 1992). Knowing that chimpanzees could not vocalize more than a few words, University of Nevada researchers Allen Gardner and Beatrice Gardner (1969) tried to teach sign language words to a chimp named Washoe, as though she were a deaf human child. After four years, Washoe could use 132 signs. At age 31, Washoe had a vocabulary of 181 signs (Sanz & Jensvold, 1997). The Gardners' announcement of the success of their efforts aroused enormous scientific and public interest. One *New York Times* reporter, having learned sign language from his deaf parents, visited Washoe and exclaimed, "Suddenly I realized I was conversing with a member of another species in my native tongue."

Although apes usually signed just single words, they sometimes strung signs together to form intelligible sentences. Washoe signed, "You me go out, please."

Seeing a doll floating in her water, Washoe signed, "Baby in my drink."

During the 1970s, further evidence of "ape language" surfaced. Although apes usually signed just single words, they sometimes strung signs together to form intelligible sentences. Washoe signed, "You me go out, please." Apes even appeared to combine words creatively. Washoe designated a swan as a "water bird." Koko, a gorilla trained by Francine Patterson (1978) in California, reportedly described a long-nosed Pinocchio doll as an "elephant baby." Lana, a chimpanzee that "talks" by punching buttons wired to a computer that translates her punchings into English, wanted her trainer's orange. She had no word for *orange*, but she did know her colors and the word for *apple*, so she improvised: "?Tim give apple which-is orange" (Rumbaugh, 1977).

As ape language reports accumulated, it seemed that apes might indeed be "little lower than human." Their vocabularies and sentences are simple, rather like those of a 2-year-old child. Yet the apes do seem to share what we humans have considered our unique ability.

Another "talking" chimpanzee Lana has learned to speak by punching word symbols on a computer keyboard. When she presses a key, the symbol lights up.

But Can Apes Really Talk?

By the late 1970s, fascination with "talking apes" turned toward cynicism: Were the chimps language champs or were the researchers chumps? The ape language researchers were making monkeys out of themselves, said the skeptics, who raised the following arguments:

- Apes gain their limited vocabularies only with great difficulty. They are hardly like speaking or signing children, who effortlessly soak up dozens of new words a week. Saying that apes can learn language because they can sign words is like saying humans can fly because they can jump.
- Chimps can make signs or push buttons in sequence to get a reward, just as Moscow circus bears can learn to ride unicycles. But pigeons, too, can peck a sequence of keys to get grain (Straub & others, 1979). No one says the pigeon is "talking."
- Apes can certainly use symbols meaningfully. But "Give orange me give eat orange me eat orange . . ." is a far cry from the exquisite syntax of a 3-year-old (Pinker, 1995). To the child, "you tickle" and "tickle you" communicate different ideas. A chimp might sign the phrases interchangeably.
- After training a chimp whom he named Nim Chimsky, Herbert Terrace (1979) concluded that much of chimpanzees' signing is nothing more than imitation of their trainers' signs.

But is this language? The ability of chimpanzees to express themselves in American Sign Language (ASL) raises questions about the very nature of language. Here, the trainer is asking, "What is this?" The sign in response is "Baby." Does the response constitute language?

- Presented with ambiguous information, people tend to see what they want or expect to see. (Recall the demonstrations of perceptual set in Chapter 4.) Interpreting chimpanzee signs as language may be little more than wishful thinking on the part of their trainers, claimed Terrace. (When Washoe signed *water bird*, she perhaps was separately naming *water* and *bird*.)

"Chimps do not develop language," surmises linguist Steven Pinker (1995). "But that is no shame on them; humans would surely do no better if trained to hoot and shriek like chimps, to perform the waggle-dance of the bee, or any of the other wonderful feats in nature's talent show."

In science as in politics, controversy stimulates progress. The provocative claim that "apes share our capacity for language" and the skeptical rejoinder that "apes no use language" (as Washoe might have put it) have moved psychologists toward a greater appreciation of apes' remarkable capabilities, and of our own. Everyone agrees that humans alone possess language, if by the term we mean verbal or signed expression of complex grammar. If we mean, more simply, the ability to communicate through a meaningful sequence of symbols, then apes are indeed capable of language.

"Although humans make sounds with their mouths and occasionally look at each other, there is no solid evidence that they actually communicate with each other."

"[Our] egocentric view that [we are] unique from all other forms of animal life is being jarred to the core."

Duane Rumbaugh and Sue Savage-Rumbaugh (1978)

Although chimpanzees do not have our facility for language, their thinking and communicating abilities continue to impress their trainers. After her second infant died, a depressed Washoe repeatedly asked "Baby?" and became withdrawn when told "Baby dead, baby gone, baby finished." Two weeks later, caretaker Roger Fouts (1992, 1997) had better news for Washoe: "I have baby for you." Washoe reacted to the signed news with instant excitement, her hair on end, swaggering and panting while signing over and again, "Baby, my baby." When Fouts then introduced the foster infant, Loulis, it took several hours for them to warm to each other, whereupon Washoe broke the ice by signing, "Come baby" and cuddling Loulis. In the months that followed, Loulis picked up 68 signs simply by observing Washoe and three other language-trained chimps.

Moreover, Washoe, Loulis, and the others now sign spontaneously, as when asking one another to *chase*, *tickle*, *hug*, *come*, or *groom*. People who sign can eavesdrop on these chimp-to-chimp conversations with near-perfect agreement about what the chimps are saying, 90 percent of which pertains to social interaction, reassurance, or play (Fouts & Bodamer, 1987). The chimps are even modestly bilingual; they can translate spoken English words into signs (Shaw, 1989–1990).

Most stunning, however, is the discovery by Sue Savage-Rumbaugh and her colleagues (1993) that pygmy chimpanzees can learn to comprehend the semantic nuances of spoken English. Kanzi, one such chimp with the grammatical abilities of a 2½-year-old, happened onto language while observing his adoptive mother being language trained. Kanzi behaves intelligently whether asked, "Can you show me the light?" or "Can you bring me the [flash]light?" or "Can you turn the light on?" Kanzi also knows the spoken words *snake*, *bite*, and *dog*. Given stuffed animals and asked, for the first time, to "make the dog bite the snake," he put the snake to the dog's mouth. For chimps as for humans, early life is a critical time for learning language. If raised without early exposure to speech or word symbols, the chimps are unable as adults to gain language competence (Rumbaugh & Savage-Rumbaugh, 1994).

Do our ideas come first and wait for words to name them? Or are our thoughts conceived in words and unthinkable without them?

So, trained apes' language capabilities are modest by human standards. Yet their impressive cognitive powers seem indeed to make them "little lower than human." If Kanzi "had a vocal tract, he would be talking," exclaims Duane Rumbaugh (1994). Realizing this, we see once again how animal research can increase our respect for the creatures studied. Believing that animals could not think, Descartes and other philosophers argued that they were living robots without moral rights. Animals, it has been said at one time or another, cannot plan, conceptualize, count, use tools, show compassion, or use language (Thorpe, 1974). Today, we know better. We have seen primates exhibit insight, show family loyalty, communicate with one another, display altruism, transmit cultural patterns across generations, and comprehend the syntax of human speech. Working out the moral implications of all this is an unfinished task for our own thinking species.

Thinking and Language

7. What is the relationship between thinking and language?

Thinking and language intricately intertwine. Asking which comes first is one of psychology's chicken-and-egg questions. Do our ideas come first and wait for words to name them? Or are our thoughts conceived in words and unthinkable without them?

linguistic relativity Whorf's hypothesis that language determines the way we think.

Language Influences Thinking

Linguist Benjamin Lee Whorf contended that language determines the way we think. According to Whorf's (1956) **linguistic relativity** hypothesis, different languages impose different conceptions of reality: "Language itself shapes a man's basic ideas." The Hopi, Whorf noted, have no past tense for their verbs. Therefore, he contended, a Hopi could not so readily *think* about the past.

Whorf's relativity hypothesis would probably not occur to people who speak only one language and view that language as simply a vehicle for thought. But to those who speak two dissimilar languages, such as English and Japanese, it seems obvious that a person thinks differently in different languages (Brown, 1986). Unlike English, which has a rich vocabulary for self-focused emotions such as anger, Japanese has many words for interpersonal emotions such as sympathy (Markus & Kitayama, 1991). Many bilinguals report that they even have a different sense of self, depending on which language they are using (Matsumoto, 1994). After immigrating from Asia to North America, bilinguals may reveal different personalities when taking the same personality test in their two languages (Dinges & Hull, 1992). Learn a language and you learn about a culture. When a language becomes extinct—the likely fate of most of the world's 5000 remaining languages—the world loses the culture and thinking that hangs on that language.

"All words are pegs to hang ideas on."

Henry Ward Beecher
Proverbs From Plymouth Pulpit
1887

"To call forth a concept, a word is needed."

Antoine Lavoisier
Elements of Chemistry
1789

It is too strong to say that language *determines* the *way* we think. A New Guinean without our words for shapes and colors nevertheless perceives them much as we do (Rosch, 1974). But our words do influence *what* we think (Hardin & Banaji, 1993). We therefore do well to choose our words carefully. When people referred to women as *girls*—as in "the girls at the office"—it perpetuated a view of women's having lower status, did it not? Or consider the generic use of the pronoun *he*. Does it make any difference whether I write "A child learns language as *he* interacts with *his* caregivers" or "Children learn language as *they* interact with *their* caregivers"? Some argue that it makes no difference because every reader knows that "the masculine gender shall be deemed and taken to include females" (as the British Parliament declared in 1850).

But is the generic *he* always taken to include females? Twenty studies have consistently found that it is not (Henley, 1989). For example, Janet Hyde (1984) asked children to finish stories for which she gave them a first line, such as "When a kid goes to school, ______ often feels excited on the first day." When Hyde used *he* in the blank, the children's stories were nearly always about males. "He or she" in the blank resulted in female characters about one-third of the time. Studies with adolescents and adults in North America and New Zealand have found similar effects of the generic *he* (Hamilton, 1988; Martyna, 1978; Ng, 1990). Sentences about "the artist and his work" tend to conjure up images of a man. Similarly, ambiguous actions taken by a "chairman of the board" seem to reveal an assertive and independent personality. The same actions taken by a "chairperson of the board" seem to reveal a more caring and warm personality (McConnell & Fazio, 1996).

A safe sign We have outfielder William Hoy to thank for baseball sign language. The first deaf player to join the major leagues, in 1892, he invented hand signals for "Strike!" "Safe!" (shown here) and "Yerr Out!" (Pollard, 1992). Such gestures worked so well that referees in all sports now use invented signs, and fans are fluent in sports sign language.

Consider, too, that people use generic pronouns selectively, as in "the doctor . . . he" and "the secretary . . . she" (MacKay, 1983). If *he* and *his* were truly gender-free, we shouldn't skip a beat when hearing that "a nurse must answer his calls" or that "man, like other mammals, nurses his young." That we are startled indicates that *his* carries a gender connotation that clashes with our idea of *nurse*.

The power of language to influence thought makes vocabulary building a crucial part of education. To expand language is to expand the ability to think. In young children, thinking develops hand in hand with language (Gopnik & Meltzoff, 1986). What is true for preschoolers is true for everyone: *It pays to increase your word power.* That is why most textbooks, including this one, introduce new words—to teach new ideas and new ways of thinking.

Increased word power helps explain what McGill University researcher Wallace Lambert (1992; Lambert & others, 1993) calls the "bilingual advantage." Bilingual children in Canada, Switzerland, Israel, South Africa, and Singapore outperform monolinguals on intelligence tests. Knowing this, Lambert helped devise a Canadian program that enables English-speaking children to be immersed in French. (From 1981 to 1991, the number of non-Quebec Canadian children immersed in French quadrupled from 65,000 to 250,000 [Columbo, 1994].) For most of their first three school years, the English-speaking children are taught by a French-speaking teacher; not until the fifth and sixth grades do they receive half their instruction in English. Not surprisingly, the children attain a natural French fluency unrivaled by other methods of language teaching. Moreover, compared with similarly capable children in control conditions, they do so without detriment to their English fluency, and with increased aptitude scores, math scores, and appreciation for French Canadian culture.

Is the generic* he *always taken to include females? Twenty studies have consistently found that it is not.

So, for English-speaking Canadians, immersion followed by bilingual education pays dividends. Does bilingual education for children in a linguistic minority also pay dividends? Advocates of "English-only" education doubt it. They argue that bilingual programs are expensive, ineffective, and detrimental to non–English-speaking children's assimilation into their English-based cultures. But studies find that such children benefit from bilingual education, especially in "two-way" schools where they, together with English-speaking children, experience half their classes in English and half in their native language. Compared with non–English-speaking children dropped into English-only schools, those in the two-way schools tend to develop higher self-esteem. They drop out less frequently. And they eventually attain higher levels of academic achievement and English proficiency (Hamers & Blanc, 1989; Padilla & Benavides, 1992; Thomas & Collier, 1997).

Increasing word power through sign language has also had great benefits for deaf people, who for thousands of years were viewed as incompetent to inherit property, marry, be educated, or have challenging work (Sacks, 1990). Since the spread of signed instruction, the deaf have shown that, when exposed to signing as preschoolers and then schooled in their language, they become fully literate. Deaf children with native sign fluency—learned, for example, as children of signing deaf parents—outperform other signing deaf children on measures of intelligence and academic achievement (Isham & Kamin, 1993). For both the deaf and the hearing, language transforms experience. Language connects us to the past and the future. Language fuels our imagination. Language links us to one another.

A thoughtful art Piano playing engages thinking without language. In the absence of a piano, mental practice can sustain one's skill.

Thinking Without Language

When you are alone, do you talk to yourself? Is "thinking" simply conversing with yourself? Without a doubt, words convey ideas. But are there not times when ideas precede words? To turn on the cold water in your bathroom, in which direction do you turn the handle?

To answer this question, you probably thought not in words but with a mental picture. Indeed, we often think in images. Artists think in images. So do composers, poets, mathematicians, athletes, and scientists. Albert Einstein reported that he achieved some of his greatest insights through visual images and only later put them into words.

Liu Chi Kung placed second in the 1958 Tchaikovsky competition—the piano Olympics—and was imprisoned a year later during China's cultural revolution. Soon after his release, after seven years without touching a piano, he was back on tour and critics judged his musicianship better than ever. How did

The interplay of thought and language The traffic runs both ways between thinking and language. Thinking affects our language, which affects our thought.

he do it without practice? "I did practice," said Liu, "every day. I rehearsed every piece I had ever played, note by note, in my mind" (Garfield, 1986).

For Olympic athletes, "mental practice has become a standard part of training," reports Richard Suinn (1997). Golf great Jack Nicklaus has said that he would "watch a movie" in his head before each shot. Georgia Nigro (1984) demonstrated the wisdom of mental practice in a laboratory test. She had people actually throw 24 darts at a target, then had half the people throw 24 darts mentally, and, finally, had all the people throw another 24 darts. Only those who had mentally practiced showed any improvement.

Moreover, remember a lesson from earlier chapters: Much information processing occurs outside of consciousness, beyond language. Inside the ever-active brain, many streams of activity flow in parallel, functioning automatically, remembered implicitly, only occasionally surfacing as conscious words. So, yes, there is much cognition without language.

What, then, should we say about the relationship between thinking and language? We have seen that language influences thinking. But if thinking did not also affect language, there would never be any new words. New words express new ideas. The basketball term *slam dunk* was coined after the act itself had become fairly common. So, let us simply say that *thinking affects our language, which then affects our thought.*

Psychological research on thinking and language mirrors the mixed reviews given our species in literature and religion. The human mind is simultaneously capable of striking intellectual failures and of vast intellectual power. Some misjudgments have disastrous consequences, so we do well to appreciate our capacity for error. Yet our heuristics often serve us well, and they certainly are efficient. Moreover, our ingenuity at problem solving and our extraordinary power of language surely, among the animals, rank humankind as almost "infinite in faculties."

REHEARSE IT!

7. Children progress from babbling to sentences of two and then four, five, six, or more words. The one-word stage of speech development is usually reached at about

a. 4 months. **c.** 1 year.
b. 6 months. **d.** 2 years.

8. B. F. Skinner believed that we learn language the same way we learn other behaviors—through association, imitation, and reinforcement. Skinner's behaviorist view is most helpful in explaining

a. the onset of babbling.
b. the speech behavior of deaf infants.
c. the seemingly effortless mastery of grammatical rules by very young children.
d. why children learn their household's language.

9. According to Noam Chomsky, we are biologically prepared to acquire language and are born with a readiness to learn the grammatical rules of the language we hear. He believes all we need to acquire language is

a. instruction in grammar.
b. exposure to language in early childhood.
c. reinforcement for babbling and other early verbal behaviors.
d. imitation and drill.

10. There is much controversy over whether apes can be taught to use language in the way that humans do. However, most researchers of ape sign language agree that apes can

a. communicate through symbols.
b. reproduce most human speech sounds.
c. create new sentences and meanings.
d. surpass a human 3-year-old in language skills.

11. According to Benjamin Lee Whorf, our language determines the way we perceive and think about the world. His linguistic relativity hypothesis suggests an explanation for why

a. a person who learns a second language thinks differently in that language.
b. children have a built-in readiness to learn grammatical rules.
c. apes are able to communicate through sign language.
d. artists, athletes, and others are able to think in visual images.

intelligence the mental abilities needed to select, adapt to, and shape environments. It involves the abilities to profit from experience, solve problems, reason, and successfully meet challenges and achieve goals.

mental age a measure of intelligence test performance devised by Binet; the chronological age typical of a given level of performance. Thus, a child who does as well as the average 8-year-old is said to have a mental age of 8.

Intelligence

So far, we have considered how humans, in general, think and communicate. But do we humans not differ from one another in our intellectual capacities? No controversy in psychology has been more heated than the question of whether there exists in each person a general intellectual capacity that can be measured and quantitifed as a number. School boards, courts, and scientists debate the usefulness and fairness of intelligence and aptitude tests. Should such tests be used to rank individuals and to determine whether to admit them to a particular college or to hire them in a particular job? Do groups differ in native intelligence?

Let's therefore consider: What is intelligence? How is it assessed? And to what extent does it result from nature (heredity) rather than nurture (environment)? Is intelligence testing society's best means of identifying those who would benefit from special opportunities? Or is intelligence testing a potent discriminatory weapon camouflaged as science?

The Origins of Intelligence Testing

8. *When and why were intelligence tests created?*

Alfred Binet "The scale, properly speaking, does not permit the measure of intelligence, because intellectual qualities . . . cannot be measured as linear surfaces are measured." (Binet & Simon, 1905)

Intelligence is a concept intended to explain why some people perform better than others on cognitive tasks. Robert Sternberg (1997) speaks for many experts in viewing **intelligence** as the mental abilities needed to select, adapt to, and shape environments. Intelligent behavior reflects a capacity to learn from experience, to solve problems, and to reason clearly. To understand the concept of intelligence, it helps first to know the history of intelligence testing.

Alfred Binet: Predicting School Achievement

The modern intelligence-testing movement began at the turn of the twentieth century when the French government passed a law requiring that all children attend school. Teachers soon faced a distressing range of individual differences. Some children seemed incapable of benefiting from the regular school curriculum and in need of special classes. But how could the schools objectively identify children with special needs?

The government was justifiably reluctant to trust teachers' subjective judgments of children's learning potential. Academic slowness might merely reflect inadequate prior education. Also, teachers might prejudge children on the basis of their social backgrounds. To minimize bias, France's minister of public education in 1904 commissioned Alfred Binet (1857–1911) and others to study the problem.

Binet and his collaborator, Théodore Simon, began by assuming that all children follow the same course of intellectual development but that some develop more rapidly. On tests, therefore, a "dull" child should perform as does a typical younger child, and a "bright" child as does a typical older child.

Binet and Simon set out to measure what came to be called a child's **mental age**, the chronological age typical of a given level of performance. The average 9-year-old has a mental age of 9. But many 9-year-olds have mental ages below or above 9. Children below average, such as 9-year-olds who perform at the level of a typical 7-year-old, would struggle with schoolwork considered normal for their age.

Binet hoped his test would be used to improve children's education, but he also feared it would be used to label children and limit their opportunities.

To measure mental age, Binet and Simon developed varied reasoning and problem-solving questions that might predict school achievement. By testing "bright" and "backward" Parisian schoolchildren on these questions, Binet and Simon succeeded: They found items that did predict how well the children handled schoolwork. Binet hoped his test would be used to improve children's education, but he also feared it would be used to label children and limit their opportunities (Gould, 1981).

Lewis Terman: The Innate IQ

What Binet viewed as merely a practical guide for identifying slow learners who needed special help was soon seen by others to be a numerical measure of inherited intelligence. After Binet's death in 1911, Stanford University professor Lewis Terman (1877–1956) decided to use Binet's test. He soon found, however, that the Paris-developed age norms worked poorly with California schoolchildren. So Terman revised the test. He adapted some of Binet's original items, added others, established new age norms, and extended the upper end of the test's range from teenagers to "superior adults." Terman gave his revision the name it retains today—the **Stanford-Binet**.

For such tests, German psychologist William Stern derived the famous **intelligence quotient**, or **IQ**. The IQ was simply a person's mental age divided by chronological age and multiplied by 100 to get rid of the decimal point:

$$\text{IQ} = \frac{\text{mental age}}{\text{chronological age}} \times 100$$

Thus, an average child, whose mental and chronological ages are the same, has an IQ of 100. But an 8-year-old who answers questions as would a typical 10-year-old has an IQ of 125.

Most current intelligence tests, including the Stanford-Binet, no longer compute an IQ. The original IQ formula works fairly well for children but not for adults. Consider: Should a 40-year-old who does as well on the test as an average 20-year-old be assigned an IQ of only 50? Obviously, something is out of whack. Today's intelligence tests therefore produce a mental ability score based on the test-taker's performance relative to the average performance of others the same age. As on the original Stanford-Binet, current tests define this score so that 100 is average, with about two-thirds of all people scoring between 85 and 115. Although there is no longer any intelligence *quotient*, the term "IQ" still lingers in everyday vocabulary as a shorthand expression for "intelligence test score."

"You did very well on your IQ test. You're a man of 49 with the intelligence of a man of 53."

"The IQ test was invented to predict academic performance, nothing else. If we wanted something that would predict life success, we'd have to invent another test completely."

Social Psychologist Robert Zajonc (1984b)

What Is Intelligence?

9. ***Is intelligence a single general ability, or is it formed from several distinct abilities?***

Reading all the conflicting ideas about intelligence can leave you feeling as Alice in Wonderland felt after reading "Jabberwocky": "Somehow it seems to fill my head with ideas—only I don't exactly know what they are." So let's see if we can refine the concept.

One General Ability or Several Specific Abilities?

We all know some people talented in science, others in creative writing, and still others in art, music, or dance. Perhaps you have known a talented artist who is dumbfounded by the simplest mathematical problems, or a brilliant

Stanford Binet the widely used American revision (by Terman at Stanford University) of Binet's original intelligence test.

intelligence quotient (IQ) defined originally as the ratio of mental age (*ma*) to chronological age (*ca*) multiplied by 100 (thus, IQ = $ma/ca \times 100$). On contemporary intelligence tests, the average performance for a given age is assigned a score of 100.

factor analysis a statistical procedure that identifies clusters of related items (called *factors*) on a test; used to identify different dimensions of performance that underlie one's total score.

general intelligence (*g*) a general intelligence factor that Spearman and others believed underlies specific mental abilities and is therefore measured by every task on an intelligence test.

savant syndrome a condition in which a person otherwise limited in mental ability has an amazing specific skill, such as in computation or drawing.

math student who has little aptitude for literary discussion. We may therefore wonder whether people's mental abilities are too diverse to justify labeling them with the single word *intelligence* or quantifying them with a number from some single scale.

To find out whether there might be a general ability factor that runs throughout our specific mental abilities, psychologists study how various abilities relate to one another. A statistical method called **factor analysis** allows researchers to identify clusters of test items that measure a common ability. For example, people who do well on vocabulary items often do well on paragraph comprehension. This cluster helps define a verbal intelligence factor. Other clusters include a spatial ability factor and a reasoning ability factor.

Charles Spearman (1863–1945), who helped develop factor analysis, believed there is also a **general intelligence**, or ***g***, factor that underlies the specific factors. People often have special abilities that stand out, Spearman allowed. But those who score high on one factor, such as verbal intelligence, typically score higher than average on other factors, such as spatial or reasoning ability. So there is at least a small tendency for different abilities to come in the same package. Spearman believed that this commonality, the *g* factor, underlies all of our intelligent behavior, from excelling in school to navigating the sea.

Howard Gardner (1983, 1993, 1995) is a modern representative of the view that intelligence nevertheless comes in different packages. He notes that brain damage may diminish one type of ability but not others. Gardner also studies reports of people with exceptional abilities, including those who excel in only one. People with **savant syndrome**, for example, score at the low end on intelligence tests but have an island of brilliance—some incredible ability, as in computation, drawing, or musical memory (Figure 8.8). These people may have virtually no language ability, yet may be able to compute numbers as quickly and accurately as an electronic calculator, or identify almost instantly the day of the week that corresponds to any given date in history.

Using such evidence, Gardner argues that we do not have *an* intelligence but instead have *multiple* intelligences, each independent of the others. In addition to the verbal and mathematical aptitudes assessed by the standard tests, he identifies distinct aptitudes for musical accomplishment, for spatially analyzing the visual world, for mastering movement skills (as in dance), and for insight-

Figure 8.8 **Savant syndrome** Although hardly able to talk coherently, Britain's Stephen Wiltshire can draw intricate scenes after just one good look. This is a drawing of St. Mark's in Venice, Italy. By age 13, Stephen was famous for his ability to "draw, with greatest ease, any street he had seen; but he could not, unaided, cross one by himself." (Sacks, 1995)

emotional intelligence the ability to perceive, express, understand, and regulate emotions.

aptitude tests tests designed to predict a person's future performance. Aptitude is the capacity to learn.

achievement tests tests designed to assess what a person has learned.

Wechsler Adult Intelligence Scale (WAIS) the most widely used intelligence test, it contains verbal and performance (nonverbal) subtests.

fully understanding ourselves, others, and our natural environment. As exemplars of these alternative intellects he offers poet T. S. Eliot, scientist Albert Einstein, composer Igor Stravinsky, artist Pablo Picasso, dancer Martha Graham, psychiatrist Sigmund Freud, leader Mahatma Gandhi, and naturalist Charles Darwin. According to Gardner, the computer programmer, the poet, the street-smart adolescent who becomes a crafty executive, and the point guard on the basketball team exhibit different kinds of intelligence. A general intelligence score is therefore like the overall rating of a city—which doesn't give you much specific information about its schools, roads, or nightlife.

Wouldn't it be wonderful if the world were so just, responds intelligence researcher Sandra Scarr (1989), that being weak in any area would be compensated by genius in some other area? Alas, the world is not just, for there remains some tendency for different skills to correlate. For example, people with mental disadvantages often have lesser physical abilities as well; thus, we hold Special Olympics to give them a chance to enjoy fair competition.

Robert Sternberg and his colleagues (1993, 1995) agree with Gardner that intelligence is not a single entity. Instead of identifying "multiple intelligences," they distinguish among three aspects of intelligence:

- *Academic problem-solving skills* These are the skills assessed by intelligence tests, which present well-defined problems having a single right answer.
- *Practical intelligence* This type of intelligence is often required for everyday tasks, which are frequently ill-defined, with multiple solutions.
- *Creative intelligence* This type of intelligence is demonstrated in reacting to novel situations.

Intelligence tests predict school grades reasonably well but predict vocational success less well. Managerial success, for example, depends less on the academic abilities assessed by an intelligence test score (assuming the score is average or above) than on a shrewd ability to manage oneself, one's tasks, and other people. Sternberg and Wagner's test of practical managerial intelligence measures whether the test-taker knows how to write effective memos, how to motivate people, when to delegate tasks and responsibilities, how to read people, and how to promote their own careers. Business executives who score high on this test tend to earn higher salaries and receive better performance ratings than do those who score low. People who demonstrate keen practical intelligence may or may not have distinguished themselves in school. In a similar finding, Stephen Ceci and Jeffrey Liker (1986) report that racetrack fans' expertise in handicapping horses—a practical but complex cognitive task—is unrelated to their intelligence test scores.

"You're wise, but you lack tree smarts."

Emotional Intelligence

Also distinct from academic intelligence is what Nancy Cantor and John Kihlstrom (1987) first called *social intelligence*—the know-how involved in comprehending social situations and managing oneself successfully. A critical part of social intelligence is what Peter Salovey and John Mayer (1990; Mayer & Salovey, 1993, 1995, 1997) call **emotional intelligence**—the ability to perceive, express, understand, and regulate emotions. Emotionally intelligent people are self-aware. They can manage their emotions without being hijacked by overwhelming depression, anxiety, or anger. They can delay gratification in pursuit of big rewards rather than being overtaken by their impulses. Their empathy allows them to read others' emotions. They handle others' emotions skillfully—knowing what to say to a grieving friend, how to encourage colleagues, how to manage conflicts. Simply said, they are emotionally smart, and thus they often succeed in careers, marriages, and parenting where other academically smarter (but emotionally less intelligent) people fail.

Emotionally intelligent people are self-aware. They can manage their emotions without being hijacked by overwhelming depression, anxiety, or anger.

Given the significance of practical, creative, and emotional intelligence, researchers are now wondering: Can we assess these success-enabling alternative intelligences? Can we teach practical and emotional intelligence to schoolchildren? Can we stimulate their creative problem-solving abilities and their abilities to read and manage emotions (Goleman, 1995)? These questions define a new frontier in the study of intelligence (the capacity for goal-directed, adaptive behavior).

In defense of academic smarts—the *g* factor—other researchers point to studies in which intelligence scores *do* predict both occupational status and job performance (Hunt, 1995; Jensen, 1993; Schmidt & Hunter, 1993). Intelligence matters most in mentally demanding jobs. Meteorology more than meter reading requires intelligence to excel. However, once admitted to a vocation, those who become highly successful have other traits as well—they are conscientious, well-connected, and doggedly energetic. Thus, high intelligence does more to get you into a profession (via the schools and training programs that take you there) than it does to make you successful, once there.

So it seems that the academic aptitude tapped by intelligence tests is indeed central to our lives. Yet personal competence in everyday living requires much that traditional intelligence tests do not measure. We might, then, liken mental abilities to physical abilities. Athleticism is not one thing but many. The ability to run fast is distinct from brute strength, which is distinct from the eye-hand coordination required to throw a ball on target. A champion weightlifter rarely has the potential to be a skilled ice skater. Yet there remains some tendency for good things to come packaged together—for running speed and throwing accuracy to correlate, thanks to general athletic ability. Likewise, intelligence involves several distinct abilities, which cluster together in the same individual often enough to define a small general intelligence factor.

Matching patterns Block design puzzles test the ability to analyze patterns. Wechsler's individually administered intelligence test comes in forms suited for adults (WAIS) and children (WISC).

Assessing Intelligence

10. *What types of tests are there?*

What is intelligence? Movie hero Forrest Gump's answer, "Stupid is as stupid does," catches the spirit of psychology's simplest answer: Intelligent is as intelligent does, on an intelligence test. In other words, intelligence is whatever intelligence tests measure. So, what are these tests, and what makes a test credible?

By this point in your life, you've faced dozens of different tests of your mental abilities: elementary school tests of basic reading and math skills, course examinations, intelligence tests, driver's license examinations, and college entrance examinations, to mention just a few. Psychologists classify such tests as either **aptitude tests**, intended to *predict* your ability to learn a new skill, or **achievement tests**, intended to *reflect* what you have learned. Thus, a college entrance exam, which seeks to predict your ability to do college work, is an aptitude test. Exams covering what you have learned in this course are achievement tests.

The actual differences between aptitude tests and achievement tests are not so clear-cut. Your achieved vocabulary influences your score on most aptitude tests. Similarly, your aptitudes for learning and test-taking influence your grades on tests of your course achievement. Most tests, whether labeled aptitude or achievement, assess both ability and its development. Distinguishing aptitude and achievement is a practical matter: We use aptitude tests to predict future performance and achievement tests to assess current performance.

Today's most widely used intelligence test, the **Wechsler Adult Intelligence Scale (WAIS)**, was created by psychologist David Wechsler, who, as a 6-year-old

VERBAL

General Information
What day of the year is Independence Day?

Similarities
In what way are *wool* and *cotton* alike?

Arithmetic Reasoning
If eggs cost 60 cents a dozen, what does 1 egg cost?

Vocabulary
Tell me the meaning of corrupt.

Comprehension
Why do people buy fire insurance?

Digit Span
Listen carefully, and when I am through, say the numbers right after me.

7 3 4 1 8 6

Now I am going to say some more numbers, but I want you to say them backward.

3 8 4 1 6

PERFORMANCE

Picture Completion
I am going to show you a picture with an important part missing. Tell me what is missing.

'85

SUN	MON	TUE	WED	THU	FRI	SAT
1	2	3	4	5	6	7
8	9	10	11	12	13	14
15	16	17	18	19	20	21
22	23	24	25	26	27	28
29	30					

Picture Arrangement
The pictures below tell a story. Put them in the right order to tell the story.

Block Design
Using the four blocks, make one just like this.

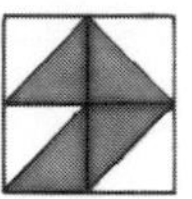

Object Assembly
If these pieces are put together correctly, they will make something. Go ahead and put them together as quickly as you can.

Digit-Symbol Substitution

Code

△	○	▱	✕	8
1	2	3	4	5

Test

△	8	✕	○	△	▱	8	✕	△	8

Figure 8.9 **Sample items from the Wechsler Adult Intelligence Scale (WAIS) subtest** (From Thorndike & Hagen, 1977)

Romanian boy, was among the Eastern European immigrants of the early 1900s who were mistakenly classified as feeble-minded because they did not know their new culture. Later he developed a similar test for school-age children, called the Wechsler Intelligence Scale for Children (WISC), and still later a test for preschool children. The WAIS consists of 11 subtests, as illustrated in Figure 8.9. It yields not only an overall intelligence score, as does the Stanford-Binet, but also separate "verbal" and "performance" (nonverbal) scores. Striking differences between the two scores alert the examiner to possible learning problems. For example, a verbal score much lower than the same person's performance score might indicate a reading or language disability. The tests also provide clues to cognitive strengths that a teacher or an employer might build upon.

Principles of Test Construction

11. *What three principles of test construction apply in evaluating a psychological test?*

To be widely accepted, psychological tests must meet three criteria: They must be *standardized, reliable*, and *valid*. The Stanford-Binet and Wechsler tests meet these requirements.

standardization defining meaningful scores by comparison with the performance of a pretested "standardization group."

normal curve the symmetrical bell-shaped curve that describes the distribution of many physical and psychological attributes. Most scores fall near the average, and fewer and fewer scores lie near the extremes.

reliability the extent to which a test yields consistent results, as assessed by the consistency of scores on two halves of the test, on alternate forms of the test, or on retesting.

Standardization

Knowing how many questions you got right on an intelligence test would tell us almost nothing. To evaluate your performance, we need a basis for comparing it with others' performance. To enable meaningful comparisons, test-makers first give the test to a representative sample of people. When other individuals take the test following the same procedures, we can then compare their scores with the standards defined by the sample group. This process of defining meaningful scores relative to a pretested group is called **standardization**.

Recall that Terman and his colleagues recognized that items developed for Parisians did not provide a satisfactory standard for evaluating Americans. So they revised the test and standardized the new version by testing 2300 native-born, white Americans of differing socioeconomic levels. Ironically, they used this standard to evaluate nonwhite American and immigrant groups (Van Leeuwen, 1982).

Standardized test results typically form a *normal distribution*, a bell-shaped pattern of scores that forms the **normal curve** (Figure 8.10). Whether we are measuring people's heights, weights, or mental aptitudes, most scores tend to cluster around the average. On an intelligence test, we call this average score 100. As we move out from the average (toward either extreme) we find fewer and fewer people. Within each age group, the Stanford-Binet and the Wechsler tests assign any person a score according to how much that person's performance deviates above or below the average. As Figure 8.10 shows, a performance higher than all but 2 percent of all scores earns an intelligence score of 130. A raw score that is comparably *below* 98 percent of all the scores earns an intelligence score of 70.

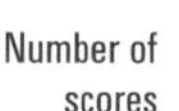

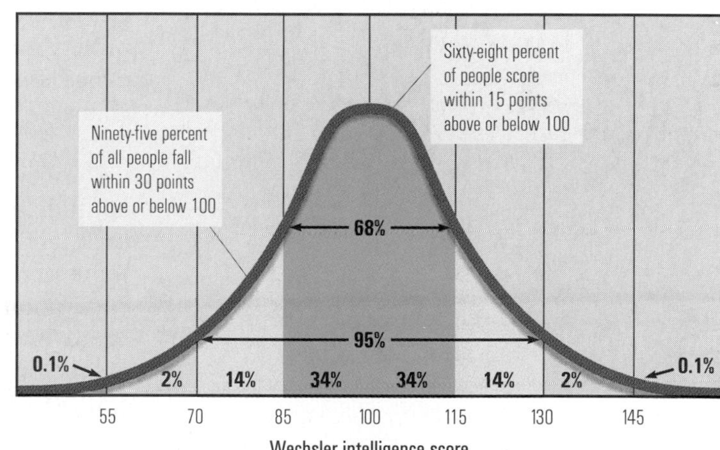

Figure 8.10 The normal curve Scores on aptitude tests tend to form a normal, or bell-shaped, curve. For example, the Wechsler scale calls the average score 100.

Reliability

Comparing your test scores to those of the standardizing group still won't tell us much about you unless the test has **reliability**. A good test must yield dependably consistent scores. To check a test's reliability, researchers retest people using the same test or another form of it. If the two scores generally agree, or *correlate*, the test is reliable. Alternatively, the researcher may split a test in half and see whether scores derived from odd and even questions agree.

The higher the correlation between the *test-retest* or the *split-half* scores, the higher the test's reliability. The tests we have considered so far—the Stanford-Binet, the WAIS, and the WISC—all have reliabilities of about +.9, which is very high. In retests, people's scores tend to match their first score closely.

validity the extent to which a test measures or predicts what it is supposed to. (See also *content validity* and *predictive validity*.)

content validity the extent to which a test samples the behavior that is of interest (such as a driving test that samples driving tasks).

criterion the behavior (such as college grades) that a test is designed to predict; thus, the measure used in defining whether the test has predictive validity.

predictive validity the success with which a test predicts the behavior it is designed to predict; it is assessed by computing the correlation between test scores and the criterion behavior. (Also called *criterion-related validity*.)

creativity the ability to produce novel and valuable ideas.

Validity

High reliability does not ensure a test's **validity**—the extent to which the test actually measures what it is supposed to measure or predicts what it is supposed to predict. If you use a shrunken tape measure to measure people's heights, your data would have high reliability (consistency) but low validity. How, then, can we determine whether a test is valid? For some tests, it is enough that they have **content validity**, which means the test taps the pertinent behavior. The road test for a driver's license has content validity because it samples the tasks a driver routinely faces. Your course exams have content validity if they assess your mastery of a representative sample of course material.

We evaluate other tests in terms of how well they agree with some **criterion**, an independent measure of what the test aims to assess. For some tests, the criterion is future performance. For example, aptitude tests must have **predictive validity** (also called *criterion-related validity*), which means they predict future achievement.

Are general aptitude tests as predictive as they are reliable? As critics are fond of noting, the answer is plainly no. The predictive power of aptitude tests is fairly strong in the early grades, but later it weakens. A better predictor of future grades is past grades, which reflect both aptitude and motivation. More generally, the best predictor of future behavior is a large sample of past behaviors of the same sort.

Creativity and Intelligence

12. *What factors affect creativity?*

Creativity is the ability to produce ideas that are both novel and valuable. The outlets for creativity vary by culture. Samoan culture encourages creativity in dance, Balinese culture in music, the African Ashanti culture in wood carvings (Lubart, 1990). In each, creativity means expressing familiar themes in novel ways.

Results from tests of intelligence and creativity suggest that a certain level of aptitude is necessary but not sufficient for creativity. In general, people with high intelligence scores do well on creativity tests. ("How many uses can you think of for a brick?") But beyond a certain level—a score of about 120—the correlation between intelligence scores and creativity disappears. Exceptionally creative architects, mathematicians, scientists, and engineers usually score no higher on intelligence tests than do their less creative peers (MacKinnon & Hall, 1972). So there is clearly more to creativity than intelligence scores. Studies of creative people suggest five other components of creativity (Sternberg, 1988; Sternberg & Lubart, 1991, 1992):

After picking up a Nobel prize in Stockholm, physicist Richard Feynman stopped in Queens, New York, to look at his high school record. "My grades were not as good as I remembered," he reported, "and my IQ was [a good, though unexceptional] 124" (Faber, 1987).

- The first is *expertise*—a well-developed base of knowledge. "Chance favors only the prepared mind," observed Louis Pasteur. The more ideas, images, and phrases we have to work with, through our accumulated learning, the more chances we have to combine these mental building blocks in novel ways.
- *Imaginative thinking skills* provide the ability to see things in new ways, to recognize patterns, to make connections. To be creative you must first master the basic elements of a problem, then redefine or explore the problem in a new way. Copernicus first developed expertise regarding the solar system and its planets and then defined the system as revolving around the Sun, not the Earth.

CLOSE-UP

Extremes of Intelligence

One way to glimpse the validity and significance of any test is to compare people who score at the two extremes of the normal curve. The two groups should differ noticeably, and they do.

In one famous project begun in 1921, Lewis Terman studied more than 1500 California schoolchildren with IQ scores over 135. Contrary to the popular myth that intellectually gifted children are frequently maladjusted because they are "in a different world" from their nongifted peers, Terman's high-scoring children were unusually healthy, well adjusted, and academically successful. When restudied over the next six decades, most of these people had attained high levels of education (Goleman, 1980). Their vocational success varied, yet the group included many doctors, lawyers, professors, scientists, and writers. Terman's whiz kids remind one of Jean Piaget, who by age 7 was devoting his free time to studying birds, fossils, and machines; who by age 15 began publishing scientific articles on mollusks; and who later went on to become this century's most famous developmental psychologist (Hunt, 1993).

At the other extreme are people whose intelligence test scores fall below 70. To be labeled as having **mental retardation**, a child must have both a low test score *and* difficulty adapting to the normal demands of independent living. Only about 1 percent of the population meets both criteria, with males outnumbering females by 50 percent (American Psychiatric Association, 1994). As Table 8.2 indicates, most such mentally challenged individuals can, with support, live in mainstream society.

A gifted child At age 10, Lenny Ng became the youngest child to score a perfect 800 on the SAT math test. At age 16, his math project won a $20,000 scholarship in the 1993 Westinghouse Science Talent Search. At age 20, he was a second-year math graduate student at MIT after graduating with highest honors from Harvard and winning a national math competition.

Table 8.2 Degrees of Mental Retardation

Level	Typical Intelligence Scores	Percentage of the Retarded	Adaptation to Demands of Life
Mild	50–70	85%	May learn academic skills up to sixth-grade level. Adults may, with assistance, achieve self-supporting social and vocational skills.
Moderate	35–49	10	May progress to second-grade level academically. Adults may contribute to their own support by labor in sheltered workshops.
Severe	20–34	3–4	May learn to talk and to perform simple work tasks under close supervision but are generally unable to profit from vocational training.
Profound	Below 20	1–2	Require constant aid and supervision.

Source: Reprinted with permission from the Diagnostic and Statistical Manual of Mental Disorders, Fourth Edition. Copyright 1994 American Psychiatric Association.

Mental retardation sometimes results from known physical causes. One such case is **Down syndrome**, a disorder caused by an extra chromosome in the person's genetic makeup. Most people with Down syndrome are either mildly or moderately retarded.

During the last two centuries, the pendulum of opinion about how best to care for individuals with mental retardation has made a complete swing. Until the mid-nineteenth century, they were cared for at home. Many of those with the most severe disabilities died, but people with milder forms of retardation often found a place in a farm-based society. Then, residential schools for slow learners were established. By the twentieth century, many of these institutions had become warehouses, providing residents no privacy, little attention, and no hope. Parents often were told to separate themselves permanently from their impaired child before they became attached.

In the last half of the twentieth century, the pendulum swung back to normalization—allowing people to live in their own communities as normally as their functioning permits. We educate children with mild retardation in less restrictive environments, and we integrate, or *mainstream*, many into regular classrooms. Most grow up with their own families and then move into a protected living arrangement, such as a group home. The hope, and often the reality, is a happier and more dignified life.

mental retardation a condition of limited mental ability (as indicated by an intelligence test score below 70) that produces difficulty in adapting to the demands of life; varies from mild to profound.

Down syndrome a condition of retardation and associated physical disorders caused by an extra chromosome in one's genetic makeup.

Everyone held up their crackers as David threw the cheese log into the ceiling fan.

- *A venturesome personality* tolerates ambiguity and risk, perseveres in overcoming obstacles, and seeks new experiences rather than following the pack. Inventors, for example, have a knack for persisting after failures, as Thomas Edison did in trying countless substances for his light bulb filament.
- The *intrinsic motivation* principle of creativity is the fourth component. As psychologist Teresa Amabile points out, "People will be most creative when they feel motivated primarily by the interest, enjoyment, satisfaction, and challenge of the work itself—rather than by external pressures" (Amabile & Hennessey, 1992). Creative people focus not so much on extrinsic motivators—meeting deadlines, impressing people, or making money—as on the intrinsic pleasure and challenge of their work.
- A *creative environment* sparks, supports, and refines creative ideas. After studying the careers of 2026 prominent scientists and inventors, Dean Keith Simonton (1992) noted that the most eminent among them were not lone geniuses. Rather they were mentored, challenged, and supported by their relationships with colleagues. Such people often have the emotional intelligence needed to network effectively with peers.

REHEARSE IT!

12. Intelligence quotient, or IQ, was originally defined as the ratio of mental age to chronological age multiplied by 100. By this definition, a 6-year-old child with a measured mental age of 6 would have an IQ of 100. Likewise, a 6-year-old with a measured mental age of 9 would have an IQ of

a. 67.
b. 133.
c. 86.
d. 150.

13. Savant syndrome is retardation combined with incredible ability in one specific area. The existence of savant syndrome seems to support

a. Sternberg's distinction among three aspects of intelligence.
b. Spearman's notion of general intelligence, or *g* factor.
c. Gardner's theory of multiple intelligences.
d. Binet's conception of mental age.

14. Intelligence tests predict school grades reasonably well but are less successful at predicting achievement in other areas. Robert Sternberg has therefore identified three aspects of intelligence, which are

a. spatial, academic, and artistic intelligence.
b. musical, athletic, and academic intelligence.
c. academic, practical, and creative intelligence.
d. emotional, practical, and spatial intelligence.

15. Emotionally intelligent people are characterized by

a. the tendency to seek immediate gratification.
b. the ability to understand their own emotions but not those of others.
c. high practical intelligence.
d. self-awareness.

16. Aptitude and achievement tests are tests of mental abilities. Aptitude tests are designed to ___________, whereas achievement tests are designed to ___________.

a. predict ability to learn; reflect what has been learned
b. assess adaptive behavior; identify level of intelligence
c. uncover undeveloped skills; objectively evaluate adaptability
d. measure performance; differentiate slow learners from all others

17. The Wechsler Adult Intelligence Scale (WAIS) yields an overall intelligence score as well as separate verbal and performance (nonverbal) scores. The WAIS is best able to tell us

a. what part of an individual's intelligence is determined by genetic inheritance.
b. whether the test-taker will succeed in a job.
c. how the test-taker compares with other adults in vocabulary and arithmetic reasoning.
d. whether the test-taker has specific skills for music and the performing arts.

18. The Stanford-Binet, the Wechsler Adult Intelligence Scale, and the Wechsler Intelligence Scale for Children are known to have very high reliability (about +.9). This means that

a. a pretest has been given to a representative sample.
b. the test yields consistent results, for example on retesting.
c. the test measures what it is supposed to measure.
d. the results of the test will be distributed on a bell-shaped curve.

19. Creativity is the ability to produce novel and valuable ideas. Which of the following is not a characteristic of a creative person?

a. expertise
b. extrinsic motivation
c. a venturesome personality
d. imaginative thinking skills

Genetic and Environmental Influences on Intelligence

13. *Is intellect influenced more by heredity or environment?*

Intelligence seems to run in families. But why? Are intellectual abilities mostly inherited? Or primarily molded by one's environment?

Few of psychology's issues arouse such passion or have such serious political implications. Consider: If we mainly inherit our differing mental abilities, and if success reflects those abilities, then people's socioeconomic standing will correspond to their inborn differences. Thus, those on top may believe their innate mental superiority justifies their social positions.

"I am, somehow, less interested in the weight and convolutions of Einstein's brain than in the near certainty that people of equal talent have lived and died in cotton fields and sweatshops."

Stephen Jay Gould
The Panda's Thumb
1980

If, on the other hand, mental abilities are primarily nurtured by the environments that raise and school us, then children from disadvantaged environments can expect to lead disadvantaged lives. In this case, people's standing will result from their unequal opportunities, a situation that many regard as basically unjust. Setting aside such political implications as best we can, let's examine the evidence.

Genetic Influences

Do people who share the same genes also share comparable mental abilities? As you can see from Figure 8.11, which summarizes many studies, the answer is clearly yes. In support of the genetic contribution to intelligence, researchers cite two sets of findings:

- The IQ scores of identical twins reared together are virtually as similar as those of the same person taking the same test twice. Fraternal twins, who share only half their genes, are much less similar in IQ scores.
- Even identical twins whose parents do not dress or treat them identically are virtual carbon copies of one another in IQ score (Loehlin & Nichols, 1976).

Figure 8.11 Intelligence: Nature and nurture The most genetically similar people have the most similar intelligence scores. Remember: 1.0 indicates a perfect correlation; zero indicates no correlation at all. (Data from McGue & others, 1993)

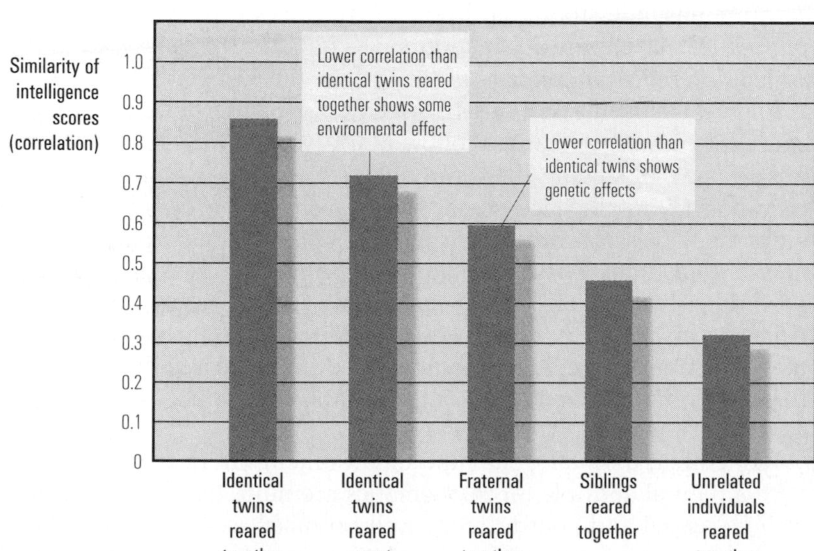

heritability the proportion of variation among individuals that we can attribute to genes. The heritability of a trait may vary, depending on the range of populations and environments studied.

Likewise, identical twins who have been reared separately have similar IQ scores—similar enough to lead twin researcher Thomas Bouchard (1996a, b) to estimate that "about 70 percent" of intelligence score variation "can be attributed to genetic variation." (Other researchers have offered estimates nearer 50 percent.)

But there is also some evidence pointing to an effect of environment. Fraternal twins, who are genetically no more alike than any other siblings but who are treated more alike because they are the same age, tend to score more alike than other siblings.

Our genes shape the experiences that shape us.

Seeking to disentangle genes and environment, researchers have also asked whether adopted children and their siblings, thanks to their shared environment, share similar aptitudes. During childhood, the intelligence test scores of adoptive siblings correlate modestly. But with age, their mental similarities disappear as the effect of common rearing wanes; by adulthood, the correlation is roughly zero (McGue & others, 1993). Such findings contradict the widely held belief that, as we accumulate life experience, the environmental influence on traits such as intelligence increases. In fact, the opposite seems true: With age, genetic influences become more apparent. Adoptive children's cognitive abilities become more like those of their biological parents and less like those of their adoptive parents (Plomin & others, 1997).

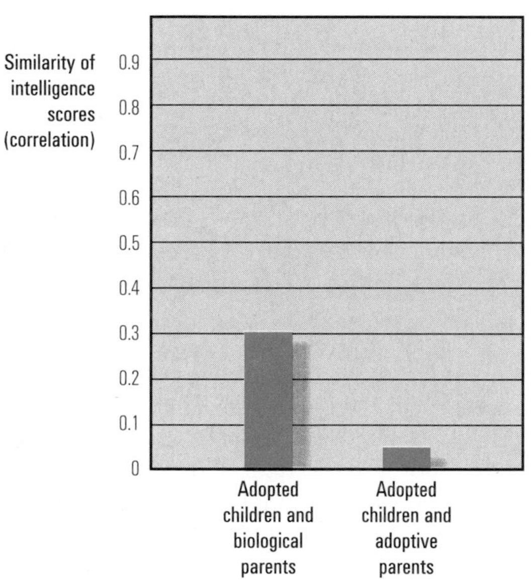

Figure 8.12 **The correlations of intelligence test scores between 245 adopted Colorado children and their adoptive and biological parents** By age 7, the adopted children had intelligence test scores more like those of their biological parents. (From Fulker & others, 1988)

Researchers have also compared the intelligence test scores of adopted children with those of their biological parents, from whom they received their genes, and those of their adoptive parents, who provided their home environment. As Figure 8.12 illustrates, adopted children's scores more closely resemble those of their biological parents than those of their adoptive parents. Of course, it also matters whether one is adopted into an impoverished environment or an enriched one (Turkheimer, 1991). Yet as Sandra Scarr (1989) noted, being reared "together in the same adoptive home does not make you intellectually similar to your brothers and sisters; being genetically related by half of your genes does."

Recall from Chapter 2 the meaning of **heritability**. To say that the heritability of intelligence—the variation in intelligence test scores attributable to genetic factors—is roughly 50+ percent does *not* mean that your genes are responsible for 50+ percent of your intelligence and that your environment is responsible for the rest. Rather, it means that we can attribute to heredity 50+ percent *of the variation in intelligence within a group of people*. This point is so often misunderstood that I repeat: We can never say what percentage of an *individual's* intelligence is inherited. Heritability refers instead to the extent to which *differences among people* are attributable to genes.

Even this conclusion must be qualified, because heritability can vary from study to study. If we were to follow Mark Twain's proposal to raise boys in barrels to age 12, feeding them through a hole, they would emerge with lower-than-normal intelligence scores. Yet, given their equal environments, their individual IQ score differences at age 12 could be explained only by their heredity. In other words, heritability for their differences would be near 100 percent. *As environments become more equal, heredity as a source of differences necessarily becomes more important.* On the other hand, compare people with similar heredities who are raised in drastically different environments (barrels versus advantaged homes), and heritability—differences due to genes—will be low.

Think about it: As society succeeds in creating equality of opportunity, it will also increase the heritability of achievement. Perfect environmental equality would create 100 percent heritability—because genes alone would have to account for any remaining human differences.

Remember, too, that genes and environment interact. For example, students with a natural aptitude for mathematics are more likely to select math courses in high school and later to score well on math aptitude tests—thanks *both* to their natural math aptitude *and* to their math experience. Our genes shape the experiences that shape us.

Environmental Influences

We have seen that our genes make a difference. Even if we were all raised in the same intellectually stimulating environment, we still would not have the same aptitudes. But we have also seen that heredity doesn't tell the whole story. Within the limits dictated by our genes, our life experiences matter.

Human environments are rarely as impoverished as the dark and barren cages inhabited by deprived rats that develop thinner-than-normal brain cortexes (see Chapter 3). Yet severe life experiences also leave marks on humans, as psychologist J. McVicker Hunt (1982) observed in a destitute Iranian orphanage in Tehran, where the typical child could not sit up unassisted at age 2 or walk at age 4. What care the infants received was not in response to their crying, cooing, or other behaviors. The infants were therefore not developing any sense of personal control over their environment, and so were becoming passive "glum lumps." Extreme deprivation was bludgeoning native intelligence.

High-quality preschool programs improve emotional intelligence—creating better attitudes toward learning and reducing school dropouts and criminality.

Aware of the benefits of responsive caregiving, Hunt began a program of "tutored human enrichment." For instance, he trained caregivers to play vocal games with the infants. First, they imitated the babies' babbling. Then they led the babies in vocal follow-the-leader by shifting from one familiar sound to another. Then they began to teach sounds from the Persian language.

The results were dramatic. All 11 infants who received these language-fostering experiences could name more than 50 objects and body parts by 22 months. So charming had the infants become that most were adopted—an unprecedented success for the orphanage.

Hunt's findings testify to the importance of environment. There is no doubt that severe disadvantage takes a toll on children (Ramey & Ramey, 1992). And when the infant malnutrition associated with severe poverty is relieved with nutritional supplements, poverty's effect on physical and cognitive development lessens (Brown & Pollitt, 1996).

But do such findings indicate a way to "give your child a superior intellect"? Some popular books claim that with intensive preschool training this is possible, but most experts are doubtful (Phillips & Stipek, 1993). Although Sandra Scarr (1984) agrees that neglectful upbringing can have grave long-term consequences, she points out that "as long as an infant has normal human contact and normal exposure to sights, sounds, human speech, and so forth, the baby will thrive." As for future intelligence, "Parents who are very concerned about providing special educational lessons for their babies are wasting their time."

"There is a large body of evidence indicating that there is little if anything to be gained by exposing middle-class children to early education."

Developmental Psychologist Edward F. Zigler (1987)

Hunt would probably agree with Scarr that extra instruction has little effect on the intellectual development of children from stimulating environments. But he was optimistic when it came to children from disadvantaged environments. Indeed, his 1961 book, *Intelligence and Experience*, helped launch Project Head Start in 1965. Head Start is a U.S. government–funded preschool program serving some 750,000 children, most of whom come from families below the poverty level. It aims to enhance children's chances for success in school and beyond by boosting their cognitive and social skills.

Does it succeed? Researchers study Head Start and other preschool programs by comparing equivalent children who do experience the program with those who don't. Their findings indicate that high-quality programs for disadvantaged children produce at least short-term cognitive gains, even on intelligence tests (Haskins, 1989). Quality programs also increase school readiness, decreasing the likelihood of a child's repeating a grade or being placed in special education. The aptitude benefits dissipate over time (reminding us that life experience *after* Head Start matters, too). The effect of education doesn't end with the preschool years. Psychologist Edward Zigler,

Getting a head start To increase readiness for schoolwork and expand children's notions of where school might lead them, Project Head Start offers educational activities. Here children in a classroom learn about colors and those on a field trip learn what firefighters do.

the program's first director, believes there are other long-term benefits (Zigler & Muenchow, 1992). High-quality preschool programs improve emotional intelligence—creating better attitudes toward learning and reducing school dropouts and criminality.

Group Differences in Intelligence Test Scores

14. ***How, and why, do ethnic and gender groups differ in aptitude test performance?***

If there were no group differences in aptitude scores, psychologists could politely debate hereditary and environmental influences in their ivory towers. But there are group differences. What are they? And what shall we make of them?

Ethnic Similarities and Differences

Fueling this discussion are two disturbing but agreed-upon facts:

- Racial groups differ in their average scores on intelligence tests.
- High-scoring people (and groups) are more likely to attain high levels of education and income.

A statement by 52 intelligence researchers explains: "The bell curve for whites is centered roughly around IQ 100; the bell curve for American blacks roughly around 85; and those for different subgroups of Hispanics roughly midway between those for whites and blacks" (Avery & others, 1994). Comparable results come from other academic aptitude tests. The black-white difference has diminished somewhat in recent years, and among children has dropped to 10 points in some recent studies (Neisser & others, 1996). Yet the test-score gap persists.

There are differences among other groups as well. European New Zealanders outscore native Maori New Zealanders. Israeli Jews outscore Israeli Arabs.

Most Japanese outscore the stigmatized Japanese minority, the Burakumin. And hearing people outscore those born deaf (Braden, 1994; Steele, 1990; Zeidner, 1990).

Everyone further agrees that such *group* differences provide little basis for judging individuals. Women outlive men by six years, but knowing someone's sex doesn't tell us with any precision how long that person will live. Even Charles Murray and Richard Herrnstein (1994), whose writings have drawn attention to black-white differences, reminded us that "millions of blacks have higher IQs than the average white."

If heredity contributes to individual differences in intelligence, does it also contribute to group differences? It's conceivable, and a few psychologists speculate that different climates and survival challenges could have led to racial differences in aptitudes (Lynn, 1991; Rushton, 1990, 1995). But it's also clear that, as in our earlier barrel-versus-home-reared boys example, group differences in a heritable trait may be entirely environmental. Consider one of nature's experiments: Allow some children to grow up hearing their culture's dominant language, while others, born deaf, do not. Then give them an intelligence test rooted in that language, and (no surprise) those with expertise in the test's language will score highest. Although individual performance differences may be substantially genetic, the group difference is not (Figure 8.13).

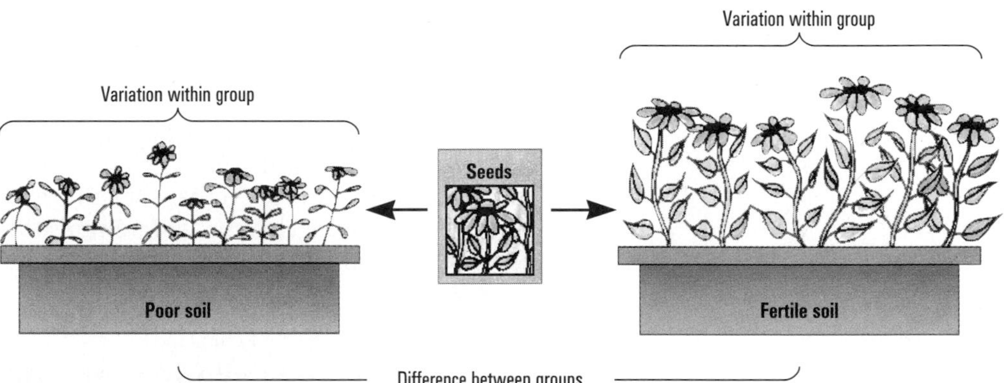

Figure 8.13 **Group differences and environmental impact** Even if the variation between members within a group reflects genetic differences, the average difference between groups may be wholly due to the environment. Imagine that seeds from the same mixture are sown in poor and fertile soil. Although height differences within each pot will be genetic, the height difference between the two groups will be environmental. (From Lewontin, 1976)

Consider, too, how even highly heritable traits might be environmentally modified: If each identical twin were exactly as tall as his or her co-twin, heritability would be 100 percent. Imagine that we then separated some young twins and gave only half of them a nutritious diet, and that the well-nourished twins all grew to be exactly 3 inches taller than their counterparts—an environmental effect comparable to that actually observed in both Britain and America, where adolescents are several inches taller than their counterparts were half a century ago (Angoff, 1987; Lynn, 1987). What would the heritability of height be now for our well-nourished twins? Still 100 percent, because the variation in height within the group would remain entirely predictable from the heights of their malnourished identical siblings. So even perfect heritability within groups would not eliminate the possibility of a strong environmental impact on the group differences.

So, is there evidence that the racial gap may be similarly environmental? Consider these findings:

- Genetics research reveals that under the skin, the races are remarkably alike (Cavalli-Sforza & others, 1994; Lewontin, 1982). Individual differences within a race are much greater than between-race differences. The average genetic difference between two Icelandic villagers or between two Kenyans

The intelligence test performance of today's better-fed and better-educated population exceeds that of the 1930s population by the same margin that the test performance of the average white today exceeds that of the average black.

greatly exceeds the difference between Icelanders and Kenyans. Moreover, looks can deceive. Europeans and Africans are genetically closer than are Africans and Aboriginal Australians.

- Asian students outperform North American students on math achievement and aptitude tests. But this difference appears to be a recent phenomenon and may reflect conscientiousness rather than competence. Asian students also attend school 30 percent more days per year and spend much more time in and out of school studying math (Geary & others, 1996; Stevenson, 1992).
- The intelligence test performance of today's better-fed and better-educated population exceeds that of the 1930s population by the same margin that the test performance of the average white today exceeds that of the average black (Ceci & Williams, 1997; Flynn, 1987). No one attributes the generational group difference to genetics.
- White and black infants have scored equally well on an infant intelligence measure (preference for looking at novel stimuli—a predictor of future intelligence scores [Fagan, 1992]).
- In different eras, different ethnic groups have experienced golden ages—periods of remarkable achievement. Twenty-five hundred years ago it was the Greeks and the Egyptians, then the Romans; in the eighth and ninth centuries, genius seemed to reside in the Arab world; 500 years ago it was the Aztec Indians and the peoples of northern Europe. Today, people marvel at Asians' technological genius. Cultures rise and fall over centuries; genes do not. That fact makes it difficult to attribute a natural superiority to any race.

"Do not obtain your slaves from Britain, because they are so stupid and so utterly incapable of being taught."

Cicero
106–43 B.C.

As educational opportunities moved toward more equality between 1977 and 1996, the black-white difference in combined Scholastic Assessment Test (SAT) scores (verbal + math) shrank 23 percent (College Board, 1987, 1996). Motivate children with rewards for correct answers on intelligence tests and the racial difference shrinks even more (Bradley-Johnson & others, 1984).

Gender Similarities and Differences

In science, as in everyday life, differences, not similarities, excite interest. Compared with the anatomical and physiological similarities between men and women, our sex differences are relatively minor. Yet it is the differences we find exciting. Similarly, in the psychological domain, gender similarities dwarf gender differences, but the differences often capture our attention. To some, it is news that there is no gender gap in average verbal ability as assessed by tests of vocabulary, reading comprehension, and solving analogies (Hyde & Linn, 1988). But most people find differences more newsworthy. Girls are better spellers: At the end of high school, only 30 percent of males spell better than the average female (Lubinski & Benbow, 1992). Boys outnumber girls at the low extremes (Halpern, 1997). Boys tend to talk later and stutter more often. In remedial reading classes, boys outnumber girls three to one (Finucci & Childs, 1981). In high school, underachieving boys outnumber girls by two to one (McCall & others, 1992).

Math and Spatial Aptitudes

In math grades, the average girl typically equals or surpasses the average boy (ETS, 1992; Kimball, 1989). And on math tests given to more than 3 million representatively sampled people in 100 independent studies, males and females obtained nearly identical average scores (Hyde & others, 1990). But

World Math Olympics champs After outscoring 350,000 of their U.S. peers, these boys all had perfect scores in competition with math whizzes from 68 other countries.

again—despite greater diversity within the genders than between them—group differences make the news. Although females have an edge in math computation, males in various cultures score higher in math problem solving (Hedges & Nowell, 1995; Lummis & Stevenson, 1990). For example, male high school seniors average 45 points higher on the 200- to 800-point SAT math test (literally meaning that they average four more correct answers on the 60-question test). Because U.S. National Merit Scholarships are based on SAT scores, only about 35 percent of these awards have gone to girls (despite girls' generally higher grades).

The score differences are sharpest at the extremes. Among precocious 12-year-olds scoring extremely high on SAT math, boys have outnumbered girls 13 to 1 (Lubinski & Benbow, 1992). In the national Putnam math contest for collegians, the top 5 finishers during the competition's first 56 years have included 279 men and, finally in 1997, 1 woman (Arenson, 1997). In other Western countries, virtually all math prodigies participating in the International Mathematics Olympiad have been males. Female math prodigies have, however, reached the top levels in non-Western countries such as China (Halpern, 1991). The average male edge seems most reliable in tests like the one shown in Figure 8.14, which involve speedily rotating three-dimensional objects in one's mind (Masters & Sanders, 1993; Voyer & others, 1995). Such spatial ability helps when fitting suitcases into a car trunk, playing chess, or doing certain types of geometry problems.

Working from an evolutionary perspective, David Geary (1995, 1996) and Irwin Silverman and Marion Eals (1992) speculate that skills in navigating within three-dimensional space also helped our ancestral fathers in tracking their prey and navigating their way home. In contrast, the survival of our ancestral mothers was enhanced by keen memory for the location of edible plants—a legacy that lives today in women's superior memory for objects and their location.

In studies of over 100,000 American adolescents, girls also modestly surpassed boys in memory for picture associations (Hedges & Nowell, 1995). And year after year, young women among the nearly 200,000 students taking Germany's Test for Medical Studies have surpassed their male counterparts in remembering facts from short medical cases (Stumpf & Jackson, 1994). (My wife, who remembers many of my experiences for me, tells me that if she died I'd be a man without a past.)

Do natural sex differences therefore explain why most mathematicians and more than 9 in 10 rated chess players and American architects, engineers, and mapmakers are men? Or why the world chess body has therefore found it necessary to hold separate competitions for men and women? Exposure to high levels of male sex hormones during the prenatal period does enhance spatial abilities (Berenbaum & others, 1995). But social expectations also shape boys' and girls' interests and abilities (Crawford & others, 1995; Eccles & others, 1990). Traditionally, math and science have been considered masculine subjects. For example, many parents send their sons to computer camps and give their daughters more encouragement in English. Thus, the male edge in math problem solving

Which two circles contain a configuration of blocks identical to the one in the circle at the left?

Standard

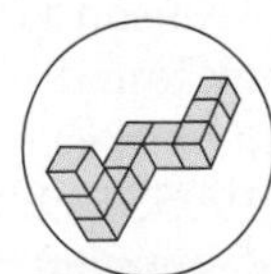

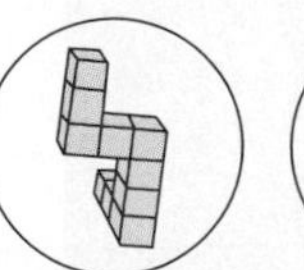

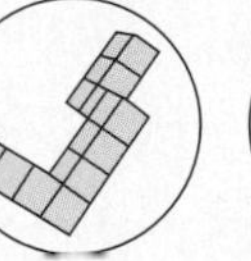

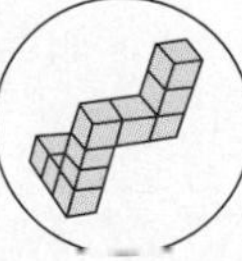

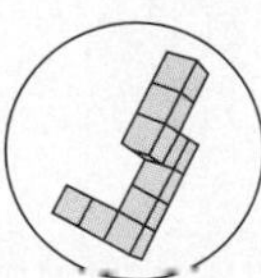

Figure 8.14 **The mental rotation test** This is a test of spatial abilities. Which two responses show a different view of the standard? (From Vandenberg & Kuse, 1978) (See page 307 for answers.)

"Math class is tough."

Talking Barbie Doll, 1992
(The toy was taken off the market after complaints.)

grows with age, becoming detectable only after elementary school. But as more and more girls are encouraged to develop their abilities in math and science, the gender gap is narrowing. Among representative national samples of high school juniors taking the Preliminary Scholastic Assessment Test (PSAT), the male edge has nearly disappeared since 1960 (Linn & Hyde, 1991).

Some people are much better emotion detectors than others are, and women are better at it then men.

Emotion-Detecting Ability

Recall that part of emotional intelligence is empathic accuracy in reading others' emotions. Some of us are more sensitive to emotional cues. Robert Rosenthal, Judith Hall, and their colleagues (1979) discovered this by showing hundreds of people brief film clips of portions of a person's emotionally expressive face or body, sometimes with a garbled voice added. For example, after a two-second scene revealing only the face of an upset woman, the researchers asked whether the woman was criticizing someone for being late or was talking about her divorce. Rosenthal and Hall reported that some people are much better emotion detectors than others are, and that women are better at it than men.

Some psychologists speculate that women's emotion-detecting ability helped our ancestral mothers read emotions in their infants and would-be lovers, which may in turn have fueled cultural tendencies to encourage women's empathic skills. Such skills may, as Chapter 3 noted, explain women's somewhat greater responsiveness in both positive and negative emotional situations.

The Question of Bias

15. *Are intelligence tests biased and discriminatory?*

Knowing about group differences in intelligence test scores leads us to wonder whether intelligence tests are biased. The answer depends on how we define *bias*. One meaning is that the tests detect not only innate differences in intelligence but also differences caused by cultural experiences. In this sense, everyone agrees that intelligence tests are biased. No one claims that heritability is 100 percent responsible for any test score. An intelligence test measures a person's developed abilities at a particular time. These abilities necessarily reflect that person's experiences *and* environment.

Another meaning of *bias* hinges on whether a test is less valid for some groups than for others. If the SAT accurately predicts the college achievement of one race but not that of another, then the test would be biased. The near-consensus among psychologists, as summarized by the National Research Council's Committee on Ability Testing, is that the major aptitude tests are *not* biased in this statistical meaning of the term (Rowe & others, 1994; Wigdor & Garner, 1982). The predictive validity of the SAT or of a standard intelligence test is roughly the same for blacks and whites and for rich and poor. If an intelligence test score of 95 predicts C grades, the rough prediction usually applies equally to all ethnic and economic groups.

Untestable compassion Intelligence test scores are only one part of the picture of a whole person. They don't measure the abilities, talent, and commitment of, for example, people who devote their lives to helping others.

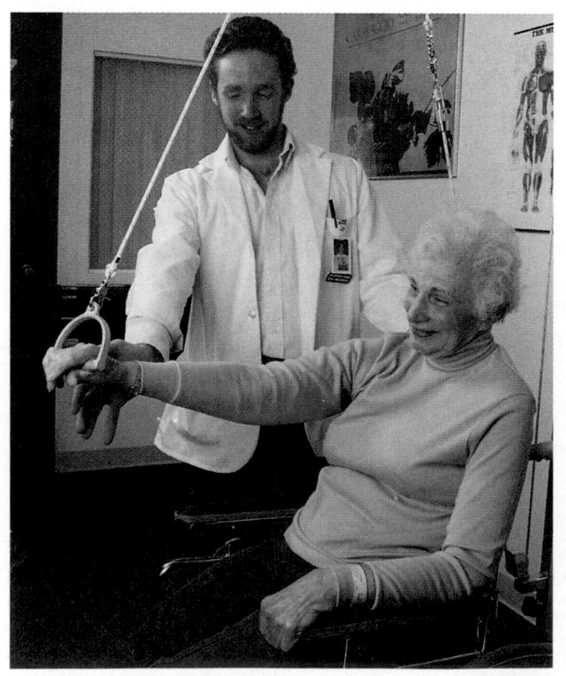

To predict school performance accurately, an aptitude test must mirror any gender or racial bias in school teaching and testing. Among students given a difficult math test by Steven Spencer and his colleagues (1997), men outperformed equally capable women—except when the women had been led to expect that women usually do as well as men on the test. Otherwise, the women apparently felt apprehensive and despairing when the going got tough. Claude Steele and Joshua Aronson (1996) observed the same self-fulfilling effect of negative beliefs. They found black students' verbal aptitude scores were lower when they took tests under conditions designed to make black students feel threatened. Steele (1995, 1997) concluded that if you tell students they probably won't succeed (as remedial "minority support" programs often do), this stereotype will eventually erode their performance both on aptitude tests and in school. Over time, such students may "disidentify" with school achievement and look for self-esteem elsewhere. University programs that instead challenge minority students to believe in their potential produce markedly higher grades and lower dropout rates.

An intelligence test measures a person's developed abilities at a particular time. These abilities necessarily reflect that person's experiences and environment.

So what can we conclude about aptitude tests and bias? The tests do seem biased in one sense—sensitivity to performance differences caused by cultural experience. But they are not biased in another—statistical prediction for different groups.

What time is it now? On page 274, did you underestimate or overestimate how quickly you would finish the chapter?

Does this mean the tests are discriminatory? Again, the answer can be yes or no. In one sense, yes, their purpose is to discriminate—to distinguish among individuals. In another sense, their purpose is to reduce discrimination by reducing reliance on subjective criteria for school and job placement—criteria such as who you know, what you look like, or how much the interviewer happens to like "your kind of person." Banning aptitude tests would force the people who decide on admissions and jobs to rely more on other considerations, such as their personal opinions. Civil service tests, for example, were devised to discriminate more fairly and objectively, by reducing the political, racial, and ethnic discrimination that preceded their use.

Answers to the mental rotation test on page 305: the first and fourth alternatives.

Perhaps, then, our aim should be threefold. First, we should realize the benefits that Alfred Binet foresaw for intelligence tests—to enable schools to recognize who might best benefit from early intervention. At the same time, we must remain alert to Binet's fear that test scores may be misinterpreted as literal measures of a person's worth and fixed potential. And finally, we must remember that *intelligence test scores reflect only one aspect of personal competence.* Our practical, creative, and emotional intelligence matter, too, as do other forms of talent and character. The competence that intelligence tests sample is important but far from all-inclusive. The spatial ability of the carpenter differs from the logical ability of the computer programmer, which differs from the verbal ability of the poet. Differences are not deficits. Because there are many ways of being successful, our personal and cultural differences—regardless of their origins—are variations on the human theme of adaptability.

"Almost all the joyful things of life are outside the measure of IQ tests."

Madeleine L'Engle
A Circle of Quiet
1972

20. A current view is that between 50 and 60 percent of intelligence score variation among individuals can be attributed to heredity. The strongest support for the hereditary influence on intelligence is the finding that

a. identical twins, but not other siblings, have nearly identical IQ scores.
b. the correlation between IQ scores of fraternal twins is higher than that for other siblings.
c. unrelated people living in the same environment tend not to have similar IQ scores.
d. the IQ scores of adopted children do not closely correlate with those of their biological or adoptive parents.

21. The heritability of a trait may vary, depending on the range of populations and environments studied. To say that the heritability of intelligence is 60 percent means that 60 percent of

a. intelligence is due to genetic factors.
b. the similarities among groups of people are attributable to genes.
c. the variation in intelligence within a group of people is attributable to genetic factors.
d. intelligence is due to the mother's genes and the rest is due to the father's genes.

22. Within the limits set by heredity, experiences help shape intelligence. The experience that has the clearest, most profound effect on intellectual development is

a. being enrolled in a Head Start program.
b. growing up in an economically disadvantaged home or neighborhood.
c. being raised in a very neglectful home or institution.
d. being exposed to very stimulating toys and lessons in infancy.

REVIEWING ■ *Thinking, Language, and Intelligence*

Our cognitive system receives, perceives, and retrieves information, which we then use to think and communicate, sometimes wisely, sometimes foolishly. In this chapter we have explored **cognition**—how we form concepts, solve problems, make decisions and judgments, use language, and exhibit intelligence.

Thinking

1. ***What are the functions of concepts?***

Concepts are one of the building blocks of thinking. They serve to simplify and order the world by organizing it into a hierarchy of categories. Concepts often form around **prototypes**, or best examples of a category.

2. ***What strategies do we use to solve problems, and what obstacles hinder our problem solving?***

When faced with new situations for which no well-learned response suffices, we may use any of several strategies, such as trial and error, **algorithms**, and rule-of-thumb **heuristics**. **Insight**, a sudden and often novel realization, can also offer solutions to problems. We do, however, face certain obstacles to successful problem solving. The **confirmation bias** predisposes us to verify rather than challenge our hypotheses. And **fixations** such as **functional fixedness** may prevent our taking a needed fresh perspective on a problem.

3. ***How are our decisions and judgments influenced by heuristics, overconfidence, and framing?***

Our use of heuristics, such as the **representativeness** and **availability heuristics**, provides highly efficient but occasionally misleading guides for making quick decisions and forming intuitive judgments. Our tendencies to seek confirmation of our hypotheses and to use quick and easy heuristics can blind us to our vulnerability to error, a phenomenon known as **overconfidence**. **Framing**—the way a question is presented—can significantly affect our thinking.

4. ***How do our preexisting beliefs influence our decision making?***

As the **belief perseverance** phenomenon indicates, we sometimes cling to our ideas after their basis has been discredited, because the explanation for their apparent validity lingers in our minds. In general, people tend to accept as more logical those conclusions that agree with their beliefs.

Language

5. ***When do children acquire language, and how does it develop?***

Among the marvels of nature is a child's ability to acquire **language**. The ease with which children progress from the **babbling stage** through the **one-word stage** to the **telegraphic speech** of the **two-word stage** and beyond has sparked a lively debate concerning how they do it. Behaviorist B. F. Skinner proposed that we learn language by the familiar principles of imitation and reinforcement. Challenging this claim, linguist Noam Chomsky argues that children are biologically prepared to learn words and use grammar. For mastery of grammar, the learning that occurs during life's first few years is, however, critical.

6. ***Is language unique to humans, or do other species also have language?***

Another vigorously debated issue is whether language is a uniquely human ability. Several teams of psychologists provoked enormous interest by teaching various apes, including a number of chimpanzees, to communicate with humans by using sign language or by pushing buttons wired to a computer. The animals have developed considerable vocabularies and are able to string words together to express meaning and requests. Skeptics point out significant differences between apes and humans in their facility with language, especially in their respective abilities to order words grammatically. Nevertheless, these studies have revealed that apes possess considerable cognitive ability.

7. ***What is the relationship between thinking and language?***

Language facilitates and expresses our thoughts. There is no disputing that words convey ideas and that different languages can embody different ways of thinking. Although the **linguistic relativity** hypothesis suggests that language *determines* thought, it is more accurate to say that language *influences* thought. Studies of the effects of using the generic pronoun *he* and the ability of vocabulary enrichment to enhance thinking reveal the influence of words.

However, some ideas, such as the ability to perceive and remember different colors, do not depend on language. We sometimes think in images rather than in words, and we invent new words to describe new ideas. So we might say that our thinking affects our language, which then affects our thought.

Intelligence

8. ***When and why were intelligence tests created?***

Intelligence can be defined as the mental abilities needed to select, adopt to, and shape environments. In the early 1900s, French psychologist Alfred Binet and his colleague Théodore Simon developed questions in an attempt to measure **mental age** and thus to help predict children's future progress in the Paris school system. Lewis Terman of Stanford University adapted Binet's test and offered his **Stanford-Binet** as a way to direct people toward occupations for which they were deemed well suited. William Stern derived the **intelligence quotient (IQ)** to define performance on Terman's test.

9. ***Is intelligence a single general ability, or is it formed from several distinct abilities?***

Psychologists agree that people have specific abilities, such as verbal and mathematical aptitudes. However, they debate whether a **general intelligence (*g*)** factor runs through all these specific abilities. **Factor analysis** and studies of special conditions, such as the **savant syndrome**, have identified clusters of mental aptitudes. Howard Garder has identified multiple intelligences, and Robert Sternberg specifies three components of intelligence: academic, practical, and creative. **Emotional intelligence** has recently been described as the ability to describe, understand, and control emotions.

10. ***What types of tests are there?***

Tests function either as **aptitude tests** (designed to predict ability to learn a particular skill) or **achievement tests** (designed to assess current competence). The most widely used test is the **Wechsler Adult Intelligence Scale (WAIS)**.

11. ***What three principles of test construction apply in evaluating a psychological test?***

A good test must be **standardized**, so that any person's performance can be meaningfully compared with others'; **reliable**, so it yields dependably consistent scores; and **valid**, so it measures what it is supposed to measure (**content validity**) or predicts, on the basis of a specified **criterion**, what it is supposed to predict (**predictive validity**). Test scores usually fall into a bell-shaped distribution, the **normal curve**. The average score is assigned an arbitrary number (such as 100 on an intelligence test). Aptitude tests are highly reliable, but their validity is more modest (as judged by their predictions of academic success).

At the extremes of the bell curve are the gifted and those with **mental retardation**. One cause of mental retardation is **Down syndrome**.

12. ***What factors affect creativity?***

Intelligence correlates weakly with **creativity**. Creative people generally have a reasonable level of intelligence, but also a developed expertise, imaginative thinking skills, a venturesome personality, intrinsic motivation, and a supportive environment.

13. ***Is intellect influenced more by heredity or environment?***

Studies of twins, family members, and adopted children point to a significant hereditary contribution to intelligence scores. **Heritability**, differences attributable to genes, increases as environmental differences decrease. These studies, plus others that compare children reared in extremely impoverished or in enriched environments or in different cultures, indicate that life experiences also significantly influence intelligence test performance.

14. ***How, and why, do ethnic and gender groups differ in aptitude test performance?***

Like individuals, groups vary in intelligence test scores. Hereditary variation *within* a group need not signify a hereditary explanation of *between*-group differences. In the case of the racial gaps in test scores, the evidence suggests that environmental differences are largely, perhaps entirely, responsible. Girls have tended to score higher on spelling tests, boys on math aptitude tests (though not in math grades). Although some psychologists believe that a gender difference in spatial ability explains the gender gap in math performance, the difference is shrinking as more girls develop their math ability.

15. ***Are intelligence tests biased and discriminatory?***

If by "biased" one means sensitive to differences caused by cultural experience, then aptitude tests are necessarily biased. But if one means what psychologists commonly mean—that a test predicts less validly for one group than for another—then the current tests considered in this chapter seem not to be biased. Indeed, tests are designed specifically to avoid more subjective forms of discrimination.

CRITICAL THINKING EXERCISE by Richard O. Straub

Now that you have read and reviewed Chapter 8, take your learning a step further by testing your critical thinking skills on the following perspective-taking exercise.

Attempts to explain language development have sparked a spirited intellectual controversy. At the heart of this controversy is the nature-nurture debate. Behaviorist B. F. Skinner believed that we can explain how babies acquire language entirely with principles of learning, such as the *association* of objects with the sounds of words, the *imitation* of language modeled by others, and the *reinforcement* of correct use of words and syntax by parents and teachers. Linguist Noam Chomsky, who favors the nature position, believes that much of our language capacity is inborn. According to this perspective, just as "learning" to walk is programmed according to a timetable of biological maturation, so children are prewired to begin to babble and talk.

In this exercise, review each of the following examples of language use by children and decide whether it *best* supports the position of B. F. Skinner or Noam Chomsky. Then explain your reasoning.

1. While Marie and her mother are looking at a book together, Marie's mother shows her a picture of an animal and says "cow." Marie says "cow," and her mother praises her for her correct utterance. Two pages later, Marie spontaneously points to a picture and correctly identifies it as a cow.

   Position supported:

   Explanation:

2. When his day care teacher asks 2-year-old Jack what he did last Saturday, he responds with "We goed to the zoo." His teacher smiles, marveling at the fact that all children Jack's age make this type of grammatical error.

   Position supported:

   Explanation:

3. Nicole, who is deaf and was not exposed to sign language until age 3, lacks the manual linguistic skills of deaf children born to deaf-signing parents.

   Position supported:

   Explanation:

4. Twelve-year-old Malcolm, who emigrated to the United States at age 4, understands English grammar much better than 20-year-old Maya, who was first exposed to English at age 12.

   Position supported:

   Explanation:

Check your progress on becoming a critical thinker by comparing your answers to the sample answers found in Appendix B.

REHEARSE IT ANSWER KEY

1. a., **2.** b., **3.** c., **4.** d., **5.** b., **6.** d., **7.** c., **8.** d., **9.** b., **10.** a., **11.** a., **12.** d., **13.** c., **14.** c., **15.** d., **16.** a., **17.** c., **18.** b., **19.** b., **20.** a., **21.** c., **22.** c.

CHAPTER

9

Motivation

In everyday conversation, the question "What motivated you to do that?" is a way of asking "What *caused* your behavior? *Why* did you act that way?" To psychologists, a **motivation** is a need or desire that serves to *energize* behavior and to *direct* it toward a goal. Like intelligence, motivation is a hypothetical concept. We infer motivation from behaviors we observe. Consider motivation in these situations:

- David Mandel (1983), a former Nazi concentration camp inmate, recalls how a starving "father and son would fight over a piece of bread. Like dogs." One father, whose 20-year-old son stole his bread from under his pillow while he slept, went into a deep depression, asking over and again how his son could do such a thing. The next day the father died. "Hunger does something to you that's hard to describe. I can't believe it myself today, so how can I expect anyone else to understand it?"
- In the Old Testament's *Song of Solomon* love poems, a man and a woman express their intense sexual passion for one another. "I am sick with love," she declares. "O that his left hand were under my head, and that his right hand embraced me!" He, in turn, pronounces her "delectable." "You are stately as a palm tree, and your breasts are like its clusters. I say I will climb the palm tree and lay hold of its branches."
- In Texas, a school truant officer discovers Alfredo Gonzales, age 14, picking fruit and sends him off to the first day of school in his life. Although placed at the lowest skill level and paddled for asking questions in Spanish—he knows no English—Alfredo decides "I could do better." Indeed, today he is a highly educated college administrator who works to motivate youth to wake up, as he did, to "their own potential and to gain a desire to achieve it."

In this chapter, we explore motivation by focusing on these three motives—hunger, sex, and achievement. Although other identifiable motives exist (including thirst, curiosity, and a need for approval), a close look at these three reveals the interplay between nature (the physiological "push") and nurture (the cognitive and cultural "pulls").

Motivational Concepts

1. ***What theoretical perspectives have helped psychologists understand motivation?***

Instincts

Early in this century, as the influence of Charles Darwin's evolutionary theory grew, it became fashionable to classify all sorts of behaviors as instincts. If people criticized themselves, it was because of their "self-abasement instinct." If they boasted, it reflected their "self-assertion instinct." After scanning 500 books, one sociologist compiled a list of 5759 supposed human instincts! Before long, the instinct-naming fad collapsed under its own weight. For rather than *explaining* human behaviors, the early instinct theorists were simply *naming* them. It was like "explaining" a bright child's low grades by labeling the child an "underachiever." To name a behavior is *not* to explain it.

To qualify as an **instinct**, a complex behavior must have a fixed pattern throughout a species and be unlearned (Tinbergen, 1951). Such behaviors are common in other species (recall imprinting in birds and the return of salmon to their birthplace). Human behavior, too, exhibits certain innate tendencies, including simple fixed patterns such as an infant's rooting and sucking reflexes. Most psychologists, though, view human behavior as directed by physiological needs *and* psychological wants.

Same motive; different wiring The more complex the nervous system, the more adaptable the organism. Both the weaver bird and the woman satisfy their need for shelter in ways that reflect their inherited capacities. The bird's behavior pattern is fixed: It can build only this kind of nest. The woman's behavior is flexible: She can learn whatever skills she needs to build a house.

Although instinct theory failed to explain human motives, the underlying assumption that genes predispose species-typical behavior is as strong as ever. We saw this in Chapter 6's discussion of our biological predisposition to learn aversions to snakes, cliffs, and other dangerous objects. And we will see this in later discussions of how evolution might influence our helping behaviors, our romantic attractions, and our gender differences. Evolutionary psychology (the study of how natural selection shaped our motivations and behaviors) is now in its heyday.

Drives and Incentives

When the original instinct theory of motivation collapsed, it was replaced by **drive-reduction theory**—the idea that a physiological need creates an aroused state that *drives* the organism to reduce the need by, say, eating or drinking. With few exceptions, when a physiological need increases, so does a psychological drive—an aroused, motivated state.

The physiological aim of drive reduction is **homeostasis**—the maintenance of a steady internal state. An example of homeostasis (literally "staying the same") is the body's temperature-regulation system, which works like a thermostat. Both systems operate through feedback loops: Sensors feed room temperature to a control device. If room temperature cools, the control device switches on the furnace. Likewise, if body temperature cools, blood vessels constrict to conserve warmth, and we feel driven to put on more clothes or seek a warmer environment. Similarly, if the water level in our cells drops, sensors detect our need for water and we feel thirsty.

Not only are we *pushed* by our "need" to reduce drives, we also are *pulled* by **incentives**—positive or negative stimuli that lure or repel us. This is one way our individual learning histories influence our motives. Depending on our learning, the aroma of fresh roasted peanuts (or toasted ants), the sight of someone we find attractive, and the threat of disapproval can all motivate our

motivation a need or desire that energizes and directs behavior.

instinct a complex behavior that is rigidly patterned throughout a species and is unlearned.

drive-reduction theory the idea that a physiological need creates an aroused tension state (a drive) that motivates an organism to satisfy the need.

homeostasis a tendency to maintain a balanced or constant internal state; the regulation of any aspect of body chemistry, such as blood glucose, around a particular level.

incentive a positive or negative environmental stimulus that motivates behavior.

behavior. Our internal needs energize and direct our behavior, but so do these external incentives. The lure of money may energize us quite apart from any need-based drive.

When there is both a need and an incentive, we feel strongly driven. The food-deprived person who smells baking bread feels a strong hunger drive. In the presence of that drive, the baking bread becomes a compelling incentive. For each motive, we can therefore ask, "How is it pushed by our inborn physiological needs and pulled by incentives in the environment?"

Optimum Arousal

Rather than reducing a physiological need or minimizing tension, some motivated behaviors *increase* arousal. Well-fed animals will leave their shelter to explore, seemingly in the absence of any need-based drive. For taking such risks, animals may, however, gain information and resources (Renner, 1992).

Curiosity drives monkeys to monkey around trying to figure out how to unlock a latch that opens nothing, or how to open a window that allows them to see outside their room (Butler, 1954). It drives the 9-month-old infant who investigates every accessible corner of the house. It drives the scientists whose work this text discusses. And it drove the voyagers who first ventured across and beneath the oceans. Asked why he wanted to climb Mount Everest, George Mallory answered, "Because it is there." Those who, like Mallory, enjoy high arousal are most likely to enjoy intense music, novel foods, and risky behaviors (Zuckerman, 1979).

Driven by curiosity Children and baby monkeys are fascinated by things they have never handled before. Their drive to explore the relatively unfamiliar is one of several motives that do not fill any immediate physiological need.

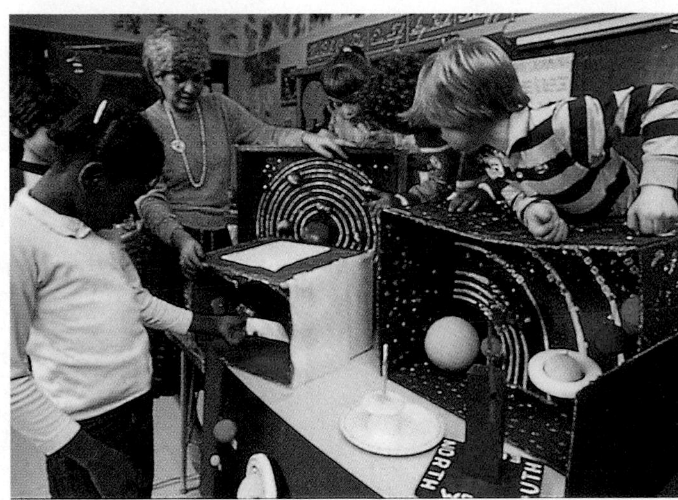

When placed in an extremely bland environment during "sensory restriction" experiments, people become more open to any available stimulation, including persuasive or therapeutic messages (Suedfeld, 1980). When stressed, the peace and quiet of prolonged quiet—lying in a room with unchanging sound and light—may sound like welcome relief. Yet facing hour after hour of monotony, we feel driven to experience stimulation. Without it, we feel bored and look for a way to increase arousal to some optimum level. With too much stimulation, we feel stressed and look for a way to decrease arousal.

hierarchy of needs Maslow's pyramid of human needs, beginning at the base with physiological needs that must first be satisfied before higher-level safety needs and then psychological needs become active.

A Hierarchy of Motives

2. *What is the basic idea behind Maslow's hierarchy of needs?*

Some needs take priority over others. At this moment, with your needs for air and water satisfied, other motives—such as your desire to achieve—energize and direct your behavior. Let your need for water go unsatisfied and your thirst will preoccupy you. But if you were deprived of air, your thirst would disappear.

Abraham Maslow (1970) described these priorities as a **hierarchy of needs** (Figure 9.1). At its base are our physiological needs, such as for food and water. Only if these needs are met are we prompted to meet our need for safety, and then to meet the uniquely human needs to give and receive love and to enjoy self-esteem. Beyond this, said Maslow (1971), lies the highest of human needs: to actualize one's full potential. (More on self-esteem and self actualization in Chapter 11.)

Maslow's hierarchy is somewhat arbitrary. Moreover, the order of such needs is not universally fixed. People have starved themselves to make a political statement. Nevertheless, the simple idea that some motives are more compelling than others does provide a framework for thinking about motivation.

Let's now consider the three representative motives, beginning at the basic, physiological level with hunger and working up through sexual motivation to the higher-level need to achieve. At each level, we shall see how environmental factors interact with what is physiologically given.

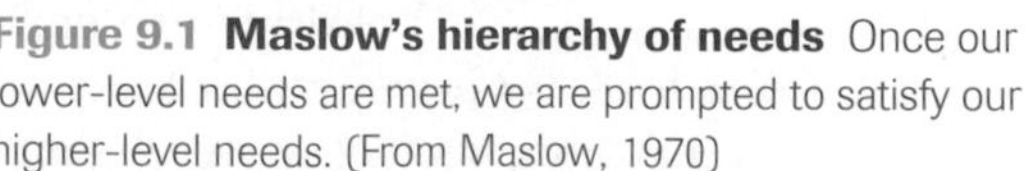

Figure 9.1 Maslow's hierarchy of needs Once our lower-level needs are met, we are prompted to satisfy our higher-level needs. (From Maslow, 1970)

REHEARSE IT!

1. Although instinct theory fails to explain most human behavior, the existence of simple fixed patterns such as an infant's rooting and sucking suggest some innate tendencies in humans. Indeed, the underlying assumption of instinct theory—that __________—is as strong as ever.

a. physiological needs arouse psychological states
b. genes predispose species-typical behavior
c. physiological needs increase arousal
d. external needs energize and direct behavior

2. Drive reduction motivates many behaviors necessary for survival. A need, or deprivation (for example, a lack of water), leads to an aroused state or drive; this in turn motivates the organism to act to reduce this drive (drink a glass of water) and restore internal stability. Drive reduction also motivates behaviors such as

a. eating and breathing.
b. satisfaction of curiosity.
c. nest building and other instincts.
d. pursuit of stimulation.

3. The aim of drive reduction is internal stability. For example, if we are too hot, we perspire; if we are dehydrated, we feel thirsty—and drink. The maintenance of a balanced internal state is called

a. instinct. **c.** a hierarchy of needs.
b. sensory restriction. **d.** homeostasis.

4. Motivated behaviors satisfy a variety of needs. Experiments on sensory restriction indicate that one such need can be to

a. reduce physiological needs.
b. minimize tension.
c. increase arousal.
d. ensure stability.

5. Behavior is also influenced by incentives in the environment. For example, a pile of leaves in the driveway may motivate you to get out the rake; your neighbor's disapproval may motivate you to turn down your radio. To explain the effects of external incentives, we must refer to

a. biological needs.
b. instinct.
c. individual learning histories.
d. homeostasis.

6. According to Abraham Maslow, we are not prompted to satisfy psychological needs, such as the need to be accepted or loved, until we have satisfied more basic needs. The most basic needs are physiological needs, including the need for food, water, and oxygen; just above these are

a. safety needs.
b. self-esteem needs.
c. belongingness needs.
d. psychological needs.

Hunger

A vivid demonstration of the supremacy of physiological needs followed reports of starvation in World War II prison camps and occupied areas. To learn more about the results of semistarvation, scientist Ancel Keys and his colleagues (1950) solicited volunteers for an experiment. More than 100 conscientious objectors to the war applied, and from them the researchers selected 36 men. First, they fed the men just enough to maintain their initial weight. Then, for six months, they cut this food level in half.

The effects soon became visible. Without thinking about it, the men began conserving energy; they appeared listless and apathetic. Their body weights dropped rapidly, eventually stabilizing at about 25 percent below their starting weights. The psychological effects were even more dramatic. Consistent with Maslow's idea of a needs hierarchy, the men became obsessed with food. They talked food. They daydreamed food. They collected recipes, read cookbooks, and feasted their eyes on delectable forbidden foods. Meanwhile, they lost their former interests in sex and social activities. They became preoccupied with their unfulfilled basic needs. As one participant reported, "If we see a show, the most interesting part of it is contained in scenes where people are eating. I couldn't laugh at the funniest picture in the world, and love scenes are completely dull."

"Nobody wants to kiss when they are hungry."
Dorothea Dix (1801–1887)

Scott Arthur Masear

"You're my best student, Beth, but I think this diet is having a negative effect on your work."

The Physiology of Hunger

3. *What physiological factors cause us to feel hungry?*

Keys' semistarved subjects felt hunger in response to signals from a homeostatic system designed to maintain normal body weight and an adequate nutrient supply. But precisely what is it that triggers hunger? Is it the pangs of an empty

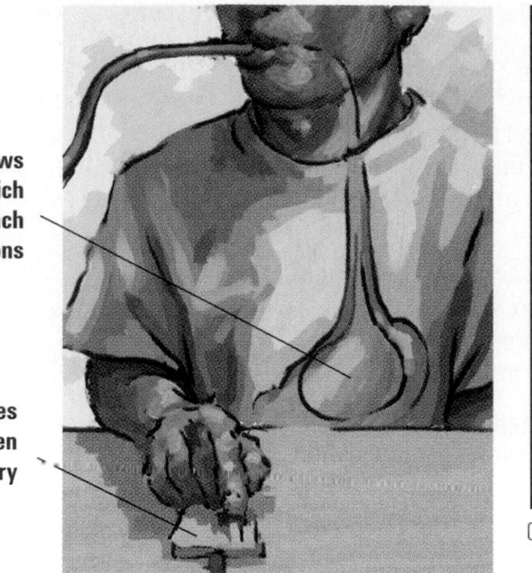

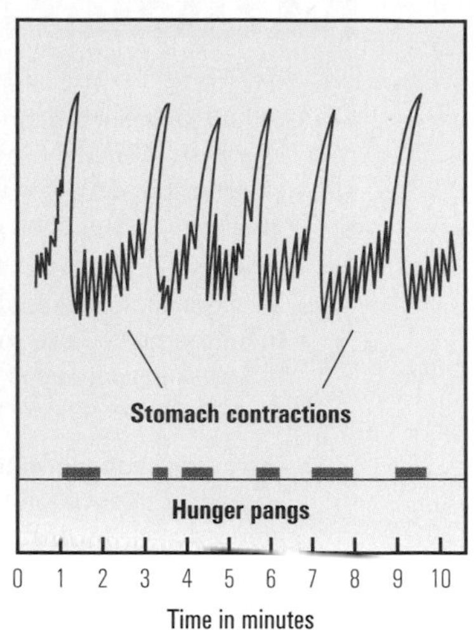

Figure 9.2 Monitoring stomach contractions Using this procedure, Washburn showed that stomach contractions (transmitted by the stomach balloon) accompany our feelings of hunger (indicated by a key press). (From Cannon, 1929)

stomach? So it feels. And so it seemed after A. L. Washburn, working with Walter Cannon (Cannon & Washburn, 1912), intentionally swallowed a balloon. When inflated in his stomach, the balloon transmitted Washburn's stomach contractions to a recording device (Figure 9.2). While his stomach was being monitored, Washburn pressed a key each time he felt hungry. The result: Washburn was having stomach contractions whenever he felt hungry. Some diet aids reduce this empty stomach feeling by filling the stomach with indigestible fibers that swell as they absorb water.

"The full person does not understand the needs of the hungry."

Irish Proverb

Alas, there is more to hunger than the pangs of an empty stomach. Researchers discovered this a quarter-century later when they removed some rats' stomachs and attached their esophagi to their small intestines (Tsang, 1938). Without stomach pangs, did hunger persist? Did the rats continue to eat regularly? Indeed they did. Hunger persists similarly in humans whose ulcerated or cancerous stomachs have been removed. In fact, one can feel hungry even on a full stomach. Animals that fill their stomachs by eating low-calorie food will eat more than animals that consume a less filling, high-calorie diet (McHugh & Moran, 1978). If the pangs of an empty stomach are not the only source of our hunger, what else matters?

Body Chemistry

Changes in body chemistry also affect hunger. People and other animals automatically regulate their caloric intake to maintain a stable body weight. This suggests that the body is somehow, somewhere, keeping tabs on its available resources. One such resource is the blood sugar **glucose**. Increases in the hormone insulin diminish blood glucose, partly by converting it to stored fat. When the blood glucose level drops, hunger increases.

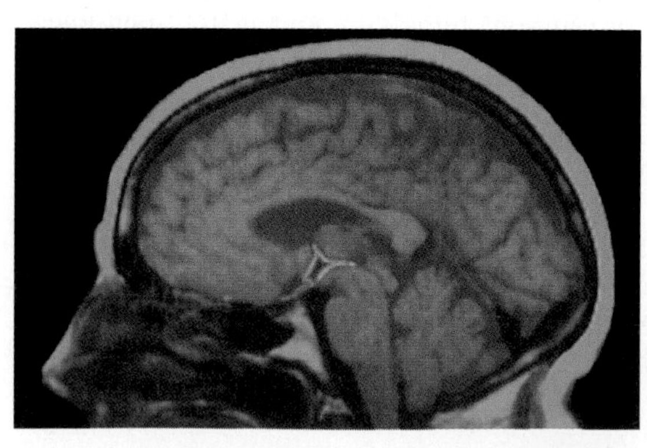

Figure 9.3 The hypothalamus As we saw in Chapter 2, the hypothalamus (colored red) performs various body maintenance functions, including control of hunger. Blood vessels supply the hypothalamus, enabling it to respond to our current blood chemistry as well as to incoming neural information about the body's state.

The Brain and Set Point

Low blood glucose triggers hunger. But you do not consciously feel your blood chemistry. Rather, the brain automatically monitors information on your body's internal state. Signals from the stomach, the intestines, and the liver (indicating whether glucose is being deposited or withdrawn) all signal the brain to motivate eating or not. But where in the brain are these messages integrated? During the 1940s and 1950s, researchers located hunger controls within the hypothalamus, a small but complex neural traffic intersection buried deep in the brain (Figure 9.3).

glucose the form of sugar that circulates in the blood and provides the major source of energy for body tissues. When its level is low, we feel hunger.

set point the point at which an individual's "weight thermostat" is supposedly set. When the body falls below this weight, an increase in hunger and a lowered metabolic rate may act to restore the lost weight.

basal metabolic rate the body's resting rate of energy expenditure.

Actually, there are two distinct hypothalamic centers that help control eating. Experiments during the 1960s suggested that activity along the sides of the hypothalamus, known as the *lateral hypothalamus*, brings on hunger. When electrically stimulated there, a well-fed animal would begin to eat; when the area was destroyed, even a starving animal had no interest in food. Activity in the lower middle of the hypothalamus, known as the *ventromedial hypothalamus*, depresses hunger. Stimulate this area and an animal will stop eating; destroy it and the animal's stomach and intestines will process food more rapidly, causing it to eat more often and to become grossly fat (Duggan & Booth, 1986; Hoebel & Teitelbaum, 1966). This discovery explained why certain patients, with tumors near the base of the brain (in what we now realize is the hypothalamus), will eat excessively and become fat (Miller, 1995).

How do these complementary areas of the hypothalamus work? One theory is that they influence how much glucose is converted to fat and how much is left available to fuel immediate activity (and minimize hunger). After ventromedial lesions, rats produce more fat and use less fat for energy, rather like a miser who runs a bit of extra money to the bank and resists taking any out (Pinel, 1993). Recent experiments also suggest that a distributed brain system monitors the body's state and reports to the hypothalamus, which processes the information and sends it along to the frontal lobes, which decide behavior (Winn, 1995).

Our bodies are astonishingly good at regulating our weight, much better than we could be through conscious efforts to control food intake precisely.

An older theory is that manipulating these two areas of the hypothalamus alters the body's "weight thermostat," which predisposes us to keep our body at a particular weight level, called its **set point** (Keesey & Corbett, 1983). When semistarved rats fall below their normal weight, biological pressures act to restore the lost weight: Hunger increases and energy expenditure decreases. If body weight rises—as happens when rats are force-fed—hunger decreases and energy expenditure increases. This stable weight toward which semistarved and overstuffed rats return is their set point.

Our bodies regulate weight much as rats' bodies do—through the control of food intake and energy output. If our body weight rises above our set point, we tend not to feel so hungry; if our weight drops below, we tend to eat more. To maintain its set-point weight, the body also adjusts its **basal metabolic rate**—its rate of energy expenditure in maintaining basic body functions when the body is at rest. By the end of their 24 weeks of semistarvation, the subjects in the World War II experiment had stabilized at three-quarters of their normal weight—while eating half of what they previously did. The stabilization resulted from reduced energy expenditure, achieved partly by physical lethargy and partly by a 29 percent drop in their basal metabolic rate.

Evidence for the brain's control of eating A lesion near the ventromedial (middle) area of the hypothalamus caused this rat's weight to triple. At 92.05 grams, it weighs about three times more than normal.

As we will see in the discussion of obesity and weight control, our heredity influences our body type and set point. Some researchers, however, doubt that the body has a precise set point that drives hunger. They believe that slow, sustained changes in body weight can, however, alter one's set point. Hunger, they say, is determined by too many factors, including learned incentives, for that to be true. Body weight settles around a level at which all these factors reach an equilibrium.

Despite the day-to-day variations in our eating, our bodies are astonishingly good at regulating our weight, much better than we could be through conscious efforts to control food intake precisely. Over the next 40 years you will eat about 20 tons of food. If during those years you increase your daily intake by just .01 ounce more than the amount required for your energy needs, you will gain 24 pounds (Martin & others, 1991). With astonishing precision, our bodies automatically balance energy intake and expenditure.

PEANUTS

The Psychology of Hunger

4. What psychological factors contribute to hunger?

Our eagerness to eat is both pushed by our physiological state—our body chemistry and hypothalamic activity—and pulled by our learned responses to external incentives.

External Incentives and Hunger

Like Pavlov's dogs, people learn to salivate in anticipation of appealing foods. Some people are especially responsive to appealing foods. When food is abundant, such people tend to gain the most weight.

Consider the 9- to 15-year-old girls studied by Judith Rodin and Joyce Slochower (1976) at an eight-week summer camp. During the first week of camp, some girls could not resist munching readily visible M&M's, even after a full meal. These girls were typical of a category the researchers called *externals*—people whose eating is triggered more by the presence of food than by internal factors. In the seven weeks that followed, the "external" girls gained the most weight.

In a delicious demonstration of how internal and external factors interact, Rodin (1984) invited other research subjects to her laboratory for lunch after they had gone 18 hours without food. While blood samples were being taken, a large, juicy steak was wheeled in, crackling as it finished grilling. As the hungry subjects sat watching, hearing, and smelling the soon-to-be-eaten steak, Rodin monitored their rising blood insulin levels and their accompanying feelings of hunger. When stimulated by the sight, sound, and aroma of the steak, "externals" had the greatest insulin increase and accompanying hunger response. This illustrates how certain individuals' psychological experience of an external incentive (the steak) can affect their internal physiological state.

Taste Preferences: Biology or Culture?

An acquired taste For Alaskan Eskimos, but not for most other North Americans, whale blubber is a tasty treat. People everywhere learn to enjoy the fatty, bitter, or irritating foods prescribed by their culture.

Body chemistry and environmental factors influence not only when we feel hunger but what we are hungry for—our taste preferences. When feeling tense or depressed, do you crave sweet or starchy carbohydrate-laden foods? Carbohydrates help boost levels of the neurotransmitter serotonin, which has calming effects. Given the drug fenfluramine, which similarly increases serotonin, carbohydrate cravers lose their cravings. This suggests that stress-related cravings might be treatable by providing food substitutes that mimic biochemical effects (Hall, 1987).

Our preferences for sweet and salty tastes are genetic and universal. Other taste preferences are conditioned, as when people given highly salted foods develop a liking for excess salt (Beauchamp, 1987) or when people develop an aversion to a food eaten before becoming violently ill. (The frequency of children's illnesses provides many chances for them to learn food aversions.)

Culture affects taste, too. Bedouins enjoy eating the eye of a camel, which most North Americans would find repulsive. Similarly, most North Americans and Europeans shun dog, rat, and horse meat, all of which are prized elsewhere, but welcome beef, which Hindus wouldn't think of eating. Such preferences vary with exposure (Pliner & Pelchat, 1991; Rozin, 1976). We humans have a natural dislike of many things unfamiliar, including novel foods (especially

CLOSE-UP

Eating Disorders

Psychological influences on eating behavior are strikingly evident in those for whom normal homeostatic pressures are overwhelmed by a motive for abnormal thinness. Consider two eating disorder cases.

Mary is a 5′ 3″ 15-year-old who, having reached 100 pounds, decided she needed to lose weight to enhance her attractiveness. After gradually reducing her food intake to a few vegetables a day and then adding a vigorous exercise program, she now weighs a mere 80 pounds. Yet she still feels and perceives herself as "fat" and plans to continue dieting. Mary has been having difficulty sleeping, has at times been depressed, and no longer has regular menstrual periods. She is socially inactive, but she is very successful academically. Mary does not regard herself as ill or needing treatment.

Alice is a 5′ 9″, 160-pound 17-year-old who says she has always been a little chubby. For the last five years, she has often eaten in binges, followed by vomiting. She will eat a quart of ice cream or an entire pie and then, to control her weight, make herself vomit in secret. Alice wants to date, but she doesn't, partly because she is so self-conscious about her looks. She has at times taken diet pills to try to lose weight.

Mary is diagnosed as having **anorexia nervosa**—a disorder in which a person becomes significantly underweight (typically, 15 percent or more) yet feels fat and is obsessed with losing weight. Even when emaciated, the person continues to limit food intake. The disorder usually develops in adolescence, 9 times out of 10 in females.

Alice's condition, which is more common, is **bulimia nervosa**—a disorder marked by repeated binge-purge episodes of overeating followed by vomiting or laxative use. Bulimia patients eat as some alcoholics drink—in spurts, sometimes under the influence of friends who also are binging (Crandall, 1988). Most binge-purge eaters are women in their late teens or twenties. Like those with anorexia, they are preoccupied with food (craving sweet and high-fat foods), are fearful of becoming overweight, and are depressed or anxious (Hinz & Williamson, 1987). The depression and shame are felt most keenly during and following binges. About half of those with anorexia also display the binge-purge-depression symptoms of bulimia. But unlike anorexia, bulimia is marked by weight fluctuations within or above normal ranges. This makes the condition easy to hide.

Researchers report that the families of bulimia patients have a higher-than-usual incidence of alcoholism, obesity, and depression. Anorexia patients often come from a family that is competitive, high-achieving, and protective (Pate & others, 1992; Yates, 1989, 1990). They set high standards, fret about falling short of expectations, and are intensely concerned with how others perceive them (Heatherton & Baumeister, 1991; Striegel-Moore & others, 1993). Eating disorders do *not*, however, provide (as some have speculated) a telltale sign of childhood sexual abuse (Kinzl & others, 1994; Pope & others, 1992, 1994; Rorty & others, 1994).

Genetics also may influence susceptibility to eating disorders. When one twin has bulimia, the chances of the other twin's sharing the disorder are much greater if they are identical rather than fraternal twins (Fichter & Noegel, 1990). People with eating disorders may also have abnormal supplies of certain neurotransmitters that put them at risk for anxiety or depression (Fava & others, 1989).

"Diana remained throughout a very insecure person at heart, almost childlike in her desire to do good for others, so she could release herself from deep feelings of unworthiness, of which her eating disorders were merely a symptom."

Charles, Earl of Spencer, euologizing his sister, Princess Diana
1997

There is, however, a cultural explanation for the fact that anorexia and bulimia occur mostly in women and mostly in weight-conscious cultures. Mothers of girls with eating disorders are themselves often focused on their own weight and on their daughters' weight and appearance (Pike & Rodin, 1991). Anorexia nervosa always begins as a weight-loss diet, and the self-induced vomiting of bulimics nearly always begins after a dieter has broken diet restrictions and gorged. Facing a diet, the bulimic's body revolts, overcoming willpower as it demands food to restore lost fat. Those whose natural set-point weight is well above their thin-ideal weight are especially vulnerable (Seligman, 1994).

Although ideals of beauty have varied over the centuries, women in every era have struggled to make their bodies conform to the ideal of their day. Thus, the sickness of today's eating disorders lies not just within the victims but also within their weight-obsessed culture—a culture that says, in countless ways, "Fat is bad," that motivates millions of women to be "always dieting," and that encourages eating binges by pressuring women to live in a constant state of semistarvation. Virtually all young adult women rate their ideal figures as thinner than their current figures (Raudenbush & Zellner, 1997). "You can't be too rich or too thin," declared the Duchess of Windsor. As obesity researchers Susan Wooley and Orland Wooley (1983) noted, "An increasingly stringent cultural standard of thinness for women has been accompanied by a steadily increasing incidence of serious eating disorders in women."

anorexia nervosa an eating disorder in which a normal-weight person (usually an adolescent female) diets and becomes significantly (15 percent or more) underweight, yet, still feeling fat, continues to starve.

bulimia nervosa an eating disorder characterized by private, "binge-purge" episodes of overeating, usually of highly caloric foods, followed by vomiting or laxative use.

novel animal-based rather than vegetarian foods). Rats, too, prefer long-familiar foods (Sclafani, 1995). This "neophobia" surely was adaptive for our ancestors, serving to protect them from potentially toxic substances. In experiments, people have tried novel fruit drinks or ethnic foods. With repeated exposure, their appreciation for the new taste typically increases; moreover, exposure to one set of novel foods increases willingness to try another (Pliner, 1982; Pliner & others, 1993).

Obesity and Weight Control

5. *What factors predispose some people to become and remain obese?*

Government guidelines encourage an under-25 body mass index (BMI), defined as

$$\frac{\textit{weight in kg (pounds} \times .45)}{\textit{squared height in meters } [(\textit{inches} \div 39.4)^2]}$$

In the United States, 59 percent of men and 49 percent of women have BMIs over 25. Some experts define obesity as a BMI of 30 or more (Haney, 1996).

People wonder: Why do some people gain while others eat the same amount and remain slim? Why do so few overweight people win the battle of the bulge? And what hope is there for the one-third of Americans who, according to the National Center for Health Statistics, are overweight?

First, the good news about fat. Fat is an ideal form of stored energy that provides the body with a high-caloric fuel reserve to carry it through periods when food is scarce—a common occurrence in the feast-or-famine existence of our prehistoric ancestors. Eating three or more meals every day is a relatively recent phenomenon and a luxury hundreds of millions of people still do not enjoy. In circumstances of alternating feast and famine, overeating and storing the excess as fat is adaptive; it prepares the body to withstand famine. This may explain why in most developing societies today, as in Europe in earlier centuries—in fact, wherever people face famine—obesity is a sign of affluence and social status (Furnham & Baguma, 1994).

To promote health by discouraging smoking, many governments now heavily tax cigarettes. Would you concur with the suggestion of Kelly Brownell (1994), director of Yale's Center for Eating and Weight Disorders, to slap a similar tax on fatty foods?

Cultures without a thin-ideal for women also are cultures without eating disorders. For example, Ghanaians idealize a larger body size than do Americans—and experience fewer eating disorders (Cogan & others, 1996). The same differences exist between African-American and European-American women (Parker & others, 1995).

Rubens' "The Garden of Love" In other times and places, fatter bodies have been idealized.

The bad news is that in those parts of the world where food and sweets are now abundantly available, the adaptive tendency to store fat has become maladaptive. Being slightly overweight poses no health risks. But the National Institutes of Health reports that genuine obesity increases the risk of diabetes, high blood pressure and heart disease, gallstones, arthritis, and certain types of cancer. This is more true for apple-shaped people who carry their weight in pot bellies than for pear-shaped people with ample hips and thighs (Greenwood, 1989). In some animals, a restricted-calorie diet prolongs youthful vitality and life expectancy (Weindruch, 1996).

Obesity is not just a threat to physical health. Being perceived as obese can affect how you are treated and how you feel about yourself. People often stereotype the obese as slow, lazy, and sloppy (Crandall, 1994, 1995; Ryckman & others, 1989). Widen people's images on a video monitor (making them look fatter) and they suddenly seem less sincere and friendly and more obnoxious and mean (Gardner & Tockerman, 1994).

The obese—sometimes victims of ridicule and job discrimination—know the stereotype. In studies of patients who were especially unhappy with their weight—those who had lost an average of 100 pounds after short-cutting digestion with intestinal bypass surgery—8 in 10 said their children had asked them not to attend school functions. And 9 in 10 said they would rather have a leg amputated than be obese again (Rand & Macgregor, 1990, 1991). Another study followed 370 obese 16- to 24-year-olds (Gortmaker & others, 1993). When restudied seven years later, two-thirds of the women were still obese.

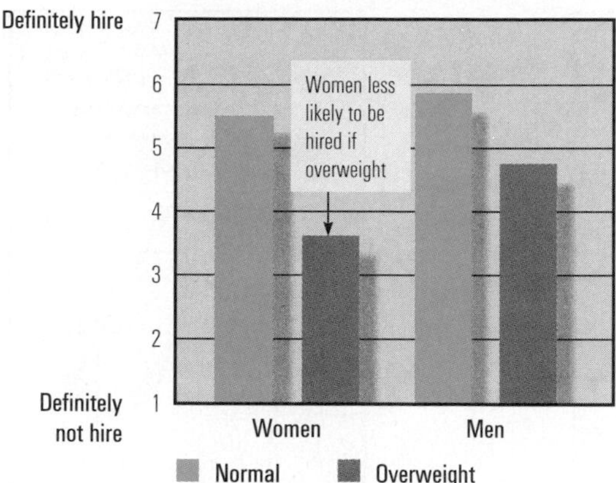

Figure 9.4 Gender and weight discrimination When women applicants were made to look overweight, university students were less willing to think they would hire them. Among men applicants, weight mattered less. (Data from Pingitore & others, 1994)

They also were less likely to be married, and they were making less money than a comparison group of some 5000 other women. Even after correcting for aptitude test scores, race, and parental income, the obese women's incomes were $7000 a year below average.

In one clever experiment, Regina Pingitore and her colleagues (1994) videotaped job interviews in which professional actors appeared as either normal-weight applicants or as overweight applicants. In one condition, they wore make-up and prostheses that made them look 30 pounds heavier. When appearing overweight, the same person, using the same lines, intonation, and gestures, was rated as less worthy of hiring. The weight bias was especially strong against women applicants (Figure 9.4).

The Physiology of Obesity

Many people think fat people are gluttons. They see obesity as a matter of choice or as reflecting a personality problem—as a maladjusted way of reducing anxiety, dealing with guilt, or gratifying an "oral fixation." If being obese signifies either a lack of self-discipline or a personality problem, then who would want to hire, date, or associate with such people? And if obese people believe such things about themselves, how could they feel anything but unworthy and undesirable? (Surprisingly, in studies to date, obese people have not suffered a notably higher rate of depression [Friedman & Brownell, 1995].)

Research on the physiology of obesity challenges the image of fat, weak-willed gluttons. Consider the arithmetic of weight gain: People get fat by consuming more calories than they expend, and the energy equivalent of a pound of fat is 3500 calories. Dieters have therefore been told that they will lose a pound for every 3500-calorie reduction in their diet. Surprise: This conclusion turns out to be false. To see why, consider the physiology of fat.

Fat Cells

The immediate determinants of body fat are the size and number of fat cells. A typical adult has about 30 billion of these miniature fuel tanks, half of which lie near the skin's surface. A fat cell can vary from relatively empty, like a deflated balloon, to overly full. In an obese person, fat cells may swell to two or three times their normal size and then divide. Once the number of fat cells increases—due to genetic predisposition, early childhood eating patterns, or adult overeating—it never decreases. On a diet, fat cells may shrink, but they do not disappear (Sjöstrum, 1980).

The unyielding nature of our fat cells is but one way in which, once we become fat, our bodies maintain fat. Another way is that fat tissue has a low basal metabolic (energy expenditure) rate. Compared with other tissue, fat takes less food energy to maintain. Thus, once we become fat, we require less food to maintain our weight than we did to attain it.

"Your skin is enlarged."

Set Point and Metabolism

There is another reason that most obese people find it so difficult to lose weight permanently. Their bodies' "weight thermostats" are set to maintain body weight within a higher-than-average range. When weight drops below the set-point range, hunger increases and metabolism decreases.

As many a dieter can testify, the drop in basal metabolic rate can be particularly frustrating. After the rapid weight losses that occur during the initial three weeks or so of a rigorous diet, further weight loss comes slowly. In one classic experiment (Bray, 1969), obese patients whose daily food intake was reduced from 3500 to 450 calories lost only 6 percent of their weight—partly because

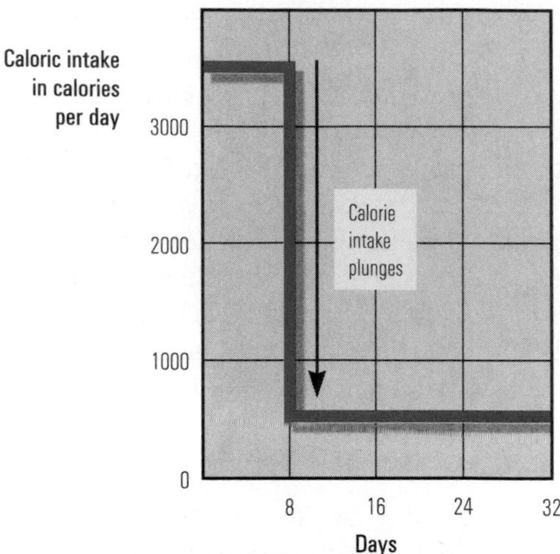

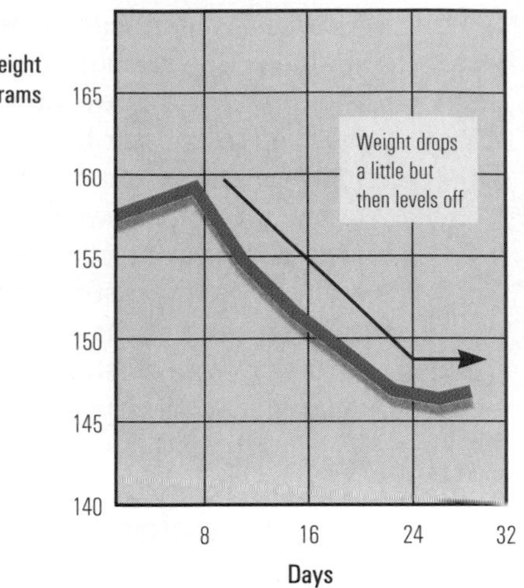

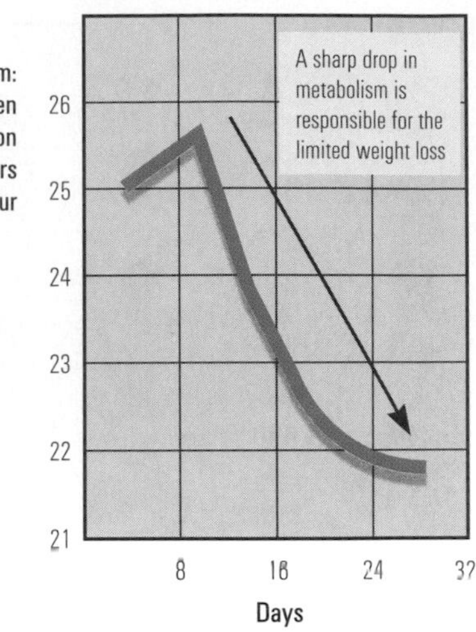

Figure 9.5 The effects of a severe diet on obese patients' body weight and metabolism After 7 days on a 3500-calorie diet, six obese patients were given only 450 calories a day for the next 24 days. Body weight declined only 6 percent and then leveled off, because basal metabolic rate dropped about 15 percent. (From Bray, 1969)

their basal metabolic rates dropped about 15 percent (Figure 9.5). Thus, the body adapts to starvation by burning off fewer calories and adapts to extra calories by burning off more. That is why reducing your food intake by 3500 calories may not reduce your weight by 1 pound. And that is why when a diet ends and the body is still conserving energy, amounts of food that only maintained weight before the diet may now increase it.

Individual differences in basal metabolic rate explain why—contrary to the stereotype of the overweight glutton—it is possible for two people of the same height, age, and activity level to maintain the same weight, even if one of them eats much more than the other does. Or why it is possible for a person to eat less than another similarly active person, yet weigh more. This appears true despite findings that people—obese people, especially—tend to overestimate their physical activity and underestimate their caloric intake (Brownell & Wadden, 1992; Lichtman & others, 1992).

The Genetic Factor

Studies of adoptees and twins reveal a genetic influence on body weight. Consider:

- Despite shared family meals, the body weights of adopted siblings fail to correlate either with one another or with those of their adoptive parents: Rather, people's weights resemble those of their biological parents (Grilo & Pogue-Geile, 1991).
- Identical twins have closely similar weights, even when reared apart (Plomin & others, 1997; Stunkard & others, 1990). Being overweight is therefore *not* simply a matter of scarfing too many hot fudge sundaes. And losing weight is not simply a matter of mind over platter.

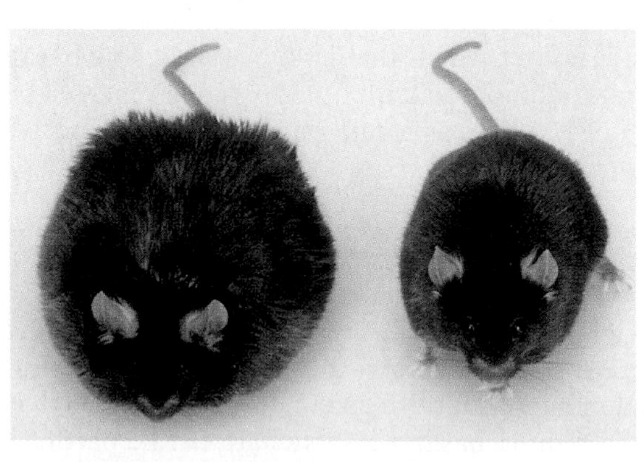

Fat-signaling hormone The obese mouse at left has a defective gene for producing the fat-signaling hormone, leptin. When the genetically similar mouse at right was treated with leptin, it shed 40 percent of its body weight.

Recent experiments reveal a mechanism for weight control. As a normal mouse's fat cells become bloated, its genes produce a protein, leptin. To estimate body fat, the brain monitors leptin levels in the blood. Increased leptin therefore signals the brain to curb eating and increase activity. So researchers injected obese mice, which produce less leptin, with daily doses of leptin. The mice then ate less, became more active, and lost weight (Halaas & others, 1995). This discovery excites wondering: Might injections of leptin similarly serve as virtual fat

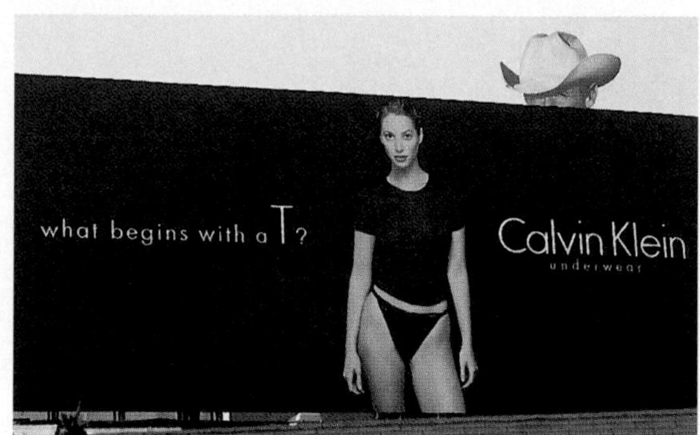

The lean look Contemporary clothing ads and films present an ideal of thinness that most women cannot attain. The message is so pervasive in our culture that even those of flawless appearance are often worried about their bodily "imperfections."

The classic Barbie fashion doll's proportions when adjusted to a 5′7″ height: 32–16–29 (Norton & others, 1996). In 1997, Mattell decided to reshape Barbie into a more realistic image.

for humans, fooling the brain into making a fat body thinner? Or, as newer research suggests, are the leptin receptors of obese humans insensitive to leptin (Considine & others, 1996)? If so, might a slightly different drug be designed that activates insensitive leptin receptors? Or might we look forward to a drug that blocks hypothalamic receptors that activate eating (Gerald & others, 1996)? Given the huge potential market for such drugs, the race to define them is on.

Genes are not the whole story, however. Diet or exercise rather than genes must explain why obesity is six times more common among lower-class than among upper-class women, more common among Americans than among Europeans, and more common among Americans today than in 1900. (Compared with their counterparts in the early 1900s, people are eating a higher-fat diet and expending fewer calories.) Ironically, the growing pudginess of Americans coincides with an increasing idealization of the thin-and-fit look. Consider:

- U.S. models of a generation ago weighed 8 percent less than the average woman; today they weigh 23 percent less—which makes the average model thinner than 95 percent of women (Wolf, 1991). Most of today's models and actresses have hardly more than half the 22 to 26 percent body fat of an average woman (Brownell, 1991). When young women view magazine pictures of ultra-thin models, they report increased feelings of shame, guilt, and body dissatisfaction (Stice & Shaw, 1994).
- In 1950, department-store mannequins looked nearly like real women. Since then, they have lost about 3 inches around their hips, which now average only 31 inches—quite unlike today's average young adult woman's 37 inches. In fact, women with as little body fat as these mannequins likely would not menstruate (University of California, 1993).
- While the average North American woman weighs *more* than her counterpart of 40 years ago and obesity rates are increasing, today's average Miss America contestant weighs about 15 pounds *less*.

Losing Weight

Perhaps you shake your head in sympathy with obese people: "Slim chance they (or we) have of becoming and staying thin. If they lose weight on a diet, their metabolism slows and their hungry fat cells cry out, 'Feed me!'" Indeed, the condition of an obese person's body reduced to average weight is much like that of a semistarved body. Held under normal set point, each body "thinks" it is starving. Having lost weight, formerly obese people look normal, but their fat cells may be abnormally small, their metabolism slow, and, like the semistarved subjects we met earlier, their minds obsessed with food.

"After years of research, after tens of millions of dieters, after tens of billions of dollars, no one has found a diet that keeps the weight off in any but a small fraction of dieters."

Martin E. P. Seligman
What You Can Change and What You Can't
1994

All this explains why most people who succeed on a weight-loss program eventually gain back nearly all of the weight (Garner & Wooley, 1991; Wing & Jeffery, 1979). One study followed 207 obese patients who had lost large amounts of weight during a two-month hospital fast (Johnson & Drenick, 1977). Half gained back all the lost weight within three years, and virtually all were again obese within nine years. Programs that modify life-style and ongoing eating behavior have better carryover to postdiet weight management. Yet participants in these programs, too, typically regain much of their lost weight (Figure 9.6, page 324). When cultural ideals of slimness collide with hunger, hunger usually wins. Commercial weight-loss programs can justifiably proclaim that they help people lose weight, *temporarily*. For most people, however, the only long-term result is a thinner wallet.

Nonetheless, the battle of the bulge rages as intensely as ever. It is especially intense in North America, where weight concern and dieting are a greater preoccupation than in, say, Australia or developing countries (Rothblum, 1990; Tiggemann & Rothblum, 1988). Americans spend $30 billion a year trying to lose

Figure 9.6 Weight change and weight-loss programs Behavior-management weight-loss programs promote weight loss, but most lost weight is regained. (From Brownell & Jeffery, 1987)

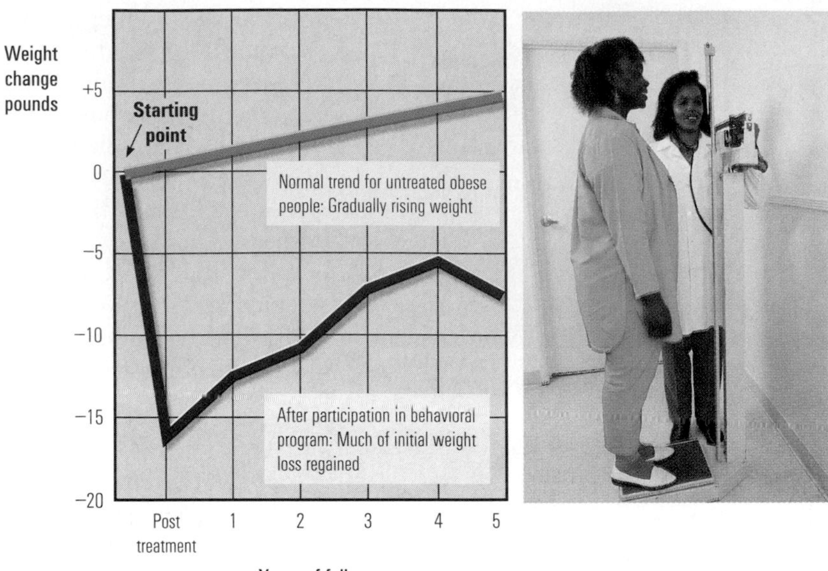

weight (Gura, 1997). In one poll, 45 percent of men and 63 percent of women said they would like to lose weight (Gallup, 1996). Asked if they would rather "be five years younger or weigh 15 pounds less," 29 percent of men and 48 percent of women preferred losing the weight (*Responsive Community*, 1996). The gender difference is even larger for teenagers: 15 percent of boys and 44 percent of girls are trying to lose weight (Centers for Disease Control, 1991).

Janet Polivy and Peter Herman (1987) believe that widespread, chronic dieting among basically normal-weight girls and women represents the seeds of eating disorder on a massive scale.

With fat cells, set points, metabolism, and genetic factors all tirelessly conspiring to make losing weight a big problem, what advice can psychology offer to those who wish to shed excess pounds? The most important advice seems to be that we should begin a diet only if we feel motivated and self-disciplined enough to restrict our eating or exercise permanently. For most people, permanent weight loss requires making a career of staying thin—a lifelong change in eating habits combined with gradually increased exercise. In fact, sustained exercise can be a weapon against the body's normal metabolic slowdown when dieting. One of the few predictors of successful long-term weight loss is exercise during and after dieting (Brownell & Wadden, 1991, 1992; Foreyt & others, 1996).

Although preserving weight loss is a constant challenge, Stanley Schachter (1982) was less pessimistic than most obesity researchers about the likelihood of doing it successfully. He recognizes the overwhelming rate of failure among people in structured weight-loss programs. But he also notes that these are a special group of people, probably people who have been unable to help themselves. Moreover, the failure rates recorded for these programs are based on single attempts at weight loss. Perhaps when people try repeatedly to lose weight, more of them do eventually succeed. When Schachter interviewed a haphazard sample of people, he found that one-fourth of them had at one time been significantly overweight and had tried to slim down. Of these, 6 out of 10 had *succeeded*: They weighed at least 10 percent less than their maximum prediet weight (an average loss of 35 pounds) and were no longer obese. And a 1993 survey of 90,000 *Consumer Reports* readers found 25 percent of dieters claiming enduring weight loss.

Bottom Liners

"It works as well as most other diet plans. . . . I've lost over $200 in less than three weeks."

Two other studies reveal less encouraging results: Fewer than a third of formerly overweight people were no longer overweight (Jeffery & Wing, 1983; Rzewnicki & Forgays, 1987). But the findings do hint that prospects for losing weight may be somewhat brighter than the dismal conclusions drawn from following patients who undergo a single weight-loss program.

THINKING CRITICALLY

Helpful Hints for Dieters

Minimize exposure to tempting food cues. Keep tempting foods out of the house or out of sight. Stay out of the sweets shops. Go to the supermarket only on a full stomach.

Take steps to boost your basal metabolic rate. Inactive people are often overweight (Figure 9.7). Sustained exercise, such as brisk walking, running, and swimming, not only empties fat cells, builds muscle, and makes you feel better, it can also temporarily speed up basal metabolism (Kolata, 1987; Thompson & others, 1982).

Modify both your basal metabolic rate and your hunger by changing the food you eat. Findings suggest that complex carbohydrates (pasta, grains, potatoes) increase basal metabolic rate and are less readily converted to body fat than are the same calories eaten as fats (Rodin, 1979, 1985). Complex carbohydrates and fructose (the sugar in fruits) stimulate less of a hunger-producing insulin jump than does refined sugar (sucrose).

Don't starve all day and eat one big meal at night. This eating pattern, common among overweight people, slows metabolism.

Beware of the binge. Among people who consciously restrain their eating, drinking alcohol or feeling anxious or depressed can unleash the urge to eat (Herman & Polivy, 1980). Once the diet is broken, the person often thinks "what the heck" and then binges (Polivy & Herman, 1985, 1987). A lapse then becomes a full collapse. Remember, most people occasionally lapse. Remind yourself that you've succeeded before and continue with your plan.

Set realistic goals. Targeting an ambitiously low weight usually dooms a dieter to eventual defeat. Setting a realistic objective for exercise and moderate weight loss can promote effort and persistence.

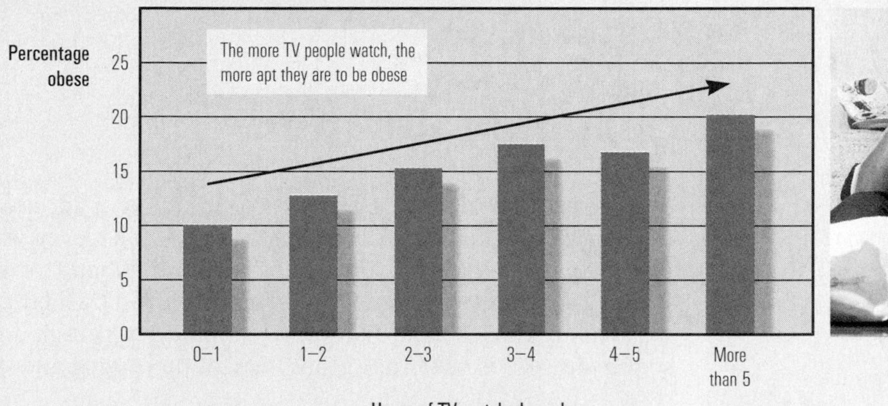

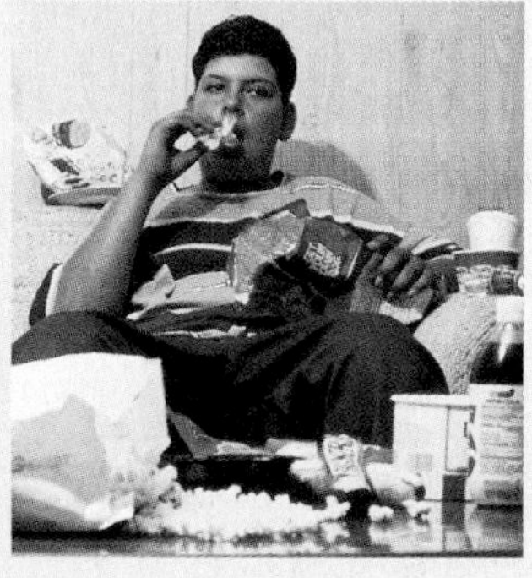

Figure 9.7 Couch potatoes beware: A correlational study of TV watching and obesity In one study of 6671 12- to 17-year-olds, obesity was more common among those who watched the most television. Of course, overweight people may avoid activity, preferring to sit and watch TV. But the association between TV watching and obesity remained when many other factors were controlled, suggesting that inactivity and snacking while watching TV do contribute to obesity. Also, as life-styles have become more sedentary and TV watching has increased, so has the percentage of overweight people in Britain, North America, and elsewhere. (From Vines, 1995)

Oprah Winfrey's yo-yo dieting illustrates both the difficulty of keeping weight off and the contemporary obsessions with women's weight. The weight she was:

1984–1987:	*About 200 pounds*
1988–1989:	*Loses 67 pounds*
1990:	*Regains 70 pounds*
1992:	*Peaks at 235 pounds*
1993:	*Loses 72 pounds*
1994:	*Loses 15 pounds more; runs 26.2 mile marathon*
1995:	*66 percent of* McCalls *(August) readers think* this time *she'll not regain the weight*

There is, however, another option for overweight people, the one chosen by 13 percent of the people Schachter interviewed—simply to accept one's weight. We all do well to note what researchers have *not* identified as causes of obesity: guilt, hostility, oral fixation, or any similar personality maladjustment. Nor is obesity simply a matter of a lack of willpower. If dieters are more likely to binge when under stress or after breaking their diets, this may be largely a consequence of their constant dieting. "Fat is not a four-letter word," proclaims the National Association to Aid Fat Acceptance. Although such statements disregard the health risks linked with significant obesity, they do convey a valid point: It is surely better to accept oneself as a little chubby than to diet and binge and feel continually out of control and guilty. Fans loved Oprah Winfrey before she lost 67 pounds. They loved her when she shed them again. And they will love her still, chubby or not.

7. The hypothalamus, a structure deep within the brain, controls feelings of hunger and fullness, in part by evaluating changes in blood chemistry. Hunger occurs in response to high blood insulin and
   - **a.** high blood glucose.
   - **b.** low blood glucose.
   - **c.** decreased energy expenditure.
   - **d.** stimulation of any part of the hypothalamus.
8. Our bodies tend to stay at a particular weight level, or set point. Changes in the basal metabolic rate help keep us at this weight. For example, when our weight falls below the set point, we feel hungrier (and eat more) and lethargic (and reduce our energy expenditure). The operation of this "weight thermostat" is an example of
   - **a.** homeostasis.
   - **b.** an eating disorder.
   - **c.** individual learning.
   - **d.** binge-purge episodes.
9. Both anorexia nervosa and bulimia nervosa are eating disorders characterized by excessive weight loss. Which of the following is true regarding bulimia nervosa?
   - **a.** People with bulimia continue to want to lose weight even when they are underweight.
   - **b.** Bulimia is marked by weight fluctuations within or above normal ranges.
   - **c.** Bulimia patients often come from middle-class families that are competitive, high-achieving, and protective.
   - **d.** If one twin is diagnosed with bulimia, the chances of the other twin's sharing the disorder are greater if they are fraternal rather than identical twins.
10. Obese people find it very difficult to lose weight permanently. This is due to several factors, including the fact that
    - **a.** with dieting, fat cells shrink and then disappear.
    - **b.** the set point of obese people is lower than average.
    - **c.** with dieting, basal metabolic rate increases.
    - **d.** there is a genetic influence on body weight.

Sexual Motivation

Sex is part of life. Had this not been so for all your ancestors, you would not be reading this book. Sexual motivation is nature's clever way of making people procreate, thus enabling our species' survival. When two people feel attracted, they hardly stop to think of themselves as guided by their genes. As the pleasure we take in eating is nature's inventive method of getting our body nourishment, so the pleasure of sex is our genes' way of preserving and spreading themselves.

"Maybe . . . it starts with a kiss."

Prenatal photographer Lennart Nilsson, answering the question "When does life begin?"

Describing Sexual Behavior

Before looking at what energizes and directs sexual arousal, let's consider the behavior patterns that a theory of sexual motivation must explain.

Unable to answer his students' questions about people's sexual practices and driven by his own sexual curiosity, Indiana University biologist Alfred Kinsey and his colleagues (1948, 1953) set out to find some answers. Kinsey's confidential interviews with 18,000 people—85 percent conducted by himself or his associate Wardell Pomeroy—asked more than 350 rapid-fire questions. Social scientists were quick to point out what Kinsey readily acknowledged—that his nonrandom sample contained an overrepresentation of well-educated, white urbanites.

As the pleasure we take in eating is nature's inventive method of getting our body nourishment, so the pleasure of sex is our genes' way of preserving and spreading themselves.

Because we do not know whether Kinsey's sample accurately represented the nation's sexual practices in the 1940s, let alone those of today, it can be misleading to report his precise findings. Moreover, Kinsey and Pomeroy's questions were posed in a way that encouraged (some say, demanded) admission of sexual activity. They never asked subjects *whether* they had engaged in a particular activity, they asked them *when* they had first engaged in it (thus making it easier for people to divulge their behavior). Pomeroy (1972, pp. 113, 124, 127) reported that he and Kinsey "went on the broad assumption that everybody had done everything." If Kinsey or Pomeroy doubted a subject's denial, they might

Alfred Kinsey The controversial biologist, shown here conducting one of his interviews, did not begin with sexually explicit questions. Rather, he first helped people feel at ease by asking nonthreatening questions about family background, health, and education.

respond, "Yes, I know you have never done that, but how old were you the *first* time you did it?" or even "Look, I don't give a damn what you've done, but if you don't tell me the straight of it, it's better that we stop this history right here. Now, how old were you the first time this or that happened?"

By today's standards of random sampling and nonleading questioning, Kinsey's tactics, and thus his results, are suspect. Yet his surveys were surely less misleading than some of the haphazard sexual surveys that have been reported more recently in the popular press. Recall from Chapter 1 that when popular "sex reports" begin with a biased sample of people (such as subscribers to selected magazines) and receive replies from only 3 percent of this nonrandom sample, there is good reason to doubt the generality of their findings.

Better information is now becoming available. Despite the media image of rampant marital infidelity—an image reinforced by media psychologist Joyce Brothers' (1990) pronouncement that two-thirds of married men and half of married women have affairs—four more recent surveys of randomly sampled U.S. adults provide a different view (Greeley, 1991; Laumann & others, 1994; Leigh & others, 1993; Smith, 1990). Nearly 9 in 10 married adults claim (even when responding anonymously) to have had sex only with their spouse during their present marriage. And 94 to 98 percent say they have been faithful during the past year. Apparently faithful attractions greatly outnumber fatal attractions. Moreover, disapproval of extramarital sex, at 91 percent, runs as high as ever among adult Americans (Smith, 1996).

The Physiology of Sex

Like hunger, sexual arousal depends on the interplay of internal and external stimuli. To understand sexual motivation, we must consider both.

The Sexual Response Cycle

6. *What stages mark the human sexual response?*

The headlines created by Kinsey's 1940s surveys reappeared after some 1960s studies in which scientists recorded the physiological responses of volunteers who masturbated or had intercourse. With the help of 382 female and 312 male volunteers—a somewhat atypical sample, consisting only of people able and willing to display arousal and orgasm while being observed in a laboratory—gynecologist-obstetrician William Masters and his collaborator Virginia Johnson (1966) monitored or filmed more than 10,000 sexual "cycles."

Their description of the **sexual response cycle** identified four stages, similar in men and women. During the initial *excitement phase*, the genital areas become engorged with blood, causing the man's penis to become partially erect and the woman's clitoris to swell and the inner lips covering her vagina to open up. Her vagina also expands and secretes lubricant, and her breasts and nipples may enlarge.

A nonsmoking 50-year-old male has about a 1-in-a-million chance of a heart attack during any hour. This increases to merely 2 in a million during the hour following sex (with no increase for those who exercise regularly). Compared with risks associated with heavy exertion or anger (see Chapter 10), this risk seems not worth losing sleep (or sex) over (Muller & others, 1996).

In the *plateau phase*, excitement peaks as breathing, pulse, and blood pressure rates continue to increase. The penis becomes fully engorged and some fluid (frequently containing enough live sperm to enable conception) may appear at the tip of the penis. Vaginal secretion continues to increase, the clitoris retracts, and orgasm feels imminent.

sexual response cycle the four stages of sexual responding described by Masters and Johnson—excitement, plateau, orgasm, and resolution.

Masters and Johnson observed muscle contractions all over the body during *orgasm*; these were accompanied by further increases in breathing, pulse, and blood pressure rates. A woman's arousal and orgasm facilitate conception by helping propel semen from the penis, positioning the uterus to receive sperm, and drawing the sperm farther inward. A woman's orgasm therefore not only reinforces intercourse, which is essential to natural reproduction, it also

refractory period a resting period after orgasm, during which a man cannot achieve another orgasm.

estrogen a sex hormone, secreted in greater amounts by females than by males. In nonhuman female mammals, estrogen levels peak during ovulation, promoting sexual receptivity.

increases retention of deposited sperm (Furlow & Thornhill, 1996). In the excitement of the moment, men and women are hardly aware of all this but are more aware of the rhythmic genital contractions that create a pleasurable feeling of sexual release. The feeling apparently is much the same for both sexes. In one study, a panel of experts could not reliably distinguish between descriptions of orgasm written by men and those written by women (Vance & Wagner, 1976).

After orgasm, the body gradually returns to its unaroused state as the engorged genital blood vessels release their accumulated blood in fairly short order. (It's like the nasal tickle that goes away rapidly if you have sneezed, slowly otherwise.) During this *resolution phase*, the male enters a **refractory period**, lasting from a few minutes to a day or more, during which he is incapable of another orgasm. A female does not have so lengthy a refractory period, which may make it possible for her to have another orgasm if restimulated during or soon after resolution (Figure 9.8)

Figure 9.8 **The sexual response cycle in men and in women** (Adapted from Masters & Johnson, 1966)

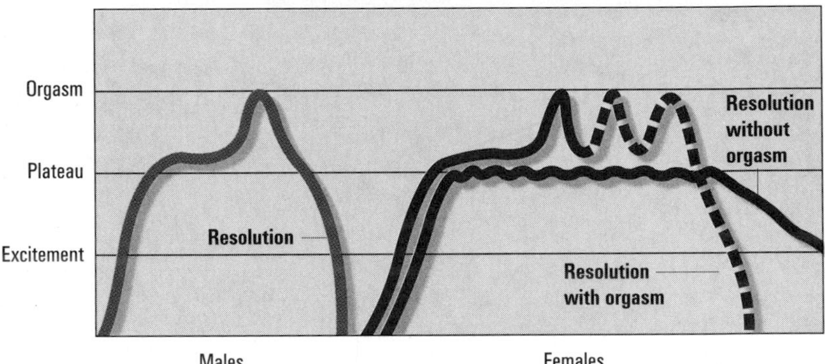

Hormones and Sexual Behavior

7. *What role do hormones play in human sexuality?*

Sex hormones have two effects: They direct the development of male and female sex characteristics, and (especially in nonhuman animals) they activate sexual behavior. In most mammals, nature neatly synchronizes sex with fertility. The female becomes sexually receptive ("in heat") when production of the female hormone **estrogen** peaks at ovulation. (In experiments, researchers stimulate receptivity by injecting female animals with estrogen.) Male hormone levels are more constant, and researchers cannot so easily manipulate the sexual behavior of male animals by hormone treatments (Feder, 1984). Nevertheless, castrated male rats—having lost their testes, which manufacture the male sex hormone testosterone—gradually lose much of their interest in receptive females, and they gradually regain it if injected with testosterone.

Hormones don't so neatly control human sexual behavior. Women's sexual desire is only slightly higher at ovulation (Harvey, 1987; Meuwissen & Over, 1992). Women's sexual desire also differs from that of other mammalian females in being more responsive to testosterone level than to estrogen level (Andersen & Cyranowski, 1995).

In men, normal fluctuations in testosterone levels, from man to man and hour to hour, have little effect on sexual drive (Byrne, 1982). Indeed, hormone fluctuations are partly a response to sexual stimulation. When James Dabbs and his colleagues (1987) had male collegians converse separately with a male and with a female student, the men's testosterone levels rose with the social arousal, but especially after talking with the female. Like the effect of the crackling steak on insulin level, sexual arousal can be a cause as well as a consequence of increased testosterone levels.

Drawing by Mankoff; 1993 The New Yorker Magazine, Inc.

"Fill'er up with testosterone."

Although normal short-term hormonal changes have little effect on desire, large hormone shifts have a big effect over the life span. A person's interest in dating and sexual stimulation usually increases with the pubertal surge in sex hormones. If the hormonal surge is precluded—as happened with prepubertal boys who were castrated during the 1600s and 1700s to preserve their soprano voices for Italian opera—the normal development of sex characteristics and sexual desire does not occur (Peschel & Peschel, 1987). Among adult men who suffer castration, sex drive typically falls along with declining testosterone levels (Hucker & Bain, 1990). Likewise, male sex offenders lose much of their sexual urge when voluntarily taking Depo-Provera, a drug that reduces testosterone level to that of a prepubertal boy (Money & others, 1983). And in later life, the typical frequency of sexual fantasies and intercourse declines as sex hormone levels decline (Leitenberg & Henning, 1995).

Hormones influence sexual arousal via the hypothalamus, which both monitors variations in blood hormone levels and activates the appropriate neural circuits. In rats, destroying a key area of the hypothalamus may end sexual activity; stimulating this area, either electrically or by directly inserting minute quantities of hormones, may activate sexual behavior.

To summarize, we might compare human sex hormones, especially testosterone, to the fuel in a car. Lacking fuel, the car will not run. But if the fuel level is minimally adequate, adding more fuel to the gas tank won't change how the car runs. The analogy is imperfect, because the interaction between hormones and sexual motivation is two-way. However, the analogy correctly suggests that biology is a necessary but not sufficient explanation of human sexual behavior. The hormonal fuel is essential, but so are the psychological stimuli that turn on the engine, keep it running, and shift it into high gear.

The Psychology of Sex

8. ***How do internal and external factors interact to stimulate sexual arousal?***

Hunger and sex are different sorts of motives. Hunger responds to a *need*. If we do not eat, we die. Sex is not in this sense a need. If we do not have sex, we may feel like dying, but we do not die. There are nevertheless similarities between hunger and sexual motivation. Both depend on internal physiological factors. And both are influenced by external stimuli.

External Stimuli

"Ours is a society which stimulates interest in sex by constant titillation. . . . Cinema, television, and all the formidable array of our marketing technology project our very effective forms of titillation and our prejudices about man as a sexy animal into every corner of every hovel in the world."

Germaine Greer (1984)

Many studies confirm that men become aroused when they see, hear, or read erotic material. More surprising to many people (because sexually explicit materials are sold mostly to men) is that most women—at least the less inhibited women who volunteer to participate in such studies—report nearly as much arousal to the same stimuli (Stockton & Murnen, 1992).

In one such study, psychologist Julia Heiman (1975) had sexually experienced university volunteers attach instruments that detected arousal (changes in penis circumference or in vaginal color). Then the students listened to one of four tapes: a sexually explicit erotic tape, a romantic tape (of a couple expressing love without physical contact), a combined erotic-romantic tape, or a neutral control tape. Which do you suppose the men were most aroused by? And the women? Both found the tape of explicit sex most arousing, especially when a woman initiated the sex and the depiction centered on her responses.

People may find such arousal either pleasing or disturbing. (Those who find it disturbing often limit their exposure to such materials, just as those wishing to

sexual disorder a problem that consistently impairs sexual arousal or functioning.

control hunger limit their exposure to tempting cues.) With repeated exposure, the emotional response to any erotic stimulus often "habituates" (lessens). During the 1920s, when women's hemlines first reached the knee, the exposed leg was a mildly erotic stimulus, as were once modest (by today's standards) two-piece swim suits and movie scenes of a mere kiss.

Some sexually explicit materials can have adverse effects. Depictions of women being sexually coerced—and enjoying it—tend to increase viewers' acceptance of the false idea that women enjoy rape, and they tend to increase male viewers' willingness to hurt women (see pages 518–519). Images of sexually attractive women and men may also lead people to devalue their own partners and relationships. After male collegians view TV or magazine depictions of sexually attractive women, they often find an average woman, or their own girlfriends or wives, less attractive (Kenrick & others, 1989; Kenrick & Gutierres, 1980; Weaver & others, 1984). Viewing X-rated sex films similarly tends to diminish people's satisfaction with their own sexual partners (Zillmann, 1989). Some sex researchers fear that reading or viewing erotica may create expectations that few men and women can hope to live up to.

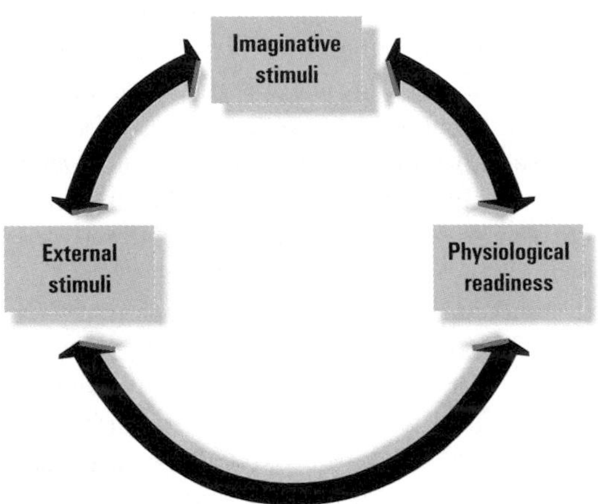

Figure 9.9 Forces affecting sexual motivation Sexual motivation results from the interplay of physiology, environment, and imagination. (From Byrne, 1982)

Imagined Stimuli

Sexual motivation arises from the interplay of physiology and environment. But the stimuli inside our heads—our imaginations—also influence sexual arousal and desire (Figure 9.9). The brain, it has been said, is our most significant sex organ. People who, because of a spinal cord injury, have no genital sensation can still feel sexual desire (Willmuth, 1987). Consider, too, the erotic potential of dreams. As noted in Chapter 5, genital arousal accompanies all types of dreams, even though most dreams have no sexual content. But in nearly all men and some 40 percent of women (Wells, 1986), dreams sometimes do contain sexual imagery that leads to orgasm. In men, these nocturnal emissions ("wet dreams") are more likely when orgasm has not occurred recently.

Wide-awake people become sexually aroused not only by memories of prior sexual activities but also by fantasies. Fantasies need not correspond to actual behavior. In one survey of masturbation-related fantasies (Hunt, 1974), 19 percent of women and 10 percent of men reported imagining being taken by someone overwhelmed with desire for them. Fantasy is not reality, however. To paraphrase Susan Brownmiller (1975), for women there's a big difference between fantasizing that Leonardo DiCaprio just won't take no for an answer and having a hostile stranger actually force himself on you.

"There is no difference between being raped and being run over by a truck except that afterward men ask if you enjoyed it."

Marge Piercy
"Rape Poem"
1976

About 95 percent of both men and women say they have had sexual fantasies. But men (whether gay or straight) fantasize about sex more often, more physically, and less romantically—and prefer less personal and faster-paced sexual content in books and videos (Leitenberg & Henning, 1995). Sexual fantasies do *not* indicate sexual problems or dissatisfaction. (If anything, sexually active people have more sexual fantasies.)

Sexual Disorders and Therapy

Masters and Johnson sought not only to describe the human sexual response cycle but also to understand and treat the inability to complete it. **Sexual disorders** are problems that consistently impair sexual functioning. Some involve sexual motivation, especially lack of sexual energy and arousability. Men, for example, may experience *premature ejaculation* (before they or their partners wish) or *impotence* (the inability to have or maintain an erection). Women more often than men experience low sexual desire or *orgasmic disorder* (infrequently or never experiencing orgasm).

What causes such problems? The idea that personality disorders are to blame has been largely discounted. Men who experience premature ejaculation are similar, even in their sexual arousal patterns, to men who do not; they simply ejaculate at lower levels of sexual arousal—something that often occurs with young men who have had long periods of sexual abstinence (Grenier & Byers, 1995; Spiess & others, 1984).

When Barbara Andersen (1983) reviewed research on the diagnosis and treatment of orgasmic disorder in women, she, too, could find no associated personality traits. Furthermore, she reported that treating orgasmic disorder through traditional psychotherapy (as though it were a disorder of personality) has been unsuccessful. She did, however, report a nearly 100 percent success rate with a behavioral treatment that trains women to enjoy their bodies and to give themselves orgasms, with a vibrator if necessary. Women who undergo such training are then sometimes able to generalize their new sexual responsiveness to interactions with their mates (Rosen & Leiblum, 1995; O'Donohue & others, 1997). Some success has also been reported in training men to control their premature ejaculations by repeatedly stimulating the penis and then stopping stimulation (or even firmly squeezing the head of the penis) when the urge to ejaculate arises. Alternatively, men can reduce their excitability by masturbating (LoPicolo & Stock, 1986).

Gender and Sexuality

9. *How do men's and women's sexual attitudes and behaviors differ?*

Across 177 studies of some 130,000 people, men are much more accepting of casual sex and they report masturbating much more often. This is among the largest of gender differences.

"With few exceptions anywhere in the world," report cross-cultural psychologist Marshall Segall and his colleagues (1990, p. 244), "males are more likely than females to initiate sexual activity." Across 177 studies of some 130,000 people, men are much more accepting of casual sex and they report masturbating much more often (Oliver & Hyde, 1993). This is among the largest of gender differences. A few other examples of gender differences in sexuality:

- In a Canadian survey of 2350 adults-only video store customers, 80 percent were males (though half claimed to engage a partner in watching the movies [Jenish, 1993]). Similarly, if you guessed that a hard-core pornography reader was male and a romance novel reader was female, you would usually be right (Malamuth, 1996).
- In a 1996 survey of 251,000 entering American college students, 54 percent of men but only 32 percent of women agreed that "if two people really like each other, it's all right for them to have sex even if they've known each other for a very short time" (Sax & others, 1996).
- In a careful survey of 3432 U.S. 18- to 59-year-olds, 48 percent of the women but only 25 percent of the men cited affection as a reason for first intercourse. And how often do they think about sex? "Every day" or "several times a day," acknowledged 19 percent of the women and 54 percent of the men (Laumann & others, 1994).

Sally Forth

sexual orientation an enduring sexual attraction toward members of either one's own gender (homosexual orientation) or the other gender (heterosexual orientation).

- Such gender differences characterize both heterosexual and homosexual people, as does a similar mating psychology. Like heterosexual men, gay men report more interest in uncommitted sex than lesbians report, and also more responsiveness to visual sexual stimuli and more concern with their partner's physical attractiveness (Bailey & others, 1994).

Gender differences in attitudes carry over to differences in behavior. Casual hit-and-run sex is most frequent among males with traditional masculine attitudes (Pleck & others, 1993). Russell Clark and Elaine Hatfield (1989) observed the striking gender difference in sexuality when in 1978 they sent some average-looking student research assistants strolling across the Florida State University quadrangle. Spotting an attractive person of the other sex, a researcher would approach and say, "I have been noticing you around campus and I find you to be very attractive. Would you go to bed with me tonight?" The women all declined, some with obvious irritation ("What's wrong with you, creep, leave me alone"). But 75 percent of the men (who perhaps felt less physically threatened) readily agreed, often with comments such as "Why do we have to wait until tonight?" Somewhat astonished by their result, Clark and Hatfield repeated their study in 1982 and twice more during the late-1980s AIDS era (Clark, 1990). Each time, virtually no women, but half or more of the men, agreed to go to bed with a stranger.

Men also have a lower threshold for misperceiving warmth as a sexual come-on. In study after study, men more often than women attribute a woman's friendliness to sexual interest (Abbey, 1987; Johnson & others, 1991). Such "misattribution" of a woman's cordiality as a "come-on" helps explain men's greater sexual assertiveness (Kenrick & Trost, 1987). The unfortunate results can range from sexual harassment to date rape (Kanekar & Nazareth, 1988; Muehlenhard, 1988; Shotland, 1989).

As Chapter 14 will explain, there is a possible evolutionary explanation for women's more relational and men's more recreational approach to sex. Compared with eggs, sperm are cheap. Moreover, while a woman incubates and nurses one infant, a male can spread his genes by impregnating other females. Our natural yearnings, argue evolutionary psychologists, are our genes' way of reproducing themselves. In our ancestral history, females most often sent their genes into the future by pairing wisely, men by pairing widely. "Humans are living fossils—collections of mechanisms produced by prior selection pressures," says David Buss (1995). But remember, say critics, cultural expectations also bend the genders. If socialized to value lifelong commitment, men may sexually bond with one partner; if socialized to accept casual sex, women may willingly have sex with many partners.

Sexual Orientation

10. ***What factors do and do not appear linked with sexual orientation?***

To motivate is to energize and direct behavior. So far, we have considered the energizing of sexual motivation but not its direction. We express the direction of our sexual interest in our **sexual orientation**—our enduring sexual attraction toward members of a particular gender. As far as we know, all cultures in all times have been predominantly heterosexual (Bullough, 1990). Yet cultures vary in their attitude toward homosexuality. Whether a culture condemns and punishes homosexuality or views it as an acceptable alternative, homosexuality survives and heterosexuality prevails.

Sexual orientation in some ways is like handedness: Most people are one way, some the other. A very few are truly ambidextrous. Regardless, the way one is endures.

Homosexual people often recall childhood play preferences like those of the other sex (Bailey & Zucker, 1995). But most homosexual people report not becoming aware of same-gender sexual feelings until during or shortly after puberty, and not thinking of themselves as gay or lesbian until around age 20 (Garnets & Kimmel, 1990).

How many people are exclusively homosexual? Until recently, the popular press assumed a homosexuality rate of 10 percent. But in both Europe and the United States, more than a dozen national surveys in the early 1990s explored sexual orientation, using methods that protected the respondents' anonymity. Their results agree in suggesting that a more accurate figure is about 3 or 4 percent of men and 1 to 2 percent of women (Laumann & others, 1994; Smith, 1996). Less than 1 percent of the respondents reported being actively bisexual, but a larger number of adults reported having had an isolated homosexual experience. And most people said they had had an occasional homosexual fantasy.

"It has been maintained for years that we each use only about 10 percent of our brain capacity; that the condom failure rate is 10 percent; and until just last year, that 10 percent of Americans are homosexual. Such statistics are partly artifacts, I suspect, of our decimal system; in a base 12 system, we'd no doubt show a similar affinity for statistics that were multiples of 8.333 percent."

John Allen Paulos
"Counting on Dyscalculia"
1993

Although health experts find it helpful to know sexual statistics, numbers do not decide issues of human rights. Similarly, it's helpful in manufacturing school desks to know that about 10 percent of people are left-handed. But whether left-handers are 3 percent or 10 percent of the population doesn't answer the moral question of whether lefties should enjoy equal rights.

What does it feel like to be homosexual in a heterosexual culture? One way for heterosexual people to understand is to imagine how they would feel if they were to be ostracized or fired for openly admitting or displaying their feelings toward someone of the other sex; if they were to overhear people making crude jokes about heterosexual people; if most movies, TV shows, and advertisements portrayed (or implied) homosexuality; and if their family members were pleading with them to change their heterosexual life-style and to enter into a homosexual marriage.

Facing such reactions, homosexual people often struggle with their sexual orientation. At first, they may try to ignore or deny their desires, hoping they will go away. But they don't. Then they may try to change, through psychotherapy, willpower, or prayer. But the feelings typically persist, as do those of heterosexual people—who are similarly incapable of becoming homosexual (Haldeman, 1994). Eventually, homosexuals may accept their orientation—by electing celibacy (as do some heterosexuals); by engaging in promiscuous sex (a choice more commonly made by men than by women); or by entering into a committed, long-term love relationship (a choice more often made by women than by men) (Peplau, 1982; Weinberg & Williams, 1974).

Personal values affect sexual orientation less than other forms of sexual behavior. Compared with people who attend church only rarely, for example, those who attend regularly are one-third as likely to have cohabited before marriage and report having had many fewer sexual partners. But they are just as likely to be homosexual (Smith, 1996).

Most psychologists today view sexual orientation as neither willfully chosen nor willfully changed. Sexual orientation in some ways is like handedness: Most people are one way, some the other. A very few are truly ambidextrous. Regardless, the way one is endures. Nor is sexual orientation linked with psychological disorder or sexual crime. "Child molester" is not a sexual orientation. Some homosexuals do abuse children, but most child molesters are heterosexual males (Gonsiorek, 1982). These facts led the American Psychiatric Association in 1973 to drop homosexuality from its list of "mental illnesses."

Understanding Sexual Orientation

Note that the scientific question is not "What causes homosexuality?" (or "What causes heterosexuality?") but "What causes differing sexual orientations?" In pursuit of answers, psychological science compares the backgrounds and physiology of people whose sexual orientations differ.

If our sexual orientation is indeed something we do not choose and cannot change, then where do these preferences come from? How do we move toward either a heterosexual or a homosexual orientation? Is homosexuality linked with problems in a child's relationships with parents, such as with a domineering mother and an ineffectual father or a possessive mother and a hostile father? As children, were many homosexuals molested, seduced, or otherwise sexually victimized by an adult homosexual? Are children who observe homosexual role models (such as parents) more likely to become homosexual?

Consider the findings of lengthy Kinsey Institute interviews with nearly 1000 homosexuals and 500 heterosexuals (Bell & others, 1981; Hammersmith, 1982). The investigators assessed nearly every imaginable psychological cause

Erick has two moms Maria Christina Vlassidis (left) and Marie Tatro (center) tell playmates of their son Erick, 8, that they are both his moms. Both women, who are lesbians, attend school conferences and support other aspects of his life. Studies suggest that being reared by lesbian or gay parents does not appreciably affect a child's sexual orientation.

of homosexuality—parental relationships, childhood sexual experiences, peer relationships, dating experiences. Their findings: Homosexuals were no more likely than heterosexuals to have been smothered by maternal love, neglected by their father, or sexually abused. More recent studies have also found that sons of homosexual men were *not* more likely to become gay if they lived with their gay dad, and that 9 in 10 children of lesbian mothers developed into heterosexuals (Bailey & others, 1995; Golombok & Tasker, 1996). If even being reared by a homosexual parent has no appreciable influence on sexual orientation, then having a gay or lesbian teacher or bus driver also seems unlikely to have an appreciable influence.

Homosexual people do, however, appear more often in certain populations:

- In America's dozen largest cities, the percentage of men identifying themselves as gay jumps to 9 percent, compared with only 1 percent in rural areas (Binson & others, 1995; Laumann & others, 1994).
- One study of the biographies of 1004 eminent people found homosexual and bisexual people overrepresented (11 percent of the sample), especially among poets (24 percent), fiction writers (21 percent), and artists and musicians (15 percent) (Ludwig, 1995).
- For uncertain reasons, men who have older brothers are somewhat more likely to be gay, report Ray Blanchard and his colleagues (1995, 1996a,b, 1997). Assuming the odds of homosexuality are roughly 3 percent among first sons, they rise to 4 percent among second sons and 5 percent for third sons.

So, what determines sexual orientation? One theory proposes that people develop same-sex erotic attachments if segregated by gender at the time their sex drive matures (Storms, 1981). But even in a tribal culture in which homosexual behavior is expected of all boys before marriage, heterosexuality prevails (Money, 1987). (As this illustrates, homosexual *behavior* does not always indicate a homosexual *orientation*.) Another theory proposes the opposite: that people develop romantic attachments to those who *differ* from, and thus are more fascinating than, the peers they associated with while growing up (Bell, 1982). The bottom line from a half-century's theory and research: If there are environmental factors that influence sexual orientation, we do not yet know what they are. If someone were to ask me, "What can I do to influence my child's sexual orientation?" my answer would have to be "I haven't a clue."

The Brain and Sexual Orientation

New research indicates that sexual orientation is at least partly physiological. Researcher Simon LeVay (1991) discovered this while studying sections of the hypothalamus taken from deceased heterosexual and homosexual people. As a gay scientist, LeVay wanted to do "something connected with my gay identity," but he knew he had to avoid biasing the results. So he did the study "blind," without knowing which donors were gay. After nine months of peering through his microscope at a cell cluster he thought might be important, LeVay sat down one morning and broke the codes. His discovery: The cell cluster was reliably larger in heterosexual men than in women and homosexual men. As the brain difference became apparent, "I was almost in a state of shock. . . . I took a walk by myself on the cliffs over the ocean. I sat for half an hour just thinking what this might mean" (LeVay, 1994).

***It should not surprise us that brains differ with sexual orientation. Remember our maxim:* Everything psychological is simultaneously biological.**

It should not surprise us that brains differ with sexual orientation. Remember our maxim: Although we find it convenient to talk separately of psychological and biological explanations, *everything psychological is simultaneously biological.* The critical questions are, can this finding be replicated? If so, when does the brain difference begin? At conception? In the womb? During childhood or

> ***"Gay men simply don't have the brain cells to be attracted to women."***
>
> Simon Levay
> *The Sexual Brain*
> 1993

adolescence? Does experience produce the difference? Or do genes or prenatal hormones (or genes via prenatal hormones)?

LeVay does not view this little neural center as a sexual orientation center; rather, he sees it as an important part of the neural pathway engaged in sexual behavior. Moreover, he acknowledges that it's possible that sexual behavior patterns influence the brain's anatomy. (In fish, rats, birds, and humans, brain structures are known to vary with experience.) But he believes it more likely that brain anatomy influences sexual orientation. Laura Allen and Roger Gorski (1992) offered a similar conclusion after discovering that a section of the fibers connecting right and left hemispheres is one-third larger in homosexual men than in heterosexual men. "The emerging neuroanatomical picture," notes Brian Gladue (1994), "is that, in some brain areas, homosexual men are more likely to have female-typical neuroanatomy than are heterosexual men."

Genes and Sexual Orientation

> ***"Studies indicate that male homosexuality is more likely to be transmitted from the mother's side of the family."***
>
> Robert Plomin, John Defries, Gerald McClearn, and Michael Rutter
> *Behavioral Genetics*
> 1997

The evidence suggests that genetic influence plays a role (Whitam & others, 1993). One research team studied the twin brothers of homosexual men. Among their identical twin brothers, 52 percent were homosexual, as were 22 percent of fraternal twin brothers (Bailey & Pillard, 1991, 1995). In a follow-up study of homosexual women, a similar 48 percent of their identical twins were homosexual, as were 16 percent of their fraternal twins (Bailey & others, 1993). With half the identical twin pairs differing, we know that genes aren't the whole story. Moreover, a new study using a diverse sample of Australian twins found somewhat lower rates of sexual similarity—although, again, identical twins were more likely than fraternal twins to share homosexual feelings (Bailey & others, 1997). This is the sort of pattern we expect to see when genes are having an *influence*. Moreover, with a single transplanted gene, scientists can now cause male fruit flies to display homosexual behavior (Zhang & Odenwald, 1995).

Prenatal Hormones and Sexual Orientation

The elevated rate of similar homosexual orientation even in fraternal twins might also result from their sharing the same prenatal environment. In animals, abnormal prenatal hormone conditions have altered the sexual orientation of a fetus. German researcher Gunter Dorner (1976, 1988) pioneered this research by manipulating a fetal rat's exposure to male hormones, thereby "inverting" its sexual behavior toward rats of the other sex. Female sheep will likewise show homosexual behavior if their pregnant mothers are injected with testosterone during a critical gestation period (Money, 1987).

> ***"Were it not for delicately balanced combinations of genetic, neurological, hormonal, and environmental factors, largely occurring prior to birth, each and every one of us would be homosexual."***
>
> Lee Ellis and M. Ashley Ames (1987)

Atypical prenatal hormones may produce similar results in humans. A critical period for the human brain's neural-hormonal control system may exist between the middle of the second and fifth months after conception (Ellis & Ames, 1987; Gladue, 1990; Meyer-Bahlburg, 1995). It seems that exposure to the hormone levels typically experienced by female fetuses during this time may predispose the person (whether female or male) to be attracted to males in later life. Some tests reveal that homosexual men have spatial abilities like those typical of heterosexual women—a pattern consistent with the hypothesis that homosexuals were exposed to atypical prenatal hormones (Gladue, 1994; McCormick & Witelson, 1991). Curiously, gay men also have fingerprint patterns rather like those of heterosexual women. Most people have more fingerprint ridges on their right hand. Jeff Hall and Doreen Kimura (1994) observed that this right-versus-left difference is less true of females and gay males than of heterosexual males—a difference that these researchers believe is due to prenatal hormones.

Because the physiological evidence is preliminary and controversial, some scientists remain skeptical. Rather than specifying sexual orientation, perhaps biological factors predispose a temperament that influences sexuality "in the context of individual learning and experience" (Byne & Parsons, 1993). Perhaps, theorizes Daryl Bem (1996), genes code for prenatal hormones and brain anatomy, which predispose *temperaments* that lead children to prefer sex-typical or sex-atypical activities and friends. These preferences may lead children later to feel attracted to whichever sex feels different. Boys with feminine interests may find masculine males exotic. This could explain why, in personal ads, gay men tend to seek masculine partners and lesbians feminine partners (Bailey & others, 1997). The dissimilar-seeming sex (one's own, for homosexual people) becomes associated with anxiety and other forms of arousal, which eventually gets transformed into romantic arousal. The exotic becomes erotic.

"Biological theories of sexual orientation are far more promising than any current alternatives."

J. Michael Bailey and Richard C. Pillard (1994)

Regardless of the process, the consistency of the genetic, prenatal, and brain findings has swung the pendulum toward a physiological explanation. Nature more than nurture, most psychiatrists now believe, predisposes sexual orientation (Vreeland & others, 1995). If biological influences prove critical (perhaps especially in certain environmental contexts), it would explain why sexual orientation is so difficult to change.

Still, some people wonder: Should the cause of sexual orientation matter? Maybe it shouldn't, but people's assumptions matter. Those who believe (as most homosexual people believe) that sexual orientation is a biological given—an enduring identity, not a choice—express more accepting attitudes toward homosexual persons (Allen & others, 1996; Furnham & Taylor, 1990; Whitley, 1990). In American surveys, agreement that homosexuality is "something that people are born with" doubled from 16 to 31 percent between 1983 and 1993. Over roughly the same period, support for equal job rights for homosexuals increased from 59 to 80 percent (Moore, 1993). Between 1982 and 1996, agreement that "homosexuality should be an acceptable alternative lifestyle" also increased, from 34 to 44 percent (Gallup, 1996). Accepting attitudes are most common among women and those with a gay or lesbian friend or relative (Herek & Capitanio, 1996; Kite & Whitley, 1996).

To gay and lesbian activists, the new biological research is a double-edged sword (Diamond, 1993). If sexual orientation, like skin color and sex, is genetically influenced, that offers a further rationale for civil rights protection. Moreover, it may alleviate parents' concerns about their children having gay teachers and role models. It does, however, raise the haunting possibility that genetic markers of sexual orientation could someday be identified through fetal testing, and the fetus aborted.

Sex and Human Values

11. *What roles do personal values play in sex research and sex education?*

Recognizing that values are both personal and cultural, most sex researchers and educators strive to keep their writings on sexuality value-free. But can the study of sexual behavior and what motivates it really be free of values? Those who think not say that the very words we use to describe behavior often reflect our personal values. When sex researchers label sexually restrained individuals as "erotophobic" and as having "high sex guilt," they express their own values. Whether we label sexual acts we do not practice as "perversions," "deviations," or part of an "alternative sexual life-style" depends on our attitudes toward the behaviors. Labels both describe and evaluate.

A sharing of love For most adults, a sexual relationship fulfills not only a biological motive, but a social need for intimacy.

When education about sex is separated from the context of human values, some students may get the idea that sexual intercourse is merely recreational activity. Diana Baumrind (1982), a University of California child-rearing expert, has observed that adolescents interpret sex education that pretends to be "value-free" as meaning that adults are neutral about adolescent sexual activity. Such an implication is unfortunate, she added, because "promiscuous recreational sex poses certain psychological, social, health, and moral problems that must be faced realistically."

CLOSE-UP

The Need to Belong

We humans feel motivated to eat and have sex. Being what Aristotle called "the social animal," we also have a need to affiliate with others and even to become strongly attached to certain others in enduring, close relationships. Human beings, contended the personality theorist Alfred Adler, have an "urge to community" (Ferguson, 1989). Roy Baumeister and Mark Leary (1995) assembled evidence for this deep *need to belong.*

Aiding Survival

Social bonds boosted our ancestors' survival rate. By keeping children close to their caregivers, attachments served as a powerful survival impulse. As adults, those who formed attachments were more likely to come together to reproduce and to stay together to nurture their offspring to maturity.

Cooperation in groups also enhanced survival. In solo combat, our ancestors were not the toughest predators. But as hunters they learned that six hands were better than two. Those who foraged in groups also gained protection from predators and enemies. If those who felt a need to belong survived and reproduced most successfully, their genes would in time predominate. The inevitable result: an innately social creature. People in every society on earth belong to groups (and, as Chapter 14 explains, prefer and favor "us" over "them").

Wanting to Belong

The need to belong colors our thoughts and emotions. We spend much time thinking about our actual and hoped-for relationships. When relationships form, we often feel joy. Falling in mutual love, people have been known to get cheek-aches from their irrepressible grins. Asked, "What is necessary for your happiness?" or "What is it that makes your life meaningful?" most people mention—before anything else—satisfying close relationships with family, friends, or romantic partners (Berscheid, 1985). Happiness hits close to home.

Increasing Social Acceptance

Much of our social behavior aims to increase our belonging—our social acceptance and inclusion. To avoid rejection, we generally conform to group standards and seek to make favorable impressions (more on this in Chapter 14). To win friendship and esteem, we monitor our behavior, hoping to create the right impressions. Seeking love and belonging, we spend billions on clothes, cosmetics, and diet and fitness aids—all motivated by our quest for acceptance.

Like sexual motivation, which feeds both love and exploitation, the need to belong feeds both deep attachments and menacing threats. Out of our need to define a "we" come loving families, faithful friendships, and team spirit, but also teen gangs, ethnic rivalries, and fanatic nationalism.

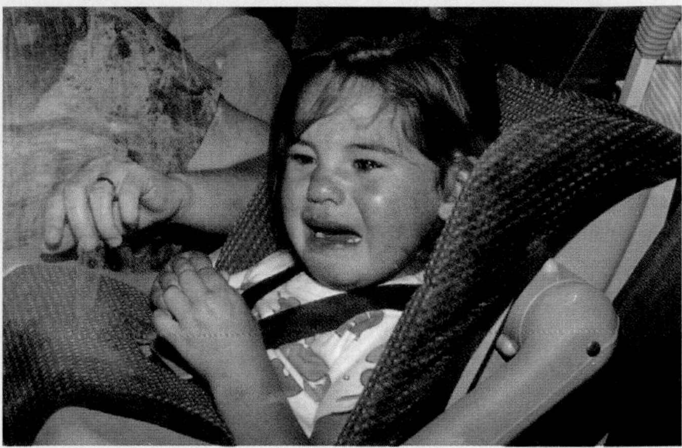

The need to belong Separated from friends or family—isolated in prison, alone at a new school, living in a foreign land—most people feel keenly their lost connections with important others. Wrenched from the only family she has ever known, by a 1993 court decision in an adoption dispute, 2½-year-old Jessica DeBoer sobs en route to her biological parents' home hundreds of miles away. As social animals, we all have something of Jessica within us—a sense of who we belong to, of who is "us."

Maintaining Relationships

People resist breaking social bonds. For most of us, familiarity breeds liking, not contempt. Thrown together at school, at summer camp, on a vacation cruise, people resist the group's dissolution. Hoping to maintain the relationships, they promise to call, to write, to come back for reunions. Parting, they feel distress. Attachments can even keep people in abusive relationships; the fear of being alone may seem worse than the pain of emotional or physical abuse.

When something threatens or dissolves our social ties, negative emotions overwhelm us. Exile, imprisonment, and solitary confinement are progressively more severe forms of punishment. Recently bereaved people often feel that life is empty and pointless and are more at risk for illness. Children reared in institutions without a sense of belonging to anyone, or locked away at home under extreme neglect, become pathetic creatures—withdrawn, frightened, speechless. Adults who are denied others' acceptance and inclusion may feel depressed. Anxiety, jealousy, loneliness, and guilt all involve threatened disruptions of our need to belong. People suffer even when bad relationships break. In one 16-nation survey, separated and divorced people were half as likely as married people to declare themselves "very happy" (Inglehart, 1990). After such separations, feelings of loneliness and anger are commonplace. Such evidence supports Baumeister and Leary's (1995) contention that "human beings are fundamentally and pervasively motivated by a need to belong."

Sex is a socially significant act. . . . Sex at its human best is life-uniting and love-renewing.

"The relationship between women and men should be characterized not by patronizing behavior or exploitation, but by love, partnership, and trustworthiness. . . . Sexuality should express and reinforce a loving relationship lived by equal partners."

Towards a Global Ethic
1993 Parliament of the World's Religions

Researchers have found that teenagers who have had formal sex education are no more likely to engage in premarital sex than those who have not (Furstenberg & others, 1985; Zelnik & Kim, 1982). Moreover, we enrich our lives by knowing ourselves, by realizing that others share our feelings, by understanding what is likely to please or displease our loved one. Witness the crumbling of falsehoods about homosexuality. Witness the growing realization that some types of sexually explicit material can lead people to devalue or hurt others.

Perhaps we can agree that the knowledge provided by sex research is preferable to ignorance, yet also agree that researchers' values should be stated openly, enabling us to debate them and to reflect on our own values. We might also remember that scientific research on sexual motivation does not aim to define the personal meaning of sex in our own lives. One can know every available fact about sex that the initial spasms of male and female orgasm come at 0.8-second intervals, that the female nipples expand 10 millimeters at the peak of sexual arousal, that systolic blood pressure rises some 60 points and the respiration rate to 40 breaths per minute—but fail to understand the human significance of sexual intimacy.

Surely one significance of sexual intimacy is its expression of our deeply social nature. Sex is a socially significant act. Men and women can achieve orgasm alone, yet most people find greater satisfaction while embracing their loved one. There is a yearning for closeness in sexual motivation. Sex at its human best is life-uniting and love-renewing.

REHEARSE IT!

11. In the 1940s, Alfred Kinsey and his colleagues used questionnaires to investigate human sexual behavior. Their results have been criticized because

- **a.** their sample was not large enough.
- **b.** their sample was not representative of the population as a whole.
- **c.** they asked leading questions.
- **d.** both *b.* and *c.* are true.

12. In describing the sexual response cycle, Masters and Johnson noted that

- **a.** a plateau phase follows orgasm.
- **b.** men experience a refractory period during which they cannot experience orgasm.
- **c.** the feeling that accompanies orgasm is stronger in men than in women.
- **d.** testosterone is released in the female as well as in the male.

13. Daily and monthly fluctuations in hormone levels do not greatly affect sexual desire in humans. Over the life span, however, hormonal changes have significant effects. A striking effect of hormonal changes on human sexual behavior is the

- **a.** arousing influence of erotic materials.
- **b.** sharp rise in sexual interest at puberty.
- **c.** increase in women's sexual desire at the time of ovulation.
- **d.** increase in testosterone levels in castrated males.

14. Sexual behavior is motivated by internal biological factors, by external stimuli, and by imaginative stimuli. An example of an external stimulus that might influence sexual behavior is

- **a.** blood level of testosterone.
- **b.** the onset of puberty.
- **c.** a sexually explicit film.
- **d.** an erotic fantasy or dream.

15. Sexual disorders are problems that consistently impair sexual functioning. In some cases, they involve sexual motivation, especially lack of arousability. The cause of such problems is

- **a.** personality traits, because psychotherapy has been used successfully to treat such problems.
- **b.** genetic factors, because no treatment has successfully eliminated the problem.
- **c.** physiological factors, because exercise has been found to help people with such problems.
- **d.** unknown, although behavioral therapy has been used successfully to treat such problems.

16. One of the most significant gender differences involves attitudes and behaviors related to sexual activity. Which of the following is true regarding this gender difference?

- **a.** Women are more likely than men to cite affection as a reason for first intercourse.
- **b.** Men are less likely than women to rent "adults-only" videos.
- **c.** Women are more likely than men to perceive warmth as a sexual come-on.
- **d.** Men are less likely than women to agree that sex is acceptable between two people even if they have known each other only a short time.

17. Sexual orientation refers to our enduring sexual attraction to members of a particular gender. Current research suggests several possible contributors to sexual orientation, including all but which of the following?

- **a.** certain cell clusters in the hypothalamus
- **b.** gender segregation during the time the sex drive matures
- **c.** a section of fibers connecting the right and left hemispheres of the brain
- **d.** exposure to hormone levels typically experienced by female fetuses

achievement motivation a desire for significant accomplishment; for mastery of things, people, or ideas; for control; for attaining a high standard.

Achievement Motivation

12. *Who has the greatest need to achieve? Why?*

The biological perspective on motivation—the idea that physiological needs drive us to satisfy those needs—provides only a partial explanation of what energizes and directs our behavior. Hunger and sex have both psychological and physiological components. Moreover, there are motives that, unlike hunger and sex, seem not to satisfy any physical need. Billionaires may be motivated to make ever more money, movie stars to become ever more famous, politicians to achieve ever more power, daredevils to seek ever greater thrills. Such motives seem not to diminish when they are fed. The more we achieve, the more we may need to achieve.

Identifying Achievement Motivation

What is your greatest achievement to date? What is your greatest future ambition—to attain fame? Fortune? Creative accomplishment? Security? Love? Power? Wisdom? Spiritual wholeness?

Think of someone you know who strives to succeed by excelling at any task where evaluation is possible. Now think of someone who is less disciplined and driven. Psychologist Henry Murray (1938) defined the first person's high need for achievement, or **achievement motivation**, as a desire for significant accomplishment, for mastering skills or ideas, for control, and for rapidly attaining a high standard.

To study this motive, we first need a way to measure it. But how? Recall from the semistarvation studies that people driven by hunger begin to fantasize about food. Our sexual orientation is similarly reflected in our prevalent sexual fantasies. Do these examples suggest a way to assess a person's need to achieve?

Superstar achievers were distinguished not so much by their extraordinary natural talent as by their extraordinary daily discipline. When their preparation met an opportunity, the result was success.

Murray and investigators David McClelland and John Atkinson presumed that people's fantasies would reflect their achievement concerns. So they asked subjects to invent stories about ambiguous pictures. If, when shown the daydreaming boy in Figure 9.10, a subject commented that the boy was preoccupied with his pursuit of a goal, that he imagined himself performing a heroic act, or that he was feeling pride in some success, the story was scored as indicating achievement concerns. McClelland and Atkinson regarded people whose stories consistently included such themes as having a high need for achievement.

Would you expect people whose stories express high achievement to prefer tasks that are easy, moderately challenging, or very difficult? People whose stories suggest low achievement motivation tend to choose either very easy or very difficult tasks, where failure is either unlikely or not embarrassing (Geen, 1984). Those whose stories express high achievement motivation tend to prefer moderately difficult tasks, where success is attainable yet attributable to their skill and effort. In a ring-toss game they often stand at an intermediate distance from the stake; this enables some successes, yet provides a suitable challenge. When things get difficult, people with a strong need to achieve persist more (Cooper, 1983). By contrast, high school underachievers persist less in completing college degrees, holding on to jobs, and maintaining their marriages (McCall, 1994).

Figure 9.10 What is this boy daydreaming about? By analyzing responses to ambiguous photos like this, motivation researchers have sought clues to people's level of achievement motivation.

As you might expect from their persistence and eagerness for realistic challenge, people with high achievement motivation do achieve more. One study followed the lives of 1528 California children whose intelligence scores were in the top 1 percent. When researchers 40 years later compared those who were most and least successful professionally, they found a motivational difference. Those who were most successful were more ambitious, energetic, and persistent. As children, they had more active hobbies. As adults, they participated in more groups and favored participating in sports over passively watching (Goleman, 1980). Another study of outstanding athletes, scholars, and artists found that all were highly motivated and self-disciplined, willing to dedicate hours every day to the pursuit of their goals (Bloom, 1985). These superstar achievers were distinguished not so much by their extraordinary natural talent as by their extraordinary daily discipline. When their preparation met an opportunity, the result was success.

intrinsic motivation a desire to perform a behavior for its own sake and to be effective.

extrinsic motivation a desire to perform a behavior due to promised rewards or threats of punishment.

industrial/organizational psychology a subfield of psychology that studies and advises on workplace behavior. Industrial/organizational (I/O) psychologists help organizations select and train employees, boost morale and productivity, and design products and assess responses to them.

Analyses of the life histories of great scientists, philosophers, political leaders, writers, and musicians confirm the importance of disciplined motivation. Great achievers, consumed by a passion to perfect their gift, often are continuously productive from an early age, notes Dean Keith Simonton (1994)—so much so that a small proportion of contributors to any field produce most of its achievements. Although intelligence is distributed like a bell curve, achievements are not—and that tells us that achievement involves much more than raw ability.

Sources of Achievement Motivation

Why, despite similar potentials, does one person become more motivated to achieve than another? Highly motivated children often have parents who encourage their independence from an early age and praise and reward them for their successes (Teevan & McGhee, 1972). Such parents encourage them to dress and feed themselves and to do well in school, and they express delight when their children achieve. Theorists speculate that the high achievement motivation displayed by such children has *emotional* roots, as children learn to associate achievement with positive emotions. There may also be *cognitive* roots, as children learn to attribute their achievements to their own competence and effort, raising their expectations (Dweck & Elliott, 1983).

"They can because they think they can."

Virgil
Aeneid
19 B.C.

Intrinsic Motivation and Achievement

13. *What is intrinsic motivation, and how can it be nurtured?*

In the classroom, at the workplace, and on the athletic field, two types of achievement motivation operate. **Intrinsic motivation** is the desire to be effective and to perform a behavior for its own sake. Intrinsically motivated people approach work or play seeking enjoyment, interest, self-expression, or challenge. **Extrinsic motivation** is seeking external rewards and avoiding punishments.

To sense the difference between extrinsic and intrinsic motivation, you might reflect on your own current experience. Are you feeling pressured to get this reading finished before a deadline? Worried about your course grade? Eager for rewards that depend on your doing well? If yes, then you are extrinsically motivated (as, to some extent, almost all students are). Are you also finding the course material interesting? Does learning it enable you to feel more competent? If there were no grade at stake, might you be curious enough to want to learn the material for its own sake? If yes, intrinsic motivation also fuels your efforts.

In sports, as in other activities, excessive external pressures and incentives can undermine intrinsic enjoyment. Researcher Dean Ryan (1980) studied university football players. He found that those on athletic scholarships (who were, in a sense, playing for pay) enjoyed their play less than did the nonscholarship players. Apparently, pay and pressure turn play into work. However, rewards can increase intrinsic motivation if their effect is to inform the players of their athletic competence (as with a "most improved player" award).

The image of achievement What motivates a person to study to the level of a Ph.D., learn five languages, and become a leading expert in international issues—as did Madeleine Albright, before becoming the U.S. United Nations representative and then secretary of state?

So, should coaches emphasize extrinsic pressures, rewards, and competition? Studies by motivation researchers Edward Deci and Richard Ryan indicate that it depends on the goal (1985, 1992). For some, as for legendary football coach Vince Lombardi, "Winning isn't everything; it's the only thing." If so, it may pay to control the players with pressures and rewards for winning. But what if the goal is—as it should be for most programs of physical education, fitness, and amateur sports—the promotion of an enduring interest and participation in physical activity? In that case, as Deci and Ryan observed, "External pressures, competitive emphasis, and evaluative feedback are in contradiction to this goal." Thus, if children's soccer coaches want their players to continue playing in the future, they should focus not on the urgency of winning but on the joy of playing one's best.

Tiger Woods on intrinsic motivation "I remember a daily ritual that we had: I would call Pop at work to ask if I could practice with him. He would always pause a second or two, keeping me in suspense, but he'd always say yes. . . . In his own way, he was teaching me initiative. You see, he never pushed me to play" (quoted in *USA Weekend*, 1997).

Motivating People

14. ***What motivational strategies are most effective at home, school, and work?***

The growing field of **industrial/organizational psychology** includes studies of how managers might best:

- promote teamwork and group achievement.
- match people with jobs by identifying motivated, well-suited personnel.
- make jobs suit people by creating work environments that boost morale and output.
- evaluate performance and create incentives for excellence.

What every leader (manager, coach, or teacher) wants to know is "How can I manage in ways that enhance people's motivation, productivity, satisfaction?" (Satisfied workers aren't always more productive, but they are less likely to be absent or to quit.) Effective leaders cultivate intrinsic motivation, attend to people's motives, set goals, and choose an appropriate leadership style.

Cultivate Intrinsic Motivation

Given that intrinsic motivation stimulates achievement, especially in situations where people work independently (as students, executives, and scientists often do), how might we encourage it? The consistent answers, from hundreds of studies: First, provide tasks that challenge and trigger curiosity (Malone & Lepper, 1986). Second, avoid snuffing out people's sense of self-determination with an overuse of controlling extrinsic rewards (Deci & Ryan, 1987).

Note that we can use extrinsic rewards in two ways: to *control* ("If you clean up your room, you can have some ice cream") or to *inform* someone of successes ("That was outstanding—we congratulate you"). Attempts to *control* people's behaviors through rewards and surveillance may be successful as long as these controls are present. If they are taken away, interest in the activity often drops. Ironically, teachers who try hardest to boost their students' achievement on competency tests tend to be most controlling, thus undermining their students' intrinsic interest. On the other hand, rewards that *inform* people that their efforts are paying off can boost their feelings of competence and intrinsic motivation.

There is an important practical principle here. Because the controlling use of rewards undermines intrinsic motivation (and creativity—see page 296), parents, teachers, and managers should take care not to be overcontrolling. It is important to expect, support, challenge, and inform, but if you want to encourage internally motivated, self-directed achievements, do not overly control.

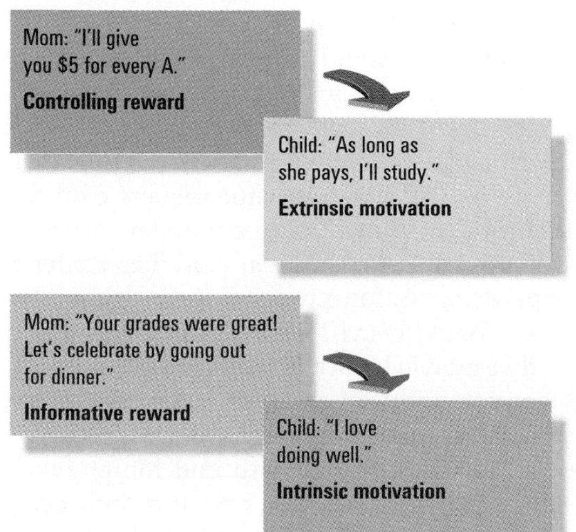

Rewards The type of reward affects motivation.

Attend to People's Motives

Effective managerial styles vary with the people managed. To motivate people, Martin Maehr and Larry Braskamp (1986; Braskamp, 1987) have advised managers to assess their people's motives and adjust their managerial style accordingly. Challenge employees who value *accomplishment* to try new activities and to exhibit excellence. Give those who value *recognition* the attention they desire. Place those who value *affiliation* in a unit that has a family feeling and shares decision making. Motivate those who value power with competition and opportunities for triumphant success. Different strokes for different folks, but for each a way to motivate.

Toys "R" everywhere Hiring Japanese top executives who know their own culture and listening to what they have to say has enabled Toys "R" Us and some other Western firms to succeed in Japanese markets.

Set Specific, Challenging Goals

In study after study, specific, challenging goals have motivated higher achievement, especially when combined with progress reports (Locke & Latham, 1990; Mento & others, 1987; Tubbs, 1986). Clear objectives, such as those you might set in planning your course work, serve to direct attention, promote effort, and stimulate creative strategies. When people find a goal reasonable, their reaching it or not affects their self-evaluation (White & others, 1995). So, to motivate high productivity, effective leaders work with people to define explicit goals and elicit commitments, and they provide feedback on progress.

Choose an Appropriate Leadership Style

Whether a directive or a democratic leadership style works best depends on the situation and the leader. The best leadership style for leading a discussion is not the best style for leading troops on a charge (Fiedler, 1981). Moreover, different leaders are suited to different styles. Some excel at **task leadership**—setting standards, organizing work, and focusing attention on goals. Being goal-oriented, task leaders are good at keeping a group centered on its mission. Typically, they have a directive style, which can work well if the leader is bright enough to give good orders (Fiedler, 1987).

"Good leaders don't ask more than their constituents can give, but they often ask—and get—more than their constituents intended to give or thought it was possible to give."

John W. Gardner
Excellence
1984

Other managers excel at **social leadership**—mediating conflicts and building the sort of team spirit that makes for high performance (Evans & Dion, 1991). Social leaders often have a democratic style: They delegate authority and welcome the participation of team members. Many experiments show that social leadership is good for morale. Subordinates usually feel more satisfied and motivated when they can participate in decision making (Burger, 1987; Spector, 1986).

John Williams and Deborah Best (1990, p. 15) have suggested an imaginary scenario in which we hear about two people: One is "adventurous, autocratic, coarse, dominant, forceful, independent, and strong." The other is "affectionate, dependent, dreamy, emotional, submissive, and weak." Did you picture the first person as a man and the second as a woman? If so, you are not alone. The world around, people perceive the first set of traits as more descriptive of men, the second set as more descriptive of women. As leaders, men indeed tend to be directive, even autocratic, and women tend to be more democratic (Eagly & Johnson, 1990). When people interact, men are more likely to utter opinions, women to express support (Aries, 1987; Wood, 1987). In everyday behavior, men are more likely to act as powerful people do—to talk assertively, to interrupt, to initiate touching, to smile less, to stare (J. Hall, 1987; Major & others, 1990). Thus, women more often excel at social leadership, men at task leadership (Eagly & Karau, 1991).

Michael Jordan on goal setting "I knew exactly where I wanted to go and I focused on getting there. . . . Whether it's golf, basketball, business, family life, or even baseball, I set goals—realistic goals—and I focus on them." (from *I Can't Accept Not Trying*, 1994)

In recent years many businesses have begun to increase employee participation in making decisions, a management style common in Sweden and Japan (Naylor, 1990; Sundstrom & others, 1990). Ironically, a major influence on the "Japanese-style participative management" now increasingly popular in North America was MIT social psychologist Kurt Lewin. Lewin and his students demonstrated the effects of worker participation on productivity in laboratory and factory experiments. Shortly before World War II, Lewin visited Japan and explained his findings to industrial and academic leaders (Nisbett & Ross, 1991).

Because effective leadership styles vary with the situation and the person, the once-popular "great person" theory of leadership—that all great leaders share certain traits—fell out of favor. However, Peter Smith and Monir Tayeb (1989) have compiled data from studies in India, Taiwan, and Iran indicating that effective managers in coal mines, banks, and government offices often exhibit a high degree of *both* task and social leadership. As achievement-minded

task leadership goal-oriented leadership that sets standards, organizes work, and focuses attention on goals.

social leadership group-oriented leadership that builds teamwork, mediates conflict, and offers support.

people, effective managers care about how work is progressing, yet they are sensitive to their subordinates' needs. Effective leaders of laboratory groups, work teams, and large corporations also tend to exude a self-confident "charisma" (House & Singh, 1987; Shamir & others, 1993). Their charisma involves a *vision* of some goal, an ability to *communicate* it clearly and simply, and enough optimism and faith in their group to *inspire* others to follow. Such leadership motivates others to identify with and commit themselves to the group's mission.

In this chapter, we have seen that identifiable physiological mechanisms drive some motives, such as hunger (though external incentives and learned tastes matter, too). Other motives, such as achievement, are more obviously driven by psychological factors, such as an intrinsic quest for mastery and the external rewards of recognition. What unifies all such motives is their common effect: the energizing and directing of behavior. Without motivation—without hunger, thirst, sex, curiosity, an urge to belong, a drive to achieve—life would be dull and aimless. Motivation adds purpose—and zing—to life.

REHEARSE IT!

18. Achievement motivation is defined as a desire for significant accomplishment, for mastering skills or ideas, for control, and for rapidly attaining a high standard. Given a choice of tasks, high achievers would select one that is

a. very difficult, so they have an excuse for failure.
b. very easy, so that they can avoid failure.
c. moderately challenging, so that their success will be attributed to their skill and effort.
d. extremely difficult, so that when they do complete the task, they can feel superior to others performing the same task.

19. Psychologists identify two types of achievement motivation: extrinsic and intrinsic. Intrinsic motivation is a desire to perform a behavior because it is enjoyable and leads to feelings of mastery. For a violinist, an example of an intrinsic motive is the desire to

a. earn enough to maintain an extravagant life-style.
b. be promoted to concertmaster.
c. perfect a difficult piece of music.
d. obtain a positive grade or evaluation.

20. Task leadership is goal-oriented, while social leadership is group-oriented. Research indicates that effective managers exhibit

a. only task leadership.
b. only social leadership.
c. task leadership for building teams and social leadership for setting standards.
d. both task and social leadership, depending on the situation and the person.

REVIEWING ■ *Motivation*

Motivation is the energizing and directing of our behavior, as exemplified in our yearning for food, our longing for sexual intimacy, our need to belong, and our desire to achieve.

Motivational Concepts

1. *What theoretical perspectives have helped psychologists understand motivation?*

Under Darwin's influence, early theorists viewed behavior as controlled by biological forces, such as **instincts**. But when it became clear that people were naming, not explaining, various behaviors by calling them instincts, psychologists turned to a **drive-reduction theory** of motivation. Most physiological needs create aroused psychological states that drive us to reduce or satisfy those needs. The aim of *drive reduction* is internal stability, or **homeostasis**. Thus, drive reduction motivates survival behaviors such as eating and drinking. Rather than reducing a physiological need or tension state, some motivated behaviors increase arousal. Curiosity-driven behaviors, for example, suggest that too little as well as too much stimulation can motivate people to seek an optimum level of arousal. Not only are we pushed by our internal drives, we are pulled by external **incentives**. Depending on our personal and cultural experiences, some stimuli (for example, certain foods or erotic images) will arouse our desires.

2. ***What is the basic idea behind Maslow's hierarchy of needs?***

Maslow's **hierarchy of needs** expresses the idea that, until satisfied, some motives are more compelling (that is, more basic) than others. At the base of his hierarchy are physiological needs and at the top are self-actualization needs.

Hunger

3. ***What physiological factors cause us to feel hungry?***

Hunger's inner push primarily originates not from the stomach's contractions but from variations in body chemistry. For example, we are likely to feel hungry when our blood **glucose** levels are low. This information is monitored by the hypothalamus, which regulates the body's weight as it influences our feelings of hunger and fullness. To maintain weight at its **set point**, the body also adjusts its **basal metabolic rate** of energy expenditure.

4. ***What psychological factors contribute to hunger?***

Especially in "external" people, the sight and smell of food can trigger hunger and eating, partly by stimulating a rise in insulin level. Our preferences for certain tastes are partly genetic and universal, but also partly learned in a cultural context. The effect of psychological factors on eating behavior is most obvious in those who suffer **anorexia nervosa** and **bulimia nervosa**.

5. ***What factors predispose some people to become and remain obese?***

Fat is a concentrated fuel reserve stored in fat cells. Under genetic influence, the number and size of these cells determine one's body fat. Obese people find it difficult to lose weight permanently because the number of fat cells is not reduced by a diet, because the energy expenditure necessary for tissue maintenance is lower in fat than in other tissues, and because the overall basal metabolic rate decreases when body weight drops below the set point. Those who nevertheless wish to diet should minimize exposure to food cues, boost energy expenditure through exercise, and make a lifelong change in eating patterns.

Sexual Motivation

6. ***What stages mark the human sexual response?***

Biologically, the human **sexual response cycle** normally follows a pattern of excitement, plateau, orgasm, and resolution. During the resolution phase, males enter a **refractory period** during which another orgasm is not possible.

7. ***What role do hormones play in human sexuality?***

Sex hormones such as **estrogen** and testosterone help our bodies develop and function as either male or female. In many nonhuman animals, hormones also help to stimulate sexual activity, but in humans, they influence sexual behavior more loosely, especially once minimally sufficient hormone levels are present.

8. ***How do internal and external factors interact to stimulate sexual arousal?***

External stimuli can trigger sexual arousal in both men and women. Sexually explicit materials may also lead people to perceive their partners as comparatively less appealing and to devalue their relationships. In combination with the internal hormonal push and the external pull of sexual stimuli, imagined stimuli (fantasies) help trigger sexual arousal. Some **sexual disorders** respond well to behavioral treatment, which assumes that people can learn to modify their sexual responses.

9. ***How do men's and women's sexual attitudes and behaviors differ?***

One of the largest reported gender differences is women's generally greater disapproval of and lesser willingness to engage in casual, uncommitted sex.

10. ***What factors do and do not appear linked with sexual orientation?***

One's heterosexual or homosexual orientation seems neither willfully chosen nor able to be willfully changed. Evidence discounts certain environmental explanations of **sexual orientation**. Preliminary new evidence links sexual orientation with genetic influences, prenatal hormones, and the size of certain brain structures.

11. **What roles do personal values play in sex research and sex education?**

Sex research and education are not value-free. Sex-related values should therefore be discussed openly, recognizing the social significance of sexual expression.

Achievement Motivation

12. ***Who has the greatest need to achieve? Why?***

Some human behaviors are energized and directed without satisfying any apparent biological need. Achieving personal goals, for example, may be motivated by a person's social needs for competence and independence. People with a high need to achieve tend to prefer moderately challenging tasks and tend to persist in accomplishing them. Many **achievement-motivated** children have parents and teachers who encourage and affirm independent achievement rather than overly controlling them with external rewards and threats.

13. ***What is intrinsic motivation, and how can it be nurtured?***

Intrinsic motivation is the desire to be effective and to perform a behavior for its own sake. Rewards that boost people's sense of competence or inform them of improvement may increase intrinsic motivation. Rewards used to control behavior (**extrinsic motivation**) do not.

14. ***What motivational strategies are most effective at home, school, and work?***

As a result of studies in **industrial/organizational psychology**, researchers have found that people's performance can be improved by increasing their intrinsic motivation; by adjusting leadership style to complement individual motives; by setting specific, challenging goals; and by practicing effective, goal-oriented **task leadership** and group-oriented **social leadership**.

CRITICAL THINKING EXERCISE by Richard O. Straub

Now that you have read and reviewed Chapter 9, take your learning a step further by testing your critical thinking skills on the following pattern-recognition exercise.

Rochelle has always felt very competitive with other people, especially her older and only sibling, Doreen. Doreen is less competitive than Rochelle and is motivated more by a desire to perform to the best of her ability than by comparing herself with others. Rochelle has always received lower grades in school than Doreen, who receives consistently high scores. Rochelle claims this is because she intentionally selects more difficult classes and instructors than her sister's. Doreen responds that she picks instructors who are challenging yet fair, while her sister picks either impossibly difficult or ridiculously easy instructors.

Rochelle has often followed in her older sister's footsteps as Doreen developed new interests. For example, Doreen recently took up the guitar. On her own initiative, she began taking lessons and diligently practicing for an hour each day. Her proud parents frequently praised her for her discipline and musical progress. Not to be outdone, Rochelle decided to start playing the guitar as well. After a week or two, however, her interest in practicing began to wane. To increase their daughter's motivation, Rochelle's parents announced that for one month they would reward both daughters' efforts by giving them one dollar for each hour they practiced. The additional incentive seemed effective for Rochelle, who increased her practice time to nearly match Doreen's. Much to her parents' surprise, however, Doreen's interest level and practice time actually decreased when they offered the monetary incentive. At the end of the month, the puzzled parents withdrew the reward for practicing. Three weeks later, neither Rochelle nor Doreen seemed very interested in playing the guitar.

1. What principles of motivation might help explain why Rochelle and Doreen differ in the level of their school performance?
2. What principles of motivation might help explain why the monetary reward for practicing influenced Rochelle and Doreen differently?
3. What advice would you offer to Doreen and Rochelle's parents if they wished to renew their daughters' interest in playing the guitar?

Check your progress on becoming a critical thinker by comparing your answers to the sample answers found in Appendix B.

REHEARSE IT ANSWER KEY

1. b., **2.** a., **3.** d., **4.** c., **5.** c., **6.** a., **7.** b., **8.** a., **9.** b., **10.** d., **11.** d.,

12. b., **13.** b., **14.** c., **15.** d., **16.** a., **17.** b., **18.** c., **19.** c., **20.** d.

FOR FURTHER INFORMATION

You can find further information on industrial/organizational psychology on the following pages:

CHAPTER
10

Emotions, Stress, and Health

Feelings—powerful, spontaneous, sometimes unforgettable. No one needs to tell you that feelings add color to your life, that in times of stress they can disrupt your life or save it. Of all the species, we humans seem the most emotional (Hebb, 1980). More often than any other creature, we express fear, anger, sadness, joy, and love.

Fiction characters help us imagine life without emotion. *Star Trek's* Mr. Spock embodied cool, rational, emotionless intelligence. So did Data, the human-appearing android in *Star Trek: The Next Generation*. Data's brilliance and cool logic gave him superhuman analytical intelligence. Yet he realized something was missing. He could write poetry, but without the passions of the heart it fell flat. Data's intellectual curiosity made him wonder about fear, anger, and joy. Try as he might, he could not create such feelings, for Data was all cognition, no emotion.

1. ***What are the components of an emotion?***

Where do emotions come from? What are their ingredients? Imagine that, while walking home along a deserted street late at night, you hear the rumble of an engine and think that someone on a motorcycle is stalking you. Your heart begins to race, your pace quickens, you wonder about the cyclist's intent, and you feel scared. As this illustrates, **emotions** are a mix of (1) physiological arousal (heart pounding), (2) expressive behaviors (quickened pace), and (3) conscious experience (interpreting the person's intent and feeling fearful). The puzzle is how these three pieces fit together: Did you first notice your heart racing, your speeded-up walking, and then feel afraid? Or did your sense of fear come first, stirring your heart and legs to respond? Before trying to answer these questions, let's examine the individual pieces of the emotion puzzle—its physiology, expression, and conscious experience.

The Physiology of Emotion

2. ***What physiological changes accompany emotional arousal?***

Arousal

Emotion physically arouses you. Some physical responses are so obvious that you easily notice them. As you hear the motorcycle's rumble, your muscles tense, your stomach develops butterflies, your mouth becomes dry.

Emotional arousal Elated excitement and panicky fear involve similar physiological arousal. That allows us to flip rapidly between the two emotions.

Not only emotion, but most psychological phenomena (vision, sleep, memory, sex, and so forth) can be approached these ways—physiologically, behaviorally, and cognitively.

"Fear lends wings to his feet."

Virgil
Aeneid
19 B.C.

One explanation of sudden death caused by a voodoo "curse" is that the terrified person's parasympathetic nervous system, which calms the body, overreacts to the extreme arousal by slowing the heart to a stop (Seligman, 1974).

Your body also mobilizes for action in less noticeable ways. To provide energy, your liver pours extra sugar into your bloodstream. To help burn the sugar, your respiration increases to supply needed oxygen. Your digestion slows, diverting blood from your internal organs to your muscles. With blood sugar driven into the large muscles, running becomes easier. Your pupils dilate, letting in more light. To cool your stirred-up body, you perspire. If you were wounded, your blood would clot more quickly. Think of this after your next crisis: Without any conscious effort, your body's response to danger was wonderfully coordinated and adaptive—preparing you to fight or flee.

As we learned in Chapter 2, our *autonomic nervous system* controls our arousal (Figure 10.1). Its sympathetic division activates arousal by directing the adrenal glands atop the kidneys to release the stress hormones epinephrine (adrenaline) and norepinephrine (noradrenaline). The surge in epinephrine and norepinephrine increases heart rate, blood pressure, and blood sugar levels. When the crisis passes, the parasympathetic neural centers become active, calming the body. Even after the parasympathetic division inhibits further release of stress hormones, those already in the bloodstream linger awhile, so arousal diminishes gradually.

Figure 10.1 **Emotional arousal**

Autonomic nervous system controls physiological arousal

Sympathetic division (arousing)		Parasympathetic division (calming)
Pupils dilate	EYES	Pupils contract
Decreases	SALIVATION	Increases
Perspires	SKIN	Dries
Increases	RESPIRATION	Decreases
Accelerates	HEART	Slows
Inhibits	DIGESTION	Activates
Secrete stress hormones	ADRENAL GLANDS	Decrease secretion of stress hormones

emotion a response of the whole organism, involving (1) physiological arousal, (2) expressive behaviors, and (3) conscious experience.

Prolonged arousal, produced by sustained stress, taxes the body (more on this later in this chapter). Yet in many situations arousal is adaptive. Too little arousal (say, sleepiness) can be as disruptive as extremely high levels of arousal. When you're taking an exam, it pays to be moderately aroused—alert but not trembling with nervousness.

Although performance is usually best when arousal is moderate, the level of arousal for optimal performance varies for different tasks. With easy or well-learned tasks, peak performance comes with relatively high arousal, which enhances the dominant, usually correct, response. With more difficult or unrehearsed tasks, the optimal arousal is somewhat lower (Figure 10.2). Runners, who are performing a well-learned task, usually achieve their peak performances when highly aroused by competition. Basketball players shooting free throws—a less automatic skill—may not perform quite as well if a packed fieldhouse makes them hyperaroused (Sokoll & Mynatt, 1984). Likewise, students who feel great anxiety during exams perform more poorly than equally able but more confident students. Training anxious students how to relax before an exam often enables them to perform better (Hembree, 1988).

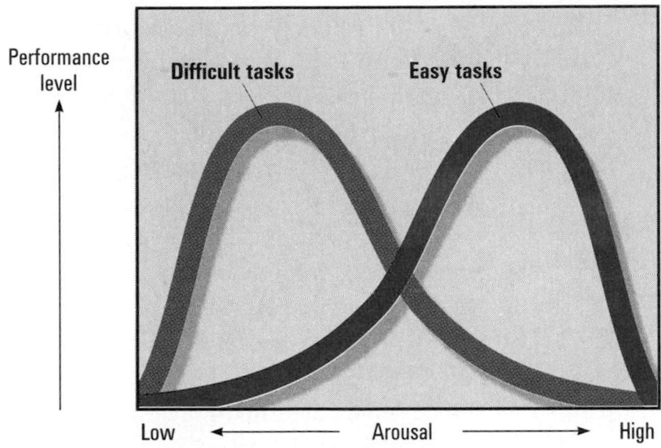

Figure 10.2 Arousal and performance Performance peaks at lower levels of arousal for difficult tasks, and at higher levels for easy or well-learned tasks.

Physiological States Accompanying Specific Emotions

Imagine conducting an experiment exploring physiological signs of arousal. In each of four rooms, you have someone watching a movie: In the first they are viewing a horror show; in the second, an anger-provoking film; in the third, a sexually arousing film; in the fourth, an utterly boring film. From the control center you monitor each person's physiological responses. By examining the perspiration, breathing, and heart rates of the viewers, could you tell who was frightened, who was angry, who was sexually aroused, and who was bored?

"No one ever told me that grief felt so much like fear. I am not afraid, but the sensation is like being afraid. The same fluttering in the stomach, the same restlessness, the yawning. I keep on swallowing."

C. S. Lewis
A Grief Observed
1961

With training, you could probably pick out the bored viewer from the other three. Discerning physiological differences among fear, anger, and sexual arousal is much harder (Cacioppo & others, 1997; Zillmann, 1986).

Fear, anger, and sexual arousal certainly *feel* different (and, as we shall see, cognitively they *are* different). A terrified person may feel a clutching, sinking sensation in the chest and a knot in the stomach. An angry person may feel "hot under the collar" and will probably experience a pressing, inner tension. The sexually stimulated person will experience a genital response. Despite their similar arousal, frightened and angered people also *look* different—"paralyzed with fear" and "ready to explode." Knowing this, can we pinpoint some distinct physiological indicators of each emotion?

Fear and rage are sometimes accompanied by differing finger temperatures and hormone secretions (Ax, 1953; Levenson, 1992). Different emotions also arise through different brain circuits (Kalin, 1993; Panksepp, 1982). As we saw on page 53, stimulate one area of a cat's limbic system and it will pull back in terror at the sight of a mouse. Stimulate another limbic area and the cat will look enraged—pupils dilated, fur and tail erect, claws out, hissing furiously.

In 1966, a young man named Charles Whitman killed his wife and mother and then climbed to the top of a tower at the University of Texas and shot 38 people. An autopsy later revealed a tumor in his limbic system.

As people experience negative emotions such as disgust, the right hemisphere becomes more electrically active. One man, having lost part of his right frontal lobe in brain surgery, became, his not-unhappy wife reported, less irritable and more affectionate (Goleman, 1995). The left hemisphere activates when processing positive emotions (Davidson & others, 1990, 1992). For some infants and adults, the left frontal lobe shows more activity than the right. These

THINKING CRITICALLY

Lie Detection

Given the physical indicators of emotion, might we, like Pinocchio, give some telltale sign whenever we lie? The *lie detector*, or **polygraph**, was once used mainly in law enforcement and national security work. But by the mid-1980s, 2 million Americans annually were reportedly being tested, usually by corporations trying to screen applicants for honesty or to uncover employee theft (Holden, 1986a).

Just what does the polygraph do? It does not literally detect lies. Rather, it measures several of the arousal responses that accompany emotion, such as changes in breathing, pulse rate, blood pressure, and perspiration. While you try to relax, the examiner measures your physiological responses as you answer questions. Some of these, called control questions, are designed to make anyone a little nervous. If asked, "In the last 20 years, have you ever taken something that didn't belong to you?" many people will tell a white lie and say no, causing arousal that the polygraph would detect. If your physiological reactions to the critical questions ("Did you ever steal anything from your previous employer?") are weaker than to the control questions, the examiner infers you are telling the truth. The assumption is that only a thief becomes agitated when denying a theft (Figure 10.3).

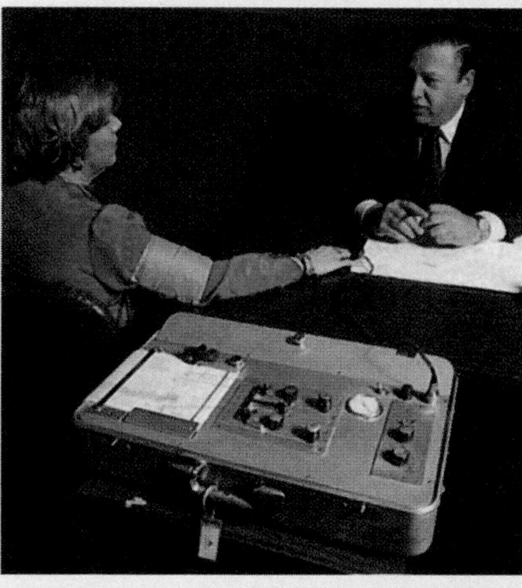

Who's lying? Can polygraph tests like this identify liars, or are its promoters putting something over on a gullible public? To learn more about this disputed issue, read on.

But there is a problem: An innocent person might also respond with heightened tension to the accusations implied by the relevant questions. When a Yakima, Washington, mother of a 4-year-old boy was accused by her ex-husband's new wife of sexually abusing her son, she gladly accepted a police offer of a polygraph test "to prove her innocence." Asked, "Did you take Tommy's penis in your mouth?" the accused mother understandably reacted with greater perspiration and blood pressure than when asked "Have you ever told a lie to get out of trouble?" (Physiologically, the fear of being disbelieved looks a lot like the fear of being caught lying.) This revealed her guilt, explained the police-sergeant-turned-polygrapher to the jury. (Fortunately for the mother, her attorney managed to locate a scientific expert who persuaded the jury that, by itself, this was not credible evidence of guilt.) Many rape victims similarly "fail" lie detector tests when reacting emotionally while telling the truth about their assailant (Lykken, 1992).

The major adversary of lie detector tests is University of Minnesota psychologist David Lykken (1983, 1991). He notes that because physiological response is much the same from one emotion to another, the polygraph cannot distinguish among anxiety, irritation, and guilt—they all appear as arousal. Thus, these tests err about one-third of the time. They more often label the innocent guilty—when the relevant question upsets the honest person—than the guilty innocent (Figure 10.4). Good advice, then, would be never to take a lie detector test if you are innocent.

Although too error-prone for use in testing applicants and employees, the polygraph can serve more appropriately as a tool in criminal investigation. Police sometimes use the polygraph to induce confessions by criminals whom they scare into thinking that any lies will be transparent. In a recent survey, however, more than 9 in 10 psychophysiologists and research psychologists agreed that savvy criminals and spies could beat the test by augmenting their arousal to control questions, such as by biting their tongue (Iacono & Lykken, 1997).

A more effective approach uses the *guilty knowledge test*, which assesses a suspect's physiological responses to details of a

individuals are typically more cheerful and less readily threatened or depressed than are those with more active right frontal lobes.

So, although emotions as varied as fear and anger involve a similar general autonomic arousal (thanks to the sympathetic nervous system), there are real, if subtle, physiological differences that help explain why we experience them so differently. Moreover, the physical accompaniments of emotion appear innate and universal—the same in a Sumatran village as in a North American village (Levenson & others, 1991).

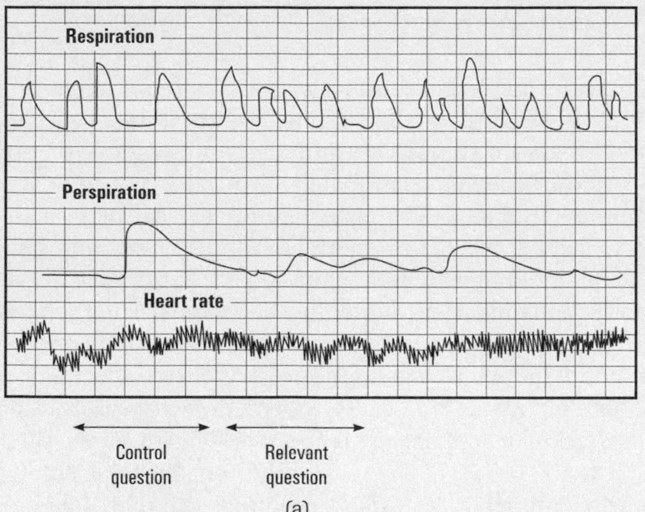

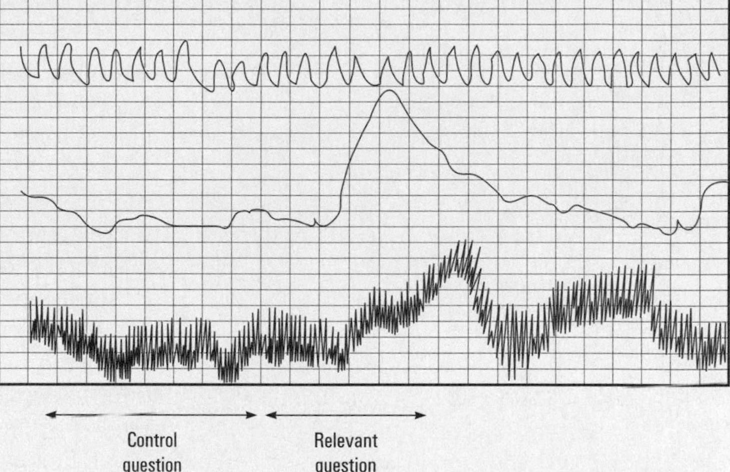

Figure 10.3 Physiological responses to a lie detector test (a) This is the record of a witness who supported an accused murderer's alibi. She reacted more strongly when answering no to a control question, "Up to age 18, did you ever deceive anyone?" than when answering yes to the relevant question, "Was [the accused] at another location at the time of the murder?" As a result, the examiner concluded she was telling the truth. **(b)** This is the record of an accused murderer judged to be lying when he pleaded self-defense. He reacted less strongly in answering no to the control question, "Up to age 18, did you ever physically harm anyone?" than when answering yes to the relevant question, "Did [the deceased] threaten to harm you in any way?" (From Raskin, 1982)

crime known only to the police and the guilty person. If a camera and money were stolen, the polygraph examiner could see whether the suspect reacts strongly to such details as the specific brand name of the camera and the dollar amounts. Presumably, only a guilty person would have such responses. Given enough such specific probes, an innocent person will seldom be wrongly accused.

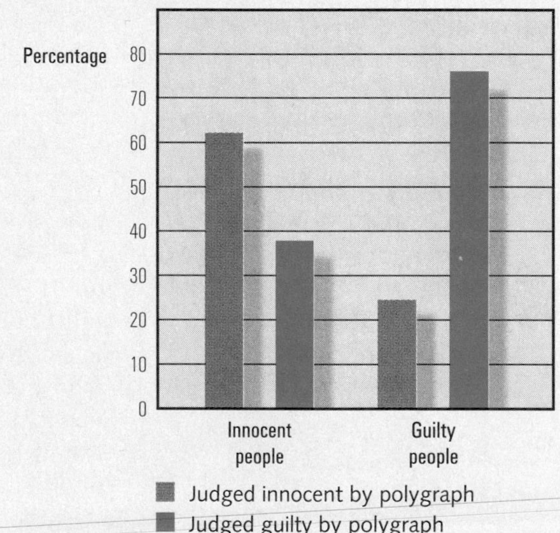

Figure 10.4 How often do lie detectors lie? Benjamin Kleinmuntz and Julian Szucko (1984) had polygraph experts study the polygraph data of 50 theft suspects who later confessed to being guilty and 50 suspects whose innocence was later established by someone's confession. Had the polygraph experts been the judges, more than one-third of the innocent would have been declared guilty, and almost one-fourth of the guilty would have been declared innocent.

polygraph a machine that is commonly used in attempts to detect lies and that measures several of the physiological responses accompanying emotion (such as perspiration, heart rate, blood pressure, and breathing changes).

Expressing Emotion

3. ***How do we communicate nonverbally? Are nonverbal expressions of emotion universally understood?***

There is another, simpler method of deciphering people's emotions: We read their bodies, listen to their tone of voice, and study their faces.

Nonverbal Communication

A silent language of emotion The art of nonverbal communication reached a pinnacle early in the twentieth century as silent films became widely available. For a nickel, enraptured audiences could watch performers mime a wide range of unmistakable emotions. Here Chester Conklin woos a woman on horseback while Louise Fazenda fumes.

"Your face, my thane, is a book where men may read strange matters."

Lady Macbeth to her husband in William Shakespeare's *Macbeth*

All of us communicate nonverbally as well as verbally. If irritated, we may tense our bodies, press our lips together, and turn away. With a gaze, an averted glance, or a stare, we can communicate intimacy, submission, or dominance (Kleinke, 1986). Among couples passionately in love, eye-gazing is typically prolonged and mutual (Rubin, 1970). Would intimate gazes stir such feelings between strangers? To find out, Joan Kellerman, James Lewis, and James Laird (1989) asked unacquainted male-female pairs to gaze intently for two minutes either at one another's hands or into one another's eyes. After separating, the eye-gazers reported feeling a greater tingle of attraction and affection.

Most of us are good enough at reading nonverbal cues to decipher the emotions in an old silent film. We are especially good at detecting nonverbal threats. In a crowd of faces, a single angry face will "pop out" faster than a single happy one (Hansen & Hansen, 1988). By exposing different parts of emotion-laden faces, Robert Kestenbaum (1992) discovered that we read fear and anger mostly from the eyes, happiness from the mouth.

Some of us are more sensitive than others to these cues. Robert Rosenthal, Judith Hall, and their colleagues (1979) discovered this by showing hundreds of people brief film clips of portions of a person's emotionally expressive face or body, sometimes with a garbled voice added. For example, after a two-second scene revealing only the face of an upset woman, the researchers would ask whether the woman was criticizing someone for being late or was talking about her divorce. Rosenthal and Hall reported that some people are much better emotion detectors than others are. Introverts tend to do better at reading others' emotions, although extraverts are themselves easier to read (Ambady & others, 1995). As we noted in Chapter 8, women also are better at it than men.

Women and men also differ in the emotions they express best, as Erik Coats and Robert Feldman (1996) demonstrated. They asked students to recall and talk about times when they were happy, sad, and angry. They then showed silent five-second videos of their reports of the three emotional states to participants who acted as judges. The judges correctly discerned women's happy recall nearly two-thirds of the time, but they were able to spot it less than half the time when observing men. Men, however, slightly surpassed women in conveying their anger.

Armed with high-tech equipment, psychologists are now linking various emotions with specific facial muscles (Figure 10.5). Hard-to-control facial muscles reveal signs of emotions you may be trying to conceal. Lifting just the inner part of your eyebrows, which few people do consciously, reveals distress or worry. Eyebrows raised and pulled together signal fear. A feigned smile, such as one we make for a photographer, often continues for more than four or five seconds, by which time most authentic expressions have faded. Feigned smiles also get switched on and off more abruptly than a genuine smile (Bugental, 1986).

E-mail letters and Internet discussions lack nonverbal cues to status, personality, age, and emotion. Nobody knows what you look or sound like, or anything about your background—you are judged solely on your words.

Our brains are rather amazing emotion-detectors. Elisha Babad, Frank Bernieri, and Robert Rosenthal (1991) discovered just *how* amazing after videotaping teachers talking to unseen schoolchildren. A mere 10-second clip of either the teacher's voice or face provided enough clues for both young and old viewers to determine whether the teacher liked and admired the child he or she was addressing. Although teachers may think they can conceal their feelings and stay objective, their students can sense what their expressions and gestures reveal.

Subtle facial indicators of emotion may someday enable a new behavioral approach to lie detection. For example, given mild emotional stimuli, electrodes attached to your facial muscles can now detect your hidden reactions (Tassinary &

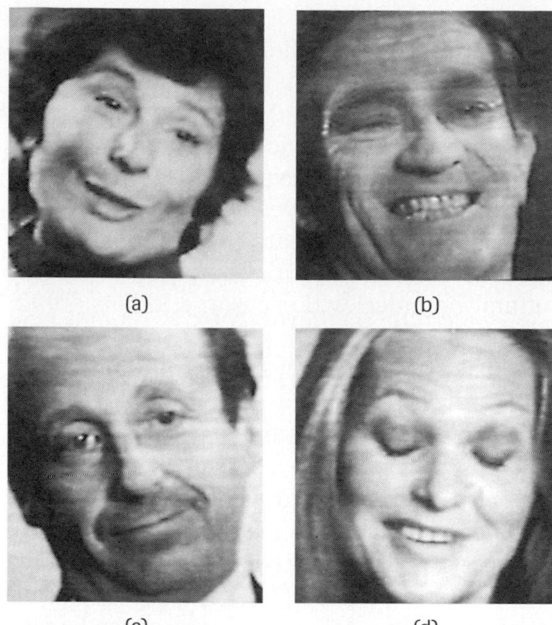

Figure 10.5 Smiles as indicators of emotions Paul Ekman's system for classifying a particular smile consists of a specific code for each of the 80 facial muscles used to create it. Notice how different these smiles are. **(a)** A smile that masks anger (the woman has just been told she is being dismissed). **(b)** An overly polite smile (the man is telling a patient to enjoy her hospital stay). **(c)** A smile softening verbal criticism ("I'd appreciate it if you wouldn't come to rehearsal drunk"). And **(d)** a reluctant, compliant smile ("I guess I don't have any choice, so OK").

Cacioppo, 1992). Your face may not look any different, but voltage changes on the skin reveal underlying micromuscular smiles or frowns.

The growing awareness that we communicate through the body's silent language has led to studies of how job applicants and interviewers communicate (or miscommunicate) nonverbally. Popular guidebooks and articles offer advice on how to interpret nonverbal signals when negotiating a business deal, selling a product, or flirting with someone. It pays to be able to read feelings that "leak through" via subtle facial expressions, body movements, and postures. Fidgeting, for example, may reveal anxiety or boredom. More specific interpretations of postures and gestures are risky. Different expressions may convey the same emotion: Either a cold stare or the avoidance of eye contact may signify hostility. And a given expression can convey very different emotions: Folded arms, for example, can signify either irritation or relaxation.

Such gestures, facial expressions, and tones of voice are all absent in computer-based communication. E-mail communications sometimes include sideways "emoticons," such as ;-) for a knowing wink and :-(for a frown. But e-mail letters and Internet discussions otherwise lack nonverbal cues to status, personality, age, and emotion. Nobody knows what you look or sound like, or anything about your background—you are judged solely on your words. Thus, when first meeting an e-mail pen pal face to face, people are often surprised at the person they encounter.

Culture and Emotional Expression

The meaning of gestures varies with the culture. Some years ago, psychologist Otto Klineberg (1938) observed that in Chinese literature people clapped their hands to express worry or disappointment, laughed a great "Ho-Ho" to express anger, and stuck out their tongues to show surprise. Similarly, the North American "thumbs up" and "A-OK" signs would be interpreted as insults in certain other cultures. (When U.S. President Nixon made the latter sign in Brazil he didn't realize he was saying "Let's have sex.") Just how important cultural definitions of gestures can be was demonstrated in 1968, when North Korea photographed supposedly happy officers from a captured U.S. Navy spy ship. In the photo, three of the men made the obscene middle-finger gesture; they had explained to their captors it was a "Hawaiian good luck sign" (Fleming & Scott, 1991).

Do facial expressions also have different meanings in different cultures? To find out, two investigative teams—one led by Paul Ekman and Wallace Friesen

Understanding gestures Volunteers working with international visitors during the 1996 Olympics were briefed on the cultural meanings of gestures.

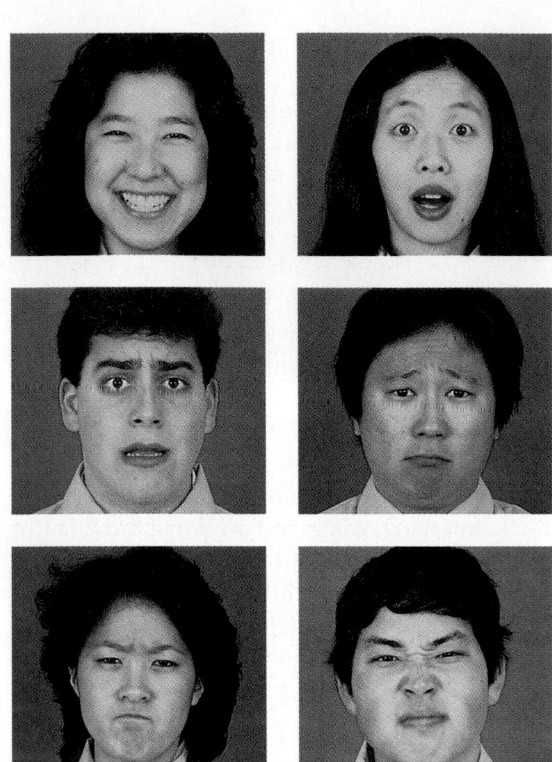

Figure 10.6 Culture-specific or culturally universal expressions? As people of differing cultures and races, do our faces speak differing languages? Which face expresses disgust? Anger? Fear? Happiness? Sadness? Surprise? The answers are on page 356. (From Matsumoto and Ekman, 1988)

"For news of the heart, ask the face."

Guinean Proverb

While weightless, astronauts' fluids move toward their upper body and their faces become puffy. This makes nonverbal communication more difficult, increasing the risks of misunderstanding, especially among multinational crews (Gelman, 1989).

(1975, 1987, 1994), the other by Carroll Izard (1977, 1994)—showed photographs of different facial expressions to people in different parts of the world and asked them to guess the emotion. You can try this yourself. Match the six emotions with the six faces of Figure 10.6.

You probably did pretty well regardless of your ethnic background. A smile's a smile the world around. Ditto for the other basic expressions. (There is no culture where people frown when they are happy.) Despite some differences (Russell, 1991, 1995), cultures and languages also share many similarities in how they categorize emotions—as anger, fear, and so on. The physiological indicators of emotion also cross cultural boundaries (Levenson & others, 1992; Mesquita & Frijda, 1992).

Do people from different cultures make and interpret facial expressions similarly because they experience similar influences, such as American movies, the BBC, and CNN? Apparently not. Ekman and his team asked isolated people in New Guinea to display various emotions in response to such statements as "Pretend your child has died." When the researchers showed videotapes of the New Guineans' facial reactions to North American collegians, the students could easily read them. Children's facial expressions—even those of blind children who have never seen a face—are also universal (Eibl-Eibesfeldt, 1971). The world over, children cry when distressed, shake their heads when defiant, and smile when happy.

The discovery that the facial muscles speak a fairly universal language would have come as no surprise to pioneering emotion researcher Charles Darwin (1809–1882). He speculated that in prehistoric times, before our ancestors communicated in words, their ability to convey threats, greetings, and submission with facial expressions helped them survive. That shared heritage, he believed, is why all humans express the basic emotions with similar facial expressions. A sneer, for example, retains elements of an animal's teeth-baring snarl.

Smiles, too, are social phenomena, not just emotional reflexes. Bowlers don't smile when they score a strike—they smile when they turn to face their companions (Jones & others, 1991; Kraut & Johnston, 1979). Even euphoric winners of Olympic gold medals typically smile not when awaiting their ceremony but when interacting with officials and facing the crowd and cameras (Fernádez-Dols & Ruiz-Belda, 1995).

It has also been adaptive for us to *interpret* faces in particular contexts. (Recall the aggressive or frightened monster from page 152.) People judge an angry face set in a frightening situation as afraid. They judge a fearful face set in a painful situation as pained (Carroll & Russell, 1996). Movie directors harness the phenomenon by creating contexts and mood music that amplify our perceptions of particular emotions.

Emotional expressions may enhance survival in other ways, too. Surprise raises the eyebrows and widens the eyes, which take in more information. Disgust wrinkles the nose, closing the nose from foul odors.

Although cultures share a universal facial language for basic emotions, they differ in how, and how much, they express emotion. In cultures that encourage individuality, as in Western Europe, Australia, New Zealand, and North America, emotional displays often are intense and prolonged. People focus on their own goals and attitudes and express themselves accordingly. Watching a film of someone's hand being cut, Americans grimace (whether alone or with other viewers). In contrast, Japanese viewers hide their emotions in the presence of others (Triandis, 1994). Asians rarely and briefly display negative or self-aggrandizing emotions that might disrupt communal feeling within close-knit groups (Markus & Kitayama, 1991; Matsumoto & others, 1988). Moreover, in Asian and other cultures that emphasize social connections and interdependence, displays of emotions such as sympathy, respect, and shame are more common than in the West.

Smiles are social phenomena, not just emotional reflexes. Bowlers don't smile when they score a strike—they smile when they turn to face their companions.

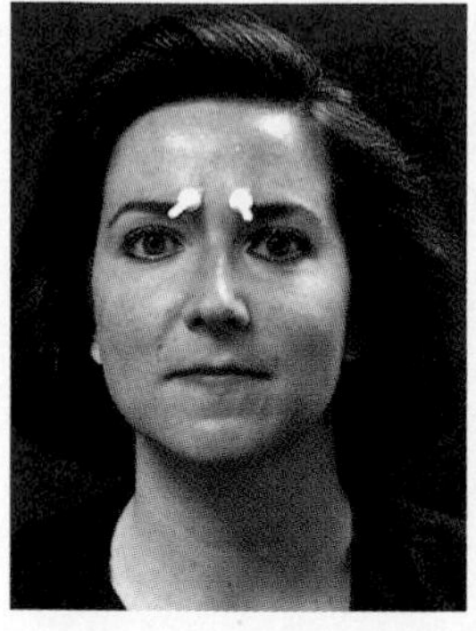
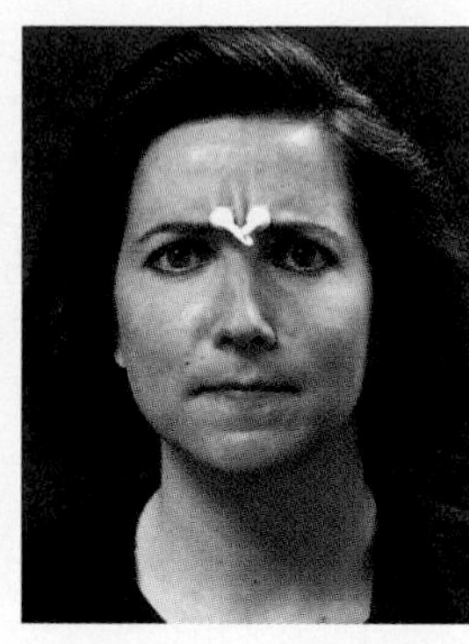

Figure 10.7 How to make people frown without telling them to frown Randy Larsen, Margaret Kasimatis, and Kurt Frey's (1992) solution: Attach two golf tees above the eyebrows and ask the subjects to make the tee tips touch. With "sad face" muscles activated, subjects felt sadder while viewing scenes of war, sickness, and starvation.

"Refuse to express a passion and it dies. . . . If we wish to conquer undesirable emotional tendencies in ourselves, we must . . . go through the outward movements of those contrary dispositions which we prefer to cultivate."

William James
Principles of Psychology
1890

Smile warmly on the outside and you feel better on the inside. Scowl and the whole world seems to scowl back.

The Effects of Facial Expressions

4. Do our facial expressions influence our feelings?

Expressions not only communicate emotion, they also amplify and regulate it. In his 1872 book, *The Expression of the Emotions in Man and Animals*, Darwin contended that "the free expression by outward signs of an emotion intensifies it. . . . He who gives way to violent gestures will increase his rage" (p. 365).

Was Darwin right? I was driving in my car one day when the song "Put on a Happy Face" came on the radio. How phony, I thought. But I tested Darwin's hypothesis anyway, as you can, too. Fake a big grin. Now scowl. Can you feel the difference?

The subjects in dozens of experiments have felt a difference. For example, James Laird and his colleagues (1974, 1984, 1989) subtly induced students to make a frowning expression by asking them to "contract these muscles" and "pull your brows together" (supposedly to help the researchers attach facial electrodes). The results? The students reported feeling a little angry. Students similarly induced to smile felt happier, found cartoons more humorous, and recalled happier memories than did the frowners. People instructed to mold their faces in ways that mimicked expressions of other basic emotions also experienced those emotions. For example, they reported feeling more fear than anger, disgust, or sadness when made to construct an expression of fear: "Raise your eyebrows. And open your eyes wide. Move your whole head back, so that your chin is tucked in a little bit, and let your mouth relax and hang open a little" (Duclos & others, 1989). Going through the motions awakens the emotions.

The effect is subtle, yet detectable in the absence of competing emotions. Consider these findings:

- If subtly manipulated into furrowing their brows (see Figure 10.7), people feel sadder while looking at sad photos.
- Saying the speech sounds *e* and *ah*, which activate smiling muscles, puts people—believe it or not—in a better mood than saying the German *ü* (rather like saying the English "e" and "y" together), which activates muscles associated with negative emotions (Zajonc & others, 1989).
- Just activating one of the smiling muscles by holding a pen in the teeth (rather than with the lips, which activates a frowning muscle) is enough to make cartoons seem more amusing (Strack & others, 1988). A heartier smile, made not just with the mouth but with raised cheeks as well, works even better (Ekman & others, 1990).

Smile warmly on the outside and you feel better on the inside. Scowl and the whole world seems to scowl back. Why might this be so? Paul Ekman and his colleagues (1983) designed an experiment to find out. Their subjects were professional actors trained in the Stanislavsky method, in which they physically (and psychologically) "become" the characters they are playing. The actors were asked to assume an expression and then hold it for 10 seconds while the researchers measured their heart rates and finger temperatures. When they made a fearful expression, their heart rate increased some 8 beats per minute and finger temperature was steady. When making an angry expression, both heart rate and finger temperature increased, as though the actor were indeed "hot-headed." Our facial expressions, it seems, send signals to our autonomic nervous system, which then responds accordingly. This experiment also confirms that subtly different body states do underlie different emotions.

Which smile makes Paul Ekman feel happy? The smile on the right, which engages the face muscles of a natural smile.

If assuming an emotional expression triggers a feeling, then imitating others' expressions should help us feel what they are feeling. Again, the laboratory evidence is supportive. Kathleen Burns Vaughn and John Lanzetta (1981) asked

Answers to the question in Figure 10.6: From left to right: happiness, surprise, fear, sadness, anger, disgust.

some students but not others to make a pained expression whenever an electric shock was apparently delivered to someone they were watching. With each apparent shock, the grimacing observers perspired more and had a faster heart rate than the other observers. So one small way to become more empathic—to feel what others feel—is to let your own face mimic the other person's expression. Acting as another acts helps us feel what another feels.

REHEARSE IT!

1. Emotions such as fear and anger involve a general autonomic arousal that is orchestrated by the sympathetic nervous system. In many situations, arousal is adaptive. For example, with a challenging task, such as taking an exam, performance is likely to be best when arousal is
a. very high.
b. moderate.
c. low.
d. diminishing.

2. Although feelings of fear and anger involve a similar general autonomic arousal, they involve different brain areas. For example, stimulate one area of a cat's ________ and the cat draws back in terror; stimulate another area and the cat hisses with rage.
a. cortex
b. hypothalamus
c. reticular formation
d. limbic system

3. We can successfully interpret nonverbal threats and certain other silent messages regardless of the national origin of the sender. However, some nonverbal behaviors are *not* universal. People in different cultures are most likely to differ in their interpretations of
a. adults' facial expressions.
b. children's facial expressions.
c. smiles.
d. postures and gestures.

4. When people are induced to assume fearful expressions, they will feel their heart rates increase. This suggests that the autonomic nervous system responds to
a. signals from the facial muscles.
b. conscious feelings of emotion.
c. physiological responses involved in deception.
d. electrical stimulation.

Experiencing Emotion

The ingredients of emotion include not only physiological arousal and expressive behavior but also our conscious experience. Psychologists have asked people to report their experiences of different emotions. Estonians, Poles, Greeks, Chinese, and Canadians all seem to place emotions along two dimensions—pleasant versus unpleasant, and intensely aroused versus sleepy (Russell & others, 1989). On the intensity scale, for example, *terrified* is more frightened than *afraid*, *enraged* is angrier than *angry*, *delighted* is happier than *happy*. To these two dimensions, we might add a third: duration. Among Americans and Japanese, at least, the emotions of joy and sadness typically endure longer than anger and guilt, which outlast fear and disgust (Matsumoto & others, 1988).

Psychologists have sought to identify emotions that are facially and experientially distinct. Carroll Izard (1977) isolated 10 such basic emotions (joy, interest-excitement, surprise, sadness, anger, disgust, contempt, fear, shame, and guilt), most of which are present in infancy (**Figure 10.8**). Izard reported that other emotions are combinations of these 10. Although Phillip Shaver and his colleagues (1996) believe that love, too, may be a basic emotion, Izard viewed it as a mixture of joy and interest-excitement.

In this chapter, we focus on two important emotions: anger and happiness. What functions do they serve? And what influences our experience of them?

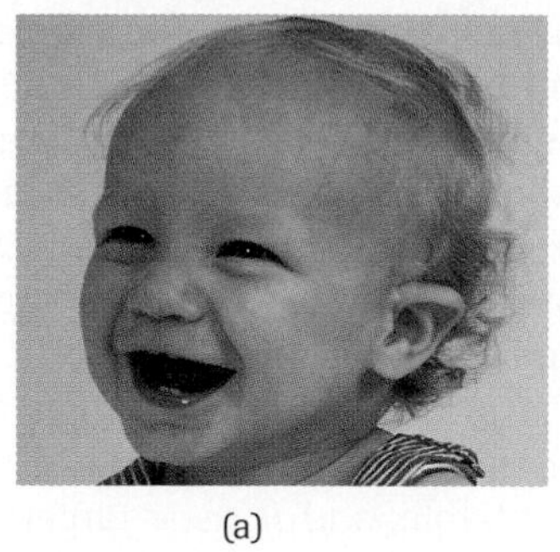

(a)

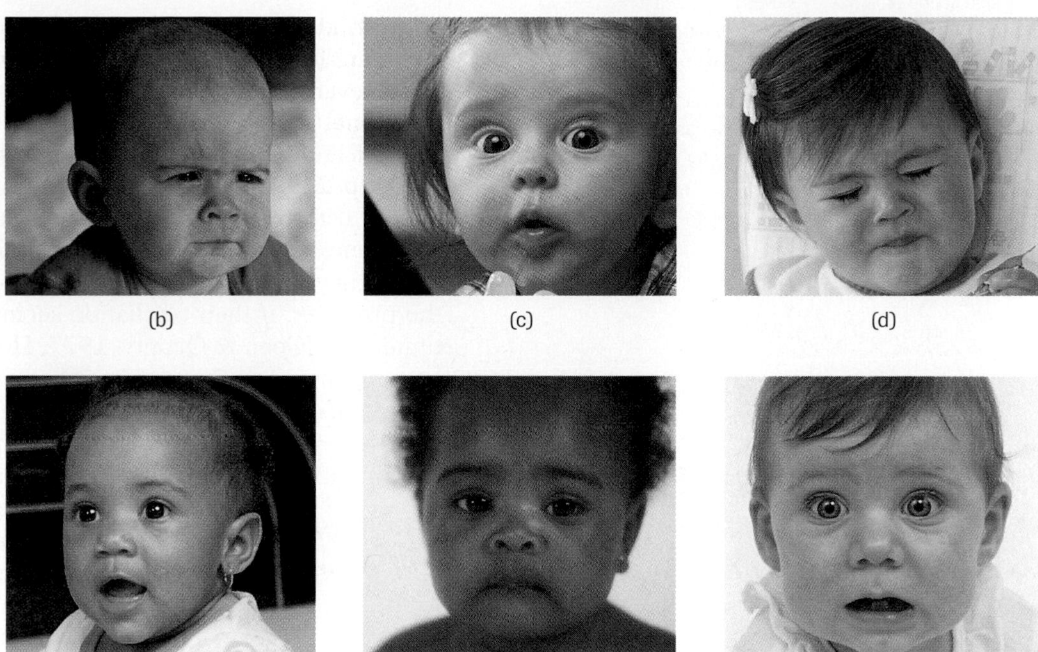

(b) (c) (d) (e) (f) (g)

Figure 10.8 Infants' naturally occurring emotions To identify the emotions present from birth, Carroll Izard analyzed the facial expressions of very young infants. Shown here are **(a)** joy (mouth forming smile, cheeks lifted, twinkle in eye); **(b)** anger (brows drawn together and downward, eyes fixed, mouth squarish); **(c)** interest (brows raised or knitted, mouth softly rounded, lips may be pursed); **(d)** disgust (nose wrinkled, upper lip raised, tongue pushed outward); **(e)** surprise (brows raised, eyes widened, mouth rounded in oval shape); **(f)** sadness (brow's inner corners raised, mouth corners drawn down); and **(g)** fear (brows level, drawn in and up, eyelids lifted, mouth corners retracted).

Anger

5. *What are the causes and consequences of anger?*

Anger is said by the sages to be "a short madness" (Horace, 65–8 B.C.) that "carries the mind away" (Virgil, 70–19 B.C.) and that can be "many times more hurtful than the injury that caused it" (Thomas Fuller, 1654–1734). But other sages say "noble anger" (William Shakespeare, 1564–1616) "makes any coward brave" (Cato, 234–149 B.C.) and "brings back . . . strength" (Virgil).

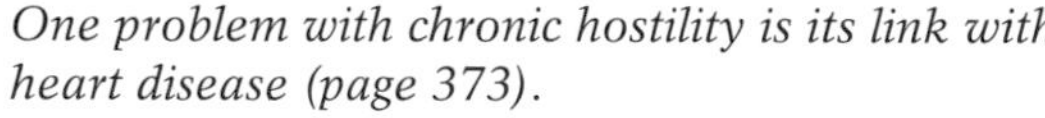

One problem with chronic hostility is its link with heart disease (page 373).

What makes us angry? To find out, James Averill (1983) asked many people to recall or keep careful records of their experiences with anger. Most reported becoming at least mildly angry several times a week; some became angry several times a day. Often the anger was a response to friends' or loved ones' perceived misdeeds. Anger was especially common when another person's act seemed willful, unjustified, and avoidable. But blameless annoyances—foul odors, high temperatures, a traffic jam, aches and pains—also have the power to make us angry (Berkowitz, 1990).

"Anger will never disappear so long as thoughts of resentment are cherished in the mind."

The Buddha
500 B.C.

What do people do with their anger? And what *should* they do with it? When anger fuels physically or verbally aggressive acts that we later regret, it is maladaptive. But Averill's subjects recalled that when they were angry they often reacted assertively rather than hurtfully. Their anger frequently led them to talk things over with the offending person, thereby lessening the aggravation. Such controlled expressions of anger are more adaptive than either hostile outbursts or internalized angry feelings.

Popular books and articles on aggression sometimes advise that even hostile outbursts can be better than keeping anger pent up. When irritated, should we go ahead and curse, tell a person off, or retaliate? Are "recovery movement" leaders right to encourage our raging at our dead parents, imaginatively cursing the former boss, or confronting our childhood abuser?

Such encouragement to vent your rage typifies individualized cultures, but it would seldom be heard in cultures where people's identity is more group-centered. People who keenly sense their *inter*dependence see anger as a threat to group harmony (Markus & Kitayama, 1991). In Tahiti, for instance, people

catharsis emotional release. In psychology, the catharsis hypothesis maintains that "releasing" aggressive energy (through action or fantasy) relieves aggressive urges.

feel-good, do-good phenomenon people's tendency to be helpful when already in a good mood.

subjective well-being self-perceived happiness or satisfaction with life. Used along with measures of objective well-being (for example, physical and economic indicators) to evaluate people's quality of life.

learn to be considerate and gentle. From infancy on in Japan, expressions of anger are less common than in Western cultures.

But even in Western cultures, the "vent your anger" advice presumes that emotional expression provides emotional release, or **catharsis**. "Catharsis is magnificent to experience and impressive to behold," notes Martin Seligman (1994, p. 239). The catharsis hypothesis maintains that we reduce anger by releasing it through aggressive action or fantasy. Experimenters report that this sometimes occurs. When people retaliate against someone who has provoked them, they may indeed calm down—*if* their counterattack is directly against the provoker, *if* their retaliation seems justifiable, and *if* their target is not intimidating (Geen & Quanty, 1977; Hokanson & Edelman, 1966). In short, expressing anger can be *temporarily* calming *if* it does not leave us feeling guilty or anxious.

Although "blowing off steam" may temporarily calm an angry person, it may also amplify underlying hostility.

Despite the afterglow—people sometimes feel better for hours afterward—catharsis usually fails to cleanse one's rage. More often, expressing anger breeds more anger. For one thing, it may provoke retaliation, thus escalating a minor conflict into a major confrontation. For another, expressing anger can magnify anger. (Recall Darwin's suggestion that violent gestures increase anger.) Ebbe Ebbesen and his colleagues (1975) saw this when they interviewed 100 frustrated engineers and technicians just laid off by an aerospace company. Some were asked questions that released hostility, such as, "What instances can you think of where the company has not been fair with you?" When these people later filled out a questionnaire that assessed their attitudes toward the company, did this opportunity to "drain off" their hostility reduce it? Quite the contrary. Compared with those who had not vented their anger, those who had let it all out exhibited *more* hostility.

Thus, although "blowing off steam" may temporarily calm an angry person, it may also amplify underlying hostility. When angry outbursts do calm us, they may be reinforcing and therefore habit forming. If stressed managers can drain off some of their tension by berating employees, then the next time they feel tense with irritation they may be more likely to explode again. Similarly, the next time you are angry you are likely to do whatever has relieved your anger in the past.

So what's the best way to handle anger? Experts have offered two suggestions. First, bring down the level of physiological arousal of anger by waiting. "It is true of the body as of arrows," noted Carol Tavris (1982), "what goes up must come down. Any emotional arousal will simmer down if you just wait long enough." Second, deal with anger in a way that involves neither being chronically angry over every little annoyance nor passively sulking, which is merely rehearsing your reasons for anger. Don't be like those who, stifling their feelings over a series of provocations, finally overreact to a single incident (Baumeister & others, 1990). Vent the anger by exercising, playing an instrument, or confiding your feelings to a friend or a diary.

A cool culture Caregivers who turn abusive against other family members are rare in Micronesia. This photo of community life on Pulap Island suggests one possible reason: Family life takes place in the open in the South Pacific. Relatives and neighbors who witness angry outbursts can step in before the emotion gets out of hand and turns into child, spouse, or elder abuse.

Anger can benefit relationships when it expresses a grievance in ways that promote reconciliation rather than retaliation. Civility means not only keeping silent about trivial irritations but also communicating important ones clearly and assertively. A nonaccusing statement of feeling—perhaps letting one's housemate know that "I get irritated when you leave your dirty dishes for me to clean up"—can help resolve the conflicts that cause anger.

Happiness

6. *What are the causes and consequences of happiness?*

"How to gain, how to keep, how to recover happiness is in fact for most men at all times the secret motive for all they do," observed William James (1902, p. 76). Understandably so, for one's state of happiness or unhappiness colors everything else. People who are happy perceive the world as safer (Johnson & Tversky, 1983), make decisions more easily (Isen & Means, 1983), rate job applicants more favorably (Baron, 1987), and report greater satisfaction with their whole lives (Schwarz & Clore, 1983). When your mood is gloomy, life as a whole seems depressing. Let your mood brighten, and suddenly your relationships, your self-image, and your hopes for the future all seem more promising.

Moreover— and this is one of psychology's most consistent findings—when we feel happy we are more willing to help others. In study after study, a mood-boosting experience (such as finding money, succeeding on a challenging task, or recalling a happy event) made people more likely to give money, pick up someone's dropped papers, volunteer time, and so forth. It's called the **feel-good, do-good phenomenon** (Salovey, 1990).

Despite the significance of happiness, psychology has more often focused on negative emotions. From 1967 through 1995, *Psychological Abstracts* (a guide to psychology's literature) included 5119 articles mentioning anger, 38,459 mentioning anxiety, and 49,028 mentioning depression. For every 21 articles on these topics, only one dealt with the positive emotions of joy (402), life satisfaction (2357), or happiness (1710).

When your mood is gloomy, life as a whole seems depressing. Let your mood brighten, and suddenly your relationships, your self-image, and your hopes for the future all seem more promising.

There is, of course, good reason to focus on negative emotions, which can make our lives miserable and drive us to seek help. But researchers are becoming increasingly interested in **subjective well-being**, assessed either as feelings of happiness (sometimes defined as a high ratio of positive to negative feelings) or as a sense of satisfaction with life. During the 1980s, annual research output on subjective well-being nearly quadrupled (Myers, 1993).

"Everything important has been said before."
Philosopher Alfred North Whitehead
1861–1947

On this subject, as on so many others, whatever psychological research reveals will have been anticipated by someone. The sages of the ages have given us any number of contradictory maxims: that happiness comes from knowing the truth, and from preserving illusions; from living for the present, and from living for the future; from being with others, and from living in peaceful solitude (Tatarkiewicz, 1976). The list goes on, but the scientific task is clear: to ask which of these competing ideas fit reality. Sifting the actual predictors of happiness from the merely plausible hunches requires research.

In their research on happiness, psychologists have studied influences upon both our temporary moods and our long-term life satisfaction. Studying people's reports of daily moods confirms that stressful events—an argument, a sick child, a car problem—trigger bad moods. No surprise there. But by the next day, the gloom nearly always lifts (Affleck & others, 1994; Bolger & others, 1989; Stone & Neale, 1984). If anything, people tend to rebound from bad days to a *better*-than-usual good mood the following day. When in a bad mood, can you usually depend on rebounding within a day or two? Are your times of elation similarly hard to sustain? In the long run, our emotional ups and downs tend to balance.

"Weeping may tarry for the night, but joy comes with the morning."
Psalms 30:5

Apart from prolonged grief over the loss of a loved one or lingering anxiety after a trauma (such as child abuse, rape, or the terrors of war), even tragedy is not permanently depressing. The finding is surprising but reliable. People who become blind or paralyzed usually recover near-normal levels of day-to-day happiness. Consider these findings:

"If I couldn't know the joy of dancing, I could know the ecstasy of creating."

Christy Brown
My Left Foot
1954

- Able-bodied University of Illinois students described themselves as happy 50 percent of the time, unhappy 22 percent of the time, and neutral 29 percent of the time. To within 1 percentage point, students with disabilities rated their emotions identically (Chwalisz & others, 1988).
- Students perceive their friends with disabilities as just as happy as their other friends (Allman, 1989).
- In one survey of 128 people with all four limbs paralyzed, most acknowledged having considered suicide after their injury. However, more than a year later, only 10 percent rated their quality of life as poor; most described it as good or excellent (Whiteneck & others, 1985). When 233 emergency room caregivers imagined how they would feel about themselves years after such an injury, only 39 percent guessed they would feel "satisfied with myself, on the whole." But that is how 95 percent of the actual patients felt (Gerhart & others, 1994). And 98 percent of them agreed that "I feel I am a person of worth."
- Learning that one is HIV-positive is devastating. Yet after five weeks of adapting to the grim news, those who tested positive felt less emotionally distraught than they expected (Sieff & others, 1997). As this finding illustrates, people seem to overestimate the long-term emotional consequences of very bad news.

Faced with adversity In 1995, an accident transformed *Superman* actor Christopher Reeve into an immobile person needing others to feed, dress, and care for him. "Maybe I should just check out," he told his wife, Dana, shortly after the accident. But within four months he reported in a Barbara Walters interview "genuine joy in being alive."

The effect of dramatically positive events is similarly temporary. Once their rush of euphoria wears off, state lottery winners typically find their overall happiness unchanged (Brickman & others, 1978). Other research confirms that there is much more to well-being than being well-off. Many people (including most new collegians, as Figure 10.9 suggests) believe they would be happier if they had more money. They probably would be—temporarily. But in the long run, increased affluence hardly affects happiness. Within most affluent countries, people with lots of money are not much happier than those with just enough to afford life's necessities. Wealth is like health: Its utter absence breeds misery, yet having it is no guarantee of happiness.

"No happiness lasts for long."

Seneca
Agamemnon
A.D. 60

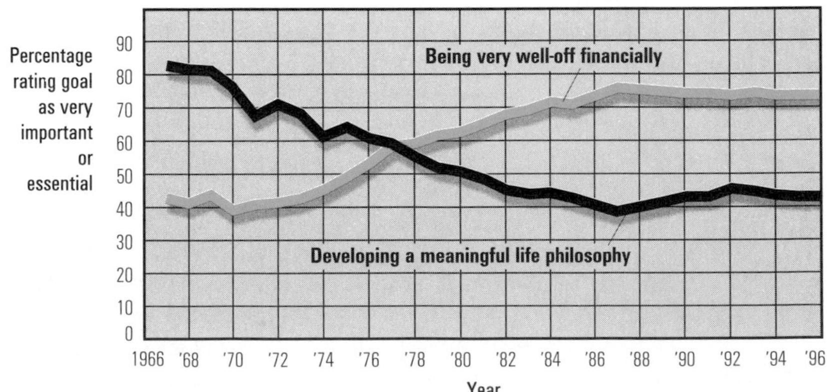

Figure 10.9 **How materialistic are entering college students?** From 1970 through most of the 1980s, annual surveys of more than 200,000 entering U.S. college students revealed an increasing desire for wealth. Just before this book went to press, 1997 data became available: 75 percent of college students rated financial well-being as very important; 41 percent rated a meaningful life philosophy as most important. (From Sax & others, 1996; Dey & others, 1991)

During the last four decades, the average U.S. citizen's buying power has doubled. The 1957 per-person after-tax income, inflated to 1995 dollars, was $8500; by 1996, thanks partly to the rich getting richer and to women's increasing employment, it was almost $20,000. Did this doubled wealth—enabling twice as many cars per capita, and color TVs, VCRs, personal computers, air conditioning, and answering machines galore—also buy more happiness? As

adaptation-level phenomenon our tendency to form judgments (of sounds, of lights, of income) relative to a "neutral" level defined by our prior experience.

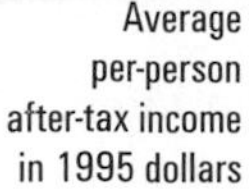

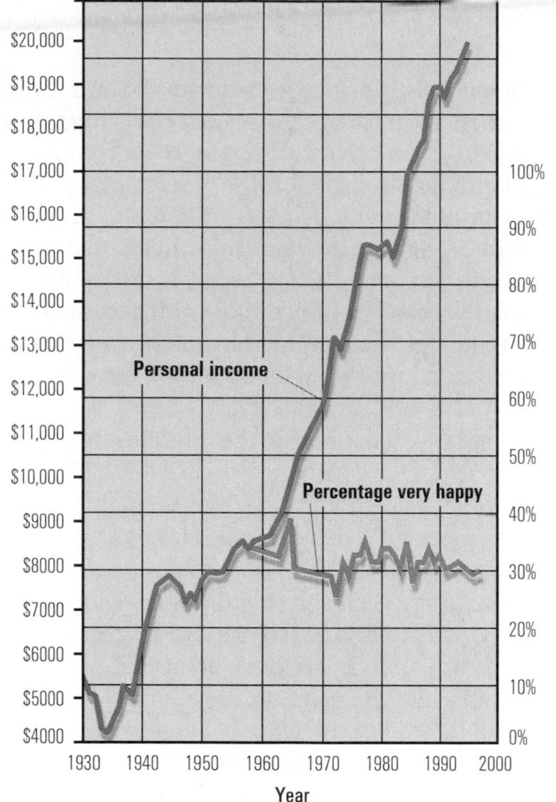

Figure 10.10 Does money buy happiness? It surely helps us to avoid certain types of pain. Yet, though buying power has doubled since the 1950s, the average American's reported happiness has remained almost unchanged. (Happiness data from Niemi & others, 1989, and T. Smith, 1997; income data from *Historical Statistics of the U.S.* and *Economic Indicators.*)

Figure 10.10 shows, the average American is now twice as rich but no happier. In 1957, some 35 percent said they were "very happy," as did slightly fewer—30 percent—in 1996. Indeed, judging by the doubled divorce rate, tripled teen-suicide rate, quintupled juvenile violence, and mushrooming depression (page 443), contemporary Americans seem to be more often miserable. The same is true of the European countries and Japan. In all these countries, people enjoy better nutrition, health care, education, and science and are somewhat happier than people in very poor countries, yet increasing real incomes have *not* produced increasing happiness. The findings lob a bombshell at modern materialism: *Economic growth in affluent countries has provided no apparent boost to morale or social well-being.*

Two psychological principles explain why, for all but the very poor, more money buys no more than a temporary surge of happiness, and why our emotions seem attached to elastic bands that pull us back from highs or lows. In its own way, each principle suggests that happiness is relative.

The Adaptation-Level Principle: Happiness Is Relative to Our Prior Experience

"Continued pleasures wear off. . . . Pleasure is always contingent upon change and disappears with continuous satisfaction."

Dutch Psychologist Nico Frijda (1988)

The **adaptation-level phenomenon** describes our tendency to judge various stimuli relative to what we have previously experienced. As psychologist Harry Helson explained, we adjust our "neutral" levels—the points at which sounds seem neither loud nor soft, temperatures neither hot nor cold, events neither pleasant nor unpleasant—based on our experience. We then notice and react to variations up or down from these levels. Adaptation researcher Allen Parducci (1995) recalls a striking example: "On the Micronesian island of Ponope, which is almost on the equator, I was told of a bitter night back in 1915 when the temperature dropped to a record-breaking 69 degrees [Fahrenheit; 21 degrees Celcius]!"

So, could we ever create a permanent social paradise on earth? Donald Campbell (1975) answered no: If you woke up tomorrow to your utopia—perhaps a world with no bills, no ills, all *A*'s, someone who loves you unreservedly—you would, for a time, feel euphoric. But you would soon recalibrate your adaptation level. Before long you would again sometimes feel gratified (when achievements surpass expectations), sometimes feel deprived (when they fall below), and sometimes feel neutral. That helps explain why, despite the realities of triumph and tragedy, million-dollar lottery winners and paraplegics report similar levels of happiness.

The point to remember: Satisfaction and dissatisfaction, success and failure—all are relative to our recent experience.

"I've got the bowl, the big yard, I know I should be happy."

The Relative Deprivation Principle: Happiness Is Relative to Others' Attainments

Happiness is relative not only to our past experience but also to our comparisons with others. We are always comparing ourselves with others. And whether we feel good or bad depends on who those others are. We are smart or agile only when others are slow-witted or clumsy.

relative deprivation the perception that one is worse off relative to those with whom one compares oneself.

An example: To explain the frustration expressed by U.S. Air Corps soldiers during World War II, researchers formulated the concept of **relative deprivation**—the sense that we are worse off than others with whom we compare ourselves. Despite a relatively rapid promotion rate for the group, many soldiers were frustrated about their own promotion rates (Merton & Kitt, 1950). Apparently, seeing so many others being promoted inflated the soldiers' expectations. And when expectations soar above attainments, the result is disappointment. When the Oakland Athletics signed baseball outfielder José Canseco to a $4.7 million annual salary, his fellow outfielder Rickey Henderson became openly dissatisfied with his $3 million salary and refused to show up on time for spring training (King, 1991).

"I have also learned why people work so hard to succeed: It is because they envy the things their neighbors have. But it is useless. It is like chasing the wind. . . . It is better to have only a little, with peace of mind, than be busy all the time with both hands, trying to catch the wind."

Ecclesiastes 4:4

"Our poverty became a reality. Not because of our having less, but by our neighbors having more."

Will Campbell
Brother to a Dragonfly
1977

Such comparisons help us understand why the middle- and upper-income people in a given country, who can compare themselves with the relatively poor, tend to be slightly more satisfied with life than their less fortunate compatriots. Nevertheless, once a person reaches a moderate income level, further increases do little to increase happiness. Why? Because as people climb the ladder of success they mostly compare themselves with peers who are at or above their current level (Gruder, 1977; Suls & Tesch, 1978). For Rickey Henderson, José Canseco was the standard of comparison. For average people, athletes' salaries are emotionally irrelevant. "Beggars do not envy millionaires, though of course they will envy other beggars who are more successful," noted Bertrand Russell (1930, p. 90). Thus "Napoleon envied Caesar, Caesar envied Alexander, and Alexander, I daresay, envied Hercules, who never existed. You cannot, therefore, get away from envy by means of success alone, for there will always be in history or legend some person even more successful than you are" (pp. 68–69).

The effect of comparison with others helps us understand why students of a given level of academic ability tend to have a higher academic self-concept if they attend a school where most other students are not exceptionally able (Marsh & Parker, 1984). If you were near the top of your class in high school, you might feel inferior upon entering a college where everyone was near the top of their class.

By "counting our blessings" when we compare ourselves with those less fortunate, we can, however, increase our satisfaction. As comparing ourselves with those who are better-off creates envy, so comparing ourselves with those less well-off boosts contentment. Marshall Dermer and his colleagues (1979) demonstrated this by asking University of Wisconsin-Milwaukee women to study others' deprivation and suffering. After viewing vivid depictions of how grim life was in Milwaukee in 1900, or after imagining and then writing about various personal tragedies, such as being burned and disfigured, the women expressed greater satisfaction with their own lives. Similarly, when mildly depressed people read about someone who is even more depressed, they feel somewhat better (Gibbons, 1986).

When downward comparisons lead upward
Comparing ourselves with those worse off can sometimes prompt us not only to count our blessings but to share them. Self-made millionaire Eugene Lang (center) did just that during an address to the graduating class of the public grade school he had attended in Harlem. After reflecting on their poverty, he suddenly offered to pay the college costs of any who graduated from high school. (With his active support during the next four years, most did graduate from high school and over half went on to college.)

Predictors of Happiness

If, as the adaptation-level phenomenon implies, our emotions tend to balance around normal, then why do some people seem so filled with joy and others so gloomy day after day? What makes one person normally happy and another less so? Research reveals several predictors of happiness (Table 10.1). Remember, though, that knowing that two variables correlate does not tell us whether one causes the other. For example, many studies indicate that religiously active people tend to report greater happiness and life satisfaction. Is happiness conducive to faith? Or does faith enhance happiness?

Whether at work or leisure, most of us derive greatest enjoyment from engaging, challenging activities. Mihaly Csikszentmihalyi (pronounced chick-SENT-me-hi; 1990) and his colleagues discovered this after giving research volunteers a pager. When beeped, the people would note what they were doing and how they were feeling. Usually, they felt happier if mentally engaged by work or active leisure than if passively vegetating. Ironically, the less expensive (and usually more involving) a leisure activity is, the more absorbed and happy people are while doing it. People are happier when gardening than when sitting on a

"I could cry when I think of the years I wasted accumulating money, only to learn that my cheerful disposition is genetic."

Table 10.1 Happiness Is . . .

Researchers Have Found That Happy People Tend to	However, Happiness Seems Not Much Related to Other Factors, Such as
Have high self-esteem	Age
Be optimistic and outgoing	Race
Have close friendships or a satisfying marriage	Gender (women are more often depressed, but also more often joyful)
Have work and leisure that engages their skills	Educational level
Have a meaningful religious faith	Parenthood (having children or not)
Sleep well and exercise	Physical attractiveness

Source: Summarized from Myers (1993) and Myers & Diener (1995, 1996).

power boat. They're happier when talking to friends than when watching TV. Happy adolescents and young adults also are more likely to be focused on personal strivings and close relationships than on money and prestige (Kasser & Ryan, 1996; Perkins, 1991). So, happy are those whose work and leisure and friendships absorb them, enabling them unself-consciously to "flow" in focused activity.

Satisfying tasks and relationships affect our happiness, but within limits imposed by our genetic leash. From their study of 254 identical and fraternal twins, David Lykken and Auke Tellegen (1996) estimated that 50 percent of the difference among people's happiness ratings is heritable. Even identical twins raised apart often are similarly happy. Depending on our outlooks and recent experiences, our happiness fluctuates around our "happiness set point," which disposes some people to be ever upbeat, and others down.

REHEARSE IT!

5. In some situations, venting anger—"blowing up"—seems to calm a person temporarily. In other cases, acting angry increases hostility. Experts suggest that to bring down anger, a good first step is to
- **a.** retaliate verbally or physically.
- **b.** wait or "simmer down."
- **c.** express anger in action or fantasy.
- **d.** review the grievance silently.

6. After graduating from college, you get a job and move into a large metropolitan city. At first, you find the street noise irritatingly loud, but after a while, it no longer bothers you, thus illustrating the
- **a.** relative deprivation principle.
- **b.** adaptation-level principle.
- **c.** feel-good, do-good phenomenon.
- **d.** catharsis principle.

7. A philosopher notes that one cannot escape envy by means of success alone: There will always be someone more successful, more accomplished, or richer with whom to compare oneself. In psychology this observation is embodied in the
- **a.** relative deprivation principle.
- **b.** adaptation-level principle.
- **c.** list of predictors of happiness.
- **d.** feel-good, do-good phenomenon.

8. When happy and unhappy people are compared, researchers find that happy people are optimistic, outgoing, and likely to have satisfying close relationships. One of the most consistent findings of psychological research is that happy people are also
- **a.** more likely to express anger.
- **b.** generally luckier than others.
- **c.** concentrated in the wealthier nations.
- **d.** more likely to help others.

9. Age, race, and gender seem not to be predictably related to subjective feelings of happiness or well-being. However, researchers have found that happy people tend to
- **a.** have children.
- **b.** score high on intelligence tests.
- **c.** have a meaningful religious faith.
- **d.** complete high school and some college education.

James-Lange theory the theory that our experience of emotion is our awareness of our physiological responses to emotion-arousing stimuli.

Cannon-Bard theory the theory that an emotion-arousing stimulus simultaneously triggers (1) physiological responses and (2) the subjective experience of emotion.

two-factor theory Schachter's theory that to experience emotion one must (1) be physically aroused and (2) cognitively label the arousal.

Theories of Emotion

We have seen that emotions arise from the interplay of physiological arousal, expressive behavior, and conscious experiences. How this interplay occurs has sparked two controversies, however. The first is an old debate: Does your heart pound because you are afraid, or are you afraid because you feel your heart pounding? The second concerns the link between our thinking and feeling: Does cognition always precede emotion?

The James-Lange and Cannon-Bard Theories

7. *What issue distinguishes the James-Lange and Cannon-Bard theories of emotion?*

Common sense tells most of us that we cry because we are sad, lash out because we are angry, tremble because we are afraid. To pioneering psychologist William James this commonsense view of emotion was 180 degrees out of line. According to James, "We feel sorry because we cry, angry because we strike, afraid because we tremble" (1890, p. 1066). After you evade an oncoming car in your lane, you may notice your racing heart and *then* feel shaken with fright. Your feeling of fear follows your body's response. James's idea, which was also proposed by Danish physiologist Carl Lange, is therefore called the **James-Lange theory**.

The James-Lange theory struck U.S. physiologist Walter Cannon (1871–1943) as implausible. Cannon thought the body's responses were not distinct enough to evoke the different emotions. Does a racing heart signal fear, anger, or love? Also, changes in heart rate, perspiration, and body temperature seemed too slow to trigger sudden emotion. Cannon, and later another physiologist, Philip Bard, concluded that physiological arousal and the emotional experience occur simultaneously: The emotion-arousing stimulus is routed simultaneously to the cortex, causing the subjective awareness of emotion, and to the sympathetic nervous system, causing the body's arousal. Thus, this **Cannon-Bard theory** implies that your heart begins pounding *as* you experience fear; one does not cause the other.

Common sense tells most of us that we cry because we are sad, lash out because we are angry, tremble because we are afraid. To pioneering psychologist William James this commonsense view of emotion was 180 degrees out of line.

As long as the evidence suggested that the arousal of one emotion is much the same as another, the James-Lange assumption that we experience our emotions through differing body states seemed improbable. With new evidence showing subtle physiological distinctions among the emotions, the James-Lange theory became more plausible. As James struggled with his own feelings of depression and grief, he came to believe that we can control emotions by going "through the outward motions" of whatever emotion one wants to experience. "To feel cheerful," he advised, "sit up cheerfully, look around cheerfully, and act as if cheerfulness were already there." The last few decades' findings concerning emotional effects of facial expressions (pages 355–356) are precisely what James might have predicted.

"Whenever I feel afraid
I hold my head erect
And whistle a happy tune."

Richard Rodgers and Oscar Hammerstein
The King and I
1958

Let's check your understanding of the James-Lange and Cannon-Bard theories. Imagine that your brain could not sense your heart pounding or your stomach churning. According to each theory, how would this affect your experienced emotions?

Cannon and Bard would have expected you to experience emotions normally, because they believed emotions occur separately from (though simultaneously with) the body's arousal. James and Lange would have expected greatly diminished emotions because they believed that to experience emotion you must first perceive your body's arousal.

The condition you imagined actually exists in people with severed spinal cords. Psychologist George Hohmann (1966) interviewed 25 soldiers who received such injuries in World War II. He asked them to recall emotion-arousing incidents that occurred before and after their spinal injuries. Those with injuries in the lower part of the spine, who had lost sensation only in their legs, reported little change in their emotions. Those who could feel nothing below the neck reported a considerable decrease in emotional intensity (as James and Lange would have expected). These soldiers said they might act much the same as before in emotion-arousing situations, but as one confessed about his anger, "It just doesn't have the heat to it that it used to. It's a mental kind of anger." On the other hand, emotions expressed mostly in body areas above the neck are felt more intensely by those with spinal cord injury. Virtually all the men Hohmann interviewed reported increases in weeping, lumps in the throat, and getting choked up when saying good-bye, worshipping, or watching a touching movie.

"Every moment is more intense."

Paralyzed actor Christopher Reeve
1995

Although such evidence breathed new life into the James-Lange theory, most researchers agree with Cannon and Bard that our experienced emotions also involve cognition (Averill, 1993). Whether we fear the man behind us on the dark street depends entirely on whether we interpret his actions as hostile or friendly. So with James and Lange we can say that our arousal is an important ingredient of emotion. And with Cannon and Bard we can say that there is more to the experience of emotion than reading our physiology.

Cognition and Emotion

8. *What is the relationship between thinking and feeling?*

Now, the second and newer controversy: Put simply, what is the connection between what we *think* and how we *feel*? Which is the chicken and which the egg? Do emotions always grow from thoughts? Are our feelings always subject to our mind's appraisal of a situation? Or can we experience emotion apart from thinking? This issue has practical implications for self-improvement.

Schachter's Two-Factor Theory of Emotion

Most psychologists today believe that our cognitions—our perceptions, memories, and interpretations—are an essential ingredient of emotion. One such theorist is Stanley Schachter, who has proposed a **two-factor theory**, in which emotions have two ingredients: physical arousal and a cognitive label. Like James and Lange, Schachter presumed that our experience of emotion grows from our awareness of our body's arousal. But like Cannon and Bard, Schachter also believed that emotions are physiologically similar. Thus, in his view, an emotional experience requires a conscious interpretation of the arousal (Figure 10.11, page 366).

Sometimes our arousal response to one event spills over into our response to the next event.

Sometimes our arousal response to one event spills over into our response to the next event. Imagine that after an invigorating run you arrive home to find a message that you got the longed-for job. With arousal lingering from the run, would you feel more elated than if you received this news after awakening from a nap?

To find out, Schachter and Jerome Singer (1962) aroused college men with injections of the hormone epinephrine. Picture yourself as one of their subjects: After receiving the injection, you go to a waiting room, where you find yourself with another person (actually an accomplice of the experimenters)

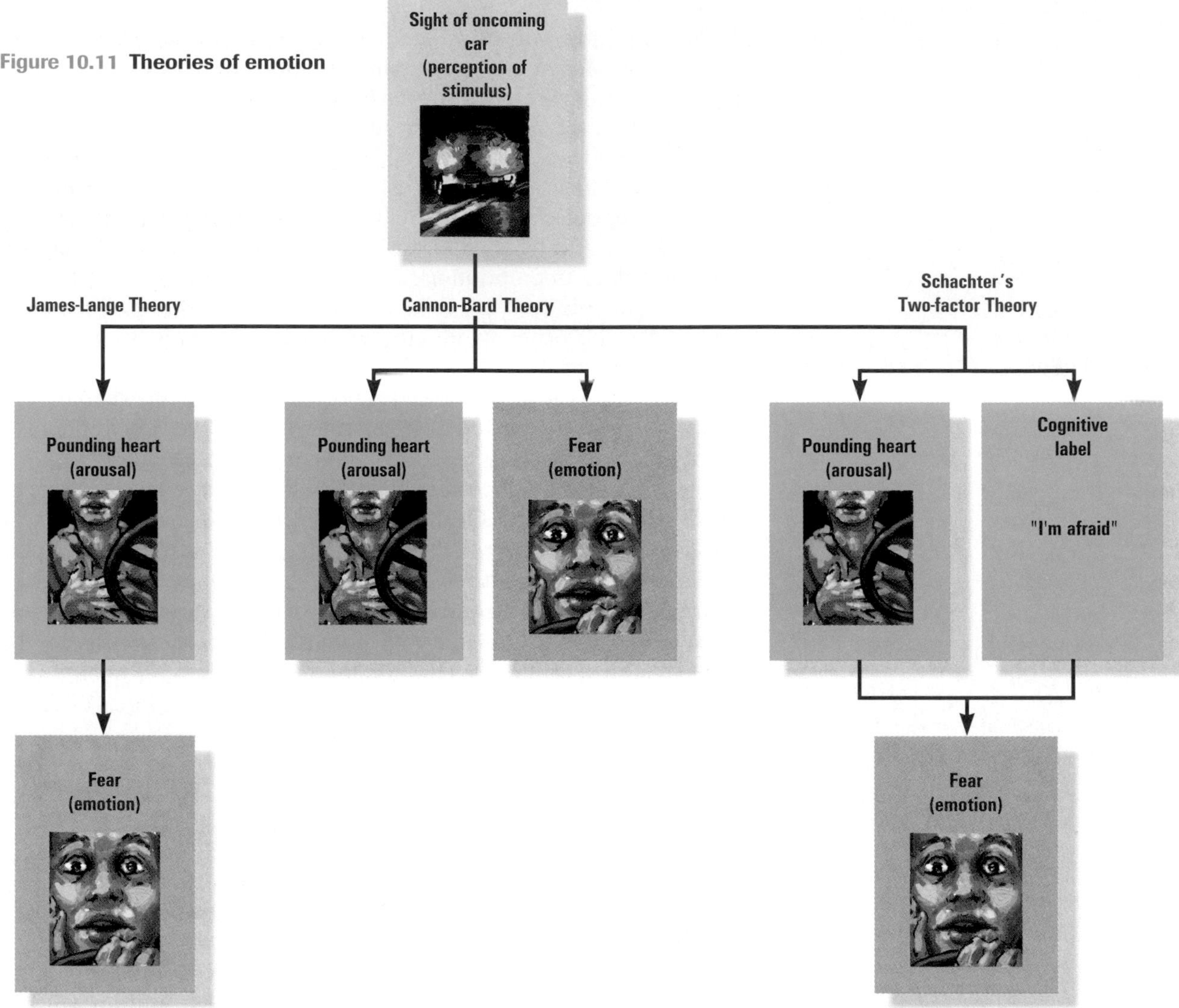

Figure 10.11 **Theories of emotion**

who is acting either euphoric or irritated. As you observe this person, you begin to feel your heart race, your body flush, and your breathing become more rapid. If told to expect these effects from the injection, what would you feel? Schachter and Singer's subjects felt little emotion—because they attributed their arousal to the drug. But if told the injection would produce no effects, what would you feel? Perhaps you would react, as another group of subjects did, by "catching" the apparent emotion of the person you are with—becoming happy if the accomplice is acting euphoric, and testy if the accomplice is acting irritated.

This discovery—that a stirred-up state can be experienced as one emotion or another very different one, depending on how we interpret and label it—has been replicated in dozens of experiments. Although emotional arousal is not as undifferentiated as Schachter believed, arousal can intensify just about any emotion (Reisenzein, 1983; Sinclair & others, 1994). Insult people who have just been aroused by pedaling an exercise bike or watching a rock concert film and they will find it easy to misattribute their arousal to the provocation. Their feelings of anger will be greater than those of similarly provoked people who were not previously aroused. Arousal from emotions as diverse as anger, fear, and sexual excitement can spill from one emotion to another (Zillmann, 1986). In anger-provoking

A stirred-up state can be experienced as one emotion or another very different one, depending on how we interpret and label it.

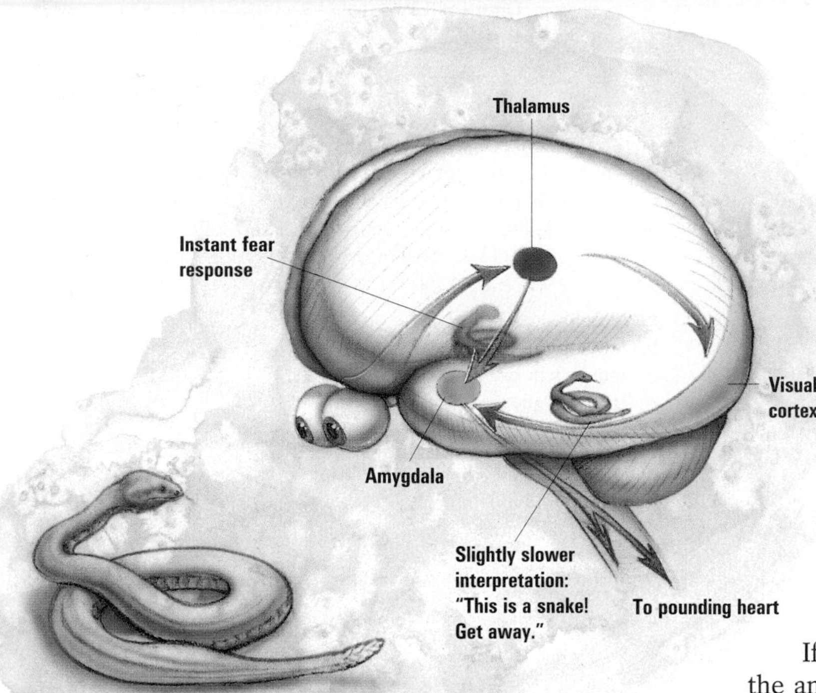

Figure 10.12 **The brain's shortcut for emotions** Sensory input may be routed both to the cortex and directly to the amygdala for a more instant emotional reaction.

situations, sexually aroused people react with more hostility; and the arousal that lingers after an intense argument or a frightening experience may intensify sexual passion (Palace, 1995).

So, arousal fuels emotion and cognition channels it. This can be seen in successful Olympic gymnasts and exam takers—who, more than their less successful competitors, label arousal as energizing, as giving them an edge, rather than as threatening (Raglin, 1992). Professors and public speakers similarly welcome prelecture arousal as meaning they are "up" or "on" rather than flat.

Must Cognition Precede Emotion?

So, to experience an emotion, must we first label our arousal? If Robert Zajonc (pronounced ZI-yence; 1980, 1984a) is right, the answer is no. He argues that our emotional reactions are sometimes quicker than our interpretations of a situation; we therefore feel some emotions *before* we think. For example, in earlier chapters, we noted that when people repeatedly view stimuli flashed too briefly for them to perceive and recall, they nevertheless come to prefer these stimuli. Without being consciously aware of having seen the stimuli, they rather like them. A subliminally flashed smiling or angry face can also prime us to feel better or worse about a follow-up stimulus (Murphy & others, 1995). (Can you recall liking something or someone immediately, without at first knowing why?)

Research on neurological processes shows how we can experience emotion before cognition. Some neural pathways involved in emotion bypass the cortical areas involved in thinking. One such pathway runs from the eye or ear via the thalamus to the amygdala, an emotional control center (LeDoux, 1994, 1996). This shortcut enables a quick, precognitive emotional response before the intellect intervenes. After the cortex has further interpreted a threat, the thinking brain can take over (Figure 10.12). In the forest, we jump at a nearby twig-cracking sound, leaving the cortex to decide later whether it was made by a predator or just the wind. Such evidence supports Zajonc's belief that *some* of our emotional reactions involve no deliberate thinking and that cognition is not always necessary for emotion. The heart is not always subject to the mind.

Emotion researcher Richard Lazarus (1984, 1991) disagrees. He concedes that our brains process and react to vast amounts of information without our conscious awareness, and he willingly grants that some emotional responses do not require *conscious* thinking. Nevertheless, he has pointed out, even instantaneously felt emotions require some sort of quick cognitive appraisal of the situation; otherwise, how do we *know* what we are reacting to? The appraisal may be effortless and we may not be conscious of it, but it is still a mental function (Figure 10.13). Emotions arise when we *appraise* an event as beneficial or harmful to our well-being.

For us, the important conclusion concerns what Lazarus and Zajonc agree on: Some emotional responses—especially simple likes, dislikes, and fears—involve no conscious thinking. We may fear the spider, even if we "know" it is harmless. After conditioning, Little Albert was afraid of furry objects (Chapter 6). Such responses are hard to alter by changing our thinking.

Other emotions—including moods such as depression and complex feelings such as hatred and love—are greatly affected by our interpretations, memories, and expectations. For these emotions, as we will see in Chapter 13, learning to *think* more positively about ourselves and the world around us makes us *feel* better.

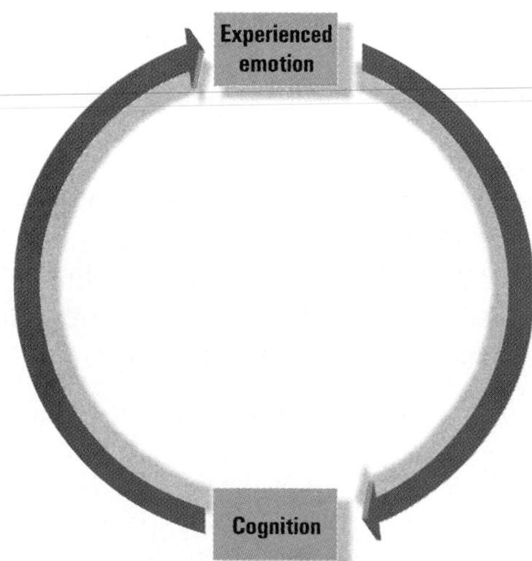

Figure 10.13 **Emotion and cognition feed each other** But which is the chicken and which the egg? Lazarus believes that, although emotions influence thinking, our cognitive appraisal of a situation always precedes emotion. Zajonc contends that some of our emotional reactions precede cognitive processing.

REHEARSE IT!

10. Two important theories of emotion are the James-Lange theory and the Cannon-Bard theory. The James-Lange theory states that our experience of an emotion is a consequence of our physiological response to a stimulus; we are afraid because our heart pounds. The Cannon-Bard theory proposes that the physiological response (like heart pounding) and the subjective experience of, say, anger

a. are unrelated.
b. occur simultaneously.
c. occur in the opposite order (with feelings of fear first).
d. are regulated by the thalamus.

11. Assume that after spending an hour on a treadmill, you receive a letter saying that your scholarship to college has been approved. The two-factor theory of emotion would predict that your physical arousal will

a. weaken your happiness.
b. intensify your happiness.
c. transform your happiness into relief.
d. have no particular effect on your happiness.

12. Research suggests that we can experience an aroused state as one of several different emotions, depending on how we interpret and label the arousal. If physically aroused by swimming, then heckled by an onlooker, we may interpret our arousal as anger and

a. become less physically aroused.
b. feel angrier than usual.
c. feel less angry than usual.
d. feel sexually aroused.

13. Robert Zajonc maintains that some of our emotional reactions occur before we have had the chance to label or interpret them. Richard Lazarus disagrees. The two psychologists differ about whether emotional responses occur in the absence of

a. physical arousal.
b. the hormone epinephrine.
c. cognitive processing.
d. learning.

Stress and Health

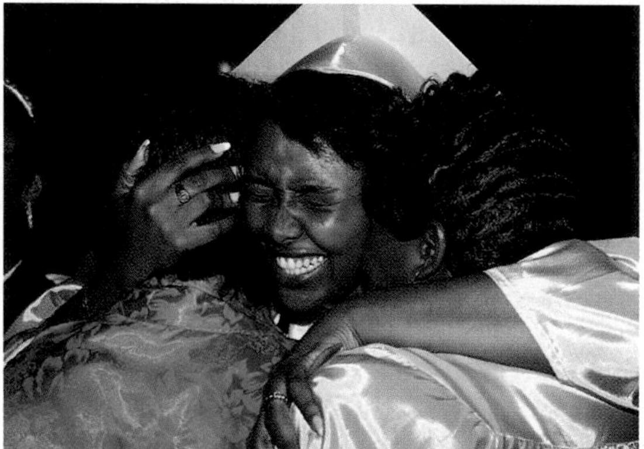

The faces of stress Challenging positive events, such as graduating into the working world, can be stressful. But most stresses arise from negative events, such as a loved one's death.

Walking along the path toward his Rocky Mountain campsite, Karl hears a rustle at his feet. As he glimpses a rattlesnake, his body mobilizes for fight or flight: His muscles tense, his adrenaline flows, his heart pounds. Then flee he does, racing to the security of camp. Once there, Karl's muscles gradually relax and his heart rate and breathing ease.

Karen leaves her suburban apartment one morning and, delayed by road construction, arrives at the parking lot of the commuter train station just in time to see the 8:05 pull away. Catching the next train, she arrives in the city late and elbows her way through crowds of rush-hour pedestrians. Once at her bank office, she apologizes to her first client, who wonders where Karen has been and why his quarterly investment report is not ready. Karen does her best to mollify the client. Afterward, she notices her tense muscles, clenched teeth, and churning stomach.

Karl's response to stress saved his life; Karen's, if chronic, could increase her risk of heart disease, high blood pressure, and other stress-linked health problems. Moreover, feeling under pressure, she might sleep and exercise less and smoke and drink more, further endangering her long-term health.

Stress and Stressors

9. *What is stress?*

Stress is a slippery concept. People sometimes use the word *stress* to describe threats or challenges ("Karen was under a lot of stress"), other times to describe our responses ("When Karl saw the rattler, he experienced acute stress"). Most psychologists would define Karen's missed train as a "stressor," Karl's physical and emotional responses as a "stress reaction," and the process by which Karen and Karl related to their environments as

stress the process by which we appraise and bodily respond to certain events, called *stressors*, that we appraise as threatening or challenging.

general adaptation syndrome (GAS) Selye's concept of the body's adaptive response to stress as composed of three stages—alarm, resistance, exhaustion.

Worldwide, reports the World Health Organization, nearly a quarter of health-care contacts are prompted by psychological problems (Sartorius, 1994).

stress. Thus, stress is not just a stimulus or a response. It is the process by which we appraise and cope with environmental threats and challenges (Figure 10.14).

When perceived as challenges, stressors can have positive effects by arousing and motivating us to conquer problems. Championship athletes, successful entertainers, and great teachers and leaders all thrive and excel when aroused by a challenge. More often, stressors threaten our resources—our status and security on the job, our loved ones' health or well-being, our deeply held beliefs, our self-image (Hobfoll, 1989). And when such stress is severe or prolonged, it may also harm.

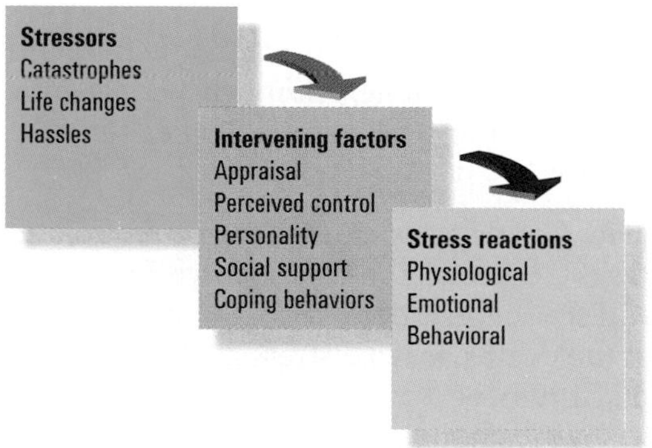

Figure 10.14 The stress process How we react to stressors depends on who we are and how we appraise and cope with them. For example, criticism that an easygoing optimist perceives as a challenge may seem a dire threat to a temperamental pessimist.

The Stress Response System

Although medical interest in stress dates back to Hippocrates (460–377 B.C.), it was not until the 1920s that Walter Cannon (1929) confirmed that the stress response is part of a unified mind–body system. He observed that extreme cold, lack of oxygen, and emotion-arousing incidents all trigger an outpouring of epinephrine (adrenaline) and norepinephrine (noradrenaline). These stress hormones enter the bloodstream from sympathetic nerve endings in the inner part of the adrenal glands. As we saw in this chapter's earlier discussion of emotional arousal, this is but one part of the sympathetic nervous system's response. When alerted by any of a number of brain pathways, the sympathetic nervous system increases heart rate and respiration, diverts blood to skeletal muscles, and releases fat from the body's stores—all to prepare the body for what Cannon called *fight or flight*. All in all, this stress response struck Cannon as wonderfully adaptive.

Canadian scientist Hans Selye's (1936, 1976) 40 years of research on stress extended Cannon's findings and helped make stress a major concept in both psychology and medicine. Selye studied animals' reactions to various other stressors, such as electric shock, surgical trauma, and immobilizing restraint. He discovered that the body's adaptive response to stress is so general—like a single burglar alarm that sounds no matter what intrudes—that he called it the **general adaptation syndrome (GAS)**.

Figure 10.15 Selye's general adaptation syndrome After a trauma, the body enters an alarm phase of temporary shock. From this it rebounds, as stress resistance rises. If the stress is prolonged, wear and tear may lead to exhaustion.

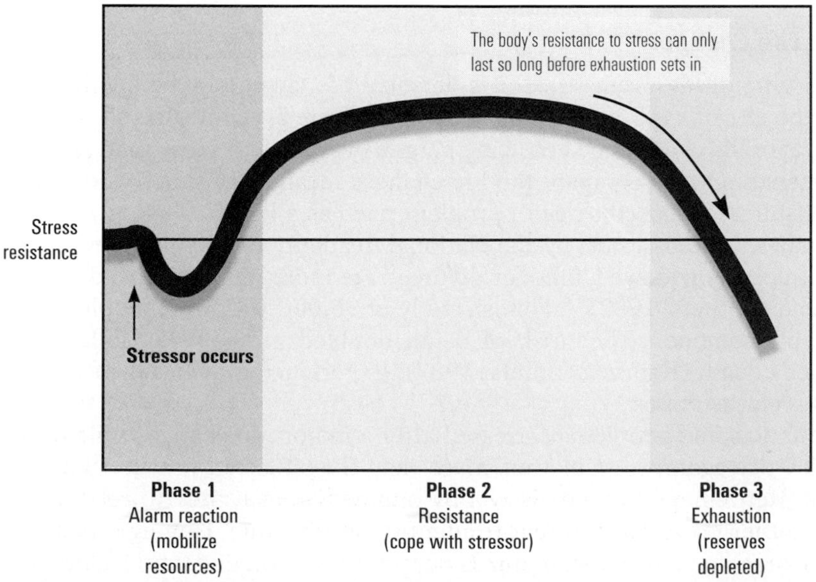

The body's resistance to stress can only last so long before exhaustion sets in
Stress resistance
Stressor occurs
Phase 1 Alarm reaction (mobilize resources)
Phase 2 Resistance (cope with stressor)
Phase 3 Exhaustion (reserves depleted)

Selye saw the GAS as having three phases (Figure 10.15). Let's say you suffer a physical or emotional trauma. In Phase 1, you experience an *alarm reaction* due to the sudden activation of your sympathetic nervous system. Your heart rate zooms, blood is diverted to your skeletal muscles, and you feel the faintness of shock. With your resources mobilized you are now ready to fight the challenge during Phase 2, *resistance*. Your temperature, blood pressure, and respiration remain high, and there is a sudden outpouring of hormones. If persistent, the stress may eventually deplete your body's reserves during Phase 3, *exhaustion*. With exhaustion, you are more vulnerable to illness or even, in extreme cases, collapse and death.

Newer research reveals subtle differences in the body's reactions to different stressors. Nevertheless, few medical experts today quarrel with Selye's basic point: Prolonged stress can produce physical deterioration. Such findings lead to the practical concerns of today's health psychologists: What causes stress? What are the effects of stress? And how can we alleviate those effects?

Stressful Life Events

10. *What provokes stress?*

How stressed we feel depends on how we appraise events. One person alone in a house dismisses its creaking sounds and experiences no stress; someone else suspects an intruder and becomes alarmed. One person regards a new job as a welcome challenge; someone else appraises it as risking failure. Research has focused on our responses to three types of stressors: catastrophes, significant life changes, and daily hassles.

Catastrophes

Catastrophes are unpredictable, large-scale events such as war and natural disasters that nearly everyone appraises as threatening. Although people often provide one another with aid and comfort after such events, the health consequences can be significant. Two examples:

- On the day of its 1994 earthquake, Los Angeles experienced a fivefold increase in sudden-death heart attacks—especially in the first two hours after the quake and near its epicenter. Physical exertion (running, lifting debris) was a factor in only 13 percent of the deaths, leaving stress as the likely trigger for the others (Muller & Verrier, 1996).
- In the year following the crash of a 747 jumbo jet at Lockerbie, Scotland, police officers—after being pressed into recovering human remains and patrolling the disaster zone—suffered a 38 percent increase in short-term illnesses (Paton, 1992).

Toxic stress Researchers have found that catastrophes such as flooding increase psychological disorders.

Do community disasters usually produce effects this great? After digesting data from 52 studies of catastrophic floods, hurricanes, and fires, Anthony Rubonis and Leonard Bickman (1991) found the typical effect more modest but nonetheless genuine. In disaster's wake, rates of psychological disorders such as depression and anxiety rose an average 17 percent. The nuclear accident at Three Mile Island produced similar stress symptoms in area residents (Baum & Fleming, 1993). Refugees fleeing their homeland also suffer increased rates of psychological disorder. Their stress stems from the trauma of uprooting and family separation and from the challenges of adjusting to a foreign culture, with its differing language, ethnicity, climate, and social norms (Williams & Berry, 1991). In all these cases, the health consequences often come only after prolonged stress.

Significant Life Changes

The second type of life-event stressor is personal life changes—the death of a loved one, the loss of a job, a marriage or divorce. Some psychologists study the health effects of life changes by following people over time to see if such events precede illnesses. Others compare the life changes recalled by those who have or have not suffered a specific health problem, such as a heart attack. A review of these studies, commissioned by the National Academy of Sciences, revealed that people recently widowed, fired, or divorced are more vulnerable to disease (Dohrenwend & others, 1982). A Finnish study of 96,000 widowed people confirmed the phenomenon: Their risk of death doubled in the week following their partner's death (Kaprio & others, 1987). Experiencing a cluster of crises puts one even more at risk.

Why, then, do some people feel stressed after a major life change while others do not? Once again, what matters more than the situation itself is our appraisal of it. Retirement may be viewed by one person as a time to relax and enjoy, by another person as a threat to identity and income. Having an abortion creates stress for women who morally oppose abortion and who lack their

No end in sight "It's not the large things that send a man to the madhouse . . . no, it's the continuing series of small tragedies . . . not the death of his love but the shoelace that snaps with no time left" (Charles Bukowski, cited by Lazarus in Wallis, 1983).

partner's or parents' support. Yet most women who appraise abortion differently do not experience severe distress after abortion (Adler & others, 1990; Major & others, 1990; Russo, 1992). The events of our lives flow through a psychological filter. Stress arises less from events per se than from how we appraise them.

Daily Hassles

As we noted earlier, our happiness stems less from enduring good fortune than from our response to daily events—a longed-for date, a gratifying letter, your team's winning the big game.

The principle works for negative events, too. Everyday annoyances may be the most significant sources of stress (Kohn & Macdonald, 1992; Lazarus, 1990; Ruffin, 1993). These daily hassles include rush-hour traffic, aggravating housemates, long lines at the bank or store, too many things to do, and misplacing things. Although some people can simply shrug them off, others are "driven up the wall" by such inconveniences. Thus, 6 in 10 people say they feel "great stress" at least once a week (Harris, 1987).

Over time, these little stressors can add up and take a toll on health and well-being. Among urban ghetto residents, many of whom endure the daily stresses that accompany poverty, unemployment, solo parenting, and overcrowding, hypertension (elevated blood pressure) rates are high. And from 1990 to 1993, following the collapse of socialism in the former Soviet Union, Russia experienced mushrooming divorce, murder, suicide, and rates of stress-related disease. During that period, life expectancy for Russian men plummeted nearly 5 years, to 58.9 years (Holden, 1996). In contrast to these high-stress groups, there is a *low* rate of heart attacks among those who live the relatively peaceful monastic life (Henry & Stephens, 1977).

Perceived Control

Catastrophes, important life changes, and daily hassles and conflicts are especially stressful when we appraise them as both negative *and* uncontrollable. Perceiving a loss of control, we are vulnerable to ill health. Elderly nursing home patients who have little perceived control over their activities tend to decline faster and die sooner than do those given more control over their activities (Rodin, 1986). Given control over their work environments—by being able to adjust office furnishings and control interruptions and distractions—workers, too, experience less stress (O'Neill, 1993).

A related factor that influences our stress vulnerability is optimism. Psychologists Michael Scheier and Charles Carver (1992) report that optimists—people who agree with statements such as, "In uncertain times, I usually expect the best"—cope better with stressful events and enjoy better health. During the last month of a semester, students previously identified as optimistic report less fatigue and fewer coughs, aches, and pains. Optimists also respond to stress with smaller increases in blood pressure, and they recover faster from heart bypass surgery. One study that followed 2428 middle-aged Finnish men for up to 10 years discovered that the number of deaths among men with a bleak, hopeless outlook was more than double that found among their optimistic counterparts (Figure 10.16).

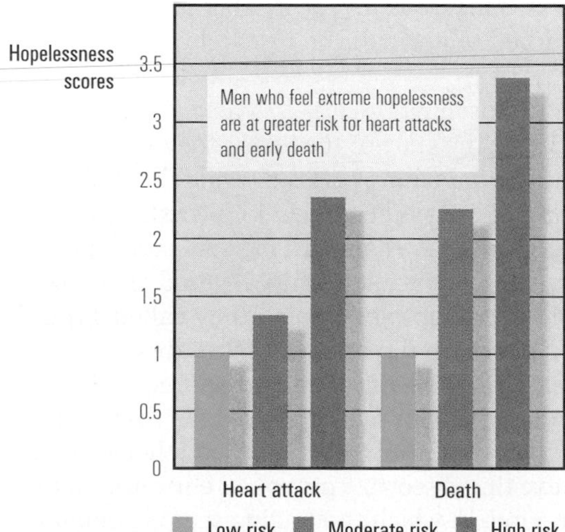

Figure 10.16 Toxic hopelessness Compared with Finnish middle-aged men scoring low in hopelessness, those scoring high were 2 to 4 times more vulnerable to a heart attack over the ensuing six years and 3 to 4 times more likely to die. (Data from Everson & others, 1996)

Why do perceived loss of control and pessimism predict health problems? Animal studies show—and human studies confirm—that losing control provokes an outpouring of stress hormones. When rats cannot control shock or when humans feel unable to control their environment, cortisol levels rise and immune responses drop (Rodin, 1986). Captive animals therefore experience more stress and are more vulnerable to disease than are wild animals (Roberts, 1988). The crowding that occurs in high-density neighborhoods, prisons, and

coronary heart disease the clogging of the vessels that nourish the heart muscle; the leading cause of death in the United States.

Type A Friedman and Rosenman's term for competitive, hard-driving, impatient, verbally aggressive, and anger-prone people.

Type B Friedman and Rosenman's term for easygoing, relaxed people.

psychophysiological illness literally, "mind-body" illness; any stress-related physical illness, such as hypertension and headaches.

college dorms is another source of diminished feelings of control—and of increased levels of stress hormones and blood pressure (Fleming & others, 1987; Ostfeld & others, 1987).

Stress and Heart Disease

11. *Who is most vulnerable to heart disease?*

Although infrequent before the twentieth century, **coronary heart disease**—the clogging of the vessels that nourish the heart muscle—became by the 1950s North America's leading cause of death. In addition to family history of the disease, many behavioral and physiological factors increase the risk of heart disease—smoking, obesity, a high-fat diet, physical inactivity, elevated blood pressure, and elevated cholesterol level. The psychological factors of stress and personality also play a big role.

In 1956, cardiologists Meyer Friedman, Ray Rosenman, and their colleagues stumbled upon an indication of how big a role (Friedman & Ulmer, 1984). While studying the eating behavior of white, San Francisco Junior League women and their husbands, Friedman and Rosenman discovered that the women consumed as much cholesterol and fat as their husbands did, yet they were far less susceptible to heart disease. Was it because of their female sex hormones? No, the researchers surmised, because African-American women with the same sex hormones but facing more stress are as prone to heart disease as their husbands are.

The Junior League president thought she knew the answer. "If you really want to know what is going to give our husbands heart attacks, I'll tell you. It's stress," she said sadly, "the stress they have to face in their businesses, day in, day out. Why, when my husband comes home at night, it takes at least one martini just to unclench his jaws."

To test the idea that stress increases vulnerability to heart disease, Friedman and Rosenman measured the blood cholesterol level and clotting speed of 40 tax accountants. From January through March, both of these coronary warning indicators were completely normal. Then, as the accountants began scrambling to finish their clients' tax returns before the April 15 filing deadline, their cholesterol and clotting measures rose to dangerous levels. In May and June, with the deadline past, the measures returned to normal. The researchers' hunch had paid off: Stress predicted heart attack risk.

The stage was set for Friedman and Rosenman's classic 9-year study of more than 3000 healthy men aged 35 to 59. At the start of the study, they interviewed each man for 15 minutes about his work and eating habits. During the interview, they noted the man's manner of talking and other behavioral patterns. Those who seemed the most reactive, competitive, hard-driving, impatient, time-conscious, supermotivated, verbally aggressive, and easily angered they called **Type A**. A roughly equal number who were more easygoing they called **Type B**. Which group do you suppose turned out to be the most coronary-prone?

In both India and America, Type A bus drivers are literally hard-driving: They brake, pass, and honk their horns more often than their more easygoing Type B colleagues (Evans & others, 1987).

By the time the study was complete, 257 of the men had suffered heart attacks, 69 percent of whom were Type A. Moreover, not one of the "pure" Type Bs—the most mellow and laid-back of their group—had suffered a heart attack.

As often happens in science, this exciting discovery provoked enormous public interest. But after the honeymoon period, in which the finding seemed definitive and revolutionary, other researchers began asking, Is the finding reliable? If so, what is the toxic component of the Type A profile: The time-consciousness? The competitiveness? The anger?

Why may Type A people be more prone to heart disease? Further research found that reactive Type A individuals are more often "combat ready." When harassed

Bannerman © 7/94.

"The fire you kindle for your enemy often burns you more than him."

Chinese proverb

or challenged, their active sympathetic nervous system redistributes bloodflow to the muscles and away from the internal organs such as the liver, which removes cholesterol and fat from the blood. Thus, their blood may contain excess cholesterol and fat that later deposit around the heart. Further stress—sometimes conflicts triggered by their own abrasiveness—may trigger the altered heart rhythms that, in those with weakened hearts, can cause sudden death (Kamarck & Jennings, 1991). In such ways, the hearts and minds of people interact.

Newer research reveals that the Type A's toxic core is not a fast-paced life but rather negative emotions—especially the anger associated with an aggressively reactive temperament (Miller & others, 1996; Williams, 1993). The effect of an anger-prone personality appears most noticeably in studies in which interviewers assess verbal assertiveness and emotional intensity. (If you pause in the middle of a sentence, an intense, anger-prone person may jump in and finish it for you.) Among young and middle-aged adults, those who react with anger over little things are the most coronary-prone. One study followed Duke University law students over 25 years. Those inclined to be hostile and cynical were five times more likely than their gentler, trusting classmates to die by middle age (Williams, 1989). As Charles Spielberger and Perry London (1982) put it, rage "seems to lash back and strike us in the heart muscle."

Anger isn't the only toxic emotion. Depression, too, can be lethal. Centers for Disease Control researchers studied adults who were feeling a sense of hopelessness or at least mild depression. Compared with those without such feelings, these downhearted people were more vulnerable to heart disease in the ensuing 12 years. This was true even after controlling for differences in age, sex, smoking, and other factors linked to heart ailments (Anda & others, 1993). In the years following a heart attack, depressed people have a quadrupled risk of further heart problems (Pratt & others, 1996; Frasure-Smith & others, 1995). The depression that follows a spouse's death also increases one's risk of having a heart attack or stroke (National Academy of Sciences, 1984).

The toxic effects of negative emotions help explain why about a quarter of medical inpatients suffer a mood or anxiety disorder, and why 4 in 10 chronically ill patients suffer or have suffered a psychiatric disorder (Cohen & Rodriguez, 1995; Katon & Sullivan, 1990). Negative emotions have physical consequences, and they may also lead to poor health practices and health-related decisions.

Stress and Susceptibility to Disease

12. How does stress make us vulnerable to disease?

Not so long ago, the term *psychosomatic* described psychologically caused physical symptoms. To laypeople, the term implied that the symptoms were unreal—they were "merely" psychosomatic. To avoid such connotations and to better describe the genuine physiological effects of psychological states, most experts today refer instead to **psychophysiological illnesses**. These illnesses, which include certain forms of hypertension and headaches, are stress-related. A person under stress may retain excess sodium and fluids, which, together with constriction of the arteries' muscle walls, contributes to increased blood pressure (Light & others, 1983).

Stress and the Immune System

Evidence that psychophysiological ailments are real comes from hundreds of new experiments that reveal the nervous and endocrine systems' influence on the immune system. The immune system is a complex surveillance system that

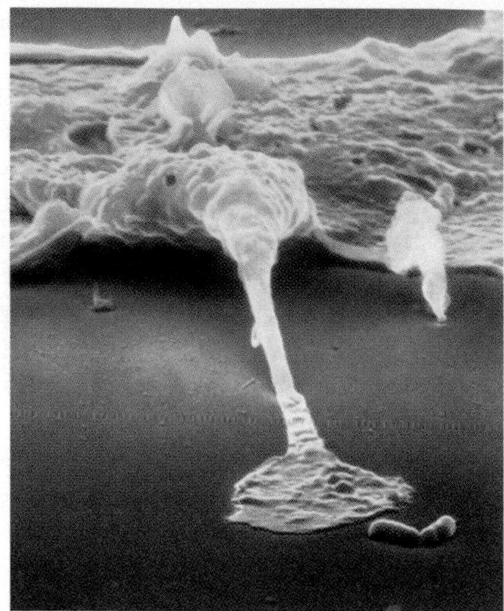

The immune system in action A large macrophage (at top) is about to trap and ingest a tiny bacterium (lower right). Macrophages constantly patrol the body in search of invaders, such as this *Escherichia coli* bacterium, and for debris, such as worn-out red blood cells.

defends the body by isolating and destroying bacteria, viruses, and other foreign substances. It includes two types of white blood cells, called **lymphocytes**. *B lymphocytes* form in the *b*one marrow and release antibodies that fight bacterial infections. *T lymphocytes* form in the *t*hymus and other lymphatic tissue and attack cancer cells, viruses, and foreign substances—even "good" ones, such as transplanted organs. Another agent of the immune system is the *macrophage* ("big eater"), which identifies, pursues, and ingests harmful invaders. Age, nutrition, genetics, body temperature, and stress all influence the immune system's activity.

The immune system can err in two directions. Responding too strongly, it may attack the body's own tissues, causing arthritis or an allergic reaction. Or it may underreact, allowing, say, a dormant herpes virus to erupt or cancer cells to multiply. Women are immunologically stronger than men (Morell, 1995). This makes them less susceptible to infections. But it also makes them more susceptible to self-attacking diseases, such as lupus and multiple sclerosis.

The immune system is not a headless horseman. Rather, it exchanges information with the brain and the hormone-secreting endocrine system. The brain regulates the secretion of stress hormones, which in turn suppress the disease-fighting lymphocytes. Thus, when animals are physically restrained, given unavoidable electric shocks, or subjected to noise, crowding, cold water, social defeat, or maternal separation, their immune systems become less active (Maier & others, 1994). One study monitored immune responses in 43 monkeys over 6 months (Cohen & others, 1992). Twenty-one were stressed by being housed with new roommates—three or four new monkeys—each month. (To empathize with the monkeys, recall the stress of leaving home to attend school or summer camp, and imagine having to repeat this experience weekly.) Compared with monkeys left in stable groups, the socially disrupted monkeys experienced weakened immune systems.

Does stress similarly suppress the immune system of humans? Consider:

The immune system is not a headless horseman. Rather, it exchanges information with the brain and the hormone-secreting endocrine system.

- Accumulating evidence shows that stress lowers the body's resistance to upper respiratory infections as well as to herpes (Cohen, 1996).
- In three separate *Skylab* missions, the immune systems of the astronauts showed reduced effectiveness immediately after the stress of reentry and splashdown (Kimzey, 1975; Kimzey & others, 1976).
- Marital spats are not good for health. As 90 healthy newlywed couples spent a half hour discussing problem areas in their marriage, some became angrier than others—and suffered more immune system suppression during the next day (Kiecolt-Glaser & others, 1993).
- Students' disease-fighting mechanisms are weaker during high-stress times, such as exam weeks, and on days when they are upset (Jemmott & Magloire, 1988; Stone & others, 1987). In one experiment, a stressful experience increased the severity of symptoms experienced by volunteers who were knowingly infected with a cold virus (Dixon, 1986). In another, 47 percent of subjects living stress-filled lives developed colds after a virus was dropped in their noses, but only 27 percent of those living relatively free of stress caught colds (Cohen & others, 1991, 1993, 1995).
- The National Academy of Sciences (1984) reports that the grief and depression that follow the death of a spouse decrease immune defenses (which helps explain the increase in disease among those recently widowed). In fact, depression of any sort tends to suppress the immune system (Herbert & Cohen, 1993; Weisse, 1992). Thus, in one study of leukemia patients preparing to undergo bone marrow transplants, 12 of 13 depressed patients died within a year. Among the many more who were not depressed, 39 percent were still alive after two years (Colon & others, 1991).

"When the heart is at ease, the body is healthy."

Chinese proverb

lymphocytes the two types of white blood cells that are part of the body's immune system: *B lymphocytes* form in the *b*one marrow and release antibodies that fight bacterial infections; *T lymphocytes* form in the *t*hymus and, among other duties, attack cancer cells, viruses, and foreign substances.

Supporting survival Can support groups help reduce emotional distress? Can they delay the course of cancer? One experiment has suggested that they can. Other research, currently under way, will reveal whether this finding is replicable.

The stress effect on immunity makes physiological sense (Maier & others, 1994). Stress, as we have seen, involves an aroused fight-or-flight response. Stress diverts energy to the muscles and brain, mobilizing the body for action. The immune response to disease is a competing energy system. It takes energy to fight infections, produce inflammations, and maintain fevers. Thus, when diseased, the body reduces muscular energy output by inactivity and increased sleep. Stress diverts energy from the disease-fighting system, rendering the person more vulnerable to illness.

Stress and Cancer

Stress and negative emotions such as depression also have been linked to cancer. To explore a possible connection between stress and cancer, experimenters have implanted tumor cells into rodents or given them cancer-producing substances. Those rodents also exposed to uncontrollable stress, such as inescapable shocks, are more prone to cancer (Sklar & Anisman, 1981). With their immune systems weakened by stress, their tumors developed sooner and grew larger.

Several investigators have reported that people, too, are at increased risk for cancer a year or so after experiencing depression, helplessness, or bereavement. For example, cancer occurs more often than usual among those widowed, divorced, or separated. One study of the husbands of women with terminal breast cancer pinpointed a possible reason: During the first 2 months after their wives' deaths, the bereaved men's lymphocyte responses dropped (Schleifer & others, 1979).

Another study gave a personality test to 2018 middle-aged men employed by the Western Electric Company in 1958. During the next 20 years, 7 percent of those not depressed and 12 percent of those somewhat depressed died of cancer (Persky & others, 1987). A large Swedish study revealed that people with a history of workplace stress had a 5.5 times greater risk of colon cancer than those who reported no such problems (Courtney & others, 1993). In both these studies, the cancer difference was not attributable to differences in age, smoking, drinking, or physical characteristics.

What is more, ever-nice cancer patients who bottle up their negative emotions have less chance of survival than do those who verbalize their feelings (O'Leary, 1990; Temoshok, 1992). A UCLA survey of 649 cancer specialists, who had treated more than 100,000 cancer patients, supported the idea that patients' attitudes matter. Four in five of these physicians rated "a positive approach to the challenge of the illness" and a "strong will to live" as important contributors to longevity (Cousins, 1989).

"A cheerful heart is a good medicine, but a downcast spirit dries up the bones."

Proverbs 17:22

In the first weeks after receiving their diagnosis, cancer patients and those carrying the AIDS virus are understandably anxious and depressed (Andersen, 1989; Antoni & others, 1991). Might promoting their fighting spirit aid their survival? Can hope boost the body by alleviating negative emotions that suppress the cancer-fighting immune system?

With cancer patients, several studies suggest yes. Mastectomy patients who display a determination to conquer their breast cancer survive longer than do those who are stoic or feel hopeless (Hall & Goldstein, 1986; Pettingale & others, 1985). A study of 86 women undergoing breast cancer therapy at Stanford University Medical School found that those who participated in weekly group therapy survived an average of 37 months, double the 19-month average survival rate among the randomly assigned nonparticipants (Spiegel & others, 1989). The investigator, psychiatrist David Spiegel (1993), was stunned. He expected the support groups to alleviate cancer-related emotional distress, but he was intending to show that more positive emotions would not influence the course of cancer. At least half a dozen research teams are now repeating his

"I didn't give myself cancer."

Mayor Barbara Boggs Sigmund
Princeton, New Jersey
1939–1990

study. If Spiegel's finding proves reliable, it will surely reinforce efforts to train physicians to communicate with patients in ways that minimize resignation and sustain hope.

One danger in publicizing reports on attitudes and cancer is that they may lead some patients to blame themselves for their cancer—"If only I had been more expressive, relaxed, and hopeful." A corollary danger is a "wellness macho" among the healthy, who credit their health to their healthy character and lay a guilt trip on the ill: "She has cancer? That's what you get for holding your feelings in and being so nice." Dying thus becomes the ultimate failure.

In noting the link between emotions and cancer, we must remember that stress does not create cancer cells. Rather, it affects their growth by weakening the body's natural defenses against a few proliferating, malignant cells. Although a relaxed, hopeful state may enhance these defenses, we must be aware of the thin line that divides science from wishful thinking. The physiological processes at work in advanced cancer or AIDS are not likely to be derailed by avoiding stress or by a relaxed but determined spirit (Kessler & others, 1991).

We must also remember that our emotional reactivity is partly inherited (recall page 93). As theologian Reinhold Niebuhr recognized in his "serenity prayer," we do well to accept those things about ourselves that we cannot change, to change those things that we can, and to seek wisdom to discern the difference. By studying the interplay among emotions, the brain, and the immune system, health psychologists seek the wisdom needed to distinguish between pseudoscientific hocus-pocus and the genuine effects of emotions on health.

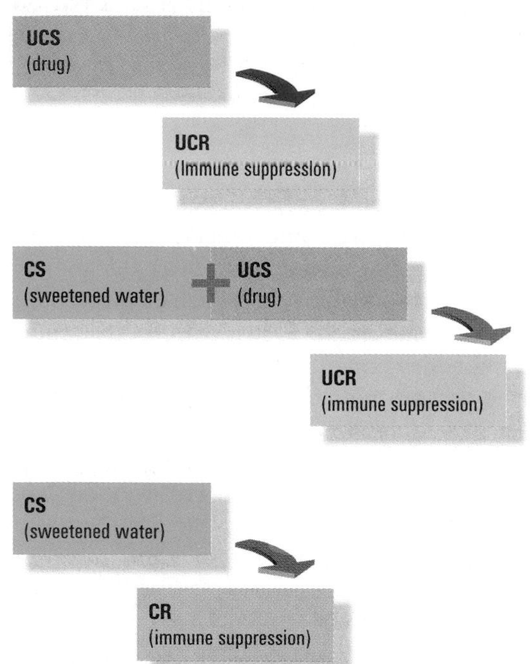

Figure 10.17 **The conditioning of immune suppression** After Ader and Cohen associated sweetened water with a drug that causes immune suppression in rats, the inert substance alone triggered the conditioned immune response.

Conditioning the Immune System

A hay fever sufferer sees the flower on the restaurant table and, not realizing it is plastic, begins to sneeze. Such experiences hint that stress is not the only psychological influence on the body's ailments. Simple classical conditioning may be an added influence. This raises an intriguing question: If conditioning affects the body's overt physiological responses, might it affect the immune system as well?

Psychologist Robert Ader and immunologist Nicholas Cohen (1985) discovered that the answer is yes. Ader came upon this discovery while researching taste aversion in rats. He paired the rats' drinking of saccharin-sweetened water with injections of a drug that happened to suppress immune functioning. After repeated pairings, sweetened water alone triggered immune suppression, as if the drug had been given (Figure 10.17). Such conditioned immune suppression can triple an animal's likelihood of growing a tumor when fed a carcinogen (Blom & others, 1995).

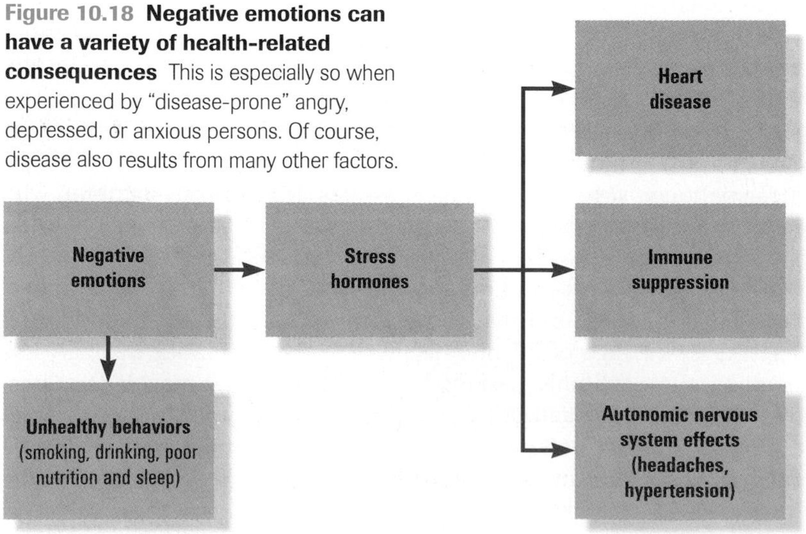

Many questions about the role of the immune system and how to harness its healing potential remain unanswered. If it is possible to condition the immune system's suppression, should it not also be possible to condition its enhancement? Might this be one way in which placebos—treatments that have no biochemical effect—promote healing? Can a placebo sometimes elicit the same healthful state produced by an actual drug? Research now under way may soon answer such questions.

For now, we can view the toll that stress sometimes takes on our resistance to disease (Figure 10.18) as a price we pay for the adaptive benefits of stress. Stress invigorates our lives by arousing and motivating us. An unstressed life would hardly be challenging or productive. Moreover, spending our resources in fighting or fleeing an external threat aids our immediate survival. But it does so at the cost of diminished resources for fighting internal threats to our body's health. When the stress is

Figure 10.18 **Negative emotions can have a variety of health-related consequences** This is especially so when experienced by "disease-prone" angry, depressed, or anxious persons. Of course, disease also results from many other factors.

Negative emotions
Stress hormones
Heart disease
Immune suppression
Autonomic nervous system effects (headaches, hypertension)
Unhealthy behaviors (smoking, drinking, poor nutrition and sleep)

momentary, the cost is negligible. When uncontrollable aggravations persist, however, the cost may become considerable.

This new research provides yet another reminder of one of contemporary psychology's overriding themes: *Mind and body interact continuously—everything psychological is simultaneously physiological.* Because psychological states are physiological events, they influence other parts of our physiological system. Just *thinking* about biting into an orange section—the sweet, tangy juice from the pulpy fruit flooding across your tongue—can trigger salivation. As the Indian sage Santi Parva recognized more than 4000 years ago, "Mental disorders arise from physical causes, and likewise physical disorders arise from mental causes."

REHEARSE IT!

14. The physiologist Walter Cannon described the role of the sympathetic nervous system in preparing the body for fight or flight. Hans Selye extended Cannon's findings by describing the body's adaptive response to stress in general. Selye's general adaptation syndrome (GAS) consists of an alarm reaction followed by

a. fight or flight.
b. resistance and exhaustion.
c. challenge and recovery.
d. stressful life events.

15. In the months following a catastrophe, such as an earthquake or a nuclear accident, there is a higher than usual number of short-term illnesses and stress-related psychological disorders. Following widowhood, there is an increased risk of illness and death. These findings suggest that

a. daily hassles have adverse health consequences.
b. experiencing a very stressful event increases one's vulnerability to illness and death.
c. the amount of stress felt is directly related to the number of stressors involved.
d. having a negative outlook has an adverse effect on recovery from illness.

16. Stressors are events that we appraise as threatening or challenging. Research suggests that the most significant sources of stress are

a. catastrophes.
b. traumatic events, such as the loss of a loved one.
c. daily hassles.
d. threatening events that we witness.

17. The stress we experience depends on how we perceive the events of our lives. A person (or animal) is most likely to find an event stressful and to suffer reduced immunity and other adverse health effects if the event seems

a. painful or harmful.
b. predictable and negative.
c. uncontrollable and negative.
d. both repellent and attractive.

18. Cardiologists Meyer Friedman, Ray Rosenman, and their colleagues observed that heart attacks were more frequent in Type A men—in those who appeared to be hard-driving, verbally aggressive, and anger-prone. The component of Type A behavior linked most closely to coronary heart disease is

a. living a fast-paced life-style.
b. working in a competitive area.
c. meeting deadlines and challenges.
d. feeling angry and negative much of the time.

19. Evidence suggests that disease-fighting mechanisms are weakened during times of high stress, for example, following the death of a loved one. Stress hormones suppress the lymphocytes, which ordinarily attack bacteria, viruses, cancer cells, and other foreign substances. The stress hormones are released mainly in response to a signal from the

a. lymphocytes and macrophages.
b. brain.
c. upper respiratory tract.
d. adrenal glands.

20. Research has shown people are at increased risk for cancer a year or so after experiencing depression, helplessness, or bereavement. In describing this link between emotions and cancer, researchers are quick to point out that

a. accumulated stress that is not relieved by positive emotions poses the greatest threat to people who are genetically vulnerable to cancer.
b. anger is the negative emotion most closely linked to cancer.
c. stress does not create cancer cells, but it weakens the body's natural defenses against them.
d. feeling optimistic about chances of survival ensures that a cancer patient will get well.

21. In testing taste aversion in rats, researchers paired the rats' drinking of saccharin-sweetened water with injections of a drug that suppressed immune functioning. After repeated pairings, sweetened water *alone* triggered immune suppression. These results suggest that

a. the immune system is under the direct control of the hypothalamus.
b. classical conditioning may influence the body's ailments.
c. placebos are as effective as actual drugs in treating the body's ailments.
d. external threats diminish our body's ability to fight internal threats.

aerobic exercise sustained exercise that increases heart and lung fitness; may also alleviate depression and anxiety.

biofeedback a system for electronically recording, amplifying, and feeding back information regarding a subtle physiological state, such as blood pressure or muscle tension.

Promoting Health

Traditionally, people have sought out medical doctors for the diagnosis and treatment of disease. That, say health psychologists, is like ignoring a car's maintenance and going to a mechanic only when the car breaks down. Now that we realize that our attitudes and behaviors affect our health, attention is focusing more and more on health maintenance—on ways of coping with stress, preventing illness, and promoting well-being.

Coping With Stress

13. ***How do people cope with stress, and what stress management techniques are effective?***

Coping with stress can mean confronting or escaping the problem and taking steps to prevent its recurrence. Coping can involve fight or flight, repelling the challenge or avoiding it, solving the problem or mentally distancing oneself from it. Yet stressors are an unavoidable part of life. This fact, coupled with the growing awareness that recurring stress correlates with heart disease, lowered immunity, and other bodily ailments, gives us a clear message. If the stress cannot be eliminated by changing or ignoring the situation, we had best learn to manage it. Stress management includes aerobic exercise, biofeedback, relaxation, and social support.

Now that we realize that our attitudes and behaviors affect our health, attention is focusing more and more on health maintenance—on ways of coping with stress, preventing illness, and promoting well-being.

Aerobic Exercise

Aerobic exercise is sustained exercise that increases heart and lung fitness. Clearly, such exercise strengthens the body. Does it also boost the spirit?

Exercise and Mood

Many studies suggest that aerobic exercise can reduce stress, depression, and anxiety. One-third of U.S. adults exercise regularly, and studies indicate that they also cope better with stressful events, exhibit more self-confidence, and are less often depressed than those who exercise less (Brown, 1991; Hogan, 1989; *Prevention*, 1995). But if we state this observation the other way around—that stressed and depressed people exercise less—cause and effect become unclear.

Experiments resolve the ambiguity by randomly assigning stressed, depressed, or anxious people either to aerobic exercise treatments or to other treatments. In one such experiment, Lisa McCann and David Holmes (1984) assigned one-third of a group of mildly depressed female college students to a program of aerobic exercise and another third to a treatment of relaxation exercises; the remaining third, a control group, received no treatment. As Figure 10.19 shows, 10 weeks later the women in the aerobic exercise program reported the greatest decrease in depression. Many of them had, quite literally, run away from their troubles.

More than 100 other studies confirm that exercise reduces depression and anxiety (Long & van Stavel, 1995; Petruzzello & others, 1991; Scott & Pepperell, 1992). Repeated surveys, some by government health agencies, reveal that Canadians and Americans are more self-confident, self-disciplined, and psychologically resilient if physically fit (Stephens,

"Is there anyone here who specializes in stress management?"

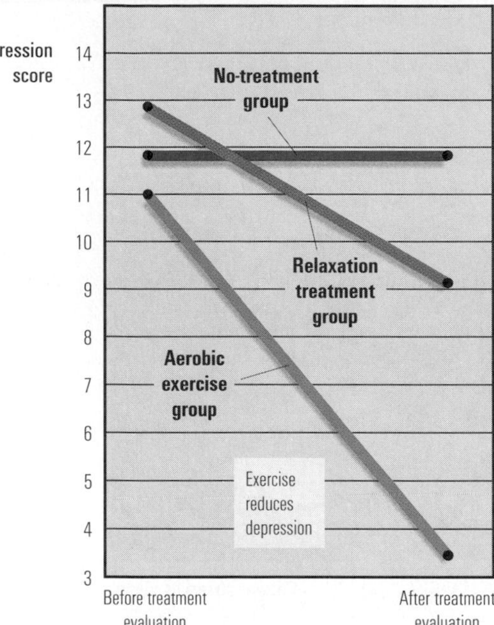

Figure 10.19 Aerobic exercise and depression Mildly depressed college women who participated in an aerobic exercise program showed markedly reduced depression, compared with those who did relaxation exercises or received no treatment. (From McCann & Holmes, 1984)

1988). Even a 10-minute walk stimulates 2 hours of increased well-being by raising energy levels and lowering tension (Thayer, 1987, 1993).

Researchers are now wondering *why* aerobic exercise alleviates the effects of stress and negative emotions. They know that exercise strengthens the heart, increases blood volume, and lowers both blood pressure and the blood pressure reaction to stress (Perkins & others, 1986; Roviario & others, 1984). Exercise also orders up chemicals from our body's internal pharmacy by increasing production of mood-boosting neurotransmitters such as norepinephrine, serotonin, and the endorphins. Perhaps the emotional benefits of exercise are a side effect of increased body arousal and warmth or of the muscle relaxation and sounder sleep that occur afterward. Or perhaps a sense of accomplishment and an improved physique enhance one's emotional state.

Exercise and Health

Other research reveals that exercise also benefits health.

- One 16-year study of 17,000 middle-aged Harvard alumni found that those who exercised regularly were likely to live longer (Paffenbarger & others, 1986).
- A study of 15,000 Control Data Corporation employees found that those who exercised had 25 percent fewer hospital days than those who did not (Anderson & Jose, 1987).
- A digest of data from 43 studies revealed that, compared with inactive adults, people who exercise suffer half as many heart attacks (Powell & others, 1987). Exercise makes the muscles hungry for the "bad fats" that contribute to clogged arteries (Barinaga, 1997).
- A review of 200 studies reveals that exercise modestly enhances cognitive abilities such as reasoning and memory (Etnier & others, 1997).

By one estimate, moderate exercise adds two years to one's expected life. "Perhaps God does not subtract the time spent exercising from your allotted time on earth," jests Martin Seligman (1994, p. 193). The "mood boost" is reaping dividends. Off your duffs, couch potatoes.

The mood boost Aerobic exercise such as jogging appears to counteract depression partly by increasing arousal (replacing depression's low-arousal state) and by doing naturally what Prozac does—increasing the brain's serotonin activity. (Jacobs, 1994)

Biofeedback and Relaxation

When a few psychologists started experimenting with ways to train people to bring their heart rate and blood pressure under conscious control, many of their colleagues thought them foolish. These functions are, after all, controlled by the autonomic ("involuntary") nervous system. Then, in the late 1960s, experiments by respected psychologists began to make the doubters wonder. Neal Miller, for one, found that rats could modify their heartbeat if given pleasurable brain stimulation when their heartbeat increased or decreased. Later research revealed that some paralyzed humans could also learn to control their blood pressure (Miller & Brucker, 1979).

Miller was experimenting with **biofeedback**, a system of recording, amplifying, and feeding back information about subtle physiological responses. Biofeedback instruments have been likened to a mirror (Norris, 1986). The instruments no more control one's body than a mirror combs one's hair. Rather,

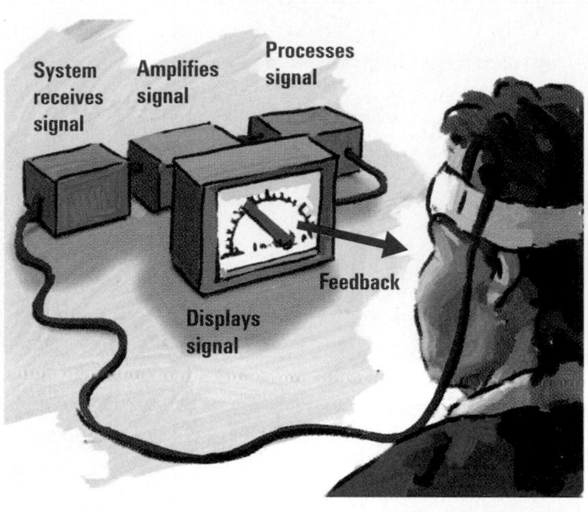

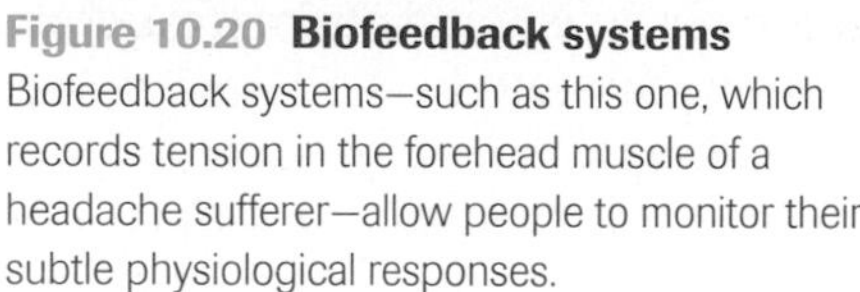

Figure 10.20 Biofeedback systems
Biofeedback systems—such as this one, which records tension in the forehead muscle of a headache sufferer—allow people to monitor their subtle physiological responses.

by reflecting the results of a person's own efforts, they allow the person to assess which techniques are most effective in controlling a particular physiological response.

In the example in Figure 10.20, a sensor records tension in the forehead muscle of a headache sufferer. A computer processes this physiological information and instantly feeds it back to the person in some easily understood signal. As the person relaxes the forehead muscle, the pointer on the display screen (or in some systems, an audible tone) may go lower. The patient's task is to learn to control the pointer or the tone and thereby learn to control the tension in the forehead muscle and the accompanying headaches.

If relaxation is an important part of biofeedback, then might relaxation exercises alone be a natural antidote to stress?

Initially, biofeedback researchers and practitioners reported that people could learn to increase their production of alpha brain waves, warm their hands, and lower their blood pressure—all signs of a more relaxed state. These studies triggered both excitement and some 4000 studies, including more than 400 in Russia alone (Sokhadze & Shtark, 1991). After a decade of study, researchers stepped back to assess the results and decided the initial claims for biofeedback were overblown and oversold (Miller, 1985). Biofeedback does enable some people to influence their finger temperature and forehead-muscle tension, and it can help somewhat in reducing the intensity of migraine headaches and chronic pain (King & Montgomery, 1980; Qualls & Sheehan, 1981; Turk & others, 1979). (Biofeedback works best on tension headaches, declared a 1995 National Institutes of Health panel.) But other, simpler methods of relaxation, which require no expensive equipment, produce many of the same benefits.

Learning the "relaxation response" Relaxation training is a component of many stress-reduction programs. At Boston's Deaconess Hospital, hypertension patients learn meditation techniques that counteract stress.

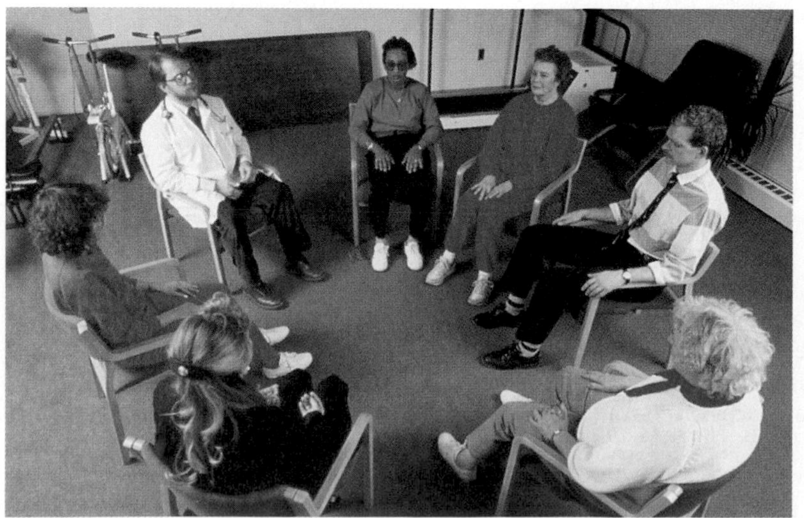

If relaxation is an important part of biofeedback, then might relaxation exercises alone be a natural antidote to stress? Cardiologist Herbert Benson (1976 to 1996) became intrigued with this possibility when he found that experienced meditators could decrease their blood pressure, heart rate, and oxygen consumption and raise their fingertip temperature. You can experience the essence of this *relaxation response*, as Benson calls it, right now: Assume a comfortable position, breathe deeply, and relax your muscles from foot to face. Now, concentrate on a single word or a phrase. (About 80

Meditation—a modern phenomenon with a long history: "Sit down alone and in silence. Lower your head, shut your eyes, breathe out gently, and imagine yourself looking into your own heart. . . . As you breathe out, say 'Lord Jesus Christ, have mercy on me'. . . . Try to put all other thoughts aside. Be calm, be patient and repeat the process very frequently."

Gregory of Sinai
Died 1346

percent of Benson's patients choose to focus on a favorite prayer.) Close your eyes and let other thoughts drift away when they intrude as you repeat your phrase continually for 10 to 20 minutes. Simply by setting aside a quiet time or two each day, many people report enjoying greater tranquility. Stress worsens pain, infertility, and insomnia, and it also suppresses the immune system. Meditative relaxation counteracts all these effects, Benson reports. One astonishing study assigned 73 residents of homes for the elderly either to daily meditation or to none. After 3 years, one-fourth of the nonmeditators had died, while all the meditators were still alive (Alexander & others, 1989).

If Type A heart attack victims could be taught to relax, might their risk of another attack be reduced? To find out, Meyer Friedman and his colleagues randomly assigned hundreds of middle-aged heart attack survivors in San Francisco to one of two groups. The first group received standard advice from cardiologists concerning medications, diet, and exercise habits. The second group received similar advice plus continuing support and counseling on life-style modification—how to slow down and relax by walking, talking, and eating more slowly; by smiling at others and laughing at themselves; by admitting mistakes; by taking time to enjoy life; and by renewing their religious faith. As Figure 10.21 indicates, during the ensuing 3 years, the second group experienced half as many repeat heart attacks as the first group. This, wrote the exuberant Friedman, is an unprecedented, spectacular reduction in heart attack recurrence. A smaller-scale British study similarly divided heart attack–prone people into control and life-style-modification groups (Eysenck & Grossarth-Maticek, 1991). During the next 13 years, it also found a 50 percent reduction in death rate among those trained to alter their thinking and life-style.

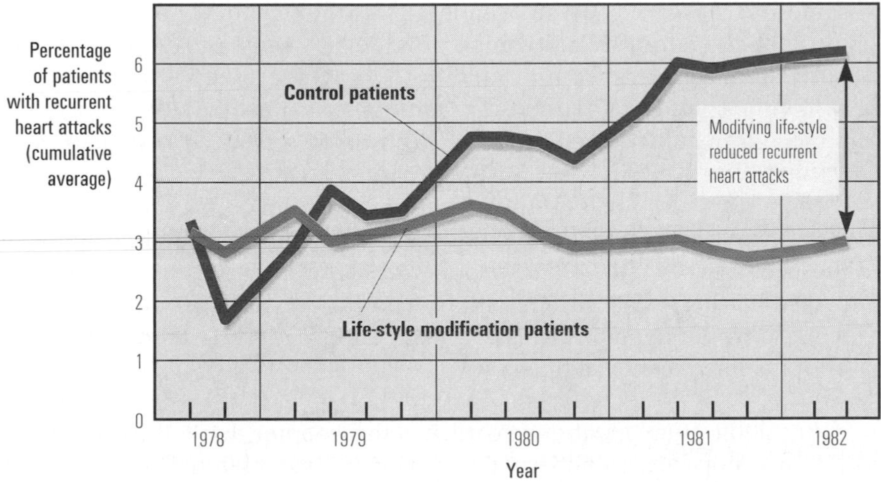

Figure 10.21 Recurrent heart attacks and life-style modification The San Francisco Recurrent Coronary Prevention Project offered heart attack survivors counseling from a cardiologist. Those who were also guided in modifying their Type A life-style suffered fewer repeat heart attacks. (From Friedman & Ulmer, 1984)

Social Support

Linda and Emily had much in common. When interviewed for a study conducted by UCLA social psychologist Shelley Taylor (1989), both Los Angeles women had married, raised three children, suffered comparable breast tumors, and recovered from surgery and 6 months of chemotherapy. But there was a difference. Linda, a widow in her early fifties, was living alone, her children scattered in Atlanta, Boston, and Europe. "She had become odd in ways that people sometimes do when they are isolated," reported Taylor. "Having no one with whom to share her thoughts on a daily basis, she unloaded them somewhat inappropriately with strangers, including our interviewer."

Interviewing Emily was difficult in a different way. Phone calls interrupted. Her children, all living nearby, were in and out of the house, dropping things off with a quick kiss. Her husband called from his office for a brief chat. Two dogs roamed the house, greeting visitors enthusiastically. All in all, Emily "seemed a serene and contented person, basking in the warmth of her family."

Humans aren't the only source of stress-buffering comfort. After stressful events, Medicare patients who have a dog or other companionable pet are less likely to visit their doctor (Siegel, 1990).

Three years later, the researchers tried to reinterview the women. Linda, they learned, had died 2 years before. Emily was still lovingly supported by her family and friends and was as happy and healthy as ever.

Because no two cancers are identical, we can't be certain that different social situations led to Linda's and Emily's fates. But they do illustrate a conclusion drawn from several large studies: Social support—feeling liked, affirmed, and encouraged by intimate friends and family—promotes happiness and health.

If this result seems obvious, imagine why close relationships could contribute to *illness*. Relationships are often fraught with stress, especially in crowded living conditions lacking privacy (Evans & others, 1989). "Hell is others," wrote Jean-Paul Sartre. Peter Warr and Roy Payne (1982) at the University of Sheffield asked a representative sample of British adults what, if anything, had emotionally strained them the day before. "Family" was their most frequent answer. Even when well-meaning, family intrusions can be stressful. And stress, as we have seen, contributes to heart disease, hypertension, and a suppressed immune system.

Social support—feeling liked, affirmed, and encouraged by intimate friends and family—promotes happiness and health.

On balance, however, close relationships more often contribute to health and happiness. Asked what prompted yesterday's times of pleasure, the same British sample, by an even larger margin, again answered "family." For most of us, family relationships provide not only our greatest heartaches but also our greatest comfort and joy. No wonder people with few close ties to family, friends, and groups are almost twice as likely to come down with a cold after being experimentally exposed to a cold virus (Cohen & others, 1997).

"Woe to one who is alone and falls and does not have another to help."

Ecclesiastes 4:10

Moreover, seven massive investigations, each following thousands of people for several years, reveal that close relationships affect health. Compared with those having few social ties, people are less likely to die prematurely if supported by close relationships with friends, family, or fellow members of church, work, or other support groups (Cohen, 1988; House & others, 1988; Nelson, 1988). Some recent examples:

- Recall the study mentioned earlier in this chapter that followed leukemia patients preparing to undergo bone marrow transplants. Two years later, only 20 percent of those who said they had little social support from their family or friends were still alive. Among those who felt strong emotional support, the 2-year survival rate was 54 percent (Colon & others, 1991).
- A study of 1234 heart attack patients found nearly a doubled rate of a recurring attack within 6 months among those living alone (Case & others, 1992).
- A study of 1965 heart disease patients revealed a 5-year survival rate of 82 percent among those married or having a confidant, but only 50 percent among those having no one (Williams & others, 1992).
- A 70-year study following 1528 California children with high IQ scores found that those whose parents did not divorce during their childhood out-

Friendships are good medicine Several long-term studies of thousands of people have found that individuals with close supportive relationships are less likely than socially isolated people to die prematurely.

PSYCHOLOGY APPLIED

Spirituality, Religion, and Health

Throughout history, humans have suffered ills and sought healing. In response, the two healing traditions—religion and medicine—historically have joined hands in care of the sick. Religious and healing efforts were often conducted by the same person; the priest was also the medicine man. Maimonides was a twelfth-century rabbi and a renowned physician. Hospitals were first established in monasteries, then spread by missionaries.

As medical science matured, however, healing and religion diverged. Rather than asking God to spare their children from smallpox, people began vaccinating them. Rather than seeking a spiritual healer when burning with bacterial fever, they turned to antibiotics.

This wall of separation between religion and medicine is now breaking down again. "Spirituality" has made a comeback. Pollster George Gallup (1994) detects "the search for spiritual moorings" as a "dominant trend" in the mid-1990s. At one point, 6 of the 10 bestselling American books explored spiritual matters. Since 1995, Harvard Medical School has annually attracted some 2000 health professionals from across North America to its conferences on "Spirituality and Healing in Medicine." New books such as *Religion and the Clinical Practice of Psychology* (American Psychological Association, 1996) and *Religion and Health* (Oxford University Press, forthcoming) are appearing. Detecting a renewed convergence of religion and medicine, *Time* magazine devoted a 1996 cover story to "Faith and Healing."

Is there fire underneath all this smoke? Do religion and spirituality actually relate to health, as polls show 4 in 5 Americans believe (Matthews, 1997)? Some 200 studies have sought to correlate "the faith factor" with health and healing (Koenig, 1997; Matthews & Larson, 1997). Among the suggestive findings are these:

- Jeremy Kark and his colleagues (1996) compared the death rates over a 16-year period for 3900 Israelis either in one of 11 religiously orthodox or in one of 11 matched, nonreligious collective settlements (kibbutz communities). The researchers reported that "belonging to a religious collective was associated with a strong protective effect" not explained by age or economic differences: In every age group, those belonging to the religious communities were about half as likely as their nonreligious counterparts to have died. This is roughly comparable to the gender difference in mortality. (According to studies in Great Britain and the United States, in every age group about 60 women die for every 100 men [Chance News, 1997].)
- An earlier study of 91,909 persons in one Maryland county found that those who attended religious services weekly were less likely to die during the study period than those who did not—53 percent less from coronary disease, 53 percent less due to suicide, and 74 percent less from cirrhosis (Comstock & Partridge, 1972).
- A Dartmouth Medical School team followed 232 people who had undergone open heart surgery (Oxman & others, 1995). In the ensuing six months, 12 percent of those who never or rarely attended religious services died, as did 5 percent of those who attended more often, and 0 percent of those who said they were "deeply religious."

Such findings demand explanation. In part, they seem due to the healthier life-styles of religiously active people—who smoke and drink less (Levin, 1994, 1996). Health-oriented, vegetarian Seventh Day Adventists have a longer-than-usual life expectancy (Berkel & de Waard, 1983). Religiously orthodox Israelis eat somewhat less fat than their nonreligious compatriots.

But such differences are not great enough to explain the dramatically reduced mortality in the religious kibbutzim, argued the Israeli researchers. The religious communities also appeared to offer stress protection and enhanced well-being, possibly resulting from a coherent worldview, an amplified sense of belonging, highly stable marriages (divorce is almost nonexistent), and the rest and meditation associated with frequent prayer and Sabbath observance. Similarly, more than 350,000 local faith communities in North America provide social support networks for their active participants, who also draw solace and hope from their faith during times of stress.

Although the religion-health correlations typically leave cause and effect ambiguous, Harold Pincus (1997), deputy medical director of the American Psychiatric Association, believes these findings "have made clear that anyone involved in providing health care services . . . cannot ignore . . . the important connections between spirituality, religion, and health."

lived children of divorce by about 4 years (Schwartz & others, 1995). Controlling for the family's economic status and the child's personality did little to diminish the family-stability factor.

"I get by with a little help from my friends."

John Lennon and Paul McCartney
Sgt. Pepper's Lonely Hearts Club Band
1967

Close relationships also provide the opportunity to confide painful feelings. In one study, health psychologists James Pennebaker and Robin O'Heeron

(1984) contacted the surviving spouses of people who had committed suicide or died in car accidents. Those who bore their grief alone had more health problems than those who openly expressed it. Talking about our troubles can be "open heart therapy."

Actively suppressing thoughts can cause them to bubble up intrusively, preoccupying the person (Wegner, 1990). Disclosing suppressed thoughts may stop the cycle. In a simulated confessional, Pennebaker asked volunteers to share with a hidden experimenter some upsetting events that had been preying on their minds. He asked some of the volunteers to describe a trivial event before they divulged the troubling one. Physiological measures revealed that their bodies remained tense the whole time they talked about the trivial event; they relaxed only when they later confided the cause of their turmoil. Even writing about personal traumas in a diary can help. When volunteers in other experiments did this, they had fewer health problems during the ensuing four to six months (Pennebaker, 1990). As one subject explained, "Although I have not talked with anyone about what I wrote, I was finally able to deal with it, work through the pain instead of trying to block it out. Now it doesn't hurt to think about it."

Suppressed traumas sometimes eat away at us and affect our physical health. Consider:

- When Pennebaker surveyed more than 700 undergraduate women, he found that about 1 in 12 reported a traumatic sexual experience in childhood. Compared with women who had experienced nonsexual traumas, such as parental death or divorce, the sexually abused women—especially those who had kept their secret to themselves—reported more headaches and stomach ailments.
- After the 1989 San Francisco Bay Area earthquake, residents talked nonstop about the upheaval for about two weeks. Then the talking died down as people tired of hearing others' opinions and feelings. ("Thank you for not sharing your earthquake experience," read one popular T-shirt.) But for another month people kept thinking about the quake. During this inhibition phase—when people kept ruminating but with less disclosure of their anxieties and feelings—hostility, nightmares, and health problems peaked (Pennebaker & Harber, 1993).
- Pennebaker and his colleagues (1989) also invited 33 Holocaust survivors to spend 2 hours recalling their experiences. Many did so in intimate detail never before disclosed. Most watched and showed family and friends a videotape of their recollections in the weeks following. Again, those who were most self-disclosing had the most improved health 14 months later. Although talking about a stressful event can temporarily arouse people, it calms them in the long run (Mendolia & Kleck, 1993). Confiding is good for the soul.

Sustained emotional reactions to stressful events can be debilitating. However, the level of stress experienced depends on the person and the environment. Nothing is stressful until we appraise it as such. Thus, our personalities and interpretations influence how we react emotionally when stressful things happen. Moreover, the toxic impact of stressful events can be buffered by a relaxed, healthy life-style and by the comfort and aid provided by supportive friends and family (Figure 10.22).

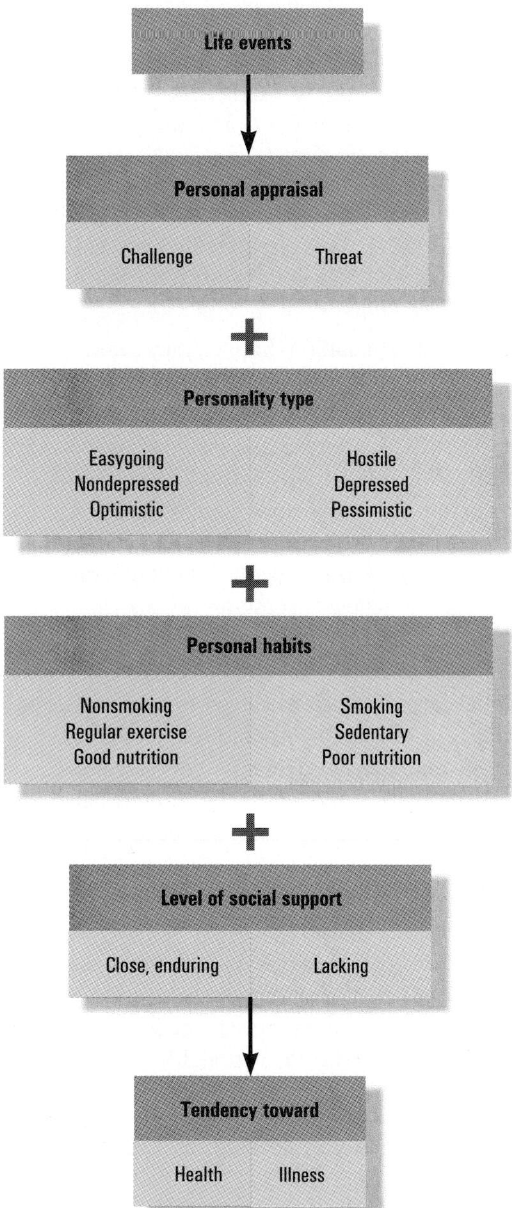

Figure 10.22 **Coping with stress** Life events can be debilitating or not. It all depends on how we appraise them and whether the stresses are buffered by a stress-resistant disposition, healthy habits, and enduring social support.

REHEARSE IT!

22. A number of studies reveal that aerobic exercise raises energy levels and helps alleviate depression and anxiety. The reasons for these emotional effects of exercise are unclear. One explanation is that exercise triggers the release of mood-boosting neurotransmitters such as norepinephrine, serotonin, and
- **a.** the placebos.
- **b.** the endorphins.
- **c.** epinephrine.
- **d.** acetylcholine.

23. Neal Miller found that rats could learn to control their heartbeat when they were rewarded with pleasurable brain stimulation for doing so. Later research showed that some paralyzed humans could also learn to control blood pressure through biofeedback. Biofeedback was thought to help people exercise control over functions that are usually controlled by
- **a.** the autonomic nervous system.
- **b.** conscious thought.
- **c.** the immune system.
- **d.** external stimuli.

24. Biofeedback is a system for electronically recording, amplifying, and feeding back information about physiological states that we are usually not conscious of—including finger temperature and forehead-muscle tension. Using a biofeedback system to control finger temperature is most similar to
- **a.** programming a computer to control appliances.
- **b.** using an automatic pilot to fly a plane.
- **c.** using a mirror to practice a dance.
- **d.** using training wheels to learn to ride a bicycle.

25. Long-term studies of thousands of people have shown that people who have close relationships—a strong social support system—are less likely to die prematurely than those who do not. These studies provide evidence that
- **a.** social ties can be a source of stress.
- **b.** people who lose a close relationship are at risk for illness.
- **c.** Type A behavior is responsible for many premature deaths.
- **d.** social support has a beneficial effect on health.

REVIEWING ■ *Emotions, Stress, and Health*

1. ***What are the components of an emotion?***

Emotions are psychological responses of the whole organism that involve an interplay among (1) physiological arousal, (2) expressive behaviors, and (3) conscious experience.

The Physiology of Emotion

2. ***What physiological changes accompany emotional arousal?***

In an emergency, the sympathetic nervous system automatically mobilizes the body for fight or flight, directing the adrenal glands to release hormones that in turn increase heart rate, blood pressure, and blood sugar level. Other changes include tensed muscles, dry mouth, dilated pupils, slowed digestion, and increased sweating. In day-to-day life, our performance on a task is usually best when arousal is moderate, though this varies with the difficulty of the task. The physical arousal that occurs with one emotion is in most ways indistinguishable from that which occurs with another. However, scientists have discovered subtle differences in the brain pathways and hormones associated with different emotions.

The physiological responses that accompany emotion are measured by a **polygraph** in order to detect whether a person is lying. Lie detectors err about a third of the time and are more likely to label the innocent guilty than the reverse.

Expressing Emotion

3. ***How do we communicate nonverbally? Are nonverbal expressions of emotion universally understood?***

Much of our communication is through the silent language of the body. Even very thin (seconds-long) videotaped slices of behavior can reveal feelings. Gestures appear to be culturally determined, but facial expressions, such as those of happiness and fear, are common the world over.

4. ***Do our facial expressions influence our feelings?***

Expressions not only communicate emotion to others, they also amplify our own emotions and signal our bodies to respond accordingly.

Experiencing Emotion

5. ***What are the causes and consequences of anger?***

Anger is most often aroused by events that are not only frustrating or insulting but also interpreted as willful, unjustified, and avoidable. Although blowing off steam (**catharsis**) may be temporarily calming, it does not, in the long run, reduce anger. Expressing anger can actually arouse more anger.

6. ***What are the causes and consequences of happiness?***

A good mood boosts people's perceptions of the world and their willingness to help others (the **feel-good, do-good phenomenon**). A person's self-perceived happiness or satisfaction with life is his or her **subjective well-being**. The moods triggered by the day's good or bad events seldom last beyond that day. Even significant good events, such as a substantial raise in income, seldom increase happiness for long. We can explain the relativity of happiness with the **adaptation-level phenomenon** and **relative deprivation** principle. Nevertheless, some people are usually happier than others, and researchers have identified factors that predict such happiness.

Theories of Emotion

7. ***What issue distinguishes the James-Lange and Cannon-Bard theories of emotion?***

One of the oldest theoretical controversies regarding emotion is whether we feel emotion after we notice our body responses (as **James and Lange** proposed) or at the same time that our bodies respond (as **Cannon and Bard** believed).

8. ***What is the relationship between thinking and feeling?***

A more recent controversy among emotion researchers concerns whether we can experience human emotions apart from cognition. Can we feel before we think? Stanley Schachter's **two-factor theory** of emotion contends that the cognitive labels we put on our states of arousal are an essential ingredient of emotion. Richard Lazarus agrees that cognition is essential: Many important emotions arise from our interpretations or inferences. Robert Zajonc, however, believes that some simple emotional responses occur instantly, not only outside our conscious awareness but before any cognitive processing occurs. The issue has practical implications: To the degree that emotions are rooted in thinking, we can hope to change them by changing our thinking.

Stress and Health

9. ***What is stress?***

Stress is the process by which we appraise and respond to events that challenge or threaten us. Walter Cannon viewed stress as a "fight-or-flight" system. Hans Selye saw it as a three-stage **general adaptation syndrome (GAS)**, including the alarm, resistance, and exhaustion stages.

10. ***What provokes stress?***

Modern research on stress has assessed the health consequences of cataclysmic events, significant life changes, and daily hassles. Events are especially stressful when perceived as both negative and uncontrollable. Optimists cope more successfully with stress and enjoy better health.

11. ***Who is most vulnerable to heart disease?***

Coronary heart disease, North America's number one cause of death, has been linked with the competitive, hard-driving, impatient, and (especially) anger-prone **Type A** personality. Under stress, the body of a reactive, hostile person secretes more of the hormones that accelerate the narrowing of the heart's artery walls. **Type B** personalities are more relaxed and easygoing.

12. ***How does stress make us vulnerable to disease?***

In addition to contributing to heart disease and a variety of **psychophysiological illnesses**, stress can suppress the immune system, inhibiting the activities of its B and T **lymphocytes** and macrophages, making a person more vulnerable to infections and cancer. New experiments indicate that the immune system's responses can be influenced by conditioning.

Promoting Health

13. ***How do people cope with stress, and what stress management techniques are effective?***

Among the components of stress management programs are **aerobic exercise**, **biofeedback**, and relaxation. Although the degree of mind control over the body that can be gained through biofeedback has fallen short of early expectations, biofeedback has become one accepted method for helping people control ailments such as tension headaches. Simple relaxation exercises offer some of the same benefits. Counseling Type A heart attack survivors to slow down and relax has helped them lower their rate of recurring attacks. Social support also helps people cope, partly by buffering the impact of stress.

CRITICAL THINKING EXERCISE by Richard O. Straub

Now that you have read and reviewed Chapter 10, take your learning a step further by testing your critical thinking skills on the following scientific problem-solving exercise.

Participants in a recent study were shown an erotic movie while they were in each of three phases of recovery from aerobic exercise. They first pedaled an exercise bicycle intensely enough to produce significant physical arousal. During each of the three recovery phases, the participants were asked (1) whether they still felt physically aroused from the exercise and (2) how sexually excited by the film they felt. Their actual physical arousal (heart rate) was measured throughout the experiment. During the first two phases of recovery, all of the participants still showed signs of actual physical arousal, although by the second phase, they said they no longer felt physically aroused from the exercise. By the third phase, they no longer showed signs of physical arousal from the exercise. All participants reported feeling significantly more sexually excited by the film during the second phase of exercise recovery than they did during the first and third phases.

1. How well would the James-Lange theory explain the results of this experiment? What variations in reported feelings of sexual excitement would this theory have predicted in the three phases of exercise recovery?
2. How well would the Cannon-Bard theory explain the results of this experiment? What variations in reported feelings of sexual excitement would this theory have predicted in the three phases of exercise recovery?
3. How well would Schachter's two-factor theory explain the results of this experiment? What variations in reported feelings of sexual excitement would this theory have predicted in the three phases of exercise recovery?

Check your progress on becoming a critical thinker by comparing your answers to the sample answers found in Appendix B.

REHEARSE IT ANSWER KEY

1. b., **2.** d., **3.** d., **4.** a., **5.** b., **6.** b., **7.** a., **8.** d., **9.** c., **10.** b., **11.** b., **12.** b., **13.** c., **14.** b., **15.** b., **16.** c., **17.** c., **18.** d., **19.** b., **20.** c., **21.** b., **22.** b., **23.** a., **24.** c., **25.** d.

CHAPTER 11

Personality

Novelist William Faulkner was a master at creating characters with vivid personalities.[1] One of his creations, Ike McCaslin, appears at various ages in more than a dozen novels and short stories. Ike is highly principled, and consistently so. At age 10 he feels a deep reverence for the wilderness and its creatures. At 21 he forfeits a "tainted" inheritance. In his late seventies he counsels his nephew to use his land responsibly. Ike the adult is an extension of Ike the child.

Another Faulkner character, Jason Compson, is a selfish, whining 4-year-old at the beginning of *The Sound and the Fury*, and a selfish, screaming 34-year-old as the novel closes. As head of the Compson household, he verbally abuses family members and household servants. Lying, threatening, conniving, he is a self-centered child who becomes a self-centered adult.

1. *What is personality?*

Faulkner's characters, as they appear and reappear throughout his fiction, exhibit the distinctiveness and consistency that define personality. The preceding chapters have emphasized how we are similar—how we all develop, perceive, learn, remember, think, and feel. This chapter emphasizes our individuality. Your individual **personality** is your characteristic pattern of thinking, feeling, and acting. If your behavior pattern is strikingly distinctive and consistent—if, say, you are always outgoing, whether at a party or in a classroom—people are likely to say that you have a "strong" personality.

Actually, much of this book deals with personality. In earlier chapters, we considered biological influences on personality, personality development across the life span, and personality-related aspects of learning, motivation, emotion, and health. In later chapters we will study disorders of personality and social influences on personality.

In this chapter we explore and evaluate four major perspectives on personality:

- Sigmund Freud's *psychoanalytic* theory, which proposes that childhood sexuality and unconscious motivations influence personality.

---

[1]Faulkner scholar Nancy Nicodemus assisted with these examples.

personality an individual's characteristic pattern of thinking, feeling, and acting.

free association in psychoanalysis, a method of exploring the unconscious in which the person relaxes and says whatever comes to mind, no matter how trivial or embarrassing.

psychoanalysis Freud's theory of personality that attributes our thoughts and actions to unconscious motives and conflicts; the techniques used in treating psychological disorders by seeking to expose and interpret unconscious tensions.

unconscious according to Freud, a reservoir of mostly unacceptable thoughts, wishes, feelings, and memories. According to contemporary psychologists, information processing of which we are unaware.

preconscious information that is not conscious but is retrievable into conscious awareness.

id contains a reservoir of unconscious psychic energy that, according to Freud, strives to satisfy basic sexual and aggressive drives. The id operates on the *pleasure principle*, demanding immediate gratification.

ego the largely conscious, "executive" part of personality that, according to Freud, mediates among the demands of the id, superego, and reality. The ego operates on the *reality principle*, satisfying the id's desires in ways that will realistically bring pleasure rather than pain.

"There is no man who is not, at each moment, what he has been and what he will be."

Oscar Wilde
1854–1900

- The *trait* perspective, in which researchers identify personality dimensions that account for our consistent behavior patterns.
- The *humanistic* approach, which focuses on our inner capacities for growth and self-fulfillment.
- The *social-cognitive* approach, which emphasizes how we shape and are shaped by our environment.

The Psychoanalytic Perspective

Ask 100 people on the street to name a notable deceased psychologist, suggests Keith Stanovich (1996, p. 1), and "Sigmund Freud would be the winner hands down." Although Freud's current influence in psychological science is slight, his notoriety continues to color people's perception of psychology and his influence lingers in literary and film interpretation, psychiatry, and pop psychology. So who was Freud, and what did he teach?

Well before entering the University of Vienna in 1873, the youthful Sigmund Freud showed signs of independence and brilliance. He had a prodigious memory. He so loved serious reading that he once ran up a bookstore debt beyond his means, feeding his insatiable interest in plays, poetry, and philosophy. As a teen he often took his evening meal in his tiny bedroom, to lose no time from his studies.

After graduating from medical school, Freud set up a private practice, specializing in nervous disorders. Before long, however, he faced patients whose disorders made no neurological sense. A patient might have lost all feeling in her hand—yet there is no sensory nerve that, if damaged, would numb the entire hand and nothing else. Freud's search for a cause for such disorders set his mind running in a direction that was destined to change human self-understanding.

Exploring the Unconscious

2. *What role do unconscious dynamics play in Freud's theory of personality?*

While experimenting with hypnosis, Freud "discovered" the unconscious. He decided that the loss of feeling in one's hand might be caused by a fear of touching one's genitals; that blindness or deafness might be caused by not wanting to see or hear something that aroused intense anxiety. He then turned to **free association**—in which he merely told the patient to relax and say whatever came to mind, no matter how embarrassing or trivial. Freud believed that free association produced a chain of thought leading into the patient's unconscious, thereby retrieving and releasing painful unconscious memories, often from childhood. Freud called his theory and associated techniques **psychoanalysis**.

Underlying Freud's psychoanalytic conception of personality was his belief that the mind is like an iceberg—mostly hidden. Our conscious awareness is the part of the iceberg that floats above the surface. Below the surface is the much larger, **unconscious** region containing thoughts, wishes, feelings, and memories, of which we are largely unaware. Some of these thoughts we store temporarily in a **preconscious** area, from which we can retrieve them into conscious awareness. Of greater interest to Freud was the mass of unacceptable passions and thoughts that he believed we *repress*, or forcibly block from our consciousness because

Sigmund Freud (1856–1939) "I was the only worker in a new field."

Freud's consulting room Freud's office was rich with antiquities from around the world, including artwork related to his ideas about unconscious motives. His famous couch, piled high with pillows, placed patients in a comfortable reclining position facing away from him to help them focus inward.

"Good morning, beheaded—uh, I mean beloved."

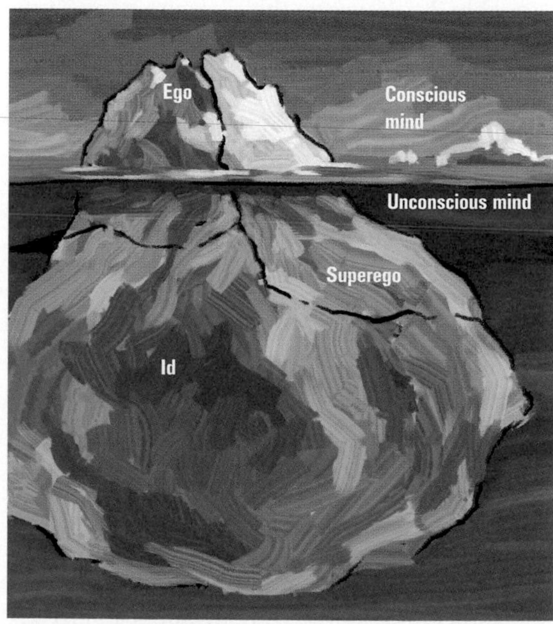

Figure 11.1 Freud's idea of the mind's structure For Freud, consciousness was like an iceberg's visible tip. Note that the id was totally unconscious, but ego and superego operated both consciously and unconsciously. (Adapted from Freud, 1933, page 111)

they would be too painful to acknowledge. Freud believed that, although we are not consciously aware of them, these troublesome feelings and ideas powerfully influence us. In his view, our unacknowledged impulses express themselves in disguised forms—the work we choose, the beliefs we hold, our daily habits, our troubling symptoms. In such ways, the unconscious seeps into our thoughts and actions.

For Freud the determinist, nothing was ever accidental. He believed he glimpsed the seepage of the unconscious not only in people's free associations, beliefs, habits, and symptoms but also in their dreams and slips of the tongue and pen while reading, writing, and speaking. Consider his example of a financially stressed patient who, not wanting any large pills, said, "Please do not give me any bills, because I cannot swallow them." Similarly, jokes were a way to express repressed sexual and aggressive tendencies. Freud viewed dreams as the "royal road to the unconscious." The remembered content of dreams (their *manifest content*—see page 181) he believed to be a censored expression of the dreamer's unconscious wishes (the dream's *latent content*). By analyzing people's dreams, Freud believed he could reveal the nature of their inner conflicts and release their inner tensions.

Personality Structure

3. *How did Freud view personality structure and development, and how did he think people defended themselves against anxiety?*

For Freud, human personality—including its emotions and strivings—arises from a conflict between our aggressive, pleasure-seeking biological impulses and the social restraints against them. In his view, personality results from our efforts to resolve this basic conflict—to express these impulses in ways that bring satisfaction without also bringing guilt or punishment.

Freud theorized that the conflict centers on three interacting systems: id, ego, and superego (Figure 11.1). These abstract psychological concepts are, said Freud, "useful aids to understanding" the mind's dynamics.

The **id** has a reservoir of unconscious psychic energy that constantly strives to satisfy basic drives to survive, reproduce, and aggress. The id operates on the *pleasure principle*: If not constrained by reality, it seeks immediate gratification. Think of newborn infants, who, governed by the id, cry out for satisfaction the moment they feel a need, caring nothing for the outside world's conditions and demands.

As the **ego** develops, the young child learns to cope with the real world. The ego operates on the *reality principle*, which seeks to gratify the id's impulses in

"Fifty is plenty."
"Hundred and fifty."

realistic ways that will bring long-term pleasure rather than pain or destruction. (Imagine what would happen if, lacking an ego, we expressed our unrestrained sexual or aggressive impulses whenever we felt them.) The ego, which contains our partly conscious perceptions, thoughts, judgments, and memories, is the personality "executive." It is a mediator, balancing the impulsive demands of the id, the restraining demands of the superego, and the real-life demands of the external world.

Beginning around age 4 or 5, Freud theorized, a child's ego recognizes the demands of the newly emerging **superego**. The superego is a voice of conscience that forces the ego to consider not only the real but the ideal. Its sole focus is on how one *ought* to behave. The superego strives for perfection, judging actions and producing positive feelings of pride or negative feelings of guilt. Someone with an exceptionally strong superego may be virtuous yet, ironically, guilt-ridden; another with a weak superego may be wantonly self-indulgent and remorseless. Because the superego's demands often oppose the id's, the ego struggles to reconcile the two. The chaste student who is sexually attracted to someone may satisfy both id and superego by joining a volunteer organization to work with the desired person.

superego the part of personality that, according to Freud, represents internalized ideals and provides standards for judgment (the conscience) and for future aspirations.

psychosexual stages the childhood stages of development (oral, anal, phallic, latency, genital) during which, according to Freud, the id's pleasure-seeking energies focus on distinct erogenous zones.

Oedipus [ED-uh-puss] **complex** according to Freud, a boy's sexual desires toward his mother and feelings of jealousy and hatred for the rival father.

identification the process by which, according to Freud, children incorporate their parents' values into their developing superegos.

fixation according to Freud, a lingering focus of pleasure-seeking energies at an earlier psychosexual stage, where conflicts were unresolved.

defense mechanisms in psychoanalytic theory, the ego's protective methods of reducing anxiety by unconsciously distorting reality.

repression in psychoanalytic theory, the basic defense mechanism that banishes anxiety-arousing thoughts, feelings, and memories from consciousness.

regression defense mechanism whereby an individual retreats, when faced with anxiety, to a more infantile psychosexual stage where some psychic energy remains fixated.

reaction formation defense mechanism by which the ego unconsciously switches unacceptable impulses into their opposites. Thus, people may express feelings that are the opposite of their anxiety-arousing unconscious feelings.

projection the defense mechanism by which people disguise their own threatening impulses by attributing them to others.

rationalization defense mechanism that offers self-justifying explanations in place of the real, more threatening, unconscious reasons for one's actions.

displacement defense mechanism that shifts sexual or aggressive impulses toward a more acceptable or less threatening object or person, as when redirecting anger toward a safer outlet.

Personality Development

Analysis of his patients' histories convinced Freud that personality forms during life's first few years. Again and again his patients' symptoms seemed rooted in unresolved conflicts from early childhood. He concluded that children pass through a series of **psychosexual stages** during which the id's pleasure-seeking energies focus on distinct pleasure-sensitive areas of the body called *erogenous zones*.

During the *oral stage*, which lasts throughout the first 18 months, the infant's sensual pleasures focus on sucking, biting, and chewing.

During the *anal stage*, from about 18 months to 3 years, the sphincter muscles become sensitive and controllable, and bowel and bladder retention and elimination become a source of gratification.

During the *phallic stage*, from roughly 3 to 6 years, the pleasure zone shifts to the genitals. Freud believed that during this stage boys seek genital stimulation and develop both unconscious sexual desires for their mother and jealousy and hatred for their father, whom they consider a rival. Given these feelings, boys would also feel guilt and a lurking fear of punishment from their father, perhaps by castration. Freud called this collection of feelings the **Oedipus** [ED-uh-puss] **complex** after the Greek legend of Oedipus, who unknowingly killed his father and married his mother. Although some psychoanalysts believed that girls experience a parallel *Electra complex*, Freud (1931, page 229) said no: "It is only in the male child that we find the fateful combination of love for the one parent and simultaneous hatred for the other as a rival."

Children eventually cope with threatening feelings, said Freud, by repressing them and by identifying with (trying to become like) the rival parent. It's as if something inside the child decides, "If you can't beat 'em (the parent of the same sex), join 'em." Through this **identification** process, children's superegos gain strength as they incorporate many of their parents' values. Freud believed that identification with the same-sex parent provides what Chapter 3 called our *gender identity*—our sense of being male or female.

With their sexual feelings repressed and redirected, children enter a *latency stage*. Freud maintained that during latency, extending from around age 6 to puberty, sexuality is dormant and children play mostly with peers of the same sex.

At puberty, latency gives way to the final stage, the *genital stage*, as the person begins to experience sexual feelings toward others.

In Freud's view, maladaptive behavior in the adult results from conflicts unresolved during earlier psychosexual stages. At any point in the oral, anal, or

Identification Freud believed that children cope with threatening feelings of competition with their same-sex parent by identifying with that parent.

phallic stage, strong conflict can lock, or **fixate**, the person's pleasure-seeking energies in that stage. For example, people who were either orally overindulged or deprived (perhaps by abrupt, early weaning) might fixate at the oral stage. Orally fixated adults are said to exhibit either passive dependence (like that of a nursing infant) or an exaggerated denial of this dependence—perhaps by acting tough and uttering biting sarcasm. They might also continue to seek oral gratification through excessive smoking and eating. Similarly, those who never quite resolve the anal conflict between the desire to eliminate at will and the demands of toilet training may be either messy and disorganized (*anal expulsive*) or highly controlled and compulsively neat (*anal retentive*). In such ways, believed Freud, the twig of personality is bent at an early age.

Defense Mechanisms

To live in social groups, we cannot act out our sexual and aggressive impulses willy-nilly. We must control them. When the ego fears losing control of the inner war between the demands of the id and the superego, the result is a dark cloud of unfocused anxiety. Anxiety, said Freud, is the price we pay for civilization. Anxiety is hard to cope with, as when we feel unsettled but are unsure why. Freud proposed that the ego protects itself against anxiety with **defense mechanisms**, which reduce or redirect anxiety in various ways, all of them distorting reality. Some examples:

Repression banishes anxiety-arousing thoughts and feelings from consciousness. According to Freud, repression underlies the other defense mechanisms, all of which disguise threatening impulses and keep them from reaching consciousness. Freud believed that repression explains why we do not remember our childhood lust for our parent of the other sex. However, he also believed that repression is often incomplete, with the repressed urges seeping out in dream symbols and slips of the tongue.

In Freud's view, maladaptive behavior in the adult results from conflicts unresolved during earlier psychosexual stages.

We also cope with anxiety through **regression**—retreating to an earlier, more infantile stage of development. Thus, when facing the anxious first days of school, a child may regress to the oral comfort of thumb-sucking. Juvenile monkeys, when anxious, retreat to infantile clinging to their mothers or to one another (Suomi, 1987). Even homesick new college students may long for the security and comfort of home.

In **reaction formation**, the ego unconsciously makes unacceptable impulses look like their opposites. En route to consciousness, the unacceptable proposition "I hate him" becomes "I love him." Timidity becomes daring. Feelings of inadequacy become bravado.

Regression Faced with a mild stress, children and young monkeys will regress, retreating to the comfort of earlier behaviors.

Projection disguises threatening impulses by attributing them to others. Thus, "He doesn't trust me" may be a projection of the actual feeling "I don't trust him" or "I don't trust myself." An El Salvadoran saying captures the idea: "The thief thinks everyone else is a thief."

The familiar mechanism of **rationalization** lets us unconsciously generate self-justifying explanations so we can hide from ourselves the real reasons for our actions. Thus, habitual drinkers may say they drink with their friends "just to be sociable." Students who fail to study may rationalize, "All work and no play makes Jack [or Jill] a dull person."

Displacement diverts one's sexual or aggressive impulses toward an object more psychologically acceptable than the one that aroused them. Children who can't express anger against their parents may displace their anger onto the family pet. Students upset over an exam may snap at a roommate.

"The lady doth protest too much, methinks."
William Shakespeare
Hamlet
1600

Sublimation is the transformation of unacceptable impulses into socially valued motivations. Freud suggested that Leonardo da Vinci's paintings of Madonnas were a sublimation of his longing for intimacy with his mother, who was separated from him at an early age.

Note that all these defense mechanisms function indirectly and unconsciously, reducing anxiety by disguising our threatening impulses. We would never say, "I'm feeling anxious; I'd better project my sexual or hostile feelings onto someone else." Defense mechanisms would not work if we recognized them. As the body unconsciously defends itself against disease, so also, believed Freud, does the ego unconsciously defend itself against anxiety.

Freud's Descendants and Dissenters

4. *How did Freud's followers differ from him?*

Freud's controversial writings soon attracted followers, mostly young, ambitious physicians who formed an inner circle around their strong-minded leader. These pioneering psychoanalysts and others, whom we now call neo-Freudians, accepted Freud's basic ideas: the personality structures of id, ego, and superego; the importance of the unconscious; the shaping of personality in childhood; and the dynamics of anxiety and the defense mechanisms. But they veered away from Freud in two important ways. First, they placed more emphasis on the role of the conscious mind in interpreting experience and coping with the environment. And second, they doubted that sex and aggression were all-consuming motivations. Instead, they placed more emphasis on loftier motives and on social interaction, as the following examples illustrate.

"The female . . . acknowledges the fact of her castration, and with it, too, the superiority of the male and her own inferiority; but she rebels against this unwelcome state of affairs."
Sigmund Freud
Female Sexuality
1931

Alfred Adler and Karen Horney [HORN-eye] agreed with Freud that childhood is important. But they believed that childhood *social*, not sexual, tensions are crucial for personality formation. Adler, who himself struggled to overcome childhood illnesses and accidents, said that much of our behavior is driven by an effort to conquer childhood feelings of inferiority, feelings that trigger strivings for superiority and power. (It was Adler who proposed the still-popular

Alfred Adler "The individual feels at home in life and feels his existence to be worthwhile just so far as he is useful to others and is overcoming feelings of inferiority" (*Problems of Neurosis*, 1964).

Karen Horney "The view that women are infantile and emotional creatures, and as such, incapable of responsibility and independence is the work of the masculine tendency to lower women's self-respect" (*Feminine Psychology*, 1932).

Carl Jung "We can keep from a child all knowledge of earlier myths, but we cannot take from him the need for mythology" (*Symbols of Transformation*, 1912).

sublimation in psychoanalytic theory, the defense mechanism by which people rechannel their unacceptable impulses into socially approved activities.

collective unconscious Carl Jung's concept of a shared, inherited reservoir of memory traces from our species' history.

projective test a personality test such as the Rorschach or TAT, that provides ambiguous stimuli designed to trigger projection of one's inner dynamics.

Thematic Apperception Test (TAT) a projective test in which people express their inner feelings and interests through the stories they make up about ambiguous scenes.

idea of the "inferiority complex.") Horney said that childhood anxiety, caused by the dependent child's sense of helplessness, triggers the desire for love and security. In countering Freud's assumptions that women have weak superegos and suffer "penis envy," Horney sought to balance the bias she detected in this masculine view of psychology.

Unlike other neo-Freudians, Carl Jung—Freud's disciple-turned-dissenter—placed less emphasis on social factors and agreed with Freud that the unconscious exerts a powerful influence. But to Jung [YOONG], the unconscious contains more than a person's repressed thoughts and feelings. There is also a **collective unconscious**, he believed, a common reservoir of images derived from our early ancestors' universal experiences. Jung said that the collective unconscious explains why, for many people, spiritual concerns are deeply rooted and why people in different cultures share certain myths and images, such as mother as a symbol of nurturance. (Today's psychologists discount the idea of inherited experiences. But many do believe that our shared evolutionary history shaped some universal dispositions.)

Since Freud died in 1939, some of his ideas have been incorporated into *psychodynamic theory*. "Most contemporary dynamic theorists and therapists are not wedded to the idea that sex is the basis of personality," notes Drew Westen (1996). They "do not talk about ids and egos, and do not go around classifying their patients as oral, anal, or phallic characters." What they do assume, with Freud, is that much of mental life is unconscious, that childhood shapes our personalities and ways of becoming attached to others, and that we often struggle with inner conflicts among our wishes, fears, and values.

Assessing the Unconscious

5. *How do projective tests assess personality, and are they considered valid?*

Those who study personality or provide therapy need ways to evaluate personality characteristics. Different personality theories have developed different methods of assessment.

Freud's theory maintains that the significant influences on personality arise from the unconscious, which contains residues from early childhood experiences. The interpretation of dreams, he said, provided the road into the unconscious mind. Psychoanalysts therefore dismiss objective assessment tools, such as agree-disagree or true-false questionnaires, as merely tapping the conscious surface. Their tool of choice would be a sort of psychological x-ray—a test that can see through our surface pretensions and reveal our hidden conflicts and impulses.

The TAT This psychologist presumes that the hopes, fears, and interests expressed in this boy's descriptions of a series of ambiguous pictures in the Thematic Apperception Test (TAT) are projections of his inner feelings.

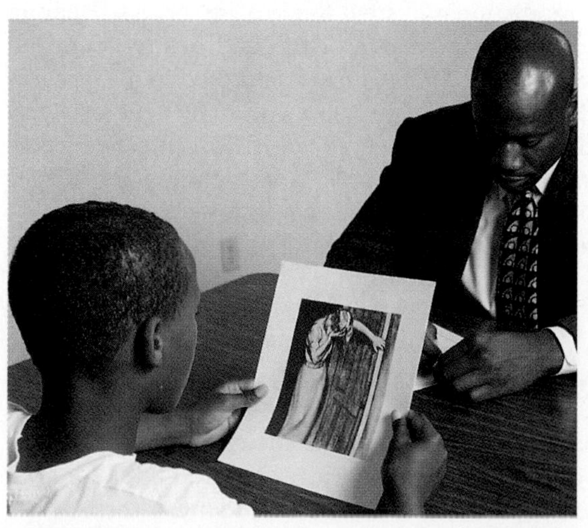

Projective tests aim to provide such a view by presenting an ambiguous stimulus and then asking test-takers to describe it or tell a story about it. The stimulus has no inherent significance, so any meaning people read into it presumably reflects a projection of their interests and conflicts. Henry Murray (1933) demonstrated a possible basis for such a test at a house party hosted by his 11-year-old daughter. Murray got the children to play a frightening game called "Murder." When shown some photographs after the game, the children perceived the photos as more malicious than they had before the game. These children, it seemed to Murray, had *projected* their inner feelings into the pictures.

A few years later, Murray introduced the **Thematic Apperception Test (TAT)**—a test in which people view ambiguous pictures and then make up stories about them. As you may recall from page 339, one use of such story telling has been to assess achievement motivation. Shown a daydreaming boy, those

The Rorschach test In this projective test, people say what a series of symmetrical inkblots look like. Some who use this test are confident that the interpretation of ambiguous stimuli will reveal unconscious aspects of the test-taker's personality. Others use it as an icebreaker or to supplement other information.

"The forward thrust of the antlers shows a determined personality, yet the small sun indicates a lack of self-confidence. . . ."

"If a professional psychologist is 'evaluating' you in a situation in which you are at risk and asks you for responses to ink blots . . . walk out of that psychologist's office."

Robyn Dawes
House of Cards: Psychology and Psychotherapy Based on Myth
1994

Rorschach inkblot test the most widely used projective test, a set of 10 inkblots, designed by Hermann Rorschach; seeks to identify people's inner feelings by analyzing their interpretations of the blots.

who imagine him fantasizing an achievement are presumed to be projecting their own goals.

Various projective tests ask test-takers to draw a person, to complete sentences ("My mother . . ."), or to provide the first word that comes to mind after the examiner says a test word. Most widely used is the famous **Rorschach inkblot test**, introduced in 1921 by Swiss psychiatrist Hermann Rorschach [ROAR-shock]. The test assumes that what we see in its 10 inkblots reflects our inner feelings and conflicts. If we see fierce animals or weapons, the examiner may infer we have aggressive tendencies.

Is this a reasonable assumption? If so, can a psychologist use the Rorschach to understand one's personality and diagnose an emotional disorder? Recall from Chapter 8's discussion of intelligence tests that the two primary criteria of a good test are reliability (consistency of results) and validity (predicting what it's supposed to). On those criteria, how good is the Rorschach?

Most researchers have considered it not very good (Peterson, 1978). There has been no one accepted system for scoring and interpreting the test. So unless two raters were trained in the same scoring system, their agreement on the results of any given test would be minimal. Nor has the test been very successful at predicting behavior or at discriminating between groups (for example, identifying who is suicidal and who is not).

Although not as popular as it once was, the Rorschach remains one of the most widely used psychological instruments (Piotrowski & Keller, 1989). Some clinicians continue to be confident of the test's validity—not as a device that by itself can provide a diagnosis but as a source of suggestive leads that supplement other information. Other clinicians believe the test is an icebreaker and a revealing interview technique. A new research-based, computer-aided scoring and interpretation tool is improving agreement among raters and enhancing the test's validity—though not yet with enough evidence to satisfy critics (Exner, 1993; Shontz & Green, 1992; Wood & others, 1996). This scoring system, however, assumes the blots actually do look like certain things, though the test assumes they do not (Dawes, 1994). Moreover, Freud himself probably would have been uncomfortable with trying to assign each patient a test score and would have been more interested in the therapist–patient interactions that take place during the test.

Evaluating the Psychoanalytic Perspective

6. ***How do Freud's ideas hold up today?***

Knowing what you do about Freud's ideas, listen now to his critics. Bear in mind that we critique Freud from the perspective of the end of the twentieth century, a perspective that is itself subject to revision. Freud died in 1939 without the benefit of all that we have since learned about human development, thinking, and emotion and without today's research tools. To criticize Freud's theories by comparing them with current concepts is like comparing Henry Ford's Model T with today's Escort, say Freud's admirers. To his critics, however, Freud's ideas are psychology's historical equivalent to astronomy's flat-earth theory.

Freud's Ideas in the Light of Modern Research

Recent research contradicts many of Freud's specific ideas. Today's developmental psychologists view our development as lifelong, not fixed in childhood. They also question Freud's idea that conscience and gender identity form as the child resolves the Oedipus complex at age 5 or 6. Children gain their gender identity earlier and become strongly masculine or feminine even without a same-sex parent present (Frieze & others, 1978). Freud's ideas about childhood sexuality arose from his rejection of stories of childhood sexual abuse told by his female patients—stories that some scholars believe he suggested or coerced and then attributed to their own childhood sexual wishes and conflicts (Powell & Boer, 1994). Today, we understand how Freud's questioning might have created false memories, and we also know that childhood sexual abuse does happen. Freud's ideas about the natural superiority of men have been thoroughly discounted.

"I agree that we see further when we stand on the shoulders of giants like [William] James. But not Freud. When we stand on his shoulders, we only discover that we're looking further in the wrong direction."

John F. Kihlstrom (1997)

As we saw in Chapter 5, new ideas about why we dream dispute Freud's belief that dreams disguise and fulfill wishes. Even slips of the tongue can be explained as competition between similar verbal choices in our memory network. Someone who says "I don't want to do that—it's a lot of brothel" may simply be blending "brother" and "trouble" (Foss & Hakes, 1978). Researchers find little support for Freud's idea that people protect themselves against painful self-knowledge by projecting their own unrecognized negative impulses onto others (Holmes, 1978, 1981). And Jerome Kagan (1989b) notes that history has been equally unkind to another of Freud's ideas—that sexual repression causes psychological disorder. From Freud's time to ours, sexual repression has diminished but psychological disorders have not.

Is Repression a Myth?

Sigmund Freud's entire psychoanalytic theory rests on his assumption that the human mind often *represses* painful experiences, banishing them into the unconscious. Freud and his legions of followers also assumed that with therapeutic assistance, people could *recover* such experiences years later and gain insight and healing as they do so.

Traumatic events, such as rape and torture, haunt survivors, who experience unwanted flashbacks. They are seared onto the soul.

Freud thought that if we could somehow uncover our past experiences, we would find them intact, like long-lost books in a dusty attic. If only we could recover and resolve the painful repressed memories of our childhood, emotional healing would follow. Under Freud's influence, repression has been used to explain hypnotic phenomena and many psychological disorders. It is also one of popular psychology's most widely accepted concepts. In one survey, 88 percent of university students believed that painful experiences commonly get pushed out of awareness and into the unconscious (Garry & others, 1994).

Actually, contend many of today's researchers, repression, if it ever occurs, is a rare mental response to terrible trauma. "Repression folklore is . . . partly refuted, partly untested, and partly untestable," says Elizabeth Loftus (1995). Consider: If the human mind indeed commonly banishes painful experiences, how do we explain these odd findings?

- Shouldn't we expect children who have witnessed a parent's murder to repress the experience? But no, one study of sixteen 5- to 10-year-old children who had this horrific experience found that not one repressed the memory (Malmquist, 1986).
- Shouldn't survivors of Nazi death camps have banished the atrocities from consciousness? But no, with rare exceptions they remember all too well—although many do benefit from disclosing and talking through their experiences (Helmreich, 1992, 1994; Pennebaker, 1990).
- Shouldn't we expect children who have been terrorized while their school bus was hijacked or pinned down by sniper fire to repress the experience? But no, in separate incidents all remembered it (Pope & Hudson, 1995).

- Shouldn't we expect victims and observers to black out the image of the horrific collapse of two hotel skywalks in which 114 died and more than 200 were injured? But no, not only do they recall it, nearly 90 percent later said they remembered it repeatedly (Wilkinson, 1983).
- Shouldn't battle-scarred veterans suffer amnesia for their worst experiences? But no, apart from concussion-related amnesia, such forgetting seems not to occur. Folklore regarding recovered battlefield memories is either unconfirmed or related to therapists' use of suggestive techniques, reports David Holmes (1990, 1994).
- Shouldn't people who have kept a diary of everyday life events later recall negative events significantly less well than positive events? But no, "the memory for the two types of events [is] almost the same," report Charles Thompson and his colleagues (1996).

There do appear to be rare exceptions—one death camp survivor reportedly forgot for over 30 years the snatching and shooting of her infant son (Kraft, 1996). Some researchers believe that extreme, prolonged stress, such as the stress some severely abused children experience, might disrupt memory by damaging the hippocampus (Schacter, 1996). But the far more common reality is that high stress enhances memory and that negative emotional events are therefore remembered well (Christianson, 1992; Shobe & Kihlstrom, 1997). In fact, too well: These and other traumatic events, such as rape and torture, haunt survivors, who experience unwanted flashbacks. They are seared onto the soul.

After studying 400 hours of recollections by 120 witnesses to the Holocaust, psychologist Robert Kraft (1996) reported that "the nearly universal response is persistent, intrusive, extended, vivid memory for personally-experienced events." "You see the babies," said survivor Sally H. (1979). "You see the screaming mothers. You see hanging people. You sit and you see that face there. It's something you don't forget."

The Unconscious Mind

History has been kinder to Freud's "iceberg" view of the mind, at least in part. We now know that we indeed have limited access to all that goes on in our minds (Erdelyi, 1985, 1988; Kihlstrom, 1990; Lewicki & others, 1992). However, the "iceberg" notion held by today's research psychologists differs from Freud's—so much so, argues Anthony Greenwald (1992), that it is time to abandon Freud's view of the unconscious. As we saw in earlier chapters, many researchers think of the unconscious not as seething passions and repressive censoring but as cooler information processing that occurs without our awareness. To them, the unconscious involves

More than we realize, we fly on autopilot.

- the schemas that automatically control our perceptions and interpretations.
- the priming by stimuli to which we have not consciously attended.
- the right hemisphere activity that enables the split-brain patient's left hand to carry out an instruction the patient cannot verbalize.
- the parallel processing of different aspects of vision and thinking.
- the implicit memories that operate without conscious recall, even among those with amnesia.
- the emotions that activate instantly, before conscious analysis.
- the self-concept and stereotypes that automatically and unconsciously influence how we process information about ourselves and others (Bargh, 1997).

> ***"Two passengers leaned against the ship's rail and stared at the sea. 'There sure is a lot of water in the ocean,' said one. 'Yes,' answered his friend, 'we've only seen the top of it.'"***
>
> Psychologist George A. Miller (1962)

More than we realize, we fly on autopilot. This understanding of unconscious information processing is more like the pre-Freudian view of an underground stream of thought from which spontaneous creative ideas surface.

Freud's Ideas as Scientific Theory

> ***"Sigmund Freud is an empirical void."***
>
> Anonymous

Psychologists also criticize Freud's theory for its scientific shortcomings. Recall from Chapter 1 that good scientific theories explain observations and offer testable hypotheses. Freud's theory rests on few objective observations and offers few hypotheses to verify or reject. (For Freud, his own recollections and interpretations of patients' free associations, dreams, and slips were evidence enough.)

The most serious problem with Freud's theory is that it offers after-the-fact explanations of any characteristic (of one person's smoking, another's fear of horses, another's sexual orientation) yet fails to *predict* such behavior and traits. If you feel angry at your mother's death, you illustrate the theory because "your unresolved childhood dependency needs are threatened." If you do not feel angry, you again illustrate the theory because "you are repressing your anger." That, said Calvin Hall and Gardner Lindzey (1978, p. 68), "is like betting on a horse after the race has been run."

> ***"We are arguing like a man who should say, 'If there were an invisible cat in that chair, the chair would look empty; but the chair does look empty; therefore there is an invisible cat in it.'"***
>
> C. S. Lewis
> *Four Loves*
> 1958

Yet Freud's supporters point out that to criticize Freudian theory for not making testable predictions is like criticizing baseball for not being an aerobic exercise. Is it fair to fault something for not being what it was never intended to be? Unlike many later psychoanalysts, Freud never claimed that psychoanalysis was predictive science. He merely claimed that, looking back, psychoanalysts could find meaning in our state of mind (Rieff, 1979). Freud's supporters also note that some of his ideas *are* enduring. It was Freud who drew our attention to the unconscious and the irrational, to our defenses against anxiety, to the importance of human sexuality, and to the tension between our biological impulses and our social well-being. It was Freud who challenged our self-righteousness, punctured our pretensions, and reminded us of our potential for evil.

Freud's legacy lives on. Some ideas that many people assume to be true—that childhood experiences mold personality, that many behaviors have disguised motives—are Freud's legacy. His early 1900s concepts penetrate our 1990s language. Without realizing their source, we may speak of *ego*, *repression*, *projection*, *complex* (as in "inferiority complex"), *sibling rivalry*, and *fixation*. "Freud's premises may have undergone a steady decline in currency within academia for many years," notes Martin Seligman (1994), "but Hollywood, the talk shows, many therapists, and the general public still love them."

REHEARSE IT!

1. According to Freud, we block thoughts, wishes, feelings, and memories that are unacceptable or unbearably painful from consciousness. The blocked material surfaces in disguised forms, for example, in physical symptoms, dreams, or slips of the tongue. This unconscious blocking of unacceptable thoughts is
   - **a.** free association.
   - **b.** repression.
   - **c.** anxiety.
   - **d.** reaction formation.
2. According to Freud's view of personality structure, the "executive" system, the __________, seeks to gratify the impulses of the __________ in more realistic ways.
   - **a.** id; ego
   - **b.** ego; superego
   - **c.** ego; id
   - **d.** id; superego
3. Freud proposed an Oedipus complex, which is resolved through a process called identification, during which the child incorporates parental values. This process is closely associated with the development of the "voice of conscience," the part of the personality that internalizes ideals and that Freud called the
   - **a.** ego.
   - **b.** superego.
   - **c.** reality principle.
   - **d.** sublimation.
4. According to the psychoanalytic view of development, the oral, anal, and phallic stages are followed by a latency stage during which sexuality is largely dormant or submerged. The latency stage extends roughly through
   - **a.** the preschool years.
   - **b.** the early school years.
   - **c.** adolescence.
   - **d.** infancy.
5. Defense mechanisms identified by Freud include regression (in which a person copes with anxiety by retreating to an earlier stage of development) and projection (in which a person disguises threatening impulses by attributing them to others). There are many other defense mechanisms. All of them have in common some distortion or disguising of reality, and all of them are
   - **a.** conscious.
   - **b.** unconscious.
   - **c.** preconscious.
   - **d.** rationalizations.
6. In general, neo-Freudians such as Adler and Horney accepted many of Freud's views but they placed more emphasis on
   - **a.** development throughout the life span.
   - **b.** the collective unconscious.
   - **c.** the role of the id.
   - **d.** social interactions.
7. Projective tests are personality tests that present test-takers with an ambiguous stimulus and ask them to respond to it, for example, by describing it or telling a story about it. One well-known projective test, which uses inkblots as stimuli, was created by
   - **a.** the neo-Freudians.
   - **b.** Henry Murray.
   - **c.** Carl Jung.
   - **d.** Hermann Rorschach.
8. Many of Freud's specific ideas—for example, his ideas on the formation of gender identity and the function of dreams—have been modified by the neo-Freudians or challenged by recent research. However, psychodynamic psychologists would agree with Freud about
   - **a.** the existence of unconscious mental processes.
   - **b.** the Oedipus and Electra complexes.
   - **c.** the predictive value of Freudian theory.
   - **d.** adult psychological problems being the result of inadequate psychosexual development.

The Trait Perspective

7. How do trait theorists view personality?

Psychoanalytic theory attempts to explain personality in terms of the dynamics that underlie behavior. It peers beneath the surface in search of hidden motives. In 1919, Gordon Allport, a curious 22-year-old psychology student, interviewed Freud in Vienna and discovered just how preoccupied the founder of psychoanalysis was with finding hidden motives, even in Allport's own behavior during the interview. That experience ultimately led Allport to do what Freud did not do—to describe personality in terms of fundamental **traits**—people's characteristic behaviors and conscious motives. Meeting Freud, said Allport, "taught me that [psychoanalysis], for all its merits, may plunge too deep, and that psychologists would do well to give full recognition to manifest motives before probing the unconscious." Allport therefore defined personality in terms of identifiable behavior patterns. He was concerned less with *explaining* individual traits than with *describing* them.

How do psychologists describe and classify personalities? An analogy may help. Imagine that you want to describe and classify apples. Someone might correctly say that every apple is unique. Still, you might find it useful to begin by classifying apples as distinct *types*—Granny Smith, McIntosh, Red or Yellow Delicious, and so forth.

trait a characteristic pattern of behavior or a disposition to feel and act, as assessed by self-report inventories and peer reports.

Based on children's physiological and psychological reactivity, Jerome Kagan (1989) has classified children's temperaments as either shy-inhibited or fearless-uninhibited types. Some health psychologists classify people as intense, *Type A*, or as laid back, *Type B*, personalities (pages 372–373).

More popular today, especially in business and career counseling, is an effort to classify people according to Carl Jung's personality types, based on their responses to 126 questions written by Isabel Briggs Myers (1987) and her mother, Kathleen Briggs. The *Myers-Briggs Type Indicator* is quite simple. It offers choices, such as "Do you usually value sentiment more than logic, or value logic more than sentiment?" Then it counts the test-taker's preferences, labels them as indicating, say, a "feeling" or "thinking" type, and feeds them back to the person in complimentary terms. Feeling types, for example, are told they are sensitive to values and "sympathetic, appreciative, and tactful"; thinking types are told they "prefer an objective standard of truth" and are "good at analyzing." Most people therefore agree with their announced type profile, which mirrors their declared preferences. They may also accept it as a basis for being matched with work partners and tasks that supposedly suit their temperaments. A National Research Council report, however, noted that the test's use has outrun research on its value as a predictor of job performance and that "the popularity of this instrument in the absence of proven scientific worth is troublesome" (Druckman & Bjork, 1991, p. 101; see also Pittenger, 1993).

Exploring Traits

Whoopi the extravert On stage, Whoopi Goldberg seems as outgoing as her stage name implies. (She was born Caryn Johnson.) Trait labels such as extraversion can describe our temperaments and typical behaviors.

Classifying people as one or another distinct personality type fails to fully capture their individuality. So how else could we describe their personalities? To return to our apple analogy, we might describe an apple along several trait dimensions—as relatively large or small, red or yellow, sweet or sour. By placing people on several trait dimensions simultaneously, psychologists can describe countless individual personality variations. (Remember from Chapter 4 that variations on just three color dimensions—hue, saturation, and brightness—create many thousands of colors.)

What trait dimensions describe personality? Allport and his associate H. S. Odbert (1936) literally counted all the words in an unabridged dictionary with which one could describe people. The list numbered almost 18,000! How, then, could psychologists condense the list to a manageable number of basic traits?

One way has been to propose traits, such as anxiety, that some theory regards as basic. A newer technique is *factor analysis*, the statistical procedure described in Chapter 8 to identify clusters of test items that tap basic components of intelligence (such as spatial ability, reasoning ability, or verbal skill). Imagine that people who describe themselves as outgoing also tend to say that they like excitement and practical jokes and that they do not like quiet reading. Such a statistically correlated cluster of behaviors reflects a basic trait, or factor—in this case, a trait called *extraversion*.

Studies comparing identical and fraternal twins, comparing identical twins reared apart, and comparing adoptees with their adoptive and biological parents, all remind us: Personality forms under the influence of genes.

British psychologists Hans Eysenck and Sybil Eysenck [EYE-zink] believe that we can reduce many of our normal individual variations to two or three genetically influenced dimensions, including *extraversion-introversion* and *emotional stability-instability* (Figure 11.2, page 402). Their *Eysenck Personality Questionnaire* has been given to people in 35 countries around the world, from China to Uganda to Russia. When people's answers are analyzed, the extraversion and emotionality factors inevitably emerge as basic personality dimensions (Eysenck, 1990, 1992). Extraverts, the researchers contend, seek stimulation because their normal levels of brain arousal are relatively low. Emotionally stable people

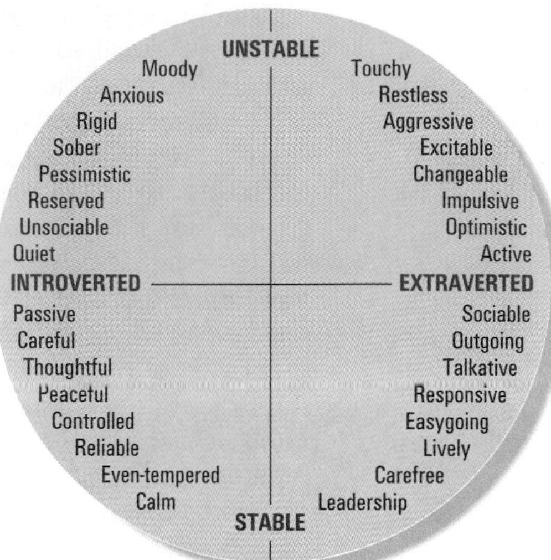

Figure 11.2 Two personality factors Mapmakers can tell us a lot by using two axes (north-south and east-west). Hans Eysenck and Sybil Eysenck use two primary personality factors—extraversion-introversion and stability-instability—as axes for describing personality variation. Varying combinations define other, more specific traits. (From Eysenck & Eysenck, 1963)

react calmly because their autonomic nervous systems are not as reactive as those of unstable people.

Many other trait theorists, too, view personality traits as biologically rooted. Jerome Kagan attributes differences in children's shyness and inhibition to their autonomic nervous system reactivity. Studies comparing identical and fraternal twins, comparing identical twins reared apart, and comparing adoptees with their adoptive and biological parents, all remind us: Personality forms under the influence of genes (pages 71–73). Our genes have much to say about the temperament and the behavioral style that help define our personality—more, it seems, than the way our parents handled us (although parents also have an influence and are mighty important for other things, such as beliefs and values).

Most researchers believe that the Eysencks' dimensions are important but that they don't tell the whole story of someone's personality. A slightly expanded set of factors—dubbed the *Big Five*—does a better job (Goldberg, 1993; John, 1990; Wiggins, 1996). If a test specifies where you are on the five dimensions of Table 11.1, it has said much of what there is to say about your personality. Around the world, people describe others in terms roughly consistent with the Big Five—how agreeable they are, how extraverted they are, and so forth. The Big Five is not the last word, but it's currently our best approximation of the basic trait dimensions. If you could ask five questions about the personality of a stranger—say, a blind date you were soon to meet—querying where the person is on these five dimensions would be most revealing.

Table 11.1 The "Big Five" Personality Factors

Trait Dimension	Description
Emotional stability	Calm versus anxious Secure versus insecure Self-satisfied versus self-pitying
Extraversion	Sociable versus retiring Fun-loving versus sober Affectionate versus reserved
Openness	Imaginative versus practical Preference for variety versus preference for routine Independent versus conforming
Agreeableness	Soft-hearted versus ruthless Trusting versus suspicious Helpful versus uncooperative
Conscientiousness	Organized versus disorganized Careful versus careless Disciplined versus impulsive

Source: Adapted from McCrae & Costa (1986, p. 1002).

Assessing Traits

8. *How do we assess traits?*

Assessment techniques derived from trait concepts do not reveal hidden personality dynamics (which is the intent of projective tests). Rather, they profile a person's behavior patterns. Many trait scales provide quick assessments of a single trait, such as extraversion, anxiety, or self-esteem. Alternatively, psychologists can assess several traits at once by administering **personality inventories**—longer questionnaires on which people respond to items covering a wide range of feelings and behaviors.

The most extensively researched and widely used personality inventory is the **Minnesota Multiphasic Personality Inventory (MMPI)**. Although it assesses

personality inventory a questionnaire (often with true-false or agree-disagree items) on which people respond to items designed to gauge a wide range of feelings and behaviors; used to assess selected personality traits.

Minnesota Multiphasic Personality Inventory (MMPI) the most widely researched and clinically used of all personality tests. Originally developed to identify emotional disorders (still considered its most appropriate use), this test is now used for many other screening purposes.

empirically derived test a test (such as the MMPI) developed by testing a pool of items and then selecting those that discriminate between groups.

"abnormal" personality tendencies rather than normal personality traits, the MMPI illustrates a good way of developing a personality inventory. One of its creators, Starke Hathaway (1960), compared his effort to that of Alfred Binet. Binet, as you may recall from Chapter 8, developed the first intelligence test by selecting items that discriminated children who would have trouble progressing normally in French schools. The MMPI items, too, were **empirically derived**. That is, from a large pool of items Hathaway and his colleagues selected those that discriminated particular diagnostic groups. They then grouped the questions according to what they measured into 10 clinical scales.

They initially gave hundreds of true-false statements ("No one seems to understand me"; "I get all the sympathy I should"; "I like poetry") to groups of psychologically disordered patients and to "normal" people. They retained any statement—no matter how silly it sounded—on which the patient group's answer differed from that of the normal group. "Nothing in the newspaper interests me except the comics" may seem senseless, but it just so happened that depressed people were more likely to answer "true." (Nevertheless, pundits have had fun spoofing the MMPI with their own mock items, such as: "Weeping brings tears to my eyes," "Frantic screams make me nervous," and "I stay in the bathtub until I look like a raisin" [Frankel & others, 1983].)

Today's new "MMPI-2," renormed on a full cross-section of Americans and containing revised items, still contains 10 clinical scales (Figure 11.3). Like its predecessor, it has several validity scales, including the so-called lie scale that assesses the extent to which a person is faking to make a good impression (by responding "false" to statements such as "I get angry sometimes"). And it has 15 content scales assessing, for instance, work attitudes, family problems, and anger.

In contrast to the subjectivity of projective tests, personality inventories are scored objectively—so objectively that a computer can administer and score them. (The computer can also provide descriptions of people who previously responded similarly.) Objectivity does not, however, guarantee validity. For example, sophisticated test-takers taking the MMPI for employment purposes can give fake answers to create a good impression. (They consistently answer in socially desirable ways, except on such items as "I get angry sometimes," for which nearly anyone would admit to being imperfect.) Moreover, the ease of computerized testing tempts untrained administrators—including many

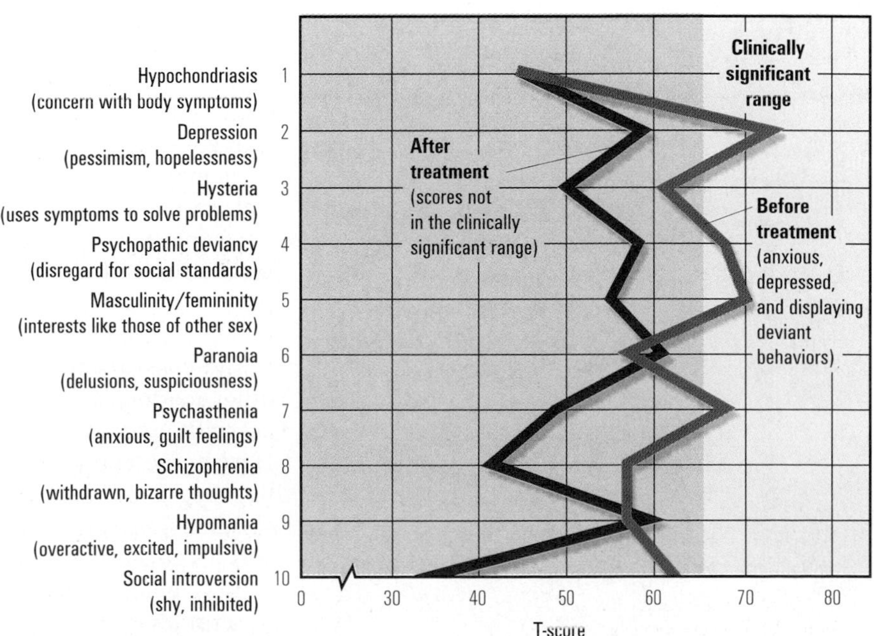

Figure 11.3 Minnesota Multiphasic Personality Inventory (MMPI) test profile Scores on the MMPI scales are converted to a "T-scale" in which the average score is 50; about two-thirds of people fall between 40 and 60. High T-scores suggest a psychological disorder. This graph plots the scores of Ed, a depressed and anxious young man, before and after psychotherapy. (Adapted from Butcher, 1990)

personnel officers, educational admissions officers, and physicians—to use the test in ways for which it has not been validated (Matarazzo, 1983). Nevertheless, for better or worse, the objectivity of the MMPI contributes to its popularity and to its translation into more than 100 languages.

Evaluating the Trait Perspective

9. Does research support the consistency of personality traits?

Are our personality traits stable and enduring? Or does our behavior depend on where we are and whom we are with? William Faulkner created characters, llke the self-centered Jason Compson, whose personality traits were consistent across various times and places. The Italian playwright Luigi Pirandello had a different view. For him, personality was ever-changing, tailored to the particular role or situation. In one of Pirandello's plays, Lamberto Laudisi describes himself to Signora Sirelli: "I am really what you take me to be; though, my dear madam, that does not prevent me from also being really what your husband, my sister, my niece, and Signora Cini take me to be—because they also are absolutely right!" To which she responds, "In other words you are a different person for each of us."

"There is as much difference between us and ourselves, as between us and others."
Michel de Montaigne
Essays
1588

The Person-Situation Controversy

Who, then, represents human personality, Faulkner's consistent Jason Compson or Pirandello's inconsistent Laudisi? Both. Our behavior is influenced by the interaction of our inner disposition with our environment. Still, the question lingers: Which is *more* important? Are we *more* as Faulkner or as Pirandello imagined us to be? Forced to choose, most people would probably side with Faulkner. Until the late 1960s, most psychologists would have, too. Isn't it obvious that some people are dependably conscientious and others unreliable, some cheerful and others dour, some outgoing and others shy?

Roughly speaking, the temporary, external influences on behavior are the focus of social psychology, and the enduring, inner influences are the focus of personality psychology. In actuality, behavior always depends on the interaction of persons with situations.

In considering this *person-situation controversy*, we seek genuine personality traits that persist over time *and* across situations. If friendliness is a trait, friendly people must act friendly at different times and places. Do they? In Chapter 3, we considered research that has followed lives through time. We noted that some scholars (especially those who study infants) are impressed with personality change; others are struck by personality stability during adulthood. If people's personalities are assessed in young adulthood and then assessed again several decades later, their characteristics persist. Interests may change—the avid collector of tropical fish may become the avid gardener. Careers may change—the determined salesperson may become a determined social worker. Relationships may change—the hostile spouse may start over with a new partner. But most people recognize their traits as their own, note Robert McCrae and Paul Costa (1994), "and it is well that they do. A person's recognition of the inevitability of his or her one and only personality is . . . the culminating wisdom of a lifetime." Faulkner would not have been surprised.

The consistency of specific *behaviors* from one situation to the next is another matter. As Walter Mischel (1968, 1984) has pointed out, people do not act with predictable consistency. In one of the first studies to reveal this, Hugh Hartshorne and Mark May (1928) gave thousands of children opportunities to lie, cheat, and steal while at home, at play, and in the classroom. Were some children consistently honest, others dishonest? Generally not. "Most children will deceive in certain situations and not in others," the researchers reported. A child's "lying, cheating, and stealing as measured by the test situations used in these studies are only very loosely related" (p. 411). More than a half-century later, Mischel's studies of college students' conscientiousness revealed a similar

Drawing by Miller; © 1984 The New Yorker Magazine, Inc.

"Mr. Coughlin over there was the founder of one of the first motorcycle gangs."

finding. There was virtually no relation between a student's being conscientious on one occasion (say, showing up for class on time) and being similarly conscientious on another occasion (say, turning in assignments on time). Pirandello would not have been surprised.

Mischel has also pointed out that people's scores on personality tests only mildly predict their behaviors. For example, people's scores on an extraversion test do not neatly predict how sociable they actually will be on any given occasion. If we remember such results, says Mischel, we will be more cautious about labeling and pigeonholing individuals. We will be more restrained when asked to predict whether someone is likely to violate parole, commit suicide, or be an effective employee. Years in advance, science can tell us the phase of the moon for any given date, but we may never be able to predict exactly how you will feel and act tomorrow.

In defense of traits, Seymour Epstein (1983a,b) maintained that trying to predict a specific act on the basis of a personality test result is like trying to predict your answer to a specific aptitude question on the basis of an intelligence test result. Your answer to any given question is unpredictable because it depends on so many variables (your reading of the question, your understanding of the topic, your concentration level at the moment, luck). Your *average* accuracy over many questions on several tests is more predictable. Similarly, people's *average* outgoingness, happiness, or carelessness over *many* situations is predictable, Epstein observed. When rating someone's shyness or agreeableness, this consistency enables people who know someone well to agree (Kenrick & Funder, 1988). As our best friends can verify, we *do* have personality traits—and some are genetically influenced traits, we now know. Moreover, our traits are socially significant. They influence our health, our thinking, and our job performance (Deary & Matthews, 1993; Hogan & others, 1996).

Consistency of Expressive Style

In unfamiliar, formal situations—perhaps when eating in the home of a person from another culture—our traits may remain hidden as we attend carefully to social cues. In familiar, informal situations—just hanging out with old friends—we feel less constrained, allowing our traits to emerge (Buss, 1989). In such situations, our expressive styles are impressively consistent. Thus, we often form lasting impressions within a few moments of meeting someone and noting the person's animation, manner of speaking, and gestures. Nalini Ambady and Robert Rosenthal (1992, 1993) videotaped 13 Harvard University graduate students teaching undergraduate courses. Observers then viewed three thin slices of each teacher's behavior—mere 10-second clips from the beginning, middle, and end of a class—and rated each teacher's level of confidence, activeness, warmth, and so forth. These behavior ratings, based on 30 *seconds* of teaching from an entire semester, predicted amazingly well the teacher's average student ratings at the semester's end. Observing even thinner slices—three 2-second clips—yielded ratings that still correlated as high as +.72 with the student evaluations. Some people's first impressions, derived from expressive behavior, predicted other people's lasting impressions!

Our expressive styles are impressively consistent. Thus, we often form lasting impressions within a few moments of meeting someone and noting the person's animation, manner of speaking, and gestures.

To sum up, we can say that at any moment the immediate situation powerfully influences a person's behavior, especially when the situation makes clear demands. We can better predict drivers' behavior at traffic lights from knowing the color of the lights than from knowing the drivers' personalities. However, averaging our behavior across many occasions reveals that we do have distinct personality traits. Moreover, we can quickly perceive individual differences in some traits, such as expressiveness.

REHEARSE IT!

9. Trait theory describes personality in terms of characteristic behaviors, or traits, such as agreeableness or extraversion. A pioneering trait theorist was
   a. Sigmund Freud.
   b. Alfred Adler.
   c. Gordon Allport.
   d. Henry Murray.

10. Hans Eysenck and Sybil Eysenck define personality in terms of two primary factors—extraversion-introversion and stability-instability. Most researchers today believe that the Eysenck dimensions are too limiting and prefer the so-called Big Five personality factors. Which of the following is *not* one of the Big Five?
    a. conscientiousness
    b. anxiety
    c. extraversion
    d. agreeableness

11. Trait theorists assess personality by developing a profile of a person's traits. For example, they administer personality inventories, long questionnaires that ask people to report their characteristic feelings and behaviors. The most widely used of all personality inventories is the
    a. extraversion-introversion scale.
    b. TAT.
    c. MMPI.
    d. Rorschach.

12. The items of the MMPI were empirically derived. This means, for example, that the designers of the test figured out which responses indicated schizophrenia by
    a. taking case histories before and after the test.
    b. analyzing the content of the items in the light of their understanding of the disorder.
    c. comparing the responses of people known to have schizophrenia with the responses of "normal" people.
    d. assessing the degree of deception, using validity scales.

13. People's scores on personality tests are only mildly predictive of their behavior. Such tests best predict
    a. a person's behavior on a specific occasion.
    b. a person's average behavior across many situations.
    c. behavior involving a single trait, such as conscientiousness.
    d. behavior that depends on situation or context.

The Humanistic Perspective

10. ***What is the central focus of the humanistic perspective?***

By 1960, some personality psychologists had become discontented with Freud's negativity and with trait psychology's objectivity. In contrast to Freud's study of the base motives of "sick" people, the focus of these *humanistic psychologists* was the strivings of "healthy" people for self-determination and self-realization. In contrast to trait psychologists, who developed profiles, they emphasized the whole person, beyond encapsulation as so many test scores.

Abraham Maslow "Any theory of motivation that is worthy of attention must deal with the highest capacities of the healthy and strong person as well as with the defensive maneuvers of crippled spirits" (*Motivation and Personality*, 1970).

Exploring the Self

Two pioneering theorists—Abraham Maslow (1908–1970) and Carl Rogers (1902–1987)—illustrate the humanistic emphases on human potential and seeing the world through the person's (not the researcher's) eyes.

Abraham Maslow's Self-Actualizing Person

Maslow proposed that we are motivated by a hierarchy of needs (page 314). If our physiological needs are met, we become concerned with personal safety; if we achieve a sense of security, we then seek to love, to be loved, and to love ourselves; with our love needs satisfied, we seek self-esteem. Having achieved self-esteem, we ultimately seek **self-actualization**, the process of fulfilling our potential.

Maslow (1970) developed his ideas by studying healthy, creative people rather than troubled clinical cases. He based his description of self-actualization on a study of people who seemed notable for their rich and productive lives—Abraham Lincoln and Eleanor Roosevelt among them. These people shared certain characteristics. Maslow reported they were self-aware and self-accepting, open and spontaneous, loving and caring, and not paralyzed by others' opinions. Secure in their sense of who they were, their interests were problem-centered rather than self-centered. Often they focused their energies on a particular task, which they regarded as their mission in life. Most enjoyed a few deep relationships rather than many superficial ones. Many had been moved by spiritual or personal *peak experiences* that surpassed ordinary consciousness.

These are mature adult qualities, said Maslow, ones found in those who have learned enough about life to be compassionate, to have outgrown their mixed feelings toward their parents, to have found their calling, to have "acquired enough courage to be unpopular, to be unashamed about being openly virtuous, etc." Maslow's work with college students led him to speculate that those likely to become self-actualizing adults were likable, caring, "privately affectionate to those of their elders who deserve it," and "secretly uneasy about the cruelty, meanness, and mob spirit so often found in young people."

Carl Rogers' Person-Centered Perspective

Fellow humanistic psychologist Carl Rogers agreed with much of Maslow's thinking. Rogers believed that people are basically good and are endowed with self-actualizing tendencies. Each of us is like an acorn, primed for growth and fulfillment, unless thwarted by an environment that inhibits growth. Rogers (1980) surmised that a growth-promoting climate required three conditions—genuineness, acceptance, and empathy.

According to Rogers, people nurture our growth by being *genuine*—by being open with their own feelings and being transparent and self-disclosing.

People also nurture growth by being *accepting*—by offering us what Rogers called **unconditional positive regard**. This is an attitude of grace, an attitude that values us even knowing our failings. Have you ever experienced the relief of having dropped your pretenses, confessed your worst feelings, and discovered that you were still accepted? We sometimes enjoy this gratifying experience in a good relationship, a close family, or an intimate friendship in which we no longer feel a need to explain ourselves and are free to be spontaneous without fear of losing the other's esteem.

The picture of empathy Being open and sharing confidences is easier when the listener shows real understanding, by feeling what we feel. Within such relationships people can relax and fully express their true selves.

Finally, people nurture growth by being *empathic*—by sharing and mirroring our feelings and reflecting our meanings. "Rarely do we listen with real understanding, true empathy," said Rogers. "Yet listening, of this very special kind, is one of the most potent forces for change that I know."

Genuineness, acceptance, and empathy are the water, sun, and nutrients that enable people to grow like vigorous oak trees, according to Rogers. For "as persons are accepted and prized, they tend to develop a more caring attitude toward themselves" (Rogers, 1980, p. 116). As persons are empathically heard, "it becomes possible for them to listen more accurately to the flow of inner experiencings."

Rogers believed that genuineness, acceptance, and empathy nurture growth not only in the relationship between therapist and client but also between parent and child, leader and group, teacher and student—in fact, between any two human beings. He would have been pleased by a finding published shortly after his death: Preschool children whose parents exhibit such attitudes usually become creative adolescents (Harrington & others, 1987).

For Maslow, and even more for Rogers, a central feature of personality is one's **self-concept**—all the thoughts and feelings we have in response to the question, "Who am I?" If our self-concept is positive, we tend to act and perceive the world positively. If it is negative—if in our own eyes we fall far short of our "ideal self"—said Rogers, we feel dissatisfied and unhappy. A worthwhile goal for therapists, parents, teachers, and friends is therefore, he said, to help others know, accept, and be true to themselves.

self-actualization according to Maslow, the ultimate psychological need that arises after basic physical and psychological needs are met and self-esteem is achieved; the motivation to fulfill one's potential.

unconditional positive regard according to Rogers, an attitude of total acceptance toward another person.

self-concept all our thoughts and feelings about ourselves, in answer to the question, "Who am I?"

Assessing the Self

Humanistic psychologists sometimes assess personality with questionnaires that evaluate people's self-concepts. One questionnaire, inspired by Carl Rogers, asks people to describe themselves both as they ideally would like to be and as they actually are. When the ideal and the actual self are nearly alike, said Rogers, the self-concept is positive. Thus, to assess his clients' personal growth during therapy, he looked for successively closer ratings of actual and ideal self.

Other humanistic psychologists believe that any standardized assessment of personality is depersonalizing, that even a questionnaire detaches the psychologist from the living human. Rather than forcing the person to respond to narrow categories, these humanistic psychologists believe that interviews and intimate conversation enable a better understanding of each person's unique experiences.

Research on the Self

11. *What have we learned from research on the self?*

Psychology's concern with people's sense of self dates back at least to William James, who devoted more than 100 pages to the topic in his 1890 *Principles of Psychology*. By 1943, Gordon Allport lamented that the self had become "lost to view." Although humanistic psychology's emphasis on the self did not instigate much scientific research, it did help renew the concept of self and keep it alive. Now, more than a century after James, the self is one of Western psychology's most vigorously researched topics. Every year, new studies galore appear on self-esteem, self-disclosure, self-awareness, self-monitoring, and so forth.

One example of the thinking about self is the concept of *possible selves* put forth by Hazel Markus and her colleagues (Inglehart & others, 1989; Markus & Nurius, 1986). Your possible selves include your visions of the self you dream of becoming—the rich self, the thin self, the loved and admired self. They also include the self you fear becoming—the unemployed self, the alcoholic self, the academically failed self. Such possible selves motivate us by laying out specific goals and giving us the energy to work toward them. Olympian Carl Lewis concentrated on the achievements of Olympic hero Jesse Owens to give form to his aspirations. Similarly, University of Michigan students in a combined undergraduate/medical school program earn higher grades if they undergo the program with a clear vision of themselves as successful doctors. The biggest dreams often give birth to the greatest achievements.

What possible future selves do you envision? To what extent do these imagined selves motivate you now?

Possible selves By giving them a chance to try out many possible selves, pretend games offer children important opportunities to grow emotionally, socially, and cognitively. Although this young boy may not grow up to be a physician, playing adult roles will certainly bear fruit in terms of an expanded vision of what he might become.

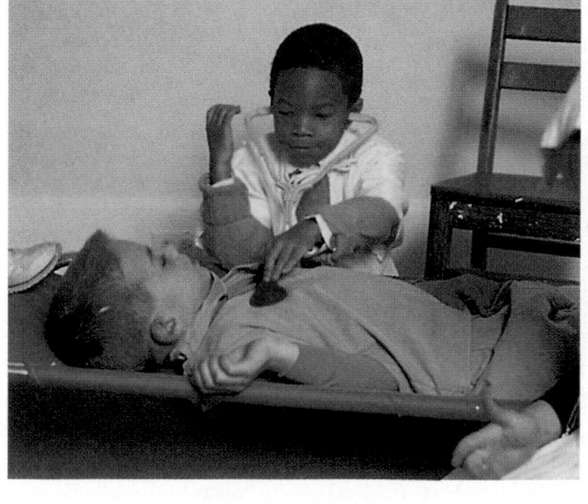

Underlying this research is an assumption (shared by humanistic psychologists) that the self, as organizer of our thoughts, feelings, and actions, is a pivotal center of personality. Research studies confirm the benefits of positive self-esteem but also hint at the hazards of pride.

The Benefits of Self-Esteem

High **self-esteem**—a feeling of self-worth—pays dividends. People who feel good about themselves (who strongly agree with self-affirming questionnaire statements) have fewer sleepless nights, succumb less easily to pressures to conform, are less likely to use drugs, are more persistent at difficult tasks, and are just plain happier (Brockner & Hulton, 1978; Brown, 1991).

People with low self-esteem don't necessarily see themselves as worthless or wicked, but they do lack good things to say about themselves. Such low self-esteem exacts costs. Unhappiness and despair often coexist with low self-esteem. People who feel they are falling short of their hopes are vulnerable to depression. Those whose self-image falls short of what they think they *ought* to be are vulnerable to anxiety (Higgins, 1987). Psychotherapy researcher Hans

self-esteem one's feelings of high or low self-worth.

Strupp (1982) noted that "As soon as one listens to a patient's story, one encounters unhappiness, frustration, and despair. . . . Basic to all these difficulties are impairments in self-acceptance and self-esteem."

Low self-esteem comes in different forms. Those vulnerable to depression often feel they are falling short of their *hopes*. Those vulnerable to anxiety often feel they are falling short of what they *ought* to be (Higgins, 1987). For such people the pain of anticipated social rejection, experienced as low self-esteem, is sometimes adaptive. As with other forms of pain, it may aid survival—by motivating them to behave in ways that sustain their inclusion within a supportive group (Leary & others, 1995). When acting appropriately, they can be comfortable with themselves, knowing they will not be left alone.

The correlational links between low self-esteem and life problems have other possible interpretations. Psychologists William Damon (1995), Robyn Dawes (1994), and Martin Seligman (1994) doubt that self-esteem is really "the armor that protects kids" from life problems. Maybe it's the other way around: Problems and failures may cause low self-esteem. Maybe self-esteem reflects reality. Maybe feeling good *follows* doing well. Maybe it's a side effect of meeting challenges and surmounting difficulties. If so, they say, the best boost to self-esteem may come less from our repeatedly telling children how wonderful they are than from their own hard-won achievements.

LOW SELF-ESTEEM

However, an *effect* of low self-esteem appears in experiments. Temporarily deflate people's self-image (say, by telling them they did poorly on an aptitude test or by disparaging their personality) and they will be more likely to disparage other people or to express heightened racial prejudice. People who are negative about themselves also tend to be thin-skinned and judgmental (Baumeister, 1993; Baumgardner & others, 1989; Pelham, 1993). Although some "love their neighbors as themselves," others loathe their neighbors as themselves. In experiments, those made to feel insecure often become excessively critical, as if to impress others with their own brilliance (Amabile, 1983). Such findings are consistent with Maslow's and Rogers' presumptions that a healthy self-image pays dividends. Accept yourself and you'll find it easier to accept others.

Culture and Self-Esteem

Is it true, as so many assume, that ethnic minorities, people with disabilities, and women live handicapped by impoverished self-esteem? The accumulated evidence says no. African-Americans do *not* suffer lower self-esteem. In the words of social psychologists Jennifer Crocker and Brenda Major (1989): "A host of studies conclude that Blacks have levels of self-esteem equal to or higher than that of Whites." The National Institute of Mental Health's 1980s study of *Psychiatric Disorders in America* similarly reveals that the rates of depression and alcoholism among African and Hispanic Americans are roughly comparable to those among other Americans (if anything, America's ethnic minorities suffer slightly less depression—see page 457).

Is it true, as so many assume, that ethnic minorities, people with disabilities, and women live handicapped by impoverished self-esteem? The accumulated evidence says no.

How could this be? Despite discrimination and sometimes lower social status, members of various "stigmatized" groups (people of color, those with disabilities, women) seem to maintain self-esteem in three ways, according to Crocker and Major:

- They value the things at which they excel.
- They attribute problems to prejudice.
- They do what everyone else does—they compare themselves to those in their own group.

These findings help us understand why, despite the realities of prejudice, all such groups report roughly comparable levels of happiness.

self-serving bias a readiness to perceive oneself favorably.

individualism giving priority to one's own goals over group goals and defining one's identity in terms of personal attributes rather than group identifications.

collectivism giving priority to the goals of one's group (often one's extended family or work group) and defining one's identity accordingly.

The Pervasiveness of Self-Serving Bias

Carl Rogers (1958) once objected to the religious doctrine that humanity's problems arise from excessive self-love, or pride. He noted that most people he had known "despise themselves, regard themselves as worthless and unlovable." Mark Twain had the idea: "No man, deep down in the privacy of his heart, has any considerable respect for himself."

Actually, most of us have a good reputation with ourselves. In studies of self-esteem, even low-scoring people respond in the midrange of possible scores (Baumeister & others, 1989). (A "low" self-esteem person responds to statements such as "I have good ideas" with qualifying adjectives such as *somewhat* or *sometimes*.) Moreover, one of psychology's most provocative yet firmly established recent conclusions concerns our potent **self-serving bias**—our readiness to perceive ourselves favorably (Brown, 1991; Myers, 1996). Consider these findings:

"To love oneself is the beginning of a life-long romance."

Oscar Wilde
An Ideal Husband
1895

People accept more responsibility for good deeds than for bad, and for successes than for failures. Athletes often privately credit their victories to their own prowess and their losses to bad breaks, lousy officiating, or the other team's exceptional performance. After receiving poor exam grades, most students in a half-dozen studies criticized the exam, not themselves. On insurance forms, drivers have explained accidents in such words as: "An invisible car came out of nowhere, struck my car, and vanished." "As I reached an intersection, a hedge sprang up, obscuring my vision, and I did not see the other car." "A pedestrian hit me and went under my car." The question "What have I done to deserve this?" is one we ask of our troubles, not our successes—those, we assume we deserve.

"It is only our bad temper that we put down to being tired or worried or hungry. We put our good temper down to ourselves."

C. S. Lewis
1898–1963

Most people see themselves as better than average. This is true for nearly any subjective and socially desirable dimension. In national surveys, most business executives say they are more ethical than their average counterpart. In several studies, 90 percent of business managers and more than 90 percent of college professors rated their performance as superior to that of their average peer. In Australia, 86 percent of people rate their job performance as above average, and only 1 percent as below average. Although the phenomenon is notably less striking in Asia, where people value modesty, self-serving biases have been observed worldwide: among Dutch, Australian, and Chinese students; Japanese drivers; Indian Hindus; and French people of all walks of life. The world, it seems, is Garrison Keillor's Lake Wobegon writ large—a place where "all the women are strong, all the men are good-looking, and all the children are above average."

"The [self-]portraits that we actually believe, when we are given freedom to voice them, are dramatically more positive than reality can sustain."

Shelley Taylor
Positive Illusions
1989

PEANUTS

Self-serving bias flies in the face of today's pop psychology. "All of us have inferiority complexes," wrote John Powell (1989, p. 15). "Those who seem not to have such a complex are only pretending." But additional findings remove any doubts (Myers, 1999):

- We remember and justify our past actions in self-enhancing ways.
- We exhibit an inflated confidence in the accuracy of our beliefs and judgments.
- We overestimate how desirably *we* would act in situations where most people behave less than admirably.
- We often seek out favorable, self-enhancing information.
- We are quicker to believe flattering descriptions of ourselves than unflattering ones, and we are impressed with psychological tests that make us look good.
- We exhibit group pride—a tendency to see our group (our school, our country, our race) as superior.

Moreover, pride does often go before a fall. Self-serving perceptions underlie conflicts ranging from other-blaming marital discord to self promoting ethnic snobbery. It was national self-righteousness that led both the Americans and Soviets during the arms race to say, "Your weapons threaten us, ours are only for defense." No wonder religion and literature so often warn against the perils of excessive pride.

So, if self-serving bias prevails, why do so many people disparage themselves? For at least two reasons. Sometimes people's self-directed put-downs are subtly strategic: They elicit reassuring strokes. Saying "No one likes me" may at least elicit "But not everyone has met you!" At other times, such as before a game or an exam, self-disparaging comments prepare us for possible failure. The coach who extols the superior strength of the upcoming opponent makes a loss understandable, a victory noteworthy.

"If you compare yourself with others, you may become vain and bitter; for always there will be greater and lesser persons than yourself."

"Desiderata"
Found in Old St. Paul's Church, London
1692

Even so, it's true: All of us some of the time, and some of us much of the time, *do* feel inferior—especially when we compare ourselves with those who are a step or two higher on the ladder of status, looks, income, or agility. The deeper and more frequently we have such feelings, the more unhappy, even depressed, we are. But for most people—the 98 percent who at anytime are *not* suffering depression (Diener, 1993; Gotlib, 1992)—thinking has a naturally positive bias.

For most people—the 98 percent who at anytime are not *suffering depression—thinking has a naturally positive bias.*

We can therefore affirm what humanistic psychologists rightly emphasize: For the individual, self-affirming thinking is generally adaptive. To a point, even our positive illusions are beneficial. They maintain our self-confidence, protect against anxiety and depression, and sustain our sense of well-being. "Life is the art of being well-deceived," observed the English essayist William Hazlitt.

Recognizing both the perils of self-righteousness and the dividends of positive self-esteem, psychologists Roy Baumeister (1989), Jonathan Brown (1991), and Shelley Taylor (1989) have all suggested that humans function best with modest self-enhancing illusions. Like the Japanese and European magnetic levitation trains, Brown noted, we function optimally when riding just off the rails—not so high that we gyrate and crash, yet not so in touch that we grind to a halt.

Culture and the Individual Self

12. *What distinguishes the individualist and collectivist views of self?*

If someone were to rip away your social connections, making you a solitary refugee in a foreign land, how much of your identity would remain intact? The answer might depend in large part on whether your culture nurtures the independent self that marks **individualism** or the interdependent self that marks **collectivism**.

For individualists, a great deal of their identity would remain intact—the very core of their being, their sense of "me," their awareness of their personal convictions and values. Although individualism varies from person to person, cross-cultural psychologists have mostly studied how it varies by culture, ranging from the extreme collectivism of rural Asia to the extreme individualism of the United States (Hofstede, 1980; Triandis, 1994). Individualistic persons and

A Cheesehead first Like athletes who take more pleasure in their team's victory than in their own performance, collectivists find satisfaction in advancing their group's interests, even at the expense of personal needs. But even individualists sometimes identify with things larger than themselves, as with this fan ardently supporting "his" football team in Wisconsin.

cultures give priority to personal goals and define their identity mostly in terms of their personal attributes. They strive for personal control and individual achievement.

For collectivists, being set adrift in a foreign land might entail a much greater loss of identity. Cut off from family, groups, and loyal friends, collectivists would lose connections that have defined who they are. In a collectivist culture, a social network provides one's bearings. What's important is not "me" but "we." Collectivists give priority to the goals of their groups—often their family, clan, or work group—and define their identity accordingly. By their group identifications, collectivists gain a sense of belonging, a set of values, a network of caring individuals, an assurance of security.

Compared with American students, students in Japan, China, and India are much less likely to complete the sentence "I am . . ." with personal traits ("I am sincere," "I am confident") and are much more likely to declare their social identities ("I am a Keio University student," "I am the third son in my family") (Cousins, 1989; Dhawan & others, 1995; Triandis, 1989a,b). For Westerners, individual identity is primary; for Asians, collective identity is more often primary.

The contrast between more individualistic and collectivistic cultures appears in people's names. Individualist cultures give priority to personal identity, by putting the personal name first ("Christine Brune"). Collectivist cultures often give priority to one's family identity ("Hui Harry"). Family loyalty also appears in popular Chinese songs, which much more often than Western popular songs express positive feelings for one's parents. To those who are from individualistic cultures, a typical Chinese song may sound quaint (Rothbaum & Xu, 1995):

> *I am mamma's short poem*
> *Composed of mother's painstaking effort,*
> *Mamma has suffered so much pain for me . . .*
> *How much I wish there would be good news tomorrow*
> *To repay mother's deep feeling for me.*

To a rural Chinese person, songs like "I Gotta Be Me" would seem equally odd.

No wonder, says Harry Triandis (1989b), that modern world colonization was led not by Asians, who were reluctant to cut social and family ties, but by the more individualist Europeans. And no wonder that countries colonized by Europeans willing to leave friends and family are today highly individualistic.

Being more self-contained, individualists easily move in and out of social groups. They feel relatively free to switch churches, to leave one job for another, or even to leave their extended families and migrate to a new place. Marriage is for as long as they both shall love. In contrast, collectivists may act shy in new groups and are more easily embarrassed (Singelis & Sharkey, 1995). They have deeper, more stable attachments to their familiar groups and friends. Relationships are long-term. Thus, loyalties run strong between employer and employees.

Because they value communal solidarity, people in collectivist cultures place a premium on maintaining harmony and allowing others to save face. Direct confrontation and blunt honesty are rare, as are expressions of personal egotism. What people say reflects not only what they feel (their inner attitudes) but also what they presume others feel (Kashima & others, 1992). Elders and superiors command respect. To preserve group spirit, people avoid touchy topics, defer to others' wishes, and display a polite, self-effacing humility (Kitayama & Markus, in press; Markus & Kitayama, 1991). People remember those who have done them favors and make reciprocation a social art. The collectivist self is not independent but *inter*dependent (Table 11.2). Among collectivists—especially those influenced by the Confucian idea of self as embedded in "a web of interrelatedness"—no person is an island (Kim & Lee, 1994).

Collectivism By identifying with family and other groups, these yak herders in India gain a sense of "we," a set of values, a network of care.

Individualism and collectivism each offer benefits—at a cost. People in competitive, individualistic cultures have more personal freedom, take more pride in personal achievements, are less geographically bound to their families, and enjoy more privacy. Their less-unified cultures offer a smorgasbord of lifestyles and invite individuals to construct their own identities. Innovation and creativity are celebrated, and human rights are respected. Such may help explain Ed Diener, Marissa Diener, and Carol Diener's (1995) finding that peo-

Table 11.2 Value Contrasts Between Individualism and Collectivism

Concept	Individualism	Collectivism
Self	Independent (identity from individual traits)	Interdependent (identity from belonging)
Life task	Discover and express one's uniqueness	Maintain connections, fit in
What matters	Me—personal achievement and fulfillment; rights and liberties	We—group goals and solidarity; social responsibilities and relationships
Coping method	Change reality	Accommodate to reality
Morality	Defined by individuals (self-based)	Defined by social networks (duty-based)
Relationships	Many, often temporary or casual; confrontation acceptable	Few, close and enduring; harmony valued
Attributing behavior	Behavior reflects one's personality and attitudes	Behavior reflects social norms and roles

Source: Adapted from Thomas Schoeneman (1994) and Harry Triandis (1994).

ple in individualistic cultures report greater happiness than do those in collectivist cultures. When individualists pursue their own ends and all goes well, life can seem rewarding.

But such benefits can come at the price of more frequent loneliness, more divorce, more homicide, and more stress-related disease (Popenoe, 1993; Triandis et al., 1988). Collectivists demand less romance and personal fulfillment in marriage, which puts the marriage relationship under less pressure (Dion & Dion, 1993). In one survey, "keeping romance alive" was rated as important to a good marriage by 78 percent of American women and 29 percent of Japanese women (*American Enterprise*, 1992).

In recent decades, Western individualism has increased, and the priority placed on social obligations and family ties has decreased (Yankelovich, 1994). Martin Seligman (1988) has argued that "rampant individualism carries with it two seeds of its own destruction. First, a society that exalts the individual to the extent ours now does will be ridden with depression. . . . Second, and perhaps most important, is meaninglessness [which occurs when there is no] attachment to something larger than you are."

Evaluating the Humanistic Perspective

13. *What impact has the humanistic perspective had on psychology?*

One thing said of Freud can also be said of the humanistic psychologists: Their impact has been pervasive. Their ideas have influenced counseling, education, child-rearing, and management. They have also influenced—sometimes in ways they did not intend—much of today's popular psychology.

One thing said of Freud can also be said of the humanistic psychologists: Their impact has been pervasive. Their ideas have influenced counseling, education, child-rearing, and management.

Through popular psychology many of us absorb some of what Maslow and Rogers taught—that a positive self-concept is the key to happiness and success, that acceptance and empathy help nurture positive feelings about oneself, and that people are basically good and capable of self-improvement. One study found that, by a 4-to-1 margin, Americans believe "human nature is basically good" rather than "fundamentally perverse and corrupt" (NORC, 1985). Humanistic psychologists can also take satisfaction in the changed response to one of the MMPI items: Among those in the 1930s normal standardization sample, only 9 percent agreed that "I am an important person"; in the mid-1980s, more than half agreed (Holden, 1986b). Responding to a 1989 Gallup poll, 85 percent of Americans rated "having a good self-image or self-respect" as *very* important; 0 percent rated it unimportant. And 89 percent of people responding to a 1992 *Newsweek* Gallup poll rated self-esteem as very important for "motivating a person to work hard and succeed." Humanistic psychology's message has been heard.

Perhaps one reason that message has been so well received is that its emphasis on the individual self reflects and reinforces Western cultural values. As self-reliant individualism has grown, with increased priority given to personal identity and aspirations, the popular media have celebrated the rugged individual. Movie plots feature rugged heroes who, true to themselves, buck social convention or take the law into their own hands. Popular songs proclaim that "I Did It My Way" and remind us that to love yourself is "The Greatest Love of All" (Schoeneman, 1994).

The prominence of the humanistic perspective also set off a backlash of criticism. First, said the critics, its concepts are vague and subjective. Consider the description of self-actualizing people as open, spontaneous, loving, self-accepting, and productive. Is this really a scientific description? Or is it merely a description of Maslow's personal values and ideals? What Maslow did, noted M. Brewster Smith (1978), was to offer impressions of his own personal heroes. Imagine another theorist who began with a different set of heroes—perhaps Napoleon, Alexander the Great, and John D. Rockefeller, Sr. This theorist would likely describe self-actualizing people as "undeterred by the needs of others," "motivated to achieve," and "obsessed with power."

Action requires enough realism to fuel concern and enough optimism to provide hope. Humanistic psychology, say the critics, encourages the needed hope but not the equally necessary realism about evil.

Second, some object to the idea that, as Carl Rogers put it, "The only question which matters is, 'Am I living in a way which is deeply satisfying to me, and which truly expresses me?'" (quoted by Wallach & Wallach, 1985). These critics have argued that the individualism encouraged by humanistic psychology—trusting and acting on one's feelings, being true to oneself, fulfilling oneself—may promote self-indulgence, selfishness, and an erosion of moral restraints (Campbell & Specht, 1985; Wallach & Wallach, 1983). Indeed, it is those who focus not on themselves but beyond themselves who are most likely to experience social support, to enjoy life, and to cope effectively with stress (Crandall, 1984).

Humanistic psychologists rebut such objections. They counter that belligerence, hostility, and insensitivity are often traceable to a poor self-concept. Moreover, they argue, a secure, nondefensive self-acceptance is actually the first step toward loving others.

A final accusation leveled against the humanistic psychologists is that of failing to appreciate the reality of our human capacity for evil. Faced with assaults on the environment, overpopulation, and threats of nuclear war, we may develop apathy from either of two rationalizations. One is a naive optimism that denies the threat ("People are basically good; everything will work out"). The other is a dark despair ("It's hopeless; why try?"). Action requires enough realism to fuel concern and enough optimism to provide hope. Humanistic psychology, say the critics, encourages the needed hope but not the equally necessary realism about evil.

However, even within humanistic psychology there is debate over whether people are basically good. Carl Rogers clearly thought so. Although aware of the "incredible amount" of cruel, destructive behavior in the world, he did "not find that this evil is inherent in human nature." Given growth-promoting conditions, "I have never known an individual to choose the cruel or destructive path" (Rogers, 1981). Evil, in his view, springs not from human nature but from toxic cultural influences, including "the constricting, destructive influence of our educational system, the injustice of our distribution of wealth, [and] our cultivated prejudices against individuals who are different."

"We do pretty well when you stop to think that people are basically good."

Fellow humanistic psychologist Rollo May dissented from Rogers' optimism. Of course the cultural context matters, he said. But "Who makes up the culture except persons like you and me? The culture is evil as well as good because we, the human beings who constitute it, are evil as well as good." May agreed with critics who see people joining the humanistic movement seeking "a community of like-minded persons who also are playing possum to the evils about us." Accepting the reality of human evil requires "the age-old religious truths of mercy and forgiveness," he said, "and it leaves no place for self-righteousness" (May, 1982).

REHEARSE IT!

14. Abraham Maslow theorized that human beings are motivated by a hierarchy of needs. When basic physiological and psychological needs are satisfied, he wrote, people become motivated to fulfill their potential through self-actualization. Maslow based his ideas on

a. Freudian theory.
b. his experiences with patients.
c. a series of laboratory experiments.
d. his study of healthy, creative people.

15. According to Carl Rogers, a growth-promoting environment is one that offers genuineness, acceptance, and empathy. The total acceptance Rogers advocated is called

a. self-concept.
b. unconditional positive regard.
c. self-actualization.
d. the "ideal self."

16. Researchers have found that high self-esteem is beneficial, noting that people who feel good about themselves have fewer sleepless nights, are less likely to use drugs, and are happier, for example. On the other hand, low self-esteem is linked with life problems. How should this link between low self-esteem and life problems be interpreted?

a. Life problems cause low self-esteem.
b. The answer isn't clear because the link is correlational and does not indicate cause and effect.
c. Low self-esteem leads to life problems.
d. Because of the self-serving bias, we must assume that external factors cause low self-esteem.

17. Researchers have found that people tend to accept responsibility for their successes or good qualities and blame circumstances or luck for their failures. This is an example of

a. low self-esteem.
b. self-actualization.
c. self-serving bias.
d. empathy.

18. Individualists and collectivists have differing identities. Compared with collectivists, individualists more often define themselves in terms of their

a. family connections.
b. nationality.
c. social roles.
d. personal achievements.

19. The humanistic perspective is most concerned with the potential for human growth and self-fulfillment; ideas of the humanistic psychologists have found their way into counseling, education, child-rearing, and popular psychology. The humanistic perspective has been so well received because

a. its emphasis on the individual fits well with the erosion of moral restraints in modern society.
b. it feeds people's optimism about the good in human nature.
c. it negates the idea that humans have a basic capacity for evil.
d. its emphasis on the individual self reflects and reinforces Western cultural values.

The Social-Cognitive Perspective

14. *What factors does the social-cognitive perspective emphasize?*

Our fourth major perspective on personality derives from psychological principles of learning, cognition, and social behavior. Called the *social-cognitive perspective* by psychologist Albert Bandura (1986), and the *cognitive social learning perspective* by others, its proponents emphasize the importance of external events and how we interpret them. Like learning theorists, social-cognitive theorists believe that we learn many of our behaviors either through conditioning or by observing others and modeling our behavior after theirs. They also emphasize the importance of mental processes: What we think about our situation affects our behavior.

reciprocal determinism the interacting influences between personality and environmental factors.

personal control our sense of controlling our environments rather than feeling helpless.

external locus of control the perception that chance or outside forces beyond one's personal control will determine one's fate.

internal locus of control the perception that one controls one's own fate.

learned helplessness the hopelessness and passive resignation an animal or human learns when unable to avoid repeated aversive events.

Exploring Behavior in Situations

Instead of focusing solely on how our environment controls us (behaviorism), social-cognitive theorists focus on how we and our environment interact: How do we interpret and respond to external events? How do our schemas, our memories, and our expectations influence our behavior patterns?

Reciprocal Influences

Bandura (1986) called the process of influencing and being influenced by our environment **reciprocal determinism**. "Behavior, internal personal factors, and environmental influences," he said, "all operate as interlocking determinants of each other" (Figure 11.4). For example, children's TV-viewing habits (past behavior) influence their viewing preferences (personal factor), which influence how television (environmental factor) affects their current behavior. The influences are mutual.

Consider three specific ways in which persons and environments interact:

1. ***Different people choose different environments.*** The school you attend, the reading you do, the television programs you watch, the music you listen to, the friends you associate with—all are part of an environment you have chosen, based partly on your dispositions (Ickes & others, 1997). *You choose it and it then shapes you.*
2. ***Our personalities shape how we interpret and react to events.*** Anxious people, for example, are more likely to be attuned to potentially threatening events than are nonanxious people (Eysenck & others, 1987). Thus, anxious people perceive the world as more threatening, and they react accordingly.
3. ***Our personalities help create situations to which we react.*** Many experiments reveal that how we view and treat people influences how they in turn treat us. If we expect someone to be angry with us, we may ignore the person, touching off the very behavior we expect.

Figure 11.4 **Reciprocal determinism** The social-cognitive perspective proposes that our personalities are shaped by the interaction of personal/cognitive factors (our thoughts and feelings), our environment, and our behaviors.

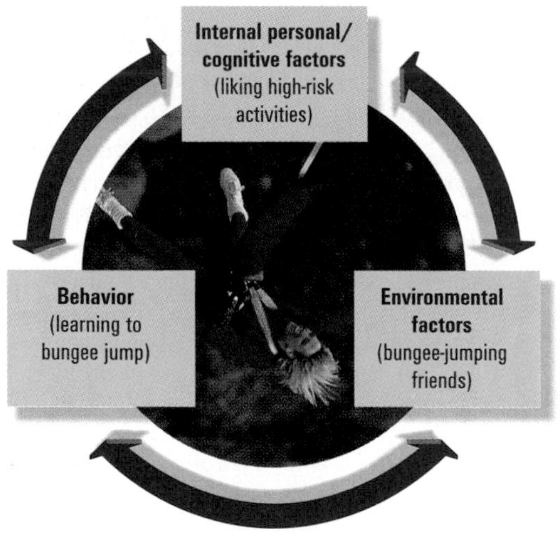

In such ways, we are both the products and the architects of our environments. If all this has a familiar ring, it may be because it parallels and reinforces a pervasive theme in psychology and in this book: *Behavior emerges from the interplay of external and internal influences.* Boiling water turns an egg hard and a potato soft. A threatening environment turns one person into a hero, another into a scoundrel. *At every moment*, our behavior is determined by our genes, our experiences, and our personalities.

Personal Control

15. *What are the causes and consequences of personal control?*

In studying how we interact with our environment, social-cognitive psychologists emphasize our sense of **personal control**—whether we learn to see ourselves as controlling, or as controlled by, our environments. Psychologists have two basic ways to study the effect of personal control (or any personality factor). One: *Correlate* people's feelings of control with their behaviors and achievements. Two: *Experiment*, by raising or lowering people's sense of control and noting the effects. Let's take these one at a time.

Locus of Control

Consider your own feelings of control. Do you feel that your life is beyond your control? That the world is run by a few powerful people? That getting a good job depends mainly on being in the right place at the right time? Or do you more strongly believe that what happens to you is your own doing? That the average person can influence government decisions? That being a success is a matter of hard work, not luck?

Hundreds of studies have compared people who differ in their perceptions of control. On the one side are those who have what psychologist Julian Rotter called an **external locus of control**—the perception that chance or outside forces determine their fate. On the other are those who perceive an **internal locus of control** and believe that to a great extent they control their own destinies. In study after study, "internals" achieve more in school, act more independently, and feel less depressed than do "externals" (Findley & Cooper, 1983; Lefcourt, 1982; Presson & Benassi, 1996). Moreover, they are better able to delay gratification and cope with various stresses, including marital problems (Miller & others, 1986).

Learned Helplessness Versus Personal Control

Helpless, oppressed people often perceive control to be external, and this perception may deepen their feelings of resignation. This is precisely what researcher Martin Seligman (1975, 1991) and others found in experiments with both animals and people. When dogs were strapped in a harness and given repeated shocks, with no opportunity to avoid them, they learned a sense of helplessness. When later placed in another situation where they *could* escape the punishment by merely leaping a hurdle, the dogs cowered without hope. Faced with repeated traumatic events over which they have no control, people, too, come to feel helpless, hopeless, and depressed. This passive resignation is called **learned helplessness** (Figure 11.5). In contrast, animals able to escape the shocks in the first situation learn personal control and easily escape shocks in the new situation.

Figure 11.5 **Learned helplessness** When animals and people experience no control over repeated bad events, they often learn helplessness.

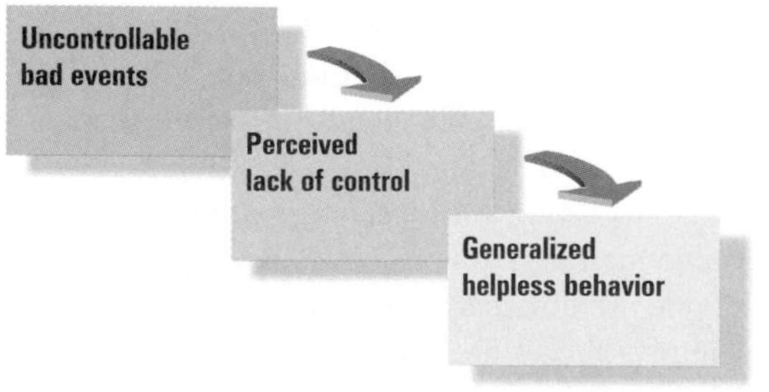

In prisons, even in factories, colleges, and well-meaning nursing homes, people given little control experience a similar lowering of morale and increased stress. Part of the shock we feel in an unfamiliar culture is a sense of diminished control when we are unsure of how people in the new environment will respond (Triandis, 1994). Measures that increase control—allowing prisoners to move chairs and control room lights and the TV, having workers participate in decision making, offering nursing home patients choices about their environment—noticeably improve health and morale (Miller & Monge, 1986; Ruback & others, 1986; Wener & others, 1987). In one famous study of nursing home patients, 93 percent of those encouraged to exert more control became more alert, active, and happy (Rodin, 1986). As researcher Ellen Langer (1983, p. 291) concluded, "Perceived control is basic to human functioning." She recommended that "for the young and old alike," we create environments that enhance a sense of control and personal efficacy.

The verdict of these studies is reassuring: People thrive under conditions of democracy, personal freedom, and empowerment. Small wonder that the citizens of stable democracies report higher levels of happiness (Inglehart, 1990). Shortly before the democratic revolution in the former East Germany, psychologists Gabriele Oettingen and Martin Seligman (1990) compared the telltale body language of working-class men in East and West Berlin bars. Compared with their counterparts on the other side of the Wall, the empowered West Berliners much more often laughed, sat upright rather than slumped, and had upward- rather than downward-turned mouths. To paraphrase the Roman philosopher Seneca, happy are those who choose their own path.

Control affects well-being Nursing home residents who can arrange their own possessions, control other aspects of their daily lives, and pursue their own interests are more vigorous and happy than those who do not have these opportunities.

Optimism

One measure of how helpless or effective you feel is where you stand on the trait dimension of optimism-pessimism. How do you characteristically explain negative and positive events? Perhaps you have known students whose *attributional style* is negative—who attribute poor performance to their lack of ability ("I can't do this") or to situations beyond their control ("bad" teachers, textbooks, or exam questions). Such students are more likely to persist in getting low grades than are students who adopt the more hopeful attitude that effort, good study habits, and self-discipline can make a difference (Noel & others, 1987; Peterson & Barrett, 1987).

THINKING CRITICALLY

Pseudo-Assessment—How to Be a "Successful" Astrologer or Palm Reader

How should we evaluate alternative ways of assessing personality? Does the alignment of the stars and planets at the time of one's birth give a clue? Is one's handwriting revealing? Do our palms expose deep secrets?

While astronomers scoff at the naiveté of astrology, psychologists ask a different question: Does it work? Are birth dates correlated with character traits? Given someone's birth date, can astrologers surpass chance when asked to identify the person from a short lineup of different personality descriptions? Can people pick out their own horoscopes from a lineup of horoscopes? The consistent answers have been: no, no, no, and no (British Psychological Society, 1993; Carlson, 1985; Kelly, 1997). Graphologists, who make predictions from handwriting samples, have similarly been found to do no better than chance when trying to guess people's occupations, based on several pages of their handwriting (Beyerstein & Beyerstein, 1992; Dean & others, 1992).

How, then, do astrologers and the like persuade thousands of newspapers worldwide and millions of people to buy their advice? Ray Hyman (1981), palm reader turned research psychologist, has revealed the suckering methods of astrologers, palm readers, and crystal-ball gazers.

Their first technique, the "stock spiel," builds on the observation that each of us is in some ways like no one else and in other ways like everyone. That some things are true of us all enables the "seer" to offer statements that seem impressively accurate: "I sense that you're nursing a grudge against someone; you really ought to let that go." "You worry about things more than you let on, even to your best friends." "You are adaptable to social situations and your interests are wide-ranging."

Such generally true statements can be combined into a personality description. Imagine that you take a personality test and then receive the following character sketch:

> You have a strong need for other people to like and to admire you. You have a tendency to be critical of yourself. . . . You pride yourself on being an independent thinker and do not accept other opinions without satisfactory proof. You have found it unwise to be too frank in revealing yourself to others. At times you are extraverted, affable, sociable; at other times you are introverted, wary, and reserved. Some of your aspirations tend to be pretty unrealistic. (Forer, 1949)

In experiments, college students have received stock assessments like this one, drawn from statements in a newsstand astrology book. When they think the bogus feedback was prepared just for them and when it is generally favorable, they nearly always rate the description as either "good" or "excellent" (Davies, 1997). Peter Glick and his co-workers (1989) found that even skeptics of astrology, when given a flattering description attributed to an astrologer, begin to think that "maybe there's something to this astrology business after all."

French psychologist Michael Gauguelin placed an ad in a Paris newspaper offering a free personal horoscope. Ninety-four percent of those receiving the horoscope later praised the description as accurate. Actually, all had received the horoscope of France's Dr. Petiot, a notorious mass murderer (Kurtz, 1983).

This acceptance is called *the Barnum effect*, named in honor of master showman P. T. Barnum's dictum, "There's a sucker born every minute." So powerful is the Barnum effect that, given a choice between this stock spiel and an individualized personality description actually based on a real test, most people choose the phony description as being more accurate. Astrologers and palm readers sprinkle their assessments with stock statements.

A second technique used by seers is to "read" our clothing, physical features, nonverbal gestures, and reactions to what they are saying. Imagine yourself as the character reader who was visited by a young woman in her late twenties or early thirties.

"We just haven't been flapping them hard enough."

In one study of optimism and behavior, Seligman and Peter Schulman (1986) compared sales made by new life insurance representatives who were more or less optimistic in their outlooks. Those who put an optimistic spin on setbacks—by seeing them as flukes or as suggesting a new approach rather than viewing them as signs of incompetence—sold more policies during their first year and were half as likely to quit. Seligman's finding came to life for him when Bob Dell, one of the optimistic recruits who began selling for Metropolitan Life after taking Seligman's optimism test, later dialed him up and sold him a policy.

Health, too, benefits from a basic optimism. As we saw in Chapter 10, a depressed hopelessness dampens the body's disease-fighting immune system. In repeated studies, optimists have been found to outlive pessimists or to live with fewer illnesses.

If positive thinking in the face of adversity pays dividends, so, too, can a dash of realism. Anxiety over contemplated failure can actually fuel energetic efforts to avoid the dreaded fate (Cantor & Norem, 1989; Goodhart, 1986; Showers, 1992). Overconfident students often perform less well than their equally able peers who, fearing they are going to bomb on the upcoming exam, proceed to study furiously and get fabulous grades. Edward Chang (1996) reports that,

Hyman described the woman as "wearing expensive jewelry, a wedding band, and a black dress of cheap material. The observant reader noted that she was wearing shoes which were advertised for people with foot trouble." Do these clues suggest anything?

Drawing on these observations, the character reader proceeded to amaze his client with his insights. He assumed that the woman had come to see him, as did most of his female customers, because of a love or financial problem. The black dress and the wedding band led him to reason that her husband had died recently. The expensive jewelry suggested that she had been financially comfortable during marriage, but the cheap dress suggested that her husband's death had left her impoverished. The therapeutic shoes signified that she was now standing on her feet more than she was used to, implying that she had been working to support herself since her husband's death.

If you are not as shrewd as this character reader (who correctly guessed that the woman was wondering if she should remarry in the hope of ending her economic hardship), no matter, according to Hyman. Just tell people what they want to hear. Memorize some Barnum statements from astrology and fortune-telling manuals and use them liberally. Tell people it is their responsibility to cooperate by relating your message to their specific experiences. Later they will recall that you predicted the specific events. Phrase statements as questions, and when you detect a positive response assert the statement strongly. Be a good listener, and later, in different words, reveal to people what they earlier revealed to you. If you dupe them, they will come.

Better yet, beware of fortune-tellers, who, by exploiting people with these techniques, become fortune-takers.

compared with European-American students, Asian-American students express somewhat greater pessimism—which he suspects partially explains their more impressive academic achievements. Success requires enough optimism to provide hope, but also enough pessimism to prevent complacency.

Excessive optimism can also blind us to real risks. Neil Weinstein (1980, 1982, 1996) has shown how our natural positive-thinking bias can promote "an unrealistic optimism about future life events." Most college students perceive themselves as less likely than their average classmate to develop drinking problems, drop out of school, or have a heart attack by age 40. Most late adolescents see themselves as much less vulnerable than their peers to the AIDS virus (Abrams, 1991).

"O God, give us grace to accept with serenity the things that cannot be changed, courage to change the things which should be changed, and the wisdom to distinguish the one from the other."

Reinhold Niebuhr
"The Serenity Prayer"
1943

Given such illusory optimism, documented in nearly 200 research reports, people may fail to take sensible precautions. Most young Americans know that half of U.S. marriages end in divorce, but they are confident that *theirs* will not (Lehman & Nisbett, 1985). Most cigarette smokers smoke high-tar brands, but only 17 percent believe their brand to have a more hazardous tar level than most others (Segerstrom & others, 1993). Compared with other women at their university, sexually active undergraduate women—especially those who do *not* consistently use effective contraception—perceive themselves as *less* vulnerable to unwanted pregnancy (Burger & Burns, 1988). Those who optimistically venture into ill-fated relationships, deny the effects of smoking, or engage in unprotected sex remind us that, like pride, blind optimism may go before a fall.

Assessing Behavior in Situations

16. *How do social-cognitive researchers evaluate personality?*

Social-cognitive researchers explore the effect of differing situations on people's behavior patterns and attitudes. They study, for example, how viewing aggressive or nonaggressive models affects behavior. They assess the impact of dehumanizing situations on people's attitudes. And they examine the consistency of people's personalities in varying circumstances.

An ambitious example of such research, and one that predates social-cognitive theory, is the U.S. Army's World War II strategy for assessing candidates for spy missions. Rather than using paper-and-pencil tests, army psychologists subjected the candidates to simulated undercover conditions. They tested their ability to handle stress, solve problems, maintain leadership, and withstand intense interrogation without blowing their covers. Although time-consuming and expensive, the assessment of behavior in a realistic situation helped predict later success on real spy missions (OSS Assessment Staff, 1948).

Business, military, and educational organizations are continuing this strategy in their evaluations of several hundred thousand persons each year in some 2000 assessment centers (Bray & Byham, 1991). AT&T observes prospective managers doing simulated managerial work. Many colleges assess potential faculty members' teaching abilities by observing them teach. The army assesses its soldiers by observing them during military exercises.

These procedures exploit the principle that the best means of predicting people's future behavior is not a personality test or an interviewer's intuition. Rather, it is their past behavior patterns in similar situations (Mischel, 1981). As long as the situation and the person remain much the same, the best predictor of future job performance is past job performance; the best predictor of future grades is past grades; the best predictor of future aggressiveness is past aggressiveness; the best predictor of drug use in young adulthood is drug use in high school. If you can't check the person's past behavior, the next-best thing is to create an assessment situation that simulates the task demands so you can see how the person handles them.

Evaluating the Social-Cognitive Perspective

17. *How does the social-cognitive perspective hold up under criticism?*

The social-cognitive perspective sensitizes researchers to how situations affect, and are affected by, individuals. More than the other perspectives, this perspective builds from psychological research on learning and cognition.

One criticism is that the theory focuses so much on the situation that it fails to appreciate the person's inner traits. Where is the person in this view of personality, ask the dissenters (Carlson, 1984); and where are human emotions? True, the situation guides our behavior. But in many instances our unconscious motives, our emotions, and our pervasive traits shine through, say the critics. Consider Percy Ray Pridgen and Charles Gill, who faced the same situation: They jointly won a $90 million lottery jackpot (Harriston, 1993). Upon learning the winning numbers, Pridgen began trembling uncontrollably, then huddled with a friend behind a bathroom door while confirming the win, then sobbed. Gill told his wife and then went to sleep.

And that brings us back to where we began our review of these personality theories: Each perspective summarized in Table 11.3 can teach us something.

Table 11.3 The Four Perspectives on Personality

Perspective	Behavior Springs From	Assessment Techniques	Evaluation
Psychoanalytic	Unconscious conflicts between pleasure-seeking impulses and social restraints	Projective tests aimed at revealing unconscious motivations	A speculative, hard-to-test theory with enormous cultural impact
Trait	Expressing biologically influenced dispositions, such as extraversion or introversion	Personality inventories that assess the strengths of different traits	A descriptive approach criticized as sometimes underestimating the variability of behavior from situation to situation
Humanistic	Processing conscious feelings about oneself in the light of one's experiences	(a) Questionnaire assessments of self-concept (b) Empathic interviews	A humane theory that reinvigorated contemporary interest in the self; criticized as subjective and sometimes naively self-centered and optimistic
Social-cognitive	Reciprocal influences between people and their situations, colored by perceptions of control	(a) Correlational and experimental studies of people's feelings of control (b) Observations of people's behavior in particular situations	An interactive theory that integrates research on learning, cognition, and social behavior; criticized as under-estimating the importance of emotions and enduring traits

The psychoanalytic perspective draws our attention to the unconscious and irrational aspects of human existence. The trait perspective systematically describes and classifies important personality components. The humanistic perspective reminds us of the importance of our sense of self and of our potential for self-actualization. The social-cognitive perspective applies psychology's basic concepts of learning and thinking and teaches us that we always act in the context of situations that we help to create.

"Nature is always more subtle, more intricate, more elegant than what we are able to imagine."

Carl Sagan
"Science—Who Cares?"
1991

Seldom in life does a single perspective on any issue give us a complete picture of another human being. Human personality reveals its different aspects when we view it from different perspectives. Each perspective enlarges our vision of the whole person.

REHEARSE IT!

20. Albert Bandura, a social-cognitive theorist, believes that interacting with our environment involves reciprocal determinism, or mutual influences among personal factors, environmental factors, and behavior. An example of an environmental factor is

a. the presence of books in a home.
b. a preference for outdoor play.
c. the ability to read at a fourth-grade level.
d. the fear of violent action on television.

21. Researchers have found that when elderly patients are given an active part in the management of their care and surroundings, their morale and health tend to improve. The assumption is that the patients do better when they perceive

a. learned helplessness.
b. an external locus of control.
c. an internal locus of control.
d. reciprocal determinism.

22. Martin Seligman described an attitude of passive resignation, which he called learned helplessness. Working with animals and people, Seligman identified the circumstances under which learned helplessness develops. For example, a dog will respond with learned helplessness if it has received repeated shocks and has had

a. the opportunity to escape.
b. no control over the shocks.
c. pain or discomfort.
d. no food or water prior to the shocks.

23. A goal of many personality theories is to be able to predict a person's behavior in a particular situation. A theory that is very sensitive to the way people affect, and are affected by, particular situations, but that says little about enduring traits, is the __________ theory.

a. psychoanalytic
b. trait
c. humanistic
d. social-cognitive

24. We have reviewed four perspectives on personality: the psychoanalytic, trait, humanistic, and social-cognitive perspectives. What conclusion can we draw regarding the four perspectives?

a. The usefulness of each depends on the behavior being studied.
b. Together, they provide an enlarged picture of the whole person.
c. The trait and social-cognitive perspectives are currently the most useful for understanding personality.
d. They need to be supplemented by a biological perspective on personality.

REVIEWING ■ *Personality*

1. *What is personality?*

Like intelligence, **personality** is an abstract concept that cannot be seen, touched, or directly measured. To psychologists, personality is one's relatively distinctive and consistent pattern of thinking, feeling, and acting. We have examined four major perspectives on personality, each valuable for the light it sheds on our complex behavior patterns.

The Psychoanalytic Perspective

2. *What role do unconscious dynamics play in Freud's theory of personality?*

Sigmund Freud believed that the mind was like an iceberg, with the **unconscious** region below the surface and the **preconscious** close enough to the surface for its contents to be retrievable. Treatment of emotional disorders led him to believe they resulted from unconscious dynamics of personality, dynamics that he sought to analyze through the techniques of **free association** and dream analysis. He referred to his theory and techniques as **psychoanalysis**.

3. *How did Freud view personality structure and development, and how did he think people defended themselves against anxiety?*

Freud saw personality as composed of a reservoir of pleasure-seeking psychic impulses (the **id**), a reality-oriented executive (the **ego**), and an internalized set of ideals (the **superego**).

Freud believed that children develop through several formative **psychosexual stages**, which he labeled the oral, anal, phallic, latency, and genital stages. During the phallic stage, boys may experience an **Oedipus complex**. To cope with threatening feelings about their parents, boys and girls **identify** with the same-sex parent, which provides their gender identity. He suggested that people's later personalities were influenced by how they resolved conflicts associated with these stages and whether they remained **fixated** at any stage.

To cope with anxiety caused by the tensions between the demands of id and superego, the ego has protective, reality-distorting **defense mechanisms**: **repression**, **regression**, **reaction formation**, **projection**, **rationalization**, **displacement**, and **sublimation**. Of these, Freud believed, repression is the most basic.

4. *How did Freud's followers differ from him?*

Neo-Freudians, among them Alfred Adler and Karen Horney, accepted many of Freud's ideas but placed more emphasis on conscious experience and on social motivations other than sex and aggression, such as feelings of inferiority and anxiety. Carl Jung expanded Freud's concept of the unconscious to include a **collective unconscious** that he believed all humans inherit.

5. *How do projective tests assess personality, and are they considered valid?*

Psychoanalytic assessment aims to reveal the unconscious aspects of personality. Although some critics question the reliability and validity of **projective tests**, such as the **Thematic Apperception Test (TAT)** and the **Rorschach inkblots**, many clinicians continue to use the Rorschach.

6. *How do Freud's ideas hold up today?*

Critics say many of Freud's specific ideas are implausible, unvalidated, or contradicted by new research, and that his theory offers only after-the-fact explanations. Nevertheless, Freud drew psychology's attention to the unconscious, to the struggle to cope with anxiety and sexuality, and to the conflict between biological impulses and social restraints. His cultural impact has been enormous.

The Trait Perspective

7. *How do trait theorists view personality?*

Rather than explain the hidden aspects of personality, **trait** theorists have described the predispositions that underlie our actions. Through factor analysis, these theorists have isolated distinct dimensions of personality: for example, the Big Five trait dimensions—emotional stability, extraversion, openness, agreeableness, and conscientiousness.

8. *How do we assess traits?*

To assess traits, psychologists have devised objective **personality inventories** such as the **empirically derived MMPI**. Computerized testing has made these inventories widely available; however, they are still most helpful when used to assess those who are emotionally troubled.

9. *Does research support the consistency of personality traits?*

Critics of trait theory question the consistency with which traits are expressed. Although people's traits do seem to persist through time, human behavior varies widely from situation to situation. Nevertheless, people's average behavior across different situations is fairly consistent.

The Humanistic Perspective

10. *What is the central focus of the humanistic perspective?*

Humanistic psychologists have sought to turn psychology's attention to the growth potential of healthy people, as seen through the individual's own experiences and self-concept. Abraham Maslow believed that if basic human needs are fulfilled, people will strive to actualize their highest potential. To describe **self-actualization**, he studied some exemplary personalities and summarized his impressions of their qualities. To nurture growth in others, Carl Rogers advised psychologists to use **unconditional positive regard** by being genuine, accepting, and empathic. In such a climate, people can develop a deeper self-awareness and a more realistic and positive **self-concept**. Humanistic psychologists assess personality through questionnaires that rate self-concept and by seeking to understand others' subjective personal experiences in therapy.

11. *What have we learned from research on the self?*

Through studies of **self-esteem** and **self-serving bias**, we know that self-esteem is an adaptive quality and that most people do perceive and explain themselves favorably.

12. ***What distinguishes the individualist and collectivist views of self?***

    Individuals and cultures vary in whether they give priority to "me" or "we"—to personal control and individual achievement or to social connections and solidarity. Self-reliant **individualism** defines identity in terms of personal goals and attributes; socially connected **collectivism** gives priority to group goals and to one's social identity and commitments.

13. ***What impact has the humanistic perspective had on psychology?***

    Humanistic psychology's critics complain that its concepts are vague and subjective, its values self-centered, and its assumptions naively optimistic. Nevertheless, humanistic psychology has helped to renew psychology's interest in the concept of self.

The Social-Cognitive Perspective

14. ***What factors does the social-cognitive perspective emphasize?***

    The social-cognitive perspective applies principles of social learning and cognition to personality, with particular emphasis on the ways in which our personalities are influenced by our interaction with the environment. Bandura's **reciprocal determinism** emphasizes how personal-cognitive factors interact with the environment.

15. ***What are the causes and consequences of personal control?***

    By studying variations among people in their perceived **personal control** and in their experiences of **learned helplessness** or mastery and competence, researchers have found that people with an **internal locus of control** are better able than those with an **external locus of control** to cope with life.

16. ***How do social-cognitive researchers evaluate personality?***

    Social-cognitive researchers study how people's behaviors and beliefs both affect and are affected by their situations. They have found that the best way to predict someone's behavior in a given situation is to observe that person's behavior in similar situations.

17. ***How does the social-cognitive perspective hold up under criticism?***

    Though faulted for underemphasizing the importance of unconscious dynamics and inner traits, the social-cognitive perspective builds on psychology's well-established concepts of learning and cognition and reminds us of the power of social situations.

CRITICAL THINKING EXERCISE by Richard O. Straub

Now that you have read and reviewed Chapter 11, take your learning a step further by testing your critical thinking skills on the following exercise.

Darren is a first-year college student who has a biting, sarcastic manner. He has a pessimistic outlook on life and feels that the world is run by a few powerful people. When he received a poor grade on a recent exam, Darren blamed the instructor and claimed the test was unfair. He stopped attending lectures, gave up studying for the course, and will probably drop it. He is experiencing similar difficulties in his other courses.

Darren always dreamed of doing well in college. Now he is despondent over his failure and believes his professors hate him. Most of all, he is concerned that if he fails in school his parents will no longer love him.

1. How might Darren's problems be explained from the psychoanalytic perspective?
2. How might Darren's problems be explained by a trait theorist?
3. How might Darren's problems be explained by a humanistic theorist?
4. How might Darren's problems be explained by a social-cognitive theorist?
5. Which perspective most closely represents your own belief about Darren's problems? Why?

Check your progress on becoming a critical thinker by comparing your answers to the sample answers found in Appendix B.

REHEARSE IT ANSWER KEY

1. b., **2.** c., **3.** b., **4.** b., **5.** b., **6.** d., **7.** d., **8.** a., **9.** c., **10.** b., **11.** c.,

12. c., **13.** b., **14.** d., **15.** b., **16.** b., **17.** c., **18.** d., **19.** d., **20.** a.,

21. c., **22.** b., **23.** d., **24.** b.

CHAPTER
12

Psychological Disorders

I felt the need to clean my room at home in Indianapolis every Sunday and would spend four to five hours at it. I would take every book out of the bookcase, dust and put it back. At the time I loved doing it. Then I didn't want to do it anymore, but I couldn't stop. The clothes in my closet hung exactly two fingers apart. . . . I made a ritual of touching the wall in my bedroom before I went out because something bad would happen if I didn't do it the right way. I had a constant anxiety about it as a kid, and it made me think for the first time that I might be nuts.

Marc, suffering obsessive-compulsive disorder (From Summers, 1996)

Whenever I get depressed it's because I've lost a sense of self. I can't find reasons to like myself. I think I'm ugly. I think no one likes me. . . . I become grumpy and short-tempered. Nobody wants to be around me. I'm left alone. Being alone confirms that I am ugly and not worth being with. I think I'm responsible for everything that goes wrong.

Greta, suffering depression (From Thorne, 1993, p. 21)

Voices, like the roar of a crowd came. I felt like Jesus; I was being crucified. It was dark. I just continued to huddle under the blanket, feeling weak, laid bare and defenseless in a cruel world I could no longer understand.

Stuart, suffering schizophrenia (From Emmons & others, 1997)

People are fascinated by the exceptional, the unusual, and the abnormal. "The sun shines and warms and lights us and we have no curiosity to know why this is so," observed Ralph Waldo Emerson, "but we ask the reason of all evil, of pain, and hunger, and [unusual] people."

Why a fascination with disturbed people? Perhaps in them we see something of ourselves. At various moments, all of us feel, think, or act as disturbed people do much of the time. We, too, get anxious, depressed, withdrawn, suspicious, deluded, or antisocial, although less intensely and enduringly. Studying psychological disorders may therefore at times evoke an eerie sense of self-recognition that illuminates our own personality dynamics. "To study the abnormal is the best way of understanding the normal," proposed William James (1842–1910).

psychological disorder a condition in which behavior is judged to be atypical, disturbing, maladaptive, and unjustifiable.

Another reason for our curiosity is that so many of us have felt, either personally or through friends or family members, the bewilderment and pain of a psychological disorder. In all likelihood, you or someone you care about has been disabled by unexplained physical symptoms, overwhelmed by irrational fears, or paralyzed by the feeling that life is not worth living. Each year there are nearly 1.9 million inpatient admissions to U.S. mental hospitals and psychiatric units (Bureau of the Census, 1996). Some 2.4 million others, often troubled but not disabled, seek help as outpatients from mental health organizations and clinics. Many more—15 percent of Americans, according to one government study—are judged to need such help (Robins & Regier, 1991). Such problems are not peculiar to the United States. No known culture is free of the two terrible maladies this chapter examines in depth—depression and schizophrenia (Draguns, 1990a,b). Some 400 million people worldwide suffer psychological disorders, according to the World Health Organization's mental health director (Sartorius, 1994). As members of the human family, few of us go through life unacquainted with the reality of psychological disturbance.

"We are all mad at some time or another."

Battista Mantuanus
Eclogues
1500

Perspectives on Psychological Disorders

1. ***What criteria are used to judge a person's behavior as disordered?***

Most people would agree that someone who is too depressed to get out of bed for weeks at a time suffers a psychological disorder. But what about those who, having experienced a loss, are unable to resume their usual social activities? Where should we draw the line between normality and abnormality? How should we *define* psychological disorders? Equally important, how should we *understand* disorders—as sicknesses that need to be diagnosed and cured, or as natural responses to a troubling environment? Finally, how might we *classify* psychological disorders? Can we do so in a way that allows us to help disturbed people and not merely stigmatize them with labels?

A benign obsession Although British street cleaner Snowy Farr's eccentric behavior may indeed be atypical, clinicians would not label it disordered because it is neither particularly disturbing nor maladaptive.

Defining Psychological Disorders

Mental health workers label behavior **psychologically disordered** when they judge it to be *atypical, disturbing, maladaptive,* and *unjustifiable*. The emotions and perceptions of Marc, Greta, and Stuart are "*ab*normal" (atypical). Being different from most other people in one's culture is *part* of what it takes to define a psychological disorder.

But there is more to a disorder than being atypical. Olympic gold medalists are abnormal in their physical abilities, and they are heroes. To be considered disordered, an atypical behavior must also be one that other people find *disturbing*.

Standards of acceptability for behaviors vary. In some cultures, people routinely behave in ways (such as going about naked) that in other cultures would be grounds for arrest. In at least one cultural context—wartime—even mass killing may be viewed as heroic. One person's homicidal "terrorist" is another person's "freedom fighter." Standards of acceptability also vary over time. Sex experts William Acton, writing in the late 1800s, and William Masters and Virginia Johnson, writing in the late 1900s, all knew that some women have orgasms during intercourse while others don't (Wakefield, 1992). For Acton, orgasm was the disorder (resulting from overstimulation); for Masters and Johnson, lack of orgasm was the disorder (resulting from inadequate stimulation). On December 9, 1977, homosexuality was a disease in the United States. By day's end on December 10, the "disease" had been officially eradicated (Greenberg, 1997). The American Psychiatric Association had dropped homosexuality as a disorder (because it was no longer believed connected with psychological problems). Later it added tobacco dependence (because it deemed smoking both addictive and self-destructive).

Maladaptiveness is a key element in defining a disorder: The behaviors must be distressing or disabling or put one at greatly increased risk of suffering or death.

Atypical and disturbing behaviors are more likely to be considered disordered when judged as harmful. Indeed, many clinicians define disorders as behaviors that are *maladaptive*—as when a smoker's nicotine dependence produces physical damage. Accordingly, even typical behaviors, such as the occasional despondency that many college students feel, may signal a psychological disorder if they become disabling. Thus, maladaptiveness is a key element in defining a disorder: The behaviors must be distressing or disabling or put one at greatly increased risk of suffering or death.

"If a man is in a minority of one, we lock him up."

Oliver Wendell Holmes
1841–1935

Finally, abnormal behavior is most likely to be considered disordered when others find it rationally *unjustifiable*. Stuart claimed to hear voices, and people presumed he was deranged. But actress Shirley MacLaine could wear a crystal on her neck and say, "See the outer bubble of white light watching you. It is part of you," and not be considered disordered because enough people found her rational (Friedrich, 1987).

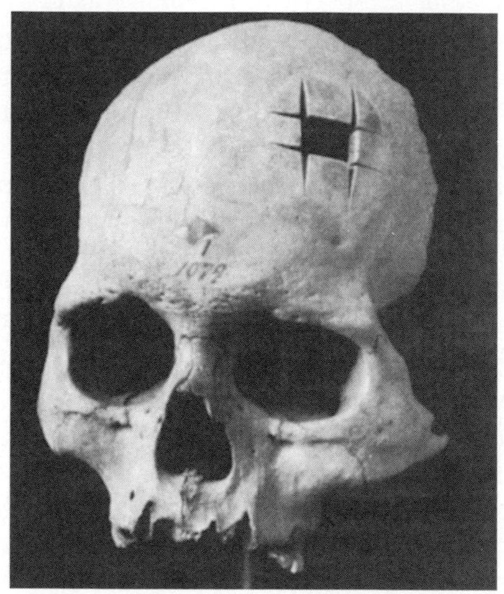

An ancient cure The hole chipped in this ancient skull found in Peru may have been designed to open the cranium to allow evil spirits to escape. One wonders whether the patient survived the cure.

Understanding Psychological Disorders

To explain puzzling behavior, people in earlier times often presumed that strange forces—the movements of the stars, godlike powers, or evil spirits—were at work. "The devil made him do it," you might have said, if you had lived during the Middle Ages. The cure might have been to get rid of the evil force—by placating the great powers or exorcising the demon. Until the last two centuries, "mad" people were sometimes caged in zoolike conditions or given "therapies" appropriate to a demon. A disordered person might have been beaten, burned, and castrated. The therapy might have included pulling teeth, removing lengths of intestines, and cauterizing the clitoris. Some even had their own blood removed and replaced with transfusions of animal blood (Farina, 1982). We have fortunately come a long way since the days of such brutal treatment.

The Medical Perspective

2. ***What is the medical model of psychological disorders, and why do critics question it?***

In response to such brutal treatment, reformers such as Philippe Pinel (1745–1826) in France insisted that madness was not demon possession but a sickness in response to severe stresses and inhumane conditions. For Pinel and other reformers, treatment meant boosting patients' morale by unchaining them, talking with them, and replacing brutality with gentleness, isolation with activity, and filth with fresh air and sun.

"Who in the rainbow can draw the line where the violet tint ends and the orange tint begins? Distinctly we see the difference of the colors, but where exactly does the one first blendingly enter into the other? So with sanity and insanity?"

Herman Melville
Billy Budd, Sailor
1924

When it was later discovered that syphilis infects the brain and distorts the mind, people also came to believe in physical causes for disorders and to search for medical treatments. Today, this medical perspective is familiar to us in the medical terminology of the mental *health* movement: A mental *illness* (also called a psycho*pathology*) needs to be *diagnosed* on the basis of its *symptoms* and *cured* through *therapy*, which may include *treatment* in a psychiatric *hospital.* In the 1800s, the assumption of this **medical model**—that psychological disorders are sicknesses—provided the impetus for much-needed reform. The "sick" were unchained and hospitals replaced asylums.

The medical perspective has gained credibility from recent discoveries. As we will see, genetically influenced abnormalities in brain structure and biochemistry contribute to a number of disorders. Two of the most troubling, depression and schizophrenia, are often treated medically. As we will also see, psychological factors, such as traumatic stress, also play an important role.

The Bio-Psycho-Social Perspective

Today's psychologists contend that *all* behavior, whether called normal or disordered, arises from the interaction of nature (genetic and physiological factors) and nurture (past and present experiences). To presume that a person is "mentally ill" attributes the condition solely to an internal problem—to a "sickness" that must be found and cured. Maybe there *is* no deep, internal problem. Maybe there is instead a growth-blocking difficulty in the person's environment, in the person's current interpretations of events, or in the person's bad habits and poor social skills.

"It's no measure of health to be well adjusted to a profoundly sick society."

Krishnamurti (1895–1986)

When Native Americans were banished from their ancestral lands, forced into poverty on barren reservations, and deprived of personal control, the result was a rate of alcoholism more than five times that of other Americans (May, 1986). Because only some Native Americans become alcoholic, the medical model would attribute such alcoholism to individual "sickness." A contemporary psychological perspective would emphasize the interaction between an individual's vulnerability and a hope-eroding environment.

Evidence of environmental effects comes from links between disorder and culture. Some major disorders such as depression and schizophrenia are universal. From Asia to Africa and across the Americas, the core symptoms of schizophrenia include irrationality and incoherent speech (Brislin, 1993; Draguns, 1990b). Other disorders are culture-bound (Beardsley, 1994; Carson & others, 1988). Different cultures have different sources of stress and produce different ways of coping. Anorexia nervosa and bulimia nervosa, for example, are disorders mostly of Western cultures (page 320). *Susto*, marked by severe anxiety, restlessness, and fear of black magic, is a disorder found in Latin America. *Taijin-kyofusho*, which combines social anxiety with easy blushing and fear of eye contact, appears in Japan. Such disorders may share an underlying dynamic (anxiety), yet culturally differ in symptoms (an eating problem or a type of fear).

Most mental health workers today assume that disorders are indeed influenced by genetic predispositions and physiological states. And by inner psychological dynamics. And by social and cultural circumstances. To get the whole picture, we need an interdisciplinary **bio-psycho-social perspective** (Figure 12.1).

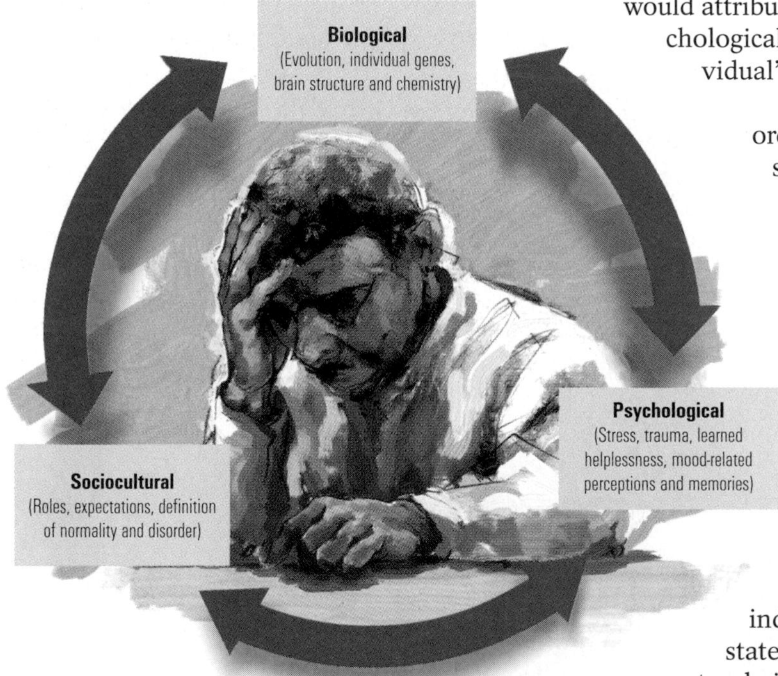

Figure 12.1 The bio-psycho-social perspective Psychologists study how biological, psychological, and sociocultural factors interact to produce specific psychological disorders.

Classifying Psychological Disorders

3. *Why are psychological disorders classified, and what system is used?*

In biology and the other sciences, classification creates order. To classify an animal as a mammal says a great deal—that it is warm-blooded, has hair or fur, and nourishes its young with milk. In psychiatry and psychology, too, classification

"I'm always like this, and my family was wondering if you could prescribe a mild depressant."

orders and describes clusters of symptoms. To classify a person's disorder as "schizophrenia" suggests that the person talks incoherently, hallucinates or has delusions (bizarre beliefs), shows either little emotion or inappropriate emotion, or is socially withdrawn. Thus, the diagnostic term provides a handy shorthand for describing a complex disorder.

In psychiatry and psychology, diagnostic classification ideally aims to describe a disorder, to predict its future course, to imply appropriate treatment, and to stimulate research into its causes. Indeed, to study a disorder we must first name and describe it. The current authoritative scheme for classifying psychological disorders is the American Psychiatric Association's *Diagnostic and Statistical Manual of Mental Disorders (Fourth Edition)*, nicknamed **DSM-IV**. This 1994 volume and accompanying case illustrations provide the basis for much of the material in this chapter. DSM-IV was developed in coordination with the tenth edition of the World Health Organization's *International Classification of Diseases* (ICD-10).

The very idea of "diagnosing" people's problems in terms of their "symptoms" presumes a mental "illness." Some practitioners are not enthralled with this medical terminology, but most find DSM-IV a helpful and practical tool. It is also a financially necessary one: Most North American health insurance companies require a DSM-IV diagnosis before they will pay for therapy.

The DSM describes disorders and their prevalence without presuming to explain their causes. Thus, the once-popular term *neurosis* is no longer a diagnostic category. DSM-IV does mention **neurotic disorders**—psychological disorders that, although distressing, still allow one to think rationally and function socially. But even this term is so vague that psychologists now use it minimally, usually as a contrast to the more bizarre and debilitating **psychotic disorders**, marked by irrationality.

For the DSM-IV categories to be valid, they must first be reliable. If one psychiatrist or psychologist diagnoses someone as having, say, "catatonic schizophrenia," what are the chances that another mental health worker will independently give the same diagnosis? With the DSM-IV's diagnostic guidelines, the chances are good. The guidelines work by asking clinicians a series of objective questions about observable behaviors, such as, "Is the person afraid to leave home?" In one study, 16 psychologists used this structured-interview procedure to diagnose 75 psychiatric patients as suffering from (1) depression, (2) generalized anxiety, or (3) some other disorder (Riskind & others, 1987). Without knowing the first psychologist's diagnosis, another psychologist viewed a videotape of each interview and offered a second opinion. For 83 percent of the patients, the two opinions agreed.

Labeling Psychological Disorders

4. *Why do clinicians assign diagnostic labels to patients? Why do some psychologists criticize such labeling?*

Most clinicians believe that classification helps in describing, treating, and researching the causes of psychological disorders. Critics, however, say that these labels at best are arbitrary and at worst are value judgments that masquerade as science. It is better, they say, to study the roots of specific symptoms, such as delusions or hallucinations, than to study catchall categories, such as schizophrenia (Persons, 1986). Moreover, once we label a person, we view that person differently (Farina, 1982). Labels create preconceptions that can bias our perceptions and interpretations.

In the most controversial demonstration of the biasing power of diagnostic labels, David Rosenhan (1973) and seven of his friends and Stanford University

medical model the concept that diseases have physical causes that can be diagnosed, treated, and, in most cases, cured. When applied to psychological disorders, the medical model assumes that these "mental illnesses" can be diagnosed on the basis of their symptoms and cured through therapy, which may include treatment in a psychiatric hospital.

bio-psycho-social perspective a contemporary perspective which assumes that biological, sociocultural, and psychological factors combine and interact to produce psychological disorders.

DSM-IV the American Psychiatric Association's *Diagnostic and Statistical Manual of Mental Disorders (Fourth Edition)*, a widely used system for classifying psychological disorders.

neurotic disorders former term for psychological disorders that are usually distressing but allow one to think rationally and function socially.

psychotic disorders psychological disorders in which a person loses contact with reality, experiencing irrational ideas and distorted perceptions.

"One of the unpardonable sins, in the eyes of most people, is for a man to go about unlabelled. The world regards such a person as the police do an unmuzzled dog, not under proper control."

T. H. Huxley
Evolution and Ethics
1893

colleagues went to mental hospital admissions offices, complaining of "hearing voices" that were saying "empty," "hollow," and "thud." Apart from this complaint and giving false names and occupations, they truthfully answered all the questions. All eight were diagnosed as mentally ill.

That these normal people were misdiagnosed is not surprising. As one psychiatrist noted, if someone swallowed blood, went to an emergency room, and spat it up, would we fault the doctor for diagnosing a bleeding ulcer? What followed the diagnosis was more startling. After admission, the "patients" exhibited no further symptoms. Yet the clinicians were able to "discover" the causes of their disorders after analyzing their (quite normal) life histories. One person was said to be reacting to mixed emotions about his parents. Furthermore, before being released (an average of 19 days later), the "patients'" normal behaviors, such as taking notes, were often misinterpreted as symptoms.

Other studies confirm that labels affect how we perceive one another. Ellen Langer and her colleagues (1974, 1980) had people rate an interviewee they thought was either normal (a job applicant) or out of the ordinary (a psychiatric or cancer patient). All raters saw the identical videotape. Those who watched unlabeled interviewees perceived them as normal; those who watched supposed-patients perceived them as "different from most people." Therapists (who thought they were evaluating a psychiatric patient) perceived the interviewee as "frightened of his own aggressive impulses," a "passive, dependent type," and so forth. A label can serve a useful purpose. But as Rosenhan discovered, it can also have "a life and an influence of its own."

Labels can also stigmatize people in others' eyes. U.S. Senator Thomas Eagleton experienced this in 1972, when he was dumped as the Democratic party's vice-presidential candidate after it was discovered he had been treated for depression with electroconvulsive therapy. The same stigma surfaced when a female associate of psychologist Stewart Page (1977) called 180 people in Toronto who were advertising furnished rooms for rent. When she merely asked if the room was still available, the answer was nearly always yes. When she said she was about to be released from a mental hospital, the answer three times out of four was no (as it was when she said she was calling for her brother who was about to be released from jail). When some of those who answered no were called by a second person who simply asked if the room was still available, the advertiser nearly always revealed that it was. Surveys in Western Europe have uncovered similar attitudes toward those labeled mentally ill. But as people come to understand psychological disorders as diseases of the brain, not failures of character, the stigma seems to be lifting (Solomon, 1996). More and more public figures are feeling free to "come out" and speak with candor about their struggles with disorders such as depression.

Labels not only bias perceptions, they can also change reality. When teachers are told certain students are "gifted," when students expect someone to be "hostile," or when interviewers check to see whether someone is "extraverted," they may act in ways that elicit the very behavior expected.

If people also form their impressions of psychological disorder from the media, then lingering stereotypes are hardly surprising. Television researcher George Gerbner (1985) reported that 1 in 5 prime-time and daytime programs depicts a psychologically disordered person, and 7 in 10 of such programs portray this character as violent or criminal. Movies, too, stereotype mental patients, sometimes as homicidal (Anthony Hopkins' role in *Silence of the Lambs*) or as freaks (Woody Allen as *Zelig*) (Hyler & others, 1991; Wahl, 1992). As alleged Unabomber Theodore Kaczynski vividly illustrated, some people diagnosed with schizophrenia are indeed more likely than other people to commit violent crime, and some disordered people are amoral and antisocial (Eronen & others, 1996; Monahan, 1992; Tiihonen and others, 1997). However, at least 9 in 10 disordered people are *not* dangerous; instead, they are anxious, depressed, or withdrawn.

Labels not only bias perceptions, they can also change reality. When teachers are told certain students are "gifted," when students expect someone to be "hostile," or when interviewers check to see whether someone is "extraverted," they may act in ways that elicit the very behavior expected (Snyder, 1984). Someone who was led to think you are nasty may treat you coldly, provoking you to respond as a nasty person would. Labels can serve as self-fulfilling prophecies.

But let us also remember the benefits of diagnostic labels. As Robert Spitzer (1975), a chief author of the current diagnostic system explained, "There is a purpose to psychiatric diagnosis. It is to enable mental health professionals to (a) communicate with each other about the subject matter of their concern, (b) comprehend the pathological processes involved in psychiatric illness, and (c) control psychiatric outcomes."

REHEARSE IT!

1. Although some psychological disorders are culture-bound, others are universal. For example, in every known culture there are people who suffer

a. bulimia nervosa.
b. anorexia nervosa.
c. schizophrenia.
d. susto.

2. To be labeled "disordered," a behavior must usually be atypical, disturbing, unjustified, and maladaptive. For example, we all wash our hands; physicians may well wash their hands 100 times a day. But if a person washes his or her hands 100 times a day for no apparent reason and is unable to do much else, the behavior will be labeled disordered because it is, among other things,

a. unjustified and maladaptive.
b. not explained by the medical model.
c. harmful to others.
d. untreatable.

3. In the past, people considered to be mad or insane were beaten, punished, or caged. A more modern approach is to equate psychological disorders with sickness and to refer the "mentally ill" to hospitals, where they can be treated as patients. This more modern approach is called the

a. social-cultual perspective.
b. psychological model.
c. medical model.
d. diagnostic model.

4. Many psychologists adhere to the idea that mental illness is a sickness arising from an internal problem. Others contend that other factors may be involved—for example, a growth-blocking difficulty in the person's environment or the person's bad habits and poor social skills. Psychologists who take this approach to mental illness are said to be advocates of the ________ perspective.

a. medical
b. biomedical
c. bio-psycho-social
d. social-cultural

5. The American Psychiatric Association's system of classifying psychological disorders is found in the DSM-IV. The DSM-IV system is more reliable than its predecessors; one study found that psychologists using the manual's structured-interview procedure agreed on a diagnosis for more than 80 percent of patients. The DSM-IV has improved reliability because it helps mental health workers base their diagnoses on

a. a few well-defined categories.
b. in-depth histories of the patients.
c. the patients' observable behaviors.
d. the theories of Pinel, Freud, and others.

6. Labels such as "schizophrenia" and "generalized anxiety" may be useful in clinical situations. In other contexts, however, labels create preconceptions and biases. From watching television dramas you would never guess that most people with psychological disorders, when encountered in the real world, seem

a. antisocial and amoral.
b. violent or homicidal.
c. accomplished in the arts and literature.
d. anxious, depressed, or withdrawn.

Anxiety Disorders

5. *What behaviors characterize anxiety disorders?*

Anxiety is part of life. When speaking in front of a class, when peering down from a ledge, when waiting to play in a big game, any one of us might feel anxious. At one time or another, most of us feel enough anxiety that we fail to make eye contact or we avoid talking to someone—"shyness," we call it. Fortunately for most of us, our occasional uneasiness is not intense and persistent. If it becomes so, we may have one of the **anxiety disorders**, marked by distressing, persistent anxiety or maladaptive behaviors that reduce anxiety. In this section we focus on **generalized anxiety disorder**, in which a person is unexplainably and

anxiety disorders psychological disorders characterized by distressing, persistent anxiety or maladaptive behaviors that reduce anxiety.

generalized anxiety disorder an anxiety disorder in which a person is continually tense, apprehensive, and aroused.

phobia an anxiety disorder marked by a persistent, irrational fear and avoidance of a specific object or situation.

obsessive-compulsive disorder an anxiety disorder characterized by unwanted repetitive thoughts (obsessions) and/or actions (compulsions).

panic disorder an anxiety disorder marked by a minutes-long episode of intense dread in which a person experiences terror and accompanying chest pain, choking, or other frightening sensations.

continually tense and uneasy; **phobias**, in which a person feels irrationally afraid of a specific object or situation; and **obsessive-compulsive disorder**, in which a person is troubled by repetitive thoughts or actions.

Generalized Anxiety Disorder

Tyrone, a 27-year-old electrician, seeks help, complaining of dizziness, sweating palms, heart palpitations, and ringing in his ears. He feels edgy and sometimes finds himself shaking. With reasonable success he hides his symptoms from his family and co-workers. Nevertheless, he has had few social contacts since the symptoms began two years ago. Worse, he occasionally has to leave work. His family doctor and neurologist can find no physical problem.

Tyrone's unfocused, out-of-control, negative feelings suggest a generalized anxiety disorder. The symptoms of this disorder are commonplace; their persistence is not. The sufferers are continually tense and jittery, worried about bad things that might happen, and experience all the symptoms of autonomic nervous system arousal (racing heart, clammy hands, stomach butterflies, sleeplessness). The tension and apprehension may leak out through furrowed brows, twitching eyelids, or fidgeting. One of the worst characteristics of a generalized anxiety disorder is that the person cannot identify, and therefore cannot avoid, its cause. To use Freud's term, the anxiety is "free-floating."

As some 1 in 75 people with **panic disorder** know, anxiety may at times suddenly escalate into a terrifying *panic attack*—a minutes-long episode of intense fear that something horrible is about to happen to them. Heart palpitations, shortness of breath, choking sensations, trembling, or dizziness typically accompany the panic. One woman in the audience at her son's kindergarten "graduation" reported suddenly feeling "hot and as though I couldn't breathe. My heart was racing and I started to sweat and tremble and I was sure I was going to faint. Then my fingers started to feel numb and tingly and things seemed unreal. It was so bad I wondered if I was dying and asked my husband to take me to the emergency room. By the time we got there (about 10 minutes) the worst of the attack was over and I just felt washed out" (Greist & others, 1986, p. 33).

The experience is unpredictable and so frightening that the sufferer often comes to fear the fear itself and to avoid situations where panic has struck. *Agoraphobia* is fear or avoidance of situations in which escape or help might not be available when panic strikes. Given such fear, people may avoid being outside the home, being in a crowd, or traveling in a plane or train or on an elevator.

"He who fears all snares falls into none."

Publius Syrus
Sententiae
43 B.C.

Phobias

Fear is an adaptive response. Fear prepares our bodies to flee danger. Fear of real or imagined enemies binds people together as families, tribes, and nations. Fear of injury protects us from harm. Fear of punishment or retaliation constrains us from harming one another.

Phobias *focus* anxiety on some specific object, activity, or situation. (See Figure 12.2 for one ranking of some common and less common fears.) Phobias—irrational fears that disrupt behavior—are a common psychological disorder that people often accept and live with. Some *specific phobias* are incapacitating, however. Marilyn, a 28-year-old homemaker, so fears thunderstorms that she feels anxious as soon as a weather forecaster mentions possible storms later in the week. If her husband is away and a storm is forecast, she sometimes stays with a close relative. During a storm, she hides from windows and buries her head to avoid seeing the lightning. She is otherwise healthy and happy.

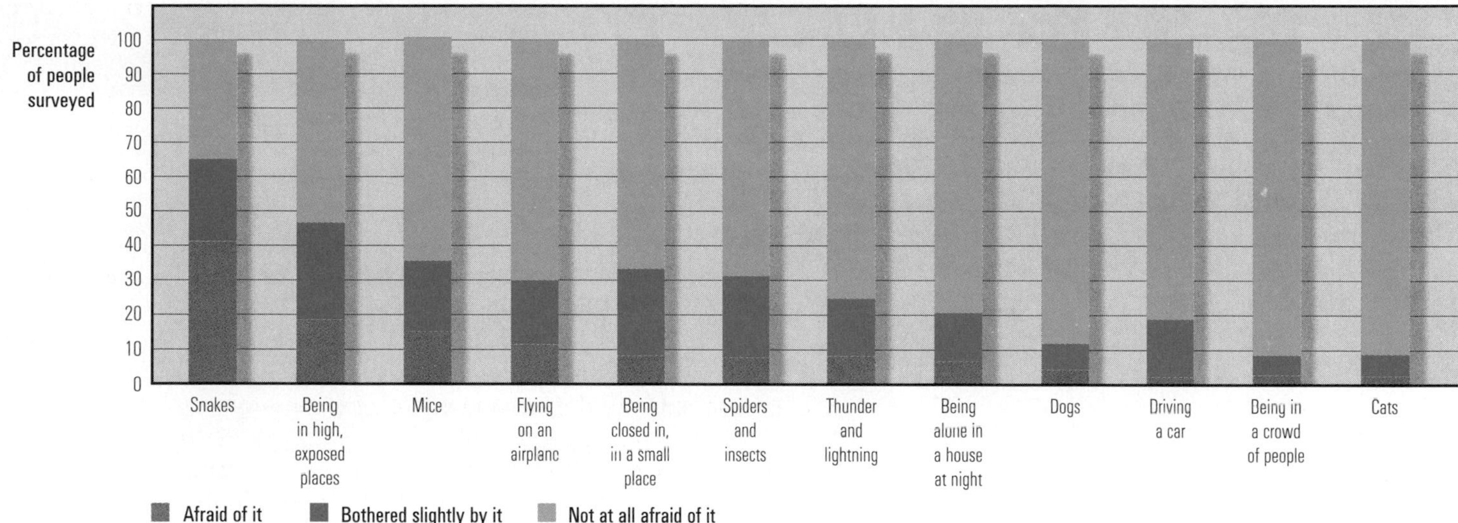

Figure 12.2 Some common and uncommon fears This national survey ranked the relative fear levels of Americans to some sources of anxiety. A fear becomes a phobia if it provokes a compelling but irrational desire to avoid the dreaded object or situation. (From *Public Opinion*, 1984)

Other people suffer from irrational fears of specific animals or insects, or of such things as heights, blood, or tunnels. Sometimes it is possible to avoid the fear-arousing stimulus: One can hide during thunderstorms or avoid high places. With a *social phobia*, an intense fear of being scrutinized by others, the anxious person will avoid potentially embarrassing social situations. The person may avoid speaking up, eating out, or going to parties—or will sweat, tremble, or have diarrhea when doing so. Compared with the other disorders discussed in this chapter, phobias appear at a younger age—often by the early teens (Burke & others, 1990).

Obsessive-Compulsive Disorder

As with generalized anxiety and phobias, we can see aspects of our own behavior in obsessive-compulsive disorder. We may at times be obsessed with senseless or offensive thoughts that will not go away. Or we may engage in compulsive, rigid behavior—rechecking a locked door, stepping over cracks in the sidewalk, or lining up our books and pencils "just so" before studying.

Obsessive thoughts and compulsive behaviors cross the fine line between normality and disorder when they become so persistent that they interfere with the way we live or when they cause distress. Checking to see that the door is locked is normal; checking the door 10 times is not. Hand washing is normal; hand washing so often that one's skin becomes raw is not. (Table 12.1, page 434, offers more examples.) At some time during their lives, often during their late teens or twenties, 2 to 3 percent of people cross that line from normal preoccupations and fussiness to debilitating disorder (Karno & others, 1988). The obsessive thoughts become so haunting, the compulsive rituals so senselessly time-consuming, that effective functioning becomes impossible.

One such person was billionaire Howard Hughes. Hughes would compulsively dictate the same phrases over and over again. Under stress, he developed an obsessive fear of germs. He became reclusive and insisted that his assistants carry out elaborate hand-washing rituals and wear white gloves when handling documents he would later touch. He ordered tape around doors and windows and forbade his staff to touch or even look at him. "Everybody carries germs around with them," he explained. "I want to live longer than my parents, so I avoid germs" (Fowler, 1986).

"He always times '60 Minutes.'"

Table 12.1 Common Obsessions and Compulsions Among 70 Children and Adolescents With Obsessive-Compulsive Disorder

Thought or Behavior	Percentage Reporting Symptom
Obsessions (repetitive thoughts)	
Dirt, germs, or toxins	40
Something terrible happening (fire, death, illness)	24
Symmetry, order, or exactness	17
Compulsions (repetitive behaviors)	
Excessive hand washing, bathing, toothbrushing, or grooming	85
Repeating rituals (in/out of a door, up/down from a chair)	51
Checking doors, locks, appliances, car brake, homework	46

Source: Adapted from Rapoport, 1989.

Explaining Anxiety Disorders

6. ***How do psychologists explain anxiety disorders?***

Freud's psychoanalytic perspective assumed that, beginning in childhood, intolerable impulses, ideas, and feelings get repressed, and that this submerged mental energy sometimes produces mystifying symptoms such as anxiety. However, today's psychologists have turned away from Freud to two contemporary perspectives—learning and biological.

The Learning Perspective

The learning perspective explains anxiety disorders by applying principles of conditioning and observational learning.

Fear Conditioning

Researchers have linked general anxiety with classical conditioning of fear. In the laboratory, they have created chronically anxious, ulcer-prone rats by giving them unpredictable electric shocks (Schwartz, 1984). Like the rape victim who reported feeling anxious when entering her old neighborhood (page 214), the animals are apprehensive in their lab environment. For many victims of post-traumatic stress disorder, anxiety swells with any reminder of their trauma. Such experiences might help explain why anxious people are hyperattentive to possible threats (Mineka & Sutton, 1992).

When experimental shocks become predictable—when preceded by a particular conditioned stimulus—the animals' fear focuses on *that* stimulus and they relax in its absence. Recall from Chapter 6 that dogs learn to fear neutral stimuli associated with shock, that infants come to fear furry objects associated with frightening noises, and that adults can become terrified of incidental stimuli linked with traumatic experiences. As infants become mobile they experience falls and near-falls—and become increasingly afraid of heights (Campos & others, 1992).

Through such conditioning, the short list of naturally painful and frightening events can multiply into a long list of human fears—fear of spiders, fear of closed spaces, fear of driving. My car was once struck by another whose driver missed a

The Wounds of War: Post-Traumatic Stress Disorder

During the fighting in Vietnam, Jack's platoon was repeatedly under fire. In one ambush, his closest friend was killed while standing a few feet away. Jack himself killed one of his enemies in a brutal assault. Years later, images of these events intrude as flashbacks and nightmares. He still jumps at the sound of a cap gun or the backfire of a car. When annoyed by family or friends, he lashes out in ways he seldom did before Vietnam. To calm his continuing anxiety, he drinks more than he should.

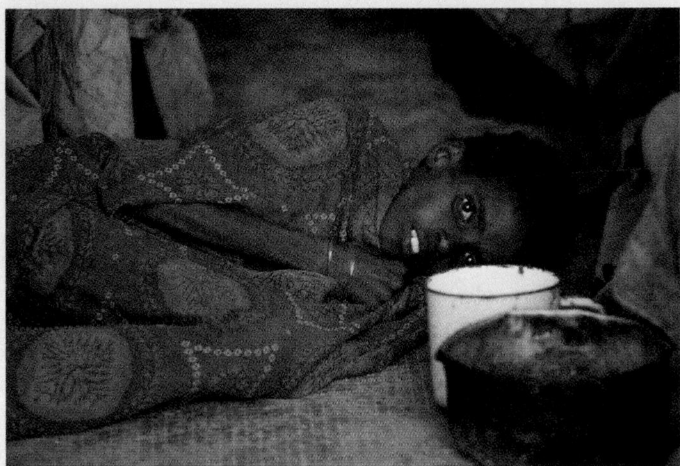

The aftermath of trauma The ravages of war, as experienced by this famine survivor at a Somalian feeding center, can linger as stress-related symptoms.

Such has been the experience of many combat veterans and sexual assault victims. Traumatic stress—experiencing or witnessing severely threatening, uncontrollable events with a sense of fear, helplessness, or horror—can produce *post-traumatic stress disorder*, symptoms of which include haunting memories and nightmares, social withdrawal, and anxiety or depression (Goodman & others, 1993; Kaylor & others, 1987; Wilson & others, 1988). After witnessing atrocities or living in life-threatening circumstances, children of the world's war zones and violent neighborhoods show similar symptoms (Garbarino, 1991). Their sense of basic trust erodes; many experience fearful wariness, troubled sleep, nightmares, and a sense of hopelessness about their future. This "learned helplessness" appears to make children who have repeatedly suffered abuse more vulnerable to post-traumatic stress if assaulted as adults (Mineka & Zinbarg, 1996).

To pin down the frequency of post-traumatic stress disorder, the U.S. Centers for Disease Control (1988) compared 7000 Vietnam combat veterans with 7000 noncombat veterans who served during the same years. Combat stress more than doubled a veteran's risk of alcohol abuse, depression, or anxiety.

Studies of U.S. and Israeli soldiers reveal that the more terrifying and prolonged the battle experience, the greater the psychological casualties (King & King, 1991; Solomon, 1990). The roughly 15 percent rate of post-traumatic stress symptoms among all Vietnam veterans was halved among those who never saw combat and tripled among those who experienced heavy combat. More than a decade after the war, one study located 2095 identical twins among Vietnam-era veterans (Goldberg & others, 1990). Compared with co-twins who served in noncombat roles in Vietnam, those who experienced heavy combat were 5.4 times more likely to be suffering post-traumatic stress disorder.

Researchers have also found that psychological disorders and suicide attempts were most common among vets who felt responsible for a trauma because they had either killed someone or failed to prevent a death (Fontana & others, 1992). Many still experience nightmares, have trouble sleeping and concentrating, and find themselves easily startled. This is especially so for those exposed to savage mutilation, torture, or the sight of a friend's death. Much as they might wish to avoid or suppress the memory, it intrudes.

Despite such symptoms, some psychologists believe post-traumatic stress disorder is a fad diagnosis. The disorder, these skeptics say, actually is infrequent (Young, 1995). Most combat-stressed veterans live productive lives. Most rescuers, such as all the Sioux City firefighters who rescued people and charred bodies from a flaming 1989 DC-10 crash, cope well afterwards (Gist & others, 1998). Most political dissidents who survive many dozens of torture episodes do *not* later exhibit post-traumatic stress disorder (Mineka & Zinbarg, 1996). And, although suffering some lingering stress symptoms, most American Jews who survived the Holocaust trauma—starvation, beatings, lost freedom, the murders of loved ones—went on to live productive lives. In fact, compared with other American Jews of the same age, these survivors have been *less* likely to have seen a psychotherapist (18 percent versus 31 percent) and *more* likely to have had stable marriages (83 percent versus 62 percent). Moreover, virtually none have committed criminal acts. Researcher William Helmreich (1992, p. 276) reflects on their successes:

> The story of the survivors is one of courage and strength, of people who are living proof of the indomitable will of human beings to survive and of their tremendous capacity for hope. It is not a story of remarkable people. It is a story of just how remarkable people can be.

stop sign. For months afterward, I felt a twinge of unease with the approach of any car from a side street. Perhaps Marilyn's phobia was similarly conditioned during a terrifying or painful experience associated with a thunderstorm.

Stimulus Generalization

Conditioned fears may remain long after we have forgotten the experiences that produced them (Jacobs & Nadel, 1985). Moreover, some fears arise from stimulus generalization. A person who fears heights after a fall may be afraid of airplanes without ever having flown.

An emotional high Although we humans seem biologically predisposed to fear heights—certainly an adaptive response—this construction worker seems fearless. The biological perspective helps us understand why most people would be terrified in this situation.

Reinforcement

Avoiding or escaping the feared situation reduces anxiety, thus reinforcing the phobic behavior. Feeling anxious or fearing panic attacks, a person may go or stay inside (Antony & others, 1992). Compulsive behaviors similarly reduce anxiety. If washing your hands relieves your feelings of unease, you will likely wash your hands again when the feelings return.

Observational Learning

Someone might also learn fear through observational learning—by observing others' fears. As we saw in Chapter 10, wild monkeys transmit their fear of snakes to their offspring; human parents similarly transmit their fears to their children.

The Biological Perspective

Evolution

We humans seem biologically prepared to develop fears of heights, storms, snakes, and insects—dangers our ancestors faced. Compulsive acts typically exaggerate behaviors that contributed to our species' survival. Grooming gone wild becomes hair pulling. Washing up becomes ritual hand washing. Checking territorial boundaries becomes checking and rechecking a door known to be locked (Rapoport, 1989).

The human mind was road tested in the Stone Age. Most phobias therefore focus on objects that, for our ancestors, presented occasional dangers: spiders, snakes, closed spaces, heights, storms. It is easy to condition and hard to extinguish fears of such stimuli (Davey, 1995; Ohman, 1986). Many of our modern fears may also have an evolutionary explanation. Fear of flying may come from our biological past, which predisposes us to fear confinement and heights.

Most phobias focus on objects that, for our ancestors, presented occasional dangers: spiders, snakes, closed spaces, heights, storms. It is easy to condition and hard to extinguish fears of such stimuli.

Moreover, consider what people tend *not* to learn to fear. World War II air raids produced remarkably few lasting phobias. As the air blitz continued, the British, Japanese, and German populations became not more panicked but more indifferent to planes not in their immediate neighborhood (Mineka & Zinbarg, 1996). Evolution does not prepare us to learn to fear bombs dropping from the sky.

Genes

Some people more than others seem genetically predisposed to particular fears and high anxiety. Identical twins often develop similar phobias, in some cases even when raised separately (Carey, 1990; Eckert & others, 1981). One pair of 35-year-old identical female twins independently developed claustrophobia. They also became so fearful of water that each would gingerly wade backward into the ocean, only up to the knees. Among monkeys, fearfulness runs in families. Individual monkeys react more strongly to stress if their close biological relatives are anxiously reactive (Suomi, 1986). Among humans, vulnerability to anxiety disorder rises when the afflicted relative is an identical twin (Barlow, 1988; Kendler & others, 1992; Roy & others, 1995).

Physiology

Generalized anxiety disorder, panic attacks, and even obsessions and compulsions are biologically measurable as an overarousal of brain areas involved in impulse control and habitual behaviors. PET scans of persons with obsessive-compulsive disorder reveal unusually high activity in an area of the frontal lobes just above the eyes (Figure 12.3) and in a more primitive area deep in the brain (Rauch & Jenike, 1993; Resnick, 1992). Some antidepressant drugs dampen this activity by affecting the availability of the neurotransmitter serotonin. This helps control obsessive-compulsive behavior.

Figure 12.3 **A PET scan of the brain of a person with obsessive-compulsive disorder** The scan reveals abnormally high metabolic activity (red areas) in the frontal lobes, seen at the top of the photo. This is visible in a region of the left hemisphere's frontal lobe involved in directing attention.

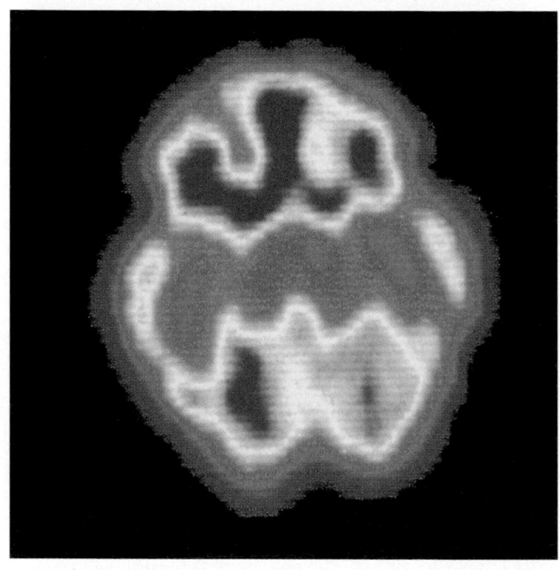

Dissociative Disorders

7. What are dissociative disorders, and why are they controversial?

Among the most intriguing disorders are the rare **dissociative disorders**, in which a person appears to experience a sudden loss of memory or change in identity. When a situation becomes too stressful, people are said to dissociate themselves from it. Their conscious awareness becomes separated from painful memories, thoughts, and feelings. (Note that this explanation presumes the existence of repressed memories, which have recently been questioned, as discussed in Chapters 7 and 11.)

Certain symptoms of dissociation are not so rare. Now and then, many people have experienced a sense of being unreal, of being separated from one's body, of watching oneself as in a movie. Facing trauma, such detachment may actually protect a person from being overwhelmed by emotion. Only when such experiences are severe and prolonged do they suggest a dissociative disorder.

Dissociative Amnesia

Amnesia, the failure to recall events, can be caused by head injuries or alcoholic intoxication. Princess Di's injured body guard was understandably unable to recall the moments before their accident. But **dissociative amnesia**, some psychologists believe, usually begins as a response to intolerable psychological stress. One 18-year-old victim was rescued from his sailboat by the Coast Guard and brought to a hospital. He knew he had gone sailing with friends and that he was a college student, but he said he could not recall what had happened to his friends. Moreover, he kept forgetting he was in a hospital; each reminder surprised him. Later, aided by a drug that relaxed him, he formed a memory: A ferocious storm had washed his companions overboard.

As this case illustrates, the forgetfulness of amnesia is selective: The young man seemed to forget what was intolerably painful. Those with amnesia may be somewhat disoriented and may forget who they are, but they will remember how to drive, count, and talk. Typically, the amnesia vanishes as abruptly as it began and rarely recurs.

dissociative disorders disorders in which conscious awareness becomes separated (dissociated) from previous memories, thoughts, and feelings. See *dissociative amnesia, dissociative fugue,* and *dissociative identity disorder.*

dissociative amnesia selective memory loss said to be brought on by extreme stress.

dissociative fugue [FEWG] a dissociative disorder in which flight from one's home and identity accompanies amnesia.

dissociative identity disorder a rare dissociative disorder in which a person exhibits two or more distinct and alternating personalities. Also called *multiple personality disorder*.

Dissociative Fugue

Like amnesia, **dissociative fugue** (pronounced FEWG, meaning "flight") involves presumed forgetting, but it also involves fleeing one's home and identity for days, months, or years. Gene Smith, a midlevel manager, had been passed over for promotion, faulted by his supervisor, and rejected by his 18-year-old son, who during a violent argument called him a "failure." Two days later, Smith disappeared. A month later and 200 miles away, police brought a man who said he was "Burt Tate" to the emergency room. Tate had been hurt in a fight at a diner, where he had been working as a short-order cook since drifting into town a month earlier. He claimed not to recall where he had lived or worked before that. He admitted that was strange but did not seem upset by it. After a missing-person check, Mrs. Smith confirmed that Burt Tate was Gene Smith. Though noticeably anxious when faced with his wife, he denied recognizing her. When "awakening" from a fugue state, people such as Gene Smith remember their old identities but typically deny remembering what occurred during the fugue. Skeptics wonder if such patients may be feigning memory loss for strategic reasons.

Dissociative Identity Disorder

Even more mysterious and controversial is the massive dissociation of self from ordinary consciousness in those with *multiple personality disorder*, now called **dissociative identity disorder**. These people have two or more distinct personalities that alternately control the person's behavior. One is usually restrained and dull, another more impulsive and uninhibited. The person with this disorder may be prim and proper one moment and loud and flirtatious the next. Each personality has its own voice and mannerisms, and the original one typically denies awareness of the other(s).

Although people diagnosed as having multiple personalities are usually not violent, there have been cases in which the person reportedly became dissociated into a "good" and a "bad" or aggressive personality—a modest version of the Dr. Jekyll/Mr. Hyde split immortalized in Robert Louis Stevenson's story. Freud would have said that, rid of the original "good" personality's awareness, the wanton second personality is free to discharge forbidden impulses. One unusual case that for a time seemed to support this interpretation involved Kenneth Bianchi, who was on trial for the "Hillside Strangler" rapes and murders of 10 California women. During a hypnosis session with Bianchi, psychologist John Watkins (1984) "called forth" a hidden personality: "I've talked a bit to Ken, but I think that perhaps there might be another part of Ken that I haven't talked to, another part that maybe feels somewhat differently from the part that I've talked to. . . . Would you talk with me, Part, by saying, 'I'm here'?" Bianchi answered "Yes" and engaged in the following interchange:

The "Hillside Strangler" Kenneth Bianchi is shown here at his trial.

Watkins: *Part, are you the same thing as Ken, or are you different in any way?*
Bianchi: *I'm not him.*
Watkins: *You're not him? Who are you? Do you have a name?*
Bianchi: *Steve. You can call me Steve.*

When speaking as Steve, Bianchi stated that he hated Ken because Ken was nice and that he (Steve), aided by a cousin, had murdered women. He also claimed that Ken knew nothing about his existence and that Ken was innocent of the murders.

Was Bianchi's second personality a ruse, simply a way of disavowing responsibility for his actions? (Bianchi, who was later convicted, was a practiced liar who had read about multiple personality in psychology books.) Exploring our capacity for personality shifts, Nicholas Spanos (1986, 1994, 1996) asked college students to pretend they were accused murderers being examined by a psychiatrist. When given the same hypnotic treatment Bianchi received, most spontaneously expressed a second personality.

This discovery made Spanos wonder: Are dissociative identities simply a more extreme version of our normal human capacity to vary the "selves" we present—as when displaying a goofy, loud-mouthed self while hanging out with friends, and a subdued, respectful self around grandparents. Are clinicians who discover multiple personalities merely triggering fantasy-prone people's enactment of a role? If so, can such people then convince themselves of the authenticity of their own role enactments? Are they like actors, who commonly report "losing themselves" in their roles? (Recall from Chapter 5 that Spanos also raised these questions about the hypnotic state. Given that most multiple personality patients are highly hypnotizable, whatever explains one condition—dissociation or role playing—may help explain the other.)

"Pretense may become reality."
Chinese Proverb

Those who accept dissociative identity as a genuine disorder find support in the distinct brain and body states associated with differing personalities (Putnam, 1991). Handedness, too, sometimes switches with personality (Henninger, 1992). In one study, ophthalmologists detected shifting visual acuity and eye-muscle balance as patients switched personalities. Such changes did not occur among control subjects trying to simulate multiple personality (Miller & others, 1991).

Skeptics nevertheless find it suspicious that the disorder has just recently become rather popular. In North America, the number of diagnoses exploded from only two reported cases per decade from 1930 to 1960 to more than 20,000 in the 1980s (McHugh, 1995a). The average number of personalities displayed also has mushroomed—from 3 to 12 per patient (Goff & Sims, 1993). This is just what one would expect after the role of multiple personality was well publicized in books and films of that time, including *The Three Faces of Eve* and *Sybil*. Moreover, most clinicians have never encountered a case of dissociative identity and the disorder is almost nonexistent outside North America, although in other cultures some people are said to be "possessed" by an alien spirit (Aldridge-Morris, 1989; Kluft, 1991). In Britain, the diagnosis—which some consider "a wacky American fad" (Cohen, 1995)—is rare. In India and Japan it is essentially nonexistent.

Are dissociative identities simply a more extreme version of our normal human capacity to vary the "selves" we present—as when displaying a goofy, loud-mouthed self while hanging out with friends, and a subdued, respectful self around grandparents?

To skeptics, these findings point to a cultural phenomenon—a disorder created by therapists in a particular social context (Merskey, 1992). Skeptics note how some therapists go fishing for it: "Have you ever felt like another part of you does things you can't control? Does this part of you have a name? Can I talk to the angry part of you?" Once patients permit a therapist to "talk to the part of you that says those angry things," they have begun acting out the fantasy. Moreover, say skeptics, "it is no coincidence" that multiple personality studies began among hypnosis practitioners (Goff, 1993).

With the dissociative disorders, as with the anxiety disorders, the psychoanalytic and learning perspectives view the symptoms as ways of dealing with anxiety. Psychoanalysts see them as defenses against the anxiety caused by the eruption of unacceptable impulses. Learning theorists see them as behaviors reinforced by anxiety reduction.

Others view dissociative disorders as what psychiatrist Frank Putnam (1995) calls "posttraumatic disorders"—a natural, protective response to "histories of childhood trauma." People diagnosed as having dissociative identity disorder are mostly women who reportedly suffered physical, sexual, or emotional abuse as children (Gleaves, 1996). Perhaps, then, multiple personalities are the desperate efforts of the traumatized to flee inward. Perhaps alternative personalities allow traumatic repressed memories to resurface. Maladaptive as they may be, perhaps such psychological disorders express our human struggle to cope with the stresses of life.

"Though this be madness, yet there is method in 't."

William Shakespeare
Hamlet
1600

Or perhaps, say skeptics, the condition is either contrived by fantasy-prone, emotionally variable people or constructed out of the therapist-patient interaction. "This epidemic will end in the way that the witch craze ended in Salem," predicts psychiatrist Paul McHugh (1995b). "The [multiple personality] phenomena will be seen as manufactured, the 'repressed memory' explanation will be recognized as misguided, and psychiatrists will become immunized against the practices that generated these artifacts."

REHEARSE IT!

7. When anxiety is so distressing, uncontrollable, or persistent that it results in maladaptive behavior, the person is said to have an anxiety disorder. If a person's anxiety takes the form of an irrational fear of a specific object or situation—for example, an irrational fear of dogs, thunderstorms, or closed spaces—the disorder is called

- **a.** a phobia.
- **b.** a panic attack.
- **c.** generalized anxiety.
- **d.** obsessive-compulsive disorder.

8. The experience of anxiety often involves physical symptoms, such as trembling, dizziness, chest pains, or choking sensations. An episode of intense dread, which is typically accompanied by such symptoms and by feelings of terror, is called

- **a.** generalized or chronic anxiety.
- **b.** a social phobia.
- **c.** a panic attack.
- **d.** an obsessive fear.

9. Marina has always been concerned with cleanliness and neatness. Her mother never had to remind her to clean up her room. When Marina became consumed with the need to clean the entire house and refused to participate in any other activities, her family consulted a therapist, who diagnosed her as having

- **a.** obsessive-compulsive disorder.
- **b.** generalized anxiety disorder.
- **c.** a phobia.
- **d.** dissociative fugue.

10. Rats subjected to unpredictable shocks in the laboratory become chronically anxious. To the learning researcher this suggests that anxiety is a response to

- **a.** a phobia.
- **b.** biological factors.
- **c.** the pressures of the superego.
- **d.** helplessness.

11. Psychologists have different ideas about the causes of phobias. For example, some psychologists stress the importance of biological predispositions, noting that we seem predisposed to fear certain stimuli. Psychologists of the learning perspective, on the other hand, maintain that phobias are

- **a.** the result of individual genetic makeup.
- **b.** a way of repressing unacceptable impulses.
- **c.** conditioned fears.
- **d.** a symptom of having been abused as a child.

12. Amnesia and fugue involve gaps in awareness—for example, sudden loss of memory. These psychological disorders are called

- **a.** anxiety disorders.
- **b.** dissociative disorders.
- **c.** mood disorders.
- **d.** memory disorders.

Mood Disorders

8. *What behaviors characterize mood disorders?*

The emotional extremes of **mood disorders** come in two principal forms: (1) *major depressive disorder*, in which the person experiences prolonged hopelessness and lethargy until eventually rebounding to normality; and (2) *bipolar disorder* (formerly called *manic depressive disorder*), in which the person alternates between depression and *mania*, an overexcited, hyperactive state.

mood disorders psychological disorders characterized by emotional extremes. See *major depressive disorder, bipolar disorder*, and *mania*.

major depressive disorder a mood disorder in which a person, for no apparent reason, experiences two or more weeks of depressed moods, feelings of worthlessness, and diminished interest or pleasure in most activities.

mania a mood disorder marked by a hyperactive, wildly optimistic state.

bipolar disorder a mood disorder in which the person alternates between the hopelessness and lethargy of depression and the overexcited state of mania.

Major Depressive Disorder

Perhaps you know what depression feels like. If you are like most college students, at some time during this year—more likely the dark months of winter than the bright days of summer—you will probably experience a few of the symptoms of depression (Beck & Young, 1978). You may feel deeply discouraged

For some people, recurring depression during winter's dark months constitutes a seasonal affective disorder. *For others, winter darkness means more blue moods. The figures below give the percentage of Americans answering yes when asked "Have you cried today?"*

Month	*Men*	*Women*
August	*4%*	*7%*
December	*8%*	*21%*

Source: Time/CNN survey, 1994

about the future, dissatisfied with your life, or isolated from others. You may lack the energy to get things done or even to force yourself out of bed; be unable to concentrate, eat, or sleep normally; or even wonder if you would be better off dead. Perhaps academic success came easily to you in high school, and now you find that disappointing grades jeopardize your goals. Perhaps you feel lonely and isolated as a "nontraditional" student—returning after attending to other work or family commitments. Perhaps social difficulties, such as loneliness or the breakup of a romance, have plunged you into despair. And maybe your brooding has at times only worsened your self-torment.

If so, you are not alone. Depression is the "common cold" of psychological disorders—an expression that effectively describes its pervasiveness but not its seriousness. Although phobias are more common, depression is the number one reason why people seek mental health services.

Depression can be an appropriate response to profoundly sad events, such as a significant loss or bereavement. To feel bad in reaction to painful events is to be in touch with reality. In such times, depression is like a car's low-oil-pressure light—a signal that warns us to stop and take protective measures. Depression is a sort of psychic hibernation: It slows us down, avoids attracting predators, and evokes support. To grind to a halt and ruminate, as depressed people do, is to reassess one's life when feeling threatened. Biologically speaking, the purpose of life is not happiness but survival and reproduction. From this perspective, there is sense to suffering.

But when does this response become seriously maladaptive? The line separating life's normal "downs" from major depression is difficult to define. Joy, contentment, sadness, and despair are different points on a continuum, points at which any of us may be found at any given moment. On that continuum, between the temporary blue moods we all experience and the crushing impact of major depression, is a condition called *dysthymic disorder*—a down-in-the-dumps mood that fills most of the day, nearly every day, for two years or more. Although less disabled than people with major depression, those with dysthymic disorder tend to experience chronic low energy and self-esteem, have difficulty concentrating or making decisions, and sleep and eat too much or too little.

Depression is like a car's low-oil-pressure light—a signal that warns us to stop and take protective measures.

Major depressive disorder occurs when signs of depression (including lethargy, feelings of worthlessness, or loss of interest in family, friends, and activities) last two weeks or more without any notable cause. The difference between a blue mood after bad news and a mood disorder is like the difference between gasping for breath for a few minutes after a hard run and being chronically short of breath.

"My life had come to a sudden stop. I was able to breathe, to eat, to drink, to sleep. I could not, indeed, help doing so; but there was no real life in me."

Leo Tolstoy
My Confession
1887

Bipolar Disorder

With or without therapy, episodes of major depression usually end. Depressed people typically rebound—usually by returning to their previous behavior patterns. However, some people rebound to or from the opposite emotional extreme—a euphoric, hyperactive, wildly optimistic state of **mania**. If depression is living in slow motion, mania is fast forward. Alternation between depression and mania signals **bipolar disorder**. During the manic phase of bipolar disorder, the person is typically overtalkative, overactive, elated (though easily irritated if crossed), has little need for sleep, and shows fewer sexual inhibitions. Speech is loud, flighty, and hard to interrupt.

One of mania's maladaptive symptoms is grandiose optimism and self-esteem, which may lead to reckless spending and investment sprees. Although people in a manic state find advice irritating, they need protection from their own poor judgment. In milder forms, however, the energy and free-flowing

"All the people in history, literature, art, whom I most admire: Mozart, Shakespeare, Homer, El Greco, St. John, Chekhov, Gregory of Nyssa, Dostoevsky, Emily Brontë: not one of them would qualify for a mental-health certificate."

Madeleine L'Engle
A Circle of Quiet
1972

Bipolar disorder History offers many examples of creative bipolar people, from Walt Whitman and Ernest Hemingway to actress Margot Kidder, shown here.

thinking of mania can fuel creativity. Bipolar disorder is especially common among creative artists (Jamison, 1993, 1995). George Frideric Handel (1685–1759), who many believe suffered a mild form of bipolar disorder, composed his nearly four-hour-long *Messiah* during three weeks of intense, creative energy (Keynes, 1980). Creative professionals who rely on precision and logic (architects, designers, journalists) are less vulnerable to bipolar disorder than are those who rely on emotional expression and vivid imagery (poets, novelists, entertainers), reports Arnold Ludwig (1995).

It is as true of emotions as all else: What goes up comes down. Before long, the elated mood either returns to normal or plunges into a brief depression. Though as maladaptive as major depression, bipolar disorder is much less common, occurring in about 1 percent of the population. Unlike major depression, it afflicts as many men as women.

Explaining Mood Disorders

9. *What causes mood disorders?*

Because depression profoundly affects so many people, it has been the subject of thousands of studies. Psychologists are working to develop a theory of mood disorders that will suggest ways to treat or prevent them. Researcher Peter Lewinsohn and his colleagues (1985) summarized the facts that any theory of depression must explain. Among them are the following:

- ***Many behavioral and cognitive changes accompany depression.*** Depressed people are inactive and unmotivated. They also are especially sensitive to negative happenings, expect negative outcomes, and are more likely to recall negative information. When the depression lifts, these behavioral and cognitive accompaniments disappear.
- ***Depression is widespread.*** Its commonality suggests that its causes, too, must be common.
- ***Compared with men, women are twice as vulnerable to major depression, even more so if they have been depressed before*** (Figure 12.4). In general, women are most vulnerable to passive disorders—internalized states, such as depression, anxiety, and inhibited sexual desire. Men's disorders are more active—alcohol abuse, antisocial conduct, lack of impulse control (see Table 12.3, page 457). Curiously, among college students the gender difference in depression is quite small (Regeth & Lewis, 1995).
- ***Most major depressive episodes last less than 3 months.*** Although therapy can speed recovery, most people suffering major depression return to normal without professional help. The plague of depression comes and, a few weeks or months later, it usually goes.
- ***Stressful events related to work, marriage, and close relationships often precede depression.*** A family member's death, a wage cut, or a physical assault increase one's risk of depression (Shrout & others, 1989). National samples of Israelis, whose tiny nation is a living stress laboratory, revealed greater feelings of depression after the outbreak of the 1982 Israel-Lebanon war (Hobfoll & others, 1989). Note, too, the high rate of depression among people in strife-torn Beirut (Figure 12.4)

About 50 percent of those who recover from depression will suffer another episode within two years. Recovery is more likely to be enduring the longer patients stay well, the fewer their previous episodes, the less stress they experience, and the more social support they have (Belsher & Costello, 1988).

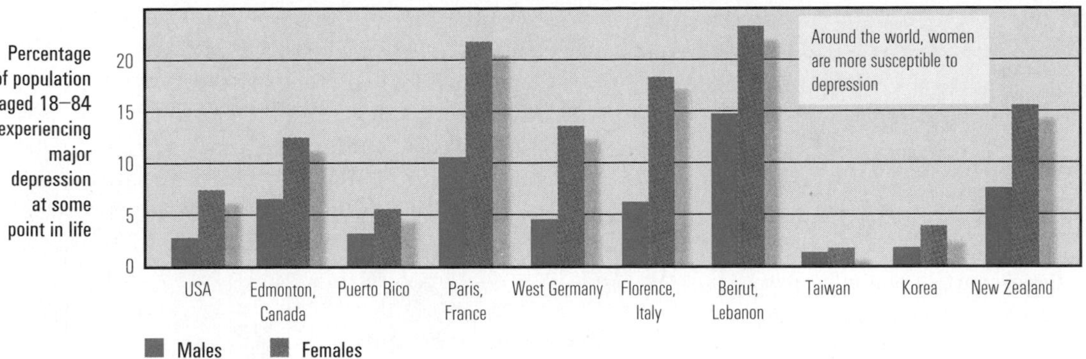

Figure 12.4 Gender and depression Interviews with 38,000 adults in 10 countries confirm what many smaller studies have found: Women have double men's risk of major depression. Note, too, that lifetime risk of depression varies by culture—from 1.5 percent in Taiwan to 19 percent in Beirut. (Data from Weissman & others, 1996)

To these facts we can add one more: With each new generation, the rate of depression is increasing and the disorder is striking earlier (now often in the late teens). It's true not only in Canada and the United States but also in Germany, Italy, France, Lebanon, New Zealand, Taiwan, and Puerto Rico (Cross-National Collaborative Group, 1992). In North America, today's young adults are three times as likely as their grandparents to report recently—or ever—suffering depression (despite the grandparents' having had many more years at risk). In one National Institute of Mental Health study of 18,244 Americans, only 1 percent of those born before 1905 had suffered major depression by age 75. Of those born since 1955, 6 percent had been depressed by age 25. The increase appears genuine, *not* primarily a result of younger adults' greater willingness to admit depression. The increasing rate of depression appears in a dramatic rise in the proportion of psychiatric patients with mood disorders. In a survey of North American psychiatric teaching hospitals, mood disorder diagnoses rose from 10 percent of patients in 1972 to 44 percent in 1990 (Stoll & others, 1993).

With each new generation, the rate of depression is increasing and the disorder is striking earlier (now often in the late teens).

As you might expect, researchers understand and interpret these facts in ways that reflect their different perspectives. To explain depression, psychoanalytic theory applies Freud's ideas about the importance of early childhood experiences and unconscious impulses. It suggests that depression occurs when significant losses evoke feelings associated with losses experienced in childhood. Loss of a romantic relationship or a job might evoke feelings associated with the loss of the intimate relationship with one's mother. Alternatively, unresolved anger toward one's parents might be turned inward against the self. Today's bio-psycho-social perspective is replacing these Freudian explanations of depression with biological and cognitive explanations.

The Biological Perspective

Most of the mental health research dollars of late have funded explorations of biological influences on mood disorders. Depression is a whole-body disorder, involving genetic predispositions, biochemical imbalances, melancholy mood, and negative thoughts.

Genetic Influences

We have long known that mood disorders run in families. The risk of major depression and bipolar disorder increases if you have a parent or sibling who became depressed before age 30 (Pauls & others, 1992; Weissman & others, 1986). If one identical twin is diagnosed as suffering major depressive disorder, the chances are about 1 in 2 that at some time the other twin will be, too. If one identical twin has bipolar disorder, the chances are 7 in 10 that the other twin will at some point be diagnosed similarly. Among fraternal twins, the corresponding odds are just under 1 in 5 (Tsuang & Faraone, 1990). The greater similarity of identical twins' depressive tendencies even occurs among twins reared apart (DiLalla & others, 1996). Moreover, adopted people who suffer a mood disorder often have close biological relatives who suffer mood disorders, become alcoholic, or commit suicide (Wender & others, 1986).

Gene-hunters' pursuit of bipolar-DNA links Linkage studies seek to identify aberrant genes in family members suffering the disorder. These Pennsylvania Amish family members—an isolated population sharing a common life-style and some vulnerability to the disorder—have been among the volunteer subjects.

CLOSE-UP

Suicide

"But life, being weary of these worldly bars,
Never lacks power to dismiss itself."

William Shakespeare
Julius Caesar
1599

Each year some three-quarters of a million wearied, despairing people worldwide will say no to life by electing a permanent solution to what may be a temporary problem (Retterstøl, 1993). In retrospect, families and friends may recall signs they believe should have forewarned them—verbal hints, giving away possessions, or withdrawal and preoccupation with death. Most people who kill themselves have been depressed. One-third have tried suicide before.

Few people who talk of suicide or think suicidal thoughts (a number that includes one-third of all adolescents and college students) actually attempt suicide, and few of those who attempt it succeed in killing themselves (Centers for Disease Control, 1989; Westefeld & Furr, 1987). Still, most individuals who do commit suicide have talked of it. And any who do threaten suicide are at least sending a signal of their desperate or despondent feelings.

To find out who commits suicide, researchers have compared the suicide rates of different groups.

- ***National differences*** The suicide rates of England, Italy, and Spain are little more than half those of Canada, Australia, and the United States; Austrian, Danish, and Finnish suicide rates are nearly double (Bureau of the Census, 1996).
- ***Racial differences*** In the United States, whites are twice as likely as blacks to kill themselves (Bureau of the Census, 1996).
- ***Gender differences*** Women are much more likely than men to attempt suicide. Depending on the country, however, men are two to four times more likely to succeed (Figure 12.5).

Figure 12.5 **Suicide rates by gender and age** In the United States, suicide rates are higher among males than among females. The highest rates of all are found among older men. (From Bureau of the Census, 1996)

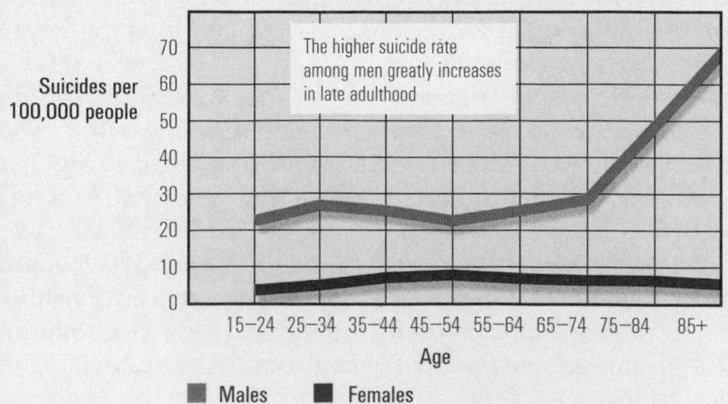

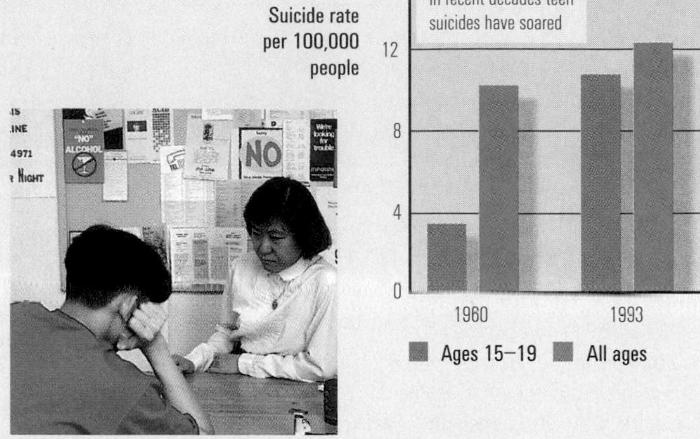

Figure 12.6 **Increasing rates of teen suicide** Teen suicide has soared since 1960. (From National Center for Health Statistics)

(Men are more likely to use foolproof methods, such as firing a bullet into the head, the method of choice in 6 of 10 U.S. suicides.)

- ***Age differences*** Due partly to improved reporting (Gist & Welch, 1989), the known suicide rate among 15- to 19-year-olds has more than doubled in the United States since 1950. It now nearly equals the traditionally higher suicide rate among adults (Figure 12.6). In Canada, the suicide rate among 15- to 18-year-olds has increased sixfold since 1955 (NFFRE, 1996).
- ***Other group differences*** Suicide rates are much higher among the rich, the nonreligious, and those who are single, widowed, or divorced (Hoyer & Lund, 1993; Stack, 1992; Stengel, 1981). In both the United States and Australia, the teen suicide surge is almost entirely among males (Hassan & Carr, 1989).

People who commit suicide often do so not while in the depths of depression, when energy and initiative are lacking, but when they begin to rebound and become capable of following through. Teenage suicides may follow a traumatic event, such as a romantic breakup or a guilt-provoking antisocial act; they are often linked with drug and alcohol abuse (Fowler & others, 1986; Kolata, 1986). Compared with people who suffer no disorder, alcoholics are roughly 100 times more likely to commit suicide, as some 3 percent of them do (Murphy & Wetzel, 1990). Even among those who have attempted suicide, alcoholics are five times more likely than nonalcoholics eventually to kill themselves (Beck & Steer, 1989). Among the elderly, suicide is sometimes chosen as an alternative to future suffering. In people of all ages, suicide is not necessarily an act of hostility or revenge, as many people think, but may be a way of switching off unendurable pain (Shneidman, 1987).

Social suggestion may trigger the final act. Following highly publicized suicides and TV programs featuring suicide, known suicides increase. So do fatal auto "accidents" and private airplane crashes (page 497).

A search for the genes that put people at risk for depression is now under way. At least 15 groups worldwide are sleuthing the genes that make one vulnerable to bipolar disorder (Veggeberg, 1996). To tease out the genes that may be implicated, researchers use *linkage analysis*. First, they find families that have had the disorder across several generations. Then they draw blood from both affected and unaffected family members and examine their DNA, looking for differences.

The Depressed Brain

Genes act by directing biochemical events that, down the line, influence behavior. The biochemical key is the neurotransmitters, those messenger molecules that shuttle signals between nerve cells. Norepinephrine, a neurotransmitter that increases arousal and boosts mood, is overabundant during mania and scarce during depression. A second neurotransmitter, serotonin, appears scarce during depression. Drugs that alleviate mania reduce norepinephrine; drugs that relieve depression tend to increase norepinephrine or serotonin supplies by blocking either their reuptake (as Prozac, Zoloft, and Paxil do with serotonin) or their chemical breakdown. Repetitive physical exercise, such as jogging, also increases serotonin and helps reduce depression (Jacobs, 1994).

Figure 12.7 The ups and downs of bipolar disorder PET scans show that brain energy consumption rises and falls with the patient's emotional switches. Red areas are where the brain rapidly consumes glucose. (Courtesy of Drs. Lewis Baxter and Michael E. Phelps, UCLA School of Medicine)

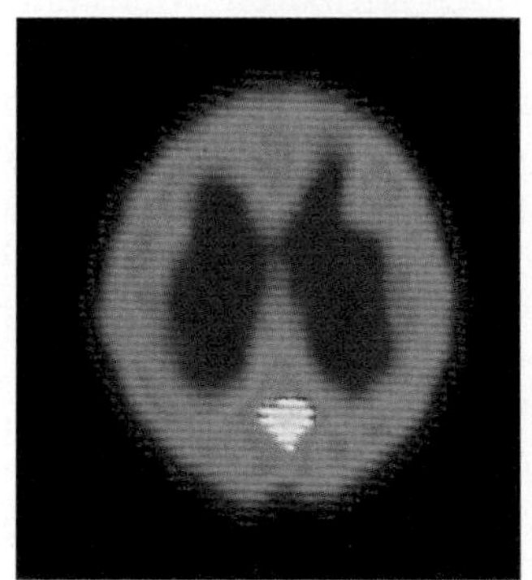

Depressed state
(17-May-83)

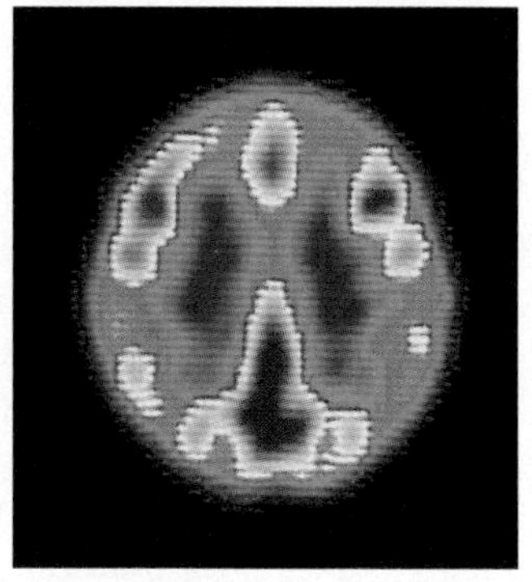

Manic state
(18-May-83)

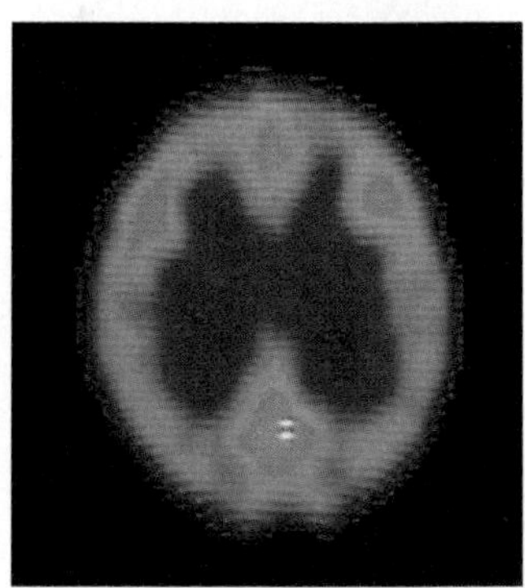

Depressed state
(27-May-83)

Using modern scanning machines, researchers are also spotting neurological signs of depression. Many studies have found the brains of depressed people to be less active, indicating a slowed-down state (Figure 12.7). The left frontal lobe, which is active during positive emotions, is likely to be inactive (Davidson, 1992). MRI scans have even shown the frontal lobes to be 7 percent smaller in severely depressed patients (Coffey & others, 1993).

Brain chemistry
Cognition
Mood

Figure 12.8 Depression—an ailing mind in an ailing body Altering any one component of the chemistry-cognition-mood circuit can alter the others.

The Social-Cognitive Perspective

Some people slide into depression for no obvious reason, even when life has been going well. Often, however, biological factors accompany psychological reactions to experience (Figure 12.8). The mind's negative thoughts somehow influence biochemical events that in a vicious cycle amplify depressing thoughts.

Recent research reveals how *self-defeating beliefs* feed the vicious cycle. Depressed people view life through dark glasses. Their intensely negative assumptions about themselves, their situations, and their futures lead them to magnify bad experiences and minimize good ones. Listen to Norman, a Canadian college professor recalling his depression:

> I [despaired] of ever being human again. I honestly felt subhuman, lower than the lowest vermin. Furthermore, I was self-deprecatory and could not understand why anyone would want to associate with me, let alone love me. . . . I was positive that I was a fraud and a phony and that I didn't deserve my Ph.D. I didn't deserve to have tenure; I didn't deserve to be a Full Professor. . . . I didn't deserve the research grants I had been awarded; I couldn't understand how I had written books and journal articles . . . I must have conned a lot of people. (Endler, 1982, pp. 45–49)

Self-defeating beliefs may arise from *learned helplessness.* As we saw in Chapter 11, both dogs and humans act depressed, passive, and withdrawn after experiencing uncontrollable painful events. Women more often than men have been abused or made to feel helpless, which may help explain why women have been twice as vulnerable to depression as have men (Nolen-Hoeksema, 1990, and see page 442). (Another explanation is that men more often suppress their negative feelings, act them out, or drown them in alcohol.)

Negative Thoughts Feed Negative Moods

> ***"I have learned to accept my mistakes by referring them to a personal history which was not of my making."***
>
> B. F. Skinner (1983)

Why do life's unavoidable failures lead some people, but not others, to become depressed? The difference lies partly with people's *attributions* of blame. We have some choice of whom or what to blame for our failures. If you fail a test and blame yourself, you may feel stupid and depressed. If you externalize the blame—perhaps attributing your failure to an unfair test—you are more likely to feel angry.

Depressed people tend to explain bad events in terms that are *stable* ("It's going to last forever"), *global* ("It's going to affect everything I do"), and *internal* ("It's all my fault"). Lyn Abramson, Gerald Metalsky, and Lauren Alloy (1989) theorize that the result of these pessimistic, overgeneralized, self-blaming attributions is a depressing sense of hopelessness. If you tend to see bad grades, social rejection, and work problems as inevitable and your own fault, and if you ruminate about such things, then when bad events happen you will experience a bad case of the blues.

Martin Seligman (1991, 1995) has argued that depression is common among young Westerners because of epidemic hopelessness, which stems from the rise of individualism and the decline of commitment to religion and family. When facing failure or rejection, contends Seligman, the self-focused individual takes on personal responsibility for problems and has nothing to fall back on for hope. In non-Western cultures, where close-knit relationships and cooperation are the norm, major depression is less common and less tied to self-blame over personal failure. In Japan, for example, depressed people instead tend to report feeling shame over letting others down (Draguns, 1990a).

Negative Moods Feed Negative Thoughts

There is, however, a chicken-and-egg problem with the social-cognitive explanation of depression. Self-defeating beliefs, self-blame, and negative attributions surely do support depression. But do they *cause* depression, any more

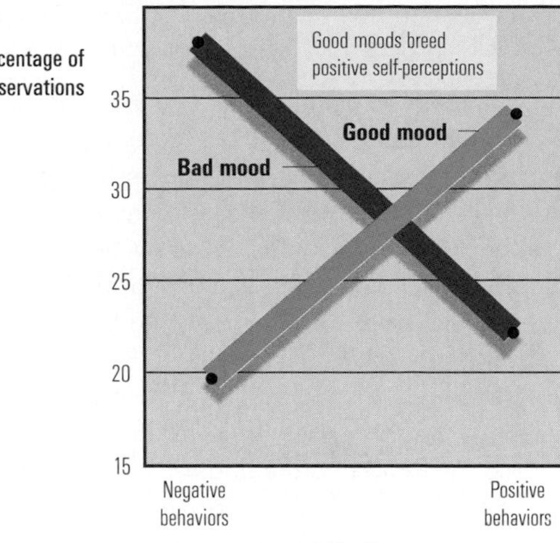

Figure 12.9 The mood effect A happy or depressed mood strongly influences people's rating of their own behavior. In this experiment, those in a hypnotically induced good mood detected many more positive than negative behaviors. The reverse was true for those in a bad mood. (From Forgas & others, 1984)

than a speedometer's reading 70 mph causes a car's speed? Peter Barnett and Ian Gotlib (1988) note that such cognitions are *indicators* of depression. Depressing thoughts *coincide* with a depressed mood. But before or after being depressed, people's thoughts are less negative. Perhaps this is because, as we noted in our discussion of state-dependent memory (pages 251–252), a depressed mood triggers negative thoughts. If you temporarily put people in a bad or sad mood, their memories, judgments, and expectations are suddenly more pessimistic.

Joseph Forgas and his associates (1984) provided a striking demonstration of the mood effect. Subjects who had been put in a good or bad mood via hypnosis then watched a videotape of themselves talking with someone the day before. The happy subjects detected in themselves more positive than negative behaviors; the unhappy subjects more often saw themselves behaving negatively (Figure 12.9). Thus, even when viewing themselves on videotape, people judge themselves more negatively when they feel depressed.

Depression's Vicious Cycle

"A recipe for severe depression is preexisting pessimism encountering failure," notes Martin Seligman (1991, p. 78). Depression is often brought on by stressful experiences—losing a job, getting divorced or rejected, physical trauma—anything that disrupts your sense of who you are and why you are a worthy human being (Hamilton & others, 1993; Kendler & others, 1993). Such brooding after failure can be adaptive; insights gained during times of depressed inactivity may later enable better strategies for interacting with the world. But depression-prone people respond to bad events in an especially self-focused, self-blaming way (Pyszczynski & others, 1991; Wood & others, 1990a,b). Their self-esteem fluctuates more rapidly up with boosts and down with threats (Butler & others, 1994). When down, their brooding amplifies negative feelings, which in turn trigger depression's other cognitive and behavioral symptoms.

This phenomenon also helps explain women's doubled risk of depression. When trouble strikes, women tend to think, men tend to act. A woman may ruminate and act anxious or depressed, whereas a man may distract himself by drinking, delving into work, and playing and watching sports (Seligman, 1994).

Depressed people are at high risk for divorce and job loss, thus compounding their depression.

None of us is immune to the dejection, diminished self-esteem, and negative thinking brought on by rejection or defeat. As Edward Hirt and his colleagues (1992) demonstrated, even small losses can temporarily sour our thinking. They studied some avid Indiana University basketball fans who seemed to regard the team as an extension of themselves. After the fans were depressed by watching their team lose, or elated by a victory, the researchers asked them to predict the team's future performance, and their own. After a loss, the fans offered bleaker assessments not only of the team's future but also of their own likely performance at throwing darts, solving anagrams, and getting a date. When things aren't going our way, it may seem as though they never will.

"Man never reasons so much and becomes so introspective as when he suffers, since he is anxious to get at the cause of his sufferings."

Luigi Pirandello
Six Characters in Search of an Author
1922

When bad events happen, those who ruminate and catastrophize with pessimistic, self-blaming thoughts are more at risk for depression. In research demonstrating this effect, Susan Nolen-Hoeksema and Jannay Morrow (1991) happened to assess Stanford University students' moods and ruminations 2 weeks before the 1989 earthquake devastated much of their area. Those identified as prone to brood over negative events showed more symptoms of depression both 10 days and 7 weeks after the earthquake. If you have an optimistic way of interpreting events, a failure or stress is unlikely to provoke depression

CLOSE-UP

Loneliness

Loneliness—the painful awareness that one's social relationships are deficient—is both a contributor to depression and its own problem. The deficiency stems from a mismatch between one's actual and desired social contacts. One person may feel lonely when isolated and another may feel lonely in a crowd.

Aloneness often breeds loneliness. People who are alone—unmarried, unattached, and often young—are more likely to feel lonely. Dutch psychologist Jenny de Jong-Gierveld (1987) has speculated that the emphasis on individual fulfillment and the downgrading of stable relationships and commitment to others are "loneliness-provoking factors." Work-related moves also make for fewer long-term family and social ties and increased loneliness (Dill & Anderson, 1998).

People commonly experience one or more of four types of loneliness (Beck & Young, 1978). To be lonely is to feel *excluded* from a group you would like to belong to; to feel *unloved* and uncared about by those around you; to feel *constricted* and unable to share your private concerns with anyone; or to feel *alienated*, or different, from those in your community.

Like depressed people, lonely people tend to blame themselves, attributing their deficient social relationships to their own inadequacies (Snodgrass, 1987). There may be a basis for this self-blame: Chronically lonely people tend to be shy, self-conscious, and lacking in self-esteem, and to be perceived as less socially competent and attractive (Cheek & Melchior, 1990; Lau & Gruen, 1992; Vaux, 1988). They often find it hard to introduce themselves, make phone calls, and participate in groups (Rook, 1984; Spitzberg & Hurt, 1987). In addition, their belief in their social unworthiness restricts their noticing and remembering positive feedback and their taking steps that would reduce their loneliness (Frankel & Prentice-Dunn, 1990). Thus, factors that work to create and maintain the cycle of depression can also produce a cycle of loneliness.

(Seligman, 1991). Even if you do get depressed, you are more likely to recover quickly (Metalsky & others, 1993; Needles & Abramson, 1990).

So, there is two-way traffic between depressed mood and negative thinking. Depression causes self-focused negative thinking, and a self-focused, self-blaming style of explaining events puts one at risk for depression when bad events strike.

Another source of depression's vicious cycle is its social consequences. Being withdrawn, self-focused, and complaining elicits rejection (Gotlib & Hammen, 1992; Segrin & Dillard, 1992). In one study, researchers Stephen Strack and James Coyne (1983) noted that "depressed persons induced hostility, depression, and anxiety in others and got rejected. Their guesses that they were not accepted were not a matter of cognitive distortion." Weary of the depressed person's fatigue, hopeless attitude, and lethargy, a spouse may threaten to leave or a boss may begin to question the person's competence. Indeed, depressed people are at high risk for divorce and job loss, thus compounding their depression. Misery may love another's company, but company does not love another's misery.

Figure 12.10 The vicious cycle of depression This cycle can be broken at any point. Chapter 13 describes some therapeutic techniques. (Adapted from Lewinsohn & others, 1985)

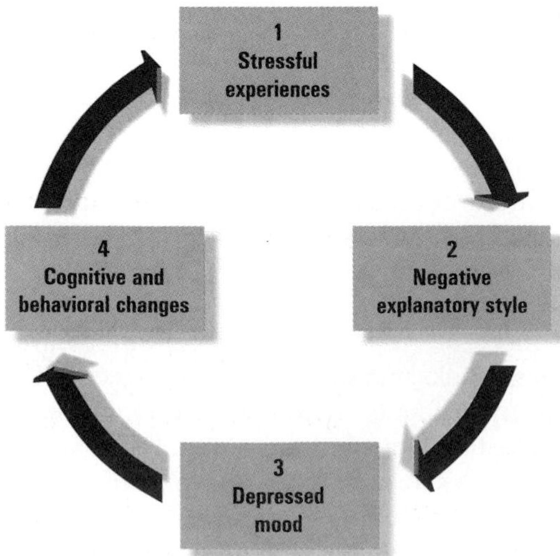

We can now assemble the pieces of the depression puzzle (Figure 12.10): (1) Stressful events interpreted through (2) a ruminating, pessimistic explanatory style create (3) a hopeless, depressed state that (4) hampers the way the person thinks and acts. This, in turn, fuels (1) more negative experiences. It's a cycle we can all recognize. Bad moods feed on themselves: When we *feel* down, we *think* negatively and remember bad experiences. On the brighter side, we can break the cycle of depression at any of these points—by moving to a different environment, by reversing our self-blame and negative attributions, by turning our attention outward, or by engaging in more pleasant activities and more competent behavior.

Winston Churchill called depression a "black dog" that periodically hounded him. Poet Emily Dickinson was so afraid of bursting into tears in public that she spent much of her adult life in seclusion (Patterson, 1951). Abraham Lincoln was so withdrawn and brooding as a young man that his friends feared he might take his own life (Kline, 1974). As each of these lives reminds us, people can and do struggle through depression. Most regain their capacity to love, to work, and even to succeed at the highest levels.

13. Dissociative identity disorder is relatively rare. An example of a disorder that is so common it has been called the "common cold" of psychological disorders is

a. amnesia. **c.** bipolar disorder.
b. depression. **d.** schizophrenia.

14. With bipolar disorder, the person alternates between the lethargy of depression and the overexcited state of mania. Although bipolar disorder is as maladaptive as depression, it is much less common and it affects

a. all ethnic groups equally.
b. primarily scientists and doctors.
c. as many men as women.
d. younger people more than older people.

15. Depression affects many people, often following a stressful event, such as divorce or job change. In a depressive episode, a person tends to be inactive and unmotivated and overly sensitive to negative happenings. In most cases the depressive episode lasts

a. less than three months. **c.** six months to one year.
b. six months. **d.** two years.

16. Depression tends to run in families. It can often be alleviated by drugs that block the reuptake of the neurotransmitters nor-epinephrine and serotonin. These statements suggest that an explanation for depression may well be found in

a. psychoanalytic theory. **c.** stressful events.
b. learned helplessness. **d.** biological factors.

17. Depressed people are more likely than others to blame themselves, rather than external factors, for their failures. Such self-defeating beliefs often arise from feelings of helplessness or futility. Psychologists who emphasize the importance of negative perceptions, beliefs, and thoughts in depression are working within the _________ perspective.

a. psychoanalytic **c.** behavioral
b. biological **d.** social-cognitive

Schizophrenia

10. *What behaviors characterize schizophrenia?*

If depression is the common cold of psychological disorders, chronic schizophrenia is the cancer. About 1 in 100 people will develop schizophrenia, joining the millions across the world who have suffered one of humanity's most dreaded disorders. It typically strikes during adolescence or young adulthood. It knows no national boundaries, and it affects males and females about equally.

Symptoms of Schizophrenia

Literally translated, **schizophrenia** means "split mind." It refers not to a multiple personality split but rather to a split from reality that shows itself in disorganized thinking, disturbed perceptions, and inappropriate emotions and actions.

Disorganized Thinking

Imagine trying to communicate with Maxine, a young woman whose thoughts spill out in no logical order. Her biographer, Susan Sheehan (1982, p. 25), observed her saying aloud to no one in particular,

> This morning, when I was at Hillside [Hospital], I was making a movie. I was surrounded by movie stars. The X-ray technician was Peter Lawford. The security guard was Don Knotts. That Indian doctor in Building 40 was Lou Costello. I'm Mary Poppins. Is this room painted blue to get me upset? My grandmother died four weeks after my eighteenth birthday.

As this strange monologue illustrates, the schizophrenia patient's thinking is fragmented, bizarre, and distorted by false beliefs, called **delusions** ("I'm Mary

schizophrenia a group of severe psychotic disorders characterized by disorganized and delusional thinking, disturbed perceptions, and inappropriate emotions and actions.

delusions false beliefs, often of persecution or grandeur, that may accompany psychotic disorders.

Poppins"). Jumping from one idea to another may occur even within sentences, creating a sort of "word salad." One young man begged for "a little more allegro in the treatment" and suggested that "liberationary movement with a view to the widening of the horizon" will "ergo extort some wit in lectures." Those with *paranoid* tendencies are particularly prone to delusions of persecution.

Many psychologists believe disorganized thoughts result from a breakdown in selective attention. Recall from Chapter 5 that we normally have a remarkable capacity for selective attention—for, say, giving our undivided attention to one voice at a party while filtering out competing sensory stimuli. Schizophrenia sufferers have impaired attention (Gjerde, 1983). Thus, an irrelevant stimulus or an extraneous part of the preceding thought easily distracts them. Minute stimuli, such as the grooves on a brick or the inflections of a voice, may distract attention from the whole scene or from the speaker's meaning. As one former schizophrenia patient recalled, "What had happened to me . . . was a breakdown in the filter, and a hodge-podge of unrelated stimuli were distracting me from things which should have had my undivided attention" (MacDonald, 1960, p. 218).

Disturbed Perceptions

A person with schizophrenia may perceive things that are not there. Such *hallucinations* (sensory experiences without sensory stimulation) are usually auditory. The person may hear voices that make insulting statements or give orders. The voices may tell the patient that she is bad or that he must burn himself with a cigarette lighter. Less commonly, people see, feel, taste, or smell things that are nonexistent. Such hallucinations have been compared to dreams breaking into waking consciousness. When the unreal seems real, the resulting perceptions are at best bizarre and at worst terrifying.

Inappropriate Emotions and Actions

The emotions of schizophrenia are often utterly inappropriate. Maxine's emotions seemed split off from reality. She laughed after recalling her grandmother's death. On occasion, she became angry for no apparent reason or cried

Art by people diagnosed with schizophrenia Commenting on the kind of artwork shown here, poet John Ashbery wrote: "The lure of the work is strong, but so is the terror of the unanswerable riddles it proposes."

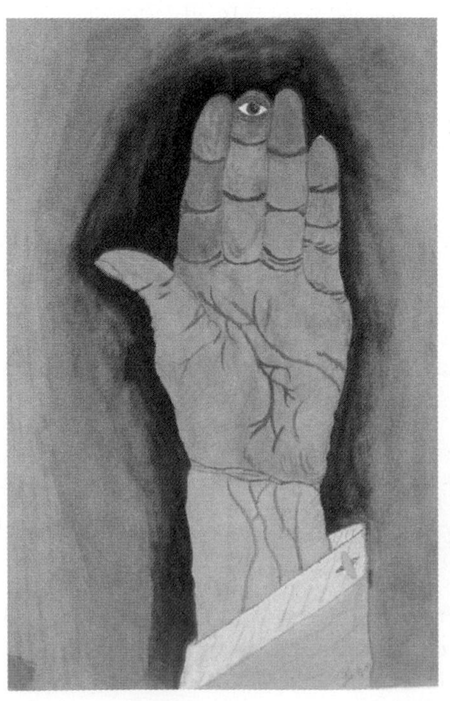

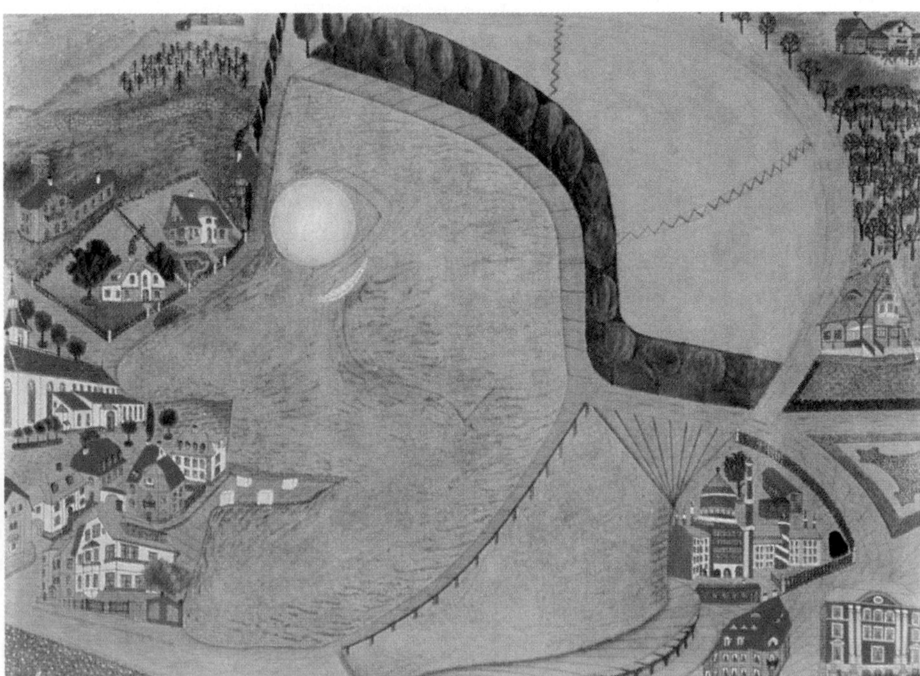

when others laughed. Other victims of schizophrenia sometimes lapse into *flat affect*, a zombielike state of apparent apathy.

Motor behavior also may be inappropriate. The person may perform senseless, compulsive acts, such as continually rocking or rubbing an arm. Those who exhibit *catatonia* may remain motionless for hours on end and then become agitated.

As you can imagine, disorganized thinking, disturbed perceptions, and inappropriate emotions and actions disrupt social relationships. During their most severe periods, people with schizophrenia live in a private inner world, preoccupied with illogical ideas and unreal images. Although some people suffer from schizophrenia only intermittently, others remain socially withdrawn and isolated throughout much of their lives. Rarely is schizophrenia a one-time episode that is "cured," never to return.

Types of Schizophrenia

We have described schizophrenia as if it were a single disorder. Actually, it is a cluster of disorders that have common features but also some distinguishing symptoms. Schizophrenia patients with *positive symptoms* are disorganized and deluded in their talk or are prone to inappropriate laughter, tears, or rage. Those with *negative symptoms* have toneless voices, expressionless faces, or mute and rigid bodies. Because schizophrenia is more than one disorder (Table 12.2), there could be more than one cause.

Table 12.2 Subtypes of Schizophrenia

Paranoid: Preoccupation with delusions or hallucinations

Disorganized: Disorganized speech or behavior, or flat or inappropriate emotion

Catatonic: Immobility (or excessive, purposeless movement), extreme negativism, and/or parrotlike repeating of another's speech or movements

Undifferentiated or *residual*: Schizophrenia symptoms without fitting one of the above types

Sometimes, as in the case of Maxine, schizophrenia develops gradually, emerging from a long history of social inadequacy (which partially explains why those predisposed to schizophrenia often end up in the lower socioeconomic levels, or even as homeless people). Other times it appears suddenly, seemingly as a reaction to stress. There is a rule that holds true around the world (World Health Organization, 1979): When the schizophrenia is a slow-developing process (called *chronic*, or *process*, schizophrenia), recovery is doubtful. When, in reaction to particular life stresses, a previously well-adjusted person develops schizophrenia rapidly (*acute*, or *reactive*, schizophrenia), recovery is much more likely. Those with chronic schizophrenia often exhibit the negative symptom of withdrawal. The outlook is better for those exhibiting positive symptoms—they more often have a reactive condition that responds to drug therapy (Fenton & McGlashan, 1991, 1994; Fowles, 1992).

Understanding Schizophrenia

11. ***What causes schizophrenia?***

Schizophrenia is not only the most dreaded psychological disorder but also one of the most heavily researched. Most current research studies link schizophrenia with brain abnormalities and genetic predispositions.

Brain Abnormalities

The idea that imbalances in brain chemistry might underlie schizophrenia has long intrigued scientists. Strange behaviors, they knew, could have strange chemical causes. The saying "mad as a hatter" refers to the psychological deterioration of British hatmakers whose brains, it was later discovered, were slowly poisoned as they moistened the brims of mercury-laden felt hats with their lips (Smith, 1983). As we saw on page 197, scientists are beginning to understand the mechanism by which chemicals such as LSD produce hallucinations. These discoveries hint that schizophrenia symptoms might have a biochemical key.

CLOSE-UP

Experiencing Schizophrenia

These recollections by a person who recovered from schizophrenia illustrate some of the thoughts and feelings of those who suffer the positive symptoms of schizophrenia. Note the hallucinations and the delusions of persecution and grandeur.

One night I was invited to listen to a talk by a worker in the foreign service. I was suspicious of him and thought he thought I was a Communist spy. I didn't say anything. I just leaned over and stared at him.

I thought the Government was spying on my room with a telescope in a building across the street. I thought people were loading down my food in the cafeteria with salt. In criminology class I thought the professor and the other students were laughing about me. I thought they were directing the poisoning of my food in the cafeteria. When I went to the cafeteria my hand shook as the waitress poured what I thought was poisonous coffee into my cup. I thought everyone in the cafeteria knew I was going to die. They all thought it was too bad but I was so evil it was necessary.

On a Saturday I drank lemonade to try to neutralize the poison. Then I would take showers to try to sweat the poison out. I was so nervous I could hardly think. I thought I might only have hours left to live. I thought of taking a bus home to my parents. But no, I thought, it was too late for that.

One day when my strange behavior landed me in a jail cell, the walls began to buzz like bees. I felt there were thousands of bees in the walls buzzing. The buzzing went on and on. There was no relief. It was maddening. Finally, I felt my father's hand rest on my head and I felt peace.

When someone asks me to explain schizophrenia I tell them, you know how sometimes in your dreams you are in them yourself and some of them feel like real nightmares? My schizophrenia was like I was walking through a dream. But everything around me was real. At times, today's world seems so boring and I wonder if I would like to step back into the schizophrenic dream, but then I remember all the scary and horrifying experiences.

Source: Excerpted and paraphrased with permission from Stuart Emmons, Craig Geisler, Kalman J. Kaplan, and Martin Harrow, *Living with Schizophrenia* (Muncie, IN: Taylor & Francis, 1997).

Dopamine Overactivity

One such key to schizophrenia involves the neurotransmitter dopamine. When researchers examined patients' brains after death, they found an excess of receptors for dopamine—in fact, a sixfold excess for the so-called D4 dopamine receptor (Seeman & others, 1993; Wong & others, 1986). Such a high level may intensify brain signals, the researchers speculate, creating schizophrenia's positive symptoms. As we might therefore expect, drugs that block dopamine receptors often lessen schizophrenia symptoms. Drugs that increase dopamine levels, such as amphetamines and cocaine, sometimes intensify schizophrenia symptoms (Swerdlow & Koob, 1987). Such dopamine overactivity may be what makes schizophrenia victims overreact to irrelevant external and internal stimuli.

Brain Anatomy

Modern brain-scanning techniques reveal that many people with chronic schizophrenia have abnormal brain activity. Some have abnormally low brain activity in the frontal lobes (Pettegrew & others, 1993; Resnick, 1992). One recent study took PET scans of brain activity while people were hallucinating (Silbersweig & others, 1995). When they heard a voice or saw something, the brain became vigorously active in several core regions, including the thalamus—a structure deep in the brain that filters and directs incoming sensation up to the cortex.

Enlarged, fluid-filled areas and a corresponding shrinkage of cerebral tissue seem characteristic of schizophrenia, especially in men (Cannon & Marco, 1994; Elkis & others, 1995). The greater the shrinkage, the worse the thought disorder tends to be (Shenton & others, 1992). The thalamus, too, is smaller than normal, which may explain why people with schizophrenia have difficulty filtering sensory input and focusing attention (Andreasen & others, 1994). The bottom line of various brain studies, reports Nancy Andreasen (1997), is that schizophrenia involves not a single brain abnormality but problems with several brain regions and their interconnections.

Naturally, scientists wonder what causes these brain abnormalities. One possibility is a prenatal problem. People conceived during the peak of the Dutch wartime famine later displayed a doubled rate of schizophrenia (Susser & others, 1996). A midpregnancy viral infection that might impair fetal brain development is another possible culprit (Waddington, 1993). Can you imagine some ways to test this prenatal viral infections idea?

Scientists exploring this possibility have asked the following questions:

- ***Are people at increased risk of schizophrenia if, during the middle of their fetal development, their country experienced a flu epidemic?*** The repeated answer is yes (Mednick & others, 1994; Murray & others, 1992; Wright & others, 1995).
- ***Are those born during the winter and spring months—after the fall-winter flu season—also at increased risk?*** The answer is yes, at 5 to 15 percent increased risk (Pulver & others, 1992; Torrey & others, 1977, 1993, 1996; Wright & Murray, 1993).
- ***In the southern hemisphere, where the seasons are the reverse of the northern hemisphere, are the months of above-average schizophrenia births similarly reversed?*** Again, the answer is yes. In Australia, for example, people born between August and October are at greater risk—unless they migrated from the northern hemisphere, in which case their risk is greater if they were born between January and March (McGrath & others, 1995).
- ***As infectious disease rates have declined, has there been a correlated decline in the later incidence of schizophrenia?*** Once again, the answer is yes (Eagles, 1991).

Although schizophrenia has other causes as well (as genetics research makes plain), these converging lines of evidence suggest that prenatal viral infections do play a contributing role.

Genetic Factors

Might people also inherit a predisposition to certain brain abnormalities? The evidence strongly suggests that some do. The 1-in-100 odds of any person's being diagnosed with schizophrenia become 1 in 10 among those who have an afflicted sibling or parent and close to 1 in 2 among those who have an afflicted identical twin (Figure 12.11). Although there are barely more than a dozen such known cases, it appears that an identical twin of a schizophrenia victim retains that 1-in-2 chance, whether the twins are reared together or apart (Plomin & others, 1997).

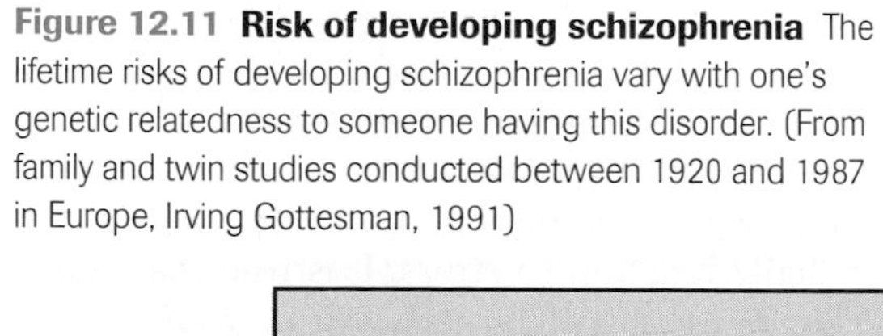
Figure 12.11 Risk of developing schizophrenia The lifetime risks of developing schizophrenia vary with one's genetic relatedness to someone having this disorder. (From family and twin studies conducted between 1920 and 1987 in Europe, Irving Gottesman, 1991)

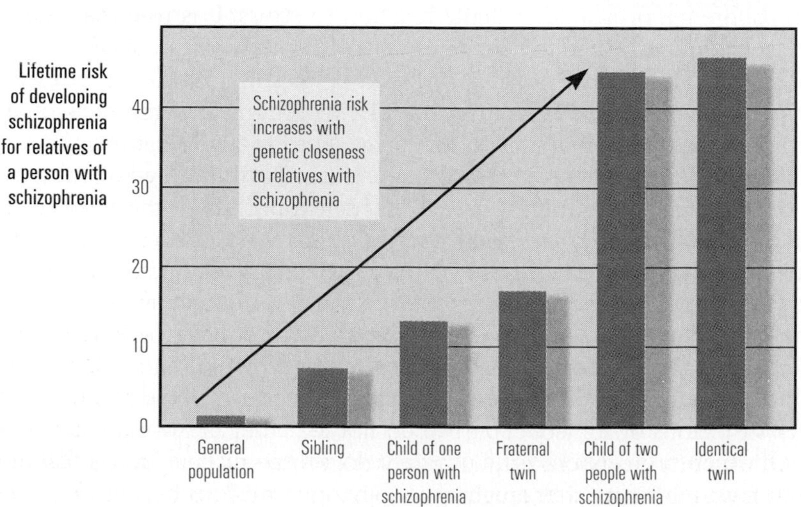

Curiously, though, even with identical twins there may be a prenatal environmental component. About 60 percent of identical twins share the same placenta. (They usually also have opposite, mirror-imaged, handedness to their co-twin.) If you have an identical twin with schizophrenia, and if you shared a placenta, you are also more likely to share the disorder. Twins who have the same placenta are more likely to experience the same prenatal viruses (Davis & others, 1995a,b). So it's possible that shared germs as well as shared genes produce identical twin similarities.

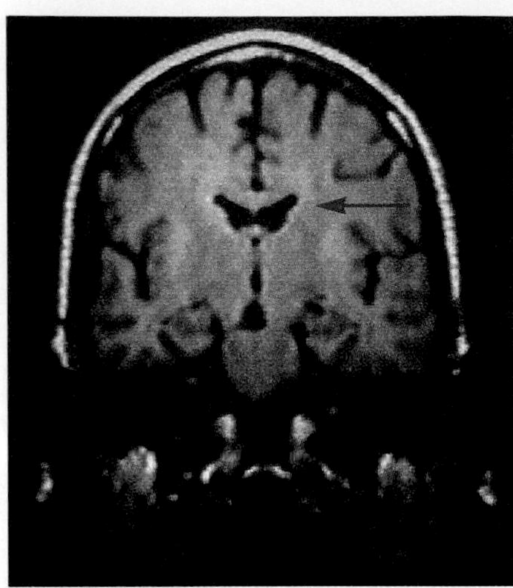

No schizophrenia

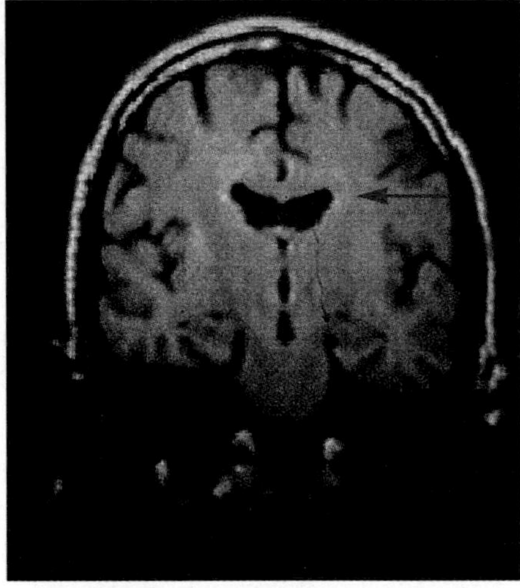

Schizophrenia

Schizophrenia in twins When twins differ, only the one afflicted with schizophrenia typically has enlarged, fluid-filled cranial cavities (Suddath & others, 1990). The difference between the twins implies some nongenetic factor, such as a virus, is also at work.

Adoption studies, however, confirm that the genetic link is real (Gottesman, 1991). Children adopted by someone who develops schizophrenia seldom "catch" the disorder. Rather, adopted children have an elevated risk if a biological parent is diagnosed with schizophrenia. Moreover, several linkage studies have implicated chromosomes 6 and 22 as the site of genes that make some people susceptible to schizophrenia (DeAngelis, 1997; Lander & Kruglyak, 1995).

The genetic contribution to schizophrenia is beyond question. But the genetic role is not so straightforward as the inheritance of eye color. After all, about half the twins who share identical genes with a person who has schizophrenia do *not* develop the disorder. Thus, behavior geneticists Susan Nicol and Irving Gottesman (1983) concluded that some people "have a genetic predisposition to the disorder but that this predisposition by itself is not sufficient for the development of schizophrenia."

Given the genetic influences upon disorders such as schizophrenia and bipolar disorder, might scientists develop genetic tests that reveal who is at risk? If so, will people in the future subject their embryos to genetic testing (and gene repair or abortion if they are at risk for a psychological or physical malady)? Or might they take their egg and sperm to the genetics lab for screening before combining them to produce an embryo? Or might children be tested for genetic risks and given appropriate preventive treatments? Although there is a growing possibility of such tests, the patterns of inheritance seem too complex to expect that a single gene abnormality will prove predictive (Gottesman, 1993). But given the explosion in gene and brain research technologies, scientists are optimistic that schizophrenia will soon be much better understood.

Psychological Factors

If genetically predisposed physiological abnormalities do not by themselves cause schizophrenia, neither do psychological factors alone. It remains true, as Nicol and Gottesman (1983) have noted, that "no environmental causes have been discovered that will invariably, or even with moderate probability, produce schizophrenia in persons who are not related to a schizophrenic."

Nevertheless, if genes predispose some people to *react* to particular experiences by developing schizophrenia, then there must be identifiable triggering experiences. Researchers have asked: Can stress trigger schizophrenia? Can difficulties in family communications be a contributing factor?

The answer to each question is a strong maybe. The psychological triggers of schizophrenia have proved elusive, partly because they may vary with the type of schizophrenia and its speed of onset—whether it is a slow-developing, chronic schizophrenia, or a sudden, acute reaction to stress. It is true that young people with schizophrenia tend to have unusually disturbed communications with their parents. But is this a cause or a result of their disorder? It is true that stressful experiences, biochemical abnormalities, and schizophrenia's symptoms often occur together. But as the bio-psycho-social perspective emphasizes, the traffic between brain biochemistry and psychological experiences runs both ways, so cause and effect are difficult to sort out. It is true that schizophrenic withdrawal often occurs in adolescence or early adulthood, coinciding with the stresses of having to become independent, assert oneself, and achieve social success and intimacy. So is schizophrenia the maladaptive coping reaction of biologically vulnerable people?

Most of us can relate more easily to the ups and downs of mood disorders than to the strange thoughts, perceptions, and behaviors of schizophrenia. Sometimes our thoughts do jump around, but we do not talk nonsensically. Occasionally we feel unjustly suspicious of someone, but we do not fear that the world is plotting against us. Often our perceptions err, but rarely do we see or hear things that are not there. We have felt regret after laughing at someone's misfortune, but we rarely

personality disorders psychological disorders characterized by inflexible and enduring behavior patterns that impair social functioning.

antisocial personality disorder a personality disorder in which the person (usually a man) exhibits a lack of conscience for wrongdoing, even toward friends and family members. May be aggressive and ruthless or a clever con artist.

The Genain quadruplets The odds of any four people picked at random all being diagnosed with schizophrenia are 1 in 100 million. But Nora, Iris, Myra, and Hester Genain have the disease. Two of the sisters have more severe forms of the disorder than the others, suggesting the influence of environmental as well as biological factors.

giggle in response to bad news. At times we just want to be alone, but we do not live in social isolation. However, millions of people around the world do talk strangely, suffer delusions, hear nonexistent voices, see things that are not there, laugh or cry at inappropriate times, or withdraw into private imaginary worlds. Because this is true, the quest to solve the cruel puzzle of schizophrenia continues.

Does a full moon trigger "madness" in some people? James Rotton and I. W. Kelly (1985) examined data from 37 studies that related lunar phase to crime, homicides, crisis calls, and mental hospital admissions. Their conclusion: There is virtually no evidence of "moon madness." Nor does lunar phase correlate with suicides, assaults, emergency room visits, or traffic disasters (Byrnes & Kelly, 1992; Kelly & others, 1990; Martin & others, 1992).

Personality Disorders

12. *What characteristics are typical of personality disorders?*

Personality disorders are inflexible and enduring patterns of behavior that impair one's social functioning. A person with a *histrionic personality disorder* displays shallow, attention-getting emotions. Histrionic individuals go to great lengths to gain others' praise and reassurance. Those with *narcissistic personality disorder* exaggerate their own importance, aided by success fantasies. They find criticism hard to accept, often reacting with rage or shame. Those with *borderline personality disorder* have an unstable identity, unstable relationships, and unstable emotions. If personality is one's enduring pattern of thinking, feeling, and acting, then a markedly unstable sense of self defines a "borderline personality."

The most frequent of these disorders, and the most troubling to society, is the **antisocial personality disorder**. The person (formerly called a *sociopath* or a *psychopath*) is typically a male whose lack of conscience becomes plain before age 15, as he begins to lie, steal, fight, or display unrestrained sexual behavior. About half of such children become antisocial adults—unable to keep a job, irresponsible as a spouse and parent, and assaultive or otherwise criminal (Farrington, 1991). When the antisocial personality combines a keen intelligence with amorality, the result may be a charming and clever con artist—or worse.

Despite their antisocial behavior, most criminals do not fit the description of antisocial personality disorder. Most criminals show responsible concern for their friends and family members; antisocial personalities feel little and fear little. In extreme cases, the results can be tragic. Henry Lee Lucas reported that at age 13 he strangled a woman who refused to have sex with him. He at one time confessed to having bludgeoned, suffocated, stabbed, shot, or mutilated some 360 women, men, and children during his 32 years of crime. During the last 6 years of his reign of terror, Lucas teamed with Elwood Toole, who reportedly slaughtered about 50 people whom he "didn't think was worth living anyhow." It ended when Lucas confessed to stabbing and dismembering his 15-year-old common-law wife, who was Toole's niece.

The antisocial personality expresses little regret over violating others' rights. "Once I've done a crime, I just forget it," said Lucas. Toole was equally matter-of-fact: "I think of killing like smoking a cigarette, like another habit" (Darrach & Norris, 1984).

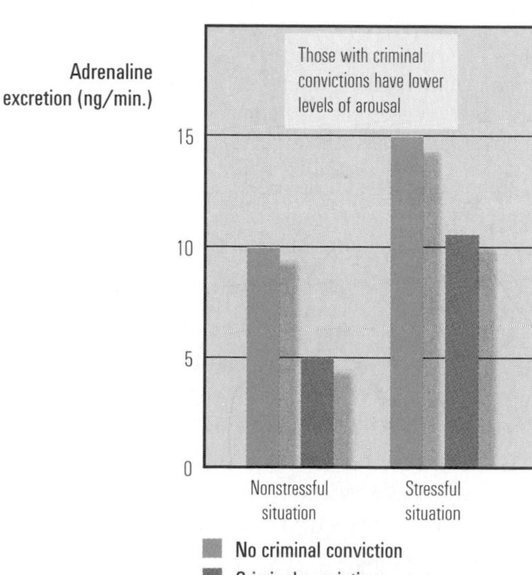

Figure 12.12 Cold-blooded arousability and risk of crime Levels of the stress hormone adrenaline were measured in two groups of 13-year-old Swedish boys. In both stressful and nonstressful situations, those who were later convicted of a crime (as 18- to 26-year-olds) showed relatively low arousal. (From Magnusson, 1990)

As with mood disorders and schizophrenia, the antisocial personality disorder is woven of biological as well as psychological strands. Although there is no single gene that codes for a complex behavior such as crime, twin and adoption studies reveal that biological relatives of certain individuals are at increased risk for criminality (Brennan & Mednick, 1993; DiLalla & Gottesman, 1991; Lyons & others, 1995). Their genetic vulnerability appears as a fearless approach to life. When they await aversive events, such as electric shocks or loud noises, they show little autonomic nervous system arousal (Hare, 1975). Even as youngsters, before committing any crime, they react with lower levels of stress hormones than do others their age (Figure 12.12).

Some studies have detected the early signs of antisocial behavior in children as young as ages 3 to 6 (Caspi & others, 1996; Tremblay & others, 1994). Boys who later became aggressive or antisocial as adolescents tended, as young children, to have been impulsive, uninhibited, unconcerned with social rewards, and low in anxiety. If channeled in more productive directions, such fearlessness may lead to courageous heroism or adventurism. Lacking a sense of social responsibility, the same disposition produces a cool con artist or killer (Lykken, 1995).

Perhaps a biologically based fearlessness, as well as early environment, helps explain the reunion of long-separated sisters Joyce Lott, 27, and Mary Jones, 29—in a South Carolina prison where both were sent on drug charges. After a newspaper story about their reunion, their long-lost half-brother Frank Strickland called. He explained it would be a while before he could come see them—because he, too, was in jail, on drug, burglary, and larceny charges (Shepherd & others, 1990).

Genetics alone is hardly the whole story of crime, however. Relative to 1960, the average American in 1995 was twice as likely to be murdered, four times as likely to report being raped, four times as likely to report being robbed, and five times as likely to report being assaulted (FBI *Uniform Crime Reports*). Violent crime is also surging in other Western nations. Yet the human gene pool has hardly changed. Or consider the British social experiment begun in 1787, exiling 160,000 criminals to Australia. The descendants of these exiles, carrying their ancestors' supposed "criminal genes," have helped create a civilized democracy whose crime rate is slightly *lower* than Britain's (*World Atlas*, 1993). Genetic predispositions do put some individuals more at risk for antisocial conduct than others; biological as well as environmental influences explain why 5 to 6 percent of offenders commit 50 to 60 percent of crimes (Lyman, 1996). But we must look to sociocultural factors to explain the modern epidemic of violence.

REHEARSE IT!

18. Schizophrenia patients often show disorganized thinking and disturbed perceptions. They may speak illogically and may hear voices urging self-destruction. Hearing voices in the absence of any auditory stimulation is an example of a(n)

a. delusion or false belief.
b. inappropriate emotion.
c. word salad.
d. hallucination.

19. Schizophrenia is actually a cluster of disorders characterized by positive or negative symptoms. A person with positive symptoms is most likely to experience

a. catatonia.
b. delusions.
c. withdrawal.
d. flat emotion.

20. Stressful events, faulty family communications, and, especially, inherited abnormalities in brain chemistry and structure are all possible factors in the development of schizophrenia. Chances for recovery are best when

a. onset is sudden, in response to stress.
b. deterioration occurs gradually, during childhood.
c. no environmental causes can be identified.
d. there is a detectable brain abnormality.

21. Unlike other psychological disorders, personality disorders need not involve any apparent anxiety, depression, or loss of contact with reality. A personality disorder, such as antisocial personality, is characterized by

a. the presence of multiple personalities.
b. disorganized thinking.
c. enduring and maladaptive personality traits.
d. mood disturbances.

Rates of Psychological Disorders

13. *How common are the psychological disorders we have discussed?*

How prevalent are the various disorders discussed in this chapter? Who is most vulnerable to them? At what times of life? To answer such questions, the U.S. National Institute of Mental Health (NIMH) undertook during the 1980s a short census of

Table 12.3 **Percentage of Americans Who Have Ever Experienced Psychological Disorders**

	Ethnicity			Gender		
Disorder	White	Black	Hispanic	Men	Women	Totals
Alcohol abuse or dependence	13.6%	13.8%	16.7%	23.8%	4.6%	13.8%
Generalized anxiety	3.4	6.1	3.7	2.4	5.0	3.8
Phobias	9.7	23.4	12.2	10.4	17.7	14.3
Obsessive-compulsive disorder	2.6	2.3	1.8	2.0	3.0	2.6
Mood disorder	8.0	6.3	7.8	5.2	10.2	7.8
Schizophrenia	1.4	2.1	0.8	1.2	1.7	1.5
Antisocial personality	2.6	2.3	3.4	4.5	0.8	2.6

Source: Data from Robins & Regier, 1991. Similar gender differences, though with somewhat higher rates of disorder, come from the U.S. National Comorbidity Survey (Kessler & others, 1994).

psychological disorders. In five different regions of the country researchers conducted lengthy, structured interviews with a representative sample of people—all told, nearly 20,000 people—and then projected their findings to the entire U.S. population. After asking hundreds of questions that probed for symptoms—"Has there ever been a period of two weeks or more when you felt like you wanted to die?"—the researchers estimated both the current and the lifetime prevalence of various disorders.

How many people suffer, or have suffered, a psychological disorder? More than most of us suppose. Reporting on the NIMH study, Lee Robins and Darrel Regier (1991, p. 329) noted that "one or more of the psychiatric disorders . . . had been experienced at some time in their lives by 32 percent of American adults, and 20 percent had an active disorder." These surprisingly high rates reflect the inclusion of institutionalized as well as community samples, and they surely also reflect how well many people manage to hide disorders such as a phobia, alcohol abuse, or depression. Table 12.3 shows the relative prevalence of most of the disorders we have considered among three ethnic groups and among men and women.

The incidence of serious psychological disorders is doubly high among those below the poverty line (Centers for Disease Control, 1992). Like so many other correlations, the poverty-disorder association raises the chicken-and-egg question: Does poverty cause disorders? Or do disorders cause poverty? It's both, though the answer varies with the disorder. Schizophrenia understandably leads to poverty. Yet the stresses and demoralization of poverty can also precipitate disorders, especially depression in women and substance abuse in men (Dohrenwend & others, 1992).

The poverty-disorder association raises the chicken-and-egg question: Does poverty cause disorders? Or do disorders cause poverty?

Those who experience a psychological disorder usually do so by early adulthood. "Over 75 percent of our sample with any disorder had experienced its first symptoms by age 24," reported Robins and Regier (1991, p. 331). The symptoms of antisocial personality and of phobia appear earliest, by a median age of 8 and 10, respectively. Symptoms of alcohol abuse, obsessive-compulsive disorder, bipolar disorder, and schizophrenia appear at a median age near 20. Major depression often hits somewhat later, at a median age of 25. Such findings make clear the need for research and treatment to help the growing number of people, especially teenagers and young adults, who suffer the bewilderment and pain of a psychological disorder.

Although mindful of the pain, we can also be encouraged by the many successful people—including Leonardo da Vinci, Isaac Newton, and Leo Tolstoy—who pursued brilliant careers while enduring psychological difficulties. The bewilderment, fear, and sorrow caused by psychological disorders are real. But, as the next chapter shows, hope is also real.

REHEARSE IT!

22. On the basis of an NIMH report, researchers note that 32 percent of American adults have experienced a psychiatric disorder at some time in their lives. Despite differences in the prevalence of disorders among ethnic groups and between men and women, all groups are vulnerable. One factor that crosses ethnic and gender lines and is closely correlated with serious psychological disorder is

a. age.
b. education.
c. poverty.
d. religious faith.

REVIEWING ■ *Psychological Disorders*

Perspectives on Psychological Disorders

1. ***What criteria are used to judge a person's behavior as disordered?***

   Between normality and abnormality lies not a gulf but a fine and somewhat arbitrary line. Where we draw the line between normality and **psychological disorder** depends on how atypical, disturbing, maladaptive, and unjustifiable a person's behavior is.

2. ***What is the medical model of psychological disorders, and why do critics question it?***

   The **medical model's** assumption that psychological disorders are mental "illnesses" has displaced earlier views that demons and evil spirits were to blame. However, critics question the medical model's labeling of psychological disorders as sicknesses. They argue that the disorders are socially defined and that some disorders are found only in certain cultures. Most mental health workers today believe that disorders are influenced by genetic predisposition, physiological states, psychological dynamics, and social circumstances (the **bio-psycho-social perspective**).

3. ***Why are psychological disorders classified, and what system is used?***

   Many psychiatrists and psychologists believe that a system for naming and describing psychological disorders facilitates treatment and research. The current edition of the *Diagnostic and Statistical Manual of Mental Disorders* (**DSM-IV**) provides an authoritative classification scheme. When DSM-IV refers to **neurotic disorders**, it does so as a contrast to the more severe **psychotic disorders**.

4. ***Why do clinicians assign diagnostic labels to patients? Why do some psychologists criticize such labeling?***

   Diagnostic labels facilitate mental health professionals' communications and research. Critics point out that for these benefits we pay the price of stigmatizing people and creating self-fulfilling prophecies. Labels also create preconceptions that bias our perceptions of people's past and present behavior and unfairly stigmatize them.

Anxiety Disorders

5. ***What behaviors characterize anxiety disorders?***

   Those who suffer an **anxiety disorder** may for no apparent reason feel uncontrollably tense and uneasy (**generalized anxiety disorder**). They may be irrationally afraid of a specific object or situation (**phobia**) or troubled by repetitive thoughts and actions (**obsessive-compulsive disorder**). Some people also experience episodes of intense dread, known as **panic disorder**.

6. ***How do psychologists explain anxiety disorders?***

   Freud's psychoanalytic perspective views anxiety disorders as the discharging of repressed impulses. The learning perspective sees them as a product of fear conditioning and observational learning. The biological perspective considers possible evolutionary, genetic, and physiological influences.

Dissociative Disorders

7. ***What are dissociative disorders, and why are they controversial?***

   Under stress, a person's conscious awareness may become dissociated (separated) from previous memories, thoughts, and feelings. **Dissociative disorders** manifest themselves in different ways. **Dissociative amnesia** involves selective forgetting in response to stress. **Dissociative fugue** involves not only forgetting one's identity but also fleeing one's home. Most mysterious of all dissociative disorders are cases of **dissociative identity** (*multiple personality*). The afflicted person is said to have two or more distinct personalities, with the original typically unaware of the other(s). Skeptics question whether this disorder may be a cultural phenomenon, finding it suspicious that the disorder has just recently become popular and is virtually nonexistent outside North America.

Mood Disorders

8. ***What behaviors characterize mood disorders?***

   Mood disorders come in two principal forms. In **major depressive disorder**, the person—without apparent reason—descends for weeks or months into deep unhappiness, lethargy, and feelings of worthlessness before rebounding to normality. In the less common **bipolar disorder**, the person alternates between the hopelessness and lethargy of depression and the hyperactive, wildly optimistic, impulsive phase of **mania**.

9. ***What causes mood disorders?***

   Current research on depression is vigorously exploring two sets of influences. The first focuses on genetic predispositions and neurotransmitter abnormalities. The second views the cycle of depression from a social-cognitive perspective, in the light of a vicious cycle of self-defeating beliefs, learned helplessness, negative attributions, and stressful experiences.

Schizophrenia

10. ***What behaviors characterize schizophrenia?***

    Schizophrenia shows itself in disorganized thinking (nonsensical talk and **delusions**, which may stem from a breakdown of selective attention); disturbed perceptions (including *hallucinations*); and inappropriate emotions and actions. It is rarely a one-time episode. Schizophrenia is a set of disorders that emerge either gradually from a chronic history of social inadequacy (in which case the outlook is dim) or suddenly in reaction to stress (in which case the prospects for recovery are brighter).

11. ***What causes schizophrenia?***

    As they have for depression, researchers have identified brain abnormalities (such as excess dopamine receptors) that seem linked with certain forms of schizophrenia. Prenatal viral infections are one possible cause. Twin and adoption studies also point to a genetic predisposition that, in conjunction with environmental factors, may bring about schizophrenia.

Personality Disorders

12. ***What characteristics are typical of personality disorders?***

    Personality disorders are enduring, maladaptive personality traits. For society, the most troubling of these is the remorseless and fearless **antisocial personality**.

Rates of Psychological Disorders

13. ***How common are the psychological disorders we have discussed?***

    A 1980s National Institute of Mental Health survey of nearly 20,000 institutionalized and community residents revealed that 1 in 3 American adults has at some time experienced a psychological disorder, and that 1 in 5 does so currently. The three most common disorders are phobias, mood disorders (with women outnumbering men 2 to 1), and alcohol abuse or dependence (with men outnumbering women 5 to 1).

CRITICAL THINKING EXERCISE by Richard O. Straub

Now that you have read and reviewed Chapter 12, take your learning a step further by testing your critical thinking skills on the following perspective-taking exercise.

Since her divorce three months ago, 65-year-old Fiona has constantly felt tired, has had difficulty sleeping and eating, and has lost all interest in her family, friends, and usual activities. Once proud of her accomplishments and optimistic about her future, Fiona now believes that everything she has ever done, or will do, is worthless. Although her husband was far from a perfect partner, Fiona is convinced that the divorce really was her fault. Her once-close friends, weary of Fiona's self-absorbed and hopeless attitude, have stopped calling her. The family physician referred Fiona to a psychiatrist, who prescribed an antidepressant. The drug seemed to help somewhat, but Fiona, worried that she would become addicted, stopped taking it regularly. Fiona's son-in-law is concerned about her dejected attitude. Her daughter, however, insists that there is no cause for alarm. She says that her mother is simply growing old—that the listlessness is reminiscent of her maternal grandmother's behavior at the same age.

1. Should Fiona's daughter be more concerned about her mother's behavior, or is she correct in attributing it to aging? Explain your reasoning.
2. How might Fiona's behavior be classified by a clinical psychologist?
3. How might Fiona's behavior be explained according to (a) the biological and (b) the social-cognitive perspective?
4. Which diagnostic perspective most closely represents your own belief about Fiona's condition? Why?

Check your progress on becoming a critical thinker by comparing your answers to the sample answers found in Appendix B.

REHEARSE IT ANSWER KEY

1. c., **2.** a., **3.** c., **4.** c., **5.** c., **6.** d., **7.** a., **8.** c., **9.** a., **10.** d., **11.** c.,

12. b., **13.** b., **14.** c., **15.** a., **16.** d., **17.** d., **18.** d., **19.** b., **20.** a.,

21. c., **22.** c.

FOR FURTHER INFORMATION

You can find further information in this text regarding psychological disorders on the following pages:

CHAPTER 13

Therapy

The history of treating psychological disorders reveals how mystifying and intractable these problems are. We have treated psychological disorders with a bewildering variety of methods, harsh and gentle: by cutting holes in the head and by giving warm baths and massages; by restraining, bleeding, or "beating the devil" out of people; by placing them in sunny, serene environments; by administering drugs and electric shocks; and by talking—talking about childhood experiences, about current feelings, about maladaptive thoughts and behaviors.

The transition from brutal to gentler treatments occurred thanks to the efforts of reformers such as Philippe Pinel in France and Dorothea Dix in the United States, Canada, and Scotland. Both advocated the construction of mental hospitals offering more humane methods of treatment. As we shall see, the introduction of therapeutic drugs and community-based treatment programs has, however, largely emptied mental health hospitals since the mid-1950s.

Today's favored treatment depends on the therapist's viewpoint. Those who believe that psychological disorders are learned will tend to favor psychological therapies. Those who view disorders as biologically rooted are likely to advocate medication as well. Those who believe that disorders are responses to social conditions will, in addition, want to reform the "sick" environment.

We can classify therapies into two main categories: The *psychological therapies* involve structured interaction (usually verbal) between a trained professional and a client with a problem. The *biomedical therapies* directly affect the nervous system.

The Psychological Therapies

Psychological therapy, or **psychotherapy**, is "a planned, emotionally charged, confiding interaction between a trained, socially sanctioned healer and a sufferer" (Frank, 1982). From among the 250 or more types of psychotherapy (Parloff, 1987), we will consider the most influential. These derive from psychology's major personality theories: psychoanalytic, humanistic, behavioral, and cognitive. We will also consider the use of these techniques in group therapies.

Each technique is distinctive, but there are common threads. Therapists who view disorders as an interplay of bio-psycho-social influences may welcome a

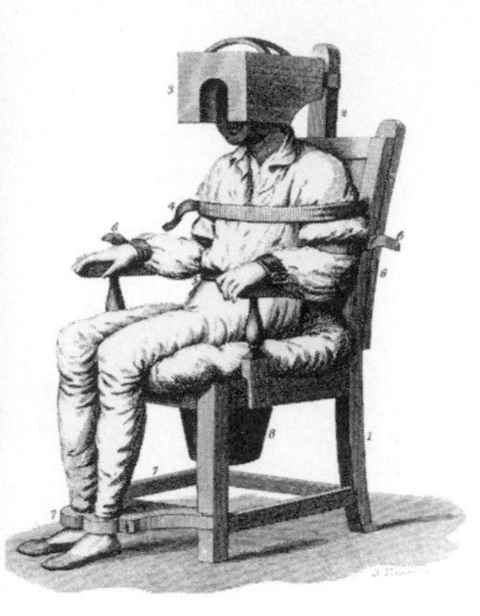

The history of treatment William Hogarth's (1697–1764) engraving (left) of St. Mary of Bethlehem hospital in London (commonly called Bedlam) depicts the treatment of mental disorders in the eighteenth century. Visitors paid to gawk at the patients as if they were viewing zoo animals. The chair (right) was designed by Benjamin Rush (1746–1813) "for the benefit of maniacal patients." Rush, a founder of the movement for more humane treatment of the mentally ill, believed that they required restraint to regain their sensibilities.

Dorothea Dix (1802–1887) "I . . . call your attention to the state of the Insane Persons confined within this Commonwealth, in cages."

combination of treatments. Indeed, half of psychotherapists describe themselves as taking an **eclectic approach** (a so-called *psychotherapy integration)*—as using a blend of therapies (Beitman & others, 1989; Castonguay & Goldfried, 1994). Depending on the client and the problem, an eclectic therapist will use a variety of techniques.

Psychoanalysis

1. *What are the aims and methods of psychoanalysis?*

Although most of today's therapists do not practice therapy as Sigmund Freud did, his psychoanalytic techniques survive. **Psychoanalysis** is part of our modern vocabulary, and its assumptions influence many other therapies.

Aims

As we noted when considering Freud's theory in Chapters 11 and 12, psychoanalysis assumes that many psychological problems are fueled by childhood's residue of supposedly repressed impulses and conflicts. Psychoanalysts try to bring these repressed feelings into conscious awareness, where the patient can deal with them. By gaining insight into the origins of the disorder—by fulfilling the ancient imperative to "know thyself" in a deep way—the patient "works through" the buried feelings. The theory presumes that healthier, less anxious living becomes possible when patients release the energy they had previously devoted to id-ego-superego conflicts.

Classical psychoanalysis The placement of the analyst's chair out of view is thought to minimize distraction and make it easy for the patient—relaxed on a couch—to verbalize whatever comes to mind.

Methods

Psychoanalysis is historical reconstruction. Its goal is to unearth the past in hope of unmasking the present. But how?

When Freud discarded hypnosis as unreliable, he turned to *free association*. Imagine yourself as a patient using the free association technique. The analyst invites you to relax, perhaps by lying on a couch. He or she will probably sit out of your line of vision, helping you focus attention on your internal thoughts and feelings. Beginning with a childhood memory, a dream, or a recent experience, you say aloud whatever comes to your mind from moment to moment. It sounds easy, but soon you notice how often you edit your thoughts as you speak, omitting material that seems trivial, irrelevant, or shameful. Even in the

psychotherapy an emotionally charged, confiding interaction between a trained therapist and someone who suffers from psychological difficulties.

eclectic approach an approach to psychotherapy that, depending on the client's problems, uses or integrates techniques from various forms of therapy. (Also called *psychotherapy integration.*)

psychoanalysis Sigmund Freud's therapeutic technique. Freud believed the patient's free associations, resistances, dreams, and transferences—and the therapist's interpretations of them—released previously repressed feelings, allowing the patient to gain self-insight.

resistance in psychoanalysis, the blocking from consciousness of anxiety-laden material.

interpretation in psychoanalysis, the analyst's noting supposed dream meanings, resistances, and other significant behaviors in order to promote insight.

transference in psychoanalysis, the patient's transfer to the analyst of emotions linked with other relationships (such as love or hatred for a parent).

safe presence of the analyst, you may pause momentarily before uttering an embarrassing thought. You may make a joking remark or change the subject to something less threatening. Sometimes your mind may go blank or you may find yourself unable to remember important details.

To the psychoanalyst, these blocks in the flow of your free associations indicate **resistance**. They hint that anxiety lurks and that you are repressing sensitive material. The analyst will want to explore these sensitive areas by making you aware of your resistances and by interpreting their underlying meaning. The analyst's **interpretations**—suggestions of underlying wishes, feelings, and conflicts—aim to provide people with *insight*. If offered at the right moment, the analyst's interpretation—of, say, your not wanting to talk about your mother—may illuminate what you are avoiding. You may then discover what your resistances mean and how they fit with other pieces of your psychological puzzle.

Freud believed that another clue to repressed impulses is your dreams' *latent content* (page 182). Thus, after inviting you to report a dream, the analyst may offer a dream analysis, suggesting its hidden meaning.

During many such sessions you will probably disclose more of yourself to your analyst than you have ever revealed to anyone. Because psychoanalytic theory emphasizes the formative power of childhood experiences, much of what you reveal will pertain to your earliest memories. You will also probably find yourself experiencing strong positive or negative feelings for your analyst. Such feelings may express the dependency or mingled love and anger that you earlier experienced toward family members or other important people in your life. When this happens, Freud would say you are actually *transferring* your strongest feelings from those other relationships to the analyst. Analysts and other therapists believe that this **transference** exposes long-repressed feelings, giving you a belated chance to work through them with your analyst's help. By examining your feelings toward the analyst, you may also gain insight into your current relationships.

Much of psychoanalysis is built on the assumption that repressed memories exist.

Woody Allen, after awakening from suspended animation in Sleeper: *"I haven't seen my analyst in 200 years. He was a strict Freudian. If I'd been going all this time, I'd probably almost be cured by now."*

Note how much of psychoanalysis is built on the assumption that repressed memories exist. That assumption, as we noted in Chapter 7, is now questioned. This challenge to an assumption that is basic to so much of professional and popular psychology is provoking intense debate.

Critics also say that psychoanalysts' interpretations are hard to refute. If, in response to the analyst's suggested interpretation, you say, "Yes! I see now," your acceptance confirms the analyst's interpretation. If you emphatically say, "No! That doesn't ring true," your denial may be taken to reveal more resistance, which would also confirm the interpretation. Psychoanalysts acknowledge that it's hard to prove or disprove their interpretations. But they insist that interpretations often are a great help to patients.

Traditional psychoanalysis is slow and expensive. It requires up to several years of several sessions a week with a highly trained and well-paid analyst. (Three times a week for just two years at $100 or more per hour comes to about $30,000.) Only those with a high income can afford such treatment.

Although there are relatively few traditional psychoanalysts, psychoanalytic assumptions influence many therapists, especially those who make *psychodynamic* assumptions. Psychodynamic therapists try to understand patients' current symptoms by exploring their childhood experiences. They probe for supposed repressed, emotion-laden information. They seek to help people gain insight into the unconscious roots of problems and work through newly resurrected feelings. Although influenced by Freud's psychoanalysis, these therapists may talk to people face to face (rather than out of the line of vision), once a week (rather than several times weekly), and for only a few weeks or months (rather than several years).

Face-to-face therapy In this type of therapy session the couch has disappeared. But the influence of psychoanalytic theory probably has not, especially if the therapist probes for the origin of the patient's symptoms by seeking information from the patient's childhood.

No brief therapy excerpt can exemplify the lengthy process of probing the past. But we can illustrate psychodynamic therapists' goal of enabling insight via their interpretations. In the following interaction, therapist David Malan responds to all that he has heard from a depressed patient by suggesting insights into her problems. Note how Malan interprets the woman's earlier remarks and suggests that her relationship with him reveals a characteristic pattern of behavior (1978, pp. 133–134).

> **Malan:** *I get the feeling that you're the sort of person who needs to keep active. If you don't keep active, then something goes wrong. Is that true?*
>
> **Patient:** *Yes.*
>
> **Malan:** *I get a second feeling about you and that is that you must, underneath all this, have an awful lot of very strong and upsetting feelings. Somehow they're there but you aren't really quite in touch with them. Isn't this right? I feel you've been like that as long as you can remember.*
>
> **Patient:** *For quite a few years, whenever I really sat down and thought about it I got depressed, so I tried not to think about it.*
>
> **Malan:** *You see, you've established a pattern, haven't you? You're even like that here with me, because in spite of the fact that you're in some trouble and you feel that the bottom is falling out of your world, the way you're telling me this is just as if there wasn't anything wrong.*

Humanistic Therapies

2. *What are the basic themes of humanistic therapy, such as Rogers' person-centered approach?*

As we noted in Chapter 11, the humanistic perspective emphasizes people's inherent potential for self-fulfillment. Not surprisingly, then, humanistic therapists aim to boost self-fulfillment by helping people grow in self-awareness and self-acceptance. Unlike psychoanalytic therapists, humanistic therapists tend to focus on

- the *present* and *future* instead of the past. They explore feelings as they occur, rather than achieving insights into the childhood origins of the feelings.
- *conscious* rather than unconscious thoughts.
- taking immediate *responsibility* for one's feelings and actions rather than uncovering hidden determinants.
- promoting *growth* and fulfillment instead of curing illness. Thus, those in therapy are "clients" rather than "patients."

The most widely used humanistic technique is Carl Rogers' (1961, 1980) **person-centered therapy**. A person-centered therapist focuses on the client's conscious self-perceptions rather than on the therapist's own interpretations. The therapist listens, without judgment or interpretation, and refrains from directing the client toward certain insights. This strategy has earned person-centered therapy the label *nondirective* therapy.

Believing that most people already possess the resources for growth, Rogers encouraged therapists to exhibit *genuineness*, *acceptance*, and *empathy*. When therapists drop their facades and genuinely express their true feelings, when they enable their clients to feel unconditionally accepted, and when they empathically sense and reflect their clients' feelings, the clients may increase in self-understanding and self-acceptance. As Rogers (1980, p. 10) explained,

"We're encouraging people to become involved in their own rescue."

Active listening The late Carl Rogers (right) empathizes with a client during a group therapy session.

Hearing has consequences. When I truly hear a person and the meanings that are important to him at that moment, hearing not simply his words, but him, and when I let him know that I have heard his own private personal meanings, many things happen. There is first of all a grateful look. He feels released. He wants to tell me more about his world. He surges forth in a new sense of freedom. He becomes more open to the process of change.

I have often noticed that the more deeply I hear the meanings of the person, the more there is that happens. Almost always, when a person realizes he has been deeply heard, his eyes moisten. I think in some real sense he is weeping for joy. It is as though he were saying, "Thank God, somebody heard me. Someone knows what it's like to be me."

"We have two ears and one mouth that we may listen the more and talk the less."

Zeno (335–263 B.C.)
Diogenes Laertius

"Hearing" refers to Rogers' technique of **active listening**—echoing, restating, and seeking clarification of what the person expresses (verbally or nonverbally) and acknowledging the expressed feelings. Active listening is now an accepted part of therapeutic counseling practices in many schools, colleges, and clinics. The counselor listens attentively and interrupts only to restate and confirm the client's feelings, to accept what the client is expressing, or to seek clarification. In counseling a male client, Rogers illustrates active listening:

Client: *I just ain't no good to nobody, never was, and never will be.*

Rogers: *Feeling that now, hm? That you're just no good to yourself, no good to anybody. Never will be any good to anybody. Just that you're completely worthless, huh?—Those really are lousy feelings. Just feel that you're no good at all, hm?*

Client: *Yeah. (Muttering in low, discouraged voice) That's what this guy I went to town with just the other day told me.*

Rogers: *This guy that you went to town with really told you that you were no good? Is that what you're saying? Did I get that right?*

Client: *M-hm.*

Rogers: *I guess the meaning of that if I get it right is that here's somebody that—meant something to you and what does he think of you? Why, he's told you that he thinks you're no good at all. And that just really knocks the props out from under you. (Client weeps quietly.) It just brings the tears. (Silence of 20 seconds)*

Client: *(Rather defiantly) I don't care though.*

Rogers: *You tell yourself you don't care at all, but somehow I guess some part of you cares because some part of you weeps over it. (Meador & Rogers, 1984, p. 167)*

person-centered therapy a humanistic therapy, developed by Carl Rogers, in which the therapist uses techniques such as active listening within a genuine, accepting, empathic environment to facilitate clients' growth.

active listening empathic listening in which the listener echoes, restates, and clarifies. A feature of Rogers' person-centered therapy.

As this brief excerpt illustrates, the person-centered counselor seeks to provide a psychological mirror that helps clients see themselves more clearly. But can a therapist be a perfect mirror, without selecting and interpreting what is reflected? Rogers conceded that one cannot be *totally* nondirective. Nevertheless,

"You say, 'Off with her head,' but what I'm hearing is, 'I feel neglected.'"

he believed that the therapist's most important contribution is to accept and understand the client. Given a nonjudgmental, grace-filled environment that provides *unconditional positive regard*, people internalize unconditional positive self-regard; they may accept even their worst traits and feel valued and whole.

If you want to listen more actively in your own relationships, three hints may help:

1. *Paraphrase*—Check your understanding by summarizing the speaker's words in your own words.
2. *Invite clarification*—"What might be an example of that?" may encourage the speaker to say more.
3. *Reflect feelings*—"That must be frustrating" might mirror what you're sensing from the speaker's body language and intensity.

REHEARSE IT!

1. All of the psychological therapies involve verbal interactions between a trained professional and a client with a problem. A therapist who encourages clients to relate their dreams and searches for the unconscious roots of their problems is drawing from

- **a.** psychoanalysis.
- **b.** humanistic therapies.
- **c.** person-centered therapy.
- **d.** nondirective therapy.

2. According to psychoanalytic theory, a patient's emotional relationship with the therapist mirrors other important relationships in the patient's life—for example, an early relationship with a parent. In psychoanalysis, the development of strong feelings for the therapist is an important part of the therapeutic process and is called

- **a.** transference.
- **b.** resistance.
- **c.** interpretation.
- **d.** empathy.

3. Humanistic therapists focus on present experience—on becoming aware of feelings as they arise and taking responsibility for them. Compared with psychoanalytic therapists, humanistic therapists are more likely to emphasize

- **a.** hidden or repressed feelings.
- **b.** childhood experiences.
- **c.** psychological disorders.
- **d.** self-fulfillment and growth.

4. Especially important to Carl Rogers' person-centered therapy is the technique of active listening. The therapist who practices active listening

- **a.** engages in free association.
- **b.** exposes the patient's resistances.
- **c.** restates and clarifies the client's statements.
- **d.** directly challenges the client's self-perceptions.

Behavior Therapies

3. *What are the assumptions and techniques of the behavior therapies?*

All the therapies we have considered so far assume that, for nonpsychotic people at least, psychological problems diminish as self-awareness grows. The psychoanalyst expects problems to subside as people gain insight into their unresolved and unconscious tensions. So does the humanistic therapist, as people "get in touch with their feelings." Behavior therapists, however, doubt that self-awareness is the key. They assume that the problem behaviors *are* the problems. You can, for example, become aware of why you are highly anxious during exams and still be anxious. Instead of trying to alleviate distressing behaviors by resolving a presumed underlying problem, **behavior therapy** applies well-established learning principles to eliminate the unwanted behavior. To treat phobias or sexual disorders, behavior therapists do not delve deep below the surface looking for inner causes. Rather, they try to replace problem thoughts and maladaptive behaviors with more constructive ways of thinking and acting.

Behavior therapists doubt that self-awareness is the key. They assume that the problem behaviors are *the problems.*

behavior therapy therapy that applies learning principles to the elimination of unwanted behaviors.

counterconditioning a behavior therapy procedure that conditions new responses to stimuli that trigger unwanted behaviors; based on classical conditioning. Includes *systematic desensitization* and *aversive conditioning.*

systematic desensitization a type of counterconditioning that associates a pleasant relaxed state with gradually increasing anxiety-triggering stimuli. Commonly used to treat phobias.

Classical Conditioning Techniques

One cluster of behavior therapies derives from principles developed in Pavlov's conditioning experiments (pages 207–211). As Pavlov and others showed, we learn various behaviors and emotions through classical conditioning. So, are maladaptive symptoms conditioned responses? If, say, a claustrophobic fear of elevators is a learned response to the stimulus of being in an enclosed space, then might one unlearn the fear by counterconditioning the fear response? **Counterconditioning** pairs the trigger stimulus with a new response that is incompatible with fear. For example, if we repeatedly pair the enclosed space of the elevator with a relaxed response, the fear response may be displaced.

One classical conditioning therapy was developed by learning theorist O. H. Mowrer for chronic bed-wetters. The child sleeps on a liquid-sensitive pad connected to an alarm. Moisture on the pad triggers the alarm, awakening the child. With repetition, this association of urinary relaxation with awakening stops the bed-wetting. In three out of four cases the treatment is effective and the success provides a boost to the child's self-image (Christophersen & Edwards, 1992; Houts & others, 1994).

Consider this: What might a psychoanalyst say about this therapy for bed-wetting? How might a behavior therapist reply?

Two specific counterconditioning techniques are *systematic desensitization* and *aversive conditioning*.

Systematic Desensitization

Picture this scene reported in 1924 by Mary Cover Jones, an associate of the behaviorist John B. Watson: Three-year-old Peter is petrified of rabbits and other furry objects. (Unlike Little Albert's laboratory-conditioned fear of white rats, described in Chapter 6, Peter's fear arose during the course of his life at home and is more intense.) Jones aims to replace Peter's fear of rabbits with a conditioned response that is incompatible with fear. Her strategy is to associate the fear-evoking rabbit with the pleasurable, relaxed response associated with eating.

As the hungry child begins eating his midafternoon snack, Jones introduces a caged rabbit on the other side of the huge room. Peter hardly notices as he eagerly munches his crackers and drinks his milk. On succeeding days, she gradually moves the rabbit closer and closer. Within two months, Peter tolerates the rabbit in his lap and strokes it while he eats. Moreover, his fear of other furry objects subsides as well, having been "countered," or replaced, by a relaxed state that cannot coexist with fear (Fisher, 1984; Jones, 1924).

THE FAR SIDE

Professor Gallagher and his controversial technique of simultaneously confronting the fear of heights, snakes, and the dark.

Unfortunately for those who might have been helped by her counterconditioning procedures, Jones' story of Peter and the rabbit did not immediately become part of psychology's lore. It was not until more than 30 years later that psychiatrist Joseph Wolpe (1958, 1982) refined her technique into what has become the most widely used method of behavior therapy: **systematic desensitization**. Wolpe assumed, as did Jones, that you cannot simultaneously be anxious and relaxed. Therefore, if you can repeatedly relax when facing anxiety-provoking stimuli, you can gradually eliminate your anxiety. The trick is to proceed gradually.

Let's see how this might work with a common phobia. Imagine yourself afraid of public speaking. A behavior therapist might first ask your help in constructing a hierarchy of anxiety-triggering speaking situations. Your anxiety hierarchy could range from mildly anxiety-provoking situations, such as speaking up in a small group of friends, to panic-provoking situations, such as having to address a large audience.

The therapist would then train you to relax. Using *progressive relaxation*, you learn to relax one muscle group after another, until you achieve a drowsy state of complete relaxation and comfort. Then the therapist asks you to imagine, with

aversive conditioning a type of counterconditioning that associates an unpleasant state (such as nausea) with an unwanted behavior (such as drinking alcohol).

your eyes closed, a mildly anxiety-arousing situation: You are having coffee with a group of friends and are deciding whether to speak up. If imagining the scene causes you to feel any anxiety, you signal your tension by raising your finger, and the therapist instructs you to switch off the mental image and go back to deep relaxation.

This imagined scene is repeatedly paired with relaxation until you can feel no trace of anxiety while imagining it. The therapist progresses up your anxiety hierarchy, using the relaxed state to desensitize you to each imagined situation. After several therapy sessions, you practice the imagined behaviors in actual situations, beginning with relatively easy tasks and gradually moving to more anxiety-filled ones (Figure 13.1). Conquering your anxiety in an actual situation, not just in your imagination, raises your self-confidence (Foa & Kozak, 1986; Williams, 1987). Eventually, you may even become a confident public speaker.

More aggressive than systematic desensitization is "flooding," an extinction procedure that forces a person to confront feared stimuli. When dogs are forced to face situations in which they have previously received shocks, it floods them with fear, which then begins to extinguish. People, too, when guided to experience or vividly imagine feared situations often come to realize that no real danger exists.

Therapists sometimes combine systematic desensitization with other techniques. For clients with phobias, they may have someone model appropriate behavior in a fear-arousing situation. If you were afraid of snakes, you would first observe someone handling a snake. Then you would be coaxed in gradual steps to approach, touch, and handle it yourself (Bandura & others, 1969). By applying this principle of observational learning, therapists have helped people overcome disruptive fears of snakes, spiders, and dogs.

Notice that the systematic desensitization and modeling procedures make no attempt to help you achieve insight into your fear's underlying cause. If you are afraid of heights, the therapist will not spend much time probing when you first experienced this fear or what may have caused it. Nor do behavior therapists worry that eliminating your fear of heights will leave an

Figure 13.1 **Systematic desensitization of a phobia** Beverly, who is terribly afraid of spiders, is gradually able to relax—as shown by her decreasing pulse rate—first at the image of a spider (frames 1–2), then in the presence of a toy spider (frame 3), a dead spider (frames 4–5), and a live one (frames 6–8). (Adapted from Gilling & Brightwell, 1982)

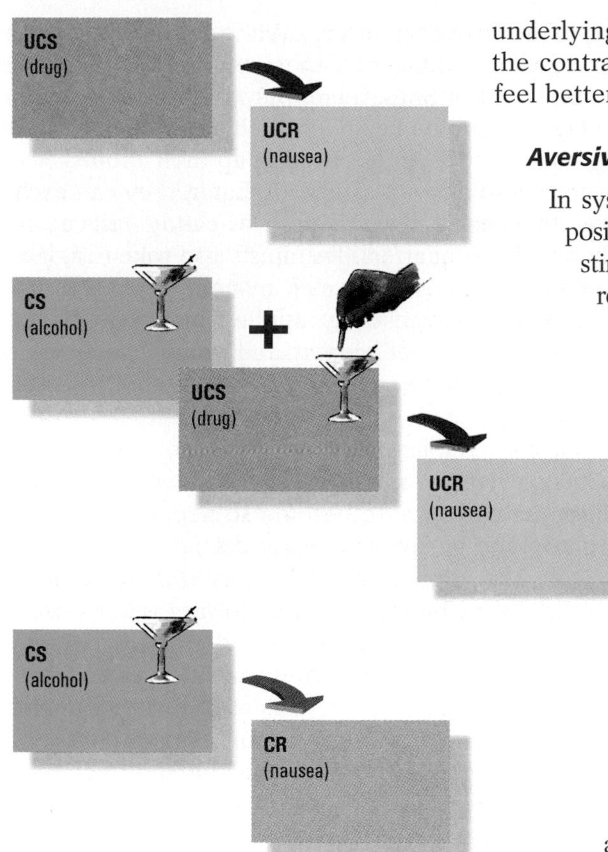

Figure 13.2 **Aversion therapy for alcoholics** After repeatedly drinking an alcoholic beverage mixed with a drug that produces severe nausea, some patients develop at least a temporary conditioned aversion to alcohol.

underlying problem that may now be expressed as, say, a fear of elevators. On the contrary, they find that overcoming maladaptive behaviors helps people feel better about themselves.

Aversive Conditioning

In systematically desensitizing a patient, the therapist seeks to substitute a positive (relaxed) response for a negative (fearful) response to a harmless stimulus. In **aversive conditioning**, the therapist tries to replace a positive response to a harmful stimulus (such as alcohol) with a negative response. Thus, aversive conditioning is the reverse of systematic desensitization.

The procedure is simple: It associates unpleasant feelings with the unwanted behavior. To treat nail biting, one can paint the fingernails with a yucky-tasting clear nail polish (Baskind, 1997). In treating an alcoholic, aversion therapists offer appealing drinks laced with a drug that produces severe nausea. By linking the drinking of alcohol with violent nausea, the therapist seeks to transform the alcoholic's reaction to alcohol from positive to negative (see Figure 13.2, and recall the taste-aversion experiments with rats and coyotes in Chapter 6). Similarly, by giving child molesters electric shocks as they view photos of nude children, aversion therapists aim to eliminate the molesters' sexual response to children. Similarly, by giving withdrawn and self-abusing autistic children harmless "aversives," such as a spray of cold water in the face, therapists hope to suppress self-injury while reinforcing more appropriate behavior. Because this therapy involves an unpleasant experience, it is practiced sparingly, with the appropriate consent. Arthur Wiens and Carol Menustik (1983) studied 685 alcoholic patients who completed an aversion therapy program at a Portland, Oregon, hospital. One year later, after returning for several booster treatments of alcohol-sickness pairings, 63 percent were still successfully abstaining. But after three years, only 33 percent had remained abstinent.

Does aversive conditioning work? In the short run it may. But, as we saw in Chapter 6, the problem is that cognition influences conditioning. People know that outside the therapist's office they can drink without fear of nausea or engage in sexually deviant behavior without fear of shock. The person's ability to discriminate between the aversive conditioning situation and all other situations can limit the treatment's effectiveness.

Operant Conditioning

Voluntary behaviors are strongly influenced by their consequences. This simple fact enables behavior therapists to reinforce desired behaviors and to withhold reinforcement for, or to punish, undesired behaviors.

As we saw in Chapter 6, voluntary behaviors are strongly influenced by their consequences. This simple fact enables behavior therapists to reinforce desired behaviors and to withhold reinforcement for, or to punish, undesired behaviors. Using operant conditioning to solve specific behavior problems has raised hopes for some cases thought to be hopeless. Retarded children have been taught to care for themselves. Socially withdrawn autistic children have learned to interact. People with schizophrenia have been helped to behave more rationally in their hospital ward.

In extreme cases, the treatment must be intensive. For 19 withdrawn, uncommunicative, 3-year-old autistic children in one study, it involved a 2-year, 40-hour-a-week shaping program by their parents (Lovaas, 1987). The combination of positive reinforcement of desired behaviors and the ignoring or punishing of aggressive and self-abusive behaviors worked wonders. By first grade, 9 of the 19 children were functioning successfully in school and exhibiting normal intelligence. Only 1 of 40 comparable children who did not undergo this treatment showed similar improvement.

Token reinforcement Operant conditioning has proved to be a powerful tool in teaching people with severe mental disabilities. At the Brooklyn Development Center (New York), clients receive tokens for learning, maintaining, or improving a skill. They can then take the tokens to the center's "store," where volunteers "sell" them different items.

The rewards used to modify behavior vary. With some people, the reinforcing power of attention or praise is sufficient. Others require more concrete rewards, such as food. In institutional settings, therapists may create a **token economy**. When patients display appropriate behavior, such as getting out of bed, washing, dressing, eating, talking coherently, cleaning up their rooms, or playing cooperatively, they receive a token or plastic coin. Later, they can exchange their accumulated tokens for various rewards, such as candy, television watching, trips to town, or better living quarters. Therapists use tokens as positive reinforcers to shape behavior in the step-by-step manner described on page 217. Token economies have been successfully applied in various settings (classrooms, hospitals, homes for the delinquent) and among members of various populations (disturbed children, those with mental disabilities, schizophrenia patients).

Critics of such *behavior modification* express two concerns. One concern is practical: What happens when the reinforcers stop, as when the person leaves the institution? Might the person have become so dependent on the extrinsic rewards that the appropriate behaviors quickly disappear? If so, how can behavior therapists make the appropriate behaviors durable? First, they may wean patients from the tokens by shifting them toward other rewards, such as social approval, that are more typical of life outside the institution. They may also train patients to behave in ways that are intrinsically rewarding. For example, as a withdrawn person becomes more socially competent, the intrinsic satisfactions of social interaction may help the person maintain the behavior.

The second concern is ethical: Is it right for one human to control another's behavior? Those who set up token economies typically deprive people of something they desire and then decide which behaviors they will reinforce. To critics, the whole behavior modification process has an authoritarian taint. Advocates reply that control already exists; rewards and punishments are already maintaining destructive behavior patterns. So why not reinforce adaptive behavior instead? They argue that treatment with positive rewards is more humane than being institutionalized or punished and that the right to effective treatment and to an improved life justifies temporary deprivation.

The depressed person interprets a suggestion as criticism, disagreement as dislike, praise as flattery, friendliness as pity.

Cognitive Therapies

4. What are the goals and techniques of the congitive therapies?

We have seen how behavior therapists treat specific fears and problem behaviors. But how do they deal with major depression or general anxiety? One can reinforce healthier behaviors and train people to avoid "high-risk" situations. Still, when anxiety has no focus, outlining a hierarchy of anxiety-triggering situations is difficult. The cognitive revolution that has so changed psychology during the last four decades has influenced how therapists treat these less clearly defined psychological problems (Figure 13.3).

The **cognitive therapies** assume that our thinking colors our feelings (Figure 13.4). Between the event and our response falls the mind. As we noted in Chapter 12, self-blaming and overgeneralized explanations of bad events are an integral part of the vicious cycle of depression. The depressed person interprets a suggestion as criticism, disagreement as dislike, praise as flattery, friendliness as pity. Ruminating on such thoughts sustains the bad mood. (That explains why distracting oneself, perhaps by getting absorbed in a task, can alleviate a bad mood [Erber & Tesser, 1992; Lyubomirsky & Nolen-Hoeksema, 1994].) If depressing thinking patterns are learned, then surely they can be replaced. Thus, cognitive therapists try in various ways to teach people new, more constructive ways of thinking.

Figure 13.3 **The cognitive revolution** Half of all faculty in accredited clinical psychology Ph.D. programs now align themselves with a cognitive or cognitive-behavioral therapy orientation. (Data from Mayne & others, 1994)

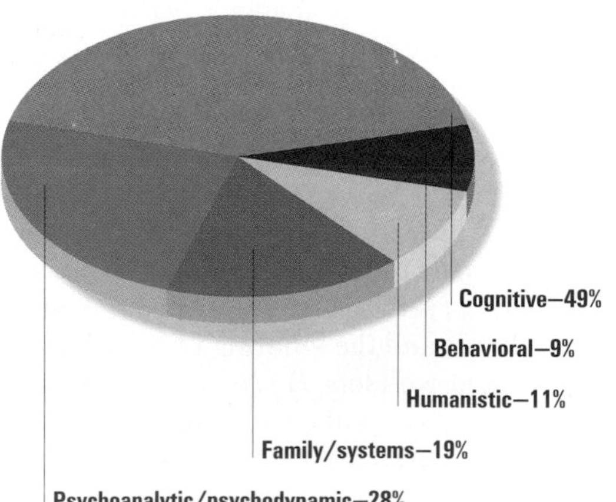

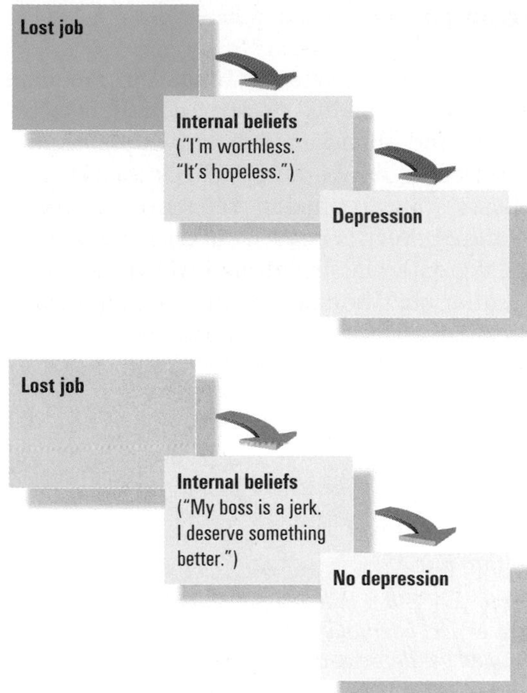

Figure 13.4 **A cognitive perspective on psychological disorders** The person's emotional reactions are produced not directly by the event but by the person's thoughts in response to the event.

Rational-Emotive Therapy

According to Albert Ellis (1962, 1987, 1993), the creator of **rational-emotive therapy** (also called *rational-emotive behavior therapy*), many problems arise from irrational thinking. For example, he describes a disturbed woman and suggests how therapy might challenge her illogical, self-defeating assumptions (1984, p. 198):

> [She] does not merely believe it is *undesirable* if her love partner is rejecting. She tends to believe, also, that (1) it is *awful*; (2) she *cannot stand* it; (3) she *should not*, must not be rejected; (4) she will *never* be accepted by any desirable partner; (5) she is a *worthless person* because one lover has rejected her; and (6) she *deserves to be damned* for being so worthless. Such common covert hypotheses are nonsensical. . . . They can be easily elicited and demolished by any scientist worth his or her salt; and the rational-emotive therapist is exactly that: an exposing and nonsense-annihilating scientist.

Does this sound like the opposite of the warm, caring, reflective acceptance of feelings expressed by Carl Rogers? It very nearly is. Ellis intends to "make mincemeat" of people's illogical ideas—that we must be loved by everyone, that we must be thoroughly competent and successful at everything, that it is a disaster when things do not go as we wish. Change people's thinking by revealing the "absurdity" of their self-defeating ideas, he believes, and you will change their self-defeating feelings and actions. Let's eavesdrop as tart-tongued Ellis exhibits his confrontational style with a 25-year-old female client who suffers feelings of guilt, unworthiness, and depression (1989, p. 219):

> **Ellis:** *The same crap! It's always the same crap. Now if you would look at the crap—instead of "Oh, how stupid I am! He hates me! I think I'll kill myself!"—then you'd get better right away.*
>
> **Client:** *You've been listening! (laughs)*
>
> **Ellis:** *Listening to what?*
>
> **Client:** *(laughs) Those wild statements in my mind, like that, that I make.*
>
> **Ellis:** *That's right! Because I know that you have to make those statements—because I have a good theory. And according to my theory, people couldn't get upset unless they made those nutty statements to themselves. . . . Even if I loved you madly, the next person you talk to is likely to hate you. So I like brown eyes and he likes blue eyes, or something. So you're then dead! Because you really think: "I've got to be accepted! I've got to act intelligently!" Well, why?*
>
> **Client:** *(very soberly and reflectively) True.*
>
> **Ellis:** *You see?*
>
> **Client:** *Yes.*
>
> **Ellis:** *Now, if you will learn that lesson, then you've had a very valuable session. Because you don't have to upset yourself. As I said before: If I thought you were the worst [expletive] who ever existed, well that's my opinion. And I'm entitled to it. But does it make you a turd?*
>
> **Client:** *(reflective silence)*
>
> **Ellis:** *Does it?*
>
> **Client:** *No.*
>
> **Ellis:** *What makes you a turd?*
>
> **Client:** *Thinking that you are.*
>
> **Ellis:** *That's right! Your belief that you are. That's the only thing that could ever do it. And you never have to believe that. See? You control your thinking. I control my thinking—my belief about you. But you don't have to be affected by that. You always control what you think.*

token economy an operant conditioning procedure that rewards desired behavior. A patient exchanges a token of some sort, earned for exhibiting the desired behavior, for various privileges or treats.

cognitive therapy therapy that teaches people new, more adaptive ways of thinking and acting; based on the assumption that thoughts intervene between events and our emotional reactions.

rational-emotive therapy a confrontational cognitive therapy, developed by Albert Ellis, that vigorously challenges people's illogical, self-defeating attitudes and assumptions. Also called *rational-emotive behavior therapy* by Ellis, emphasizing a behavioral "homework" component.

Cognitive Therapy for Depression

Like Ellis, cognitive therapist Aaron Beck was originally trained in Freudian techniques. As Beck analyzed his depressed patients' dreams, he found recurring negative themes of loss, rejection, and abandonment that extended into their waking thoughts. So in his form of cognitive therapy, Beck and his colleagues (1979) seek to reverse clients' catastrophizing beliefs about themselves, their situations, and their futures. Beck shares with Ellis the goal of getting depressed people to take off the dark glasses through which they view life. But his technique is a kinder, gentler questioning that aims to help people discover their irrationalities (Beck & others, 1979, pp. 145–146):

Patient: *I agree with the descriptions of me but I guess I don't agree that the way I think makes me depressed.*

Beck: *How do you understand it?*

Patient: *I get depressed when things go wrong. Like when I fail a test.*

Beck: *How can failing a test make you depressed?*

Patient: *Well, if I fail I'll never get into law school.*

Beck: *So failing the test means a lot to you. But if failing a test could drive people into clinical depression, wouldn't you expect everyone who failed the test to have a depression? . . . Did everyone who failed get depressed enough to require treatment?*

Patient: *No, but it depends on how important the test was to the person.*

Beck: *Right, and who decides the importance?*

Patient: *I do.*

Beck: *And so, what we have to examine is your way of viewing the test (or the way that you think about the test) and how it affects your chances of getting into law school. Do you agree?*

Patient: *Right.*

Beck: *Do you agree that the way you interpret the results of the test will affect you? You might feel depressed, you might have trouble sleeping, not feel like eating, and you might even wonder if you should drop out of the course.*

Patient: *I have been thinking that I wasn't going to make it. Yes, I agree.*

Beck: *Now what did failing mean?*

Patient: *(tearful) That I couldn't get into law school.*

Beck: *And what does that mean to you?*

Patient: *That I'm just not smart enough.*

Beck: *Anything else?*

Patient: *That I can never be happy.*

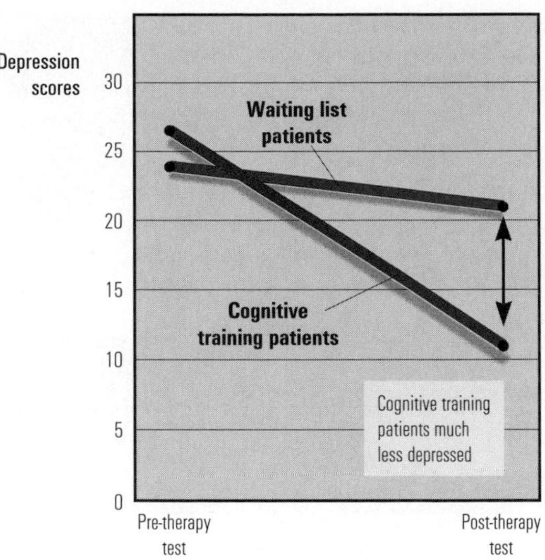

Figure 13.5 **Cognitive therapy for depression** After undergoing a program that trained them to think more like nondepressed people—by noticing and taking personal credit for good events and by not taking blame for or overgeneralizing from bad events—patients' depression dropped dramatically. (From Rabin & others, 1986)

Beck: *And how do these* thoughts *make you feel?*

Patient: *Very unhappy.*

Beck: *So it is the meaning of failing a test that makes you very unhappy. In fact, believing that you can never be happy is a powerful factor in producing unhappiness. So, you get yourself into a trap—by definition, failure to get into law school equals "I can never be happy."*

Another variety of cognitive therapy builds on the finding that depressed people do not exhibit the self-serving bias common in nondepressed people (page 448). Instead, they often attribute their failures to themselves and attribute their successes to external circumstances. Thus, Adele Rabin and her colleagues (1986) explained to 235 depressed adults the advantages of interpreting events as nondepressed people do. She then trained them to reform their habitually negative patterns of thinking and labeling. For example, she gave the patients homework assignments that required them to record each day's positive events and to write down how they contributed to each. Compared with depressed people who remained on a waiting list to receive therapy, those who went through the positive thinking exercises became much less depressed (Figure 13.5). The more people change their negative thinking styles, the more their depression lifts (Seligman, 1989).

Changed thinking after cognitive therapy also reduces the risk of relapse (Hollon & others, 1992). Changed thinking *before* depression hits can also help "vaccinate" those at risk. Teams led by Martin Seligman (1996; Gillham & others, 1995) are helping at-risk children—those who have suffered mild depression or whose parents are in conflict—learn how to dispute their pessimistic, negative thoughts and to think and act more positively. Once children experience a depressive episode, it often becomes their way of reacting to bad events. But not so for the 10- to 12-year-old children in one of the Seligman team's studies. Two years after receiving cognitive training, the participants were half as likely as those in a control group to be moderately or severely depressed. "Our results suggest," conclude the hopeful researchers, "that children can be taught cognitive and social skills that will buffer them against the alarmingly high rate of depression that occurs during puberty."

The more people change their negative thinking styles, the more their depression lifts.

Cognitive therapists often combine the reversal of self-defeating thinking with efforts to modify behavior. *Cognitive-behavior therapy* aims to make people aware of their irrational negative thinking, to replace it with new ways of thinking and talking, *and* to practice the more positive approach in everyday settings.

Because we often think in words, getting people to change what they *say* to themselves is an effective way to change their thinking. Perhaps you can identify with the anxious students who before an exam make matters worse with self-defeating thoughts: "This exam is probably going to be impossible. All these other students seem so relaxed and self-confident. I wish I were better prepared. Anyhow, I'm so nervous I'll forget everything." To change such negative patterns, Donald Meichenbaum (1977, 1985) offers "stress inoculation training." He trains people to restructure their thinking in stressful situations. Sometimes it may be enough simply to say more positive things to oneself: "Relax. The exam may be hard, but it will be hard for everyone else, too. I studied harder than most people. Besides, I don't need a perfect score to get a good grade."

Group and Family Therapies

5. *In what group contexts do people receive therapy?*

Except for traditional psychoanalysis, the therapies we have considered may also occur in therapist-led small groups. Although it does not provide the same degree of therapist involvement with each client, group therapy saves therapists'

Family therapy This type of therapy often acts as a preventive mental health strategy. The therapist helps family members understand how the ways they relate to each other create problems. The treatment emphasis is not on changing the individuals but rather on changing their relationships and interactions.

time and clients' money—and usually is no less effective than individual therapy (Fuhriman & Burlingame, 1994). More important, the social context allows people both to discover that others have problems similar to their own and to try out new ways of behaving. As you have perhaps experienced, receiving honest feedback—being reassured that you look poised even though you feel anxious and self-conscious, for example—can be very helpful. And it can be a relief to find that you are not alone—to learn that others, despite their apparent composure, share your problems and your feelings of loneliness, inadequacy, or anger.

Such has been the experience of a wide range of people, from cancer patients to dieters to recovering alcoholics (Yalom, 1985). Many participate in *self-help* and *support groups*—for substance abusers, divorced people, gamblers, the bereaved, and those simply seeking personal growth. In an individualistic age, with more and more people living alone or feeling isolated, the popularity of support groups also reflects a longing for community and connectedness. More than 100 million Americans belong to small religious, interest, or self-help groups that meet regularly—and 9 in 10 report that group members "support each other emotionally" (Gallup, 1994). The grandparent of self-help groups, Alcoholics Anonymous (AA), reportedly has 60,000 chapters in 112 countries. Its famous 12-step strategy, emulated by many other self-help groups, asks members to admit their powerlessness, to seek help from a higher power and from one another, and (the twelfth step) to take the message to others in need of it. In one 8-year, $27 million investigation, alcoholics seeking treatment reduced their drinking sharply and to roughly the same degree whether randomly assigned to a therapy based on AA principles and AA participation or to cognitive-behavior therapy or a "motivational therapy" (Project Match, 1997).

One special type of group interaction, **family therapy**, assumes that no person is an island. We live and grow in relation to others, especially our families. We struggle to differentiate ourselves from our families, but we also need to connect with them emotionally. Some problem behaviors arise from the tension between these two tendencies, which often creates family stress. Thus, patients often come to therapists seeking help in their relationships with family members.

Unlike most psychotherapy, which focuses on what happens inside the person's own skin, family therapists work with family groups to heal relationships and to mobilize family resources. Their aim is to help family members discover the role they play within their family's social system. A child's rebellion, for example, affects and is affected by other family tensions. Family therapists also attempt—usually with some success, research suggests (Hazelrigg & others, 1987; Shadish & others, 1993)—to open up communication within the family or to help family members discover new ways of preventing or resolving conflicts.

family therapy therapy that treats the family as a system. It views an individual's unwanted behaviors as influenced by or directed at other family members; encourages family members toward positive relationships and improved communication.

REHEARSE IT!

5. Behavior therapies apply learning principles to the treatment of problems such as sexual disorders, phobias, and alcoholism. In treating people with these problems, the goal of the behavior therapist is to
   a. identify and treat the underlying causes of the problem.
   b. improve learning and insight.
   c. eliminate the unwanted behavior.
   d. improve communication and social sensitivity.
6. Behavior therapists assume that phobias and other maladaptive behaviors are conditioned responses. Behaviorists attempt either to extinguish these responses or to countercondition a client by conditioning a new response to stimuli that trigger maladaptive or unwanted responses. Two counterconditioning techniques are systematic desensitization and
   a. positive reinforcement.
   b. aversive conditioning.
   c. rational-emotive therapy.
   d. token economy.
7. The technique of systematic desensitization, developed by Joseph Wolpe, teaches people to relax in the presence of progressively more anxiety-provoking stimuli. Systematic desensitization has been found to be especially effective in the treatment of
   a. phobias.
   b. depression.
   c. alcoholism.
   d. bed-wetting.
8. Some institutions, such as homes for people who are mentally retarded or delinquent, use a token economy to shape behavior. They hand out tokens, which may later be exchanged for other rewards, to a person who displays a desired behavior or takes a step in the right direction. The token economy is an application of
   a. classical conditioning.
   b. counterconditioning.
   c. cognitive therapy.
   d. operant conditioning.
9. Cognitive therapists assume that our internal beliefs and characteristic ways of thinking strongly influence our responses to events. They treat emotional problems by teaching people new, more constructive ways of thinking. An example of a cognitive therapy is rational-emotive therapy, which was developed by
   a. Carl Rogers.
   b. Joseph Wolpe.
   c. Albert Ellis.
   d. Aaron Beck.
10. A new form of cognitive therapy teaches people to stop attributing failures to personal inadequacy, and success to external circumstances. This form of cognitive therapy has been shown to be especially effective in treating
    a. mental retardation.
    b. phobias.
    c. alcoholism.
    d. depression.
11. Psychotherapy is in large part an individual process, although most therapies may occur in therapist-led small groups. The social context of this group therapy tells people that others have problems similar to theirs and allows them to act out alternative behaviors. One type of group therapy, family therapy, serves as a
    a. source of psychoanalysis.
    b. preventive mental health strategy.
    c. self-help group.
    d. type of behavior therapy.

Evaluating Psychotherapies

6. *What does research on psychotherapy reveal about its effectiveness?*

Advice columnist Ann Landers frequently advises her troubled letter writers to get professional help. One response urged the writer "not to give up. Hang in there until you find [a psychotherapist] who fills the bill. It's worth the effort." She advised the same day's second letter writer, "There are many excellent mental health facilities in your city. I urge you to make an appointment at once" (Farina & Fisher, 1982). Therapy advocate Tipper Gore (1994) would concur: "The data show high levels of success in treating large numbers of people suffering [mental illnesses]." Many people share Ann Landers' and Tipper Gore's confidence in psychotherapy's effectiveness. The National Institute of Mental Health estimates that 15 percent of Americans seek help for psychological and addictive disorders each year (Figure 13.6).

Before 1950, the main mental health providers were psychiatrists. Since then, the demand has outgrown the psychiatric profession, and most psychotherapy is now done by clinical and counseling psychologists; clinical social workers; pastoral, marital, abuse, and school counselors; and psychiatric nurses. Much of it is done through *community mental health* programs, which provide outpatient therapy, crisis phone lines, and halfway houses for those making the transition from hospitalization to independent living. Is the faith that Ann Landers and millions of others worldwide place in these therapists justified?

Figure 13.6 To whom do people turn? The National Institute of Mental Health reports that 19 million Americans a year seek help for psychological difficulties. About 2 in 5 seek out a mental health worker, such as a psychologist or psychiatrist. (Data from Regier & others, 1993)

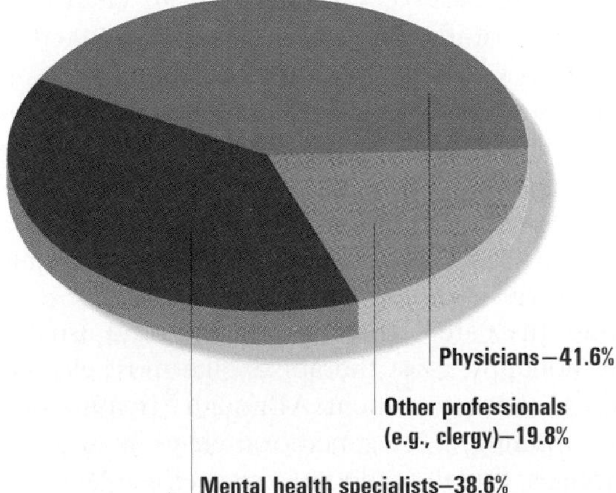

Is Psychotherapy Effective?

The question, though simply put, is not simply answered. For one thing, measuring therapy's effectiveness is not like taking your body's temperature. If you and I were to undergo psychotherapy, how would we gauge its effectiveness? By how we feel about our progress? How our therapist feels about it? How our friends and family feel about it? How our behavior has changed?

Clients' Perceptions

If clients' testimonials were the only yardstick, we could strongly affirm the effectiveness of psychotherapy. Research indicates that 3 out of 4 clients report themselves satisfied, and 1 in 2 say they are "very satisfied" (Lebow, 1982). When 2900 readers of *Consumer Reports* (1995; Kotkin & others, 1996; Seligman, 1995) reported on their experiences with mental health professionals, 89 percent were at least "fairly well satisfied." And 9 in 10 who recalled feeling *fair* or *very poor* when beginning therapy now were feeling *very good, good,* or at least *so-so.* We have their word for it—and who should know better?

If clients' testimonials were the only yardstick, we could strongly affirm the effectiveness of psychotherapy. Research indicates that 3 out of 4 clients report themselves satisfied.

We should not dismiss these testimonials lightly. People enter therapy because they are suffering, and most leave feeling better about themselves. But there are several reasons why client testimonials do not persuade psychotherapy's skeptics:

- **People often enter therapy in crisis.** When, with the normal ebb and flow of events, the crisis passes, people may attribute their improvement to the therapy.
- **Clients may need to believe the therapy was worth the effort.** To admit investing time and money in something ineffective is like admitting to having one's car serviced repeatedly by a mechanic who never fixed it. Self-justification is a powerful human motive.
- **Clients generally like their therapists and speak kindly of them.** Even if the clients' problems remain, say the therapy critics, "they work hard to find something positive to say. The therapist had been very understanding, the client had gained a new perspective, he learned to communicate better, his mind was eased, anything at all so as not to have to say treatment was a failure" (Zilbergeld, 1983, p. 117).

Clinicians' Perceptions

If clinicians' perceptions accurately reflected therapeutic effectiveness, we would have even more reason to celebrate. Case studies of successful treatment abound. Furthermore, every therapist treasures compliments from clients as they say goodbye or later express their gratitude. The problem is that clients justify entering psychotherapy by emphasizing their woes, justify leaving therapy by emphasizing their well-being, and stay in touch only if satisfied. Therapists are aware of failures, but they are mostly the failures of *other* therapists—those whose clients, having experienced only temporary relief, are now seeking a new therapist for their recurring problems. Thus, the same person with the same recurring difficulty—the same old weight problem, depression, or marital difficulty—may represent "success" stories in several therapists' files.

Because people enter therapy when they are extremely unhappy, and usually leave when they are less extremely unhappy, most therapists, like most clients, testify to therapy's success—regardless of the treatment. Although "treatments" have varied widely, from chains to counseling, every generation views its own approach as more enlightened. Testimonials, therefore, do not prove effectiveness.

PSYCHOLOGY APPLIED

A Consumer's Guide to Psychotherapists

When should a person seek the help of a mental health professional? Life for everyone is marked by a mix of serenity and stress, blessing and bereavement, good moods and bad. It is only when troubling thoughts and emotions interfere with normal living that we should consider talking to a professional. The American Psychological Association offers these common trouble signals:

- Feelings of hopelessness
- Deep and lasting depression
- Self-destructive behavior such as alcohol and drug abuse
- Disruptive fears
- Sudden mood shifts
- Thoughts of suicide
- Compulsive rituals such as hand washing
- Sexual difficulties

If you are looking for a therapist, you may wish to shop around by having a preliminary consultation with two or three therapists. You can describe your problem and learn each therapist's treatment approach. You can ask questions about the therapist's values, credentials (see table below), and fees. And you can assess your feelings about each therapist.

Therapists and Their Training

Type	Description
Psychiatrists	Physicians who specialize in the treatment of psychological disorders. Not all psychiatrists have had extensive training in psychotherapy, but as M.D.s they can prescribe medications. Thus, they tend to see those with the most serious problems. Many have a private practice.
Clinical psychologists	Most are psychologists with a Ph.D. and expertise in research, assessment, and therapy, supplemented by a supervised internship. About half work in agencies and institutions, half in private practice.
Clinical or psychiatric social workers	A two-year Master of Social Work graduate program plus postgraduate supervision prepares some social workers to offer psychotherapy, mostly to people with everyday personal and family problems. About half have earned the National Association of Social Workers' designation of clinical social worker.
Counselors	Marriage and family counselors specialize in problems arising from family relations. Pastoral counselors provide counseling to countless people. Abuse counselors work with substance abusers and with spouse and child abusers and their victims.

Outcome Research

How, then, can we objectively measure the effectiveness of psychotherapy? What types of people and problems are best helped, and by what type of psychotherapy? The questions have both academic and personal relevance. If you or someone you care about feels anxious or depressed, or suffers some psychological disorder, how likely is it that psychotherapy will help?

If you or someone you care about feels anxious or depressed, or suffers some psychological disorder, how likely is it that psychotherapy will help?

In the hope of better assessing psychotherapy's effectiveness, psychologists have turned to controlled research studies. Similar research in the 1800s transformed medicine from concocted treatments (bleeding, purging, infusions of plant and metal substances) into a science. The transformation occurred when skeptical physicians began to realize that many patients got better on their own, that most of the fashionable treatments were doing no good, and that sorting sense from nonsense required closely following illnesses—with and without a particular treatment. Typhoid fever patients, for example, often improved after a treatment such as bleeding. That convinced most physicians that the treatment worked. It was not until a control group was given mere bed rest—and 70 percent were observed to improve after five weeks of fever—that physicians were shocked to learn that their treatments were, at best, worthless (Thomas, 1992).

In psychology, the opening volley in what became a spirited debate over such research was fired by British psychologist Hans Eysenck (1952). He summarized studies showing that after undergoing psychotherapy, two-thirds of those suffering nonpsychotic disorders improve markedly. To this day, no one disputes that optimistic estimate.

So why are we still debating psychotherapy's effectiveness? Because Eysenck also reported similar improvement among *untreated* persons, such as those who were on waiting lists. With or without psychotherapy, he said, roughly two-thirds improved noticeably. Time was a great healer.

"Fortunately, [psycho]analysis is not the only way to resolve inner conflicts. Life itself still remains a very effective therapist."

Karen Horney
Our Inner Conflicts
1945

The avalanche of criticism prompted by Eysenck's conclusions revealed shortcomings in his analyses. Also, Eysenck could find only 24 studies of psychotherapy outcomes to analyze in 1952. Today, there are hundreds. The best of these studies randomly assign people on a waiting list to therapy or to no therapy. Afterward, researchers evaluate.

In the first statistical digest of these studies, Mary Lee Smith and her colleagues (1980) combined the results of 475 investigations. For psychotherapists, the welcome result was that "the evidence overwhelmingly supports the efficacy of psychotherapy" (p. 183). Figure 13.7 depicts their finding—that the average therapy client ends up better off than 80 percent of the untreated individuals on waiting lists. The claim is more modest than it first appears—by definition, about 50 percent of untreated people also are better off than the average untreated person. Nevertheless, Smith and her collaborators concluded that "psychotherapy benefits people of all ages as reliably as schooling educates them, medicine cures them, or business turns a profit" (p. 183).

Newer research summaries confirm this optimism (Lipsey & Wilson, 1993; Shadish & others, 1997). In one ambitious study, the National Institute of Mental Health compared three depression treatments: cognitive therapy, interpersonal therapy (which focuses on social relations), and a standard drug therapy. Twenty-eight experienced therapists at research sites in Norman, Oklahoma; Washington, D.C.; and Pittsburgh, Pennsylvania, were trained in one of the three methods and randomly assigned their share of the 239 depressed patients

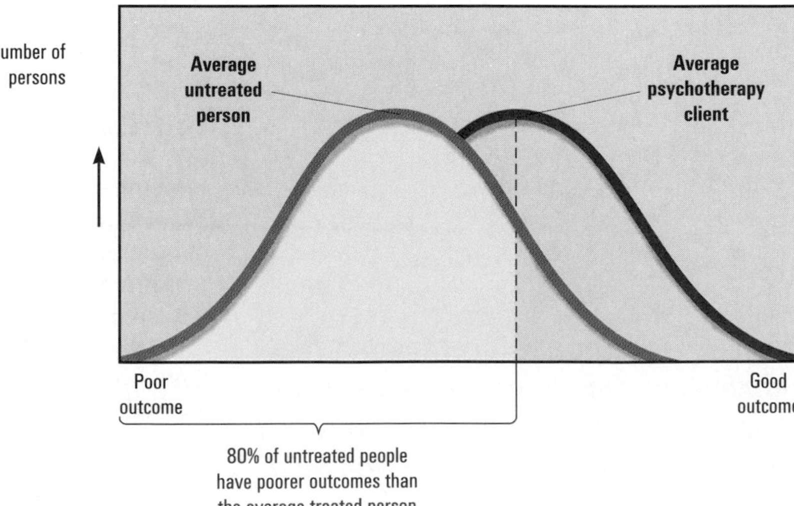

Figure 13.7 **Treatment versus no treatment** These two normal distribution curves based on data from 475 studies show the improvement of untreated people and psychotherapy clients. The outcome for the average therapy client surpassed that for 80 percent of the untreated people. (Adapted from Smith & others, 1980)

who participated. Patients in all three groups improved more than did those in a control group who received merely an inert medication and supportive attention, encouragement, and advice. Among patients who completed a full 16-week treatment program, the depression had lifted for slightly more than half of those in each treatment group—but for only 29 percent of those in the control group (Elkin & others, 1989). This verdict echoes the results of the earlier outcome studies: *Those not undergoing therapy often improve, but those undergoing therapy are more likely to improve.*

Often, however, the improvement was not permanent. Only 1 in 4 patients undergoing psychotherapy and 1 in 6 undergoing drug therapy both recovered and experienced no relapse within 18 months (Shea & others, 1992). So, extravagant expectations that psychotherapy will transform your life and personality seem unwarranted. Still, Eysenck's pessimism also seems unwarranted. *On average*, psychotherapy is somewhat effective—and is also cost-effective when compared with the greater costs of medical care for psychologically related ailments (Turkington, 1987). The annual cost of psychological disorders and substance abuse—including crime, accidents, lost work, and treatment—is staggering. Thus, just as an investment in prenatal and well-baby care *reduces* long-term costs, so will an investment in almost any effective treatment for psychological problems. Anything that boosts employees' psychological well-being will reduce medical costs, improve work efficiency, and diminish absenteeism. Studies by health insurers show that mental health treatment can more than pay for itself with reduced medical costs (American Psychological Association, 1991).

But note that "on average" refers to no one therapy in particular. It is like saying, "Surgery is somewhat effective," or like reassuring lung-cancer patients that "on the average" medical treatment of health problems is effective. What people want to know is not the effectiveness of therapy in general but the effectiveness of particular treatments for their particular problems.

In general, therapy is most effective when the problem is clear-cut (Singer, 1981). Those who suffer phobias, who are unassertive, or who are frustrated by sexual performance problems can hope for improvement. Those who suffer chronic schizophrenia or who wish to change their whole personality are unlikely to benefit from psychotherapy alone (Zilbergeld, 1983). The more specific the problem, the more hope there is.

The Relative Effectiveness of Different Therapies

People considering therapy want to know *which* psychotherapy will be most effective for their problem. Despite claims of superiority by advocates of different types of therapy, comparisons of therapies reveal no clear winner (Smith and Glass, 1977, 1980; Wampold & others, 1997). No one type of therapy has proved consistently superior. (*Consumer Reports* [1995] readers were equally satisfied no matter what type of therapy they received and whether treated by a psychiatrist, psychologist, or social worker.) Moreover—and more astonishing—it has made no discernible difference whether the therapy was group or individual or how well trained and experienced the therapist was. It seems as though the dodo bird in *Alice in Wonderland* was right: "Everyone has won and all must have prizes."

Some therapies are, however, well suited to particular disorders. With specific behavior problems such as phobias, compulsions, or sexual disorders, behavioral conditioning therapies achieve especially favorable results (Bowers & Clum, 1988; Giles, 1983). With depression, the cognitive therapies prove most successful (Dobson, 1989; Shapiro & Shapiro, 1982). Just as physicians offer particular treatments for specific medical problems, rather than treating every complaint with the same drug or surgical procedure, so psychotherapists increasingly offer particular treatments for specific psychological problems.

"Different sores have different salves."

English Proverb

"I utilize the best from Freud, the best from Jung, and the best from my Uncle Marty, a very smart fellow."

Commonalities Among Psychotherapies

Some clinicians suggest a reason why no one therapeutic method proves generally superior or inferior to another. Despite their differences, each therapy's effectiveness may derive from underlying commonalities. Jerome Frank (1982), Marvin Goldfried (Goldfried & Padawer, 1982), and Hans Strupp (1986) studied common ingredients of various therapies and suggested that they all offer at least three benefits: hope for demoralized people; a new perspective on oneself and the world; and an empathic, trusting, caring relationship. These "nonspecific" factors aren't all that therapy offers, but they are important aspects (Barker & others, 1988; Jones & others, 1988; Roberts & others, 1993). They are part of what the growing numbers of self-help and support groups offer their members. And they have been part of what traditional healers offer (Jackson, 1992). Healers—special people to whom others disclose their suffering—have for centuries listened to understand and to empathize, reassure, advise, console, interpret, or explain.

Hope for Demoralized People

People who seek therapy typically feel anxious, depressed, devoid of self-esteem, and incapable of turning things around. What any therapy offers is the expectation that, with commitment from the patient, things can and will get better. Apart from the particular therapeutic technique, this belief may itself promote improved morale, new feelings of self-efficacy, and diminished symptoms (Prioleau & others, 1983). This benefit of a person's belief in a treatment is the *placebo effect.* As we saw in Chapter 1, a placebo is an inert treatment often used as a control treatment in drug experiments. The placebo has no effect apart from a person's belief in it. In psychotherapy experiments, the placebo treatment may be listening to inspirational tapes, attending group discussions, or taking a fake pill.

The finding that improvement is greater for placebo-treated people than for untreated people (although not as great as for those receiving actual psychotherapy) suggests that one reason therapies help is that they offer hope. Said differently, therapy outcomes vary with the client's attitude—the client's motivation, confidence, and commitment. Each therapy, in its individual way, may harness the client's own healing powers. And that, says psychiatrist Jerome Frank, helps us understand why all sorts of treatments—including some folk healing rites known to be powerless apart from the patient's belief—may in their own time and place produce cures.

"All successful therapy has two things in common: It is forward-looking and it requires assuming responsibility. Therapy that reviews childhood endlessly has a century-long history of being ineffective. All therapy that works for depression, anxiety, and sexual problems focuses on exactly what is going wrong now and on how to correct it."

Martin E. P. Seligman
What You Can Change and What You Can't
1994

A New Perspective

Every therapy offers people a plausible explanation of their symptoms and an alternative way of looking at themselves or responding to their worlds. Therapy also offers new experiences that help people change their views of themselves and their behaviors. Armed with a believable fresh perspective, they may approach life with a new attitude.

An Empathic, Trusting, Caring Relationship

To say that all therapies are about equally effective is not to say all *therapists* are equally effective. Regardless of their therapeutic technique, effective therapists are empathic people who seek to understand another's experience; whose care and concern the client feels; and whose respectful listening, reassurance, and advice earn the client's trust and respect. In the National Institute of Mental Health depression-treatment study, the most effective therapists were those who were perceived as most empathic and caring, and who established the closest

A caring relationship Effective therapists form a bond of trust with their patients.

therapeutic bonds with their clients (Blatt & others, 1996). Indeed, some believe that warmth and empathy are hallmarks of healers everywhere, whether psychiatrists, witch doctors, or shamans (Torrey, 1986).

The notion that all therapies offer *hope* through the *fresh perspective* offered by a *caring person* gains support from a meta-analysis of 39 studies. Each study compared treatment offered by professional therapists with treatment offered by laypeople. These laypeople included friendly professors, people who had had a few hours' training in empathic listening skills, and college students supervised by a professional clinician. The result? The "paraprofessionals," as we call these briefly trained people, typically proved as effective as the professionals (Christensen & Jacobson, 1994). Although most of the problems they treated were mild, trained paraprofessionals were—believe it or not—as effective as professionals even when dealing with more disturbed adults, such as those diagnosed as seriously depressed.

To recap, people who seek help usually improve. So do many of those who do not undergo psychotherapy, and that is a tribute to our human resourcefulness and to our capacity to care for one another. Nevertheless, though the therapist's orientation and experience appear not to matter much, those who receive some psychotherapy usually improve more than those who do not. Mature, articulate people with specific emotional or behavioral problems often improve the most.

Part of what all therapies offer is hope, a fresh way of looking at life, and an empathic, caring relationship. That may explain why the empathy and friendly counsel of paraprofessionals are often as helpful as professional psychotherapy. And that may also explain why people who feel supported by close relationships—who enjoy the fellowship and friendship of caring people—are less likely to need or seek therapy (Frank, 1982; O'Connor & Brown, 1984).

Culture and Values in Psychotherapy

All therapies offer hope, and nearly all therapists attempt to enhance their clients' sensitivity, openness, personal responsibility, and sense of purpose (Jensen & Bergin, 1988). But on certain matters of moral and cultural diversity, therapists may differ from one another and from their clients (Kelly, 1990). In Canada and the United States, for example, about 1 in 25 people declare themselves atheists or agnostics, as do (depending on the survey) one-fifth to one-half of psychiatrists and clinical psychologists (Gallup, 1993; Jensen, 1991; Lukoff & others, 1992). In Britain, two-thirds of psychiatrists say they are atheists (Neeleman & Persaud, 1995). That raises an issue: What values prevail in psychotherapy? What values *should* prevail? Should it matter that highly religious persons prefer religiously similar therapists (Worthington & others, 1996)?

Albert Ellis, the rational-emotive therapist, and Allen Bergin, co-editor of the *Handbook of Psychotherapy and Behavior Change*, illustrate how sharply values can differ. Ellis (1980) assumes that "no one and nothing is supreme," that "self-gratification" should be encouraged, and that "unequivocal love, commitment, service, and . . . fidelity to any interpersonal commitment, especially marriage, leads to harmful consequences." Bergin (1980) assumes the opposite—that "because God is supreme, humility and the acceptance of divine authority are virtues," that "self-control and committed love and self-sacrifice are to be encouraged," and that "infidelity to any interpersonal commitment, especially marriage, leads to harmful consequences." Bergin and Ellis disagree more radically than most therapists regarding what values are healthiest. In so doing, however, they illustrate what they agree on: that psychotherapists' personal beliefs and values influence their practice. Knowing that clients tend to adopt their therapists' values (Worthington & others, 1996), Bergin and Ellis also agree that therapists should divulge their values more openly.

Value differences also can become significant when a therapist from one culture meets a client from another. In North America, Europe, and Australia, for example, most therapists reflect their culture's individualism (by giving priority to personal desires and identity). Clients who are immigrants from Asian countries, which expect people to be mindful of others' expectations, may therefore have difficulty with therapies that require them to think independently. Such differences help explain the reluctance of some minority populations to use mental health services (Sue, 1990). Recognizing that therapists and clients may differ in values, in communication styles, and in language, many therapy training programs are now providing training in cultural sensitivity and recruiting members of underrepresented culture groups.

REHEARSE IT!

12. The question "Is psychotherapy effective?" has been the subject of hundreds of scientific studies and innumerable personal accounts. The most enthusiastic or optimistic view of psychotherapy comes from

- **a.** outcome research.
- **b.** psychologist Hans Eysenck.
- **c.** reports of clinicians and clients.
- **d.** a government study of treatment for depression.

13. On average, troubled people who undergo therapy are more likely to improve than those who do not, and therapy tends to be most effective when the problem is clear-cut and specific. Studies show that ________________ therapy is most effective overall.

- **a.** behavior
- **b.** humanistic
- **c.** individual as opposed to group
- **d.** no one type of

14. Psychologists have observed that people's belief that a treatment will help them is often sufficient to cause some improvement. A neutral treatment, such as an inert pill, that results in improved morale and diminished symptoms is called

- **a.** a placebo effect.
- **b.** preventive mental health.
- **c.** an empathic perspective.
- **d.** clinical treatment.

The Biomedical Therapies

Psychotherapy is one way to treat psychological disorders. The other is physically changing the brain's functioning—by altering its chemistry with drugs, by overloading its circuits with electroconvulsive shock, or by disconnecting its circuits through psychosurgery. Although psychologists can provide "talking" therapies, only psychiatrists (as medical doctors) offer most biomedical therapies.

Drug Therapies

7. What are the most common forms of drug therapy?

By far the most widely used biomedical treatments today are the drug therapies. When introduced in the 1950s, drug therapy greatly reduced the need for psychosurgery or hospitalization. Discoveries in **psychopharmacology** (the study of drug effects on mind and behavior) revolutionized the treatment of severely disordered people, liberating hundreds of thousands from confinement in mental hospitals. Thanks to drug therapy—and to political and legal efforts to minimize involuntary hospitalization and to return hospitalized people to their communities, aided by community mental health programs—the resident population of state and county mental hospitals in the United States today is but 20 percent of what it was 40 years ago (Figure 13.8).

Another way to treat psychological disorders is physically changing the brain's functioning—by altering its chemistry with drugs, by overloading its circuits with electroconvulsive shock, or by disconnecting its circuits through psychosurgery.

For those still unable to care for themselves, however, release from hospitals has meant not liberation but homelessness. If home is the place where, as

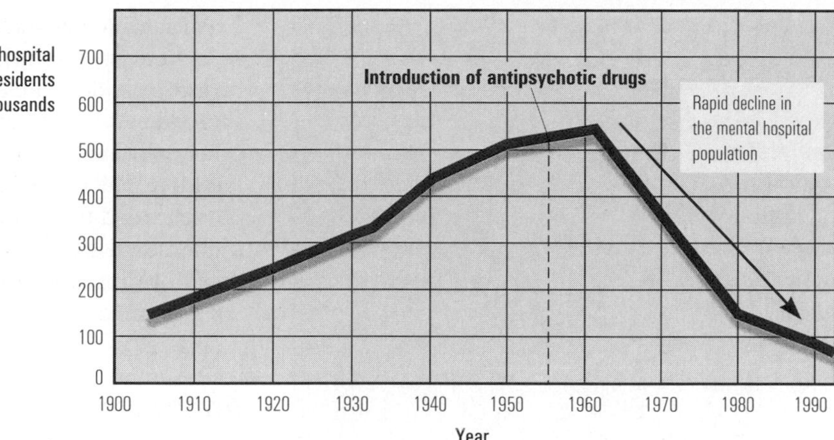

Figure 13.8 The emptying of U.S. mental hospitals After the widespread introduction of antipsychotic drugs, starting in about 1955, the number of residents in state and county mental hospitals declined sharply. But in the rush to deinstitutionalize the mentally ill, many people who were ill-equipped to care for themselves were left homeless on city streets. (Data from the National Institute of Mental Health and the U.S. Bureau of the Census, 1996)

Robert Frost said, when you go there, they have to take you in, then some 200,000 disordered Americans and many thousands of Europeans have no place to call home (Fichter & others, 1996; Leshner, 1992). Studies suggest that about one-third of the homeless suffer disabling psychological disorders (Fischer & Breakey, 1991; Levine & Rog, 1990; McCarty & others, 1991). And that doesn't include alcohol or drug abuse, which also plague at least 1 in 3 homeless people. Furthermore, 25 percent of today's homeless are female—unlike the 1950s, when only 3 percent of the homeless in major cities were female (Rossi, 1990).

With almost any new treatment, including drug therapy, there is a first wave of enthusiasm as many people apparently improve. But that enthusiasm often diminishes after researchers subtract the rate of (1) normal recovery among untreated persons and (2) recovery due to the placebo effect, which arises from the positive expectations of patients and mental health workers alike. So, to evaluate the effectiveness of any new drug, researchers use the *double-blind technique*. Half the patients receive the drug, the other half a similar-appearing placebo. Neither the staff nor the patients know who gets which. In double-blind studies, several types of drugs have proved useful in treating psychological disorders.

"The mentally ill were out of the hospital, but in many cases they were simply out on the streets, less agitated but lost, still disabled but now uncared for."

Lewis Thomas
Late Night Thoughts on Listening to Mahler's Ninth Symphony
1983

Antipsychotic Drugs

The revolution in drug therapy for psychological disorders began when it was accidentally discovered that certain drugs, used for other medical purposes, also calmed psychotic patients. These antipsychotic drugs, such as chlorpromazine (sold as Thorazine), provide most help to schizophrenia patients experiencing the positive symptoms of auditory hallucinations and paranoia by dampening their responsiveness to irrelevant stimuli (Lenzenweger & others, 1989). Patients with the negative symptoms of apathy and withdrawal often do not respond well to these antipsychotic drugs. A newer drug, clozapine (marketed as Clozaril), does sometimes enable "awakenings" in such people. It also sometimes helps those who have positive symptoms but haven't responded to other drugs. Although clozapine has a toxic effect on white blood cells in 1 or 2 percent of cases—thus necessitating regular blood tests—it is currently the most effective schizophrenia treatment (Skelton & others, 1995). Researchers are testing possible cousin drugs that would offer the same benefits without the blood problem.

The molecules of antipsychotic drugs are similar enough to molecules of the neurotransmitter dopamine to occupy its receptor sites and block its activity (Pickar & others, 1984; Taubes, 1994). (Clozapine also blocks serotonin activity.) The finding that most antipsychotic drugs block dopamine receptors reinforces the idea that an overactive dopamine system contributes to schizophrenia.

psychopharmacology the study of the effects of drugs on mind and behavior.

Herself renewed Drugs that block serotonin activity, as clozapine does, help some people live independently. One such person was Daphne Moss, who—freed from her paranoid delusions that her parents were witches—began teaching school. She went from "hating the sunshine in the morning to loving it."

Antipsychotics such as Thorazine are powerful drugs that can produce sluggishness, tremors, and twitches similar to those of Parkinson's disease, which is marked by too little dopamine (Kaplan & Saddock, 1989). (Clozapine, thankfully, has few such side effects.) What is an effective dose for some people may be an overdose for others. Asians, for example, seem to require lower doses than do Caucasians (Holden, 1991). By carefully monitoring the dosage and its effects, therapist and patient tread the fine line between relieving the symptoms and causing extremely unpleasant side effects. In this way, and with the help of supportive people, hundreds of thousands of people with schizophrenia who had been consigned to the back wards of mental hospitals have returned to jobs and to near-normal lives.

Antianxiety Drugs

Among the most heavily prescribed and abused drugs are the antianxiety agents, such as Valium and Librium. Like alcohol, these drugs depress central nervous system activity. Because they reduce tension and anxiety without causing excessive sleepiness, they have been prescribed even for minor emotional stresses. Used in combination with other therapy, an antianxiety drug can help a person learn to cope with frightening situations and fear-triggering stimuli.

The criticism sometimes made of the behavior therapies—that they reduce symptoms without resolving underlying problems—is also made of antianxiety drugs. Unlike the behavior therapies, they may even be used as a continuing treatment. Routinely "popping a Valium" at the first sign of tension can produce psychological dependence on the drug. When heavy users stop taking the drug, they may experience increased anxiety and insomnia, driving them back to the drug for relief.

Antidepressant Drugs

The [antidepressant] drug effect is often modest. Aerobic exercise, which helps calm anxious people and energize depressed people, does about as much good, and with positive side effects.

As the antianxiety drugs calm anxious people down, the antidepressants sometimes lift depressed people up. The boost is due partly to a nice placebo effect—the new hope that patients gain when taking a drug they believe will help them—and partly to the drug's physical effect (Sapirstein & Kirsch, 1996).

Most of these drugs increase the availability of the neurotransmitters norepinephrine or serotonin, which elevate arousal and mood and appear scarce during depression. Consider fluoxetine, which 20 million users worldwide know as Prozac, the world's most widely prescribed psychiatric drug (Horgan, 1996). Prozac blocks the reabsorption and removal of serotonin from synapses (Figure 13.9). Prozac and its cousins Zoloft and Paxil are therefore called serotonin-reuptake-inhibitor drugs. Other antidepressants work by blocking the reabsorption of both norepinephrine and serotonin or by inhibiting an enzyme that breaks down neurotransmitters such as serotonin. These drugs, however, have more potential side effects, such as dry mouth, weight gain, or dizzy spells.

Patients who begin taking antidepressants do not wake up the next day singing "Oh, what a beautiful morning!" Although the influence of antidepressants on neurotransmission occurs within hours, their full psychological effect often requires four weeks, sometimes aided by cognitive therapy to help the patient reverse a now-habitual negative thinking style. Moreover, after allowing for natural recovery ("spontaneous remission") and a placebo effect, the drug effect is often modest (Greenberg & others, 1992, 1994). Aerobic exercise, which helps calm anxious people and energize depressed people, does about as much good, and with positive side effects (see page 378).

Although the drug effects are less exciting than many news stories would have us believe, they also are less frightening than other stories have suggested. Some people taking Prozac, for example, have committed suicide, but their numbers seem

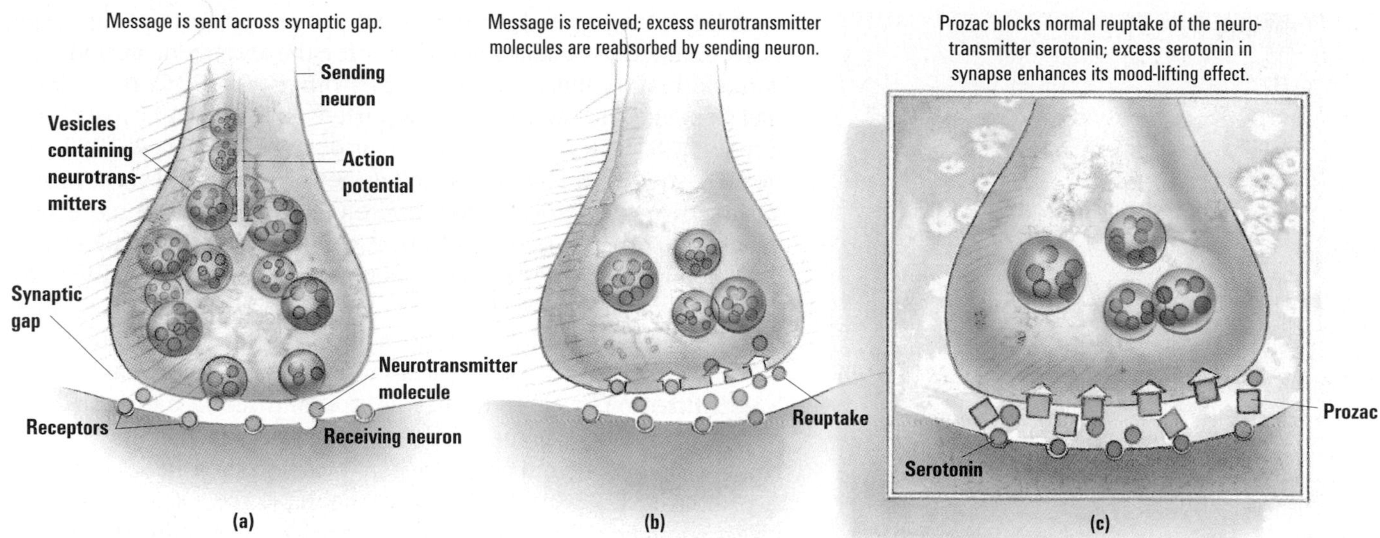

Figure 13.9 Biology of antidepressants

fewer than we would expect from millions of depressed people not taking the medication. Prozac users who commit suicide are like cellular phone users who get brain cancer. Given the millions of people taking Prozac and using cellular phones, alarming anecdotes tell us nothing. The question critical thinkers want answered is this: Do these groups suffer an elevated *rate* of suicide and brain cancer? The answer in each case appears to be no (Paulos, 1995; Tollefson & others, 1993, 1994).

For those suffering the manic-depressive mood swings of a bipolar disorder, the simple salt **lithium** can be an effective mood stabilizer. An Australian physician, John Cade, discovered this in the 1940s when he administered lithium to a severely manic patient. Although his reason for doing so was misguided—he thought lithium had calmed excitable guinea pigs when actually it made them sick—Cade found that in less than a week the patient became perfectly well (Snyder, 1986). With continued lithium use, the emotional highs and lows typically level. After suffering mood swings for years, about 7 in 10 people with bipolar disorder benefit from a long-term daily dose of this cheap salt (Solomon & others, 1995).

Current drug therapies reduce or increase activity at all the receptors for a given neurotransmitter. This has been likened to watering one's garden by flooding it. Drug researchers hope that the next generation of therapeutic drugs will target specific receptors that control specific symptoms, rather like watering individual plants. If so, such drugs may offer greater potency with fewer side effects (Goleman, 1996).

Electroconvulsive Therapy

8. *How effective are electroconvulsive therapy and psychosurgery?*

A more controversial brain manipulation occurs through shock treatment, or **electroconvulsive therapy (ECT)**. When ECT was first introduced in 1938, the wide-awake patient was strapped to a table and jolted with roughly 100 volts of electricity to the brain, producing racking convulsions and brief unconsciousness. ECT therefore gained a barbaric image that lingers to the present. Today, however, patients first receive a general anesthetic so they are not conscious and a muscle relaxant to prevent injury from convulsions. Then a psychiatrist momentarily electrically shocks the unconscious patient's brain. Within 30 minutes the patient awakens and remembers nothing of the treatment or of the hours preceding it.

Psychiatrists usually limit ECT to severely depressed patients. (It is usually ineffective in treating other psychological disorders.) After three such treatments

lithium a chemical that provides an effective drug therapy for the mood swings of bipolar (manic-depressive) disorders.

electroconvulsive therapy (ECT) a biomedical therapy for severely depressed patients in which a brief electric current is sent through the brain of an anesthetized patient.

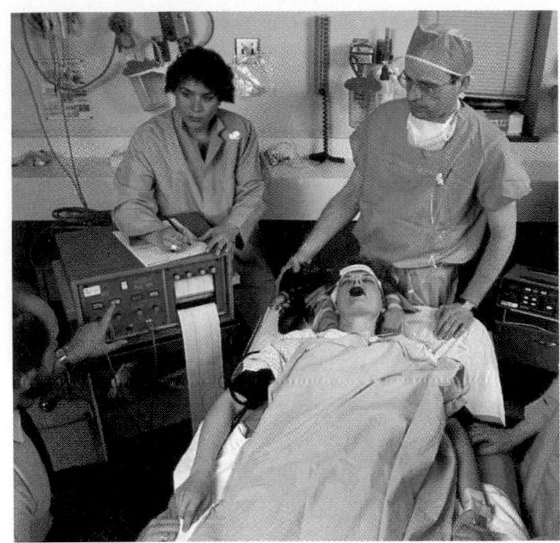

Electroconvulsive therapy Although ECT is controversial, it is the preferred treatment for depression that does not respond to drug therapy.

The medical use of electricity is an ancient practice. Physicians treated the Roman Emperor Claudius (10 B.C.–A.D. 54) for headaches by pressing electric eels to his temples.

each week for two to four weeks, 80 percent or more of depressed people improve markedly—with memory loss for the treatment period but without discernible brain damage (Bergsholm & others, 1989; Coffey, 1993). "A miracle had happened in two weeks," reported noted research psychologist Norman Endler (1982) after ECT alleviated his deep depression. A 1985 panel of the National Institutes of Health, as well as newer research reviews, confirm that ECT is an effective treatment for severely depressed patients who have not responded to drug therapy (Consensus Conference, 1985; Parker & others, 1992). Thus, reports the American Psychiatric Association (1990), ECT has regained respectability as a "major treatment" for depression.

How does ECT work? After more than 50 years, no one knows for sure (Kapur & Mann, 1993). Perhaps electrical shock increases the release of norepinephrine, a neurotransmitter that elevates arousal and mood and seems in short supply during depression. Or perhaps the shock-induced seizures cause the brain to react by calming neural centers where overactivity produces depression.

Although ECT is credited with saving many from suicide, its Frankenstein-like image continues. No matter how impressive the results, the idea of electrically shocking people into convulsions still strikes many as barbaric, especially given our ignorance about why ECT works. Moreover, ECT-treated patients, like other formerly depressed patients, are vulnerable to relapse (Table 13.1). Nevertheless, electroconvulsive therapy is, in the minds of many psychiatrists and patients, a lesser evil than depression's misery, anguish, and risk of suicide. One recipient likened ECT to smallpox vaccine, which was saving lives before we knew how it worked.

Table 13.1 Comparing Treatments for Depression

	Cognitive Therapy	Antidepressant Drugs	Electroconvulsive Therapy
Percent marked improvement	60–80%	60–80%	80%
Relapse rate	moderate	moderate to high	moderate to high
Side effects	none	moderate	severe
Time scale	months	weeks	days
Overall	very good	useful to very good	useful to very good

Source: Adapted from Martin E. P. Seligman, *What you can change and what you can't* (New York: Knopf, 1994).

Psychosurgery

Because its effects are irreversible, **psychosurgery**—surgery that removes or destroys brain tissue to change behavior—is the most drastic and the least-used biomedical intervention. In the 1930s, Portuguese physician Egas Moniz developed what became the best-known psychosurgical operation: the **lobotomy**. Moniz found that cutting the nerves connecting the frontal lobes with the emotion-controlling centers of the inner brain calmed uncontrollably emotional and violent patients. After shocking the patient into a coma, a neurosurgeon would hammer an icepicklike instrument through each eye socket into the brain, then wiggle it to sever connections running up to the frontal lobes. If a bit crude, the whole procedure was at least easy and cheap, taking only about 10 minutes. During the 1940s and 1950s, tens of thousands of severely disturbed people were "lobotomized," and Moniz was honored with a Nobel prize (Valenstein, 1986).

psychosurgery surgery that removes or destroys brain tissue in an effort to change behavior.

lobotomy a now-rare psychosurgical procedure once used to calm uncontrollably emotional or violent patients. The procedure cut the nerves that connect the frontal lobes to the emotion-controlling centers of the inner brain.

Although the intention was simply to disconnect emotion from thought, the effect was often more drastic: The lobotomy produced a permanently lethargic, immature, impulsive personality. During the 1950s, after some 35,000 people had been lobotomized in the United States alone, calming drugs became available and psychosurgery was largely abandoned. Today, lobotomies are almost never performed. Other psychosurgery is used only in extreme cases. For example, if a patient suffers uncontrollable seizures, surgeons can deactivate the specific nerve clusters that cause or transmit the convulsions. Because such beneficial operations are irreversible, however, neurosurgeons perform them only as a last resort.

The effectiveness of the biomedical therapies reminds us of a fundamental lesson: We find it convenient to talk of separate psychological and physiological influences, but *everything psychological is physiological.* Every thought and feeling depends on the functioning brain. Every creative idea, every moment of joy or anger, every period of depression emerges from the electrochemical activity of the living brain. But the influence is two-way. Thus, when therapy relieves obsessive-compulsive behavior, PET scans reveal a calmer brain (Schwartz & others, 1996).

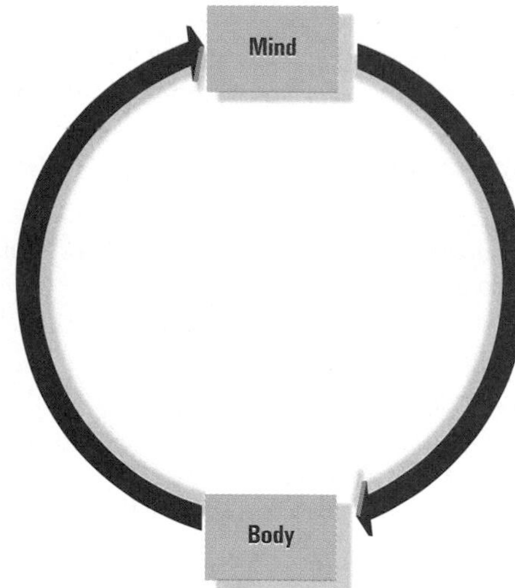

Mind-body interaction The biomedical therapies assume that mind and body are a unit: Affect one and you will affect the other.

Preventing Psychological Disorders

9. *What is the rationale for preventive mental health programs?*

Psychotherapies and biomedical therapies tend to locate the cause of psychological disorders within the disordered person. We infer that people who act cruelly must be cruel and that people who act "crazy" must be "sick." We attach labels to such people, thereby distinguishing them from "normal" folks. It follows, then, that we try to treat "abnormal" people by giving them insight into their problems, by changing their thinking, or by controlling them with drugs.

There is an alternative viewpoint: We could interpret many psychological disorders as understandable responses to a disturbing and stressful society. According to this view, it is not just the person who needs treatment, but also the person's social context. Better to prevent a problem by reforming a sick situation than to wait for a problem to arise and then treat it.

A story about the rescue of a drowning person from a rushing river illustrates this viewpoint: Having successfully administered first aid to the first victim, the rescuer spots another struggling person and pulls her out, too. After a half dozen repetitions, the rescuer suddenly turns and starts running away while the river sweeps yet another floundering person into view. "Aren't you going to rescue that fellow?" asks a bystander. "Heck no," the rescuer replies. "I'm going upstream to find out what's pushing all these people in."

"It is better to prevent than to cure."

Peruvian Folk Wisdom

Preventive mental health is upstream work. It seeks to prevent psychological casualties by identifying and alleviating the conditions that cause them. George Albee (1986) believes there is abundant evidence that poverty, meaningless work, constant criticism, unemployment, racism, and sexism undermine people's sense of competence, personal control, and self-esteem. Such stresses increase their risk of depression, alcoholism, and suicide.

Albee contends that those who care about preventing psychological casualties should therefore support programs that alleviate poverty, discrimination, and other demoralizing situations. We eliminated smallpox not by treating the afflicted but by inoculating the unafflicted. We conquered yellow fever by controlling mosquitos. Prevention of psychological problems means empowering those who have learned an attitude of helplessness, changing environments that breed loneliness, renewing the disintegrating family, and bolstering parents' and teachers' skills at nurturing children's self-esteem. Indeed, "Everything aimed at improving the human condition, at making life more fulfilling and meaningful, may be considered part of primary prevention of mental or emotional disturbance" (Kessler & Albee, 1975, p. 557).

"Mental disorders arise from physical ones, and likewise physical disorders arise from mental ones."

The Mahabharata
c. A.D. 200

There is more to the psychological disorders story than bad environments. Anxiety disorders, major depression, bipolar disorder, and schizophrenia are known biological events. Yet Albee reminds us again of one of this book's themes: *A human being is an integrated bio-psycho-social system.* For years we have trusted our bodies to physicians and our minds to psychiatrists and psychologists. That neat separation no longer seems valid. Chemical imbalances can produce schizophrenia and depression. And anger, depression, and stress, as Chapter 10 shows, can threaten our physical health. *"Mens sana in corpore sano,"* says an ancient Latin adage: A healthy mind in a healthy body.

REHEARSE IT!

15. Certain antipsychotic drugs are used to calm schizophrenia patients so that they can live outside the hospital. The drugs often bring relief from auditory hallucinations and other troubling symptoms. However, they can have unpleasant side effects, most notably

a. hyperactivity.
b. convulsions and momentary memory loss.
c. sluggishness, tremors, and twitches.
d. paranoia.

16. Valium and Librium, which depress central nervous system activity, are among the most heavily prescribed and abused drugs. These drugs are referred to as ____________ drugs.

a. antipsychotic
b. antianxiety
c. antidepressant
d. antineurotic

17. The antidepressant drugs seem to increase the availability of the neurotransmitters norepinephrine or serotonin, which appear to be scarce during depression. One antidepressant drug that often brings relief to patients suffering the manic-depressive mood swings of bipolar disorder is

a. dopamine.
b. Librium.
c. lithium.
d. Valium.

18. Two controversial biomedical therapies are electroconvulsive therapy (shock treatment) and lobotomy (a type of psychosurgery). Lobotomy, once used to treat uncontrollably violent patients, is no longer an accepted treatment. Electroconvulsive therapy, however, remains in use as a treatment for

a. depression.
b. severe depression.
c. schizophrenia.
d. anxiety disorders.

19. Being poor or unemployed undermines a person's self-esteem and sense of competence. An approach that seeks to alleviate poverty and other demoralizing situations that put people at high risk for developing psychological disorders is

a. biomedical therapy.
b. the humanistic approach.
c. empathy and active listening.
d. preventive mental health.

REVIEWING ■ *Therapy*

The Psychological Therapies

Treatment for psychological disorders encompasses both the psychological therapies, involving structured interactions, and the biomedical therapies, which alter neural functions. The major **psychotherapies** derive from the familiar psychoanalytic, humanistic, behavioral, and cognitive perspectives on psychology. Today, many therapists employ an **eclectic approach**, using a variety of therapies, depending on the patient's needs.

1. ***What are the aims and methods of psychoanalysis?***

Psychoanalysts try to help people gain insight into the unconscious origins of their disorders and to work through the accompanying feelings. To do so, an analyst draws on techniques such as free association and the **interpretation** of patients' dreams, **resistances**, and **transference** to the therapist of long-repressed feelings. Like psychoanalytic theory, **psychoanalysis** is criticized for after-the-fact interpretations and for being time-consuming and costly. Although traditional psychoanalysis is not practiced widely, its influence can be seen in the work of psychodynamic therapists who explore childhood experiences, who assume that defense mechanisms repress emotion-laden information, and who seek to help their clients achieve insight into the root of their problems.

2. ***What are the basic themes of humanistic therapy, such as Rogers' person-centered approach?***

Unlike psychoanalysts, humanistic therapists focus on clients' current conscious feelings and on their taking responsibility for their own growth. Carl Rogers, in his **person-centered therapy**, used **active listening** to express genuineness, acceptance, and empathy.

3. ***What are the assumptions and techniques of the behavior therapies?***

Behavior therapists worry less about promoting self-awareness and more about directly modifying problem behaviors. Thus, they may **countercondition** behaviors through **systematic desensitization** or **aversive conditioning**. Or they may apply operant conditioning principles with behavior modification techniques such as, in institutional settings, **token economies**.

4. ***What are the goals and techniques of the cognitive therapies?***

The **cognitive therapies**, such as Ellis' **rational-emotive therapy** and Beck's cognitive therapy for depression, aim to change self-defeating thinking by training people to look at themselves in new, more positive ways. Cognitive behavior therapy also helps clients to regularly practice new ways of thinking and talking.

5. ***In what group contexts do people receive therapy?***

Many therapeutic techniques can also be applied in a group context. Self-help and support groups, such as Alcoholics Anonymous, engage many millions of people. **Family therapy** treats the family as an interactive system from which problems may arise.

Evaluating Psychotherapies

6. ***What does research on psychotherapy reveal about its effectiveness?***

Because the positive testimonials of clients and therapists cannot prove that therapy is actually effective, psychologists have conducted hundreds of outcome studies of psychotherapy. These studies indicate that (1) people who remain untreated often improve; (2) those who receive psychotherapy are somewhat more likely to improve, regardless of what kind of therapy they receive and for how long; (3) mature, articulate people with specific behavior problems often receive the greatest benefits from therapy; but (4) placebo treatments or the sympathy and friendly counsel of "paraprofessionals" also tend to produce more improvement than occurs in untreated people. Different types of psychotherapy offer certain commonalities, such as new hope, a fresh perspective, and an empathic, caring relationship. Therapists do, however, differ in the values that influence their aims.

The Biomedical Therapies

7. ***What are the most common forms of drug therapy?***

As a result of discoveries in **psychopharmacology**, drugs have become the most widely used biomedical therapy. Antipsychotic drugs, used in treating schizophrenia, block dopamine activity; antianxiety drugs depress central nervous system activity; antidepressant drugs increase the availability of serotonin and norepinephrine; and **lithium** is a mood stabilizer prescribed for those with bipolar disorder.

8. ***How effective are electroconvulsive therapy and psychosurgery?***

Although controversial, a growing body of evidence indicates that **electroconvulsive therapy (ECT)** is an effective treatment for many severely depressed people who do not respond to drug therapy. Brain surgery has been found to alleviate specific problems, but the effects of radical psychosurgical procedures such as the **lobotomy** are irreversible and potentially drastic. Thus, **psychosurgery** is seldom performed.

Preventing Psychological Disorders

9. ***What is the rationale for preventive mental health programs?***

Advocates of preventive mental health argue that many psychological disorders could be prevented. Their aim is to change oppressive, esteem-destroying environments into more benevolent, nurturing environments that foster individual growth and self-confidence.

CRITICAL THINKING EXERCISE by Richard O. Straub

Now that you have read and reviewed Chapter 13, take your learning a step further by testing your critical thinking skills on the following practical problem-solving exercise.

Deborah is very satisfied with the large amount of time and money she has invested in psychotherapy. When she began therapy, her life was in crisis and she was desperate for help in overcoming her depressed, pessimistic attitude. After shopping around, she finally found an understanding cognitive therapist who made her feel she could get her life back on track. After three months of psychotherapy, Deborah is once again enjoying her life and attributes her recovery to the psychotherapy.

Vincent is a middle-aged manager of an auto parts store. He is under a lot of pressure at work, has a very negative attitude about life, and "blows up" frequently at minor family annoyances. Although he admits that he is depressed and complains to his family a lot, he doesn't feel there is anything wrong with him. His family disagrees and is concerned that he is increasingly showing signs of psychologically disordered behavior. At their insistence, Vincent reluctantly agrees to see a psychotherapist. He picks a name at random from the phone book and grudgingly endures several weeks of "overpriced gibberish" to appease his family. Despite the good efforts of the psychotherapist, who attempts to countercondition Vincent's maladaptive behaviors, Vincent shows no improvement following psychotherapy.

1. Assuming their initial problems were equally serious, what could account for Deborah's and Vincent's very different experiences with psychotherapy?
2. Deborah now swears by cognitive therapy, whereas Vincent is very critical of behavior therapy. Are their recommendations acceptable as scientific evidence regarding the effectiveness of psychotherapy? Why or why not?

Check your progress on becoming a critical thinker by comparing your answers to the sample answers found in Appendix B.

REHEARSE IT ANSWER KEY

1. a., **2.** a., **3.** d., **4.** c., **5.** c., **6.** b., **7.** a., **8.** d., **9.** c., **10.** d., **11.** b., **12.** c., **13.** d., **14.** a., **15.** c., **16.** b., **17.** c., **18.** b., **19.** d.

CHAPTER
14

Social Psychology

"We cannot live for ourselves alone," remarked the novelist Herman Melville, for "our lives are connected by a thousand invisible threads." **Social psychologists** explore these connections by scientifically studying how we *think about*, *influence*, and *relate* to one another.

Social Thinking

Especially when the unexpected occurs, we analyze why people act as they do. Does her warmth reflect romantic interest in me, or is that how she relates to everyone? Does his absenteeism signify laziness or a stressful work atmosphere?

Attributing Behavior to Persons or to Situations

1. ***How do we tend to explain others' behavior? How do we explain our own behavior?***

After studying how people explain others' behavior, Fritz Heider (1958) proposed an **attribution theory**. Heider noted that people usually attribute others' behavior either to their internal dispositions or to their external situations. A teacher, for example, may wonder whether a child's hostility reflects an aggressive personality (*a dispositional attribution*) or whether the child is reacting to stress or abuse (*a situational attribution*).

In class, we notice that Julie doesn't say much; over coffee, Jack talks nonstop. Attributing their behaviors to their personal dispositions, we decide that Julie is shy and Jack is outgoing. Because people do have enduring personality traits, such attributions are sometimes valid. However, we often overestimate the influence of personality and underestimate the influence of situation. In class, Jack may be as quiet as Julie. Catch Julie at a party and you may hardly recognize your quiet classmate. Underestimating such situational influences is known as the **fundamental attribution error**.

An experiment by David Napolitan and George Goethals (1979) illustrates the phenomenon. They had Williams College students talk, one at a time, with a

social psychology the scientific study of how we think about, influence, and relate to one another.

attribution theory the theory that we tend to give a causal explanation for someone's behavior, often by crediting either the situation or the person's disposition.

fundamental attribution error the tendency for observers, when analyzing another's behavior, to underestimate the impact of the situation and to overestimate the impact of personal disposition.

attitude a belief and feeling that predisposes one to respond in a particular way to objects, people, and events.

young woman who acted either aloof and critical or warm and friendly. Beforehand, they told half the students the woman's behavior would be spontaneous. They told the other half the truth—that she had been instructed to *act* friendly (or unfriendly). What effect do you suppose this information had?

None. The students disregarded the information. If the woman acted friendly, they inferred she really was a warm person. If she acted unfriendly, they inferred she really was a cold person. In other words, they attributed her behavior to her personal disposition *even when told that her behavior was situational*—that she was merely acting that way for purposes of the experiment.

You, too, have surely committed the fundamental attribution error. In judging, say, whether your psychology instructor is shy or outgoing, you have perhaps by now inferred that he or she has an outgoing personality. But you know your instructor only from the classroom, a situation that demands outgoing behavior. Catch the instructor in a different situation and you might be surprised (as some of my students are when confronting me in a pick-up basketball game). Outside their assigned roles, professors seem less professorial, presidents less presidential, servants less servile.

Recall from Chapter 11 that personality psychologists study the enduring, inner determinants of behavior that help to explain why different people act differently in a given situation. Social psychologists study the social influences that help explain why the same person will act differently in different situations.

The instructor, on the other hand, observes his or her own behavior in many different situations—in the classroom, in meetings, at home—and so might say, "Me, outgoing? It all depends on the situation. In class or with good friends, yes, I'm outgoing. But at conventions I'm really rather shy."

So, when explaining *our own* behavior, we are sensitive to how our behavior changes with the situations we encounter. When explaining *others'* behavior, particularly after observing them in only one type of situation, we often commit the fundamental attribution error: We disregard the situation and leap to unwarranted conclusions about their personality traits. We do so partly because we have learned to focus our attention more on the person than on the situational context. Meanwhile, the person's own attention focuses more on the situation to which he or she is reacting. Reverse the perspectives of actor and observer—by having each view a videotape replay of the situation from the other's perspective—and this reverses the attributions (Lassiter & Irvine, 1986; Storms, 1973). By seeing the world from the actor's perspective, the observers better appreciate the situation. Given an observer's point of view, the actors better appreciate their own personal style.

Outside their assigned roles, professors seem less professorial, presidents less presidential, servants less servile.

The Effects of Attribution

In everyday life we often struggle to explain others' actions. To what should we attribute them? A jury must decide whether a shooting was malicious or in self-defense. An unhappy wife and husband each ponder why the other behaves so selfishly. An interviewer must judge whether the applicant's geniality is genuine. When we make such judgments, our attributions—either to the person or to the situation—have important consequences (Fincham & Bradbury, 1993; Fletcher & others, 1990). Happily married couples attribute their spouse's tart-tongued remark to a temporary situation ("She must have had a bad day at work"). Unhappily married persons attribute the same remark to a mean disposition ("Why did I marry such a hostile person?").

"Otis, shout at that man to pull himself together."

Or consider the political effects of attribution: How do you explain poverty or unemployment? Researchers in Britain, India, Australia, and the United States (Furnham, 1982; Pandey & others, 1982; Wagstaff, 1982; Zucker & Weiner, 1993) report that political conservatives tend to attribute such social problems to the personal dispositions of the poor and unemployed themselves: "People generally get what they deserve. Those who don't work are often freeloaders. People who take initiative can still get ahead." "Society is not to blame for crime, criminals are," said one U.S. presidential candidate (Dole, 1996). Political liberals (and social scientists) are more likely to blame past and present situations: "If you or I had to live with the same poor education, lack of opportunity, and discrimination, would we be any better off?"

In evaluating employees, managers must also make attributions. They are likely to attribute the poor performance of workers to personal factors, such as low ability or lack of motivation. Workers who are doing poorly on a job recognize situational influences: inadequate supplies, poor working conditions, difficult co-workers, impossible demands (Rice, 1985).

The practical point to remember: Our attributions—to individuals' dispositions or to their situations—have real consequences.

Attitudes and Actions

Social psychology's single most important concept has been that of *attitudes*. **Attitudes** are beliefs and feelings that predispose our reactions to objects, people, and events. If we *believe* that someone is mean, we may *feel* dislike for the person and *act* unfriendly. "Change the way people think," said South African civil rights martyr Steve Biko, "and things will never be the same."

Do Our Attitudes Guide Our Actions?

2. *Under what conditions do our attitudes guide our behavior?*

"Thinking is easy, acting difficult, and to put one's thoughts into action, the most difficult thing in the world."

German poet Goethe
1749–1832

Although most persuasive appeals assume that changed attitudes can indeed change behavior, dozens of studies during the 1960s challenged this idea (Wicker, 1971). Moreover, studies of people's attitudes and behaviors regarding cheating, religion, and racial minorities revealed that folks often talk and act a different game.

But the seeming hypocrisy did startle social psychologists, most of whom shared Biko's belief that there is a close connection between thought and action, character and conduct, private words and public deeds. So they conducted many follow-up studies during the 1970s and 1980s (Kraus, 1991; Wallace & others, 1996). These studies reveal that our attitudes *will* guide our actions if:

- **Outside influences on what we say and do are minimal.** Social pressures may blur the underlying connection between our attitudes and actions by affecting either what we say or what we do (Figure 14.1). In 1990, four weeks before a U.S. congressional election, President George Bush and political leaders from both main parties asked members of the U.S. House of Representatives to pass a compromise deficit-reducing budget. Privately, most members of Congress agreed that the painful cuts and tax increases were essential to the nation's health: Among those retiring or unopposed for reelection, and thus facing little external pressure, 86 percent voted for the bill. For others, voting their privately held attitude was more difficult. Among the 36 representatives who were about to face angry voters in close races back home, there were no profiles in courage: All 36 voted against it.
- **The attitude is specifically relevant to the behavior.** People readily profess *general* attitudes that contradict their behavior. They proclaim love while yelling at their mate, cherish honesty while cheating on their income tax returns, and value good health while smoking and not exercising. Attitudes about the specific act do, however, guide action. Attitudes toward exercise predict exercising behavior.

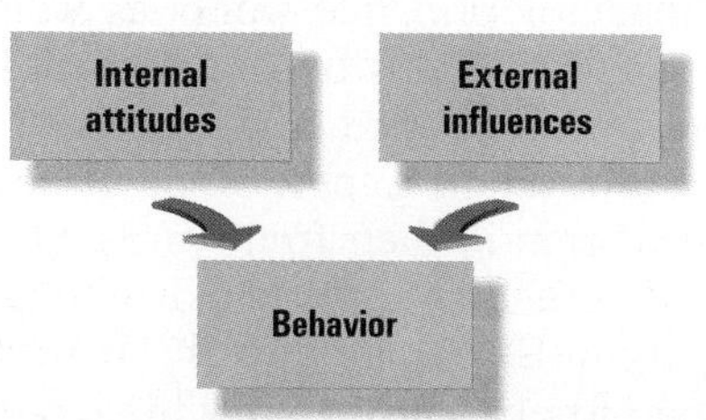

Figure 14.1 Attitudes, external influences, and behavior Our behavior is affected by our inner attitudes as well as by external social influences.

foot-in-the-door phenomenon the tendency for people who have first agreed to a small request to comply later with a larger request.

role a set of expectations about a social position, defining how those in the position ought to behave.

cognitive dissonance theory the theory that we act to reduce the discomfort (dissonance) we feel when two of our thoughts (cognitions) are inconsistent. For example, when we become aware that our attitudes and our actions clash, we can reduce the resulting dissonance by changing our attitudes.

- **We are keenly aware of our attitudes.** When we mindlessly follow habit or social expectations, our attitudes lie dormant. If something makes us self-conscious or reminds us of how we feel, we are truer to our convictions. For example, Martha Powell and Russell Fazio (1984) report that repeating an attitude makes it come to mind more quickly. Moreover, attitudes that come quickly to mind are more likely to guide our behavior (Fazio, 1990). When we know and are conscious of what we believe, we are true to ourselves.

Do Our Actions Affect Our Attitudes?

3. *Under what conditions does our behavior affect our attitudes?*

So, attitudes will affect behavior under certain circumstances: when other influences are minimal, when the attitude is specific to the behavior, and when people are mindful of their attitudes. Now consider a more surprising principle: People also come to believe in what they have stood up for. Many streams of evidence confirm that *attitudes follow behavior*. Here are two.

The Foot-in-the-Door Phenomenon

During the Korean War, many captured U.S. soldiers were imprisoned in war camps run by Chinese communists. Without using brutality, the captors secured the collaboration of hundreds of their prisoners in various activities. Some merely ran errands or accepted favors. Others made radio appeals and false confessions. Still others informed on fellow prisoners and divulged military information. When the war ended, 21 prisoners chose to stay with the communists. More returned home "brainwashed"—convinced that communism was a good thing for Asia.

People come to believe in what they have stood up for. Many streams of evidence confirm that attitudes follow behavior.

A key ingredient of the Chinese "thought-control" program was its effective use of the **foot-in-the-door phenomenon**—a tendency for people who agree to a small request to comply later with a larger one. The Chinese harnessed this phenomenon by gradually escalating their demands on the prisoners, beginning with harmless requests (Schein, 1956). Having "trained" the prisoners to speak or write trivial statements, the communists then asked them to copy or create something more important, noting, perhaps, the flaws of capitalism. The prisoners then participated in group discussions, wrote self-criticisms, or uttered public confessions. Once they had done so, perhaps to gain privileges, the prisoners then often adjusted their beliefs toward consistency with their public acts.

The point is simple, says Robert Cialdini (1993): To get people to agree to something big, "Start small and build." And be wary of those who would exploit you with the tactic. This chicken-and-egg spiral of actions feeding attitudes feeding actions enables behavior to escalate. A trivial act makes the next act easier. Succumb to a temptation and you will find the next temptation harder to resist.

Fortunately, the attitudes-follow-behavior principle works as well for good deeds as for bad. The foot-in-the-door tactic helps boost charitable contributions, blood donations, and product sales. In one experiment, researchers posing as safety-drive volunteers asked Californians to permit the installation of a large, poorly lettered "Drive Carefully" sign in their front yards. Only 17 percent consented. Other home owners were first approached with a small request: Would they display a 3-inch-high "Be a Safe Driver" sign? Nearly all readily agreed. When reapproached two weeks later to allow the large, ugly sign in their front yards, 76 percent consented (Freedman & Fraser, 1966).

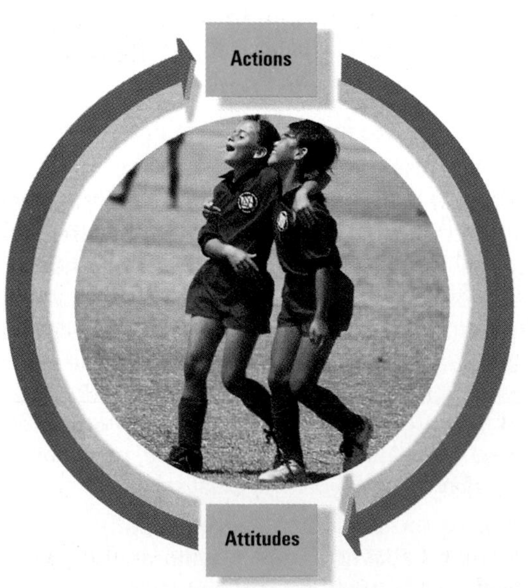

Attitudes follow behavior Cooperative actions, such as those performed by people on sports teams, feed mutual liking. Such attitudes, in turn, promote positive behavior.

In the years immediately following the introduction of school desegregation and the passage of the Civil Rights Act of 1964, white Americans expressed diminishing racial prejudice. And as Americans in different regions came to act more alike—thanks to more uniform national standards against discrimination—they began to think more alike. Experiments confirm that moral action has positive effects on the actor and that doing favors for another person often leads to greater liking of the person. We love people for the good we do them as well as for the good they do us. Evil acts shape the self, but so do moral acts.

Role Playing Affects Attitudes

In psychology, as in the theater, a **role** refers to a cluster of prescribed actions—the behaviors we expect of those who occupy a particular social position. When you adopt a new role—when you become a college student, a newlywed, or a new employee—you strive to follow the social prescriptions. At first, the behaviors may feel phony, because you are *acting* the role. The first weeks in the military feel artificial—as if one is pretending to be a soldier. The first weeks of a marriage may feel like "playing house." Before long, however, your behavior no longer feels forced. What began as play-acting in the theater of life becomes *you*.

Researchers have confirmed this effect by assessing people's attitudes before and after they adopt a new role. Sometimes this occurs in laboratory situations, sometimes in everyday situations, such as before and after taking a job. In one laboratory study, college students volunteered to spend time in a simulated prison devised by psychologist Philip Zimbardo (1972). Some he randomly designated as guards; he gave them uniforms, billy clubs, and whistles and instructed them to enforce certain rules. The remainder became prisoners; they were locked in barren cells and forced to wear humiliating outfits. After a day or two in which the volunteers self-consciously "played" their roles, the simulation became real—too real. Most of the guards developed disparaging attitudes, and some devised cruel and degrading routines. One by one, the prisoners broke down, rebelled, or became passively resigned, causing Zimbardo to call the study off after only six days.

In real life, the military junta then in power in Greece was training another group of men to become torturers (Staub, 1989). The men's indoctrination into their roles occurred in small steps. First, the trainee stood guard outside the interrogation cells—the "foot in the door." Next, he stood guard inside. Only then was he ready to become actively involved in the questioning and torture. As the nineteenth-century writer Nathaniel Hawthorne noted, "No man, for any considerable period, can wear one face to himself and another to the multitude without finally getting bewildered as to which may be true." Behavior affects attitudes. What we do, we gradually become.

Social roles are powerful Initially, both the obedient recruit and the abusive sergeant may have consciously adopted the behavior expected of them. In time, they may become the characters they are playing.

Why Do Our Actions Affect Our Attitudes?

Without doubt, then, actions can affect attitudes, sometimes turning prisoners into collaborators, doubters into believers, or mere acquaintances into friends. But why? One explanation is that we feel motivated to justify our actions. When aware that our attitudes and actions don't coincide, we experience tension, called *cognitive dissonance*. To relieve this tension, according to the **cognitive dissonance theory** proposed by Leon Festinger, people often bring their attitudes into line with their actions. It's as if people rationalize, "If I chose to do it (or say it), I must believe in it." The less coerced and more responsible we feel for a troubling act, the more dissonance we feel. The more dissonance we feel, the more motivated we are to find consistency, such as by changing our attitudes to help justify the act.

Dozens of experiments have confirmed cognitive dissonance by making people feel responsible for behavior that is inconsistent with their attitudes and that has foreseeable consequences. As a subject in one of these experiments, you might agree for a measly $2 to help a researcher by writing an essay that supports something you don't believe in (perhaps a tuition increase). Feeling responsible for the statements (which are not consistent with your attitudes), you likely would feel dissonance, especially if you thought an administrator would be reading your essay. How would you reduce the uncomfortable dissonance? One way would be to start believing your phony words. Let your pretense become your reality.

> ***"Sit all day in a moping posture, sigh, and reply to everything with a dismal voice, and your melancholy lingers. . . . If we wish to conquer undesirable emotional tendencies in ourselves, we must . . . go through the outward movements of those contrary dispositions which we prefer to cultivate."***
>
> William James
> *Principles of Psychology*
> 1890

The attitudes-follow-behavior principle has some heartening implications. Although we cannot directly control all our feelings, we can influence them by altering our behavior. If we are unloving, we can become more loving by behaving as if we were so—by doing thoughtful things, expressing affection, giving affirmation. If we are down in the dumps, we can do as cognitive therapists advise and talk in more positive, self-accepting ways with fewer self–put-downs. *The point to remember:* Changing our behavior can change how we think and feel. Just do it.

REHEARSE IT!

1. In explaining a person's behavior we tend to make the fundamental attribution error—we overestimate the impact of internal factors (such as disposition or personality) and underestimate the impact of the situation in which the behavior occurs. Thus, if we encounter a person seemingly high on drugs, we might attribute the person's behavior to

a. moral weakness or an addictive personality.
b. peer pressure.
c. the easy availability of the drug on city streets.
d. society's acceptance of drug use.

2. Whether our actions are really guided by our attitudes depends on several factors. For example, attitudes that are specifically relevant to a behavior are most likely to predict that behavior. Thus, we could best predict whether someone will vote in a mayoral election if we knew the person's attitude on

a. the value of democracy.
b. the benefits of efficient city government.
c. corruption in municipal affairs.
d. the importance of this particular election.

3. During the Korean War, the Chinese "brainwashed" soldiers to think that communism was a good thing for Asia. A key ingredient in their "thought-control" program was their ability to make use of the tendency of people who have first agreed to a small request to comply later with a larger request. This tendency is called

a. the fundamental attribution error.
b. the foot-in-the-door phenomenon.
c. the behavior-follows-attitudes principle.
d. role playing.

4. When we are aware that there is a discrepancy between our attitudes and our behavior, cognitive dissonance theory predicts that we will act to reduce the discomfort or dissonance we feel. The theory explains why

a. people who act against their attitudes tend to change their attitudes.
b. attitudes predict actions when social pressures are minimized.
c. changing an attitude—through persuasion—often fails to result in behavioral changes.
d. people are hypocritical, talking one way and acting another.

Social Influence

Social psychology's great lesson is the enormous power of social influence on our attitudes, beliefs, decisions, and actions. This influence can be seen in our conformity, compliance, and group behavior. Suicides, bomb threats, airplane hijackings, and UFO sightings all have a curious tendency to come in clusters. Armed with principles of social influence, advertisers and salespeople aim to sway our decisions to buy, to donate, to vote. Isolated with others who share their grievances, dissenters may gradually become rebels and rebels may become terrorists. During a lengthy stay in another part of the world, we may struggle with the new cultural norms. Let's examine the pull of these social strings. How strong are they? How do they operate?

conformity adjusting one's behavior or thinking to coincide with a group standard.

Conformity and Obedience

4. *What do experiments on conformity and compliance reveal about the power of social influence?*

Behavior is contagious. One person giggles, coughs, or yawns, and others in the group are soon doing the same. A cluster of people stand gazing upward, and passersby pause to do likewise. Laughter, even canned laughter, can be infectious. Bartenders and street musicians know to "seed" their tip cups with money to suggest that others have given.

Sometimes the effects of suggestibility are more serious. Sociologist David Phillips and his colleagues (1985, 1989) found that known suicides increase following a highly publicized suicide. So do fatal auto accidents and private airplane crashes (some of which disguise suicides)—and they do so only in areas where the suicide is publicized. Following film star Marilyn Monroe's suicide on August 6, 1962, the number of August suicides in the United States exceeded the usual count by 200. In Germany and the United States, suicide increases have also followed fictional suicides on soap operas and on dramas dealing with suicide (Gould & Shaffer, 1986; Hafner & Schmidtke, 1989; Phillips, 1982). Such copycat suicides help explain the clusters of teenage suicides that occasionally occur in some communities.

Suicides, bomb threats, airplane hijackings, and UFO sightings all have a curious tendency to come in clusters.

Group Pressure and Conformity

Suggestibility is a subtle type of **conformity**—adjusting our behavior or thinking to bring it into line with some group standard. To study conformity, Solomon Asch (1955) devised a simple test. As a participant in the study, you arrive at the experiment location in time to take a seat at a table where five people are already seated. The experimenter asks which of three comparison lines is identical to a standard line (Figure 14.2). You see clearly that the answer is Line 2 and await your turn to say so after the others. Your boredom with this experiment begins to show when the next set of lines proves equally easy.

Now comes the third trial, and the correct answer seems just as clear-cut, but the first person gives what strikes you as a wrong answer: "Line 3." When the second person and then the third and fourth give the same wrong answer, you sit up straight and squint. When the fifth person agrees with the first three, you feel your heart begin to pound. The experimenter then looks to you for your answer. Torn between the unanimity of your five fellow subjects and the evidence of your own eyes, you feel tense and much less sure of yourself than you were moments ago. You hesitate before answering, wondering whether you should suffer the discomfort of being viewed as an oddball. What answer do you give?

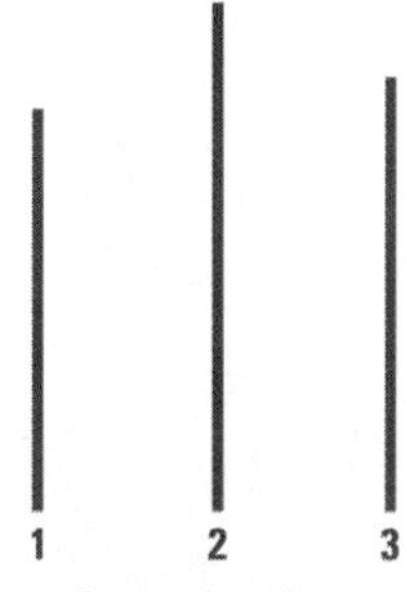

Figure 14.2 **Asch's conformity experiments** Which of the three comparison lines is equal to the standard line? What do you suppose most people would say after hearing five others say, "Line 3"? In this photo from one of Asch's experiments, the subject (center) shows the severe discomfort that comes from disagreeing with the responses of other group members.

normative social influence influence resulting from a person's desire to gain approval or avoid disapproval.

norm an understood rule for accepted and expected behavior. Norms prescribe "proper" behavior.

informational social influence influence resulting from one's willingness to accept others' opinions about reality.

In the experiments conducted by Asch and others after him, thousands of college students have experienced this conflict. Answering such questions alone, they erred less than 1 percent of the time. But it was a different story when several others—confederates working for the experimenter—answered incorrectly. Asch reports that more than one-third of the time his "intelligent and well-meaning" college subjects were then "willing to call white black" more than one-third of the time by going along with the group.

Conditions That Strengthen Conformity

Asch's procedure became the model for later investigations. Although experiments have not always found such a high degree of blind conformity, they reveal that conformity increases when

- we are made to feel incompetent or insecure.
- the group has at least three people. (Further increases in the group size yield not much more conformity.)
- the group is unanimous. (The support of a single fellow dissident greatly increases our social courage.)
- we admire the group's status and attractiveness.
- we have made no prior commitment to any response.
- others in the group observe our behavior.
- our culture strongly encourages respect for social standards.

Thus, we might predict the behavior of Marina, an eager but insecure new member of a prestigious sorority: Noting that the 40 other members appear unanimous in their plans for an upcoming fund-raiser, Marina is unlikely to voice her dissent.

Reasons for Conforming

Why do we clap when others clap, eat as others eat, believe what others believe, even see what others see? Frequently, it is to avoid rejection or to gain social approval. In such cases, we are responding to what social psychologists call **normative social influence**. We are sensitive to social **norms**—understood rules for accepted and expected behavior—because the price we pay for being different may be severe. Marco Lokar knows. During the 1991 Persian Gulf War, Lokar, an Italian, was the only Seton Hall University basketball player who chose not to display an American flag on his uniform. As the team traveled about, the fans' abusive responses to his nonconforming behavior became unbearable, so he quit the team and returned to Italy.

"Have you ever noticed how one example–good or bad–can prompt others to follow? How one illegally parked car can give permission for others to do likewise? How one racial joke can fuel another?"

Marian Wright Edelman
The Measure of Our Success
1992

But respecting norms is not the only reason we conform: The group may provide valuable information. Only a very stubborn person will *never* listen to others. When we accept others' opinions about reality, we are responding to **informational social influence**. "Those who never retract their opinions love themselves more than they love truth," observed Joseph Joybert, an eighteenth-century French essayist.

We perceive social influence as negative or positive, depending on our values. When influence supports what we approve, we applaud those who are "open-minded" and "sensitive" enough to be "responsive." When influence supports what we disapprove, we scorn the "submissive conformity" of those who comply with others' wishes. As we saw in Chapter 11, cultures vary in the value they place on individualism or collectivism. Western Europeans and those in most English-speaking countries tend to prize individualism more than conformity and obedience. In experiments conducted in 17 countries, conformity rates have been lower in individualistic cultures (Bond & Smith, 1996).

Stanley Milgram (1933–1984) The late social psychologist's obedience experiments now "belong to the self-understanding of literate people in our age" (Sabini, 1986).

Obedience

Social psychologist Stanley Milgram (1974) knew that people often comply with social pressures. But how would they respond to outright commands? To find out, he undertook what have become social psychology's most famous and controversial experiments. Imagine yourself as one of the nearly 1000 participants in Milgram's 20 experiments.

Responding to an advertisement, you come to Yale University's psychology department to participate in an experiment. Professor Milgram's assistant explains that the study concerns the effect of punishment on learning. You and another person draw slips from a hat to see who will be the "teacher" (which your slip says) and who will be the "learner." The learner is then led to an adjoining room and strapped into a chair that is wired through the wall to an electric shock machine. You sit down in front of the machine, which has switches labeled with voltages. Your task: to teach and then test the learner on a list of word pairs. You are to punish the learner for wrong answers by delivering brief electric shocks, beginning with a switch labeled "15 Volts—Slight Shock." After each error by the learner, you are to move up to the next higher voltage. With each flick of a switch, lights flash, relay switches click on, and an electric buzzing fills the air.

If you comply with the experimenter's instructions, you hear the learner grunt when you flick the third, fourth, and fifth switches. After you activate the eighth switch (labeled "120 Volts—Moderate Shock"), the learner shouts that the shocks are painful. After the tenth switch ("150 Volts—Strong Shock"), he cries, "Experimenter, get me out of here! I won't be in the experiment anymore! I refuse to go on!" You draw back when you hear these pleas, but the experimenter prods you: "Please continue—the experiment requires that you continue." If you still resist, he insists, "It is absolutely essential that you continue," or "You have no other choice, you *must* go on."

If you obey, you hear the learner's protests escalate to shrieks of agony as you continue to raise the shock level with each succeeding error. After the 330-volt level, the learner refuses to answer and soon falls silent. Still, the experimenter pushes you toward the final, 450-volt switch, ordering you to ask the questions and, if no correct answer is given, to administer the next shock level.

How far do you think you would follow the experimenter's commands? When Milgram surveyed people before conducting the experiment, most declared they would stop playing such a sadistic role soon after the learner first indicated pain and certainly before he shrieked in agony. This also was the prediction made by each of 40 psychiatrists whom Milgram asked to guess the outcome. When Milgram actually conducted the experiment with men aged 20 to 50, he was astonished to find that 63 percent complied fully—right up to the last switch.

Did the "teachers" figure out the hoax—that no shock was being delivered? Did they guess that the learner was a confederate who only pretended to feel the shocks? Did they realize that the experiment was really testing their willingness to comply with commands to inflict punishment? No, the teachers typically displayed genuine agony: They sweated, trembled, laughed nervously, and bit their lips.

Milgram's use of deception and stress triggered a debate over his research ethics. In his own defense, Milgram pointed out that, after the participants learned of the deception and actual research purposes, virtually none regretted taking part. When 40 of the "teachers" who had agonized most were later interviewed by a psychiatrist, none appeared to be suffering emotional aftereffects. All in all, said Milgram, the experiments provoked less stress than university students experience when facing and sometimes failing big exams (Blass, 1996).

Perhaps the participants obeyed because the learners' protests were not convincing. To preclude this possibility, Milgram repeated the experiment, with 40 new teachers. This time his confederate mentioned a "slight heart condition" while being strapped into the chair, and then he complained and screamed more intensely as the shocks became more punishing. Still, 65 percent of the new teachers complied fully (Figure 14.3).

In later experiments, Milgram discovered that subtle details of a situation powerfully influence people. When he varied the social conditions, the proportion of fully compliant subjects varied from 0 to 93 percent. Obedience was highest when

- the person giving the orders was close at hand and was perceived to be a legitimate authority figure.
- the authority figure was supported by a prestigious institution. (Milgram got somewhat less compliance when he dissociated his experiments from Yale University.)
- the victim was depersonalized or at a distance, even in another room. (Similarly, in combat with an enemy they can see, many soldiers either do not fire their rifles or do not aim them properly. Such refusals to kill are rare among those who operate the more distant weapons of artillery or aircraft [Padgett, 1989].)
- there were no role models for defiance; that is, no other subjects were seen disobeying the experimenter.

The power of legitimate, close-at-hand authorities is dramatically apparent in stories of those who received orders to carry out the atrocities of the Holocaust. In the summer of 1942, nearly 500 middle-aged German reserve police officers were dispatched to Jozefow, Poland, in German-occupied territory. On July 13, the group's visibly upset commander informed his recruits, mostly family men, that they had been ordered to round up the village's Jews, who were said to be aiding the enemy. Able-bodied men were to be sent to work camps, and all the rest were to be shot on the spot. Given a chance to refuse participation in the executions, only about a dozen immediately refused. Within 17 hours, the remaining 485 officers killed 1500 helpless women, children, and elderly Jews by shooting them in the back of the head as they lay face down. Faced with the pleadings of the victims, and seeing the gruesome results, some 20 percent of the officers did eventually dissent, managing either to miss their victims or to wander away and hide until the slaughter was over (Browning, 1992). But in real life, as in Milgram's experiments, the disobedient were the minority.

Figure 14.3 Milgram's follow-up obedience experiment In a repeat of the earlier experiment, 65 percent of the adult male "teachers" fully obeyed the experimenter's commands to continue. This was despite the "learner's" earlier mention of a heart condition and despite hearing cries of protest after 150 volts and agonized protests after 330 volts. (Data from Milgram, 1974)

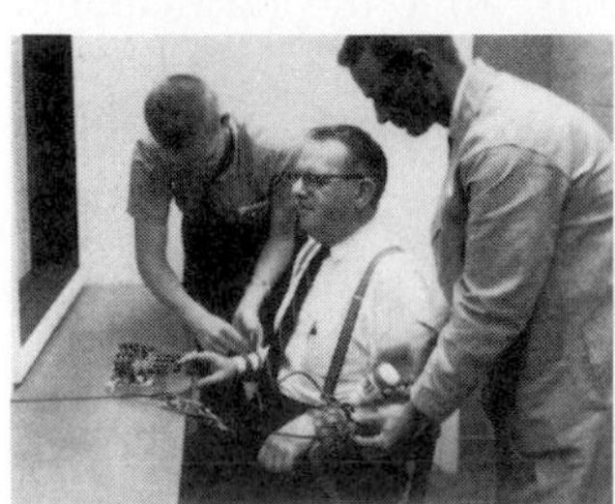

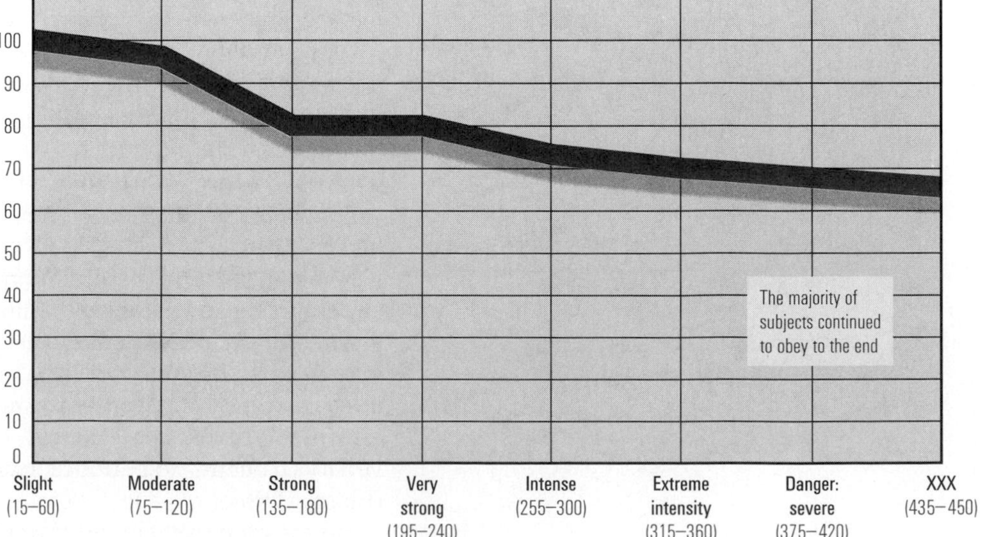

Standing up for democracy Some individuals—roughly one in three in Milgram's experiments—resist social coercion, as did this unarmed man in Beijing, by single-handedly challenging an advancing line of tanks the day after the 1989 Tiananmen Square student uprising was crushed.

Meanwhile, in the French village of Le Chambon, French Jews destined for deportation to Germany were being sheltered by villagers who openly defied orders to cooperate with the "New Order." The villagers' ancestors had themselves been persecuted and their pastors had been teaching them to "resist whenever our adversaries will demand of us obedience contrary to the orders of the Gospel" (Rochat, 1993). Ordered by police to give a list of sheltered Jews, the head pastor modeled defiance: "I don't know of Jews, I only know of human beings." Without realizing how long and terrible the war would be, or how much punishment and poverty they would suffer, the resisters made an initial commitment to resist. Supported by their beliefs, their role models, their interaction with one another, and their own initial acts, they remained defiant to the war's end.

Lessons From the Conformity and Obedience Studies

What do the Asch and Milgram experiments teach us about ourselves? How does judging the length of a line or flicking a shock switch relate to everyday social behavior? Recall from Chapter 1 that psychological experiments aim not to re-create the literal behaviors of everyday life but to capture and explore the underlying processes that shape those behaviors. Asch and Milgram devised experiments in which the subjects had to choose between adhering to their own standards and being responsive to others, a dilemma we all face frequently.

In Milgram's experiments, subjects were also torn between what they should respond to—the pleas of the victim or the orders of the experimenter. Their moral sense warned them not to harm another, but it also prompted them to obey the experimenter and to be a good research participant. With kindness and obedience on a collision course, obedience usually won.

Social influences can be strong enough to make people conform to falsehoods or capitulate to cruelty.

These experiments demonstrate that social influences can be strong enough to make people conform to falsehoods or capitulate to cruelty. "The most fundamental lesson of our study," Milgram noted, is that "ordinary people, simply doing their jobs, and without any particular hostility on their part, can become agents in a terrible destructive process" (1974, p. 6). Milgram entrapped his subjects not by asking them first to zap "learners" with enough electricity to make their hair stand on end. Rather, he exploited the foot-in-the-door effect, beginning with a little tickle of electricity and escalating step by step. In the subjects' minds, the little action became justified, making the next act tolerable. In Jozefow, in Le Chambon, and in Milgram's experiments, those who resisted often did so early. With the first acts of compliance or resistance, attitudes began to follow and justify behavior.

"I was only following orders."

Adolf Eichmann
Director of Nazi deportation of Jews to concentration camps

So it happens when people succumb, gradually, to evil. In any society, great evils sometimes grow out of people's compliance with little evils. The Nazi leaders suspected that most German civil servants would resist shooting or gassing Jews directly, but they found them surprisingly willing to handle the paperwork of the Holocaust (Silver & Geller, 1978). Likewise, when Milgram asked 40 men to administer the learning test while someone else did the shocking, 93 percent complied. Contrary to our images of devilish villains, evil doesn't require monstrous characters; it's enough to have ordinary people corrupted by an evil situation.

Drawing by Mel Yauk.

"Drive off the cliff, James, I want to commit suicide."

Group Influence

How do groups affect our behavior? To find out, social psychologists study the various influences that operate in the simplest of groups—one person in the presence of another—and those that operate in more complex groups, such as families, teams, and committees.

THINKING CRITICALLY

Social Influence

Many social influences are so subtle that we don't notice them. Or if we do, we think ourselves immune. "Yes, TV affects others," most people say, "but not me." Peer examples don't intimidate us. Role models don't sway us. Ads don't persuade us. For we are not slaves to fads, fashions, and opinions; we are true to ourselves.

Or so we think. The reality, as social influence research has a thousand times demonstrated, is that the influence others have on us, and we on them, is real, though often unnoticed. The extent to which influences go unnoticed, even by those looking for them, appears in studies of "facilitated communication" with autistic children. *Autism*, a pervasive disorder that appears during the preschool years, is marked by apparent indifference to others, minimal intelligible speech, and restricted interests and activities. Hoping to break down the walls that isolate such children, a facilitator holds or steadies the arm of an autistic child, who uses one finger to type words on a keyboard.

The technique is said to have produced breathtaking results with thousands of children, who suddenly begin typing intelligible words (sometimes elaborate sentences) which supposedly report their experiences and feelings. In several dozen cases where a person other than the parent was a facilitator, children have typed accusations of sexual abuse by their parents.

These spectacular findings and serious accusations led some people to question who was doing the communicating and the accusing—the child or the facilitator? To find out, Douglas Wheeler and his colleagues (1993) had 12 autistic children view pictures of everyday objects (a shoe, a book, a comb) and then type what they saw. When their facilitators saw the same picture, the children often typed the correct answer. When the facilitators saw a different picture, or no picture, the children were *never* correct (Figure 14.4).

More than two dozen other experiments have produced similar results, some by not allowing the facilitator to see the keyboard (Jacobson & others, 1995). Facilitated communication proponents reply (as have ESP—extrasensory perception—proponents) that the pressure of the testing situation obliterates the delicate phenomenon. But to the researchers, the more logical conclusion is the one reluctantly drawn by some of the shocked facilitators: The communication comes not from the child but from the facilitator (who misattributes the action to the child). The results stunned the well-meaning facilitators. Until the controlled experiment, they had no awareness of their influence on the child's movements. In this situation, as in so many others, human influence is subtle, unnoticed, even disbelieved, yet very real.

Figure 14.4 Testing facilitated communication The child responds after the facilitator and child see the same or different pictures. (Adapted from Wheeler & others, 1993)

Individual Behavior in the Presence of Others

5. ***In what ways are we affected by the mere presence of others?***

Appropriately, social psychology's first experiments focused on the simplest of all questions about social behavior: How are we influenced by the mere presence of others—by people watching us or joining us as we engage in various activities?

Social Facilitation

Having noticed that cyclists' racing times were faster when they competed against each other than when competing with a clock, Norman Triplett (1898) guessed that the presence of others boosts performance. To test his hypothesis,

social facilitation improved performance of tasks in the presence of others; occurs with simple or well-learned tasks but not with tasks that are difficult or not yet mastered.

social loafing the tendency for people in a group to exert less effort when pooling their efforts toward attaining a common goal than when individually accountable.

Triplett had adolescents wind a fishing reel as rapidly as possible. He discovered that they wound faster in the presence of someone who worked simultaneously on the same task. This stronger performance in the presence of others is known as **social facilitation**. For example, after a light turns green, drivers take about 15 percent less time to travel the first 100 yards when another car is beside them at the intersection than when they are alone (Towler, 1986). But on tougher tasks (learning nonsense syllables or solving complex multiplication problems), people perform less well when observers or others working on the same task are present.

Table 14.1 Home Advantage in Major Team Sports

Sport	Games Studied	Home Team Winning Percentage
Baseball	23,034	53.5%
Football	2,592	57.3
Ice hockey	4,322	61.1
Basketball	13,596	64.4
Soccer	37,202	69.0

From Courneya & Carron, 1992

Further studies revealed why others' presence sometimes helps and sometimes hinders performance (Guerin, 1986; Zajonc, 1965). When observed by others, people become aroused. This arousal strengthens the most likely response—the correct one on an easy task, an incorrect one on a difficult task. Thus, when observed, people perform well-learned tasks more quickly and accurately and unmastered tasks less quickly and accurately. James Michaels and his associates (1982) found that expert pool players who made 71 percent of their shots when alone made 80 percent when four people came to watch them. Poor shooters, who made 36 percent of their shots when alone, made only 25 percent when watched. The energizing effect of an enthusiastic audience probably contributes to the home advantage enjoyed by various sports teams. Studies of more than 80,000 college and professional athletic events in Canada, the United States, and England reveal that home teams win about 6 in 10 games (somewhat fewer for baseball and football, somewhat more for basketball and soccer—see Table 14.1).

The point to remember: What you do well, you are likely to do even better in front of an audience, especially a friendly audience; what you normally find difficult may seem impossible when others are watching.

Social facilitation also helps explain a funny effect of crowding: Comedy records that are mildly amusing to people in an uncrowded room seem funnier to people in a densely packed room (Aiello & others, 1983; Freedman & Perlick, 1979). As comedians and actors know, a "good house" is a full one. The arousal triggered by crowding amplifies other reactions, too. If sitting close, participants in experiments like a friendly person more, an unfriendly person less (Schiffenbauer & Schiavo, 1976; Storms & Thomas, 1977).

Social facilitation Skilled athletes often find they are "on" before an audience. What they do well, they do even better when people are watching.

Social Loafing

The social facilitation experiments test the effect of others' presence on performance on an individual task, such as shooting pool. What happens to performance when people perform the same task as a group? In a team tug-of-war, for example, do you suppose the effort that a person puts forth would be more than, less than, or the same as the effort he or she would exert in a one-on-one tug-of-war?

To find out, Alan Ingham and his fellow researchers (1974) asked blindfolded University of Massachusetts students to "pull as hard as you can" on a rope. When Ingham fooled the students into believing three others were also pulling behind them, they exerted only 82 percent as much effort as when they knew they were pulling alone.

To describe the diminished effort by those submerged in a group, Bibb Latané and his colleagues (1981; Jackson & Williams, 1988) coined the term **social loafing**. In 78 experiments conducted in the United States, India, Thailand, Japan, China, and Taiwan, social loafing occurred on various tasks, though it was especially common among men in individualistic cultures (Karau & Williams, 1993). In one such experiment, blindfolded subjects seated in a group clapped or shouted as loud as they could while listening through headphones to the sound of loud clapping or shouting. When told they were doing it with

deindividuation the loss of self-awareness and self-restraint occurring in group situations that foster arousal and anonymity.

group polarization the enhancement of a group's prevailing attitudes through discussion within the group.

groupthink the mode of thinking that occurs when the desire for harmony in a decision-making group overrides a realistic appraisal of alternatives.

the others, the subjects produced about one-third less noise than when they thought their individual efforts were identifiable.

Why? First, people acting as part of a group feel less accountable and therefore worry less about what others think. Second, they may view their contribution as dispensable (Harkins & Szymanski, 1989; Kerr & Bruun, 1983). As many leaders of organizations know, if group members share equally in the group's benefits regardless of how much they contribute, they may slack off and "free-ride" on the other group members' efforts.

Deindividuation

So, the presence of others can arouse people (as in the social facilitation experiments) or can diminish their feelings of responsibility (as in the social loafing experiments). Sometimes the presence of others both arouses people *and* diminishes their sense of responsibility. The result can be uninhibited behavior ranging from a food fight in the dining hall or screaming at a basketball referee to vandalism or rioting. Abandoning normal restraints to the power of the group is termed **deindividuation**. To be deindividuated is to be less self-conscious and less restrained when in a group situation.

Whether in a mob, at a rock concert, at a dance, or at worship, to lose self-consciousness (to become deindividuated) is to become more responsive to the group experience.

Deindividuation often occurs when group participation makes people feel aroused and anonymous. In one experiment, New York University women dressed in depersonalizing Ku Klux Klan–style hoods delivered twice as much electric shock to a victim as did identifiable women (Zimbardo, 1970). (As in all such experiments, the "victim" did not actually receive the shocks.) Similarly, tribal warriors who depersonalize themselves with face paints or masks are more likely than those with exposed faces to kill, torture, or mutilate captured enemies (Watson, 1973). Whether in a mob, at a rock concert, at a dance, or at worship, to lose self-consciousness (to become deindividuated) is to become more responsive to the group experience.

Effects of Group Interaction

6. *What are group polarization and groupthink?*

We have examined the conditions under which the presence of others can

- make easy tasks easier and difficult tasks harder.
- tempt people to free-ride on the efforts of others and motivate them to cycle faster.
- enhance humor and fuel mob violence.

Research shows how group interaction, too, can have both bad and good effects.

Group Polarization

Educational researchers have noted that, over time, initial differences between groups of college students often grow. If the first-year students at College *X* tend to be more intellectually oriented than those at College *Y*, that difference will probably be amplified by the time they are seniors. Similarly, if the political conservatism of students who join fraternities and sororities is greater than that of students who do not, the gap in the political attitudes of the two groups will probably widen as they progress through college (Wilson & others, 1975).

This enhancement of a group's prevailing tendencies—called **group polarization**—occurs when people within a group discuss attitudes that most of them

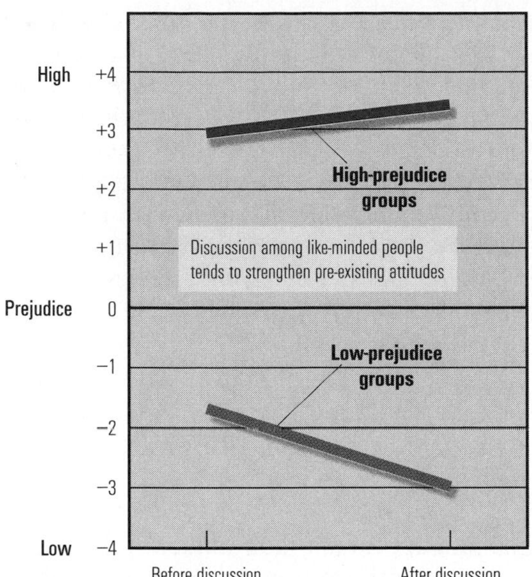

Figure 14.5 Group polarization If a group is like-minded, discussion strengthens its prevailing opinions. Talking over racial issues increased prejudice in a high-prejudice group of high school students and decreased it in a low-prejudice group. (Data from Myers & Bishop, 1970)

"One's impulse to blow the whistle on this nonsense was simply undone by the circumstances of the discussion."

Arthur M. Schlesinger, Jr. (1965, p. 255)

favor or oppose. For example, George Bishop and I discovered that when highly prejudiced high school students discussed racial issues, their attitudes became more prejudiced. When low-prejudice students discussed the same issues, they became more tolerant (Figure 14.5).

Group polarization can have beneficial results, as when it amplifies a sought-after spiritual awareness or strengthens the resolve of those in a self-help group. But it can also have dire consequences. From their analysis of terrorist organizations around the world, psychologists Clark McCauley and Mary Segal (1987) note that the terrorist mentality does not erupt suddenly. Rather, it arises among people who have come together because of a grievance and who become more and more extreme as they interact in isolation from moderating influences.

Groupthink

Does group interaction ever distort important group decisions? Social psychologist Irving Janis thought so when he first read the account by historian Arthur M. Schlesinger, Jr., of how U.S. President John F. Kennedy and his advisers blundered into an ill-fated plan to invade Cuba with 1400 CIA-trained Cuban exiles. When the invaders were easily captured and soon linked to the U.S. government, Kennedy wondered in hindsight, "How could we have been so stupid?"

To find out, Janis (1982) studied the decision-making procedures that led to the fiasco. He discovered that the high morale of the recently elected president and his advisers fostered a sense that the plan would succeed. To preserve the good group feeling, dissenting views were suppressed or self-censored, especially after the president voiced his enthusiasm for the scheme. Since no one spoke sharply against the idea, everyone assumed there was a consensus in favor of it. To describe this harmonious but unrealistic group thinking, Janis coined the term **groupthink**.

Janis and others then examined other historical fiascos—the failure to anticipate the 1941 Japanese attack on Pearl Harbor, the escalation of the Vietnam War, the U.S. Watergate cover-up, the Chernobyl nuclear reactor accident (Reason, 1987), and the U.S. space shuttle *Challenger* explosion (Esser & Lindoerfer, 1989). They discovered that in these cases, too, groupthink was fed by overconfidence, conformity, self-justification, and group polarization. Buoyed by a string of successful space shuttle launches, the NASA (National Aeronautics and Space Administration) management team approached the 1985 *Challenger* mission brimming with confidence but frustrated by launch delays. When the rocket booster's engineers opposed the launch because of dangers posed by freezing temperatures, group pressures to go ahead effectively silenced their warnings. Unless the engineers could *prove* that the rocket seals would not hold, the management group would not agree to another delay. Moreover, managers shielded the NASA executive who made the final "Go" decision from information about the warnings. Wrongly assuming that support was unanimous, he launched the *Challenger* on its one-way flight to annihilation.

Despite such fiascos and tragedies, Janis also knew that, with some types of problems, two heads are better than one. So he also studied instances in which U.S. presidents and their advisers collectively made good decisions. Examples were the Truman administration's formulation of the Marshall Plan, which offered assistance to Europe after World War II, and the Kennedy administration's actions to keep the Soviets from installing missiles in Cuba. In such instances—and in the business world, too, Janis believed—groupthink is prevented by a leader who welcomes various opinions, invites experts' critiques of developing plans, or even assigns people to identify possible problems. As the suppression of dissent bends a group toward bad decisions, so open debate often shapes good decisions.

"Truth springs from argument among friends."

Philosopher David Hume
1711–1776

culture the enduring behaviors, ideas, attitudes, and traditions shared by a large group of people and transmitted from one generation to the next.

personal space the buffer zone we like to maintain around our bodies.

gender role a set of expected behaviors for males and for females.

In affirming the power of social influence, we must not overlook our power as individuals. *Social control* (the power of the situation) and *personal control* (the power of the individual) interact. People aren't billiard balls. When feeling pressured, we may react by doing the opposite of what is expected, thereby reasserting our sense of freedom (Brehm & Brehm, 1981). Moreover, many of the situations that influence us are ones we helped create. If we expect people to be uncooperative and hostile, we may treat them in ways that elicit such behavior. Thus, our expectations may become *self-fulfilling prophecies*. In one experiment, men talked more charmingly by phone to women they believed to be beautiful. This led the women to respond more warmly—confirming the men's idea that attractive people are likeable (Snyder & others, 1977).

Minority Influence

7. *Can a minority sway a majority?*

The power of committed individuals also appears in their influence over their groups. Social history is often made by a minority that sways the majority. Were this not so, communism would be an obscure theory, Christianity would be a small Middle Eastern sect, and Rosa Parks' refusal to sit at the back of the bus would not have ignited the civil rights movement. Technological history, too, is often made by innovative minorities who overcome the majority's resistance to change. To many folks, the railroad was a nonsensical idea; some farmers feared that train noise would prevent hens from laying eggs. People derided Robert Fulton's steamboat as "Fulton's Folly." As Fulton later said, "Never did a single encouraging remark, a bright hope, a warm wish, cross my path." Much the same reaction greeted the printing press, the telegraph, the incandescent lamp, and the typewriter (Cantril & Bumstead, 1960).

Holding consistently to a minority opinion will not make you popular, but it may make you influential.

To better understand how minorities can sway majorities, European social psychologists led by Serge Moscovici (1985) have investigated groups in which one or two individuals consistently express a controversial attitude or an unusual perceptual judgment. They have repeatedly found that a minority that unswervingly holds to its position is far more successful in swaying the majority than is a minority that waffles. Holding consistently to a minority opinion will not make you popular, but it may make you influential. This is especially so if your self-confidence stimulates others to consider why you react as you do. Although people often follow the majority view publicly, they may privately develop sympathy for the minority view. Even when a minority's influence is not yet visible, it may be persuading some members of the majority to rethink their views (Wood & others, 1994). Thus, the combined powers of social thinking and social influence are enormous; but so are the powers of the committed individual.

Gandhi As the life of Mahatma Gandhi powerfully testifies, a consistent and persistent minority voice can sometimes sway the majority. The nonviolent appeals and fasts of the Hindu nationalist and spiritual leader were instrumental in winning India's independence from Britain in 1947.

Cultural Influences

8. *How do cultural norms and gender roles affect our behavior?*

The readers of this book are a diverse community, reaching from Africa to Australia and from Singapore to Sweden. Our varying **cultures** exert a powerful, long-lasting influence on our behaviors, ideas, attitudes, and traditions. Riding along with a unified culture is like riding a bike with the wind: As the wind carries us along, we hardly notice it's there. When we try riding *against* it we feel its force, as when moving to or visiting another part of the world. Face-to-face with a different culture, people become aware of the cultural winds. Visiting Europe, most North Americans are struck by the smallness of the cars, the left-handed use of the fork, the uninhibited attire on the beaches. Stationed in Saudi Arabia, European and American soldiers alike realized the liberality of their home cultures. Visiting North America, visitors from some cultures struggle to understand why people wear their dirty *street* shoes in the house, or why people find it fun to eat a picnic lunch out in the bush amid flies and ants.

"Live with vultures, become a vulture; live with crows, become a crow."

Laotian Proverb

Cultural Norms

All cultural groups evolve norms—their rules for accepted and expected behavior. Muslims use only the right hand's fingers for eating. The Japanese have norms for taking shoes off, for giving and opening gifts, and for showing respect to one's social superiors.

Sometimes social expectations seem oppressive. "Why should it matter how I dress?" However, norms also grease the social machinery. Prescribed, well-learned behaviors free us from self-preoccupation. Knowing when to clap or bow, which fork to pick up first at a dinner party, and what sorts of gestures and compliments are appropriate, we can relax and enjoy one another without fear of embarrassment or insult. Likewise, having a well-understood norm for greeting people in one's culture—by shaking hands or kissing each cheek—precludes awkward moments deciding whether to lead with one's hand or cheek.

Culture influences personal space Behavior that is seen as appropriate in one culture may violate the norms of another group. In Arab countries, such as Morocco, people typically require less personal space than do members of some European and North American groups.

When cultures collide, their differing norms often bemuse or befuddle. If someone invades our **personal space**—the portable buffer zone we like to maintain around our bodies—we feel uncomfortable. Scandinavians, most Americans, and the British prefer more personal space than do Latin Americans, Arabs, and the French (Sommer, 1969). At a social gathering, a Mexican seeking a comfortable conversation distance may waltz around a room with a backpedaling American. (You can demonstrate this at a party by playing space invader as you talk with someone.) To the American, the Mexican may seem intrusive; to the Mexican, the American may seem cold and standoffish.

Cultures also vary in their expressiveness. People whose roots are in northern European culture often perceive people from Mediterranean cultures as warm and charming but inefficient. The Mediterraneans, in turn, see the northern Europeans as efficient but cold and preoccupied with punctuality (Triandis, 1981).

Cultures vary in their pace of life, too. The British businessperson may feel frustrated by a Latin American client who arrives 30 minutes late for lunch. People from time-conscious Japan—where bank clocks keep exact time, pedestrians walk briskly, and postal clerks fill requests speedily—may find themselves growing impatient when visiting Indonesia, where clocks keep less exact time and the pace of life is slower (Levine, 1990). In adjusting to their host countries, U.S. Peace Corps volunteers reported that, after the language difference, two of their greatest culture shocks were the slower pace of life and the differing punctuality of the people (Spradley & Phillips, 1972).

An exercise in culture People in individualistic Western cultures sometimes see the Japanese as straitjacketed by their culture's norms. But from the Japanese perspective, the same tradition expresses a "serenity that comes to people who know exactly what to expect from each other." (Weisz & others, 1984)

Gender Roles

A whole set of norms defines our culture's **gender roles**—our expectations about the way men and women behave. Traditionally, men initiate dates, drive the car, and pick up the check; women cook the meals, buy and care for the children's clothes, and do the shopping. In the United States, for example, married mothers do 90 percent of the laundry and 13 percent of the car maintenance (Acock & Demo, 1994). And I don't have to tell you which parent, about 90 percent of the time in two-parent families, stays home with a sick child, arranges for the baby-sitter, or calls the doctor (Maccoby, 1995). Such formulas smooth social relations, saving awkward decisions about who does what. But they do so at a cost: If we deviate from such conventions, we may feel anxious.

Gender roles have tended not to offer equal rights and power. "There are no human societies in which women dominate men," notes Felicia Pratto (1996). As of 1997, women were 11.7 percent of the world's national legislators (Briscoe, 1997). They were also 3 percent of United Nations ambassadors, less than 1 percent of the presidents and prime ministers of the world's countries, and 0 percent of the Nobel awardees in economics since the prize began in 1901 (Sivard, 1995). Even on Israel's communal farms, the kibbutzim, where children were reared together—dressed, bathed, and given toys without regard to gender—boys grew up to do mostly masculine things and to dominate the leadership roles. Girls, though legally equal, played more with dolls and in adulthood sought more contact with children (Wilson, 1993).

Evolution may predispose men to the assertiveness and toughness that serve their reproductive goals, and women to the interpersonal skills that serve their reproductive goals (Archer, 1996). But we know that gender roles are not rigidly fixed by evolution, because they vary across cultures. Among the industrialized countries, gender roles vary. Women fill 48 percent of managerial positions in Switzerland, 28 percent in Austria, 17 percent in the United States, 3 percent in Ghana, and 2 percent in South Korea (Triandis, 1994). In North America, medicine and dentistry have been predominantly male occupations; in Russia, most medical doctors are women, as are most dentists in Denmark.

Gender roles vary over time as well as across cultures:

- As we began this century, only one country—New Zealand—granted women the right to vote. As we end it, only one democracy—Kuwait—did not (Briscoe, 1995).
- In 1938, only 1 in 5 Americans approved of "a married woman earning money in business or industry if she has a husband capable of supporting her"; by 1996, 4 in 5 approved (Niemi & others, 1989; Smith, 1997).
- In the flick of an apron, the number of U.S. college women hoping to be full-time homemakers plunged during the late 1960s and early 1970s (Figure 14.6).
- Since 1968, women's assertiveness has also increased (Twenge, 1996).
- In developing countries, too, gender roles are changing. Between 1970 and 1992, girls' enrollment in schools rose from 38 to 68 percent, shrinking the gender gap (UNICEF, 1996).

Cultural influences are huge, but cultures can change.

"So—against odds, women inch forwards."

Eleanor Roosevelt
1946

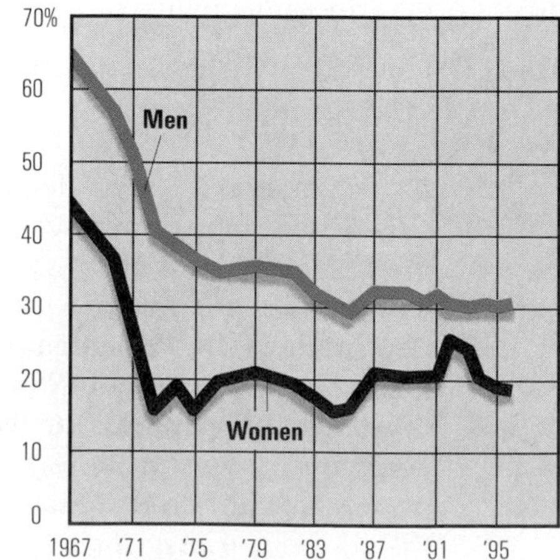

Figure 14.6 Changing attitudes about gender roles U.S. college students' endorsement of the traditional view of women's role has declined dramatically over the past three decades. (From Sax & others, 1996; Dey & others, 1991)

REHEARSE IT!

5. Conformity involves adjusting our thinking and behavior toward others in the group. Conformity studies have found that a person is most likely to conform to a group if

a. the group members have diverse opinions.
b. the person feels competent and secure.
c. the group consists of at least three people.
d. other group members will not observe the person's behavior.

6. In a classic experiment on obedience, Stanley Milgram tested his subjects' willingness to comply with a command to deliver painful high-voltage shocks to another person. Although no shocks were given, the subjects believed they were—and more than 60 percent complied with the experimenter's instruction to deliver stronger and stronger shocks. In subsequent experiments, Milgram's obedience studies showed that the rate of compliance was highest when

a. the victim was at a distance.
b. the experimenter was in another room.
c. other subjects refused to go along with the experimenter.
d. the subjects believed the victim had a heart condition.

7. In the presence of others we become aroused: Before an audience, a swimmer swims faster. Social facilitation—improved performance in the presence of others—occurs with

a. any physical task. **c.** a well-learned task.
b. new learning. **d.** competitive sports only.

8. When people are part of a group working toward a common goal, their individual efforts are diminished. Latané and his colleagues called this

a. minority influence. **c.** social loafing.
b. social facilitation. **d.** group polarization.

9. In a group situation that fosters arousal and anonymity, a person sometimes loses self-consciousness and self-control. This phenomenon, called deindividuation, is best illustrated by

a. improved performance in front of an audience.
b. unrestrained behavior at a mass rally.
c. evasion of responsibility in a group clean-up effort.
d. denial of one's own perceptions in the face of an opposing consensus.

10. If a group is like-minded, discussion strengthens its prevailing opinion. This effect is called

a. groupthink. **c.** group polarization.
b. minority influence. **d.** social facilitation.

11. Group interaction has the potential of distorting important group decisions. For example, when a group's desire for harmony overrides its realistic appraisal of alternatives, ________ has occurred.

a. group polarization **c.** social facilitation
b. groupthink **d.** deindividuation

12. In psychology, personal space refers to the portable buffer zone we like to maintain around our bodies. This space varies according to cultural norms. Which of the following prefer *less* personal space than the others?

a. Americans **c.** Arabs
b. British **d.** Scandinavians

13. Gender roles vary across cultures and over time. "Gender role" refers to our

a. sense of being male or female.
b. expectations about the way men and women behave.
c. biological sex.
d. beliefs about how men and women should earn a living.

Social Relations

Having sampled how we *think* about and *influence* one another, we come finally to social psychology's third focus—how we *relate* to one another. We will ponder the bad and the good: from prejudice, aggression, and conflict to attraction, altruism, and peacemaking.

Prejudice

Prejudice means prejudgment. It is an unjustifiable and usually negative attitude toward a group—typically a different cultural, ethnic, or gender group. Like all attitudes, **prejudice** is a mixture of beliefs (often overgeneralized and called **stereotypes**), emotions (hostility, envy, or fear), and predispositions to action (to discriminate). To *believe* that overweight people are gluttonous, to *feel* disgust for an overweight person, and to be hesitant to hire or date an overweight person is to be prejudiced.

Like other forms of prejudgment, prejudices are schemas that influence how we notice and interpret events. In one study, most whites perceived a white

prejudice an unjustifiable (and usually negative) attitude toward a group and its members. Prejudice generally involves stereotyped beliefs, negative feelings, and a predisposition to discriminatory action.

stereotype a generalized (often overgeneralized) belief about a group of people.

man shoving a black man as "horsing around." The same shove by the black man to the white was more often seen as "violent" (Duncan, 1976). Our preconceived ideas about people bias our impressions of their behavior. Prejudgments color perceptions.

How prejudiced are people? To find out, we can assess what they say and what they do. To judge by what Americans say, racial and gender attitudes have changed dramatically in the last half-century (Figure 14.7). Nearly everyone agrees that children of all races should attend the same schools and that women and men should receive the same pay for the same job.

As blatant prejudice wanes, subtle prejudice lingers. In socially intimate settings (dating, dancing, marrying), many people admit they would feel uncomfortable with someone of another race. (Although the percentage of interracial marriages in the United States has increased sixfold since 1960, this still represents only 2.4 percent of all married couples.) This fact helps explain why, in a survey of students at 390 colleges and universities, 53 percent of African-American students felt excluded from school activities (Hurtado & others, 1994). (Similar feelings were reported by 24 percent of Asian-Americans, 16 percent of Mexican-Americans, and 6 percent of European-Americans.) On National Basketball Association teams, where 80 percent of the 1997 players and all the top 15 scorers were African-American, a similar majority–minority dynamic can lead some white minority players to feel lonely or disrespected (Waller, 1998).

Elsewhere, hate still rages openly—between Israel's Palestinians and Jews, Bosnia's Serbs and Muslims, Rwanda's Tutsis and Hutus. In Europe and North America, "hate talk" and "hate crimes" still occasionally victimize immigrants, racial minorities, and homosexuals.

Around the world, gender prejudice and discrimination persist, too. Worldwide, two-thirds of children without basic schooling are girls. Thus, there are some 350 million illiterate men and 600 million illiterate women (United Nations, 1991, 1993). In Saudi Arabia, women are not allowed to drive. In Western countries, we pay more to those (usually men) who take care of our garbage than to those (usually women) who take care of our children. Despite gender equality in intelligence scores, people perceive their fathers as more intelligent than their mothers (Furnham & Rawles, 1995).

Nowhere are female infants left out on a hillside to die of exposure, as was the practice in ancient Greece. Yet even today boys are often valued more than their sisters. Because testing now enables sex-selective abortions, South Korean male births exceed female births by 14 percent (instead of the normal 5 percent). In China, male births during 1992 exceeded female births by 18 percent. Among China's preschoolers there are now nearly 120 boys for every 100 girls

Does perception change with race? The Italian clothing manufacturer Benetton asked this question with altered photographs in their company magazine. Skin color and facial features are, however, mere frosting on the physiological cake. On average, any two randomly chosen humans are 99.8 percent alike in the alphabetic sequence in their genetic code. Only 6 percent of their 0.2 percent difference is racial; 9 percent represents ethnic difference within races (for example, between French and Italians); 85 percent is individual differences within one's group. (Hoffman, 1994; Vines, 1995)

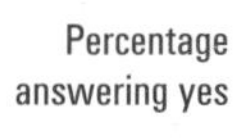

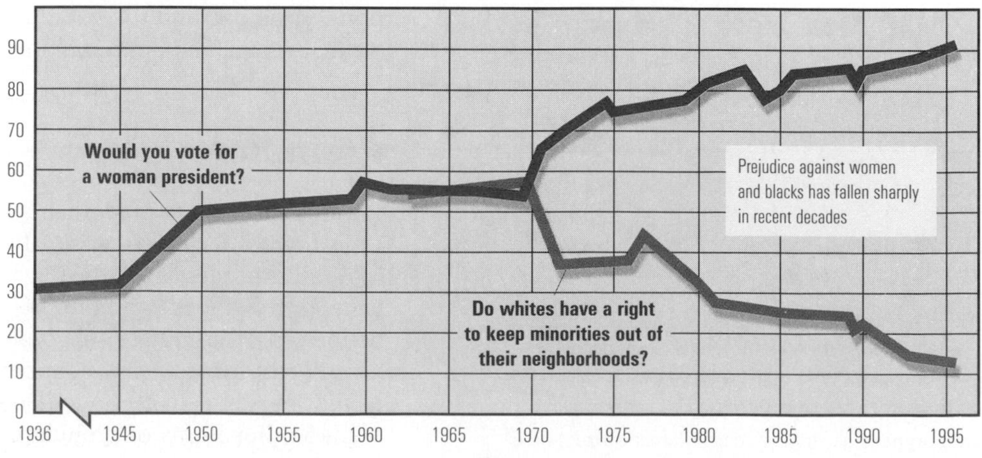

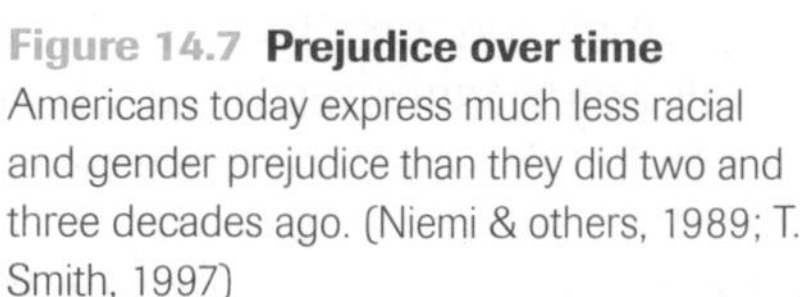

Figure 14.7 **Prejudice over time** Americans today express much less racial and gender prejudice than they did two and three decades ago. (Niemi & others, 1989; T. Smith, 1997)

ingroup bias the tendency to favor one's own group.

scapegoat theory the theory that prejudice provides an outlet for anger by providing someone to blame.

(Herbert, 1997; Kristof, 1993). Sex-selective neglect and abortions have resulted in China and India together having 76 million fewer females than they should have (Klasen, 1994). (You read that right: 76 *million* "missing women.")

Why does prejudice arise? Inequalities, social divisions, and emotional scapegoating are partly responsible. But so are the natural cognitive mechanisms by which we simplify our worlds.

"Unhappily the world has yet to learn how to live with diversity."

Pope John Paul II
Address to the United Nations
1995

Social Inequalities

9. *What are the social and emotional roots of prejudice?*

When some people have money, power, and prestige and others do not, the "haves" usually develop attitudes that justify things as they are. In the extreme case, slave owners perceived slaves as innately lazy, ignorant, and irresponsible—as having the very traits that "justified" enslaving them. More commonly, women are perceived as unassertive but sensitive and therefore suited for the caretaking tasks they often perform (Hoffman & Hurst, 1990). In short, prejudice rationalizes inequalities.

Discrimination also increases prejudice through the reactions it provokes in its victims, another example of a self-fulfilling prophecy. In his classic 1954 book, *The Nature of Prejudice*, Gordon Allport noted that being a victim of discrimination can produce either self-blame or anger. Both reactions may create new grounds for prejudice through the classic *blame-the-victim* dynamic. If the circumstances of ghetto life breed a higher crime rate, someone can then use the higher crime rate to justify continuing the discrimination that helped to create the ghetto.

"You cannot oppress people for over three centuries and then say it is all over and expect them to put on suits and ties and become decent attaché-carrying citizens and go to work on Wall Street."

Shelby Steele
"The New Segregation"
1992

Us and Them: Ingroup and Outgroup

The social definition of who you are—your ethnicity, gender, religion, academic major—also implies who you are not. Mentally drawing a circle that defines "us" excludes "them." Such group identifications typically promote an **ingroup bias**—a favoring of one's own group. Even an arbitrary us-them distinction—created by grouping people with the toss of a coin—leads people to show favoritism to their own group when dividing rewards (Tajfel, 1982; Wilder, 1981).

The urge to distinguish enemies from friends predisposes prejudice against strangers. To Greeks of the classical era, all non-Greeks were "barbarians." Most citizens in the coalition of countries fighting in the 1991 Persian Gulf War felt more pain over the few hundred dead Allied soldiers than over the reported 100,000 Iraqi dead. In Africa, where some 700 traditional societies cluster into fewer than 50 nations, people typically like and admire their own group and direct their hostility toward other groups (Segall & others, 1990). Most children believe their school is better than the other schools in town. Even chimpanzees have been seen to wipe clean the spot where they were touched by a chimp from another group (Goodall, 1986).

"All good people agree,
And all good people say
All nice people, like us, are We
And everyone else is They.
But if you cross over the sea
Instead of over the way
You may end by (think of it)
looking on We
As only a sort of They."

Rudyard Kipling
"We and They"
1926

Scapegoating

Prejudice springs not only from the divisions of society but also from the passions of the heart. Prejudice may express anger: When things go wrong, finding someone to blame can provide a target for one's anger. Evidence for this **scapegoat theory** of prejudice comes from high prejudice levels among economically frustrated people and from experiments in which a temporary frustration intensifies prejudice. Nazi leader Hermann Rausching once explained the

"If the Tiber reaches the walls, if the Nile does not rise to the fields, if the sky doesn't move or the Earth does, if there is famine, if there is plague, the cry is at once: 'The Christians to the lion!'"

Tertullian
Apologeticus
A.D. 197

Nazis' need to scapegoat: "If the Jew did not exist, we should have to invent him" (quoted by Koltz, 1983). Passions produce prejudice.

In addition to providing a handy emotional outlet for anger, despised outgroups can also boost ingroup members' self-esteem. In experiments, students who experience failure or are made to feel insecure will often restore their self-esteem by disparaging a rival school or another person (Cialdini & Richardson, 1980; Crocker & others, 1987). To boost our own sense of status, it helps to have others to denigrate. For this reason, a rival's misfortune sometimes provides a twinge of pleasure.

Cognitive Roots of Prejudice

10. *What are the cognitive roots of prejudice?*

Prejudice springs from the divisions of society, the passions of the heart, and also from the mind's natural workings. Stereotyped beliefs are a by-product of how we cognitively simplify the world.

Do racial stereotypes influence perceptions? Augustana College's black students' and white students' reactions to the O. J. Simpson "not guilty" criminal trial verdict mirrored racial differences in perceptions of his guilt or innocence (based partly on stereotypes of white police officers as honest or as oppressive).

Categorization

One way we simplify our world is to categorize things. A chemist classifies molecules as organic and inorganic. A mental health professional classifies people's psychological disorders by types. In categorizing people into groups we often stereotype them. Stereotypes may contain a germ of truth, yet they also bias our perceptions. Jeff Stone and his colleagues (1997) demonstrated this by having Princeton University students listen to a radio broadcast of a university basketball game, evaluating the performance of one player. Those introduced to him with a photo of a black player gave him a better performance evaluation than did those who had been shown a photo of a white player.

Categorization also biases our perceptions of diversity. Although we view ourselves as individuals, we overestimate the similarity of people within groups other than our own. "They"—the members of some other group—seem to look and act alike, but "we" are diverse (Bothwell & others, 1989). If we could see ourselves from a penguin's perspective, we would all look alike—much as penguins all look alike to us (though not to their fellow penguins). We are keenly sensitive to differences within our group, less so to differences within other groups. To those in one ethnic group, members of another often seem more alike in appearance, personality, and attitudes than they are.

We overestimate the similarity of people within groups other than our own. "They"—the members of some other group—seem to look and act alike, but "we" are diverse.

Vivid Cases

As noted in Chapter 8's discussion of the availability heuristic, we often judge the frequency of events by instances that readily come to mind. If asked whether black men jump higher than white men, those who think of Michael Jordon may overgeneralize that "yes, white men can't jump."

In an experiment with University of Oregon students, Myron Rothbart and his colleagues (1978) showed how we overgeneralize from vivid, memorable cases. They divided the students into two groups and showed them information about 50 men. The first group's list included 10 men arrested for nonviolent crimes, such as forgery. The second group's list included 10 men arrested for violent crimes, such as assault. When both groups later recalled how many men on their list had committed any sort of crime, the second group overestimated how many there were. Vivid (violent) cases, being readily available to memory, influence our judgments of a group.

just-world phenomenon the tendency of people to believe the world is just and that people therefore get what they deserve and deserve what they get.

aggression any physical or verbal behavior intended to hurt or destroy.

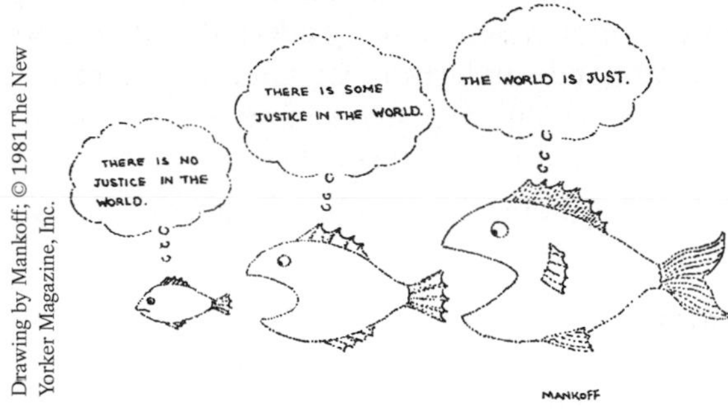

Drawing by Mankoff; © 1981 The New Yorker Magazine, Inc.

The Just-World Phenomenon

We noted earlier that people often justify their prejudice by blaming its victims. Bystanders may also blame victims, by assuming that the world is just and that people get what they deserve. In experiments, merely observing someone receive painful shocks has led many people to think less of the victim (Lerner, 1980). This **just-world phenomenon** reflects an idea we commonly teach our children—that good is rewarded and evil is punished. From this it is a short leap to assume that those who succeed must be good and those who suffer must be bad. Such reasoning enables the rich to see their own wealth, and the poor's misfortune, as justly deserved. As one German civilian is said to have remarked when visiting the Bergen-Belsen concentration camp shortly after World War II, "What terrible criminals these prisoners must have been to receive such treatment."

Hindsight bias is also at work here (Carli & Leonard, 1989). Have you ever heard people say that rape victims, abused spouses, or people with AIDS got what they deserved? An experiment by Ronnie Janoff-Bulman and her collaborators (1985) illustrates victim-blaming. When given an account of a date that ended with the woman's being raped, people perceived the woman as partly to blame. In hindsight, they thought, "She should have known better." (Victim-blaming also reassures people that it couldn't happen to them.) Others who were given the same account, without the rape, did not perceive the woman as inviting rape. Only when victimized was she faulted for her behavior.

Aggression

The most destructive force in our social relations is aggression. In psychology, *aggression* has a more precise meaning than it does in everyday usage. The assertive, persistent salesperson is not aggressive. Nor is the dentist who makes you wince with pain. But the person who passes along a vicious rumor about you and the attacker who mugs you are aggressive. **Aggression** is any physical or verbal behavior intended to hurt or destroy, whether done out of hostility or as a calculated means to an end.

Time and again, we have seen that behavior emerges from the interaction of biology and experience. Research on aggression reinforces that theme. For a gun to fire, the trigger must be pulled; with some people, as with hair-trigger guns, it doesn't take much to trip an explosion. Let us look first at biological factors that influence our thresholds for aggressive behavior. Then we'll examine the psychological factors that pull the trigger.

In only 25 years in the United States, guns have caused 800,000 suicidal, homicidal, and accidental deaths. Compared with people of the same sex, race, age, and neighborhood, those who keep a gun in the home (ironically, often for protection) are 2.7 times more likely to be murdered—nearly always by a family member or close acquaintance (Kellermann & others, 1993).

The Biology of Aggression

11. ***What biological factors influence aggressive behavior?***

According to one view, argued by Sigmund Freud and others, our species has a volcanic potential to erupt in aggression. Freud thought that we harbor not only positive survival instincts but also a self-destructive "death instinct" that we usually displace toward others as aggression or release in socially approved activities such as painting or sports.

Although aggression varies too widely from culture to culture and person to person to be considered an unlearned instinct, biology does influence aggression. Stimuli that influence aggressive behavior operate through our biological system. We can look for biological influences at three levels—genetic, neural, and biochemical. Our genes engineer our individual nervous systems, which operate electrochemically.

Genetic Influences

Animals have been bred for aggressiveness—sometimes for sport, sometimes for research. Twin studies suggest that genes influence human aggression as well (Raine, 1993; Rushton & others, 1986). If one identical twin admits to "having a violent temper," the other twin will often independently admit the same. Fraternal twins are much less likely to respond similarly.

Neural Influences

Animal and human brains have neural systems that produce aggressive behavior when stimulated (Moyer, 1983). Consider:

- The domineering leader of a caged monkey colony had a radio-controlled electrode implanted in a brain area that, when stimulated, inhibits aggression. When researchers placed the button that activates the electrode in the colony's cage, one small monkey learned to push it every time the boss became threatening.
- A mild-mannered woman had an electrode implanted in her brain's limbic system (in the amygdala) by neurosurgeons seeking to diagnose a disorder. Because the brain has no sensory receptors, she was unable to feel the stimulation. But at the flick of a switch she snarled, "Take my blood pressure. Take it now," and then stood up and began to strike the doctor.
- Intensive evaluation of 15 death-row inmates revealed that all 15 had suffered a severe head injury. Researcher Dorothy Lewis and her colleagues (1986) infer that many condemned criminals suffer unrecognized neurological disorders.

"It's a guy thing."

So, does the brain have a "violence center" that produces aggression when stimulated? Actually, no one spot in the brain controls aggression, because aggression is a complex behavior that occurs in particular contexts. Rather, the brain has neural systems that facilitate aggression, making it more likely, given provocation and no deterrents.

Biochemical Influences

Hormones, alcohol, and other substances in the blood influence the neural systems that control aggression. A raging bull will become a gentle Ferdinand when castration reduces its testosterone level. The same is true of castrated mice. When injected with testosterone, the castrated mice again become aggressive. However, the traffic between hormones and behavior is two-way. Testosterone heightens dominance and aggressiveness, but dominating or defeating behavior also boosts testosterone levels (Gladue & others, 1989).

> ***"We could avoid two-thirds of all crime simply by putting all able-bodied young men in cryogenic sleep from the age of 12 through 28."***
>
> David T. Lykken
> *The Antisocial Personalities*
> 1995

Although humans are less sensitive to hormonal changes, violent criminals tend to be muscular young males with lower-than-average intelligence scores, low levels of the neurotransmitter serotonin, and higher-than-average testosterone levels (Dabbs, 1992; Pendick, 1994; Wilson & Herrnstein, 1985). Drugs that sharply reduce their testosterone levels subdue their aggressive tendencies. With age, testosterone levels—and aggressiveness—diminish. Among teenage boys and adult men, high testosterone levels correlate with delinquency, hard drug use, and aggressive, bullying responses to frustration (Berman & others, 1993; Dabbs & Morris, 1990; Olweus & others, 1988).

> ***"He that is naturally addicted to Anger, let him Abstain from Wine; for it is but adding Fire to Fire."***
>
> Seneca
> *De Ira*
> A.D. 49

For both biological and psychological reasons, alcohol unleashes aggressive responses to frustration (Bushman, 1993; Ito & others, 1996; Taylor & Chermack, 1993). (Just *thinking* you've imbibed alcohol has some effect; but so, too, does unknowingly ingesting alcohol slipped into a drink.) Police data and prison surveys reinforce conclusions from experiments on alcohol and aggression. Aggression-prone people are more likely to drink and to become violent when intoxicated (White & others, 1993). People who have been drinking commit about 50 percent of sexual assaults and other violent crimes (Abbey & others, 1993, 1996; Seto & Barbaree, 1995).

frustration-aggression principle the principle that frustration—the blocking of an attempt to achieve some goal—creates anger, which can generate aggression.

Deindividuation + competition + alcohol = aggression A 1985 riot at a soccer game in Brussels left 38 dead and 437 injured. Aroused by the competition and loaded with alcohol, English fans lost all restraint when provoked by Italian fans. They attacked the Italians, who retreated and were then crushed against a wall.

The Psychology of Aggression

12. *What psychological factors influence aggressive behavior?*

Biological factors influence the ease with which the aggression trigger pulls. But what psychological factors do the pulling?

Aversive Events

Although suffering sometimes builds character, it may also bring out the worst in us. Studies in which animals or humans experience unpleasant events reveal that those made miserable often make others miserable (Berkowitz, 1983, 1989).

Being blocked short of a goal also increases people's readiness to aggress. This phenomenon is called the **frustration-aggression principle**: Frustration creates anger, which may in some people generate aggression, especially in the presence of an aggressive cue, such as a gun. Frustrations are instances of aversive events. Like frustration, other aversive stimuli—physical pain, personal insults, foul odors, hot temperatures, cigarette smoke, and a host of others—can also evoke hostility. For example, violent crime and spouse abuse occur more often in summer than winter, in hot years than in cooler years, in hot cities than in cooler cities, and on hotter days than on colder days (Anderson, 1989, and Figure 14.8).

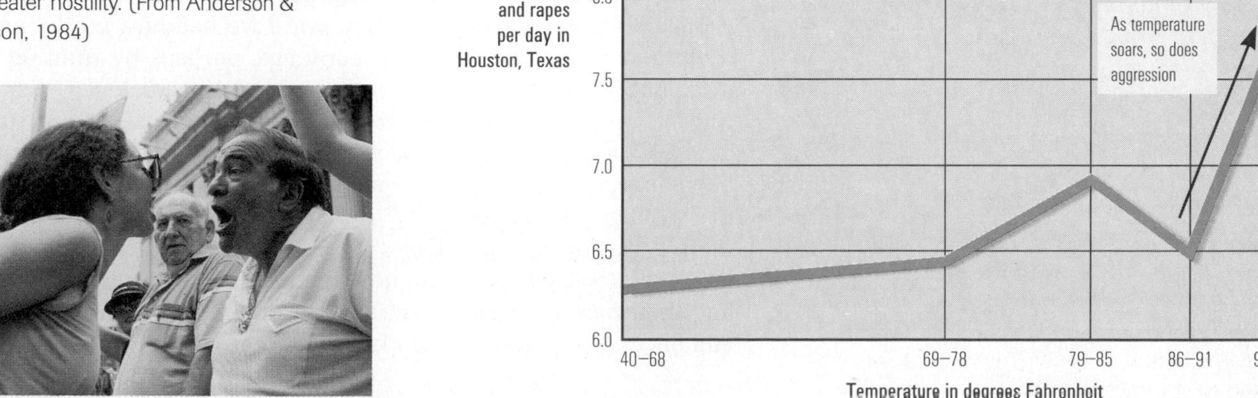

Figure 14.8 **Uncomfortably hot weather and aggressive reactions** Between 1980 and 1982 in Houston, murders and rapes were more common on days over 91°F, as shown in the graph. This finding is consistent with those from laboratory experiments in which people working in a hot room reacted to provocations with greater hostility. (From Anderson & Anderson, 1984)

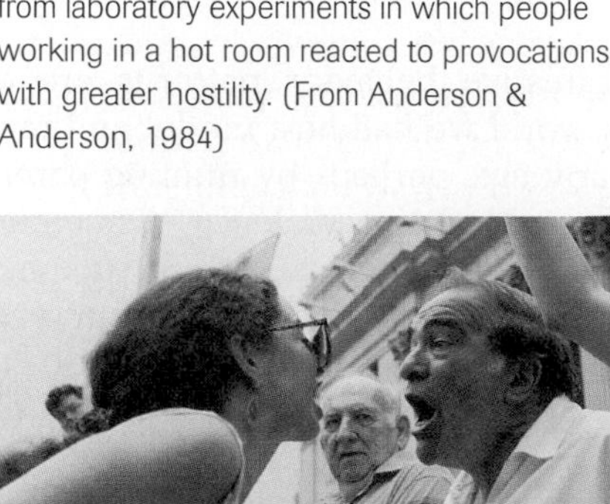

"Why do we kill people who kill people to show that killing people is wrong?"

National Coalition to Abolish the Death Penalty 1992

Learning to Express and Inhibit Aggression

Aggression may be a natural response to aversive events, but learning can alter natural reactions. Animals naturally eat when they are hungry. But if appropriately rewarded or punished, they can be taught either to overeat or to starve.

Aggressive reactions are more likely in situations where experience has taught us that aggression pays. Children whose aggression successfully intimidates other children may become more aggressive.

Aggressive behavior can be learned through direct rewards. Adults who have fought successfully to retain control of their "turf" become increasingly vicious. Aggression can also be learned through observation. Children who grow up observing aggressive models often imitate the behaviors they see. Parents of delinquent youngsters typically discipline with beatings, thus modeling aggression as a method of dealing with problems (Patterson & others, 1982, 1992). They also frequently cave into (reward) their children's tears and temper tantrums.

Different cultures model, reinforce, and evoke differing tendencies toward violence. For example, crime rates are higher in countries marked by a great disparity between rich and poor (Triandis, 1994). Richard Nisbett (1993) and Dov Cohen (1996) show how cultural values can also differ within a country. They analyzed violence among whites in southern U.S. towns settled by Scots-Irish herders whose tradition emphasized "manly honor," the use of arms to protect one's flock, and a history of coercive slavery. To this day, their cultural descendants have triple the homicide rates and are more supportive of physically punishing children, of warfare initiatives, and of uncontrolled gun ownership than are whites in New England towns settled by Puritan, Quaker, and Dutch farmer-artisans.

Social influence also appears in high violence rates among cultures and families that experience minimal father care (Triandis, 1994). For example, the U.S. Bureau of Justice Statistics reports that 70 percent of imprisoned juveniles did not grow up with two parents (Beck & others, 1988). (Because an absent parent is usually a father, most grew up with minimal father care.) The correlation between father absence and violence in the United States holds for all races, income levels, and locations (Prothrow-Stith, 1991; Staub, 1993). The correlation also appears over time. In 1960, just over 1 in 10 children did not live with two parents, and only 16,000 juveniles were arrested for violent crime. In 1995, more than 3 in 10 children did not live with two parents, and a similar-sized juvenile population produced more than 100,000 arrests for violent crime.

That many individuals lead gentle, even heroic, lives amid social stresses reminds us that individuals differ. The person matters. That people differ over time and place reminds us that environments differ. Situations matter. Aggressive behavior, like all behavior, arises from the interaction of persons and situations.

Once established, however, aggressive behavior patterns are difficult to change. To foster a kinder, gentler world we had best model and reward sensitivity and cooperation from an early age, perhaps by training parents how to discipline without modeling violence. Modeling violence—screaming and hitting—is precisely what exasperated parents often do. Parent-training programs advise a more positive approach. They encourage parents to reinforce desirable behaviors and to frame statements positively ("When you finish loading the dishwasher, you can go play," rather than "If you don't load the dishwasher, there'll be no playing.") One "aggression-replacement program" that brought down re-arrest rates of juvenile offenders and gang members taught the youth and their parents communication skills, trained them in how to control anger, and encouraged more thoughtful moral reasoning (Goldstein & Glick, 1994).

Television Watching and Aggression

Parents are hardly the only aggression models. During their first 18 years, most children spend more time watching television than they spend in school. In the United States, the average household has a TV on 51 hours a week (Elliot, 1996). In urban homes across the world, including those of South America and Asia, television is now commonplace. In Beijing, for example, the percentage of homes with television skyrocketed from 32 percent in 1980 to 95 percent by the end of the decade (Lull, 1988). With more than 1 billion TV sets now in homes around the world, CNN reaching 150 countries, and MTV videos seen from Alaska to Bangladesh, television is creating a global pop culture (Lippman, 1992). One can watch American programs in Perth or Prague and hear Mariah Carey and Garth Brooks from New Delhi to Newfoundland. But television does not reflect the world we live in. On evening dramas broadcast in the United States during the 1980s and early 1990s and often exported to the rest of the world, only one-third of the characters were women. Fewer than 3 percent were visibly old. One percent were Hispanic. Only 1 in 10 was married (Gerbner, 1993).

"The problem with television is that the people must sit and keep their eyes glued to a screen: the average American family hasn't time for it. Therefore the showmen are convinced that . . . television will never be a serious competitor of [radio] broadcasting."

The New York Times
1939

In 1993, U.S. network programs offered about 3 violent acts per hour during prime time, and 18 per hour during children's Saturday morning programs (Gerbner & others, 1993). During the last 20 years the average child has viewed some 8000 TV murders and 100,000 other acts of violence before finishing elementary school (Huston & others, 1992). If one includes cable programming and video rentals, the violence numbers escalate. (Popular rental films like *Die Hard*, with its 264 deaths, are much more violent than major network programs.) An analysis of more than 3000 network and cable programs aired during 1996–1997 revealed that nearly 6 in 10 featured violence, that 74 percent of the violence went unpunished, that 58 percent did not show the victims' pain, and that nearly half the incidents involved justified violence and nearly half involved an attractive perpetrator. These conditions, taken together, define the recipe for the violence viewing effect described below (Donnerstein, 1998).

Does viewing televised aggression influence some people to commit aggression? Was the judge who in 1993 tried two British 10-year-olds for their murder of a 2-year-old right to suspect that one possible influence was the aggressors' exposure to "violent video films"? To answer such questions, researchers have conducted correlational and experimental studies (Hearold, 1986; Wood & others, 1991).

THE FAR SIDE

Drawing by Gary Larson: "The Far Side" cartoon is reprinted by permission of Chronicle Features, San Francisco.

In the days before television

Correlational studies link young children's viewing of violence and their combativeness as teenagers and young adults (Eron, 1987; Turner & others, 1986). In the United States and Canada, a doubling of homicide rates between 1957 and 1974 coincided with the introduction and spread of television. Moreover, census regions that were late in acquiring television showed the homicide jump correspondingly later. Among white South Africans, who were first introduced to television in 1975, a similar near-doubling of the homicide rate did not begin until after 1975 (Centerwall, 1989). "There is absolutely no doubt," concluded the 1993 American Psychological Association Commission on Violence and Youth, "that higher levels of viewing violence on television are correlated with increased acceptance of aggressive attitudes and increased aggressive behavior."

But as we know from Chapter 1, correlation does not imply causation. So these correlational studies do not prove that viewing violence *causes* aggression (Freedman, 1988; McGuire, 1986). Maybe aggressive children prefer violent programs. Maybe children of neglectful or abusive parents are both more aggressive and more often left in front of the TV. Or maybe television simply reflects, rather than affects, violent trends.

To pin down causation, experimenters have randomly assigned some viewers to view violence and others to view entertaining nonviolence. Does viewing

TV's greatest effect may stem from what it displaces. Children and adults who spend four hours a day watching television spend four fewer hours in active pursuits—talking, studying, playing, reading, or socializing with friends. What would you have done with your extra time if you had never watched television, and how might you therefore be different?

"Thirty seconds worth of glorification of a soap bar sells soap. Twenty-five minutes worth of glorification of violence sells violence."

U.S. Senator Paul Simon
Remarks to the Communitarian Network
1993

CALVIN AND HOBBES

murder and mayhem make people react more cruelly when irritated? "The consensus among most of the research community," reported the National Institute of Mental Health (1982), "is that violence on television does lead to aggressive behavior by children and teenagers who watch the programs." The violence effect stems from a combination of factors—from *arousal* by the violent excitement, from the strengthening of violence-related *ideas*, from the erosion of one's *inhibitions*, and from *imitation* (Geen & Thomas, 1986). One research team observed a sevenfold increase in violent play immediately after children viewed the "Power Rangers" (Boyatzis & others, 1995). Boys' aggressive acts often precisely imitated the characters' flying karate kicks and other violent acts.

Television's unreal world, in which acts of aggression greatly outnumber acts of affection, can also affect our *thinking* about the real world. Those who avidly watch prime-time crime regard the world as more dangerous (Gerbner & others, 1993; Heath & Petraitis, 1987; Singer & Singer, 1986). Prolonged exposure to violence also desensitizes viewers; they become more indifferent to it when later viewing a brawl, whether on TV or in real life (Rule & Ferguson, 1986). While spending three evenings watching sexually violent movies, male viewers in one experiment became progressively less bothered by the raping and slashing. Three days later, they also expressed less sympathy for domestic violence victims than did research participants who had not been exposed to the films, and they rated the victims' injuries as less severe (Mullin & Linz, 1995). Indeed, as Edward Donnerstein and his co-researchers (1987) suggested, an evil psychologist could hardly imagine a better way to make people indifferent to brutality than to expose them to an escalating series of scenes, from fights to killings to the mutilations in slasher movies. Watching cruelty fosters indifference.

Sexual Aggression and the Media

A woman's risk of rape has varied across cultures and times (Koss & others, 1994). Over the last 30 years, America's reported rape rate has quadrupled. Recent surveys of both women and men reveal that unreported rapes—four in five committed by dates or acquaintances—greatly outnumber those reported (Schafran, 1995). In other surveys, about one-fifth of women report that a man has forced them to do something sexually, about one-half report some form of unwanted sexual coercion, and most report experiencing verbal sexual harassment (Craig & others, 1989; Laumann & others, 1994; Sandberg & others, 1985). Similar levels of sexual coercion have been reported in Canadian, Australian, and New Zealand surveys (Koss & others, 1994; Patton & Mannison, 1995).

What factors might explain the modern epidemic of sexual aggression? Alcohol consumption—often linked with aggression—has not increased. We do know that sexually coercive men typically are sexually unrestrained and hostile in their relationships with women (Figure 14.9). Might changes in the media have contributed to such tendencies?

Coinciding with the increase in sexual aggression has been, thanks to the home video business, easier access to *R*-rated "slasher films" and *X*-rated films. Content analyses reveal that *X*-rated films mostly depict quick, casual sex between strangers, but that scenes of rape and sexual exploitation of women by men are also common (Cowan & others, 1988; NCTV, 1987; Yang & Linz, 1990).

Rape scenes often portray the victim at first fleeing and resisting her attacker, then becoming aroused and finally driven to ecstasy. Most men are not sexually aroused (as measured by a "penile plethysmograph") while viewing rape depictions. But convicted rapists are. So are normal men if they have been drinking or if, after being aroused by exercise, a woman's insults anger them (Barbaree & Marshall, 1991). In less graphic form, the same unrealistic script—she resists,

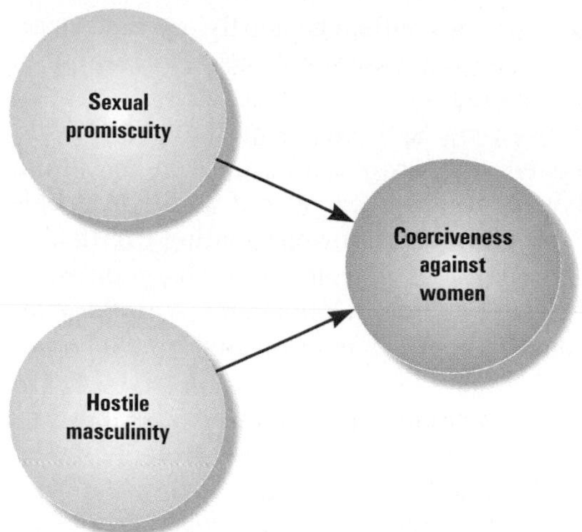

Figure 14.9 Men who sexually coerce women The recipe for coercion against women combines an impersonal approach to sex with hostile and traditionally masculine attitudes. (Adapted from Neil Malamuth, 1996)

In follow-up studies, Zillmann (1989) found that after massive exposure to X-rated sexual films, men and women became more accepting of extramarital sex, of women's sexual submission to men, and of a man's seducing a 12-year-old girl. As people heavily exposed to televised crime perceive the world as more dangerous, so people heavily exposed to pornography see the world as more sexual.

Pornography means different things to different people. Following Webster's dictionary, some define pornography as erotic depictions intended to excite sexual arousal. Others define it as sexual materials that exploit, degrade, or subordinate women.

Some media critics have also worried about media models of an "impulsive sexuality" that encourage uncommitted sex (a predictor of sexual violence) and father-absent families (a predictor of juvenile violence).

he persists, she melts—is commonplace in TV scenes and in romance novels. The woman who first thwarts the insistent man ends up passionately kissing him. In *Gone With the Wind*, Scarlett O'Hara is carried to bed screaming and wakes up singing. Most rapists accept this "rape myth"—the idea that some women invite or enjoy rape and get "swept away" while being "taken" (Brinson, 1992). (In actuality, rape is not only traumatic, it also frequently harms women's reproductive and sexual health [Golding, 1996].)

Laboratory experiments reveal that repeated viewing of *X*-rated films (even if nonviolent) makes one's own partner seem less attractive (page 330), makes women's friendliness seem more sexual, and makes sexual aggression seem less serious (Harris, 1994). In one such experiment, Dolf Zillmann and Jennings Bryant (1984) showed undergraduates six brief, sexually explicit films a week for six weeks. A control group viewed nonerotic films during the same six-week period. Three weeks later, both groups read a newspaper report about a man convicted but not yet sentenced for raping a hitchhiker. When asked to suggest an appropriate prison term, those who had viewed sexually explicit films recommended sentences half as long as those recommended by the control group.

In search of possible media effects on men's willingness to aggress against women, experimenters examined the effect of film viewing on men's acceptance of the rape myth. Neil Malamuth and James Check (1981) compared reactions of University of Manitoba men who were shown either two nonsexual movies or two movies depicting a man sexually overpowering a woman. A week later, when surveyed by a different experimenter, those who had seen the films with mild sexual violence were more accepting of violence against women and reported themselves a little more likely to rape if assured they could get away with it. Further experiments showed that viewing slasher movies, such as *The Texas Chainsaw Massacre*, can also lead viewers to trivialize rape.

Other experiments have explored the effect of violent versus nonviolent films on men's willingness to deliver supposed electric shocks to women who earlier provoked them. (Although such experiments cannot study actual sexual violence, they can assess a man's willingness to hurt a woman.) These experiments suggest that it's not eroticism but depictions of sexual *violence* (whether in *R*-rated slasher films or *X*-rated films) that most directly affect men's acceptance and performance of aggression against women. A 1986 conference of 21 social scientists, including many of the researchers who conducted these experiments, produced a consensus (Surgeon General, 1986): "Pornography that portrays sexual aggression as pleasurable for the victim increases the acceptance of the use of coercion in sexual relations." Contrary to much popular opinion, viewing such depictions does not provide an outlet for bottled-up impulses. Rather, "in laboratory studies measuring short-term effects, exposure to violent pornography increases punitive behavior toward women."

TV Violence, Pornography, and Society

Significant behaviors such as violence usually have many determinants, making any single explanation an oversimplification. Asking what causes violence is therefore like asking what causes cancer. Those who study the effects of asbestos exposure on cancer rates may remind us that asbestos is indeed a cancer cause, but only one among many. Likewise, report Neil Malamuth and his colleagues (1991, 1995), several factors can create a predisposition to sexual violence; they include not only the media but also child abuse, dominance motives, and disinhibition by alcohol. Still, if media depictions of violence can disinhibit and desensitize; if viewing sexual violence fosters hostile, domineering attitudes and behaviors; and if viewing pornography leads viewers to trivialize rape, devalue their partners, and engage in uncommitted sex, then media influence is not a minor issue.

conflict a perceived incompatibility of actions, goals, or ideas.

social trap a situation in which the conflicting parties, by rationally pursuing their self-interests, become caught in mutually destructive behavior.

Social psychologists attribute the media's influence partly to the *social scripts* they provide. When we find ourselves in new situations, uncertain how to act, we rely on social scripts provided by our culture. After so many episodes of "Power Rangers," followed by Sylvester Stallone and Arnold Schwarzenegger action films, youngsters may acquire a script—a mental tape for how to act—that gets played when they face real-life conflicts. Challenged, they may "act like a man" by intimidating or eliminating the threat. Likewise, after viewing 15 sexual innuendoes and acts per prime-time TV hour—nearly all involving impulsive, short-term relationships—youths may acquire sexual scripts they later enact in real-life relationships (Sapolsky & Tabarlet, 1991).

"If we expect families to teach children not to solve their problems with guns and violence, we need cultural and media signals and public policies that demonize rather than glamorize and support violence."

Children's Defense Fund
1992

Might public consciousness be raised by making people aware of the information you have just been reading? In the 1940s, movies often depicted African-Americans as childlike, superstitious buffoons. Today, such images are offensive. In the 1960s and 1970s, entertainment from rock music to movies such as *Easy Rider* glamorized drug use. Responding to a tidal change in cultural attitudes, the entertainment industry now more often portrays drugs as dangerous. Even gratuitous cigarette smoking largely disappeared until the 1990s, whereupon its reappearance was accompanied by a new surge in teen smoking rates. Responding to growing public concern about violence and the media, television violence levels declined in the early 1990s (Gallup, 1993; Gerbner & others, 1993). The growing sensitivity to violence has raised hopes that, without violating artistic freedom, society might someday look back with embarrassment on the days when movies "entertained" people with scenes of torture, mutilation, and sexual coercion.

"What we're trying to do is raise the level of awareness of violence against women and pornography to at least the level of awareness of racist and Ku Klux Klan literature."

Gloria Steinem (1988)

Conflict

13. *What social processes fuel conflict?*

We live in surprising times. With astonishing speed, democratic movements have swept away totalitarian rule in Eastern European countries, and hopes for a new world order have displaced the Cold War chill. Yet world spending for arms and armies continues to drain $2 billion per day from spending for housing, nutrition, education, and health. Knowing that, as the UNESCO motto declares, wars begin in human minds, psychologists have wondered what causes destructive conflict. How might the perceived threats of social diversity be replaced by a spirit of cooperation?

To a social psychologist, a **conflict** is a seeming incompatibility of actions, goals, or ideas. The elements of conflict are much the same at all levels, from nations in an arms race to cultural disputes within a society to individuals in marital strife. In each situation, people become enmeshed in a destructive social process that produces results no one wants. Among these destructive processes are social traps and distorted perceptions.

A social trap In the Atlantic waters off Newfoundland, those who fished knew that their individual catch was their livelihood and, by itself, hardly depleted the whole fish population. Such reasoning by everyone, including outsiders, depleted fish stocks. The result: Newfoundland's fishing fleet sits idle and an economy is in ruins during a 1990s fishing moratorium. This unemployed fisherman has been forced to use his boat for firewood.

Social Traps

In some situations, we can enhance our collective well-being by pursuing our personal interests. As capitalist Adam Smith wrote in *The Wealth of Nations* (1776), "It is not from the benevolence of the butcher, the brewer, or the baker that we expect our dinner, but from their regard to their own interest." In other situations, the parties involved may become caught up in mutually harmful behavior as they pursue their own ends. Such situations are **social traps**.

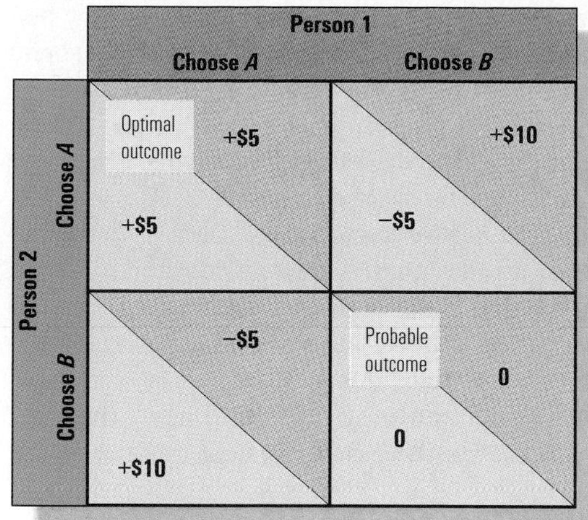

Figure 14.10 Social trap game matrix By pursuing our self-interest and not trusting others, we can end up losers. To illustrate this, imagine playing the game above. The pink triangles show the outcomes for Person 1, which depend on the choices made by both persons. If you were Person 1, would you choose *A* or *B*? (This game is called a "non-zero-sum game" because the outcomes need not add up to zero; both sides can win or both can lose.)

Consider the simple game matrix in Figure 14.10, which is similar to those used in experiments with thousands of people. In this game, both sides can win or both can lose, depending on the players' individual choices. Pretend that you are Person 1, and that you and Person 2 will each receive the amount shown after you separately choose either *A* or *B*. (You might invite someone to look at the matrix with you and take the role of Person 2.) Which do you choose—*A* or *B*?

As you ponder the game, you will discover that you and Person 2 are caught in a dilemma. If you both choose *A*, you both benefit, making $5 each. Neither of you benefits if you both choose *B*, for neither of you make anything. Nevertheless, on any single trial you serve your own interests if you choose *B*: You can't lose, and you might make $10. But the same is true for the other person. Hence, the social trap: As long as you both pursue your own immediate best interest and choose *B*, you will both end up with nothing—the typical result—when you could have made $5.

Many real-life situations similarly pit people's individual interests against their communal well-being. Individual whalers reason that the few whales they take will not threaten the species and that if they didn't take them, others would anyway. The result: A species of whales becomes endangered. The individual car owner and homeowner reasons, "It would cost me comfort or money to buy a more fuel-efficient car and furnace. Besides, the fossil fuels I burn don't add much to the greenhouse gases." When others reason similarly, the collective result threatens disaster—global warming.

Social traps challenge us to find ways of reconciling our right to pursue our personal well-being with our responsibility for the well-being of all. Psychologists are therefore exploring ways to convince people to cooperate for their mutual betterment—through agreed-upon *regulations*, through better *communication*, and through promoting *awareness* of our responsibilities toward community, nation, and the whole of humanity (Dawes, 1980; Linder, 1982; Sato, 1987). Under such conditions, people more often cooperate, whether playing laboratory games or playing the real game of life.

Enemy Perceptions

Psychologists have noted a curious tendency for those in conflict to form diabolical images of each other. These distorted images are so similar that we call them *mirror-image perceptions*: As we see them—as untrustworthy and evil intentioned—so they see us. Thus, during the early 1980s, the U.S. government viewed the communist support of guerrillas trying to overthrow the government of El Salvador as evidence of an "evil empire" at work. Meanwhile, the Soviets saw the U.S. support of guerrillas trying to overthrow the government of Nicaragua as the work of "imperialist warmongers." As enemies change, so do perceptions. In American minds and media, the "bloodthirsty, cruel, treacherous" Japanese of World War II later became our "intelligent, hardworking, self-disciplined, resourceful allies" (Gallup, 1972).

Psychologists have noted a curious tendency for those in conflict to form diabolical images of each other. These distorted images are so similar that we call them mirror-image perceptions.

We have considered the psychological roots of biased perceptions. The *self-serving bias* leads each party to accept credit for good deeds and to shuck the blame for bad deeds (Chapter 11). Although two nations admit to a buildup of military forces, the *fundamental attribution error* leads each to see the other's actions as arising from an aggressive disposition and to view its own buildup as necessary self-defense. Information about each other's actions is then filtered, interpreted, and remembered through preconceived *stereotypes*. Group interaction among like-minded policymakers may *polarize* these tendencies, lead-

"Why do you see the speck that is in your brother's eye, but do not notice the log that is in your own eye?"

Jesus
Luke 6:41–42

ing to *groupthink*, whereby each sees its own group as more moral, thereby justifying retaliation. In Soviet-U.S. relations, such biases resulted in the social perceptions that fueled the arms race: Each side (1) wished for mutual arms reduction, but (2) wanted above all to avoid disarming while the other armed, and (3) perceived the other side as wanting above all to gain an arms advantage (Plous, 1993).

Another result of such perceptions is a vicious cycle of hostility. If Victor believes Samantha is annoyed with him, he may snub her, causing her to act in ways that justify his perception. As with individuals, so with countries. Perceptions confirm themselves by influencing the other country to react in ways that seem to justify them. The self-fulfilling prophecy rides again.

Now that we've considered the bad side of our social relations—prejudice, aggression, and conflict—let's focus on the positive side of social relations—attraction, altruism, and peacemaking.

14. Experiments show that when people are temporarily frustrated, they express more intense prejudice. When things go wrong, prejudice provides an outlet for our anger–and gives us someone to blame. This effect is best described by

a. ingroup bias.
b. scapegoat theory.
c. Freud's theory on the death instinct.
d. the just-world phenomenon.

15. Stereotypes are a natural by-product of our usual ways of thinking. For example, we tend to judge the frequency of events in terms of cases that come readily to memory. Thus, if several well-publicized murders are committed by members of a particular group, we tend to react with fear and suspicion toward all members of the group. In other words, we

a. blame the victim.
b. overgeneralize from vivid, memorable cases.
c. create a scapegoat.
d. categorize people incorrectly.

16. Aggression is physical or verbal behavior that is intended to hurt someone. We find biological influences on aggression at three levels: the genetic, the neural, and the biochemical. Evidence of a biochemical influence on aggression is the finding that

a. aggressive behavior varies widely from culture to culture.
b. animals can be bred for aggressiveness.
c. stimulation of an area of the brain's limbic system produces aggressive behavior.
d. a higher-than-average level of the hormone testosterone is associated with violent behavior in males.

17. Studies show that delinquent young people tend to have parents who relied on beatings to enforce discipline. This demonstrates that aggression can be

a. learned through direct rewards.
b. triggered by exposure to violent media.
c. learned through observation of aggressive models.
d. caused by hormone changes at puberty.

18. There is considerable controversy about the effects of heavy exposure to television programs showing violence. However, most experts would agree that repeated viewing of television violence

a. makes all viewers significantly more aggressive.
b. has little effect on viewers.
c. dulls the viewer's sensitivity to violence.
d. makes viewers angry and frustrated.

19. A 1986 conference of social scientists who studied the effects of pornography on ordinary adult men generally agreed that violent pornography

a. has little effect on most viewers.
b. is the primary cause of reported and unreported rapes.
c. leads viewers to be more accepting of coercion in sexual relations.
d. has no short-term effects, other than arousal and entertainment.

20. Conflicts often arise from destructive social processes. In many situations, individuals, in rationally pursuing their self-interests, get caught up in a behavior that harms both themselves and others. This destructive social process is called

a. gameplaying.
b. mirror-image perception.
c. a social trap.
d. the fundamental attribution error.

mere exposure effect the phenomenon that repeated exposure to novel stimuli increases liking of them.

Attraction

Pause a moment and think about your relationships with two people—a close friend and someone who has stirred in you feelings of romantic love. What factors lead to friendship and romance? What factors help us sustain these relationships?

We endlessly wonder how we can win others' affection and what makes our own affections flourish or fade. Do birds of a feather flock together or do opposites attract? Does familiarity breed contempt or liking? Does absence make the heart grow fonder or is out of sight out of mind? Social psychology suggests some answers.

Familiarity breeds acceptance When this rare white penguin was born in the Sydney, Australia, zoo, his tuxedoed peers ostracized him. Zookeepers thought they would need to dye him black to gain acceptance. But after three weeks of contact, the other penguins came to accept him.

The Psychology of Attraction

14. *What psychological factors promote attraction?*

What is the psychological chemistry that binds two people together in that special sort of friendship that helps one cope with all other relationships? Consider three ingredients of our liking for one another.

Proximity

Before friendships become close, they must begin. Proximity—geographic nearness—is perhaps the most powerful predictor of friendship. Proximity provides opportunities for aggression, but much more often it breeds liking. Study after study reveals that people are most likely to like, and even to marry, those who live in the same neighborhood, who sit nearby in class, who work in the same office, who share the same parking lot. Look around.

Why is proximity so conducive to liking? Obviously, part of the answer is the greater availability of those we often meet. But there is more to it than that. For one thing, repeated exposure to novel stimuli—be they nonsense syllables, musical selections, geometric figures, Chinese characters, human faces, or the letters of our own name—increases our liking for them (Moreland & Zajonc, 1982; Nuttin, 1987). This phenomenon, which is now exploited by advertisers, we call the **mere exposure effect**. Within certain limits (Bornstein, 1989), familiarity breeds fondness. Richard Moreland and Scott Beach (1992) demonstrated this by having four equally attractive women silently attend a 200-student class for 0, 5, 10, or 15 class sessions. At the end of the class, students were shown slides of each woman and asked to rate their attractiveness. The most attractive? The ones they'd seen most often. The phenomenon will come as no surprise to the young Taiwanese man who wrote more than 700 letters to his girlfriend, urging her to marry him. She did marry—the mail carrier (Steinberg, 1993).

For our ancestors, the mere exposure phenomenon was adaptive. What was familiar was generally safe and approachable. What was unfamiliar was more often

The mere exposure effect The mere exposure effect applies even to ourselves. Because the human face is not perfectly symmetrical, the face we see in the mirror is not the same as the one our friends see. Most of us prefer the familiar mirror image, whereas our friends like the reverse (Mita & others, 1977). Minister of State Jim Bolger known to New Zealanders is shown at left. The person Bolger sees in the mirror each morning is shown at right, and that's the photo he would probably prefer.

dangerous and threatening. Robert Zajonc (1998) concludes that evolution has hard-wired into us the tendency to bond with those who are familiar and to be wary of those who are unfamiliar. Gut-level prejudice against those culturally different may thus be a primitive, automatic emotional response (Devine, 1995).

Physical Attractiveness

Once proximity affords you contact, what most affects your first impressions: The person's sincerity? Intelligence? Personality? Hundreds of experiments reveal that it is something far more superficial: appearance.

"Personal beauty is a greater recommendation than any letter of introduction."

Aristotle
Apothegems
330 B.C.

For people taught that "beauty is only skin deep" and that "appearances can be deceiving," the power of physical attractiveness is unnerving. In one early study, Elaine Hatfield and her co-workers (Walster & others, 1966) randomly matched new University of Minnesota students for a "Welcome Week" dance. Before the dance, all took a battery of personality and aptitude tests. On the night of the blind date, the couples danced and talked for more than two hours and then took a brief intermission to rate their dates. What determined whether they liked each other? So far as the researchers could determine, only one thing mattered: physical attractiveness (which had been rated by the researchers beforehand). Both the men and the women liked good-looking dates best. Although women are more likely than men to *say* that another's looks don't affect them, a man's looks do affect women's behavior (Feingold, 1990; Sprecher, 1989; Woll, 1986).

"Love comes in at the eye."

William Butler Yeats
"A Drinking Song"
1909

People's physical attractiveness has wide-ranging effects. It predicts their dating frequency, their feelings of popularity, and others' initial impressions of their personalities. We perceive attractive people, even children and those of our own sex, to be happier, more sensitive, more successful, and more socially skilled, though not more honest or compassionate (Eagly & others, 1991; Feingold, 1992; Hatfield & Sprecher, 1986). Attractive and well-dressed people are more likely to make a favorable impression on potential employers (Cash & Janda, 1984; Solomon, 1987). To judge from their gazing times, even babies prefer attractive over unattractive faces (Langlois & others, 1987).

That looks are important may seem unfair and unenlightened. Two thousand years ago the Roman statesman Cicero felt the same way: "The final good and the supreme duty of the wise person is to resist appearance." Cicero might be reassured by two other findings about attractiveness.

First, people's attractiveness is surprisingly unrelated to their self-esteem and happiness (Diener & others, 1995; Major & others, 1984). One reason may be that, except after comparing themselves with superattractive people, few people view themselves as unattractive (Thornton & Moore, 1993). (Thanks, perhaps, to the mere exposure effect, most of us become accustomed to our faces.) Another reason is that strikingly attractive people are sometimes suspicious that praise may be simply a reaction to their looks. When less attractive people are praised for their work, they are more likely to accept it as sincere (Berscheid, 1981).

"The thin, narrow-shouldered ectomorph who was yesterday's spinster librarian is today's high fashion model; the plump and buxom endomorph who was a Victorian romantic ideal today is eating cottage cheese and grapefruit, and weighing in every Tuesday at Weight Watchers."

Phyllis Bronstein-Burrows (1981)

Cicero might also find comfort in knowing that attractiveness judgments are relative. The standards by which judges crown "Miss Universe" hardly apply to the whole planet. Rather, beauty is in the eye of the culture—most accepted standards of beauty are influenced by one's place and time. Hoping to look attractive, people in different cultures have pierced their noses, lengthened their necks, bound their feet, dyed their skin and hair, gorged themselves to achieve a full figure or liposuctioned fat to achieve a slim one, strapped on leather garments to make their breasts seem smaller or surgically filled their breasts with silicone and put on Wonder Bras to make them look bigger. In North America, the ultra-thin ideal of the Roaring Twenties gave way to the soft, voluptuous Marilyn Monroe ideal of the 1950s, to be replaced by the lean, athletic ideal of the 1990s.

Some aspects of attractiveness, however, do cross place and time. It comes as no surprise to evolutionary psychologists that men in 37 cultures, from Australia to Zambia, judge women as more attractive if they have a youthful

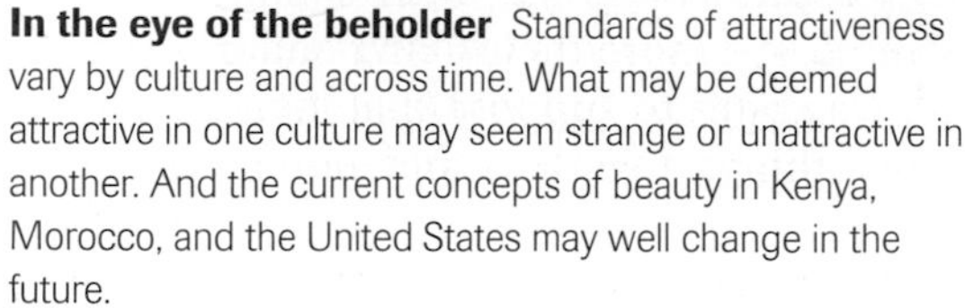

In the eye of the beholder Standards of attractiveness vary by culture and across time. What may be deemed attractive in one culture may seem strange or unattractive in another. And the current concepts of beauty in Kenya, Morocco, and the United States may well change in the future.

appearance (Figure 14.11). Psychologists say that men drawn to healthy, fertile-appearing women have stood a better chance of sending their genes into the future. From yesterday's Stone Age figurines to today's *Playboy* centerfolds and Miss America winners—and regardless of cultural variations in ideal weight—men feel most attracted to women whose waists are roughly a third narrower than their hips—a sign of youthful fertility (Singh, 1993).

Women also feel attracted to healthy-looking men, but especially to those who seem mature, dominant, and affluent (Singh, 1995). Such attributes connote, say the evolutionary psychologists, a capacity to support and protect (Buss, 1996; Schmitt & Buss, 1996). Henry Kissinger, an adviser to U.S. presidents, had the same idea: "Power is the world's greatest aphrodisiac." Evolutionary psychologists also are unsurprised that each sex tends to advertise the qualities that maximize its odds of attracting desirable partners: women by spending time and money on appearance, men by trying to establish their status and dominance. In singles ads, for example, women tend to offer looks and seek status; men do the reverse (Rajecki & others, 1991).

"Love is a dirty trick played on us to achieve the continuation of the species."

Novelist W. Somerset Maugham
1874–1965

Cultural standards aside, attractiveness also depends on our feelings about the person. In a Rodgers and Hammerstein musical, Prince Charming asks Cinderella, "Do I love you because you're beautiful, or are you beautiful because I love you?" Chances are it is both. As we see someone again and again, and come to like the person, physical imperfections grow less noticeable and attractiveness grows more apparent (Beaman & Klentz, 1983; Gross & Crofton, 1977). As Shakespeare put it in *A Midsummer Night's Dream*, "Love looks not with the eyes, but with the mind." Until you got to know him, E.T. was as ugly as Darth Vader.

"Love has ever in view the absolute loveliness of that which it beholds."

George MacDonald
Unspoken Sermons
1867

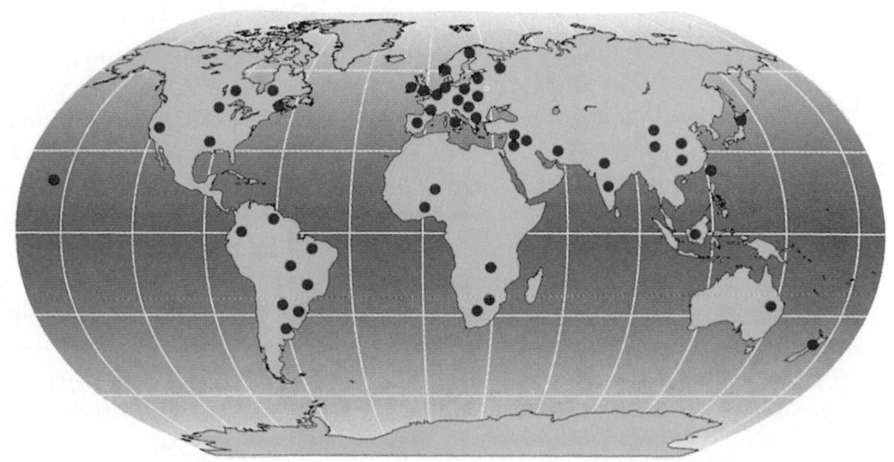

Figure 14.11 Worldwide mating preferences David Buss and an international team of collaborators surveyed the mating preferences of 10,047 people in 37 countries. Men everywhere preferred attractive physical features suggesting youth and health—and reproductive potential. Women everywhere preferred men with resources and social status (from Buss, 1994b). This gender difference, evolutionary psychologists believe, is the result of natural selection favoring those whose choices help perpetuate their genes.

"Pardon me, but I can't help noticing that we share similar tastes in tropical-fruit-flavored chewing gum."

Similarity

Let's say that proximity has brought you into contact with someone and that your appearance has made a favorable first impression. What now influences whether acquaintances develop into friends? For example, as you get to know someone better, is the chemistry better if you are opposites or if you are alike?

It makes a good story—extremely different types living in harmonious union: Rat, Mole, and Badger in *The Wind in the Willows*, Frog and Toad in Arnold Lobel's books. The stories delight us by expressing what we seldom experience, for we tend *not* to like dissimilar people (Rosenbaum, 1986). In real life, opposites retract. Birds that flock together usually *are* of a feather. Friends and couples are far more likely to share common attitudes, beliefs, and interests (and, for that matter, age, religion, race, education, intelligence, smoking behavior, and economic status) than are randomly paired people. Much as you and I may dismiss such differences, seeing ourselves as one human family in a global village, we can't hang out with 6 billion people. Moreover, the greater people's likeness, the more their liking endures (Byrne, 1971). Journalist Walter Lippmann was right to suppose that love is best sustained "when the lovers love many things together, and not merely each other." Similarity breeds content.

Proximity, attractiveness, and similarity are not the only determinants of attraction. We also like those who like us, especially when our self-image is low. When we believe someone likes us, we respond to them more warmly, which leads them to like us even more (Curtis & Miller, 1986). To be liked is powerfully rewarding.

Indeed, a simple reward theory of attraction—that we will like those whose behavior is rewarding to us and that we will continue relationships that offer more rewards than costs—can explain all the findings we have considered so far. When a person lives or works in close proximity with someone else, it costs less time and effort to develop the friendship and enjoy its benefits. Attractive people are aesthetically pleasing, and associating with them can be socially rewarding. Those with similar views reward us by validating our own.

Romantic Love

15. ***What is the distinction between passionate and companionate love?***

Occasionally, people progress from initial impressions to friendship to the more intense, complex, and mysterious state of romantic love. Elaine Hatfield (1988) distinguishes two types of love: temporary passionate love and a more enduring companionate love.

Passionate Love

Noting that arousal is a key ingredient of **passionate love**, Hatfield suggests that the two-factor theory of emotion (page 365) can help us understand this intense positive absorption in another. The theory assumes that (1) emotions have two ingredients—physical arousal plus cognitive appraisal—and that (2) arousal from any source can enhance one emotion or another, depending on how we interpret and label the arousal.

In tests of this theory, college men have been aroused by fright, by running in place, by viewing erotic materials, or by listening to humorous or repulsive monologues. They are then introduced to an attractive woman and asked to rate her (or their girlfriend). Unlike unaroused men, those who are stirred up attribute some of their arousal to the woman or girlfriend and feel more attracted to her (Carducci & others, 1978; Dermer & Pyszczynski, 1978; White & Kight, 1984).

passionate love an aroused state of intense positive absorption in another, usually present at the beginning of a love relationship.

companionate love the deep affectionate attachment we feel for those with whom our lives are intertwined.

HI & LOIS

Outside the laboratory, Donald Dutton and Arthur Aron (1974, 1989) went to two bridges across British Columbia's rocky Capilano River. One was a swaying footbridge 230 feet above the rocks; the other was a low, solid bridge. An attractive young female accomplice intercepted men coming off each bridge, sought their help in filling out a short questionnaire, and then offered her phone number in case they wanted to hear more about her project. Far more of those who had just crossed the high bridge—which left their hearts pounding—accepted the number and later called the woman. To be revved up and to associate some of that arousal with a desirable person is to feel the pull of passion. As lovers who take a thrilling roller coaster ride together know, adrenaline makes the heart grow fonder.

Companionate Love

Inevitably, the passion of romantic love subsides. The intense absorption in the other, the thrill of the romance, the giddy "floating on a cloud" feeling fades. JUST MARRIED becomes just married. Recognizing the short duration of passionate love, some societies have deemed such feelings an irrational reason for marrying. Better, such cultures say, to choose (or have someone choose for you) a partner with compatible backgrounds and interests. Non-Western cultures, where people rate love as less important for marriage decisions, indeed have lower divorce rates (Levine & others, 1995).

Recognizing the short duration of passionate love, some societies have deemed such feelings an irrational reason for marrying.

So, are the French correct in saying that "love makes the time pass and time makes love pass"? Or can friendship and commitment keep a relationship going after the passion cools? Hatfield notes that if love matures it becomes a steadier **companionate love**—a deep, affectionate attachment. There may be adaptive wisdom to this change from passion to affection. Passionate love often produces children, whose survival is aided by the parents' waning obsession with one another. Social psychologist Ellen Berscheid and her colleagues (1984) note that the failure to appreciate passionate love's limited half-life can doom a relationship: "If the inevitable odds against eternal passionate love in a relationship were better understood, more people might choose to be satisfied with the quieter feelings of satisfaction and contentment."

"When two people are under the influence of the most violent, most insane, most delusive, and most transient of passions, they are required to swear that they will remain in that excited, abnormal, and exhausting condition continuously until death do them part."

George Bernard Shaw
Man and Superman
1903

Passionate love to companionate love The quality of love changes as a relationship matures from passionate absorption to affectionate attachment.

One key to a gratifying and enduring relationship is **equity**: Both partners receive in proportion to what they give. When equity exists—when both partners freely give and receive, when they share decision making—their chances for sustained and satisfying companionate love are good (Gray-Little & Burks, 1983; Van Yperen & Buunk, 1990). Mutually sharing self and possessions, giving and getting emotional support, promoting and caring about one another's welfare, are at the core of every type of loving relationship (Sternberg & Grajek, 1984). It's true for lovers, for parent and child, and for intimate friends.

"When a match has equal partners then I fear not."

Aeschylus
Prometheus Bound
478 B.C.

Another vital ingredient of loving relationships is intimacy. A strong friendship or marriage permits **self-disclosure**, a revealing of intimate details about ourselves—our likes and dislikes, our dreams and worries, our proud and shameful moments. "When I am with my friend," noted the Roman statesman Seneca, "me thinks I am alone, and as much at liberty to speak anything as to think it." Self-disclosure breeds liking, and vice versa (Collins & Miller, 1994). As one person reveals a little, the other reciprocates, the first person reveals more, and on and on, as friends or lovers move to deeper intimacy. Given self-disclosing intimacy plus mutually supportive equality, the odds favor enduring companionate love.

Altruism

Altruism—an unselfish regard for others' welfare—is another powerful example of positive social interactions. Altruism became a major concern of social psychologists after an especially vile act of sexual violence. A knife-wielding stalker repeatedly stabbed Kitty Genovese, then raped her as she lay dying outside her Queens, New York, apartment at 3:30 A.M. on March 13, 1964. "Oh, my God, he stabbed me!" Genovese screamed into the early-morning stillness. "Please help me!" Windows opened and lights went on as 38 of her neighbors heard her screams. Her attacker fled and then returned to stab her eight more times and rape her again. Not until he departed for good did anyone so much as call the police, at 3:50 A.M.

"Probably no single incident has caused social psychologists to pay as much attention to an aspect of social behavior as Kitty Genovese's murder."

R. Lance Shotland (1984)

Bystander Intervention

16. *What is the bystander effect?*

Reflecting on the Genovese murder and other such tragedies, most commentators lamented the bystanders' "apathy" and "indifference." Rather than blaming them, social psychologists John Darley and Bibb Latané (1968b) attributed onlooker inaction to an important situational factor—the presence of others. Given the right circumstances, they suspected, most of us might behave similarly.

After staging emergencies under various conditions, Darley and Latané assembled their findings into a decision scheme: We will help only if the situation enables us first to *notice* the incident, then to *interpret* it as an emergency, and finally to *assume responsibility* for helping (Figure 14.12).

At each step, the presence of other bystanders turns people away from the path that leads to helping. In the laboratory and on the street, people in groups of strangers are more likely than solitary individuals to keep their eyes on what they are doing or where they are going. If they notice an unusual situation, they may infer from the blasé reactions of the other passersby that the situation is not an emergency. "The person lying on the sidewalk must be drunk," they think, and move on.

But sometimes, as with the Genovese murder, the emergency is unambiguous and people still fail to help. The witnesses looking out through their windows noticed the incident, correctly interpreted the emergency, yet failed to assume responsibility. To find out why, Darley and Latané (1968a) simulated a physical emergency in their laboratory. University students participated in a

equity a condition in which people receive from a relationship in proportion to what they give to it.

self-disclosure revealing intimate aspects of oneself to others.

altruism unselfish regard for the welfare of others.

bystander effect the tendency for any given bystander to be less likely to give aid if other bystanders are present.

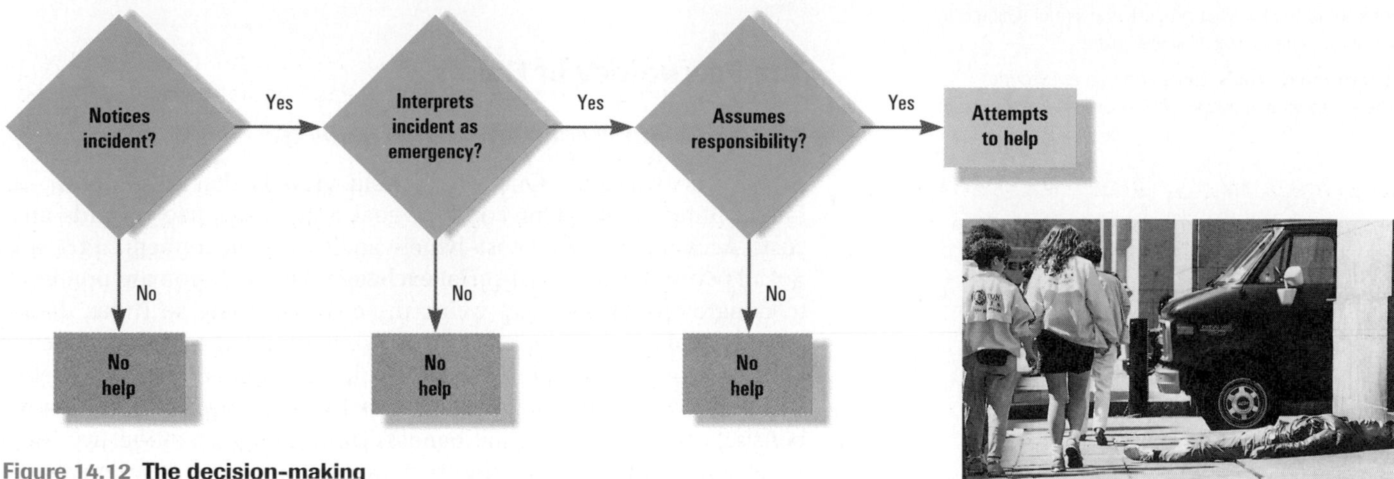

Figure 14.12 The decision-making process for bystander intervention Before helping, one must first notice an emergency, then correctly interpret it, and then feel responsible. (From Darley & Latané, 1968b)

discussion over an intercom. Each student was in a separate cubicle, and only the person whose microphone was switched on could be heard. One of the students was an accomplice of the experimenters. When his turn came, he called for help and made sounds as though he were having an epileptic seizure.

How did the other students react? As Figure 14.13 shows, those who believed they were the only person who could hear the victim—and therefore thought they bore total responsibility for helping—usually went to his aid. Those who thought others could also hear were more likely to react as did Kitty Genovese's neighbors. When more people shared responsibility for helping, any single listener was less likely to help.

In hundreds of additional experiments, psychologists have studied the factors that influence bystanders' willingness to relay an emergency phone call, aid a stranded motorist, donate blood, pick up dropped books, contribute money, and give time. For example, Latané, James Dabbs (1975), and 145 collaborators took 1497 elevator rides in three cities and "accidentally" dropped coins or pencils in front of 4813 fellow passengers. The women coin-droppers were more likely to receive help than were the men—a gender difference often reported by other researchers (Eagly & Crowley, 1986). But the major finding was the **bystander effect**: Any particular bystander was less likely to give aid with other bystanders present. When one other person was on the elevator, those who dropped the coins were helped 40 percent of the time. When there were six passengers, help came less than 20 percent of the time.

From their observations of behavior in tens of thousands of such "emergencies," altruism researchers have discerned some additional patterns. The *best* odds of our helping someone occur when

- we have just observed someone else being helpful.
- we are not in a hurry.
- the victim appears to need and deserve help.
- the victim is in some way similar to us.
- we are in a small town or rural area.
- we are feeling guilty.
- we are focused on others and not preoccupied.
- we are in a good mood.

This last result, that happy people are helpful people, is one of the most consistent findings in all of psychology. No matter how people are cheered—whether by being made to feel successful and intelligent, by thinking happy thoughts, by finding money, or even by receiving a posthypnotic suggestion—they become more generous and more eager to help (Carlson & others, 1988).

Figure 14.13 Responses to a simulated physical emergency When people thought they alone heard the calls for help from a person they believed to be having an epileptic seizure, they usually helped. But when they thought four others were also hearing the calls, fewer than a third responded. (From Darley & Latané, 1968a)

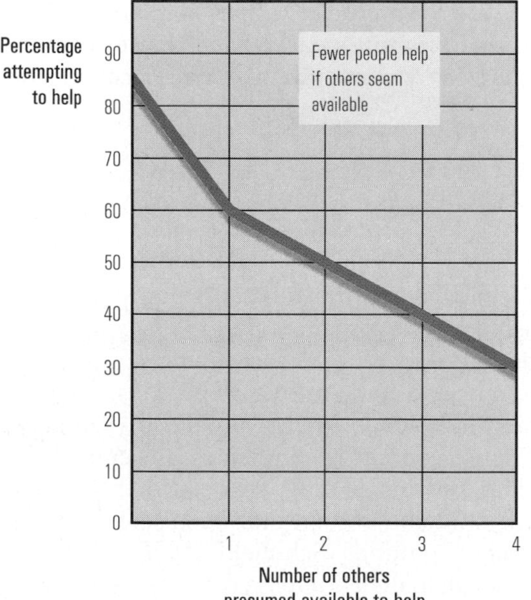

"Oh, make us happy and you make us good!"

Robert Browning
The Ring and the Book
1868

social exchange theory the theory that our social behavior is an exchange process, the aim of which is to maximize benefits and minimize costs.

superordinate goals shared goals that override differences among people and require their cooperation.

The Psychology of Helping

17. *What other factors influence helping?*

So *why* do we help? One widely held view is that self-interest underlies all human interactions: Our constant goal is to maximize rewards and minimize costs. Accountants call it cost–benefit analysis. Philosophers call it utilitarianism. Social psychologists call it **social exchange theory**. If you are pondering whether to donate blood, you may weigh the costs of doing so (time, discomfort, and anxiety) against the benefits (reduced guilt, social approval, good feelings). If the anticipated rewards of helping exceed the anticipated costs, you help.

Social expectations also influence helping. They prescribe how we ought to behave, often to our mutual benefit. Through socialization, we learn the *reciprocity norm*, the expectation that we should return help, not harm, to those who have helped us. In our relations with others of similar status, the reciprocity norm compels us to give (in favors, gifts, or social invitations) about as much as we receive. With young children and others who cannot give as much as they receive, we also learn a *social responsibility norm*—that we should help those who need our help, even if the costs outweigh the benefits. In repeated Gallup surveys, people who each week attend church or synagogue services often exhibit the social responsibility norm: They report volunteering more than twice as many hours in helping the poor and infirm than do those who rarely or never attend religious services (Hodgkinson & Weitzman, 1992). They also give away three times as much money.

Peacemaking

18. *What circumstances facilitate the resolution of conflict?*

How can we transform antagonisms fed by prejudice, aggression, and various conflicts into constructive attitudes that promote peace? Such transformations are most likely in situations characterized by cooperation, communication, and conciliation.

Cooperation

Does it help to put two conflicting parties into close contact so they might get to know and like each other? It depends. When the contact is noncompetitive and between parties of equal status, such as fellow store clerks, it may help. Initially prejudiced co-workers of different races have, in such circumstances, usually learned to accept one another. Among Europeans, friendly contact with ethnic minorities leads to less prejudice (Pettigrew, 1969, 1997). However, mere contact is sometimes not enough. In most desegregated middle and junior high schools in the United States, white and black students resegregate themselves in the lunchrooms and on the school grounds (Schofield, 1986).

Mere contact was not enough to defuse intense conflicts instigated by researcher Muzafer Sherif (1966). He placed 22 Oklahoma City boys in two separate areas of a Boy Scout camp. He then put the two groups through a series of competitive activities, with prizes going to the victors. Before long, each group became intensely proud of itself and hostile to the other group's "sneaky," "smart-alecky stinkers." Food wars broke out during meals. Cabins were ransacked. Fistfights had to be broken up by the camp staff. When Sherif brought the two groups together, they avoided one another, except to taunt and threaten.

Superordinate goals override differences
Cooperative efforts to achieve shared goals are an effective way to break down social barriers.

"You cannot shake hands with a clenched fist."

Indira Gandhi
1971

Nevertheless, within a few days Sherif transformed these young enemies into jovial comrades by giving them **superordinate goals**—shared goals that overrode their differences and that could be achieved only through cooperation. A planned disruption of the camp water supply necessitated that all 22 boys work together to restore water. Renting a movie in those pre-VCR days required their pooled resources. A truck stalled until all the boys pulled and pushed together to get it moving. Having used isolation and competition to make strangers into enemies, Sherif used shared predicaments and goals to reconcile the enemies and make them friends. What reduced conflict was not contact itself, but *cooperative* contact.

Members of interracial groups who work together on projects and play together on athletic teams typically come to feel friendly toward those of the other race. So do those who engage in cooperative classroom learning.

Extending these findings, Samuel Gaertner and his co-workers (1989) report that cooperation has especially positive effects when it leads people to define a new, inclusive group that dissolves their former subgroups. Seat the members of two groups not on opposite sides, but alternately around the table. Give them a new, shared name. Have them work together. Such experiences change "us and them" into "we." People once perceived as in another group now are part of one's own group.

During the 1970s, several teams of educational researchers simultaneously wondered: If cooperative contacts between members of rival groups encourage positive attitudes, could we apply this principle in multicultural schools? Could we promote interracial friendships by replacing competitive classroom situations with cooperative ones? And could cooperative learning maintain or even enhance student achievement? Many experiments confirm that in all three cases, the answer is yes (Johnson & Johnson, 1989, 1994; Slavin, 1989). Members of interracial groups who work together on projects and play together on athletic teams typically come to feel friendly toward those of the other race. So do those who engage in cooperative classroom learning. So encouraging are these results that more than 25,000 teachers have introduced interracial cooperative learning into their classrooms (Kohn, 1987). Working with fellow students in all their diversity sets the stage, declared the Carnegie Council on Adolescent Development (1989), for "adult work life and for citizenship in a multicultural society."

"I am prepared this day to declare myself a citizen of the world, and to invite everyone everywhere to embrace this broader vision of our interdependent world, our common quest for justice, and ultimately for Peace on Earth."

Father Theodore Hesburgh
The Human Imperative
1974

The power of cooperative activity to make friends of former enemies has led psychologists to urge increased international exchange and cooperation (Klineberg, 1984). As we engage in mutually beneficial trade, as we work to protect our common destiny on this fragile planet, and as we become more aware that our hopes and fears are shared, we can change misperceptions into a solidarity based on common interests. Although we will never love all our differences or be pals with everyone, we can, as we work toward shared goals, grow to accept and value human diversity.

Communication

In the social trap game matrix we considered earlier, people usually are distrustful and pursue their individual interests as a defense against exploitation. But when the players are allowed to discuss the dilemma and negotiate, cooperation increases (Jorgenson & Papciak, 1981).

When conflicts become intense, a third-party mediator—a marriage counselor, labor mediator, diplomat, community volunteer—may facilitate communication (Rubin & others, 1994). Mediators help each party to voice its viewpoint and to understand the other's. By helping each side think about the other's underlying needs and goals, the mediator aims to replace a competitive *win-lose* orientation with a cooperative *win-win* orientation that aims at a mutually beneficial resolution. A classic example concerns the two friends who, after quarreling over an orange, agreed to split it, whereupon one squeezed his half for juice while the other used the peel from her half to make a cake. If only the two had understood each other's motives, they could have hit on the win-win solution of one having all the juice, the other all the peel.

GRIT Graduated and Reciprocated Initiatives in Tension-Reduction—a strategy designed to decrease international tensions.

Such understanding and cooperative resolution is most needed, yet least likely, in times of anger or crisis (Bodenhausen & others, 1994; Tetlock, 1988). When conflicts intensify, images become more stereotyped, communication becomes more difficult, and judgments become more rigid.

Neutral third parties may also suggest proposals that would be dismissed if offered by either side. People often "reactively devalue" a concession offered by an adversary ("if they're willing to give that up, they must not value it"); the same concession may seem less like a token gesture when suggested by a third party. Lee Ross and Constance Stillinger (1991) showed how this works. They found that a nuclear disarmament proposal that Americans dismissed when attributed to the Soviet Union seemed more acceptable when attributed to a neutral third party.

Conciliation

When tension and suspicion peak, cooperation and communication may become impossible. Each party is likely to threaten, coerce, or retaliate. In the weeks before the Persian Gulf War, President Bush threatened, in the full glare of publicity, to "kick Saddam's ass." Saddam Hussein communicated in kind, threatening to make Americans "swim in their own blood."

Under such conditions, is there an alternative to war or surrender? Social psychologist Charles Osgood (1962, 1980) has advocated a strategy of "Graduated and Reciprocated Initiatives in Tension-Reduction," nicknamed **GRIT**. In applying GRIT, one side first announces its recognition of mutual interests and its intent to reduce tensions. It then initiates one or more small, conciliatory acts. Without weakening one's retaliatory capability, this modest beginning opens the door for reciprocation by the other party. Should the enemy respond with hostility, one reciprocates in kind. But so, too, with any conciliatory response. Thus, President Kennedy's gesture of stopping atmospheric nuclear tests began a series of reciprocated conciliatory acts that culminated in the 1993 atmospheric test-ban treaty.

Civilization advances not by cultural isolation—maintaining walls around ethnic enclaves—but by tapping the knowledge, the skills, and the arts that are each culture's legacy to the whole human race.

In laboratory experiments, GRIT has been the most effective strategy known for increasing trust and cooperation (Lindskold & others, 1978–1988). Even during intense personal conflict, when communication has been nonexistent, a small conciliatory gesture—a smile, a touch, a word of apology—may work wonders. Conciliations allow both parties to begin edging down the tension ladder to a safer rung where communication and mutual understanding can begin.

And how good that such can happen, for civilization advances not by cultural isolation—maintaining walls around ethnic enclaves—but by tapping the knowledge, the skills, and the arts that are each culture's legacy to the whole human race. Thomas Sowell (1991) notes that, thanks to cultural sharing, every modern society is enriched by a cultural mix. We have China to thank for paper and printing and for the magnetic compass that opened the great explorations. We have Egypt to thank for trigonometry. We have the Islamic world and India's Hindus to thank for our Arabic numerals, which, except for numbering kings and queens, really are superior to the Roman numerals they replaced. While celebrating and claiming these cultural legacies, we can also welcome the enrichment of today's social diversity. We can view ourselves as individual instruments in a human orchestra. And we can therefore affirm our own culture's heritage while building bridges of communication, understanding, and cooperation across cultural traditions.

"To begin with, I would like to express my sincere thanks and deep appreciation for the opportunity to meet with you. While there are still profound differences between us, I think the very fact of my presence here today is a major breakthrough."

REHEARSE IT!

21. Repeated exposure to a stimulus—including a new human face—increases our liking of the stimulus. This *mere exposure effect* helps explain why proximity is a powerful predictor of friendship and marriage, and why, for example, people tend to marry someone

a. about as attractive as themselves.
b. who lives or works nearby.
c. of similar religious or ethnic background.
d. who has similar attitudes and habits.

22. Male subjects who are aroused by various stimuli and then introduced to an attractive woman tend to attribute their arousal to the woman, and to report positive feelings toward her. This supports the two-factor theory of emotion, which assumes that emotions such as passionate love consist of physical arousal plus

a. a reward. **c.** companionate love.
b. proximity. **d.** our interpretation of that arousal.

23. Companionate love is described as a deep, affectionate attachment. Vital to the maintenance of such loving relationships are (is)

a. equity and self-disclosure. **c.** intense positive absorption.
b. physical attraction. **d.** proximity and similarity.

24. Psychologists have studied the factors that determine whether a bystander will come to the aid of a stranger in an "emergency." They have found that people who are in a good mood are most likely to extend their help. Perhaps the most important finding, though, is the bystander effect, which states that a particular bystander is less likely to give aid if

a. the victim is similar to him or her in appearance.
b. there is no one else present.
c. other bystanders are present.
d. the incident occurs in a deserted or rural area.

25. Social exchange theory contends that all social behavior is aimed at maximizing benefits and minimizing costs. Social expectations also influence helping. For example, through socialization, we are taught that we should help those who need our help. This is called

a. the reciprocity norm. **c.** the social responsibility norm.
b. altruism. **d.** bystander intervention.

26. Social psychologists have attempted to define the circumstances that facilitate conflict resolution. One way of fostering cooperation is by providing contentious groups with superordinate goals, which are

a. the goals of friendly competition.
b. shared goals that override differences.
c. goals for winning at negotiations.
d. goals for reducing conflict through increased contact.

REVIEWING ▪ *Social Psychology*

Social psychologists study how people think about, influence, and relate to one another.

Social Thinking

1. ***How do we tend to explain others' behavior? How do we explain our own behavior?***

According to **attribution theory**, we generally explain people's behavior by attributing it either to internal dispositions or to external situations. In accounting for others' actions, we tend to underestimate the influence of the situation, thus committing the **fundamental attribution error**. When we explain our own behavior, however, we more often point to the situation and not to ourselves.

2. ***Under what conditions do our attitudes guide our behavior?***

Attitudes predict behavior only under certain conditions, as when other influences are minimized, when the attitude is specific to the behavior, and when people are aware of their attitudes.

3. ***Under what conditions does our behavior affect our attitudes?***

Studies of the **foot-in-the-door phenomenon** and of **role** playing reveal that our actions can also modify our attitudes, especially when we feel responsible for those actions. **Cognitive dissonance theorists** explain that behavior shapes attitudes because people feel discomfort when their actions go against their feelings and beliefs; they reduce the discomfort by bringing their attitudes more into line with what they have done.

Social Influence

4. ***What do experiments on conformity and compliance reveal about the power of social influence?***

Solomon Asch and others learned that under certain conditions people will **conform** to a group's judgment even when it is clearly incorrect. In Milgram's famous experiments, people who were torn between obeying an experimenter and responding to another's pleas usually chose to obey orders, even though obedience appeared to involve harming another person. These classic experiments demonstrate the potency of social forces, and they highlight the fact that we conform either to gain social approval by adhering to social **norms** (**normative social influence**) or because we depend on the information that others provide (**informational social influence**).

5. ***In what ways are we affected by the mere presence of others?***

Experiments on **social facilitation** indicate that the presence of others can arouse individuals, slightly boosting their performance on easy tasks but hindering it on difficult ones. When people pool their efforts toward a group goal, **social loafing** may occur as individuals free-ride on others' efforts. When people are aroused and made anonymous by a group, they may become less self-aware and self-restrained, a psychological state known as **deindividuation**.

6. ***What are group polarization and groupthink?***

Discussions with like-minded others often produce **group polarization**, an enhancement of the group's prevailing attitudes. This is one cause of **groupthink**, the tendency for harmony- seeking groups to make unrealistic decisions after suppressing unwelcome information.

7. ***Can a minority sway a majority?***

The power of the group is great, but so can be the power of a minority, especially when its views are expressed consistently.

8. ***How do cultural norms and gender roles affect our behavior?***

Cultural rules for accepted and expected behavior vary in ways that befuddle people. **Cultures** differ, for example, in their requirements for **personal space**, their expressiveness, their pace of life, and the strength of their role expectations. They also differ in their **gender roles**—the behaviors expected of males and females.

Social Relations

9. ***What are the social and emotional roots of prejudice?***

Prejudice is a mixture of beliefs (often **stereotypes**), emotions, and predispositions to action. It often arises as those who enjoy social and economic superiority attempt to justify the status quo. Even the temporary assignment of people to groups can cause an **ingroup bias**. Prejudice may also serve the emotional functions of draining off the anger caused by frustration and of boosting self-esteem. The **scapegoat theory** explains how finding someone to blame for a frustrating situation provides on outlet for anger.

10. ***What are the cognitive roots of prejudice?***

Research reveals how our ways of processing information—for example, by overestimating similarities when we categorize people or by noticing and remembering vivid cases—work to create stereotypes. In addition, favored social groups often rationalize their higher status by the **just-world phenomenon**.

11. ***What biological factors influence aggressive behavior?***

Aggressive behavior, like all behavior, is a product of nature and nurture. Although psychologists dismiss the idea that **aggression** is instinctual, aggressiveness is genetically influenced. Moreover, certain areas of the brain, when stimulated, activate or inhibit aggression, and these neural areas are biochemically influenced.

12. ***What psychological factors influence aggressive behavior?***

A variety of psychological factors also influence aggression. Aversive events create frustration, which leads to anger and possibly to aggression, according to the **frustration-aggression principle**. Such stimuli are especially likely to trigger aggression in those rewarded for their own aggression or those who have learned aggression from role models or have repeatedly observed violent media portrayals of aggressive models. Such factors desensitize people to cruelty and prime them to behave aggressively when provoked. Media influences may also cultivate the rape myth and make sexual aggression seem less terrible.

13. ***What social processes fuel conflict?***

Conflicts between individuals and cultures often arise from destructive social processes. These include **social traps**, in which each party, by protecting and pursuing its self-interest, creates an outcome that no one wants. The spiral of conflict also feeds and is fed by distorted mirror-image perceptions, in which each party views itself as moral and the other as untrustworthy and evil-intentioned.

14. ***What psychological factors promote attraction?***

Three factors are known to influence our liking for one another. *Proximity*—geographical nearness—is conducive to attraction, partly because **mere exposure** to novel stimuli enhances liking. *Physical attractiveness* influences social opportunities and the way one is perceived. As acquaintanceship moves toward friendship, *similarity* of attitudes and interests greatly increases liking.

15. ***What is the distinction between passionate and companionate love?***

Passionate love can be viewed as a temporary, aroused state that we cognitively label as love. The strong affection of **companionate love**, which often emerges as a relationship matures, is enhanced by an **equitable** relationship and by intimate **self-disclosure**.

16. ***What is the bystander effect?***

Studies of **altruism** have explored both helping in emergencies and planned helping. In response to incidents of bystander nonintervention in emergencies, social psychologists undertook experiments that revealed a **bystander effect**: Any given bystander is less likely to help if others are present. The bystander effect is especially apparent in situations where the presence of others inhibits one's noticing the event, interpreting it as an emergency, or assuming responsibility for helping. Many factors, including mood, also influence willingness to help someone in distress.

17. ***What other factors influence helping?***

Social exchange theory proposes that our social behaviors—even our helpful acts—maximize our benefits (which may include our own good feelings) and minimize our costs. Our desire to help is also affected by social norms, which prescribe reciprocating the help we have received and being socially responsible toward those in need.

18. ***What circumstances facilitate the resolution of conflict?***

Enemies sometimes become friends, especially when the circumstances favor cooperation to achieve **superordinate goals**, understanding through communication, and reciprocated conciliatory gestures (**GRIT**).

CRITICAL THINKING EXERCISE by Richard O. Straub

Now that you have read and reviewed Chapter 14, take your learning a step further by testing your critical thinking skills on the following pattern-recognition exercise (adapted from Zechmeister & Johnson, 1992).

Write down three characteristics or descriptions that you associate with each of the following groups of people.

Physicians	______________
Athletes	______________
Artists	______________
Vegetarians	______________
College Students	______________
Lawyers	______________

With which of these groups do you most closely identify? With which do you least identify? The group with which you most closely identify can be considered one of your ingroups; the one that you feel most unlike is one of your outgroups.

1. Was it easier to come up with descriptions for your ingroup or for your outgroup?
2. Are your descriptions of your ingroup and outgroup equally favorable? If not, why do you think this is so?
3. In the answer key in Appendix B you will find ingroup and outgroup descriptions made by a group of college students. Before looking at it, decide whether your ingroup or your outgroup descriptions are more likely to match those of the other college students. How would you explain this phenomenon?

Check your progress on becoming a critical thinker by comparing your answers to the sample answers found in Appendix B.

REHEARSE IT ANSWER KEY

1. a., **2.** d., **3.** b., **4.** a., **5.** c., **6.** a., **7.** c., **8.** c., **9.** b., **10.** c., **11.** b., **12.** c., **13.** b., **14.** b., **15.** b., **16.** d., **17.** c., **18.** c., **19.** c., **20.** c., **21.** b., **22.** d., **23.** a., **24.** c., **25.** c., **26.** b.

FOR FURTHER INFORMATION

For further information in this text on culture and multicultural experience, see:

For further information in this text on the psychology of women and men, see:

Statistical Reasoning

APPENDIX A

Science fiction writer H. G. Wells predicted that "statistical thinking will one day be as necessary for efficient citizenship as the ability to read and write." That day has arrived. Today's statistics are tools that help us see and interpret what the unaided eye might miss.

Unaided by statistics, top-of-the-head estimates often misread reality and mislead the public. Someone throws out a big round number, which others echo. Before long the big round number becomes a public myth. A few examples:

- 1 percent of Americans (2.6 million) are homeless. Or is it 300,000, as earlier estimated by the federal government? Or 600,000, as estimated by the Urban Institute (Crossen, 1994)?
- 10 percent of people are homosexual. Or is it 2 to 3 percent, as suggested by various national surveys (Chapter 9)?
- We ordinarily use but 10 percent of our brain. Or is it closer to 100 percent? (Which 90 percent, or even 10 percent, would you be willing to sacrifice?)
- Two-thirds of married men and half of married women have had an affair. Or is it more like only 1 in 7, as suggested in careful surveys in several countries (Chapter 1)?

The point to remember: Doubt big, round, undocumented numbers.

Describing Data

Researchers or not, we all make observations or gather data that we must organize and interpret. Let's see how we might effectively do this.

Distributions

Laura is a U.S. college admissions officer. Attempting to predict which currently enrolled students will succeed at her school, she sorts through their high school grades, aptitude scores, biographical statements, recommendation letters, and

Table A.1 Laura's Sample Data

Student	Precollege GPA	College GPA	SAT	Family Income	Student	Precollege GPA	College GPA	SAT	Family Income
Andrea	2.1	1.6	950	$ 15,000	Mark	3.6	4.0	1370	$ 45,000
Bubba	2.9	2.8	720	20,000	Nicole	2.9	2.2	875	35,000
Cindy	3.7	3.6	1350	30,000	Nobuyuki	3.2	2.1	1180	25,000
Dang Cho	3.1	3.9	1100	20,000	Ralph	2.7	2.8	1065	35,000
Ezekiel	3.4	3.1	1100	40,000	Renae	3.9	3.3	1130	20,000
Fiona	2.9	2.6	775	20,000	Rochelle	2.3	2.5	725	30,000
Gamal	2.7	3.3	750	25,000	Rowland	2.8	2.5	700	40,000
Hope	2.0	2.4	800	45,000	Tammy	3.0	3.5	1270	20,000
Huong	3.5	2.7	1010	70,000	Tiffany	3.1	2.7	810	25,000
Jae-Min	3.9	3.5	1375	475,000	Timothy	3.5	2.9	900	90,000
Kraig	3.4	3.7	820	30,000	Todd	3.8	3.2	940	20,000
Larry	3.1	2.5	1105	15,000	Wilbur	2.6	2.1	750	30,000
Malachi	3.4	3.3	800	50,000	Xandria	3.5	3.3	1020	20,000
Manuel	3.3	3.3	1120	25,000	Xin	4.0	3.8	1400	45,000
Maria	3.5	3.6	900	710,000	Yolanda	3.1	2.8	900	30,000

subsequent college grades. But there is too much information to remember. Moreover, she knows that impressions are swayed by remembered information, often the vivid or extreme instances. So she starts by laying out the basic data on a small random sample of students (Table A.1).

She is first interested in how these students did in high school. So she displays their precollege grade point averages (GPAs) as a bar graph (Figure A.1). By showing the number of GPAs within a particular interval as a bar, Laura can see approximately where any particular student's GPA falls relative to the others. She can also express any student's ranking as a **percentile rank**, which states the percentage of scores that fall below a particular score. A student whose percentile rank is 99 has a GPA that exceeds those of 99 percent

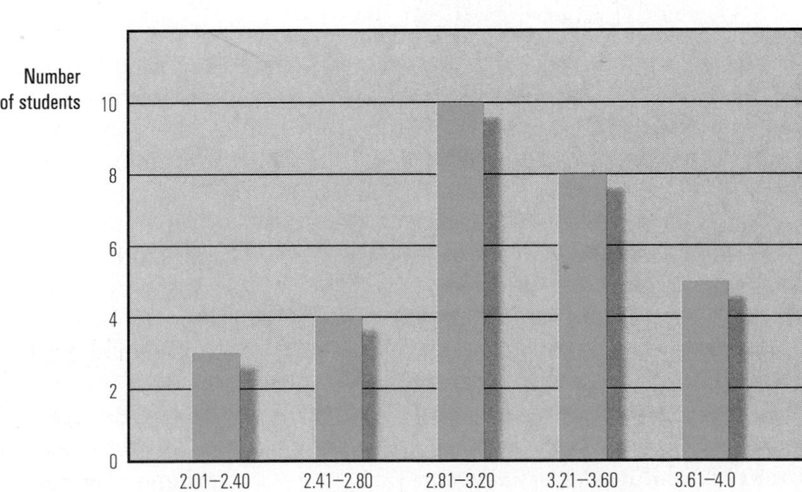

Figure A.1 **Bar graph** High school GPAs of 30 students.

percentile rank the percentage of the scores in a distribution that fall below a given score.

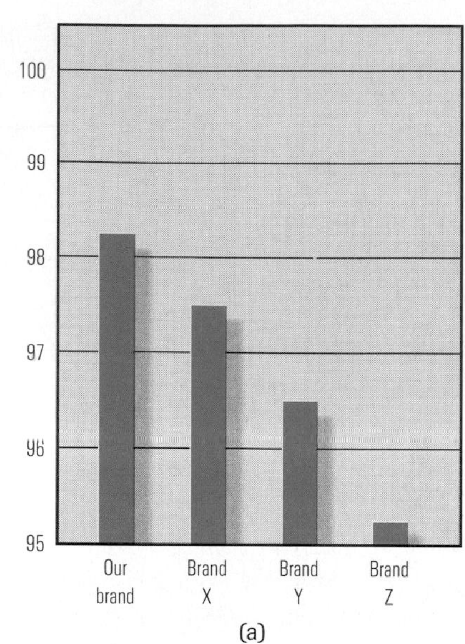

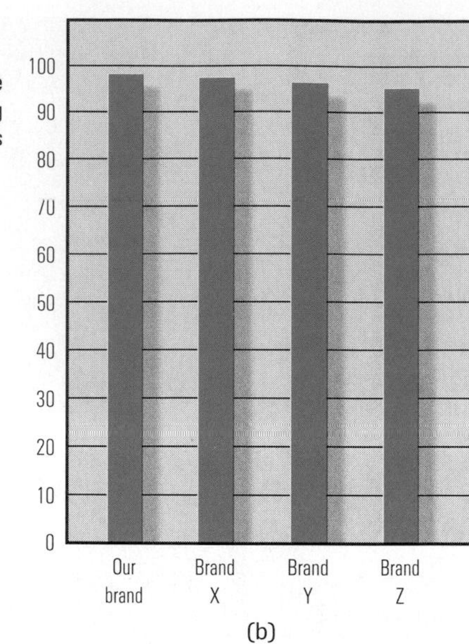

Figure A.2 Read the scale labels An American truck manufacturer offered graph **(a)**—with actual brand names included—to suggest the much greater durability of its trucks. Note, however, how the apparent difference shrinks as the vertical scale changes in graph **(b)**.

of all the students. (You can never have a percentile rank of 100. Your score can never exceed those of 100 percent of the people because you are one of them.)

A note of caution: Take care when reading statistical graphs. Depending on what people want to emphasize, they can design the graph to make the same difference look small or big (Figure A.2). *The point to remember*: When looking at statistical graphs in books and magazines and on television ads and news broadcasts, think critically. Always read the scale labels and note their range.

Take care when reading statistical graphs. Depending on what people want to emphasize, they can design the graph to make the same difference look small or big.

Central Tendencies

Laura wonders: What are typical precollege grades and family income levels among her college's students? That is, what is a representative or *central tendency*? For any distribution of scores there are three commonly used measures of the central tendency. The simplest is the **mode**, the most frequently occurring score. The most commonly reported is the **mean**, or arithmetic average—the total sum of all the scores divided by the number of scores. (From calculating your grade point average, you are familiar with the mean.) The **median** is the middle score—the 50th percentile; if you arrange all the scores in order from the highest to the lowest, half will be above the median and half will be below it.

The point to remember: Always note which measure of central tendency is reported. Then, if it is a mean, consider whether a few atypical scores could be distorting it.

Measures of central tendency neatly summarize data. Laura can report, for example, that her student sample has a mean precollege GPA of 3.16. But consider what happens to the mean when a distribution is lopsided or *skewed* (rather than symmetrical). As Figure A.3 shows with the family income data, the mode, median, and mean tell different stories. This is because the mean is biased by a few extreme scores (in this case, the two families with very high incomes). To say her students have a mean family income of $70,000 is true but misleading. Understanding this, you can see how a British newspaper could accurately run the headline "Income for 62% Is Below Average" (Waterhouse, 1993). Because the bottom *half* of British income earners receive only a *quarter* of the national income cake, most British people, like most people everywhere, make less than the mean.

"The poor are getting poorer, but with the rich getting richer it all averages out in the long run."

If Microsoft founder Bill Gates were to move to a town with 24,000 penniless people, his 1997 net worth of $24 billion would instantly make its average (mean) resident a millionaire.

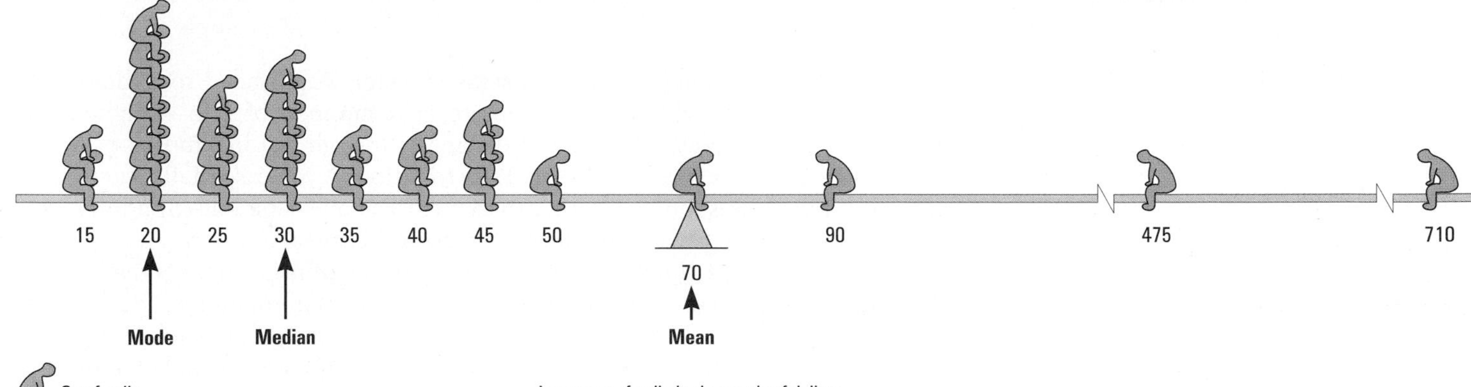

Figure A.3 A skewed distribution This graphic representation of the distribution of incomes illustrates the three measures of central tendency—mode, median, and mean. Note how just a few high incomes make the mean—the fulcrum point that balances the incomes above and below—deceptively high.

Variation

Knowing the value of an appropriate measure of central tendency can tell us a great deal. But it also helps to know how similar or diverse the scores are. Thus, Laura wonders: How much do my students vary from one another?

Averages derived from scores with low variability are more reliable than averages based on scores with high variability. Consider a basketball player who scored between 13 and 17 points in each of her first 10 games in a season. Knowing this, we would be more confident that she would score near 15 points in her next game than if her scores had varied from 5 to 25 points.

The **range** of scores—the gap between the lowest and highest scores—provides only a crude estimate of variation because just one extreme score in an otherwise uniform group will create a deceptively large range. The $695,000 income range in Laura's sample is misleadingly large ($710,000 – $15,000) because all but the two highest incomes range between $15,000 and $90,000.

The more standard measure of how much scores deviate from one another is the **standard deviation**. It better gauges whether scores are packed together or dispersed, because it uses information from each score. The standard deviation is important and not hard to compute: (1) Calculate the difference, or deviation, between each score and the mean; (2) square these deviations; (3) find their average; and (4) find the square root of this average.

As an example, consider Peter, the punter (kicker) on his U.S. college football team. To keep track of his progress, he records the distance of each of his punts. He does not trust his gut-level impression of how consistent his punting is. After his first football game, Peter therefore calculates the standard deviation for his four punts (Table A.2).

Table A.2 Standard Deviation

Punting Distance (in Yards)	Deviation From Mean (40 Yards)	Deviation Squared
36	−4	16
38	−2	4
41	+1	1
45	+5	25
Mean = 160/4 = 40	Sum of (deviations)² = 46	

$$\text{Standard deviation} = \sqrt{\frac{\text{Sum of (deviations)}^2}{\text{Number of scores}}} = \sqrt{\frac{46}{4}} = 3.4 \text{ yards}$$

mode the most frequently occurring score in a distribution.

mean the arithmetic average of a distribution, obtained by adding the scores and then dividing by the number of scores.

median the middle score in a distribution; half the scores are above it and half are below it.

range the difference between the highest and lowest scores in a distribution.

standard deviation a measure of score variability; computed by (1) calculating the deviation of each score from the mean, (2) squaring those deviations, (3) finding their average, and (4) finding the square root of this average.

normal curve (normal distribution) a symmetrical, bell-shaped curve that describes the distribution of many types of data; most scores fall near the mean (68 percent fall within 1 standard deviation of it) and fewer and fewer near the extremes.

scatterplot a graphed cluster of dots, each of which represents the values of two variables (such as one student's high school GPA and college GPA). The slope of the points suggests the degree and direction of the relationship between the two variables. (Also called a *scattergram* or *scatter diagram*.)

correlation coefficient a statistical measure of the extent to which two factors vary together, and thus of how well either factor predicts the other. Scores with a *positive correlation coefficient* go up and down together (as with high school and college GPAs). A *negative correlation coefficient* indicates that one score falls as the other rises (as in the relationship between self-esteem and depression).

To grasp the meaning of this statistic, Peter would need to understand how scores tend to be distributed. In nature, large numbers of data—heights, weights, intelligence scores, grades, punt distances (though not incomes)—often form a roughly symmetrical, bell-shaped distribution. Most cases fall near the mean, and fewer cases fall near either extreme. This bell-shaped distribution is so typical that we call the curve it forms the **normal curve**.

As Figure A.4 shows, a useful property of the normal curve is that roughly 68 percent of the cases fall within 1 standard deviation on either side of the mean (in Peter's case, within 3.4 yards of his 40-yard average). About 95 percent of cases fall within 2 standard deviations. Thus, Chapter 8 notes that about 68 percent of people taking an intelligence test will score within ±15 points of 100. About 95 percent will score within ±30 points.

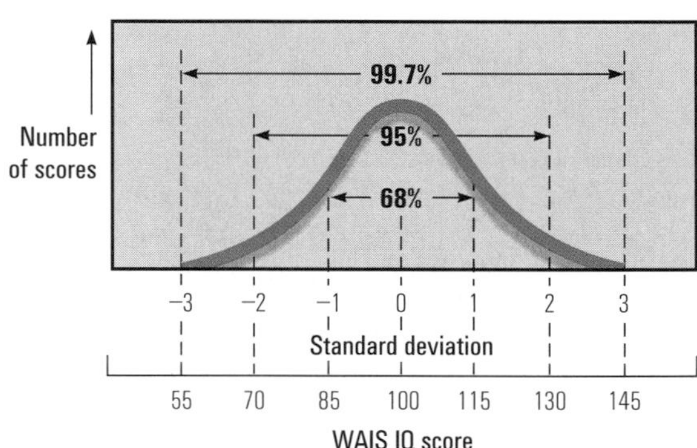

Figure A.4 The normal curve Large samples of data often form a normal, or bell-shaped, curve in which 68 percent of the cases fall within 1 standard deviation of the mean and 95 percent fall within 2 standard deviations. For example, on an intelligence test such as the WAIS, we assign the mean a value of 100 and 1 standard deviation equals 15 points. Therefore 68 percent of the scores fall between 85 and 115, and 95 percent fall between 70 and 130 on this test.

Correlation

In this book we often ask how much two things relate: How closely related are the personality scores of identical twins? How well do intelligence test scores predict achievement? How often does stress lead to disease? To get a feel for whether one set of scores relates to a second set, we can display the data as a **scatterplot**. Figure A.5(a) depicts the actual relationship between Scholastic Assessment Test scores and college GPAs for Laura's 30 students. Each point on the graph represents these two numbers for one student. Figure A.5(b) is a scatterplot of the relationship between these students' precollege and college GPAs.

The **correlation coefficient** is a statistical measure of how strongly related any two sets of scores are. Its possible range is as follows:

- **+1.00**, which means that one set of scores increases in direct proportion to the other's increase.
- **0.00**, meaning that the scores are unrelated.
- **−1.00**, which means that one set of scores goes up precisely as the other goes down.

Figure A.5 Scatterplots Plot **(a)** shows, for 30 actual students, the relationship between total Scholastic Assessment Test scores (verbal plus mathematical) and college GPAs. Plot **(b)** shows the closer relationship between precollege and college GPAs for 30 college students. Each point represents the data for one student.

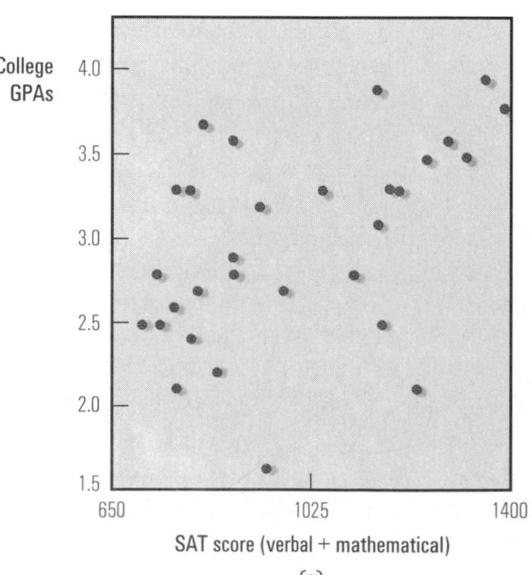

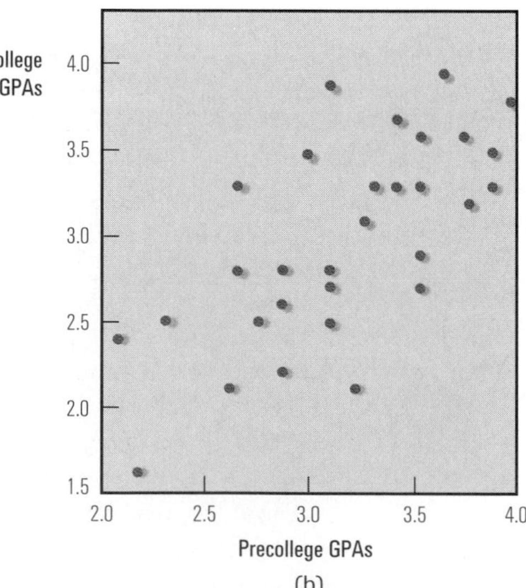

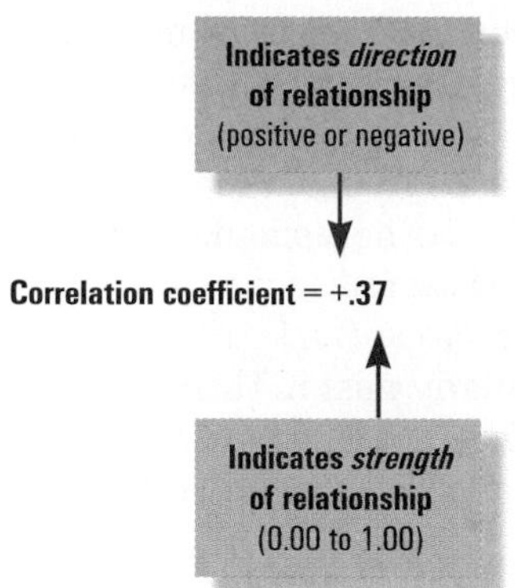

How to read a correlation coefficient

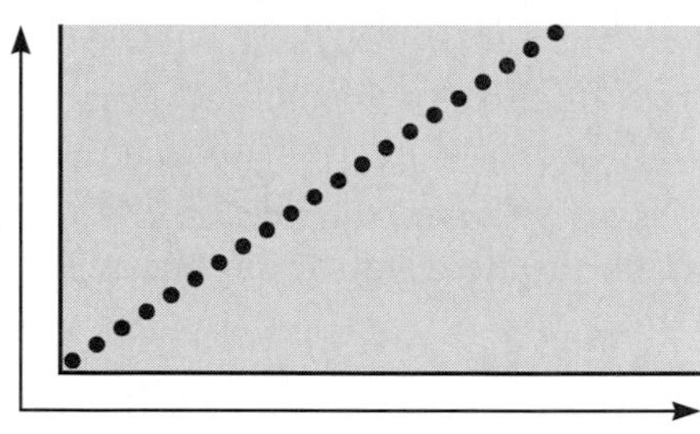

Perfect positive correlation (+1.00)

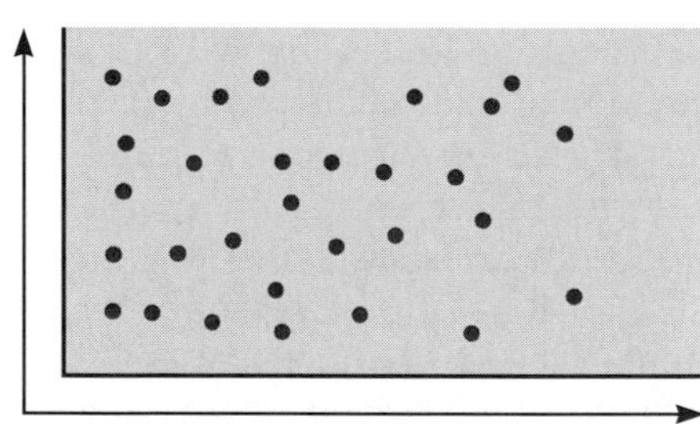

No relationship (0.00)

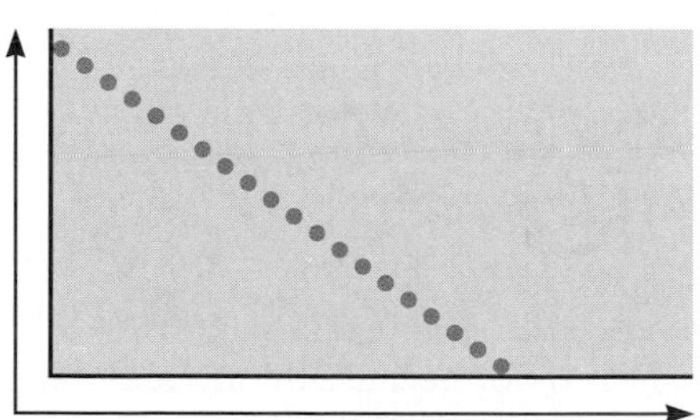

Perfect negative correlation (−1.00)

(Note that a correlation's being negative has nothing to do with its strength or weakness; a negative correlation means two things relate inversely [in opposite directions]. A weak correlation, indicating little or no relationship, is one that has a coefficient near zero.) Now look again at the scatterplots in Figure A.5. Do the correlations look positive or negative?

In each scatterplot in Figure A.5, the upward, oval-shaped slope of the cluster of points as one moves to the right shows that the two sets of scores tend to rise together. This means the correlations are positive: a +.50 correlation for the SAT–college GPA relationship shown in Figure A.5(a) and a stronger +.69 for the precollege GPA–college GPA relationship shown in Figure A.5(b). High SAT scores and, especially, high precollege grades, predict high college grades. (The high school–college GPA relationship, incidentally, illustrates the common finding that the best predictor of people's future behavior is usually their behavior in similar situations in the past. The best predictor of future grades is past grades, which reflect both aptitude and motivation. Still, people do sometimes change.)

Statistics can help us see what the naked eye sometimes misses. To demonstrate this for yourself, try to discern what relationship, if any, exists between two sets of scores not yet organized into a scatterplot. Alessandra wonders whether men's heights correlate with their temperaments. She measures the heights of 20 men, has someone else independently assess their temperaments (from zero for extremely calm to 100 for highly reactive), and obtains the data in Table A.3, page 542.

With all the relevant data right in front of you, can you tell whether there is (1) a positive correlation between height and reactive temperament, (2) very little or no correlation, or (3) a negative correlation?

Comparing the columns in Table A.3, most people detect very little relationship between height and temperament. In fact, the correlation in this imaginary example is moderately positive, +.57, as you could see if you made a scatterplot of the data. If we fail to see a relationship when data are presented as systematically as in this table, how much less likely are we to notice such a relationship in everyday life? To see what is right in front of us, we sometimes need statistical illumination. People can easily see evidence of gender discrimination when given statistically summarized information about job level, seniority, performance, gender, and salary. But they often see no discrimination when the same information dribbles in, case by case (Twiss & others, 1989).

The point to remember: Although the correlation coefficient tells us nothing about cause and effect, it *can* help us see the world more clearly by revealing the actual extent to which two things relate.

Correlations not only make visible the relationships that we might otherwise miss; they also restrain our "seeing" nonexistent relationships. As Chapter 1 explained, a perceived correlation that does not really exist is an *illusory correlation*. When we *believe* there is a relationship between two things, we are likely to *notice* and *recall* instances that confirm our belief. If we believe that dreamt events are forecasts of actual events, we may notice and recall confirming instances more than disconfirming instances. The result is an illusory correlation.

Illusory correlations feed an *illusion of control*—that chance events are subject to our personal control. Gamblers, remembering their lucky rolls, may come to believe they can influence the roll of the dice by again throwing gently for low numbers and hard for high numbers. The illusion that uncontrollable events correlate with our actions is also fed by a statistical phenomenon called **regression toward the mean**. Average results are more typical than extreme results. Thus, after an unusual event, things tend to return toward their average level; extraordinary happenings tend to be followed by more ordinary ones.

regression toward the mean the tendency for extremes or unusual scores to fall back (regress) toward the average.

Table A.3 **Height and Temperament of 20 Men**

Subject	Height in Inches	Temperament
1	80	75
2	63	66
3	61	60
4	79	90
5	74	60
6	69	42
7	62	42
8	75	60
9	77	81
10	60	39
11	64	48
12	76	69
13	71	72
14	66	57
15	73	63
16	70	75
17	63	30
18	71	30
19	68	84
20	70	39

Examples are abundant: Basketball players who make or miss all their shots in the first half of the game are likely to "regress" (fall back) to their more usual performance level during the second half. Students who score much lower or higher on an exam than they usually do are likely, when retested, to regress toward their average. Unusual ESP subjects who defy chance when first tested nearly always lose their "psychic powers" when retested (a phenomenon parapsychologists have called the "decline effect").

The point may seem obvious, yet we regularly miss it. Thus, we sometimes attribute what may be a normal statistical regression (the expected falling back to normal) to something we have done. Consider these examples:

- After a sudden crime wave, the town council initiates a "stop crime" drive and the crime rate then returns to previous levels. The drive may therefore appear more successful than it was.
- Coaches who yell at their players after an unusually bad first half may feel rewarded for having done so when the team's performance improves (returns to normal) during the second half.
- Scientists who win a Nobel prize often have diminished accomplishments thereafter, leading some to wonder whether winning a Nobel hinders creativity.
- Some people also believe there is a "*Sports Illustrated* jinx"—that athletes whose peak performances get them on the cover of the magazine will then suffer a decline in their performance.

In each of these cases, it is possible that the effect is genuine. It is more likely, however, that each represents the natural tendency for behavior to regress from the unusual to the more usual.

Failure to recognize regression is the source of many superstitions and of some ineffective practices as well. When day-to-day behavior has a large element of chance fluctuation, we may notice that others' behavior improves (regresses toward average) after we criticize them for very bad performance, and that it worsens (regresses toward average) after we warmly praise them for an exceptionally fine performance. Ironically, then, regression toward the average can mislead us into feeling rewarded for having criticized others and into feeling punished for having praised them (Tversky & Kahneman, 1974).

The point to remember: When a fluctuating behavior returns to normal, there is no need to invent fancy explanations for why it does so. Regression toward the mean is probably at work.

"Once you become sensitized to it, you see regression everywhere."

Psychologist Daniel Kahneman (1985)

Statistical Inference

Data are "noisy." One group's average score (women's salaries) could conceivably differ from another's (men's salaries) not because of any real difference but merely due to chance fluctuation in the people sampled. So how confidently can we infer that an observed difference is reliable?

When Is It Safe to Generalize From a Sample?

In deciding whether to generalize from our samples, three principles are worth keeping in mind. Let's look at each.

1. **Representative samples are better than biased samples.** As Chapter 1 explained, the best basis for generalizing is not from the exceptional, memorable

cases one finds at the extremes but from a representative sample of cases. No research involves a representative sample of the whole human population. Thus, it pays to keep in mind what population a study has sampled.

2. **Less-variable observations are more reliable than those that are more variable.** As we noted in the example of the basketball player whose scores were consistent, an average is more reliable when it comes from scores with low variability.
3. **More cases are better than fewer.** An eager high school senior visits two college campuses, each for a day. At the first, the student randomly attends three classes and discovers each instructor to be witty and engaging. At the next campus, the three sampled instructors seem dull and uninspiring. Returning home, the student tells friends about the "great teachers" at the first school and the "bores" at the second school. Again, we know it but we ignore it: Small samples provide less reliable estimates of the average than do large samples. The proportion of heads in samples of 10 coin tosses varies more than in samples of 100 tosses.

Said differently, *averages based on more cases are more reliable* (less variable) than averages based on only a few cases. Knowing this, answer a question posed by Christopher Jepson, David Krantz, and Richard Nisbett (1983) to University of Michigan introductory psychology students:

> The registrar's office at the University of Michigan has found that usually about 100 students in Arts and Sciences have a 4.00 GPA at the end of their first term at the University. However, only about 10 to 15 students graduate with a 4.00 GPA. What do you think is the most likely explanation for the fact that there are more 4.00 GPAs after one term than at graduation?

How did you answer? Most of the students in the study came up with plausible causes for the drop in GPA, such as, "Students tend to work harder at the beginning of their college careers than toward the end." Fewer than a third recognized the statistical phenomenon clearly at work: Averages based on fewer courses are more variable, which guarantees a greater number of extremely low and high GPAs at the end of the first term.

The point to remember: Don't be overly impressed by a few anecdotes. Generalizations based on only a few cases are unreliable.

When Is a Difference Significant?

We can have most confidence when generalizing from samples that (1) are representative of the population we wish to study, (2) give us consistent rather than highly variable data, and (3) are large rather than small. These principles extend to the inferences we make about differences between groups.

Statistical tests help us by indicating the reliability of differences. You needn't understand how statistics are computed to understand the logic behind them: When *averages* from two samples are each *reliable* measures of their respective populations (as when each is based on many observations that have small variability), then the difference between the samples is likely to be reliable as well. When the *difference* between the averages for the two samples is *large*, we have even more confidence that the difference between them reflects a real difference in their populations.

In short, *when the sample averages are reliable and the difference between them is large*, we say the difference has **statistical significance**. This simply means that the difference probably reflects a real difference and is not due to chance variation between the samples. In judging statistical significance, psychologists are conservative. They are like juries who must assume innocence

statistical significance a statistical statement of how likely it is that an obtained result occurred by chance.

PEANUTS

unless guilt is proven, because they would rather risk setting free a guilty person than convicting an innocent person. For most psychologists, proof beyond a reasonable doubt means not making much of a finding unless the odds of its occurring by chance are less than 5 percent (an arbitrary criterion).

When reading about research, you should remember that, given large enough or homogeneous enough samples, a difference between them may be "statistically significant" yet have little practical significance. For example, comparisons of the intelligence test scores among several hundred-thousand first-born and later-born individuals shows a highly significant tendency for first-born individuals within a family to have average scores that are higher than those of their later-born siblings—but only by one or two points (Zajonc & Markus, 1975). Although the difference is statistically significant, it has little practical significance. Some psychologists therefore advocate alternatives to significance testing (Hunter, 1997). Better, they say, to use other ways to express a finding's magnitude and reliability.

The point to remember: Statistical significance indicates the *likelihood* that a result will happen by chance. It does not indicate the *importance* of the result.

REVIEWING ▪ *Statistical Reasoning*

To be an educated person today is to be able to apply simple statistical principles to everyday reasoning. One needn't remember complicated formulas to think more clearly and critically about data.

From our consideration of how we can organize and describe data—by constructing distributions and computing measures of central tendency, variation, correlation, statistical **percentile ranks**, and significance—we derived seven important points to remember when assessing studies that use statistical reasoning:

1. Doubt big, round, undocumented numbers.
2. Always note which measure of central tendency (**mean, median**, or **mode**) is reported. Then, if it is a mean, consider whether a few atypical scores could be distorting it.
3. When looking at statistical graphs in books and magazines and on television ads and news broadcasts, think critically: Always read the scale labels and note their **range**. Use of **standard deviations** provides a more reliable measure of variation. Many types of data form a **normal curve**.
4. Although the **correlation coefficient** (often depicted on a **scatterplot**) does not tell cause and effect, it *can* help us see the world more clearly by revealing the actual extent to which two things relate.
5. When a fluctuating behavior returns to normal, there is no need to invent fancy explanations for why it does so. **Regression toward the mean** is probably at work.
6. Don't be overly impressed by a few anecdotes. Generalizations based on only a few cases are unreliable.
7. **Statistical significance** indicates the *likelihood* that a result will occur by chance. It does not indicate the importance of the result.

Sample Answers to Critical Thinking Exercises

APPENDIX B

Most psychology courses have two major goals: (1) to help you acquire a basic understanding of psychology's knowledge base, and (2) to help you learn to think like a psychologist. The second goal—learning to think like a psychologist—involves critical thinking. Critical thinking can be regarded as a special set of "thinking skills that promote conscious, purposeful, and active involvement of the thinker with new ideas" (Halonen, 1994). Included among these skills are careful observation, asking questions, seeing connections among ideas, and the ability to analyze arguments and the evidence on which they are based.

The critical thinking exercises in this textbook have been designed to help you develop your ability to think critically as you learn about psychology.[1] Each exercise emphasizes one of six categories of critical thinking: *pattern recognition, practical problem solving, creative problem solving, scientific problem solving, psychological reasoning*, and *perspective taking*.

As the foundation for all other forms of critical thinking, *pattern recognition* is the ability to use psychological concepts to describe behavior patterns and events, especially when there are discrepancies between your expectations of what is normal in a certain situation and what actually occurs.

When events or behaviors are unexpected, they may constitute a problem. *Practical problem solving* is the ability to use psychological concepts to develop a plan of action that will lead to the problem's solution.

Creative problem solving is the ability to make novel connections between previously unrelated ideas. This type of critical thinking often leads to new insights about behavior and mental phenomena.

Psychologists employ the scientific method to develop comprehensive and systematic explanations of behavior and mental phenomena. At the heart of this is *scientific problem solving*, which seeks to uncover relationships among the many factors, or variables, involved in producing behavior.

Psychological information is transmitted through persuasive arguments that state a relationship between some aspect of behavior, such as intelligence, and another factor, such as age. *Psychological reasoning* is thinking critically about such arguments, especially the evidence on which they are based.

[1] The model for these exercises comes from J. S. Halonen (1994), *Critical thinking companion for introductory psychology*. New York: Worth Publishers.

The final category of critical thinking is *perspective taking*, which refers to the ability to recognize the ways in which each person's thinking is shaped by his or her values and past experiences.

You should now be ready to expand your critical thinking skills by completing the exercises prepared for each chapter of your textbook. For some chapters, the exercise presents a hypothetical situation that you will need to think through. For others, you will be asked to evaluate arguments that are derived from actual psychological research. And for still other chapters, your understanding of psychological concepts will be tested by asking you to apply them to a new situation. Carefully read the passage for each exercise and then answer the questions that follow.

Polish your critical thinking skills by applying them to each of your college courses, and to other aspects of life as well. Learn to think critically about advertising, political speeches, and the material presented in popular periodicals.

CHAPTER 1 *Thinking Critically With Psychology*

Scientific Problem Solving

1. **Focal behavior:** Reading ability among first graders.
2. **Hypothesis:** Children who watch "Sesame Street" develop greater reading ability than children who watch cartoons.
3. **Independent variable:** Type of television program (educational versus cartoon).
4. **Dependent variable:** Reading test score.
5. **Controlled variables:**
   a. Television program content (educational versus noneducational) during the daily, 1-hour period of exposure.
   b. Ages of subjects.
   c. Reading ability measured over the same time period.
6. **Uncontrolled variables:**
   a. Absence of random assignment leaves alternative explanations for reading improvement in the educational television group. As volunteers, the "Sesame Street" subjects may have been more highly motivated to have their children succeed in reading than the cartoon subjects, who were drafted.
   b. Reading ability of subjects in the two groups was not measured *before* the experiment began. At the outset, the "Sesame Street" subjects may have had higher reading scores than the cartoon subjects.
   c. Knowledge of the teacher's hypothesis (by both students and their parents) may have influenced the results so that the experimental group outperformed the control group.
   d. Other daily activities, such as reading to parents or watching other television programs, might have differentially influenced the reading skills in the two groups.
7. **Valid test of hypothesis?** No. Since so many variables were not controlled, virtually nothing can be concluded from this study. A more valid test would have *randomly assigned* volunteers, who were *not informed* of the teacher's hypothesis and who had been pretested and matched for comparable reading ability to the two groups.

CHAPTER 2 *Biology and Behavior*

Pattern Recognition

Brain Structures	How the Structures Are Involved in Musical Performance
Lower-Level Structures	
Medulla	This structure controls heartbeat, breathing, and other vital systems that keep the musician's body functioning while he or she plays.
Thalamus	By routing sensory information from the musician's eyes, ears, and fingertips to higher brain regions, this structure facilitates the musician's seeing, hearing, touching, decision making, and coordination.
Reticular formation	By helping to control arousal, this structure is crucial in maintaining the musician's attention to the task.
Hippocampus	This structure is involved in the formation of memories for musical theory, as well as of memories of how to play the musical instrument.
Cerebellum	This structure helps coordinate movements involved in playing the instrument.
Structures of the Cerebral Cortex	
Motor cortex	This area is involved in organizing the body movements necessary for playing the instrument.
Sensory cortex	This area is involved in processing incoming sensory information from the musician's fingertips.
Association areas	These areas are involved in the planning and decision making inherent in reading music and playing the instrument.
Corpus callosum	This area is involved in combining information processed by the left and right hemispheres so that the performance reflects the integrated activity of both sides of the brain.

CHAPTER 3 *The Developing Person*

Creative Problem Solving

Erikson describes the crises of infancy and toddlerhood as those of trust versus mistrust and autonomy versus shame and doubt, respectively. If their needs are dependably met, infants and toddlers develop a sense of basic trust; if their needs are not met, they may become doubting, suspicious, or pessimistic as they grow older. The quality of the child's caregiving is an important factor in promoting healthy development during this stage, as is the stability and safety of the home environment. In addition, cultural values that promote or discourage autonomy in infants, as well as the child's gender and temperament, may cause parents to encourage independence more in certain children than in others.

Erikson describes the crises of the preschool and elementary school years as those of initiative versus guilt and competence versus inferiority, respectively. As children strive to develop competence in the skills valued by society, the actions and attitudes of parents, caregivers, and teachers have a powerful effect. When social and cultural expectations are realistic and forgiving, when tasks are structured so that success is likely, and when curiosity and initiative are encouraged, children will come to view themselves as both productive and industrious. When expectations are impossibly high, or when efforts result in failure or criticism, children may come to view themselves as inadequate and inferior.

Physical ability is an important factor in development during childhood. Physically challenged children, who find it increasingly difficult to keep up with their peers, may experience self-doubt and lose confidence in their abilities. Conversely, children who have a special skill, such as excelling at a particular sport or playing a musical instrument, may find it easier to achieve a sense of competence during this stage of development.

Erikson describes the crises of adolescence and young adulthood as identity versus role confusion and intimacy versus isolation, respectively. Those who successfully meet these challenges establish their own goals and values and begin to develop intimate relationships with others; those who struggle may become confused about who they are and feel alienated and lonely. Supportive peers and nurturing parents help by allowing the young person to try out different roles and experiment with various related identities. Social, ethnic, and cultural norms assist by providing recognized developmental milestones along the way. Graduation ceremonies, driver's licenses, and "coming of age" celebrations help young people announce to the world (and to themselves) who they are. Unfortunately, there are many potential obstacles to psychosocial development during these years. These include family circumstances (such as divorce, poverty, or abusive relationships), personal choices (such as early sexual behavior, drug experimentation, and other high-risk behaviors), and even historical circumstances (such as war or famine) that limit the developing person's options in achieving identity and intimacy.

Erikson describes the crises of middle adulthood and late adulthood as generativity versus stagnation and integrity versus despair, respectively. Those who feel productive in their contributions to work, family, and the world emerge with a sense of purpose (generativity) and personal satisfaction in the meaningfulness of their lives (integrity). Those who feel that their work and lives have been unimportant or who have been forced to redefine their identities following divorce, the death of a loved one, or the loss of a job may look back on their lives with bitterness. Health, financial security, career success, as well as specific choices that the individual made earlier in life regarding parenting and intimacy, are important factors in determining whether these final challenges of the life span are met successfully.

CHAPTER 4 *Sensation and Perception*

Practical Problem Solving

Figure-Ground: This grouping principle enables us to perceive any object, called the *figure*, as distinct from its surroundings, called the *ground*. Web text, buttons, and graphics (the "figures") need to be bright and obvious against uncomplicated backgrounds (the "grounds"). Your viewers will miss important information if it has to compete for attention with a background that is either too busy or that does not provide enough contrast with the "figures" (for instance, if colors are too similar, figure can't easily be distinguished from ground).

Similarity: If figures look similar to each other, we group them together. Understanding this principle will help you provide consistency across the pages of a Web site. This should make your viewers feel more comfortable and help them locate what they are looking for more easily. For example, you may want to use the company logo as a consistent element on each page of the Web site. On a more basic level, consistent paragraph formatting, text size, fonts, and color can all be used to increase readability and the ease of navigation through a Web site.

Relative Brightness: Because nearby objects reflect more light to our eyes, dimmer objects seem farther away. You can use this principle to your advantage by effectively using light, shade, and shadow to add the visual appeal of three-dimensional Web graphics and text.

Size-Distance Relationship: Perceiving an object's general size provides us with cues to its distance. As with any two-dimensional representation of depth, Web graphics rely on size constancy and the size-distance relationship to convey the perceptual impression of nearness to and farness from the viewer. Effective Web page designs scale the size of graphics to indicate the importance of particular topics. Larger graphics appear closer and more important. Smaller graphics appear farther away and less important.

Culture and Perception: Cultural background influences nearly every aspect of perception, from how our eyes scan a page, to our sensitivity to monocular depth cues, to our emotional response to color. So you will want to pay close attention, for example, to the placement of items at your site. In Western cultures people read from top to bottom and from left to right. You will want to place the more important items near the top of a page, and keep in mind that the top left corner will get the most immediate attention. Well-positioned text and graphic elements capitalize on these tendencies to promote smooth eye flow (top to bottom and left to right) and subordination (read this first, read this next).

The effective use of color also illustrates cultural influences on perception. In the United States, for example, "cool colors" such as blue and green are perceived as soothing, while "warm colors" such as red and orange are perceived as more stimulating. As another example, the color red is often used to indicate danger, while green may represent financial information. So, you will want to incorporate colors into your site *carefully*, based on the messages you wish to convey and the emotional response you wish to evoke.

CHAPTER 5 *States of Consciousness*

Creative Problem Solving

1. Because insomnia complainers typically overestimate their loss of sleep, you might reasonably doubt the severity of your aunt's problem. In addition, the fact that she apparently is not irritable, unable to concentrate, or suffering from other common effects of sleep deprivation suggests that she may be exaggerating her sleep loss. You might help alleviate your aunt's anxiety by informing her that laboratory studies reveal that insomnia complainers underestimate the amount they sleep by nearly 50 percent. It is likely that she *thinks* she is sleeping very little because she is remembering only her waking moments.

   Being middle aged, your aunt should be reminded that occasional awakenings are more likely than when she was younger, and that developmental changes in circadian arousal are quite normal. Older adults such as your aunt are more likely to feel at their best during the morning hours, with their alertness and performance efficiency declining as the day wears on.

2. In addition to reassuring your aunt that her problem is probably not worth fretting over, you should advise her that her napping, late-night exercising, and alcohol use may be contributing to her perceived sleep problems. To

promote better sleep, she should avoid napping during the day, exercise regularly but not in the evening, avoid alcoholic drinks (which suppress REM sleep), and try to maintain a regular sleep/waking schedule.

3. As for your aunt's belief that she has stopped dreaming, you can safely reassure her that even people who claim they never dream will almost always report a dream if they are awakened when their eye movements and bodily arousal indicate REM sleep. And even if she is dreaming less, tell her that she needn't worry that lost dreams will lead to psychological problems. Freud's theory that dreams provide a psychic safety valve has little support from contemporary psychologists, who emphasize instead the role of REM sleep in information processing.

   To prove that she hasn't lost her ability to dream, your aunt might set an alarm to awaken her 15 minutes earlier one morning. Because REM periods are longer near a person's normal waking time, an early alarm is likely to arouse your aunt during a dream and improve her recollection.

4. Freud believed that by fulfilling our unconscious wishes, dreams discharge otherwise unacceptable feelings. According to this theory, a person who could not dream would therefore have no "psychic safety valve." The unresolved inner conflicts presumably would surface in other undesirable ways in the person's behavior and mental processes.

   A physiological psychologist would probably emphasize the role of REM sleep in providing the brain with periodic stimulation. The absence of such stimulation might lead to deterioration in the brain's neural circuitry and result in lapses of memory, poor attention span, or other mental difficulties.

   A cognitive psychologist would probably point to the role of REM sleep in information processing and memory. Without REM, people might have more difficulty learning new information, retaining and retrieving knowledge, and coping with stressful experiences.

CHAPTER 6 *Learning*

Pattern Recognition

1. For children who learn to wake up without special training, the sensation of a wet bed or diaper functions as a UCS that elicits awakening, which is the UCR. Bladder tension (unless painful) is an initially neutral stimulus that becomes associated with the UCS. Over time, bladder tension becomes a CS and will cause the child to awaken before the bed or diaper is wet. This learned awakening is the CR.

2. For children who are trained with the special sheet and bell, the UCS is the bell that causes them to wake up; the UCR is waking up in response to the bell; the CS is bladder tension; and the CR is waking up in response to bladder tension.

3. Although the classical conditioning explanation for this example makes sense based on the evidence, an explanation based on operant conditioning is also possible. Although in very young children waking up is normally a reflexive act (and therefore subject to classical conditioning), in older children it might be considered a *voluntary* act (and therefore subject to operant conditioning). Children may learn to wake up because this behavior operates on the environment to produce rewarding stimuli, such as the pleasurable sensation of relieving one's bladder.

CHAPTER 7 *Memory*

Practical Problem Solving

1. The police are trying to identify the car-jacker. For some reason, they suspect that Raymond committed the crime, and they are attempting to obtain more evidence by jogging Naomi's eyewitness memory.
2. Naomi was probably initially unable to identify the gunman because the fleeting glimpse did not allow her to encode the details of his appearance. The confusion of the moment may also have prevented Naomi from rehearsing her mental image of the perpetrator, allowing her memory to decay quickly. Moreover, seeing hundreds of mug-book photographs so soon after the crime could have retroactively interfered with whatever real memory Naomi had of the gunman's appearance. Finally, the mug book may not actually have contained the gunman's photograph.
3. The misleading questioning and repeated exposure to Raymond's photograph may have caused Naomi to misremember the actual event and to reconstruct her memory of it to include Raymond's involvement. Seeing the lineup of men several weeks later, Naomi may have been unable to discriminate her eyewitness memory from her memory of the mug-book photographs. This would also account for Naomi's newfound confidence in the accuracy of her memory.

CHAPTER 8 *Thinking, Language, and Intelligence*

Perspective Taking

1. **Position supported:** B. F. Skinner's

   Explanation: Marie's utterances can be explained by three principles of learning: *imitation*, *association*, and *reinforcement*. The first time she said "cow," she may merely have been imitating her mother's utterance. The fact that she later spontaneously identified a cow indicates that she had formed an association between the picture and word, and had been reinforced (by her mother's praise) for demonstrating her new knowledge.
2. **Position supported:** Noam Chomsky's

   Explanation: Jack's grammatical error ("goed") is an example of overgeneralizing a grammatical rule (adding *–ed* to form the past tense of a regular verb). Because it is unlikely that Jack has ever heard his parents or teacher make this error, principles of learning cannot explain this utterance. Because all children make this type of error, the existence of a common underlying biological language acquisition device is implicated.
3. **Position supported:** B. F. Skinner's

   Explanation: Nicole's deficiency in signing demonstrates the impact of early experience in language development.
4. **Position supported:** Noam Chomsky's

   Explanation: Because Malcolm and Maya have presumably been exposed to English for the same number of years, principles of learning cannot explain the difference in their fluency. Chomsky would say that Maya was exposed to English too late in life for her inborn language acquisition device to benefit fully.

CHAPTER 9 *Motivation*

Pattern Recognition

1. Assuming that Rochelle and Doreen have roughly equal ability, there must be another explanation for the difference in their school performance. Doreen's high grades, her motivation to select moderately challenging classes where success is attainable yet attributable to her own efforts, and her desire to do *her* best rather than compare herself to others point to a high level of achievement motivation. Rochelle's preference for very easy or very difficult tasks is typical of people with a lower need for achievement. In such situations, failure is either unlikely or unembarrassing because it is attributable to the impossibility of the task rather than the individual's performance.
2. Initially, practicing the guitar was its own reward for Doreen; extrinsic rewards were unnecessary. The monetary reward her parents later provided may have *overjustified* guitar playing, turning it into a form of work and lessening Doreen's intrinsic enjoyment and, thus, her motivation for practicing. Rochelle's primary motive for learning the guitar apparently involved competing with her sister. This is an example of extrinsic motivation rather than motivation to master a skill for its own sake. The monetary reward offered by her parents provided an additional extrinsic incentive, to which Rochelle responded by increasing her practice time. When Doreen began to lose interest in practicing and the monetary reward was withdrawn, the extrinsic basis for Rochelle's motivation was lost. As a result, Rochelle lost interest in playing the guitar.
3. The parents would be wise to recognize the different levels of achievement motivation in their daughters and to individualize their treatment in order to capitalize on this difference. As an independent "self-starter," Doreen will probably respond more to rewards that are informative rather than controlling. Praise and encouragement rather than extrinsic rewards will be more effective in boosting Doreen's feelings of competence and intrinsic motivation. For Rochelle, the parents first need to clarify their goal. If they want to do everything in their power to improve Rochelle's proficiency on the guitar, they might capitalize on her competitiveness by placing her in group classes where comparisons with others are inevitable. If they want to cultivate intrinsic motivation, they would do well to encourage greater independence in Rochelle by challenging her to reach her own potential as a musician and frequently praising her for her successes.

CHAPTER 10 *Emotions, Stress, and Health*

Scientific Problem Solving

1. The James-Lange theory proposes that the experience of emotion derives from our awareness of our physiological responses to emotion-arousing stimuli. It also equates different emotions with specific body states. Assuming that sexual excitement can be triggered by the physical changes induced by exercise, this theory would predict greater reported feelings of sexual excitement during the first two phases of exercise recovery, when the subjects were actually physically aroused, than during the third phase, when the subjects were no longer aroused. The fact that sexual excitement was low during the first phase of recovery, when physical arousal was high, seems to conflict with the theory.

2. The Cannon-Bard theory proposes that an emotion-arousing stimulus simultaneously triggers physical arousal and the subjective experience of emotion. Assuming that the film was an emotion-arousing stimulus, this theory would predict greater reported feelings of sexual excitement during all three phases of the experiment, because subjects viewed the film in each phase. However, this explanation is inconsistent with the finding that subjects reported being sexually excited only during the second phase of the experiment. The theory offers no explanation of why the emotional experiences of subjects during Phases 1 and 2 differed.

3. According to Schachter's two-factor theory, to experience an emotion one must be physically aroused and cognitively label that arousal as an emotion. Of the three theories, this one seems to explain the results of the experiment most fully. During the first phase, subjects were physically aroused, and a potential "emotional" explanation for their arousal (the film) was available. Because they *perceived* that they were still aroused from the exercise, however, subjects during this phase attributed their arousal to the exercise rather than to sexual excitement. By the third phase, the subjects had fully recovered from the exercise and lacked the physical arousal necessary to trigger the emotion-attribution process. In Phase 2, the subjects were physically aroused but did not subjectively perceive this arousal. According to the two-factor theory, this unexplained arousal was therefore attributed to sexual excitement from the film.

CHAPTER 11 *Personality*

Perspective Taking

1. A psychoanalyst might explain Darren's problems as being rooted in unresolved childhood conflicts. His sarcastic manner might indicate that he was orally overindulged as a child and is fixated in the oral stage of psychosexual development. A psychoanalyst might also say that Darren's ego is attempting to defend itself from anxiety by offering a self-justifying explanation for his poor performance on the exam ("the test was unfair") in place of the real, more threatening reason for failure ("I was unprepared").

2. A trait theorist would probably describe Darren's personality in terms of characteristic behaviors and motives. According to the Big Five personality factors, for example, Darren might be described as anxious and self-pitying (emotional stability), sober and reserved (extraversion), suspicious and undisciplined (agreeableness and conscientiousness, respectively).

3. A humanistic theorist might explain Darren's pessimism and sarcastic manner as the result of low self-esteem and perhaps not having his basic needs met as his personality was formed. Humanistic theorists might also suggest that Darren has a negative self-concept because his ideal self (a successful college student) differs from his actual self (an academic failure). His unwillingness to accept responsibility for his failure might be described as a self-serving bias.

4. A social-cognitive theorist would probably point to the reciprocal influences among Darren's past behavior, internal personal factors, and external experiences in shaping his personality. His anxiety and unwillingness to accept responsibility for failure suggest that he perceives the world as threatening and himself as being controlled by his environment. Darren's hopeless attitude and external locus of control may have resulted from repeated experiences with undesirable events over which he had no control.

CHAPTER 12 *Psychological Disorders*

Perspective Taking

1. Fiona's daughter should be more concerned; she may by wrongly attributing to old age what is really psychologically disordered behavior. Fiona's behavior satisfies at least three of the criteria for such a label: it is atypical, disturbing, and maladaptive. Furthermore, although triggered by the stress of her divorce, her symptoms have persisted too long and are too extreme to be considered a normal, justifiable response to a stressful event. Fiona's daughter is also misinterpreting the biological evidence: The grandmother's similar symptoms and the effectiveness of antidepressant medication are further evidence for a psychological disorder.

2. A clinical psychologist would argue that Fiona is showing classic symptoms of *major depressive disorder*, including poor appetite, insomnia, lethargy, feelings of worthlessness, and loss of interest in family and friends. He or she would also point out that these symptoms have persisted much longer than would normally be expected following a stressful event.

3. (a) A biologically oriented therapist would cite two pieces of evidence: (1) Since her mother seems to have suffered depression in late middle age, Fiona may have a genetic predisposition to this condition; and (2) the fact that an antidepressant drug made her feel less depressed suggests Fiona's depression may be caused by a biochemical imbalance.

   (b) From the social-cognitive perspective, Fiona's depression is fueled by a vicious cycle of overgeneralized, self-focused, negative thinking. She has explained a stressful experience (her divorce) in terms that are *stable* and *global* ("Everything I have ever done, or will do, is worthless") and *internal* ("The divorce is my fault"). The hopelessness resulting from these self-blaming attributions has elicited social rejection, hampered her behavior, and is likely to lead to further negative experiences.

CHAPTER 13 *Therapy*

Practical Problem Solving

1. There are several possible reasons why psychotherapy was apparently effective for Deborah but not for Vincent. One is that cognitive therapies, such as Deborah's, have proven most successful in treating depression. Behavior therapies, such as the counterconditioning Vincent experienced, have proven to be more effective in treating specific behavior problems, such as phobias, compulsions, or sexual disorders. A second reason is that Deborah actively sought and entered therapy at a time of personal crisis, whereas Vincent felt that there was nothing unusual about his behavior or attitude. Deborah's depression may have lifted partly as a result of the passage of time and the lessening of the crisis. A third reason is that Deborah chose her therapist carefully, and she worked with someone who offered her hope that things would improve. Vincent picked his therapist randomly, maintained a skeptical attitude throughout therapy, and never admitted he needed help. Thus, Deborah's belief in her treatment could have created a powerful placebo effect that harnessed her own healing powers and led to improvement. Finally, Deborah invested considerably more time and money in her therapy than Vincent did. This would probably result in a stronger need to justify the therapy and, thus, a more favorable evaluation of its effectiveness.

2. Clients' perceptions of the effectiveness of psychotherapy are not acceptable as scientific evidence. One reason is that people who are suffering nonpsychotic disorders often improve whether or not they receive treatment. Psychotherapy clients who would have improved anyway might misattribute their improvement to therapy. Furthermore, people who go into therapy with the expectation that it will be effective may fall victim to the confirmation bias and remember only information that confirms their expectation.

CHAPTER 14 *Social Psychology*

Pattern Recognition

1. If, like many people, you found it more difficult to generate descriptions of outgroups, this may be the result of your relatively limited contact with members of such groups.
2. If your ingroup descriptions were more favorable than your outgroup descriptions, you may be expressing a tendency to favor one's own group, called the ingroup bias.
3. When 50 college students were asked to describe each of these groups, their top five descriptions were as follows:

   Physicians: (1) intelligent/smart; (2) caring/understanding/compassionate; (3) wealthy/rich; (4) busy/hardworking; (5) well-educated

   Athletes: (1) athletic/fit/strong; (2) driven/highly motivated/dedicated; (3) competitive; (4) agile/quick; (5) glorified/famous/popular and egotistical/proud

   Artists: (1) creative; (2) bizarre/strange; (3) free-spirited/nonconforming/individualistic; (4) liberal/tolerant/open-minded; (5) talented/gifted

   Vegetarians: (1) healthy/health-conscious; (2) environmentally or ecologically conscious; (3) limited in diet/picky about food; (4) caring/sensitive; (5) liberal

   College Students: (1) fun/wild/exciting; (2) stressed/pressured/fatigued; (3) intelligent/bright; (4) diligent/dedicated/studious; (5) poor/broke and open-minded/tolerant/liberal

   Lawyers: (1) articulate/convincing/persuasive; (2) deceptive/dishonest; (3) wealthy/rich; (4) intelligent/smart; (5) strong-willed/powerful and ambitious/success-oriented

If your outgroup descriptions match better with the above than your ingroup descriptions, it may reflect the human tendency to form stereotyped beliefs in order to simplify the world. In categorizing people into groups, we see the members of the outgroup as all alike, whereas the members of the ingroup are viewed as much more diverse.

Glossary

A

absolute threshold the minimum stimulation needed to detect a particular stimulus. (p. 127)

accommodation the process by which the eye's lens changes shape to focus the image of objects on the retina. (p. 131)

acetylcholine [ah-seat-el-KO-leen] **(ACh)** a neurotransmitter that, among its functions, triggers muscle contraction. (p. 42)

achievement motivation a desire for significant accomplishment; for mastery of things, people, or ideas; for control; for attaining a high standard. (p. 339)

achievement tests tests designed to assess what a person has learned. (p. 293)

acquisition the initial stage in classical conditioning; the phase associating a neutral stimulus with an unconditioned stimulus so that the neutral stimulus comes to evoke a conditioned response. (p. 209)

action potential a neural impulse; a brief electrical charge that travels down an axon. The action potential is generated by the movement of positively charged atoms in and out of channels in the axon's membrane. (p. 40)

active listening empathic listening in which the listener echoes, restates, and clarifies. A feature of Rogers's person-centered therapy. (p. 465)

adaptation-level phenomenon our tendency to form judgments (of sounds, of lights, of income) relative to a "neutral" level defined by our prior experience. (p. 360)

adolescence the transition period from childhood to adulthood, extending from puberty to independence. (p. 99)

adrenal [ah-DREEN-el] **glands** a pair of endocrine glands just above the kidneys. The adrenals secrete the hormones epinephrine (adrenaline) and norepinephrine (noradrenaline), which help to arouse the body in times of stress. (p. 68)

aerobic exercise sustained exercise that increases heart and lung fitness; may also alleviate depression and anxiety. (p. 378)

aggression any physical or verbal behavior intended to hurt or destroy. (p. 513)

algorithm a methodical, logical rule or procedure that guarantees solving a particular problem. Contrasts with the usually speedier—but also more error-prone—use of *heuristics*. (p. 269)

alpha waves the relatively slow brain waves of a relaxed, awake state. (p. 174)

altruism unselfish regard for the welfare of others. (p. 528)

Alzheimer's disease a progressive and irreversible brain disorder characterized by gradual deterioration of memory, reasoning, language, and, finally, physical functioning. (p. 112)

amnesia the loss of memory. (p. 246)

amphetamines drugs that stimulate neural activity, causing speeded-up body functions and associated energy and mood changes. (p. 194)

amygdala [ah-MIG-dah-la] two almond-shaped neural clusters that are components of the limbic system and are linked to emotion. (p. 53)

anorexia nervosa an eating disorder in which a normal-weight person (usually an adolescent female) diets and becomes significantly (15 percent or more) underweight, yet, still feeling fat, continues to starve. (p. 319)

antisocial personality disorder a personality disorder in which the person (usually a man) exhibits a lack of conscience for wrongdoing, even toward friends and family members. May be aggressive and ruthless or a clever con artist. (p. 455)

anxiety disorders psychological disorders characterized by distressing, persistent anxiety or maladaptive behaviors that reduce anxiety. (p. 431)

aphasia impairment of language, usually caused by left hemisphere damage either to Broca's area (impairing speaking) or to Wernicke's area (impairing understanding). (p. 59)

applied research scientific study that aims to solve practical problems. (p. 7)

aptitude tests tests designed to predict a person's future performance. Aptitude is the capacity to learn. (p. 293)

association areas areas of the cerebral cortex that are not involved in primary motor or sensory functions; rather, they are involved in higher mental functions such as learning, remembering, thinking, and speaking. (p. 58)

associative learning learning that certain events occur together. The events may be two stimuli (as in classical conditioning) or a response and its consequences (as in operant conditioning). (p. 206)

attachment an emotional tie with another person; shown in young children by their seeking closeness to the caregiver and showing distress on separation. (p. 91)

attitude a belief and feeling that predisposes one to respond in a particular way to objects, people, and events. (p. 493)

attribution theory the theory that we tend to give a causal explanation for someone's behavior, often by crediting either the situation or the person's disposition. (p. 491)

audition the sense of hearing. (p. 138)

automatic processing unconscious encoding of incidental information such as space, time, and frequency and of well-learned information such as word meanings. (p. 234)

autonomic [aw-tuh-NAHM-ik] **nervous system** the part of the peripheral nervous system that controls the glands and the muscles of the internal organs (such as the heart). Its sympathetic division arouses; its parasympathetic division calms. (p. 45)

availability heuristic estimating the likelihood of events based on their availability in memory; if instances come readily to mind (perhaps because of their vividness), we presume such events are common. (p. 272)

aversive conditioning a type of counterconditioning that associates an unpleasant state (such as nausea) with an unwanted behavior (such as drinking alcohol). (p. 469)

axon the extension of a neuron, ending in branching terminal fibers, through which messages are sent to other neurons or to muscles or glands. (p. 40)

B

babbling stage beginning at 4 months, the stage of speech development in which the infant spontaneously utters various sounds at first unrelated to the household language. (p. 278)

barbiturates drugs that depress the activity of the central nervous system, reducing anxiety but impairing memory and judgment. (p. 194)

basal metabolic rate the body's resting rate of energy expenditure. (p. 317)

basic research pure science that aims to increase the scientific knowledge base. (p. 7)

basic trust according to Erik Erikson, a sense that the world is predictable and trustworthy; said to be formed during infancy by appropriate experiences with responsive caregivers. (p. 94)

behavior genetics the study of the power and limits of genetic and environmental influences on behavior. (p. 70)

behavior therapy therapy that applies learning principles to the elimination of unwanted behaviors. (p. 466)

behaviorism the view that psychology (1) should be an objective science that (2) studies behavior without reference to mental processes. Most research psychologists today agree with (1) but not with (2). (p. 214)

belief perseverance clinging to one's initial conceptions after the basis on which they were formed has been discredited. (Confirmation bias—searching for belief-support information— contributes to belief perseverance.) (p. 275)

binocular cues depth cues, such as retinal disparity and convergence, that depend on the use of two eyes. (p. 148)

bio-psycho-social perspective a contemporary perspective which assumes that biological, sociocultural, and psychological factors combine and interact to produce psychological disorders. (p. 428)

biofeedback a system for electronically recording, amplifying, and feeding back information regarding a subtle physiological state, such as blood pressure or muscle tension. (p. 379)

biological psychology a branch of psychology concerned with the links between biology and behavior. (Some biological psychologists call themselves *behavioral neuroscientists, neuropsychologists, behavior geneticists, physiological psychologists,* or *biopsychologists.*) (p. 39)

bipolar disorder a mood disorder in which the person alternates between the hopelessness and lethargy of depression and the overexcited state of mania. (p. 441)

blind spot the point at which the optic nerve leaves the eye, creating a "blind" spot because no receptor cells are located there. (p. 132)

bottom-up processing analysis that begins with the sense receptors and works up to the brain's integration of sensory information. (p. 125)

brainstem the oldest part and central core of the brain, beginning where the spinal cord swells as it enters the skull; it is responsible for automatic survival functions. (p. 48)

Broca's area an area of the frontal lobe, in the left hemisphere for most people, that directs the muscle movements involved in speech. (p. 60)

bulimia nervosa an eating disorder characterized by private, "binge-purge" episodes of overeating, usually of highly caloric foods, followed by vomiting or laxative use. (p. 319)

bystander effect the tendency for any given bystander to be less likely to give aid if other bystanders are present. (p. 529)

C

Cannon-Bard theory the theory that an emotion-arousing stimulus simultaneously triggers (1) physiological responses and (2) the subjective experience of emotion. (p. 364)

case study an observation technique in which one person is studied in depth in the hope of revealing universal principles. (p. 14)

catharsis emotional release. In psychology, the catharsis hypothesis maintains that "releasing" aggressive energy (through action or fantasy) relieves aggressive urges. (p. 358)

central nervous system (CNS) the brain and spinal cord. (p. 44)

cerebellum [sehr-uh-BELL-um] the "little brain" attached to the rear of the brainstem; it helps coordinate voluntary movement and balance. (p. 52)

cerebral [seh-REE-bruhl] **cortex** the intricate fabric of interconnected neural cells that covers the cerebral hemispheres; the body's ultimate control and information-processing center. (p. 55)

chromosomes threadlike structures made of DNA molecules that contain the genes. (p. 69)

chunking organizing items into familiar, manageable units; often occurs automatically. (p. 238)

circadian rhythm [ser-KAY-dee-an] the biological clock; cyclical bodily rhythms (for example, of temperature and wakefulness). (p. 173)

classical conditioning a type of learning in which an organism comes to associate stimuli. A neutral stimulus that signals an unconditioned stimulus (UCS) begins to produce a response that anticipates and prepares for the unconditioned stimulus. (Also called *Pavlovian conditioning*.) (p. 207)

clinical psychology a branch of psychology that studies, assesses, and treats people with psychological disorders. (p. 7)

cochlea [KOHK-lee-uh] a coiled, bony, fluid-filled tube in the inner ear through which sound waves trigger nerve impulses. (p. 139)

cognition all the mental activities associated with thinking, knowing, and remembering. (pp. 86, 267)

cognitive dissonance theory the theory that we act to reduce the discomfort (dissonance) we feel when two of our thoughts (cognitions) are inconsistent. For example, when we become aware that our attitudes and our actions clash, we can reduce the resulting dissonance by changing our attitudes. (p. 495)

cognitive map a mental representation of the layout of one's environment. For example, after exploring a maze, rats act as if they have learned a cognitive map of it. (p. 222)

cognitive therapy therapy that teaches people new, more adaptive ways of thinking and acting; based on the assumption that thoughts intervene between events and our emotional reactions. (p. 470)

collective unconscious Carl Jung's concept of a shared, inherited reservoir of memory traces from our species' history. (p. 395)

collectivism giving priority to the goals of one's group (often one's extended family or work group) and defining one's identity accordingly. (p. 411)

color constancy perceiving familiar objects as having consistent color, even if changing illumination alters the wavelengths reflected by the object. (p. 137)

companionate love the deep affectionate attachment we feel for those with whom our lives are intertwined. (p. 527)

concept a mental grouping of similar objects, events, or people. (p. 268)

concrete operational stage in Piaget's theory, the stage of cognitive development (from about 6 or 7 to 11 years of age) during which children gain the mental operations that enable them to think logically about concrete events. (p. 89)

conditioned response (CR) in classical conditioning, the learned response to a previously neutral conditioned stimulus (CS). (p. 208)

conditioned stimulus (CS) in classical conditioning, an originally neutral stimulus that, after association with an unconditioned stimulus (UCS), comes to trigger a conditioned response. (p. 208)

cones receptor cells that are concentrated near the center of the retina and that function in daylight or in well-lit conditions. The cones detect fine detail and give rise to color sensations. (p. 132)

confirmation bias a tendency to search for information that confirms one's preconceptions. (p. 270)

conflict a perceived incompatibility of actions, goals, or ideas. (p. 520)

conformity adjusting one's behavior or thinking to coincide with a group standard. (p. 497)

consciousness our awareness of ourselves and our environment (p. 170)

conservation the principle (which Piaget believed to be a part of concrete operational reasoning) that properties such as mass, volume, and number remain the same despite changes in the forms of objects. (p. 87)

content validity the extent to which a test samples the behavior that is of interest (such as a driving test that samples driving tasks). (p. 296)

continuous reinforcement reinforcing the desired response every time it occurs. (p. 219)

control condition the condition of an experiment that contrasts with the experimental treatment and serves as a comparison for evaluating the effect of the treatment. (p. 24)

convergence a binocular cue for perceiving depth; the extent to which the eyes converge inward when looking at an object. (p. 150)

coronary heart disease the clogging of the vessels that nourish the heart muscle; the leading cause of death in the United States. (p. 372)

corpus callosum [KOR-pus kah-LOW-sum] the large band of neural fibers connecting the two brain hemispheres and carrying messages between them. (p. 63)

correlation a statistical measure that indicates the extent to which two factors vary together and thus how well either factor predicts the other. (p. 17)

correlation coefficient a statistical measure of the extent to which two factors vary together, and thus of how well either factor predicts the other. Scores with a *positive correlation coefficient* go up and down together (as with high school and college GPAs). A *negative correlation coefficient* indicates that one score falls as the other rises (as in the relationship between self-esteem and depression). (p. 540)

counterconditioning a behavior therapy procedure that conditions new responses to stimuli that trigger unwanted behaviors; based on classical conditioning. Includes *systematic desensitization* and *aversive conditioning*. (p. 467)

creativity the ability to produce novel and valuable ideas. (p. 296)

criterion the behavior (such as college grades) that a test (such as the SAT) is designed to predict; thus, the measure used in defining whether the test has predictive validity. (p. 296)

critical period an optimal period shortly after birth when an organism's exposure to certain stimuli or experiences produces proper development. (p. 92)

critical thinking thinking that does not blindly accept arguments and conclusions. Rather, it examines assumptions, discerns hidden values, evaluates evidence, and assesses conclusions. (p. 9)

cross-sectional study a study in which people of different ages are compared with one another. (p. 113)

crystallized intelligence one's accumulated knowledge and verbal skills; tends to increase with age. (p. 114)

CT (computed tomography) scan a series of x-ray photographs taken from different angles and combined by computer into a composite representation of a slice through the body. Also called *CAT scan*. (p. 50)

culture the enduring behaviors, ideas, attitudes, and traditions shared by a large group of people and transmitted from one generation to the next. (pp. 29, 506)

D

defense mechanisms in psychoanalytic theory, the ego's protective methods of reducing anxiety by unconsciously distorting reality. (p. 393)

deindividuation the loss of self-awareness and self-restraint occurring in group situations that foster arousal and anonymity. (p. 504)

déjà vu that eerie sense that "I've experienced this before." Cues from the current situation may subconsciously trigger retrieval of an earlier experience. (p. 251)

delta waves the large, slow brain waves associated with deep sleep. (p. 174)

delusions false beliefs, often of persecution or grandeur, that may accompany psychotic disorders. (p. 449)

dendrite the bushy, branching extensions of a neuron that receive messages and conduct impulses toward the cell body. (p. 40)

dependent variable the experimental factor—in psychology, the behavior or mental process—that is being measured; the variable that may change in response to manipulations of the independent variable. (p. 25)

depressants drugs (such as alcohol, barbiturates, and opiates) that reduce neural activity and slow body functions. (p. 193)

depth perception the ability to see objects in three dimensions although the images that strike the retina are two-dimensional; allows us to judge distance. (p. 148)

developmental psychology a branch of psychology that studies physical, cognitive, and social change throughout the life span. (p. 79)

difference threshold the minimum difference that a person can detect between two stimuli 50 percent of the time. We experience the difference threshold as a just noticeable difference. (Also called *just noticeable difference* or *jnd*.) (p. 128)

discrimination in classical conditioning, the ability to distinguish between a conditioned stimulus and other stimuli that do not signal an unconditioned stimulus. (p. 210)

displacement defense mechanism that shifts sexual or aggressive impulses toward a more acceptable or less threatening object or person, as when redirecting anger toward a safer outlet. (p. 393)

dissociation a split in consciousness, which allows some thoughts and behaviors to occur simultaneously with others. (p. 188)

dissociative amnesia selective memory loss said to be brought on by extreme stress. (p. 437)

dissociative disorders disorders in which conscious awareness becomes separated (dissociated) from previous memories, thoughts, and feelings. See *dissociative amnesia*, *dissociative fugue*, and *dissociative identity disorder*. (p. 437)

dissociative fugue [fewg] a dissociative disorder in which flight from one's home and identity accompanies amnesia. (p. 438)

dissociative identity disorder a rare dissociative disorder in which a person exhibits two or more distinct and alternating personalities. Also called *multiple personality disorder*. (p. 438)

DNA (deoxyribonucleic acid) a complex molecule containing the genetic information that makes up the chromosomes. (p. 69)

double-blind procedure an experimental procedure in which both the subject and the research staff are ignorant (blind) about whether the subject has received the treatment or a placebo. Commonly used in drug-evaluation studies. (p. 27)

Down syndrome a condition of retardation and associated physical disorders caused by an extra chromosome in one's genetic makeup. (p. 297)

drive-reduction theory the idea that a physiological need creates an aroused tension state (a drive) that motivates an organism to satisfy the need. (p. 313)

DSM-IV the American Psychiatric Association's *Diagnostic and Statistical Manual of Mental Disorders (Fourth Edition)*, a widely used system for classifying psychological disorders. (p. 429)

E

echoic memory a momentary sensory memory of auditory stimuli; if attention is elsewhere, sounds and words can still be recalled within 3 or 4 seconds. (p. 242)

eclectic approach an approach to psychotherapy that depends on the client's problems, uses or integrates techniques from various forms of therapy. (Also called *psychotherapy integration*.) (p. 462)

effortful processing encoding that requires attention and conscious effort. (p. 234)

ego the largely conscious, "executive" part of personality that, according to Freud, mediates among the demands of the id, superego, and reality. The ego operates on the *reality principle*, satisfying the id's desires in ways that will realistically bring pleasure rather than pain. (p. 391)

egocentrism in Piaget's theory, the inability of the preoperational child to take another's point of view. (p. 88)

electroconvulsive therapy (ECT) a biomedical therapy for severely depressed patients in which a brief electric current is sent through the brain of an anesthetized patient. (p. 485)

electroencephalogram (EEG) an amplified recording of the waves of electrical activity that sweep across the brain's surface. These waves are measured by electrodes placed on the scalp. (p. 50)

embryo the developing human organism from about 2 weeks after fertilization through the second month. (p. 81)

emotion a response of the whole organism, involving (1) physiological arousal, (2) expressive behaviors, and (3) conscious experience. (p. 347)

emotional intelligence the ability to perceive, express, understand, and regulate emotions. (p. 292)

empirically derived test a test (such as the MMPI) developed by testing a pool of items and then selecting those that discriminate between groups. (p. 403)

encoding the processing of information into the memory system, for example by extracting meaning. (p. 233)

endocrine [EN-duh-krin] **system** the body's "slow" chemical communication system; a set of glands that secrete hormones into the bloodstream. (p. 67)

endorphins [en-DOR-fins] "morphine within"—natural, opiate-like neurotransmitters linked to pain control and to pleasure. (p. 43)

equity a condition in which people receive from a relationship in proportion to what they give to it. (p. 528)

estrogen a sex hormone, secreted in greater amounts by females than by males. In nonhuman female mammals, estrogen levels peak during ovulation, promoting sexual receptivity. (p. 328)

evolutionary psychology the study of the evolution of behavior using the principles of natural selection, which presumably favor behavioral tendencies that contribute to the preservation and spread of one's genes. (p. 70)

experiment a research method in which the investigator manipulates one or more factors (independent variables) to observe their effect on some behavior or mental process (the dependent variable) while controlling other relevant factors by random assignment of subjects. (p. 23)

experimental condition the condition of an experiment that exposes subjects to the treatment (to one version of the "independent variable"). (p. 24)

explicit memory memory of facts and experiences that one can consciously know and "declare." (Also called *declarative memory*.) (p. 247)

external locus of control the perception that chance or outside forces beyond one's personal control will determine one's fate. (p. 417)

extinction the diminishing of a conditioned response; occurs in classical conditioning when an unconditioned stimulus (UCS) does not follow a conditioned stimulus (CS). (p. 209)

extrasensory perception (ESP) the controversial claim that perception can occur apart from sensory input. Said to include *telepathy, clairvoyance,* and *precognition*. (p. 160)

extrinsic motivation a desire to perform a behavior due to promised rewards or threats of punishment. (p. 340)

F

factor analysis a statistical procedure that identifies clusters of related items (called *factors*) on a test; used to identify different dimensions of performance that underlie one's total score. (p. 291)

false consensus effect the tendency to overestimate the extent to which others share our beliefs and behaviors. (p. 15)

family therapy therapy that treats the family as a system. Views an individual's unwanted behaviors as influenced by or directed at other family members; encourages family members toward positive relationships and improved communication. (p. 474)

fantasy-prone personality someone who imagines and recalls experiences with lifelike vividness and who spends considerable time fantasizing. (p. 172)

feature detectors nerve cells in the brain that respond to specific features of the stimulus, such as shape, angle, or movement. (p. 134)

feel-good, do-good phenomenon people's tendency to be helpful when already in a good mood. (p. 359)

fetal alcohol syndrome (FAS) physical and cognitive abnormalities in children caused by a pregnant woman's heavy drinking. In severe cases, symptoms include noticeable facial misproportions. (p. 81)

fetus the developing human organism from 9 weeks after conception to birth. (p. 81)

figure-ground the organization of the visual field into objects (the *figures*) that stand out from their surroundings (the *ground*). (p. 147)

fixation the inability to see a problem from a new perspective; an impediment to problem solving. (pp. 270, 393)

fixed-interval schedule in operant conditioning, a schedule of reinforcement that reinforces a response only after a specified time has elapsed. (p. 220)

fixed-ratio schedule in operant conditioning, a schedule of reinforcement that reinforces a response only after a specified number of responses. (p. 219)

flashbulb memory a clear memory of an emotionally significant moment or event. (p. 232)

fluid intelligence one's ability to reason speedily and abstractly; tends to decrease during late adulthood. (p. 114)

foot-in-the-door phenomenon the tendency for people who have first agreed to a small request to comply later with a larger request. (p. 494)

formal operational stage in Piaget's theory, the stage of cognitive development (normally beginning about age 12) during which people begin to think logically about abstract concepts. (p. 90)

framing the way an issue is posed; how an issue is framed can significantly affect decisions and judgments. (p. 274)

fraternal twins twins who develop from separate zygotes. They are genetically no closer than brothers and sisters, but they share the fetal environment. (p. 71)

free association in psychoanalysis, a method of exploring the unconscious in which the person relaxes and says whatever comes to mind, no matter how trivial or embarrassing. (p. 390)

frequency the number of complete wavelengths that pass a point in a given time (for example, per second). (p. 138)

frontal lobes the portion of the cerebral cortex lying just behind the forehead; involved in speaking and muscle movements and in making plans and judgments. (p. 55)

frustration-aggression principle the principle that frustration—the blocking of an attempt to achieve some goal—creates anger, which can generate aggression. (p. 515)

functional fixedness the tendency to think of things only in terms of their usual functions; an impediment to problem solving. (p. 271)

fundamental attribution error the tendency for observers, when analyzing another's behavior, to underestimate the impact of the situation and to overestimate the impact of personal disposition. (p. 491)

G

gate-control theory the theory that the spinal cord contains a neurological "gate" that blocks pain signals or allows them to pass on to the brain. The "gate" is opened by the activity of pain signals traveling up small nerve fibers and is closed by activity in larger fibers or by information coming from the brain. (p. 142)

gender in psychology, the characteristics, whether biologically or socially influenced, by which people define male and female. (p. 80)

gender identity one's sense of being male or female. (p. 97)

gender role a set of expected behaviors for males and for females. (p. 507)

gender schema theory the theory that children learn from their cultures a concept of what it means to be male and female and that they adjust their behavior accordingly. (p. 98)

gender-typing the acquisition of a traditional masculine or feminine role. (p. 97)

general adaptation syndrome (GAS) Selye's concept of the body's adaptive response to stress as composed of three stages—alarm, resistance, exhaustion. (p. 369)

general intelligence (*g*) a general intelligence factor that Spearman and others believed underlies specific mental abilities and is therefore measured by every task on an intelligence test. (p. 291)

generalization the tendency, once a response has been conditioned, for stimuli similar to the conditioned stimulus to evoke similar responses. (p. 210)

generalized anxiety disorder an anxiety disorder in which a person is continually tense, apprehensive, and aroused. (p. 431)

genes the biochemical units of heredity that make up the chromosomes; a segment of DNA capable of synthesizing a protein. (p. 69)

gestalt an organized whole. Gestalt psychologists emphasize our tendency to integrate pieces of information into meaningful wholes. (p. 147)

glial cells non-neural nervous system cells that support, nourish, and protect neurons. (p. 55)

glucose the form of sugar that circulates in the blood and provides the major source of energy for body tissues. When its level is low, we feel hunger. (p. 316)

GRIT Graduated and Reciprocated Initiatives in Tension-Reduction—a strategy designed to decrease international tensions. (p. 532)

grouping the perceptual tendency to organize stimuli into coherent groups. (p. 147)

group polarization the enhancement of a group's prevailing attitudes through discussion within the group. (p. 504)

groupthink the mode of thinking that occurs when the desire for harmony in a decision-making group overrides a realistic appraisal of alternatives. (p. 505)

H

hallucinations false sensory experiences, such as seeing something in the absence of an external visual stimulus. (p. 174)

hallucinogens psychedelic ("mind-manifesting") drugs, such as LSD, that distort perceptions and evoke sensory images in the absence of sensory input. (p. 193)

heritability the proportion of variation among individuals that we can attribute to genes. The heritability of a trait may vary, depending on the range of populations and environments studied. (pp. 73, 300)

heuristic a rule-of-thumb strategy that often allows us to make judgments and solve problems efficiently; usually speedier but also more error-prone than *algorithms*. (p. 269)

hidden observer Hilgard's term for a hypnotized subject's awareness of experiences, such as pain, that go unreported during hypnosis. (p. 190)

hierarchy of needs Maslow's pyramid of human needs, beginning at the base with physiological needs that must first be satisfied before higher-level safety needs and then psychological needs become active. (p. 314)

hindsight bias the tendency to believe, after learning an outcome, that one would have foreseen it. (Also known as the I-knew-it-all-along phenomenon.) (p. 10)

hippocampus a neural center located in the limbic system that helps process explicit memories for storage. (p. 247)

homeostasis a tendency to maintain a balanced or constant internal state; the regulation of any aspect of body chemistry, such as blood glucose, around a particular level. (p. 312)

hormones chemical messengers, mostly those manufactured by the endocrine glands, that are produced in one tissue and affect another. (p. 67)

hue the dimension of color that is determined by the wavelength of light; what we know as the color names *blue, green*, and so forth. (p. 130)

hypnosis a social interaction in which one person (the hypnotist) suggests to another (the subject) that certain perceptions, feelings, thoughts, or behaviors will spontaneously occur. (p. 183)

hypothalamus [hi-po-THAL-uh-muss] a neural structure lying below (*hypo*) the thalamus; it directs several maintenance activities (eating, drinking, body temperature), helps govern the endocrine system via the pituitary gland, and is linked to emotion. (p. 53)

hypothesis a testable prediction, often implied by a theory. (p. 13)

I

iconic memory a momentary sensory memory of visual stimuli; a photographic or picture-image memory lasting no more than a few tenths of a second. (p. 242)

id contains a reservoir of unconscious psychic energy that, according to Freud, strives to satisfy basic sexual and aggressive drives. The id operates on the *pleasure principle*, demanding immediate gratification. (p. 391)

identical twins twins who develop from a single zygote (fertilized egg) that splits in two, creating two genetic replicas. (p. 71)

identification the process by which, according to Freud, children incorporate their parents' values into their developing superegos. (p. 392)

identity one's sense of self; according to Erikson, the adolescent's task is to solidify a sense of self by testing and integrating various roles. (p. 104)

illusory correlation the perception of a relationship where none exists. (p. 18)

imagery mental pictures; a powerful aid to effortful processing, especially when combined with semantic encoding. (p. 237)

implicit memory retention without conscious recollection (of skills and dispositions). (Also called *nondeclarative memory*.) (p. 247)

imprinting the process by which certain animals form attachments during a critical period very early in life. (p. 92)

incentive a positive or negative environmental stimulus that motivates behavior. (p. 312)

independent variable the experimental factor that is manipulated; the variable whose effect is being studied. (p. 25)

individualism giving priority to one's own goals over group goals and defining one's identity in terms of personal attributes rather than group identifications. (p. 411)

industrial/organizational psychology a subfield of psychology that studies and advises on workplace behavior. Industrial/organizational (I/O) psychologists help organizations select and train employees, boost morale and productivity, and design products and assess responses to them. (p. 341)

informational social influence influence resulting from one's willingness to accept others' opinions about reality. (p. 498)

ingroup bias the tendency to favor one's own group. (p. 511)

inner ear the innermost part of the ear, containing the cochlea, semicircular canals, and vestibular sacs. (p. 139)

insight a sudden and often novel realization of the solution to a problem; it contrasts with strategy-based solutions. (p. 269)

insomnia a sleep disorder involving recurring problems in falling or staying asleep. (p. 179)

instinct a complex behavior that is rigidly patterned throughout a species and is unlearned. (p. 312)

intelligence the mental abilities needed to select, adapt to, and shape environments. It involves the abilities to profit from experience, solve problems, reason, and successfully meet challenges and achieve goals. (p. 289)

intelligence quotient (IQ) defined originally as the ratio of mental age (*ma*) to chronological age (*ca*) multiplied by 100 (thus, $IQ = ma/ca \times 100$). On contemporary intelligence tests, the average performance for a given age is assigned a score of 100. (p. 290)

intensity the amount of energy in a light or sound wave, which we perceive as brightness or loudness, as determined by the wave's amplitude. (p. 130)

internal locus of control the perception that one controls one's own fate. (p. 417)

interneurons central nervous system neurons that internally communicate and intervene between the sensory inputs and motor outputs. (p. 44)

interposition a monocular cue for perceiving distance; we perceive an object partially blocking our view of another object as closer. (p. 150)

interpretation in psychoanalysis, the analyst's noting supposed dream meanings, resistances, and other significant behaviors in order to promote insight. (p. 463)

intimacy in Erikson's theory, the ability to form close, loving relationships; a primary developmental task in late adolescence and early adulthood. (p. 105)

intrinsic motivation a desire to perform a behavior for its own sake and to be effective. (p. 340)

J

James-Lange theory the theory that our experience of emotion is our awareness of our physiological responses to emotion-arousing stimuli. (p. 364)

just-world phenomenon the tendency of people to believe the world is just and that people therefore get what they deserve and deserve what they get. (p. 513)

K

kinesthesis [kin-ehs-THEE-sehs] the system for sensing the position and movement of individual body parts. (p. 145)

L

language our spoken, written, or gestured words and the ways we combine them to communicate meaning. (p. 277)

latent content according to Freud, the underlying but censored meaning of a dream (as distinct from its manifest content). Freud believed that a dream's latent content functions as a safety valve. (p. 182)

latent learning learning that occurs but is not apparent until there is an incentive to demonstrate it. (p. 222)

law of effect Thorndike's principle that behaviors followed by favorable consequences become more likely. (p. 216)

learned helplessness the hopelessness and passive resignation an animal or human learns when unable to avoid repeated aversive events. (p. 417)

learning a relatively permanent change in an organism's behavior due to experience. (p. 205)

lesion [LEE-zhuhn] tissue destruction. A brain lesion is a naturally or experimentally caused destruction of brain tissue. (p. 48)

limbic system a doughnut-shaped system of neural structures at the border of the brainstem and cerebral hemispheres; associated with emotions such as fear and aggression and drives such as those for food and sex. Includes the hippocampus, amygdala, and hypothalamus. (p. 52)

linear perspective a monocular cue for perceiving distance; we perceive the converging of what we know to be parallel lines as indicating increasing distance. (p. 150)

linguistic relativity Whorf's hypothesis that language determines the way we think. (p. 286)

lithium a chemical that provides an effective drug therapy for the mood swings of bipolar (manic-depressive) disorders. (p. 485)

lobotomy a now-rare psychosurgical procedure once used to calm uncontrollably emotional or violent patients. The procedure cut the nerves that connect the frontal lobes to the emotion-controlling centers of the inner brain. (p. 486)

longitudinal study research in which the same people are restudied and retested over a long period. (p. 113)

long-term memory the relatively permanent and limitless storehouse of the memory system. (p. 233)

long-term potentiation (LTP) an increase in a synapse's firing potential after brief, rapid stimulation. Believed to be a neural basis for learning and memory. (p. 245)

LSD (*lysergic acid diethylamide*) a powerful hallucinogenic drug; also known as acid. (p. 197)

lymphocytes the two types of white blood cells that are part of the body's immune system: *B lymphocytes* form in the *b*one marrow and release antibodies that fight bacterial infections; *T lymphocytes* form in the *t*hymus and, among other duties, attack cancer cells, viruses, and foreign substances. (p. 374)

M

major depressive disorder a mood disorder in which a person, for no apparent reason, experiences two or more weeks of depressed moods, feelings of worthlessness, and diminished interest or pleasure in most activities. (p. 441)

mania a mood disorder marked by a hyperactive, wildly optimistic state. (p. 441)

manifest content according to Freud, the remembered story line of a dream (as distinct from its latent content). (p. 181)

maturation biological growth processes that enable orderly changes in behavior, relatively uninfluenced by experience. (p. 83)

mean the arithmetic average of a distribution, obtained by adding the scores and then dividing by the number of scores. (p. 538)

median the middle score in a distribution; half the scores are above it and half are below it. (p. 538)

medical model the concept that diseases have physical causes that can be diagnosed, treated, and, in most cases, cured. When applied to psychological disorders, the medical model assumes that these "mental illnesses" can be diagnosed on the basis of their symptoms and cured through therapy, which may include treatment in a psychiatric hospital. (p. 428)

medulla [muh-DUL-uh] the base of the brainstem; controls heartbeat and breathing. (p. 48)

memory the persistence of learning over time through the storage and retrieval of information. (p. 231)

menarche [meh-NAR-key] the first menstrual period. (p. 100)

menopause the time of natural cessation of menstruation; also refers to the biological changes a woman experiences as her ability to reproduce declines. (p. 110)

mental age a measure of intelligence test performance devised by Binet; the chronological age typical of a given level of performance. Thus, a child who does as well as the average 8-year-old is said to have a mental age of 8. (p. 289)

mental retardation a condition of limited mental ability (as indicated by an intelligence score below 70) that produces difficulty in adapting to the demands of life; varies from mild to profound. (p. 297)

mere exposure effect the phenomenon that repeated exposure to novel stimuli increases liking of them. (p. 523)

middle ear the chamber between the eardrum and cochlea containing three tiny bones (hammer, anvil, and stirrup) that concentrate the vibrations of the eardrum on the cochlea's oval window. (p. 139)

Minnesota Multiphasic Personality Inventory (MMPI) the most widely researched and clinically used of all personality tests. Originally developed to identify emotional disorders (still considered its most appropriate use), this test is now used for many other screening purposes. (p. 402)

misinformation effect incorporating misleading information into one's memory of an event. (p. 256)

mnemonics [nih-MON-iks] memory aids, especially those techniques that use vivid imagery and organizational devices. (p. 238)

mode the most frequently occurring score in a distribution. (p. 538)

modeling the process of observing and imitating a behavior. (p. 226)

monocular cues distance cues, such as linear perspective and overlap, available to either eye alone. (p. 148)

mood-congruent memory the tendency to recall experiences that are consistent with one's current good or bad mood. (p. 252)

mood disorders psychological disorders characterized by emotional extremes. See *major depressive disorder*, *bipolar disorder*, and *mania*. (p. 440)

motivation a need or desire that energizes and directs behavior. (p. 311)

motor cortex an area that is located at the rear of the frontal lobes and that controls voluntary movements. (p. 56)

motor neurons the neurons that carry outgoing information from the central nervous system to the muscles and glands. (p. 44)

MRI (magnetic resonance imaging) a technique that uses magnetic fields and radio waves to produce computer-generated images that distinguish among different types of soft tissue; allows us to see structures within the brain. (p. 51)

myelin [MY-uh-lin] **sheath** a layer of fatty tissue segmentally encasing the fibers of many neurons; makes possible vastly greater transmission speed of neural impulses. (p. 40)

N

narcolepsy a sleep disorder characterized by uncontrollable sleep attacks. The sufferer may lapse directly into REM sleep, often at inopportune times. (p. 179)

naturalistic observation observing and recording behavior in naturally occurring situations without trying to manipulate and control the situation. (p. 17)

nature-nurture issue the longstanding controversy over the relative contributions of genes and experience to the development of psychological traits and behaviors. (p. 5)

near-death experience an altered state of consciousness reported after a close brush with death (such as through cardiac arrest); often similar to drug-induced hallucinations. (p. 197)

nerves neural "cables" containing many axons. These bundled axons, which are part of the peripheral nervous system, connect the central nervous system with muscles, glands, and sense organs. (p. 44)

nervous system the body's speedy, electrochemical communication system, consisting of all the nerve cells of the peripheral and central nervous systems. (p. 44)

neuron a nerve cell; the basic building block of the nervous system. (p. 40)

neurotic disorders former term for psychological disorders that are usually distressing but allow one to think rationally and function socially. (p. 429)

neurotransmitters chemical messengers that traverse the synaptic gaps between neurons. When released by the sending neuron, neurotransmitters travel across the synapse and bind to receptor sites on the receiving neuron, thereby influencing whether it will generate a neural impulse. (p. 41)

night terrors a sleep disorder characterized by high arousal and an appearance of being terrified; unlike nightmares, night terrors occur during Stage 4 sleep, within 2 or 3 hours of falling asleep, and are seldom remembered. (p. 180)

norm an understood rule for accepted and expected behavior. Norms prescribe "proper" behavior. (p. 498)

normal curve the symmetrical bell-shaped curve that describes the distribution of many physical and psychological attributes. Most scores fall near the average, and fewer and fewer scores lie near the extremes. (Also called normal distribution.) (pp. 295, 540)

normative social influence influence resulting from a person's desire to gain approval or avoid disapproval. (p. 498)

O

object permanence the awareness that things continue to exist even when not perceived. (p. 86)

observational learning learning by observing and imitating the behavior of others. (p. 226)

obsessive-compulsive disorder an anxiety disorder characterized by unwanted repetitive thoughts (obsessions) and/or actions (compulsions). (p. 432)

occipital [ahk-SIP-uh-tuhl] **lobes** the portion of the cerebral cortex lying at the back of the head; includes the visual areas, which receive visual information from the opposite visual field. (p. 55)

Oedipus [ed-uh-puss] **complex** according to Freud, a boy's sexual desires toward his mother and feelings of jealousy and hatred for the rival father. (p. 392)

one-word stage the stage in speech development, from about age 1 to 2, during which a child speaks mostly in single words. (p. 279)

operant behavior behavior that operates on the environment, producing consequences. (p. 216)

operant conditioning a type of learning in which behavior is strengthened if followed by reinforcement or diminished if followed by punishment. (p. 216)

operational definition a statement of the procedures (operations) used to define research variables. (p. 25)

opiates opium and its derivatives, such as morphine and heroin; they depress neural activity, temporarily lessening pain and anxiety. (p. 195)

opponent-process theory the theory that opposing retinal processes (red-green, yellow-blue, white-black) enable color vision. For example, some cells are stimulated by green and inhibited by red; others are stimulated by red and inhibited by green. (p. 136)

optic nerve the nerve that carries neural impulses from the eye to the brain. (p. 132)

overconfidence the tendency to be more confident than correct—to overestimate the accuracy of one's beliefs and judgments. (p. 274)

P

panic disorder an anxiety disorder marked by a minutes-long episode of intense dread in which a person experiences terror and accompanying chest pain, choking, or other frightening sensations. (p. 432)

parallel processing processing several aspects of a problem simultaneously; the brain's natural mode of information processing for many functions, including vision. (p. 134)

parapsychology the study of paranormal phenomena, including ESP. (p. 160)

parasympathetic nervous system the division of the autonomic nervous system that calms the body, conserving its energy. (p. 45)

parietal [puh-RYE-uh-tuhl] **lobes** the portion of the cerebral cortex lying at the top of the head and toward the rear; includes the sensory cortex. (p. 55)

partial reinforcement reinforcing a response only part of the time; results in slower acquisition of a response but much greater resistance to extinction than does continuous reinforcement. (p. 219)

passionate love an aroused state of intense positive absorption in another, usually present at the beginning of a love relationship. (p. 526)

percentile rank the percentage of the scores in a distribution that fall below a given score. (p. 537)

perception the process of selecting, organizing, and interpreting sensory information, enabling us to recognize meaningful objects and events. (p. 125)

perceptual adaptation in vision, the ability to adjust to an artificially displaced or even inverted visual field. (p. 155)

perceptual constancy perceiving objects as unchanging (having consistent lightness, color, shape, and size) even as illumination and retinal images change. (p. 151)

perceptual set a mental predisposition to perceive one thing and not another. (p. 156)

peripheral nervous system (PNS) the sensory and motor neurons that connect the central nervous system (CNS) to the rest of the body. (p. 44)

personal control our sense of controlling our environments rather than feeling helpless. (p. 416)

personal space the buffer zone we like to maintain around our bodies. (p. 507)

person-centered therapy a humanistic therapy, developed by Carl Rogers, in which the therapist uses techniques such as active listening within a genuine, accepting, empathic environment to facilitate clients' growth. (p. 464)

personality an individual's characteristic pattern of thinking, feeling, and acting. (p. 389)

personality disorders psychological disorders characterized by inflexible and enduring behavior patterns that impair social functioning. (p. 455)

personality inventory a questionnaire (often with true-false or agree-disagree items) on which people respond to items designed to gauge a wide range of feelings and behaviors; used to assess selected personality traits. (p. 402)

PET (positron emission tomography) scan a visual display of brain activity that detects where a radioactive form of glucose goes while the brain performs a given task. (p. 50)

phobia an anxiety disorder marked by a persistent, irrational fear and avoidance of a specific object or situation. (p. 432)

physical dependence a physiological need for a drug, marked by unpleasant withdrawal symptoms when the drug is discontinued. (p. 191)

pitch a tone's highness or lowness; depends on frequency. (p. 138)

pituitary gland the endocrine system's most influential gland. Under the influence of the hypothalamus, the pituitary regulates growth and controls other endocrine glands. (p. 68)

placebo [pluh-SEE-bo] an inert substance or condition that may be administered instead of a presumed active agent, such as a drug, to see if it triggers the effects believed to characterize the active agent. (p. 27)

plasticity the brain's capacity for modification, as evident in brain reorganization following damage (especially in children) and in experiments on the effects of experience on brain development. (p. 62)

polygraph a machine that is commonly used in attempts to detect lies and that measures several of the physiological responses accompanying emotion (such as perspiration, heart rate, blood pressure, and breathing changes). (p. 350)

population all the cases in a group, from which samples may be drawn for a study. (p. 15)

posthypnotic amnesia supposed inability to recall what one experienced during hypnosis; induced by the hypnotist's suggestion. (p. 184)

posthypnotic suggestion a suggestion, made during a hypnosis session, to be carried out after the subject is no longer hypnotized; used by some clinicians to help control undesired symptoms and behaviors. (p. 186)

preconscious information that is not conscious but is retrievable into conscious awareness. (p. 390)

predictive validity the success with which a test predicts the behavior it is designed to predict; it is assessed by computing the correlation between test scores and the criterion behavior. (Also called *criterion-related validity*.) (p. 296)

prejudice an unjustifiable (and usually negative) attitude toward a group and its members. Prejudice generally involves stereotyped beliefs, negative feelings, and a predisposition to discriminatory action. (p. 509)

preoperational stage in Piaget's theory, the stage (from about 2 to 6 or 7 years of age) during which a child learns to use language but does not yet comprehend the mental operations of concrete logic. (p. 87)

primary reinforcer an innate reinforcer, such as one that satisfies a biological need. (p. 218)

primary sex characteristics the body structures (ovaries, testes, and external genitalia) that make sexual reproduction possible. (p. 100)

priming the activation, often unconsciously, of particular associations in memory. (p. 250)

proactive interference the disruptive effect of prior learning on the recall of new information. (p. 253)

projection the defense mechanism by which people disguise their own threatening impulses by attributing them to others. (p. 393)

projective test a personality test, such as the Rorschach or TAT, that provides ambiguous stimuli designed to trigger projection of one's inner dynamics. (p. 395)

prosocial behavior positive, constructive, helpful behavior. The opposite of antisocial behavior. (p. 227)

prototype the best example of a category; matching new items to the prototype provides a quick and easy method for including items in a category (as when comparing feathered creatures to a prototypical bird, such as a robin). (p. 269)

psychiatry a branch of medicine dealing with psychological disorders; practiced by physicians who sometimes provide medical (for example, drug) treatments as well as psychological therapy. (p. 7)

psychoactive drug a chemical substance that alters perceptions and mood. (p. 191)

psychoanalysis Sigmund Freud's therapeutic technique. Freud believed the patient's free associations, resistances, dreams, and transferences—and the therapist's interpretations of them—released previously repressed feelings, allowing the patient to gain self-insight. (pp. 390, 462)

psychological dependence a psychological need to use a drug, such as to relieve negative emotions. (p. 191)

psychological disorder a condition in which behavior is judged to be atypical, disturbing, maladaptive, and unjustifiable. (p. 426)

psychology the science of behavior and mental processes. (p. 3)

psychopharmacology the study of the effects of drugs on mind and behavior. (p. 482)

psychophysics the study of relationships between the physical characteristics of stimuli, such as their intensity, and our psychological experience of them. (p. 126)

psychophysiological illness literally, "mind-body" illness; any stress-related physical illness, such as hypertension and headaches. (p. 373)

psychosexual stages the childhood stages of development (oral, anal, phallic, latency, genital) during which, according to Freud, the id's pleasure-seeking energies focus on distinct erogenous zones. (p. 392)

psychosurgery surgery that removes or destroys brain tissue in an effort to change behavior. (p. 486)

psychotherapy an emotionally charged, confiding interaction between a trained therapist and someone who suffers from psychological difficulties. (p. 461)

psychotic disorders psychological disorders in which a person loses contact with reality, experiencing irrational ideas and distorted perceptions. (p. 429)

puberty the period of sexual maturation, during which a person becomes capable of reproducing. (p. 100)

punishment an aversive event that *decreases* the behavior that it follows. (p. 220)

R

random assignment assigning subjects to experimental and control conditions by chance, thus minimizing preexisting differences between those assigned to the different groups. (p. 24)

random sample a sample that fairly represents a population because each member has an equal chance of inclusion. (p. 16)

range the difference between the highest and lowest scores in a distribution. (p. 539)

rational-emotive therapy a confrontational cognitive therapy, developed by Albert Ellis, that vigorously challenges people's illogical, self-defeating attitudes and assumptions. Also called *rational-emotive behavior therapy* by Ellis, emphasizing a behavioral "homework" component. (p. 471)

rationalization defense mechanism that offers self-justifying explanations in place of the real, more threatening, unconscious reasons for one's actions. (p. 393)

reaction formation defense mechanism by which the ego unconsciously switches unacceptable impulses into their opposites. Thus, people may express feelings that are the opposite of their anxiety-arousing unconscious feelings. (p. 393)

recall a measure of memory in which the person must retrieve information learned earlier, as on a fill-in-the-blank test. (p. 249)

reciprocal determinism the interacting influences between personality and environmental factors. (p. 416)

recognition a measure of memory in which the person need only identify items previously learned, as on a multiple-choice test. (p. 249)

reflex a simple, automatic, inborn response to a sensory stimulus, such as the knee-jerk response. (p. 46)

refractory period a resting period after orgasm, during which a man cannot achieve another orgasm. (p. 328)

regression defense mechanism in which individual retreats, when faced with anxiety, to a more infantile psychosexual stage where some psychic energy remains fixated. (p. 393)

regression toward the mean the tendency for extremes of unusual scores to fall back (regress) toward the average. (p. 541)

rehearsal the conscious repetition of information, either to maintain it in consciousness or to encode it for storage. (p. 235)

reinforcer in operant conditioning, any event that *strengthens* the behavior it follows. (p. 217)

relative brightness a monocular cue for perceiving distance; dimmer objects appear more distant. (p. 151)

relative deprivation the perception that one is worse off relative to those with whom one compares oneself. (p. 362)

relative height a monocular cue for perceiving distance; higher objects appear more distant. (p. 150)

relative motion a monocular cue for perceiving distance; when we move, objects at different distances change their relative positions in our visual image, with those closest moving most. (Also called *motion parallax*.) (p. 150)

relative size a monocular cue for perceiving distance; when we assume two objects are the same size, the one that produces the smaller image appears more distant. (p. 150)

relearning a memory measure that assesses the amount of time saved when learning material for a second time. (p. 249)

reliability the extent to which a test yields consistent results, as assessed by the consistency of scores on two halves of the test, on alternate forms of the test, or on retesting. (p. 295)

REM rebound the tendency for REM sleep to increase following REM sleep deprivation (created by repeated awakenings during REM sleep). (p. 183)

REM sleep rapid eye movement sleep, a recurring sleep stage during which vivid dreams commonly occur. Also known as *paradoxical sleep* because the muscles are relaxed (except for minor twitches) but other body systems are active. (p. 174)

replication repeating the essence of a research study, usually with different subjects in different situations, to see whether the basic finding generalizes to other subjects and circumstances. (p. 13)

representativeness heuristic a rule of thumb for judging the likelihood of things in terms of how well they seem to represent, or match, particular prototypes; may lead one to ignore other relevant information. (p. 271)

repression in psychoanalytic theory, the basic defense mechanism that banishes anxiety–arousing thoughts, feelings, and memories from consciousness. (pp. 254, 393)

resistance in psychoanalysis, the blocking from consciousness of anxiety-laden material. (p. 463)

respondent behavior behavior that occurs as an automatic response to some stimulus. (p. 216)

reticular formation a nerve network in the brainstem that plays an important role in controlling arousal. (p. 49)

retina the light-sensitive inner surface of the eye, containing the receptor rods and cones plus layers of neurons that begin the processing of visual information. (p. 131)

retinal disparity a binocular cue for perceiving depth: the greater the disparity (difference) between the two images the retina receives of an object, the closer the object is to the viewer. (p. 149)

retrieval the process of getting information out of memory storage. (p. 233)

retroactive interference the disruptive effect of new learning on the recall of old information. (p. 253)

rods retinal receptors that detect black, white, and gray; necessary for peripheral and twilight vision, when cones don't respond. (p. 132)

role a set of expectations about a social position, defining how those in the position ought to behave. (p. 495)

rooting reflex a baby's tendency, when touched on the cheek, to open the mouth and search for the nipple. (p. 82)

Rorschach inkblot test the most widely used projective test, a set of 10 inkblots, designed by Hermann Rorschach; seeks to identify people's inner feelings by analyzing their interpretations of the blots. (p. 396)

S

savant syndrome a condition in which a person otherwise limited in mental ability has an amazing specific skill, such as in computation or drawing. (p. 291)

scapegoat theory the theory that prejudice provides an outlet for anger by providing someone to blame. (p. 511)

scatterplot a graphed cluster of dots, each of which represents the values of two variables (such as one student's high school GPA and college GPA). The slope of the points suggests the degree and direction of the relationship between the two variables. (Also called a *scattergram* or *scatter diagram.*) (p. 540)

schema a concept or framework that organizes and interprets information. (p. 86)

schizophrenia a group of severe psychotic disorders characterized by disorganized and delusional thinking, disturbed perceptions, and inappropriate emotions and actions. (p. 449)

secondary reinforcer a conditioned reinforcer; an event that gains its reinforcing power through its association with a primary reinforcer. (p. 218)

secondary sex characteristics nonreproductive sexual characteristics, such as female breasts and hips, male voice quality, and body hair. (p. 100)

selective attention the focusing of conscious awareness on a particular stimulus, as in the cocktail party effect. (p. 170)

self-actualization according to Maslow, the ultimate psychological need that arises after basic physical and psychological needs are met and self-esteem is achieved; the motivation to fulfill one's potential. (p. 406)

self-concept all our thoughts and feelings about ourselves, in answer to the question, "Who am I?" (p. 407)

self-disclosure revealing intimate aspects of oneself to others. (p. 528)

self-esteem one's feelings of high or low self-worth. (p. 408)

self-serving bias a readiness to perceive oneself favorably. (p. 410)

sensation the process by which our sensory receptors and nervous system receive and represent stimulus energies from our environment. (p. 125)

sensorimotor stage in Piaget's theory, the stage (from birth to about 2 years of age) during which infants know the world mostly in terms of their sensory impressions and motor activities. (p. 86)

sensory adaptation diminished sensitivity as a consequence of constant stimulation. (p. 129)

sensory cortex the area that is located at the front of the parietal lobes and that registers and processes body sensations. (p. 57)

sensory interaction the principle that one sense may influence another, as when the smell of food influences its taste. (p. 143)

sensory memory the immediate, initial recording of sensory information in the memory system. (p. 234)

sensory neurons neurons that carry incoming information from the sense receptors to the central nervous system. (p. 44)

serial position effect our tendency to recall best the last and first items in a list. (p. 236)

set point the point at which an individual's "weight thermostat" is supposedly set. When the body falls below this weight, an increase in hunger and a lowered metabolic rate may act to restore the lost weight. (p. 317)

sexual disorder a problem that consistently impairs sexual arousal or functioning. (p. 330)

sexual orientation an enduring sexual attraction toward members of either one's own gender (homosexual orientation) or the other gender (heterosexual orientation). (p. 332)

sexual response cycle the four stages of sexual responding described by Masters and Johnson—excitement, plateau, orgasm, and resolution. (p. 327)

shaping an operant conditioning procedure in which reinforcers guide behavior toward closer and closer approximations of a desired goal. (p. 216)

short-term memory activated memory that holds a few items briefly, such as the seven digits of a phone number while dialing, before the information is stored or forgotten. (p. 233)

skeletal nervous system the division of the peripheral nervous system that controls the body's skeletal muscles. (p. 45)

Skinner box a chamber containing a bar or a key that an animal can manipulate to obtain a food or water reinforcer, with attached devices to record the animal's rate of bar pressing or key pecking. Used in operant conditioning research. (p. 216)

sleep apnea a sleep disorder characterized by temporary cessations of breathing during sleep and consequent momentary reawakenings. (p. 179)

social clock the culturally preferred timing of social events such as marriage, parenthood, and retirement. (p. 115)

social exchange theory the theory that our social behavior is an exchange process, the aim of which is to maximize benefits and minimize costs. (p. 530)

social facilitation improved performance of tasks in the presence of others; occurs with simple or well-learned tasks but not with tasks that are difficult or not yet mastered. (p. 503)

social leadership group-oriented leadership that builds teamwork, mediates conflict, and offers support. (p. 342)

social learning theory the theory that we learn social behavior by observing and imitating and by being rewarded or punished. (p. 97)

social loafing the tendency for people in a group to exert less effort when pooling their efforts toward attaining a common goal than when individually accountable. (p. 503)

social psychology the scientific study of how we think about, influence, and relate to one another. (p. 492)

social trap a situation in which the conflicting parties, by rationally pursuing their self-interests, become caught in mutually destructive behavior. (p. 520)

source amnesia attributing to the wrong source an event that we experienced, heard about, read about, or imagined. (Also called *source misattribution.*) Source amnesia, along with the misinformation effect, is at the heart of many false memories. (p. 257)

spacing effect the tendency for distributed study or practice to yield better long-term retention than is achieved through massed study or practice. (p. 235)

split brain a condition in which the two hemispheres of the brain are isolated by cutting the connecting fibers (mainly those of the corpus callosum) between them. (p. 63)

spontaneous recovery the reappearance, after a rest period, of an extinguished conditioned response. (p. 210)

SQ3R a study method incorporating five steps: *S*urvey, *Q*uestion, *R*ead, *R*ehearse, *R*eview. (p. 34)

standard deviation a measure of score variability; computed by (1) calculating the deviation of each score from the mean, (2) squaring those deviations, (3) finding their average, and (4) finding the square root of this average. (p. 539)

standardization defining meaningful scores by comparison with the performance of a pretested "standardization group." (p. 295)

Stanford-Binet the widely used American revision (by Terman at Stanford University) of Binet's original intelligence test. (p. 290)

statistical significance a statistical statement of how likely it is that an obtained result occurred by chance. (p. 543)

stereotype a generalized (often overgeneralized) belief about a group of people. (p. 509)

stimulants drugs (such as caffeine, nicotine, and the more powerful amphetamines and cocaine) that excite neural activity and speed up body functions. (p. 193)

storage the retention of encoded information over time. (p. 233)

stranger anxiety the fear of strangers that infants commonly display, beginning by about 8 months of age. (p. 91)

stress the process by which we appraise and bodily respond to certain events, called *stressors*, that we appraise as threatening or challenging. (p. 369)

subjective well-being self-perceived happiness or satisfaction with life. Used along with measures of objective well-being (for example, physical and economic indicators) to evaluate people's quality of life. (p. 359)

sublimation in psychoanalytic theory, the defense mechanism by which people rechannel their unacceptable impulses into socially approved activities. (p. 394)

subliminal below one's absolute threshold for conscious awareness. (p. 127)

superego the part of personality that, according to Freud, represents internalized ideals and provides standards for judgment (the conscience) and for future aspirations. (p. 392)

superordinate goals shared goals that override differences among people and require their cooperation. (p. 531)

survey a technique for ascertaining the self-reported attitudes or behaviors of people, usually by questioning a representative, random sample of them. (p. 15)

sympathetic nervous system the division of the autonomic nervous system that arouses the body, mobilizing its energy in stressful situations. (p. 45)

synapse [SIN-aps] the junction between the axon tip of the sending neuron and the dendrite or cell body of the receiving neuron. The tiny gap at this junction is called the *synaptic gap* or *cleft.* (p. 41)

systematic desensitization a type of counterconditioning that associates a pleasant relaxed state with gradually increasing anxiety-triggering stimuli. Commonly used to treat phobias. (p. 467)

T

task leadership goal-oriented leadership that sets standards, organizes work, and focuses attention on goals. (p. 342)

telegraphic speech during the two-word stage, speech patterns in which the child speaks like a telegram—"go car"—using mostly nouns and verbs and omitting "auxiliary" words. (p. 279)

temperament a person's characteristic emotional reactivity and intensity. (p. 92)

temporal lobes the portion of the cerebral cortex lying roughly above the ears; includes the auditory areas, each of which receives auditory information primarily from the opposite ear. (p. 55)

teratogens agents, such as chemicals and viruses, that can reach the embryo or fetus during prenatal development and cause harm. (p. 81)

testosterone the most important of the male sex hormones. Both males and females have it, but the additional testosterone in males stimulates the growth of the male sex organs in the fetus and the development of the male sex characteristics during puberty. (p. 80)

thalamus [THAL-uh-muss] the brain's sensory switchboard, located on top of the brainstem; it directs messages to the sensory receiving areas in the cortex and transmits replies to the cerebellum and medulla. (p. 49)

THC the major active ingredient in marijuana; triggers a variety of effects, including mild hallucinations. (p. 198)

Thematic Apperception Test (TAT) a projective test in which people express their inner feelings and interests through the stories they make up about ambiguous scenes. (p. 395)

theory an explanation using an integrated set of principles that organizes and predicts observations. (p. 13)

threshold the level of stimulation required to trigger a neural impulse. (p. 41)

token economy an operant conditioning procedure that rewards desired behavior. A patient exchanges a token of some sort, earned for exhibiting the desired behavior, for various privileges or treats. (p. 470)

tolerance the diminishing effect with regular use of the same dose of a drug, requiring the user to take larger and larger doses before experiencing the drug's effect. (p. 191)

top-down processing information processing guided by higher-level mental processes, as when we construct perceptions drawing on our experience and expectations. (p. 125)

trait a characteristic pattern of behavior or a disposition to feel and act, as assessed by self-report inventories and peer reports. (p. 400)

transference in psychoanalysis, the patient's transfer to the analyst of emotions linked with other relationships (such as love or hatred for a parent). (p. 463)

two-factor theory Schachter's theory that to experience emotion one must (1) be physically aroused and (2) cognitively label the arousal. (p. 365)

two-word stage beginning about age 2, the stage in speech development during which a child speaks mostly two-word statements. (p. 279)

Type A Friedman and Rosenman's term for competitive, hard-driving, impatient, verbally aggressive, and anger-prone people. (p. 372)

Type B Friedman and Rosenman's term for easygoing, relaxed people. (p. 372)

U

unconditional positive regard according to Rogers, an attitude of total acceptance toward another person. (p. 407)

unconditioned response (UCR) in classical conditioning, the unlearned, naturally occurring response to the unconditioned stimulus (UCS), such as salivation when food is in the mouth. (p. 208)

unconditioned stimulus (UCS) in classical conditioning, a stimulus that unconditionally— naturally and automatically—triggers a response. (p. 208)

unconscious according to Freud, a reservoir of mostly unacceptable thoughts, wishes, feelings, and memories. According to contemporary psychologists, information processing of which we are unaware. (p. 390)

V

validity the extent to which a test measures or predicts what it is supposed to. (See also *content validity* and *predictive validity*.) (p. 296)

variable-interval schedule in operant conditioning, a schedule of reinforcement that reinforces a response at unpredictable time intervals. (p. 220)

variable-ratio schedule in operant conditioning, a schedule of reinforcement that reinforces a response after an unpredictable number of responses. (p. 220)

vestibular sense the sense of body movement and position, including the sense of balance. (p. 145)

visual capture the tendency for vision to dominate the other senses, as when we perceive voices in films as coming from the screen we see rather than from the projector behind us. (p. 138)

visual cliff a laboratory device for testing depth perception in infants and young animals. (p. 148)

W

wavelength the distance from the peak of one light or sound wave to the peak of the next. Electromagnetic wavelengths vary from the short blips of cosmic rays to the long pulses of radio transmission. (p. 130)

Weber's law the principle that, for a difference to be perceived, two stimuli must differ by a constant minimum percentage (rather than a constant amount). (p. 129)

Wechsler Adult Intelligence Scale (WAIS) the WAIS is the most widely used intelligence test; contains verbal and performance (nonverbal) subtests. (p. 293)

Wernicke's area an area of the left temporal lobe involved in language comprehension. (p. 60)

withdrawal the discomfort and distress that follow discontinuing the use of an addictive drug. (p. 191)

X

***X* chromosome** the sex chromosome found in both men and women. Females have two *X* chromosomes; males have one. An *X* chromosome from each parent produces a female. (p. 80)

Y

***Y* chromosome** the sex chromosome found only in males. When paired with an *X* sex chromosome from the mother, it produces a male child. (p. 80)

Young-Helmholtz trichromatic (three-color) theory the theory that the retina contains three different color receptors—one most sensitive to red, one to green, one to blue—which when stimulated in combination can produce the perception of any color. (p. 136)

Z

zygote the fertilized egg; it enters a 2-week period of rapid cell division and develops into an embryo. (p. 81)

References

Aas, H., & Klepp, K-I. (1992). Adolescents' alcohol use related to perceived norms. *Scandinavian Journal of Psychology, 33,* 315–325. (p. 201)

Abbey, A. (1987). Misperceptions of friendly behavior as sexual interest: A survey of naturally occurring incidents. *Psychology of Women Quarterly, 11,* 173–194. (p. 332)

Abbey, A. (1991). Acquaintance rape and alcohol consumption on college campuses: How are they linked? *Journal of American College Health, 39,* 165–169. (p. 193)

Abbey, A., Ross, L. T., & McDuffie, D. (1993). Alcohol's role in sexual assault. In R. R. Watson (Ed.), *Drug and alcohol abuse reviews, vol 5: Addictive behaviors in women.* Totowa, NJ: Humana Press. (p. 514)

Abbey, A., Ross, L. T., McDuffie, D., & McAuslan, P. (1996). Alcohol and dating risk factors for sexual assault among college women. *Psychology of Women Quarterly, 20,* 147–169. (p. 514)

Abrams, D. (1991). AIDS: What young people believe and what they do. Paper presented at the British Association for the Advancement of Science conference. (p. 419)

Abrams, D. B., & Wilson, G. T. (1983). Alcohol, sexual arousal, and self-control. *Journal of Personality and Social Psychology, 45,* 188–198. (p. 194)

Abramson, L. Y., Metalsky, G. I., & Alloy, L. B. (1989). Hopelessness depression: A theory-based subtype. *Psychological Review, 96,* 358–372. (p. 446)

Acitelli, L. K., & Antonucci, T. C. (1994). Gender differences in the link between marital support and satisfaction in older couples. *Journal of Personality and Social Psychology, 67,* 688–698. (p. 116)

Acock, A. C., & Demo, D. H. (1994). *Family diversity and well-being.* Thousand Oaks, CA: Sage. (p. 507)

Adair, J. G., Paivio, A., & Ritchie, P. (1996). Psychology in Canada. *Annual Review of Psychology, 47,* 341–370. (p. 7)

Adelmann, P. K., Antonucci, T. C., Crohan, S. F., & Coleman, L. M. (1989). Empty nest, cohort, and employment in the well-being of midlife women. *Sex Roles, 20,* 173–189. (p. 118)

Ader, R., & Cohen, N. (1985). CNS-immune system interactions: Conditioning phenomena. *Behavioral and Brain Sciences, 8,* 379–394. (p. 376)

Adler, N. E., David, H. P., Major, B. N., Roth, S. H., Russo, N. F., & Wyatt, G. E. (1990). Psychological responses after abortion. *Science, 248,* 41–44. (p. 371)

Adolphs, R., Tranel, D., Damasio, H., & Damasio, A. (1994). Impaired recognition of emotion in facial expressions following bilateral damage to the human amygdala. *Nature, 372,* 669–672. (p. 53)

Advertising Age (1958, February 10). "Phone now," said CBC subliminally—but nobody did. P. 8. (p. 128)

Affleck, G., Tennen, H., Urrows, S., & Higgins, P. (1994). Person and contextual features of daily stress reactivity: Individual differences in relations of undesirable daily events with mood disturbance and chronic pain intensity. *Journal of Personality and Social Psychology, 66,* 329–340. (p. 350)

Aiello, J. R., Thompson, D. D., & Brodzinsky, D. M. (1983). How funny is crowding anyway? Effects of room size, group size, and the introduction of humor. *Basic and Applied Social Psychology, 4,* 193–207. (p. 503)

Ainsworth, M. D. S. (1973). The development of infant-mother attachment. In B. Caldwell & H. Ricciuti (Eds.), *Review of child development research* (Vol. 3). Chicago: University of Chicago Press. (p. 92)

Ainsworth, M. D. S. (1979). Infant-mother attachment. *American Psychologist, 34,* 932–937. (p. 93)

Ainsworth, M. D. S. (1989). Attachments beyond infancy. *American Psychologist, 44,* 709–716. (p. 92)

Albee, G. W. (1986). Toward a just society: Lessons from observations on the primary prevention of psychopathology. *American Psychologist, 41,* 891–898. (p. 487)

Alcock, J. E. (1981). *Parapsychology: Science or magic?* Oxford: Pergamon. (p. 251)

Alcock, J. E. (1985, Spring). Parapsychology: The "spiritual" science. *Free Inquiry,* pp. 25–35. (p. 164)

Aldrich, M. S. (1989). Automobile accidents in patients with sleep disorders. *Sleep, 12,* 487–494. (p. 179)

Aldridge-Morris, R. (1989). *Multiple personality: An exercise in deception.* Hillsdale, NJ: Erlbaum. (p. 439)

Alexander, C. N., Langer, E. J., Newman, R. I., Chandler, H. M., & Davies, J. L. (1989). Transcendental meditation, mindfulness, and longevity: An experimental study with the elderly. *Journal of Personality and Social Psychology*, *57*, 950–964. (p. 381)

Alkon, D. L., Amaral, D. G., Baer, M. F., Black, J., Carew, T. J., Cohen, N. J., Disterhoft, J. F., Eichenbaum, H., Golski, S., Gorman, L. K., Lynch, G., McNaughton, B. L., Mishkin, M., Moyer, J. R. Jr., Olds, J. L., Olton, D. S., Otto, T., Squire, L. R., Staubli, U., Thompson, L. T., & Wible, C. (1991). Learning and memory. *Brain Research Reviews*, *16*, 193–220. (p. 245)

Allard, F., & Burnett, N. (1985). Skill in sport. *Canadian Journal of Psychology*, *39*, 294–312. (p. 239)

Allen, J. B., Repinski, D. J., Ballard, J. C., & Griffin, B. W. (1996). Beliefs about the etiology of homosexuality may influence attitudes toward homosexuals. Paper presented to the American Psychological Society convention. (p. 336)

Allen, L. S., & Gorski, R. A. (1992). Sexual orientation and the size of the anterior commisure in the human brain. *Proceedings of the National Academy of Sciences*, *89*, 7199–7202. (p. 335)

Allman, A. L. (1989). Subjective well-being of students with and without disabilities. Paper presented at the Midwestern Psychological Association convention. (p. 360)

Allport, G. W., & Odbert, H. S. (1936). Trait-names: A psycho-lexical study. *Psychological Monographs*, *47*(1). (p. 401)

Alwin, D. F. (1990). Historical changes in parental orientations to children. In N. Mandell (Ed.), *Sociological studies of child development* (Vol. 3). Greenwich, CT: JAI Press. (p. 95)

Amabile, T. M. (1983). *The social psychology of creativity.* New York: Springer-Verlag. (p. 409)

Amabile, T. M., & Hennessey, B. A. (1992). The motivation for creativity in children. In A. K. Boggiano & T. S. Pittman (Eds.), *Achievement and motivation: A social-developmental perspective.* New York: Cambridge University Press. (p. 298)

Ambady, N., Hallahan, M., & Rosenthal, R. (1995). On judging and being judged accurately in zero-acquaintance situations. *Journal of Personality and Social Psychology*, *69*, 518–529. (p. 352)

Ambady, N., & Rosenthal, R. (1992). Thin slices of expressive behavior as predictors of interpersonal consequences: A meta-analysis. *Psychological Bulletin*, *111*, 256–274. (p. 405)

Ambady, N., & Rosenthal, R. (1993). Half a minute: Predicting teacher evaluations from thin slices of nonverbal behavior and physical attractiveness. *Journal of Personality and Social Psychology*, *64*, 431–441. (p. 405)

American Enterprise (1992, January/February). Women, men, marriages & ministers. P. 106. (p. 413)

American Psychiatric Association. (1990). *The practice of ECT: Recommendations for treatment, training, and privileging.* Washington, DC: American Psychiatric Press. (p. 486)

American Psychiatric Association. (1994). *Diagnostic and statistical manual of mental disorders (Fourth Edition)*. Washington, DC: American Psychiatric Press. (p. 297)

American Psychological Association. (1991). Medical cost offset. Washington, DC: American Psychological Association Practice Directorate. (p. 479)

American Psychological Association. (1992). Ethical principles of psychologists and code of conduct. *American Psychologist*, *47*, 1597–1611. (p. 33)

Anda, R., Williamson, D., Jones, D., Macera, C., Eaker, E., Glassman, A., & Marks, J. (1993). Depressed affect, hopelessness, and the risk of ischemic heart disease in a cohort of U.S. adults. *Epidemiology*, *4*, 285–294. (p. 373)

Andersen, B. L. (1983). Primary orgasmic dysfunction: Diagnostic considerations and review of treatment. *Psychological Bulletin*, *93*, 105–136. (p. 331)

Andersen, B. L. (1989). Health psychology's contribution to addressing the cancer problem: Update on accomplishments. *Health Psychology*, 8, 683–703. (p. 375)

Andersen, B. L., & Cyranowski, J. M. (1995). Women's sexuality: Behaviors, responses, and individual differences. *Journal of Consulting and Clinical Psychology*, *63*, 891–906. (p. 328)

Anderson, C. A. (1989). Temperature and aggression: Ubiquitous effects of heat on occurrence of human violence. *Psychological Bulletin*, **106**, 74–96. (p. 515)

Anderson, C. A., & Anderson, D. C. (1984). Ambient temperature and violent crime: Tests of the linear and curvilinear hypotheses. *Journal of Personality and Social Psychology*, *46*, 91–97. (p. 515)

Anderson, C. A., Lepper, M. R., & Ross, L. (1980). Perseverance of social theories: The role of explanation in the persistence of discredited information. *Journal of Personality and Social Psychology*, *39*, 1037–1049. (p. 276)

Anderson, D. R., & Jose, W. S., II (1987, December). Employee lifestyle and the bottom line: Results from the StayWell evaluation. *Fitness in Business*, pp. 86–91. (p. 379)

Anderson, P. B., & Mathieu, D. A. (1996). College students' high-risk sexual behavior following alcohol consumption. *Journal of Sex & Marital Therapy*, *22*, 259–263. (p. 193)

Anderson, R. C., Pichert, J. W., Goetz, E. T., Schallert, D. L., Stevens, K. V., & Trollip, S. R. (1976). Instantiation of general terms. *Journal of Verbal Learning and Verbal Behavior*, *15*, 667–679. (p. 250)

Andreasen, N. C. (1997). Linking mind and brain in the study of mental illnesses: A project for a scientific psychopathology. *Science*, *275*, 1586–1593. (p. 453)

Andreasen, N. C., & others (1994). Thalamic abnormalities in schizophrenia visualized through magnetic resonance image averaging. *Science*, *266*, 294–298. (p. 452)

Angoff, W. H. (1987). The nature-nurture debate, aptitudes, and group differences. Presidential address to American Psychological Association Division 5. (p. 303)

Antoni, M. H., LaPerriere, A., Schneiderman, N., & Fletcher, M. A. (1991). Stress and immunity in individuals at risk for AIDS. *Stress Medicine*, 7, 35–44. (p. 375)

Antony, M. M., Brown, T. A., & Barlow, D. H. (1992). Current perspectives on panic and panic disorder. *Current Directions in Psychological Science*, *1*, 79–82. (p. 436)

Antrobus, J. (1991). Dreaming: Cognitive processes during cortical activation and high afferent thresholds. *Psychological Review*, *98*, 96–121. (p. 182)

Archer, J. (1996). Sex differences in social behavior: Are the social role and evolutionary explanations compatible? *American Psychologist*, *51*, 909–917. (p. 508)

Arenson, K. W. (1997, May 4). Romanian woman breaks male grip on top math prize. *Grand Rapids Press*, p. A7 (*New York Times* news service). (p. 305)

Aries, E. (1987). Gender and communication. In P. 671ver & C. Henrick (Eds.), *Review of Personality and Social Psychology*, 7, 177–200. (p. 342)

Arnold, R. B. (1991, October 7). A star cries incest. *People*, pp. 84–88. (p. 260)

Asch, S. E. (1955). Opinions and social pressure. *Scientific American*, *193*, 31–35. (p. 497)

Aserinsky, E. (1988, January 17). Personal communication. (p. 174)

Astin, A. W., Korn, W. S., & Berz, E. R. (1989). *The American freshman: National norms for Fall 1989.* Los Angeles: American Council on Education and UCLA. (p. 117)

Atkinson, R. (1988). *The teenage world: Adolescent self-image in ten countries.* New York: Plenum Press. (p. 96)

Atwell, R. H. (1986, July 28). Drugs on campus: A perspective. *Higher Education & National Affairs*, p. 5. (p. 194)

Averill, J. R. (1983). Studies on anger and aggression: Implications for theories of emotion. *American Psychologist*, *38*, 1145–1160. (p. 357)

Averill, J. R. (1993). William James's other theory of emotion. In M. E. Donnelly (Ed.), *Reinterpreting the legacy of William James.* Washington, DC: American Psychological Association. (p. 365)

Avery, R. D., & others (1994, December 13). Mainstream science on intelligence. *Wall Street Journal*, editorial page. (p. 302)

Ax, A. F. (1953). The physiological differentiation of fear and anger in humans. *Psychosomatic Medicine*, *15*, 433–442. (p. 349)

Axel, R. (1995, October). The molecular logic of smell. *Scientific American*, pp. 154–159. (p. 144)

Axinn, W. G., & Thornton, A. (1992). The relationship between cohabitation and divorce: Selectivity or causal influence? *Demography*, *29*, 357–374. (p. 117)

Azar, B. (1995, May). Several genetic traits linked to alcoholism. *APA Monitor*, pp. 21–22. (p. 200)

Babad, E., Bernieri, F., & Rosenthal, R. (1991). Students as judges of teachers' verbal and nonverbal behavior. *American Educational Research Journal*, *28*, 211–234. (p. 352)

Bachman, J., Wadsworth, K., O'Malley, P., Johnston, L., & Schulenberg, J. (1997). *Smoking, drinking, and drug use in young adulthood: The impact of new freedoms and new responsibilities.* Mahwah, NJ: Erlbaum. (p. 200)

Backus, J. (1977). *The acoustical foundations of music* (2nd ed.). New York: Norton. (p. 139)

Baddeley, A. D. (1982). *Your memory: A user's guide.* New York: Macmillan. (p. xvi, 235)

Bahrick, H. P. (1984). Semantic memory content in permastore: 50 years of memory for Spanish learned in school. *Journal of Experimental Psychology: General*, *111*, 1–29. (p. 243)

Bahrick, H. P., Bahrick, P. O., & Wittlinger, R. P. (1975). Fifty years of memory for names and faces: A cross-sectional approach. *Journal of Experimental Psychology: General*, *104*, 54–75. (p. 249)

Bahrick, H. P., & Hall, L. K. (1991). Lifetime maintenance of high school mathematics content. *Journal of Experimental Psychology: General*, *120*, 20–33. (p. 235)

Bailey, J. M., Bobrow, D., Wolfe, M., & Mikach, S. (1995). Sexual orientation of adult sons of gay fathers. *Developmental Psychology*, *31*, 124–129. (p. 334)

Bailey, J. M., Dunne, M. P., & Martin, N. G. (1997). Sex differences in the distribution and determinants of sexual orientation in a national twin sample. Unpublished manuscript, Northwestern University, Evanston, IL. (p. 335)

Bailey, J. M., Gaulin, S., Agyei, Y., & Gladue, B. A. (1994). Effects of gender and sexual orientation on evolutionarily relevant aspects of human mating psychology. *Journal of Personality and Social Psychology*, *66*, 1081–1093. (p. 332)

Bailey, J. M., Kim, P. Y., & Linsenmeier, J. A. W. (1997). Butch, femme, or straight acting? Partner preferences of gay men and lesbians. *Journal of Personality and Social Psychology*, *73*, 960–973. (p. 336)

Bailey, J. M., & Pillard, R. C. (1991). A genetic study of male sexual orientation. *Archives of General Psychiatry*, *48*, 1089–1096. (p. 335)

Bailey, J. M., & Pillard, R. C. (1994, January). The innateness of homosexuality. *Harvard Mental Health Letter*, pp. 4–6. (p. 336)

Bailey, J. M., & Pillard, R. C. (1995). Genetics of human sexual orientation. *Annual Review of Sex Research*, *6*, 126–150. (p. 335)

Bailey, J. M., Pillard, R. C., Neale, M. C., & Agyei, Y. (1993). Heritable factors influence sexual orientation in women. *Archives of General Psychiatry*, *50*, 217–223. (p. 335)

Bailey, J. M., & Zucker, K. J. (1995). Childhood sex-typed behavior and sexual orientation: A conceptual analysis and quantitative review. *Developmental Psychology*, *31*, 43–55. (p. 332)

Baillargeon, R. (1992). The object concept revisited. In C. Granrud (Ed.), *Visual perception and cognition in infancy. Carnegie-Mellon Symposia on Cognition*, Vol. 23. Hillsdale, NJ: Erlbaum. (p. 87)

Baillargeon, R. (1994). How do infants learn about the physical world? *Current Directions in Psychological Science*, *3*, 133–140. (p. 87)

Baker, E. L. (1987). The state of the art of clinical hypnosis. *International Journal of Clinical and Experimental Hypnosis*, *35*, 203–214. (p. 186)

Balakrishan, T. R., Rao, K. V., Lapierre-Adamcyk, E., & Krotki, K. J. (1987). A hazard model analysis of the covariates of marriage dissolution in Canada. *Demography*, *24*, 395–406. (p. 117)

Ball, W., & Tronick, E. (1971). Infant responses to impending collision: Optical and real. *Science*, *171*, 818–820. (p. 148)

Baltes, P. B. (1993). The aging mind: Potential and limits. *The Gerontologist*, *33*, 580–594. (p. 114)

Baltes, P. B. (1994). Life-span developmental psychology: On the overall landscape of human development. Invited address, American Psychological Association convention. (p. 114)

Bandura, A. (1977). *Social learning theory*. Englewood Cliffs, NJ: Prentice-Hall. (p. 226)

Bandura, A. (1986). *Social foundations of thought and action: A social-cognitive theory.* Englewood Cliffs, NJ: Prentice-Hall. (pp. 415, *416)*

Bandura, A., Blanchard, E. B., & Ritter, B. (1969). Relative efficacy of desensitization and modeling approaches for inducing behavioral, affective, and attitudinal changes. *Journal of Personality and Social Psychology*, *13*, 173–199. (p. 468)

Bandura, A., Ross, D., & Ross, S. A. (1961). Transmission of aggression through imitation of aggressive models. *Journal of Abnormal and Social Psychology*, *63*, 575–582. (p. 226)

Bannon, L. (1995, October 25). Beastly gossip. *Grand Rapids Press*, pp. A1, A4 (reprinted from *Wall Street Journal*). (p. 157)

Barbaree, H. E., & Marshall, W. L. (1991). The role of male sexual arousal in rape: Six models. *Journal of Consulting and Clinical Psychology*, *59*, 621–630. (p. 518)

Bargh, J. A. (1997). The automaticity of everyday life. In R. S. Wyer, Jr. (ed.), *Advances in social cognition*, vol. 10. Mahwah, NJ: Erlbaum. (p. 398)

Barinaga, M. (1992a). The brain remaps its own contours. *Science*, *258*, 216–218. (p. 62)

Barinaga, M. (1997). Visual system provides clues to how the brain perceives. *Science*, *275*, 1583–1585. (p. 147)

Barinaga, M. B. (1997). How exercise works its magic. *Science*, *276*, 1325. (p. 379)

Barker, S. L., Funk, S. C., & Houston, B. K. (1988). Psychological treatment versus nonspecific factors: A meta-analysis of conditions that engender comparable expectations for improvement. *Clinical Psychology Review*, *8*, 579–594. (p. 480)

Barlow, D. H. (1988). *Anxiety and its disorders: The nature and treatment of anxiety and panic.* New York: Guilford. (p. 437)

Barnett, A. (1990). Air safety: End of the golden age? *Chance*, *1*(2), pp. 8–12. (p. 273)

Barnett, A. (1996, June 9). Quoted by Adam Bryan, "Fly me; Why no airline brags: "We're the safest." *New York Times*, Section 4, p. 1. (p. 273)

Barnett, P. A., & Gotlib, I. H. (1988). Psychosocial functioning and depression: Distinguishing among antecedents, concomitants, and consequences. *Psychological Bulletin*, *104*, 97–126. (p. 447)

Barnier, A. J., & McConkey, K. M. (1992). Reports of real and false memories: The relevance of hypnosis, hypnotizability, and context of memory test. *Journal of Abnormal Psychology*, *101*, 521–527. (p. 185)

Baron, R. A. (1987). Interviewer's mood and reaction to job applicants: The influence of affective states on applied social judgments. *Journal of Applied Social Psychology*, *17*, 911–926. (p. 359)

Baron, R. A. (1988). Negative effects of destructive criticism: Impact on conflict, self-efficacy, and task performance. *Journal of Applied Psychology*, *73*, 199–207. (p. 224)

Barry, D. (1995, September 17). Teen smokers, too, get cool, toxic, waste-blackened lungs. *Asbury Park Press*, p. D3. (p. 201)

Barry, D. (1996, August 11). Syndicated column. (p. 99)

Baruch, G. K., & Barnett, R. (1986). Role quality, multiple role involvement, and psychological well-being in midlife women. *Journal of Personality and Social Psychology*, *51*, 578–585. (p. 118)

Bashore, T. R. (1994). Some thoughts on neurocognitive slowing. *Acta Psychologica*, *86*, 295–325. (p. 111)

Baskind, D. E. (1997, December 14). Personal communication, from Delta College. (p. 469)

Bass, E., & Davis, L. (1988). *The courage to heal.* New York: Harper & Row. (p. 259)

Bass, L. E., & Kane-Williams, E. (1993). Stereotype or reality: Another look at alcohol and drug use among African American children. U.S. Department of Health and Human Services, *Public Health Reports*, *108* (Supplement 1), 78–84. (p. 201)

Bat-Chava, Y. (1993). Antecedents of self-esteem in deaf people: A meta-analytic review. *Rehabilitation Psychology*, *38*(4), 221–234. (p. 140)

Bat-Chava, Y. (1994). Group identification and self-esteem of deaf adults. *Personality and Social Psychology Bulletin*, *20*, 494–502. (p. 140)

Baum, A., & Fleming, I. (1993). Implications of psychological research on stress and technological accidents. *American Psychologist*, *48*, 665–672. (p. 370)

Baumeister, R. F. (1989). The optimal margin of illusion. *Journal of Social and Clinical Psychology*, *8*, 176–189. (pp. 274, *411)*

Baumeister, R. F. (1993). Understanding the inner nature of low self-esteem: Uncertain, fragile, protective, and conflicted. In R. F. Baumeister (Ed.), *Self-esteem: The puzzle of low self-regard.* New York: Plenum. (p. 409)

Baumeister, R. F., & Leary, M. R. (1995). The need to belong: Desire for interpersonal attachments as a fundamental human motivation. *Psychological Bulletin*, *117*, 497–529. (p. 337)

Baumeister, R. F., Stillwell, A., & Wotman, S. R. (1990). Victim and perpetrator accounts of interpersonal conflict: Autobiographical narratives about anger. *Journal of Personality and Social Psychology*, *59*, 994–1005. (p. 358)

Baumeister, R. F., & Tice, D. M. (1986). How adolescence became the struggle for self: A historical transformation of psychological development. In J. Suls & A. G. Greenwald (Eds.), *Psychological perspectives on the self* (Vol. 3). Hillsdale, NJ: Erlbaum. (p. 99)

Baumeister, R. F., Tice, D. M., & Hutton, D. G. (1989). Self-presentational motivations and personality differences in self-esteem. *Journal of Personality*, *57*, 547–579. (p. 410)

Baumgardner, A. H. (1990). To know oneself is to like oneself: Self-certainty and self-affect. *Journal of Personality and Social Psychology*, *58*, 1062–1072. (p. 104)

Baumgardner, A. H., Kaufman, C. M., & Levy, P. E. (1989). Regulating affect interpersonally: When low esteem leads to greater enhancement. *Journal of Personality and Social Psychology*, *56*, 907–921. (p. 409)

Baumrind, D. (1982). Adolescent sexuality: Comment on Williams' and Silka's comments on Baumrind. *American Psychologist*, *37*, 1402–1403. (p. 336)

Beaman, A. L., & Klentz, B. (1983). The supposed physical attractiveness bias against supporters of the women's movement: A meta-analysis. *Personality and Social Psychology Bulletin*, *9*, 544–550. (p. 525)

Beardsley, L. M. (1994). Medical diagnosis and treatment across cultures. In W. J. Lonner & R. Malpass (Eds.), *Psychology and culture.* Boston: Allyn & Bacon. (p. 428)

Beardsley, T. (1996, July). Waking up. *Scientific American*, pp. 14, 18. (p. 178)

Beauchamp, G. K. (1987). The human preference for excess salt. *American Scientist*, *75*, 27–33. (p. 318)

Beck, A. J., Kline, S. A., & Greenfeld, L. A. (1988). Survey of youth in custody, 1987. U.S. Department of Justice, Bureau of Justice Statistics Special Report. (p. 516)

Beck, A. T., Rush, A. J., Shaw, B. F., & Emery, G. (1979). *Cognitive therapy of depression.* New York: Guilford Press. (p. 472)

Beck, A. T., & Steer, R. A. (1989). Clinical predictors of eventual suicide: A 5– to 10–year prospective study of suicide attempters. *Journal of Affective Disorders*, *17*, 203–209. (p. 444)

Beck, A. T., & Young, J. E. (1978, September). College blues. *Psychology Today*, pp. 80–92. (pp. 440, 448)

Begg, I. M., Needham, D. R., & Bookbinder, M. (1993). Do backward messages unconsciously affect listeners? No. *Canadian Journal of Experimental Psychology*, *47*, 1–14. (p. 128)

Beilin, H. (1992). Piaget's enduring contribution to developmental psychology. *Developmental Psychology*, *28*, 191–204. (p. 90)

Beitman, B. D., Goldfried, M. R., & Norcross, J. C. (1989). The movement toward integrating the psychotherapies: An overview. *American Journal of Psychiatry*, *146*, 138–147. (p. 462)

Bell, A. P. (1982, November/December). Sexual preference: A postscript. (SIECUS Report, *11, No. 2) Church and Society,* pp. 34–37. (p. 334)

Bell, A. P., Weinberg, M. S., & Hammersmith, S. K. (1981). *Sexual preference: Its development in men and women.* Bloomington: Indiana University Press. (p. 333)

Beloff, J. (1985, Spring). Science, religion and the paranormal. *Free Inquiry*, pp. 36–41 (p. 164)

Belsher, G., & Costello, C. G. (1988). Relapse after recovery from unipolar depression: A critical review. *Psychological Bulletin*, *104*, 84–96. (p. 442)

Belsky, J., Lang, M., & Huston, T. L. (1986). Sex typing and division of labor as determinants of marital change across the transition to parenthood. *Journal of Personality and Social Psychology*, *50*, 517–522. (p. 118)

Bem, D. J. (1996). Exotic becomes erotic: A developmental theory of sexual orientation. *Psychological Review*, *103*, 320–335. (p. 336)

Bem, D. J., & Honorton, C. (1994). Does psi exist? Replicable evidence for an anomalous process of information transfer. *Psychological Bulletin*, *115*, 4–18. (p. 163)

Bem, S. (1993). *The lenses of gender.* New Haven: Yale University Press. (p. 98)

Bem, S. L. (1987). Masculinity and femininity exist only in the mind of the perceiver. In J. M. Reinisch, L. A. Rosenblum, & S. A. Sanders (Eds.), *Masculinity/femininity: Basic perspectives.* New York: Oxford University Press. (p. 98)

Bennett, N. G., Blanc, A. K., & Bloom, D. E. (1988). Commitment and the modern union: Assessing the link between premarital cohabitation and subsequent marital stability. *American Sociological Review*, *53*, 127–138. (p. 117).

Bennett, W., & DiIulio, J. (1996). *Body count.* New York: Simon & Schuster. (p. 201)

Benson, H. (1996). *Timeless healing: The power and biology of belief.* New York: Scribner. (p. 380)

Benson, H., & Klipper, M. Z. (1976). *The relaxation response.* New York: Morrow. (p. 380)

Benson, H., & Proctor, W. (1984). *Beyond the relaxation response: How to harness the healing power of your personal beliefs.* New York: Times Books. (p. 380)

Benson, H., & Proctor, W. (1987). *Your maximum mind.* New York: Times Books/Random House. (p. 380)

Benson, P. L. (1992, Spring). Patterns of religious development in adolescence and adulthood. *PIRI Newsletter*, 2–9. (p. 105)

Benson, P. L., Sharma, A. R., & Roehlkepartain, E. C. (1994). *Growing up adopted: A portrait of adolescents and their families.* Minneapolis: Search Institute. (p. 73)

Berenbaum, S. A., & Hines, M. (1992). Early androgens are related to childhood sex-typed toy preferences. *Psychological Science*, *3*, 203–206. (p. 80)

Berenbaum, S. A., Korman, K., & Leveroni, C. (1995). Early hormones and sex differences in cognitive abilities. *Learning and Individual Differences*, *7*, 303–321. (p. 305)

Bergin, A. E. (1980). Psychotherapy and religious values. *Journal of Consulting and Clinical Psychology*, *48*, 95–105. (p. 481)

Bergsholm, P., Larsen, J. L., Rosendahl, K., & Holsten, F. (1989). Electroconvulsive therapy and cerebral computed tomography. *Acta Psychiatrica Scandinavia*, *80*, 566–572. (p. 486)

Berk, L. E. (1994, November). Why children talk to themselves. *Scientific American*, pp. 78–83. (p. 89)

Berkel, J., & de Waard, F. (1983). Mortality pattern and life expectancy of Seventh Day Adventists in the Netherlands. *International Journal of Epidemiology*, *12*, 455–459. (p. 383)

Berkowitz, L. (1983). Aversively stimulated aggression: Some parallels and differences in research with animals and humans. *American Psychologist*, *38*, 1135–1144. (p. 515)

Berkowitz, L. (1989). Frustration-aggression hypothesis: Examination and reformulation. *Psychological Bulletin*, *106*, 59–73. (p. 515)

Berkowitz, L. (1990). On the formation and regulation of anger and aggression: A cognitive-neoassociationistic analysis. *American Psychologist*, *45*, 494–503. (p. 357)

Berman, M., Gladue, B., & Taylor, S. (1993). The effects of hormones, Type A behavior pattern, and provocation on aggression in men. *Motivation and Emotion*, *17*, 125–138. (p. 514)

Berndt, T. J. (1992). Friendship and friends' influence in adolescence. *Current Directions in Psychological Science*, *1*, 156–159. (p. 105)

Berry, D. S., & McArthur, L. Z. (1986). Perceiving character in faces: The impact of age-related craniofacial changes on social perception. *Psychological Bulletin*, *100*, 3–18. (p. 210)

Berscheid, E. (1981). An overview of the psychological effects of physical attractiveness and some comments upon the psychological effects of knowledge of the effects of physical attractiveness. In G. W. Lucker, K. Ribbens, & J. A. McNamara (Eds.), *Psychological aspects of facial form* (Craniofacial growth series). Ann Arbor: Center for Human Growth and Development, University of Michigan. (p. 524)

Berscheid, E. (1985). Interpersonal attraction. In G. Lindzey & E. Aronson (Eds.), *The handbook of social psychology*. New York: Random House. (p. 337)

Berscheid, E., Gangestad, S. W., & Kulakowski, D. (1984). Emotion in close relationships: Implications for relationship counseling. In S. D. Brown & R. W. Lent (Eds.), *Handbook of counseling psychology*. New York: Wiley. (p. 527)

Beyerstein, B., & Beyerstein, D. (Eds.) (1992). *The write stuff: Evaluations of graphology.* Buffalo, NY: Prometheus Books. (p. 418)

Bhatt, R. S., Wasserman, E. A., Reynolds, W. F., Jr., & Knauss, K. S. (1988). Conceptual behavior in pigeons: Categorization of both familiar and novel examples from four classes of natural and artificial stimuli. *Journal of Experimental Psychology: Animal Behavior Processes*, *14*, 219–234. (p. 217)

Binet, A., & Simon, T. (1905; reprinted 1916). New methods for the diagnosis of the intellectual level of subnormals. In A. Binet & T. Simon, *The development of intelligence in children.* Baltimore: Williams & Wilkins. (p. 289)

Binson, D., Michaels, S., Stall, R., Coates, T. J., Gagnon, J. H., & Catania, J. A. (1995). Prevalence and social distribution of men who have sex with men: United States and its urban centers. *Journal of Sex Research*, *32*, 245–254. (p. 334)

Bishop, G. D. (1991). Understanding the understanding of illness: Lay disease representations. In J. A. Skelton & R. T. Croyle (Eds.), *Mental representation in health and illness.* New York: Springer-Verlag. (p. 269)

Bjork, R. A. (1978). The updating of human memory. In G. H. Bower (Ed.), *The psychology of learning and motivation* (Vol. 12). New York: Academic Press. (p. 240)

Bjorklund, D. F., & Green, B. L. (1992). The adaptive nature of cognitive immaturity. *American Psychologist*, *47*, 46–54. (p. 89)

Blackmore, S. (1991, Fall). Near-death experiences: In or out of the body? *Skeptical Inquirer*, pp. 34–45. (p. 197)

Blackmore, S. (1993). *Dying to live.* Amherst, NY: Prometheus Books. (p. 197)

Blanchard, R., & Bogaert, A. F. (1996a). Homosexuality in men and number of older brothers. *American Journal of Psychiatry*, *153*, 27–31. (p. 334)

Blanchard, R., & Bogaert, A. F. (1996b). Biodemographic comparisons of homosexual and heterosexual men in the Kinsey interview data. *Archives of Sexual Behavior*, *25*, 551–579. (p. 334)

Blanchard, R., & Klassen, P. (1997). H-Y antigen and homosexuality in men. *Journal of Theoretical Biology*, *185*, 373–378. (p. 334)

Blanchard, R., Zucker, K. J., Bradley, S. J., & Hume, C. S. (1995). Birth order and sibling sex ratio in homosexual male adolescents and probably prehomosexual feminine boys. *Developmental Psychology*, *31*, 22–30. (p. 334)

Blass, T. (1996). Stanley Milgram: A life of inventiveness and controversy. In G. A. Kimble, C. A. Boneau, & M. Wertheimer (eds.), *Portraits of pioneers in psychology*, Vol. II. Washington, DC and Mahwah, NJ: American Psychological Association and Lawrence Erlbaum Publishers. (p. 499)

Blatt, S. J., Sanislow, C. A., III, Zuroff, D. C., & Pilkonis, P. (1996). Characteristics of effective therapists: Further analyses of data from the National Institute of Mental Health Treatment of Depression Collaborative Research Program. *Journal of Consulting and clinical Psychology*, *64*, 1276–1284. (p. 481)

Blom, J. M. C., Tamarkin, L., Shiber, J. R., & Nelson, R. J. (1995). Learned immunosuppression is associated with an increased risk of chemically-induced tumors. *Neuroimmunomodulation*, *2*, 92–99. (p. 527)

Bloom, B. S. (Ed.). (1985). *Developing talent in young people.* New York: Ballantine. (p. 339)

Bloom, F. E. (1993, January/February). What's new in neurotransmitters. *BrainWork*, pp. 7–9. (p. 42)

Blum, K., Cull, J. G., Braverman, E. R., & Comings, D. E. (1996). Reward deficiency syndrome. *American Scientist*, *84*, 132–145. (p. 54)

Bodenhausen, G. V., Sheppard, L. A., & Kramer, G. P. (1994). Negative affect and social judgment: The differential impact of anger and sadness. *European Journal of Social Psychology*, *24*, 45–62. (p. 532)

Boesch-Achermann, H., & Boesch, C. (1993). Tool use in wild chimpanzees: New light from dark forests. *Current Directions in Psychological Science*, *2*, 18–21. (p. 270)

Bohman, M., & Sigvardsson, S. (1990). Outcome in adoption: Lessons from longitudinal studies. In D. Brodzinsky & M. Schechter (eds.), *The psychology of adoption.* New York: Oxford University Press. (p. 73)

Bolger, N., DeLongis, A., Kessler, R. C., & Schilling, E. A. (1989). Effects of daily stress on negative mood. *Journal of Personality and Social Psychology*, *57*, 808–818. (p. 359)

Bond, C. F., Jr., Pitre, U., & Van Leeuwen, M. D. (1991). Encoding operations and the next-in-line effect. *Personality and Social Psychology Bulletin*, *17*, 435–441. (p. 235)

Bond, M. H. (1988). Finding universal dimensions of individual variation in multi-cultural studies of values: The Rokeach and Chinese values surveys. *Journal of Personality and Social Psychology*, *55*, 1009–1015. (p. 96)

Bond, R., & Smith, P. B. (1996). Culture and conformity: A meta-analysis of studies using Asch's (1952b, 1956) line judgment task. *Psychological Bulletin*, *119*, 111–137. (p. 498)

Boring, E. G. (1930). A new ambiguous figure. *American Journal of Psychology*, *42*, 444–445. (p. 156)

Bornstein, M. H. (1989). Stability in early mental development: From attention and information processing in infancy to language and cognition in childhood. In M. G. Bornstein & N. A. Krasnegor (Eds.), *Stability and continuity in mental development: Behavioral and biological perspectives.* Hillsdale, NJ: Erlbaum. (pp. 92, 523)

Bornstein, M. H., Tal, J., Rahn, C., Galperin, C. Z., Pecheux, M-G., Lamour, M., Toda, S., Azuma, H., Ogino, M., & Tamis-LeMonda, C. S. (1992a). Functional analysis of the contents of maternal speech to infants of 5 and 13 months in four cultures: Argentina, France, Japan, and the United States. *Developmental Psychology*, *28*, 593–603. (p. 97)

Bornstein, M. H., Tamis-LeMonda, C. S., Tal, J., Ludemann, P., Toda, S., Rahn, C. W., Pecheux, M-G., Azuma, H., Vardi, D. (1992b). Maternal responsiveness to infants in three societies: The United States, France, and Japan. *Child Development*, *63*, 808–821. (p. 97)

Bornstein, R. F., Galley, D. J., Leone, D. R., & Kale, A. R. (1991). The temporal stability of ratings of parents: Test-retest reliability and influence of parental contact. *Journal of Social Behavior and Personality*, *6*, 641–649. (p. 252)

Boroditsky, R., Fisher, W., & Sand, M. (1995, July). Teenagers and contraception. Section of The Canadian contraception study. *Journal of the Society of Obstetricians and Gynaecologists of Canada*, Special Supplement, pp. 22–25. (p. 107)

Bothwell, R. K., Brigham, J. C., & Malpass, R. S. (1989). Cross-racial identification. *Personality and Social Psychology Bulletin*, *15*, 19–25. (p. 512)

Bouchard, T. J., Jr. (1981, December 6). Interview on *Nova: Twins* [program broadcast by the Public Broadcasting Service]. (p. 71)

Bouchard, T. J., Jr. (1996a). IQ similarity in twins reared apart: Finding and responses to critics. In R. Sternberg & C. Grigorenko (eds.), *Intelligence: Heredity and environment.* New York: Cambridge University Press. (p. 300)

Bouchard, T. J., Jr. (1996b). Behavior genetic studies of intelligence, yesterday and today: The long journey from plausibility to proof. *Journal of Biosocial Science*, *28*, 527–555. (p. 300)

Bouchard, T. J., Jr., Lykken, D. T., McGue, M., Segal, N. L., & Tellegen, A. (1990). Sources of human psychological differences: The Minnesota study of twins reared apart. *Science*, *250*, 223–228. (pp. 17, 71)

Bower, G. H. (1983). Affect and cognition. *Philosophical Transaction: Royal Society of London, Series B*, *302*, 387–402. (p. 251)

Bower, G. H. (1986). Prime time in cognitive psychology. In P. Eelen (Ed.), *Cognitive research and behavior therapy: Beyond the conditioning paradigm.* Amsterdam: North Holland Publishers. (p. 250)

Bower, G. H., & Clark, M. C. (1969). Narrative stories as mediators for serial learning. *Psychonomic Science*, *14*, 181–182. (p. 238)

Bower, G. H., Clark, M. C., Lesgold, A. M., & Winzenz, D. (1969). Hierarchical retrieval schemes in recall of categorized word lists. *Journal of Verbal Learning and Verbal Behavior*, *8*, 323–343. (p. 239)

Bower, G. H., & Morrow, D. G. (1990). Mental models in narrative comprehension. *Science, 247,* 44–48. (pp. 236–237)

Bowers, K. S. (1984). Hypnosis. In N. Endler & J. M. Hunt (Eds.), *Personality and behavioral disorders* (2nd ed.). New York: Wiley. (p. 184)

Bowers, K. S. (1987, July). Personal communication. (p. 185)

Bowers, K. S. (1990). Unconscious influences and hypnosis. In J. E. Singer (Ed.), *Repression and dissociation: Implications for personality theory, psychopathology, and health.* Chicago: University of Chicago Press. (p. 190)

Bowers, K. S., & LeBaron, S. (1986). Hypnosis and hypnotizability: Implications for clinical intervention. *Hospital and Community Psychiatry, 37,* 457–467. (p. 188)

Bowers, T. G., & Clum, G. A. (1988). Relative contribution of specific and nonspecific treatment effects: Meta-analysis of placebo-controlled behavior therapy research. *Psychological Bulletin, 103,* 315–323. (p. 479)

Bowlby, J. (1979). *The making and breaking of affectional bonds.* London: Tavistock. (p. 92)

Boyatzis, C. J., Matillo, G. M., & Nesbitt, K. M. (1995). Effects of the 'Mighty Morphin Power Rangers' on children's aggression with peers. *Child Study Journal, 25,* 45–55. (p. 518)

Boynton, R. M. (1979). *Human color vision.* New York: Holt, Rinehart & Winston. (p. 136)

Braden, J. P. (1994). *Deafness, deprivation, and IQ.* New York: Plenum. (pp. 140, *303)*

Bradley, D. R., Dumais, S. T., & Petry, H. M. (1976). Reply to Cavonius. *Nature, 261,* 78. (p. 147)

Bradley-Johnson, S., Johnson, C. M., Shanahan, R. H., Rickert, V. L., & Tardona, D. R. (1984). Effects of token reinforcement on WISC-R performance of black and white, low-socioeconomic second graders. *Behavioral Assessment, 6,* 365–373. (p. 304)

Brainerd, C. J. (1996). Piaget: A centennial celebration. *Psychological Science, 7,* 191–195. (p. 85)

Bransford, J. D., & Johnson, M. K. (1972). Contextual prerequisites for understanding: Some investigations of comprehension and recall. *Journal of Verbal Learning and Verbal Behavior, 11,* 717–726. (p. 237)

Braskamp, L. A. (1987). Spectrum: Utility for educational selection and organizational development. Paper presented at the American Psychological Association convention. (p. 341)

Braun, S. (1996). New experiments underscore warnings on maternal drinking. *Science, 273,* 738–739. (p. 81)

Bray, D. W., & Byham, W. C. (1991, Winter). Assessment centers and their derivatives. *Journal of Continuing Higher Education,* pp. 8–11. (p. 420)

Bray, G. A. (1969). Effect of caloric restriction on energy expenditure in obese patients. *Lancet, 2,* 397–398. (pp. 321, 322)

Brehm, S., & Brehm, J. W. (1981). *Psychological reactance: A theory of freedom and control.* New York: Academic Press. (p. 506)

Breland, K., & Breland, M. (1961). The misbehavior of organisms. *American Psychologist, 16,* 661–664. (p. 223)

Brennan, P. A., & Mednick, S. A. (1993). Genetic perspectives on crime. *Acta Psychiatrica Scandinavia, Suppl. 370,* 19–26. (p. 455)

Brenner, M. (1973). The next-in-line effect. *Journal of Verbal Learning and Verbal Behavior, 12,* 320–323. (p. 235)

Brewer, C. L. (1996). Personal communication. (p. 6)

Brewer, W. F. (1977). Memory for the pragmatic implications of sentences. *Memory & Cognition, 5,* 673–678. (p. 236)

Brickman, P., Coates, D., & Janoff-Bulman, R. J. (1978). Lottery winners and accident victims: Is happiness relative? *Journal of Personality and Social Psychology, 36,* 917–927. (p. 360)

Briere, J., & Runtz, M. (1993). Childhood sexual abuse: Long-term sequelae and implications for psychological assessment. *Journal of Interpersonal Violence, 8,* 312–330. (p. 260)

Bril, B. (1986). Motor development and cultural attitudes. In H. T. A. Whiting & M. G. Wade (Eds.), *Themes in motor development.* Dordrecht, Netherlands: Martinus Nijhoff. (p. 84)

Brinson, S. L. (1992). The use and opposition of rape myths in prime-time television dramas. *Sex Roles, 27,* 359–375. (p. 519)

Briscoe, D. (1995, August 27). Women's share of power slips since the late 1980s. Associated Press (*Grand Rapids [Mich.] Press,* p. A16). (p. 508)

Briscoe, D. (1997, February 16). Women lawmakers still not in charge. Associated Press (*Grand Rapids [Mich.] Press,* p. A23). (p. 508)

Brislin, R. (1993). *Understanding culture's influence on behavior.* Fort Worth, TX: Harcourt Brace. (p. 428)

British Psychological Society (1993). Ethical principles for conducting research with human participants. *The Psychologist: Bulletin of the British Psychological Society, 6,* 33–36. (p. 33)

British Psychological Society (1993). Graphology in personnel assessment. Leicester, England: British Psychological Society. (p. 418)

Brockner, J., & Hulton, A. J. B. (1978). How to reverse the vicious cycle of low self-esteem: The importance of attentional focus. *Journal of Experimental Social Psychology, 14,* 564–578. (p. 408)

Brodzinsky, D. M., & Schechter, M. D. (Eds.) (1990). *The psychology of adoption.* New York: Oxford University Press. (p. 73)

Bronstein-Burrows, P. (1981). *Introductory psychology: A course in the psychology of both sexes.* Paper presented at the meeting of the American Psychological Association. (p. 524)

Brooks-Gunn, J. (1989). Adolescents as daughters and as mothers: A developmental perspective. In I. Sigel & G. Brody (Eds.), *Family research.* Hillsdale, NJ: Erlbaum. (p. 101)

Brooks-Gunn, J., & Furstenberg, F. F., Jr. (1989). Adolescent sexual behavior. *American Psychologist, 44,* 249–257. (p. 108)

Brothers, J. (1990, February 18). Why wives have affairs. *Parade,* pp. 4–7. (p. 327)

Brown, E. L., & Deffenbacher, K. (1979). *Perception and the senses.* New York: Oxford University Press. (p. 141)

Brown, J. D. (1991). Accuracy and bias in self-knowledge. In C. R. Snyder & D. F. Forsyth (Eds.), *Handbook of social and clinical psychology: The health perspective.* New York: Pergamon Press. (pp. 408, 410, 411)

Brown, J. D. (1991). Staying fit and staying well: Physical fitness as a moderator of life stress. *Journal of Personality and Social Psychology, 60,* 555–561. (p. 378)

Brown, J. L., & Pollitt, E. (1996, February). Malnutrition, poverty and intellectual development. *Scientific American,* pp. 38–43. (p. 301)

Brown, R. (1986). Linguistic relativity. In S. H. Hulse & B. F. Green, Jr. (Eds.), *One hundred years of psychological research in America.* Baltimore: Johns Hopkins University Press. (p. 286)

Brown, R., & Kulik, J. (1982). Flashbulb memories. In U. Neisser (Ed.), *Memory observed.* San Francisco: Freeman. (p. 232)

Brown, S. W., Garry, M., Loftus, E., Silver, B., DuBois, K., & DuBreuil, S. (1996). People's beliefs about memory: Why don't we have better memories? Paper presented at the American Psychological Society convention. (pp. 187, 244)

Brownell, K. D. (1991). Dieting and the search for the perfect body: Where physiology and culture collide. *Behavior Therapy*, *22*, 1–12. (p. 323)

Brownell, K. D. (1994, December 15). Get slim with higher taxes. *New York Times*, p. A29. (p. 320)

Brownell, K. D., & Jeffery, R. W. (1987). Improving long-term weight loss: Pushing the limits of treatment. *Behavior Therapy*, *18*, 353–374. (p. 324)

Brownell, K. D., & Wadden, T. A. (1991). The heterogeneity of obesity: Fitting treatments to individuals. *Behavior Therapy*, *22*, 153–177. (p. 324)

Brownell, K. D., & Wadden, T. A. (1992). Etiology and treatment of obesity: Understanding a serious, prevalent, and refractory disorder. *Journal of Consulting and Clinical Psychology*, *60*, 505–517. (pp. 322, 324)

Browning, C. (1992). *Ordinary men: Reserve police battalion 101 and the final solution in Poland*. New York: HarperCollins. (p. 500)

Brownmiller, S. (1975). *Against our will: Men, women, and rape*. New York: Simon and Schuster. (p. 330)

Bryant, F. B., & Brockway, J. H. (1997). Hindsight bias in reaction to the O. J. Simpson verdict. *Basic and Applied Social Psychology*, *19*, 225–241. (p. 11)

Buehler, R., Griffin, D., & Ross, M. (1994). Exploring the "planning fallacy": Why people underestimate their task completion times. *Journal of Personality and Social Psychology*, *67*, 366–381. (p. 274)

Bugelski, B. R., Kidd, E., & Segmen, J. (1968). Image as a mediator in one-trial paired-associate learning. *Journal of Experimental Psychology*, *76*, 69–73. (p. 238)

Bugental, D. B. (1986). Unmasking the "polite smile": Situational and personal determinants of managed affect in adult-child interaction. *Personality and Social Psychology Bulletin*, *12*, 7–16. (p. 352)

Bullard, T. E. (1987). *UFO abductions: The measure of a mystery. Vol. 2: Catalogue of cases*. Mount Ranier, MD: Fund for UFO Research. Cited by L. S. Newman & R. F. Baumeister, (1996). Toward an explanation of the UFO abduction phenomenon: Hypnotic, elaboration, extraterrestrial sadomasochism, and spurious memories. *Psychological Inquiry*, *7*, 99–126. (p. 186)

Bullough, V. (1990). The Kinsey scale in historical perspective. In D. P. McWhirter, S. A. Sanders, & J. M. Reinisch (Eds.), *Homosexuality/heterosexuality: Concepts of sexual orientation*. New York: Oxford University Press. (p. 332)

Bumpass, L. L., & Sweet, J. A. (1989). National estimates of cohabitation. *Demography*, *26*, 615–625. (p. 117)

Buquet, R. (1988). Le reve et les deficients visuels (Dreams and the visually-impaired). *Psychanalyse-a-l'Universite*, *13*, 319–327. (p. 181)

Bureau of the Census (1996). *Statistical abstract of the United States 1996*. Washington, DC: U.S. Government Printing Office. (pp. 107, 116, 117, 444, 526)

Burger, J. M. (1987). Increased performance with increased personal control: A self-presentation interpretation. *Journal of Experimental Social Psychology*, *23*, 350–360. (p. 342)

Burger, J. M., & Burns, L. (1988). The illusion of unique invulnerability and the use of effective contraception. *Personality and Social Psychology Bulletin*, **14**, *264–270. (p. 420)*

Burish, T. G., & Carey, M. P. (1986). Conditioned aversive responses in cancer chemotherapy patients: Theoretical and developmental analysis. *Journal of Counseling and Clinical Psychology*, *54*, 593–600. (p. 213)

Burke, K. C., Burke, J. D., Regier, D. A., & Rae, D. S. (1990). Age at onset of selected mental disorders in five community populations. *Archives of General Psychiatry*, *47*, 511–518. (p. 433)

Busch, C. M., Zonderman, A. B., & Costa, P. T. (1994). Menopausal transition and psychological distress in a nationally representative sample: Is menopause associated with psychological distress? *Journal of Aging and Health*, *6*, 209–228. (p. 110)

Bushman, B. J. (1993). Human aggression while under the influence of alcohol and other drugs: An integrative research review. *Current Directions in Psychological Science*, *2*, 148–152. (p. 514)

Buss, D. (1994b). The strategies of human mating. *American Scientist*, *82*, 238–249. (p. 525)

Buss, D. M. (1991). Evolutionary personality psychology. *Annual Review of Psychology*, *42*, 459–491. (p. 31)

Buss, D. M. (1995). Evolutionary psychology: A new paradigm for psychological science. *Psychological Inquiry,* **6**, 1–30. (p. 332)

Buss, D. M. (1996). Sexual conflict: Evolutionary insights into feminism and the "battle of the sexes." In D. M. Buss & N. M. Malamuth (eds.), *Sex, power, conflict: Evolutionary and feminist perspectives*. New York: Oxford University Press. (p. 525)

Butcher, J. N. (1990). *The MMPI–2 in psychological treatment*. New York: Oxford University Press. (p. 403)

Butler, A. C., Hokanson, J. E., & Flynn, H. A. (1994). A comparison of self-esteem lability and low trait self-esteem as vulnerability factors for depression. *Journal of Personality and Social Psychology*, *66*, 166–177. (p. 447)

Butler, R. A. (1954, February). Curiosity in monkeys. *Scientific American*, pp. 70–75. (p. 313)

Byne, W., & Parsons, B. (1993). Human sexual orientation: The biologic theories reappraised. *Archives of General Psychiatry*, *50*, 228–239. (p. 335)

Byrne, D. (1971). *The attraction paradigm*. New York: Academic Press. (p. 526)

Byrne, D. (1982). Predicting human sexual behavior. In A. G. Kraut (Ed.), *The G. Stanley Hall Lecture Series* (Vol. 2). Washington, DC: American Psychological Association. (pp. 209, 328, 330)

Byrne, R. W. (1991, May/June). Brute intellect. *The Sciences*, pp. 42–47. (p. 282)

Byrnes, G., & Kelly, I. W. (1992). Crisis calls and lunar cycles: A twenty-year review. *Psychological Reports*, *71*, 779–785. (p. 455)

Cacioppo, J. T., Berntson, G. G., Klein, D. J., & Poehlmann, K. M. (1997). The psychophysiology of emotion across the lifespan. *Annual Review of Gerontology and Geriatrics*, *17*, in press. (p. 349)

Cahill, L. (1994). (Beta)-adrenergic activation and memory for emotional events. *Nature*, *371*, 702–704. (p. 246)

Cameron, P., & Biber, H. (1973). Sexual thought throughout the lifespan. *Gerontologist*, *13*, 144–147. (p. 171)

Campbell, D. T. (1975). On the conflicts between biological and social evolution and between psychology and moral tradition. *American Psychologist, 30,* 1103–1126. (p. 361)

Campbell, D. T., & Specht, J. C. (1985). Altruism: Biology, culture, and religion. *Journal of Social and Clinical Psychology, 3*(1), 33–42. (p. 414)

Campbell, S. (1986). *The Loch Ness Monster: The evidence.* Willingborough, Northamptonshire, U.K.: Acquarian Press. (p. 157)

Camper, J. (1990, February 7). Drop pompom squad, U. of I. rape study says. *Chicago Tribune,* p. 1. (p. 193)

Campos, J. J., Bertenthal, B. I., & Kermoian, R. (1992). Early experience and emotional development: The emergence of wariness and heights. *Psychological Science, 3,* 61–64. (pp. 148, 131)

Cannon, T. D., & Marco, E. (1994). Structural brain abnormalities as indicators of vulnerability to schizophrenia. *Schizophrenia Bulletin, 20,* 89–102. (p. 452)

Cannon, W. B. (1929). *Bodily changes in pain, hunger, fear, and rage.* New York: Branford. (pp. 316, 369)

Cannon, W. B., & Washburn, A. (1912). An explanation of hunger. *American Journal of Physiology, 29,* 441–454. (p. 316)

Cantor, N., & Kihlstrom, J. F. (1987). *Personality and social intelligence.* Englewood Cliffs, NJ: Prentice-Hall. (p. 292)

Cantor, N., & Norem, J. K. (1989). Defensive pessimism and stress and coping. *Social Cognition, 7,* 92–112. (p. 418)

Cantril, H., & Bumstead, C. H. (1960). *Reflections on the human venture.* New York: New York University Press. (p. 506)

Carducci, B. J., Cosby, P. C., & Ward, D. D. (1978). Sexual arousal and interpersonal evaluations. *Journal of Experimental Social Psychology, 14,* 449–457. (p. 526)

Carey, G. (1990). Genes, fears, phobias, and phobic disorders. *Journal of Counseling and Development, 68,* 628–632. (p. 436)

Carli, L. L., & Leonard, J. B. (1989). The effect of hindsight on victim derogation. *Journal of Social and Clinical Psychology, 8,* 331–343. (p. 513)

Carlson, M. (1995, August 29). Quoted by S. Blakeslee, In brain's early growth, timetable may be crucial. *New York Times,* pp. C1, C3. (p. 94)

Carlson, M., Charlin, V., & Miller, N. (1988). Positive mood and helping behavior: A test of six hypotheses. *Journal of Personality and Social Psychology, 55,* 211–229. (p. 529)

Carlson, R. (1984). What's social about social psychology? Where's the person in personality research? *Journal of Personality and Social Psychology, 47,* 1304–1309. (p. 420)

Carlson, S. (1985). A double-blind test of astrology. *Nature, 318,* 419–425. (p. 418)

Carnegie Council on Adolescent Development. (1989, June). *Turning points: Preparing American youth for the 21st century.* (The report of the Task Force on Education of Young Adolescents.) New York: Carnegie Corporation. (p. 531)

Carroll, J. M., & Russell, J. A. (1996). Do facial expressions signal specific emotions? Judging emotion from the face in context. *Journal of Personality and Social Psychology, 70,* 205–218. (p. 354)

Carson, R. C., Butcher, J. N., & Coleman, J. C. (1988). *Abnormal psychology and modern life* (8th ed.). Glenview, IL: Scott, Foresman. (p. 428)

Cartwright, R. D. (1978). *A primer on sleep and dreaming.* Reading, MA: Addison-Wesley. (p. 175)

Case, R. B., Moss, A. J., Case, N., McDermott, M., & Eberly, S. (1992). Living alone after myocardial infarction: Impact on prognosis. *Journal of the American Medical Association, 267,* 515–519. (p. 382)

Cash, T., & Janda, L. H. (1984, December). The eye of the beholder. *Psychology Today,* pp. 46–52. (p. 524)

Caspi, A., & Moffitt, T. E. (1991). Individual differences are accentuated during periods of social change: The sample case of girls at puberty. *Journal of Personality and Social Psychology, 61,* 157–168. (p. 101)

Caspi, A., Moffitt, T. E., Newman, D. L., & Silva, P. A. (1996). Behavioral observations at age 3 years predict adult psychiatric disorders: Longitudinal evidence from a birth cohort. *Archives of General Psychiatry, 53,* 1033–1039. (p. 455)

Castonguay, L. G., & Goldfried, M. R. (1994). Psychotherapy integration: An idea whose time has come. *Applied & Preventive Psychology, 3,* 159–172. (p. 462)

Cattell, R. B. (1963). Theory of fluid and crystallized intelligence: A critical experiment. *Journal of Educational Psychology, 54,* 1–22. (p. 114)

Cavalli-Sforza, L., Menozzi, P., & Piazza, A. (1994). *The history and geography of human genes.* Princeton, NJ: Princeton University Press. (p. 303)

Ceci, S. J. (1993). Cognitive and social factors in children's testimony. Master Lecture, American Psychological Association convention. (pp. 258, *259)*

Ceci, S. J., & Bruck, M. (1993). Child witnesses: Translating research into policy. *Social Policy Report* (Society for Research in Child Development), 7(3), 1–30. (p. 258)

Ceci, S. J., & Bruck, M. (1995). *Jeopardy in the courtroom: A scientific analysis of children's testimony.* Washington, DC: American Psychological Association. (p. 258)

Ceci, S. J., Huffman, M. L. C., Smith, E., & Loftus, E. F. (1994). Repeatedly thinking about a non-event: Source misattributions among preschoolers. *Consciousness and Cognition, 3,* 388–407. (p. 259)

Ceci, S. J., & Liker, J. K. (1986). A day at the races: A study of IQ, expertise, and cognitive complexity. *Journal of Experimental Psychology: General, 115,* 255–266. (p. 292)

Ceci, S. J., & Williams, W. M. (1997). Schooling, intelligence, and income. *American Psychologist, 52,* 1051–1058. (p. 304)

Centers for Disease Control. (1989). Results from the national adolescent student health survey. *Morbidity and Mortality Weekly Report, 38*(9), 147–150. (p. 435, 444)

Centers for Disease Control. (1991). Body-weight perceptions and selected weight-management goals and practices of high school students—United States, 1990. *Morbidity and Mortality Weekly Report, 40,* 741, 747–750. (p. 324)

Centers for Disease Control. (1992, January 3). Sexual behavior among high school students—United States, 1990. *Morbidity and Mortality Weekly Report, 40,* Nos. 51 & 52, 885–888. (p. 108)

Centers for Disease Control. (1992, September 16). Serious mental illness and disability in the adult household population: United States, 1989. *Advance Data* No. 218 from *Vital and Health Statistics,* National Center for Health Statistics. (p. 457)

Centerwall, B. S. (1989). Exposure to television as a risk factor for violence. *American Journal of Epidemiology, 129,* 643–652. (p. 517)

Cerella, J. (1985). Information processing rates in the elderly. *Psychological Bulletin, 98,* 67–83. (p. 112)

Chalmers, R. (1995, September 19). Sizing sizzle of mutuals. *Edmonton Journal*, p. E1. (p. 22)

Chamove, A. S. (1980). Nongenetic induction of acquired levels of aggression. *Journal of Abnormal Psychology*, *89*, 469–488. (p. 227)

Chance News (1997, 30 December). Gender and mortality statistics. *Chance News,* 6.13 (from Dart.Chance@Dartmouth.edu). (p. 383)

Chang, E. C. (1996). Cultural differences in optimism, pessimism, and coping: Preditors of subsequent adjustment in Asian American and Caucasian American college students. *Journal of Counseling Psychology*, *43*, 113–123. (p. 418)

Chase, W. G., & Simon, H. A. (1973). Perception in chess. *Cognitive Psychology*, *4*, 55–81. (p. 239)

Chaves, J. F. (1989). Hypnotic control of clinical pain. In N. P. Spanos & J. F. Chaves (Eds.), *Hypnosis: The cognitive-behavioral perspective.* Buffalo, NY: Prometheus Books. (p. 188)

Cheek, J. M., & Melchior, L. A. (1990). Shyness, self-esteem, and self-consciousness. In H. Leitenberg (Ed.), *Handbook of social and evaluation anxiety.* New York: Plenum. (pp. 96, 448)

Cherfas, J. (1990). Two bomb attacks on scientists in the U.K. *Science*, *248*, 1485. (p. 32)

Cherlin, A. J., Furstenberg, F. F., Jr., Chase-Landale, P. L., Kiernan, K. E., Robins, P. K., Morrison, D. R., & Teitler, J. O. (1991). Longitudinal studies of effects of divorce on children in Great Britain and the United States. *Science*, *252*, 1386–1389. (p. 95)

Cherlin, A. J., Kiernan, K. E., & Chase-Lansdale, P. L. (1995). Parental Divorce in Childhood and Demographic Outcomes in Young Adulthood. *Demography*, *32*, 299–316. (p. 85)

Chess, S., & Thomas, A. (1987). *Know your child: An authoritative guide for today's parents.* New York: Basic Books. (p. 92)

Chomsky, N. (1959). Review of B. F. Skinner's *Verbal behavior. Language*, *35*, 26–58. (p. 280)

Chomsky, N. (1972). *Language and mind.* New York: Harcourt Brace Jovanovich. (p. 277)

Chomsky, N. (1987). Language in a psychological setting. Sophia Linguistic Working Papers in Linguistics, No. 22, Sophia University, Tokyo. (p. 280)

Christensen, A., & Jacobson, N. S. (1994). Who (or what) can do psychotherapy: The status and challenge of nonprofessional therapies. *Psychological Science*, *5*, 8–14. (p. 481)

Christianson, S. A. (1992). Emotional stress and eyewitness memory: A critical review. *Psychological Bulletin*, *112*, 284–309. (p. 398)

Christophersen, E. R., & Edwards, K. J. (1992). Treatment of elimination disorders: State of the art 1991. *Applied & Preventive Psychology*, *1*, 15–22. (p. 467)

Chwalisz, K., Diener, E., & Gallagher, D. (1988). Autonomic arousal feedback and emotional experience: Evidence from the spinal cord injured. *Journal of Personality and Social Psychology*, *54*, 820–828. (p. 360)

Cialdini, R. B. (1993). *Influence: Science and practice* (3rd ed.). New York: Harper Collins. (p. 494)

Cialdini, R. B., & Richardson, K. D. (1980). Two indirect tactics of image management: Basking and blasting. *Journal of Personality and Social Psychology*, *39*, 406–415. (p. 512)

Clark, R. D., III (1990). The impact of AIDS on gender differences in willingness to engage in casual sex. *Journal of Applied Social Psychology*, *20*, 771–782. (p. 332)

Clark, R. D., III, & Hatfield, E. (1989). Gender differences in willingness to engage in casual sex. *Journal of Psychology and Human Sexuality*, *2*, 39–55. (p. 332)

Coats, E. J., & Feldman, R. S. (1996). Gender differences in nonverbal correlates of social status. *Personality and Social Psychology Bulletin*, *22*, 1014–1022. (p. 352)

Coe, W. C. (1989a). Posthypnotic amnesia: Theory and research. In N. P. Spanos & J. F. Chaves (Eds.), *Hypnosis: The cognitive-behavioral perspective.* Buffalo, NY: Prometheus Books. (p. 184)

Coe, W. C. (1989b). Hypnosis: The role of sociopolitical factors in a paradigm clash. In N. P. Spanos & J. F. Chaves (Eds.), *Hypnosis: The cognitive-behavioral perspective.* Buffalo, NY: Prometheus Books. (p. 190)

Coffey, C. E. (Ed.) (1993). *Clinical science of electroconvulsive therapy.* Washington, DC: American Psychiatric Press. (p. 486)

Coffey, C. E., Wilkinson, W. E., Weiner, R. D., Parashos, I. A., Djang, W. T., Webb, M. C., Figiel, G. S., & Spritzer, C. E. (1993). Quantitative cerebral anatomy in depression: A controlled magnetic resonance imaging study. *Archives of General Psychiatry*, *50*, 7–16. (p. 445)

Cogan, J. C., Bhalla, S. K., Sefa-Dedeh, A., & Rothblum, E. D. (1996). A comparison study of United States and African students on perceptions of obesity and thinness. *Journal of Cross-Cultural psychology*, *27*, 98–113. (p. 320)

Cohen, D. (1995, June 17). Now we are one, or two, or three. *New Scientist*, pp. 14–15. (p. 439)

Cohen, D. (1996). Law, social policy, and violence: The impact of regional cultures. *Journal of Personality and Social Psychology*, *70*, 961–978. (p. 516)

Cohen, G., Conway, M. A., & Maylor, E. A. (1994). Flashbulb memories in older adults. *Psychology and Aging*, *9*, 454–463. (p. 113)

Cohen, S. (1988). Psychosocial models of the role of social support in the etiology of physical disease. *Health Psychology*, *7*, 269–297. (p. 382)

Cohen, S. (1996). Psychological stress, immunity, and upper respiratory infections. *Current Directions in Psychological Science*, *5*, 86-90. (p. 374)

Cohen, S., Doyle, W. J., Skinner, D. P., Rabin, B. S., & Gwaltney, Jr., J. M. (1997). Social ties and susceptibility to the common cold. *Journal of the American Medical Association*, *277*, 1940–1944. (p. 382)

Cohen, S., Doyle, W. J., Skoner, D. P., Fireman, P., Gwaltney, J. M., Jr., & Newson, J. T. (1995). State and trait negative affect as predictors of objective and subjective symptoms of respiratory viral infections. *Journal of Personality and Social Psychology*, *68*, 159–169. (p. 374)

Cohen, S., Kaplan, J. R., Cunnick, J. E., Manuck, S. B., & Rabin, B. S. (1992). Chronic social stress, affiliation, and cellular immune response in nonhuman primates. *Psychological Science*, *3*, 301–304. (p. 374)

Cohen, S., & Rodriguez, M. S. (1995). Pathways linking affective disturbances and physical disorders. *Health Psychology*, *14*, 374–380. (p. 373)

Cohen, S., Tyrrell, D. A. J., & Smith, A. P. (1991). Psychological stress and susceptibility to the common cold. *New England Journal of Medicine*, *325*, 606–612. (p. 374)

Cohen, S., Tyrrell, D. A. J., & Smith, A. P. (1993). Negative life events, perceived stress, negative affect, and susceptibility to the common cold. *Journal of Personality and Social Psychology*, *64*, 131–140. (p. 374)

Coile, D. C., & Miller, N. E. (1984). How radical animal activists try to mislead humane people. *American Psychologist, 39,* 700–701. (p. 32)

Cole, N. S. (1995, March 22). Personal correspondence, from Educational Testing Service, Princeton, NJ 08541. (p. 346)

Coleman, J. C. (1980). *The nature of adolescence.* London: Methuen. (p. 100)

Coleman, P. D., & Flood, D. G. (1986). Dendritic proliferation in the aging brain as a compensatory repair mechanism. In D. F. Swaab, E. Fliers, M. Mirmiram, W. A. Van Gool, & F. Van Haaren (Eds.), *Progress in brain research* (Vol. 20). New York: Elsevier. (p. 112)

College Board (1987). *1987 profile of SAT and achievement test takers.* New York: The College Entrance Examination Board. (p. 304)

College Board (1996, August 22). *News from The College Board.* New York: The College Entrance Examination Board. (p. 304)

Colley, A. (1995, August). Psychology, science and women. *The Psychologist,* pp. 346–352. (p. 7)

Collins, N. L., & Miller, L. C. (1994). Self-disclosure and liking: A meta-analytic review. *Psychological Bulletin, 116,* 457–475. (p. 527)

Colombo, J. (1982). The critical period concept: Research, methodology, and theoretical issues. *Psychological Bulletin, 91,* 260–275. (p. 92)

Colon, E. A., Callies, A. L., Popkin, M. K., & McGlave, P. B. (1991). Depressed mood and other variables related to bone marrow transplantation survival in acute leukemia. *Psychosomatics, 32,* 420–425. (pp. 374, 382)

Comstock, G. W., & Partridge, K. B. (1972). Church attendance and health. *Journal of Chronic Disease, 25,* 665–672. (p. 383)

Consensus Conference. (1985). Electroconvulsive therapy. *Journal of the American Medical Association, 254,* 2103–2108. (p. 486)

Considine, R. V., Sinha, M. K., Madhur, K., Heiman, M. L., & Kriauciunas (1996). Serum immunoreactive-leptin concentrations in normal-weight and obese humans. *New England Journal of Medicine, 334,* 292–295. (p. 323)

Consumer Reports (1995, November). Does therapy help? Pp. 734–739. (pp. 476, 479)

Conway, M., & Ross, M. (1984). Getting what you want by revising what you had. *Journal of Personality and Social Psychology, 47,* 738–748. (p. 254)

Cook, E. W., III, Hodes, R. L., & Lang, P. J. (1986). Preparedness and phobia: Effects of stimulus content on human visceral conditioning. *Journal of Abnormal Psychology, 95,* 195–207. (p. 212)

Cooper, G. D., Adams, H. B., & Scott, J. C. (1988). Studies in REST: I. Reduced environmental stimulation therapy (REST) and reduced alcohol consumption. *Journal of Substance Abuse Treatment, 5,* 61–68. (p. 178)

Cooper, W. H. (1983). An achievement motivation nomological network. *Journal of Personality and Social Psychology, 44,* 841–861. (p. 339)

Coren, S. (1993). *The left-hander syndrome: The causes and consequences of left-handedness.* New York: Vintage Books. (p. 66)

Coren, S. (1996). *Sleep thieves: An eye-opening exploration into the science and mysteries of sleep.* New York: Free Press. (pp. 176, 178, 179)

Corina, D. P., Vaid, J., & Bellugi, U. (1992). The linguistic basis of left hemisphere specialization. *Science, 255,* 1258–1260. (p. 64)

Costa, P. T., Jr., & McCrae, R. R. (1989). Personality continuity and the changes of adult life. In M. Storandt & G. R. VandenBos (Eds.), *The adult years: Continuity and change.* Washington, DC: American Psychological Association. (p. 121)

Courneya, K. S., & Carron, A. V. (1992). The home advantage in sports competitions: A literature review. *Journal of Sport and Exercise Psychology, 14,* 13–27. (p. 503)

Courtney, J. G., Longnecker, M. P., Theorell, T., & de Verdier, M. G. (1993). Stressful life events and the risk of colorectal cancer. *Epidemiology, 4,* 407–414. (p. 375)

Cousins, N. (1989). *Head first: The biology of hope.* New York: Dutton. (p. 375)

Cousins, S. D. (1989). Culture and self-perception in Japan and the United States. *Journal of Personality and Social Psychology, 56,* 124–131. (p. 412)

Cowan, G., Lee, C., Levy, D., & Snyder, D. (1988). Dominance and inequality in X-rated videocassettes. *Psychology of Women Quarterly, 12,* 299–311. (p. 518)

Cowan, N. (1988). Evolving conceptions of memory storage, selective attention, and their mutual constraints within the human information-processing system. *Psychological Bulletin, 104,* 163–191. (p. 242)

Cowan, N. (1994). Mechanisms of verbal short-term memory. *Current Directions in Psychological Science, 3,* 185–189. (p. 242)

Cowart, B. J. (1981). Development of taste perception in humans: Sensitivity and preference throughout the life span. *Psychological Bulletin, 90,* 43–73. (p. 143)

Craig, M. E., Kalichman, S. C., & Follingstad, D. R. (1989). Verbal coercive sexual behavior among college students. *Archives of Sexual Behavior, 18,* 421–434. (p. 518)

Craig, O., & Shields, J. (1996, July 14). For pity's sake. *The Sunday Times,* Section 3, pages 1–2. (p. 210)

Craik, F. I. M., & Watkins, M. J. (1973). The role of rehearsal in short-term memory. *Journal of Verbal Learning and Verbal Behavior, 12,* 599–607. (p. 236)

Crandall, C. S. (1988). Social contagion of binge eating. *Journal of Personality and Social Psychology, 55,* 588–598. (p. 319)

Crandall, C. S. (1994). Prejudice against fat people: Ideology and self-interest. *Journal of Personality and Social Psychology, 66,* 882–894. (p. 320)

Crandall, C. S. (1995). Do parents discrminate against their heavy-weight daughters? *Personality and Social Psychology Bulletin, 21,* 724–735. (p. 320)

Crandall, J. E. (1984). Social interest as a moderator of life stress. *Journal of Personality and Social Psychology, 47,* 164–174. (p. 414)

Crawford, M., Chaffin, R., & Fitton, L. (1995). *Learning and Individual Differences, 7,* 341–362. (p. 305)

Crocker, J., & Major, B. (1989). Social stigma and self-esteem: The self-protective properties of stigma," *Psychological Review, 89,* 608–630. (p. 409).

Crocker, J., Thompson, L. L., McGraw, K. M., & Ingerman, C. (1987). Downward comparison, prejudice, and evaluation of others: Effects of self-esteem and threat. *Journal of Personality and Social Psychology, 52,* 907–916. (p. 512)

Crook, T. H., & West, R. L. (1990). Name recall performance across the adult life-span. *British Journal of Psychology, 81,* 335–340. (pp. 112, 113)

Cross-National Collaborative Group (1992). The changing rate of major depression. *Journal of the American Medical Association, 268*, 3098–3105. (p. 443)

Crossen, C. (1994). *Tainted truth: The manipulation of fact in America.* New York: Simon & Schuster. (p. 536)

Crowell, J. A., & Waters, E. (1994). Bowlby's theory grown up: The role of attachment in adult love relationships. *Psychological Inquiry, 5*, 1–22. (p. 92)

CSICOP (1994, December). Psychics fail once again. *Skeptical Briefs*, p. 9. (p. 162)

Csikszentmihalyi, M. (1990). *Flow: The psychology of optimal experience.* New York: Harper & Row. (pp. 271, *362)*

Curtis, R. C., & Miller, K. (1986). Believing another likes or dislikes you: Behaviors making the beliefs come true. *Journal of Personality and Social Psychology, 51*, 284–290. (p. 526)

Dabbs, J. M., Jr. (1992). Testosterone measurements in social and clinical psychology. *Journal of Social and Clinical Psychology, 11*, 302–321. (p. 514)

Dabbs, J. M., Jr., & Morris, R. (1990). Testosterone, social class, and antisocial behavior in a sample of 4,462 men. *Psychological Science, 1*, 209–211. (p. 514)

Dabbs, J. M., Jr., Ruback, R. B., & Besch, N. F. (1987). Male saliva testosterone following conversations with male and female partners. Paper presented at the American Psychological Association convention. (p. 328)

Damasio, H., Grabowski, T., Frank, R., Galaburda, A. M., & Damasio, A. R. (1994). The return of Phineas Gage: Clues about the brain from the skull of a famous patient. *Science, 264*, 1102–1105. (p. 59)

Damon, W. (1995). *Greater expectations: Overcoming the culture of indulgence in America's homes and schools.* New York: Free Press. (pp. 85, 409)

Darley, J. M., & Latané, B. (1968a). Bystander intervention in emergencies: Diffusion of responsibility. *Journal of Personality and Social Psychology, 8*, 377–383. (pp. 528, 529)

Darley, J. M., & Latané, B. (1968b, December). When will people help in a crisis? *Psychology Today*, pp. 54–57, 70–71. (pp. 528, 529)

Darrach, B., & Norris, J. (1984, August). An American tragedy. *Life*, pp. 58–74. (p. 455)

Darwin, C. (1859/1988). *The origin of species.* Vol. 15 of *The Works of Charles Darwin*, edited by P. H. Barrett & R. B. Freeman. New York: New York University Press. (p. 69)

Daum, I., & Schugens, M. M. (1996). On the cerebellum and classical conditioning. *Psychological Science, 5*, 58–61. (p. 248)

Davey, G. C. L. (1992). Classical conditioning and the acquisition of human fears and phobias: A review and synthesis of the literature. *Advances in Behavior Research and Therapy, 14*, 29–66. (p. 213)

Davey, G. C. L. (1995). Preparedness and phobias: Specific evolved associations or a generalized expectancy bias? *Behavioral and Brain Sciences, 18*, 289–297. (p. 436)

Davidson, R. J. (1992). Emotion and affective style: Hemispheric substrates. *Psychological Science, 3*, 39–43. (pp. 349, 445)

Davidson, R. J., Ekman, P., Saron, C. D., Senulis, J. A., & Friesen, W. V. (1990). Approach-withdrawal and cerebral asymmetry: Emotional expression and brain physiology I. *Journal of Personality and Social Psychology, 58*, 330–341. (p. 349)

Davies, D. R., Matthews, G., & Wong, C. S. K. (1991). Aging and work. *International Review of Industrial and Organizational Psychology, 6*, 149–211. (p. 115)

Davies, M. F. (1997). Positive test strategies and confirmatory retrieval processes in the evaluation of personality feedback. *Journal of Personality and Social Psychology, 73*, 574–583. (p. 418)

Davis, J. O., & Phelps, J. A. (1995a). Twins with schizophrenia: Genes or germs? *Schizophrenia Bulletin, 21*, 13–18. (p. 453)

Davis, J. O., Phelps, J. A., & Bracha, H. S. (1995b). Prenatal development of monozygotic twins and concordance for schizophrenia. *Schizophrenia Bulletin, 21*, 357–366. (p. 453)

Dawes, R. M. (1980). Social dilemmas. *Annual Review of Psychology, 31*, 169–193. (p. 521)

Dawes, R. M. (1994). *House of cards: Psychology and psychotherapy built on myth.* New York: Free Press. (pp. 396, *409)*

Dawson, N. V., Arkes, H. R., Siciliano, C., Blinkhorn, R., Lakshmanan, M., & Petrelli, M. (1988). Hindsight bias: An impediment to accurate probability estimation in clinicopathologic conferences. *Medical Decision Making, 8*, 259–264. (p. 11)

Day, R. H. (1984). The nature of perceptual illusions. *Interdisciplinary Science Reviews, 9*, 47–58. (p. 153)

Dean, G. A., Kelly, I. W., Saklofske, D. H., & Furnham, A. (1992). Graphology and human judgment. In B. Beyerstein & D. Beyerstein (Eds.), *The write stuff: Evaluations of graphology.* Buffalo, NY: Prometheus Books. (p. 418)

DeAngelis, T. (1997, January). Chromosomes contain clues on schizophrenia. *APA Monitor*, p. 26. (p. 454)

Deary, I. J., & Matthews, G. (1993). Personality traits are alive and well. *The Psychologist: Bulletin of the British Psychological Society, 6*, 299–311. (p. 405)

de Boysson-Bardies, B., Halle, P., Sagart, L., & Durand, C. (1989). A cross linguistic investigation of vowel formats in babbling. *Journal of Child Language, 16*, 1–17. (p. 278)

Deci, E. L., & Ryan, R. M. (1985). *Intrinsic motivation and self-determination in human behavior.* New York: Plenum Press. (p. 340)

Deci, E. L., & Ryan, R. M. (1987). The support of autonomy and the control of behavior. *Journal of Personality and Social Psychology, 53*, 1024–1037. (p. 341)

Deci, E. L., & Ryan, R. M. (1992). The initiation and regulation of intrinsically motivated learning and achievement. In A. K. Boggiano & T. S. Pittman (Eds.), *Achievement and motivation: A social-developmental perspective.* New York: Cambridge University Press. (p. 340)

de Cuevas, J. (1990, September-October). "No, she holded them loosely." *Harvard Magazine*, pp. 60–67. (p. 280)

de Jong-Gierveld, J. (1987). Developing and testing a model of loneliness. *Journal of Personality and Social Psychology, 53*, 119–128. (p. 448)

Delgado, J. M. R. (1969). *Physical control of the mind: Toward a psychocivilized society.* New York: Harper & Row. (p. 57)

DeLoache, J. S. (1987). Rapid change in the symbolic functioning of very young children. *Science, 238*, 1556–1557. (p. 87)

DeLoache, J. S. (1995). Early understanding and use of symbols: The model model. *Current Directions in Psychological Science, 4*, 109–113. (p. 88)

Dement, W. (1990). In the PBS film, *Sleep alert.* Quoted by *Behavior Today*, March 12, p. 8. (p. 177)

Dement, W. (1997, September). What all undergraduates should know about how their sleeping lives affect their waking lives. http://www-leland.stanford.edu/~dement/sleepless.html (p. 177)

Dement, W. C. (1978). *Some must watch while some must sleep.* New York: Norton. (pp. 174, 178, 179)

Dement, W. C., & Wolpert, E. A. (1958). The relation of eye movements, body mobility, and external stimuli to dream content. *Journal of Experimental Psychology*, *55*, 543–553. (p. 181)

Dempster, F. N. (1988). The spacing effect: A case study in the failure to apply the results of psychological research. *American Psychologist*, *43*, 627–634. (p. 235)

Denes-Raj, V., Epstein, S., & Cole, J. (1995). The generality of the ratio-bias phenomenon. *Personality and Social Psychology Bulletin*, *21*, 1083–1092. (p. 275)

Dennett, D. (1996, September 9). Quoted by Ian Parker, Richard Dawkins' evolution. *The New Yorker*, pp. 41–45. (p. 2)

Denton, K., & Krebs, D. (1990). From the scene to the crime: The effect of alcohol and social context on moral judgment. *Journal of Personality and Social Psychology*, *59*, 242–248. (p. 193)

D'Eon, J. L. (1989). Hypnosis in the control of labor pain. In N. P. Spanos & J. F. Chaves (Eds.), *Hypnosis: The cognitive-behavioral perspective.* Buffalo, NY: Prometheus Books. (p. 188)

Dermer, M., Cohen, S. J., Jacobsen, E., & Anderson, E. A. (1979). Evaluative judgments of aspects of life as a function of vicarious exposure to hedonic extremes. *Journal of Personality and Social Psychology*, *37*, 247–260. (p. 362)

Dermer, M., & Pyszczynski, T. A. (1978). Effects of erotica upon men's loving and liking responses for women they love. *Journal of Personality and Social Psychology*, *36*, 1302–1309. (p. 526)

Deutsch, J. A. (1972, July). Brain reward: ESP and ecstasy. *Psychology Today*, pp. 46–48. (p. 54)

Deutsch, M. (1991). Egalitarianism in the laboratory and at work. In R. Vermunt & H. Steensma (Eds.), *Social justice in human relations.* New York: Plenum. (p. 224)

DeValois, R. L., & DeValois, K. K. (1975). Neural coding of color. In E. C. Carterette & M. P. Friedman (Eds.), *Handbook of perception: Vol. V. Seeing.* New York: Academic Press. (p. 136).

Devine, P. G. (1995). Prejudice and outgroup perception. In A. Tesser (ed.), *Advanced social psychology*. New York: McGraw-Hill. (p. 523)

de Waal, F. B. M. (1995, March). Bonobo sex and society. *Scientific American*, pp. 82–88. (p. 69)

Dey, E. L., Astin, A. W., & Korn, W. S. (1991). *The American freshman: Twenty-five year trends.* Los Angeles: Higher Education Research Institute, UCLA. (pp. 360, *508)*

Dhawan, N., Roseman, I. J., Naidu, R. K., Thapa, K., & Rettek, S. I. (1995). Self-concepts across two cultures: India and the United States. *Journal of Cross-Cultural Psychology*, *26*, 606–621. (p. 412)

Diaconis, P., & Mosteller, F. (1989). Methods for studying coincidences. *Journal of the American Statistical Association*, *84*, 853–861. (p. 20)

Diamond, J. (1986). Variation in human testis size. *Nature*, *320*, 488–489. (p. 70)

Diamond, J. (1989, May). The great leap forward. *Discover*, pp. 50–60. (p. 277)

Diener, E. (1993). Most Americans are happy. Unpublished manuscript, University of Illinois. (p. 411)

Diener, E., Diener, M., & Diener, C. (1995). Factors predicting the subjective well-being of nations. *Journal of Personality and Social Psychology*, *69*, 851–864. (pp. 412, 524)

DiLalla, D. L., Carey, G., Gottesman, I. I., & Bouchard, T. J., Jr. (1996). Heritability of MMPI personality indicators of psychopathology in twins reared apart. *Journal of Abnormal Psychology*, *105*, 491–499. (pp. 72, 443)

DiLalla, L. F., & Gottesman, I. I. (1991). Biological and genetic contributors to violence—Widom's untold tale. *Psychological Bulletin*, *109*, 125–129. (p. 455)

Dill, J. C., & Anderson, C. A. (1998). Loneliness, shyness, and depression: The etiology and interrelationships of everyday problems in living. In T. Joiner & J. C. Coyne (eds.), *Recent advances in interpersonal approaches to depression.* Washington, D.C.: American Psychological Association. (p. 448)

Dindia, K., & Allen, M. (1992). Sex differences in self-disclosure: A meta-analysis. *Psychological Bulletin*, *112*, 106–124. (p. 105)

Dinges, N. G., & Hull, P. (1992). Personality, culture, and international studies. In D. Lieberman (Ed.), *Revealing the world: An interdisciplinary reader for international studies.* Dubuque, IA: Kendall-Hunt. (p. 286)

Dion, K. K., & Dion, K. L. (1993). Individualistic and collectivistic perspectives on gender and the cultural context of love and intimacy. *Journal of Social Issues*, *49*, 53–69. (p. 413)

Dixon, B. (1986, April). Dangerous thoughts: How we think and feel can make us sick. *Science*, *86*, pp. 63–66. (p. 374)

Dobson, K. S. (1989). A meta-analysis of the efficacy of cognitive therapy for depression. *Journal of Consulting and Clinical Psychology*, *57*, 414–419. (p. 479)

Dodd, M. (1996, September 19). $500,000 ball raises skepticism. *USA Today*, p. 9C. (p. 161)

Dohrenwend, B. P., Levav, I., Shrout, P. E., Schwartz, S., Naveh, G., Link, B. G., Skodol, A. E., & Stueve, A. (1992). Socioeconomic status and psychiatric disorders: The causation-selection issue. *Science*, *255*, 946–952. (p. 457)

Dohrenwend, B., Pearlin, L., Clayton, P., Hamburg, B., Dohrenwend, B. P., Riley, M., & Rose, R. (1982). Report on stress and life events. In G. R. Elliott & C. Eisdorfer (Eds.), *Stress and human health: Analysis and implications of research* (A study by the Institute of Medicine/National Academy of Sciences). New York: Springer. (p. 370)

Dole, R. (1996, April 20). Quoted by M. Duffy, Look who's talking. *Time*, p. 48. (p. 493)

Dolezal, H. (1982). *Living in a world transformed.* New York: Academic Press. (p. 156)

Domhoff, G. W. (1996). *Finding meaning in dreams: A quantitative approach.* New York: Plenum. (p. 181)

Domjan, M. (1992). Adult learning and mate choice: Possibilities and experimental evidence. *American Zoologist*, *32*, 48–61. (p. 209)

Domjan, M. (1994). Formulation of a behavior system for sexual conditioning. *Psychonomic Bulletin & Review*, *1*, 421–428. (p. 209)

Donnerstein, E. (1998). Why do we have those new ratings on television. Invited address to the National Institute on the Teaching of Psychology. (p. 517)

Donnerstein, E., Linz, D., & Penrod, S. (1987). *The question of pornography.* New York: Free Press. (p. 518)

Dorner, G. (1976). *Hormones and brain differentiation.* Amsterdam: Elsevier Scientific. (p. 335)

Dorner, G. (1988). Neuroendocrine response to estrogen and brain differentiation in heterosexuals, homosexuals, and transsexuals. *Archives of Sexual Behavior, 17,* 57–75. (p. 335)

Doty, R. L., Shaman, P., Applebaum, S. L., Giberson, R., Siksorski, L., & Rosenberg, L. (1984). Smell identification ability: Changes with age. *Science, 226,* 1441–1443. (p. 111)

Draguns, J. G. (1990a). Normal and abnormal behavior in cross-cultural perspective: Specifying the nature of their relationship. *Nebraska Symposium on Motivation 1989, 37,* 235–277. (pp. 426, 446)

Draguns, J. G. (1990b). Applications of cross-cultural psychology in the field of mental health. In R. W. Brislin (Ed.), *Applied cross-cultural psychology.* Newbury Park, CA: Sage. (pp. 426, 428)

Druckman, D., & Bjork, R. A. (1991). *In the mind's eye: Enhancing human performance.* National Academy Press: Washington, DC. (p. 401)

Druckman, D., & Bjork, R. A. (eds.) (1994). *Learning, remembering, believing: Enhancing human performance.* Washington, DC: National Academy Press. (pp. 184, 185, 188)

Druckman, D., & Swets, J. A. (Eds.). (1988). *Enhancing human performance: Issues, theories, and techniques.* Washington, DC: National Academy Press. (p. 162)

Duclos, S. E., Laird, J. D., Sexter, M., Stern, L., & Van Lighten, O. (1989). Emotion-specific effects of facial expressions and postures on emotional experience. *Journal of Personality and Social Psychology, 57,* 100–108. (p. 355)

Duggan, J. P., & Booth, D. A. (1986). Obesity, overeating, and rapid gastric emptying in rats with ventromedial hypothalamic lesions. *Science, 231,* 609–611. (p. 317)

Duncan, B. L. (1976). Differential social perception and attribution of intergroup violence: Testing the lower limits of stereotyping of blacks. *Journal of Personality and Social Psychology, 34,* 590–598. (p. 510)

Duncan, G. J., Hill, M. S., & Hoffman, S. D. (1988). Welfare dependence within and across generations. *Science, 239,* 467–471. (p. 273)

Duncker, K. (1945). On problem solving. *Psychological Monographs, 58* (Whole no. 270). (p. 271)

Dunn, J., & Plomin, R. (1990). *Separate lives: Why siblings are so different.* New York: Basic Books. (p. 72)

Dutton, D. G., & Aron, A. (1989). Romantic attraction and generalized liking for others who are sources of conflict-based arousal. *Canadian Journal of Behavioural Sciences, 21,* 246–257. (p. 527)

Dutton, D. G., & Aron, A. P. (1974). Some evidence for heightened sexual attraction under conditions of high anxiety. *Journal of Personality and Social Psychology, 30,* 510–517. (p. 527)

Dweck, C. S., & Elliott, E. S. (1983). Achievement motivation. In P. Mussen & E. M. Hetherington (Eds.), *Handbook of child psychology* (Vol. IV). New York: Wiley. (p. 340)

Eagles, J. M. (1991). Is schizophrenia disappearing? *British Journal of Psychiatry, 158,* 834–835. (p. 453)

Eagly, A. H., Ashmore, R. D., Makhijani, M. G., & Kennedy, L. C. (1991). What is beautiful is good, but . . .: A meta-analytic review of research on the physical attractiveness stereotype. *Psychological Bulletin, 110,* 109–128. (p. 524)

Eagly, A. H., & Crowley, M. (1986). Gender and helping behavior: A meta-analytic review of the social psychological literature. *Psychological Bulletin, 100,* 283–308. (p. 529)

Eagly, A. H., & Johnson, B. T. (1990). Gender and leadership style: A meta-analysis. *Psychological Bulletin, 108,* 233–256. (p. 342)

Eagly, A. H., & Karau, S. J. (1991). Gender and the emergence of leaders: A meta-analysis. *Journal of Personality and Social Psychology, 60,* 685–710. (p. 342)

Ebbesen, E. B., Duncan, B., & Konecni, V. J. (1975). Effects of content of verbal aggression on future verbal aggression: A field experiment. *Journal of Experimental Social Psychology, 11,* 192–204. (p. 358)

Ebbinghaus, H. (1885). *Über das Gedachtnis.* Leipzig: Duncker & Humblot. Cited in R. Klatzky (1980), *Human memory: Structures and processes.* San Francisco: Freeman. (p. 243)

Eccles, J. S., Jacobs, J. E., & Harold, R. D. (1990). Gender role stereotypes, expectancy effects, and parents' socialization of gender differences. *Journal of Social Issues, 46,* 183–201. (p. 305)

Eckensberger, L. H. (1994). Moral development and its measurement across cultures. In W. J. Lonner & R. Malpass (Eds.), *Psychology and culture.* Boston: Allyn and Bacon. (p. 103)

Eckert, E. D., Heston, L. L., & Bouchard, T. J., Jr. (1981). MZ twins reared apart: Preliminary findings of psychiatric disturbances and traits. In L. Gedda, P. Paris, & W. D. Nance (Eds.), *Twin research: Vol. 3. Pt. B. Intelligence, personality, and development.* New York: Alan Liss. (p. 436)

Edison, T. A. (1948). *The diary and sundry observations of Thomas Alva Edison,* edited by D. D. Runes. New York: Philosophical Library. Cited by S. Coren (1996). *Sleep Thieves.* New York: Free Press. (p. 176)

Edwards, C. P. (1981). The comparative study of the development of moral judgment and reasoning. In R. H. Munroe, R. L. Munroe, & B. B. Whiting (Eds.), *Handbook of cross-cultural human development.* New York: Garland Press. (p. 103)

Edwards, C. P. (1982). Moral development in comparative cultural perspective. In D. A. Wagner & H. W. Stevenson (Eds.), *Cultural perspectives on child development.* San Francisco: Freeman. (p. 103)

Ehrhardt, A. A. (1987). A transactional perspective on the development of gender differences. In J. M. Reinisch, L. A. Rosenblum, & S. A. Sanders (Eds.), *Masculinity/femininity: Basic perspectives.* New York: Oxford University Press. (p. 80)

Ehrlichman, H., & Halpern, J. N. (1988). Affect and memory: Effects of pleasant and unpleasant odors on retrieval of happy and unhappy memories. *Journal of Personality and Social Psychology, 55,* 769–779. (p. 145)

Eibl-Eibesfeldt, I. (1971). *Love and hate: The natural history of behavior patterns.* New York: Holt, Rinehart & Winston. (p. 354)

Eich, E. (1990). Learning during sleep. In R. B. Bootzin, J. F. Kihlstrom, & D. L. Schacter (Eds.), *Sleep and cognition.* Washington, DC: American Psychological Association. (p. 181)

Eich, E. (1995). Searching for mood dependent memory. *Psychological Science, 6,* 67–75. (p. 251)

Eich, J. E. (1980). The cue-dependent nature of state-dependent retrieval. *Memory and Cognition, 8,* 157–173. (p. 194)

Eisenberg, N., & Lennon, R. (1983). Sex differences in empathy and related capacities. *Psychological Bulletin, 94,* 100–131. (p. 105)

Ekman, P. (1994). Strong evidence for universals in facial expressions: A reply to Russell's mistaken critique. *Psychological Bulletin, 115,* 268–287. (pp. 353, 354)

Ekman, P., Davidson, R. J., & Friesen, W. V. (1990). The Duchenne smile: Emotional expression and brain physiology II. *Journal of Personality and Social Psychology*, *58*, 342–353. (p. 355)

Ekman, P., & Friesen, W. V. (1975). *Unmasking the face.* Englewood Cliffs, NJ: Prentice-Hall. (pp. 353, 354)

Ekman, P., Friesen, W. V., O'Sullivan, M., Chan, A., Diacoyanni-Tarlatzis, I., Heider, K., Krause, R., LeCompte, W. A., Pitcairn, T., Ricci-Bitti, P. E., Scherer, K., Tomita, M., & Tzavaras, A. (1987). Universals and cultural differences in the judgments of facial expressions of emotion. *Journal of Personality and Social Psychology*, *53*, 712–717. (pp. 353, 354)

Ekman, P., Levenson, R. W., & Friesen, W. V. (1983). Autonomic nervous system activity distinguishes among emotions. *Science*, *221*, 1208–1210. (p. 355)

Elkin, I., Shea, T., Watkins, J. T., Imber, S. D., Sotsky, S. M., Collins, J. F., Glass, D. R., Pilkonis, P. A., Leber, W. R., Docherty, J. P., Fiester, S. J., & Parloff, M. B. (1989). National Institute of Mental Health treatment of depression collaborative research program. *Archives of General Psychiatry*, *46*, 971–983. (p. 479)

Elkind, D. (1970). The origins of religion in the child. *Review of Religious Research*, *12*, 35–42. (p. 101)

Elkind, D. (1978). *The child's reality: Three developmental themes.* Hillsdale, NJ: Erlbaum. (p. 101)

Elkis, H., Friedman, L., Wise, A., & Meltzer, H. Y. (1995). Meta-analyses of studies of ventricular enlargement and cortical sulcal prominence in mood disorders: Comparisons with controls or patients with schizophrenia. *Archives of General Psychiatry*, *52*, 735–746. (p. 452)

Elliot, A. (1996, January 18). Personal communication for Nielsen Media Research Director of Communications via e-mail (Anne_Elliot@tvratings.com). (p. 517)

Ellis, A. (1962). *Reason and emotion in psychotherapy.* Secaucus, NJ: Citadel Press. (p. 471)

Ellis, A. (1980). Psychotherapy and atheistic values: A response to A. E. Bergin's "Psychotherapy and religious values." *Journal of Consulting and Clinical Psychology*, *48* 635–639. (pp. 471, 481)

Ellis, A. (1987). The impossibility of achieving consistently good mental health. *American Psychologist*, *42*, 364–375. (p. 471)

Ellis, A. (1989). Rational-emotive therapy. In R. J. Corsine & D. Wedding (Eds.), *Current psychotherapies* (4th ed.). Itasca, IL: Peacock. (p. 471)

Ellis, A. (1993). Changing rational-emotive therapy (RET) to rational emotive behavior therapy (REBT). *The Behavior Therapist*, *16*, 257–258. (p. 471)

Ellis, A., & Becker, I. M. (1982). *A guide to personal happiness.* North Hollywood, CA: Wilshire Book Co. (p. 215)

Ellis, H. C., & Ashbrook, P. W. (1989). The "state" of mood and memory research: A selective review. *Journal of Social Behavior and Personality*, *4*, 1–21. (p. 251)

Ellis, L., & Ames, M. A. (1987). Neurohormonal functioning and sexual orientation: A theory of homosexuality-heterosexuality. *Psychological Bulletin*, *101*, 233–258. (p. 335)

Emde, R. N., Plomin, R., Robinson, J., Corley, R., DeFries, J., Fulker, D. W., Reznick, J. S., Campos, J., Kagan, J., & Zahn-Waxler, C. (1992). Temperament, emotion, and cognition at fourteen months: The MacArthur Longitudinal Twin Study. *Child Development*, *63*, 1437–1455. (p. 93)

Emery, C. E., Jr. (1995, September/October). Telephone psychics: Friends or phonies? *Skeptical Inquirer*, pp. 14–17. (p. 160)

Emmons, S., Geisler, C., Kaplan, K. J., & Harrow, M. (1997). *Living with schizophrenia.* Muncie, IN: Taylor and Francis (Accelerated Development). (pp. 425, *452)*

Empson, J. A. C., & Clarke, P. R. F. (1970). Rapid eye movements and remembering. *Nature*, *227*, 287–288. (p. 182)

Endler, N. S. (1982). *Holiday of darkness: A psychologist's personal journey out of his depression.* New York: Wiley. (p. 446, 486)

Engen, T. (1987). Remembering odors and their names. *American Scientist*, *75*, 497–503. (p. 145)

Epstein, S. (1983a). Aggregation and beyond: Some basic issues on the prediction of behavior. *Journal of Personality*, *51*, 360–392. (p. 405)

Epstein, S. (1983b). The stability of behavior across time and situations. In R. Zucker, J. Aronoff, & A. I. Rabin (Eds.), *Personality and the prediction of behavior.* San Diego: Academic Press. (p. 405)

Erber, R., & Tesser, A. (1992). Task effort and the regulation of mood: The absorption hypothesis. *Journal of Experimental Social Psychology*, *28*, 339–359. (p. 470)

Erdelyi, M. H. (1985). *Psychoanalysis: Freud's cognitive psychology.* New York: Freeman. (p. 398)

Erdelyi, M. H. (1988). Repression, reconstruction, and defense: History and integration of the psychoanalytic and experimental frameworks. In J. Singer (Ed.), *Repression: Defense mechanism and cognitive style.* Chicago: University of Chicago Press. (p. 398)

Erel, O., & Burman, B. (1995). Interrelatedness of marital relations and parent-child relations: A meta-analytic review. *Psychological Bulletin*, *118*, 108–132. (p. 118)

Eron, L. D. (1987). The development of aggressive behavior from the perspective of a developing behaviorism. *American Psychologist*, *42*, 435–442. (p. 517)

Eronen, M., Tihonen, J., & Hakola, P. (1996). Schizophrenia and homicidal behavior. *Schizophrenia Bulletin*, *22*, 83–89. (p. 430)

Esser, J. K., & Lindoerfer, J. S. (1989). Groupthink and the space shuttle *Challenger* accident: Toward a quantitative case analysis. *Journal of Behavioral Decision Making*, *2*, 167–177. (p. 505)

Etnier, J. L., Salazar, W., Landers, D. M., Petruzzello, S. J., Han, M., & Nowell, P. (1997). The influence of physical fitness and exercise upon cognitive functioning: A meta-analysis. *Journal of Sport & Exercise Psychology*, *19*, 249–277. (p. 379)

ETS (1992). Three reports shed new light on gender differences in testing. *ETS Developments*, *37*(3), 4–7. (p. 304)

Evans, C. R., & Dion, K. L. (1991). Group cohesion and performance: A meta-analysis. *Small Group Research*, *22*, 175–186. (p. 342)

Evans, G. W., Palsane, M. N., & Carrere, S. (1987). Type A behavior and occupational stress: A cross-cultural study of blue-collar workers. *Journal of Personality and Social Psychology*, *52*, 1002–1007. (p. 372)

Evans, G. W., Palsane, M. N., Lepore, S. J., & Martin, J. (1989). Residential density and psychological health: The mediating effects of social support. *Journal of Personality and Social Psychology*, *57*, 994–999. (p. 382)

Everson, S. A., & others (1996). Hopelessness and risk of mortality and incidence of myocardial infarction and cancer. *Psychosomatic Medicine*, *58*, 113–121. (p. 371)

Exner, J. E. (1993). *The Rorschach: A comprehensive system, Vol. 1. Basic foundations* (3rd ed.). New York: Wiley. (p. 396)

Eysenck, H. J. (1952). The effects of psychotherapy: An evaluation. *Journal of Consulting Psychology, 16*, 319–324. (p. 478)

Eysenck, H. J. (1990, April 30). An improvement on personality inventory. *Current Contents: Social and Behavioral Sciences, 22*(18), 20. (p. 401)

Eysenck, H. J. (1992). Four ways five factors are *not* basic. *Personality and Individual Differences, 13*, 667–673. (p. 401)

Eysenck, H. J., & Grossarth-Maticek, R. (1991). Creative novation behaviour therapy as a prophylactic treatment for cancer and coronary heart disease: Part II—Effects of treatment. *Behaviour Research and Therapy, 29*, 17–31. (p. 381)

Eysenck, M. W., MacLeod, C., & Mathews, A. (1987). Cognitive functioning and anxiety. *Psychological Research, 49*, 189–195. (p. 416)

Eysenck, S. B. G., & Eysenck, H. J. (1963). The validity of questionnaire and rating assessments of extraversion and neuroticism, and their factorial stability. *British Journal of Psychology, 54*, 51–62. (p. 402)

Faber, N. (1987, July). Personal glimpse. *Reader's Digest*, p. 34. (p. 296)

Fackelmann, K. (1997, March 22). Marijuana on trial. *Science News*, pp. 178–179, 183. (p. 198)

Fagan, J. F., III (1992). Intelligence: A theoretical viewpoint. *Current Directions in Psychological Science, 1*, 82–86. (p. 304)

Fantz, R. L. (1961, May). The origin of form perception. *Scientific American*, pp. 66–72. (p. 82)

Farina, A. (1982). The stigma of mental disorders. In A. G. Miller (Ed.), *In the eye of the beholder.* New York: Praeger. (pp. 427, 429)

Farina, A., & Fisher, J. D. (1982). Beliefs about mental disorders: Findings and implications. In G. Weary & H. L. Mirels (Eds.), *Integrations of clinical and social psychology.* New York: Oxford University Press. (p. 475)

Farrington, D. P. (1991). Antisocial personality from childhood to adulthood. *The Psychologist: Bulletin of the British Psychological Society, 4*, 389–394. (p. 455)

Fava, M., Copeland, P. M., Schweiger, U., & Herzog, D. B. (1989). Neurochemical abnormalities of anorexia nervosa and bulimia nervosa. *American Journal of Psychiatry, 146*, 963–971. (p. 319)

Fazio, R. H. (1990). Multiple processes by which attitudes guide behavior: The MODE model as an integrative framework. In M. P. Zanna (Ed.), *Advances in experimental social psychology* (Vol. 23). San Diego, CA: Academic Press. (p. 494)

Feder, H. H. (1984). Hormones and sexual behavior. *Annual Review of Psychology, 35*, 165–200. (p. 328)

Feeney, D. M. (1987). Human rights and animal welfare. *American Psychologist, 42*, 593–599. (p. 32)

Feeney, J. A., & Noller, P. (1990). Attachment style as a predictor of adult romantic relationships. *Journal of Personality and Social Psychology, 58*, 281–291. (p. 94)

Fehr, B., & Russell, J. A. (1991). The concept of love viewed from a prototype perspective. *Journal of Personality and Social Psychology, 60*, 425–438. (p. 269)

Feingold, A. (1990). Gender differences in effects of physical attractiveness on romantic attraction: A comparison across five research paradigms. *Journal of Personality and Social Psychology, 59*, 981–993. (p. 524)

Feingold, A. (1992). Good-looking people are not what we think. *Psychological Bulletin, 111*, 304–341. (p. 524)

Fenton, W. S., & McGlashan, T. H. (1991). Natural history of schizophrenia subtypes: II. Positive and negative symptoms and long-term course. *Archives of General Psychiatry, 48*, 978–986. (p. 451)

Fenton, W. S., & McGlashan, T. H. (1994). Antecedents, symptom progression, and long-term outcome of the deficit syndrome in schizophrenia. *American Journal of Psychiatry, 151*, 351–356. (p. 451)

Ferguson, E. D. (1989). Adler's motivational theory: An historical perspective on belonging and the fundamental human striving. *Individual Psychology, 45*, 354–361. (p. 337)

Fernandez, E., & Turk, D. C. (1989). The utility of cognitive coping strategies for altering pain perception: A meta-analysis. *Pain, 38*, 123–135. (p. 143)

Fernandez-Dols, J-M., & Ruiz-Belda, M-A. (1995). Are smiles a sign of happiness? Gold medal winners at the Olympic Games. *Journal of Personality and Social Psychology, 69*, 1113–1119. (p. 354)

Fichter, M. M., & Noegel, R. (1990). Concordance for bulimia nervosa in twins. *International Journal of Eating Disorders, 9*, 255–263. (p. 319)

Fichter, M. M., & others (1996). Mental illness in a representative sample of homeless men in Munich, Germany. *European Archives of Psychiatry and Clinical Neuroscience, 246*, 185–196. (p. 483)

Fiedler, F. E. (1981). Leadership effectiveness. *American Behavioral Scientist, 24*, 619–632. (p. 342)

Fiedler, F. E. (1987, September). When to lead, when to stand back. *Psychology Today*, pp. 26–27. (p. 342)

Field, T. M., Schanberg, S. M., Scafidi, F., Bauer, C. R., Vega-Lahr, N., Garcia, R., Nystrom, J., & Kuhn, C. M. (1986). Tactile/kinesthetic stimulation effects on preterm neonates. *Pediatrics, 77*, 654–658. (p. 84)

Fincham, F. D., & Bradbury, T. N. (1993). Marital satisfaction, depression, and attributions: A longitudinal analysis. *Journal of Personality and Social Psychology, 64*, 442–452. (p. 492)

Findley, M. J., & Cooper, H. M. (1983). Locus of control and academic achievement: A literature review. *Journal of Personality and Social Psychology, 44*, 419–427. (p. 417)

Fink, G. R., Markowitsch, H. J., Reinkemeier, M., Bruckbauer, T., Kessler, J., & Heiss, W-D. (1996). Cerebral representation of one's own past: Neural networks involved in autobiographical memory. *Journal of Neuroscience, 16*, 4275–4282. (p. 248)

Finkel, L. H., & Sajda, P. (1994). Constructing visual perception. *American Scientist, 82*, 224–237. (p. 160)

Finucci, J. M., & Childs, B. (1981). Are there really more dyslexic boys than girls? In A. Ansara, N. Geschwind, A. Galaburda, M. Albert, & N. Gartrell (Eds.), *Sex differences in dyslexia.* Towson, MD: The Orton Dyslexia Society. (p. 304)

Fischer, P. J., & Breakey, W. R. (1991). The epidemiology of alcohol, drug, and mental disorders among homeless persons. *American Psychologist, 46*, 1115–1128. (p. 483)

Fischhoff, B. (1982). Debiasing. In D. Kahneman, P. Slovic, & A. Tversky (Eds.), *Judgment under uncertainty: Heuristics and biases.* New York: Cambridge University Press. (p. 274)

Fischhoff, B., Slovic, P., & Lichtenstein, S. (1977). Knowing with certainty: The appropriateness of extreme confidence. *Journal of Experimental Psychology: Human Perception and Performance, 3*, 552–564. (p. 274)

Fisher, H. E. (1993, March/April). After all, maybe it's biology. *Psychology Today*, pp. 40–45. (p. 116)

Fisher, H. T. (1984). Little Albert and Little Peter. *Bulletin of the British Psychological Society*, *37*, 269. (p. 467)

Fleming, I., Baum, A., & Weiss, L. (1987). Social density and perceived control as mediator of crowding stress in high-density residential neighborhoods. *Journal of Personality and Social Psychology*, *52*, 899–906. (p. 372)

Fleming, J. H., & Scott, B. A. (1991). The costs of confession: The Persian Gulf War POW tapes in historical and theoretical perspective. *Contemporary Social Psychology*, *15*, 127–138. (p. 353)

Fletcher, G. J. O., Fitness, J., & Blampied, N. M. (1990). The link between attributions and happiness in close relationships: The roles of depression and explanatory style. *Journal of Social and Clinical Psychology*, *9*, 243–255. (p. 492)

Flynn, J. R. (1987). Massive IQ gains in 14 nations: What IQ tests really measure. *Psychological Bulletin*, *101*, 171–191. (p. 304)

FMS (1996). *Frequently asked questions about the False Memory Syndrome Foundation* (available at http://www.csicop.org/~fitz/fmsf/faq.html) (accessed September 13, 1996). (p. 260)

Foa, E. B., & Kozak, M. J. (1986). Emotional processing of fear: Exposure to corrective information. *Psychological Bulletin*, *99*, 20–35. (p. 468)

Folkman, S., Chesney, M., Collette, L., Boccellari, A., & Cooke, M. (1996). Postbereavement depressive mood and its prebereavement predictors in HIV+ and HIV- gay men. *Journal of Personality and Social Psychology*, *70*, 336–348. (p. 119)

Foltved, P. (1996). The psychological profession in Denmark. In A. Schorr & S. Saari (eds.), *Psychology in Europe: Facts, figures, realities*. Gottingen: Hogrefe & Huber. (p. 7)

Fong, G. T., Frantz, D. H., & Nisbett, R. E. (1986). The effects of statistical training on thinking about everyday problems. *Cognitive Psychology*, *18*, 253–292. (p. 28)

Fontana, A., Rosenheck, R., & Brett, E. (1992). War zone traumas and posttraumatic stress disorder symptomatology. *Journal of Nervous and Mental Disease*, *180*, 748–755. (p. 435)

Foree, D. D., & LoLordo, V. M. (1973). Attention in the pigeon: Differential effects of food-getting versus shock-avoidance procedures. Journal of Comparative and Physiological Psychology, 85, 551–558. (p. 222)

Forer, B. R. (1949). The fallacy of personal validation: A classroom demonstration of gullibility. *Journal of Abnormal and Social Psychology*, *44*, 118–123. (p. 418)

Foreyt, J. P., Walker, S., Poston, C., II, & Goodrick, G. K. (1996). Future directions in obesity and eating disorders. *Addictive Behaviors*, *21*, 767–778. (p. 324)

Forgas, J. P., Bower, G. H., & Krantz, S. E. (1984). The influence of mood on perceptions of social interactions. *Journal of Experimental Social Psychology*, *20*, 497–513. (pp. 252, *447)*

Forgatch, M. S. (1995, March). Reported by W. W. Gibbs, Seeking the criminal element. *Scientific American*, pp. 100–107. (p. 18)

Fortune (1995, March 6). Infomercials 1994: The greatest hits. Page 20. (p. 160)

Foss, D. J., & Hakes, D. T. (1978). *Psycholinguistics: An introduction to the psychology of language*. Englewood Cliffs, NJ: Prentice-Hall. (p. 397)

Fouts, R. (1997). *Next of kin: What chimpanzees have taught me about who we are*. New York: Morrow. (p. 285)

Fouts, R. S. (1992). Transmission of a human gestural language in a chimpanzee mother-infant relationship. *Friends of Washoe*, *12/13*, pp. 2–8. (p. 285)

Fouts, R. S., & Bodamer, M. (1987). Preliminary report to the National Geographic Society on: "Chimpanzee intrapersonal signing." *Friends of Washoe*, 7(1), 4–12. (p. 285)

Fowler, M. J., Sullivan, M. J., & Ekstrand, B. R. (1973). Sleep and memory. *Science*, *179*, 302–304. (p. 254)

Fowler, R. C., Rich, C. L., & Young, D. (1986). San Diego suicide study: II. Substance abuse in young cases. *Archives of General Psychiatry*, *43*, 962–965. (p. 444)

Fowler, R. D. (1986, May). Howard Hughes: A psychological autopsy. *Psychology Today*, pp. 22–33. (p. 433)

Fowles, D. C. (1992). Schizophrenia: Diathesis-stress revisited. *Annual Review of Psychology*, *43*, 303–336. (p. 451)

Fox, J. L. (1984). The brain's dynamic way of keeping in touch. *Science*, *225*, 820–821. (p. 57)

Fozard, J. L., & Popkin, S. J. (1978). Optimizing adult development: Ends and means of an applied psychology of aging. *American Psychologist*, *33*, 975–989. (p. 111)

Frank, J. D. (1982). Therapeutic components shared by all psychotherapies. In J. H. Harvey & M. M. Parks (Eds.), *The Master Lecture Series: Vol. 1. Psychotherapy research and behavior change*. Washington, DC: American Psychological Association. (pp. 461, 480, 481)

Frank, M. G., & Gilovich, T. (1988). The dark side of self and social perception: Black uniforms and aggression in professional sports. *Journal of Personality and Social Psychology*, *54*, 74–85. (pp. 23, 24)

Frank, S. J. (1988). Young adults' perceptions of their relationships with their parents: Individual differences in connectedness, competence, and emotional autonomy. *Developmental Psychology*, *24*, 729–737. (p. 107)

Frankel, A., & Prentice-Dunn, S. (1990). Loneliness and the processing of self-relevant information. *Journal of Social and Clinical Psychology*, *9*, 303–315. (p. 475)

Frankel, A., Strange, D. R., & Schoonover, R. (1983). CRAP: Consumer rated assessment procedure. In G. H. Scherr & R. Liebmann-Smith (Eds.), *The best of The Journal of Irreproducible Results*. New York: Workman Publishing. (p. 403)

Frankenburg, W., Dodds, J., Archer, P., Shapiro, H., & Bresnick, B. (1992). The Denver II: A major revision and restandardization of the Denver Developmental Screening Test. *Pediatrics*, *89*, 91–97. (p. 84)

Frasure-Smith, N., Lesperance, F., & Talajic, M. (1995). The impact of negative emotions on prognosis following myocardial infarction: Is it more than depression? *Health Psychology*, *14*, 388–398. (p. 373)

Fredrickson, B. L., & Kahneman, D. (1993). Duration neglect in retrospective evaluations of affective episodes. *Journal of Personality and Social Psychology*, *65*, 45–55. (p. 237)

Freedman, J. L. (1978). *Happy people*. San Diego: Harcourt Brace Jovanovich. (p. 119)

Freedman, J. L. (1988). Television violence and aggression: What the evidence shows. In S. Oskamp (Ed.), *Television as a social issue*. Newbury Park, CA: Sage. (p. 517)

Freedman, J. L., & Fraser, S. C. (1966). Compliance without pressure: The foot-in-the-door technique. *Journal of Personality and Social Psychology, 4*, 195–202. (p. 494)

Freedman, J. L., & Perlick, D. (1979). Crowding, contagion, and laughter. *Journal of Experimental Social Psychology*, 15, 295–303. (p. 503)

Freeman, W. J. (1991, February). The physiology of perception. *Scientific American*, pp. 78–85. (p. 135)

Freud, S. (1931; reprinted 1961). Female sexuality. In J. Strachey (Trans.), *The standard edition of the complete psychological works of Sigmund Freud.* London: Hogarth Press. (p. 392)

Freud, S. (1933). *New introductory lectures on psycho-analysis.* New York: Carlton House. (p. 391)

Freud, S. (1935; reprinted 1960). *A general introduction to psychoanalysis.* New York: Washington Square Press. (p. 116)

Freyd, P. (1996, September 13). Personal correspondence via e-mail. (p. 260)

Friedman, M. A., & Brownell, K. D. (1995). Psychological correlates of obesity: Moving to the next research generation. *Psychological Bulletin, 117*, 3–20. (p. 321)

Friedman, M., & Ulmer, D. (1984). *Treating Type A behavior—and your heart.* New York: Knopf. (pp. 372, 381)

Friedrich, O. (1987, December 7). New age harmonies. *Time*, pp. 62–72. (p. 427)

Frieze, I. H., Parsons, J. E., Johnson, P. B., Ruble, D. N., & Zellman, G. L. (1978). *Women and sex roles: A social psychological perspective.* New York: Norton. (p. 397)

Frijda, N. H. (1988). The laws of emotion. *American Psychologist, 43*, 349–358. (p. 361)

Fritsch, G., & Hitzig, E. (1870; reprinted 1960). On the electrical excitability of the cerebrum. In G. Von Bonin (Trans.), *Some papers on the cerebral cortex.* Springfield, IL: Charles C. Thomas. (p. 56)

Fromkin, V., & Rodman, R. (1983). *An introduction to language* (3rd ed.). New York: Holt, Rinehart & Winston. (p. 279)

Fry, A. F., & Hale, S. (1996). Processing speed, working memory, and fluid intelligence: Evidence for a developmental cascade. *Psychological Science*, 7, 237–241. (p. 111)

Fuhriman, A., & Burlingame, G. M. (1994). Group psychotherapy: Research and practice. In A. Fuhriman & G. M. Burlingame (eds.), *Handbook of group psychotherapy.* New York: Wiley. (p. 474)

Fulker, D. W., DeFries, J. C., & Plomin, R. (1988). Genetic influence on general mental ability increases between infancy and middle childhood. *Nature, 336*, 767–769. (p. 300)

Fuller, M. J., & Downs, A. C. (1990). Spermarche is a salient biological marker in men's development. Poster presented at the American Psychological Society convention. (p. 101)

Funder, D. C., & Block, J. (1989). The role of ego-control, ego-resiliency, and IQ in delay of gratification in adolescence. *Journal of Personality and Social Psychology, 57*, 1041–1050. (p. 103)

Furlow, F. B., & Thornhill, R. (1996, January/February). The orgasm wars. *Psychology Today*, pp. 42–46. (p. 328)

Furnham, A. (1982). Explanations for unemployment in Britain. *European Journal of Social Psychology, 12*, 335–352. (p. 551)

Furnham, A. (1993). A comparison between psychology and non-psychology students' misperceptions of the subject. *Journal of Social Behavior and Personality, 8*, 311–322. (p. 185)

Furnham, A., & Baguma, P. (1994). Cross-cultural differences in the evaluation of male and female body shapes. *International Journal of Eating Disorders, 15*, 81–89. (p. 320)

Furnham, A., & Rawles, R. (1995). Sex differences in the estimation of intelligence. *Journal of Social Behavior and Personality, 10*, 741–748. (p. 510)

Furnham, A., & Taylor, L. (1990). Lay theories of homosexuality: Aetiology, behaviours, and 'cures.' *British Journal of Social Psychology, 29*, 135–147. (p. 336)

Furstenberg, F. F., Jr., Moore, K. A., & Peterson, J. L. (1985). Sex education and sexual experience among adolescents. *American Journal of Public Health, 75*, 1331–1332. (p. 338)

Gabbay, F. H. (1992). Behavior-genetic strategies in the study of emotion. *Psychological Science, 3*, 50–55. (p. 93)

Gabrieli, J. D. E., Desmond, J. E., Demb, J. E., Wagner, A. D., Stone, M. V., Vaidya, C. J., & Glover, G. H. (1996). Functional magnetic resonance imaging of semantic memory processes in the frontal lobes. *Psychological Science*, 7, 278–283. (p. 248)

Gaertner, S. L., Mann, J., Murrell, A., & Dovidio, J. F. (1989). Reducing intergroup bias: The benefits of recategorization. *Journal of Personality and Social Psychology, 57*, 239–249. (p. 531)

Galambos, N. L. (1992). Parent-adolescent relations. *Current Directions in Psychological Science, 1*, 146–149. (p. 106)

Galanter, E. (1962). Contemporary psychophysics. In R. Brown, E. Galanter, E. H. Hess, & G. Mandler (Eds.), *New directions in psychology.* New York: Holt, Rinehart & Winston. (p. 127)

Gallup, G. G., Jr., & Suarez, S. D. (1985). Alternatives to the use of animals in psychological research. *American Psychologist, 40*, 1104–1111. (p. 32)

Gallup, G. H. (1972). *The Gallup poll: Public opinion 1935–1971* (Vol. 3). New York: Random House. (p. 521)

Gallup, G. H., Jr. (1994, October). Millions finding care and support in small groups. *Emerging Trends*, pp. 2–5. (p. 474)

Gallup, G. H., Jr. (1994, December). A nation in recovery. *PRRC Emerging Trends*, pp. 1–2. (p. 383)

Gallup, G. H., Jr., & Newport, F. (1991, Winter). Belief in paranormal phenomena among adult Americans. *Skeptical Inquirer*, pp. 137–146. (p. 187)

Gallup Organization. (1993). Other hemsipheres may think our religion is alien and exotic. *PRRC Emerging Trends, 15*, 1–3. (p. 481)

Gallup Organization. (1996, April). Majority disapprove of homosexual marriages. *Emerging Trends* (Princeton Religion Research Center), p. 2. (p. 336)

Gallup Poll Monthly (1992, October). The first presidential debate: Perot makes best impression; Bush falls short. P. 11. (p. 157)

Gallup Poll Monthly (1996, July). Currently use alcohol? P. 27. (p. 199)

Gallup Poll Monthly (1996, March). Would you like to lose weight, put on weight, or stay at your present weight? P. 43. (p. 324)

Gallup Report. (1989, March/April). Commercial aviation. Pp. 32–33. (p. 273)

Garbarino, J., Kostelny, K., & Dubrow, N. (1991). What children can tell us about living in danger. *American Psychologist, 46*, 376–383. (p. 435)

Garcia, J., & Gustavson, A. R. (1997, January). Carl R. Gustavson (1946–1996): Pioneering wildlife psychologist. *APS Observer*, pp. 34–35. (p. 212)

Garcia, J., & Koelling, R. A. (1966). Relation of cue to consequence in avoidance learning. *Psychonomic Science*, *4*, 123–124. (p. 212)

Gardner, H. (1983). *Frames of mind: The theory of multiple intelligences.* New York: Basic Books. (p. 291)

Gardner, H. (1993). *Creating minds.* New York: Basic Books. (p. 291)

Gardner, H. (1995). Perennial antinomies and perpetual redrawings: Is there progress in the study of mind? In R. L. Solso & D. W. Massaro (Eds.), *The science of the mind: 2001 and beyond.* New York: Oxford University Press. (p. 291)

Gardner, R. A., & Gardner, B. I. (1969). Teaching sign language to a chimpanzee. *Science*, *165*, 664–672. (p. 283)

Gardner, R. M., & Tockerman, Y. R. (1994). A computer-TV video methodology for investigating the influence of somatotype on perceived personality traits. *Journal of Social Behavior and Personality*, *9*, 555–563. (p. 320)

Garfield, C. (1986). *Peak performers: The new heroes of American business.* New York: Morrow. (p. 288)

Garner, D. M., & Wooley, S. C. (1991). Confronting the failure of behavioral and dietary treatments for obesity. *Clinical Psychology Review*, *11*, 729–780. (p. 323)

Garnets, L., & Kimmel, D. (1990). Lesbian and gay dimensions in the psychological study of human diversity. Master lecture, American Psychological Association convention. (p. 333)

Garry, M., & Loftus, E. F., & Brown, S. W. (1994). Memory: A river runs through it. *Consciousness and Cognition*, *3*, 438–451. (p. 397)

Garry, M., Manning, C. G., Loftus, E. F., & Sherman, S. J. (1996). Imagination inflation: Imagining a childhood event inflates confidence that it occurred. *Psychonomic Bulletin & Review*, *3*, 208–214. (p. 256)

Gawin, F. H. (1991). Cocaine addiction: Psychology and neurophysiology. *Science*, *251*, 1580–1586. (p. 196)

Gazzaniga, M. S. (1967, August). The split brain in man. *Scientific American*, pp. 24–29. (pp. 62, 63)

Gazzaniga, M. S. (1983). Right hemisphere language following brain bisection: A 20-year perspective. *American Psychologist*, *38*, 525–537. (p. 64)

Gazzaniga, M. S. (1988). *Mind matters: How mind and brain interact to create our conscious lives.* Boston: Houghton Mifflin. (p. 63)

Gazzaniga, M. S. (1988). Organization of the human brain. *Science*, *245*, 947–952. (p. 191)

Gazzaniga, M. S. (1992). *Nature's mind: The biological roots of thinking, emotions, sexuality, language, and intelligence.* New York: Basic Books. (p. 62)

Geary, D. C. (1995). Sexual selection and sex differences in spatial cognition. *Learning and Individual Differences*, *7*, 289–301. (p. 305)

Geary, D. C. (1996). Sexual selection and sex differences in mathematical abilities. *Behavioral and Brain Sciences*, *19*, 229–247. (p. 305)

Geary, D. C., Salthouse, T. A., Chen, G-P., & Fan, L. (1996). Are East Asian versus American differences in arithmetical ability a recent phenomenon? *Developmental Psychology*, *32*, 254–262. (p. 304)

Geen, R. G. (1984). Human motivation: New perspectives on old problems. In A. M. Rogers & C. J. Scheirer (Eds.), *The G. Stanley Hall Lecture Series* (Vol. 4). Washington, DC: American Psychological Association. (p. 339)

Geen, R. G., & Quanty, M. B. (1977). The catharsis of aggression: An evaluation of a hypothesis. In L. Berkowitz (Ed.), *Advances in experimental social psychology* (Vol. 10). New York: Academic Press. (p. 358)

Geen, R. G., & Thomas, S. L. (1986). The immediate effects of media violence on behavior. *Journal of Social Issues*, *42*(3), *7–28. (p. 518)*

Geldard, F. A. (1972). *The human senses* (2nd ed.). New York: Wiley. (p. 136)

Gelman, D. (1989, May 15). Voyages to the unknown. *Newsweek*, pp. 66–69. (p. 354)

George (1996, December). What does America believe? P. 117. (p. 187)

Gerald, C., Walker, M. W., Criscione, L., & Gustafson, E. L. (1996). A receptor subtype involved in neuropeptide-Y-induced food intake. *Nature*, *382*, 168–171. (p. 323)

Gerard, R. W. (1953, September). What is memory? *Scientific American*, pp. 118–126. (p. 245)

Gerbner, G. (1985). Dreams that hurt: Mental illness in the mass media. Keynote address to the First Rosalynn Carter Symposium on Mental Health Policy, Emory University School of Medicine, Atlanta. (p. 430)

Gerbner, G. (1990). Stories that hurt: Tobacco, alcohol, and other drugs in the mass media. In H. Resnik (Ed.), *Youth and drugs: Society's mixed messages.* Rockville, MD: Office for Substance Abuse Prevention, U.S. Department of Health and Human Services. (p. 200)

Gerbner, G. (1993, June). Women and minorities on television: A study in casting and fate. A report to the Screen Actors Guild and the American Federation of Radio and Television Artists. (p. 517)

Gerbner, G., Morgan, M., & Signorielli, N. (1993). Television violence profile No. 16: The turning point from research to action. Annenberg School for Communication, University of Pennsylvania. (pp. 517, 518, 520)

Gerhart, K. A., Koziol-McLain, J., Lowenstein, S. R., & Whiteneck, G. G. (1994). Quality of life following spinal cord injury: Knowledge and attitudes of emergency care providers. *Annals of Emergency Medicine*, *23*, 807–812. (p. 360)

Gerrard, M., & Luus, C. A. E. (1995). Judgments of vulnerability to pregnancy: The role of risk factors and individual differences. *Personality and Social Psychology Bulletin*, *21*, 160–171. (p. 108)

Gest, S. D. (1997). Behavioral inhibition: Stability and associations with adaptation from childhood to early adulthood. *Journal of Personality and Social Psychology*, *72*, 467–475. (p. 93)

Gfeller, J. D., Lynn, S. J., & Pribble, W. E. (1987). Enhancing hypnotic susceptibility: Interpersonal and rapport factors. *Journal of Personality and Social Psychology*, *52*, 586–595. (p. 189)

Giambra, L. M. (1974). Daydreaming across the life span: Late adolescent to senior citizen. *Aging and Human Development*, *5*, 115–140. (p. 171)

Gibbons, F. X. (1986). Social comparison and depression: Company's effect on misery. *Journal of Personality and Social Psychology*, *51*, 140–148. (p. 362)

Gibbs, W. W. (1996, June). Mind readings. *Scientific American*, pp. 34–36. (p. 57)

Gibson, E. J., & Walk, R. D. (1960, April). The "visual cliff." *Scientific American*, pp. 64–71. (p. 148)

Gibson, H. B. (1979). The 'Royal Nonesuch' of parapsychology. *Bulletin of the British Psychological Society*, *32*, 65–67. (p. 202)

Gibson, H. B. (1995, April). Recovered memories. *The Psychologist*, pp. 153–154. (p. 185)

Giles, D. E., Dahl, R. E., & Coble, P. A. (1994). Childbearing, developmental, and familial aspects of sleep. In J. M. Oldham & M. B. Riba (Eds.), *Review of Psychiatry*, (Vol. 13). Washington, DC: American Psychiatric Press. (p. 175)

Giles, T. R. (1983). Probable superiority of behavioral interventions—II: Empirical status of the equivalence of therapies hypothesis. *Journal of Behavior Therapy and Experimental Psychiatry*, *14*, 189–196. (p. 479)

Gillham, J. E., Reivich, K. J., Jaycox, L.H., & Seligman, M. E. P. (1995). Prevention of depressive symptoms in schoolchildren: Two-year follow-up. *Psychological Science*, *6*, 343–351. (p. 473)

Gilligan, C. (1982). *In a different voice: Psychological theory and women's development.* Cambridge, MA: Harvard University Press. (p. 105)

Gilligan, C., Lyons, N. P., & Hanmer, T. J. (Eds.). (1990). *Making connections: The relational worlds of adolescent girls at Emma Willard School.* Cambridge, MA: Harvard University Press. (p. 105)

Gilling, D., & Brightwell, R. (1982). *The human brain.* New York: Facts on File. (p. 468)

Gilovich, T. (1991). *How we know what isn't so: The fallibility of human reason in everyday life*. New York: Free Press. (pp. 18, 19)

Gilovich, T. D. (1996). The spotlight effect: Exaggerated impressions of the self as a social stimulus. Unpublished manuscript, Cornell University. (p. 89)

Gilovich, T., & Medvec, V. H. (1995). The experience of regret: What, when, and why. *Psychological Review*, *102*, 379–395. (p. 119)

Gilovich, T., Vallone, R., & Tversky, A. (1985). The hot hand in basketball: On the misperception of random sequences. *Cognitive Psychology*, *17*, 295–314. (p. 22)

Giros, B., Jaber, M., Jones, S. R., Wrightman, R. M., & Caron, M. G. (1996). Hyperlocomotion and indifference to cocaine and amphetamine in mice lacking the dopamine transporter. *Nature*, *379*, 606–612. (p. 196)

Gist, R., Lubin, B., & Redburn, B. G. (1998). Psychosocial, ecological, and community perspectives on disaster response. *Journal of Personal & Interpersonal Loss*, *3*, 25-51. (p. 435)

Gist, R., & Welch, Q. B. (1989). Certification change versus actual behavior change in teenage suicide rates, 1955–1979. *Suicide and Life Threatening Behavior*, *19*, 277–288. (p. 444)

Gjerde, P. F. (1983). Attentional capacity dysfunction and arousal in schizophrenia. *Psychological Bulletin*, *93*, 57–72. (p. 450)

Gladue, B. A. (1990). Hormones and neuroendocrine factors in atypical human sexual behavior. In J. R. Feierman (Ed.), *Pedophilia: Biosocial dimensions*. New York: Springer-Verlag. (p. 335)

Gladue, B. A. (1994). The biopsychology of sexual orientation. *Current Directions in Psychological Science*, *3*, 150–154. (p. 335)

Gladue, B. A., Boechler, M., & McCaul, K. D. (1989). Hormonal response to competition in human males. *Aggressive Behavior*, *15*, 409–422. (p. 514)

Gleaves, D. H. (1996). The sociocognitive model of dissociative identity disorder: A reexamination of the evidence. *Psychological Bulletin*, *120*, 42–59. (p. 439)

Glenn, N. D. (1975). Psychological well-being in the postparental stage: Some evidence from national surveys. *Journal of Marriage and the Family*, *37*, 105–110. (p. 118)

Glick, P., Gottesman, D., & Jolton, J. (1989). The fault is not in the stars: Susceptibility of skeptics and believers in astrology to the Barnum effect. *Personality and Social Psychology Bulletin*, *15*, 572–583. (p. 418)

Godden, D. R., & Baddeley, A. D. (1975). Context-dependent memory in two natural environments: On land and underwater. *British Journal of Psychology*, *66*, 325–331. (pp. xvi, 250, *251)*

Goff, D. C. (1993). Reply to Dr. Armstrong. *Journal of Nervous and Mental Disease*, *181*, 604–605. (p. 439)

Goff, D. C., & Simms, C. A. (1993). Has multiple personality disorder remained consistent over time? *Journal of Nervous and Mental Disease*, *181*, 595–600. (p. 439)

Gold, M., & Yanof, D. S. (1985). Mothers, daughters, and girlfriends. *Journal of Personality and Social Psychology*, *49*, 654–659. (p. 106)

Goldberg, J., True, W. R., Eisen, S. A., & Henderson, W. G. (1990). A twin study of the effects of the Vietnam War on posttraumatic stress disorder. *Journal of the American Medical Association*, *263*, 1227–1232. (p. 435)

Goldberg, L. R. (1993). The structure of phenotypic personality traits. *American Psychologist*, *48*, 26–34. (p. 402)

Goldfried, M. R., & Padawer, W. (1982). Current status and future directions in psychotherapy. In M. R. Goldfried (Ed.), *Converging themes in psychotherapy: Trends in psychodynamic, humanistic, and behavioral practice.* New York: Springer. (p. 480)

Golding, J. M. (1996). Sexual assault history and women's reproductive and sexual health. *Psychology of Women Quarterly*, *20*, 101–121. (p. 519)

Goldman, D. (1996). Why mice drink. *Nature Genetics*, *13*, 137–138. (p. 200)

Goldstein, A. P., & Glick, B. (1994). Aggression replacement training: Curriculum and evaluation. *Simulation and Gaming*, *25*(1), 9. (p. 516)

Goleman, D. (1980, February). 1,528 little geniuses and how they grew. *Psychology Today*, pp. 28–53. (pp. 297, 339)

Goleman, D. (1995). *Emotional intelligence*. New York: Bantam. (pp. 293, 349)

Goleman, D. (1996, November 19). Research on brain leads to pursuit of designer drugs. *New York Times*, pp. C1, C3. (p. 485)

Golombok, S., & Tasker, F. (1996). Do parents influence the sexual orientation of their children? Findings from a longitudinal study of lesbian families. *Developmental Psychology*, *32*, 3–11. (p. 334)

Golub, S. (1983). *Menarche: The transition from girl to woman.* Lexington, MA: Lexington Books. (p. 101)

Gonsiorek, J. C. (1982). Summary and conclusions. In W. Paul, J. D. Weinrich, J. C. Gonsiorek, & M. E. Hotvedt (Eds.), *Homosexuality: Social, psychological, and biological issues.* Beverly Hills, CA: Sage. (p. 333)

Goodall, J. (1986). *The chimpanzees of Gombe: Patterns of behavior.* Cambridge, MA: Harvard University Press. (p. 511)

Goodchilds, J. (1987). Quoted by Carol Tavris, Old age is not what it used to be. *The New York Times Magazine: Good Health Magazine*, September 27, pp. 24–25, 91–92. (p. 110)

Goodhart, D. E. (1986). The effects of positive and negative thinking on performance in an achievement situation. *Journal of Personality and Social Psychology*, *51*, 117–124. (p. 418)

Goodman, G. S., Rudy, L., Bottoms, B. L., & Aman, C. (1990). Children's concerns and memory: Issues of ecological validity in the study of children's eyewitness testimony. In R. Fivush & J. A. Hudson (Eds.), *Knowing and remembering in young children*. New York: Cambridge University Press. (p. 258)

Goodman, L. A., Koss, M. P., & Russo, N. F. (1993). Violence against women: Mental health effects. Part II. Conceptualizations of post-traumatic stress. Applied & Preventive Psychology, 2, 123–130. (p. 435)

Goodwin, C. J. (1991). Misportraying Pavlov's apparatus. *American Journal of Psychology*, *104*, 135–141. (p. 208)

Gopnik, A., & Meltzoff, A. N. (1986). Relations between semantic and cognitive development in the one-word stage: The specificity hypothesis. *Child Development*, *57*, 1040–1053. (p. 286)

Goranson, R. E. (1978). *The hindsight effect in problem solving*. Unpublished manuscript, cited by G. Wood (1984), Research methodology: A decision-making perspective. In A. M. Rogers & C. J. Scheirer (Eds.), *The G. Stanley Hall Lecture Series* (Vol. 4). Washington, DC: American Psychological Association. (p. 12)

Gore, A., Jr. (1992). *Earth in the balance: Ecology and the human spirit*. Boston: Houghton-Mifflin. (p. 273)

Gore, T., interviewed by C. Greer (1994, September 11). I know there is help. *Parade*, 4–7. (p. 475)

Gortmaker, S. L., Must, A., Perrin, J. M., Sobol, A. M., & Dietz, W. H. (1993). Social and economic consequences of overweight in adolescence and young adulthood. *New England Journal of Medicine*, *329*, 1008–1012. (p. 320)

Gotlib, I. H. (1992). Interpersonal and cognitive aspects of depression. *Current Directions in Psychological Science*, *1*, 149–154. (p. 411)

Gotlib, I. H., & Hammen, C. L. (1992). *Psychological aspects of depression: Toward a cognitive-interpersonal integration*. New York: Wiley. (p. 448)

Gottesman, I. I. (1991). *Schizophrenia genesis: The origins of madness*. New York: Freeman. (pp. 454, *453)*

Gottesman, I. I. (1993). The origins of schizophrenia: Past as prologue. In R. Plomin & G. E. McClearn (Eds.), *Nature, nurture, and psychology*. Washington, DC: American Psychological Association. (p. 454)

Gottman, J. (with N. Silver) (1994). *Why marriages succeed or fail*. New York: Simon & Schuster. (p. 117)

Gould, M. S., & Shaffer, D. (1986). The impact of suicide in television movies: Evidence of imitation. *New England Journal of Medicine*, *315*, 690–694. (p. 497)

Gould, S. J. (1981). *The mismeasure of man*. New York: Norton. (p. 290)

Grady, C. L., & others (1995). Age-related reductions in human recognition memory due to impaired encoding. *Science*, *269*, 218–221. (p. 240)

Graf, P. (1990). Life-span changes in implicit and explicit memory. *Bulletin of the Psychonomic Society*, *28*, 353–358. (p. 113)

Graham, J. W., Marks, G., & Hansen, W. B. (1991). Social influence processes affecting adolescent substance use. *Journal of Applied Psychology*, *76*, 291–298. (p. 201)

Gray-Little, B., & Burks, N. (1983). Power and satisfaction in marriage: A review and critique. *Psychological Bulletin*, *93*, 513–538. (p. 527)

Greeley, A. M. (1991). *Faithful attraction*. New York: Tor Books. (pp. 16, 117, 327)

Greeley, A. M. (1994, May/June). Marital infidelity. *Society*, pp. 9–13. (p. 16)

Greenberg, G. (1997). Right answers, wrong reasons: Revisiting the deletion of homosexuality from the *DSM*. *Review of General Psychology*, *1*, 256–270. (p. 427)

Greenberg, R. P., Bornstein, R. F., Greenberg, M. D., & Fisher, S. (1992). A meta-analysis of antidepressant outcome under "blinder" conditions. *Journal of Consulting and Clinical Psychology*, *60*, 664–669. (p. 484)

Greenberg, R. P., Bornstein, R. F., Zborowski, M. J., Fisher, S., & Greenberg, M. D. (1994). A meta-analysis of fluoxetine outcome in the treatment of depression. *Journal of Nervous and Mental Disease*, *182*, 547–551. (p. 484)

Greene, R. L. (1987). Effects of maintenance rehearsal on human memory. *Psychological Bulletin*, *102*, 403–413. (p. 236)

Greenwald, A. G. (1992). New look 3: Unconscious cognition reclaimed. *American Psychologist*, *47*, 766–779. (p. 398)

Greenwald, A. G. (1992). Subliminal semantic activation and subliminal snake oil. Paper presented to the American Psychological Association Convention, Washington, DC. (p. 27)

Greenwald, A. G., & Banaji, M. R. (1995). Implicit social cognition: Attitudes, self-esteem, and stereotypes. *Psychological Review*, *102*, 4–27. (p. 171)

Greenwald, A. G., Spangenberg, E. R., Pratkanis, A. R., & Eskenazi, J. (1991). Double-blind tests of subliminal self-help audiotapes. *Psychological Science*, *2*, 119–122. (p. 26)

Greenwood, M. R. C. (1989). Sexual dimorphism and obesity. In A. J. Stunkard & A. Baum (Eds.). *Perspectives in behavioral medicine: Eating, sleeping, and sex*. Hillsdale, NJ: Erlbaum. (p. 320)

Greer, G. (1984, April). The uses of chastity and other paths to sexual pleasures. *MS*, pp. 53–60, *96. (p. 329)*

Gregory, R. L. (1968, November). Visual illusions. *Scientific American*, pp. 66–76. (p. 153)

Gregory, R. L. (1978). *Eye and brain: The psychology of seeing* (3rd ed.). New York: McGraw-Hill. (p. 155)

Gregory, R. L., & Gombrich, E. H. (Eds.). (1973). *Illusion in nature and art*. New York: Charles Scribner's Sons. (p. 158)

Greif, E. B., & Ulman, K. J. (1982). The psychological impact of menarche on early adolescent females: A review of the literature. *Child Development*, *53*, 1413–1430. (p. 100)

Greist, J. H., Jefferson, J. W., & Marks, I. M. (1986). *Anxiety and its treatment*. Washington, DC: American Psychiatric Press. (p. 432)

Grenier, G., & Byers, E. S. (1995). Rapid ejaculation: A review of conceptual, etiological, and treatment issues. *Archives of Sexual Behavior*, *24*, 447–472. (p. 331)

Grilo, C. M., & Pogue-Geile, M. F. (1991). The nature of environmental influences on weight and obesity: A behavior genetic analysis. *Psychological Bulletin*, *110*, 520–537. (p. 322)

Grobstein, C. (1979, June). External human fertilization. *Scientific American*, pp. 57–67. (p. 81)

Gross, A. E., & Crofton, C. (1977). What is good is beautiful. *Sociometry*, *40*, 85–90. (p. 525)

Grossberg, S. (1995). The attentive brain. *American Scientist*, *83*, 438–449. (p. 158)

Grossman, M., & Wood, W. (1993). Sex differences in intensity of emotional experience: A social role interpretation. *Journal of Personality and Social Psychology*, *65*, 1010–1022. (p. 105)

Gruder, C. L. (1977). Choice of comparison persons in evaluating oneself. In J. M. Suls & R. L. Miller (Eds.), *Social comparison processes*. New York: Hemisphere. (p. 362)

Guerin, B. (1986). Mere presence effects in humans: A review. *Journal of Personality and Social Psychology*, *22*, 38–77. (p. 503)

Guion, R. M. (1992). Science, pseudoscience, and silly science in applied psychology. Paper presented to the American Psychological Association convention. (p. 19)

Gulevich, G., Dement, W., & Johnson, L. (1966). Psychiatric and EEG observations on a case of prolonged (264 hours) wakefulness. *Archives of General Psychiatry*, *15*, 29–35. (p. 178)

Gura, T. (1997). Obesity sheds its secrets. *Science*, *275*, 751–753. (p. 324)

Gustavson, C. R., Garcia, J., Hankins, W. G., & Rusiniak, K. W. (1974). Coyote predation control by aversive conditioning. *Science*, *184*, 581–583. (p. 212)

Gustavson, C. R., Kelly, D. J., & Sweeney, M. (1976). Prey-lithium aversions I: Coyotes and wolves. *Behavioral Biology*, *17*, 61–72. (p. 212)

Guttmacher Institute (1993). *Facts in brief*. New York: Alan Guttmacher Institute. (p. 108)

Guttmacher Institute (1994). *Sex and America's teenagers*. New York: Alan Guttmacher Institute. (pp. 99, *108)*

H., Sally (1979, August). Videotape recording number T-3, Fortunoff Video Archive of Holocaust Testimonies. New Haven, CT: Yale University Library. (p. 398)

Haber, R. N. (1970, May). How we remember what we see. *Scientific American*, pp. 104–112. (p. 232)

Hackel, L. S., & Ruble, D. N. (1992). Changes in the marital relationship after the first baby is born: Predicting the impact of expectancy disconfirmation. *Journal of Personality and Social Psychology*, *62*, 944–957. (p. 118)

Hafner, H., & Schmidtke, A. (1989). Do televised fictional suicide models produce suicides? In D. R. Pfeffer (Ed.), *Suicide among youth: Perspectives on risk and prevention*. Washington, DC: American Psychiatric Press. (p. 497)

Halaas, J. L., & others (1995). Weight-reducing effects of the plasma protein encoded by the *obese* gene. *Science*, *269*, 543–546. (p. 322)

Halberstadt, J. B., & Niedenthal, P. M., & Kushner, J. (1995). Resolution of lexical ambiguity by emotional state. *Psychological Science*, *6*, 278–281. (p. 158)

Haldeman, D. C. (1994). The practice and ethics of sexual orientation conversion therapy. *Journal of Consulting and Clinical Psychology*, *62*, 221–227. (p. 333)

Hall, C. S., Dornhoff, W., Blick, K. A., & Weesner, K. E. (1982). The dreams of college men and women in 1950 and 1980: A comparison of dream contents and sex differences. *Sleep*, *5*, 188–194. (p. 181)

Hall, C. S., & Lindzey, G. (1978). *Theories of personality* (2nd ed.). New York: Wiley. (p. 399)

Hall, G. S. (1904). *Adolescence: Its psychology and its relations to physiology, anthropology, sex, crime, religion and education* (Vol. I). New York: Appleton-Century-Crofts. (p. 99)

Hall, J. A. (1987). On explaining gender differences: The case of nonverbal communication. In P. Shaver & C. Hendrick (Eds.), *Review of Personality and Social Psychology*, 7, 177–200. (p. 342)

Hall, J. A. Y., & Kimura, D. (1994). Dermatoglyphic assymetry and sexual orientation in men. *Behavioral Neuroscience*, *108*, 1203–1206. (p. 335)

Hall, N. R., & Goldstein, A. L. (1986, March/April). Thinking well: The chemical links between emotions and health. *The Sciences*, pp. 34–40. (p. 375)

Hall, T. (1987, September 27). Cravings: Does your body know what it needs? *The New York Times Magazine: Good Health Magazine*, pp. 23, 62–65. (pp. 105, 318)

Hallinan, J. T. (1997, January 14). State moves to end payments in repressed memory cases. Newhouse News Service release (*Grand Rapids [Mich.] Press*). (p. 259)

Halpern, D. F. (1991). Cognitive sex differences: Why diversity is a critical research issue. Paper presented to the American Psychological Association convention. (p. 305)

Halpern, D. F. (1997). Sex differences in intelligence: Implications for education. *American Psychologist*, *52*, 1091–1102. (p. 304)

Hamers, J. F., & Blanc, M. H. (1989). *Bilinguality and bilingualism*. Cambridge: Cambridge University Press. (p. 287)

Hamid, A. (1992). The developmental cycle of a drug epidemic: The cocaine smoking epidemic of 1981–1991. *Journal of Psychoactive Drugs*, *24*, 337–348. (p. 196)

Hamill, R., Wilson, T. D., & Nisbett, R. E. (1980). Insensitivity to sample bias: Generalizing from atypical cases. *Journal of Personality and Social Psychology*, *39*, 578–589. (p. 272)

Hamilton, M. C. (1988). Using masculine generics: Does generic "he" increase male bias in the user's imagery? *Sex Roles*, *19*, 785–799. (p. 286)

Hamilton, V. L., Hoffman, W. S., Broman, C. L., & Rauma, D. (1993). Unemployment, distress, and coping: A panel study of autoworkers. *Journal of Personality and Social Psychology*, *65*, 234–247. (p. 447)

Hammersmith, S. K. (1982, August). *Sexual preference: An empirical study from the Alfred C. Kinsey Institute for Sex Research*. Paper presented at the meeting of the American Psychological Association, Washington, DC. (p. 333)

Haney, D. Q. (1996, October 16). Fat now outnumber the skinny. Associated Press release (*Anchorage Daily News*). (p. 320)

Hansen, C. H., & Hansen, R. D. (1988). Finding the face-in-the-crowd: An anger superiority effect. *Journal of Personality and Social Psychology*, *54*, 917–924. (p. 352)

Hardin, C., & Banaji, M. R. (1993). The influence of language on thought. *Social Cognition*, *11*, 277–308. (p. 286)

Hare, R. D. (1975). Psychophysiological studies of psychopathy. In D. C. Fowles (Ed.), *Clinical applications of psychophysiology*. New York: Columbia University Press. (p. 455)

Harkins, S. G., & Szymanski, K. (1989). Social loafing and group evaluation. *Journal of Personality and Social Psychology, 56,* 934–941. (p. 504)

Harlow, H. F., Harlow, M. K., & Suomi, S. J. (1971). From thought to therapy: Lessons from a primate laboratory. *American Scientist, 59,* 538–549. (p. 91)

Harper's Index (1997). Reprinted in *Funny Times,* December, p. 10. (p. 226)

Harrington, D. M., Block, J. H., & Block, J. (1987). Testing aspects of Carl Rogers' theory of creative environments: Child-rearing antecedents of creative potential in young adolescents. *Journal of Personality and Social Psychology,* 52, 851–856. (p. 407)

Harris, B. (1979). Whatever happened to Little Albert? *American Psychologist, 34,* 151–160. (p. 214)

Harris, J. R. (1995). Where is the child's environment: A group socialization theory of development. *Psychological Review, 102,* 458–489. (p. 107)

Harris, J. R. (1998). *The nurture assumption.* New York: Free Press. (pp. 72, *107)*

Harris, L. (1987). *Inside America.* New York: Random House. (p. 371)

Harris, R. J. (1994). The impact of sexually explicit media. In J. Brant & D. Zillmann (Eds.), *Media effects: Advances in theory and research.* Hillsdale, NJ: Erlbaum. (p. 519)

Harriston, K. A. (1993, December 24). 1 shakes, 1 snoozes; both win $45 million. *Washington Post* release in *Tacoma News Tribune,* pp. A1, A2. (p. 420)

Hartmann, E. (1981, April). The strangest sleep disorder. *Psychology Today,* pp. 14, 16, 18. (p. 180)

Hartshorne, H., & May, M. A. (1928). *Studies in deceit.* New York: Macmillan. (p. 404)

Harvey, S. M. (1987). Female sexual behavior: Fluctuations during the menstrual cycle. *Journal of Psychosomatic Research, 31,* 101–110. (p. 328)

Haskins, R. (1989). Beyond metaphor: The efficacy of early childhood education. *American Psychologist, 44,* 274–282. (p. 301)

Hassan, R., & Carr, J. (1989). Changing patterns of suicide in Australia. *Australian and New Zealand Journal of Psychiatry, 23,* 226–234. (p. 444)

Hatfield, E. (1988). Passionate and companionate love. In R. J. Sternberg & M. L. Barnes (Eds.), *The psychology of love.* New Haven: Yale University Press. (p. 526)

Hatfield, E., & Sprecher, S. (1986). *Mirror, mirror . . . The importance of looks in everyday life.* Albany: State University of New York Press. (p. 524)

Hathaway, S. R. (1960). *An MMPI Handbook* (Vol. 1, Foreword). Minneapolis: University of Minnesota Press. (Revised edition, 1972). (p. 403)

Hayes, J. R. (1981). *The complete problem solver.* Philadelphia: Franklin Institute Press. (p. 250)

Hazelrigg, M. D., Cooper, H. M., & Borduin, C. M. (1987). Evaluating the effectiveness of family therapies: An integrative review and analysis. *Psychological Bulletin, 101,* 428–442. (p. 474)

Hearold, S. (1986). A synthesis of 1043 effects of television on social behavior. In G. Comstock (Ed.), *Public communication and behavior.* New York: Academic Press. (p. 517)

Heath, A. C., Jardine, R., & Martin, N. G. (1989). Interactive effects of genotype and social environment on alcohol consumption in female twins. *Journal of Studies on Alcohol, 50,* 38–48. (p. 200)

Heath, L., & Petraitis, J. (1987). Television viewing and fear of crime: Where is the mean world? *Basic and Applied Social Psychology, 8,* 97–123. (p. 518)

Heatherton, T. F., & Baumeister, R. F. (1991). Binge eating as escape from self-awareness. *Psychological Bulletin, 110,* 86–108. (p. 319)

Hebb, D. O. (1980). *Essay on mind.* Hillsdale, NJ: Erlbaum. 9–16. (p. 347)

Hedges, L. V., & Nowell, A. (1995). Sex differences in mental test scores, variability, and numbers of high-scoring individuals. *Science, 269,* 41–45. (p. 305)

Heider, F. (1958). *The psychology of interpersonal relations.* New York: Wiley. (p. 491)

Heiman, J. R. (1975, April). The physiology of erotica: Women's sexual arousal. *Psychology Today,* 90–94. (p. 329)

Heller, W. (1990, May/June). Of one mind: Second thoughts about the brain's dual nature. *The Sciences,* pp. 38–44. (p. 67)

Hellige, J. B. (1993). Unity of thought and action: Varieties of interaction between the left and right cerebral hemispheres. *Current Directions in Psychological Science,* 2, 21–25. (p. 66)

Helmreich, W. B. (1992). *Against all odds: Holocaust survivors and the successful lives they made in America.* New York: Simon & Schuster. (pp. 397, 435)

Helmreich, W. B. (1994). Personal correspondence. Department of Sociology, City University of New York. (p. 397)

Hembree, R. (1988). Correlates, causes, effects, and treatment of test anxiety. *Review of Educational Research, 58,* 47–77. (p. 349)

Henley, N. M. (1989). Molehill or mountain? What we know and don't know about sex bias in language. In M. Crawford & M. Gentry (Eds.), *Gender and thought: Psychological perspectives.* New York: Springer-Verlag. (p. 286)

Henninger, P. (1992). Conditional handedness: Handedness changes in multiple personality disordered subject reflect shift in hemispheric dominance. *Consciousness and Cognition, 1,* 265–287. (pp. 439, *467)*

Henry, J. P., & Stephens, P. M. (1977). *Stress, health, and the social environment.* New York: Springer-Verlag. (p. 371)

Herbert, B. (1997, November 2). China's missing girl babies. *New York Times News Service,* reprinted in *Grand Rapids Press,* p. H2. (p. 511)

Herbert, T. B., & Cohen, S. (1993). Depression and immunity: A meta-analytic review. *Psychological Bulletin, 113,* 472–486. (p. 374)

Herek, G. M., & Capitanio, J. P. (1996). "Some of my best friends": Intergroup contact, concealable stigma, and heterosexuals' attitudes toward gay men and lesbians. *Personality and Social Psychology Bulletin,* 22, 412–424. (p. 336)

Herman, C. P., & Polivy, J. (1980). Restrained eating. In A. J. Stunkard (Ed.), *Obesity.* Philadelphia: Saunders. (p. 325)

Herrmann, D. (1982). Know thy memory: The use of questionnaires to assess and study memory. *Psychological Bulletin, 92,* 434–452. (p. 263)

Herrnstein, R. J., & Loveland, D. H. (1964). Complex visual concept in the pigeon. *Science, 146,* 549–551. (p. 217)

Hershenson, M. (1989). *The moon illusion.* Hillsdale, NJ: Erlbaum. (p. 152)

Hess, D. J. (1993). *Science in the new age: The paranormal, its defenders and debunkers, and American culture.* Madison: University of Wisconsin Press. (p. 163)

Hess, E. H. (1956, July). Space perception in the chick. *Scientific American*, pp. 71–80. (p. 155)

Hetherington, E. M., & Clingempeel, W. G. (1992). Coping with marital transitions: A family systems perspective. *Monographs of the Society for Research in Child Development, 57*, 1–242. (p. 95)

Hetherington, E. M., Reiss, D., & Plomin, R. (1993). *The separate social worlds of siblings: The impact of nonshared environment on development.* Hillsdale, NJ: Erlbaum. (p. 72)

Hetherington, E. M., Stanley-Hagan, M., & Anderson, E. R. (1989). Marital transitions: A child's perspective. *American Psychologist, 44*, 303–312. (p. 95)

Higgins, E. T. (1987). Self-discrepancy: A theory relating self and affect. *Psychological Review, 94*, 319–340. (pp. 408, 409)

Hilgard, E. R. (1986). *Divided consciousness: Multiple controls in human thought and action.* New York: Wiley. (p. 190)

Hilgard, E. R. (1992). Dissociation and theories of hypnosis. In E. Fromm & M. R. Nash (Eds.), *Contemporary hypnosis research.* New York: Guilford. (p. 190)

Hines, M., & Green, R. (1991). Human hormonal and neural correlates of sex-typed behaviors. *Review of Psychiatry, 10*, 536–555. (p. 80)

Hintzman, D. L. (1978). *The psychology of learning and memory.* San Francisco: Freeman. (p. 238)

Hinz, L. D., & Williamson, D. A. (1987). Bulimia and depression: A review of the affective variant hypothesis. *Psychological Bulletin, 102*, 150–158. (p. 319)

Hirst, W., Neisser, U., & Spelke, E. (1978, June). Divided attention. *Human Nature*, pp. 54–61. (p. 190)

Hirt, E. R., Zillmann, D., Erickson, G. A., & Kennedy, C. (1992). Costs and benefits of allegiance: Changes in fans' self-ascribed competencies after team victory versus defeat. *Journal of Personality and Social Psychology, 63*, 724–738. (p. 447)

Hobfoll, S. E. (1989). Conservation of resources: A new attempt at conceptualizing stress. *American Psychologist, 44*, 513–524. (p. 369)

Hobfoll, S. E., Lomranz, J., Eyal, N., Bridges, A., & Tzemach, M. (1989). Pulse of a nation: Depressive mood reactions of Israelis to the Israel-Lebanon war. *Journal of Personality and Social Psychology, 56*, 1002–1012. (p. 442)

Hobson, J. A. (1988). *The dreaming brain.* New York: Basic Books. (p. 182)

Hobson, J. A. (1995, September). Quoted by C. H. Colt, The power of dreams. *Life*, pp. 36–49. (p. 183)

Hodgkinson, V. A., & Weitzman, M. S. (1992). *Giving and volunteering in the United States.* Washington, DC: Independent Sector. (p. 587)

Hoebel, B. G., & Teitelbaum, P. (1966). Effects of forcefeeding and starvation on food intake and body weight in a rat with ventromedial hypothalamic lesions. *Journal of Comparative and Physiological Psychology, 61*, 189–193. (p. 317)

Hoffman, C., & Hurst, N. (1990). Gender stereotypes: Perception or rationalization? *Journal of Personality and Social Psychology, 58*, 197–208. (p. 511)

Hoffman, P. (1994, November). The science of race. *Discover*, p. 4. (p. 510)

Hofstede, G. (1980). *Culture's consequences: International differences in work-related values.* Beverly Hills: Sage. (p. 411)

Hogan, J. (1989). Personality correlates of physical fitness. *Journal of Personality and Social Psychology, 56*, 284–288. (p. 378)

Hogan, R., Hogan, J., & Roberts, B. W. (1996). Personality measurement and employment decisions. *American Psychologist, 51*, 469–477. (p. 405)

Hohmann, G. W. (1966). Some effects of spinal cord lesions on experienced emotional feelings. *Psychophysiology, 3*, 143–156. (p. 365)

Hokanson, J. E., & Edelman, R. (1966). Effects of three social responses on vascular processes. *Journal of Personality and Social Psychology, 3*, 442–447. (p. 358)

Holden, C. (1980a). Identical twins reared apart. *Science, 207*, 1323–1325. (p. 71)

Holden, C. (1980b, November). Twins reunited. *Science, 80*, 55–59. (p. 71)

Holden, C. (1986a). Days may be numbered for polygraphs in the private sector. *Science, 232*, 705. (p. 350)

Holden, C. (1986b). Researchers grapple with problems of updating classic psychological test. *Science, 233*, 1249–1251. (p. 414)

Holden, C. (1991). Alcoholism gene: Coming or going? *Science, 254*, 200. (p. 200)

Holden, C. (1991). New center to study therapies and ethnicity. *Science, 251*, 748. (p. 484)

Holden, C. (1993). Wake-up call for sleep research. *Science, 259*, 305. (p. 177)

Hollon, S. D., DeRubeis, R. J., & Seligman, M. E. P. (1992). Cognitive therapy and the prevention of depression. *Applied & Preventive Psychology, 1*, 89–95. (p. 473)

Holmes, D. (1990). The evidence for repression: An examination of sixty years of research. In J. Singer (Ed.), *Repression and dissociation: Implications for personality theory, psychopathology, and health.* Chicago: University of Chicago Press. (p. 398)

Holmes, D. S. (1978). Projection as a defense mechanism. *Psychological Bulletin, 85*, 677–688. (p. 397)

Holmes, D. S. (1994). Is there evidence for repression? No. (Unexpurgated version on an article which was rewritten by the *Harvard Mental Health Letter* and published as "Is there evidence for repression? Doubtful," June, 1994, pp. 4–6.) (p. 398)

Holtgraves, T., & Skeel, J. (1992). Cognitive biases in playing the lottery: Estimating the odds and choosing the numbers. *Journal of Applied Social Psychology, 22*, 934–952. (p. 19)

Holzman, P. S., & Matthysse, S. (1990). The genetics of schizophrenia: A review. *Psychological Science, 1*, 279–286. (p. 129)

Hooper, J., & Teresi, D. (1986). *The three-pound universe.* New York: Macmillan. (p. 54)

Hooykaas, R. (1972). *Religion and the rise of modern science.* Grand Rapids, MI: Eerdmans. (p. 9)

Horgan, J. (1995, December). A sign is born. *Scientific American*, pp. 18–19. (p. 280)

Horgan, J. (1996, December). Why Freud isn't dead. *Scientific American*, pp. 106–111. (p. 484)

Horn, J. L. (1982). The aging of human abilities. In J. Wolman (Ed.), *Handbook of developmental psychology.* Englewood Cliffs, NJ: Prentice-Hall. (p. 114)

Horne, J. A. (1989). Sleep loss and "divergent" thinking ability. *Sleep, 11,* 528–536. (p. 178)

House, J. S., Landis, K. R., & Umberson, D. (1988). Social relationships and health. *Science, 241,* 540–545. (p. 382)

House, R. J., & Singh, J. V. (1987). Organizational behavior: Some new directions for I/O psychology. *Annual Review of Psychology, 38,* 669–718. (p. 343)

Houts, A. C., Berman, J. S., & Abramson, H. (1994). Effectiveness of psychological and pharmacological treatments for nocturnal enuresis. *Journal of Consulting and Clinical Psychology, 62,* 737–745. (p. 467)

Howe, M. L., & Courage, M. L. (1993). On resolving the enigma of infantile amnesia. *Psychological Bulletin, 113,* 305–326. (p. 83)

Hoyer, G., & Lund, E. (1993). Suicide among women related to number of children in marriage. *Archives of General Psychiatry, 50,* 134–137. (p. 444)

Hubel, D. H. (1979, September). The brain. *Scientific American,* pp. 45–53. (p. 129)

Hubel, D. H., & Wiesel, T. N. (1979, September). Brian mechanisms of vision. *Scientific American,* pp. 150–162. (pp. 133–134)

Hublin, Kaprio, J., Partinen, M., Heikkila, K., & Koskenvuo, M. (1997). Prevalence and genetics of sleepwalking: A population-based twin study. *Neurology, 48,* 177–181. (p. 175)

Hucker, S. J., & Bain, J. (1990). Androgenic hormones and sexual assault. In W. Marshall, R. Law, & H. Barbaree (Eds.), *The handbook on sexual assault.* New York: Plenum. (p. 329)

Hugick, L. (1989, July). Women play the leading role in keeping modern families close. *Gallup Report,* No. 286, pp. 27–34. (p. 105)

Hull, J. G., Young, R. D., & Jouriles, E. (1986). Applications of the self-awareness model of alcohol consumption: Predicting patterns of use and abuse. *Journal of Personality and Social Psychology, 51,* 790–796. (p. 194)

Hulme, C., & Tordoff, V. (1989). Working memory development: The effects of speech rate, word length, and acoustic similarity on serial recall. *Journal of Experimental Child Psychology, 47,* 72–87. (p. 242)

Hunt, E. (1995). The role of intelligence in modern society. *American Scientist, 83,* 356–368. (p. 293)

Hunt, J. M. (1982). Toward equalizing the developmental opportunities of infants and preschool children. *Journal of Social Issues, 38*(4), 163–191. (p. 301)

Hunt, M. (1974). *Sexual behavior in the 1970s.* Chicago: Playboy Press. (p. 330)

Hunt, M. (1993). *The story of psychology.* New York: Doubleday. (pp. 3, 102, 215, 297)

Hunter, J. E. (1997). Needed: A ban on the significance test. *Psychological Science, 8,* 3–7. (p. 544)

Hunter, S., & Sundel, M. (Eds.). (1989). *Midlife myths: Issues, findings, and practice implications.* Newbury Park, CA: Sage. (p. 115)

Hurtado, S., Dey, E. L., & Trevino, J. G. (1994). Exclusion or self-segregation? Interaction across racial/ethnic groups on college campuses. Paper presented at the American Educational Research Association annual meeting. (p. 568)

Huston, A. C., Donnerstein, E., Fairchild, H., Feshbach, N. D., Katz, P. A., & Murray, J. P. (1992). *Big world, small screen: The role of television in American society.* Lincoln, NE: University of Nebraska Press. (p. 517)

Hyde, J. S. (1983, November). *Bem's gender schema theory.* Paper presented at GLCA Women's Studies Conference, Rochester, IN. (p. 255)

Hyde, J. S. (1984, July). Children's understanding of sexist language. *Developmental Psychology, 20*(4), 697–706. (p. 286)

Hyde, J. S., Fennema, E., & Lamon, S. J. (1990). Gender differences in mathematics performance: A meta-analysis. *Psychological Bulletin, 107,* 139–155. (p. 304)

Hyde, J. S., & Linn, M. C. (1988). Gender differences in verbal ability: A meta-analysis. *Psychological Bulletin, 104,* 53–69. (p. 304)

Hyler, S., Gabbard, G. O., & Schneider, I. (1991). Homicidal maniacs and narcissistic parasites: Stigmatization of mentally ill persons in the movies. *Hospital and Community Psychiatry, 42,* 1044–1048. (p. 430)

Hyman, I. E., Jr., Husband, T. H., & Billings, F. J. (1995). False memories of childhood experiences. *Applied Cognitive Psychology, 9,* 181–197. (p. 256)

Hyman, I. E., Jr., & Pentland, J. (1996). The role of mental imagery in the creation of false childhood memories. *Journal of Memory and Language, 35,* 101–117. (p. 256)

Hyman, R. (1981). Cold reading: How to convince strangers that you know all about them. In K. Frazier (Ed.), *Paranormal borderlands of science.* Buffalo, NY: Prometheus. (p. 418)

Hyman, R. (1986). Maimonides dream-telepathy experiments. *Skeptical Inquirer, 11,* 91–92. (p. 162)

Hyman, R. (1994). Anomaly or artifact? Comments on Bem and Honorton. *Psychological Bulletin, 115,* 19–24. (p. 164)

Hyman, R. (1996, March/April). Evaluation of the military's twenty-year program on psychic spying. *Skeptical Inquirer,* pp. 21–23, 27. (p. 163)

Hyman, R. (1996, March/April). The evidence for psychic functioning: Claims vs. reality. *The Skeptical Inquirer,* pp. 24–26. (p. 164)

Iacono, W. G., & Lykken, D. T. (1997). The validity of the lie detector: Two surveys of scientific opinion. *Journal of Applied Psychology, 82,* 426–433. (p. 350)

Ickes, W., Snyder, M., & Garcia S. (1997). Personality influences on the choice of situations. In R. Hogan, J. Johnson, & S. Briggs (eds.), *Handbook of Personality Psychology.* San Diego: Academic Press. (p. 416)

Immen, W. (1995, July 16). Canadians ignore 'safe sex' warning. *Toronto Globe and Mail* (reprinted *Grand Rapids Press,* p. A22). (p. 108)

Ingham, A. G., Levinger, G., Graves, J., & Peckham, V. (1974). The Ringelmann effect: Studies of group size and group performance. *Journal of Experimental Social Psychology, 10,* 371–384. (p. 503)

Inglehart, M. R., Markus, H., & Brown, D. R. (1989). The effects of possible selves on academic achievement—A panel study. In J. P. Forgas & J. M. Innes (Eds.), *Recent advances in social psychology: An international perspective.* New York: Elsevier Science Publishers. (p. 408)

Inglehart, R. (1990). *Culture shift in advanced industrial society.* Princeton, NJ: Princeton University Press. (pp. 116, 119, 337, 417)

Inman, M. L., & Baron, R. S. (1996). Influence of prototypes on perceptions of prejudice. *Journal of Personality and Social Psychology, 70,* 727–739. (p. 269)

Insel, P. M., & Roth, W. T. (1976). *Health in a changing society.* Palo Alto, CA: Mayfield. (p. 110)

Irwin, M., Mascovich, A., Gillin, J. C., Willoughby, R., Pike, J., & Smith, T. L. (1994). Partial sleep deprivation reduces natural killer cell activity in humans. *Psychosomatic Medicine, 56,* 493–498. (p. 178)

Isen, A. M., & Means, B. (1983). The influence of positive affect on decision-making strategy. *Social Cognition, 2,* 28–31. (p. 359)

Isham, W. P., & Kamin, L. J. (1993). Blackness, deafness, IQ, and *g. Intelligence, 17,* 37–46. (p. 287)

ISR (1994, May). High schoolers' job may 'cost' too much. *ISR Newsletter,* p. 11 (University of Michigan). (p. 18)

Ito, T. A., Miller, N., & Pollock, V. E. (1996). Alcohol and aggression: A meta-analysis on the moderating effects of inhibitory cues, triggering events, and self-focused attention. *Psychological Bulletin, 120,* 60–82. (p. 514)

Izard, C. E. (1977). *Human emotions.* New York: Plenum Press. (pp. 354, 356)

Izard, C. E. (1994). Innate and universal facial expressions: Evidence from developmental and cross-cultural research. *Psychological Bulletin, 115,* 288–299. (p. 354)

Jackson, J. M., & Williams, K. D. (1988). Social loafing: A review and theoretical analysis. Unpublished manuscript, Fordham University. (p. 503)

Jackson, S. W. (1992). The listening healer in the history of psychological healing. *American Journal Psychiatry, 149,* 1623–1632. (p. 480)

Jacobs, B. L. (1987). How hallucinogenic drugs work. *American Scientist, 75,* 386–392. (p. 197)

Jacobs, B. L. (1994). Serotonin, motor activity, and depression-related disorders. *American Scientist, 82,* 456–463. (pp. 379, 445)

Jacobs, W. J., & Nadel, L. (1985). Stress-induced recovery of fears and phobias. *Psychological Bulletin, 92,* 512–531. (p. 436)

Jacobson, J. W., Mulick, J. A., & Schwartz, A. A. (1995). A history of facilitated communication: Science, pseudoscience, and antiscience. Science working group on facilitated communication. *American Psychologist, 50,* 750–765. (p. 502)

James, K. (1986). Priming and social categorizational factors: Impact on awareness of emergency situations. *Personality and Social Psychology Bulletin, 12,* 462–467. (p. 250)

James, W. (1890). *The principles of psychology* (Vol. 2). New York: Holt. (pp. 141, *239, 263, 359, 364, 496)*

Jameson, D. (1985). Opponent-colors theory in light of physiological findings. In D. Ottoson & S. Zeki (Eds.), *Central and peripheral mechanisms of color vision.* New York: Macmillan. (p. 137)

Jamison, K. R. (1993). *Touched with fire: Manic-depressive illness and the artistic temperament.* New York: Free Press. (p. 442)

Jamison, K. R. (1995, February). Manic-depressive illness and creativity. *Scientific American,* pp. 62–67. (p. 442)

Janis, I. L. (1982). *Groupthink: Psychological studies of policy decisions and fiascoes.* Boston: Houghton Mifflin. (p. 505)

Janis, I. L. (1986). Problems of international crisis management in the nuclear age. *Journal of Social Issues, 42*(2), 201–220. (p. 271)

Janis, I. L. (1989). *Crucial decisions: Leadership in policymaking and crisis management.* New York: Free Press. (p. 270)

Janoff-Bulman, R., Timko, C., & Carli, L. L. (1985). Cognitive biases in blaming the victim. *Journal of Experimental Social Psychology, 21,* 161–177. (p. 513)

Jarvik, L. F. (1975). Thoughts on the psychobiology of aging. *American Psychologist, 30,* 576–583. (p. 112)

Jeffrey, R. W., & Wing, R. R. (1983). Recidivism and self-cure of smoking and obesity: Data from population studies. *American Psychologist, 38,* 852. (p. 324)

Jemmott, J. B., III, & Magloire, K. (1988). Academic stress, social support, and secretory immunoglobulin A. *Journal of Personality and Social Psychology, 55,* 803–810. (p. 374)

Jenish, D. (1993, October 11). The king of porn. *Maclean's,* pp. 52–64. (p. 331)

Jenkins, J. G., & Dallenbach, K. M. (1924). Obliviscence during sleep and waking. *American Journal of Psychology, 35,* 605–612. (p. 254)

Jenkins, J. M., & Astington, J. W. (1996). Cognitive factors and family structure associated with theory of mind development in young children. *Developmental Psychology, 32,* 70–78. (p. 88)

Jensen, A. R. (1993). Psychometric *g* and achievement. In B. R. Gifford (Ed.), *Policy perspectives on educational testing.* Boston: Kluwer. (p. 293)

Jensen, J. P., & Bergin, A. E. (1988). Mental health values of professional therapists: A national interdisciplinary survey. *Professional Psychology: Research and Practice, 19,* 290–297. (p. 481)

Jepson, C., Krantz, D. H., & Nisbett, R. E. (1983). Inductive reasoning: Competence or skill. *The Behavioral and Brain Sciences, 3,* 494–501. (p. 543)

Jervis, R. (1985, April 2). Quoted in D. Goleman, Political forces come under new scrutiny of psychology. *The New York Times,* pp. C1, C4. (p. 275)

John, O. P. (1990). The "big five" factor taxonomy: Dimensions of personality in the natural language and in questionnaires. In L. A. Pervin (Ed.), *Handbook of personality: Theory and research.* New York: Guilford Press. (p. 402)

Johnson, C. B., Stockdale, M. S., & Saal, F. E. (1991). Persistence of men's misperceptions of friendly cues across a variety of interpersonal encounters. *Psychology of Women Quarterly, 15,* 463–475. (p. 332)

Johnson, D. (1990). Animal rights and human lives: Time for scientists to right the balance. *Psychological Science, 1,* 213–214. (p. 32)

Johnson, D., & Drenick, E. J. (1977). Therapeutic fasting in morbid obesity. Long-term follow-up. *Archives of Internal Medicine, 137,* 1381–1382. (p. 323)

Johnson, D. W., & Johnson, R. T. (1989). *Cooperation and competition: Theory and research.* Edina, MN: Interaction Book. (p. 531)

Johnson, D. W., & Johnson, R. T. (1994). Constructive conflict in the schools. *Journal of Social Issues, 50*(1), 117–137. (p. 531)

Johnson, E. J., & Tversky, A. (1983). Affect, generalization, and the perception of risk. *Journal of Personality and Social Psychology, 45,* 20–31. (p. 359)

Johnson, J. S., & Newport, E. L. (1991). Critical period effects on universal properties of language: The status of subjacency in the acquisition of a second language. *Cognition, 39*, 215–258. (pp. 280, 281)

Johnson, M. H. (1992). Imprinting and the development of face recognition: From chick to man. *Current Directions in Psychological Science, 1*, 52–55. (p. 92)

Johnston, L. D. (1997, December 18). Monitoring the future study of drug use. News and Information Services, University of Michigan. (pp. 196, 199)

Johnston, L. D., O'Malley, P., & Bachman, J. (1994, January 27). Drug use rises among American teen-agers. Ann Arbor: News and Information Services, University of Michigan. (p. 200)

Jones, E. E., Cumming, J. D., & Horowitz, M. J. (1988). Another look at the nonspecific hypothesis of therapeutic effectiveness. *Journal of Consulting and Clinical Psychology, 56*, 48–55. (p. 480)

Jones, M. C. (1924). A laboratory study of fear: The case of Peter. *Journal of Genetic Psychology, 31*, 308–315. (p. 467)

Jones, M. C. (1957). The later careers of boys who were early or late maturing. *Child Development, 28*, 113–128. (p. 101)

Jones, S. S., Collins, K., & Hong, H-W. (1991). An audience effect on smile production in 10-month-old infants. *Psychological Science, 2*, 45–49. (p. 354)

Jones, W. H., Carpenter, B. N., & Quintana, D. (1985). Personality and interpersonal predictors of loneliness in two cultures. *Journal of Personality and Social Psychology, 48*, 1503–1511. (p. 30)

Jorgenson, D. O., & Papciak, A. S. (1981). The effects of communication, resource feedback, and identifiability on behavior in a simulated commons. *Journal of Experimental Social Psychology, 17*, 373–385. (p. 531)

Jorm, A. F., Korten, A. E., & Henderson, A. S. (1987). The prevalence of dementia: A quantitative integration of the literature. *Acta Psychiatrica Scandinavica, 76*, 465–479. (p. 112)

Kagan, J. (1976). Emergent themes in human development. *American Scientist, 64*, 186–196. (p. 94)

Kagan, J. (1984). *The nature of the child*. New York: Basic Books. (p. 91)

Kagan, J. (1989). *Unstable ideas: Temperament, cognition, and self.* Cambridge, MA: Harvard University Press. (pp. 121, 397, 401)

Kagan, J. (1995). On attachment. *Harvard Review of Psychiatry, 3*, 104–106. (p. 92, 93)

Kagan, J., Snidman, N., & Arcus, D. M. (1992). Initial reactions to unfamiliarity. *Current Directions in Psychological Science, 1*, 171–174. (p. 93)

Kahneman, D. (1985, June). Quoted by K. McKean, Decisions, decisions. *Discover*, pp. 22–31. (p. 542)

Kahneman, D. (in press). Assessments of individual well-being: A bottom-up approach. In D. Kahneman, E. Diener, & N. Schwartz (eds.), *Understanding well-being: Scientific perspectives on enjoyment and suffering*. New York: Russell Sage Foundation. (p. 142)

Kahneman, D., Fredrickson, B. L., Schreiber, C. A., & Redelmeier, D. A. (1993). When more pain is preferred to less: Adding a better end. *Psychological Science, 4*, 401–405. (p. 142)

Kahneman, D., Knetsch, J. L., & Thaler, R. (1986). Fairness as a constraint on profit seeking: Entitlements in the market. *American Economic Review, 76*, 728–741. (p. 275)

Kahneman, D., & Tversky, A. (1972). Subjective probability: A judgment of representativeness. *Cognitive Psychology, 3*, 430–454. (p. 19)

Kail, R. (1991). Developmental change in speed of processing during childhood and adolescence. *Psychological Bulletin, 109*, 490–501. (p. 111)

Kalin, N. H. (1993, May). The neurobiology of fear. *Scientific American*, pp. 94–101. (p. 349)

Kamarck, T., & Jennings, J. R. (1991). Biobehavioral factors in sudden cardiac death. *Psychological Bulletin, 109*, 42–75. (p. 373)

Kaminer, W. (1992). *I'm dysfunctional, you're dysfunctional: The recovery movement and other self-help fashions.* Reading, MA: Addison-Wesley. (p. 192)

Kandel, D. B., & Raveis, V. H. (1989). Cessation of illicit drug use in young adulthood. *Archives of General Psychiatry, 46*, 109–116. (p. 201)

Kandel, E. R., & Schwartz, J. H. (1982). Molecular biology of learning: Modulation of transmitter release. *Science, 218*, 433–443. (p. 245)

Kanekar, S., & Nazareth, A. (1988). Attributed rape victim's fault as a function of her attractiveness, physical hurt, and emotional disturbance. *Social Behaviour, 3*, 37–40. (p. 332)

Kann, L., Warren, W., Collins, J. L., Ross, J., Collins, B., Kolbe, L. J. (1993). Results from the national school-based 1991 Youth Risk Behavior Survey and progress toward achieving related health objectives for the nation. U.S. Department of Health and Human Services, *Public Health Reports, 108* (Supplement 1), 47–55. (p. 201)

Kapitza, S. (1991, August). Antiscience trends in the U.S.S.R. *Scientific American*, pp. 32–38. (p. 164)

Kaplan, H. I., & Saddock, B. J. (Eds.). (1989). *Comprehensive textbook of psychiatry, V.* Baltimore, MD: Williams and Wilkins. (p. 484)

Kaprio, J., Koskenvuo, M., & Rita, H. (1987). Mortality after bereavement: A prospective study of 95,647 widowed persons. *American Journal of Public Health, 77*, 283–287. (p. 370)

Kapur, S., & Mann, J. J. (1993). Antidepressant action and the neurobiologic effects of ECT: Human studies. In C. E. Coffey (Ed.), *The clinical science of electroconvulsive therapy*. Washington, DC: American Psychiatric Press. (p. 486)

Karacan, I., Aslan, C., & Hirshkowitz, M. (1983). Erectile mechanisms in man. *Science, 220*, 1080–1082. (p. 175)

Karacan, I., Goodenough, D. R., Shapiro, A., & Starker, S. (1966). Erection cycle during sleep in relation to dream anxiety. *Archives of General Psychiatry, 15*, 183–189. (p. 175)

Karau, S. J., & Williams, K. D. (1993). Social loafing: A meta-analytic review and theoretical integration. *Journal of Personality and Social Psychology, 65*, 681–706. (p. 503)

Kark, J. D., Shemi, G., Friedlander, Y., Martin, O., Manor, O., & Blondheim, S. H. (1996). Does religious observance promote health? Mortality in secular vs. religious kibbutzim in Israel. *American Journal of Public Health, 86*, 341–346. (p. 383)

Karni, A., & Sagi, D. (1994). Dependence on REM sleep of overnight improvement of perceptual skills. *Science, 265*, 679–682. (p. 182)

Karno, M., Golding, J. M., Sorenson, S. B., & Burnam, A. (1988). The epidemiology of obsessive-compulsive disorder in five US communities. *Archives of General Psychiatry, 45*, 1094–1099. (p. 433)

Kashima, Y., Siegal, M., Tanaka, K., & Kashima, E. S. (1992). Do people believe behaviours are consistent with attitudes? Towards a cultural psychology of attribution processes. *British Journal of Social Psychology, 31*, 111–124. (p. 412)

Kasser, T., & Ryan, R. M. (1996). Further examining the American dream: Differential correlates of intrinsic and extrinsic goals. *Personality and Social Psychology Bulletin, 22,* 280–287. (p. 363)

Katon, W., & Sullivan, M. D. (1990). Depression and chronic medical illness. *Journal of Clinical Psychiatry, 51,* 3–11. (p. 373)

Kaufman, A. S., Reynolds, C. R., & McLean, J. E. (1989). Age and WAIS-R intelligence in a national sample of adults in the 20- to 74-year age range: A cross-sectional analysis with educational level controlled. *Intelligence, 13,* 235–253. (p. 114)

Kaufman, J., & Zigler, E. (1987). Do abused children become abusive parents? *American Journal of Orthopsychiatry, 57,* 186–192. (p. 94)

Kaufman, L., & Rock, I. (1962). The moon illusion I. *Science, 136,* 953–961. (p. 152)

Kaye, K. L., & Bower, T. G. R. (1994). Learning and intermodal transfer of information in newborns. *Psychological Science, 5,* 286–288. (p. 87)

Kaylor, J. A., King, D. W., & King, L. A. (1987). Psychological effects of military service in Vietnam: A meta-analysis. *Psychological Bulletin, 102,* 257–271. (p. 435)

Keesey, R. E., & Corbett, S. W. (1983). Metabolic defense of the body weight set-point. In A. J. Stunkard & E. Stellar (Eds.), *Eating and its disorders.* New York: Raven Press. (p. 317)

Kellerman, J., Lewis, J., & Laird, J. D. (1989). Looking and loving: The effects of mutual gaze on feelings of romantic love. *Journal of Research in Personality, 23,* 145–161. (p. 352)

Kellermann, A. L., Rivara, F. P., Rushforth, N. B., Banton, H. G., Feay, D. T., Francisco, J. T., Locci, A. B., Prodzinski, J., Hackman, B. B., & Somes, G. (1993). Gun ownership as a risk factor for homicide in the home. *New England Journal of medicine, 329,* 1084–1091. (p. 513)

Kelling, S. T., & Halpern, B. P. (1983). Taste flashes: Reaction times, intensity, and quality. *Science, 219,* 412–414. (p. 143)

Kelly, I. W. (1997). Modern astrology: A critique. *Psychological Reports, 81,* 931–962. (p. 418)

Kelly, I. W., Laverty, W. H., & Saklofske, D. H. (1990). Geophysical variables and behavior: LXIV. An empirical investigation of the relationship between worldwide automobile traffic disasters and lunar cycles: No relationship. *Psychological Reports, 67,* 987–994. (p. 455)

Kelly, T. A. (1990). The role of values in psychotherapy: A critical review of process and outcome effects. *Clinical Psychology Review, 10,* 171–186. (p. 481)

Kempe, R. S., & Kempe, C. C. (1978). *Child abuse.* Cambridge, MA: Harvard University Press. (p. 94)

Kendall-Tackett, K. A., Williams, L. M., & Finkelhor, D. (1993). Impact of sexual abuse on children: A review and synthesis of recent empirical studies. *Psychological Bulletin, 113,* 164–180. (pp. 94, 260)

Kendler, K. S., Neale, M. C., Kessler, R. C., Heath, A. C., & Eaves, L. J. (1992). Generalized anxiety disorder in women: A population-based twin study. *Archives of General Psychiatry, 49,* 267–272. (p. 437)

Kendler, K. S., Neale, M., Kessler, R., Heath, A., & Eaves, L. (1993). A twin study of recent life events and difficulties. *Archives of General Psychiatry, 50,* 789–796. (p. 447)

Kennedy, S., & Over, R. (1990). Psychophysiological assessment of male sexual arousal following spinal cord injury. *Archives of Sexual Behavior, 19,* 15–27. (p. 47)

Kenrick, D. T., & Funder, D. C. (1988). Profiting from controversy: Lessons from the person-situation debate. *American Psychologist, 43,* 23–34. (p. 405)

Kenrick, D. T., & Gutierres, S. E. (1980). Contrast effects and judgments of physical attractiveness: When beauty becomes a social problem. *Journal of Personality and Social Psychology, 38,* 131–140. (p. 330)

Kenrick, D. T., Gutierres, S. E., & Goldberg, L. L. (1989). Influence of popular erotica on judgments of strangers and mates. *Journal of Experimental Social Psychology, 25,* 159–167. (p. 330)

Kenrick, D. T., & Trost, M. R. (1987). A biosocial theory of heterosexual relationships. In K. Kelly (Ed.), *Females, males, and sexuality.* Albany: State University of New York Press. (p. 332)

Kerr, N. L., & Bruun, S. E. (1983). Dispensability of member effort and group motivation losses: Free-rider effects. *Journal of Personality and Social Psychology, 44,* 78–94. (p. 504)

Kessler, M., & Albee, G. (1975). Primary prevention. *Annual Review of Psychology, 26,* 557–591. (p. 487)

Kessler, R. C., Foster, C., Joseph, J., Ostrow, D., Wortman, C., Phair, J., & Chmiel, J. (1991). Stressful life events and symptom onset in HIV infection. *American Journal of Psychiatry, 148,* 733–738. (p. 376)

Kessler, R. C., McGonagle, K. A., Zhao, S., Nelson, C. B., Hughes, M., Eshleman, S., Wittchen, H-U., Kendler, K. S. (1994). Lifetime and 12-month prevalence of *DSM-III-R* psychiatric disorders in the United States. *Archives of General Psychiatry, 51,* 8–19. (p. 457)

Kestenbaum, R. (1992). Feeling happy versus feeling good: The processing of discrete and global categories of emotional expressions by children and adults. *Developmental Psychology, 28,* 1132–1142. (p. 352)

Keynes, M. (1980, December 20/27). Handel's illnesses. *The Lancet,* pp. 1354–1355. (p. 442)

Keys, A., Brozek, J., Henschel, A., Mickelsen, O., & Taylor, H. L. (1950). *The biology of human starvation.* Minneapolis: University of Minnesota Press. (p. 315)

Kiecolt-Glaser, J. K., Malarkey, W. B., Chee, M., Newton, T., Cacioppo, J. T., Mao, H-Y., & Glaser, R. (1993). Negative behavior during marital conflict is associated with immunological down-regulation. *Psychosomatic Medicine, 55,* 395–409. (p. 374)

Kihlstrom, J. F. (1985). Hypnosis. *Annual Review of Psychology, 36,* 385–418. (pp. 184, 188)

Kihlstrom, J. F. (1990). Awareness, the psychological unconscious, and the self. Address to the American Psychological Association convention. (pp. 255, 398)

Kihlstrom, J. F. (1990). The psychological unconscious. In L. A. Pervin (Ed.), *Handbook of personality: Theory and research.* New York: Guilford Press. (pp. 255, 398)

Kihlstrom, J. F. (1994). The social construction of memory. Paper presented to the American Psychological Society convention. (p. 257)

Kihlstrom, J. F. (1996). Quoted in *Frequently asked questions about the False Memory Syndrome Foundation* (available at http://www.csicop.org/~fitz/fmsf/faq.html (accessed September 13, 1996). (p. 260)

Kihlstrom, J. F. (1997, 11 November). Freud as giant pioneer on whose shoulders we should stand. Social psychology listserv posting (spsp@stolaf.edu). (p. 397)

Kihlstrom, J. F., & McConkey, K. M. (1990). William James and hypnosis: A centennial reflection. *Psychological Science, 1,* 174–177. (p. 190)

Kim, K. H. S., Relkin, N. R., Lee, K-M, & Hirsch, J. (1997). Distinct cortical areas associated with native and second languages. *Nature, 388*, 171–174. (p. 51)

Kim, Y., & Lee, S-H. (1994). The Confucian model of morality, justice, selfhood and society: Implications for modern society. In *The universal and particular natures of Confucianism*, The Academcy of Korean Studies. (p. 412)

Kimball, M. M. (1989). A new perspective on women's math achievement. *Psychological Bulletin, 105*, 198–214. (p. 304)

Kimble, G. A. (1981). *Biological and cognitive constraints on learning.* In L. T. Benjamin, Jr. (Ed.), *The G. Stanley Hall Lecture Series* (Vol. 1). Washington, DC: American Psychological Association. (p. 212, 215)

Kimzey, S. L. (1975). The effects of extended spaceflight on hematologic and immunologic systems. *Journal of the American Medical Women's Association, 30*(5), 218–232. (p. 374)

Kimzey, S. L., Johnson, P. C., Ritzman, S. E., & Mengel, C. E. (1976, April). Hematology and immunology studies: The second manned Skylab mission. *Aviation, Space, and Environmental Medicine*, pp. 383–390. (p. 374)

King, D. W., & King, L. A. (1991). Validity issues in research on Vietnam veteran adjustment. *Psychological Bulletin, 109*, 107–124. (p. 435)

King, N. J., & Montgomery, R. B. (1980). Biofeedback-induced control of human peripheral temperature: A critical review of the literature. *Psychological Bulletin, 88*, 738–752. (p. 380)

King, P. (1991, March 18). Bawl players. *Sports Illustrated*, pp. 14–17. (p. 362)

Kinnier, R. T., & Metha, A. T. (1989). Regrets and priorities at three stages of life. *Counseling and Values, 33*, 182–193. (p. 99)

Kinsey, A. C., Pomeroy, W., & Martin, C. (1948). *Sexual behavior in the human male.* Philadelphia: Saunders. (p. 326)

Kinsey, A. C., Pomeroy, W., Martin, C., & Gebhard, P. (1953). *Sexual behavior in the human female.* Philadelphia: Saunders. (p. 326)

Kinzl, J. F., Traweger, C., Guenther, V., & Biebl, W. (1994). Family background and sexual abuse associated with eating disorders. *American Journal of Psychiatry, 151*, 1127–1131. (p. 319)

Kirk, S. A., & Gallagher, J. J. (1989). *Educating exceptional children.* Boston: Houghton Mifflin. (p. 140)

Kirkpatrick, L. A. (1994). The role of attachment in religious belief and behavior. *Advances in Personal Relationships, 5*, 239–265. (p. 92)

Kirsch, I., & Lynn, S. J. (1995). The altered state of hypnosis. *American Psychologist, 50*, 846–858. (p. 190)

Kisor, H. (1990). *What's that pig outdoors.* New York: Hill and Wang. (p. 140)

Kitayama, S., & Markus, H. R. (in press). Construal of the self as cultural frame: Implications for internationalizing psychology. In J. D'Arms, R. G. Hastie, S. E. Hoelscher, & H. K. Jacobson (Eds.), *Becoming more international and global: Challenges for American higher education.* Ann Arbor: University of Michigan Press. (p. 412)

Kite, M. E., & Johnson, B. T. (1988). Attitudes toward older and younger adults: A meta-analysis. *Psychology and Aging, 3*, 233–244. (p. 112)

Kite, M. E., & Whitley, B. E., Jr. (1996). Sex differences in attitudes toward homosexual persons, behaviors, and civil rights: A meta-analysis. *Personality and Social Psychology Bulletin, 22*, 336–353. (p. 336)

Klasen, S. (1994). "Missing women" reconsidered. *World Development, 22*, 1061–1071. (p. 511)

Klasen, S. (1994). "Missing women" reconsidered. *World Development, 22.* (p. 511)

Klayman, J., & Ha, Y-W. (1987). Confirmation, disconfirmation, and information in hypothesis testing. *Psychological Review, 94*, 211–228. (p. 270)

Kleinke, C. L. (1986). Gaze and eye contact: A research review. *Psychological Bulletin, 100*, 78–100. (p. 352)

Kleinmuntz, B., & Szucko, J. J. (1984). A field study of the fallibility of polygraph lie detection. *Nature, 308*, 449–450. (p. 350)

Kleitman, N. (1960, November). Patterns of dreaming. *Scientific American*, pp. 82–88. (p. 174)

Klemm, W. R. (1990). Historical and introductory perspectives on brainstem-mediated behaviors. In W. R. Klemm & R. P. Vertes (Eds.), *Brainstem mechanisms of behavior.* New York: Wiley. (p. 49)

Kline, D., & Schieber, F. (1985). Vision and aging. In J. E. Birren & K. W. Schaie (Eds.), *Handbook of the psychology of aging.* New York: Van Nostrand Reinhold. (p. 111)

Kline, N. S. (1974). *From sad to glad.* New York: Ballantine Books. (p. 448)

Klineberg, O. (1938). Emotional expression in Chinese literature. *Journal of Abnormal and Social Psychology, 33*, 517–520. (p. 353)

Klineberg, O. (1984). Public opinion and nuclear war. *American Psychologist, 39*, 1245–1253. (p. 531)

Kluft, R. P. (1991). Multiple personality disorder. In A. Tasman & S. M. Goldfinger (Eds.), *Review of Psychiatry*, vol. 10. Washington, DC: American Psychiatric Press. (p. 439)

Klüver, H., & Bucy, P. C. (1939). Preliminary analysis of functions of the temporal lobes in monkeys. *Archives of Neurology and Psychiatry, 42*, 979–1000. (p. 53)

Koenig, H. G. (1997). *Is religion good for your health? The effects of religion on physical and mental health.* Binghamton, NY: Haworth Press. (p. 383)

Kohlberg, L. (1981). *The philosophy of moral development: Essays on moral development* (Vol. I). San Francisco: Harper & Row. (p. 102)

Kohlberg, L. (1984). *The psychology of moral development: Essays on moral development* (Vol. II). San Francisco: Harper & Row. (p. 102)

Kohler, I. (1962, May). Experiments with goggles. *Scientific American*, pp. 62–72. (p. 156)

Köhler, W. (1925; reprinted 1957). *The mentality of apes.* London: Pelican. (p. 269)

Kohn, A. (1987, October). It's hard to get left out of a pair. *Psychology Today*, pp. 53–57. (p. 531)

Kohn, P. M., & Macdonald, J. E. (1992). The survey of recent life experiences: A decontaminated hassles scale for adults. *Journal of Behavioral Medicine, 15*, 221–236. (p. 371)

Kolata, G. (1986). Youth suicide: New research focuses on a growing social problem. *Science, 233*, 839–841. (p. 444)

Kolata, G. (1987). Metabolic catch-22 of exercise regimens. *Science, 236*, 146–147. (p. 325)

Kolata, G. (1996, May 21). Could it be? Weather has nothing to do with your arthritis pain? *New York Times*, p. C13. (p. 18)

Kolata, G. (1996, December 10). With major math proof, brute computers show flash of reasoning power. *New York Times*, p. C1. (p. 276)

Kolb, B. (1989). Brain development, plasticity, and behavior. *American Psychologist*, *44*, 1203–1212. (p. 62)

Kolers, P. A. (1975). Specificity of operations in sentence recognition. *Cognitive Psychology*, *7*, 289–306. (p. 234)

Koltz, C. (1983, December). Scapegoating. *Psychology Today*, pp. 68–69. (p. 512)

Konishi, M. (1993, April). Listening with two ears. *Scientific American*, pp. 66–73. (p. 141)

Koslowsky, M., & Babkoff, H. (1992). Meta-analysis of the relationship between total sleep deprivation and performance. *Chronobiology International*, *9*, 132–136. (p. 178)

Koss, M. P., Heise, L., & Russo, N. P. (1994). The global health burden of rape. *Psychology of Women Quarterly*, *18*, 509–537. (p. 518)

Kotkin, M., Daviet, C., & Gurin, J. (1996). The *Consumer Reports* mental health survey. *American Psychologist*, *51*, 1080–1082. (p. 476)

Kotva, H. J., & Schneider, H. G. (1990). Those "talks"—general and sexual communication between mothers and daughters. *Journal of Social Behavior and Personality*, *5*, 603–613. (p. 108)

Kraft, C. (1978). A psychophysical approach to air safety: Simulator studies of visual illusions in night approaches. In H. L. Pick, H. W. Leibowitz, J. E. Singer, A. Steinschneider, & H. W. Stevenson (Eds.), *Psychology: From research to practice.* New York: Plenum Press. (p. 159)

Kraft, R. (1996, December 2, and 1994, July 20). Personal correspondence (from Otterbein College) regarding Holocaust memories. (p. 398)

Kraus, S. J. (1991). Attitudes and the prediction of behavior. Doctoral dissertation, Harvard University. (p. 493)

Kraut, R. E., & Johnston, R. E. (1979). Social and emotional messages of smiling: An ethological approach. *Journal of Personality and Social Psychology*, *37*, 1539–1553. (p. 354)

Krebs, D. L., & Van Hesteren, F. (1994). The development of altruism: Toward an integrative model. *Developmental Review*, *14*, 103–158. (p. 103)

Kristof, N. (1993, July 22). China faces huge surplus of males as scans hold key to missing girls. *The Guardian* (England), p. 22. (p. 511)

Krosnick, J. A., & Alwin, D. F. (1989). Aging and susceptibility to attitude change. *Journal of Personality and Social Psychology*, *57*, 416–425. (p. 121)

Krosnick, J. A., Betz, A. L., Jussim, L. J., & Lynn, A. R. (1992). Subliminal conditioning of attitudes. *Personality and Social Psychology Bulletin*, *18*, 152–162. (p. 127)

Krupa, D. J., Thompson, J. K., & Thompson, R. F. (1993). Localization of a memory trace in the mammalian brain. *Science*, *260*, 989–991. (p. 248)

Kuhl, P. K., & Meltzoff, A. N. (1982). The bimodal perception of speech in infancy. *Science*, *218*, 1138–1141. (p. 278)

Kurtz, P. (1983, Spring). Stars, planets, and people. *The Skeptical Inquirer*, pp. 65–68. (p. 418)

Kutas, M. (1990). Event-related brain potential (ERP) studies of cognition during sleep: Is it more than a dream? In R. R. Bootzin, J. F. Kihlstrom, & D. Schacter (Eds.), *Sleep and cognition*. Washington, DC: American Psychological Association. (p. 175)

Labouvie-Vief, G., & Schell, D. A. (1982). Learning and memory in later life. In B. B. Wolman (Ed.), *Handbook of developmental psychology*. Englewood Cliffs, NJ: Prentice-Hall. (p. 113)

Lacayo, R. (1995, June 12). Violent reaction. *Time*, pp. 25–39. (p. 15)

Ladd, G. T. (1887). *Elements of physiological psychology.* New York: Scribner's. (p. 169)

Laird, J. D. (1974). Self-attribution of emotion: The effects of expressive behavior on the quality of emotional experience. *Journal of Personality and Social Psychology*, *29*, 475–486. (p. 355)

Laird, J. D. (1984). The real role of facial response in the experience of emotion: A reply to Tourangeau and Ellsworth, and others. *Journal of Personality and Social Psychology*, *47*, 909–917. (p. 355)

Laird, J. D., Cuniff, M., Sheehan, K., Shulman, D., & Strum, G. (1989). Emotion specific effects of facial expressions on memory for life events. *Journal of Social Behavior and Personality*, *4*, 87–98. (p. 355)

Lambert, W. E. (1992). Challenging established views on social issues: The power and limitations of research. *American Psychologist*, *47*, 533–542. (p. 287)

Lambert, W. E., Genesee, F., Holobow, N., & Chartrand, L. (1993). Bilingual education for majority English-speaking children. *European Journal of Psychology of Education*, *8*, 3–22. (p. 287)

Lancioni, G. (1980). Infant operant conditioning and its implications for early intervention. *Psychological Bulletin*, *88*, 516–534. (p. 82)

Landauer, T. K. (1986). How much do people remember? Some estimates of the quantity of learned information in long-term memory. *Cognitive Science*, *10*, 477–493. (p. 243)

Lander, E., & Kruglyak, L. (1995). Genetic dissection of complex traits: Guidelines for interpreting and reporting linkage studies. *Nature Genetics*, *11*, 241–247. (p. 454)

Landfield, P., Cadwallader, L. B., & Vinsant, S. (1988). Quantitative changes in hippocampal structure following long-term exposure to Delta–9–tetrahydrocannabinol: Possible mediation by glucocorticoid systems. *Brain Research*, Vol. 443, 47–62. (p. 198)

Landry, D. W. (1997, February). Immunotherapy for cocaine addiction. *Scientific American*, pp. 42–45. (p. 197)

Langer, E. J. (1983). *The psychology of control.* Beverly Hills, CA: Sage. (p. 417)

Langer, E. J., & Abelson, R. P. (1974). A patient by any other name. . . : Clinician group differences in labeling bias. *Journal of Consulting and Clinical Psychology*, *42*, 4–9. (p. 430)

Langer, E. J., & Imber, L. (1980). The role of mindlessness in the perception of deviance. *Journal of Personality and Social Psychology*, *39*, 360–367. (p. 430)

Langlois, J. H., Roggman, L. A., Casey, R. J., Ritter, J. M., Rieser-Danner, L. A., & Jenkins, V. Y. (1987). Infant preferences for attractive faces: Rudiments of a stereotype? *Developmental Psychology*, *23*, 363–369. (p. 524)

Larsen, R. J., Kasimatis, M., & Frey, K. (1992). Facilitating the furrowed brow: An unobtrusive test of the facial feedback hypothesis applied to unpleasant affect. *Cognition and Emotion*, *6*, 321–338. (p. 355)

Larzelere, R. E. (1994). Corporal punishment by parents. In M. A. Mason & E. Gambrill (eds.), *Debating children's lives: Current controversies on children and adolescents*. Thousand Oaks, CA: Sage. (p. 220)

Larzelere, R. E. (1996). A review of the outcomes of parental use of nonabusive or customary physical punishment. *Pediatrics, 78,* 824–828. (p. 220)

Lashley, K. S. (1950). In search of the engram. In *Symposium of the Society for Experimental Biology* (Vol. 4). New York: Cambridge University Press. (p. 245)

Lassiter, G. D., & Irvine, A. A. (1986). Video-taped confessions: The impact of camera point of view on judgments of coercion. *Journal of Personality and Social Psychology, 16,* 268–276. (p. 492)

Latané, B. (1981). The psychology of social impact. *American Psychologist, 36,* 343–356. (p. 503)

Latané, B., & Dabbs, J. M., Jr. (1975). Sex, group size and helping in three cities. *Sociometry, 38,* 180–194. (p. 529)

Lau, S., & Gruen, G. E. (1992). The social stigma of loneliness: Effect of target person's and perceiver's sex. *Personality and Social Psychology Bulletin, 18,* 182–189. (p. 448)

Laumann, E. O., Gagnon, J. H., Michael, R. T., & Michaels, S. (1994). *The social organization of sexuality: Sexual practices in the United States.* Chicago: University of Chicago Press. (pp. 327, 331, 333, 334, 518)

Laurence, J-R., & Perry, C. (1988). *Hypnosis, will and memory: A psycho-legal history.* New York: Guilford. (p. 185)

Layton, B. D., & Turnbull, B. (1975). Belief, evaluation, and performance on an ESP task. *Journal of Experimental Social Psychology, 11,* 166–179. (p. 161)

Lazarus, R. S. (1984). On the primacy of cognition. *American Psychologist, 39,* 124–129. (p. 367)

Lazarus, R. S. (1990). Theory-based stress measurement. *Psychological Inquiry, 1,* 3–13. (p. 371)

Lazarus, R. S. (1991). Progress on a cognitive-motivational-relational theory of emotion. *American Psychologist, 46,* 352–367. (p. 367)

Leach, P. (1993). Should parents hit their children? *The Psychologist: Bulletin of the British Psychological Society, 6,* 216–220. (p. 221)

Leach, P. (1994). *Children first.* New York: Knopf. (p. 221)

Leary, M. R., Schreindorfer, L. S., & Haupt, A. L. (1995). The role of low self-esteem in emotional and behavioral problems: Why is low self-esteem dysfunctional? *Journal of Social and Clinical Psychology, 14,* 297–314. (p. 409)

Lebow, J. (1982). Consumer satisfaction with mental health treatment. *Psychological Bulletin, 91,* 244–259. (p. 476)

LeDoux, J. (1994, June). Emotion, memory and the brain. *Scientific American,* pp. 50–57. (p. 367)

LeDoux, J. (1996). *The emotional brain: The mysterious underpinnings of emotionsl life.* New York: Simon & Schuster. (p. 416)

Lefcourt, H. M. (1982). *Locus of control: Current trends in theory and research.* Hillsdale, NJ: Erlbaum. (p. 417)

Lehman, D. R., Lempert, R. O., & Nisbett, R. E. (1988). The effects of graduate training on reasoning: Formal discipline and thinking about everyday-life events. *American Psychologist, 43,* 431–442. (p. 28)

Lehman, D. R., & Nisbett, R. E. (1985). Effects of higher education on inductive reasoning. Unpublished manuscript, University of Michigan. (p. 419)

Lehman, D. R., Wortman, C. B., & Williams, A. F. (1987). Long-term effects of losing a spouse or child in a motor vehicle crash. *Journal of Personality and Social Psychology, 52,* 218–231. (p. 119)

Leibowitz, H. W. (1985). Grade crossing accidents and human factors engineering. *American Scientist, 73,* 558–562. (pp. 150–151)

Leigh, B. C. (1989). In search of the seven dwarves: Issues of measurement and meaning in alcohol expectancy research. *Psychological Bulletin, 105,* 361–373. (p. 194)

Leigh, B. C., Temple, M. T., & Trocki, K. F. (1993). The sexual behavior of US adults: Results from a national survey. *American Journal of Public Health, 83,* 1400–1408. (p. 327)

Leitenberg, H., & Henning, K. (1995). Sexual fantasy. *Psychological Bulletin, 117,* 469–496. (pp. 171, *329, 330)*

Lenzenweger, M. F., Dworkin, R. H., & Wethington, E. (1989). Models of positive and negative symptoms in schizophrenia: An empirical evaluation of latent structures. *Journal of Abnormal Psychology, 98,* 62–70. (p. 483)

Leo, J. (1991, August 19). No-fault syntax. *U.S. News and World Report,* p. 17. (p. 192)

Lerner, M. J. (1980). *The belief in a just world: A fundamental delusion.* New York: Plenum Press. (p. 513)

Leshner, A. I. (1992). *Outcasts on main street: Report of the federal task force on homelessness and severe mental illness.* Washington, DC: Interagency Council on the Homeless, Office of the Programs for the Homeless Mentally Ill, National Institute of Mental Health. (p. 483)

LeVay, S. (1991). A difference in hypothalamic structure between heterosexual and homosexual men. *Science, 253,* 1034–1037. (p. 334)

Levenson, R. W. (1992). Autonomic nervous system differences among emotions. *Psychological Science, 3,* 23–27. (p. 349)

Levenson, R. W., Ekman, P., Heider, K., & Friesen, W. V. (1991). Emotion and autonomic nervous system activity in an Indonesian culture. Unpublished manuscript, University of California, Berkeley. (p. 398)

Levenson, R. W., Ekman, P., Heider, K., & Friesen, W. V. (1992). Emotion and autonomic nervous system activity in the Minangkabau of West Sumatra. *Journal of Personality and Social Psychology, 62,* 972–988. (p. 350)

Lever, J. (1978). Sex differences in the complexity of children's play and games. *American Sociological Review, 43,* 471–483. (p. 105)

Levin, I. P., & Gaeth, G. J. (1988). How consumers are affected by the framing of attribute information before and after consuming the product. *Journal of Consumer Research, 15,* 374–378. (p. 274)

Levin, I. P., Schnittjer, S. K., & Thee, S. L. (1988). Information framing effects in social and personal decisions. *Journal of Experimental Social Psychology, 24,* 520–529. (pp. 274–275)

Levin, J. (1994). Religion and health: Is there an association, is it valid, and is it causal? *Social Science and Medicine, 38,* 1475–1482. (p. 383)

Levin, J. (1996). How religion influences morbidity and health: Reflections on natural history, salutogenesis, and host resistance. *Social Science and Medicine, 43,* 849–864. (p. 383)

Levine, A. (1990, May 7). America's youthful bigots. *U.S. News and World Report,* pp. 59–60. (p. 507)

Levine, I. S., & Rog, D. J. (1990). Mental health services for homeless mentally ill persons: Federal initiatives and current service trends. *American Psychologist, 45,* 963–968. (p. 483)

Levine, R., Sato, S., Hashimoto, T., & Verma, J. (1995). Love and marriage in eleven cultures. *Journal of Cross-Cultural Psychology, 26,* 554–571. (p. 527)

Levitt, E. E. (1986). Coercion, voluntariness, compliance and resistance: The essence of hypnosis twenty-seven years after Orne. Invited address to the American Psychological Association convention. (p. 186)

Levy, B., & Langer, E. (1992). Avoidance of the memory loss stereotype: Enhanced memory among the elderly deaf. American Psychological Association convention, Washington, DC. (p. 169)

Levy, J. (1985, May). Right brain, left brain: Fact and fiction. *Psychology Today*, pp. 38–44. (p. 66)

Lewicki, P., Hill, T., & Czyzewska, M. (1992). Nonconscious acquisition of information. *American Psychologist*, *47*, 796–801. (p. 398)

Lewinsohn, P. M., Hoberman, H., Teri, L., & Hautziner, M. (1985). An integrative theory of depression. In S. Reiss & R. Bootzin (Eds.), *Theoretical issues in behavior therapy*. Orlando, FL: Academic Press. (pp. 442, *448)*

Lewinsohn, P. M., & Rosenbaum, M. (1987). Recall of parental behavior by acute depressives, remitted depressives, and nondepressives. *Journal of Personality and Social Psychology*, *52*, 611–619. (p. 252)

Lewis, D. O., Pincus, J. H., Bard, B., Richardson, E., Prichep, L. S., Feldman, M., & Yeager, C. (1988). Neuropsychiatric, psychoeducational, and family characteristics of 14 juveniles condemned to death in the United States. *American Journal of Psychiatry*, *145*, 584–589. (p. 94)

Lewis, D. O., Pincus, J. H., Feldman, M., Jackson, L., & Bard, B. (1986). Psychiatric, neurological, and psychoeducational characteristics of 15 death row inmates in the United States. *American Journal of Psychiatry*, *143*, 838–845. (p. 514)

Lewis, M. (1992). Commentary. *Human Development*, *35*, 44–51. (p. 252)

Lewontin, R. (1976). Race and intelligence. In N. J. Block & G. Dworkin (Eds.), *The IQ controversy: Critical readings*. New York: Pantheon. (p. 303)

Lewontin, R. (1982). *Human diversity*. New York: Scientific American Library. (pp. 31, *303)*

Licata, A., Taylor, S., Berman, M., & Cranston, J. (1993). Effects of cocaine on human aggression. *Pharmacology Biochemistry and Behavior*, *45*, 549–552. (p. 197)

Lichtman, S. W., Pisarska, K., Berman, E. R., Pestone, M., Dowling, H., Offenbacher, E., Weisel, H., Heshka, S., Matthews, D. E., & Heymsfield, S. B. (1992). Discrepancy between self-reported and actual caloric intake and exercise in obese subjects. *New England Journal of Medicine*, *327*, 1893–1898. (p. 322)

Lifton, R. J. (1986). *The Nazi doctors*. New York: Basic Books. (p. 194)

Light, K. C., Koepke, J. P., Obrist, P. A., & Willis, P. W., Jr. (1983). Psychological stress induces sodium and fluid retention in men at high risk for hypertension. *Science*, *220*, 429–431. (p. 373)

Linder, D. (1982). Social trap analogs: The tragedy of the commons in the laboratory. In V. J. Derlega & J. Grzelak (Eds.), *Cooperative and helping behavior: Theories and research*. New York: Academic Press. (p. 521)

Lindsay, D. S. (1995). Psychotherapy and memories of childhood sexual abuse. Invited address to the American Psychological Assocation convention. (p. 261)

Lindskold, S. (1978). Trust development, the GRIT proposal, and the effects of conciliatory acts on conflict and cooperation. *Psychological Bulletin*, *85*, 772–793. (p. 532)

Lindskold, S. (1986). GRIT: Reducing distrust through carefully introduced conciliation. In S. Worchel & W. G. Austin (Eds.), *Psychology of intergroup relations* (2nd ed.). Chicago: Nelson-Hall. (p. 532)

Lindskold, S., & Han, G. (1988). GRIT as a foundation for integrative bargaining. *Personality and Social Psychology Bulletin*, *14*, 335–345. (p. 532)

Lindskold, S., Han, G., & Betz, B. (1986). Repeated persuasion in interpersonal conflict. *Journal of Personality and Social Psychology*, *51*, 1183–1188. (p. 532)

Lindskold, S., Walters, P. S., & Koutsourais, H. (1983). Cooperators, competitors, and response to GRIT. *Journal of Conflict Resolution*, *27*, 521–532. (p. 532)

Linn, M. C., & Hyde, J. S. (1991). Trends in cognitive and psychosocial gender differences. In R. M. Lerner, A. C. Petersen, & J. Brooks-Gunn (Eds.), *The encyclopedia of adolescence*. New York: Garland Publishing. (p. 306)

Linville, P. W., Fischer, G. W., & Fischhoff, B. (1992). AIDS risk perceptions and decision biases. In J. B. Pryor & G. D. Reeder (Eds.), *The social psychology of HIV infection*. Hillsdale, NJ: Erlbaum. (p. 275)

Lippman, J. (1992, October 25). Global village is characterized by a television in every home. *Grand Rapids Press* (*Los Angeles Times Syndicate*), p. F9. (p. 517)

Lipsey, M. W., & Wilson, D. B. (1993). The efficacy of psychological, educational, and behavioral treatment: Confirmation from meta-analyses. *American Psychologist*, *48*, 1181–1209. (p. 478)

Livingstone, M., & Hubel, D. (1988). Segregation of form, color, movement, and depth: Anatomy, physiology, and perception. *Science*, *240*, 740–749. (p. 134)

Locke, E. A., & Latham, G. P. (1990). Work motivation and satisfaction: Light at the end of the tunnel. *Psychological Science*, *1*, 240–246. (p. 342)

Loehlin, J. C., & Nichols, R. C. (1976). *Heredity, environment, and personality*. Austin: University of Texas Press. (pp. 70, 299)

Loewenstein, G., & Furstenberg, F. (1991). Is teenage sexual behavior rational? *Journal of Applied Social Psychology*, *21*, 957–986. (p. 219)

Loftus, E. (1995, March/April). Remembering dangerously. *Skeptical Inquirer*, pp. 20–29. (p. 260, 397)

Loftus, E., & Ketcham, K. (1994). *The myth of repressed memory*. New York: St. Martin's Press. (pp. 245, 258, 261, 262)

Loftus, E. F. (1979). The malleability of human memory. *American Scientist*, *67*, 313–320. (p. 256)

Loftus, E. F. (1980). *Memory: Surprising new insights into how we remember and why we forget*. Reading, MA: Addison-Wesley. (p. 185)

Loftus, E. F. (1993). The reality of repressed memories. *American Psychologist*, *48*, 518–537. (p. 262)

Loftus, E. F. (1997, September). Creating false memories. *Scientific American*, pp. 71–75. (p. 260)

Loftus, E. F., Coan, J., & Pickrell, J. E. (1996). Manufacturing false memories using bits of reality. In L. Reder (ed.), *Implicit memory and metacognition*. Mahway, NJ: Erlbaum. (p. 261)

Loftus, E. F., Levidow, B., & Duensing, S. (1992). Who remembers best? Individual differences in memory for events that occurred in a science museum. *Applied Cognitive Psychology*, 6, 93–107. (pp. 256, 258, 295, 298)

Loftus, E. F., & Loftus, G. R. (1980). On the permanence of stored information in the human brain. *American Psychologist, 35,* 409–420. (p. 244)

Loftus, E. F., Milo, E. M., & Paddock, J. R. (1995). The accidental executioner: Why psychotherapy must be informed by science. *The Counseling Psychologist, 23,* 300–309. (pp. 260)

Loftus, E. F., & Palmer, J. C. (1974). Reconstruction of automobile destruction: An example of the interaction between language and memory. *Journal of Verbal Learning and Verbal Behavior, 13,* 585–589. (pp. 255, 256)

Loftus, E. F., & Pickrell, J. (1995). The formation of false memories. *Psychiatric Annals, 25,* 720–725. (p. 256)

Loftus, G. F. (1992). When a lie becomes memory's truth: Memory distortion after exposure to misinformation. *Current Directions in Psychological Science, 1,* 121–123. (p. 256)

London, P. (1970). The rescuers: Motivational hypotheses about Christians who saved Jews from the Nazis. In J. Macaulay & L. Berkowitz (Eds.), *Altruism and helping behavior.* New York: Academic Press. (p. 227)

Long, B. C., & van Stavel, R. (1995). Effects of exercise training on anxiety: A meta-analysis. *Journal of Applied Sport Psychology, 7,* 167–189. (p. 378)

LoPiccolo, J. L., & Stock, W. E. (1986). Treatment of sexual dysfunction. *Journal of Consulting and Clinical Psychology, 54,* 158–167. (p. 331)

Lord, C. G., Lepper, M. R., & Preston, E. (1984). Considering the opposite: A corrective strategy for social judgment. *Journal of Personality and Social Psychology, 47,* 1231–1247. (p. 275)

Lord, C. G., Ross, L., & Lepper, M. (1979). Biased assimilation and attitude polarization: The effects of prior theories on subsequently considered evidence. *Journal of Personality and Social Psychology, 37,* 2098–2109. (p. 275)

Lorenz, K. (1937). The companion in the bird's world. *Auk, 54,* 245–273. (p. 92)

Lourenco, O., & Machado, A. (1996). In defense of Piaget's theory: A reply to 10 common criticisms. *Psychological Review, 103,* 143–164. (p. 90)

Lovaas, O. I. (1987). Behavioral treatment and normal educational and intellectual functioning in young autistic children. *Journal of Consulting and Clinical Psychology, 55,* 3–9. (p. 469)

Lozoff, B. (1989). Nutrition and behavior. *American Psychologist, 44,* 231–236. (p. 539)

Lu, Z.-L., Williamson, S. J., & Kaufman, L. (1992). Behavioral lifetime of human auditory sensory memory predicted by physiological measures. *Science, 258,* 1668–1670. (p. 242)

Lubart, T. I. (1990). Creativity and cross-cultural variation. *International Journal of Psychology, 25,* 39–59. (p. 296)

Lubinski, D., & Benbow, C. P. (1992). Gender differences in abilities and preferences among the gifted: Implications for the math-science pipeline. *Current Directions in Psychological Science, 1,* 61–66. (pp. 304–305)

Ludwig, A. M. (1995). *The price of greatness: Resolving the creativity and madness controversy.* New York: Guilford Press. (pp. 334, 442)

Lukoff, D., Lu, F., & Turner, R. (1992). Toward a more culturally sensitive DSM-IV: Psychoreligious and psychospiritual problems. *Journal of Nervous and Mental Disease, 180,* 673–682. (p. 481)

Lull, J. (Ed.). (1988). *World families watch television.* Newbury Park, CA: Sage. (p. 517)

Lummis, M., & Stevenson, H. W. (1990). Gender differences in beliefs and achievement: A cross-cultural study. *Developmental Psychology, 26,* 254–263. (p. 305)

Luria, A. M. (1968). In L. Solotaroff (Trans.), *The mind of a mnemonist.* New York: Basic Books. (p. 231)

Lykken, D. T. (1983, April). Polygraph prejudice. *APA Monitor,* p. 4. (p. 350)

Lykken, D. T. (1991). Science, lies, and controversy: An epitaph for the polygraph. Invited address upon receipt of the Senior Career award for Distinguished Contribution to Psychology in the Public Interest, American Psychological Association convention. (p. 350)

Lykken, D. T. (1992). Science, lies, and controversy: An epitaph for the polygraph. Invited address upon receipt of the Senior Career award for Distinguished Contribution to Psychology in the Public Interest, American Psychological Association convention. (p. 350)

Lykken, D. T. (1995). *The antisocial personalities.* Hillsdale, NJ: Erlbaum. (p. 456)

Lykken, D. T., McGue, M., Tellegen, A., & Bouchard, T. J., Jr. (1992). Emergenesis: Genetic traits that may not run in families. *American Psychologist, 47,* 1565–1577. (p. 72)

Lykken, D., & Tellegen, A. (1996). Happiness is a stochastic phenomenon. *Psychological Science, 7,* 186–189. (p. 363)

Lyman, D. R. (1996). Early identification of chronic offenders: Who is the fledgling psychopath? *Psychological Bulletin, 120,* 209–234. (p. 456)

Lynch, G., & Staubli, U. (1991). Possible contributions of long-term potentiation to the encoding and organization of memory. *Brain Research Reviews, 16,* 204–206. (p. 245)

Lynn, M. (1988). The effects of alcohol consumption on restaurant tipping. *Personality and Social Psychology Bulletin, 14,* 87–91. (p. 193)

Lynn, R. (1987). Japan: Land of the rising IQ. A reply to Flynn. *Bulletin of the British Psychological Society, 40,* 464–468. (p. 303)

Lynn, R. (1991, Fall/Winter). The evolution of racial differences in intelligence. *The Mankind Quarterly, 32,* 99–145. (p. 303)

Lynn, S. J., Lock, T. G., Myers, B., & Payne, D. G. (1997). Recalling the unrecallable: Should hypnosis be used to recover memories in psychotherapy? *Current Directions in Psychological Science, 6,* 79–83. (p. 185)

Lynn, S. J., & Rhue, J. W. (1986). The fantasy-prone person: Hypnosis, imagination, and creativity. *Journal of Personality and Social Psychology, 51,* 404–408. (p. 184)

Lynn, S. J., Rhue, J. W., & Weekes, J. R. (1990). Hypnotic involuntariness: A social cognitive analysis. *Psychological Review, 97,* 169–184. (p. 189)

Lyon, D., & Greenberg, J. (1991). Evidence of codependency in women with an alcoholic parent: Helping out Mr. Wrong. *Journal of Personality and Social Psychology, 61,* 435–439. (p. 192)

Lyons, M. J., & others (1995). Differential heritability of adult and juvenile antisocial traits. *Archives of General Psychiatry, 52,* 906–915. (p. 455)

Lytton, H., & Romney, D. M. (1991). Parents' differential socialization of boys and girls: A meta-analysis. *Psychological Bulletin, 109,* 267–296. (p. 97)

Lyubomirsky, S., & Nolen-Hoeksema, S. (1994). The effects of depressive rumination on thinking and problem solving. Unpublished manuscript, Stanford University. (p. 470)

Maas, J. B. (1998). *Power sleep: Revolutionary strategies that prepare your mind and body for peak performance.* New York: Villard. (pp. 177, 178)

Maccoby, E. E. (1990). Gender and relationships: A developmental account. *American Psychologist, 45,* 513–520. (p. 105)

Maccoby. E. E. (1995). Divorce and custody: The rights, needs, and obligations of mothers, fathers, and children. *Nebraska Symposium on Motivation, 42,* 135–172. (p. 507)

MacDonald, N. (1960). Living with schizophrenia. *Canadian Medical Association Journal, 82,* 218–221. (p. 450)

MacDonald, T. K., Zanna, M. P., & Fong, G. T. (1995). Decision making in altered states: Effects of alcohol on attitudes toward drinking and driving. *Journal of Personality and Social Psychology, 68,* 973–985. (p. 193)

MacDonald, T. K., Zanna, M. P., & Fong, G. T. (1996). Why common sense goes out the window: The effects of alcohol on intentions to use condoms. *Personality and Social Psychology Bulletin, 22,* 763–775. (p. 194)

MacDonald, T. K., Zanna, M. P., & Fong, G. T. (1998). Alcohol and intentions to engage in risky health-related behaviors: Experimental evidence for a causal relationship. In J. Adair & F. Craik (eds.), Advances in psychological science, vol. 2: Developmental, personal, and social aspects. East Sussex, UK: Psychology Press. (p. 194)

MacDonald, T. K., Zanna, M. P., & Fong, G. T. (in press). Alcohol and intentions to engage in risky health-related behaviors: Experimental evidence for a causal relationship. In J. Adair & F. Craik (eds.), *Advances in psychological science, vol. 2: Developmental, personal, and social aspects.* East Sussex, UK: Psychology Press. (p. 194)

MacFarlane, A. (1978, February). What a baby knows. *Human Nature,* pp. 74–81. (p. 82)

Macfarlane, J. W. (1964). Perspectives on personality consistency and change from the guidance study. *Vita Humana,* 7, 115–126. (pp. 99, *121)*

MacKay, D. G. (1983). Prescriptive grammar and the pronoun problem. In B. Thorne, C. Kramarae, & N. Henley (Eds.), *Language, gender and society.* Rowley, MA: Newbury House. (p. 286)

MacKinnon, D. W., & Hall, W. B. (1972). Intelligence and creativity. *Proceedings, XVIIth International Congress of Applied Psychology* (Vol. 2, pp. 1883–1888). Brussels: Editest. (p. 296)

MacLeod, C., & Campbell, L. (1992). Memory accessibility and probability judgments: An experimental evaluation of the availability heuristic. *Journal of Personality and Social Psychology, 63,* 890–902. (p. 272)

Maehr, M. L., & Braskamp, L. A. (1986). *The motivation factor: A theory of personal investment.* Lexington, MA: Lexington Books. (p. 341)

Magnusson, D. (1990). Personality research—challenges for the future. *European Journal of Personality, 4,* 1–17. (p. 455)

Mahowald, M. W., & Ettinger, M. G. (1990). Things that go bump in the night: The parsomias revisted. *Journal of Clinical Neurophysiology, 7,* 119–143. (p. 174)

Maier, S. F., Watkins, L. R., & Fleshner, M. (1994). Psychoneuroimmunology: The interface between behavior, brain, and immunity. *American Psychologist, 49,* 1004–1017. (pp. 374, *375)*

Major, B., Carrington, P. I., & Carnevale, P. J. D. (1984). Physical attractiveness and self-esteem: Attribution for praise from an other-sex evaluator. *Personality and Social Psychology Bulletin, 10,* 43–50. (p. 524)

Major, B., Cozzarelli, C., Sciacchitano, A. M., Cooper, M. L., Testa, M., & Mueller, P. M. (1990). Perceived social support, self-efficacy, and adjustment to abortion. *Journal of Personality and Social Psychology, 59,* 452–463. (p. 371)

Major, B., Schmidlin, A. M., & Williams, L. (1990). Gender patterns in social touch: The impact of setting and age. *Journal of Personality and Social Psychology, 58,* 634–643. (p. 342)

Malamuth, N. M. (1996). Sexually explicit media, gender differences, and evolutionary theory. *Journal of Communication, 46,* 8–31. (pp. 331, *519)*

Malamuth, N. M., & Check, J. V. P. (1981). The effects of media exposure on acceptance of violence against women: A field experiment. *Journal of Research in Personality, 15,* 436–446. (p. 519)

Malamuth, N. M., Linz, D., Heavey, C. L., Barnes, G., & Acker, M. (1995). Using the confluence model of sexual aggression to predict men's conflict with women: A 10-year follow-up study. *Journal of Personality and Social Psychology, 69,* 353–369. (p. 519)

Malamuth, N. M., Sockloskie, R. J., Koss, M. P., & Tanaka, J. S. (1991). Characteristics of aggressors against women: Testing a model using a national sample of college students. *Journal of Consulting and Clinical Psychology, 59,* 670–681. (p. 519)

Malan, D. H. (1978). "The case of the secretary with the violent father." In H. Davanloo (Ed.), *Basic principles and techniques in short-term dynamic psychotherapy.* New York: Spectrum. (p. 464)

Malinosky-Rummell, R., & Hansen, D. J. (1993). Long-term consequences of childhood physical abuse. *Psychological bulletin, 114,* 68–79. (p. 94)

Malkiel, B. (1985). *A random walk down Wall Street* (4th ed.). New York: Norton. (p. 274)

Malkiel, B. G. (1989a). Is the stock market efficient? *Science, 243,* 1313–1318. (p. 22)

Malkiel, B. G. (1995, June). Returns from investing in equity mutual funds 1971 to 1991. *Journal of Finance,* pp. 549–572. (p. 22, 274)

Malloy, E. A., & others (1994, June 7). Report of the Commission on Substance Abuse at Colleges and Universities, reported by *Associated Press.* (p. 194)

Malmquist, C. P. (1986). Children who witness parental murder: Post-traumatic aspects. *Journal of the American Academy of Child Psychiatry, 25,* 320–325. (p. 397)

Malone, T. W., & Lepper, M. R. (1986). Making learning fun: A taxonomy of intrinsic motivations for learning. In R. E. Snow & M. J. Farr (Eds.), *Aptitude, learning, and instruction: III. Cognitive and affective process analysis.* Hillsdale, NJ: Erlbaum. (p. 341)

Manber, R., Bootzin, R. R., Acebo, C., & Carskadon, M. A. (1996). The effects of regularizing sleep-wake schedules on daytime sleepiness. *Sleep, 19,* 432–441. (p. 179)

Mandel, D. (1983, March 13). One man's holocaust: Part II. The story of David Mandel's journey through hell as told to David Kagan. *Wonderland Magazine* (Grand Rapids Press), pp. 2–7. (p. 311)

Manning, W. G., Keefer, E. B., Newhouse, J. P., Sloss, E. M., & Wasserman, J. (1989). The taxes of sin: Do smokers and drinkers pay their way? *Journal of the American Medical Association, 261,* 1604–1609. (p. 195)

Maquet, P., Peters, J-M., Aerts, J., Delfiore, G., Degueldre, C., Luxen, A., & Franck, G. (1996). Functional neuroanatomy of human rapid-eye-movement sleep and dreaming. *Nature, 383,* 163–166. (p. 182)

Markowitsch, H. J. (1995). Which brain regions are critically involved in the retrieval of old episodic memory? *Brain Research Reviews, 21,* 117–127. (p. 248)

Markus, G. B. (1986). Stability and change in political attitudes: Observe, recall, and "explain." *Political Behavior, 8,* 21–44. (p. 257)

Markus, H., & Kitayama, S. (1991). Culture and the self: Implications for cognition, emotion, and motivation. *Psychological Review, 98,* 224–253. (pp. 286, 354, 357, 412)

Markus, H., & Nurius, P. (1986). Possible selves. *American Psychologist, 41,* 954–969. (p. 408)

Marlatt, G. A. (1991). Substance abuse: Etiology, prevention, and treatment issues. Master lecture, American Psychological Association convention. (pp. 194, 219)

Marschark, M., Richman, C. L., Yuille, J. C., & Hunt, R. R. (1987). The role of imagery in memory: On shared and distinctive information. *Psychological Bulletin, 102,* 28–41. (p. 237)

Marsh, H. W., & Parker, J. W. (1984). Determinants of student self-concept: Is it better to be a relatively large fish in a small pond even if you don't learn to swim as well? *Journal of Personality and Social Psychology, 47,* 213–231. (p. 362)

Marteau, T. M. (1989). Framing of information: Its influences upon decisions of doctors and patients. *British Journal of Social Psychology, 28,* 89–94. (p. 274)

Martin, A., Wiggs, C. L., Ungerleider, L. G., & Haxby, J. V. (1996). Neural correlates of category-specific knowledge. *Nature, 379,* 649–652. (p. 51)

Martin, R. J., White, B. D., & Hulsey, M. G. (1991). The regulation of body weight. *American Scientist, 79,* 528–541. (p. 317)

Martin, S. J., Kelly, I. W., & Saklofske, D. H. (1992). Suicide and lunar cycles: A critical review over 28 years. *Psychological Reports, 71,* 787–795. (p. 455)

Martyna, W. (1978). What does "he" mean? Use of generic masculine. *Journal of Communication, 28*(1), 131–138. (p. 286)

Maslow, A. H. (1970). *Motivation and personality* (2nd ed.). New York: Harper & Row. (pp. 314, 406, 407)

Maslow, A. H. (1971). *The farther reaches of human nature.* New York: Viking Press. (p. 305)

Masse, L. C., & Tremblay, R. E. (1997). Behavior of boys in kindergarten and the onset of substance use during adolescence. *Archives of General Psychiatry, 54,* 62–68. (p. 200)

Masters, M. S., & Sanders, B. (1993). Is the gender difference in mental rotation disappearing? *Behavior Genetics, 23,* 337–341. (p. 305)

Masters, W. H., & Johnson, V. E. (1966). *Human sexual response.* Boston: Little, Brown. (pp. 327, *328)*

Matarazzo, J. D. (1983). Computerized psychological testing. *Science, 221,* 323. (p. 404)

Matsumoto, D. (1994). *People: Psychology from a cultural perspective.* Pacific Grove, CA: Brooks/Cole. (p. 286)

Matsumoto, D., & Ekman, P. (1989). American-Japanese cultural differences in intensity ratings of facial expressions of emotion. *Motivation and Emotion, 13,* 143–157. (p. 354)

Matsumoto, D., Kudoh, T., Scherer, K., & Wallbott, H. (1988). Antecedents of and reactions to emotions in the United States and Japan. *Journal of Cross-Cultural Psychology, 19,* 267–286. (pp. 354, *356)*

Matt, G. E., Vazquez, C., & Campbell, W. K. (1992). Mood-congruent recall of affectively toned stimuli: A meta-analytic review. *Clinical Psychology Review, 12,* 227–255. (p. 251)

Matthews, D. A. (1997). Religion and spirituality in primary care. *Mind/Body Medicine,* 2, 9–19. (p. 383)

Matthews, D. A., & Larson, D. B. (1997). *The faith factor: An annotated bibliography of clinical research on spiritual subjects,* Vol. I-IV. Rockville, MD: National Institute for Healthcare Research and Georgetown University Press. (p. 383)

Matthews, K. A. (1992). Myths and realities of the menopause. *Psychosomatic Medicine, 54,* 1–9. (p. 110)

Maurer, D., & Maurer, C. (1988). *The world of the newborn.* New York: Basic Books. (p. 82)

May, C., & Hasher, L. (1997). Circadian arousal and cognition. *Journal of Experimental Psychology: Human Perception and Performance,* in press. (p. 173)

May, C. P., Hasher, L., & Stoltzfus, E. R. (1993). Optimal time of day and the magnitude of age differences in memory. *Psychological Science, 4,* 326–330. (p. 113)

May, P. A. (1986). Alcohol and drug misuse prevention programs for American Indians: Needs and opportunities. *Journal of Studies on Alcohol, 47,* 187–195. (p. 428)

May, R. (1982). The problem of evil: An open letter to Carl Rogers. *Journal of Humanistic Psychology,* 22, 10–21. (p. 415)

Mayer, J. D., & Salovey, P. (1993). The intelligence of emotional intelligence. *Intelligence, 17,* 433–442. (p. 292)

Mayer, J. D., & Salovey, P. (1995). Emotional intelligence and the construction and regulation of feelings. *Applied and Preventive Psychology, 4,* 197–208. (p. 292)

Mayer, J. D., & Salovey, P. (1997). What is emotional intelligence? In P. Salovey & D. Sluyter (eds.), *Emotional development, emotional literacy, and emotional intelligence.* New York: Basic Books. (p. 292)

Mayne, T. J., Norcross, J. C., & Sayette, M. A. (1994). Admission requirements, acceptance rates, and financial assistance in clinical psychology programs. *American Psychologist, 49,* 806–811. (p. 470)

McAneny, L. (1996, September). Large majority think government conceals information about UFOs. *Gallup Poll Monthly,* pp. 23–28. (p. 160)

McBurney, D. H. (1996). *How to think like a psychologist: Critical thinking in psychology.* Upper Saddle River, NJ: Prentice-Hall. (p. 58)

McBurney, D. H., & Collings, V. B. (1984). *Introduction to sensation and perception* (2nd ed.). Englewood Cliffs, NJ: Prentice-Hall. (pp. 153, 154)

McBurney, D. H., & Gent, J. F. (1979). On the nature of taste qualities. *Psychological Bulletin, 86,* 151–167. (p. 143)

McCall, R. B. (1994). Academic underachievers. *Current Directions in Psychological Science, 3*, 15–19. (p. 339)

McCall, R. B., Evahn, C., & Kratzer, L. (1992). High school underachievers. Newbury Park, CA: Sage. (p. 304)

McCann, I. L., & Holmes, D. S. (1984). Influence of aerobic exercise on depression. *Journal of Personality and Social Psychology, 46*, 1142–1147. (pp. 378, 379)

McCarthy, P. (1986, July). Scent: The tie that binds? *Psychology Today*, pp. 6, 10. (p. 144)

McCartney, K., Harris, M. J., & Bernieri, F. (1990). Growing up and growing apart: A developmental meta-analysis of twin studies. *Psychological Bulletin, 107*, 226–237. (p. 72)

McCarty, D., Argeriou, M., Huebner, R. B., & Lubran, B. (1991). Alcoholism, drug abuse, and the homeless. *American Psychologist, 46*, 1139–1148. (p. 483)

McCaul, K. D., & Malott, J. M. (1984). Distraction and coping with pain. *Psychological Bulletin, 95*, 516–533. (p. 143)

McCauley, C. R., & Segal, M. E. (1987). Social psychology of terrorist groups. In C. Hendrick (Ed.), *Group processes and intergroup relations.* Beverly Hills, CA: Sage. (p. 505)

McClintock, M. K., & Herdt, G. (1996). Rethinking puberty: The development of sexual attraction. *Current Directions in Psychology, 5*, 178–183. (p. 100)

McCloskey, M., Wible, C. G., & Cohen, N. J. (1988). Is there a special flashbulb-memory mechanism? *Journal of Experimental Psychology: General, 117*, 171–181. (p. 232)

McConkey, K. M. (1992). The effects of hypnotic procedures on remembering: The experimental findings and their implications for forensic hypnosis. In E. Fromm and M. R. Nash (Eds.), *Contemporary hypnosis research.* New York: Guilford Press. (p. 185)

McConkey, K. M. (1995)., Hypnosis, memory, and the ethics of uncertainty. *Australian Psychologist, 30*, 1–10. (p. 185)

McConnell, A., & Fazio, R. H. (1996). Women as men and people: Effects of gender-marked language. *Personality and Social Psychology Bulletin, 22*, 1004–1013. (p. 286)

McConnell, R. A. (1991). National Academy of Sciences opinion on parapsychology. *Journal of the American Society for Psychical Research, 85*, 333–365. (p. 160)

McCormick, C. M., & Witelson, S. F. (1991). A cognitive profile of homosexual men compared to heterosexual men and women. *Psychoneuroendocrinology, 16*, 459–473. (p. 335)

McCrae, R. R., & Costa, P. T., Jr. (1986). Clinical assessment can benefit from recent advances in personality psychology. *American Psychologist, 41*, 1001–1003. (p. 402)

McCrae, R. R., & Costa, P. T., Jr. (1990). *Personality in adulthood.* New York: Guilford. (p. 115)

McCrae, R. R., & Costa, P. T., Jr. (1994). The stability of personality: Observations and evaluations. *Current Directions in Psychological Science, 3*, 173–175. (pp. 121, *404)*

McFarland, C., & Ross, M. (1987). The relation between current impressions and memories of self and dating partners. *Psychological Bulletin, 13*, 228–238. (p. 257)

McGaugh, J. L. (1994). Quoted by B. Bower, "Stress hormones hike emotional memories." *Science News, 146*, p. 262. (p. 246)

McGhee, P. E. (1976). Children's appreciation of humor: A test of the cognitive congruence principle. *Child Development, 47*, 420–426. (p. 89)

McGrath, J., Welham, J., & Pemberton, M. (1995). Month of birth, hemisphere of birth and schizophrenia. *British Journal of Psychiatry, 167*, 783–785. (p. 453)

McGrath, M. J., & Cohen, D. G. (1978). REM sleep facilitation of adaptive waking behavior: A review of the literature. *Psychological Bulletin, 85*, 24–57. (p. 182)

McGue, M., Bouchard, T. J., Jr., Iacono, W. G., & Lykken, D. T. (1993). Behavioral genetics of cognitive ability: A life-span perspective. In R. Plomin & G. E. McClearn (Eds.), *Nature, nurture and psychology.* Washington, DC: American Psychological Association. (pp. 299, 300)

McGue, M., Pickens, R. W., & Svikis, D. S. (1992). Sex and age effects on the inheritance of alcohol problems: A twin study. *Journal of Abnormal Psychology, 202*, 3–17. (p. 200)

McGuire, W. J. (1986). The myth of massive media impact: Savings and salvagings. In G. Comstock (Ed.), *Public communication and behavior.* Orlando, FL: Academic Press. (p. 517)

McHugh, P. R. (1995a). Witches, multiple personalities, and other psychiatric artifacts. *Nature Medicine, 1*(2), 110–114. (p. 439)

McHugh, P. R. (1995b). Resolved: Multiple personality disorder is an individually and sociall created artifact. *Journal of the American Academy of Child and Adolescent Psychiatry, 34*, 957–959. (p. 440)

McHugh, P. R., & Moran, T. H. (1978). Accuracy of the regulation of caloric ingestion in the rhesus monkey. *American Journal of Physiology, 235*, R29–34. (p. 316)

McKinlay, J. B., McKinlay, S. M., & Brambilla, D. J. (1987a). Health status and utilization behavior associated with menopause. *American Journal of Epidemiology, 125*, 110–121. (p. 110)

McKinlay, J. B., McKinlay, S. M., & Brambilla, D. (1987b). The relative contributions of endocrine changes and social circumstances to depression in mid-aged women. *Journal of Health and Social Behavior, 28*, 345–363. (p. 110)

McLennan, W. (1995). *Australian social trends 1995.* Australian Bureau of Statistics. (p. 117)

Meador, B. D., & Rogers, C. R. (1984). Person-centered therapy. In R. J. Corsini (Ed.), *Current psychotherapies* (3rd ed.). Itasca, IL: Peacock. (p. 465)

Meaney, M. J., Aitken, D. H., Van Berkel, C., Bhatnagar, S., & Sapolsky, R. M. (1988). Effect of neonatal handling on age-related impairments associated with the hippocampus. *Science, 239*, 766–768. (p. 84)

Medical Institute for Sexual Health (April, 1994). Condoms ineffective against human papilloma virus. *Sexual Health Update, 2.* (p. 108)

Mednick, S. A., Huttunen, M. O., & Machon, R. A. (1994). Prenatal influenza infections and adult schizophrenia. *Schizophrenia Bulletin, 20*, 263–267. (p. 453)

Meichenbaum, D. (1977). *Cognitive-behavior modification: An integrative approach.* New York: Plenum Press. (p. 473)

Meier, R. P. (1991). Language acquisition by deaf children. *American Scientist, 79*, 60–70. (pp. 140, *282)*

Meltzoff, A. N. (1988a). Infant imitation and memory: Nine-month-olds in immediate and deferred tests. *Child Development, 59*, 217–225. (p. 226)

Meltzoff, A. N. (1988b). Infant imitation after a 1-week delay: Long-term memory for novel acts and multiple stimuli. *Developmental Psychology*, *24*, 470–476. (p. 226)

Meltzoff, A. N. (1988c). Imitation of televised models by infants. *Child Development*, *59*, 1221–1229. (p. 265)

Meltzoff, A. N., & Borton, R. W. (1979). Intermodal matching by human neonates. *Nature*, 282, 403-404. (p. 87)

Melzack, R. (1984). The myth of painless childbirth. *Pain*, *19*, 321–337. (p. 143)

Melzack, R. (1990, February). The tragedy of needless pain. *Scientific American*, pp. 27–33. (p. 191)

Melzack, R. (1992, April). Phantom limbs. *Scientific American*, pp. 120–126. (p. 142)

Melzack, R. (1993). Distinguished contribution series. *Canadian Journal of Experimental Psychology*, *47*, 615–629. (p. 142)

Melzack, R., & Wall, P. D. (1965). Pain mechanisms: A new theory. *Science*, *150*, 971–979. (p. 142)

Melzack, R., & Wall, P. D. (1983). *The challenge of pain*. New York: Basic Books. (p. 142)

Mendolia, M., & Kleck, R. E. (1993). Effects of talking about a stressful event on arousal: Does what we talk about make a difference? *Journal of Personality and Social Psychology*, *64*, 283–292. (p. 384)

Mento, A. J., Steel, R. P., & Karren, R. J. (1987). A meta-analytic study of the effects of goal setting on task performance: 1966–1984. *Organizational Behavior and Human Decision Processes*, *39*, 52–83. (p. 342)

Merskey, H. (1992). The manufacture of personalities: The production of multiple personality disorder. *British Journal of Psychiatry*, *160*, 327–340. (p. 439)

Merton, R. K. (1938; reprinted 1970). *Science, technology and society in seventeenth-century England*. New York: Fertig. (p. 9)

Merton, R. K., & Kitt, A. S. (1950). Contributions to the theory of reference group behavior. In R. K. Merton & P. F. Lazarsfeld (Eds.), *Continuities in social research: Studies in the scope and method of the American soldier.* Glencoe, IL: Free Press. (p. 362)

Mesquita, B., & Frijda, N. H. (1992). Cultural variations in emotions: A review. *Psychological Bulletin*, *112*, 179–204. (p. 354)

Messer, W. S., & Griggs, R. A. (1989). Student belief and involvement in the paranormal and performance in introductory psychology. *Teaching of Psychology*, *16*, 187–191. (p. 162)

Mestel, R. (1997, April 26). Get real, Siggi. *New Scientist*. Http://www.newscientist.com/ns/970426/siggi.html (p. 181)

Meston, C. M., Trapnell, P. D., & Gorzalka, B. B. (1996). Ethnic and gender differences in sexuality: Variations in sexual behavior between Asian and non-Asian university students. *Archives of Sexual Behavior*, *25*, 33–72. (p. 107)

Metalsky, G. I., Joiner, T. E., Jr., , Hardin, T. S., & Abramson, L. Y. (1993). Depressive reactions to failure in a naturalistic setting: A test of the hopelessness and self-esteem theories of depression. *Journal of Abnormal Psychology*, *102*, 101–109. (p. 448)

Meuwissen, I., & Over, R. (1992). Sexual arousal across phases of the human menstrual cycle. *Archives of Sexual Behavior*, *21*, 101–119. (p. 328)

Meyer-Bahlburg, H. F. L. (1995). Psychoneuroendocrinology and sexual pleasure: The aspect of sexual orientation. In P. R. Abramson & S. D. Pinkerton (eds.), *Sexual Nature/Sexual Culture*. Chicago: The University of Chicago Press. (p. 335)

Michaels, J. W., Bloomel, J. M., Brocato, R. M., Linkous, R. A., & Rowe, J. S. (1982). Social facilitation and inhibition in a natural setting. *Replications in Social Psychology*, *2*, 21–24. (p. 503)

Middlebrooks, J. C., & Green, D. M. (1991). Sound localization by human listeners. *Annual Review of Psychology*, *42*, 135–159. (p. 141)

Mikulincer, M., Babkoff, H., Caspy, T., & Sing, H. (1989). The effects of 72 hours of sleep loss on psychological variables. *British Journal of Psychology*, *80*, 145–162. (p. 177)

Milan, R. J., Jr., & Kilmann, P. R. (1987). Interpersonal factors in premarital contraception. *Journal of Sex Research*, *23*, 289–321. (p. 108)

Milgram, S. (1974). *Obedience to authority.* New York: Harper & Row. (pp. 499–501)

Miller, G. A. (1962). *Psychology: The science of mental life*. New York: Harper & Row. (p. 399)

Miller, G. A., & Gildea, P. M. (1987, September). How children learn words. *Scientific American*, pp. 94–99. (p. 277)

Miller, J. D., & Pifer, L. (1996). *Science and engineering indicators*. Washington, DC: National Science Foundation. (p. 27)

Miller, K. I., & Monge, P. R. (1986). Participation, satisfaction, and productivity: A meta-analytic review. *Academy of Management Journal*, *29*, 727–753. (p. 417)

Miller, N. E. (1983). Value and ethics of research on animals. Paper presented at the meeting of the American Psychological Association. (p. 32)

Miller, N. E. (1985, February). Rx: biofeedback. *Psychology Today*, pp. 54–59. (p. 380)

Miller, N. E. (1995). Clinical-experimental interactions in the development of neuroscience: A primer for nonspecialists and lessons for young scientists. *American Psychologist*, *50*, 901–911. (p. 317)

Miller, N. E., & Brucker, B. S. (1979). A learned visceral response apparently independent of skeletal ones in patients paralyzed by spinal lesions. In N. Birbaumer & H. D. Kimmel (Eds.), *Biofeedback and self-regulation.* Hillsdale, NJ: Erlbaum. (p. 379)

Miller, P. A., Eisenberg, N., Fabes, R. A., & Shell, R. (1996). Relations of moral reasoning and vicarious emotion to young children's prosocial behavior toward peers and adults. *Developmental Psychology*, *32*, 210–219. (p. 103)

Miller, P. C., Lefcourt, H. M., Holmes, J. G., Ware, E. E., & Saleh, W. E. (1986). Marital locus of control and marital problem solving. *Journal of Personality and Social Psychology*, *51*, 161–169. (p. 417)

Miller, S. D., Blackburn, T., Scholes, G., White, G. L., & Mamalis, N. (1991). Optical differences in multiple personality disorder: A second look. *Journal of Nervous and Mental Disease*, *179*, 132–135. (p. 439)

Miller, T. Q., Smith, T. W., Turner, C. W., Guijarro, M. L., & Hallet, A. J. (1996). A meta-analytic review of research on hostility and physical health. *Psychological Bulletin*, *119*, 322–348. (p. 373)

Millers, J. G., & Bersoff, D. M. (1995). Development in the context of everyday family relationships: Culture, interpersonal morality and adaptation. In M. Killen and D. Hart (eds.), *Morality in everyday life: A developmental perspective*. New York: Cambridge University Press. (p. 103)

Mills, M., & Melhuish, E. (1974). Recognition of mother's voice in early infancy. *Nature*, *252*, 123–124. (p. 82)

Mineka, S., & Sutton, S. K. (1992). Cognitive biases and the emotional disorders. *Psychological Science*, *3*, 65–69. (p. 434)

Mineka, S., & Zinbarg, R. (1996). Conditioning and ethological models of anxiety disorders: Stress-in-dynamic-context anxiety models. In D. Hope (ed.), *Perspectives on anxiety, panic, and fear. Nebraska symposium on motivation.* Lincoln, NE: University of Nebraska Press. (pp. 435, 436)

Mirin, S. M., & Weiss, R. D. (1989). Genetic factors in the development of alcoholism. *Psychiatric Annals*, *19*, 239–242. (p. 200)

Mischel, W. (1968). *Personality and assessment.* New York: Wiley. (p. 404)

Mischel, W. (1981). Current issues and challenges in personality. In L. T. Benjamin, Jr. (Ed.), *The G. Stanley Hall Lecture Series* (Vol. 1). Washington, DC: American Psychological Association. (p. 420)

Mischel, W. (1984). Convergences and challenges in the search for consistency. *American Psychologist*, *39*, 351–364. (p. 404)

Mischel, W., Shoda, Y., & Peake, P. K. (1988). The nature of adolescent competencies predicted by preschool delay of gratification. *Journal of Personality and Social Psychology*, *54*, 687–696. (p. 103)

Mischel, W., Shoda, Y., & Rodriguez, M. L. (1989). Delay of gratification in children. *Science*, *244*, 933–938. (pp. 103, 218)

Mita, T. H., Dermer, M., & Knight, J. (1977). Reversed facial images and the mere-exposure hypothesis. *Journal of Personality and Social Psychology*, *35*, 597–601. (p. 524)

Mitchell, T. R., Thompson, L., Peterson, E., & Cronk, R. (1997). Temporal adjustments in the evaluation of events: The "rosy view." *Journal of Experimental Social Psychology*, in press. (p. 234)

MMWR (1995, January 3). Sexual behavior among high school students: United States, *1990. Morbidity and Mortality Weekly Report*, *40*, 885–887. (p. 107)

Monaghan, P. (1992, September 23). Professor of psychology stokes a controversy on the reliability and repression of memory. *Chronicle of Higher Education*, pp. A9–A10. (p. 262)

Monahan, J. (1992). Mental disorder and violent behavior: Perceptions and evidence. *American Psychologist*, *47*, 511–521. (p. 430)

Money, J. (1987). Sin, sickness, or status? Homosexual gender identity and psychoneuroendocrinology. *American Psychologist*, *42*, 384–399. (pp. 334, *335)*

Money, J., Berlin, F. S., Falck, A., & Stein, M. (1983). *Antiandrogenic and counseling treatment of sex offenders.* Baltimore: Department of Psychiatry and Behavioral Sciences, The Johns Hopkins University School of Medicine. (p. 329)

Moody, R. (1976). *Life after life.* Harrisburg, PA: Stackpole Books. (p. 197)

Mook, D. G. (1983). In defense of external invalidity. *American Psychologist*, *38*, 379–387. (p. 29)

Moorcroft, W. (1993). *Sleep, dreaming, and sleep disorders: An introduction* (2nd ed.). Landam, MD: University Press of America. (pp. 174, 176, 178)

Moore, D. W. (1993, April). Public polarized on gay issue. *Gallup Poll Monthly*, pp. 30–34. (p. 336)

Moore, T. E. (1988). The case against subliminal manipulation. *Psychology and Marketing*, *5*, 297–316. (p. 127)

Moreland, R. L., & Beach, S. R. (1992). Exposure effects in the classroom: The development of affinity among students. *Journal of Experimental Social Psychology*, *28*, 255–276. (p. 523)

Moreland, R. L., & Zajonc, R. B. (1982). Exposure effects in person perception: Familiarity, similarity, and attraction. *Journal of Experimental Social Psychology*, *18*, 395–415. (p. 523)

Morell, V. (1995). Attacking the causes of "silent" infertility. *Science*, *269*, 775–776. (p. 108)

Morell, V. (1995). Zeroing in on how hormones affect the immune system. *Science*, *269*, 773–775. (p. 374)

Morelli, G. A., Rogoff, B., Oppenheim, D., & Goldsmith, D. (1992). Cultural variation in infants' sleeping arrangements: Questions of independence. *Developmental Psychology*, *26*, 604–613. (p. 96)

Morin, R., & Brossard, M. A. (1997, March 4). Communication breakdown on drugs. *Washington Post*, pp. A1, A6. (p. 107)

Morris, R. L. (1996, September 6). Personal correspondence, citing forthcoming data from Dalton Ph.D thesis. (p. 164)

Morris, R. L., Dalton, K., Delanoy, D. L., & Watt, C. (1995). Comparison of the sender/no sender condition in the ganzfeld. *Proceedings of the Parapsychological Association 38th Annual Convention*, pp. 244–259. Durham, NC: Parapsychological Association. (p. 164)

Morrison, D. M. (1985). Adolescent contraceptive behavior: A review. *Psychological Bulletin*, *98*, 538–568. (p. 108)

Morton, G. E. (1994). Personal communication. (p. 13)

Moscovici, S. (1985). Social influence and conformity. In G. Lindzey & E. Aronson (Eds.), *The handbook of social psychology*, 3rd ed. Hillsdale, N.J.: Erlbaum. (p. 506)

Mosher, D. L., & Anderson, R. D. (1986). Macho personality, sexual aggression, and reactions to guided imagery of realistic rape. *Journal of Research in Personality*, *20*, 77–94. (p. 193)

Moss, H. A., & Susman, E. J. (1980). Longitudinal study of personality development. In O. G. Brim, Jr., & J. Kagan (Eds.), *Constancy and change in human development.* Cambridge, MA: Harvard University Press. (p. 121)

Moyer, K. E. (1983). The physiology of motivation: Aggression as a model. In C. J. Scheier & A. M. Rogers (Eds.), *G. Stanley Hall Lecture Series* (Vol. 3). Washington, DC: American Psychological Association. (p. 514)

Muehlenhard, C. L. (1988). Misinterpreted dating behaviors and the risk of date rape. *Journal of Social and Clinical Psychology*, *6*, 20–37. (p. 332)

Mukerjee, M. (1997, January). Trends in animal research. *Scientific American*, pp. 86–93. (p. 31)

Muller, J. E., Mittleman, M. A., Maclure, M., Sherwood, J. B., & Tofler, G. H. (1996). Triggering myocardial infarction by sexual activity. *Journal of the American Medical Association*, *275*, 1405–1409. (p. 327)

Muller, J. E., & Verrier, R. L. (1996). Triggering of sudden death—Lessons from an earthquake. *New England Journal of Medicine*, *334*, 460–461. (p. 370)

Murphy, G. E., & Wetzel, R. D. (1990). The lifetime risk of suicide in alcoholism. *Archives of General Psychiatry*, *47*, 383–392. (p. 444)

Murphy, S. T., Monahan, J. L., & Zajonc, R. B. (1995). Additivity of nonconscious affect: Combined effects of priming and exposure. *Journal of Personality and Social Psychology*, *69*, 589–602. (p. 367)

Murphy, S. T., & Zajonc, R. B. (1993). Affect, cognition, and awareness: Affective priming with optimal and suboptimal stimulus exposures. *Journal of Personality and Social Psychology*, *64*, 723–739. (p. 127)

Murphy, T. N. (1982). Pain: Its assessment and management. In R. J. Gatchel, A. Baum, & J. E. Singer (Eds.), *Handbook of psychology and health: Vol. I. Clinical psychology and behavioral medicine: Overlapping disciplines.* Hillsdale, NJ: Erlbaum. (p. 142)

Murray, C., & Herrnstein, R. J. (1994, October 31). Race, genes and I.Q.—An apologia. *New Republic*, pp. 27–37. (p. 303)

Murray, H. (1938). *Explorations in personality.* New York: Oxford University Press. (p. 339)

Murray, H. A. (1933). The effect of fear upon estimates of the maliciousness of other personalities. *Journal of Social Psychology*, *4*, 310–329. (p. 395)

Murray, H. A., & Wheeler, D. R. (1937). A note on the possible clairvoyance of dreams. *Journal of Psychology*, *3*, 309–313. (p. 163)

Murray, R., Jones, P., O'Callaghan, E., Takei, N., & Sham, P. (1992). Genes, viruses, and neurodevelopmental schizophrenia. *Journal of Psychiatric Research*, *26*, 225–235. (p. 453)

Myers, D. G. (1993). *The pursuit of happiness.* New York: Avon Books. (pp. 359, *363)*

Myers, D. G. (1996). *Social psychology*, 5th ed. New York: McGraw-Hill. (p. 410)

Myers, D. G. (1999). *Social psychology,* 6th edition. New York: McGraw-Hill. (p. 410)

Myers, D. G., & Bishop, G. D. (1970). Discussion effects on racial attitudes. *Science*, *169*, 78–779. (p. 505)

Myers, D. G., & Diener, E. (1995). Who is happy? *Psychological Science*, *6*, 10–19. (p. 363)

Myers, D. G., & Diener, E. (1996, May). The pursuit of happiness. *Scientific American,* pp. 54–56. (p. 363)

Myers, I. B. (1987). *Introduction to type: A description of the theory and applications of the Myers-Briggs Type Indicator.* Palo Alto, CA: Consulting Psychologists Press. (p. 401)

Napolitan, D. A., & Goethals, G. R. (1979). The attribution of friendliness. *Journal of Experimental Social Psychology*, 15, 105–113. (p. 491)

Nash, M. (1987). What, if anything, is regressed about hypnotic age regression? A review of the empirical literature. *Psychological Bulletin*, *102*, 42–52. (p. 185)

National Academy of Science. (1984). *Bereavement: Reactions, consequences, and cure.* Washington, DC: National Academy Press. (pp. 373, 374)

National Academy of Science. (1991). *Science, medicine, and animals.* Washington, DC: National Academy Press. (p. 31)

National Academy of Sciences, Institute of Medicine. (1982). *Marijuana and health.* Washington, DC: National Academic Press. (p. 198)

National Center for Health Statistics. (1990). *Health, United States, 1989.* Washington, DC: U.S. Department of Health and Human Services. (p. 111)

National Center for Health Statistics. (1991). Family structure and children's health: United States, 1988," *Vital and Health Statistics, Series 10, No. 178*, CHHS Publication No. PHS 91–1506 by Deborah A. Dawson. (pp. 95, 96)

National Institute of Mental Health. (1982). *Television and behavior: Ten years of scientific progress and implications for the eighties.* Washington, DC: U.S. Government Printing Office. (p. 518)

National Institute on Drug Abuse. (1992). National Household survey on drug abuse: Population estimates 1991 (February 27, 1992 replacement pages). Rockville, MD: Alcohol, Drug Abuse, and mental Health Administration. (p. 196)

National Research Council. (1987). *Risking the future: Adolescent sexuality, pregnancy, and childbearing.* Washington, DC: National Academy Press. (p. 108)

National Research Council. (1990). *Human factors research needs for an aging population.* Washington, DC: National Academy Press. (pp. 111, 112)

National Safety Council. (1991). *Accident facts*. Chicago: National Safety Council. (p. 273)

Naylor, T. H. (1990). Redefining corporate motivation, Swedish style. *Christian Century*, *107*, 566–570. (p. 342)

NCTV News. (1987, July-August). More research links harmful effects to non-violent porn. National Coalition on Television Violence, p. 12. (p. 518)

Needles, D. J., & Abramson, L. Y. (1990). Positive life events, attributional style, and hopefulness: Testing a model of recovery from depression. *Journal of Abnormal Psychology*, *99*, 156–165. (p. 448)

Neeleman, J., & Persaud, R. (1995). Why do psychiatrists neglect religion? *British Journal of Medical Psychology*, *68*, 169–178. (p. 481)

Neese, R. M. (1991, November/December). What good is feeling bad? The evolutionary benefits of psychic pain. *The Sciences*, pp. 30–37. (pp. 141, *212)*

Neisser, U. (1981). John Dean's memory: A case study. *Cognition*, *9*, 1–22. (p. 233)

Neisser, U. (1982). Memorists. In U. Neisser (Ed.), *Memory observed: Remembering in natural contexts.* San Francisco: Freeman. (p. 257)

Neisser, U., Boodoo, G., Bouchard, T. J., Jr., Boykin, A. W., Brody, N., Ceci, S. J., Halpern, D. F., Loehlin, J. C., Perloff, R., Sternberg, R. J., & Urbina, S. (1996). Intelligence: Knows and unknowns. *American Psychologist*, *51*, 77–101. (p. 302)

Neisser, U., & Harsch, N. (1992). Phantom flashbulbs: False recollections of hearing the news about *Challenger*. In E. Winograd & U. Neisser (Eds.), *Affect and accuracy in recall: Studies of "flashbulb" memories.* New York: Cambridge University Press. (pp. 232, 256)

Neisser, U., Winograd, E., & Weldon, M. S. (1991). Remembering the earthquake: "What I experienced" vs. "How I heard the news." Paper presented to the Psychonomic Society convention. (p. 246)

Neitz, J., Geist, T., & Jacobs, G. H. (1989). Color vision in the dog. *Visual Neuroscience*, *3*, 119–125. (p. 136)

Nelson, K. (1973). Structure and strategy in learning to talk. *Monographs of the Society for Research in Child Development*, *38*(1 & 2, Serial No. 149). (p. 279)

Nelson, K. (1993). The psychological and social origins of autobiographical memory. *Psychological Science*, *4*, 7–13. (p. 83)

Nelson, N. (1988). *A meta-analysis of the life-event/health paradigm: The influence of social support.* Philadelphia: Temple University Ph.D. dissertation. (p. 382)

Nevin, J. A. (1988). Behavioral momentum and the partial reinforcement effect. *Psychological Bulletin*, *103*, 44–56. (p. 219)

Newcomb, M. D., & Bentler, P. M. (1988). Impact of adolescent drug use and social support on problems of young adults: A longitudinal study. *Journal of Abnormal Psychology*, *97*, 64–75. (p. 198)

Newcomb, M. D., & Harlow, L. L. (1986). Life events and substance use among adolescents: Mediating effects of perceived loss of control and meaninglessness in life. *Journal of Personality and Social Psychology, 51,* 564–577. (p. 200)

Newell, A. (1988, March 9). Quoted by D. L. Wheeler, From years of work in psychology and computer science, scientists build theories of thinking and learning. *Chronicle of Higher Education,* pp. A4, A6. (p. 13)

Newman, L. S., & Baumeister, R. F. (1996). Toward an explanation of the UFO abduction phenomenon: Hypnotic, elaboration, extraterrestrial sadomasochism, and spurious memories. *Psychological Inquiry, 7,* 99–126. (p. 186)

Newport, E. L. (1990). Maturational constraints on language learning. *Cognitive Science, 14,* 11–28. (p. 282)

NFFRE (1996). Family facts. *Family Matters, 1*(1), 8. Published by National Foundation for Family Research and Education, Calgary, AB T2P 3H5. (p. 444)

Ng, S. H. (1990). Androcentric coding of *man* and *his* in memory by language users. *Journal of Experimental Social Psychology, 26,* 455–464. (p. 286)

Niccols, G. A. (1994). Fetal alcohol syndrome: Implications for Psychologists. *Clinical Psychology Review, 14,* 91–111. (p. 81)

Nickell, J. (1996, May/June). A study of fantasy proneness int he thirteen cases of alleged encounters in John Mack's *Abduction. Skeptical Inquirer,* pp. 18–20, *54. (p. 186)*

Nickerson, R. S., & Adams, M. J. (1979). Long-term memory for a common object. *Cognitive Psychology, 11,* 287–307. (p. 240)

Nicol, S. E., & Gottesman, I. I. (1983). Clues to the genetics and neurobiology of schizophrenia. *American Scientist, 71,* 398–404. (p. 454)

Nicolaus, L. K., Cassel, J. F., Carlson, R. B., & Gustavson, C. R. (1983). Taste-aversion conditioning of crows to control predation on eggs. *Science, 220,* 212–214. (p. 212)

Niemi, R. G., Mueller, J., & Smith, T. W. (1989). *Trends in public opinion: A compendium of survey data.* New York: Greenwood Press. (pp. 361, *508, 510)*

Nigro, G. (1984). Cited by U. Neisser, The role of invariant structures in the control of movement. In M. Frese & J. Sabini (Eds.), *Goal directed behavior: The concept of action in psychology.* Hillsdale, NJ: Erlbaum. (p. 288)

Nisbett, R., & Ross, L. (1991). *The person and the situation.* New York: McGraw-Hill. (p. 342)

Nisbett, R. E. (1993). Violence and U.S. regional culture. *American Psychologist, 48,* 441–449. (p. 516)

Nisbett, R. E., & Borgida, E. (1975). Attribution and the psychology of prediction. *Journal of Personality and Social Psychology, 32,* 932–943. (p. 276)

Nisbett, R. E., & Ross, L. (1980). *Human inference: Strategies and shortcomings of social judgment.* Englewood Cliffs, NJ: Prentice-Hall. (p. 271)

Nishizawa, S. (1996). The religiousness and subjective well-being of Japanese students. Paper presented at the XXVI International Congress of Psychology. (p. 160)

Noble, E. P. (1993). The D2 dopamine receptor gene: A review of association studies in alcoholism. *Behavior Genetics, 23,* 119–129. (p. 200)

Noel, J. G., Forsyth, D. R., & Kelley, K. N. (1987). Improving the performance of failing students by overcoming their self-serving attributional biases. *Basic and Applied Social Psychology, 8,* 151–162. (p. 417)

Nolen-Hoeksema, S. (1990). *Sex differences in depression.* Stanford, CA: Stanford University Press. (p. 446)

Nolen-Hoeksema, S., & Morrow, J. (1991). A prospective study of depression and post-traumatic stress symptoms following a natural disaster: The 1989 Loma Prieta earthquake. *Journal of Personality and Social Psychology, 61,* 115–121. (p. 447)

NORC (National Opinion Research Center) (1985, October/November). Images of the world. *Public Opinion,* p. 38. (p. 413)

NORC (1997). National Opinion Research Center data archived and retrieved from http://www.icpsr.umich.edu. (p. 116)

Norman, D. A. (1988). *The psychology of everyday things.* New York: Basic Books. (p. 159)

Norris, P. A. (1986). On the status of biofeedback and clinical practice. *American Psychologist, 41,* 1009–1010. (p. 379)

Norton, K. L., Olds, T. S., Olive, S., & Dank, S. (1996). Ken and Barbie at life size. *Sex Roles, 34,* 287-294. (p. 323)

Notarius, C., & Markman, H. (1993). *We can work it out.* New York: Putnam. (p. 117)

Nuttin, J. M., Jr. (1987). Affective consequences of mere ownership: The name letter effect in twelve European languages. *European Journal of Social Psychology, 17,* 381–402. (p. 523)

O'Connor, P., & Brown, G. W. (1984). Supportive relationships: Fact or fancy? *Journal of Social and Personal Relationships, 1,* 159–175. (p. 481)

O'Donohue, W., Dopke, C. A., & Swingen, D. N. (1997). Psychotherapy for female sexual dysfunction: A review. *Clinical Psychology Review, 17,* 537–566. (p. 331)

Oetting, E. R., & Beauvais, F. (1987). Peer cluster theory, socialization characteristics, and adolescent drug use: A path analysis. *Journal of Counseling Psychology, 34,* 205–213. (p. 201)

Oetting, E. R., & Beauvais, F. (1990). Adolescent drug use: Findings of national and local surveys. *Journal of Social and Personal Relationships, 1,* 159–175. (p. 201)

Oettingen, G., & Seligman, M. E. P. (1990). Pessimism and behavioural signs of depression in East versus West Berlin. *European Journal of Social Psychology, 20,* 207–220. (p. 417)

Offer, D., Ostrov, E., Howard, K. I., & Atkinson, R. (1988). *The teenage world: Adolescents' self-image in ten countries.* New York: Plenum. (p. 106)

Ohman, A. (1986). Face the beast and fear the face: Animal and social fears as prototypes for evolutionary analyses of emotion. *Psychophysiology, 23,* 123–145. (p. 436)

Olds, J. (1958). Self-stimulation of the brain. *Science, 127,* 315–324. (p. 54)

Olds, J. (1975). Mapping the mind onto the brain. In F. G. Worden, J. P. Swazey, & G. Adelman (Eds.), *The neurosciences: Paths of discovery.* Cambridge, MA: MIT Press. (p. 54)

Olds, J., & Milner, P. (1954). Positive reinforcement produced by electrical stimulation of the septal area and other regions of rat brain. *Journal of Comparative and Physiological Psychology, 47,* 419–427. (p. 54)

O'Leary, A. (1990). Stress, emotion, and human immune function. *Psychological Bulletin, 108,* 363–382. (p. 375)

Oliner, S. P., & Oliner, P. M. (1988). *The altruistic personality: Rescuers of Jews in Nazi Europe.* New York: Free Press. (p. 227)

Oliver, M. B., & Hyde, J. S. (1993). Gender differences in sexuality: A meta-analysis. *Psychological Bulletin, 114,* 29–51. (p. 331)

Olweus, D., Mattsson, A., Schalling, D., & Low, H. (1988). Circulating testosterone levels and aggression in adolescent males: A causal analysis. *Psychosomatic Medicine, 50,* 261–272. (p. 514)

O'Malley, P. M., & Bachman, J. G. (1983). Self-esteem: Change and stability between ages 13 and 23. *Developmental Psychology, 19,* 257–268. (p. 104)

O'Neill, M. J. (1993). The relationship between privacy, control, and stress responses in office workers. Paper presented to the Human Factors and Ergonomics Society convention. (p. 371)

Orne, M. T., & Evans, F. J. (1965). Social control in the psychological experiment: Antisocial behavior and hypnosis. *Journal of Personality and Social Psychology, 1,* 189–200. (p. 186)

Osgood, C. E. (1962). *An alternative to war or surrender.* Urbana: University of Illinois Press. (p. 532)

Osgood, C. E. (1980). *GRIT: A strategy for survival in mankind's nuclear age?* Paper presented at the Pugwash Conference on New Directions in Disarmament. (p. 532)

OSS Assessment Staff. (1948). *The assessment of men.* New York: Rinehart. (p. 420)

Ostfeld, A. M., Kasl, S. V., D'Atri, D. A., & Fitzgerald, E. F. (1987). *Stress, crowding, and blood pressure in prison.* Hillsdale, NJ: Erlbaum. (p. 372)

Oxman, T. E., Freeman, D. H., Jr., & Manheimer, E. D. (1995). Lack of social participation or religious strength and comfort as risk factors for death after cardiac surgery in the elderly. *Psychosomatic Medicine, 57,* 5–15. (p. 383)

Padgett, V. R. (1989). Predicting organizational violence: An application of 11 powerful principles of obedience. Paper presented to the American Psychological Association convention. (p. 500)

Padilla, R. V., & Benavides, A. H. (eds.) (1992). *Critical perspectives on bilingual education research.* Tempe, AZ: Bilingual Press. (p. 287)

Paffenbarger, R. S., Jr., Hyde, R. T., Wing, A. L., & Hsieh, C-C. (1986). Physical activity, all-cause mortality, and longevity of college alumni. *New England Journal of Medicine, 314,* 605–612. (p. 379)

Page, S. (1977). Effects of the mental illness label in attempts to obtain accommodation. *Canadian Journal of Behavioral Science, 9,* 84–90. (p. 430)

Paikoff, R. L., & Brooks-Gunn, J. (1991). Do parent-child relationships change during puberty? *Psychological Bulletin, 110,* 47–66. (p. 106)

Paivio, A. (1986). *Mental representations: A dual coding approach.* New York: Oxford University Press. (p. 237)

Palace, E. M. (1995). Modification of dysfunctional patterns of sexual response through autonomic arousal and false physiological feedback. *Journal of Consulting and Clinical Psychology, 63,* 604–615. (p. 367)

Palladino, J. J., & Carducci, B. J. (1983). *"Things that go bump in the night": Students' knowledge of sleep and dreams.* Paper presented at the meeting of the Southeastern Psychological Association. (p. 173)

Palmer, S., Schreiber, C., & Box, C. (1991). Remembering the earthquake: "Flashbulb" memory for experienced vs. reported events. Paper presented to the Psychonomic Society convention. (p. 246)

Palumbo, S. R. (1978). *Dreaming and memory: A new information-processing model.* New York: Basic Books. (p. 182)

Pandey, J., Sinha, Y., Prakash, A., & Tripathi, R. C. (1982). Right-left political ideologies and attribution of the causes of poverty. *European Journal of Social Psychology, 12,* 327–331. (p. 492)

Panksepp, J. (1982). Toward a general psychobiological theory of emotions. *Behavioral and Brain Sciences, 5,* 407–467. (p. 349)

Parducci, A. (1995). *Happiness, pleasure, and judgment: The contextual theory and its applications.* Hillsdale, NJ: Erlbaum. (p. 361)

Parker, G., Roy, K., Hadzi, P. D., Pedic, F. (1992). Psychotic (delusional depression: A meta-analyis of physical treatments. *Journal of Affective Disorders, 24,* 17–24. (p. 486)

Parker, S., Nichter, M., Nichter, M., & Vuckovic, N. (1995). Body image and weight concerns among African American and white adolescent females: Differences that make a difference. *Human Organization, 54,* 103–114. (p. 320)

Parloff, M. B. (1987, February). Psychotherapy: An import from Japan. *Psychology Today,* pp. 74–75. (p. 461)

Pate, J. E., Pumariega, A. J., Hester, C., & Garner, D. M. (1992). Cross-cultural patterns in eating disorders: A review. *Journal of the American Academy of Child and Adolescent Psychiatry, 31,* 802–809. (p. 319)

Paton, D. (1992). Disaster research: The Scottish dimension. *The Psychologist: Bulletin of the British Psychological Society, 5,* 535–538. (p. 370)

Patterson, F. (1978, October). Conversations with a gorilla. *National Geographic,* pp. 438–465. (p. 283)

Patterson, G. R., Chamberlain, P., & Reid, J. B. (1982). A comparative evaluation of parent training procedures. *Behavior Therapy, 13,* 638–650. (pp. 221, 516)

Patterson, G. R., Reid, J. B., & Dishion, T. J. (1992). *Antisocial boys.* Eugene, OR: Castalia. (p. 516)

Patterson, R. (1951). *The riddle of Emily Dickinson.* Boston: Houghton Mifflin. (p. 448)

Paulos, J. A. (1995). *A mathematician reads the newspaper.* New York: Basic Books. (p. 485)

Pauls, D. L., Morton, L. A., & Egeland, J. A. (1992). Risks of affective illness among first-degree relatives of bipolar I old-order Amish probands. *Archives of General Psychiatry, 49,* 703–708. (p. 443)

Pavlov, I. P. (1927). In G. V. Anrep (Trans.), *Conditioned reflexes.* London: Oxford University Press. (pp. 207, 210)

Pawlik, K., & d'Ydewalle, G. (1996). Psychology and the global commons: Perspectives of international psychology. *American Psychologist, 51,* 488–495. (Updated by e-mail, 8 November 1996.) (p. 7)

Pedersen, N. L., Plomin, R., McClearn, G. E., & Friberg, L. (1988). Neuroticism, extraversion, and related traits in adult twins reared apart and reared together. *Journal of Personality and Social Psychology, 55,* 950–957. (p. 71)

Pekkanen, J. (1982, June). Why do we sleep? *Science, 82,* p. 86. (p. 178)

Pelham, B. W. (1993). On the highly positive thoughts of the highly depressed. In R. F. Baumeister (Ed.), *Self-esteem: The puzzle of low self-regard.* New York: Plenum. (p. 409)

Pendergrast, M. (1996, May). False memory—forget it. *The Psychologist*, p. 200. (p. 261)

Pendick, D. (1994, January/February). The mind of violence. *Brain Work: The Neuroscience Newsletter*, pp. 1–3, 5. (p. 514)

Penfield, W. (1969). Consciousness, memory, and man's conditioned reflexes. In K. Pigram (Ed.), *On the biology of learning*. New York: Harcourt, Brace & World. (p. 244)

Pennebaker, J. (1990). *Opening up: The healing power of confiding in others*. New York: William Morrow. (pp. 384, 397)

Pennebaker, J. W., Barger, S. D., & Tiebout, J. (1989). Disclosure of traumas and health among Holocaust survivors. *Psychosomatic Medicine*, *51*, 577–589. (p. 384)

Pennebaker, J. W., & Harber, K. D. (1993). A social stage model of collective coping: The Loma Prieta earthquake and the Persian Gulf war. *Journal of Social Issues*, *49*, 125–145. (p. 384)

Pennebaker, J. W., & O'Heeron, R. C. (1984). Confiding in others and illness rate among spouses of suicide and accidental death victims. *Journal of Abnormal Psychology*, *93*, 473–476. (pp. 383–384)

Peplau, L. A. (1982). Research on homosexual couples: An overview. *Journal of Homosexuality*, *8*(2), 3–8. (p. 333)

Peplau, L. A., & Gordon, S. L. (1985). Women and men in love: Gender differences in close heterosexual relationships. In V. E. O'Leary, R. K. Unger, & B. S. Wallston (Eds.), *Women, gender, and social psychology*. Hillsdale, NJ: Erlbaum. (p. 16)

Pepperberg, I. M. (1994). Numerical competence in an African gray parrot (*Psittacus erithacus*). *Journal of Comparative Psychology*, *108*, 36–44. (p. 282)

Perkins, H. W. (1991). Religious commitment, Yuppie values, and well-being in post-collegiate life. *Review of Religious Research*, *32*, 244–251. (p. 363)

Perkins, K. A., Dubbert, P. M., Martin, J. E., Faulstich, M. E., & Harris, J. K. (1986). Cardiovascular reactivity to psychological stress in aerobically trained versus untrained mild hypertensives and normotensives. *Health Psychology*, *5*, 407–421. (p. 379)

Perlmutter, M. (1983). Learning and memory through adulthood. In M. W. Riley, B. B. Hess, & K. Bond (Eds.), *Aging in society: Selected reviews of recent research*. Hillsdale, NJ: Erlbaum. (p. 113)

Perrett, D. I., & Emergy, N. J. (1994). Understanding the intentions of others from visual signals: Neurophysiological evidence. *Cahiers de Psychology Cognitive/Current Psychology of Cognition*, *13*, 683–694. (p. 134)

Perrett, D. I., Harries, M., Misflin, A. J., & Chitty, A. J. (1988). Three stages in the classification of body movements by visual neurons. In H. B. Barlow, C. Blakemore, & M. Weston Smith (Eds.), *Images and understanding*. Cambridge: Cambridge University Press. (p. 134)

Perrett, D. I., Hietanen, J. K., Oram, M. W., & Benson, P. J. (1992). Organization and functions of cells responsive to faces in the temporal cortex. *Philosophical Transactions of the Royal Society of London: Series B*, *335*, 23–30. (p. 134)

Persky, V. W., Kempthorne-Rawson, J., & Shekelle, R. B. (1987). Personality and risk of cancer: 20–year follow-up of the Western Electric study. *Psychosomatic Medicine*, *49*, 435–449. (p. 375)

Persons, J. B. (1986). The advantages of studying psychological phenomena rather than psychiatric diagnoses. *American Psychologist*, *41*, 1252–1260. (p. 429)

Pert, C. B. (1986, Summer). The wisdom of the receptors: Neuropeptides, the emotions, and bodymind. *Advances* (Institute for the Advancement of Health), *3*, 8–16. (p. 54)

Pert, C. B., & Snyder, S. H. (1973). Opiate receptor: Demonstration in nervous tissue. *Science*, *179*, 1011–1014. (p. 42)

Peschel, E. R., & Peschel, R. E. (1987). Medical insights into the castrati in opera. *American Scientist*, *75*, 578–583. (p. 329)

Peters, T. J., & Waterman, R. H., Jr. (1982). *In search of excellence: Lessons from America's best-run companies*. New York: Harper & Row. (p. 224)

Peterson, C., & Barrett, L. C. (1987). Explanatory style and academic performance among university freshmen. *Journal of Personality and Social Psychology*, *53*, 603–607. (p. 417)

Peterson, C., Peterson, J., & Skevington, S. (1986). Heated argument and adolescent development. *Journal of Social and Personal Relationships*, *3*, 229–240. (p. 101)

Peterson, L. R., & Peterson, M. J. (1959). Short-term retention of individual verbal items. *Journal of Experimental Psychology*, *58*, 193–198. (p. 242)

Peterson, R. (1978). Review of the Rorschach. In O. K. Buros (Ed.), *The eighth mental measurements yearbook* (Vol. I). Highland Park, NJ: Gryphon Press. (p. 396)

Petitto, L. A., & Marentette, P. F. (1991). Babbling in the manual mode: Evidence for the ontogeny of language. *Science*, *251*, 1493–1496. (pp. 278, 282)

Peto, R., Lopez, A. D., Boreham, J., Thun, M., & Heath, C., Jr. (1992). Mortality from tobacco in developed countries: Indirect estimation from national vital statistics. *Lancet*, *339*, 1268–1278. (p. 195)

Peto, R., & others (1994). *Mortality from smoking in developed countries, 1950–2000: Indirect estimates from national vital statistics*. New York: Oxford University Press. (p. 195).

Petruzzello, S. J., Landers, D. M., Hatfield, B. D., Kubitz, K. A., & Salazar, W. (1991). A meta-analysis on the anxiety-reducing effects of acute and chronic exercise. *Sports Medicine*, *11*, 143–182. (p. 378)

Pettegrew, J. W., Keshavan, M. S., & Minshew, N. J. (1993). 31P nuclear magnetic resonance spectroscopy: Neurodevelopment and schizophrenia. *Schizophrenia Bulletin*, *19*, 35–53. (p. 478)

Pettigrew, T. F. (1969). Racially separate or together? *Journal of Social Issues*, *25*, 43–69. (p. 530)

Pettigrew, T. F. (1997). Generalized intergroup contact effects on prejudice. *Personality and Social Psychology Bulletin*, *23*, 173–185. (p. 530)

Pettingale, K. W., Morris, T., Greer, S., & Haybittle, J. L. (1985, March 30). Mental attitudes to cancer: An additional prognostic factor. *Lancet*, p. 750. (p. 375)

Pfeiffer, E. (1977). Sexual behavior in old age. In E. W. Busse & E. Pfeiffer (Eds.), *Behavior and adaptation in late life* (2nd ed.). Boston: Little, Brown. (p. 112)

Phillips, D. P. (1982). The impact of fictional television stories on U.S. adult fatalities: New evidence on the effect of the mass media on violence. *American Journal of Sociology*, 87, 1340–1359. (p. 497)

Phillips, D. P. (1985). Natural experiments on the effects of mass media violence on fatal aggression: Strengths and weaknesses of a new approach. In L. Berkowitz (Ed.), *Advances in experimental social psychology* (Vol. 19). Orlando, FL: Academic Press. (p. 497)

Phillips, D. P., Carstensen, L. L., & Paight, D. J. (1989). Effects of mass media news stories on suicide, with new evidence on the role of story content. In D. R. Pfeffer (Ed.), *Suicide among youth: Perspectives on risk and prevention.* Washington, DC: American Psychiatric Press. (p. 497)

Phillips, D., & Stipek, D. (1993). Early formal schooling: Are we promoting achievement or anxiety? *Applied and Preventive Psychology, 2,* 141–150. (p. 301)

Phillips, J. L. (1969). *Origins of intellect: Piaget's theory.* San Francisco: Freeman. (p. 88)

Piaget, J. (1932). *The moral judgment of the child.* New York: Harcourt, Brace & World. (p. 102)

Piccione, C., Hilgard, E. R., & Zimbardo, P. G. (1989). On the degree of stability of measured hypnotizability over a 25–year period. *Journal of Personality and Social Psychology, 56,* 289–295. (p. 184)

Pickar, D., Labarca, R., Linnoila, M., Roy, A., Hommer, D., Everett, D., & Payl, S. M. (1984). Neuroleptic-induced decrease in plasma homovanillic acid and antipsychotic activity in schizophrenic patients. *Science, 225,* 954–957. (p. 483)

Pike, K. M., & Rodin, J. (1991). Mothers, daughters, and disordered eating. *Journal of Abnormal Psychology, 100,* 198–204. (p. 319)

Pillemer, D. G. (1995). What is remembered about early childhood events? Invited paper presentation to the American Psychological Society convention. (p. 83)

Pincus, H. A. (1997) Commentary: Spirituality, religion, and health: Expanding, and using the knowledge base. *Mind/Body Medicine, 2,* 49. (p. 383)

Pinel, J. P. J. (1993). *Biopsychology,* 2nd ed. Boston: Allyn & Bacon. (p. 317)

Pingitore, R., Dugoni, B. L., Tindale, R. S., & Spring, B. (1994). Bias against overweight job applicants in a simulated employment interview. *Journal of Applied Psychology, 79,* 909–917. (p. 321)

Pinker, S. (1990, September-October). Quoted by J. de Cuevas, "No, she holded them loosely." *Harvard Magazine,* pp. 60–67. (p. 277)

Pinker, S. (1995). The language instinct. *The General Psychologist, 31,* 63–65. (pp. 280, 283, 284)

Piotrowski, C., & Keller, J. W. (1989). Psychological testing in outpatient mental health facilities: A national study. *Professional Psychology: Research and Practice, 20,* 423–425. (p. 396)

Pittenger, D. J. (1993). The utility of the Myers-Briggs Type Indicator. *Review of Ecuational Research, 63,* 467–488. (p. 401)

Pleck, J. H., Sonenstein, F. L., & Ku, L. C. (1993). Masculinity ideology: Its impact on adolescent males' heterosexual relationships. *Journal of Social Issues, 49,* 11–29. (p. 332)

Pliner, P. (1982). The effects of mere exposure on liking for edible substances. *Appetite: Journal for Intake Research, 3,* 283–290. (p. 320)

Pliner, P., Pelchat, M., & Grabski, M. (1993). Reduction of neophobia in humans by exposure to novel foods. *Appetite, 20,* 111–123. (p. 320)

Pliner, P., & Pelchat, M. L. (1991). Neophobia in humans and the special status of foods of animal origin. *Appetite, 16,* 205–218. (p. 318)

Plomin, R., DeFries, J. C., McClearn, G. E., & Rutter, M. (1997). *Behavioral genetics.* New York: Freeman. (pp. 69, 300, 322, 453)

Plous, S. (1993). The nuclear arms race: Prisoner's dilemma or perceptual dilemma? *Journal of Peace Research, 30,* 163–179. (p. 522)

Polivy, J., & Herman, C. P. (1985). Dieting and binging: A causal analysis. *American Psychologist, 40,* 193–201. (p. 325)

Polivy, J., & Herman, C. P. (1987). Diagnosis and treatment of normal eating. *Journal of Personality and Social Psychology, 55,* 635–644. (pp. 324, 325)

Pollard, R. (1992). 100 years in psychology and deafness: A centennial retrospective. Invited address to the American Psychological Association convention, Washington, DC. (p. 286)

Polusny, M. A., & Follette, V. M. (1995). Long-term correlates of child sexual abuse: Theory and review of the empirical literature. Applied & Preventive Psychology, 4, 143–166. (p. 94)

Pomerleau, O. F., & Pomerleau, C. S. (1984). Neuroregulators and the reinforcement of smoking: Towards a biobehavioral explanation. *Neuroscience and Biobehavioral Reviews, 8,* 503–513. (p. 195)

Pomeroy, W. B. (1972). *Dr. Kinsey and the Institute for Sex Research.* New York: Harper & Row. (p. 326)

Pons, T. P., Garraghty, P. E., Ommaya, A. K., Kaas, J. H., Taub, E., & Mishkin, M. (1991). Massive cortical reorganization after sensory deafferentation in adult macaques. *Science, 252,* 1857–1860. (p. 62)

Poole, D. A., & Lindsay, D. S. (1995). Interviewing preschoolers: Effects of nonsuggestive techniques, parental coaching and leading questions on reports of nonexperienced events. *Journal of Experimental Child Psychology, 60,* 129–154. (p. 258)

Poole, D. A., Lindsay, D. S., Memon, A., & Bull, R. (1995). Psychotherapy and the recovery of memories of childhood sexual abuse: U.S. and British practitioners' opinions, practices, and experiences. *Journal of Consulting and Clinical Psychology, 63,* 426–437. (p. 260)

Poon, L. W. (1987). Myths and truisms: Beyond extant analyses of speed of behavior and age. Address to the Eastern Psychological Association convention. (p. 112)

Pope, H. G., Jr., & Hudson, J. I. (1992). Is childhood sexual abuse a risk factor for bulimia nervosa? *American Journal of Psychiatry, 149,* 455–463. (p. 319)

Pope, H. G., Jr., & Hudson, J. I. (1995). Can memories of childhood sexual abuse be repressed? *Psychological Medicine, 25,* 121–126. (p. 397)

Pope, H. G., Mangweth, B., Negrao, A. B., Hudson, J. I., & Cordias, T. A. (1994). Childhood sexual abuse and bulimia nervosa: A comparison of American, Austrian, and Brazilian women. *American Journal of Psychiatry, 151,* 732–737. (p. 319)

Pope, H. G., & Yurgelun-Todd, D. (1996). The residual cognitive effects of heavy marijuana use in college students. *Journal of the American Medical Association, 275,* 521–527. (p. 198)

Popenoe, D. (1993). The evolution of marriage and the problem of stepfamilies: A biosocial perspective. Paper presented at the National Symposium on Stepfamilies, Pennsylvania State University. (p. 413)

Porter, D., & Neuringer, A. (1984). Music discriminations by pigeons. *Journal of Experimental Psychology: Animal Behavior Processes, 10,* 138–148. (p. 217)

Posner, M. I., & Carr, T. H. (1992). Lexical access and the brain: Anatomical constraints on cognitive models of word recognition. *American Journal of Psychology, 105,* 1–26. (p. 60)

Powell, J. (1989). *Happiness is an inside job.* Valencia, CA: Tabor. (p. 410)

Powell, J. L. (1988). A test of the knew-it-all-along effect in the 1984 Presidential and statewide elections. *Journal of Applied Social Psychology, 18,* 760–773. (p. 11)

Powell, K. E., Thompson, P. D., Caspersen, C. J., & Kendrick, J. S. (1987). Physical activity and the incidence of coronary heart disease. *Annual Review of Public Health, 8,* 253–287. (p. 379)

Powell, M. C., & Fazio, R. H. (1984). Attitude accessibility as a function of repeated attitudinal expression. *Personality and Social Psychology Bulletin, 10,* 139–148. (p. 494)

Powell, R. A., & Boer, D. P. (1994). Did Freud mislead patients to confabulate memories of abuse? *Psychological Reports, 74,* 1283–1298. (p. 397)

Pratkanis, A. R. (1992). The cargo-cult science of subliminal persuasion. *Skeptical Inquirer, 16,* 260–272. (p. 127)

Pratkanis, A. R., Eskenazi, J., & Greenwald, A. G. (1994). What you expect is what you believe (but not necessarily what you get): A test of the effectiveness of subliminal self-help audiotapes. *Basic and Applied Social Psychology, 15,* 251–276. (p. 127)

Pratt, L. A., Ford, D. E., Crum, R. M., Armenian, H. K., Gallo, J. J., & Eaton, W. W. (1996). Depression, psychotropic medication, and risk of myocardial infarction: Prospective data from the Baltimore ECA follow-up. *Circulation, 94,* 3123–3129. (p. 373)

Pratto, F. (1996). Sexual politics: The gender gap in the bedroom, the cupboard, and the cabinet. In D. M. Buss & N. M. Malamuth (eds.), *Sex, power, conflict: Evolutionary and feminist perspectives.* New York: Oxford University Press. (p. 508)

Prentice, D. A., & Miller, D. T. (1993). Pluralistic ignorance and alcohol use on campus: Some consequences of misperceiving the social norm. *Journal of Personality and Social Psychology, 64,* 243–256. (p. 201)

Prescott, C. A., Hewitt, J. K., Truett, K. R., Heath, A. C., Neale, M. C., & Eaves, L. J. (1994, March). Genetic and environmental influences on lifetime alcohol-related problems in a volunteer sample of older twins. *Journal of Studies on Alcohol,* pp. 184–202. (p. 200)

Presson, P. K., & Benassi, V. A. (1996). Locus of control orientation and depressive symptomatology: A meta-analysis. *Journal of Social Behavior and Personality, 11,* 201–212. (p. 417)

Prioleau, L., Murdock, M., & Brody, N. (1983). An analysis of psychotherapy versus placebo studies. *The Behavioral and Brain Sciences, 6,* 275–310. (p. 480)

Project Match Research Group (1997). Matching alcoholism treatments to client heterogeneity: Project MATCH posttreatment drinking outcomes. *Journal of Studies on Alcohol, 58,* 7–29. (p. 474)

Prothrow-Stith, D. (1991). *Deadly consequences.* New York: Harper-Collins. (p. 516)

Public Opinion. (1984, August/September). Phears and Phobias, p. 32. (p. 433)

Public Opinion. (1987, May/June). Teen angels (report of University of Michigan survey), p. 32. (p. 100)

Pulver, A. E., Liang, K-Y., Brown, C. H., Wolyniec, P., McGrath, J., Adler, L., Tam, D., Carpenter, W. T., & Childs, B. (1992). Risk factors in schizophrenia: Season of birth, gender, and familial risk. *British Journal of Psychiatry, 160,* 65–71. (p. 453)

Putnam, F. W. (1991). Recent research on multiple personality disorder. *Psychiatric Clinics of North America, 14,* 489–502. (p. 439)

Putnam, F. W. (1995). Rebuttal of Paul McHugh. *Journal of the American Academy of Child and Adolescent Psychiatry, 34,* 963. (p. 439)

Pyszczynski, T., Hamilton, J. C., Greenberg, J., & Becker, S. E. (1991). Self-awareness and psychological dysfunction. In C. R. Snyder & D. O. Forsyth (Eds.), *Handbook of social and clinical psychology: The health perspective.* New York: Pergamon. (p. 447)

Qualls, P. J., & Sheehan, P. W. (1981). Electromyograph biofeedback as a relaxation technique: A critical appraisal and reassessment. *Psychological Bulletin, 90,* 21–42. (p. 380)

Rabin, A. S., Kaslow, N. J., & Rehm, L. P. (1986). Aggregate outcome and follow-up results following self-control therapy for depression. Paper presented at the American Psychological Association convention. (p. 473)

Raglin, J. S. (1992). Anxiety and sport performance. In J. O. Holloszy (ed.), *Exercise and sports sciences reviews,* vol. 20. Baltimore: Williams & Wilkins. (p. 415)

Raine, A. (1993). *The psychopathology of crime: Criminal behavior as a clinical disorder.* San Diego, CA: Academic Press. (p. 514)

Rajecki, D. W., Bledsoe, S. B., & Rasmussen, J. L. (1991). Successful personal ads: Gender differences and similarities in offers, stipulations, and outcomes. *Basic and Applied Social Psychology, 12,* 457–469. (p. 525)

Ramey, S. L., & Ramey, C. T. (1992). Early educational intervention with disadvantaged children—To what effect? *Applied and Preventive Psychology, 1,* 131–140. (p. 301)

Rand, C. S. W., & Macgregor, A. M. C. (1990). Morbidly obese patients' perceptions of social discrimination before and after surgery for obesity. *Southern Medical Journal, 83,* 1390–1395. (p. 320)

Randi, J. (1997, October 10). E-mail list letter from owner-jrefinfo@ssr.com (p. 163)

Rapoport, J. L. (1989, March). The biology of obsessions and compulsions. *Scientific American,* pp. 83–89. (pp. 434, 436)

Raskin, D. C. (1982). University of Utah, as shown in *Science '82,* June, 24–27. (p. 351)

Rauch, S. L., & Jenike, M. A. (1993). Neurobiological models of obsessive-compulsive disorder. *Psychomatics, 34,* 20–32. (p. 437)

Raudenbush, B., & Zellner, D. A. (1997). Nobody's satisfied: Effects of abnormal eating behaviors and actual and perceived weight status on body image satisfaction in males and females. *Journal of Social and Clinical Psychology, 16,* 95–110. (p. 319)

Reason, J. (1987). The Chernobyl errors. *Bulletin of the British Psychological Society, 40,* 201–206. (p. 505)

Reason, J., & Mycielska, K. (1982). *Absent-minded? The psychology of mental lapses and everyday errors.* Englewood Cliffs, NJ: Prentice-Hall. (p. 157)

Redelmeier, D. A., & Tversky, D. A. (1996). On the belief that arthritis pain is related to the weather. *Proceedings of the National Academy of Sciences, 93,* 2895–2896. (p. 18)

Regeth, R., & Lewis, M. (1995). Sex differences in depression: A meta-analysis. Paper presented at the Americal Psychological Society convention. (p. 442)

Regier, D. A., Narrow, W. E., Rae, D. S., Manderscheid, R. W., Locke, B. Z., & Goodwin, F. K. (1993). The de facto U.S. mental and addictive disorders service system: Epidemiologic catchment area prospective 1-year prevalence rates of disorders and services. *Archives of General Psychiatry, 50,* 85–94. (p. 475)

Reisenzein, R. (1983). The Schachter theory of emotion: Two decades later. *Psychological Bulletin, 94,* 239–264. (p. 366)

Reiser, M. (1982). *Police psychology.* Los Angeles: LEHI. (p. 162)

Remley, A. (1988, October). From obedience to independence. *Psychology Today,* pp. 56–59. (p. 96)

Renner, M. J. (1992). Curiosity and exploration. In L. R. Squire (ed.), *Encyclopedia of Learning and Memory*. New York: Macmillan. (p. 313)

Renner, M. J., & Renner, C. H. (1993). Expert and novice intuitive judgments about animal behavior. *Bulletin of the Psychonomic Society, 31*, 551–552. (p. 83)

Renner, M. J., & Rosenzweig, M. R. (1987). Enriched and impoverished environments: Effects on brain and behavior. New York: Springer-Verlag. (p. 83)

Rescorla, R. A., & Wagner, A. R. (1972). A theory of Pavlovian conditioning: Variations in the effectiveness of reinforcement and nonreinforcement. In A. H. Black & W. F. Perokasy (Eds.), *Classical conditioning II: Current theory*. New York: Appleton-Century-Crofts. (p. 211)

Resnick, M. D., & 12 others (1997). Protecting adolescents from harm: Findings from the National Longitudinal Study on Adolescent Health. *Journal of the American Medical Association, 278*, 823–832. (pp. 21, 106)

Resnick, S. M. (1992). Positron emission tomography in psychiatric illness. *Current Directions in Psychological Science, 1*, 92–98. (pp. 437, 452)

Responsive Community (1996, Fall). Age vs. weight. Page 83 (reported from a *Wall Street Journal* survey). (p. 324)

Retterstøl, N. (1993). *Suicide: A European perspective.* New York: Cambridge University Press. (p. 445)

Reveen, P. J. (1987–88). Fantasizing under hypnosis: Some experimental evidence. *The Skeptical Inquirer, 12*, 181–183. (p. 187)

Rhodes, S. R. (1983). Age-related differences in work attitudes and behavior: A review and conceptual analysis. *Psychological Bulletin, 93*, 328–367. (p. 111)

Rice, B. (1985, September). Performance review: The job nobody likes. *Psychology Today*, pp. 30–36. (p. 493)

Rice, M. E., & Grusec, J. E. (1975). Saying and doing: Effects on observer performance. *Journal of Personality and Social Psychology, 32*, 584–593. (p. 227)

Richardson, J. (1993). The curious case of coins: Remembering the appearance of familiar objects. *The Psychologist: Bulletin of the British Psychological Society, 6*, 360–366. (p. 240)

Rieff, P. (1979). *Freud: The mind of a moralist* (3rd ed.). Chicago: University of Chicago Press. (p. 399)

Ring, K. (1980). *Life at death: A scientific investigation of the near-death experience.* New York: Coward, McCann & Geoghegan. (p. 197)

Ring, K. (1992). *The omega project: Near death experiences, UFO encounters, and mind at large.* New York: Morrow. (p. 198)

Riskind, J. H., Beck, A. T., Berchick, R. J., Brown, G., & Steer, R. A. (1987). Reliability of DSM-III diagnoses for major depression and generalized anxiety disorder using the structured clinical interview for DSM-III. *Archives of General Psychiatry, 44*, 817–820. (p. 429)

Roberts, A. H., Kewman, D. G., Mercier, L., & Hovell, M. (1993). The power of nonspecific effects in healing: Implications for psychosocial and biological treatments. *Clinical Psychology Review, 13*, 375–391. (p. 480)

Roberts, L. (1988). Beyond Noah's ark: What do we need to know? *Science, 242*, 1247. (p. 371)

Robins, L., & Regier, D. (Eds.). (1991). *Psychiatric disorders in America.* New York: Free Press. (pp. 457, 526)

Robins, L. N., Davis, D. H., & Goodwin, D. W. (1974). Drug use by U.S. Army enlisted men in Vietnam: A follow-up on their return home. *American Journal of Epidemiology, 99*, 235–249. (p. 192)

Robinson, F. P. (1970). *Effective study.* New York: Harper & Row. (p. 34)

Robinson, J. L., Kagan, J., Reznick, J. S., & Corley, R. (1992). The heritability of inhibited and uninhibited behavior: A twin study. *Developmental Psychology, 28*, 1030–1037. (p. 93)

Rochat, F. (1993). How did they resist authority? Protecting refugees in Le Chambon during World War II. Paper presented at the American Psychological Association convention. (p. 501)

Rock, I., Hall, S., & Davis, J. (1994). Why do ambiguous figures reverse? *Acta Psychologica, 87*, 33–57. (p. 147)

Rock, I., & Palmer, S. (1990, December). The legacy of Gestalt psychology. *Scientific American*, pp. 84–90. (p. 148)

Rodin, J. (1979). *Obesity theory and behavior therapy: An uneasy couple?* Paper presented at the meeting of the Association for the Advancement of Behavior Therapy. (p. 325)

Rodin, J. (1984, December). A sense of control [interview]. *Psychology Today*, pp. 38–45. (p. 318)

Rodin, J. (1985). Insulin levels, hunger and food intake: An example of feedback loops in body weight regulation. *Health Psychology, 4*, 1–18. (p. 325)

Rodin, J. (1986). Aging and health: Effects of the sense of control. *Science, 233*, 1271–1276. (pp. 371, 417)

Rodin, J., & Slochower, J. (1976). Externality in the non-obese: Effects of environmental responsiveness on weight. *Journal of Personality and Social Psychology, 33*, 338–344. (p. 318)

Rodriquez De Fronseca, F., Carrera, M. R. A., Navarro, M., Koob, G. F., & Weiss, F. (1997). Activation of coriticotropin-releasing factor in the limbic system during cannabinoid withdrawal. *Science, 276*, 2050–2054. (p. 198)

Roediger, H. L., III, Wheeler, M. A., & Rajaram, S. (1993). Remembering, knowing, and reconstructing the past. In D. L. Medin (Ed.), *The psychology of learning and motivation: Advances in research and theory,* vol. 30. Orlando, FL: Academic Press. (p. 256)

Rogers, C. R. (1958). Reinhold Niebuhr's *The self and the dramas of history:* A criticism. *Pastoral Psychology, 9*, 15–17. (p. 410)

Rogers, C. R. (1961). *On becoming a person: A therapist's view of psychotherapy.* Boston: Houghton Mifflin. (p. 464)

Rogers, C. R. (1980). *A way of being.* Boston: Houghton Mifflin. (pp. 464–465)

Rogers, C. R. (1981, Summer). Notes on Rollo May. *Perspectives, 2*(1), p. 16. (p. 414)

Rogers, S. (1992–1993, Winter). How a publicity blitz created the myth of subliminal advertising. *Public Relations Quarterly*, pp. 12–17. (p. 127)

Rogers, S. (1994). Subliminal advertising: Grand scam of the 20th century. Paper presented to the American Academy of Advertising convention. (pp. 127, 151)

Rohner, R. P. (1986). *The warmth dimension: Foundations of parental acceptance-rejection theory.* Newbury Park, CA: Sage. (p. 97)

Rook, K. S. (1984). Promoting social bonding: Strategies for helping the lonely and socially isolated. *American Psychologist, 39*, 1389–1407. (p. 448)

Rorty, M., Yager, J., & Rossotto, E. (1994). Childhood sexual, physical, and psychological abuse in bulimia nervosa. *American Journal of Psychiatry, 151,* 1122–1126. (p. 319)

Rosch, E. (1974). Linguistic relativity. In A. Silverstein (Ed.), *Human communication: Theoretical perspectives.* New York: Halsted Press. (p. 286)

Rosch, E. (1978). Principles of categorization. In E. Rosch & B. L. Lloyd (Eds.), *Cognition and categorization.* Hillsdale, NJ: Erlbaum. (p. 269)

Rosen, R. C., & Leiblum, S. R. (1995). Treatment of sexual disorders in the 1990s: An integrated approach. *Journal of Consulting and Clinical Psychology, 63,* 877–890. (p. 331)

Rosenbaum, M. (1986). The repulsion hypothesis: On the nondevelopment of relationships. *Journal of Personality and Social Psychology,* 51, 1156–1166. (p. 526)

Rosenhan, D. L. (1973). On being sane in insane places. *Science, 179,* 250–258. (p. 429)

Rosenthal, R., Hall, J. A., Archer, D., DiMatteo, M. R., & Rogers, P. L. (1979). The PONS test: Measuring sensitivity to nonverbal cues. In S. Weitz (Ed.), *Nonverbal communication* (2nd ed.). New York: Oxford University Press. (pp. 306, 352)

Rosenzweig, M. R. (1984). Experience, memory, and the brain. *American Psychologist, 39,* 365–376. (p. 83)

Rosenzweig, M. R. (1992). Psychological science around the world. *American Psychologist, 47,* 718–722. (p. 7)

Ross, L., Greene, D., & House, P. (1977). The false consensus effect: An egocentric bias in social perception and attribution process. *Journal of Experimental Social Psychology, 13,* 279–301. (p. 15)

Ross, L., & Stillinger, C. (1991). Barriers to conflict resolution. *Negotiation Journal, 7,* 389–404. (p. 532)

Ross, M. (1996). Validating memories. In N. L. Stein, P. A. Ornstein, B. Tversky, & C. Brainerd (eds.), *Memory for everyday and emotional events.* Hillsdale, NJ: Erlbaum. (p. 257)

Ross, M., McFarland, C., & Fletcher, G. J. O. (1981). The effect of attitude on the recall of personal histories. *Journal of Personality and Social Psychology, 40,* 627–634. (p. 254)

Rossi, A. S., & Rossi, P. H. (1993). *Of human bonding: Parent-child relations across the life course.* Hawthorne, NY: Aldine de Gruyter. (p. 105)

Rossi, P. H. (1990). The old homeless and the new homelessness in historical perspective. *American Psychologist, 45,* 954–959. (p. 483)

Rossi, P. J. (1968). Adaptation and negative aftereffect to lateral optical displacement in newly hatched chicks. *Science, 160,* 430–432. (p. 156)

Roth, T., Roehrs, T., Zwyghuizen-Doorenbos, A., Stpeanski, E., & Witting, R. (1988). Sleep and memory. In I. Hindmarch & H. Ott (Eds.), *Benzodiazepine receptor ligans, memory and information processing.* New York: Springer-Verlag. (p. 181)

Rothbart, M., Fulero, S., Jensen, C., Howard, J., & Birrell, P. (1978). From individual to group impressions: Availability heuristics in stereotype formation. *Journal of Experimental Social Psychology, 14,* 237–255. (p. 512)

Rothbaum, F., & Xu, X. (1995). The theme of giving back to parents in Chinese and American songs. *Journal of Cross-Cultural Psychology, 26,* 698–713. (p. 412)

Rothblum, E. D. (1990). Women and weight: Fad and fiction. *Journal of Psychology, 124,* 5–24. (p. 323)

Rothstein, W. G. (1980). The significance of occupations in work careers: An empirical and theoretical review. *Journal of Vocational Behavior, 17,* 328–343. (p. 118)

Rotton, J., & Kelly, I. W. (1985). Much ado about the full moon: A meta-analysis of lunar-lunacy research. *Psychological Bulletin, 97,* 286–306. (p. 455)

Rovee-Collier, C. (1993). The capacity for long-term memory in infancy. *Current Directions in Psychological Science, 2,* 130–135. (p. 250)

Roviaro, S., Holmes, D. S., & Holmsten, R. D. (1984). Influence of a cardiac rehabilitation program on the cardiovascular, psychological, and social functioning of cardiac patients. *Journal of Behavioral Medicine, 7,* 61–81. (p. 379)

Rowe, D. C. (1990). As the twig is bent? The myth of child-rearing influences on personality development. *Journal of Counseling and Development, 68,* 606–611. (pp. 71, 107)

Rowe, D. C. (1994). *The limits of family influence.* New York: Guilford. (p. 107)

Rowe, D. C., Vazsonyi, A. T., & Flannery, D. J. (1994). No more than skin deep: Ethnic and racial similarity in developmental process. *Psychological Review, 101,* 396–413. (p. 306)

Roy, M-A., Neale, M. C., Pedersen, N. L., Mathe, A. A., & Kendler, K. S. (1995). A twin study of generalized anxiety disorder and major depression. *Psychological Medicine, 25,* 1037–1049. (p. 437)

Rozin, P. (1976). The selection of food by rats, humans and other animals. In J. Rosenblatt, R. A. Hinde, C. Beer, & E. Shaw (Eds.), *Advances in the study of behavior,* vol. 6. New York: Academic Press. (p. 318)

Rozin, P., Millman, L., & Nemeroff, C. (1986). Operation of the laws of sympathetic magic in disgust and other domains. *Journal of Personality and Social Psychology, 50,* 703–712. (p. 210)

Ruback, R. B., Carr, T. S., & Hopper, C. H. (1986). Perceived control in prison: Its relation to reported crowding, stress, and symptoms. *Journal of Applied Social Psychology, 16,* 375–386. (p. 417)

Rubin, J. Z., Pruitt, D. G., & Kim, S. H. (1994). *Social conflict: Escalation, stalemate, and settlement.* New York: McGraw-Hill. (p. 531)

Rubin, L. B. (1985). *Just friends: The role of friendship in our lives.* New York: Harper & Row. (p. 106)

Rubin, Z. (1970). Measurement of romantic love. *Journal of Personality and Social Psychology, 16,* 265–273. (p. 352)

Rubonis, A. V., & Bickman, L. (1991). Psychological impairment in the wake of disaster: The disaster-psychopathology relationship. *Psychological Bulletin, 109,* 384–399. (p. 370)

Ruchlis, H. (1990). *Clear thinking: A practical introduction.* Buffalo, NY: Prometheus Books. (p. 269)

Ruffin, C. L. (1993). Stress and health—little hassles vs. major life events. *Australian Psychologist, 28,* 201–208. (p. 371)

Rule, B. G., & Ferguson, T. J. (1986). The effects of media violence on attitudes, emotions, and cognitions. *Journal of Social Issues, 42*(3), 29–50. (p. 518)

Rumbaugh, D. M. (1977). *Language learning by a chimpanzee: The Lana project.* New York: Academic Press. (p. 283)

Rumbaugh, D. M. (1994, February 15). Remarks on *Nova: Can chimps talk?* PBS Television. (p. 285)

Rumbaugh, D. M., & Savage-Rumbaugh, S. (1978). Chimpanzee language research: Status and potential. *Behavior Research Methods & Instrumentation, 10*, 119–131. (p. 285)

Rumbaugh, D. M., & Savage-Rumbaugh, S. (1994, January/February). Language and apes. *Psychology Teacher Network*, pp. 2–5, 9. (p. 285)

Rushton, J. P. (1975). Generosity in children: Immediate and long-term effects of modeling, preaching, and moral judgment. *Journal of Personality and Social Psychology, 31*, 459–466. (p. 227)

Rushton, J. P. (1990). Race differences, r/K theory, and a reply to Flynn. *The Psychologist: Bulletin of the British Psychological Society, 5*, 195–198. (p. 303)

Rushton, J. P. (1995). *Race, evolution, and behavior: A life history perspective.* New Brunswick, NJ: Transaction Publishers. (p. 303)

Rushton, J. P., Fulker, D. W., Neale, M. C., Nias, D. K. B., & Eysenck, H. J. (1986). Altruism and aggression: The heritability of individual differences. *Journal of Personality and Social Psychology, 50*, 1192–1198. (p. 514)

Russell, B. (1930/1985). *The conquest of happiness.* London: Unwin Paperbacks. (p. 362)

Russell, J. A. (1991). Culture and the categorization of emotions. *Psychological Bulletin, 110*, 426–450. (p. 354)

Russell, J. A. (1995). Facial expressions of emotion: What lies beyond minimal universality. *Psychological Bulletin, 118*, 379–391. (p. 354)

Russell, J. A., Lewicka, M., & Niit, T. (1989). A cross-cultural study of a circumplex model of affect. *Journal of Personality and Social Psychology, 57*, 848–856. (p. 356)

Russo, N. F. (1992). Abortion, childbearing, and women's well-being. *Professional Psychology: Research and Practice, 23*, 269–280. (p. 371)

Rutter, M. (1979). Maternal deprivation, 1972–1978: New findings, new concepts, new approaches. *Child Development, 50*, 283–305. (p. 94)

Ryan, E. D. (1980). Attribution, intrinsic motivation, and athletics: A replication and extension. In C. H. Nadeau, W. R. Halliwell, K. M. Newell, & G. C. Roberts (Eds.), *Psychology of motor behavior and sport—1979.* Champaign, IL: Human Kinetics Press. (p. 340)

Ryckman, R. M., Robbins, M. A., Kaczor, L. M., & Gold J. A. (1989). Male and female raters' stereotyping of male and female physiques. *Personality and Social Psychology Bulletin, 15*, 244–251. (p. 320)

Rymer, R. (1993). *Genie: An abused child's flight from silence.* New York: HarperCollins. (p. 324)

Rzewnicki, R., & Forgays, D. G. (1987). Recidivism and self-cure of smoking and obesity: An attempt to replicate. *American Psychologist, 42*, 97–100. (p. 324)

Sabini, J. (1986). Stanley Milgram (1933–1984). *American Psychologist, 41*, 1378–1379. (p. 499)

Sacks, O. (1985). *The man who mistook his wife for a hat.* New York: Summit Books. (pp. 64, 145, 246)

Sacks, O. (1990). *Seeing voices: A journey into the world of the deaf.* New York: HarperCollins. (p. 287)

Sacks, O. (1995, January 9). Prodigies. *New Yorker*, pp. 44–65. (p. 291)

Sadato, N., & others (1996). Activation of the primary visual cortex by Braille reading in blind subjects. *Nature, 380*, 526–528. (p. 62)

Saffran, J. R., Aslin, R. N., & Newport, E. L. (1996). Statistical learning by 8-month-old infants. *Science, 274*, 1926–1928. (p. 281)

Sagan, C. (1979). *Broca's brain.* New York: Random House. (pp. 9, 48)

Sagan, C. (1987, February 1). The fine art of baloney detection. *Parade.* (p. 163)

Sagan, C., & Druyan, A. (1992). *Shadows of forgotten ancestors: A search for who we are.* New York: Random House. (p. 283)

Salovey, P. (1990, January/February). Interview. *American Scientist*, pp. 25–29. (p. 359)

Salovey, P., & Mayer, J. D. (1990). Emotional intelligence. *Imagination, cognition, and personality, 9*, 185–211. (p. 292)

Salthouse, T. A. (1992). *Mechanisms of age-cognition relations in adulthood.* Hillsdale, NJ: Erlbaum. (p. 111)

Salthouse, T. A. (1994). The nature of the influence of speed on adult age differences in cognition. *Developmental Psychology, 30*, 240–259. (p. 111)

Samuels, S., & McCabe, G. (1989). Quoted by P. Diaconis & F. Mosteller, Methods for studying coincidences. *Journal of the American Statistical Association, 84*, 853–861. (p. 20)

Sanchez, R. D., Contri, G. B., & Pardo, I. Q. (1996). Spanish psychologists on the labor market. In A. Schorr & S. Saari (eds.), *Psychology in Europe: Facts, figures, realities. Gottingen: Hogrefe & Huber.* (p. 7)

Sandberg, G. G., Jackson, T. L., & Petretic-Jackson, P. (1985). *Sexual aggression and courtship violence in dating relationships.* Paper presented at the meeting of the Midwestern Psychological Association. (p. 518)

Sanes, J, Donoghue, J., Thangaraj, V., Edelman, R. R., & Warach, S. (1995). Shared neural substrates controlling hand movements in human motor cortex. *Science, 269*, 1775–1777. (p. 57)

Sanz, C., & Jensvold, M. L. (1997). Chimpanzees' reaction to naive versus educated visitors. *Friends of Washoe, 18*(Summer/Fall), 9–14. (p. 283)

Sapadin, L. A. (1988). Friendship and gender: Perspectives of professional men and women. *Journal of Social and Personal Relationships, 5*, 387–403. (p. 106)

Sapirstein, G., & Kirsch, I. (1996). Listening to Prozac, but hearing placebo? A meta analysis of the placebo effect of antidepressant medication. Paper presented to the American Psychological Association convention. (p. 484)

Sapolsky, B. S., & Tabarlet, J. O. (1991). Sex in primetime television: 1979 versus 1989. *Journal of Broadcasting and Electronic Media, 35*, 505–516. (pp. 108, 520)

Sartorius, N. R. (1994). Description of WHO's mental health programme. In W. J. Lonner & R. Malpass (Eds.), *Psychology and culture.* Boston: Allyn and Bacon. (pp. 369, 426)

Sato, K. (1987). Distribution of the cost of maintaining common resources. *Journal of Experimental Social Psychology, 23*, 19–31. (p. 521)

Savage-Rumbaugh, E. S., Murphy, J., Sevcik, R. A., Brakke, K. E., Williams, S. L., & Rumbaugh, D. M., with commentary by Bates, E. (1993). Language comprehension in ape and child. *Monographs of the Society for Research in Child Development, 58* (no. 233), 1–254. (p. 285)

Sax, L. J., Astin, A. W., Korn, W. S., & Mahoney, K. M. (1996). *The American freshman: National norms for Fall 1996.* Los Angeles, CA: Higher Education Research Institute, UCLA. (pp. 109, 199, 331, 360, 508)

Sayre, R. F. (1979). The parents' last lessons. In D. D. Van Tassel (Ed.), *Aging, death, and the completion of being.* Philadelphia: University of Pennsylvania Press. (p. 112)

Scarr, S. (1984, May). What's a parent to do? [Conversation with E. Hall.] *Psychology Today*, pp. 58–63. (p. 301)

Scarr, S. (1989). Protecting general intelligence: Constructs and consequences for interventions. In R. J. Linn (Ed.), *Intelligence: Measurement, theory, and public policy.* Champaign: University of Illinois Press. (pp. 292, 300)

Schab, F. R. (1990). Odors and the remembrance of things past. *Journal of Experimental Psychology: Learning, Memory, and Cognition, 16*, 648–655. (p. 145)

Schab, F. R. (1991). Odor memory: Taking stock. *Psychological Bulletin, 109*, 242–251. (p. 145)

Schachter, S. (1982). Recidivism and self-cure of smoking and obesity. *American Psychologist, 37*, 436–444. (p. 324)

Schachter, S., & Singer, J. E. (1962). Cognitive, social and physiological determinants of emotional state. *Psychological Review, 69*, 379–399. (p. 365)

Schacter, D. L. (1992). Understanding implicit memory: A cognitive neuroscience approach. *American Psychologist, 47*, 559–569. (p. 247)

Schacter, D. L. (1996). *Searching for memory: The brain, the mind, and the past.* New York: Basic Books. (pp. 112, 247, 248, 257, 398)

Schafran, L. H. (1995, August 26). Rape is still underreported. *New York Times*, p. I19. (p. 518)

Schaie, K. W. (1994). The life course of adult intellectual abilities. *American Psychologist, 49*, 304–313. (p. 114)

Schaie, K. W., & Geiwitz, J. (1982). *Adult development and aging.* Boston: Little, Brown. (p. 114)

Scheerer, M. (1963, April). Problem solving. *Scientific American*, pp. 118–128. (pp. 270–271)

Scheier, M. F., & Carver, C. S. (1992). Effects of optimism on psychological and physical well-being: Theoretical overview and empirical update. *Cognitive Therapy and Research, 16*, 201–228. (p. 371)

Schein, E. H. (1956). The Chinese indoctrination program for prisoners of war: A study of attempted brainwashing. *Psychiatry, 19*, 149–172. (p. 494)

Schiavi, R. C., & Schreiner-Engel, P. (1988). Nocturnal penile tumescence in healthy aging men. *Journal of Gerontology: Medical Sciences, 43*, M146–150. (p. 175)

Schlaug, G., Jancke, L., Huang, Y., & Steinmetz, H. (1995). In vivo evidence of structural brain asymmetry in musicians. *Science, 267*, 699–701. (p. 51)

Schleifer, S. J., Keller, S. E., McKegney, F. P., & Stein, M. (1979). *The influence of stress and other psychosocial factors on human immunity.* Paper presented at the 36th Annual Meeting of the American Psychosomatic Society. (p. 375)

Schlesinger, A. M., Jr. (1965). *A thousand days.* Boston: Houghton Mifflin. (p. 505)

Schmidt, F. L., & Hunter, J. E. (1993). Tacit knowledge, practical intelligence, general mental ability, and job knowledge. *Current Directions in Psychological Science, 2*, 8–9. (p. 293)

Schmidt, G., Klusmann, D., Zeitzschel, U., & Lange, C. (1994). Changes in adolescents' sexuality between 1970 and 1990 in West-Germany. *Archives of Sexual Behavior, 23*, 489–513. (p. 109)

Schmitt, D. P., & Buss, D. M. (1996). Strategic self-promotion and competitor derogation: Sex and context effects on the perceived effectiveness of mate attraction tactics. *Journal of Personality and Social Psychology, 70*, 1185–1204. (p. 525)

Schnaper, N. (1980). Comments germane to the paper entitled "The reality of death experiences" by Ernst Rodin. *Journal of Nervous and Mental Disease, 168*, 268–270. (p. 197)

Schoeneman, T. J. (1994). *Individualism.* In V. S. Ramachandran (Ed.), *Encyclopedia of Human Behavior.* San Diego: Academic Press. (pp. 413, 414)

Schofield, J. W. (1986). Black-White contact in desegregated schools. In M. Hewstone & R. Brown (Eds.), *Contact and conflict in intergroup encounters.* Oxford: Basil Blackwell Ltd. (p. 530)

Schonfield, D., & Robertson, B. A. (1966). Memory storage and aging. *Canadian Journal of Psychology, 20*, 228–236. (p. 113)

Schooler, J. W., Gerhard, D., & Loftus, E. F. (1986). Qualities of the unreal. *Journal of Experimental Psychology: Learning, Memory, and Cognition, 12*, 171–181. (p. 256)

Schuckit, M. A., and Smith, T. L. (1996, March). An 8-year follow-up of 450 sons of alcoholic and control subjects. *Archives of General Psychiatry, 53*, 202–210. (p. 200)

Schwartz, B. (1984). *Psychology of learning and behavior* (2nd ed.). New York: Norton. (pp. 213, 434)

Schwartz, J. E., Friedman, H. S., Tucker, J. S., Tomlinson-Keasey, C., Wingard, D. L., & Criqui, M. H. (1995). Sociodemographic and psychosocial factors in childhood as predictors of adult mortality. *American Journal of Public Health, 85*, 1237–1245. (p. 383)

Schwartz, J. M., Stoessel, P. W., Baxter, L. R., Jr., Martin, K. M., & Phelps, M. E. (1996). Systematic changes in cerebral glucose metabolic rate after successful behavior modification treatment of obsessive-compulsive disorder. *Archives of General Psychiatry, 53*, 109–113. (p. 487)

Schwarz, N., & Clore, G. L. (1983). Mood, misattribution, and judgments of well-being: Informative and directive functions of affective states. *Journal of Personality and Social Psychology, 45*, 513–523. (p. 359)

Schwarz, N., Strack, F., Kommer, D., & Wagner, D. (1987). Soccer, rooms, and the quality of your life: Mood effects on judgments of satisfaction with life in general and with specific domains. *European Journal of Social Psychology, 17*, 69–79. (p. 252)

Sclafani, A. (1995). How food preferences are learned: Laboratory animal models. *Proceedings of the Nutrition Society, 54*, 419–427. (p. 320)

Scott, C., & Pepperell, P. (1992). Exercise and depression: A meta-analysis. Paper presented at the Southwestern Psychological Association convention. (p. 378)

Scott, W. A., Scott, R., & McCabe, M. (1991). Family relationships and children's personality: A cross-cultural, cross-source comparison. *British Journal of Social Psychology, 30*, 1–20. (p. 97)

Seeman, P., Guan, H-C., & Van Tol, H. H. M. (1993). Dopamine D4 receptors elevated in schizophrenia. *Nature, 365*, 441–445. (p. 452)

Segall, M. H., Dasen, P. R., Berry, J. W., & Poortinga, Y. H. (1990). *Human behavior in global perspective: An introduction to cross-cultural psychology.* New York: Pergamon. (pp. 90, 331, 511)

Segerstrom, S. C., McCarthy, W. J., Caskey, N. H., Gross, T. D., & Jarvik, M. E. (1993). Optimistic bias among cigarette smokers. *Journal of Applied Social Psychology, 23*, 1606–1618. (p. 419)

Segrin, C., & Dillard, J. P. (1992). The interactional theory of depresion: A meta-analysis of the research literature. *Journal of Social and Clinical Psychology, 11*, 43–70. (p. 448)

Seligman, M. E. P. (1974, May). Submissive death: Giving up on life. *Psychology Today*, pp. 80–85. (p. 348)

Seligman, M. E. P. (1975). *Helplessness: On depression, development and death.* San Francisco: Freeman. (p. 417)

Seligman, M. E. P. (1988, October). Boomer blues. *Psychology Today*, pp. 50–55. (p. 413)

Seligman, M. E. P. (1989). Explanatory style: Predicting depression, achievement, and health. In M. D. Yapko (Ed.), *Brief therapy approaches to treating anxiety and depression.* New York: Brunner/Mazel. (p. 473)

Seligman, M. E. P. (1991). *Learned optimism.* New York: Knopf. (pp. 169, 417, 446, 447)

Seligman, M. E. P. (1994). *What you can change and what you can't* New York: Knopf. (pp. 319, 358, 379, 399, 409, 447, 448, 480, 486)

Seligman, M. E. P. (1995). The effectiveness of psychotherapy: The *Consumer Reports* study. *American Psychologist, 50*, 965–974. (pp. 446, 476)

Seligman, M. E. P. (1996). Predicting and preventing depression. Master Lecture, American Psychological Association convention. (p. 473)

Seligman, M. E. P., & Schulman, P. (1986). Explanatory style as a predictor of productivity and quitting among life insurance sales agents. *Journal of Personality and Social Psychology, 50*, 832–838. (p. 418)

Seligman, M. E. P., & Yellen, A. (1987). What is a dream? *Behavior Research and Therapy, 25*, 1–24. (pp. 174, *182)*

Selye, H. (1936). A syndrome produced by diverse nocuous agents. *Nature, 138*, 32. (p. 369)

Selye, H. (1976). *The stress of life.* New York: McGraw-Hill. (p. 369)

Service, R. F. (1994). Will a new type of drug make memory-making easier? *Science, 266*, 218–219. (p. 245)

Seto, M. C., & Barbaree, H. E. (1995). The role of alcohol in sexual aggression. *Clinical Psychology Review, 15*, 545–566. (pp. 194, 514)

Shadish, W. R. & 13 others (1997). Evidence that therapy works in clinically representative conditions. *Journal of Consulting and clinical Psychology, 65*, 355–365. (p. 478)

Shadish, W. R., Montgomery, L. M., Wilson, P., Wilson, M. R., Bright, I., & Okwumabua, T. (1993). Effects of family and marital psychotherapies: A meta-analysis. *Journal of Consulting and Clinical Psychology, 61*, 992–1002. (p. 474)

Shamir, B., House, R. J., & Arthur, M. B. (1993). The motivational effects of charismatic leadership: A self-concept based theory. *Organizational Science, 4*, 577–594. (p. 343)

Shanks, D. (1993, 30 January). Breaking Chomsky's rules. *New Scientist*, pp. 26–29. (p. 280)

Shapiro, D. A., & Shapiro, D. (1982). Meta-analysis of comparative therapy outcome studies: A replication and refinement. *Psychological Bulletin, 92*, 581–604. (p. 479)

Shaver, P. R., & Hazan, C. (1993). Adult romantic attachment: Theory and evidence. In D. Perlman & W. Jones (Eds.), *Advances in personal relationships,* vol. 4. Greenwich, CT: JAI. (p. 94)

Shaver, P. R., Morgan, H. J., & Wu, S. (1996). Is love a basic emotion. *Personal Relationships, 3*, 81–96. (p. 356)

Shaw, H. L. (1989–90). Comprehension of the spoken word and ASL translation by chimpanzees (Pan troglodytes). *Friends of Washoe, 9*(1/2), 8–19. (p. 285)

Shawitz, B.A., & others (1995). Sex differences in the functional organization of the brain for language. *Nature, 373*, 607–609. (p. 51)

Shea, M.T., Elkin, I., Imber, S. D., Sotsky, S. M., Watkins, J.T., Collins, J. F., Pilkonis, P. A., Beckham, E., Glass, D. R., Dolan, R.T., & Parloff, M. B. (1992). Course of depressive symptoms over follow-up: Findings from the National Institute of mental Health Treatment of Depression Collaborative Research Program. *Archives of General Psychiatry, 49*, 782–787. (p. 479)

Sheehan, S. (1982). *Is there no place on earth for me?* Boston: Houghton Mifflin. (p. 449)

Shenton, M. E., Kiknis, R., Jolesz, F. A., & others (1992). Abnormalities of the left temporal lobe and thought disorder in schizophrenia: A quantitative magnetic resonance imaging study. *New England Journal of Medicine, 327*, 604–612. (p. 452)

Shepard, R. N. (1981). Psychophysical complementarity. In M. Kubovy & J. R. Pomerantz (Eds.), *Perceptual organization.* Hillsdale, NJ: Erlbaum. (p. 152)

Shepard, R. N. (1990). *Mind sights.* New York: Freeman. (pp. 33, 152, 156, 158)

Shepherd, C. (1997, April). News of the weird. *Funny Times*, p. 15. (p. 71)

Shepherd, C., Kohut, J. J., & Sweet, R. (1990). *More news of the weird.* New York: Penguin/Plume Books. (p. 456)

Sherif, M. (1966). *In common predicament: Social psychology of intergroup conflict and cooperation.* Boston: Houghton Mifflin. (p. 530)

Sherry, D., & Vaccarino, A. L. (1989). Hippocampus and memory for food caches in black-capped chickadees. *Behavioral Neuroscience, 103*, 308–318. (p. 248)

Shettleworth, S. J. (1973). Food reinforcement and the organization of behavior in golden hamsters. In R. A. Hinde & J. Stevenson-Hinde (Eds.), *Constraints on learning.* London: Academic Press. (p. 222)

Shettleworth, S. J. (1993). Where is the comparison in comparative cognition? Alternative research programs. *Psychological Science, 4*, 179–184. (p. 243)

Shneidman, E. (1987, March). At the point of no return. *Psychology Today*, pp. 54–58. (p. 444)

Shontz, F. C., & Green, P. (1992). Trends in research on the Rorschach: Review and recommendations. *Applied and Preventive Psychology, 1*, 149–156. (p. 396)

Shotland, R. L. (1984, March 12). Quoted in Maureen Dowd, 20 years after the murder of Kitty Genovese, the question remains: Why? *The New York Times,* p. B1. (p. 528)

Shotland, R. L. (1989). A model of the causes of date rape in developing and close relationships. In C. Hendrick (Ed.), *Review of Personality and Social Psychology* (Vol. 10). Newbury Park, CA: Sage. (p. 332)

Showers, C. (1992). The motivational and emotional consequences of considering positive or negative possibilities for an upcoming event. *Journal of Personality and Social Psychology, 63*, 474–484. (p. 418)

Shrout, P. E., Link, B. G., Dohrenwend, B. P., Skodol, A. E., Stueve, A., & Mirotznik, J. (1989). Characterizing life events as risk factors for depression: The role of fateful loss events. *Journal of Abnormal Psychology, 98*, 460–467. (p. 442)

Sieff, E. M., Dawes, R. M., & Loewenstein, G. F. (1997). Anticipated versus actual responses to HIV test results. *American Journal of Psychology*, in press. (p. 360)

Siegel, J. M. (1990). Stressful life events and use of physician services among the elderly: The moderating role of pet ownership. *Journal of Personality and Social Psychology, 58,* 1081–1086. (p. 382)

Siegel, R. K. (1977, October). Hallucinations. *Scientific American,* pp. 132–140. (p. 197)

Siegel, R. K. (1980). The psychology of life after death. *American Psychologist, 35,* 911–931. (p. 197)

Siegel, R. K. (1984, March 15). Personal communication. (p. 197)

Siegel, R. K. (1990). *Intoxication.* New York: Pocket Books. (pp. 191, 194, 196, 197, 198)

Siegel, R. K. Quoted by J. Hooper (1982, October), Mind tripping. *Omni,* pp. 72–82, 159–160. (p. 197)

Siegler, R. S., & Ellis, S. (1996). Piaget on childhood. *Psychological Science, 7,* 211–215. (p. 86)

Silbersweig, D. A., & others (1995). A functional neuroanatomy of hallucinations in schizophrenia. *Nature, 378,* 176–179. (p. 452)

Silva, A. J., Stevens, C. F., Tonegawa, S., & Wang, Y. (1992). Deficient hippocampal long-term potentiation in alpha-calcium-calmodulin kinase II mutant mice. *Science, 257,* 201–206. (p. 245)

Silva, C. E., & Kirsch, I. (1992). Interpretive sets, expectancy, fantasy proneness, and dissociation as predictors of hypnotic response. *Journal of Personality and Social Psychology, 63,* 847–856. (p. 184)

Silver, M., & Geller, D. (1978). On the irrelevance of evil: The organization and individual action. *Journal of Social Issues, 34,* 125–136. (p. 501)

Silverman, I., & Eals, M. (1992). Sex differences in spatial abilities: Evolutionary theory and data. In J. H. Barkow, L. Cosmides, & J. Tooby (eds.), *The adapted mind: Evolutionary psychology and the generation of culture.* New York: Oxford University Press. (p. 305)

Silverman, K., Evans, S. M., Strain, E. C., & Griffiths, R. R. (1992). Withdrawal syndrome after the double-blind cessation of caffeine consumption. *New England Journal of Medicine, 327,* 1109–1114. (p. 195)

Silverman, P. S., & Retzlaff, P. D. (1986). Cognitive stage regression through hypnosis: Are earlier cognitive stages retrievable? *International Journal of Clinical and Experimental Hypnosis, 34,* 192–204. (p. 185)

Simonton, D. K. (1988). Age and outstanding achievement: What do we know after a century of research? *Psychological Bulletin, 104,* 251–267. (p. 115)

Simonton, D. K. (1990). Creativity in the later years: Optimistic prospects for achievement. *The Gerontologist, 30,* 626–631. (p. 115)

Simonton, D. K. (1992). The social context of career success and course for 2,026 scientists and inventors. *Personality and Social Psychology Bulletin, 18,* 452–463. (p. 298)

Simonton, D. K. (1994). *Greatness: Who makes history and why.* New York: Guilford Press. (p. 340)

Simpson, J. A., Rholes, W. S., & Nelligan, J. S. (1992). Support seeking and support giving within couples in an anxiety-provoking situation: The role of attachment styles. *Journal of Personality and Social Psychology, 62,* 434–446. (p. 94)

Sinclair, R. C., Hoffman, C., Mark, M. M., Martin, L. L., & Pickering, T. L. (1994). Construct accessibility and the misattribution of arousal: Schachter and Singer revisited. *Psychological Science, 5,* 15–18. (p. 366)

Singelis, T. M., & Sharkey, W. F. (1995). Culture, self-construal, and embarrassability. *Cross-Cultural Psychology, 26,* 622–644. (p. 412)

Singer, J. L. (1975). Navigating the stream of consciousness: Research in daydreaming and related inner experience. *American Psychologist, 30,* 727–738. (p. 171)

Singer, J. L. (1976, July). Fantasy: The foundation of serenity. *Psychology Today,* pp. 32–37. (p. 172)

Singer, J. L. (1981). Clinical intervention: New developments in methods and evaluation. In L. T. Benjamin, Jr. (Ed.), *The G. Stanley Hall Lecture Series* (Vol. 1). Washington, DC: American Psychological Association. (p. 479)

Singer, J. L. (1986). Is television bad for children? *Social Science, 71,* 178–182. (p. 172)

Singer, J. L., & Singer, D. G. (1986). Family experiences and television viewing as predictors of children's imagination, restlessness, and aggression. *Journal of Social Issues, 42*(3), 7–28. (p. 518)

Singh, D. (1993). Adaptive significance of female physical attractiveness: Role of waist-to-hip ratio. *Journal of Personality and Social Psychology, 65,* 293–307. (p. 525)

Singh, D. (1995). Female judgment of male attractiveness and desirability for relationships: Role of waist-to-hip ratio and financial status. *Journal of Personality and Social Psychology, 69,* 1089–1101. (p. 525)

Sivard, R. L. (1995). *Women. . . a world survey,* 2nd ed. Washington, DC: World Priorities. (p. 508)

Sivard, R. L. (1996). *World military and social expenditures 1996,* 16th edition. Washington, DC: World Priorities. (p. 237).

Sjöstrom, L. (1980). Fat cells and body weight. In A. J. Stunkard (Ed.), *Obesity.* Philadelphia: Saunders. (p. 321)

Skaggs, W. E., & McNaughton, B. L. (1996). Replay of neuronal firing sequences in rat hippocampus during sleep following spatial experience. *Science, 271,* 1870–1873. (p. 248)

Skelton, J. A., Pepe, M. M., & Pineo, T. S. (1995). How much better is clozapine? A meta-analytic review and critical appraisal. *Experimental and Clinical Psychopharmacology, 3,* 270–279. (p. 483)

Skinner, B. F. (1953). *Science and human behavior.* New York: Macmillan. (p. 219)

Skinner, B. F. (1956). A case history in scientific method. *American Psychologist, 11,* 221–233. (p. 220)

Skinner, B. F. (1957). *Verbal behavior.* Englewood Cliffs, NJ: Prentice-Hall. (p. 279)

Skinner, B. F. (1961, November). Teaching machines. *Scientific American,* pp. 91–102. (p. 219)

Skinner, B. F. (1983, September). Origins of a behaviorist. *Psychology Today,* pp. 22–33. (pp. 223, *446)*

Skinner, B. F. (1985). *Cognitive science and behaviorism.* Unpublished manuscript, Harvard University. (p. 279)

Skinner, B. F. (1986). What is wrong with daily life in the western world? *American Psychologist, 41,* 568–574. (p. 224)

Skinner, B. F. (1988). The school of the future. Address to the American Psychological Association convention. (p. 224)

Skinner, B. F. (1989). Teaching machines. *Science, 243,* 1535. (p. 224)

Skinner, B. F. (1990). Address to the American Psychological Association convention. (p. 222)

Sklar, L. S., & Anisman, H. (1981). Stress and cancer. *Psychological Bulletin, 89,* 369–406. (p. 375)

Skov, R. B., & Sherman, S. J. (1986). Information-gathering processes: Diagnosticity, hypothesis-confirmatory strategies, and perceived hypothesis confirmation. *Journal of Experimental Social Psychology, 22,* 93–121. (p. 270)

Slavin, R. E. (1989). Cooperative learning and student achievement. In R. E. Slavin (Ed.), *School and classroom organization.* Hillsdale, NJ: Erlbaum. (p. 531)

Slovic, P. (1987). Perception of risk. *Science, 236,* 280–285. (p. 273)

Slovic, P., & Fischhoff, B. (1977). On the psychology of experimental surprises. *Journal of Experimental Psychology: Human Perception and Performance, 3,* 544–551. (p. 10)

Smart, R. G., Adlaf, E. M., & Walsh, G. W. (1991). The Ontario student drug use survey: Trends between 1977 and 1991. Toronto: Addiction Research Foundation. (p. 199)

Smith, A. (1983). Personal correspondence. (p. 451)

Smith, A. (1987). Personal communication. (p. 62)

Smith, A., & Sugar, O. (1975). Development of above normal language and intelligence 21 years after left hemispherectomy. *Neurology, 25,* 813–818. (p. 62)

Smith, K. H., & Rogers, M. (1994). Effectiveness of subliminal messages in television commercials: Two experiments. *Journal of Applied Psychology, 79,* 866–874. (p. 127)

Smith, M. B. (1978). Psychology and values. *Journal of Social Issues, 34,* 181–199. (p. 414)

Smith, M. L., & Glass, G. V. (1977). Meta-analysis of psychotherapy outcome studies. *American Psychologist, 32,* 752–760. (p. 479)

Smith, M. L., Glass, G. V., & Miller, R. L. (1980). *The benefits of psychotherapy.* Baltimore: Johns Hopkins Press. (p. 478)

Smith, P. B., & Tayeb, M. (1989). Organizational structure and processes. In M. Bond (Ed.), *The cross-cultural challenge to social psychology*. Newbury Park, CA: Sage. (p. 343)

Smith, P. F. (1995). Cannabis and the brain. *New Zealand Journal of Psychology, 24,* 5–12. (p. 198)

Smith, T. W. (1990). Adult sexual behavior in 1989: Number of partners, frequency, and risk. General Social Survey Topic Report No. 18, National Opinion Research Center, University of Chicago. (p. 327)

Smith, T. W. (1996). American sexual behavior: Trends, sociodemographic differences, and risk behavior. National Opinion Research Center GSS Topical Report No. 25 (http:www.norc.uchicago.edu/sextrend.htm) (pp. 327, 333)

Smith, T. W. (1997). Personal correspondence. Data from the General Social Survey, National Opinion Research Center, University of Chicago. (pp. 508, 510)

Smith, T. W. (1997). Personal correspondence. Data from the General Social Survey, National Opinion Research Center, University of Chicago. (pp. 361, 510)

Snarey, J. (1987, June). A question of morality. *Psychology Today,* pp. 6–7. (p. 103)

Snarey, J. R. (1985). Cross-cultural universality of social-moral development: A critical review of Kohlbergian research. *Psychological Bulletin, 97,* 202–233. (p. 103)

Snodgrass, M. A. (1987). The relationships of differential loneliness, intimacy and characterological attributional style to duration of loneliness. *Journal of Social Behavior and Personality, 2,* 173–186. (p. 448)

Snyder, M. (1984). When belief creates reality. In L. Berkowitz (Ed.), *Advances in experimental social psychology* (Vol. 18). New York: Academic Press. (p. 431)

Snyder, M., Tanke, E. D., & Berscheid, E. (1977). Social perception and interpersonal behavior: On the self-fulfilling nature of social stereotypes. *Journal of Personality and Social Psychology, 35,* 656–666. (p. 506)

Snyder, S. H. (1984). Neurosciences: An integrative discipline. *Science, 225,* 1255–1257. (p. 41)

Snyder, S. H. (1986). *Drugs and the brain.* New York: Scientific American Library. (p. 485)

Sokhadze, E. M., & Shtark, M. B. (1991). Scientific and clinical biofeedback in the USSR. *Biofeedback and Self-Regulation, 16,* 253–260. (p. 380)

Sokoll, G. R., & Mynatt, C. R. (1984). *Arousal and free throw shooting.* Paper presented at the meeting of the Midwestern Psychological Association. (p. 349)

Solomon, D. A., Keitner, G. I., Miller, I. W., Shea, M. T., & Keller, M. B. (1995). Course of illness and maintenance treatments for patients with bipolar disorder. *Journal of Clinical Psychiatry, 56,* 5–13. (p. 485)

Solomon, J. (1996, May 20). Breaking the silence. *Newsweek,* pp. 20–22. (p. 430)

Solomon, M. (1987, December). Standard issue. *Psychology Today,* pp. 30–31. (p. 524)

Solomon, Z. (1990). Does the war end when the shooting stops? The psychological toll of war. *Journal of Applied Social Psychology, 20,* 1733–1745. (p. 435)

Sommer, R. (1969). *Personal space.* Englewood Cliffs, NJ: Prentice-Hall. (pp. 17, 507)

Sonenstein, F. L. (1992). Condom use. *Science, 257,* 861. (p. 107)

Sowell, T. (1991, May/June). Cultural diversity: A world view. *American Enterprise,* pp. 44–55. (p. 532)

Spanos, N. P. (1982). A social psychological approach to hypnotic behavior. In G. Weary & H. L. Mirels (Eds.), *Integrations of clinical and social psychology.* New York: Oxford. (p. 186)

Spanos, N. P. (1986). Hypnosis, nonvolitional responding, and multiple personality: A social psychological perspective. *Progress in Experimental Personality Research, 14,* 1–62. (p. 438)

Spanos, N. P. (1987–88). Past-life hypnotic regression: A critical view. *The Skeptical Inquirer, 12,* 174–180. (p. 187)

Spanos, N. P. (1991). Hypnosis, hypnotizability, and hypnotherapy. In C. R. Snyder & D. R. Forsyth (Eds.), *Handbook of social and clinical psychology: The health perspective.* New York: Pergamon Press. (p. 188)

Spanos, N. P. (1994). Multiple identity enactments and multiple personality disorder: A sociocognitive perspective. *Psychological Bulletin, 116,* 143–165. (pp. 189, 438)

Spanos, N. P. (1996). *Multiple identities and false memories: A sociocognitive perspective.* Washington, DC: American Psychological Association Books. (pp. 188, 189, 438)

Spanos, N. P., Burgess, C. A., & Burgess, M. F. (1994). Past-life identities, UFO abductions, and Satanic ritual abuse: The social construction of memories. *International Journal of Clinical and Experimental Hypnosis, 42,* 433–446. (p. 261)

Spanos, N. P., & Coe, W. C. (1992). A Social-psychological approach to hypnosis. In E. Fromm & M. R. Nash (Eds.), *Contemporary hypnosis research.* New York: Guilford. (p. 189)

Spanos, N. P., Radtke, L., & Bertrand, L. D. (1985). Hypnotic amnesia as a strategic enactment: Breaching amnesia in highly susceptible subjects. *Journal of Personality and Social Psychology, 47,* 1155–1169. (p. 184)

Spector, P. E. (1986). Perceived control by employees: A meta-analysis of studies concerning autonomy and participation at work. *Human Relations, 39,* 1005–1016. (p. 342)

Spencer, S. J., Steele, C. M., & Quinn, D. M. (1997). Stereotype threat and women's math performance. Unpublished manuscript, Hope College. (p. 306)

Sperling, G. (1960). The information available in brief visual presentations. *Psychological Monographs, 74* (Whole No. 498). (p. 241)

Sperry, R. W. (1964). *Problems outstanding in the evolution of brain function.* James Arthur Lecture, American Museum of Natural History, New York. Cited by R. Ornstein (1977), *The psychology of consciousness* (2nd ed.). New York: Harcourt Brace Jovanovich. (pp. 63–64)

Sperry, R. W. (1968). Hemisphere deconnection and unity in conscious awareness. *American Psychologist, 23,* 723–733. (p. 63)

Sperry, R. W. (1982). Some effects of disconnecting the cerebral hemispheres. *Science, 217,* 1223–1226. (p. 66)

Sperry, R. W. (1985). Changed concepts of brain and consciousness: Some value implications. *Zygon, 20,* 41–57. (p. 135)

Spiegel, D. (1993). Social support: How friends, family, and groups can help. In D. Goleman & J. Gurin (Eds.), *Mind-body medicine: How to use your mind for better health.* Yonkers, NY: Consumer Reports Books. (p. 375)

Spiegel, D., Bloom, J. R., Kraemer, H. C., & Gottheil, E. (1989, October 14). Effect of psychosocial treatment on survival of patients with metastatic breast cancer. *The Lancet,* pp. 888–891. (p. 375)

Spielberger, C., & London, P. (1982). Rage boomerangs. *American Health, 1,* 52–56. (p. 373)

Spiess, W. F. J., Greer, J. H., & O'Donohue, W. T. (1984). Premature ejaculation: Investigation of factors in ejaculatory latency. *Journal of Abnormal Psychology, 93,* 242–245. (p. 331)

Spitzberg, B. H., & Hurt, H. T. (1987). The relationship of interpersonal competence and skill to reported loneliness across time. *Journal of Social Behavior and Personality, 2,* 157–172. (p. 448)

Spitzer, R. L. (1975). On pseudoscience in science, logic in remission, and psychiatric diagnosis: A critique of Rosenhan's "On being sane in insane places." *Journal of Abnormal Psychology, 84,* 442–452. (p. 431)

Spradley, J. P., & Phillips, M. (1972). Culture and stress: A quantitative analysis. *American Anthropologist, 74,* 518–529. (p. 507)

Sprecher, S. (1989). The importance to males and females of physical attractiveness, earning potential, and expressiveness in initial attraction. *Sex Roles, 21,* 591–607. (p. 524)

Sprecher, S., & Sedikides, C. (1993). Gender differences in perceptions of emotionality: The case of close heterosexual relationships. *Sex Roles, 28,* 511–530. (p. 105)

Springer, S. P., & Deutsch, G. (1985). *Left brain, right brain.* San Francisco: Freeman. (p. 65)

Squire, L. R. (1987). *Memory and brain.* New York: Oxford University Press. (pp. 246, 247)

Squire, L. R. (1992). Memory and the hippcampus: A synthesis from findings with rats, monkeys, and humans. *Psychological Review, 99,* 195–231. (p. 248)

Sroufe, L. A., Fox, N. E., & Pancake, V. R. (1983). Attachment and dependency in developmental perspective. *Child Development, 54,* 1615–1627. (p. 94)

Stack, S. (1992). Marriage, family, religion, and suicide. In R. Maris, A. Berman, J. Maltsberger, & R. Yufit (Eds.), *Assessment and prediction of suicide.* New York: Guilford Press. (p. 444)

Stanford University Center for Narcolepsy (1996). Available: http://www.hia.com/narcoctr/welcome.html (accessed August 26). (p. 179)

Stanovich, K. (1996). *How to think straight about psychology.* New York: HarperCollins. (p. 390)

Stattin, H., & Magnusson, D. (1990). *Pubertal maturation in female development.* Hillsdale, NJ: Erlbaum. (p. 101)

Staub, E. (1989). *The roots of evil: The psychological and cultural sources of genocide.* New York: Cambridge University Press. (p. 495)

Staub, E. (1993). Societal-cultural, familial and psychological origins of youth violence. Paper presented at the American Psychological Association convention. (p. 516)

Steele, C. (1990, May). A conversation with Claude Steele. *APS Observer,* pp. 11–17. (p. 303)

Steele, C. M. (1995, August 31). Black students live down to expectations. *New York Times.* (p. 306)

Steele, C. M. (1997). A threat in the air: How stereotypes shape intellectual identity and performance. *American Psychologist, 52,* 613–629. (p. 306)

Steele, C. M., & Aronson, J. (1996). Stereotype threat and the intellectual test performance of African Americans. *Journal of Personality and Social Psychology, 69,* 797–811. (p. 306)

Steele, C. M., & Josephs, R. A. (1990). Alcohol myopia: Its prized and dangerous effects. *American Psychologist, 45,* 921–933. (p. 194)

Stein, J. A., Newcomb, M. D., & Bentler, P. M. (1986). Stability and change in personality: A longitudinal study from early adolescence to young adulthood. *Journal of Research In Personality, 20,* 276–291. (p. 121)

Steinberg, L. (1987, September). Bound to bicker. *Psychology Today,* pp. 36–39. (p. 106)

Steinberg, N. (1993, February). Astonishing love stories (from an earlier United Press International report). *Games,* p. 47. (p. 520)

Stengel, E. (1981). Suicide. In *The new Encyclopaedia Britannica, Macropaedia* (Vol. 17, pp. 777–782). Chicago: Encyclopaedia Britannica. (p. 444)

Stephens, T. (1988). Physical activity and mental health in the United States and Canada: Evidence from four population surveys. *Preventive Medicine, 17,* 35–47. (pp. 378–379)

Stepp, L. S. (1996, July 2). Universal goals: Family, achievement and dreams. *International Herald Tribune,* p. 2. (p. 106)

Sternberg, R. J. (1988). Applying cognitive theory to the testing and teaching of intelligence. *Applied Cognitive Psychology, 2,* 231–255. (p. 296)

Sternberg, R. J. (1997). The concept of intelligence and its role in lifelong learning and success. *American Psychologist, 52,* 1030–1037. (p. 289)

Sternberg, R. J., & Grajek, S. (1984). The nature of love. *Journal of Personality and Social Psychology*, *47*, 312–329. (p. 527)

Sternberg, R. J., & Lubart, T. I. (1991). An investment theory of creativity and its development. *Human Development*, 1–31. (p. 296)

Sternberg, R. J., & Lubart, T. I. (1992). Buy low and sell high: An investment approach to creativity. *Psychological Science*, *1*, 1–5. (p. 296)

Sternberg, R. J., & Wagner, R. K. (1993). The *g*-ocentric view of intelligence and job performance is wrong. *Current Directions in Psychological Science*, *2*, 1–5. (p. 292)

Sternberg, R. J., Wagner, R. K., Williams, W. M., & Horvath, J. A. (1995). Testing common sense. *American Psychologist*, *50*, 912–927. (p. 292)

Stevenson, H. W. (1992, December). Learning from Asian schools. *Scientific American*, pp. 70–76. (p. 304)

Stice, E., & Shaw, H. E. (1994). Adverse effects of the media portrayed thin-ideal on women and linkages to bulimic symptomatology. *Journal of Social and Clinical Psychology*, *13*, 288–308. (p. 323)

Stock, R. W. (1995, July 13). Reducing the risk for older drivers. *New York Times*, p. C1. (p. 112)

Stockton, M. C., & Murnen, S. K. (1992). Gender and sexual arousal in response to sexual stimuli: A meta-analytic review. Presented at the American Psychological Society convention. (p. 329)

Stoll, A. L., Tohen, M., Baldessarini, R. J., Goodwin, D. C., Stein, S., Katz, S., Geenens, D., Swinson, R. P., Goethe, J. W., & McGlashan, T. (1993). Shifts in diagnostic frequencies of schizophrenia and major affective disorders at six North American psychiatric hospitals, 1972–1988. *American Journal of Psychiatry*, *150*, 1668–1673. (p. 443)

Stone, A. A., Cox, D. S., Valdimarsdottir, H., Jandor, L., & Neale, J. M. (1987). Evidence that secretory IgA antibody is associated with daily mood. *Journal of Personality and Social Psychology*, *52*, 988–993. (p. 374)

Stone, A. A., & Neale, J. M. (1984). Effects of severe daily events on mood. *Journal of Personality and Social Psychology*, *46*, 137–144. (p. 359)

Stone, J., Perry, Z. W., & Darley, J. M. (1997). "White men can't jump": Evidence for the perceptual confirmation of racial stereotypes following a basketball game. *Basic and Applied Social Psychology*, *19*, 291–306. (p. 512)

Stoppard, J. M., & Gruchy, C. D. G. (1993). Gender, context, and expression of positive emotion. *Personality and Social Psychology Bulletin*, *19*, 143–150. (p. 105)

Storms, M. D. (1973). Videotape and the attribution process: Reversing actors' and observers' points of view. *Journal of Personality and Social Psychology*, *27*, 165–175. (p. 492)

Storms, M. D. (1981). A theory of erotic orientation development. *Psychological Review*, *88*, 340–353. (p. 334)

Storms, M. D., & Thomas, G. C. (1977). Reactions to physical closeness. *Journal of Personality and Social Psychology*, *35*, 412–418. (p. 503)

Strack, F., Martin, L., & Stepper, S. (1988). Inhibiting and facilitating conditions of the human smile: A nonobtrusive test of the facial feedback hypothesis. *Journal of Personality and Social Psychology*, *54*, 768–777. (p. 355)

Strack, S., & Coyne, J. C. (1983). Social confirmation of dysphoria: Shared and private reactions to depression. *Journal of Personality and Social Behavior*, *44*, 798–806. (p. 448)

Strange, S. L., & Forsyth, D. R. (1993). Long-term benefits of adolescent peer groups. Paper presented at the Eastern Psychological Association convention. (p. 104)

Straub, R. O., Seidenberg, M. S., Bever, T. G., & Terrace, H. S. (1979). Serial learning in the pigeon. *Journal of the Experimental Analysis of Behavior*, *32*, 137–148. (p. 283)

Straus, M. A., & Gelles, R. J. (1980). *Behind closed doors: Violence in the American family.* New York: Anchor/Doubleday. (p. 221)

Streissguth, A. P., Aase, J. M., Clarren, S. K., Randels, S. P., LaDue, R. A., & Smith, D. F. (1991). Fetal alcohol syndrome in adolescents and adults. *Journal of the American Medical Association*, *265*, 1961–1967. (p. 81)

Strentz, H. (1986, January 1). Become a psychic and amaze your friends! *Atlanta Journal*, p. 15A. (p. 161)

Striegel-Moore, R. H., Silberstein, L. R., & Rodin, J. (1993). The social self in bulimia nervosa: Public self-consciousness, social anxiety, and perceived fraudulence. *Journal of Abnormal Psychology*, *102*, 297–303. (p. 319)

Strupp, H. H. (1982). The outcome problem in psychotherapy: Contemporary perspectives. In J. H. Harvey & M. M. Parks (Eds.), *The master lecture series: Vol. 1. Psychotherapy research and behavior change.* Washington, DC: American Psychological Association. (pp. 409, 410)

Strupp, H. H. (1986). Psychotherapy: Research, practice, and public policy (How to avoid dead ends). *American Psychologist*, *41*, 120–130. (p. 480)

Stumpf, H., & Jackson, D. N. (1994). Gender-related differences in cognitive abilities: Evidence from a medical school admissions testing program. *Personality and Individual Differences*, *17*, 335–344. (p. 305)

Stunkard, A. J., Harris, J. R., Pedersen, N. L., & McClearn, G. E. (1990). A separated twin study of the body mass index. *New England Journal of Medicine*, *322*, 1483–1487. (p. 322)

Suddath, R. L., Christison, G. W., Torrey, E. F., Casanova, M. F., & Weinberger, D. R. (1990). Anatomical abnormalities in the brains of monozygotic twins discordant for schizophrenia. *New England Journal of Medicine*, *322*, 789–794. (p. 454)

Sue, D. W. (1990). Culture-specific strategies in counseling: A conceptual framework. *Professional Psychology: Research and Practice*, *21*, 424–433. (p. 482)

Suedfeld, P. (1980). *Restricted environmental stimulation: Research and clinical applications.* New York: Wiley. (p. 313)

Suedfeld, P., & Mocellin, J. S. P. (1987). The "sensed presence" in unusual environments. *Environment and Behavior*, *19*, 33–52. (p. 198)

Suinn, R. M. (1997). Mental practice in sports psychology: Where have we been, where do we go? *Clinical Psychology: Science and Practice*, *4*, 189–207. (p. 288)

Suls, J. M., & Tesch, F. (1978). Students' preferences for information about their test performance: A social comparison study. *Journal of Experimental Social Psychology*, *8*, 189–197. (p. 362)

Summers, M. (1996, December 9). Mister clean. *People Weekly*, pp. 139–142. (p. 425)

Sundstrom, E., De Meuse, K. P., & Futrell, D. (1990). Work teams: Applications and effectiveness. *American Psychologist*, *45*, 120–133. (p. 342)

Suomi, S. J. (1986). Anxiety-like disorders in young nonhuman primates. In R. Gettleman (Ed.), *Anxiety disorders of childhood.* New York: Guilford Press. (p. 437)

Suomi, S. J. (1987). Genetic and maternal contributions to individual differences in rhesus monkey biobehavioral development. In N. A. Krasnegor & others (Eds.), *Perinatal development: A psychobiological perspective.* Orlando, FL: Academic Press. (p. 393)

Suppes, P. Quoted by R. H. Ennis (1982). Children's ability to handle Piaget's propositional logic: A conceptual critique. In S. Modgil & C. Modgil (Eds.), *Jean Piaget: Consensus and controversy.* New York: Praeger. (p. 90)

Surgeon General. (1986). *The Surgeon General's workshop on pornography and public health*, June 22–24. Report prepared by E. P. Mulvey & J. L. Haugaard and released by Office of the Surgeon General on August 4, *1986. (p. 519)*

Susser, E., & others (1996). Schizophrenia after prenatal famine. *Archives of General Psychiatry*, *53*, 25–31 (p. 453)

Sweat, J. A., & Durm, M. W. (1993). Psychics: Do police departments really use them? *Skeptical Inquirer*, *17*, 148–158. (p. 162)

Swerdlow, N. R., & Koob, G. F. (1987). Dopamine, schizophrenia, mania, and depression: Toward a unified hypothesis of cortico-stiato-pallido-thalamic function (with commentary). *Behavioral and Brain Sciences*, *10*, 197–246. (p. 452)

Taha, F. A. (1972). A comparative study of how sighted and blind perceive the manifest content of dreams. *National Review of Social Sciences*, *9*(3), 28. (p. 181)

Tajfel, H. (Ed.). (1982). *Social identity and intergroup relations.* New York: Cambridge University Press. (p. 511)

Tanda, G., Pontieri, F. E., Di Chiara, G. (1997). Cannabinoid and heroin activation of mesolimbic dopamine transmission by a common mu-1 opioid receptor mechanism. *Science*, *276*, 2048–2050. (p. 198)

Tannen, D. (1990). *You just don't understand: Women and men in conversation.* New York: Morrow. (pp. 30, *105)*

Tanner, J. M. (1978). *Fetus into man: Physical growth from conception to maturity.* Cambridge, MA: Harvard University Press. (p. 100)

Tassinary, L. G., & Cacioppo, J. T. (1992). Unobservable facial actions and emotion. *Psychological Science*, *3*, 28–33. (pp. 352–353)

Tatarkiewicz, W. (1976). *Analysis of happiness.* The Hague: Martinus Nijhoff, 1976. (p. 359)

Taubes, G. (1994). Will new dopamine receptors offer a key to schizophrenia? *Science*, *265*, 1034–1035. (p. 483)

Tavris, C. (1982, November). Anger defused. *Psychology Today*, pp. 25–35. (p. 358)

Tavris, C. (1993, January 3). Beware the incest-survivor machine. *New York Times Book Review,* pp. 1, *16–18. (p. 260)*

Taylor, S. E. (1989). *Positive illusions*. New York: Basic Books. (pp. 274, 381)

Taylor, S. P., & Chermack, S. T. (1993). Alcohol, drugs and human physical aggression. *Journal of Studies on Alcohol*, Supplement No. 11, 78–88. (p. 514)

Teevan, R. C., & McGhee, P. E. (1972). Childhood development of fear of failure motivation. *Journal of Personality and Social Psychology*, *21*, 345–348. (p. 340)

Teghtsoonian, R. (1971). On the exponents in Stevens' law and the constant in Ekinan's law. *Psychological Review*, *78*, 71–80. (p. 129)

Temoshok, L. (1992). *The Type C connection: The behavioral links to cancer and your health.* New York: Random House. (p. 375)

Terrace, H. S. (1979, November). How Nim Chimpsky changed my mind. *Psychology Today*, pp. 65–76. (p. 283)

Tesser, A., Forehand, R., Brody, G., & Long, N. (1989). Conflict: The role of calm and angry parent-child discussion in adolescent development. *Journal of Social and Clinical Psychology*, *8*, 317–330. (p. 106)

Tetlock, P. E. (1988). Monitoring the integrative complexity of American and Soviet policy rhetoric: What can be learned? *Journal of Social Issues*, *44*, 101–131. (p. 532)

Thatcher, R. W., Walker, R. A., & Giudice, S. (1987). Human cerebral hemispheres develop at different rates and ages. *Science*, *236*, 1110–1113. (p. 121)

Thayer, R. E. (1987). Energy, tiredness, and tension effects of a sugar snack versus moderate exercise. *Journal of Personality and Social Psychology*, *52*, 119–125. (p. 379)

Thayer, R. E. (1993). Mood and behavior (smoking and sugar snacking) following moderate exercise: A partial test of self-regulation theory. *Personality and Individual Differences*, *14*, 97–104. (p. 379)

Thelen, E. (1994). Three-month-old infants can learn task-specific patterns of interlimb coordination. *Psychological Science*, *5*, 280–285. (p. 84)

Thomas, A., & Chess, S. (1986). The New York Longitudinal Study: From infancy to early adult life. In R. Plomin & J. Dunn (Eds.), *The study of temperament: Changes, continuities, and challenges.* Hillsdale, NJ: Erlbaum. (p. 121)

Thomas, G. V., & Blackman, D. (1991). Are animal experiments on the way out? *The Psychologist*, *14*, 208–212. (p. 32)

Thomas, L. (1992). *The fragile species.* New York: Maxwell Macmillan. (p. 478)

Thomas, W. P., & Collier, V. P. (1997). School effectiveness for language minority students. Washington, DC: National Clearinghouse for Bilingual Education. (p. 287)

Thompson, C. P., Frieman, J., & Cowan, T. (1993). Rajan's memory. Paper presented to the American Psychological Society convention. (p. 243)

Thompson, C. P., Vogl, R. J., Walker, W. R., & Wooten, L. (1996). Involuntary memories in depressed and nondepressed individuals. Paper presented to the Psychonomic Society convention. (p. 398)

Thompson, J. K., Jarvie, G. J., Lahey, B. B., & Cureton, K. J. (1982). Exercise and obesity: Etiology, physiology, and intervention. *Psychological Bulletin*, *91*, 55–79. (p. 325)

Thorndike, A. L., & Hagen, E. P. (1977). Measurement and evaluation in psychology and education. New York: Macmillan. (p. 294)

Thorne, J., with Larry Rothstein (1993). *You are not alone: Words of experience and hope for the journey through depression.* New York: HarperPerennial. (p. 425)

Thornton, B., & Moore, S. (1993). Physical attractiveness contrast effect: Implications for self-esteem and evaluations of the social self. *Personality and Social Psychology Bulletin*, *19*, 474–480. (p. 524)

Thorpe, W. H. (1974). *Animal nature and human nature*. London: Metheun. (p. 285)

Tiggemann, M., & Rothblum, E. D. (1988). Gender differences in social consequences of perceived overweight in the United States and Australia. *Sex Roles*, *18*, 75–86. (p. 323)

Tiihonen, J., Isohanni, M., Rasanen, P., Koiranen, M., & Moring, J. (1997). Specific major mental disorders and criminality: A 26-year prospective study of the 1966 northern Finland birth cohort. *American Journal of Psychiatry, 154,* 840–845. (p. 430)

Tinbergen, N. (1951). *The study of instinct.* Oxford: Clarendon. (p. 312)

Tirrell, M. E. (1990). Personal communication. (p. 209)

Tolchin, M. (1994, April 17). Major airlines go two years without a fatality. *New York Times* report in *Grand Rapids Press,* p. A10. (p. 273)

Tollefson, G. D., & others (1994). Absence of a relationship between adverse events and suicidality during pharmacotherapy for depression. *Journal of Clinical Psychopharmacology, 14,* 163–169. (p. 485)

Tollefson, G. D., & others (1993). Evaluation of suicidality during pharmacologic treatment of mood and nonmood disorders. *Annals of Clinical Psychiatry, 5,* 209–224. (p. 485)

Tolstoy, L. (1904). *My confessions.* Boston: Dana Estes. (p. 6)

Torrey, E. F. (1986). *Witchdoctors and psychiatrists.* New York: Harper & Row. (p. 481)

Torrey, E. F., Bowler, A. E., Rawlings, R., & Terrazas, A. (1993). Seasonality of schizophrenia and stillbirths. *Schizophrenia Bulletin, 19,* 557–562. (p. 453)

Torrey, E. F., Rawlings, R. R., Ennis, J. M., Merrill, D. D., & Flores, D. S. (1996). Birth seasonality in bipolar disorder, schizophrenia, schizoaffective disorder and stillbirths. *Schizophrenia Research, 21,* 141–149. (p. 453)

Torrey, E. F., Torrey, B. B., & Peterson, M. A. (1977). Seasonality of schizophrenic births in the United States. *Archives of General Psychiatry, 34,* 1065–1070. (p. 453)

Towler, G. (1986). From zero to one hundred: Coaction in a natural setting. *Perceptual and Motor Skills, 62,* 377–378. (p. 503)

Travis, J. (1994). Glia: The brain's other cells. *Science, 266,* 970–972. (p. 55)

Treisman, A. (1987). Properties, parts, and objects. In K. R. Boff, L. Kaufman, & J. P. Thomas (Eds.), *Handbook of perception and human performance.* New York: Wiley. (p. 147)

Tremblay, R. E., Pihl, R. O., Vitaro, F., & Dobkin, P. L. (1994). Predicting early onset of male antisocial behavior from preschool behavior. *Archives of General Psychiatry, 51,* 732–739. (p. 455)

Triandis, H. C. (1981). Some dimensions of intercultural variation and their implications for interpersonal behavior. Paper presented at the American Psychological Association convention. (p. 507)

Triandis, H. C. (1989a). The self and social behavior in differing cultural contexts. *Psychological Review, 96,* 506–520. (p. 412)

Triandis, H. C. (1989b). Cross-cultural studies of individualism and collectivism. In J. J. Berman (Ed.), *Nebraska symposium on motivation 1989* (Vol. 37). Lincoln, NE: University of Nebraska Press. (p. 412)

Triandis, H. C. (1994). *Culture and social behavior.* New York: McGraw-Hill. (pp. 96, 279, 354, 411, 413, 417, 508, 516)

Triandis, H. C., Bontempo, R., Villareal, M. J., Asai, M., & Lucca, N. (1988). Individualism and collectivism: Cross-cultural perspectives on self-ingroup relationships. *Journal of Personality and Social Psychology, 54,* 323–338. (p. 413)

Trickett, P. K., & McBride-Chang, C. (1995). The developmental impact of different forms of child abuse and neglect. *Developmental Review, 15,* 311–337. (p. 94)

Trickett, P. K., & Putnam, F. W. (1993). Impact of child sexual abuse on females: Toward a developmental, psychobiological integration. *Psychological Science, 4,* 81–87. (p. 260)

Trimble, J. E. (1994). Cultural variations in the use of alcohol and drugs. In W. J. Lonner & R. Malpass (Eds.), *Psychology and culture.* Boston: Allyn & Bacon. (p. 200)

Triplett, N. (1898). The dynamogenic factors in pacemaking and competition. *American Journal of Psychology, 9,* 507–533. (p. 502)

Trolier, T. K., & Hamilton, D. L. (1986). Variables influencing judgments of correlational relations. *Journal of Personality and Social Psychology, 50,* 879–888. (p. 18)

True, R. M. (1949). Experimental control in hypnotic age regression states. *Science, 110,* 583–584. (p. 187)

Tsang, Y. C. (1938). Hunger motivation in gastrectomized rats. *Journal of Comparative Psychology, 26,* 1–17. (p. 316)

Tsuang, M. T., & Faraone, S. V. (1990). *The genetics of mood disorders.* Baltimore, MD: Johns Hopkins University Press. (p. 443)

Tubbs, M. E. (1986). Goal setting: A meta-analytic examination of the empirical evidence. *Journal of Applied Psychology, 71,* 474–483. (p. 342)

Tulving, E. (1996, August 18). Quoted in J. Gatehouse, Technology revealing brain's secrets. *Montreal Gazette,* p. A3. (p. 247)

Turk, D. C., Meichenbaum, D. H., & Berman, W. H. (1979). Application of biofeedback for the regulation of pain: A critical review. *Psychological Bulletin, 86,* 1322–1338. (p. 380)

Turkheimer, E. (1991). Individual and group differences in adoption studies of IQ. *Psychological Bulletin, 110,* 392–405. (p. 300)

Turkington, C. (1987, August). Help for the worried well. *Psychology Today,* pp. 44–48. (p. 479)

Turner, C. W., Hesse, B. W., & Peterson-Lewis, S. (1986). Naturalistic studies of the long-term effects of television violence. *Journal of Social Issues, 42*(3), 7–28. (p. 517)

Tversky, A., & Kahneman, D. (1974). Judgment under uncertainty: Heuristics and biases. *Science, 185,* 1124–1131. (pp. 271, 542)

Twenge, J. M. (1996). Sex differences in personality traits, 1940–1992. Paper presented at the Midwestern Psychological Association convention. (p. 508)

Twiss, C., Tabb, S., & Crosby, F. (1989). Affirmative action and aggregate data: The importance of patterns in the perception of discrimination. In F. Blanchard & F. Crosby (Eds.), *Affirmative action: Social psychological perspectives.* New York: Springer-Verlag. (p. 541)

Ulrich, R. E. (1991). Animal rights, animal wrongs and the question of balance. *Psychological Science, 2,* 197–201. (p. 30)

Umiltá, C., Simion, F., & Valenza, E. (1996). Newborn's preference for faces. *European Psychologist, 1,* 200–205. (p. 82)

Underwood, B. J. (1957). Interference and forgetting. *Psychological Review, 64,* 49–60. (p. 253)

UNICEF (1996). *The state of the world's children.* New York: Oxford University Press. (p. 508)

United Nations (1991). *The world's women 1970–1990: Trends and statistics.* New York: United Nations. (p. 510)

United Nations (1992). *1991 demographic yearbook.* New York: United Nations. (p. 115)

United Nations (1993). Children: A basic focus in IYF. *The Family*, No. 3., pp. 1–2. (p. 510)

University of California (1993, December). The new American body. *University of California at Berkeley Wellness Letter*, pp. 1–2. (p. 323)

Urbany, J. E., Bearden, W. O., & Weilbaker, D. C. (1988). The effect of plausible and exaggerated reference prices on consumer perceptions and price search. *Journal of Consumer Research, 15*, 95–110. (p. 275)

Valenstein, E. S. (1986). *Great and desperate cures: The rise and decline of psychosurgery*. New York: Basic Books. (pp. 486)

Vallone, R. P., Griffin, D. W., Lin, S., & Ross, L. (1990). Overconfident prediction of future actions and outcomes by self and others. *Journal of Personality and Social Psychology, 58*, 582–592. (p. 12)

Vance, E. B., & Wagner, N. N. (1976). Written descriptions of orgasm: A study of sex differences. *Archives of Sexual Behavior, 5*, 87–98. (p. 328)

Vandenberg, S. G., & Kuse, A. R. (1978). Mental rotations: A group test of three-dimensional spatial visualization. *Perceptual and Motor Skills, 47*, 599–604. (p. 305)

van den Boom, D. (1990). Preventive intervention and the quality of mother-infant interaction and infant exploration in irritable infants. In W. Koops, H. J. G. Soppe, J. L. van der Linden, P. C. M. Molenaar, & J. J. F. Schroots (Eds.), *Developmental psychology behind the dikes: An outline of developmental psychology research in The Netherlands*. The Netherlands: Uitgeverij Eburon. Cited by C. Hazan & P. R. Shaver (1994). Deeper into attachment theory. *Psychological Inquiry, 5*, 68–79. (p. 93)

van der Meer, A. L. H., van der Weel, F. R., & Lee, D. N. (1995). The functional significance of arm movements in neonates. *Science, 267*, 693–695. (p. 84)

VanderStoep, S. W., & Shaughnessy, J. J. (1997). Taking a course in research methods improves reasoning about real-life events. *Teaching of Psychology, 24*, 122–124. (p. 28)

van Drunen, P. (1996). Professional psychology in the Netherlands: History and recent trends. In A. Schorr & S. Saari (Eds.), *Psychology in Europe: Facts, figures, realities*. Gottingen: Hogrefe & Huber. (p. 7)

Van Dyke, C., & Byck, R. (1982, March). Cocaine. *Scientific American*, pp. 128–141. (p. 197)

van IJzendoorn, M. H., & Kroonenberg, P. M. (1988). Cross-cultural patterns of attachment: A meta-analysis of the strange situation. *Child Development, 59*, 147–156. (p. 92)

Van Leeuwen, M. S. (1982). IQism and the just society: Historical background. *Journal of the American Scientific Affiliation, 34*, 193–201. (p. 295)

Van Yperen, N. W., & Buunk, B. P. (1990). A longitudinal study of equity and satisfaction in intimate relationships. *European Journal of Social Psychology, 20*, 287–309. (p. 527)

Vaughn, K. B., & Lanzetta, J. T. (1981). The effect of modification of expressive displays on vicarious emotional arousal. *Journal of Experimental Social Psychology, 17*, 16–30. (p. 355)

Vaux, A. (1988). Social and personal factors in loneliness. *Journal of Social and Clinical Psychology, 6*, 462–471. (p. 448)

Veggeberg, S. K. (1996, March-April). Manic depression: Gene-Hunters' hopes rise. *Brain Work*, pp. 1–2. (p. 444)

Vekassy, L. (1977). Dreams of the blind. *Magyar Pszichologiai Szemle, 34*, 478–491. (p. 181)

Vemer, E., Coleman, M., Ganong, L. H., & Cooper, H. (1989). Marital satisfaction in remarriage: A meta-analysis. *Journal of Marriage and the Family, 51*, 713–725. (p. 116)

Venn, J. (1986). Hypnosis and the Lamaze method: A reply to Wideman and Singer. *American Psychologist, 41*, 475–476. (p. 188)

Vines, G. (1995, July 8). Genes in black and white. *New Scientist*, pp. 34–37. (p. 510)

Vines, G. (1995, July 22). Fight fat with feeling. *New Scientist*, pp. 14–15. (p. 325)

Vokey, J. R., & Read, J. D. (1985). Subliminal messages: Between the devil and the media. *American Psychologist, 40*, 1231–1239. (pp. 128, 157)

von Senden, M. (1932; reprinted 1960). In P. Heath (Trans.), *Space and sight: The perception of space and shape in the congenitally blind before and after operation*. Glencoe, IL: Free Press. (p. 155)

Voyer, D., Voyer, S., & Bryden, M. P. (1995). Magnitude of sex differences in spatial abilities: A meta-analysis and consideration of critical variables. *Psychological Bulletin, 117*, 250–270. (p. 305)

Vreeland, C. N., Gallagher, B. J., III, & McFalls, J. A., Jr. (1995). The beliefs of members of the American Psychiatric Association on the etiology of male homosexuality: A national survey. *Journal of Psychology, 129*, 507–517. (p. 336)

Waddington (1993). Neurodynamics of abnormalities in cerebral metabolism and structure in schizophrenia. *Schizophrenia Bulletin, 19*, 55–69. (p. 453)

Wagstaff, G. (1982). Attitudes to rape: The "just world" strikes again? *Bulletin of the British Psychological Society, 13*, 275–283. (p. 492)

Wahl, O. F. (1992). Mass media images of mental illness: A review of the literature. *Journal of Community Psychology, 20*, 343–352. (p. 430)

Wakefield, J. C. (1992). The concept of mental disorder: On the boundary between biological facts and social values. *American Psychologist, 47*, 373–388. (p. 426)

Wallace, D. S., Lord, C. G., & Bond, C. F., Jr. (1996). Which behaviors do attitudes predict? Review and meta-analysis of 60 years' research. Unpublished manuscript, Ohio University. (p. 493)

Wallach, M. A., & Wallach, L. (1983). *Psychology's sanction for selfishness: The error of egoism in theory and therapy*. New York: Freeman. (p. 414)

Wallach, M. A., & Wallach, L. (1985, February). How psychology sanctions the cult of the self. *Washington Monthly*, pp. 46–56. (p. 414)

Waller, D. (1995, December 11). The vision thing. *Time*, p. 48. (p. 163)

Waller, J. (1998). *Face to face: The changing state of racism across America*. New York: Plenum. (p. 510)

Wallis, C. (1983, June 6). Stress: Can we cope? *Time*, pp. 48–54. (p. 371)

Wallis, C. (1987, October 12). Back off, buddy: A new Hite report stirs up a furor over sex and love in the '80s. *Time*, pp. 68–73. (p. 16)

Walster (Hatfield), E., Aronson, V., Abrahams, D., & Rottman, L. (1966). Importance of physical attractiveness in dating behavior. *Journal of Personality and Social Psychology, 4*, 508–516. (p. 524)

Wampold, B. E., Mondin, G. W., Moody, M., Stich, F., Benson, K., & Ahn, H. (1997). A meta-analysis of outcome studies comparing bona fide psychotherapies: Empirically, "All must have prizes." *Psychological Bulletin*, *122*, 203–215. (p. 479)

Ward, C. (1994). Culture and altered states of consciousness. In W. J. Lonner & R. Malpass (Eds.), *Psychology and culture*. Boston: Allyn & Bacon. (p. 194)

Warr, P., & Payne, R. (1982). Experiences of strain and pleasure among British adults. *Social Science and Medicine*, *16*, 1691–1697. (p. 382)

Wason, P. C. (1960). On the failure to eliminate hypotheses in a conceptual task. *Quarterly Journal of Experimental Psychology*, *12*, 129–140. (p. 270)

Wason, P. C. (1981). The importance of cognitive illusions. *The Behavioral and Brain Sciences*, *4*, 356. (p. 12)

Wasserman, E. A. (1993). Comparative cognition: Toward a general understanding of cognition in behavior. *Psychological Science*, *4*, 156–161. (p. 217)

Wasserman, E. A. (1995). The conceptual abilities of pigeons. *American Scientist*, *83*, 246–255. (p. 268)

Waterhouse, R. (1993, July 19). Income for 62 percent is below average pay. *The Independent*, p. 4. (p. 538)

Waterman, A. S. (1988). Identity status theory and Erikson's theory: Commonalities and differences. *Developmental Review*, *8*, 185–208. (p. 104)

Watkins, J. G. (1984). The Bianchi (L. A. Hillside Strangler) case: Sociopath or multiple personality? *International Journal of Clinical and Experimental Hypnosis*, *32*, 67–101. (p. 438)

Watson, J. B. (1913). Psychology as the behaviorist views it. *Psychological Review*, *20*, 158–177. (pp. 170, *214)*

Watson, J. B. (1924). *Behaviorism*. New York: Norton. (p. 214)

Watson, J. B., & Rayner, R. (1920). Conditioned emotional reactions. *Journal of Experimental Psychology*, *3*, 1–14. (p. 214)

Watson, R. I., Jr. (1973). Investigation into deindividuation using a cross-cultural survey technique. *Journal of Personality and Social Psychology*, *25*, 342–345. (p. 504)

Weaver, J. B., Masland, J. L., & Zillmann, D. (1984). Effect of erotica on young men's aesthetic perception of their female sexual partners. *Perceptual and Motor Skills*, *58*, 929–930. (p. 330)

Webb, W. B. (1992). *Sleep: The gentle tyrant*. Bolton, MA: Anker Publishing. (pp. 175, 179)

Webb, W. B., & Campbell, S. S. (1983). Relationships in sleep characteristics of identical and fraternal twins. *Archives of General Psychiatry*, *40*, 1093–1095. (p. 179)

Wechsler, D. (1972). "Hold" and "Don't Hold" tests. In S. M. Chown (Ed.), *Human aging*. New York: Penguin. (p. 113)

Wechsler, H., Davenport, A., Dowdall, G., Moeykens, B., & Castillo, S. (1994). Health and behavioral consequences of binge drinking in college. *Journal of the American Medical Association*, *272*, 1672–1677. (p. 194)

Wegner, D. M. (1990). *White bears and other unwanted thoughts: Suppression, obsession, and the psychology of mental control*. New York: Penguin Books. (p. 384)

Weinberg, M. S., & Williams, C. (1974). *Male homosexuals: Their problems and adaptations*. New York: Oxford University Press. (p. 333)

Weindruch, R. (1996, January). Caloric restriction and aging. *Scientific American*, pp. 46–52. (p. 320)

Weingartner, H., Rudorfer, M. V., Buchsbaum, M. S., & Linnoila, M. (1983). Effects of serotonin on memory impairments produced by ethanol. *Science*, *221*, 472–473. (p. 246)

Weinstein, N. (1996, October 4). 1996 optimistic bias bibliography. Distributed via internet from weinstein_c@aesop.rutgers.edu. (p. 419)

Weinstein, N. D. (1980). Unrealistic optimism about future life events. *Journal of Personality and Social Psychology*, *39*, 806–820. (p. 419)

Weinstein, N. D. (1982). Unrealistic optimism about susceptibility to health problems. *Journal of Behavioral Medicine*, *5*, 441–460. (p. 419)

Weisse, C. S. (1992). Depression and immunocompetence: A review of the literature. *Psychological Bulletin*, *111*, 475–489. (p. 374)

Weissman, M. M., Merikangas, K. R., Wickramaratne, P., Kidd, K. K., Prusoff, B. A., Leckman, J. F., & Pauls, D. L. (1986). Understanding the clinical heterogeneity of major depression using family data. *Archives of General Psychiatry*, *43*, 430–434. (p. 443)

Weissman, M. M., & others (1996). Cross-national epidemiology of major depression and bipolar disorder. *Journal of the American Medical Association*, *276*, 293–299. (p. 443)

Weisz, J. R., Rothbaum, F. M., & Blackburn, T. C. (1984). Standing out and standing in: The psychology of control in America and Japan. *American Psychologist*, *39*, 955–969. (p. 507)

Weller, S. (1993). A meta-analysis of condom effectiveness in reducing sexually transmitted HIV. *Social Science and Medicine*, *36*. 1635–1644. (p. 108)

Wellman, H. M., & Gelman, S. A. (1992). Cognitive development: Foundational theories of core domains. *Annual Review of Psychology*, *43*, 337–375. (p. 87)

Wells, B. L. (1986). Predictors of female nocturnal orgasms: A multivariate analysis. *Journal of Sex Research*, *22*, 421–437. (p. 330)

Wells, G. L. (1981). Lay analyses of causal forces on behavior. In J. Harvey (Ed.), *Cognition, social behavior and the environment*. Hillsdale, NJ: Erlbaum. (p. 206)

Wender, P. H., Kety, S. S., Rosenthal, D., Schulsinger, F., Ortmann, J., & Lunde, I. (1986). Psychiatric disorders in the biological and adoptive families of adopted individuals with affective disorders. *Archives of General Psychiatry*, *43*, 923–929. (p. 443)

Wener, R., Frazier, W., & Farbstein, J. (1987, June). Building better jails. *Psychology Today*, pp. 40–49. (p. 417)

Werker, J. F. (1989). Becoming a native listener. *American Scientist*, *77*, 54–59. (p. 278)

West, P. D. B., & Evans, E. F. (1990). Early detection of hearing damage in young listeners resulting from exposure to amplified music. *British Journal of Audiology*, *24*, 89–103. (p. 139)

Westefeld, J. S., & Furr, S. R. (1987). Suicide and depression among college students. *Professional Psychology: Research and Practice*, *18*, 119–123. (p. 444)

Westen, D. (1996). Is Freud really dead? Teaching psychodynamic theory to introductory psychology. Presentation to the Annual Institute on the Teaching of Psychology, St. Petersburg Beach, Florida. (p. 395)

Wheeler, D. L., Jacobson, D. L., Paglieri, R. A., & Schwartz, A. A. (1993). An experimental assessment of facilitated communication. *Mental Retardation*, *31*, 49–60. (p. 502)

Whitam, F. L., Diamond, M., & Martin, J. (1993). Homosexual orientation in twins: A report on 61 pairs and three triplet sets. *Archives of Sexual Behavior, 22,* 187–206. (p. 335)

White, G. L., & Kight, T. D. (1984). Misattribution of arousal and attraction: Effects of salience of explanations for arousal. *Journal of Experimental Social Psychology, 20,* 55–64. (p. 526)

White, H. R., Brick, J., & Hansell, S. (1993). A longitudinal investigation of alcohol use and aggression in adolescence. *Journal of Studies on Alcohol,* Supplement No. 11, 62–77. (p. 514)

White, K. M. (1983). Young adults and their parents: Individuation to mutuality. *New Directions for Child Development, 22,* 61–76. (p. 107)

White, L., & Edwards, J. (1990). Emptying the nest and parental well-being: An analysis of national panel data. *American Sociological Review, 55,* 235–242. (p. 118)

White, P. H., Kjelgaard, M. M., & Harkins, S. G. (1995). Testing the contribution of self-evaluation to goal-setting effects. *Journal of Personality and Social Psychology, 69,* 69–79. (p. 342)

Whiten, A., & Byrne, R. W. (1988). Tactical deception in primates. *Behavioral and Brain Sciences, 11,* 233–244, 267–273. (p. 17)

Whiteneck, G. G., & others (1985). A collaborative study of high quadriplegia. Englewood, CO: Rocky Mountain Regional Spinal Cord Injury System for the National Institute of Handicapped Research. (p. 360)

Whiting, B. B., & Edwards, C. P. (1988). *Children of different worlds: The formation of social behavior.* Cambridge, MA: Harvard University Press. (p. 96)

Whitley, B. E., Jr. (1990). The relationships of heterosexuals' attributions for the causes of homosexuality to attitudes toward lesbians and gay men. *Personality and Social Psychology Bulletin, 16,* 369–377. (p. 336)

Whorf, B. L. (1956). Science and linguistics. In J. B. Carroll (Ed.), *Language, thought, and reality: Selected writings of Benjamin Lee Whorf.* Cambridge, MA: MIT Press. (p. 286)

Wickelgren, W. A. (1977). *Learning and memory.* Englewood Cliffs, NJ: Prentice-Hall. (p. 237)

Wicker, A. W. (1971). An examination of the "other variables" explanation of attitude-behavior inconsistency. *Journal of Personality and Social Psychology, 19,* 18–30. (p. 493)

Widom, C. S. (1989a). Does violence beget violence? A critical examination of the literature. *Psychological Bulletin, 106,* 3–28. (p. 94)

Widom, C. S. (1989b). The cycle of violence. *Science, 244,* 160–166. (p. 94)

Wiens, A. N., & Menustik, C. E. (1983). Treatment outcome and patient characteristics in an aversion therapy program for alcoholism. *American Psychologist, 38,* 1089–1096. (p. 469)

Wierson, M., & Forehand, R. (1994). Parent behavioral training for child noncompliance: Rationale, concepts, and effectiveness. *Current Directions in Psychological Science, 3,* 146–149. (p. 224)

Wierzbicki, M. (1993). Psychological adjustment of adoptees: A meta-analysis. *Journal of Clinical Child Psychology, 22,* 447–454. (p. 73)

Wiesel, T. N. (1982). Postnatal development of the visual cortex and the influence of environment. *Nature, 299,* 583–591. (p. 155)

Wigdor, A. K., & Garner, W. R. (1982). *Ability testing: Uses, consequences, and controversies.* Washington, DC: National Academy Press. (p. 306)

Wiggins, J. S. (ed.) (1996). *The five-factor model of personality: Theoretical perspectives.* New York: Guilford. (p. 402)

Wilder, D. A. (1981). Perceiving persons as a group: Categorization and intergroup relations. In D. L. Hamilton (Ed.), *Cognitive processes in stereotyping and intergroup behavior.* Hillsdale, NJ: Erlbaum. (p. 511)

Wilkinson, C. B. (1983). Aftermath of a disaster: The collapse of the Hyatt Regency Hotel skywalks. *American Journal of Psychiatry, 140,* 1134–1139. (p. 398)

Williams, C. L., & Berry, J. W. (1991). Primary prevention of acculturative stress among refugees. *American Psychologist, 46,* 632–641. (p. 370)

Williams, J. E. (1992). Culture and behavior: Sense and nonsense. Presidential address to the Southeastern Psychological Association convention. (p. 24)

Williams, J. E., & Best, D. L. (1990). *Measuring sex stereotypes: A multination study.* Newbury Park, CA: Sage. (p. 342)

Williams, L. M. (1994). Recall of childhood trauma: A prospective study of women's memories of child sexual abuse. *Journal of Consulting and Clinical Psychology, 62,* 1167–1176. (p. 259)

Williams, R. (1989). *The trusting heart: Great news about Type A behavior.* New York: Random House. (p. 373)

Williams, R. (1993). *Anger kills.* New York: Times Books. (p. 373)

Williams, R. B., Barefoot, J. C., Califf, R. M., Haney, T. L., Saunders, W. B., Pryor, D. B., Hlatky, M. A., Siegler, I. C., Mark, D. B. (1992). Prognostic importance of social and economic resources among medically treated patients with angiographically documented coronary artery disease. *Journal of the American Medical Association, 267,* 520–524. (p. 382)

Williams, S. L. (1987). Self-efficacy and mastery-oriented treatment for severe phobias. Paper presented to the American Psychological Association convention. (p. 468)

Willingham, W. W., Lewis, C., Morgan, R., & Ramist, L. (1990). *Predicting college grades: An analysis of institutional trends over two decades.* Princeton: Educational Testing Service. (p. 347)

Willmuth, M. E. (1987). Sexuality after spinal cord injury: A critical review. *Clinical Psychology Review, 7,* 389–412. (p. 330)

Wilson, J. G. (1993). *The moral sense.* New York: Free Press. (p. 508)

Wilson, J. P., Harel, Z., & Kahana, B. (1988). *Human adaptation to extreme stress: From the Holocaust to Vietnam.* New York: Plenum Press. (p. 435)

Wilson, J. Q., & Herrnstein, R. J. (1985). *Crime and human nature.* New York: Simon and Schuster. (p. 514)

Wilson, R. C., Gaft, J. G., Dienst, E. R., Wood, L., & Bavry, J. L. (1975). *College professors and their impact on students.* New York: Wiley. (p. 504)

Wilson, R. S. (1979). Analysis of longitudinal twin data: Basic model and applications to physical growth measures. *Acta Geneticae medicae et Gemellologiae, 28,* 93–105. (p. 85)

Wilson, S. C., & Barber, T. X. (1983). The fantasy-prone personality: Implications for understanding imagery, hypnosis, and parapsychological phenomena. In A. A. Sheikh (Ed.), *Imagery: Current theory, research, and applications.* New York: Wiley. (pp. 172, 198)

Wilson, W. R. (1979). Feeling more than we can know: Exposure effects without learning. *Journal of Personality and Social Psychology, 37,* 811–821. (p. 170)

Windholz, G. (1989, April-June). The discovery of the principles of reinforcement, extinction, generalization, and differentiation of conditional reflexes in Pavlov's laboratories. *Pavlovian Journal of Biological Science*, *26*, 64–74. (p. 210)

Windholz, G. (1997). Ivan P. Pavlov: An overview of his life and psychological work. *American Psychologist*, *52*, 941–946. (p. 209)

Wing, R. R., & Jeffrey, R. W. (1979). Outpatient treatments of obesity: A comparison of methodology and clinical results. *International Journal of Obesity*, *3*, 261–279. (p. 323)

Winn, P. (1995). The lateral hypothalamus and motivated behavior: An old syndrome reassessed and a new perspective gained. *Current Directions in Psychological Science*, *4*, 182–187. (p. 317)

Witelson, S. F. (1985). The brain connection: The corpus callosum is larger in left-handers. *Science*, *229*, 665–667. (p. 65)

Wixted, J. T., & Ebbesen, E. B. (1991). On the form of forgetting. *Psychological Science*, 2, 409–415. (p. 243)

Wolf, N. (1991). *The beauty myth: How images of beauty are used against women.* New York: Morrow. (p. 323)

Wolf, R. (1996, May/June). Believing what we see, hear, and touch: The delights and dangers of sensory illusions. *Skeptical Inquirer*, pp. 23–30. (p. 149)

Woll, S. (1986). So many to choose from: Decision strategies in videodating. *Journal of Social and Personal Relationships*, *3*, 43–52. (p. 524)

Wolpe, J. (1958). *Psychotherapy by reciprocal inhibition.* Stanford, CA: Stanford University Press. (p. 467)

Wolpe, J. (1982). *The practice of behavior therapy.* New York: Pergamon. (p. 467)

Wong, D. F., & associates. (1986). Positron emission tomography reveals elevated D2 dopamine receptors in drug-naive schizophrenics. *Science*, *234*, 1588–1563. (p. 452)

Wong, M. M., & Csikszentmihalyi, M. (1991). Affiliation motivation and daily experience: Some issues on gender differences. *Journal of Personality and Social Psychology*, *60*, 154–164. (p. 105)

Wood, G. (1979). The knew-it-all-along effect. *Journal of Experimental Psychology: Human Perception and Performance*, *4*, 345–353. (p. 10)

Wood, J. M., Bootzin, R. R., Kihlstrom, J. F., & Schacter, D. L. (1992). Implicit and explicit memory for verbal information presented during sleep. *Psychological Science*, *3*, 236–239. (p. 235)

Wood, J. M., Bootzin, R. R., Rosenhan, D., Nolen-Hoeksema, S., & Jourden, F. (1992). Effects of the 1989 San Francisco earthquake on frequency and content of nightmares. *Journal of Abnormal Psychology*, *101*, 219–224. (p. 181)

Wood, J. M., Nezworski, M. T., & Stejskal, W. J. (1996). The comprehensive system for the Rorschach: A critical examination. *Psychological Science*, *7*, 3-10. (p. 396)

Wood, J. V., Saltzberg, J. A., & Goldsamt, L. A. (1990a). Does affect induce self-focused attention? *Journal of Personality and Social Psychology*, *58*, 899–908. (p. 447)

Wood, J. V., Saltzberg, J. A., Neale, J. M., Stone, A. A., & Rachmiel, T. B. (1990b). Self-focused attention, coping responses, and distressed mood in everyday life. *Journal of Personality and Social Psychology*, *58*, 1027–1036. (p. 447)

Wood, W. (1987). Meta-analytic review of sex differences in group performance. *Psychological Bulletin*, *102*, 53–71. (p. 342)

Wood, W., Lundgren, S., Ouellette, J. A., Busceme, S., & Blackstone, T. (1994). Minority influence: A meta-analytic review of social influence processes. *Psychological Bulletin*, *115*, 323–345. (p. 506)

Wood, W., Wong, F. Y., & Chachere, J. G. (1991). Effects of media violence on viewers' aggression in unconstrained social interaction. *Psychological Bulletin*, *109*, 371–383. (p. 517)

Woodruff-Pak, D. S. (1989). Aging and intelligence: Changing perspectives in the twentieth century. *Journal of Aging Studies*, *3*, 91–118. (p. 113)

Woods, N. F., Dery, G. K., & Most, A. (1983). Recollections of menarche, current menstrual attitudes, and premenstrual symptoms. In S. Golub (Ed.), *Menarche: The transition from girl to woman.* Lexington, MA: Lexington Books. (p. 100)

Wooley, S., & Wooley, O. (1983). Should obesity be treated at all? *Psychiatric Annals*, *13*(11), 884–885, 888. (p. 319)

World atlas: A multimedia view of the world (1993). A CD-ROM, Macintosh version 3. Novato, CA: Software Toolworks. (p. 456)

World Health Organization.(1979). *Schizophrenia: An international follow-up study.* Chicester, England: Wiley. (p. 451)

Worthington, E. L., Jr. (1989). Religious faith across the life span: Implications for counseling and research. *The Counseling Psychologist*, *17*, 555–612. (p. 101)

Worthington, E. L., Jr., Kurusu, T. A., McCullogh, M. E., & Sandage, S. J. (1996). Empirical research on religion and psychotherapeutic processes and outcomes: A 10-year review and research prospectus. *Psychological Bulletin*, *119*, 448–487. (p. 481)

Wortman, C. B., & Silver, R. C. (1989). The myths of coping with loss. *Journal of Consulting and Clinical Psychology*, *57*, 349–357. (p. 119)

Wright, P., & Murray, R. M. (1993). Schizophrenia: Prenatal influenza and autoimmunity. *Annals of Medicine*, *25*, 497–502. (p. 453)

Wright, P., Takei, N., Rifkin, L., & Murray, R. M. (1995). Maternal influenza, obstetric complications, and schizophrenia. *American Journal of Psychiatry*, *152*, 1714–1720. (p. 453)

Wu, T-C., Tashkin, D. P., Djahed, B., & Rose, J. E. (1988). Pulmonary hazards of smoking marijuana as compared with tobacco. *New England Journal of Medicine*, *318*, 347–351. (p. 198)

Wyatt, J. K., & Bootzin, R. R. (1994). Cognitive processing and sleep: Implications for enhancing job performance. *Human Performance*, *7*, 119–139. (pp. 181, 235)

Wynn, K. (1992). Addition and subtraction by human infants. *Nature*, *358*, 749–759. (pp. 87, *88)*

Wynn, K. (1995). Infants possess a system of numerical knowledge. *Current Directions in Psychological Science*, *4*, 172–177. (p. 87)

Wysocki, C. J., & Gilbert, A. N. (1989). *National Geographic* survey: Effects of age are heterogeneous. *Annals of the New York Academy of Sciences*, *561*, 12–28. (p. 145)

Yalom, I. D. (1985). *The theory and practice of group psychotherapy* (3rd ed.). New York: Basic Books. (p. 474)

Yang, N., & Linz, D. (1990). Movie ratings and the content of adult videos: The sex-violence ratio. *Journal of Communication*, *40*(2), 28–42. (p. 518)

Yankelovich, D. (1994). The affluence affect. In H. J. Aaron, T. Mann, and T. Taylor (eds.), *Values and Public Policy*. Washington, DC: Brookings Institution. (p. 413)

Yankelovich Partners (1995, May/June). Growing old. *American Enterprise*, p. 108. (p. 110)

Yapko, M. D. (1994). Suggestibility and repressed memories of abuse: A survey of psychotherapists' beliefs. *American Journal of Clinical Hypnosis*, *36*, 163–171. (p. 186)

Yarnell, P. R., & Lynch, S. (1970, April 25). Retrograde memory immediately after concussion. *Lancet*, pp. 863–865. (p. 246)

Yates, A. (1989). Current perspectives on the eating disorders: I. History, psychological and biological aspects. *Journal of the American Academy of Child and Adolescent Psychiatry*, *28*, 813–828. (p. 319)

Yates, A. (1990). Current perspectives on the eating disorders: II. Treatment, outcome, and research directions. *Journal of the American Academy of Child and Adolescent Psychiatry*, *29*, 1–9. (p. 319)

Young, A. (1995). *The harmony of illusions: Inventing post-traumatic stress disorder.* Princeton: Princeton University Press. (p. 435)

Zajonc, R. B. (1965). Social facilitation. *Science*, *149*, 269–274. (p. 503)

Zajonc, R. B. (1980). Feeling and thinking: Preferences need no inferences. *American Psychologist*, *35*, 151–175. (p. 367)

Zajonc, R. B. (1984a). On the primacy of affect. *American Psychologist*, *39*, 117–123. (p. 367)

Zajonc, R. B. (1984b, July 22). Quoted by D. Goleman, Rethinking IQ tests and their value. *The New York Times,* p. D22. (p. 290)

Zajonc, R. B. (1998). Emotions. In D. Gilbert, S. T. Fiske, & G. Lindzey (eds.), *Handbook of social psychology*, 4th ed. New York: McGraw-Hill. (p. 523)

Zajonc, R. B., & Markus, G. B. (1975). Birth order and intellectual development. *Psychological Review*, *82*, 74–88. (p. 544)

Zajonc, R. B., Murphy, S. T., & Inglehart, M. (1989). Feeling and facial efference: Implications of the vascular theory of emotions. *Psychological Review*, *96*, 395–416. (p. 355)

Zeidner, M. (1990). Perceptions of ethnic group modal intelligence: Reflections of cultural stereotypes or intelligence test scores? *Journal of Cross-Cultural Psychology*, *21*, 214–231. (p. 303)

Zelnick, M., & Kim, Y. J. (1982). Sex education and its association with teenage sexual activity, pregnancy, and contraceptive use. *Family Planning Perspectives*, *14*(3), 117–126. (p. 338)

Zhang, S. D., & Odenwald, W. F. (1995). Misexpression of the white (w) gene triggers male-male courtship in Drosophila. *Proceedings of the National Academy of Sciences of the United States of America*, *92*, 5525–5529. (p. 335)

Zigler, E. F. (1987). Formal schooling for four-year-olds? No. *American Psychologist*, *42*, 254–260. (p. 301)

Zigler, E. F., & Muenchow, S. (1992). *Head start: The inside story of a great American experiment.* New York: Basic Books. (p. 301)

Zilbergeld, B. (1983). *The shrinking of America: Myths of psychological change.* Boston: Little, Brown. (pp. 476, *479)*

Zillmann, D. (1986). Effects of prolonged consumption of pornography. Background paper for *The Surgeon General's workshop on pornography and public health*, June 22–24. Report prepared by E. P. Mulvey & J. L. Haugaard and released by Office of the Surgeon General on August 4, 1986. (pp. 349, 366)

Zillmann, D. (1989). Effects of prolonged consumption of pornography. In D. Zillmann & J. Bryant (Eds.), *Pornography: Research advances and policy considerations.* Hillsdale, NJ: Erlbaum. (pp. 330, 519)

Zillmann, D., & Bryant, J. (1984). Effects of massive exposure to pornography. In N. Malamuth & E. Donnerstein (Eds.), *Pornography and sexual aggression.* Orlando, FL: Academic Press. (p. 519)

Zimbardo, P. G. (1970). The human choice: Individuation, reason, and order versus deindividuation, impulse, and chaos. In W. J. Arnold & D. Levine (Eds.), *Nebraska Symposium on Motivation*, 1969. Lincoln, NE: University of Nebraska Press. (p. 504)

Zimbardo, P. G. (1972, April). Pathology of imprisonment. *Transaction/Society*, pp. 4–8. (p. 495)

Zucker, G. S., & Weiner, B. (1993). Conservatism and perceptions of poverty: An attributional analysis. *Journal of Applied Social Psychology*, *23*, 925–943. (p. 492)

Zuckerman, M. (1979). *Sensation seeking: Beyond the optimal level of arousal.* Hillsdale, NJ: Erlbaum. (p. 313)

Illustration Credits

PREFACE:

p. xvii *(left)* Oliver Meckes/Photo Researchers; *(center)* Michael Newman/Photo Edit; *(right)* Crews/The Image Works; *(top)* Shackman/Monkmeyer.

TABLE OF CONTENTS:

p. vii Didier Givois/Agence Vandystadt/Photo Researchers; **p. viii** Tom & Dee Ann McCarthy/Rainbow; **p. ix** *(top)* Dan McCoy/Rainbow; **p. ix** *(bottom)* Jacques Chenet/Woodfin Camp & Associates; **p. x** Bob Daemmrich/Stock, Boston; **p. xi** Robert Azzi/Woodfin Camp & Associates; **p. xii** Myrleen Ferguson/Photo Edit.

CHAPTER 1

Opener p. xxxii John Boykin/Photo Edit; **p. 2** *(left)* Sally Cassidy/The Picture Cube; *(center)* Joe Carini/The Image Works; *(right)* Robert Caputo/Stock, Boston; **p. 4** Ebbinghaus: The Bettmann Archive; Binet, Wundt, Thorndike, Hall, Freud, Watson, and James: Brown Brothers; Washburn: National Library of Medicine; Calkins: Wellesley College Archives; Pavlov: Sovfoto; **p. 5** *(top)* © 1992 Rob Nelson/Black Star; *(bottom)* Robert Brenner/Photo Edit; Dion Ougust/The Image Works; **p. 7** *(left)* Laura Dwight/Photo Edit; *(center)* and *(right)* Treë; *(bottom)* Laura Dwight; **p. 8** Bob Kinmonth; **p. 10** Jim Pickerell/Stock, Boston; **p. 14** Shackman/Monkmeyer; **p. 15** Susan Kuklin/Photo Researchers; **p. 17** Courtesy of Richard Byrne and David Myers; **p. 19** *(left)* Michael Newman Jr./Photo Edit; *(right)* David Phillips/Photo Researchers; Fig. 1.3 Adapted with permission of The Free Press, a division of Simon & Schuster from *How we know what isn't so: The fallibility of human reason in everyday life* by Thomas Gilovich. Copyright © 1991 Thomas Gilovich; **p. 20** *(bottom)* UPI/Corbis-Bettmann; **p. 21** R. Sidney/The Image Works; Fig. 1.5 Adapted from Ross, B. (Jan. 1987). In K. McKean, "The orderly pursuit of pure disorder." *Discover*, pp. 72–81. Barry Ross/Copyright © 1987. Reprinted with permission of *Discover* Magazine; **p. 25** *(top)* Super Stock; *(bottom)* Smith/ Monkmeyer; Fig. 1.7 Frank, M.G. & Gilovich, T. (1988). The dark side of self and social perception: Black uniforms and aggression in professional sports. *Journal of Personality and Social Psychology, 54*, 74–85. Copyright © 1988 American Psychological Association. Reprinted by permission; **p. 29** Mark S. Wexler/Woodfin Camp & Associates; **p. 32** Jim Amos/Science Source/Photo Researchers; **p. 33** Fig. 1.9 From *Mind sights* by Roger N. Shepard, Copyright © 1990 Roger N. Shepard. Reprinted with permission of W.H. Freeman and Company.

CHAPTER 2

Opener p. 38 Ron Lowery/Graphics, Inc./Stock Market; **p. 40** Oliver Meckes/ Ottawa /Photo Researchers; **p. 42** Bob Daemmrich/Stock, Boston; **p. 48** A. Glauberman/Photo Researchers; **p. 50** *(top)* Alexander Tsiaras/Stock, Boston; **p. 50** *(bottom)* Hank Morgan/Rainbow; **p. 51** Daniel R. Weinberger, M.D. CBDB, NIMH; **p. 53** *(top)* Frank Siteman/Stock, Boston; *(bottom)* Pix*ELATION from Fran Heyl Associates; **p. 57** Courtesy of Drs. Jack Belliveau and Bruce Rosen, Massachusetts General Hospital, NMR Center; **p. 59** Hanna Damasio, M.D. University of Iowa and Science; **p. 62** Joe McNally; **p. 63** Martin M. Rotker; Figs. 2.23 Gazzaniga, M.S. (1983). Right hemisphere language following brain bisection: A 20-year perspective. *American Psychologist, 38*, 525–537; **p. 66** Robert Brenner/Photo Edit; **p. 68** Didier Givois/Agence Vandystadt/Photo Researchers; **p. 72** Bob Sacha; **p. 73** Kathleen Marie Menke/Crystal Images/Monkmeyer.

CHAPTER 3

Opener p. 78 Lou Jones; **p. 80** *(top)* Francis Leroy, Biocosmos/Science Photo Library/Photo Researchers; *(bottom)* Lennart Nilsson/Bonnier Fakta Bokforlag; **p. 81** (a-c) Petit Format/Science Source Photo Researcher, Inc.; (d) Donald Yeager/Camera MD Studios; Fig. 3.3 Johnson & Morton (1991). *Psychological Review, 98*, 164–181. Copyright © 1991 by the American Psychological Association. Reprinted with permission; **p. 83** Fig. 3.4 Conel, J. L. (1939–1963). The Postnatal development of the human cerebral cortex (Vols. I-VI) Reprinted by permission of Harvard University Press; **p. 84** *(left)* Felicia Martinez/Photo Edit; *(center left)* Shackman/Monkmeyer; *(center right)* Alan Carruthers/ Photo Researchers; *(right)* Bob Daemmrich Photos/ Stock, Boston; Fig. 3.5 Adapted from figure in "Brain changes in response to experience" by M.R. Rosenzweig, E.L. Bennett, and M.C. Diamond. Copyright © Ikuyo Tagawa Garber for Bunji Tagawa; **p. 86** Bill Anderson/Monkmeyer; **p. 87** Doug Goodman/Monkmeyer; **p. 88** Ontario Science Centre; Fig. 3.7 Wynn, K. (1992). Addition and subtraction by human infants. *Nature, 358*, 749–759. Reprinted by permission of *Nature*. Copyright © 1992 Macmillan Magazines Limited; **p. 91** *(top)* Elizabeth Crews/The Image Works; *(bottom)*

Harlow Primate Laboratory, University of Wisconsin; **p. 93** Bob Daemmrich/The Image Works; *(bottom)* Harlow Primate Laboratory, University of Wisconsin; Fig. 3.10 Kagan, J. (1976). Emergent themes in human devlopment. *American Scientist, 64*, 186–196. Reprinted by permission of *American Scientist*, Journal of Sigma XI, The Scientific Research Society; **p. 96** Sybil Shackman/Monkmeyer; **p. 98** Siteman/Monkmeyer; **p. 99** Michael Newman/Photo Edit; Fig. 3.13 Reproduced with the permission of the Alan Guttmacher Institute from *Sex and America's Teenagers*, Alan Guttmacher Institute, New York, 1994; Fig. 3.14 Reprinted by permission of the publisher from *Fetus into man: Physical growth from conception to maturity* by J.M. Tanner, Cambridge, MA.: Harvard University Press, Copyright © 1978 by J.M. Tanner; **p. 102** *(right)* Cynthia Johnson/Gamma Liaison; *(left)* Frances M. Roberts; **p. 104** *(top)* John Eastcott/YVA Momatiuk/The Image Works; *(bottom)* Esbin-Anderson/The Image Works; *(bottom right)* David Vance/The Image Bank; *(bottom left)* David Delossy/The Image Bank; **p. 105** *(right)* Copyright © 1994 David J. Sams/Stock, Boston; *(left)* Bob Daemmrich/The Image Works; Fig. 3.18 Adapted from Insel, P.M. & Roth, W.T. (1976). *Health in a changing society*. Mountain View, CA: Mayfield, p. 98; **p. 111** *(top)* Michael Newman/Photo Edit; *(bottom)* David Wells/The Image Bank; Fig. 3.19 Adapted with permission from Doty, R.L., et al. (1984). Smell identification ability: Changes with age. *Science, 226*, 1441–1443. Copyright © 1984 by the American Association for the Advancement of Science; Fig. 3.20 Stock, R. W. (1995, July 13). Reducing the risk for older drivers. *New York Times*, p. C1. Copyright © 1995 by The New York Times Co. Reprinted with permission; Fig. 3.21 Jorm A.F., Korten, A.E., & Henderson, A.S. (1987). The prevalence of dementia: A quantitative integration of the literature. *Acta Psychiatrica Scandinivica, 76*, 465–479. Copyright © 1987 Munksgaard International Publishers, Ltd., Copenhagen, Denmark; **p. 113** David Myers; Fig. 3.23 Schonfield, D. & Robertson, B. A. (1966). Memory storage and aging. *Canadian Journal of Psychology, 20*, 228–236. Copyright © 1966. Canadian Psychological Association. Reprinted with permission; Fig. 3.24 Adapted from Schaie, K. W. (1994). The life course of adult intellectual abilities. *American Psychologist, 49*, 304–313. Copyright © 1994 American Psychological Association. Adapted by permission; Fig. 3.25 Adapted from Kaufman, A. S., Reynolds, C. R., & McLean, J.E. (1989). Age and WAIS-R intelligence in a national sample of adults in the 20 to 74 year age range: A cross-sectional analysis with educational level controlled. *Intelligence, 13*, 235–253. Reprinted with permission from Ablex Publishing Corporation; Fig. 3.26 McCrae, R.R & Costa, P.T. Jr. (1990). *Personality in adulthood*. New York: Guilford Press, p. 149. Copyright © 1990 Guilford Press; **p. 116** Tom & Dee Ann McCarthy/Rainbow; **p. 117** Bumpass, L. L, & Sweet, J. A. (1989). National estimates of Cohabitation. *Demography, 26*, 615–625; **p. 118** *(left)* Joe McNally; *(center)* Bob Daemmrich/The Image Works; *(right)* Charles Harbutt/Actuality.

CHAPTER 4

Opener p. 124 Philip Gould/Corbis; **p. 126** Detail "The Forest has Eyes" by Bev Doolittle Copyright © The Greenwich Workshops, Inc. Trumbull, CT; **p. 127** Marvin Lyons/The Image Bank; **p. 131** Thomas Eisner; **p. 133** E.R. Lewis, Y.Y. Zeevi, F.S. Werblin, 1969; **p. 134** *(top)* Fritz Goro, LIFE Magazine, Copyright © 1971 Time Warner, Inc.; **p. 134** *(bottom)* Ross Kinnaird/Allsport; **p. 135** Tim Bieber/The Image Bank; **p. 136** *(top)* Fritz Goro, LIFE Magazine Copyright © 1971 Time Warner, Inc.; *(bottom)* From Richmond Products, Boca Raton, Fl; **p. 137** From Albers, J. (1975). *The Interaction of Color* (revised pocket edition) (Plate VI-3). New Haven, CT: Yale University Press. Photo courtesy of the Josef Albers Foundation; Copyright **p. 138** *(top)* Mark Burnett/Stock, Boston; *(bottom)* Richard Kaylin/Tony Stone Images; **p. 140** Jill Levine; **p. 141** Bruce Ayres/Tony Stone Images; **p. 142** Paul J. Sutton/Duomo; **p. 143** Michael Newman/Photo Edit; Fig. 4.17 Wysocki, C. J. & Gilbert, A. N. (1989). In C. Murphy & W. S. Cain (Eds.), *Proceedings of the conference on nutrition and the chemical senses in aging* (Annals of the New York Academy of Sciences), Vol. 561. New York: New York Academy of Sciences; **p. 147** Barinaga, 1997; Fig. 4.18 Bradley, D. R., Dumais, & Petry (1976). Reply to Cavonius. *Nature, 261*, 78. Reprinted with permission from Nature. Copyright © 1976 Macmillan Magazines Limited; **p. 148** *(bottom)* Enrico Ferorelli; **p. 150** *(top)* Otto Greule, Jr./Allsport USA; *(bottom)* René Magritte, *The Blank Signature*, oil on canvas, National Gallery of Art, Washington. Collection of Mr. & Mrs. Paul Mellon. Photo by Richard Carafelli; **p. 151** *(left)* Rainer Grosskopf/Tony Stone Worldwide; *(bottom)* City Art Gallery, Bristol/The Bridgeman Art Library, Superstock; **p. 152** *(bottom right)* Alan Choisnet/The Image Bank; Fig. 4.26 Shepard, R. N. (1981). Psychophysical. In M. Kubovky & J. R. Pomerantz (Eds.), *Perceptual organization* (pp. 279–341). Hillsdale, NJ: Lawrence Erlbaum. Copyright © 1981 by Lawrence Erlbaum Associates; Fig. 4.28a From *Mind sights* by Shepard. Copyright © 1990 by Roger N. Shepard. Used with permission of W.H. Freeman and Company; **p. 153** E. Schwartzenberg/The Exploratorium; Fig. 4.29a From "Visual Illusions" (November 1968, pp. 66–76) by R.L. Gregory. Copyright © 1968 by Scientific American, Inc. All rights reserved; Fig. 4.29b Day, R.H. (1984) The nature of perceptual illusions. *Interdisciplinary Science Reviews, 9*, 47–58; **p. 156** *(top)* Courtesy of Hubert Dolezal; *(bottom)* Fig. 4.32 From *Mind sights* by Roger N. Shepard. Copyright © 1990 by Roger N. Shepard. Reprinted by permission by W.H. Freeman & Company; **p. 157** *(left)* Frank Searle, Photo Adams/Sygma; **p. 157** *(right)* Dick Ruhl; **p. 158** Adapted from Gregory, R.L., & Gombrich, E.H. (Eds.) (1974). *Illusion in nature and art*. New York: Charles Scribner's Sons. Copyright © UNESCO; Fig. 4.34 From *Mind sights* by Roger N. Shepard. Copyright © 1990 by Roger N. Shepard. Reprinted by permission of W.H. Freeman and Company; **p. 159** Norman, D. 1988, The psychology of everyday things. New York: Basic Books. Reprinted with permission of Basic Books, Inc. a division of HaperCollions Publishers; **p. 164** Alva Bernadine; Fig. 4.35 Kraft, C. (1978). A psychological approach to air safety: Simulator studies of visual illusions in night approaches. In H.L. Pick, H.W. Leibowitz, J.E. Singer, A. Steinschneider, & H.W. Stevenson (Eds.), *Psychology: From research to practice*. New York: Plenum Press.

CHAPTER 5

Opener p. 168 Dan McCoy/Rainbow; **p. 170** Will & Deni McIntyre; **p. 171** *(top)* Jeff Greenberg/Photo Edit; *(bottom)* Peter Turnley/Black Star; **p. 174** Hank Morgan/Rainbow; Figs. 5.1 and 5.2 From Dement, W. (1978). *Some must watch while some must sleep*. Stanford, CA: Portable Stanford Book Series, 1972. Reprinted by permission of the Stanford Alumni Association, Stanford University; **p. 175** Ted Spagna/Science Source/Photo Researchers; Fig. 5.3 *(left)* Cartwright, R.D. (1978). *A primer on sleep and dreaming*. Reading, MA: Addison-Wesley; Fig. 5.3 *(right)* Webb, W.B. (1992). *Sleep: The gentle tyrant*, 2/e., Bolton, MA: Anker Publishing; Fig. 5.4 Adapted with permission of The Free Press, a division of Simon & Schuster from *Sleep thieves: An eye-opening exploration into the science and mysteries of sleep* by Stanley Coren. Copyright © 1996 by Stanley Coren; **p. 177** Patrick Ward/Copyright © Discover Magazine; **p. 180** Dan McCoy/Rainbow; **p. 182** Chagall, Marc. *I and the Village*. 1911. Oil on canvas, 6′ 3 5/8 × 59 5/8″ (192.1 × 151.4 cm). The Museum of Modern Art, New York. Mrs. Simon Guggenheim Fund. Photograph Copyright © 1997 The Museum of Modern Art, New York; **p. 184** James Wilson/ Woodfin Camp & Associates; **p. 187** Agnew & Sons,

London/ Bridgeman Art Library, London/Superstock; **p. 188** Joel Gordon; **p. 189** Mimi Forsyth/Monkmeyer; **p. 190** Courtesy of News and Publications Service, Stanford University; **p. 194** MADD, Minnesota State Office & Clarity Coverdale Rueff, Minneapolis; **p. 197** Fig. 5.9 From *Hallucinations* by R.K. Siegel. Copyright © 1977 Scientific American, Inc. All rights reserved.

CHAPTER 6

Opener p. 204 Elizabeth Crews/Image Works; **p. 207** Sovfoto; Fig. 6.4 Adapted from Goodwin, C. J. (1991). Misportraying Pavlov's apparatus. *American Journal of Psychology, 104*, 135–141. Copyright © 1991 by the Board of Trustees of the University of Illinois. Used with permission of the University of Illinois Press; **p. 212** *(bottom)* C. Parry/The Image Works; *(top)* Courtesy of UCLA Media; **p. 214** Brown Brothers; **p. 216** *(bottom)* Richard Wood/The Picture Cube; **p. 217** Fred Bavendam/Peter Arnold, Inc.; **p. 218** George White/Location Photography; **p. 221** Joan Liftin/Actuality; **p. 223** *(top)* Saola/Gamma Liaison; **p. 223** *(bottom)* Falk/ Monkmeyer; **p. 224** Jeff Greenberg/Photo Edit; **p. 226** *(top)* Harper's Index 1997; *(bottom)* Courtesy of Albert Bandura, Stanford University; **p. 227** *(right)* Bob Daemmrich/The Image Works; *(left)* From Meltzoff, A.N. (1988). Imitation of televised models by infants. *Child Development, 59*, 1221–1229. Photos Courtesy of A.N. Meltzoff & M. Hanak.

CHAPTER 7

Opener p. 230 Michael Siluk/Picture Cube; **p. 232** Courtesy of Hersh & Treadgold, Inc., Desktop Paging Software, Inc., and NEC, Inc.; **p. 233** Fred Ward/Black Star; **p. 234** *(top)* Gjon Mili, Life Magazine Copyright © 1950 Time Warner Inc.; *(left)* D. Young Wolff/Photo Edit; *(right)* Robert Brenner/Photo Edit; Fig. 7.3 Data from H. Ebbinghaus, 1885. Reprinted with permission of Simon & Schuster Inc. from *Your memory: A user's guide* by A. D. Baddeley. Copyright © 1982 by Multimedia Publications (UK) Ltd.; **p. 236** Bachmann/Photo Researchers; Fig. 7.4 Craik, F.I.M. & Watkins, M.J. (1973). The role of rehearsal in short-term memory. *Journal of Verbal Learning and Verbal Behavior, 12*, 599–607. Reprinted by permission of Academic Press Inc.; **p. 237** Sivard, R.l. (1996). *World military and social expenditures 1996*. Washington, DC: World Priorities; Fig. 7.5 From *The psychology of learning and memory* by Douglas L. Hintzman. Copyright © 1978 by W.H. Freeman and Company. Reprinted with permission; Fig. 7.9 Nickerson, R.S. & Adams M.J. (1979). Long-term memory for a common object. *Cognitive Psychology, 11*, 287–307. Reprinted by permission of Academic Press, Inc.; **p. 243** R. J. Erwin/Photo Researchers; Fig. 7.12 Adapted from Ebbinghaus, E. (1885). Über das Gedächtnis. Leipzig: Dunker. *Human memory: Structures and processes*, 2/e by Klatzky. Copyright © 1980 by W. H. Freeman and Company. Used with permission. **p. 244** Will & Deni McIntyre/Photo Researchers; Fig. 7.13 Adapted from Bahrick, H. P. (1984). Semantic memory content in permastore: 50 years of memory for Spanish learned in school. *Journal of Experimental Psychology: General, 113*, 1–29. Copyright © 1984 American Psychological Association. Adapted by permission; **p. 246** Fernando Sepe Jr./AP Wide World Photos, Inc.; **p. 248** From "Learning and Memory", 1994 Copyright © Cold Springs Laboratories, Courtesy of James Golomb, M.D., Dept. of Neurology, NYU School of Medicine; **p. 249** *(left)* Seth Poppel/Yearbook Archives; *(right)* Seth Poppel/Yearbook Archives; Fig. 7.16 Adapted from Bower, G. H. (1986). Prime time in cognitive psychology. In P. Eelen (Ed.), *Cognitive research and behavior therapy: Beyond the conditioning paradigm*. Amsterdam: North Holland Publishers; **p. 251** *(top)* Fred McConnaughey/Photo Researchers; Fig. 7.17 Adapted from Godden, D.R. & Baddeley, A. D. (1975). Context-dependent memory in two natural environments: On land and under water. *British Journal of Psychology, 66*, 325–331; **p. 252** Dan McCoy/Rainbow; Fig. 7.22 Loftus, E. F. (1979). The malleability of human memory. *American Scientist, 67*, 313–320. Reprinted by permission of *American Scientist*, Journal of Sigma Xi, The Scientific Research Society; **p. 262** Courtesy of Elizabeth Loftus, University of Washington; **p. 263** Flip Chalfant/The Image Bank.

CHAPTER 8

Opener p. 266 Lou Jones; **p. 269** *(left)* Daniel J. Cox/Liaison International; *(right)* J. Messerschmidt/The Picture Cube; *(bottom)* Spencer Grant/Liaison International; Figs. 8.1 and 8.3 Copyright © John Alcorn. In "Problem Solving" by M. Scheerer. *Scientific American*, 1963, Figs. 8.2 and 8.4 Duncker, K. (1945). On problem-solving. *Psychological Monographs, 58* (Whole no. 270); **p. 273** Diedra Laird/*The Charlotte Observer*; **p. 274** Copyright © 1996 Treë; **p. 275** Stanely Rowin/The Picture Cube; **p. 276** Lloyd DeGrane/NYT Pictures; **p. 277** M & E. Bernheim/Woodfin Camp & Associates; Fig. 8.5 Adapted from Werker, J.F. (1989). Becoming a native listener. *American Scientist*, 77-59. Reprinted with permission of *American Scientist*, Journal of Sygma Xi, The Scientific Research Society. Photos Courtesy of Peter McLeod, Acadia University; **p. 279** David Young-Wolff/Photo Edit; **p. 281** *(left)* Oliver Meckes/Photo Researchers; **p. 281** *(center)* Michael Newman/Photo Edit; *(right)* Crews/The Image Works; *(top)* Shackman/Monkmeyer; Fig. 8.7 Johnson, J.S. & Newport, E.L. (1989). Critical period effects in second language learning: The influence of maturational state on the acquisition of English as a second language. *Cognitive Psychology, 21*, 60–99. Reprinted by permission of Academic Press, Inc.; **p. 282** *(top)* George Ancona in Ancona, G. & Beth, M. (1989) *The Handtalk Zoo*. New York: Macmillan Publishing Company; *(bottom)* William Munoz; **p. 283** Language Research Center, Yerkes Regional Primate Research Center; **p. 284** *(top)* Paul Fusco/Magnum Photos; **p. 286** Stephen Dunn/Allsport; **p. 287** Goodwin/Monkmeyer; **p. 288** Elizabeth Crews/The Image Works; **p. 289** National Library of Medicine; **p. 291** Fig. 8.8 From Wiltshire, S. (1991) *Floating Cities*. London: Michael Joseph Ltd.; **p. 293** Lew Merrim/Monkmeyer; Fig. 8.9 *Measurement and evaluation in psychology and education*, 5/e, by Thorndike/Hagan, © 1986, pp. 233–235. Adapted by permission of Prentice Hall, Upper Saddle River, New Jersey; **p. 297** Michael O'Neill; **p. 299** Mark Richards/Photo Edit; Fig. 8.12 Fulker, D.W., DeFries, J.C. & Plomin, R. (1988). Genetic influence on general mental ability increases between infancy and middle childhood. *Nature, 336*, 767–769. Reprinted by permission of *Nature*. Copyright © 1988 Macmillan Magazines Limited; **p. 302** *(left)* Jacques Chenet/Woodfin Camp & Associates; *(right)* Susan Lapides/Design Conceptions; Fig. 8.13 Lewontin, R. (1976). Race and intelligence. In N.J. Block & G.Dworken (Eds.), *The IQ controversy: Critical readings*. New York: Pantheon. Copyright © 1976 N.J. Block & G. Dworken. Reprinted by permission; **p. 305** Courtesy Robert Allen Strawn; Fig. 8.14 Reprinted with permission of authors and publishers from Vandenberg, S.G. & Kuse, A.R. Mental rotations, group test of three-dimensional spatial visualization. *Perceptual and Motor Skills, 47*, 1978, pp. 599–604; **p. 306** J. Griffin/The Image Works.

CHAPTER 9

Opener p. 310 Superstock; **p. 312** *(bottom)* Bob Daemmrich/ The Image Works; *(top)* Tony Brandenburg/Bruce Coleman, Inc.; **p. 313** *(left)* George Ancona/International Stock; *(right)* Harlow Primate Laboratory, University of Wisconsin; **p. 314** *(top)* Wesley Hitt/Liaison International; *(center)* Michael Dwyer/Stock, Boston;

(bottom) Dale Spartas/Liaison International; Fig. 9.1 From *Motivation and personality*, 3/e by Abraham H. Maslow, Revised by Robert Frager et al. Copyright © 1954, 1987 by Harper & Row Publishers, Inc. Copyright © 1970 by Abraham H. Maslow. Reprinted by permission of Addison-Wesley Educational Publishers, Inc.; **p. 316** Pix*ELATION from Fran Heyl Associates; Fig. 9.2 Adapted from Cannon, W.B. (1929). *Bodily changes in pain, hunger, fear, and rage*. New York: Branford; **p. 317** Richard Howard; **p. 318** Richard Olsenius/Black Star; **p. 320** *The Garden of Love* (Detail), Peter Paul Reubens, The Prado, Madrid/The Bridgeman Art Library, Superstock; **p. 322** *(top)* Phyllis Picardi/Stock, Boston; Courtesy of John Sholtis, The Rockefeller University, New York, NY; **p. 323** Michael Newman/Photo Edit; **p. 324** Michael Newman/Photo Edit; Fig. 9.5 Bray, G. A. (1969). Effect of caloric restriction on energy expenditure in obese patients. *Lancet, 2*, 397 398. Copyright © 1969 by the Lancet Ltd.; Fig. 9.6 Adapted from Brownell, K.D. & Jeffrey, R.W. (1987). Improving long-term weight loss: Pushing the limits of treatment. *Behavior Therapy, 18*, 353–374. Copyright © 1987 by the Association for Advancement of Behavior Therapy. Reprinted by permission of the publisher; **p. 325** Tony Freeman/ Photo Edit; Fig. 9.7 Dietz, W.H., Jr., & Gortmaker, S.L. (1985). Do we fatten our children at the television set? Obesity and television viewing children and adolescents. Reproduced by permission of *Pediatrics, Vol. 75*, p. 807, copyright 1985; **p. 327** Photo by Dellenback reprinted by permission of the Kinsey Institute for Research in Sex, Gender, and Reproduction, Inc.; Fig. 9.8 Adapted from Masters, W.H. & Johnson, V. E. (1966). *Human sexual response*. Boston: Little, Brown & Company. Copyright © 1966 by Masters and Johnson; Fig. 9.9 Byrne, D. (1982). Predicting human sexual behavior. In A.G. Kraut, *The G. Stanley Hall Lecture Series (Vol. 2)*. Copyright © 1982 by the American Psychological Association. Reprinted by permission of the author and publisher; **p. 334** Cynthia Johnson/Time Magazine; **p. 336** Nathaniel Antman/The Image Works; **p. 337** AP/Wide World Photos, Inc.; **p. 339** McClelland, D. C. , et al (1953). *The achievement motive*. New York: Appleton-Centuy Crofts. Reprinted by permission of Irvington Publishers, New York; **p. 340** Stephen Jaffe/The Gamma Liaison Network; **p. 341** Jack Smith/ Associated Press Photo; **p. 342** *(top)* Fujifotos/The Image Works; *(bottom)* Jonathan Daniel/Allsport.

CHAPTER 10

Opener p. 346 Myrleen Cate/Photo Edit; **p. 348** © M. Grecco/Stock, Boston; **p. 350** Bernard Gottfryd/Woodfin Camp & Associates; Fig. 10.3 Courtesy of David Raskins, University of Utah, as shown in *Science*, June 1982, pp. 24–27; Fig. 10.4 Kleinmuntz, B. & Szucko, J. J. (1984). A field study of the fallibility of polygraph lie detection. *Nature, 308*, 449–450. Reprinted by permission of *Nature*. Copyright © 1984 Macmillan Journals Limited; **p. 352** Culver Pictures; **p. 353** (a-d) Dr. Paul Ekman, University of California at San Francisco; **p. 354** © 1988 Ekman & Matsumoto, Japanese and Caucasian Facial Expressions of Emotions; **p. 355** Courtesy of Louis Schakel/ Michael Kausman/The New York Times Pictures; **p. 357** (a) Tom McCarthy/Rainbow; (b) Patrick Donehue/Photo Researchers; (c) Bob Daemmrich/The Image Works; (d) Michael Newman/Photo Edit; (e) Merrim/Monkmeyer; (f) Nancy Brown/The Image Bank; (g) Marc Grimberg/The Image Bank; **p. 358** Wolfgang Kaehler; **p. 360** Mark Lennihan/AP/Wide World Photos, Inc.; Fig. 10.10 Adapted from Solomon, R.L. (1980). The opponent-process theory of acquired motivation: The costs of pleasure and the benefits of pain. *American Psychologist, 35*, 691–712. Copyright © 1980 American Psychological Association. Reprinted by permission of the author; **p. 362** Robert Deutsch/USA Today; **p. 363** Drawing by Handelsman; Copyright © 1996 The New Yorker, Inc.; **p. 368** *(top)* Arlene Collins/Monkmeyer; *(bottom)* Miro Vintoniv/Stock Boston; **p. 370** Charles Bertram/Gamma Liaison; **p. 371** Peter Glass/ Monkmeyer; **p. 374** Lennart Nilsson/Boehringer Ingelheim International GmbH; **p. 375** Gerd Ludwig/Woodfin Camp & Associates; **p. 379** *(top)* P. Fagot/Explorer/Photo Researchers; *(bottom)* LeDuc/ Monkmeyer; Fig. 10.19 Adapted from McCann, I.L., & Holmes, D.S. (1984). Influence of aerobic exercise on depression. *Journal of Personality and Social Psychology, 46*, 1142–1147. Copyright © 1984 by the American Psychological Association. Adapted by permission of the authors; **p. 380** *(top)* Dan McCoy/Rainbow; *(bottom)* Steve Liss/Time Magazine; **p. 381** Billy E. Barnes/Stock, Boston; Fig. 10.21 From *Treating Type A Behavior and Your Heart* by Meyer Friedman, M.D. and Diane Ulmer, R.N., M.S. Copyright © 1984 by Meyer Friedman. Reprinted by permission of Alfred A. Knopf, Inc.; **p. 382** Bob Daemmrich/Stock, Boston.

CHAPTER 11

Opener p. 388 Jack Fields/Corbis; **p. 390** Culver Pictures; **p. 391** *(top)* Edmund Engelman; **p. 393** *(top)* Grantpix/Monkmeyer; *(bottom left)* Rick Friedman/Black Star; *(bottom right)* Harlow Primate Laboratory, University of Wisconsin; **p. 394** *(left)* National Library of Medicine; *(center)* The Bettmann Archive; *(right)* Archives of the History of American Psychology; **p. 395** Merrim/Monkmeyer; **p. 396** Merrim/Monkmeyer; **p. 401** AP/Wide World Photos, Inc.; **p. 402** *(right)* Wolf/Monkmeyer; *(left)* Joel Gordon; Fig. 11.2 Eysenck, S. B. G. & Eysenck, H. J. (1963). The validity of questionnaire and rating assessments of extraversion and neuroticism, and their factorial stability. *British Journal of Psychology, 54*, 51–62. Fig. 1; Fig. 11.3 From *The MMPI-2 in psychological treatment* by J.N. Butcher. Copyright © 1990 by Oxford University Press, Inc. Used by permission of Oxford University Press, Inc.; **p. 406** Ted Polumbaum/Life Magazine Copyright © 1968 Time Warner, Inc.; **p. 407** Mark Antman/The Image Works; **p. 408** Sybil Shackman/Monkmeyer; **p. 412** *(top)* G. B. Rose/Gamma Liaison; *(bottom)* B. and C. Alexander/Photo Researchers; **p. 416** Stephen Wade/Allsport USA; **p. 417** Joe McNally.

CHAPTER 12

Opener p. 424 Photo Researchers; **p. 426** Tony Ray Jones/Magnum Photos; **p. 427** J. Otis Wheelock/Courtesy Dept. of Library Services American Museum of Natural History; Fig. 12.2 Roper report 84–3, February 11–25, 1984. *Public Opinion*, August/September, 25. Reprinted with permission of the American Enterprise Institute for Public Policy Research, Washington, DC; **p. 435** Jean Michel Turpin/Gamma Liaison; **p. 436** John Coletti/Stock, Boston; **p. 437** Baxter, L.R., et al. (1987). Local cerebral glucose metabolic rates in obsessive-compulsive disorder. Archives of General Psychology, 44(3), 211–218. Copyright © 1987 American Medical Association; **p. 438** AP/Wide World Photos, Inc.; **p. 442** Exley/Gamma Liaison; **p. 443** Jerry Irwin Photography; **p. 444** Shackman/Monkmeyer; **p. 445** Courtesy of Drs. Lewis Baxter and Michael E. Phelps, UCLA School of Medicine; **p. 447** Sidney/Monkmeyer; Fig. 12.9 Forgas, J.P., et al. (1984). The influence of mood on perceptions of social interactions. *Journal of Experimental and Social Psychology, 20*, 497–513. Orlando, FL: Academic Press, Journals Division; Fig. 12.10 Adapted from Lewinsohn, P.M., et al. (1985). An integrative theory of depression. In S. Reiss and R. Bootzin (Eds.), *Theoretical issues in behavior therapy*. Orlando, FL: Academic Press; **p. 450** *(right)* Berthold, L., *Untitled*. The Prinzhorn Collection, University of Heidelberg. Photos: Krannert Museum, University of Illinois at Urbana-Champaign; *(left)* August Natterer, Witch's Head. The Prinzhorn Collection, University of Heidelberg. Photos: Krannert Museum, University of Illinois at Urbana-Champaign; Fig. 12.11 Data from *Schizophrenia genesis: The origins of madness* by I.I.

Gottesman. Copyright © 1991 by W.H. Freeman and Company. Used with permission; **p. 454** From Suddath, Richard L., et al. (1990). Anatomical abnormalities in the brains of monozygotic twins discordant for schizophrenia. *The New England Journal of Medicine, 322*, 12. Copyright © 1990 by the Massachusetts Medical Society. Photo courtesy of Daniel R. Weinberger, M.D., NIH-NIMH/NSC; **p. 455** Courtesy of Genain Family; Fig. 12.12 Adapted from Magnusson, D. (1990). Personality research—challenges for the future. *European Journal of Personality, 4*, 1–17. Copyright © 1990, reprinted by permission of John Wiley & Sons, Ltd.

CHAPTER 13

Opener p. 460 Seth Resnick/Stock, Boston; **p. 462** *(top left)* The Granger Collection; *(top right)* The Bettmann Archive; *(bottom)* Richard T. Nowitz/Photo Researchers; **p. 464** Steve Goldberg/Monkmeyer; **p. 465** Michael Rougier, Life Magazine, Copyright © Time War-ner, Inc.; **p. 466** The New Yorker Magazine, Inc.; Fig. 13.1 Gilling, D. & Brightwell, R. (1982). *The human brain.* New York: Facts on File. Reprinted by permission of Little, Brown & Co. (UK); **p. 470** Joel Gordon; Fig. 13.5 Rabin, A.S. et al. (1986). Aggregate outcome and follow-up results following self-control therapy for depression. Paper presented at the American Psychological Association convention; **p. 474** Stacy Pick/Stock, Boston; **p. 477** © Richard Nowitz/Photo Researchers; Fig. 13.7 Adapted from Smith, M.L. et al. (1980). *The benefits of psychotherapy* (p. 88) Baltimore, MD: Johns Hopkins University Press. Reprinted by permission; **p. 481** Mark Antman/ The Image Works; **p. 483** Lee Snider/The Image Works; **p. 484** Lynn Johnson/Black Star; **p. 486** James Wilson/Woodfin Camp & Associates.

CHAPTER 14

Opener p. 490 Irene Bayer/Monkmeyer Press; **p. 494** D. MacDonald/Photo Edit; **p. 495** Thomas Hopker/Magnum Photos; **p. 497** William Vandivert/Scientfic American; **p. 499** Courtesy of CUNY Graduate School and University Center; **p. 500** Copyright 1965 by Stanley Milgram. From the film OBEDIENCE, distributed by Penn State, Media Sales; **p. 501** *(top)* AP/Wide World Photos, Inc.; Fig. 14.4 Adapted from Wheeler, D.L., Jacobson, D.L., Paglieri, R.A., & Schwartz, A.A. (1993). An experimental assessment of facilitated communication. *Mental Retardation, 31*, 49–60; **p. 503** Tom Pidgeon/AP Wide World Photo; **p. 506** Margaret Bourke-White, Life Magazine. Copyright © 1946 Time Warner, Inc.; **p. 507** *(bottom)* Fujifotos/ The Image Works; *(top)* Robert Azzi/Woodfin Camp & Associates; **p. 508** Monkmeyer; Fig. 14.6 Dey, E.L., et al (1991). *The American Freshman: Twenty-Five Year Trends.* Los Angeles: Higher Education Research Institute, UCLA; **p. 510** *(top and bottom)* Courtesy of *COLORS Magazine*; Fig. 14.7 Nieni, R.G., Moeller, J., & Smith, T.W. (1989) *Trends in public opinion: A compendium of survey data.* New York: Greenwood Press. Reprinted with permission; **p. 512** Larry Fischer/AP/Wide World, Inc.; **p. 515** *(top)* Presse-Sports; *(bottom)* Robert Brenner/Photo Edit; Fig. 14.8 Anderson, C.A. & Anderson, D.C. (1984). Ambient temperature and violent crime: Tests of the linear and curvilinear hypotheses. *Journal of Personality and Social Sciences, 46*, 91–97. Copyright © 1984 American Psychological Association. Reprinted with permission; Fig. 14.9 Adapted from Malamuth, N.M. (1989). Sexually violent media, thought patterns, and anti-social behavior, in G. Comstock (Ed.), *Public Communication and Behavior*, Vol. 2. San Diego, CA: Academic Press; **p. 520** Keith Gosse/The Evening Telegram; **p. 523** Rex USA ; **p. 524** Popperfoto/Archive Photos; **p. 525** *(top, left)* Margaret Gowan/Tony Stone Worldwide; *(center)* Victor Englebert/Photo Researchers; *(right)* Nancy Brown/The Image Bank; **p. 528** *(left)* Sotographs/Gamma Liaison; *(right)* Myrleen Ferguson/Photo Edit; **p. 529** Akos Szilvasi/Stock, Boston; Fig. 14.12 Darley J.M. & Latane, B. (1968b, December). When will people help in a crisis? *Psychology Today*, 54–57, 70–71, Reprinted with permission from Psychology Today Magazine. Copyright © 1968 (Sussex Publishers, Inc.); Fig. 14.13 Darley J.M. & Latane, B. (1968a). Bystander intervention in emergencies: Diffusion of responsibility. *Journal of Personality and Social Psychology, 8*, 377–383. Copyright © 1968 by the American Psychological Association. Reprinted by permission; **p. 530** Bob Daemmrich/Stock, Boston.

Name Index

A

B

F

G

M

Q

R

T

U

V

W

X

Y

Z

Subject Index

A

D

E

F

G

H

I

J

K

L

M

N

Q

R

S